Lecture Notes in Computer Science 16995

The series Lecture Notes in Computer Science (LNCS), including its subseries Lecture Notes in Artificial Intelligence (LNAI) and Lecture Notes in Bioinformatics (LNBI), has established itself as a medium for the publication of new developments in computer science and information technology research, teaching, and education.

LNCS enjoys close cooperation with the computer science R & D community, the series counts many renowned academics among its volume editors and paper authors, and collaborates with prestigious societies. Its mission is to serve this international community by providing an invaluable service, mainly focused on the publication of conference and workshop proceedings and postproceedings. LNCS commenced publication in 1973.

Lingling Ding · Yannis Manolopoulos ·
Richard Chbeir · Karam Bou-chaaya ·
Schahram Dustdar · Tran Ngoc Tuan
Editors

Web and Big Data

10th Asia-Pacific Web (APWeb) and Web-Age Information Management (WAIM) International Joint Conference, APWeb-WAIM 2026
Danang, Vietnam, September 7–9, 2026
Proceedings, Part III

Springer

Editors
Lingling Ding
Liaoning University
Shenyang, China

Richard Chbeir
Université de Pau et des Pays de l'Adour
Anglet, France

Schahram Dustdar
TU Wien
Wien, Austria

Yannis Manolopoulos
University of York
Thessaloniki, Greece

Karam Bou-chaaya
EXPLEO GROUP
Montigny-le-Bretonneux, France

Tran Ngoc Tuan
FPT University
Ho Chi Minh City, Vietnam

ISSN 0302-9743 ISSN 1611-3349 (electronic)
Lecture Notes in Computer Science
ISBN 978-981-92-5698-3 ISBN 978-981-92-5699-0 (eBook)
https://doi.org/10.1007/978-981-92-5699-0

This Springer imprint is published by the registered company Springer Nature Singapore Pte Ltd.
The registered company address is: 152 Beach Road, #21-01/04 Gateway East, Singapore 189721, Singapore

Preface

This volume (LNCS 16995) and its companion volumes (LNCS 16993 and 16994) contain the proceedings of the 10th Asia-Pacific Web (APWeb) and Web-Age Information Management (WAIM) Joint Conference on Web and Big Data, for short called APWeb-WAIM. The 10th APWeb-WAIM joint conference was held in Da Nang, Vietnam during 7–9 September 2026.

As an Asia-Pacific flagship conference focusing on research, development, and applications related to Web information management, APWeb-WAIM builds on the successes of its ancestor APWeb and WAIM conferences. Previous APWeb events were held in Beijing (1998), Hong Kong (1999), Xi'an (2000), Changsha (2001), Xi'an (2003), Hangzhou (2004), Shanghai (2005), Harbin (2006), Huangshan (2007), Shenyang (2008), Suzhou (2009), Busan (2010), Beijing (2011), Kunming (2012), Sydney (2013), Changsha (2014), Guangzhou (2015), and Suzhou (2016). On the other hand, WAIM events were held in Shanghai (2000), Xi'an (2001), Beijing (2002), Chengdu (2003), Dalian (2004), Hangzhou (2005), Hong Kong (2006), Huangshan (2007), Zhangjiajie (2008), Suzhou (2009), Jiuzhaigou (2010), Wuhan (2011), Harbin (2012), Beidaihe (2013), Macau (2014), Qingdao (2015), and Nanchang (2016). The APWeb-WAIM joint conferences were held in Beijing (2017), Macau (2018), Chengdu (2019), Tianjin (2020), Guangzhou (2021), Nanjing (2022), Wuhan (2023), Jinhua (2024), and Shenyang (2025).

Researchers and practitioners from around the world came together at this leading international forum to share innovative ideas, original research findings, case study results, and practical insights in the areas of the World Wide Web and big data. APWeb-WAIM 2026 received a total of 309 research paper submissions. After a double-blind review process (each paper received at least three review reports), the conference accepted 108 regular research papers, resulting in an acceptance rate less than 35%. In addition, the conference accepted 24 special track papers, 1 industry paper, and 9 demo papers.

Moreover, the following 3 international workshops were organized:

- 9th International Workshop on Knowledge Graph Management and Applications (KGMA), organized by Meng Wang and Xin Wang, and
- 8th International Workshop on Semi-structured Big Data Management and Applications (SemiBDMA), organized by Linlin Ding,
- 1st International Workshop on Natural Resources Survey, Monitoring, and Assessment in the Big Data Era (NRSMA), organized by Xiaohui Huang, Yuewei Wang, Xiaodao Chen, Wei Han, Fan Lei, Yunliang Chen, Jianxin Li, and Lizhe Wang.

The contributed papers address a wide range of topics, such as large language models, knowledge graphs, neural networks and learning, machine learning, time series, tree-enabled processing, prediction, traffic management, community-based issues, recommendation systems, query processing, semantic issues, trajectory management, video and image processing, crowdsourcing, security and privacy, and database engineering.

The high-quality program documented in these proceedings would not have been possible without the authors who chose the APWeb-WAIM joint conference to disseminate their findings.

In addition, the conference program included 3 plenary talks by:

- Gao Cong (Nanyang Technological University, Singapore) entitled: "From AI4DB to Databases for AI: Rethinking Data Systems in the LLM Era",
- Hai Jin (Huazhong University of Science and Technology) entitled: "A Unified Approach of Graph Computing: From Foundations to Systems and Beyond", and
- Xiaofang Zhou (Hong Kong University of Science and Technology) entitled: "Advanced Similarity Query Processing in Vector Databases".

We would like to express our gratitude to all individuals, institutions, and sponsors that supported APWeb-WAIM 2026. We are grateful to all distinguished scientists for their invaluable contributions to the conference program. We are deeply thankful to the Program Committee members for lending their time and expertise to the conference. We also acknowledge the support of the other members of the organizing committee, all of whom helped make APWeb-WAIM 2026 a success.

Special thanks are due to the industry chairs (Dang Van Cuong, Le Quang Dam, and Tran The Hung), workshop chair (Jiajia Li), tutorial chair (Shiyu Yang), demo chairs (Cao Vu Bui, and Vo Quoc Trinh), publicity chairs (Yang Cao, Bohan Li, Nguyen Thi Thu Nga, and Salma Sassi), local organizing committee chairs (Le This My Hahn, Nguyen Dang Nghia, and Luong Vuong Nguyen), CCF TCIS liaison (Xin Wang), and CCF TCDB liaison (Yueguo Chen). Finally, we are grateful to the steering committee representative (Yanchun Zhang) for his guidance and support.

With the ever-growing importance of appropriate methods in these data-rich times and the rapid development of web-related technologies, APWeb-WAIM will continue to be a flagship conference in this field.

Lingling Ding
Yannis Manolopoulos
Richard Chbeir
Schahram Dustdar
Tran Ngoc Tuan
Karam Bou-chaaya

Organization

General Chairs

Richard Chbeir	Université de Pau et Pays de l'Adour, France
Schahram Dustdar	Technical University of Vienna, Austria
Tran Ngoc Tuan	FPT University, Vietnam

Program Chairs

Ding Linlin	Liaoning University, China
Yannis Manolopoulos	University of York, Europe Campus, Greece

Industry Chairs

Dang Van Cuong	University of Da Nang, Vietnam
Le Quang Dam	Marvell Technology, Vietnam
Tran The Hung	FPT Corporation, Vietnam

Tutorials Chair

Shiyu Yang	Guangzhou University, China

Workshop Chair

Jiajia Li	Shenyang Aerospace University, China

Demo Chairs

Cao Vu Bui	FPT University, Vietnam
Vo Quoc Trinh	FPT University, Vietnam

Publicity Chairs

Nguyen This Thus Nga	FPT University, Vietnam
Bohan Li	Nanjing University of Aeronautics and Astronautics, China
Yang Cao	Institute of Science Tokyo, Japan
Salma Sassi	ECE Lyon, France

Publication Chair

Karam Bou-chaaya	Expleo Group, France

Local Organizing Committee Chairs

Le Thi My Hahn	FPT University, Vietnam
Luong Vuong Nguyen	FPT University, Vietnam
Nguyen Dang Nghia	FPT University, Vietnam

CCF TCIS Liaison

Xin Wang	Tianjin University, China

CCF TCDB Liaison

Yueguo Chen	Renmin University of China, China

APWeb-WAIM Steering Committee Representative

Yanchun Zhang	Zhejiang Normal University, China

Program Committee

Sarra Abidi	National School of Computer Science (ENSI), Tunisia
Khloud Al Jallad	Arab International University, Syria

Rui An	Shaanxi Normal University, China
Sauvik Bal	Techno India University, India
Dariusz Barbucha	Gdynia Maritime University, Poland
Emna Ben Abdallah	University of Sfax, Tunisia
Leila Ben Othman	University of Tunis El Manar, Tunisia
Nicola Bena	University of Milan, Italy
Salima Benbernou	University Paris Cité, France
Djamal Benslimane	Claude Bernard University Lyon 1, France
Xin Bi	Northeastern University, China
Ismael Bouassida Rodriguez	University of Sfax, Tunisia
Nizar Bouguila	Concordia University, Canada
Ghizlane Bourahouat	School of Information Sciences, Morocco
Taotao Cai	University of Southern Queensland, Australia
Jinli Cao	La Trobe University, Australia
Yunpeng Chai	Renmin University of China, China
Ameni Chamekh	University of Sfax, Tunisia
Ioannis Chamodrakas	National and Kapodistrian University of Athens, Greece
Tsz Nam Chan	Shenzhen University, China
Jian Chen	Chinese Academy of Sciences, China
Lu Chen	Swinburne University of Technology, Australia
Weitong Chen	Adelaide University, Australia
Xiao Chen	Hong Kong Polytechnic University, China
Zi Chen	Wuhan University of Technology, China
Dickson Chiu	University of Hong Kong, China
Paolo Crippa	Marche Polytechnic University, Italy
Ningning Cui	Chang'an University, China
Alfredo Cuzzocrea	University of Calabria, Italy
Ana da Rocha	Universidade Federal Fluminense, Brazil
Boris Delibasic	University of Belgrade, Serbia
Shizhuo Deng	Northeastern University, China
Linlin Ding	Liaoning University, China
Xiaofeng Ding	Huazhong University of Science and Technology, China
Yuefeng Du	Liaoning University, China
Jide Edu	University of Strathclyde, UK
Mounim El Yacoubi	Télécom SudParis, France
Ichrak Ennaceur	Claude Bernard University Lyon 1, France
Ziquan Fang	Zhejiang University, China
Luigi Gallo	Pegaso University, Italy
Yongfeng Ge	Victoria University, Australia
Xiangyang Gou	Peking University, China

Na Guo	Shenyang Aerospace University, China
Yu Guo	Beijing Normal University, China
Mohammed Haddad	Claude Bernard University Lyon 1, France
Petr Hajek	University of Pardubice, Czech Republic
Akram Hakiri	University of Pau and the Adour Region, France
Sami Hamdi	Jazan University, Saudi Arabia
Nourelhouda Hammouda	University of Sfax, Tunisia
Fei Hao	Shaanxi Normal University, China
Salima Harrat	Higher Normal School of Bouzareah, Algeria
Trong-Minh Hoang	Posts and Telecommunication Institute of Technology, Vietnam
Yang Hongxin	Liaoning University, China
Hao Huang	Wuhan University, China
Shan Huang	Dalian Minzu University, China
Galina Ilieva	Plovdiv University Paisii Hilendarski, Bulgaria
Wissem Inoubli	University of Artois, France
Danwen Ji	Tongji University, China
Hangxu Ji	Northeastern University, China
Ma Ji	Liaoning University, China
Wanting Ji	Liaoning University, China
Dayu Jia	Liaoning University, China
Qinghan Jin	Northeastern University, China
Zhao Jin	Huazhong University of Science and Technology, China
Slim Kallel	University of Sfax, Tunisia
Huhu Kang	Shaanxi Normal University, China
Epaminondas Kapetanios	University of Hertfordshire, UK
Ioannis Karydis	Ionian University, Greece
Aleksandra Klasnja Milicevic	University of Novi Sad, Serbia
Sarah Kohail	Zayed University, UAE
Ferdinand Kpieleh	University of Cincinnati, USA
Kalliopi Kravari	International Hellenic University, Greece
Sabeur Lajili	University of Sousse, Tunisia
Florin Leon	Gheorghe Asachi Technical University of Iaşi, Romania
Hong Va Leong	Hong Kong Polytechnic University, China
Boyang Li	Beijing Institute of Technology, China
Dong Li	Liaoning University, China
Jiajia Li	Shenyang Aerospace University, China
Jianxin Li	Edith Cowan University, Australia
Jiatong Li	Hong Kong Polytechnic University, China

Lei Li	Hong Kong University of Science and Technology (Guangzhou), China
Mo Li	Liaoning University, China
Wei Li	Harbin Engineering University, China
Wentao Li	University of Leicester, UK
Youhuan Li	Hunan University, China
Yuan Li	North China University of Technology, China
Xiang Lian	Kent State University, USA
Kangzheng Liu	Huazhong University of Science and Technology, China
Tingting Liu	Liaoning University, China
Xiaoyi Liu	Arizona State University, USA
Yu Liu	Beijing Jiaotong University, China
Jing Lu	Liaoning University, China
Jiangang Ma	Federation University Australia, Australia
Jie Ma	Xi'an Jiaotong University, China
Ke Ma	Huazhong University of Science and Technology, China
Qiang Ma	Kyoto Institute of Technology, Japan
Yuliang Ma	Northeastern University, China
Elio Masciari	University of Naples Federico II, Italy
Agon Memeti	University of Tetova, North Macedonia
Xiaoye Miao	Zhejiang University, China
Miloud Mihoubi	TÉLUQ University, Canada
Yang-Sae Moon	Kangwon National University, South Korea
Phivos Mylonas	National Technical University of Athens, Greece
Mohamad Nassar	University of New Haven, USA
Thanh Tam Nguyen	Griffith University, Australia
Tiezheng Nie	Northeastern University, China
Alexander Norta	Dymaxion Oy, Estonia
Xiao Pan	Shijiazhuang Tiedao University, China
Dimitrios Panagoulias	University of Piraeus, Greece
Jun Pang	Wuhan University of Science and Technology, China
Sanghyun Park	Yonsei University, South Korea
Yuwei Peng	Wuhan University, China
Nhan Phan	Ho Chi Minh University of Technology, Vietnam
Ahmad Qadeib Alban	Université Paris Dauphine-PSL, France
Yu-Xuan Qiu	Beijing Institute of Technology, China
Pavlo Radiuk	Khmelnytskyi National University, Ukraine
Da Ren	Hong Kong Polytechnic University, China

Boyu Ruan	Hong Kong University of Science and Technology, China
Alexander Ryjov	Lomonosov Moscow State University, Russia
Jarogniew Rykowski	Poznań University of Business and Economics, Poland
Muath Sabha	Arab American University, Palestine
Zaineb Sakhrawi	University of Sfax, Tunisia
Imad Saleh	Paris 8 University, France
Francesco Santini	University of Perugia, Italy
Stefano Sebastio	Collins Aerospace, Ireland
Jiaxing Shen	Lingnan University, China
Han Shi	Liaoning University, China
Tuo Shi	Aalto University, Finland
Yu Shidong	Liaoning University, China
Jiefu Song	IRIT, Toulouse, France
Wei Song	Wuhan University, China
Xiangyu Song	Chang'an University, China
Yumeng Song	Aalborg University, Denmark
Zhen Song	Shandong University, China
Liana Stanescu	University of Craiova, Romania
Yongjiao Sun	Northeastern University, China
Aroua Taamallah	University of Sousse, Tunisia
Chaogang Tang	China University of Mining and Technology, China
Peng Tang	Shandong University, China
Min Tao	Wuzhou University, China
Joe Tekli	Lebanese American University, Lebanon
Yiping Teng	Shenyang Aerospace University, China
Alexandra Vultureanu-Albisi	University of Craiova, Romania
Aina Wang	Liaoning University, China
Beilun Wang	Southeast University, China
Chen Wang	Liaoning University, China
Hongzhi Wang	Harbin Institute of Technology, China
Hua Wang	Victoria University, Australia
Shigang Wang	Heilongjiang University, China
Wenli Wang	Education University of Hong Kong, China
Xiaoyang Wang	University of New South Wales, Australia
Yiqi Wang	Microsoft, Australia
Yishu Wang	Northeastern University, China
Zhaokang Wang	Nanjing University of Aeronautics and Astronautics, China
Zhibin Wang	Nanjing University, China

Shi-ting Wen	NingboTech University, China
Tianxing Wu	Southeast University, China
Zhizhong Wu	Google, USA
Haoran Xu	China University of Geosciences, Beijing, China
Shuai Xu	Nanjing University of Aeronautics and Astronautics, China
Yingwei Xu	Liaoning University, China
Yajun Yang	Tianjin University, China
Yu Yang	Education University of Hong Kong, China
Zhengyi Yang	University of Sydney, Australia
Shanshan Yao	Shanxi University, China
Xin Yao	Northeastern University, China
Zhongming Yao	Aalborg University, Denmark
Shaoyi Yin	University of Toulouse, France
Muhammad Younas	Oxford Brookes University, UK
Jianke Yu	Zhejiang Gongshang University, China
Yonghong Yu	Nanjing University of Posts and Telecommunications, China
Adib Zaman	University of Cincinnati, USA
Yuxiang Zeng	Beihang University, China
Jie Zhang	Hong Kong University of Science and Technology, China
Jilian Zhang	Jinan University, China
Junhua Zhang	Northeastern University, China
Ningyu Zhang	Zhejiang University, China
Xiaohan Zhang	National Supercomputing Shenzhen Center, China
Xiaowang Zhang	Tianjin University, China
Yanfeng Zhang	Northeastern University, China
Yong Zhang	Tsinghua University, China
Chunyan Zhao	East China Normal University, China
Minghao Zhao	East China Normal University, China
Zhigao Zheng	Wuhan University, China
Zixin Zhong	Tongji University, China
Xiangmin Zhou	RMIT University, Australia
Qiang Zhu	University of Michigan – Dearborn, USA
Rui Zhu	Shenyang Aerospace University, China
Yuanxiang Zhu	Liaoning University, China
Zhaonian Zou	Harbin Institute of Technology, China

Sponsors

Springer

Connected Environment & Distributed Energy Data Management Solutions Research Group

The French Chapter of the ACM Special Interest Group on Applied Computing

FPT University Vietnam

Contents

Neural Networks and Learning

AV-MultiDet: Frame-Level Multimodal Learning for Fine-Grained Deepfake Detection and Temporal Localization 3
Ngoc-Phuong-Linh Nguyen and Tran-Ngoc-Tran Le

Continuous-Time Modeling of Crypto Limit Order Books with Liquid Neural Networks 18
Qiankang Xu, Linhan Xia, Mingzhan Yang, Jingjing Wang, Ziwei Yan, Tanren Liu, and Kai Lei

CRISP: Category-Role Informed Sheaf Propagation Network 33
Yuhao Wang, Xiangdong Zou, Kai Du, Chengbo Yu, and Hui Li

TransDyG: An Anomaly Detection Method Integrating Dynamic Graphs and Transformers 50
Yunxiang Wang, Shanhe Niu, Ruiqi Wang, Bo Jiang, Boya Yang, and Baoxu Liu

Traffic Management

EAST: Embedding-Aligned Modality Adaptation for Large Language Model-Based Traffic Forecasting 67
Siya Qiu, Liang Du, Chuxuan Zeng, Ling Deng, Qiong Luo, and Jing Tang

PQ-STM: Pattern-Aware and Query-Guided Spatiotemporal Modeling for Traffic Forecasting 83
Yangnan Xu, Hengyu Liu, Zhihong Cui, Mingxing Shao, Tiancheng Zhang, Minghe Yu, Fangling Leng, and Ge Yu

Rule-Grounded Reasoning for Traffic Video Question Answering with Regulation Knowledge Graphs 100
Daijie Zhu, Yuchen Pan, Xin Hu, Long Li, Zedong Liu, Jie Zhao, and Xiangyu Song

Spatio-Temporal Graph Prompt Interaction for Cross-Region Traffic Speed Forecasting 116
Kun Chen, Lei Zhang, Yutong Wu, Bailong Liu, Fuyang Zhang, and Zixin Zhang

Neural Networks and Learning

Balancing Informativeness and Learnability: Difficulty-Stratified Active CoT Distillation ... 135
Liangyu Wei, Baohang Zhou, Kehui Song, Xiaohan Ma, Tae-Sun Chung, Joon-Young Paik, and Rize Jin

CLEEF: A Contrastive Learning-Based Embedding Enhancement Framework with Triple-Level Adaptive Selection ... 150
Jingyu Zhang, Liqiang Xie, Zhijie Zhu, Wenheng Li, and Qianzhen Zhang

Empower Label Propagation in Heterogeneous Information Networks ... 167
Keqi Zhou, Zhiqiong Wang, Jinyi Chen, Xian Zhang, and Junchang Xin

FedSketchFair: Efficient and Fair Federated Learning Under Domain Skew via Sketch-Based Aggregation ... 184
Yuheng Chen, Meifan Zhang, and Lihua Yin

Trajectory Management

Direction-Guided Conditional Denoising for Uncertainty-Aware Pedestrian Trajectory Prediction ... 201
Yongfei Ye, Zichen Wang, Shilei Kuang, and Senzhang Wang

EVT^2: Efficient and Verifiable Trajectory Top-k Queries in Hybrid-Storage Blockchains ... 216
Yusen Mao, Zhongming Yao, Junchang Xin, Chenchen Yan, Yumeng Song, Zhongzhong Jiang, and Zhiqiong Wang

Spatial Relation Modeling for Trajectory-User Linking via Dual-View Graph Learning ... 233
Zida Liu, Lei Zhang, Yutong Wu, Bailong Liu, and Yuhan Min

STMixMamba: A Lightweight Hybrid Model for User Trajectory Forecasting in Location-Based Services ... 249
Meishan Chen, Wei He, Yonghui Xu, Wei Fang, and Lizhen Cui

Video and Image Processing

Dense Audio-Visual Event Localization with Bidirectional Temporal Cross-Modal Alignment and Boundary-Aware Cross-Scale Collaboration ... 269
Lingling Zi, Xiaoyan Zeng, and Xin Cong

High-Confidence Cross-Modal Guided Multimodal Manipulated Media Detection and Localization ... 284
Kexin Zhang

LADI: Logic-Aware Dual Injection for Instruction-Guided Image Editing via Structural-Semantic Disentanglement ... 299
Wenlei Wang, Shuai Xu, and Ali Ibrahim Abba

Recognition of Handwritten Python Code in Academic Exam Settings Using a Multi-stage OCR Pipeline ... 314
Tuan-Minh Do, Cong-Tam Phan, Hoang-Phuc Mai, Ngoc-Bao-Quang Nguyen, and Cao Vu Bui

Special Track

Adaptive Retrieval Over Dual-Layer Graph Memory for Multi-hop Question Answering ... 331
Yaru Zhao, Zhitao Chen, Xueyao Zhang, and Binyang Li

EviDS- KG: A Conflict-Aware Psychiatric Knowledge Graph Benchmark with Dempster–Shafer Evidence Representation ... 343
Kang Yao, Congcong Tian, Quanbo Cheng, Zhijie Ren, Weiwei Fu, and Jinjiang Cui

Diagnosing Override Regimes in Multi-hop RAG Choosers: Decision-Relevant AUC and Rescue-Hurt Geometry ... 355
Qihui Li, Haodong Lu, and Ruixin Kang

Graph Structure Purification: A Two-Stage Defense Against Structural Adversarial Attacks on GNN-Based Network Intrusion Detection Systems ... 369
Manh-Huy Dang, Xuan-Trang Phan-Thi, Thanh-Thao Truong, Hung-Chen Truong, and Thanh-Nam Tran

VeilSearch: Split-Vector Local Differential Privacy for Encrypted Cross-Modal Retrieval ... 381
Yingying Qi, Jiabei Wang, Xugong Qin, and Yongbin Zhou

CorrTie: Correction-Aware Tie-Breaking for Active Learning with Vision-Language Models ... 397
Duc Tai Phan, Tri Nguyen Thai, Khoa Minh Nguyen, Nhut Minh Nguyen, and Duc Ngoc Minh Dang

DACMRec: A Dual-Level Augmented Contrastive Meta-Learning Model for Next POI Recommendation ... 408
RuYue Wang, Wei He, and Zhen Feng

Hierarchical Prototype Reasoning Network for Few-Shot and Zero-Shot Learning ... 425
Tu Nguyen Anh, Nhan Huu Tran, and Vinh Dinh Nguyen

Impact of DICOM Preprocessing Strategies on Chest X-Ray Abnormality Detection ... 440
Thi-Bich-Tra Le, Ngoc-Duy Le, Tuan-Minh Do, Trung-Nguyen Hoang, Ly-Minh-Hoang Tran, and Thi-Thu-Hong Phan

Persistence-Aware Reward Design for Closed-Loop Reinforcement Learning-Based Network Intrusion Defense ... 456
Yen Vy Trinh Nguyen, Le Binh Ho, Tuan Anh Pham, Hoang Tri Nguyen, and Hoang Dinh Mai

A Multi-LLM Collaborative Framework for Chemical Warehouse Safety Assessment with Knowledge Distillation ... 471
Li Xu

A Weakly Supervised Approach to Student–Major Fit Prediction Using Latent Behavioral Factors ... 484
Tuan Phong Tran, Van Vu Nguyen, Quang Ha Nguyen, and Thuy Hang Nguyen

Assessing Uncertainty in Stock Returns: A Gaussian Mixture Distribution-Based Method ... 495
Yanlong Wang, Jian Xu, Hongkang Zhang, Shao-Lun Huang, Danny Dongning Sun, and Xiao-Ping Zhang

Diagnosing Domain Shift in Wav2Vec2-Based Cross-Corpus Speech Emotion Recognition ... 508
Hoang-Anh-Hong Trinh and Tran-Ngoc-Tran Le

REM-CaR: Retrieval-Augmented Generation Enhanced Medical Case-Based Reasoner ... 520
Zhiliang Li, Beihong Jin, Yuhui Chen, Tao Gong, and Yu Fu

FLESC: Flexible Stripeless Erasure Coding Scheme for In-Memory Storage Systems ... 537
Xiao Li, Guiwen Luo, Yaqiang Zhang, Yaqian Zhao, and Jing Wang

MADRQ: A Multi-agent Demonstration-Guided Framework for Multi-dimensional Range Query Optimization ... 551
Yabin Liu and Chaokun Wang

Panel-Aware Best-of-K Selection for Mental-Health Support Dialogue 566
Kang Yao, Quanbo Cheng, Zhijie Ren, Weiwei Fu, and Jinjiang Cui

PBSM: A Prediction-Based Switch Migration Framework for Controller Utilization Reduction in Distributed SDN 577
Firas Zobary

Structured Similar-Column Retrieval for Long-Tail Column Type Annotation 592
Changlong Wang, Huimei Tian, Zhixiong Yin, Wenhao Zhao, and Pengjuan Lu

Special and Industrial Tracks

A LLM-Powered Multi-agent System for Cross-View Integration in Digital Government Systems 607
Chang Xie, Haoyi Shang, Canqiang Li, and Keman Huang

A Blockchain-Based Framework for Fine-Grained Fair Data Trading with Verifiable Policy Compliance 617
Hai Liang, Peng Chen, Changsong Yang, Yujue Wang, Yong Ding, and Qianhong Wu

SADA: Balancing Attack Strength and Visual Fidelity in Unrestricted Adversarial Attacks 631
Hui Li, Yanrong Lu, Wencheng Yang, Ji Zhang, Taotao Cai, and Kaize Shi

Sensitive Data Protection for Text-to-SQL Tasks in Large Language Models ... 643
Weiwei Yang, Junrui Lu, Rize Jin, and Joon-Young Paik

The First 3D Integrated Web-Based Seft-Visualization Blockchain Structure 655
Anh-Khoa Ngo-Ho, Hoang-Du Thach, and Anh-Khoi Ngo-Ho

Demo Track

THESIS-CHECKER: An LLM-Based Configurable Service for Thesis Compliance Review 667
Ruixiao Huang, Ruize Gao, Weilong Ding, Zihang Yin, and Zhuofeng Zhao

DySRec: Dynamic Context-Aware Psychometric Scale Recommendation via Multi-Agent Collaboration ... 671
Yanzeng Li, Xiaoning Cao, Jialun Zhong, Jianpeng Hu, Jiangshan Tan, Ningning Liu, Feng Xiang, and Shasha Han

TraceTG: A Traceable Testing Platform for Developing a Temporal Graph Database Management System ... 676
Jinghe Song and Jiacheng Chen

iCoLoc: An Interactive System for Spatial Co-location Pattern Mining via LLM-Guided Intent and Contrastive Preference Learning ... 681
Xijia Ye, Xinran Xu, Jing Huang, Qi Han, and Xuguang Bao

PCTR-Miner: A Tourism Route Recommendation System Based on Circular Co-location Pattern Mining ... 685
Qi Han, Yao Qin, and Xuguang Bao

GCSS-Miner: A Graph-Based Co-location Siting System for EV Charging Piles ... 690
Jing Huang, Mingsai Ban, and Xuguang Bao

SKTQ: A Privacy-Preserving Continuous Spatial Keyword Top-k Query System in Cloud-Fog Environments ... 695
Xueling Hu, Yiping Teng, Bingfeng Yu, and Gang Wang

MMIL-CAD: A Multimodal MIL Visual Analytics System for Clinician-Assisted IBD Diagnosis ... 700
Tianya Zhu, Haiwei Pan, Kejia Zhang, Chunling Chen, Yajie Liu, and Xinyu Liu

IFQAIR-LLM: Intelligent Financial Question Answering Integrated with Intention Recognition Based on Large Language Model ... 704
Fangshu Chen, Junjun Sun, Junqi Pan, and Jiahui Wang

Author Index ... 709

Neural Networks and Learning

AV-MultiDet: Frame-Level Multimodal Learning for Fine-Grained Deepfake Detection and Temporal Localization

Ngoc-Phuong-Linh Nguyen and Tran-Ngoc-Tran Le(✉)

FPT University, Greenwich Vietnam, Ho Chi Minh campus, Vietnam
linhnnpgcs220260@fpt.edu.vn , tranltn2@fe.edu.vn

Abstract. The proliferation of multimodal deepfakes spanning static image forgeries, audio manipulations, video face swaps, and synchronized audio-visual fabrications demands detection systems that operate reliably across heterogeneous forgery types within a unified forensic pipeline. Existing works predominantly address a single modality or task in isolation, leaving a systematic cross-modality and cross-dataset evaluation gap in the literature. In this work, we evaluate a series of evolutionary baselines, ranging from static forensics to multimodal classification, through four progressively stronger detection pipelines: a triple stream spatial forensics model for static image detection, a gated fusion classifier for pre extracted audio visual features, an end to end cross attention multimodal classifier, and finally our core contribution: AV-MultiDet is a fully supervised multi task localization network for joint forgery classification and fine grained temporal boundary estimation. The multi-task pipeline adapts the WMMT framework to a fully-supervised end-to-end setting, introducing an EDA-driven metadata-aligned 64-frame sampling strategy that captures real-to-fake transition dynamics with sub-0.2 s boundary precision. We conduct systematic evaluation across five diverse benchmarks including FakeAVCeleb, LAV-DF, Hi-DF, PolyGlotFake, and AV-Deepfake1M++, encompassing intra-domain, cross-domain, multilingual, and large-scale distribution-shift scenarios. Our framework achieves 88.8% mAP and 93.4% AR on LAV-DF temporal localization, outperforming all weakly-supervised baselines by over 15 mAP points, while maintaining competitive cross-domain accuracy of 78% on AV-Deepfake1M++ with only 1,400 fine-tuning samples.

Keywords: Deepfake Detection · Multimodal Processing · Multitask Learning · Audio-Visual Fusion · Temporal Localization

1 Introduction

AI-generated synthetic media, commonly known as deepfakes, pose a growing threat to the integrity of web-based information ecosystems. Deepfake-related financial fraud on social networks has risen sharply in recent years, and the

L. Ding et al. (Eds.): APWeb-WAIM 2026, LNCS 16995, pp. 3–17, 2027.
https://doi.org/10.1007/978-981-92-5699-0_1

market for deepfake detection technology is expanding rapidly, which underscores the need for scalable and robust detection systems under realistic large-scale online conditions.

Modern multimodal deepfakes include static image manipulations, audio-only voice cloning, video face-swaps, and synchronized audio-visual forgeries [1]. A particularly challenging case is *partial forgery*, where manipulated segments are embedded within otherwise authentic videos. Such content requires not only binary detection but also precise *temporal localization* of forged intervals for effective content moderation, digital forensics, and trust assessment.

Existing approaches typically address a single modality or a single task. Unimodal methods [7,8] achieve strong intra-domain accuracy but degrade when manipulations span multiple modalities. Multimodal classifiers [5,11] improve robustness yet still treat each video as globally real or fake, without temporal boundaries. Weakly supervised localization methods [13,14] reduce annotation cost but lose localization precision under domain shift. To our knowledge, no prior work jointly addresses (i) multi-modality forensics across image, audio, and audio-visual streams, (ii) fine-grained temporal localization with sub-0.2 s boundary precision, and (iii) systematic cross-domain evaluation under severe distribution shift, within a single end-to-end framework.

AV-MultiDet targets large-scale online video streams, where diverse forgery types coexist and labeled target-domain data are limited. Four progressive detection pipelines are developed, covering the main forgery modalities and culminating in a fully supervised multi-task localization network. The final pipeline adapts the WMMT framework [13] to a fully supervised setting and introduces an EDA-driven, metadata-aligned 64-frame sampling strategy that captures real-to-fake transitions with sub-0.2 s boundary precision.

Our main contributions are as follows:

- A **multi-stage comparative study** that establishes baseline performances for static image forgery, gated audio-visual fusion, cross-attention multimodal classification, and multi-task temporal localization, demonstrating the necessity of fine-grained boundary estimation in multimodal deepfake forensics.
- An **end-to-end multi-task architecture** (AV-MultiDet) that combines ViT for visual artifact extraction, HuBERT for phonetic representations, and a Modality-Aware Expert Selector with a modified Temporal Property Preserving Attention (TPPA) mechanism for persistent cross-modal forgery verification.
- **Comprehensive temporal localization and cross-domain evaluation**: on LAV-DF [3], AV-MultiDet achieves 88.8% mAP and 93.4% AR, exceeding weakly supervised baselines [12–14] by more than 15 mAP points with temporal boundary MAE < 0.1 s at 25 FPS; on AV-Deepfake1M++ [1], it attains 78% accuracy and 69.2% mAP using only 1,400 fine-tuning samples, which demonstrates practical adaptability in label-scarce target domains.

The remainder of this paper is organized as follows. Section 2 reviews related work. Section 3 describes the four pipelines and the AV-MultiDet architecture. Section 4 presents the experimental setup and datasets. Section 5 reports results and ablation studies. Section 6 concludes with limitations and directions for practical deployment scenarios.

2 Related Work

2.1 Unimodal Deepfake Detection

Early research on deepfake forensics focused on unimodal methods that analyse either visual or audio signals in isolation. FaceForensics++ [10] established a large-scale visual benchmark and showed that convolutional models such as XceptionNet can effectively capture spatial artifacts from diverse face manipulations, while later work exploited temporal cues including abnormal eye-blinking [8] and blending boundaries around the face region [7]. These approaches are computationally efficient and achieve high accuracy in controlled settings, but they are inherently limited when manipulations affect multiple modalities simultaneously or when fine-grained temporal localization is required.

2.2 Multimodal Deepfake Detection

To address cross-modal inconsistencies, multimodal methods jointly process audio and visual streams. DF-TransFusion [5] integrates speech and lip movements via cross-attention, and M2TR [11] employs multi-scale transformers over spatial and frequency-domain representations, reporting strong performance on curated benchmarks such as FF++ [10] and FakeAVCeleb [4]. These studies demonstrate that combining modalities improves resilience against sophisticated forgeries, yet most models still operate at the video level and output only global real/fake decisions without frame-level temporal boundaries.

2.3 Multitask Learning and Temporal Localization

Multitask learning provides a natural framework for combining classification and localization objectives. SJEDD [17] uses a joint embedding space based on CLIP to align visual features with semantic labels and shows strong cross-dataset generalization for face forgery detection. Closer to the present work, WMMT [13] introduces a weakly supervised multimodal framework that jointly learns audio, visual, and multimodal classifiers while localizing manipulated temporal segments; on LAV-DF [3], it sets a leading benchmark for weakly supervised localization, and its cross-dataset evaluation on AV-Deepfake1M [1] highlights the difficulty of maintaining temporal precision under severe domain shift.

Despite this progress, existing multimodal systems either rely on pre-extracted features, operate in a weakly supervised regime, or lack fine-grained temporal evaluation under cross-domain conditions. In contrast, AV-MultiDet leverages a 64-frame representative sampling strategy for end-to-end multimodal learning and introduces a fully supervised multi-task architecture for joint multimodal classification and frame-level localization, systematically evaluated in both intra-domain and cross-domain settings on FakeAVCeleb [4], LAV-DF [3], and AV-Deepfake1M++ [1] . Beyond these works, recent studies from 2025–2026 explore multimodal deepfake detectors with lightweight architectures, self-supervised pretraining, and diffusion-aware forensic pipelines [6,9] emphasising real-time deployment and robustness to rapidly evolving generative models; our contribution is complementary, providing a fully supervised frame-level localization benchmark across five datasets and a systematic cross-domain analysis that offers an upper-bound perspective when rich annotations and end-to-end multimodal learning are available.

3 Methodology

To counter increasingly sophisticated deepfakes, we adopt a series of progressive baseline pipelines (Table 1) that evolves from static image forensics to multimodal audio-visual synchronization. By shifting from global multiclass classification to fine-grained anomaly localization, the system can detect subtle spoof segments that are imperceptible to humans but critical for identifying high-fidelity manipulations.

In this table, pipelines No.1–3 serve as evolutionary baselines. Specifically, No.3 (Multi-Cross) provides the fundamental multimodal fusion architecture that underpins the development of our proposed AV-MultiDet (No.4)

Table 1. Comparative performance of preliminary baseline pipelines (No. 1–3) and the proposed AV-MultiDet (No. 4)

No.	Name	Methodology	Performances	
			Intra-domain	Cross-domain
1	Hybrid Spatio-Spectral-Noise Image	Focuses on spatial forgery artifacts, including texture, blending boundaries, and lighting inconsistencies, using image backbones such as ResNet and EfficientNet.	**HiDF:** Acc: 98%	–
2	AVTripBranchs	Integrates feature vectors from both audio and visual streams during training, with particular attention to mouth-region and lip-motion cues.	**FakeAVCeleb:** Acc: 99%	**PolyGlotFake:** Acc: 71%
3	Multi-Cross	Models temporal consistency between audio and visual streams using an end-to-end architecture that receives full-face inputs to capture broader facial dynamics.	**FakeAVCeleb:** Acc: 98%	–
4	AV-MultiDet	Uses a multi-task learning framework to jointly detect forged content and localize manipulated temporal segments.	**LAV-DF:** Acc: 94% mAP: 88% mAR: 93.4%	**AV-Deepfake1M++:** Acc: 78% mAP: 69.2% mAR: 78.2%

Notes: * Few-shot model, automatically generated online

3.1 Multi-modal Baseline (Multi-cross)

Dataset and Preprocessing

We use the FakeAVCeleb dataset [4], which comprises 500 real videos and more than 19,000 manipulated samples generated by Wav2Lip, FSGAN, DeepFake, and FaceSwap. Its synchronised audio-video structure supports both unimodal and multimodal training across four categories: Real-Real, Fake-Real, Real-Fake, and Fake-Fake. Since deepfake manipulations affect not only lip synchronisation but also more subtle artifacts across the full face, we extract full-face regions rather than cropping only the mouth; each sample is represented by a fixed sequence of 16 frames with the corresponding audio segment, preserving temporal alignment between modalities. For our experiments, samples are partitioned into training, validation, and test subsets based on subject identities, ensuring no identity overlap across splits and preventing subject identity leakage.

Model Architecture

The baseline architecture, termed **Multi-Cross**, follows an end-to-end multimodal learning framework in which audio and visual streams are first processed in separate branches and then fused through cross-attention to capture cross-modal inconsistencies. The visual branch uses MTCNN to detect and crop the facial region from each frame, which is resized to 224 × 224 and encoded by a pre-trained Vision Transformer (ViT), while the audio branch uses Wav2Vec2 to extract contextual representations from raw waveforms that are temporally aligned with the visual frames. A cross-attention module then allows audio and visual features to attend to each other, producing a joint audio-visual representation that is used for video-level classification (Fig. 1).

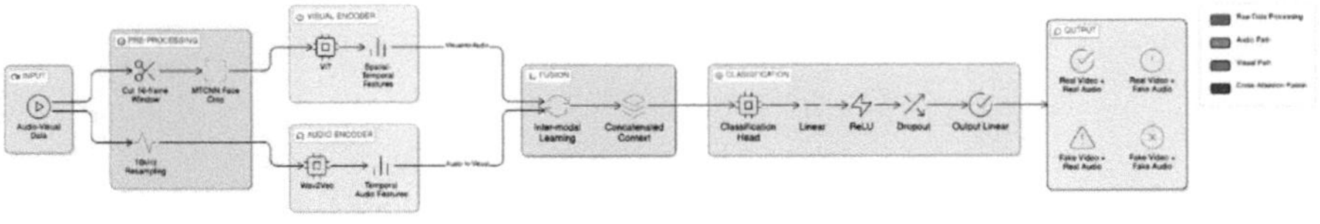

Fig. 1. Spatio-temporal cross-attention framework for the Multi-Cross baseline.

3.2 Multi-modal Classification and Localization (AV-MultiDet)

Datasets and Preprocessing

AV-MultiDet is evaluated on LAV-DF [3] and AV-Deepfake1M++ [1]. LAV-DF is a multi-task benchmark with more than 136,000 videos across four balanced categories (original, audio-only fake, video-only fake, dual-modality fake), which supports precise temporal localization of forged segments. We follow the official split provided by the dataset, using 5,000 videos for training, 2,000 for validation, and 2,000 for testing. AV-Deepfake1M++ provides over two million videos from

2,000 subjects with diverse audio-visual manipulations and serves as a challenging evaluation of cross-domain robustness; we adopt the official split with 1,000 videos for training, 400 for validation, and 2,000 for testing.

For high-precision analysis, each input video is decomposed into a visual stream and an audio stream. Instead of dividing videos into arbitrary segments, we sample a fixed window of 64 consecutive frames whose position is aligned with the forgery metadata in the dataset annotations. During training, the sampling position is chosen within a valid range derived from the annotated fake interval so that the selected clip fully covers the forged segment; if multiple forged segments are present, one segment is randomly selected in each iteration. A small temporal margin is added around the manipulation boundaries when computing the valid range, ensuring sufficient real-to-fake transition context while preventing the forged region from being positioned too close to the clip boundaries. Most manipulated segments are transient, typically 0.2–1.5 s (5–35 frames), so a 64-frame window at 25 FPS (2.56 s) provides an effective temporal horizon for capturing temporal transitions while preserving continuity. Audio features have higher temporal resolution than visual frames, so temporal pooling is applied to synchronise audio representations with the 64-frame visual window.

Model Architecture

The AV-MultiDet architecture builds on the Multi-Cross pipeline as an upgraded localization framework, inheriting several of its multimodal components while adapting them to fine-grained temporal boundary estimation through parallel feature extraction for vision and audio. The visual branch extends the original Vision Transformer (ViT) stream by combining it with a ResNet18 backbone equipped with a high-pass filter to capture both semantic content and high-frequency artifacts left by generative models, yielding a visual representation F_v. The audio branch replaces the previous Wav2Vec encoder with HuBERT to obtain deeper phonetic and acoustic features, forming an audio representation F_a.

Feature Enhancement and Fusion. A feature enhancement and fusion module models intra-modal and cross-modal dependencies. Intra-feature enhancement refines F_v and F_a separately, while inter-feature enhancement exchanges information between modalities to detect synchronisation discrepancies such as mismatched lip motion and speech, producing enriched features F'_v, F'_a, and a joint multimodal feature F'_m.

Temporal Property Preserving Attention (TPPA), inspired by the mechanism proposed in [13], extends beyond simple temporal weighting. Whereas the original TPPA primarily emphasises suspicious temporal regions through correlation-based weighting, our implementation verifies whether anomalous patterns persist consistently across neighbouring temporal contexts before reinforcing them. Given local audio-visual features, TPPA applies masked multi-head attention with positional encoding to aggregate contextual information from adjacent frames within a short temporal window, suppressing transient artifacts such as motion blur or isolated noisy frames and strengthening temporally consistent forgery cues. This design refines feature representations for more accurate frame-level boundary localization under a fully supervised end-to-end framework (Fig. 2).

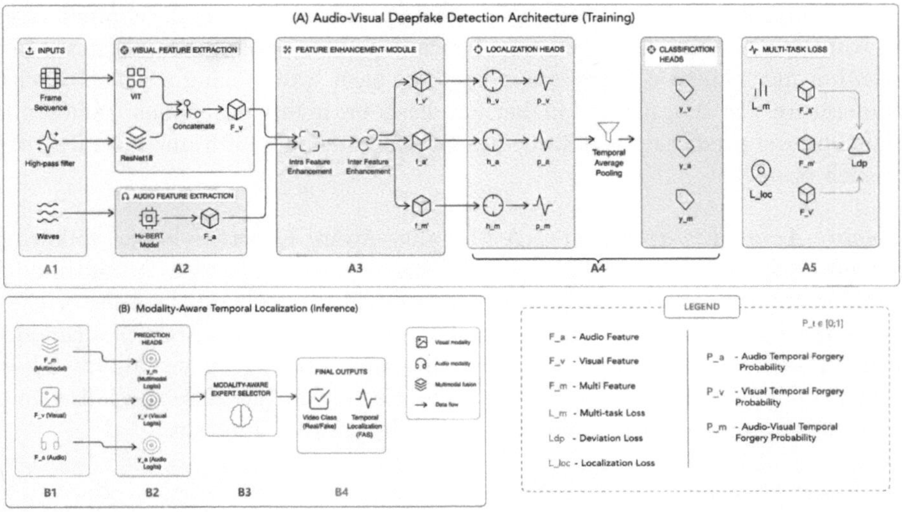

Fig. 2. Overall architecture of AV-MultiDet. (A) Training pipeline: multimodal visual and audio features are extracted, refined by the TPPA-based feature enhancement module, and jointly optimised through localization and classification heads using multi-task learning. (B) Inference pipeline: a full video is processed using sequential 64-frame windows; clip-level predictions are aggregated for video-level classification, while the highest-scoring window is further analysed to estimate frame-level forgery boundaries using the Forgery Activation Sequence (FAS).

Relation to WMMT. Our framework builds on the multi-branch classification/localization paradigm introduced by WMMT [13] and reuses the deviation-perceiving loss formulation to magnify feature discrepancies between authentic and forged regions. However, AV-MultiDet differs from WMMT in three key aspects. First, it operates in a fully supervised regime with frame-level temporal annotations instead of relying on weak video-level labels, enabling more precise boundary estimation. Second, it introduces a metadata-aligned 64-frame sampling strategy that explicitly targets real-to-fake transition dynamics and provides a representative temporal horizon for end-to-end multimodal learning. Third, it extends the original TPPA mechanism with local masked multi-head attention that verifies whether cross-modal anomalies persist consistently across neighbouring contexts before reinforcing them, rather than simply reweighting isolated high-scoring frames.

Localization and Classification Heads. After feature enhancement, three temporal localization heads h_a, h_v, and h_m operate on audio-only, visual-only, and multimodal features, respectively. Each head is implemented as a lightweight temporal block based on one-dimensional convolutions along the time axis, producing frame-level scores p_a, p_v, p_m while preserving the original temporal resolution.

Clip-level classification heads y_a, y_v, and y_m aggregate frame-level predictions via soft attention pooling. Instead of mean or max pooling, a parameter-free attention mechanism computes a weight for each frame using a softmax with temperature $\tau = 0.3$, placing higher emphasis on highly suspicious frames; the final clip-level prediction is obtained as the weighted sum of frame-level features for each branch.

Modality-Aware Expert Selector. A Modality-Aware Expert Selector, following the multitask paradigm in [13], acts as a decision gate at inference. A multimodal classifier first predicts the forgery type at the video level, and the selector then routes the sample to the most appropriate localization head: the multimodal head h_m for joint audio-visual forgeries, the visual head h_v for visual-only fakes, and the audio head h_a for audio-only fakes. Each head therefore specialises in a particular manipulation scenario and supports ablation analysis.

Multi-task Loss and Inference Strategy. The overall loss function adapts the WMMT formulation [13] and combines three components:

$$\mathcal{L}_{\text{total}} = \mathcal{L}_{\text{cls}} + \mathcal{L}_{\text{loc}} + \mathcal{L}_{\text{dp}}. \tag{1}$$

The classification loss $\mathcal{L}_{\text{cls}}$ supervises four-way video-level classification (Both Real, Both Fake, Visual Fake, Audio Fake) with branch-specific weights, the localization loss $\mathcal{L}_{\text{loc}}$ encourages accurate frame-level prediction of real and fake segments for each branch, and the deviation-perceiving loss $\mathcal{L}_{\text{dp}}$ magnifies feature discrepancies between manipulated and authentic regions and is applied only to samples that contain at least one forged modality, following the original formulation in [13].

During training, each video contributes one 64-frame segment sampled by the metadata-aligned strategy. At inference time, the full video is divided into a sequence of 64-frame windows. For each window, the model produces both a classification score and a frame-level Forgery Activation Sequence (FAS). Video-level classification is obtained by aggregating the classification scores across all windows. For temporal localization, the window with the highest classification score is selected as the candidate manipulated region, and its FAS is post-processed using adaptive thresholding, grouping consecutive positive frames, and merging neighbouring segments to determine the final manipulation boundaries.

Implementation Details

AV-MultiDet is trained with the Adam optimizer, a learning rate of 1×10^{-5}, batch size 32, and 100 epochs. The multi-task objective combines cross-entropy loss for four-way video-level classification (Both Real, Both Fake, Visual Fake,

Audio Fake), a BCEWithLogits-based localization loss for frame-level prediction of real and fake segments in each branch, and a deviation-perceiving loss following the original formulation in [13] to magnify feature discrepancies between manipulated and authentic regions. Task weights are set to 0.6 : 1.0 : 0.2 for classification, localization, and deviation-perceiving components, respectively. To improve robustness, we apply simple data augmentation: random crop, flip, and JPEG compression in the visual branch, and gain perturbation, speed perturbation, and time masking in the audio branch.

The resulting model has approximately 21.9 million trainable parameters and 199.6 million parameters in total. On a single high-end GPU, the average inference time is about 0.8 s per full-length video, with a GPU processing time of roughly 795 ms and peak memory usage around 5.4 GB per video. This footprint is well suited to offline moderation pipelines, but is not yet ideal for latency-critical edge deployment; improving throughput and reducing memory usage via model pruning, knowledge distillation, and more lightweight backbones is therefore an important direction for making the framework practical in real-time, large-scale monitoring scenarios.

4 Experiments and Results

4.1 Classification Model on FakeAVCeleb

Performance Analysis

We first evaluate the Multi-Cross baseline on FakeAVCeleb [4]. The model is trained for 50 epochs and converges rapidly, achieving stable performance on both validation and test sets. On the held-out test set, it reaches an overall accuracy of 98.6% and consistently high F1-scores across all four classes, demonstrating that the architecture can reliably distinguish between Real-Real, Real-Fake, Fake-Real, and Fake-Fake samples.

Building on these results, we extend the evaluation to a more demanding setting that requires not only video-level classification but also frame-level temporal localization of forged segments.

4.2 Multi-modal Classification and Localization on LAV-DF

Classification Performance

We evaluate AV-MultiDet on LAV-DF [3]. The multi-task architecture is trained jointly for classification and temporal localization and achieves its best performance after 31 epochs. On 2,000 full-length test videos, the model attains 94% accuracy with balanced precision and recall across all four classes, as reported in Table 2.

Ablation: Audio-Only vs Visual-Only

To quantify the contribution of each modality, we evaluate variants that use only audio or only visual input. On LAV-DF, the audio-only model achieves 0.98 F1-score, while the visual-only model degrades to 0.84, confirming that

Table 2. Classification report on the LAV-DF test set.

Class	Precision	Recall	F1-score	Support
Real–Real	0.99	0.88	0.93	500
Real–Fake	0.96	0.91	0.93	500
Fake–Real	0.88	0.97	0.92	500
Fake–Fake	0.98	0.92	0.95	500
Accuracy	–	–	0.94	2000

speech cues provide stronger supervision than visual artifacts in this dataset. This is consistent with the characteristics of LAV-DF: audio forgery introduces globally discriminative synthesis and compression artifacts, making clip-level classification relatively straightforward, whereas incorporating the visual branch introduces additional variability due to appearance changes, illumination, pose, and subtle visual artifacts, resulting in a slight trade-off in classification accuracy. Visual features alone are therefore insufficient when deepfake artifacts are subtle or visually consistent with real data, motivating the use of multimodal fusion and stronger visual encoders (Table 3).

Table 3. Ablation on LAV-DF: audio-only vs visual-only classification.

Setting	Precision	Recall	F1-score
Audio only	0.98	0.98	0.98
Visual only	0.84	0.84	0.84
Full model	0.94	0.94	0.94

Temporal Localization Metrics

Temporal localization performance is evaluated using mean Average Precision (mAP) and Average Recall (AR) across several IoU thresholds. Table 4 reports results for the full model and unimodal variants.

The full model achieves 88.8% mAP and 93.4% AR on average, clearly outperforming both unimodal variants across all IoU thresholds. Boundary-level analysis shows a mean absolute error of approximately 2.18 frames at the start and 1.24 frames at the end of forged segments, corresponding to less than 0.1 s at 25 FPS. While this mild early-start and late-end bias improves recall, it may over-flag borderline content around short manipulations, and refining the TPPA module and post-processing thresholds to reduce this asymmetry is an important direction for future work. Although audio provides highly discriminative cues for clip-level classification, precise boundary estimation is inherently more challenging because modern speech synthesis produces smooth temporal transitions; by incorporating complementary visual cues, the full model refines boundary estimation and achieves substantially better localization performance.

Table 4. Temporal localization on LAV-DF at different IoU thresholds.

	Full model		Audio only		Visual only	
IoU Threshold	AP (%)	AR (%)	AP (%)	AR (%)	AP (%)	AR (%)
0.1	95.5	98.2	65.5	66.5	54.4	66.6
0.3	92.7	96.5	63.1	64.6	48.5	60.5
0.5	87.9	93.4	60.4	63.1	36.2	49.1
0.7	79.1	85.4	58.2	61.1	18.9	32.6
Average	**88.8**	**93.4**	61.8	63.8	39.4	52.1

Comparison with Existing Localization Frameworks

Table 5 compares AV-MultiDet against representative localization methods on the LAV-DF benchmark. Prior methods such as WMMT, CoLA, and LOCO operate under a weakly supervised regime using pre-extracted features (e.g., TSN and BYOL-A), whereas AV-MultiDet is trained end-to-end with fine-grained labels. This comparison is not intended to assert mere numerical dominance; rather, it serves to establish a performance upper bound, demonstrating the potential for effectively exploiting raw multimodal information when supported by full supervision in a realistic forensic environment.

Table 5. Comparison with state-of-the-art methods on LAV-DF for temporal forgery localization. † weakly-supervised. ‡ pre-extracted features (TSN + BYOL-A); not directly comparable to end-to-end methods.

Method	Features	AP@0.5	AP@0.75	AP@0.95	AR@100	mAP
MDS	Visual‡	12.78	1.62	0.00	32.15	–
AVFusion	Audio+Visual‡	65.38	23.89	0.11	52.11	–
BA-TFD [2]	Audio+Visual‡	76.90	38.50	0.25	58.42	–
BA-TFD+ [2]	Audio+Visual‡	96.30	84.96	4.44	81.62	–
ActionFormer [15]	Visual‡	95.34	90.20	23.73	90.41	–
UMMAFormer [16]	Audio+Visual‡	**98.83**	**95.54**	**37.61**	92.48	–
CoLA† [14]	Audio+Visual‡	–	–	–	–	51.54
LOCO† [12]	Audio+Visual‡	–	–	–	–	82.65
WMMT† [13]	Audio+Visual‡	–	–	–	–	73.27
AV-MultiDet (Ours)	**End-to-end (raw)**	87.90	–	–	**93.40**	**88.80**

4.3 Cross-Domain Evaluation on AV-Deepfake1M++

Dataset Characteristics
AV-Deepfake1M++ [1] contains more than one million videos from over 2,000 subjects with diverse audio, visual, and multimodal manipulations. Compared with LAV-DF [3], its forged segments are generally shorter, videos often contain multiple manipulated intervals, and real content exhibits higher variability, noise, and compression artifacts. These differences create a strong domain shift and provide a stringent test of the modelâĂŹs robustness.

Compared with LAV-DF, its forged segments are generally shorter (often below 1 s), many videos contain multiple disjoint manipulated intervals, and real content exhibits higher variability, noise, and compression artifacts, creating a strong domain shift and a substantially harder localization scenario.

Classification and Ablation Results
For cross-domain evaluation, the model is first trained on LAV-DF and then fine-tuned on a subset of approximately 1,400 AV-Deepfake1M++ samples. After 25 epochs of adaptation, it reaches an overall accuracy of 78% on a 2,000-video test set, as summarised in Table 6.

Table 6. Classification report on the AV-Deepfake1M++ test set.

Class	Precision	Recall	F1-score	Support
Real–Real	0.93	0.44	0.60	500
Fake–Real	0.64	0.94	0.76	500
Real–Fake	0.81	0.85	0.83	500
Fake–Fake	0.90	0.89	0.90	500
Accuracy	–	–	0.78	2000

To quantify modality contributions under domain shift, we evaluate audio-only and visual-only variants on AV-Deepfake1M++. The audio-only model achieves a precision of 0.85, recall of 0.81, and F1-score of 0.81, while the visual-only model attains 0.84 precision, 0.83 recall, and 0.83 F1-score; in comparison, the full multimodal model reaches 0.89 precision, 0.78 recall, and 0.78 F1-score. These results indicate that unimodal branches retain strong classification performance under severe domain shift, whereas the joint multimodal model trades some clip-level accuracy for the richer representations needed for temporal localization.

Temporal Localization and Comparison to Baselines
Temporal localization under domain shift is evaluated using the same IoU-based mAP and AR metrics. Table 7 summarises the performance of AV-MultiDet and its unimodal variants, and Table 8 compares our model with prior work trained only on LAV-DF.

Although performance degrades relative to the intra-domain setting as the IoU threshold increases, the full model maintains substantially higher mAP

Table 7. Temporal localization on AV-Deepfake1M++ at different IoU thresholds.

	Full model		Audio only		Visual only	
IoU Threshold	AP (%)	AR (%)	AP (%)	AR (%)	AP (%)	AR (%)
0.1	85.5	93.3	60.3	65.4	58.4	66.6
0.3	81.1	89.0	48.8	56.3	55.9	63.7
0.5	69.1	77.9	22.1	35.2	50.1	58.4
0.7	41.1	52.3	2.46	10.3	33.2	43.5
Average	**69.2**	**78.2**	33.4	41.8	49.4	58.1

Table 8. Cross-domain performance on AV-Deepfake1M++ [1]. Models trained on LAV-DF [3]. † zero-shot cross-dataset evaluation without fine-tuning.

Method	Fine-tune Samples	mAP (%)	AR (%)
CoLA† [14]	0	6.50	–
LOCO† [12]	0	18.89	–
WMMT† [13]	0	13.00	63.08
AV-MultiDet (Ours)	**1,400**	**69.2**	**78.2**

and AR than its unimodal variants and achieves clearly stronger cross-domain temporal localization than prior methods. This comparison should be interpreted as an upper bound rather than a strictly fair apples-to-apples benchmark: CoLA, LOCO, and WMMT are evaluated zero-shot on AV-Deepfake1M++, whereas AV-MultiDet receives a limited adaptation budget of 1,400 fine-tuning samples. A fully fair setting would require retraining or adapting each baseline under the same label budget, which we leave to future work due to the substantial computational cost.

Qualitative Failure Patterns. The boundary-offset analysis shows that AV-MultiDet tends to trigger slightly earlier at the beginning of forged segments and to over-extend detections at the end, which improves recall but can over-flag borderline content. On LAV-DF, very short audio-only manipulations with smooth synthetic speech transitions remain challenging, leading to small temporal drifts around the ground-truth boundaries, whereas longer dual-modality forgeries are localised more reliably. Under cross-domain conditions on AV-Deepfake1M++, failures are often associated with highly compressed or noisy videos containing multiple disjoint forged intervals, where subtle visual-only artifacts may be overshadowed by stronger acoustic cues (Fig. 3).

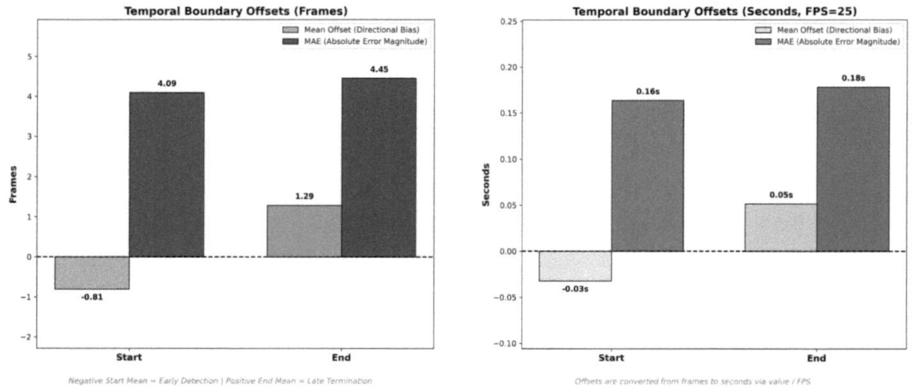

Fig. 3. Temporal boundary offset analysis in frames (left) and seconds (right).

5 Conclusion

This paper presents AV-MultiDet, a progressive four-pipeline framework for multimodal deepfake detection and fine-grained temporal localization. By unifying static image forensics, audio-visual fusion, and multi-task localization within a single multimodal benchmark, AV-MultiDet addresses the cross-modality and cross-dataset evaluation gap in existing literature. The proposed end-to-end multi-task architecture achieves 88.8% mAP and 93.4% AR on LAV-DF, outperforming all weakly supervised baselines by over 15 mAP points, while maintaining 78% cross-domain accuracy on AV-Deepfake1M++ with only 1,400 fine-tuning samples. Despite these encouraging results, several challenges remain. The proposed framework still relies on frame-level temporal annotations and exhibits a strong dependence on acoustic features, which makes subtle visual-only face-swaps without prominent audio artifacts harder to detect. Performance may further degrade under significant domain shifts or unseen deepfake generation techniques, and potential dataset bias together with future adversarial adaptation remains an important challenge for robust multimodal forensic systems. Future work will explore lightweight backbone alternatives for real-time web deployment and extend the framework to emerging diffusion-based deepfake modalities.

References

1. Cai, Z., Ghosh, S., Adatia, A.P., Hayat, M., Dhall, A., Stefanov, K.: Av-Deepfake1m: a large-scale LLM-driven audio-visual deepfake dataset. In: Proceedings of the 32nd ACM International Conference on Multimedia (2023)
2. Cai, Z., Ghosh, S., Gedeon, T., Dhall, A., Stefanov, K., Hayat, M.: “Glitch in the Matrix!âĂİ: a large scale benchmark for content driven audio-visual forgery detection and localization. Comput. Vis. Image Underst. **236**, 103818 (2023)

3. Cai, Z., Stefanov, K., Dhall, A., Hayat, M.: Do you really mean that? content driven audio-visual deepfake dataset and multimodal method for temporal forgery localization: anonymous submission paper id 73. In: 2022 International Conference on Digital Image Computing: Techniques and Applications (DICTA), pp. 1–10 (2022)
4. Khalid, H., Tariq, S., Woo, S.S.: FakeAVCeleb: a novel audio-video multimodal deepfake dataset. arXiv:abs/2108.05080 (2021)
5. Kharel, A., Paranjape, M., Bera, A.: DF-Transfusion: multimodal deepfake detection via lip-audio cross-attention and facial self-attention. arXiv:abs/2309.06511 (2023)
6. Koutlis, C., Papadopoulos, S.: AuViRe: audio-visual speech representation reconstruction for deepfake temporal localization. In: 2026 IEEE/CVF Winter Conference on Applications of Computer Vision (WACV), pp. 7168–7177 (2025)
7. Li, L., et al.: Face X-ray for more general face forgery detection (2020)
8. Li, Y., Chang, M.C., Lyu, S.: In Ictu Oculi: exposing AI created fake videos by detecting eye blinking. In: 2018 IEEE International workshop on information forensics and security (WIFS), pp. 1–7. IEEE (2018)
9. Liu, J., Wang, J., Hou, S., Ren, M., Wu, H., He, Z.: Beyond face swapping: a diffusion-based digital human benchmark for multimodal deepfake detection. arXiv:abs/2505.16512 (2025)
10. Rossler, A., Cozzolino, D., Verdoliva, L., Riess, C., Thies, J., Nießner, M.: FaceForensics++: learning to detect manipulated facial images. In: Proceedings of the IEEE/CVF International Conference on Computer Vision, pp. 1–11 (2019)
11. Wang, J., Wu, Z., Chen, J., Jiang, Y.G.: M2TR: multi-modal multi-scale transformers for deepfake detection. In: Proceedings of the 2022 International Conference on Multimedia Retrieval (2021)
12. Wu, J., Xu, W., Lu, W., Luo, X., Yang, R., Guo, S.: Weakly-supervised audio temporal forgery localization via progressive audio-language co-learning network. https://arxiv.org/abs/2505.01880 (2025)
13. Xu, W., Lu, W., Luo, X.: Weakly supervised multimodal temporal forgery localization via multitask learning. arXiv:abs/2508.02179 (2025)
14. Zhang, C., Cao, M., Yang, D., Chen, J., Zou, Y.: CoLA: weakly-supervised temporal action localization with snippet contrastive learning. In: IEEE/CVF Conference on Computer Vision and Pattern Recognition (CVPR), pp. 16005–16014 (2021)
15. Zhang, C.L., Wu, J., Li, Y.: ActionFormer: localizing moments of actions with transformers. ArXiv **abs/2202.07925** (2022)
16. Zhang, R., Wang, H., han Du, M., Liu, H., Zhou, Y., Zeng, Q.: UMMAFormer: a universal multimodal-adaptive transformer framework for temporal forgery localization. In: Proceedings of the 31st ACM International Conference on Multimedia (2023)
17. Zou, M., Yu, B., Zhan, Y., Lyu, S., Ma, K.: Semantics-oriented multitask learning for deepfake detection: a joint embedding approach. IEEE Trans. Circuits Syst. Video Technol. **35**, 9950–9963 (2024)

Continuous-Time Modeling of Crypto Limit Order Books with Liquid Neural Networks

Qiankang Xu[1], Linhan Xia[1], Mingzhan Yang[1], Jingjing Wang[1], Ziwei Yan[1], Tanren Liu[2], and Kai Lei[1(✉)]

[1] ICNLab, SECE, Shenzhen Graduate School, Peking University, Shenzhen, P. R. China
qkxu25@stu.pku.edu.cn, linhanxia@aliyun.com, bingling0812@163.com, {jingjing_wang,yanzw}@pku.edu.cn, leik@pkusz.edu.cn
[2] Sf Technology, Shenzhen, P. R. China
tanrenliu@sf-express.com

Abstract. High-frequency trading in cryptocurrency markets necessitates precise modeling of limit order book (LOB) dynamics. Compared with traditional financial assets, cryptocurrency LOBs exhibit higher volatility and more pronounced microstructural variability, posing challenges for existing predictive models. Most prior approaches adopt discrete time formulations, such as recurrent neural networks and transformer based models, which impose fixed temporal resolutions on inherently continuous and irregular market processes. This discretization may obscure fine-grained temporal patterns and limit the effectiveness of feature representation. To address these critical limitations, we introduce an innovative framework utilizing Liquid Time Constant Neural Networks (LTCs), a continuous-time neural architecture. In this paradigm, the network's internal states evolve seamlessly according to ordinary differential equations (ODEs), with adaptive time constants that dynamically respond to the incoming data stream. This design enables superior capture of high-frequency patterns, directly tackling the core problem of temporal granularity in volatile markets. Evaluations across diverse datasets reveal that our LTC-based methodology outperforms traditional models by **4% to 8%** in key metrics, including accuracy and cross-market generalization. Furthermore, we establish the benchmark for cryptocurrency LOB trend forecasting, complete with publicly accessible datasets available.

Keywords: Liquid neural network · Time series prediction · Limit order book · Benchmark evaluation

1 Introduction

High-frequency trading (HFT) has recently occupied the majority of cryptocurrencies markets [16,25], where split-second decisions are heavily based on

L. Ding et al. (Eds.): APWeb-WAIM 2026, LNCS 16995, pp. 18–32, 2027.
https://doi.org/10.1007/978-981-92-5699-0_2

accurate predictions of the trading trend derived from the limit order book (LOB) [18]. As the primary real-time indicator of market liquidity and price formation, LOB dynamics directly shape trading strategies and profitability [11]. Cryptocurrencies, however, exhibit uniquely high volatility and non-stationary behavior compared to traditional assets–Bitcoin's intraday price swings, for example, even exceed 50%, dwarfing those of most stocks or forex pairs [21]. Moreover, HFT constitutes an even larger share of trading volume in crypto markets, further amplifying their inherent instability [3]. This extreme volatility heightens both the significance and the challenges of making reliable LOB-based predictions, underscoring the need for modeling approaches specifically tailored to crypto.

Despite the centrality of LOB signals in crypto HFT, existing deep-learning methods for LOB-based crypto HFT face two major bottlenecks: first, their reliance on discrete time steps causes them to miss the ultra-high-frequency and irregular order-flow events typical of crypto LOBs, resulting in less accurate predictions [2]; second, they generalize poorly across assets–models trained on Bitcoin often perform poorly on Ethereum or other altcoins because they fail to separate asset-specific microstructure noise from general market dynamics.

To bridge these critical drawbacks of previous methods, we introduce a liquid time constant networks (LTCs) based approach. LTCs based on the continuous-time modeling of neural ordinary differential equations (Neural ODE) [2], and it can seamlessly handle data streams with irregularly spaced arrivals [7], which can better modeling high dynamic data like crypto-LOBs. Moreover, LTCs-based models have better generalization capability through dynamic causal modeling, combined with the hierarchical feedback mechanism of the biological nervous system, the core features (such as the direction of the order flow) can be explicitly distinguished from the background noise. This paper delivers three fundamental contributions in cryptocurrencies LOBs trend prediction:

1. **Benchmark Datasets:** We establish the first benchmark dataset for cryptocurrency limit order book trend prediction, comprising bid and ask observations at microsecond resolution for major assets such as BTC and ETH. Unlike existing datasets that are often restricted to coarse snapshots or short time spans, our dataset preserves fine grained market microstructure dynamics at an ultra high temporal resolution, enabling the modeling of rapid order flow variations and transient liquidity imbalances. In addition, we develop a unified pipeline for data preprocessing and evaluation, which supports fair and reproducible comparisons across predictive models in high frequency trading settings.
2. **LTCs-based approach:** Our approach leverages liquid time constant networks (LTCs), a variety of RNNs as backbone to better capture cryptocurrency LOB dynamics. Unlike traditional RNNs or Attention-based models that process data at fixed intervals, LTCs use continuous-time modeling to naturally handle the irregular, high-frequency updates in crypto markets. The key advantage lies in their adaptive time constants, which automatically

adjust to different market conditions - quickly responding to rapid order flow changes while maintaining stability during volatile periods.

3. **Comprehensive Experiments:** We employed the LTCs model together with other baseline architectures to conduct the Mid-price trend prediction(MPTP) and Market Depth Forecast(MDF) experiments on the BTC dataset. The results reveal that, for the MPTP task, LTCs achieved an average $f1$ score improvement of approximately **4% to 8%** over the other models; for the MDF task, LTCs attained an average R^2 gain in the range of **0.02 to 0.09** compared to the alternatives.Besides,We explored the impact of different feature sets across all models,including raw data,raw data + time-insensitive features and raw data + time-insensitive + time-sensitive shown.Finally,we conducted our final experiment within a cross-dataset evaluation framework: specifically, the models trained on the Bitcoin (BTC) limit order book data were subsequently tested on the Ethereum (ETH) LOB dataset to assess their generalisation capabilities.

2 Related Work

2.1 Limit Order Book Prediction

LOB is electronic collection of unexecuted limit orders in the financial market, demonstrates assets' liquidity and transaction costs which provides HFT strategy making with evidence [15]. Among them, precisely predicting the trend of LOB can assist HFT traders better seize arbitrage opportunities. The development of methods for predicting the trend of LOB has gone through three main stages: statistic based prediction, machine learning-based prediction, and hybrid model prediction.

Early LOB prediction was mainly based on statistic methods. These methods are two folds. The first fold is regression include logic regression and linear regression. Logic regression typically is employed to predict some market events like price jumps [23], and linear regression, usually been taken to predict some LOB indicators like mid-price and order balance based on handcrafted features [4,13]. Another fold is machine learning approaches. Compared with regression methods, non regression machine learning perform better in flexibility and adaptability. For instance, SVM-based methods perform better in multiple benchmark studies under HFT scenarios [10,13].

Deep-learning advances have significantly enhanced modelling of limit-order-book (LOB) dynamics, deploying architectures such as CNNs, RNNs and attention based models to forecast price movements, mid-price changes and order-flow behaviour. For instance, CNNs have been used to extract spatial patterns from LOB data:applied CNNs to predict stock-price direction using LOB snapshots [19]; introduced DeepLOB to capture multi-level spatial dependencies for mid-price prediction on NASDAQ data [22]. Meanwhile, RNNs, particularly LSTM and attention-augmented variants have been leveraged for temporal modeling: employed LSTM on sequential LOB data for price prediction [6], and combined

LSTM with attention in a bilinear network to enhance long-term dependency capture [17]. Attention-based models, such as Transformers, prioritize relevant LOB features and capture long-range dependencies, offering flexibility in high-frequency settings. Jung et al. [9] introduced a framework using Transformer [20], BERT [5], achieving state-of-the-art performance on millisecond-resolution LOBSTER data. These models demonstrate superior performance but require significant computational resources and large datasets, which may be scarce for cryptocurrency markets.Despite their advancements, traditional DL time-series models rely on discrete time sampling, which fails to capture the ultra-high dynamicity of cryptocurrency LOBs.

Besides, benchmark studying on limit order books is also an attractive research topic. A pivotal contribution is the FI-2010 dataset, introduced by [14], the first publicly available high-frequency LOB dataset for mid-price prediction. It comprises normalized time-series data for five stocks from the NASDAQ Nordic market over ten consecutive days, totaling approximately 4 million samples. Another significant benchmark dataset is HKGSAS-2020, introduced by Huang et al., [8], covering thousands of stocks in the Chinese A-share market from June to September 2020. This dataset focuses on short-term predictions of volume-weighted average price (VWAP) changes and trading volume across 12 time horizons (1 to 300 s). Comparative studies of predictive models for LOBs have leveraged these datasets to benchmark various approaches. [15] conducted a comprehensive study comparing deep learning models for stock price trend prediction using the FI-2010 dataset. They evaluated models such as Ridge Regression (RR), Single Layer Feedforward Neural Networks (SLFN), Linear Discriminant Analysis (LDA), and advanced architectures like DeepLOB and TransLOB. Similarly, [12] benchmarked deep learning models, introducing a volume-based LOB representation that outperformed traditional level-based schemes in short-term return prediction, emphasizing the importance of data representation in model performance. However, previous benchmark studies ignored the rapidly growing Crypto limit order book.

2.2 Liquid Time Constant Networks

Liquid neural networks (LNNs) [7] constitute an emerging class of continuous-time recurrent architectures specifically designed to address the inherent limitations of conventional discrete-time neural networks in modeling dynamic and sequential data. Unlike traditional recurrent neural networks or transformer-based models that rely on fixed time discretization, LNNs formulate the evolution of hidden states through ordinary differential equations with adaptive time constants, enabling the model to continuously evolve in response to streaming inputs. This property allows LNNs to naturally capture fine-grained temporal dependencies and non-stationary dynamics, making them particularly suitable for scenarios characterized by irregular sampling rates and rapidly changing environments.

In particular, Chahine et al. [1] proposed an imitation learning framework grounded in LNNs, where the model learns control policies directly from expert

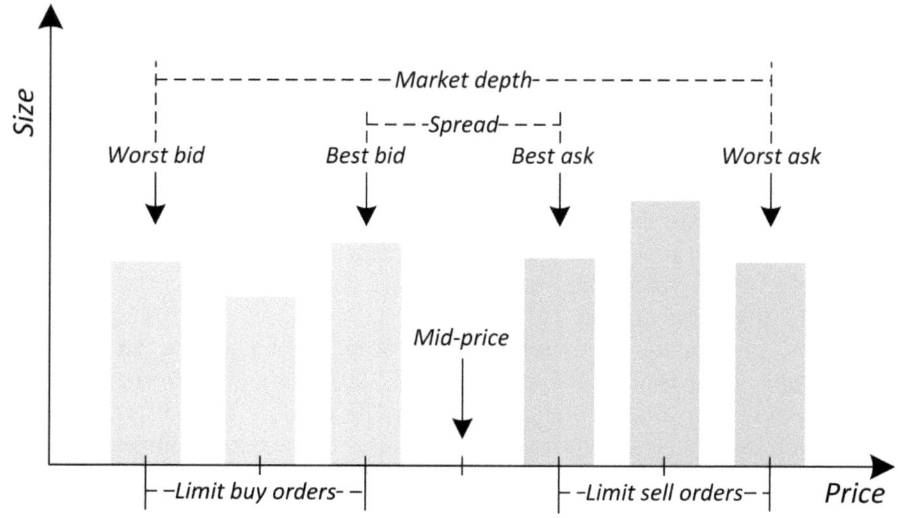

Fig. 1. Visualizing Limit Order Book Data:three *bid* and three *ask* levels of varying price and size are shown, as well as the *Mid-price*, *spread* and *market depth*.

demonstrations while preserving temporal continuity. Their results show that LNN-based agents exhibit strong robustness and generalization capabilities, especially under significant out-of-distribution (OOD) shifts, such as changes in environmental conditions or sensor noise. This highlights the advantage of LNNs in modeling complex dynamical systems where stability and adaptability are critical.

Despite these promising properties, the application of LNNs in financial domains remains largely unexplored. In particular, no existing study has systematically investigated the use of LNNs for limit order book (LOB) modeling and trend prediction. Given that LOB data exhibits high-frequency fluctuations, strong temporal dependencies, and continuous-time microstructure dynamics, the continuous-time formulation of LNNs offers a potentially powerful paradigm for capturing such intricate patterns. Therefore, extending LNNs to the LOB domain is not only a natural progression but also a promising direction for advancing high-frequency financial modeling and improving predictive performance in volatile market environments.

3 Data and Preprocessing

The limit order book (LOB) is modeled as a time series $\mathbb{L} \in \mathbb{R}^{4\times L\times T}$, where $\mathbb{L}(t) \in \mathbb{R}^{4\times L}$ is the LOB at time step $t \in [0, T]$.Specifically, the order-book at time t, denoted by $\mathbb{L}(t)$, is defined as

$$\mathbb{L}(t) = \{\, P_i^{\text{bid}}(t),\, S_i^{\text{bid}}(t),\, P_i^{\text{ask}}(t),\, S_i^{\text{ask}}(t)\}_{i\in[0,L]}$$

where T is the total number of observed time steps and L denotes the number of price levels on each side of the order book.$P_i^{\text{bid/ask}}(t)$ and $S_i^{\text{bid/ask}}(t)$ demote the price and size at level i at time t respectively.An example of LOB is shown in Fig. 1.

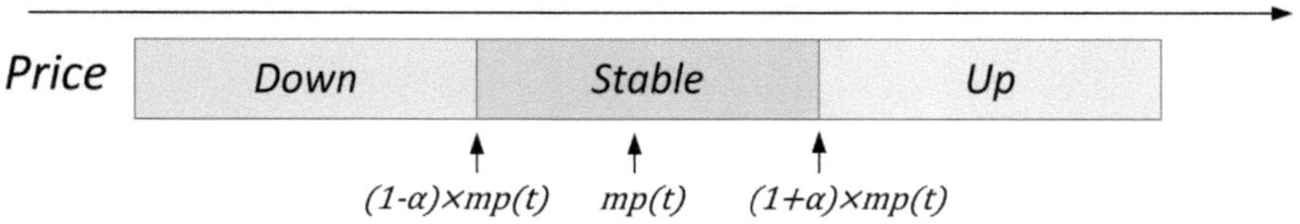

Fig. 2. By comparing the average *mid-price* to an interval defined around the current mid-price, the resulting trend may be classified into one of three categories: downward, stable, or upward.

Table 1. LOB Features. LOB Featuresconsists of three feature sets: a set of Basic LOB features, a set of Time-insensitive features, and a set of Time-sensitive features.

Feature Set	Definitions	Details
Basic LOB	$u_1 = \{P_i^{\text{bid}}, V_i^{\text{bid}}, P_i^{\text{ask}}, V_i^{\text{ask}}\}_{i=1}^{n}$	5-level LOB Data
Time-insensitive	$u_2 = \{(P_i^{\text{bid}} - P_i^{\text{ask}}), (P_i^{\text{bid}} + P_i^{\text{ask}})/2\}_{i=1}^{n}$	Spread & Mid-Price
	$u_3 = \{P_n^{\text{ask}} - P_i^{\text{ask}}, P_i^{\text{ask}} - P_n^{\text{bid}}, \lvert P_{i+1}^{\text{ask}} - P_i^{\text{ask}}\rvert, \lvert P_{i+1}^{\text{bid}} - P_i^{\text{bid}}\rvert\}_{i=1}^{n-1}$	Price Differences
	$u_4 = \left\{\frac{1}{n}\sum_{i=1}^{n} P_i^{\text{ask}}, \frac{1}{n}\sum_{i=1}^{n} P_i^{\text{bid}}, \frac{1}{n}\sum_{i=1}^{n} V_i^{\text{ask}}, \frac{1}{n}\sum_{i=1}^{n} V_i^{\text{bid}}\right\}$	Price & Volume Means
	$u_5 = \left\{\sum_{i=1}^{n}(P_i^{\text{ask}} - P_i^{\text{bid}}), \sum_{i=1}^{n}(V_i^{\text{ask}} - V_i^{\text{bid}})\right\}$	Accumulated Differences
Time-sensitive	$u_6 = \{\frac{dP_i^{\text{ask}}}{dt}, \frac{dP_i^{\text{bid}}}{dt}, \frac{dV_i^{\text{ask}}}{dt}, \frac{dV_i^{\text{bid}}}{dt}\}_{i=1}^{n}$	Price & Volume Derivation

Mid-Price Trend Prediction (MPTP). As Fig. 1 illustrates, the best bid price is the highest bid, while the best ask is the lowest ask.The mid-price,$mp(t)$,is the average of these best prices. Figure 2 presents an alternative method in which the mid-price prediction task is formulated as a classification problem, categorising trends into three classes: U (upward), D (downward) and S (stable). In line with Ntakaris et al. [14], labels are derived from raw LOB data by comparing the current mid-price to the average future mid-price:

$$\begin{cases} \textbf{U}, & \text{if avg\_mp}(k,t) > \text{mp}(t)(1+\alpha) \\ \textbf{D}, & \text{if avg\_mp}(k,t) < \text{mp}(t)(1-\alpha) \text{ where avg\_mp}(k,t) = \dfrac{1}{k}\displaystyle\sum_{i=1}^{k} mp(t+i). \\ \textbf{S}, & \text{otherwise,} \end{cases}$$

Using $\alpha = 0.001\%$ yields approximately equal distribution for each label (Table 1).

Algorithm 1. LTCs-LOB update by fused ODE Solver

Input: Sequences $L(t) \in \mathbb{R}^{N\times M}$, initial hidden state $x_0 \in \mathbb{R}^{N\times H}$; Parameter $\theta = \{\tau^{(H\times 1)}, \gamma^{(M\times H)}, \gamma_r^{(H\times H)}, \mu^{(1\times H)}, A^{(1\times H)}, N, \Delta t\}$; Steps s = number of unfolding steps.

Output: Final hidden state $x_{\text{final}} \in \mathbb{R}^{N\times H}$

1: $x \leftarrow x_0$
2: **for** $i = 1 \dots s$ **do**
3: $x \leftarrow \frac{x+\Delta t\, \sigma\left(x\gamma_r + L(t)\gamma + \mu\right) \odot A}{1+\Delta t\left(\frac{1}{\tau} + \sigma\left(x\gamma_r + L(t)\gamma+\mu\right)\right)}$
4: **end for**
5: **return** x

Market Depth Forecast (MDF). As Fig. 1 illustrates, the worst bid price is the lowest bid,while the worst ask price is the highest ask.The market depth, $md(t)$, is the average of these worst prices. At time t, our target is :

$$target_k(t) = \frac{1}{k}\sum_{i=1}^{k} md(t+i) \quad \text{where } k \text{ is the forecasting horizon.}$$

4 Liquid Time Constant Network(LTCs)

LTCs is a more stable continuous-time recurrent neural network determined by the following equation:

$$\frac{d\mathbf{x}(t)}{dt} = -\left[\tfrac{1}{\tau} + f\big(\mathbf{x}(t), \mathbf{I}(t), t, \theta\big)\right] \mathbf{x}(t) + f\big(\mathbf{x}(t), \mathbf{I}(t), t, \theta\big)\, \mathbf{A} \tag{1}$$

where $\mathbf{x}(t) \in \mathbb{R}^M$ denotes the hidden-state vector at time t, $\mathbf{I}(t) \in \mathbb{R}^N$ is the input vector at time t, τ is a scalar time constant that governs the decay rate of the hidden state, $f\big(\mathbf{x}(t), \mathbf{I}(t), t, \theta\big)$ is a nonlinear mapping which determines a state- and input-dependent gain, and $\mathbf{A} \in \mathbb{R}^M$ is the target-bias toward which the hidden state $\mathbf{x}(t)$ is driven when the gain is active.

4.1 Liquid Time-Constant

A neural network f not only governs the derivative of the hidden state $x(t)$, but also defines an input-dependent, dynamically varying time-constant:

$$\tau_{\text{sys}} = \frac{\tau}{1 + \tau\, f\big(x(t), I(t), t, \theta\big)}. \tag{2}$$

Here, the time-constant serves as a parameter that characterises both the responsiveness and coupling-sensitivity of the underlying ODE. This mechanism enables each individual element of the hidden state to instantiate specialised dynamical subsystems aligned to the input features arriving at each time-point.

Algorithm 2. Training an LTCs-based model for LOB prediction using BPTT

Inputs: Dataset of traces $\{(L^{(i)}, y^{(i)})\}_{i=1}^{len}$, where each $L^{(i)} \in \mathbb{R}^{T \times M}$; loss function $\mathcal{L}(\theta)$; LTCs-cell$= f(L, x, \theta)$; initial parameters θ_0; learning rate α; output weights W_{out} and bias b_{out}; number of epochs m

Output: Trained model parameters θ

$\theta \leftarrow \theta_0$
for $i = 1 \ldots m$ **do**
  Sample a minibatch $\{(L_b, y_b)\}$
  Initialize hidden state x
  $\mathcal{L}_{\text{batch}} \leftarrow 0$
  for $j = 1 \ldots T$ **do**
    $x = f(L_b(j), x, \theta)$
    $\hat{y}(t) = W_{\text{out}}\, x + b_{\text{out}}$
    $\mathcal{L}_{\text{batch}} \leftarrow \mathcal{L}_{\text{batch}} + \text{Loss}(y_{b,j}, \hat{y}_j)$
  end for
  $\nabla_\theta \mathcal{L}_{\text{batch}} \leftarrow \frac{\partial \mathcal{L}_{\text{batch}}}{\partial \theta}$
  Update parameters: $\theta \leftarrow \theta - \alpha \nabla_\theta \mathcal{L}_{\text{batch}}$
end for
return θ

4.2 LTCs Forward-Pass by a Fused ODE Solvers

Because the semantics of LTCs are non-linear, solving Eq.(1) analytically is far from trivial. Yet at any given time T, the system's state can still be computed by a numerical ODE solver that simulates from the initial trajectory $x(0)$ to $x(T)$. The solver discretizes the continuous simulation interval $[0, T]$ into time points $[t_0, t_1, \ldots, t_n]$. Consequently, each solver step only needs to update the neuronal states from t_i to t_{i+1}. To this end, the Fused Solver numerically unrolls a given dynamical system of the form dx/dt = f(x) by:

$$x(t_{i+1}) = x(t_i) + \Delta t\, f\big(x(t_i),\, x(t_{i+1})\big). \tag{3}$$

In particular, we replace only those occurrences of $x(t_i)$ that appear linearly in the function f with $x(t_{i+1})$. As a result, Eq. (2) can be solved symbolically for $x(t_{i+1})$. By applying the Fused Solver to the LTCs representation and solving for $x(t + \Delta t)$, we obtain:

$$x(t + \Delta t) = \frac{x(t) + \Delta t\, f\big(x(t),\, I(t),\, t,\, \theta\big)\, A}{1 + \Delta t\, \big(1/\tau + f\big(x(t),\, I(t),\, t,\, \theta\big)\big)}. \tag{4}$$

Equation (4) computes a single update state for an LTCs network. Algorithm 1 then presents how to implement such a network given a parameter space θ, under the assumption that f is an arbitrary activation function.

4.3 Training LTCs Networks by BPTT

In Neural Ordinary Differential Equations [2], the authors propose using the adjoint sensitivity method for reverse-mode automatic differentiation. However, the adjoint method may incur numerical errors when executed in reverse-mode integration.Conversely, direct back-propagation through time (BPTT) sacrifices memory efficiency in favour of fully accurate reconstruction of the forward pass during reverse-mode integration [24].Accordingly, the Liquid Time-Constant Network employs a standard back-propagation through time algorithm. Algorithm 2 details the procedure used to train the LTCs-based model for LOB prediction via BPTT.

Table 2. Mid-price Trend Prediction Results (Mean&Standard Deviation) on Basic LOB data with time-insensitive features with time-sensitive features.The best model is bolded

Model	Metrics	K=5	K=10	K=20
LTCs	$f1$	**81.53(0.5)**	**73.18(0.5)**	**64.87(0.7)**
LSTM	$f1$	76.56(0.4)	70.99(0.5)	63.84(0.4)
MLP	$f1$	71.42(1.1)	63.62(2.6)	34.44(1.6)
CNN1	$f1$	74.68(1.8)	68.33(1.6)	60.58(0.5)
CNN2	$f1$	75.20(0.4)	69.98(1.2)	60.48(1.0)
CNNLSTM	$f1$	76.99(0.7)	71.19(0.6)	61.71(1.1)
iTransformer	$f1$	78.02(0.6)	70.78(0.6)	57.74(0.3)
DEEPLOB	$f1$	77.41(0.8)	70.78(0.7)	58.93(1.5)
DAIN	$f1$	75.19(0.6)	69.05(0.7)	61.06(0.5)

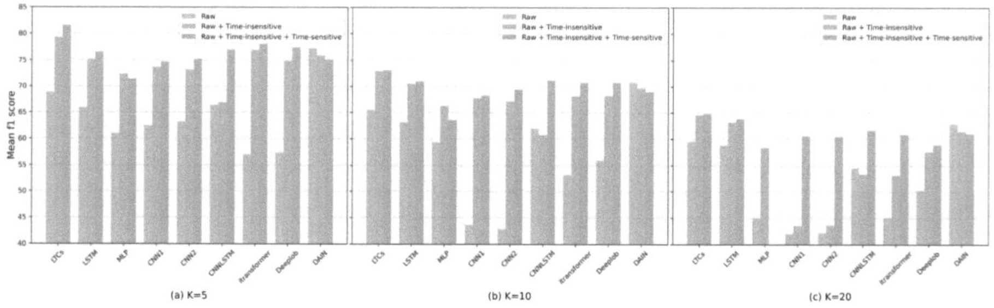

Fig. 3. These plots illustrate the incremental prediction power gained from time-insensitive and time-sensitive features under the **MPTP** experiment.

5 Experiments

Our benchmark evaluations utilize Bitcoin (BTC) and Ethereum (ETH) LOB data. For MPTP, we use F1 scores as metrics. For MDF, we use Mean Squared

Table 3. Market Depth Forecasting Results (Mean&Standard Deviation) on Basic LOB data with time-insensitive features with time-sensitive features.The best model is bolde.

Model	Metrics	K=5	K=10	K=20
LTCs	MSE	**0.264(0.004)**	**0.274(0.009)**	**0.281(0.001)**
	$CORR$	**0.860(0.002)**	**0.857(0.002)**	**0.853(0.002)**
	R^2	**0.736(0.004)**	**0.726(0.009)**	**0.720(0.012)**
LSTM	MSE	0.299(0.006)	0.295(0.010)	0.315(0.020)
	$CORR$	0.841(0.003)	0.843(0.007)	0.836(0.008)
	R^2	0.701(0.007)	0.705(0.010)	0.687(0.020)
MLP	MSE	0.322(0.008)	0.315(0.012)	0.322(0.005)
	$CORR$	0.833(0.008)	0.831(0.006)	0.828(0.004)
	R^2	0.678(0.008)	0.685(0.012)	0.679(0.005)
CNN1	MSE	0.314(0.019)	0.324(0.025)	0.327(0.016)
	$CORR$	0.833(0.011)	0.827(0.014)	0.830(0.008)
	R^2	0.685(0.019)	0.675(0.025)	0.675(0.016)
CNN2	MSE	0.315(0.005)	0.318(0.018)	0.311(0.003)
	$CORR$	0.834(0.003)	0.833(0.008)	0.839(0.006)
	R^2	0.684(0.005)	0.682(0.018)	0.691(0.003)
CNNLSTM	MSE	0.303(0.011)	0.300(0.018)	0.308(0.012)
	$CORR$	0.841(0.006)	0.843(0.005)	0.841(0.003)
	R^2	0.696(0.011)	0.700(0.018)	0.694(0.012)
iTransformer	MSE	0.282(0.004)	0.293(0.012)	0.300(0.011)
	$CORR$	0.850(0.004)	0.847(0.005)	0.843(0.003)
	R^2	0.718(0.004)	0.707(0.012)	0.702(0.011)
DEEPLOB	MSE	0.299(0.008)	0.302(0.009)	0.316(0.009)
	$CORR$	0.842(0.004)	0.839(0.005)	0.833(0.005)
	R^2	0.701(0.008)	0.698(0.009)	0.685(0.009)
DAIN	MSE	0.357(0.007)	0.355(0.014)	0.344(0.014)
	$CORR$	0.802(0.005)	0.803(0.009)	0.812(0.008)
	R^2	0.643(0.007)	0.644(0.014)	0.658(0.014)

Error (MSE), Pearson Correlation Coefficient (Corr), and Coefficient of Determination (R^2) as metrics.

5.1 Models

Our benchmark comprises two distinct tasks (MPTP and MDF). For each task, we select 9 representative models with the aim of systematically evaluating a diverse range of neural-architectures,including LTCs, MLP, CNN(CNN1), causal CNN(CNN2) ,LSTM, iTransformer and so on.This consistent advantage demonstrates the strong temporal modelling capacity and stability of the liquid-time-constant mechanism, which adapts effectively to dynamic input patterns in the LOB.

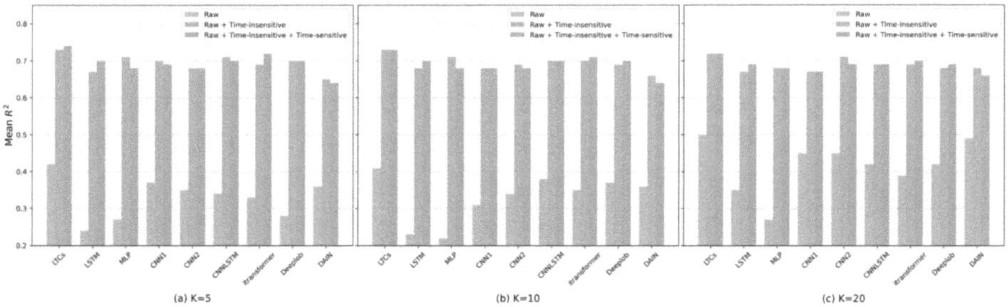

Fig. 4. These plots illustrate the incremental prediction power gained from time-insensitive and time-sensitive features under the **MDF** experiment.

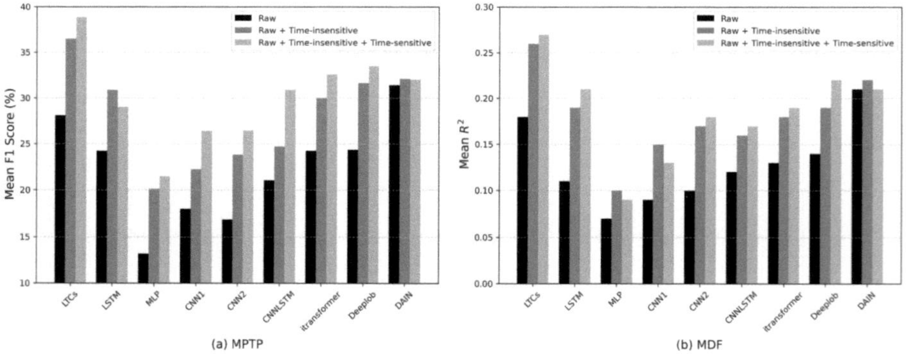

Fig. 5. These plots illustrate the cross-dataset evaluation performance where the model trained on the LOB data from currency BTC is tested on the LOB data of currency ETH to assess its generalizability beyond the training domain when the when the forecast horizon is set to $K=5$.

5.2 MPTP Results and MDF Results

Table 2 and Table 3 reports the mean $f1$ scores for all models evaluated on the mid-price trend prediction (MPTP) task and the R^2 for all models evaluated on the market depth forecast (MDF) task at forecasting horizons of K = 5,

10 and 20 using feature sets comprised of raw data, time-insensitive features and time-sensitive features shown in Fig. 1. The model LTCs achieves the highest performance across all horizons under two different tasks.When K = 5, the LTCs model achieved an improvement of approximately **3 %** to **10 %** in the MPTP experiment, and an increase of about **0.02** to **0.10** in the MDF experiment, compared with the other models.As the forecasting horizon increases, all models exhibit performance degradation, indicating the increased uncertainty and difficulty of long-term prediction. Nevertheless, LTCs maintains a consistent advantage, suggesting its stronger capability in modeling temporal dependencies and generalizing across different time scales.

5.3 Outcomes Across Varied Dataset Feature Configurations

Figure 3 and Fig. 4 illustrate the incremental prediction power gained from time-insensitive and time-sensitive features shown in Fig. 1 under the MPTP experiment and MDF experiment.The results indicate that both time-insensitive and time-sensitive features yield measurable improvements over the basic LOB feature set, thereby confirming the broad effectiveness of these additional feature categories in enhancing model performance.When only the raw features were used, the DAIN model outperformed all other models in both the MPTP and MDF tasks. However, when time-insensitive and time-sensitive features were added, DAIN did not demonstrate a significant improvement, whereas LTCs exhibited a marked performance uplift–indicating that the LTCs model is more sensitive to enriched features.These observations indicate that LTCs is more sensitive to feature enrichment and can more effectively utilize multi-scale temporal information, leading to superior performance when more informative features are available.

5.4 Cross-Dataset Evaluation

Figure 5 illustrates the outcomes of a cross-dataset evaluation in which models trained on the limit order book (LOB) data of currency BTC are tested on the LOB data of currency ETH, using a forecast horizon of K=5.The results clearly illustrate the model's cross-dataset generalization capability:When using only raw features, the DAIN model still delivered the best performance. However, upon incorporating time-insensitive and time-sensitive features, the LTCs model achieved the highest gain, demonstrating its superior generalization capability and heightened sensitivity to enriched feature sets.

This behavior can be explained by the intrinsic modeling differences between the two approaches. DAIN primarily relies on adaptive normalization to mitigate distributional shifts, which is effective when feature representations are limited but less expressive under richer feature settings. In contrast, LTCs leverages continuous-time dynamics to model temporal evolution, enabling it to learn more transferable patterns that are less dependent on dataset-specific distributions. As a result, LTCs can better capture invariant temporal structures across different markets, leading to improved cross-dataset generalization when additional informative features are introduced.

6 Conclusion

In this paper, we introduce the first standardized benchmark for cryptocurrency LOB trend prediction and propose liquid time-constant neural networks (LTCs) as a principled architecture for modeling high-frequency order-book dynamics. Our benchmark is constructed from large-scale real-world LOB data collected from Binance, covering Bitcoin (BTC) and Ethereum (ETH) markets from January to April 2025, and comprises approximately two billion event timestamps with corresponding bid and ask updates. Compared to existing datasets, this benchmark captures ultra-high-frequency microstructure dynamics and provides a unified pipeline for fair evaluation across different predictive tasks and feature settings.

Across both mid-price trend prediction (MPTP) and market depth forecasting (MDF) tasks, extensive experiments demonstrate that the proposed LTC-based approach consistently outperforms strong baselines, achieving improvements of 4% to 8% in predictive accuracy and cross-dataset generalizability. These gains can be attributed to the continuous-time formulation of LTCs, which enables adaptive modeling of temporal dynamics and more faithful representation of irregular, rapidly evolving LOB sequences. Overall, our results highlight the importance of dynamics-aware, continuous-time modeling in capturing the complex behavior of real-world high-frequency financial markets and provide a strong foundation for future research in LOB prediction.

Acknowledgment. This work was supported by the New Generation Artificial Intelligence National Science and Technology Major Project (No. 2025ZD0122304) and the Shenzhen Science and Technology Program (Nos. ZDCY20250901095900001 and SYSPG20241211173440003).

References

1. Chahine, M., et al.: Robust flight navigation out of distribution with liquid neural networks. Sci. Robot. **8**(77), eadc8892 (2023)
2. Chen, R.T., Rubanova, Y., Bettencourt, J., Duvenaud, D.K.: Neural ordinary differential equations. Adv. Neural Inf. Proces. Syst. **31** (2018)
3. Clapham, B., Haferkorn, M., Zimmermann, K.: The impact of high-frequency trading on modern securities markets: an analysis based on a technical interruption. Bus. Inf. Syst. Eng. **65**, 7–24 (2023)
4. Cont, R., Kukanov, A., Stoikov, S.: The price impact of order book events. J. Financ. Economet. **12**, 47–88 (2014)
5. Devlin, J., Chang, M.W., Lee, K., Toutanova, K.: BERT: pre-training of deep bidirectional transformers for language understanding. In: Proceedings of the 2019 Conference of the North American Chapter of the Association for Computational Linguistics: Human Language Technologies, Volume 1 (Long And Short Papers), pp. 4171–4186 (2019)

6. Dixon, M.: Sequence classification of the limit order book using recurrent neural networks. J. Comput. Sci. **24**, 277–286 (2018)
7. Hasani, R., Lechner, M., Amini, A., Rus, D., Grosu, R.: Liquid time-constant networks. In: Proceedings of the AAAI Conference on Artificial Intelligence, vol. 35, pp. 7657–7666 (2021)
8. Huang, C., Ge, W., Chou, H., Du, X.: Benchmark dataset for short-term market prediction of limit order book in china markets. J. Financ. Data Sci. **3**, 171–183 (2021)
9. Jung, J., Lee, K.: Attention-based reading, highlighting, and forecasting of the limit order book. arXiv preprint arXiv:2409.02277 (2024)
10. Kercheval, A.N., Zhang, Y.: Modelling high-frequency limit order book dynamics with support vector machines. Quant. Finance **15**, 1315–1329 (2015)
11. Li, H., Xiao, Y., Polukarov, M., Ventre, C.: Thermodynamic analysis of financial markets: measuring order book dynamics with temperature and entropy. Entropy **26**, 24 (2023)
12. Lucchese, L., Pakkanen, M.S., Veraart, A.E.: The short-term predictability of returns in order book markets: A deep learning perspective. Int. J. Forecast. **40**, 1587–1621 (2024)
13. Nousi, P., et al.: Machine learning for forecasting mid-price movements using limit order book data. IEEE Access **7**, 64722–64736 (2019)
14. Ntakaris, A., Magris, M., Kanniainen, J., Gabbouj, M., Iosifidis, A.: Benchmark dataset for mid-price forecasting of limit order book data with machine learning methods. J. Forecast. **37** (2018)
15. Prata, M., et al.: Lob-based deep learning models for stock price trend prediction: a benchmark study. Artif. Intell. Rev. **57**, 116 (2024)
16. Qin, M., Sun, S., Zhang, W., Xia, H., Wang, X., An, B.: EarnHFT: efficient hierarchical reinforcement learning for high frequency trading. In: Proceedings of the AAAI Conference on Artificial Intelligence, vol. 38 (2024)
17. Tran, D.T., Iosifidis, A., Kanniainen, J., Gabbouj, M.: Temporal attention-augmented bilinear network for financial time-series data analysis. IEEE Trans. Neural Netw. Learn. Syst. **30**, 1407–1418 (2018)
18. Tripathi, A., Dixit, A., et al.: Information content of order imbalance in an order-driven market: Indian evidence. Financ. Res. Lett. **41**, 101863 (2021)
19. Tsantekidis, A., Passalis, N., Tefas, A., Kanniainen, J., Gabbouj, M., Iosifidis, A.: Forecasting stock prices from the limit order book using convolutional neural networks. In: 2017 IEEE 19th Conference on Business Informatics (CBI), vol. 1, pp. 7–12. IEEE (2017)
20. Vaswani, A., et al.: Attention is all you need. Adv. Neural Inf. Proces. Syst. **30** (2017)
21. Wang, Y., Lu, W., Lin, M.B., Ren, R., Härdle, W.K.: Cross-exchange crypto risk: a high-frequency dynamic network perspective. Int. Rev. Financ. Anal. **94**, 103246 (2024)
22. Zhang, Z., Zohren, S., Roberts, S.: DeepLOB: deep convolutional neural networks for limit order books. IEEE Trans. Signal Process. **67**, 3001–3012 (2019)
23. Zheng, B., Moulines, E., Abergel, F.: Price jump prediction in a limit order book. J. Math. Finance **3**, 242–255 (2013)

24. Zhuang, J., Dvornek, N., Li, X., Tatikonda, S., Papademetris, X., Duncan, J.: Adaptive checkpoint adjoint method for gradient estimation in neural ODE. In: III, H.D., Singh, A. (eds.) Proceedings of the 37th International Conference on Machine Learning. Proceedings of Machine Learning Research, vol. 119, pp. 11639–11649. PMLR (2020)
25. Zong, C., Wang, C., Qin, M., Feng, L., Wang, X., An, B.: MacroHFT: memory augmented context-aware reinforcement learning on high frequency trading. In: Proceedings of the 30th ACM SIGKDD Conference on Knowledge Discovery and Data Mining, pp. 4712–4721 (2024)

CRISP: Category-Role Informed Sheaf Propagation Network

Yuhao Wang, Xiangdong Zou, Kai Du(✉), Chengbo Yu, and Hui Li

Jianghan University,Wuhan, Hubei, China
dukai@jhun.edu.cn

Abstract. Next point-of-interest (next POI) recommendation predicts the next location of a user from historical check-in trajectories. Existing methods model mobility sequences with recurrent networks, attention mechanisms, geographical constraints, and graph neural networks. Most graph-enhanced approaches, however, still use relatively fixed propagation rules, which makes it difficult to separate heterogeneous transition semantics induced by POI categories and user roles. The same restaurant, for example, may correspond to tourist dining, workday meals, or daily leisure activities, each of which may imply a different subsequent mobility intention.

We propose the Category-Role Informed Sheaf Propagation Network (CRISP) to address this issue. CRISP introduces category- and role-aware sheaf propagation for next POI recommendation. In the global POI graph, edge-level restriction maps are generated from the source category, target category, and transition weight to model category-dependent transition semantics. In the user history graph, user role families are incorporated so that the same category transition can induce different propagation behaviors across user groups. CRISP also uses Last-Step CE to align training with last-step evaluation and introduces Posterior Sequential Transition Modeling (PST) to refine final ranking with user-daypart-conditioned transition memory. Experiments on two Foursquare datasets show that CRISP achieves strong performance on early-ranking metrics and remains competitive across overall ranking metrics.

Keywords: Next POI Recommendation · Recommendation Systems · Graph Neural Networks · Sheaf Neural Networks

1 Introduction

Next point-of-interest (next POI) recommendation predicts the next location a user will visit from historical check-in trajectories. It is a fundamental task in location-based services and urban computing. Human mobility is affected by short-term trajectory context, geographical proximity, temporal regularity, long-term preference, and group-level behavioral patterns. Existing studies model

Y. Wang and X. Zou—Contributed equally to this work.

L. Ding et al. (Eds.): APWeb-WAIM 2026, LNCS 16995, pp. 33–49, 2027.
https://doi.org/10.1007/978-981-92-5699-0_3

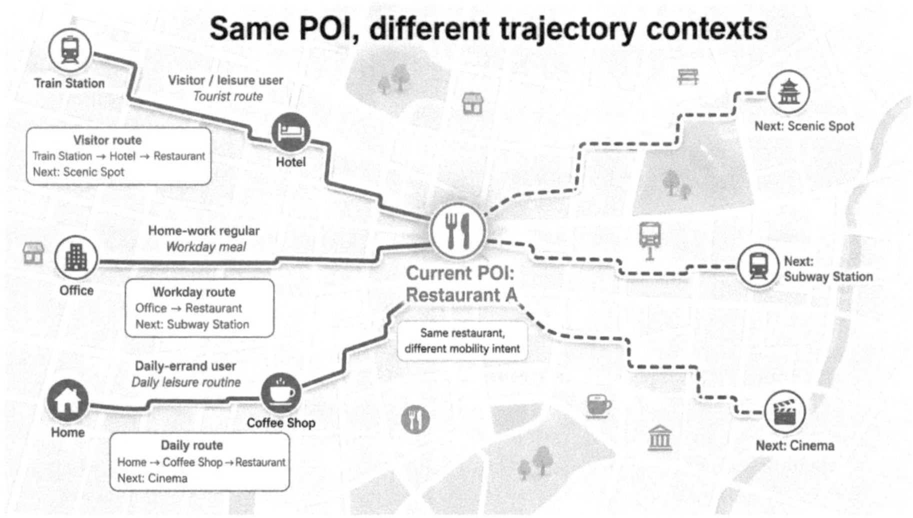

Fig. 1. The same POI can imply different mobility intentions under different category trajectories and user roles.

these factors with recurrent networks, attention mechanisms, Transformer architectures, and graph structures [2,20,22,23].

Most graph-enhanced next POI models, despite their effectiveness, still treat graph edges as relatively homogeneous connections. A POI transition edge usually represents historical co-occurrence or sequential movement, while message passing is controlled by fixed GCN-style aggregation or shared attention rules. In real mobility scenarios, the same POI or transition may carry different meanings under different trajectory contexts. As shown in Fig. 1, different users may arrive at the same restaurant through different category trajectories. A visitor route such as Train Station → Hotel → Restaurant may be followed by a scenic spot; a workday route such as Office → Restaurant may be followed by a subway station; and a daily leisure route such as Home → Coffee Shop → Restaurant may be followed by a cinema. Thus, the same target POI can imply different subsequent mobility intentions.

This example points to two forms of context heterogeneity. Transition semantics first depend on category context. Transitions from a hotel, an office, and a cinema to a restaurant share the same target category but may correspond to tourist dining, workday meals, or after-movie activities. Transition semantics also depend on user roles. Users with commuting, leisure, shopping, or mixed urban behaviors may follow different subsequent patterns even when they visit similar categories. Our data analysis on NYC and TKY confirms that category transition distributions are highly non-uniform and that user role families show clear differences in category transition patterns.

To model such heterogeneity, we propose the Category-Role Informed Sheaf Propagation Network (CRISP). The core component of CRISP is the Category-

Role Conditioned Sheaf Graph Encoder (CR-Sheaf). In the global POI graph, CR-Sheaf generates edge-specific restriction maps from source category, target category, and transition weight, transforming messages by category-dependent mobility semantics before propagation. In the user history graph, CR-Sheaf further incorporates user role families, allowing the same category transition to induce different propagation behaviors across user groups. In this way, CRISP extends fixed graph aggregation into category- and role-conditioned sheaf diffusion.

Standard next POI evaluation focuses on the last valid timestep of each trajectory, whereas many models are trained with losses over all sequence positions. We introduce Last-Step CE to reduce this training-evaluation mismatch. We also design Posterior Sequential Transition Modeling (PST), which uses user-daypart-conditioned transition memory to refine final candidate ranking. PST complements CR-Sheaf by modeling posterior sequential regularities after the neural backbone produces candidate scores.

The paper makes four main contributions. It identifies category transition heterogeneity and user-role heterogeneity as key challenges in graph-enhanced next POI recommendation. It proposes CRISP, a category-role-informed sheaf propagation network for context-aware graph propagation and posterior transition refinement. It designs CR-Sheaf, with a Category-Conditioned Global Sheaf Encoder and a Role-Family-Conditioned User Sheaf Encoder, to generate edge-level restriction maps for context-aware message passing. It further introduces Last-Step CE and PST to align optimization and final ranking with the last-step recommendation protocol. Experiments on Foursquare-NYC and Foursquare-TKY demonstrate the effectiveness of CRISP on early-ranking metrics and its competitive overall ranking performance.

2 Related Work

2.1 Sequential and Spatio-Temporal Next POI Recommendation

Next POI recommendation is widely studied as sequential mobility prediction. Early methods such as FPMC [11] and PRME [3] combine personalized preference with sequential transition regularities. Deep sequential models then capture more complex mobility dependencies. ST-RNN incorporates temporal intervals and spatial distances into recurrent transitions [7], DeepMove retrieves long-term mobility regularities with attention [2], and STGN enhances recurrent modeling with spatio-temporal gates [22]. LSTPM, Flashback, and STAN further model long-term preferences, historical hidden-state retrieval, and spatio-temporal attention [8,12,19]. Recent Transformer and state-space models, such as GETNext [20] and GeoMamba [10], model longer trajectory dependencies. These methods mainly learn transition semantics implicitly from sequences, whereas CRISP explicitly models category- and role-conditioned graph propagation.

2.2 Graph-Enhanced POI Recommendation

POI transitions, spatial proximity, and co-visitation relations naturally form graph structures. GCN and GAT provide general graph representation learning mechanisms [5,14]. In next POI recommendation, graph structures complement sequential modeling with global mobility patterns and collaborative POI relations. GETNext constructs trajectory-flow graphs for Transformer-based prediction [20]. SNPM models dynamic POI dependencies with graphs [21]. GUGEN constructs global POI graphs, distance graphs, user graphs, and neighbor representations to capture geographical and user-specific patterns [23]. ReHDM explores region-aware dynamic hypergraphs to alleviate trajectory sparsity [6]. Most graph-enhanced models still use fixed or shared propagation rules. CRISP instead generates edge-level sheaf restriction maps conditioned on category and user-role contexts.

2.3 Context Heterogeneity and Sheaf-Based Modeling

Context heterogeneity is central to mobility prediction because transition meaning depends on category, time, user behavior, and local trajectory context. Ordinary GNNs aggregate neighbor messages with shared transformations, which can be insufficient when adjacent nodes have incompatible semantics. Neural sheaf diffusion provides a general graph learning mechanism by assigning restriction maps to graph edges and comparing node signals after local transformations [1]. Its primary goal is to improve graph representation learning under heterophily and oversmoothing, and the restriction maps usually serve as task-agnostic local geometric transformations. Sheaf4Rec further introduces sheaf neural networks into graph-based recommendation, mainly focusing on user-item interaction graphs and collaborative filtering settings [9]. These methods show the usefulness of sheaf structures for heterogeneous graph relations, but they do not explicitly model sequential mobility semantics, POI category transitions, geographical movement, or user behavioral roles in next-POI recommendation.

CRISP differs from these sheaf-based models in both task formulation and restriction-map conditioning. Instead of applying a generic sheaf layer to a static graph, CRISP parameterizes restriction maps as mobility-context functions. In the global POI graph, restriction maps are conditioned on source category, target category, and transition weight. In the user-history graph, they are further conditioned on the user's offline role family. Therefore, the local sheaf space in CRISP corresponds to category-role-specific mobility semantics rather than only generic graph geometry or static user-item interaction relations. CRISP also integrates sheaf propagation with trajectory sequence encoding, last-step-aware optimization, and posterior transition-memory refinement, which are specific to the next-POI recommendation protocol.

3 Problem Definition

Let $\mathcal{U}$ denote the user set and $\mathcal{P}$ the POI set. Each POI $p \in \mathcal{P}$ has attributes such as geographical coordinates and category. A check-in record is (u, p, t), where user u visits POI p at time t.

For each user, check-ins are sorted by time and segmented into trajectories. A trajectory is

$$S_u = \{(p_1, t_1), (p_2, t_2), \ldots, (p_L, t_L)\},$$

where p_i is the visited POI and t_i is the timestamp. Given a prefix trajectory

$$S_u^{1:l} = \{(p_1, t_1), \ldots, (p_l, t_l)\},$$

next POI recommendation predicts the next POI p_{l+1}.

In addition to POI categories, we define a user role family r_u for each user using offline mobility statistics, including revisit behavior, commuting tendency, weekend activity, mobility range, and category preference. The role variable is not an external label for final prediction; it provides context for user-graph propagation. Formally, the goal is to learn

$$f(u, S_u^{1:l}, r_u, p),$$

which assigns a ranking score to each candidate POI $p \in \mathcal{P}$. Candidate POIs are ranked by score, and the top-ranked POIs are returned.

4 Method

Figure 2 shows the overall architecture of CRISP. Given a trajectory prefix $T_u^{1:l} = [x_1^u, x_2^u, \ldots, x_l^u]$ of user u, CRISP predicts the POI that the user is most likely to visit next. The input includes the POI sequence, temporal information, POI categories, user roles, global POI transition relations, geographical distance relations, user historical mobility relations, and neighboring POI context. CRISP first learns context-dependent POI and user preference representations from graph structures, then fuses them with trajectory context to generate candidate POI scores at each timestep. Finally, posterior sequential transition modeling captures user-specific subsequent-visit regularities under temporal contexts and refines final ranking.

4.1 Overview

CRISP has three components. The category-role-informed sheaf propagation module generates restriction maps from edge-level context, allowing different category transitions and user roles to induce different propagation semantics. The multi-source trajectory representation learning module then fuses global mobility patterns, geographical proximity, user historical preference, and short-term trajectory context to produce neural candidate scores. PST learns user- and daypart-conditioned posterior transition memory from training trajectories for final ranking.

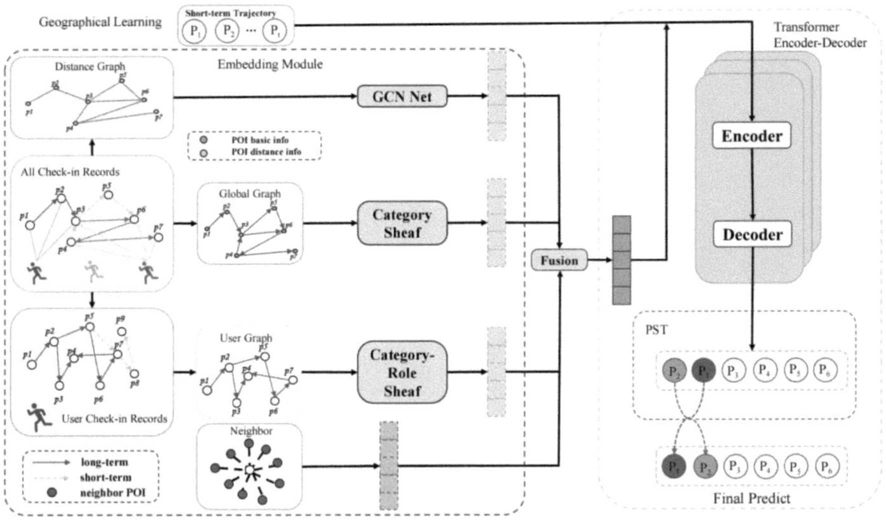

Fig. 2. Overall architecture of CRISP.

4.2 Category-Role Informed Sheaf Propagation

Figure 3 illustrates the Category-Conditioned Sheaf Encoder. In next POI recommendation, graph edges represent mobility transitions in historical trajectories. The same edge or transition type, however, can carry different meanings across contexts. For example, Hotel → Restaurant more likely indicates tourist dining, Office → Restaurant workday meals, and Home → Coffee Shop → Restaurant daily leisure routes. If all edges share one propagation rule, the model treats these transitions as homogeneous adjacency relations and weakens their semantic differences.

For each global POI graph edge, the source category, target category, and transition weight are encoded as edge context. The edge context generates source-side and target-side adapters, which align endpoint messages before comparison, aggregation, and residual update.

To model context-dependent transition semantics, CRISP uses sheaf propagation to generate edge-specific transformations. Let $\mathbf{h}_i, \mathbf{h}_j \in \mathbb{R}^d$ denote node representations and $\mathbf{z}_{ij}$ denote the context vector of edge (i, j). CRISP generates endpoint restriction vectors by

$$[\mathbf{r}_i^{ij}, \mathbf{r}_j^{ij}] = \sigma(\mathrm{MLP}(\mathbf{z}_{ij})).$$

We use diagonal restrictions, i.e., element-wise adapters, to preserve contextual transformation capacity while avoiding dense edge-specific matrices.

Before propagation, CRISP maps endpoint representations into an edge-level semantic space. The local disagreement and messages are

$$\mathbf{d}_{ij} = \mathbf{r}_i^{ij} \odot \mathbf{h}_i - \mathbf{r}_j^{ij} \odot \mathbf{h}_j, \quad \mathbf{m}_{i \leftarrow j} = -\mathbf{r}_i^{ij} \odot \mathbf{d}_{ij}, \quad \mathbf{m}_{j \leftarrow i} = \mathbf{r}_j^{ij} \odot \mathbf{d}_{ij}.$$

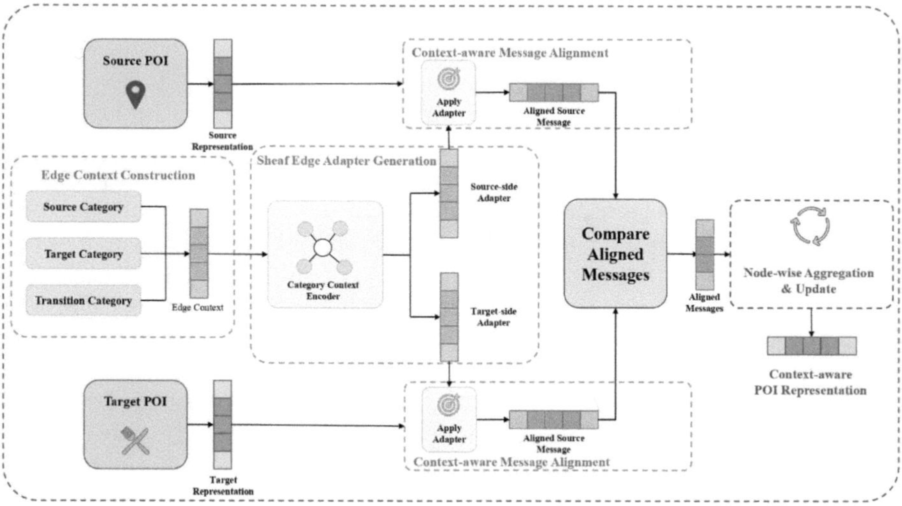

Fig. 3. Internal workflow of the Category-Conditioned Sheaf Encoder.

Messages are therefore compared after contextual alignment rather than directly aggregated in the original node space.

For node v, edge messages are aggregated and normalized by transition weights:

$$\mathbf{a}_v = \frac{\sum_{e \in \mathcal{E}(v)} w_e \mathbf{m}_{e \to v}}{\sum_{e \in \mathcal{E}(v)} w_e + \epsilon}.$$

The node representation is updated by

$$\mathbf{h}'_v = \mathbf{h}_v + \mathrm{ReLU}\left(\mathrm{Norm}(\mathbf{W}_{self}\mathbf{h}_v + \mathbf{W}_{up}\mathbf{a}_v)\right).$$

This residual update preserves POI identity while injecting context-conditioned graph information.

CRISP uses different condition vectors for global POI transitions and user historical transitions. For a global edge (p_i, p_j), the condition vector is

$$\mathbf{z}^g_{ij} = [\mathbf{e}_{c(p_i)}; \mathbf{e}_{c(p_j)}; w_{ij}],$$

where $\mathbf{e}_{c(p_i)}$ and $\mathbf{e}_{c(p_j)}$ are source and target category embeddings. This allows transitions such as Office $\to$ Restaurant and Hotel $\to$ Restaurant to induce different restriction maps.

For a user-history edge, CRISP further incorporates the user role embedding:

$$\mathbf{z}^u_{ij} = [\mathbf{e}_{c(p_i)}; \mathbf{e}_{c(p_j)}; \mathbf{e}_{r_u}; w_{ij}].$$

The role family r_u is constructed offline from historical mobility behavior rather than manually annotated or inferred from next-POI labels. For each user, we extract a mobility profile vector from training trajectories, including activity intensity, revisit regularity, category diversity, spatial mobility range, weekend, night, and commute-period activity ratios, and macro-category preference distributions. Skewed count and distance features are transformed by $\log(1 + x)$, clipped at the 1st and 99th percentiles, and standardized before clustering. We then apply K-means clustering and select the number of clusters from $\{5, 6, 7, 8\}$ according to the silhouette score. The resulting clusters are assigned interpretable role-family names according to their temporal, spatial, and semantic mobility patterns.

During model training, only the discrete role-family ID is used. The role ID is mapped to an embedding $\mathbf{e}_{r_u}$ and concatenated with the source category embedding, target category embedding, and transition weight to generate the user-history sheaf restriction maps. Thus, user roles do not serve as additional prediction labels; instead, they condition the propagation function so that the same category transition can induce different message transformations for different user groups.

Global category-conditioned propagation and user role-conditioned propagation share the same sheaf diffusion principle: both generate endpoint restriction maps from condition vectors and pass messages based on local disagreement. They differ in context source. Global transition propagation focuses on category semantics, whereas user-history propagation further includes role semantics. This unified design models context heterogeneity in both global mobility patterns and personalized user patterns.

4.3 Multi-source Trajectory Representation Learning

CRISP maps multiple mobility signals to trajectory timesteps for next POI prediction. At each timestep, the model considers global POI transition semantics, geographical distance relations, user historical mobility preference, and neighboring POI context. Global POI transition semantics come from category-conditioned sheaf propagation and capture global mobility regularities under different category transitions. Geographical distance relations describe spatial proximity among POIs. User historical mobility preference comes from role-conditioned sheaf propagation and captures long-term personalized visit patterns. Neighboring POI context complements the candidate space around the current location.

Let $\mathbf{g}_t$, $\mathbf{d}_t$, $\mathbf{u}_t$, and $\mathbf{n}_t$ denote the global transition, geographical distance, user history, and neighboring context representations at timestep t. CRISP fuses them into

$$\mathbf{x}_t = \omega_g \mathbf{g}_t + \omega_d \mathbf{d}_t + \omega_u \mathbf{u}_t + \omega_n \mathbf{n}_t,$$

where $\omega_g, \omega_d, \omega_u, \omega_n$ are learnable weights. For a trajectory of length l, the fused sequence is

$$\mathbf{X} = [\mathbf{x}_1, \mathbf{x}_2, \ldots, \mathbf{x}_l].$$

CRISP uses a causal sequence encoder to model trajectory context:

$$\mathbf{H} = \text{Transformer}(\mathbf{X}),$$

where $\mathbf{H} = [\mathbf{h}_1, \mathbf{h}_2, \ldots, \mathbf{h}_l]$ and $\mathbf{h}_t$ is the contextual hidden state at timestep t. A POI decoder generates neural scores over all candidate POIs:

$$\mathbf{s}_t^{model} = \text{Decoder}(\mathbf{h}_t).$$

CRISP also incorporates user historical visit preference as a personalized residual signal. Let $\mathbf{s}_t^{hist}$ denote candidate POI scores from user historical visit patterns. The neural prediction score is

$$\mathbf{s}_t^{neural} = \mathbf{s}_t^{model} + \mathbf{s}_t^{hist}.$$

Thus, candidate ranking depends on current trajectory context and long-term user preference.

4.4 Last-Step-Aware Training Objective

Next POI evaluation usually focuses on the last valid timestep of each trajectory. Given trajectory prefix $T_u^{1:l}$, the model is evaluated by whether it predicts p_{l+1}^u. Training with only full-sequence cross-entropy optimizes intermediate and final timesteps at the same time, which creates a mismatch with final evaluation. CRISP mitigates this mismatch with a last-step-aware objective that preserves full-sequence learning while directly optimizing the final decision position.

Let $y_t = p_{t+1}$ be the supervision label at timestep t, and let $\mathbf{s}_t^{neural}$ be the corresponding candidate POI scores. The full-sequence cross-entropy is

$$\mathcal{L}_{seq} = -\sum_{t=1}^{l} \log \frac{\exp(s_{t,y_t}^{neural})}{\sum_{p \in \mathcal{P}} \exp(s_{t,p}^{neural})}.$$

The last-step cross-entropy is applied only to the last valid prediction position:

$$\mathcal{L}_{last} = -\log \frac{\exp(s_{l,y_l}^{neural})}{\sum_{p \in \mathcal{P}} \exp(s_{l,p}^{neural})}.$$

The final objective is

$$\mathcal{L} = \mathcal{L}_{seq} + \lambda_{last}\mathcal{L}_{last},$$

where λ_{last} controls the weight of last-step supervision. This objective retains intermediate supervision and strengthens final-position ranking.

4.5 Posterior Sequential Transition Modeling

Neural scores integrate graph structures, trajectory context, and user historical preference. User mobility, however, also contains stable posterior sequential transition regularities. For example, the same user may repeatedly visit certain POIs after leaving a specific location in the evening, and mobility after workday lunch may differ from mobility after weekend leisure activities. To capture such personalized posterior transitions, CRISP introduces Posterior Sequential Transition Modeling (PST).

PST constructs conditional transition memory from training trajectories. Given user u, current POI p_t, and daypart context b_t, it counts how often candidate POI p appears as a subsequent visit:

$$M(u, b_t, p_t, p) = \text{Count}_{\mathcal{D}_{train}}(u, b_t, p_t \rightarrow p).$$

Here, b_t denotes daypart context discretized from timestamps, such as morning, afternoon, evening, or night. This memory captures which POIs a user is more likely to visit after the current POI under a temporal context.

To reduce raw count-scale effects, PST uses log-normalized posterior transition scores:

$$s_t^{pst}(p) = \log(1 + M(u, b_t, p_t, p)).$$

During inference, CRISP combines neural scores with PST posterior transition scores:

$$s_t(p) = s_t^{neural}(p) + \alpha s_t^{pst}(p),$$

where α controls the PST score weight. The final recommendation list ranks candidate POIs by $s_t(p)$.

PST does not replace the neural model. It injects user-daypart-conditioned sequential transition regularities into final ranking. The neural model learns complex contextual representations and candidate POI semantics, while PST explicitly models observable posterior transition memory from training trajectories. Their combination makes final ranking reflect both representation learning and personalized sequential transition structures.

During training, PST does not optimize model parameters; CRISP is trained with $\mathcal{L}_{seq} + \lambda_{last}\mathcal{L}_{last}$. During inference, the neural model first produces $\mathbf{s}_t^{neural}$, and PST queries transition memory using the current user, current POI, and daypart context. The final Top-K list ranks POIs with the combined score. Thus, PST complements neural representation learning at final ranking.

For PST, daypart is discretized from the current timestamp into morning, afternoon, evening, and night. The default memory key is (u, b_t, p_t), where u is the user, b_t is the source daypart, and p_t is the current POI. PST uses log-normalized transition counts from the training split. During inference, posterior correction is applied only within the top-B candidate band produced by the neural model, with $B = 50$. We use centered refinement, where the mean posterior score within the candidate band is subtracted before adding the PST score to the neural score. The default PST strength is $\alpha = 0.8$.

5 Experiments

5.1 Experimental Setup

Datasets. We conduct experiments on two public check-in datasets, Foursquare-NYC and Foursquare-TKY. Both contain users, POIs, categories, timestamps, and geographical coordinates, enabling evaluation of city-level global mobility patterns and user-level personalized mobility preferences. Following a unified preprocessing pipeline, we filter inactive users and low-frequency POIs, then split continuous check-ins into trajectory samples. Table 1 reports the preprocessed statistics.

Table 1. Statistics of the preprocessed datasets.

Dataset	Users	POIs	Categories	Check-ins	Traj.	Train	Test	Avg. Len.
NYC	873	4924	314	78950	15699	12734	2965	5.029
TKY	2124	7767	286	309135	55491	44853	10638	5.5709

Preprocessing and Split Protocol. We remove duplicate check-ins, filter low-activity users and low-frequency POIs, and segment each user's chronologically ordered check-ins into trajectories using a 24-hour window. Trajectories shorter than three check-ins are removed, and users with fewer than four trajectories are filtered out. For each user, trajectories are split in chronological order: the earlier trajectories are used for training and the later trajectories for testing. Global POI transition graphs, distance graphs, user-history graphs, role-family statistics, and PST transition memories are constructed from the training split only. This protocol avoids using future next-POI targets when constructing graph edges, role features, or posterior transition counts. The candidate POI vocabulary is fixed after preprocessing and is shared across training and testing.

Evaluation Metrics. We report Acc@K, MAP@K, and MRR. We set K to 1, 5, 10, and 20. Acc@K indicates whether the ground-truth next POI appears in the top-K list. MAP@K evaluates ranking quality within the top-K results, and MRR measures the reciprocal rank of the ground-truth POI. Since next-POI recommendation serves one-step decisions, Acc@1 and MRR directly reflect top-rank prediction ability.

Baselines. We compare CRISP with representative next POI recommendation methods, including sequential models DeepMove [2], EEDN [16], LSTPM [12], PLSPL [18], STAN [8], and HiLS [15]; graph-enhanced methods HGARN [13], AGRAN [17], GETNext [20], FPGT [4], SNPM [21], and GUGEN [23]; and the recent hierarchical graph method ReHDM [6]. ReHDM does not report Acc@20 or MAP@K, marked as –.

Implementation and Reproducibility Details. CRISP is implemented in PyTorch. We use Adam with learning rate 10^{-3}, weight decay 0, batch size 32, and train for 100 epochs. StepLR is used with decay factor 0.5 every 10 epochs. The default embedding dimensions are 100 for POIs, 150 for users, 200 for categories, and 100 for GPS features. The GCN hidden size is 128. The numbers of global graph, distance graph, and user graph layers are 5, 4, and 3, respectively. The Transformer encoder uses 4 heads and 3 layers with dropout 0.5.

The number of neighboring POIs is set to 20, and the sheaf condition dimension is 32. Unless otherwise specified, all models use the same preprocessing, split protocol, and evaluation code. Main results are averaged over three random seeds $\{1000, 1001, 1002\}$, while ablation studies keep all settings unchanged except for the removed component.

5.2 User Role Construction and Analysis

We construct user role families to provide stable long-term mobility context for user-history graph propagation. For each user, check-ins are first sorted by time. We derive temporal variables including hour, day of week, weekend indicator, night indicator, and commute-period indicator. Night is defined as 22:00–06:00, and commute periods are defined as 07:00–10:00 and 17:00–20:00. Fine-grained POI categories are further mapped to macro categories, including transport, food/coffee, nightlife, shopping, residence/work, leisure/outdoor, service/daily, and other. This macro-category mapping is used only for role construction and interpretability analysis; it does not modify the next-POI prediction labels.

The role profile of each user contains four groups of features: activity features, revisit and category-diversity features, spatial mobility features, and temporal-semantic preference features. Activity features include the number of check-ins, active days, average daily check-ins, number of trajectories, average trajectory length, and trajectory duration. Revisit and diversity features include unique POI ratio, revisit ratio, unique category ratio, normalized category entropy, dominant POI ratio, and dominant category ratio. Spatial features include average and maximum mobility radius, average Haversine distance between consecutive check-ins, 90th-percentile movement distance, and average within-trajectory movement distance. Temporal-semantic features include weekend, night, and commute-period activity ratios, as well as macro-category visit proportions.

After feature transformation, clipping, and standardization, we apply K-means clustering to obtain user role clusters. The number of clusters is selected by silhouette score, and semantically similar clusters are merged into role families such as Transit Commuters, Shopping Weekenders, Home-Work Regulars, Mixed Urban Movers, and Daily-Errand Users. The lookup table records the original user ID, the continuous model user ID, the role name, the role family, and the role-family ID. During training and inference, CRISP queries the role-family ID of each batch user and uses its embedding only in the role-conditioned user sheaf encoder.

Role families show distinct behavioral and sequential characteristics. In NYC, Home-Work Regulars and Transit Commuters account for large proportions, indicating strong commuting and regular mobility patterns. In TKY, Transit Commuters and Shopping Weekenders are more prominent, reflecting stronger transport-oriented and weekend-consumption behaviors. Role-specific category transition distributions also differ substantially. Commuter-like users, for example, concentrate more on transport-related transitions, while leisure-oriented users show more diverse food, shopping, and entertainment transitions. The mean pairwise Jensen-Shannon divergence between role-specific category transition distributions reaches 0.6153 on NYC and 0.4463 on TKY, with maximum values of 0.7692 and 0.7282. These results support role-conditioned propagation in user history graphs.

5.3 Overall Performance

Tables 2 and 3 report overall performance. Table 2 compares Acc@K on NYC and TKY; Table 3 reports MAP@K and MRR.

Table 2. Overall performance comparison in terms of Acc@K. The best result in each column is shown in bold, the second-best result is underlined, and the CRISP row is shaded in blue.

Model	Ref	Foursquare-NYC				Foursquare-TKY			
		Acc@1	**Acc@5**	**Acc@10**	**Acc@20**	**Acc@1**	**Acc@5**	**Acc@10**	**Acc@20**
DeepMove [2]	WWW 18	0.1131	0.2443	0.2963	0.3482	0.0891	0.1692	0.1935	0.2022
EEDN [16]	SIGIR 23	0.1272	0.2913	0.3215	0.3369	0.0954	0.2242	0.2717	0.2963
LSTPM [12]	AAAI 20	0.2648	0.5614	0.6677	0.7231	0.2195	0.3141	0.4297	0.5275
PLSPL [18]	TKDE 22	0.2414	0.5486	0.6416	0.6921	0.2157	0.3142	0.4314	0.5304
STAN [8]	WWW 21	0.2563	0.5412	0.6574	0.7001	0.2249	0.3911	0.5213	0.5886
HILS [15]	TMC 24	0.2860	0.5640	0.6732	0.7239	0.2410	0.4370	0.5495	0.6319
HGARN [13]	arXiv 22	0.2883	0.5646	0.6714	0.7283	0.2233	0.4298	0.5103	0.5644
AGRAN [17]	SIGIR 23	0.2134	0.5194	0.5997	0.6382	0.2302	0.4265	0.5258	0.5967
GETNext [20]	SIGIR 22	0.2792	0.5611	0.6733	0.7396	0.2539	0.4523	0.5613	0.6504
FPGT [4]	ASC 23	0.2814	0.5630	0.6771	0.7494	0.2603	0.4712	0.5765	0.6586
SNPM [21]	AAAI 23	0.2775	0.5638	0.6814	**0.7813**	0.2604	0.5095	0.5872	**0.7134**
GUGEN [23]	TMC 24	<u>0.2981</u>	<u>0.5925</u>	<u>0.6929</u>	0.7556	0.2743	0.5132	0.5916	0.6631
ReHDM [6]	IJCAI 25	0.2914	0.5686	0.6521	–	**0.3184**	<u>0.5461</u>	<u>0.6063</u>	–
CRISP	**Ours**	**0.3166**	**0.6045**	**0.6994**	<u>0.7611</u>	<u>0.3114</u>	**0.5501**	**0.6278**	<u>0.6912</u>

For Acc@K, the gains of CRISP are most visible at small K, which is consistent with the design goal of improving the final top-ranked recommendation. On Foursquare-NYC, CRISP obtains the best Acc@1, Acc@5, and Acc@10, and achieves the second-best Acc@20. On Foursquare-TKY, CRISP achieves the best Acc@5 and Acc@10, while ranking second on Acc@1 and Acc@20. These results indicate that CRISP is particularly effective in improving early-ranking next-POI recommendation performance.

For MAP@K and MRR, CRISP achieves the best MAP@5 and MAP@10 on both datasets, showing that it effectively improves the ranking quality of top candidate POIs. For MAP@20 and MRR, CRISP also remains highly competitive, obtaining the second-best MAP@20 and MRR on Foursquare-NYC and the second-best MAP@20 on Foursquare-TKY. These results further demonstrate that CRISP is especially effective for early-ranking recommendation while maintaining competitive overall ranking performance.

Table 3. Overall performance comparison in terms of MAP@K and MRR. The best result in each column is shown in bold, the second-best result is underlined, and the CRISP row is shaded in blue.

Model	Ref	Foursquare-NYC				Foursquare-TKY			
		MAP@5	MAP@10	MAP@20	MRR	MAP@5	MAP@10	MAP@20	MRR
DeepMove [2]	WWW 18	0.1615	0.1684	0.1721	0.1758	0.1478	0.1557	0.1600	0.1643
EEDN [16]	SIGIR 23	0.1868	0.1911	0.2014	0.2023	0.1643	0.1826	0.1921	0.1941
LSTPM [12]	AAAI 20	0.3601	0.3747	0.3802	0.3828	0.3026	0.3142	0.3196	0.3241
PLSPL [18]	TKDE 22	0.2936	0.3386	0.3725	0.3784	0.2139	0.2906	0.3335	0.3343
STAN [8]	WWW 21	0.3342	0.3732	0.3894	0.3901	0.2743	0.3322	0.3526	0.3553
HILS [15]	TMC 24	0.3904	0.4132	0.4182	0.4194	0.3415	0.3601	0.3702	0.3734
HGARN [13]	arXiv 22	0.3945	0.4155	0.4178	0.4219	0.3168	0.3292	0.3349	0.3385
AGRAN [17]	SIGIR 23	0.3431	0.3584	0.3715	0.3721	0.3263	0.3344	0.3584	0.3606
GETNext [20]	SIGIR 22	0.3854	0.4026	0.4086	0.4113	0.3541	0.3682	0.3732	0.3764
FPGT [4]	ASC 23	0.3793	0.4041	0.4112	0.4136	0.3622	0.3758	0.3792	0.3837
SNPM [21]	AAAI 23	0.3721	0.4172	**0.4413**	**0.4428**	0.3716	0.3786	**0.4153**	<u>0.4161</u>
GUGEN [23]	TMC 24	<u>0.4092</u>	<u>0.4226</u>	0.4276	0.4296	<u>0.3736</u>	<u>0.3842</u>	0.3892	0.3939
ReHDM [6]	IJCAI 25	–	–	–	–	–	–	–	**0.4229**
CRISP	**Ours**	**0.4213**	**0.4341**	<u>0.4383</u>	<u>0.4404</u>	**0.3909**	**0.4018**	<u>0.4064</u>	0.4097

5.4 Ablation Study

To analyze each component, we conduct ablation studies on Foursquare-NYC, as shown in Table 4. Global Category Sheaf keeps only category-conditioned global graph propagation. User Role Sheaf keeps only role-conditioned user graph propagation. CR-Sheaf combines both context-conditioned propagation types. CR-Sheaf + Last-Step CE further introduces the last-step-aware objective. CRISP is the full model with category-role-informed sheaf propagation, Last-Step CE, and PST.

Table 4. Ablation study on the Foursquare-NYC dataset. The best result in each column is shown in bold, and the second-best result is underlined.

Method	Acc@1	Acc@5	Acc@10	Acc@20	MAP@20	MRR
Global Category Sheaf	0.3048	0.5953	0.6917	<u>0.7588</u>	0.4302	0.4321
User Role Sheaf	<u>0.3070</u>	0.5896	<u>0.6957</u>	0.7547	<u>0.4313</u>	<u>0.4334</u>
CR-Sheaf	0.3063	0.5947	0.6954	0.7549	0.4301	0.4320
CR-Sheaf + Last-Step CE	0.3049	<u>0.5964</u>	0.6936	0.7558	0.4289	0.4310
CRISP	**0.3166**	**0.6045**	**0.6994**	**0.7611**	**0.4383**	**0.4404**

The ablation results support the main design of CRISP. The full model achieves the best Acc@1, Acc@5, Acc@10, Acc@20, MAP@20, and MRR, showing that the three components work best together. User Role Sheaf performs better than Global Category Sheaf on Acc@1, Acc@10, MAP@20, and MRR, which suggests that role-conditioned user history propagation provides useful personalized constraints for early ranking. Global Category Sheaf remains competitive on Acc@5 and Acc@20, showing that category-conditioned propagation contributes complementary global mobility semantics. These patterns are consistent with the motivation of combining category-role sheaf propagation, last-step-aware optimization, and PST.

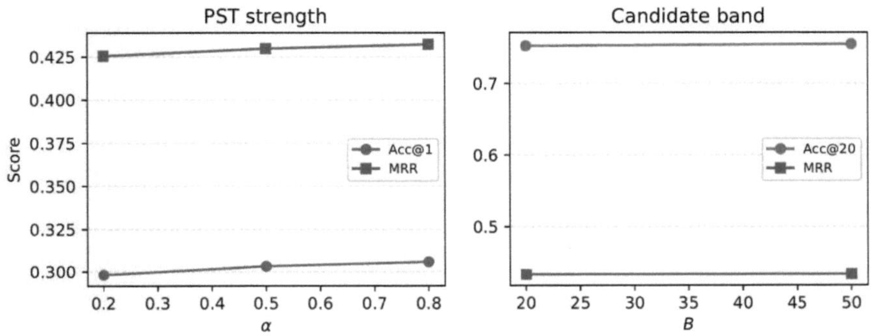

Fig. 4. PST parameter sensitivity analysis.

5.5 Parameter Analysis

We analyze the sensitivity of PST to posterior transition strength α and candidate band width B. All results are averaged over three seeds on Foursquare-NYC. As shown in Fig. 4, increasing α from 0.2 to 0.8 improves Acc@1 and MRR. This indicates that posterior transition memory needs sufficient strength to affect final ranking. For candidate band width, $B = 50$ gives a stable setting and lets PST refine plausible candidates without excessively changing the ranking space.

6 Conclusion

This paper proposes CRISP for next POI recommendation. It models context heterogeneity through category-conditioned global sheaf propagation and role-family-conditioned user sheaf propagation. This design allows graph messages to adapt to category transitions and user mobility roles. Last-Step CE aligns training with last-step evaluation, while PST refines final ranking with user-daypart-conditioned transition memory. Experiments on Foursquare-NYC and Foursquare-TKY show that CRISP improves several key early-ranking metrics and achieves competitive overall ranking performance. The ablation study further shows that category-role sheaf propagation and PST are responsible for the main gains, especially in the early-ranking range targeted by the proposed design.

References

1. Bodnar, C., Di Giovanni, F., Chamberlain, B.P., Liò, P., Bronstein, M.M.: Neural sheaf diffusion: A topological perspective on heterophily and oversmoothing in GNNs. In: Advances in Neural Information Processing Systems, vol. 35 (2022)
2. Feng, J., et al.: Deepmove: Predicting human mobility with attentional recurrent networks. In: Proceedings of the 2018 World Wide Web Conference, pp. 1459–1468 (2018). https://doi.org/10.1145/3178876.3186058
3. Feng, S., Li, X., Zeng, Y., Cong, G., Chee, Y.M., Yuan, Q.: Personalized ranking metric embedding for next new poi recommendation. In: Proceedings of the Twenty-Fourth International Joint Conference on Artificial Intelligence, pp. 2069–2075 (2015)
4. He, Y., Zhou, W., Luo, F., Gao, M., Wen, J.: Feature-based poi grouping with transformer for next point of interest recommendation. Appl. Soft Comput. **147**, 110754 (2023). https://doi.org/10.1016/j.asoc.2023.110754
5. Kipf, T.N., Welling, M.: Semi-supervised classification with graph convolutional networks. In: International Conference on Learning Representations (2017)
6. Li, X., et al.: Beyond individual and point: Next poi recommendation via region-aware dynamic hypergraph with dual-level modeling. In: Proceedings of the Thirty-Fourth International Joint Conference on Artificial Intelligence, pp. 3081–3089 (2025). https://doi.org/10.24963/ijcai.2025/343
7. Liu, Q., Wu, S., Wang, L., Tan, T.: Predicting the next location: A recurrent model with spatial and temporal contexts. In: Proceedings of the Thirtieth AAAI Conference on Artificial Intelligence, pp. 194–200 (2016). https://doi.org/10.1609/aaai.v30i1.9971
8. Luo, Y., Liu, Q., Liu, Z.: Stan: Spatio-temporal attention network for next location recommendation. In: Proceedings of The Web Conference 2021, pp. 2177–2185 (2021). https://doi.org/10.1145/3442381.3449998
9. Purificato, A., Cassarà, G., Siciliano, F., Liò, P., Silvestri, F.: Sheaf4rec: Sheaf neural networks for graph-based recommender systems. arXiv preprint arXiv:2304.09097 (2023)
10. Qin, Y., Xie, J., Xiao, Z., Zhang, M.: Geomamba: Towards multi-granular poi recommendation with geographical state space model. Proc. AAAI Conf. Artif. Intell. **39**(12), 12479–12487 (2025). https://doi.org/10.1609/aaai.v39i12.33360
11. Rendle, S., Freudenthaler, C., Schmidt-Thieme, L.: Factorizing personalized Markov chains for next-basket recommendation. In: Proceedings of the 19th International Conference on World Wide Web, pp. 811–820 (2010). https://doi.org/10.1145/1772690.1772773
12. Sun, K., Qian, T., Chen, T., Liang, Y., Nguyen, Q.V.H., Yin, H.: Where to go next: Modeling long- and short-term user preferences for point-of-interest recommendation. In: Proceedings of the AAAI Conference on Artificial Intelligence, vol. 34, pp. 214–221 (2020). https://doi.org/10.1609/aaai.v34i01.5353
13. Tang, Y., He, J., Zhao, Z.: Hgarn: Hierarchical graph attention recurrent network for human mobility prediction. arXiv preprint arXiv:2210.07765 (2022)
14. Veličković, P., Cucurull, G., Casanova, A., Romero, A., Liò, P., Bengio, Y.: Graph attention networks. In: International Conference on Learning Representations (2018)
15. Wang, C., Yuan, M., Yang, Y., Peng, K., Jiang, H.: Revisiting long- and short-term preference learning for next poi recommendation with hierarchical LSTM. IEEE Trans. Mobile Comput. **23**(12) (2024). https://doi.org/10.1109/TMC.2024.3417405

16. Wang, X., Fukumoto, F., Cui, J., Suzuki, Y., Li, J., Yu, D.: FEDN: Enhanced encoder-decoder network with local and global context learning for poi recommendation. In: Proceedings of the 46th International ACM SIGIR Conference on Research and Development in Information Retrieval, pp. 383–392 (2023) https://doi.org/10.1145/3539618.3591678
17. Wang, Z., Zhu, Y., Wang, C., Ma, W., Li, B., Yu, J.: Adaptive graph representation learning for next poi recommendation. In: Proceedings of the 46th International ACM SIGIR Conference on Research and Development in Information Retrieval, pp. 393–402 (2023). https://doi.org/10.1145/3539618.3591634
18. Wu, Y., Li, K., Zhao, G., Qian, X.: Personalized long- and short-term preference learning for next poi recommendation. IEEE Trans. Knowl. Data Eng. **34**(4), 1944–1957 (2022). https://doi.org/10.1109/TKDE.2020.3002531
19. Yang, D., Fankhauser, B., Rosso, P., Cudré-Mauroux, P.: Location prediction over sparse user mobility traces using RNNs: Flashback in hidden states. In: Proceedings of the Twenty-Ninth International Joint Conference on Artificial Intelligence, pp. 2184–2190 (2020). https://doi.org/10.24963/ijcai.2020/302
20. Yang, S., Liu, J., Zhao, K.: Getnext: Trajectory flow map enhanced transformer for next poi recommendation. In: Proceedings of the 45th International ACM SIGIR Conference on Research and Development in Information Retrieval, pp. 1144–1153 (2022). https://doi.org/10.1145/3477495.3531983
21. Yin, F., Liu, Y., Shen, Z., Chen, L., Shang, S., Han, P.: Next poi recommendation with dynamic graph and explicit dependency. In: Proceedings of the AAAI Conference on Artificial Intelligence, vol. 37, pp. 4827–4834 (2023). https://doi.org/10.1609/aaai.v37i4.25608
22. Zhao, P., et al.: Where to go next: a spatio-temporal gated network for next poi recommendation. Proc. AAAI Conf. Artif. Intell. **33**(01), 5877–5884 (2019). https://doi.org/10.1609/aaai.v33i01.33015877
23. Zuo, C., Zhang, X., Yan, L., Zhang, Z.: GUGEN: global user graph enhanced network for next poi recommendation. IEEE Trans. Mob. Comput. **23**(12), 14975–14986 (2024). https://doi.org/10.1109/TMC.2024.3455107

TransDyG: An Anomaly Detection Method Integrating Dynamic Graphs and Transformers

Yunxiang Wang[1,2], Shanhe Niu[1,2], Ruiqi Wang[1], Bo Jiang[1,2], Boya Yang[1(✉)], and Baoxu Liu[1,2]

[1] Institute of Information Engineering, Chinese Academy of Sciences, Beijing, China
{wangyunxiang,niushanhe,wangruiqi,jiangbo,yangboya,liubaoxu}@iie.ac.cn
[2] School of Cyber Security, University of Chinese Academy of Sciences, Beijing, China

Abstract. Network behavior data is inherently graph-structured, comprising user entities and their complex interactions. While anomaly detection in this context can be framed as a graph anomaly detection problem, real-world network environments are highly dynamic. Conventional detectors that rely on static graph snapshots fail to capture temporal dependencies and evolving attack patterns, resulting in limited generalization and adaptability to novel threats. To address this issue, we propose TransDyG, a dynamic graph anomaly detection framework tailored for network behavior analysis. TransDyG integrates dynamic graph representation learning with Transformer-based sequence modeling to achieve unified spatiotemporal encoding. Along the spatial dimension, Graph Neural Networks (GNNs) capture local topological structures and interaction dependencies. Along the temporal dimension, a Transformer models long-range dependencies across time steps, capturing the underlying evolution of network behaviors. It produces coherent spatiotemporal representations, enhancing the model's ability to detect complex multi-step attacks. Furthermore, by leveraging the in-context learning and generalization-by-inference capabilities of Transformers, TransDyG can rapidly adapt to emerging behavior patterns from limited examples, enabling effective few-shot detection of novel anomalies without full parameter retraining. Extensive experiments on benchmark dataset demonstrate that TransDyG accurately characterizes the evolution of anomalous behaviors and exhibits superior robustness and transferability in dynamic, open-world network settings.

Keywords: Dynamic Graphs · Transformers · Network Behavior Modeling · Anomaly Detection

L. Ding et al. (Eds.): APWeb-WAIM 2026, LNCS 16995, pp. 50–64, 2027.
https://doi.org/10.1007/978-981-92-5699-0_4

1 Introduction

Anomaly detection [1] refers to the problem of identifying patterns in data that do not conform to expected behavior. In the field of cybersecurity, these inconsistent patterns are typically referred to as anomalies or outliers. Anomaly detection is widely applied in cybersecurity for intrusion detection [2], vulnerability detection [3], anomalous behavior detection [4], and more.

Graphs are an expressive data structure naturally suited for representing interactions between entities by capturing complex relationships [5]. While most research focuses on static graphs, real-world graph data often evolves over time. For example, knowledge networks continuously acquire new concepts and connections. Modeling such dynamic graphs has thus become increasingly important. By leveraging both temporal information and relational structure, dynamic graph analysis enables more effective anomaly detection, enhancing system security and integrity.

Graph representation learning aims to utilize representation learning techniques to map graphs into a vector space, preserving both structural and semantic features of the graph. The learned vectors retain the similarity of nodes in graph-structured data, enhancing the generalization performance of models for downstream anomaly detection tasks. In recent years, the Transformer [6] has achieved significant success in Natural Language Processing (NLP) [7] and Computer Vision (CV) [8]. Recognized as one of the most powerful neural networks, it has replaced Convolutional Neural Networks (CNNs) and Recurrent Neural Networks (RNNs) as the de facto standard for numerous tasks such as language understanding, machine translation, and image segmentation. It has also made considerable breakthroughs in the field of graph representation learning.

In the field of anomaly detection, combining Transformer with graph representation learning has become a hotspot in both academia and industry. However, applying Transformer to graph data still faces several challenges, primarily including: (1) Deep Structure Awareness: In unsupervised learning, when using Transformer to model graph structure, the model can easily overfit complex "normal" patterns. Effectively identifying the topological structure of the graph and the attribute differences of nodes and edges is required. (2) Dynamic Feature Capture: Anomalies in dynamic graphs may manifest as anomalous behaviors of specific local nodes or edges, or as anomalous changes in the global network topology, necessitating the simultaneous capture of global and local features. (3) Computational Cost: Anomaly detection in dynamic graphs often involves large-scale graph data, making computational resources and time efficiency significant challenges.

To tackle these challenges, we propose a novel framework combining dynamic graphs and Transformer, named TransDyG, as illustrated in the Fig. 1. It samples attention nodes for each central node based on semantic and structural information, acquires basic graph structure information for the Transformer through shortest-path-based positional encoding, and then, based on our proposed TransDyG, integrates Transformer and dynamic graphs to simultaneously extract structural and temporal features of the graph. Finally, it detects normal and attack behaviors based on anomaly scores. Specifically, the key contributions of our research are as follows:

- **We introduce a spatiotemporal context serialization and encoding method, which converts the local neighborhood of each candidate edge into a fixed-length sequence.** It then incorporates structural roles, hop distances, and temporal offsets via learnable embeddings, allowing the Transformer to effectively model both local and global dependencies in dynamic graphs.
- **We propose a novel dynamic graph anomaly detection model named TransDyG, which integrates Transformer with dynamic graph representation learning.** By jointly encoding node, edge, and topological features into a shared embedding space, TransDyG captures both local structural dependencies and long-range temporal evolutions, enabling robust detection of complex multi-step attacks and adaptation to diverse feature distributions.
- **We evaluate TransDyG on widely used benchmark dataset for dynamic graph anomaly detection.** Experimental results demonstrate that our method achieves superior detection accuracy, robustness, and transferability compared to baselines.

2 Related Work

2.1 Anomaly Detection in Dynamic Graphs

We denote a Continuous-Time Dynamic Graph (CTDG) as $CTDG = (G, O)$, where G is a static graph representing the initial state of the dynamic graph at time t_0, and O is a set of observations/events. Each observation is a tuple of the form (event type, event, timestamp), where the event type can be edge addition, edge deletion, node addition, node deletion, node split, node merge, etc.

A Discrete-Time Dynamic Graph (DTDG) is a sequence of snapshots extracted from a dynamic graph, sampled at regular time intervals. We define a DTDG as $DTDG = \{G^1, G^2, \ldots, G^T\}$, where $G^t = \{V^t, E^t\}$ represents the graph at snapshot t, V^t is the set of nodes in G^t, and E^t is the set of edges in G^t.

We use "dynamic graph" to refer to both DTDGs and CTDGs. Compared to CTDGs, developing models for DTDGs is often simpler but may incur information loss by focusing only on specific snapshots of the graph's evolution. Notably, models developed for CTDGs can generally be applied to DTDGs, while the converse may not hold. Therefore, the dynamic graphs discussed in this paper refer to CTDGs.

Traditional graph-based anomaly detection techniques involve the application of anomaly and outlier detection methods to graph data mining, primarily including distance-based methods, information theory-based methods, deviation-based methods, and community-based methods. Dynamic graph anomaly detection focuses on identifying anomalous events within dynamic graphs. Recently, deep learning methods have made significant progress in this area. Abdaljalil et al. [9] proposed an unsupervised framework named T-StructGAD, which employs GConvGRU to capture short-term structural changes and combines it with LSTM to model long-term temporal dependencies. The GConvGRU + LSTM combination generates deep node embeddings that simultaneously incorporate structural information and temporal evolution, effectively handling the evolving nature of graphs and improving anomaly detection accuracy. Traditional graph embeddings directly use node IDs or edge attributes, which may leak privacy. AER-GAD [10] proposes an anonymized edge representation mechanism for dynamic bipartite graphs, integrating Bi-GCN and TGAT to achieve joint structure-temporal modeling under privacy protection. This method significantly reduces privacy leakage risk while maintaining high detection accuracy. AD-FG [11] transforms network traffic into graph structures and enables cross-domain collaborative anomaly detection through federated learning, emphasizing both privacy protection and model generalization. In dynamic graph anomaly detection, besides analyzing anomalies based on node and edge features, the fusion of node and edge features for analysis is increasingly being adopted. Tian et al. proposed the SAD [12] framework, based on TGAT (Temporal Graph Attention Network), to capture the structural and node/edge feature evolution over time. It employs a temporal-equipped memory bank combined with pseudo-label contrastive learning to achieve efficient semi-supervised anomaly detection in dynamic graphs. Fathony et al. [13] focus on anomaly detection in dynamic bipartite node-edge attributed graphs, emphasizing the importance of interaction relations. They fully utilize the heterogeneity of the bipartite structure and edge attributes to realize unsupervised interaction-focused anomaly detection.

2.2 Application of Transformer in Dynamic Graphs

Transformer is a neural network initially proposed by Vaswani et al. [6], which relies entirely on the attention mechanism to learn representative embeddings for various types of data. Recent works have also applied Transformer to dynamic graph tasks. GraphERT [14] pioneered the use of Transformer, seamlessly integrating graph structure learning with temporal analysis by applying Masked Language Modeling (MLM) on graph random walk sequences. TSAD [15] employs a multi-head self-attention mechanism to capture long-term dependencies among nodes, combines it with time-aware positional encoding to handle temporal evolution, and introduces cross-temporal attention to aggregate historical node representations, enhancing the modeling of periodic patterns and structural changes. AADDN [16] further incorporates Graph Attention Networks to focus on node interactions and neighborhood influences. AnomalyLLM [17] learns dynamic edge representations through contrastive pre-training, bridges the modality gap to LLM space, and performs few-shot anomalous edge detection via in-context prompting and LLM reasoning, enabling the detection of diverse anomaly types by adjusting prompts and addressing the poor generalization of traditional methods to novel anomalies.

SimpleDyG [18] reinterprets dynamic graphs as a sequence modeling problem and proposes an innovative time-alignment technique. Solely considering structural or temporal features is limited in dynamic graph detection. STCAD [19] utilizes a dynamic graph Transformer to model structure-temporal features. Its structure-temporal node encoder samples contextual subgraphs for candidate edges and extracts features at two levels: the first level employs independent structural and temporal features to capture dynamic graph characteristics; the second level captures structure-temporal coupled information. YÄślmaz et al. [20] integrate the global structural aggregation capability of GCN with the attention mechanism of GAT, first using GCN to extract global features, then employing GAT to enhance local node interactions.

3 Methodology

In this paper, we model network traffic as a dynamic graph by sliding a time window over raw packets and constructing a snapshot G_t for each interval. The goal is to detect anomalous edges: for each candidate interaction $e = (u, v, t)$, we learn a function $f(e, G_{\leq t})$ that outputs an anomaly score, where $G_{\leq t}$ denotes the graph sequence up to time t. The overall model architecture is illustrated in Fig. 1.

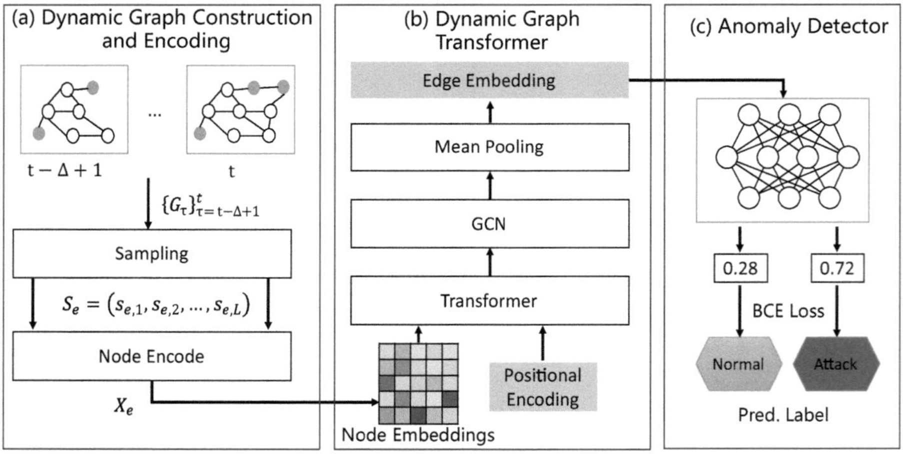

Fig. 1. Architecture of our proposed TransDyG for anomaly detection using dynamic graphs and transformer.

3.1 Dynamic Graph Construction and Edge-Context Encoding

The dynamic graph is represented as a snapshot sequence $\{G_t\}_{t=1}^{T}$, where $G_t = (V_t, E_t)$. For a candidate interaction edge $e = (u, v, t)$ at snapshot t, we extract its structural–temporal context within a time window of length Δ and serialize it into a fixed-length edge-context sequence. It jointly encodes the endpoint attributes of $e = (u, v, t)$, the k-hop local neighborhood structure, and the cross-window temporal context into a sliceable and aggregatable representation, which serves as the foundational feature for subsequent modules, including spatiotemporal representation learning, local structural aggregation, edge-representation fusion, and dynamic anomaly detection.

Edge-Context Serialization. Within the window $W_t = t - \Delta + 1, \ldots, t$, we sample the local spatiotemporal neighborhood around the endpoints u and v, denoted as

$$C(e) = \Psi\left(u, v, t, G_{\mathcal{T}}, k\right),$$

where k controls the neighborhood size and $\Psi(\cdot)$ denotes a context construction operator over multiple hops and multiple time steps. We unfold $C(e)$ into a length-L sequence according to a predefined template,

$$S_e = (s_{e,1}, s_{e,2}, \ldots, s_{e,L}).$$

Each position $s_{e,\ell}$ corresponds to a contextual slot. In practice, this sequence is mapped to three types of discrete indices:

$$p_e = (p_{e,1}, \ldots, p_{e,L}), \quad h_e = (h_{e,1}, \ldots, h_{e,L}), \quad \tau_e = (\tau_{e,1}, \ldots, \tau_{e,L}),$$

which respectively represent: (i) the position index p_e, encoding the structural role of each sequence slot; (ii) the hop-distance index h_e, indicating the hop distance of the slot relative to the central endpoints; and (iii) the temporal-distance index τ_e, specifying the time offset of the slot with respect to the current snapshot t.

Spatiotemporal Discrete Encoding. To explicitly encode three complementary cues—structural position, topological distance, and temporal offset—we introduce three learnable embedding tables:

$$E_{\text{pos}} \in \mathbb{R}^{|P| \times d}, \quad E_{\text{hop}} \in \mathbb{R}^{|H| \times d}, \quad E_{\text{time}} \in \mathbb{R}^{|T| \times d},$$

where d = `hidden_size`. For the ℓ-th slot, the input vector is obtained via additive fusion:

$$x_{e,\ell} = E_{\text{pos}}[p_{e,\ell}] + E_{\text{hop}}[h_{e,\ell}] + E_{\text{time}}[\tau_{e,\ell}].$$

We then apply layer normalization followed by dropout to obtain the input sequence

$$X_e = \text{Dropout}\big(\text{LN}\big(\big[x_{e,1}\ x_{e,2} \cdots x_{e,L}\big]\big)\big) \in \mathbb{R}^{L \times d}.$$

.

Through edge-context serialization and spatiotemporal discrete encoding operations, the model jointly encodes the endpoint information of the edge $e = (u, v, t)$, the k-hop local structure, and the cross-window temporal context into an initial spatiotemporal representation that is both sliceable and aggregatable.

3.2 Integrating Transformer and GCN for Spatiotemporal Representation and Edge Embedding

We employ a Transformer to model global interactions in the serialized edge-context sequence X_e, producing a high-order spatiotemporal representation H_e. Then, we reconstruct H_e into endpoint-centered local structural blocks via template-based slicing, and employ a lightweight GCN to aggregate information from the endpoints to their neighborhoods. We concatenate and fuse multi-view subgraphs followed by a global pooling operation, and derive a 4096-dimensional edge embedding h_e through endpoint-level concatenation and a linear projection. The resulting representation supports the construction of both normal edges and negative-sampled pseudo-anomalous edges, thereby providing a unified feature space for subsequent dynamic anomaly detection.

Transformer-Based Global Interaction Modeling. Building upon the spatiotemporal fusion, we feed X_e into a stack of Transformer encoder layers to capture high-order dependencies within the sequence, yielding a sequence-level spatiotemporal representation. Specifically,

$$H_e^{(0)} = X_e,$$
$$H_e^{(\ell)} = \text{TransformerLayer}\left(H_e^{(\ell-1)}\right), \quad \ell = 1, \ldots, L_T.$$

where $H_e^{(L_T)} \in \mathbb{R}^{L\times d}$. Within each layer, multi-head attention(MHA) establishes global interactions for any pair of slots (i, j) and perform softmax normalization.

During the serialization stage, the central endpoints and their k neighborhood slots are placed into the sequence according to a fixed template. In the subsequent local subgraph extraction stage, we apply a deterministic template-based slicing scheme to reconstruct these slots into endpoint-centered local substructure represent.

$$S(H_e; f, g, h) = \left[\, H_e[f] \;;\; H_e[g-1 : h-1] \,\right] \in \mathbb{R}^{(k+1)\times d}$$

where, $H_e[f]$ serves as the endpoint-centered representation, while $H_e[g-1 : h-1]$ corresponds to the representations of its k neighborhood slots. Then, we treat sequence positions 0 and 1 as the central tokens for endpoints u and v, respectively, and extract two views from two non-overlapping index ranges. For endpoint u (anchor, with center position 0):

$$X_u^{(1)} = S(H_e; 0, 2, k+1), \qquad X_u^{(2)} = S(H_e; 0, 2k+4, 3k+3).$$

For endpoint v (positive, with center position 1):

$$X_v^{(1)} = S(H_e; 1, k+2, 2k+1), \qquad X_v^{(2)} = S(H_e; 1, 3k+4, 4k+3).$$

This design explicitly models, for each endpoint, a local substructure composed of a central token and k neighborhood slots under two contextual views, thereby providing structured inputs for subsequent GCN-based local aggregation and edge-level fusion.

Local Structural Aggregation. We treat each endpoint-specific block $X \in \mathbb{R}^{(k+1)\times d}$ as a miniature subgraph composed of a central endpoint and its k neighborhood slots, on which we perform a lightweight graph convolution to enable local message passing and feature aggregation. Specifically, we first construct a star-topology adjacency matrix $A \in \mathbb{R}^{(k+1)\times(k+1)}$, where the central node is connected to all neighboring nodes. Under the fixed local topology, we employ a GCN with two nonlinear transformations and adjacency-based aggregation to structurally encode the local block:

$$\begin{aligned} Z &= \sigma(XW_1 + b_1), \\ Y &= AZW_2 + b_2. \end{aligned}$$

where $\sigma(\cdot) = \text{ReLU}$, and $W_1 \in \mathbb{R}^{d\times 128}$ and $W_2 \in \mathbb{R}^{128\times d}$ are learnable parameters. This procedure can be interpreted as aggregating neighborhood-slot information toward the central endpoint under the star adjacency constraint, thereby facilitating message passing and feature smoothing for local structural context. As a result, the sequence representation produced by the Transformer is further transformed into an explicit local subgraph representation. For the four endpoint-local blocks under two views $r \in \{1, 2\}$, we obtain the aggregated representations as:

$$\begin{aligned} Y_u^{(r)} &= \text{GCN}\Big(X_u^{(r)}, A\Big) \\ Y_v^{(r)} &= \text{GCN}\Big(X_v^{(r)}, A\Big)\; r \in \{1, 2\}. \end{aligned}$$

The local aggregation operation provides structurally consistent and alignable endpoint subgraph representations, which serve as inputs for subsequent multi-view fusion and edge-level representation construction.

Multi-view Fusion and Edge Representation Construction. We integrate endpoint-centric local subgraph representations obtained from different views and further map them into a fixed-dimensional edge-level embedding to support subsequent anomaly discrimination. Specifically, for endpoints u and v, let $Y_u^{(r)}, Y_v^{(r)} \in \mathbb{R}^{(k+1)\times d}$ denote the representations aggregated by the local GCN under two views $r \in \{1, 2\}$. We first concatenate them along the node-slot dimension to perform multi-view fusion, yielding the multi-view local structural representations:

$$Y_u = \Big[Y_u^{(1)}; Y_u^{(2)}\Big] \in \mathbb{R}^{2(k+1)\times d}, \qquad Y_v = \Big[Y_v^{(1)}; Y_v^{(2)}\Big] \in \mathbb{R}^{2(k+1)\times d}.$$

Next, to obtain compact endpoint-level representations, we apply global average pooling to each endpoint subgraph, producing endpoint embeddings:

$$g_u = \text{Pool}(Y_u) = \frac{1}{2(k+1)} \sum_{i=1}^{2(k+1)} Y_u[i] \in \mathbb{R}^d, \qquad g_v = \text{Pool}(Y_v) \in \mathbb{R}^d.$$

Finally, we concatenate the two endpoint embeddings and apply a linear projection followed by a nonlinear activation to perform edge-level fusion and dimensionality expansion, resulting in a 4096 dimensional edge representation:

$$h_e = ReLU\left(W_m\left[g_u; g_v\right] + b_m\right) \in \mathbb{R}^{4096}$$

where $W_m \in \mathbb{R}^{4096\times 2d}$ is learnable. It preserves multi-view local structural information at the endpoint level while compressing it into a unified edge-level representation, thereby providing stable and alignable input features for the subsequent classification head.

3.3 Dynamic Anomaly Detection

In this section, we take the edge-level representation $h_e \in \mathbb{R}^{4096}$ as input and produces a logit via an MLP. During training, the model is jointly optimized with a cross-entropy loss and an endpoint-subgraph-based margin contrastive loss. During inference, the logit is mapped to an anomaly probability through a sigmoid function. In the anomaly detection stage, we employ a lightweight multilayer perceptron (MLP) as the classification head to output the anomaly logit for each edge:

$$s_e = f_{\mathrm{MLP}}(h_e) \in \mathbb{R}.$$

We further map it to the posterior anomaly probability via a sigmoid function:

$$p_e = \sigma(s_e) = \frac{1}{1+\exp(-s_e)} \in (0,1).$$

Here, p_e quantifies the confidence that edge e is anomalous; during inference, the model directly outputs $\sigma(s_e)$ as the predicted probability. Considering that truly anomalous edges are typically scarce and expensive to annotate, we construct a pseudo-anomalous set $\widetilde{E}_t$ for each snapshot t based on the observed edge set E_t. Specifically, we adopt a negative sampling strategy that keeps the source endpoint fixed while randomly replacing the destination endpoint to generate pseudo-anomalous edges, and we discard duplicates or edges that have already appeared to ensure sample diversity and validity. Consequently, the training set at snapshot t is formulated as

$$\mathcal{D}_t = \{(e_i, y_i) \mid e_i \in E_t\} \cup \{(\widetilde{e}_j, 1) \mid \widetilde{e}_j \in \widetilde{E}_t\},$$

where the labels y_i of observed edges are provided by annotation, and all negatively sampled edges are assigned the anomalous label 1. The edge-level binary supervision is optimized using a sigmoid-activated cross-entropy loss:

$$\mathcal{L}_{\mathrm{cls}} = -\frac{1}{N}\sum_{i=1}^{N}\Big(y_i \log(p_i) + (1-y_i)\log\big(1-(p_i)\big)\Big),$$

where p_i denotes the probability predicted by the model, $y_i \in \{0,1\}$, and N is the number of training samples. To further enhance the separability of representations for connection rewiring and anomalous links, we introduce a margin-based contrastive loss that explicitly constrains the relative distances between anchor–positive and anchor–negative pairs. During training, we construct three types of endpoint-local subgraph representations $\{A_i, P_i, N_i\}$, corresponding to the anchor (endpoint u), the positive (the true endpoint v), and the negative (the replaced endpoint $\tilde{v}$), respectively. We additionally employ a margin-based contrastive loss $\mathcal{L}$con on the endpoint subgraph representations to separate normal and anomalous pairs.

$\mathcal{L}_{\text{con}}$ employs a margin-based contrastive loss, whose expression is as follows:

$$\mathcal{L}_{\text{con}} = \frac{1}{N}\sum_{i=1}^{N} \max\left(0,\ \|A_i - P_i\|_2^2 - \|A_i - N_i\|_2^2 + \delta\right)$$

The overall optimization objective is given by

$$\mathcal{L} = \mathcal{L}_{\text{cls}} + \mathcal{L}_{\text{con}}.$$

During inference, the model computes the anomaly probability for each candidate edge in a given snapshot as

$$p_e = \sigma(f_{\text{MLP}}(h_e)),$$

Without constructing negative samples. For evaluation, we compute f1 on a per-snapshot basis over the test snapshot set, and aggregate the predictions across all snapshots to obtain an overall f1, thereby quantifying both the detection performance and temporal stability of edge anomaly detection as the dynamic graph evolves over time.

4 Experiment

4.1 Dataset

The UNSW-NB15 dataset [21], developed by the Australian Centre for Cybersecurity (ACCS), serves as a contemporary benchmark for building and evaluating intrusion detection systems. It addresses the limitations of earlier datasets by simulating a realistic network environment that encompasses both normal traffic and a diverse range of generated network attacks. The dataset comprises 2,540,044 data points and includes 49 features, covering basic attributes (e.g., protocol and IP address), content-based features, and time-dependent statistical data. It also contains nine distinct attack categories: Shellcode, Generic, Worms, Fuzzers, DoS, Reconnaissance, Analysis, Backdoor, and Exploits. This diversity makes UNSW-NB15 a comprehensive reference for evaluating machine learning based network intrusion detection methods.

4.2 Experiment Setup

Baselines. We have selected eight methods as baseline methods for comparing performance. Firstly, based on machine learning methods such as random forest(RF), support vector machine(SVM), XGBoost, etc. Secondly, methods based on deep learning include convolutional neural networks(CNN), long short-term neural networks(LSTM), multi-layer perceptrons(MLP), etc. Finally, the latest method in the field of network anomaly detection was selected, CEN-DGNN, which utilizes deep graph convolutional neural networks for edge node co embedding, extracts long-range dependencies between nodes, and uses multi-dimensional edge features to obtain non local structural features and fine high-order node features; The GCN-LOF ensemble graph convolutional network and local outlier factors enhance the sensitivity of the model to rare and sparse attack patterns.

Implementation Details. The preprocessing pipeline transforms the raw UNSW-NB15 network traffic data(.csv format) into a sequence of discrete temporal graph snapshots through the following methodology:

Temporal Bucketing Strategy: Given a time bucket size of $\tau = 600 seconds$ (10 minutes), network flows are discretized into non-overlapping temporal windows, then sparse temporal buckets (empty snapshots) are removed, and remaining snapshots are reindexed to form a contiguous sequence.

Label propagation: Binary edge labels $l(u, v) \in \{0, 1\}$(normal/attack) follow a max-pooling strategy, where $l(u, v) = max\{l_1, l_2, ..., l_k\}$ for k duplicate edges.

Temporal Train-Test Split: Snapshots are chronologically partitioned into training and testing sets with default ratio $\rho_{train} = 0.5$, ensuring temporal consistency where all training snapshots precede testing snapshots.

Graph Topology Construction: For each snapshot $G_t = (V, E_t)$, the edge set E_t and corresponding edge attributes (labels, weights) are stored, along with the global neighborhood structure $\Gamma(v)$ representing all temporal neighbors of each node v across the entire dataset.

Hyperparameter Settings. Neighborhood sampling: For each central node, the top-K = 18 most relevant neighbors are selected to form a fixedâĂŚsize local subgraph. A temporal window size of 2 allows the model to incorporate edge information from both the current snapshot and the previous one.

Representation dimensions: The discrete spatiotemporal encoding, Transformer, and GCN input/output all use 512-dimensional embeddings. The GCN hidden layer dimension is 128 for extracting local structural features. After merging the representations of both endpoints of an edge, the resulting edge representation has dimension 4096, providing highâĂŚlevel features for the subsequent classifier.

Transformer module: It consists of 3 stacked encoder layers, each with 4 attention heads. The feed-forward network uses GELU activation, with a hidden dropout rate of 0.5 and an attention dropout rate of 0.3.

GCN module: It takes the 512-dim output from the Transformer, reduces it to 128-dim via the first linear layer, and then projects it back to 512-dim through a second linear layer, performing local information aggregation.

Classification MLP: The architecture is 4096 → 1024 → 1, mapping the edge representation to a single anomaly logit.

Optimizer: Adam is used with an initial learning rate of 0.0001 and an L2 weight decay of 0.0005. The batch size is set to 1024.

Regularization: High dropout rates (0.5 for hidden layers, 0.3 for attention) together with weight decay (0.0005) help mitigate overfitting.

4.3 Anomaly Detection Results

In order to comprehensively evaluate the performance of TransDyG, we selected eight representative baseline methods for comparison. As shown in the Table 1, the TransDyG model demonstrates excellent comprehensive performance. Its accuracy reaches 95.47%, recall rate is as high as 98.13%, and F1 score is 96.79%. Compared to the best performing MLP, TransDyG has increased recall by approximately 1.9%; Compared with GCN-LOF, F1 score has increased by 0.39%. Especially while maintaining high recall, TransDyG's accuracy is significantly higher than CNN, which also pursues high recall with 17.95% higher), indicating that the model achieves a better balance between detection capability and false alarm control, and overall performance is better than existing comparison methods.

Table 1. Comparison of existing methods with proposed model on UNSW-NB15 dataset.

Methods	Precision	Recall	F1-score
RF	93.79	94.08	93.93
SVM	92.34	88.20	90.22
XGBoost	93.90	93.31	93.61
CNN	77.52	98.12	86.62
LSTM	94.12	92.01	93.01
MLP	96.17	96.23	96.17
CEN-DGCNN [22]	97.50	100.00	81.01
GCN-LOF [23]	-	93.10	96.40
TransDyG(proposed)	**95.47**	**98.13**	**96.79**

4.4 Ablation Study

We further conducted ablation studies to demonstrate the effectiveness of each component in TransDyG. TransDyG (no SDE) indicates no spatiotemporal discrete encoding (using random initialization $N(0, 0.02)$ instead of), TransDyG (no LSA) indicates no local structure aggregation (using mean pooling instead of), and TransDyG (no Trans) indicates no Transformer was used (skiping the

Transformer and using embedding directly). Other experimental environments and parameter settings remain consistent. The experimental results is illustrated in Fig. 2.

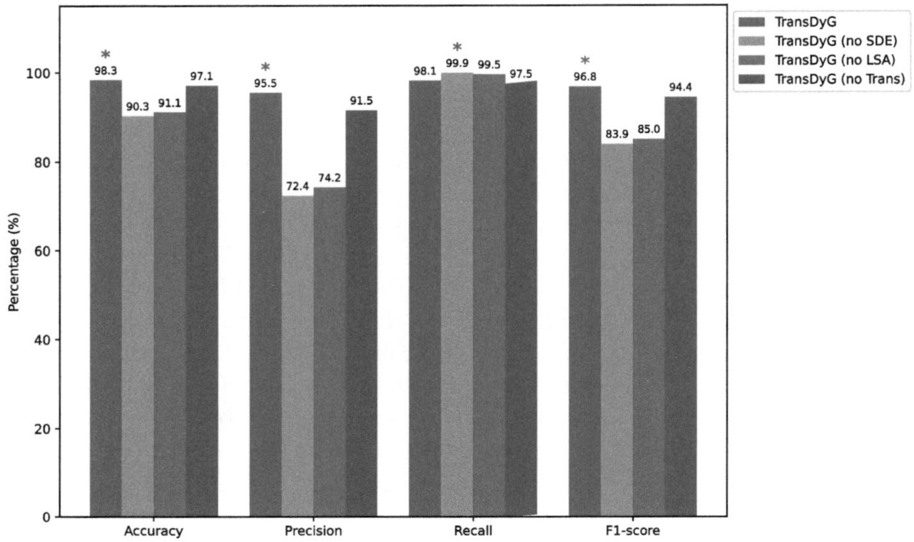

Fig. 2. Influence of different modules. "no SDE" means no spatiotemporal discrete encoding, "no LSA" means no local structure aggregation, "no Trans" means no Transformer was used.

The experimental results indicate that each component contributes to the final performance of the model. Specifically, the complete model TransDyG performs the best on all metrics. After removing SDE and LSA, the accuracy, precision, and F1 score of the model all showed a significant decrease (for example, F1 score decreased from 96.79% to 83.93% and 85.03%, respectively), indicating that spatiotemporal discrete encoding and local structure aggregation play a key role in capturing complex graph structure dynamic features. It is worth noting that after removing these two modules, the recall remains high, indicating that the model has strong coverage ability for positive cases. However, the significant decrease in Precision (to 72.36% and 74.21%, respectively) resulted in a decrease in the overall F1 score, indicating that the model generated a lot of false positives. In contrast, removing the Transformer module also caused a performance decline, but the magnitude of the decline was relatively small (F1 score decreased from 96.79% to 94.40%). This indicates that even without the global dependency modeling capability of Transformer, relying solely on other modules can still perform classification tasks well. However, the introduction of Transformer can further enhance the feature representation ability and bring better overall performance.

5 Conclusion

In this paper, we introduce TransDyG, a dynamic graph anomaly detection framework that integrates Transformer sequence modeling with GNNs to capture evolving network behaviors beyond static graphs. It constructs temporal graph snapshots from network traffic, serializes edge contexts with learnable embeddings, applies Transformer for global interactions, GCN for local aggregation, multi-view fusion, and pooling to yield compact edge representations. An MLP head, optimized via cross-entropy and contrastive losses with negative sampling, estimates anomaly probabilities effectively. Experiments on UNSW-NB15 show TransDyG outperforms baselines (Random Forest, GCN, CEN-DGCNN, GCN-LOF) in accuracy, precision, recall, and F1-score. Ablations confirm the value of its components, enabling robust novel anomaly detection with minimal retraining and strong adaptability. TransDyG advances network anomaly detection through unified spatiotemporal representations. Future directions include continuous-time graphs, heterogeneous attributes, and real-time deployment for improved scalability.

Acknowledgments. This research is supported by the Strategic Priority Research Program of the Chinese Academy of Sciences (No. XDA0460100), National Key Research and Development Program of China (No.2023YFC2206402). This work is also supported by the Program of Key Laboratory of Network Assessment Technology, the Chinese Academy of Sciences, Program of Beijing Key Laboratory of Network Security and Protection Technology.

References

1. Chandola, V., Banerjee, A., Kumar, V.: Anomaly detection: a survey. ACM Comput. Surv. (CSUR) **41**(3), 1–58 (2009)
2. Hamed, T., Dara, R., Kremer, S.C.: Network intrusion detection system based on recursive feature addition and bigram technique. Comput. Security **73**, 137–155 (2018)
3. Nguyen, V.A., Nguyen, D.Q., Nguyen, V., Le, T., Tran, Q.H. and Phung, D.:. Regvd: Revisiting graph neural networks for vulnerability detection. In: Proceedings of the ACM/IEEE 44th International Conference on Software Engineering: Companion Proceedings, pp. 178–182 (2022)
4. Nikolova, E., Jecheva, V.: Some similarity coefficients and application of data mining techniques to the anomaly-based ids. Telecommun. Syst. **50**(2), 127–135 (2012)
5. Yan, B., et al.: Graph mining for cybersecurity: a survey. ACM Trans. Knowl. Discov. Data **18**(2), 1–52 (2023)
6. Vaswani, A., et al.: Attention is all you need. In: Advances in Neural Information Processing Systems, vol. 30 (2017)
7. Chen, N., Liu, F., You, C., Zhou, P., Zou, Y.: Adaptive bi-directional attention: Exploring multi-granularity representations for machine reading comprehension. In: ICASSP 2021-2021 IEEE International Conference on Acoustics, Speech and Signal Processing (ICASSP), pp. 7833–7837. IEEE (2021)

8. Zhang, P., Liu, H., Li, C., Xie, X., Kim, S., Wang, H.: Foundation model-oriented robustness: Robust image model evaluation with pretrained models. arXiv preprint arXiv:2308.10632 (2023)
9. Abdaljalil, S., Hasan Kurban, R., Atat, E., Serpedin, K.: Qaraqe: Deep temporal and structural embeddings for robust unsupervised anomaly detection in dynamic graphs. IEEE Open J. Comput. Society (2025)
10. Fang, L., Feng, K., Gui, J., Feng, S., Aiqun, H.: Anonymous edge representation for inductive anomaly detection in dynamic bipartite graph. Proc. VLDB Endowment **16**(5), 1154–1167 (2023)
11. Zhao, Y., Liu, Z., Pang, J.: Anomaly detection in network traffic via cross-domain federated graph representation learning. Appl. Sci. **15**(11), 6258 (2025)
12. Tian, S., et al.: Sad: Semi-supervised anomaly detection on dynamic graphs. arXiv preprint arXiv:2305.13573 (2023)
13. Fathony, R., Ng, J., Chen, J.: Interaction-focused anomaly detection on bipartite node-and-edge-attributed graphs. In: 2023 International Joint Conference on Neural Networks (IJCNN), pp. 1–10. IEEE (2023)
14. Beladev, M., Katz, G., Rokach, L., Singer, U., Radinsky, K.: Graphert–transformers-based temporal dynamic graph embedding. In: Proceedings of the 32nd ACM International Conference on Information and Knowledge Management, pp. 68–77 (2023)
15. Zhang, J., Feng, K.: TSAD: Transformer-based semi-supervised anomaly detection for dynamic graphs. Mathematics **13**(19), 3123 (2025)
16. Zhao, Y.: Attention-based anomaly detection in dynamic network. Big Data Mining Anal. **9**(1), 70–86 (2025)
17. Liu, S., et al.: Anomalyllm: Few-shot anomaly edge detection for dynamic graphs using large language models. In: 2024 IEEE International Conference on Data Mining (ICDM), pp. 785–790. IEEE, (2024)
18. Yuxia, W., Fang, Y., Liao, L.: On the feasibility of simple transformer for dynamic graph modeling. In: Proceedings of the ACM Web Conference, pp. 870–880 (2024)
19. Zong, C., Zhuang, Y., Shao, J., Weiming, L.: Structural-temporal coupling anomaly detection with dynamic graph transformer. Data Min. Knowl. Disc. **40**(1), 8 (2026)
20. Yılmaz, A., Das, R.: A novel hybrid approach combining GCN and gat for effective anomaly detection from firewall logs in campus networks. Comput. Netw. **259**, 111082 (2025)
21. Ghurab, M., Gaphari, G., Alshami, F., Alshamy, R., Othman, S.: A detailed analysis of benchmark datasets for network intrusion detection system. Asian J. Res. Comput. Sci. **7**(4), 14–33 (2021)
22. Zhou, Y.: Co-embedding of edges and nodes with deep graph convolutional neural networks. Sci. Rep. **13**(1), 16966 (2023)
23. Qin, Z., Li, L., Luo, Q., Yu, X., Zhang, Q.: Enhancing intrusion detection performance using GCN-LOF: A hybrid graph-based anomaly detection approach. Comput. Netw. 111606 (2025)

Traffic Management

EAST: Embedding-Aligned Modality Adaptation for Large Language Model-Based Traffic Forecasting

Siya Qiu[1,2], Liang Du[3], Chuxuan Zeng[3], Ling Deng[3], Qiong Luo[1,2], and Jing Tang[1,2](✉)

[1] The Hong Kong University of Science and Technology, Hong Kong, China
sqiual@connect.ust.hk, luo@cse.ust.hk

[2] The Hong Kong University of Science and Technology (Guangzhou), Guangzhou, China
jingtang@ust.hk

[3] Unicom Smart Manufacturing Technology Industry (Guangdong) Co.Ltd, Shenzhen, China
{dul28,zengchuxuan,dengling1}@chinaunicom.cn

Abstract. Traditional deep learning methods for traffic forecasting typically rely on large amounts of localized training data, limiting their adaptability across regions. Large Language Models (LLMs) are known for their generalization ability, but they are trained on discrete, tokenized natural language, which creates a fundamental modality gap with continuous, multivariate traffic data. Existing LLM-based traffic forecasting methods often inject externally calculated embeddings into LLMs and extract the last hidden state to predict all future steps in a single pass. However, these methods do not address the modality gap problem and fail to exploit the token-by-token generation dynamics of LLMs. To address these limitations, we propose EAST (Embedding-Aligned Modality Adaptation for Large Language Model-Based Traffic Forecasting), a novel framework that exploits the use of visual representations for modality alignment and an auto-regressive LLM decoding strategy. We conduct extensive experiments on five real-world datasets, including three widely used land-traffic benchmarks and two newly introduced maritime traffic datasets. EAST consistently outperforms all baselines, achieving at least 8.4% lower MAE and 32.3% lower RMSE in full-shot learning, and 5.3% lower MAE and 23.6% lower RMSE in few-shot learning. These results highlight EAST's robustness and strong generalization capabilities across diverse traffic domains. The code is available at: https://github.com/sqiual/EAST.

Keywords: Large Language Models · Traffic Prediction · Spatio-Temporal Forecasting · Cross-Modal Alignment · Contrastive Learning

L. Ding et al. (Eds.): APWeb-WAIM 2026, LNCS 16995, pp. 67–82, 2027.
https://doi.org/10.1007/978-981-92-5699-0_5

1 Introduction

Traffic forecasting is essential in a lot of real-world applications, ranging from urban congestion management to global maritime route planning. While traditional deep learning models (e.g., RNNs, GNNs) [2,23] have shown remarkable traffic prediction accuracy in the area of interest, they typically rely on a large amount of training data, facing difficulties when transferring to unseen areas or domains. Recently, the prominent generalization ability of Large Language Models (LLMs) [13,18] has raised researchers' interest in their application to traffic forecasting. However, a fundamental barrier remains| LLMs are trained on discrete text tokens, whereas traffic data is continuous numerical data. Prior studies have shown that directly tokenizing such numerical data often disrupts temporal continuity and fine-grained structure, impairing generalization [17]. Therefore, the modality mismatch between textual data and traffic data poses a critical question: how can we unlock the generalization ability of LLMs for traffic forecasting by bridging the modality gap between language and traffic data?

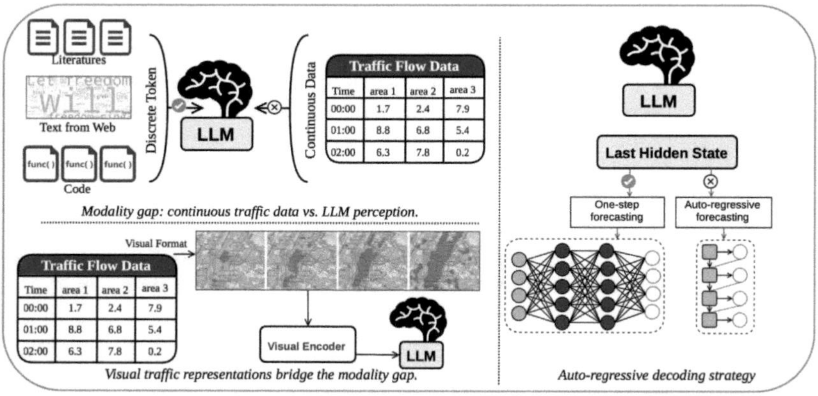

Fig. 1. Schematic overview of EAST.

Recent efforts to adapt LLMs for traffic forecasting predominantly adopt a numerical embedding injection paradigm [6,10,12]. They construct the embeddings of traffic data through an external encoder and directly inject into the intermediate LLMs model layers. Although this avoids tokenization of raw data through LLMs' self-contained embedding layers, it suffers from a modality misalignment issue, posing challenges for LLMs to understand the meaning of such embeddings.

Recent advances in Vision-Language Models (VLMs) [1,9,16] reveal that LLMs can effectively understand non-textual data| such as images and videos| when paired with visual encoders. Drawing inspiration from Time-LLM [24], we observe that traffic forecasting joint modeling of spatial development and temporal dynamics, which is analogous to video understanding and generation.

This motivates us to shift gear—instead of treating traffic data as a conventional time series, we transform it into a video-like frame sequence, where each frame encodes the spatio-temporal state of the traffic data at a distinct time step. These frame-based representations align with LLMs' pretrained visual understanding while preserving the structural and temporal integrity of traffic data.

Beyond the modality gap issue, current LLM-based traffic forecasting methods often raise another problem regarding their decoding strategies. Most approaches extract the final hidden state of the last token from the LLM and pass it through an external lightweight predictor (e.g., an MLP) to generate all future values in one step [6,8,12,24]. Though efficient, this design has two fundamental flaws: (1) Temporal Modeling Deficiency: by predicting all future embeddings in one step neglects the inter-step dependencies, which are essential for capturing temporal dynamics in sequence forecasting. (2) Architectural Misalignment: This strategy bypasses the LLM's original design| autoregressive, token-by-token generation| which underexploitates LLMs' causal inference capability.

To address the aforementioned limitations, we propose EAST (Embedding-Aligned Modality Adaptation for Large Language Model-Based Traffic Forecasting), a novel framework that employs video representations to bridge the modality gap between natural language and traffic data, and preserves the autoregressive generation nature of LLMs. EAST consists of three main components: (1) Sequence Pattern Encoder: A temporal module that captures multi-scale temporal dependencies from raw traffic sequence data, producing enriched temporal representations. (2) Spatio-temporal Video Encoder: Transforms traffic flow data into a video-like frame. It employs dual transformers to jointly model spatial interactions (intra-frame) and temporal evolutions (inter-frame). The generated video-encoded representation integrates both spatial and temporal features. (3) Multi-modal Fusion Module: Aligns the temporal and video-encoded representations in a shared latent space through contrastive learning. The resulting unified embeddings are fed into the LLM for autoregressive decoding. Figure 1 provides an overview of the workflow of EAST.

To evaluate the performance of EAST, we conduct extensive experiments on five real-world datasets, including three land-based traffic datasets| NYCtaxi, NYCbike, and TrafficNJ| and two newly proposed maritime traffic datasets| MarineFL and MarineCB. We test EAST under full-shot and few-shot forecasting settings. Experimental results demonstrate that EAST substantially improves forecasting accuracy compared to other baselines.

To summarize, the contribution of this paper are threefolds:

- We propose to transform spatio-temporal traffic sequences into video-like frames, which embeddings enables LLMs to leverage their video understanding, thus bridge the modality gap between numeric time series and language.
- We propose EAST, a LLM-based model for traffic forecasting, which includes a Sequence Pattern Encoder for raw sequence modeling, a Spatio-temporal Video Encoder for frame-based feature extraction, and a Multi-Modal Fusion module to align these modalities, enabling autoregressive traffic prediction with LLMs.

- We validate EAST's forecasting performance across five datasets from two distinct domains: land and maritime traffic, demonstrating EAST's ability to generalize under domain shifts with limited supervision in few-shot settings.

2 Related Work

2.1 LLM for Time Series Prediction

Large Language Models (LLMs) have raised significant attention due to their strong reasoning capabilities. This also brings researchers' interests in applying LLMs for time series forecasting. LLMTime [7] proposes to represent time series as strings of numerical tokens and modifies the LLM's discrete distribution framework to approximate continuous distributions for enhanced temporal modeling. LLM4TS [5] employs a two-phase fine-tuning approach: it first aligns large language models with the unique patterns of time series data, then fine-tunes them for forecasting tasks.

However, LLMs are primarily trained on textual data, which is different from time series data in modality. Recent studies focus on bridging this modality gap, and to better align time series representations with the representation space where the LLMs are trained in. STLLM [12] proposes an encoder based on Temporal Convolutional Networks (TCNs) to extract temporal features from time series data, which are subsequently fed into a partially frozen LLM for fine-tuning. STELLM [20] introduces spatio-temporal prompting by computing the graph Laplacian eigenvectors of the node adjacency matrix as spatial prompts, and retrieving similar historical patterns to form temporal prompts. Similarly, LLM-TFP [6] propose a ST-tokenizer, which generates tokens embeddings incorporating spatio-temporal properties. The token embeddings is then put forward to a frozen pre-trained BERT model, and then go through a convocational layer before outputting the prediction.

More recently, UrbanGPT [10] and UniST [21] project time series data into the natural language representation space using multi-layer perceptrons (MLPs). However, these approaches do not explicitly address the modality gap issue between time series data and natural language. To tackle this issue, TimeLLM [8] introduces a reprogramming technique that maps time series representations into the vocabulary space via a cross-attention mechanism.

2.2 VLM for Series Prediction

Recent advances in vision-language modeling (VLM) reveal LLMs' ability in visual understanding, including spatio-temporal pattern understanding, such as video. ViViT [3] adapts the Vision Transformer architecture to video data through spatiotemporal tokenization and joint attention mechanisms. Building on this, TimeSformer [4] introduces a divided attention mechanism that processes spatial and temporal dimensions separately. CLIP [16], although originally designed for static image-text alignment, has shown promise for sequential data through frame-wise feature aggregation. While Time-VLM [24] is the first work proposed to leverage images to guide madality alignment to help LLMs' understanding of time series data.

3 Problem Formulation

Traffic flow forecasting is a spatio-temporal prediction task, which predicts the traffic density of each region of an area over a period of time. Let $X \in \mathbb{R}^{T\times N\times F}$ represents the traffic data, where T is the total number of time steps, N is the number of spatial regions in the area, and F is the number of features per region (e.g., inflow, outflow, direction). For each region $n \in \{1, 2, \ldots, N\}$, the traffic temporal sequence is denoted as $x^n = [x_1^n, x_2^n, \ldots, x_T^n] \in \mathbb{R}^{T\times F}$. Given the historical observed traffic sequence up to time τ, denoted as $X_\tau = \{x_{1:\tau}^n\}_{n=1}^N$, the goal is to predict future traffic sequence from time $\tau+1$ to H: $Y_{\tau+1:\tau+T} = \{x_{\tau+1:\tau+T}^n\}_{n=1}^N$

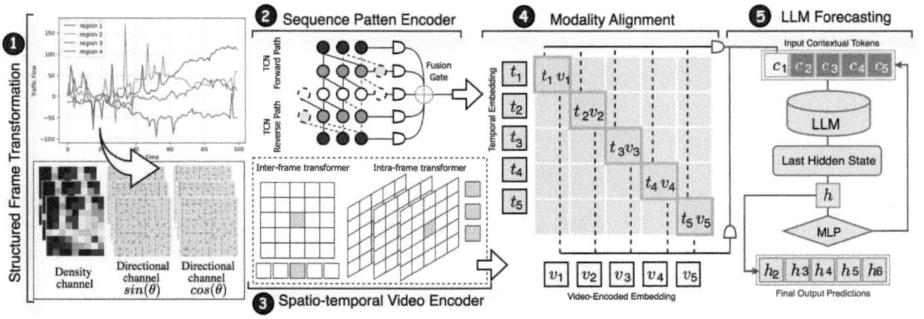

Fig. 2. Model architecture of EAST.

4 Methodology

Our model includes the following components: Sequence Pattern Encoder, Spatio-temporal Video Encoder, Multi-Modal Fusion and Auto-regressive forecasting Module. Figure 2 gives an overview of the workflow of EAST.

4.1 Sequence Pattern Encoder

The sequence pattern encoder extracts temporal patterns from raw traffic signals using a sequence of bi-directional Temporal Convolutional Network (TCN) blocks. The encoder captures multi-scale temporal dependencies across different time resolutions.

Given the input sequence of region n, denoted as $x^n \in \mathbb{R}^{\tau \times F}$, we first project it into a d-dimensional hidden space via a linear transformation:

$$\mathbf{z}^{(0)} = x^n \mathbf{W}_{\text{in}} + \mathbf{b}_{\text{in}}, \quad \mathbf{W}_{\text{in}} \in \mathbb{R}^{F \times d}, \quad \mathbf{b}_{\text{in}} \in \mathbb{R}^{d}, \tag{1}$$

where $\mathbf{z}^{(0)}$ is the initial hidden representation of our raw traffic input. Next, $\mathbf{z}^{(0)}$ is pass through L bi-directional TCN blocks. Each block $l \in \{1, \ldots, L\}$ contains two TCNs, one with a forward path and the other with a reverse path. Each TCN is convolved using a kernel with size m and dilated with rate 2^l. The temporal representations outputting from the forward and reverse paths at layer l, $\mathbf{h}_{\text{fwd}}^{(l)}$ and $\mathbf{h}_{\text{rev}}^{(l)}$, are represented as:

$$\begin{aligned}
\mathbf{h}_{\text{fwd}}^{(l)} &= \mathbf{h}_{\text{fwd}}^{(l-1)} + \sigma\left(\sum_{i=0}^{m-1} \mathbf{W}_i^{(l),\text{fwd}} \mathbf{z}_{t-(2^l \cdot i)}^{(l-1)} + \mathbf{b}^{(l),\text{fwd}}\right), \\
\mathbf{h}_{\text{rev}}^{(l)} &= \mathbf{h}_{\text{rev}}^{(l-1)} + \sigma\left(\sum_{i=0}^{m-1} \mathbf{W}_i^{(l),\text{rev}} \mathbf{z}_{t+(2^l \cdot i)}^{(l-1)} + \mathbf{b}^{(l),\text{rev}}\right),
\end{aligned} \tag{2}$$

where $\mathbf{W}^{(l),\text{fwd}}, \mathbf{W}^{(l),\text{rev}} \in \mathbb{R}^{d \times d}$ and $\mathbf{b}^{(l),\text{fwd}}, \mathbf{b}^{(l),\text{rev}} \in \mathbb{R}^{d}$ are the TCN weights and biases for the forward and reverse paths, respectively, at layer l. $\sigma(\cdot)$ denotes the Sigmoid activation function.

The forward and reverse representations are fused through a learnable gating mechanism:

$$\begin{aligned}
\mathbf{G}^{(l)} &= \sigma\left(\text{Conv1D}\left([\mathbf{h}_{\text{fwd}}^{(l)} \| \mathbf{h}_{\text{rev}}^{(l)}]\right)\right), \\
\mathbf{z}^{(l)} &= \mathbf{G}^{(l)} \odot \mathbf{h}_{\text{fwd}}^{(l)} + (1 - \mathbf{G}^{(l)}) \odot \mathbf{h}_{\text{rev}}^{(l)} + \mathbf{z}^{(l)-1},
\end{aligned} \tag{3}$$

where $\odot$ denotes the Hadamard product, $\|$ denotes feature-wise concatenation along the channel dimension. The residual connection with $\mathbf{z}^{l-1}$ stabilize the training process.

After L TCN blocks, we obtain the final temporal embedding for region n by summing the outputs from all layers:

$$\mathbf{H}_{\text{temp}}^{n} = \sum_{l=1}^{L} \mathbf{z}^{(l)} \in \mathbb{R}^{\tau \times d}. \tag{4}$$

4.2 Spatio-Temporal Video Encoder

Inspired by Time-VLM [24], which bridges univariate time-series and text via static images, we extend this paradigm to multivariate spatio-temporal data through structured frame sequences.

Traffic Data to Structured Frame Sequence Conversion. Given the input data $X \in \mathbb{R}^{\tau \times N \times F}$ from an area of N spatial regions, we further arrange the N spatial regions into a 2D spatial grid of size $H \times W$. This yields $\tilde{X} \in \mathbb{R}^{\tau \times H \times W \times F}$.

For each timestep t, we construct a three-channel image $\mathbf{I}_t \in \mathbb{R}^{3 \times H \times W}$, including a density channel $\mathbf{D}_t$, and two directional channels $\sin \theta_t$ and $\cos \theta_t$. The density channel $\mathbf{D}_t \in \mathbb{R}^{H \times W}$ encodes traffic density. The directional channels record the dominant flow direction, $\theta_t \in \mathbb{R}^{H \times W}$, of each grid in the frame.

The flow directions are initially collected in degrees. To construct the directional channels, we transfer degrees in radius, then further encode the radius with Sine and Cosine:

$$\begin{cases} \theta_t^{\mathrm{rad}} = \frac{\pi}{180} \cdot \theta_t, \\ \sin\theta_t = \sin(\theta_t^{\mathrm{rad}}), \\ \cos\theta_t = \cos(\theta_t^{\mathrm{rad}}), \end{cases} \tag{5}$$

This transformation preserves angular continuity, avoiding discontinuities at angular boundaries (i.e., 0∘and 360∘). We define the final image representation at time t as:

$$\mathbf{I}_t = [\mathbf{D}_t, \sin\theta_t, \cos\theta_t] \in \mathbb{R}^{3\times H\times W}. \tag{6}$$

By stacking image frames across all time steps, we obtain the video-like spatio-temporal frame sequence:

$$\mathcal{I}_{1:\tau} = [\mathbf{I}_1, \mathbf{I}_2, \dots, \mathbf{I}_\tau] \in \mathbb{R}^{\tau\times 3\times H\times W}. \tag{7}$$

Patch Embedding Extraction. For each frame $\mathbf{I}_t \in \mathbb{R}^{3\times H\times W}$: We apply a 2D convolutional layer with kernel size $p \times p$, stride s, and padding u to extract overlapping patches and project them into an e-dimensional embedding space to form feature map $\mathbf{v}_t \in \mathbb{R}^{e\times H'\times W'}$,

$$H' = \left\lfloor \frac{H + 2u - p}{s} \right\rfloor + 1, \quad W' = \left\lfloor \frac{W + 2u - p}{s} \right\rfloor + 1. \tag{8}$$

We flatten the spatial dimensions into patch tokens and add learnable positional embeddings on to them:

$$\mathbf{V}_t^{\mathrm{patch}} = \mathrm{Flatten}(\mathbf{v}_t) + \mathbf{P}, \quad \mathbf{P} \in \mathbb{R}^{N\times e}, \quad N = H' \times W'. \tag{9}$$

Video Encoding with Dual-Transformer Blocks. We process the flattened patch embeddings using a video encoder inspired by TimeSformer [4], which separates spatio-temporal attention into spatial and temporal attention modules individually. We employ a dual-transformer architecture to capture both intra-frame spatial and inter-frame temporal patch dependencies. The patch tokens $\mathbf{V}_t^{\mathrm{patch}}$ are processed through K dual-transformer blocks, each consisting of spatial transformer encoder followed by temporal transformer encoder.

For each block $k \in \{1, \dots, K\}$, we first apply a spatial transformer encoder independently to each frame to generate the intra-frame spatial embeddings $\mathbf{O}_{\mathrm{spa}}^{(k)}$:

$$\begin{aligned} &\mathbf{O}_{\mathrm{spa}}^{(k)} = \mathrm{Attention}(\mathbf{Q}^{(s)}, \mathbf{K}^{(s)}, \mathbf{V}^{(s)}), \\ &\mathbf{Q}^{(s)} = \mathbf{O}^{(k-1)}\mathbf{W}_q^{(s)}, \quad \mathbf{K}^{(s)} = \mathbf{O}^{(k-1)}\mathbf{W}_k^{(s)}, \quad \mathbf{V}^{(s)} = \mathbf{O}^{(k-1)}\mathbf{W}_v^{(s)}, \end{aligned} \tag{10}$$

where $\mathbf{O}^{(0)} = \mathbf{V}_t^{\mathrm{patch}}$. Next, we apply temporal transformer encoder across corresponding patch positions over the time dimension:

$$\begin{aligned} &\mathbf{O}^{(k)} = \mathrm{Attention}(\mathbf{Q}^{(t)}, \mathbf{K}^{(t)}, \mathbf{V}^{(t)}), \\ &\mathbf{Q}^{(t)} = \mathbf{O}_{\mathrm{spa}}^{(k)}\mathbf{W}_q^{(t)}, \quad \mathbf{K}^{(t)} = \mathbf{O}_{\mathrm{spa}}^{(k)}\mathbf{W}_k^{(t)}, \quad \mathbf{V}^{(t)} = \mathbf{O}_{\mathrm{spa}}^{(k)}\mathbf{W}_v^{(t)}. \end{aligned} \tag{11}$$

After K encoding blocks, we obtain the final video-encoded representation:

$$\mathbf{O}_{\text{video}} = \mathbf{O}^{(K)} \in \mathbb{R}^{\tau \times N \times e}, \tag{12}$$

which encodes both spatial patterns within frames and temporal evolution across frames.

4.3 Multi-modal Fusion and Auto-regressive Forecasting

Contrastive Alignment. Given the temporal embeddings $\mathbf{H}_{\text{temp}}$ from the Sequence Pattern Encoder and the video-encoded embeddings $\mathbf{O}_{\text{video}}$ from the Spatio-temporal Video Encoder, we first project both embeddings into a shared space $\mathbb{R}^{d_m}$, generating $\mathbf{Z}_{\text{temp}}$ and $\mathbf{Z}_{\text{video}}$:

$$\begin{aligned} \mathbf{Z}_{\text{temp}} &= \text{LayerNorm}(\mathbf{H}_{\text{temp}}\mathbf{W}_t), \quad & \mathbf{W}_t \in \mathbb{R}^{d \times d_m} \\ \mathbf{Z}_{\text{video}} &= \text{LayerNorm}(\mathbf{O}_{\text{video}}\mathbf{W}_v), \quad & \mathbf{W}_v \in \mathbb{R}^{e \times d_m}. \end{aligned} \tag{13}$$

We then apply contrastive learning to align $\mathbf{Z}_{\text{temp}}$ and $\mathbf{Z}_{\text{video}}$. Specifically, we form positive pairs as $(\mathbf{Z}^i_{\text{temp}}, \mathbf{Z}^i_{\text{video}})$, where $i = j$, indicating that both embeddings originate from the same region. Negative pairs are defined as $(\mathbf{Z}^i_{\text{temp}}, \mathbf{Z}^j_{\text{video}})$, where $i \neq j$ indicating that the embeddings originate from different regions. The contrastive loss is defined as:

$$\begin{aligned} \mathcal{L}_{\text{align}} = -\frac{1}{2(\tau)} \sum_{t=1}^{\tau} \Bigg[& \log \frac{\exp\left(s(\mathbf{z}^i_{\text{temp}}, \mathbf{z}^i_{\text{video}})/\mu\right)}{\sum_{i \neq j} \exp\left(s(\mathbf{z}^i_{\text{temp}}, \mathbf{z}^j_{\text{video}})/\mu\right)} \\ & + \log \frac{\exp\left(s(\mathbf{z}^i_{\text{video}}, \mathbf{z}^i_{\text{temp}})/\mu\right)}{\sum_{i \neq j} \exp\left(s(\mathbf{z}^i_{\text{video}}, \mathbf{z}^j_{\text{temp}})/\mu\right)} \Bigg] \end{aligned} \tag{14}$$

where $s(\cdot, \cdot)$ denotes cosine similarity and μ is a temperature scaling hyperparameter.

Gated Modality Fusion. After contrastive alignment, the aligned embeddings $\mathbf{Z}_{\text{temp}}$ and $\mathbf{Z}_{\text{video}}$ are passed through a learnable fusion gate to integrate both temporal and video-encoded information:

$$\begin{aligned} \mathbf{g} &= \sigma(\mathbf{Z}_{\text{temp}}\mathbf{W}^t_g + \mathbf{Z}_{\text{video}}\mathbf{W}^v_g + \mathbf{b}_g), \\ \mathbf{Z}_{\text{fused}} &= \mathbf{g} \odot \mathbf{Z}_{\text{temp}} + (1 - \mathbf{g}) \odot \mathbf{Z}_{\text{video}}, \end{aligned} \tag{15}$$

where $\mathbf{W}^t_g, \mathbf{W}^v_g \in \mathbb{R}^{d_m \times d_m}$ weights of the fusion gate, and σ is the Sigmoid activation function. This mechanism enables the model to adaptively evaluate the importance of embeddings at each time step.

Autoregressive LLM Decoding. To forecast future traffic data, we employ an autoregressive decoder from a transformer decoder-based large language model (LLM). The fused multi-modal embeddings $\mathbf{Z}_{\text{fused}}$, which encodes both spatial and temporal context across τ time steps, is first enriched with positional encoding $\mathbf{P}_{\text{fused}}$ to form the contextual input tokens $\mathbf{C}$:

$$\mathbf{C}_{\tau+1} = \mathbf{Z}_{\text{fused}} + \mathbf{P}_{\text{fused}} \tag{16}$$

Here, τ denotes the length of the observed traffic sequence, and the goal is to predict the future states from step $\tau + 1$ to T. At time step $t = \tau + 1$, the LLM processes the initial context $\mathbf{C}_{\tau+1}$ to generate the last hidden states:

$$\mathbf{H}_{\tau+1} = \text{LLM}(\mathbf{C}_{\tau+1}) \tag{17}$$

We extract the last hidden token $\mathbf{h}_{\tau+1} = \mathbf{H}_{\tau+1}[:, -1, :]$, and project it into the embedding space to form the first prediction embedding:

$$\mathbf{e}_{\tau+1} = \mathbf{W}_p \mathbf{h}_{\tau+1}. \tag{18}$$

For each subsequent time step $t \in \{\tau + 2, \ldots, T\}$, the decoder takes the original context $\mathbf{C}_{\tau+1}$ concatenated with previously generated embeddings $\{e_{\tau+1}, \ldots, e_{t-1}\}$ to form the input for LLM:

$$\mathbf{C}_t = [\mathbf{C}_{\tau+1} \| \mathbf{e}_{\tau+1} \| \cdots \| \mathbf{e}_{t-1}] \tag{19}$$

This updated context C_t is fed into the LLM to produce the hidden state for the next step:

$$\begin{aligned} \mathbf{H}_t &= \text{LLM}(\mathbf{C}_t) \\ \mathbf{h}_t &= \mathbf{H}_t[:, -1, :] \\ \mathbf{e}_t &= \mathbf{W}_p \mathbf{h}_t \end{aligned} \tag{20}$$

We repeat this process until the desires prediction length is reached. Once all future steps are autoregressively decoded, the sequence of embedding vectors $\{\mathbf{e}_{\tau+1}, \ldots, \mathbf{e}_T\}$ is mapped to the target space using a feedforward projection:

$$\hat{\mathbf{Y}} = \text{MLP}([\mathbf{e}_{\tau+1} \| \cdots \| \mathbf{e}_T]) \tag{21}$$

This autoregressive decoding framework allows the model to generate temporally coherent forecasts.

5 Dataset Construction

To enable diverse traffic flow prediction scenarios, we constructed two novel maritime traffic flow datasets derived from raw Automatic Identification System (AIS) data. The raw AIS data was obtained from the Office for Coastal Management [15] and consists of positional signals broadcast by vessel transponders.

We derived the traffic flow representations through the following procedure. First, two rectangular maritime regions were selected as areas of interest (AOIs). Each AOI was discretized into a uniform spatial grid with a resolution of 0.1° latitude × 0.1° longitude (approximately 1 km × 1 km at these latitudes). The first dataset, *MarineFL*, covers the sea area around Florida, bounded by 24°N to 34°N and 85°W to 75°W. The second dataset, *MarineCB*, covers a region in the Caribbean Sea, bounded by 26°N to 31°N and 96°W to 86°W.

For each grid cell and each time interval, traffic inflow and outflow were computed by counting AIS positional points moving into or out of the cell during that interval. Additionally, the dominant traffic direction within each cell was recorded. Both datasets span the period from June 1, 2024, to December 31, 2024, providing seven months of continuous traffic flow observations.

6 Experiment

6.1 Experimental Setup

We evaluate the effectiveness of EAST on five datasets, including three land-based traffic datasets| NYCtaxi, NYCbike, and TrafficNJ, and two newly proposed maritime traffic datasets| MarineFL and MarineCB. The land-based datasets record traffic flow across different regions for New York and New Jersey with an hourly time resolution. In our experimental setup, the model observes traffic flow over the past 6 h (6 time steps) to predict the flow for the next 6 h. For the maritime datasets, which capture ship traffic in the Florida coastal regions and the area around the Caribbean Sea with a 30-minute resolution, the model observes the past 6 h (12 time steps) and forecasts the subsequent 6 h.

6.2 Implementation Details and Evaluation Metrics

The Sequence Pattern Encoder consists of five bi-directional TCN (Temporal Convolutional Networks) blocks, where each block contains two TCNs, one with the forward path and the other with reverse path. The dilation factor of the convolutions increases exponentially across layers, following 2^d, where d is the layer index. The Spatio-temporal Visual Encoder includes four multi-head spatio-temporal transformer layers, each with eight attention heads. The transformer processes each input patch by dividing it into 3×3 overlapping sub-patches, which serve as visual tokens.

The LLM backbone in EAST can be any open-source decoder-only LLM (e.g., GPT-2, LLaMA-3, Vicuna). In this work, we report results using GPT-2 as the backbone. The model is trained for 50 epochs with an initial learning rate of $5e-6$ using the Adam optimizer, and optimized with the widely used RMSE losses and our contrastive loss $\mathcal{L}_{\text{align}}$ mentioned in the Methodology Section. The model performance is evaluated using the Mean Absolute Error (MAE) and the Root Mean Square Error (RMSE), between the model predictions and the ground truth values. The formulas for MAE and RMSE loss are given as follows:

$$\begin{aligned} \text{MAE} &= \frac{1}{T-\tau}\sum_{i=\tau}^{T}|\hat{y}_i - y_i|, \\ \text{RMSE} &= \sqrt{\frac{1}{T-\tau}\sum_{i=\tau}^{T}\left(\hat{y}_i - y_i\right)^2}, \end{aligned} \tag{22}$$

where $\hat{y}$ and y denote the predicted and ground truth values, and $T - \tau$ is the length of the prediction.

Table 1. Comparison of traffic flow prediction performance under full-shot learning (training with the entire dataset). The results are reported in terms of MAE and RMSE, where lower values indicate better performance. Bold values indicate the best performance, and underlined values indicate the second best.

Full-shot	MarineFL		MarineCB		NYCtaxi		NYCbike		TrafficNJ		Avg. Impv. %	
	MAE	RMSE	MAE	RMSE	MAE	RMSE	MAE	RMSE	MAE	RMSE	MAE	RMSE
DLinear	4.36	11.49	3.37	8.43	21.56	57.09	3.57	8.80	0.82	1.48	↑ 48.6%	↑ 22.0%
AutoFormer	4.58	**11.09**	3.63	8.52	18.55	49.75	3.66	8.76	0.79	1.44	↑ 44.5%	↑ 21.0%
TimeLLM	4.45	11.26	3.26	8.95	17.4	46.00	2.65	7.94	0.70	1.38	↑ 39.20%	↑ 20.30%
TimeVLM	4.19	14.70	3.03	8.53	16.49	45.21	2.94	8.24	0.65	1.28	↑ 36.6%	↑ 28.1%
GPT4TS	4.30	14.53	3.01	8.69	17.22	50.15	3.29	10.33	0.77	1.49	↑ 39.5%	↑ 32.8%
PatchTST	4.26	15.33	3.11	8.70	17.19	50.05	3.31	10.34	0.76	1.49	↑ 39.5%	↑ 34.3%
OpenCity	12.89	28.33	3.35	10.57	20.14	46.42	9.22	18.31	0.94	1.64	↑ 62.8%	↑ 60.0%
STLLM	10.27	45.52	4.04	15.33	23.46	50.50	2.63	5.76	0.90	1.43	↑ 58.0%	↑ 65.0%
UniST	4.76	18.83	3.53	9.35	**7.93**	20.10	2.17	5.60	0.51	1.02	↑ 8.4%	↑ 32.3%
OURS	**3.90**	11.20	**2.85**	**7.75**	8.18	**17.16**	**1.88**	**3.76**	**0.50**	**0.85**	-	-

Table 2. Comparison of traffic prediction performance under few-shot learning (training with 10% of the dataset). The results are reported in terms of MAE and RMSE, where lower values indicate better performance. Bold values indicate the best performance, and underlined values indicate the second best.

Few-shot 10%	MarineFL		MarineCB		NYCtaxi		NYCbike		TrafficNJ		Avg. Impv. %	
	MAE	RMSE	MAE	RMSE	MAE	RMSE	MAE	RMSE	MAE	RMSE	MAE	RMSE
DLinear	4.37	11.03	3.36	8.48	24.31	63.45	4.43	11.99	0.91	1.61	↑ 27.5%	↑ 21.0%
AutoFormer	4.57	**11.01**	3.59	8.52	22.84	59.94	4.31	11.39	0.86	1.55	↑ 25.0%	↑ 19.4%
TimeLLM	4.50	11.16	3.36	8.76	18.23	49.36	3.43	9.96	0.71	1.42	↑ 10.3%	↑ 16.4%
TimeVLM	4.39	14.76	**3.07**	8.68	17.39	48.16	3.10	9.01	0.68	1.77	↑ 5.3%	↑ 23.6%
GPT4TS	4.06	14.50	3.27	8.81	17.70	51.54	3.34	10.56	0.70	1.47	↑ 6.7%	↑ 26.0%
PatchTST	4.09	14.73	3.12	9.04	17.67	51.34	3.44	10.77	0.71	1.47	↑ 6.6%	↑ 27.4%
OpenCity	14.18	29.24	3.48	10.73	31.14	69.67	9.55	18.53	0.97	1.68	↑ 54.20%	↑ 56.50%
STLLM	10.28	42.52	5.34	20.57	26.69	56.83	3.36	6.97	1.22	1.93	↑ 42.2%	↑ 63.7%
UniST	6.01	19.01	4.19	10.63	18.68	48.31	3.05	8.99	0.76	1.45	↑ 17.1%	↑ 34.7%
OURS	**3.96**	11.21	3.20	**8.29**	**16.72**	**35.01**	**2.59**	**5.59**	**0.64**	**1.07**	-	-

6.3 Baselines

To evaluate the performance of EAST, we compare the model performance of EAST against nine baseline methods, including: (1) classical time series models (DLinear [22], AutoFormer [19], PatchTST [14]) widely adopted for traffic prediction; (2) LLM-based approaches (TimeLLM [8], TimeVLM [24], GPT4TS [25]) representing recent researches in adapting LLMs for time series forecasting; and (3) spatio-temporal models (STLLM [12], UniST [21], OpenCity [11]), which are designed explicitly for spatiotemporal data. This systematic selection enables comprehensive evaluation across established techniques.

7 Result

7.1 Main Result

We conduct extensive experiments under three settings| full-shot learning (training with 100% of the data), and few-shot learning (training with 10% and 5% of the data, respectively). The results show that across all three settings, EAST outperforms the baseline models on the majority of evaluation metrics across datasets. The detailed experimental results are summarized in Tables 1, Table 2, andTable 3.

Table 3. Comparison of traffic flow prediction performance under few-shot learning (training with 5% of the dataset). The results are reported in terms of MAE and RMSE, where lower values indicate better performance. Bold values indicate the best performance, and underlined values indicate the second best.

Few-shot 5%	MarineFL		MarineCB		NYCtaxi		NYCbike		TrafficNJ		Avg. Impv. %	
	MAE	RMSE	MAE	RMSE	MAE	RMSE	MAE	RMSE	MAE	RMSE	MAE	RMSE
DLinear	4.38	11.50	3.36	8.50	24.87	64.86	4.52	12.20	0.96	1.65	$\uparrow$ 24.3%	$\uparrow$ 21.0%
AutoFormer	4.59	11.57	3.59	8.55	25.02	65.09	4.63	12.06	1.09	1.73	$\uparrow$ 25.9%	$\uparrow$ 21.2%
TimeLLM	5.00	11.57	3.32	8.80	19.54	52.16	3.94	11.39	0.94	1.85	$\uparrow$ 11.9%	$\uparrow$ 20.4%
TimeVLM	4.65	14.78	**3.07**	9.15	18.69	54.26	3.32	9.99	**0.69**	1.37	$\uparrow$ 5.2%	$\uparrow$ 24.2%
GPT4TS	4.13	14.68	3.20	8.81	18.19	52.17	3.40	10.51	0.72	1.48	$\uparrow$ 2.7%	$\uparrow$ 24.6%
PatchTST	4.15	14.82	3.33	8.93	**17.65**	51.5	3.35	10.50	0.71	1.47	$\uparrow$ 1.2%	$\uparrow$ 25.1%
OpenCity	13.75	28.63	3.46	10.67	31.68	68.82	9.93	18.85	0.96	1.68	$\uparrow$ 51.7%	$\uparrow$ 55.0%
STLLM	10.28	42.53	5.34	20.57	27.74	59.7	3.43	7.16	1.26	2.34	$\uparrow$ 40.0%	$\uparrow$ 63.2%
UniST	5.59	18.89	5.50	13.17	19.65	52.77	3.30	8.89	0.84	1.57	$\uparrow$ 17.3%	$\uparrow$ 37.1%
OURS	**4.03**	**11.50**	3.16	**8.45**	18.14	**38.04**	**2.70**	**5.50**	0.81	**1.29**	-	-

Full-Shot Forecasting. As shown in Table 1, EAST consistently reduces the average MAE and RMSE across all five datasets when compared to baseline models. Specifically, EAST achieves MAE reductions of 36%62% and RMSE reductions of 21%65% relative to DLinear, AutoFormer, TimeLLM, TimeVLM, GPT4TS, PatchTST, STLLM, and OpenCity. Although the MAE improvement over UniST is relatively modest at 8%, the RMSE is reduced by a substantial amount of 32.3%. These results demonstrate that EAST delivers strong predictive accuracy when sufficient training data is available.

Few-Shot Forecasting. In the few-shot learning setting, we train models using only 10% and 5% of the available training data, referred to as Few-10% and Few-5% for clarity. As shown in Table 2, under the Few-10% setting, the MAE improvements are slightly smaller compared to the full-shot setting. In particular, EAST reduces MAE by 25%54% over DLinear, AutoFormer, STLLM, and OpenCity, by 10%17% over UniST and TimeLLM, and by 5%6% over TimeVLM, GPT4TS, and PatchTST. While MAE gains are smaller, the RMSE improvements remain relatively stable. EAST achieves RMSE reductions of 16%21% over DLinear, AutoFormer, and TimeLLM, and 23%63% over the remaining baselines, which is comparable to full-shot performance.

For the Few-5% setting, models are trained using only 5% of the available data. As shown in Table 3, the overall MAE improvements further decrease. Compared to STLLM and OpenCity, EAST achieves MAE reductions of 40%-51%; compared to DLinear, AutoFormer, and UniST, the MAE reductions is 17%25%; compared to TimeLLM, the reduction is 11.9%; while for TimeVLM, GPT4TS, and PatchTST, the MAE gains fall below 5%. Despite the reduced MAE improvements, the RMSE reductions remain robust. EAST achieves a 37%-63% reduction in RMSE relative to UniST, STLLM, and OpenCity, and 20%25% compared to other baselines.

8 Ablation Study

To assess the contribution of each component in EAST, we perform an ablation study by disabling individual modules. We evaluate the following variants: (1) *MLP-LLM*, where raw inputs are projected into the hidden space via an MLP and directly fed to the LLM, testing whether a simple projection is sufficient; (2) *SeqEnc-LLM*, which adds the Sequence Pattern Encoder to capture temporal dependencies before LLM input, assessing if temporal modeling alone can enable effective understanding; (3) *AlignedTemp-LLM*, which uses only the modality-aligned temporal embeddings to examine whether alignment resolves the modality gap; and (4) *AlignedVis-LLM*, which uses only aligned visual embeddings to test whether visual semantics alone are sufficient; (5) *Full EAST*. Results are summarized in Fig. 3.

From Fig. 3, we observe that *MLP-LLM* exhibits significantly higher MAE and RMSE across all four datasets, indicating that simply projecting time-series data into the LLM's hidden space via an MLP is suboptimal. The results of *SeqEnc-LLM* confirm that by incorporating a more sophisticated Sequence Pattern Encoder, the MAE and RMSE can be reduced by a substantial amount, with an average of 270% and 208%, respectively, compared to *MLP-LLM*.

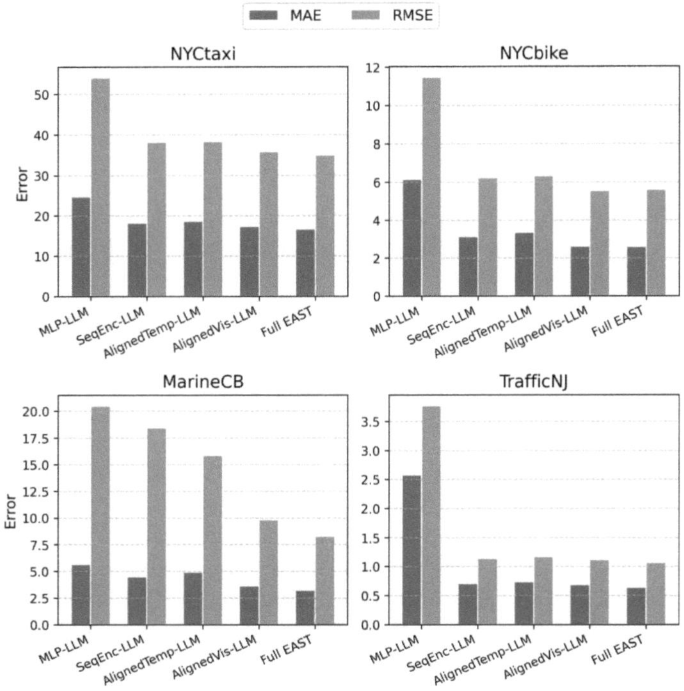

Fig. 3. Ablation study results on four datasets comparing five model variants: MLP-LLM, SeqEnc-LLM, AlignedTemp-LLM, AlignedVis-LLM, and Full EAST. The results are reported in terms of MAE and RMSE, where lower values indicate better performance.

We next examine the utility of modality alignment and multimodal fusion. *AlignedVis-LLM* outperforms *SeqEnc-LLM*| with MAE and RMSE reductions of 12.9% and 27.0%, respectively, demonstrating that modality alignment effectively enhances LLM-based forecasting. However, neither *AlignedTemp-LLM* nor *AlignedVis-LLM* matches the performance of *Full EAST*. By integrating both aligned temporal and visual embeddings, *Full EAST* reduces MAE and RMSE by 20.4% and 19.1% compared to *AlignedTemp-LLM*, and by 6.3% and 6.2% compared to *AlignedVis-LLM*. This confirms that combining modality alignment with multimodal fusion delivers the most substantial improvements.

9 Conclusion

Large Language Models (LLMs)pretrained on discrete textual data face challenges in understanding continuous traffic data. Inspired by the emergence of Vision-Language Models (VLMs), which demonstrate that LLMs can comprehend spatio-temporal data such as videos, we propose EAST (Embedding-Aligned Modality Adaptation for Large Language Model-Based Traffic Forecasting). EAST transforms traffic data into a video-like frame sequence and encodes it using a video encoder, serving as an intermediate modality to align traffic and textual data. Furthermore, EAST adheres to the original design of LLMs by employing a token-by-token decoding strategy. Experimental results validate the adaptability and generalization ability of EAST under full-shot and few-shot learning settings.

Acknowledgments. This work is partially supported by National Key R&D Program of China under Grant No. 2024YFA1012700, by the National Natural Science Foundation of China (NSFC) under Grant No. 62402410, by Guangdong Provincial Project (No. 2023QN10X025), and by Research and Development of Heterogeneous Computing Interconnection and Scheduling Software Stack (YF202400000003).

References

1. Alayrac, J.B.: Flamingo: a visual language model for few-shot learning. Adv. Neural. Inf. Process. Syst. **35**, 23716–23736 (2022)
2. Alsehaimi, B., Alzamzami, O., Alowidi, N., Ali, M.: An adaptive spatio-temporal traffic flow prediction using self-attention and multi-graph networks. Sensors **25**(1), 282 (2025)
3. Arnab, A., Dehghani, M., Heigold, G., Sun, C., Lučić, M., Schmid, C.: Vivit: A video vision transformer. In: Proceedings of the IEEE/CVF International Conference on Computer Vision, pp. 6836–6846 (2021)
4. Bertasius, G., Wang, H., Torresani, L.: Is space-time attention all you need for video understanding? In: ICML, vol. 2, p. 4 (2021)
5. Chang, C., Peng, W.C., Chen, T.F.: Llm4ts: Two-stage fine-tuning for time-series forecasting with pre-trained LLMs, CoRR (2023)
6. Cheng, H., Gong, Z., Wang, C.: LLM-TFP: Integrating large language models with spatio-temporal features for urban traffic flow prediction. Appl. Soft Comput. 113174 (2025)
7. Gruver, N., Finzi, M., Qiu, S., Wilson, A.G.: Large language models are zero-shot time series forecasters. Adv. Neural. Inf. Process. Syst. **36**, 19622–19635 (2023)
8. Jin, M., et al.: Time-LLM: Time series forecasting by reprogramming large language models. arXiv preprint arXiv:2310.01728 (2023)
9. Li, J., Li, D., Xiong, C., Hoi, S.: Blip: Bootstrapping language-image pre-training for unified vision-language understanding and generation. In: International Conference on Machine Learning, pp. 12888–12900. PMLR (2022)
10. Li, Z., et al.: Urbangpt: Spatio-temporal large language models. In: Proceedings of the 30th ACM SIGKDD Conference on Knowledge Discovery and Data Mining, pp. 5351–5362 (2024)
11. Li, Z., Xia, L., Shi, L., Xu, Y., Yin, D., Huang, C.: Opencity: Open spatio-temporal foundation models for traffic prediction. arXiv preprint arXiv:2408.10269 (2024)
12. Liu, C., et al.: Spatial-temporal large language model for traffic prediction. In: 2024 25th IEEE International Conference on Mobile Data Management (MDM), pp. 31–40. IEEE (2024)
13. Mann, B., et al.: Language models are few-shot learners. arXiv preprint arXiv:2005.14165 **1**(3), 3 (2020)

14. Nie, Y., Nguyen, N.H., Sinthong, P., Kalagnanam, J.: A time series is worth 64 words: Long-term forecasting with transformers. arXiv preprint arXiv:2211.14730 (2022)
15. Office for Coastal Management: Nationwide automatic identification system 2023 (2023). https://www.fisheries.noaa.gov/inport/item/70162
16. Radford, A., et al.: Clip: Learning transferable visual models from natural language supervision, (2019). arXiv preprint
17. Spathis, D., Kawsar, F.: The first step is the hardest: Pitfalls of representing and tokenizing temporal data for large language models. J. Am. Med. Inform. Assoc. **31**(9), 2151–2158 (2024)
18. Touvron, H., et al.: Llama: Open and efficient foundation language models. arXiv preprint arXiv:2302.13971 (2023)
19. Wu, H., Xu, J., Wang, J., Long, M.: Autoformer: Decomposition transformers with auto-correlation for long-term series forecasting. Adv. Neural. Inf. Process. Syst. **34**, 22419–22430 (2021)
20. Wu, T., Ling, Q.: Stellm: Spatio-temporal enhanced pre-trained large language model for wind speed forecasting. Appl. Energy **375**, 124034 (2024)
21. Yuan, Y., Ding, J., Feng, J., Jin, D., Li, Y.: Unist: A prompt-empowered universal model for urban spatio-temporal prediction. In: Proceedings of the 30th ACM SIGKDD Conference on Knowledge Discovery and Data Mining, pp. 4095–4106 (2024)
22. Zeng, A., Chen, M., Zhang, L., Xu, Q.: Are transformers effective for time series forecasting? In: Proceedings of the AAAI Conference on Artificial Intelligence, vol. 37, pp. 11121–11128 (2023)
23. Zhang, X.: Enhancing urban flow prediction via mutual reinforcement with multi-scale regional information. Neural Netw. **182**, 106900 (2025)
24. Zhong, S., Ruan, W., Jin, M., Li, H., Wen, Q., Liang, Y.: Time-VLM: Exploring multimodal vision-language models for augmented time series forecasting. arXiv preprint arXiv:2502.04395 (2025)
25. Zhou, T., Niu, P., Sun, L., Jin, R., et al.: One fits all: power general time series analysis by pretrained LM. Adv. Neural. Inf. Process. Syst. **36**, 43322–43355 (2023)

PQ-STM: Pattern-Aware and Query-Guided Spatiotemporal Modeling for Traffic Forecasting

Yangnan Xu[1], Hengyu Liu[2], Zhihong Cui[3], Mingxing Shao[1], Tiancheng Zhang[1(✉)], Minghe Yu[4], Fangling Leng[1], and Ge Yu[1]

[1] School of Computer Science and Engineering,Northeastern University, Shenyang, China
tczhang@mail.neu.edu.cn
[2] Department of Computer Science, Aalborg University, Aalborg, Denmark
[3] Department of Informatics,The University of Oslo, Oslo, Norway
[4] Software College, Northeastern University, Shenyang, China

Abstract. Accurate traffic forecasting is foundational to effective Intelligent Transportation System (ITS) and critical for improving urban mobility, safety, and operational efficiency. However, achieving accurate predictions remains challenging due to the complex spatiotemporal heterogeneity inherent in real-world traffic data. Existing methods typically handle this heterogeneity only implicitly, often by applying shared operations across all nodes and time steps. This limitation makes it difficult to capture diverse temporal dynamics and to distinguish function-driven spatial dependencies from those induced merely by geographic proximity, thereby limiting prediction accuracy and generalization. To address these limitations, we propose the **P**attern-aware and **Q**uery-guided **S**patio**t**emporal **M**odel (`PQ-STM`). Our framework explicitly models heterogeneity through two core modules: a Temporal Pattern-aware Module, which uses prototype similarity routing to assign each time series to a sparse set of specialized temporal units, and a Spatial Query-guided Module, which constructs stable functional queries to retrieve relevant spatial context from functionally similar nodes beyond geographic proximity. Experiments on six real-world datasets show that `PQ-STM` achieves state-of-the-art performance.

Keywords: Traffic forecasting · Spatiotemporal heterogeneity · Temporal pattern modeling · Function-guided spatial dependency

1 Introduction

Accurate traffic forecasting is a key component of Intelligent Transportation System (ITS), aiming to predict future traffic states (e.g., flow, speed) based on historical data [19]. This capability is critical to improve urban planning, traffic dispatching, and the overall safety and efficiency of transportation systems

L. Ding et al. (Eds.): APWeb-WAIM 2026, LNCS 16995, pp. 83–99, 2027.
https://doi.org/10.1007/978-981-92-5699-0_6

[8,25]. Accurate predictions allow city planners and traffic managers to proactively address potential congestion, optimize traffic signal control, and ultimately contribute to smoother commutes and more sustainable urban environments [8,19,25].

Real-world traffic data exhibits complex heterogeneity, which involves variations across spatial and temporal dimensions. Temporally, patterns at a single location change over time (e.g., peak vs. off-peak hours). Spatially, heterogeneity involves more than just differing patterns across locations (e.g., downtown vs. residential areas); critically, it reflects that the underlying dependencies are often driven by functional similarity rather than geographical proximity.

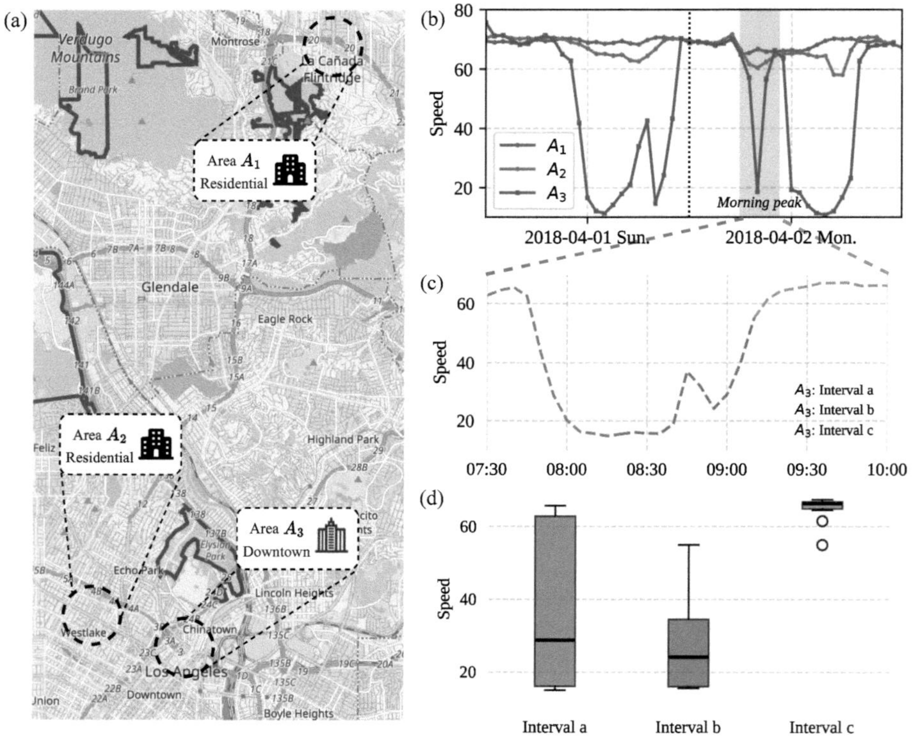

Fig. 1. An integrated view of spatio-temporal heterogeneity in real-world traffic data. (a) Locations of the three selected areas: the downtown area A_3 and the two residential areas A_1 and A_2. (b) Demonstration of spatial heterogeneity: distant residential areas A_1 and A_2 exhibit highly similar patterns, while the nearby residential A_2 and downtown A_3 show vastly different dynamics, indicating function, not proximity, drives spatial dependency. (c-d) Demonstration of temporal heterogeneity through a detailed view and statistical distributions of a single traffic event (A_3's morning peak).

Figure 1 provides an integrated example of such spatiotemporal heterogeneity: spatial dependencies are often driven by functional similarity rather than geographic proximity, while traffic patterns at a single location can shift sharply within a single event. These phenomena occur consistently throughout spatio-temporal data. However, modeling such spatio-temporal heterogeneity is non-trivial, as it poses several significant challenges.

Challenge I: How to effectively distinguish and model the diverse temporal patterns in traffic data? The challenge arises from two aspects. On the data side, traffic patterns are non-stationary, meaning they are always changing (e.g., rush hours differ from other times). On the task side, a forecasting model needs to generalize to predict future patterns it has not seen before. However, existing sequence models, from early recurrent neural networks (RNNs) [3,14] to recent transformers [7], fail to effectively address this challenge, as they usually rely on fixed shared mechanisms across all time steps. Such uniform processing overlooks the non-stationarity of traffic data and often leads to overly smoothed predictions that cannot capture sharp temporal variations.

Challenge II: How to capture the true functionally-driven spatial dependencies in traffic networks? This challenge arises from two main difficulties. On the data side, the true relationships between nodes are based on their function, but these "functional connections" are hidden. The physical road map is often a poor guide because it only shows which nodes are close to each other. On the task side, the model must handle a dual task: it needs to infer the hidden functional relationships while also making accurate predictions. However, existing spatial models, from early GNNs [11,27] relying on static proximity graphs to recent dynamic graph or attention-based methods [4,24], often fail to capture these true functional dependencies. They depend on fixed local structures or short-term traffic patterns, lacking mechanisms for a node's long-term functional role, thus struggling with spatial heterogeneity.

To overcome the aforementioned challenges, we propose the **P**attern-aware and **Q**uery-guided **S**patio-**t**emporal **M**odel (`PQ-STM`), a novel framework designed to explicitly handle spatiotemporal heterogeneity. ***To address Challenge I***, the Temporal Pattern-aware Module (TPM) performs prototype similarity routing to assign each time series to a sparse set of specialized temporal units, enabling the model to better capture diverse temporal patterns. ***To address Challenge II***, the Spatial Query-guided Module (SQM) captures function-driven spatial dependencies through stable functional queries. Each node constructs a query by combining a data-driven functional prior with a learnable node-specific residual, and uses it to retrieve relevant spatial context from functionally similar nodes regardless of geographic distance.

The main contributions of this paper are as follows:

- We propose the Temporal Pattern-aware Module (TPM), which performs prototype similarity routing to assign each time series to a sparse set of specialized temporal units, enabling the model to better capture diverse temporal patterns.
- We propose the Spatial Query-guided Module (SQM) to model spatial heterogeneity. It constructs stable functional queries from a data-driven prior

and a learnable node-specific residual, enabling each node to retrieve relevant spatial context beyond geographic proximity.

– We conduct extensive experiments on six real-world datasets. The results show that `PQ-STM` achieves state-of-the-art performance, demonstrating the effectiveness of explicitly modeling spatiotemporal heterogeneity.

2 Related Work

Our work is mainly related to deep learning-based traffic forecasting methods from two perspectives: temporal modeling and spatial modeling.

2.1 Modeling Temporal Dynamics

Capturing temporal dependencies is crucial for traffic forecasting. Early deep learning methods mainly relied on recurrent architectures such as LSTM [14] and GRU [3] to model sequential dynamics. To improve efficiency and capture multi-scale patterns, later works also incorporated temporal convolutions, as in STGCN [27]. More recently, Transformer-based models such as GMAN [28] and PDFormer [7] achieved strong performance by leveraging self-attention to model long-range dependencies.

Despite their success, these methods generally apply shared temporal operations across all inputs, which limits their ability to adapt to the non-stationary and heterogeneous nature of traffic patterns. As a result, they may fail to capture localized temporal fluctuations and struggle to model diverse temporal dynamics.

2.2 Modeling Spatial Dependencies

Modeling spatial correlations on irregular road networks is another key challenge in traffic forecasting. Early studies often used CNNs on grid-based traffic representations, while GNN-based methods such as DCRNN [11] and STGCN [27] later became the dominant paradigm by introducing graph convolutions on predefined adjacency matrices. To overcome the limitations of static graphs, subsequent works developed adaptive or dynamic graph structures, such as Graph-WaveNet [24], AGCRN [1], and DGCRN [10]. In parallel, attention-based models including ASTGCN [4] and GMAN [28] were proposed to capture global spatial dependencies.

However, both dynamic graph and attention-based methods are typically driven by short-term input states and lack an explicit mechanism to encode each node's long-term functional role. Consequently, they still struggle to model function-driven, non-local spatial dependencies under spatial heterogeneity.

3 Preliminaries

3.1 Traffic Forecasting Problem

We model a traffic network as a graph $\mathcal{G} = (V, E, A)$, where $V = \{v_1, \ldots, v_N\}$ is the set of N sensors, E denotes the road connectivity, and $A \in \mathbb{R}^{N \times N}$ is the adjacency matrix. At time step t, the traffic state over all nodes is denoted by $X_t \in \mathbb{R}^{N \times D}$, where D is the number of input features.

Given the historical observations over the past T_{his} time steps,

$$\mathcal{X} = \langle X_{t-T_{his}+1}, X_{t-T_{his}+2}, \ldots, X_t \rangle \in \mathbb{R}^{T_{his} \times N \times D},$$

the goal is to predict the target traffic variable over the next T_{pred} time steps,

$$\mathcal{Y} = \langle Y_{t+1}, Y_{t+2}, \ldots, Y_{t+T_{pred}} \rangle \in \mathbb{R}^{T_{pred} \times N}.$$

Formally, the task is to learn a mapping function $\mathcal{F}(\cdot; \theta)$:

$$\mathcal{Y} = \mathcal{F}(\mathcal{X}; \theta). \tag{1}$$

4 Methodology

In this section, we introduce the proposed Pattern-aware and Query-guided Spatiotemporal Model (`PQ-STM`), illustrated in Fig. 2. `PQ-STM` consists of three modules: (1) the **Input Embedding Layer**, which enriches raw traffic features with periodic context; (2) the **Temporal Pattern-aware Module (TPM)**, which performs prototype similarity routing to assign each time series to specialized temporal units for capturing diverse temporal patterns; and (3) the **Spatial Query-guided Module (SQM)**, which constructs stable functional queries to retrieve relevant spatial context from functionally similar nodes beyond geographic proximity. Finally, a lightweight prediction head maps the learned representation to future traffic forecasts.

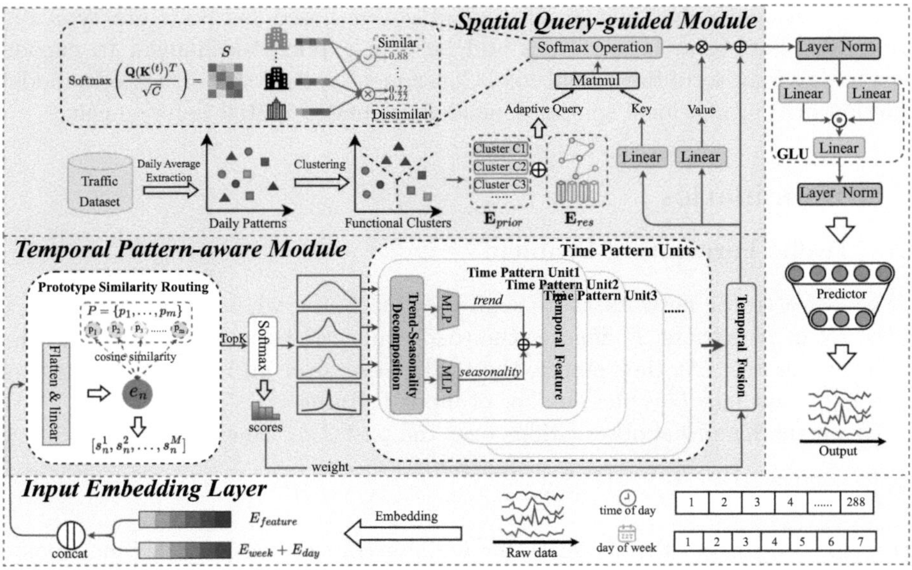

Fig. 2. The overall architecture of the PQ-STM.

4.1 Input Embedding Layer

Given the historical input sequence $\mathcal{X} \in \mathbb{R}^{T_{his} \times N \times D}$, we first project it to a dense feature embedding $\mathbf{E}_{feature} \in \mathbb{R}^{T_{his} \times N \times \varphi}$ using a fully connected layer. Following common practice in traffic forecasting [11,17], we also encode periodic context with day-of-week and time-of-day embeddings, denoted by $\mathbf{E}_{week}, \mathbf{E}_{day} \in \mathbb{R}^{T_{his} \times N \times \varphi}$. The final input representation is obtained by concatenating these embeddings along the feature dimension:

$$\mathbf{H}_{in} = \text{Concat}(\mathbf{E}_{feature}, \mathbf{E}_{week}, \mathbf{E}_{day}) \in \mathbb{R}^{T_{his} \times N \times C}, \tag{2}$$

where $C = 3\varphi$. The fused representation $\mathbf{H}_{in}$ is then fed into TPM and SQM.

4.2 Temporal Pattern-Aware Module

The Temporal Pattern-aware Module (TPM) addresses temporal heterogeneity through three components: prototype similarity routing, Time Pattern Units (TPUs), and a Temporal Fusion Unit. It first computes routing weights from the input sequence, then sparsely activates specialized TPUs through Top-K routing, and finally aggregates their outputs into a unified temporal representation.

Prototype Similarity Routing. To handle temporal heterogeneity, TPM performs prototype similarity routing to assign each input sequence to a sparse set of specialized temporal units. Given $\mathbf{H}_{in} \in \mathbb{R}^{T_{his} \times N \times C}$, routing is applied independently for each node n. Let $\mathbf{x}_n = \mathbf{H}_{in}[:, n, :] \in \mathbb{R}^{T_{his} \times C}$ denote the temporal feature sequence of node n. We summarize it into a latent vector $\mathbf{e}_n \in \mathbb{R}^C$ via

$$\mathbf{e}_n = \text{Flatten}(\mathbf{x}_n)\mathbf{W}_e + \mathbf{b}_e, \tag{3}$$

where $\mathbf{W}_e \in \mathbb{R}^{(T_{his} \times C) \times C}$ and $\mathbf{b}_e \in \mathbb{R}^C$ are learnable parameters.

We maintain a set of learnable prototypes $\mathbf{P} = \{\mathbf{p}_1, \ldots, \mathbf{p}_M\} \subset \mathbb{R}^C$, initialized by the M centroids obtained from K-Means clustering on historical sequence embeddings from the training set. The similarity between $\mathbf{e}_n$ and prototype $\mathbf{p}_i$ is computed by cosine similarity:

$$s_n^i = \frac{\mathbf{e}_n \cdot \mathbf{p}_i}{\|\mathbf{e}_n\|_2 \|\mathbf{p}_i\|_2}. \tag{4}$$

Let $\mathbf{s}_n = [s_n^1, \ldots, s_n^M]$ denote the routing score vector. To obtain sparse activation, we keep only the Top-K scores ($K \leq M$):

$$\tilde{s}_n^i = \begin{cases} s_n^i, & i \in \mathcal{I}_n, \\ -\infty, & \text{otherwise,} \end{cases}$$

where $\mathcal{I}_n$ is the index set of the Top-K elements in $\mathbf{s}_n$. The routing weights are then computed as

$$\boldsymbol{\alpha}_n = \text{Softmax}(\tilde{\mathbf{s}}_n / \tau), \tag{5}$$

where $\tau > 0$ is a learnable temperature parameter.

Time Pattern Units. Each Time Pattern Unit (TPU) refines the temporal representation of $\mathbf{x}_n \in \mathbb{R}^{T_{his} \times C}$ by following the decomposition strategy in Autoformer [21]. Specifically, $\mathbf{x}_n$ is decomposed into trend and seasonal components using a moving average (with window size l_{ma}) and replication padding:

$$\begin{aligned} \hat{\mathbf{x}}_n &= \text{AvgPool}_{l_{ma}}(\text{Padding}(\mathbf{x}_n)), \\ \mathbf{r}_n &= \mathbf{x}_n - \hat{\mathbf{x}}_n. \end{aligned} \tag{6}$$

Each TPU i applies separate linear transformations to the two components:

$$\begin{aligned} \mathbf{H}_n^{(tr,i)} &= \text{ReLU}(\hat{\mathbf{x}}_n \mathbf{W}_i^{(tr)}), \\ \mathbf{H}_n^{(se,i)} &= \text{ReLU}(\mathbf{r}_n \mathbf{W}_i^{(se)}), \\ \mathbf{H}_n^{(i)} &= \mathbf{H}_n^{(tr,i)} + \mathbf{H}_n^{(se,i)}, \end{aligned} \tag{7}$$

where $\mathbf{W}_i^{(tr)}, \mathbf{W}_i^{(se)} \in \mathbb{R}^{C \times C}$.

Temporal Fusion Unit. The Temporal Fusion Unit (TFU) aggregates TPU outputs into a unified temporal representation. Given the routing weights $\boldsymbol{\alpha}_n \in \mathbb{R}^M$ obtained by prototype similarity routing, it computes for each node n:

$$\mathbf{H}_n^{(TPM)} = \sum_{i=1}^{M} \alpha_n^i \mathbf{H}_n^{(i)}, \tag{8}$$

where $\mathbf{H}_n^{(i)} \in \mathbb{R}^{T_{his} \times C}$ denotes the output sequence of the i-th TPU for node n. With Top-K masking, only selected TPUs contribute to the aggregation. Finally, $\{\mathbf{H}_n^{(TPM)}\}_{n=1}^N$ are stacked along the spatial dimension to form $\mathbf{H}^{(TPM)} \in \mathbb{R}^{T_{his} \times N \times C}$, which is fed into the subsequent Spatial Query-guided Module.

4.3 Spatial Query-Guided Module

The Spatial Query-guided Module (SQM) addresses spatial heterogeneity by constructing stable functional queries and using them to retrieve relevant spatial context from functionally similar nodes beyond geographic proximity. It consists of three steps: data-driven functional prior construction, adaptive query construction, and function-guided spatial aggregation.

Data-Driven Functional Prior. To capture long-term functional roles, we construct a functional prior from the training data. For each node n, we compute its mean daily profile:

$$\mathbf{p}_n = \frac{1}{|\mathcal{D}|} \sum_{d \in \mathcal{D}} \mathbf{X}_n^{(d)} \in \mathbb{R}^{D_p}, \tag{9}$$

where $\mathcal{D}$ is the set of training days, $\mathbf{X}_n^{(d)}$ is the within-day traffic series of node n on day d, and D_p is the number of time steps per day. We then apply K-Means to $\{\mathbf{p}_n\}_{n=1}^N$ to partition nodes into K_s functional groups, and denote the cluster assignment of node n by c_n. Based on this assignment, we maintain a learnable prior dictionary $\mathbf{E}_{prior} \in \mathbb{R}^{K_s \times C}$, and each node retrieves its prior embedding as $\mathbf{e}_n^{prior} = \mathbf{E}_{prior}[c_n] \in \mathbb{R}^C$.

Adaptive Query Construction. To account for node-level variations within the same functional group, we introduce a learnable residual embedding matrix $\mathbf{E}_{res} \in \mathbb{R}^{N \times C}$, where $\mathbf{e}_n^{res} = \mathbf{E}_{res}[n] \in \mathbb{R}^C$ denotes the residual embedding of node n. The query of node n is constructed as

$$\mathbf{q}_n = \mathbf{e}_n^{prior} + \mathbf{e}_n^{res}. \tag{10}$$

Stacking all queries yields $\mathbf{Q} \in \mathbb{R}^{N \times C}$ for subsequent spatial aggregation.

Function-Guided Spatial Aggregation. For each time step t, we take the slice $\mathbf{H}^{(t)} = \mathbf{H}^{(\mathrm{TPM})}[t,:,:] \in \mathbb{R}^{N\times C}$ and project it into key and value matrices:

$$\mathbf{K}^{(t)} = \mathbf{H}^{(t)}\mathbf{W}_K, \quad \mathbf{V}^{(t)} = \mathbf{H}^{(t)}\mathbf{W}_V, \tag{11}$$

where $\mathbf{W}_K, \mathbf{W}_V \in \mathbb{R}^{C\times C}$ are learnable. We use the functional query matrix $\mathbf{Q} \in \mathbb{R}^{N\times C}$ directly, without an additional query projection, to preserve its stable functional semantics. The aggregation is computed with a residual connection:

$$\mathbf{Z}^{(t)} = \mathrm{Softmax}\left(\frac{\mathbf{Q}(\mathbf{K}^{(t)})^\top}{\sqrt{C}}\right)\mathbf{V}^{(t)} + \mathbf{H}^{(t)}, \tag{12}$$

where Softmax is applied row-wise over the node dimension, producing a dense $N \times N$ affinity matrix. Stacking $\{\mathbf{Z}^{(t)}\}_{t=1}^{T_{his}}$ yields $\mathbf{Z} \in \mathbb{R}^{T_{his}\times N\times C}$, and the last time step is used as the summary representation:

$$\mathbf{H}_{\mathrm{out}} = \mathbf{Z}^{(T_{his})} \in \mathbb{R}^{N\times C}. \tag{13}$$

4.4 Prediction Layer

The Prediction Layer maps the refined spatiotemporal representation $\mathbf{H}_{out} \in \mathbb{R}^{N\times C}$ to multi-step forecasts in a non-autoregressive manner. We first apply a GLU-based feed-forward block [6]. Let $\bar{\mathbf{H}} = \mathrm{LayerNorm}(\mathbf{H}_{out})$. Then

$$\mathbf{H}_{glu} = \left(\sigma(\bar{\mathbf{H}}\mathbf{W}_u) \odot (\bar{\mathbf{H}}\mathbf{W}_v)\right)\mathbf{W}_o, \tag{14}$$

where $\mathbf{W}_u, \mathbf{W}_v, \mathbf{W}_o \in \mathbb{R}^{C\times C}$ are learnable parameters, $\sigma(\cdot)$ denotes the Sigmoid function, and $\odot$ denotes element-wise multiplication. With a residual connection, the refined representation is

$$\mathbf{H}_o = \mathrm{LayerNorm}(\mathbf{H}_{glu} + \mathbf{H}_{out}) \in \mathbb{R}^{N\times C}. \tag{15}$$

Finally, an MLP maps $\mathbf{H}_o$ to the forecast:

$$\mathbf{Y} = \mathrm{MLP}(\mathbf{H}_o) \in \mathbb{R}^{N\times T_{pred}}. \tag{16}$$

5 Experiments

we evaluate `PQ-STM` on six real-world traffic datasets. We first introduce the experimental settings, including datasets, baselines, implementation details, and evaluation metrics. We then report the main comparison results, followed by ablation studies, efficiency analysis, hyperparameter analysis, and case studies.

5.1 Settings

Datasets. We evaluate PQ-STM on six real-world traffic datasets with 5-minute sampling intervals. **METR-LA** [11] and **PEMS-BAY** [11] are traffic speed datasets collected from loop detectors in Los Angeles and the San Francisco Bay Area, respectively. **PEMS03** [18], **PEMS04** [4], **PEMS07** [18], and **PEMS08** [4] are traffic flow datasets from the California Performance Measurement System (PeMS). Detailed statistics are summarized in Table 1.

For all datasets, we use the previous 12 time steps ($T_{his} = 12$) to predict the next 12 time steps ($T_{pred} = 12$). Following standard settings [4,11], METR-LA and PEMS-BAY are split into training/validation/testing sets with a ratio of 7:1:2, while the PeMS datasets are split by 6:2:2. Z-score normalization is applied using the mean and standard deviation computed from the training set.

Table 1. Statistics of the six datasets.

Dataset	Nodes	Samples	Time Range	Type
METR-LA	207	34,272	03/2012-06/2012	Speed
PEMS-BAY	325	52,116	01/2017-05/2017	Speed
PEMS03	358	26,208	09/2018-11/2018	Flow
PEMS04	307	16,992	01/2018-02/2018	Flow
PEMS07	883	28,224	05/2017-08/2017	Flow
PEMS08	170	17,856	07/2016-08/2016	Flow

Baseline Methods. We compare PQ-STM with representative STGNN-based traffic forecasting models covering different spatial modeling paradigms. These include adaptive or dynamic graph methods, such as Graph WaveNet [24], MTGNN [23], AGCRN [1], DGCRN [10], D^2STGNN [17], STDN [2], MAGE [13], MHGNet [22], and FDDSGCN [26]; attention-based models, including GMAN [28], ASTGNN [5], PDFormer [7], STAMT [12], and LLGformer [9]; as well as the retrieval-augmented model RAST [16].

Evaluation Metrics. Following prior work [5,18], we use Mean Absolute Error (MAE), Mean Absolute Percentage Error (MAPE), and Root Mean Square Error (RMSE) for evaluation. Missing values are masked during both training and testing [11,24].

Experimental Settings. All experiments are conducted on a single NVIDIA RTX A4000 GPU with 16 GB memory. We train PQ-STM using the Ranger21 optimizer [20] with an initial learning rate of 0.001 and a batch size of 64, and apply early stopping for convergence. Key architectural hyperparameters are kept fixed across datasets; detailed values are provided in our anonymous code repository: https://anonymous.4open.science/r/PQ-STM-BF90/. All experiments use fixed random seeds for reproducibility.

5.2 Experiment Results

We compare PQ-STM with all baseline methods, and the results are reported in Table 2. Overall, PQ-STM achieves the best performance on most datasets and metrics, demonstrating the effectiveness of explicitly modeling both temporal and spatial heterogeneity. We attribute this improvement to the joint design of TPM and SQM, which enables adaptive temporal pattern modeling and function-driven non-local spatial dependency modeling.

Table 2. Performance comparison of all models on four real-world datasets. **Bold** indicates the best performance, and underline indicates the second best.

Model	PEMS03			PEMS04			PEMS07			PEMS08		
	MAE	RMSE	MAPE	MAE	RMSE	MAPE	MAE	RMSE	MAPE	MAE	RMSE	MAPE
GWN	15.80	25.88	14.92%	18.54	30.09	12.71%	19.84	32.86	8.44%	14.54	23.67	9.41%
MTGNN	15.88	25.24	15.47%	18.96	31.05	13.65%	20.98	34.40	9.31%	15.12	24.23	9.65%
AGCRN	15.29	26.95	15.15%	19.83	32.26	13.97%	20.57	34.40	8.74%	15.95	25.22	10.09%
GMAN	16.52	27.18	17.36%	18.84	30.75	13.25%	20.97	34.20	9.05%	14.57	24.71	9.98%
ASTGNN	15.78	25.00	**14.79%**	18.60	30.91	12.36%	20.62	34.00	8.86%	15.00	24.70	9.50%
DGCRN	15.80	25.94	15.04%	18.80	30.65	12.82%	20.48	33.25	9.06%	14.60	24.16	9.33%
D^{2}STGNN	15.88	26.01	15.12%	18.20	**29.78**	12.28%	19.68	33.19	8.22%	14.35	24.18	9.33%
PDFormer	15.76	25.56	15.51%	18.32	29.96	12.10%	19.83	32.87	8.52%	13.58	23.51	9.04%
STAMT	15.58	25.81	16.30%	18.98	30.45	12.59%	19.67	32.85	8.59%	13.84	23.59	9.12%
STDN	15.93	27.53	17.67%	18.40	30.41	12.21%	20.08	33.73	9.29%	14.33	23.85	10.07%
MAGE	15.72	24.73	15.87%	19.76	31.05	12.64%	19.89	33.83	8.25%	13.76	24.74	9.39%
MHGNet	15.87	26.06	16.68%	19.36	31.03	12.93%	19.94	33.20	8.79%	15.58	24.41	10.05%
FDDSGCN	15.63	25.07	16.22%	19.45	30.51	12.89%	20.79	34.11	9.35%	15.40	24.75	10.40%
LLGformer	15.60	25.62	16.43%	19.03	30.50	12.74%	19.60	32.63	8.66%	15.10	24.06	10.00%
RAST	15.03	25.95	15.76%	19.86	31.93	13.18%	21.64	34.96	9.03%	15.81	25.07	10.02%
PQ-STM (ours)	**14.64**	**23.61**	15.71%	**18.17**	30.13	**11.93%**	**19.09**	**32.55**	**7.96%**	**13.41**	**23.20**	**8.83%**

5.3 Ablation Study

To evaluate the contribution of each component in PQ-STM, we conduct ablation studies on four representative datasets with the following variants:

(1) **PQ-STM w/o TE:** removes the day-of-week and time-of-day embeddings, using only raw feature embeddings as input.
(2) **PQ-STM w/o TPM:** replaces TPM with a lightweight linear temporal baseline.
(3) **PQ-STM w/o FP&NR:** removes the Functional Prior (FP) and Node Residual (NR) in SQM, and generates queries from current states, reducing the module to standard spatial self-attention.
(4) **PQ-STM w/o SQM:** replaces SQM with a standard multi-layer GCN based on the physical graph.

Table 3. Performance comparison on METR-LA and PEMS-BAY across different horizons. **Bold** and underline indicate the best and second best.

Dataset	Models	15 min			30 min			60 min		
		MAE	RMSE	MAPE(%)	MAE	RMSE	MAPE(%)	MAE	RMSE	MAPE(%)
METR-LA	GWN	2.69	5.15	6.99	3.08	6.20	8.47	3.51	7.28	9.96
	MTGNN	2.69	5.16	6.89	3.05	6.13	8.16	3.47	7.21	9.70
	AGCRN	2.85	5.53	7.63	3.20	6.52	9.00	3.59	7.45	10.47
	PDFormer	2.83	5.45	7.77	3.20	6.46	9.19	3.62	7.47	10.91
	STAMT	2.75	5.25	7.10	3.10	6.30	8.55	3.55	7.35	10.15
	MAGE	2.72	5.20	7.05	3.08	6.25	8.50	3.52	7.30	10.05
	RAST	2.85	5.45	7.50	3.22	6.55	9.15	3.65	7.60	10.60
	PQ-STM	**2.66**	**5.09**	**6.57**	**2.96**	**6.03**	**8.01**	**3.33**	**7.04**	**9.58**
PEMS-BAY	GWN	**1.30**	**2.73**	2.71	1.63	3.73	3.73	1.99	4.60	4.71
	MTGNN	1.33	2.80	2.81	1.66	3.77	3.75	1.95	4.50	4.62
	AGCRN	1.35	2.88	2.91	1.67	3.82	3.81	1.94	4.50	4.55
	PDFormer	1.32	2.83	2.78	1.64	3.79	3.71	1.91	4.43	4.51
	STAMT	1.32	2.78	2.75	1.65	3.75	3.72	1.93	4.45	4.58
	MAGE	1.31	2.76	2.73	1.64	3.74	3.74	1.92	4.48	4.60
	RAST	1.38	2.90	2.95	1.72	3.90	3.95	2.05	4.75	4.90
	PQ-STM	**1.30**	2.80	**2.55**	**1.54**	**3.66**	**3.63**	**1.87**	**4.32**	**4.23**

The complete PQ-STM consistently performs best, confirming the complementary roles of its components. Removing SQM causes the largest degradation (e.g., MAE increases by 1.00 on PEMS03 and 2.23 on PEMS07), showing that fixed-topology graph convolution cannot capture non-local function-driven dependencies. Replacing TPM with a linear temporal baseline also degrades performance (e.g., MAE increases by 0.30 on PEMS03 and 0.83 on PEMS07), highlighting the importance of adaptive temporal pattern modeling. Removing the functional prior and node-specific residual further hurts performance (e.g., MAE increases by 0.50 on PEMS03), showing that stable functional guidance is necessary beyond standard self-attention. Removing temporal embeddings also degrades performance, confirming the benefit of explicit periodic context (Fig. 3 and Table 3).

5.4 Computation Efficiency

PQ-STM achieves a favorable trade-off between forecasting accuracy and computational cost. As shown in Fig. 4, on PEMS04, PQ-STM attains strong prediction accuracy with relatively few parameters and lower training time per epoch.

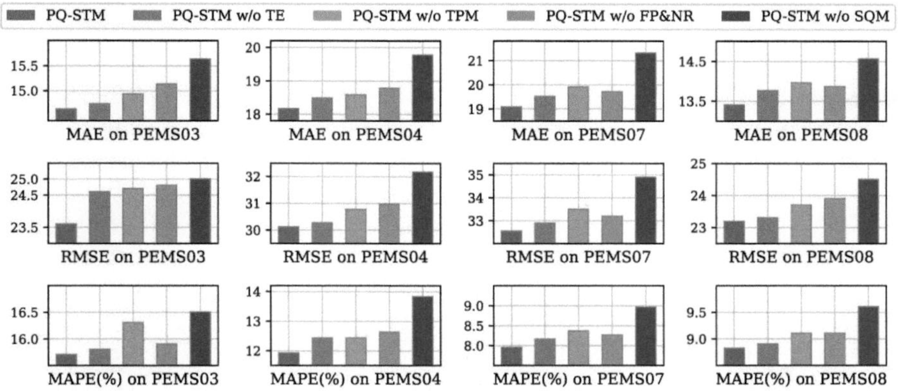

Fig. 3. Ablation study on four datasets.

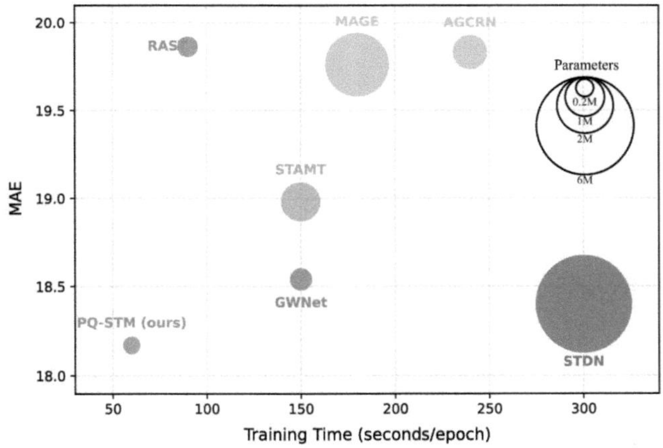

Fig. 4. Efficiency comparison on PEMS04 (batch size = 64). All models are evaluated under the same settings.

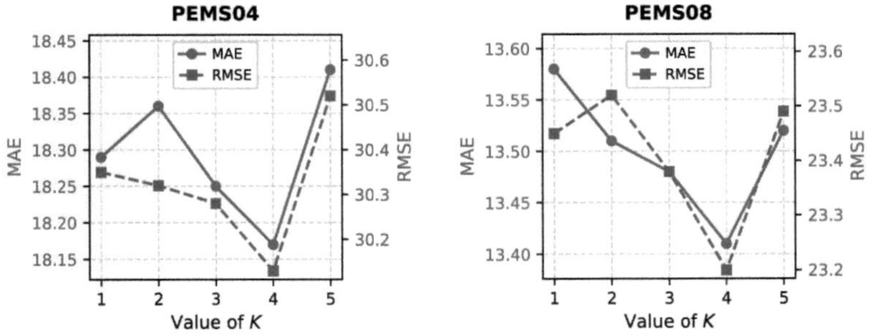

Fig. 5. Sensitivity of the Top-K routing parameter K on PEMS04 and PEMS08 (lower is better). The best results are obtained at $K = 4$.

5.5 Parameter Sensitivity

We study the impact of the Top-K parameter in prototype similarity routing by varying $K \in \{1, 2, 3, 4, 5\}$ with all other settings fixed. As shown in Fig. 5, both datasets achieve the best performance at $K = 4$. In general, very small K limits pattern coverage, whereas overly large K (e.g., $K = 5$) degrades performance due to redundant pattern mixing. Thus, we set $K = 4$ by default.

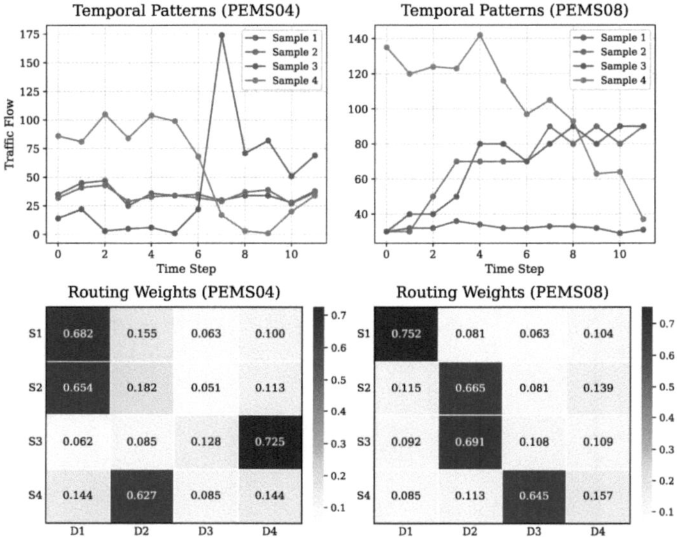

Fig. 6. Case study of TPM routing on PEMS04 and PEMS08. Stable, spiking, and declining patterns yield distinct routing preferences, while similar upward trends tend to be routed to the same unit.

5.6 Case Study

Interpreting TPM Routing. Figure 6 shows that TPM yields interpretable routing behaviors. On PEMS04, stable patterns (S1/S2) are routed mainly to D1, while the sudden peak (S3) and sharp decline (S4) are routed to D4 (0.725) and D2 (0.627), respectively. A similar trend is observed on PEMS08, where time series with similar upward trends (S2 and S3) are routed to the same unit D2. These results suggest that prototype similarity routing adaptively selects temporal units according to time-varying dynamics.

Functional Space Visualization for SQM. We analyze the METR-LA dataset as a case study. Figure 7(a) visualizes the node queries $\{\mathbf{q}_n\}$ in a 2D t-SNE [15] space, where coherent groups emerge. As shown in Fig. 7(b) and (c), geographic proximity does not necessarily imply functional similarity: Node 34

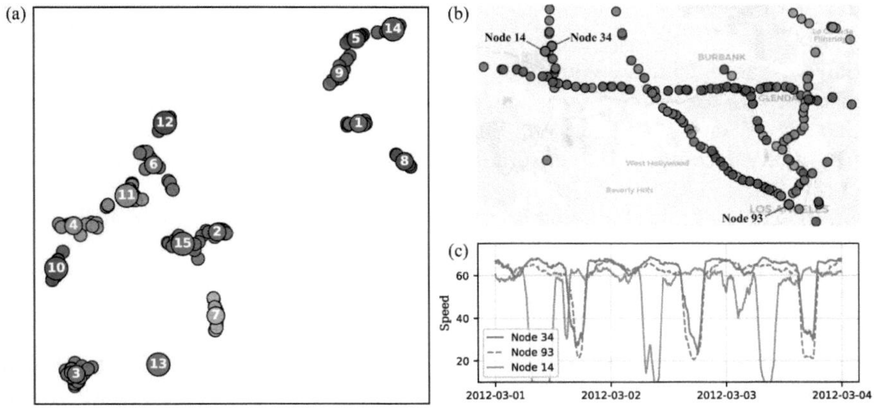

Fig. 7. SQM case study on METR-LA. (a) 2D t-SNE visualization of node queries $\{\mathbf{q}_n\}$. (b) Geographic map of selected nodes. (c) Speed time series: nearby nodes can be dissimilar (34 vs. 14), while distant nodes can be similar (34 vs. 93).

and Node 14 are spatially close but have substantially different speed profiles, whereas Node 34 and Node 93 are far apart yet exhibit highly similar temporal behaviors. These observations suggest that SQM captures meaningful functional contexts for modeling non-local dependencies beyond physical adjacency.

6 Conclusion

In this paper, we proposed the Pattern-aware and Query-guided Spatiotemporal Model (`PQ-STM`) for traffic forecasting under spatiotemporal heterogeneity. `PQ-STM` consists of two key components: (1) the Temporal Pattern-aware Module (TPM), which uses prototype similarity routing to assign each time series to a sparse set of specialized temporal units for capturing diverse temporal patterns; and (2) the Spatial Query-guided Module (SQM), which constructs stable functional queries to retrieve non-local spatial context and capture function-driven dependencies beyond geographic proximity. Extensive experiments on six real-world datasets demonstrate that `PQ-STM` achieves consistent state-of-the-art performance. These results show that explicitly modeling heterogeneity in both temporal and spatial dimensions leads to more accurate and robust spatiotemporal forecasting.

Acknowledgments. This research was funded by the National Natural Science Foundation of China (Nos. 62272093,62137001).

References

1. Bai, L., Yao, L., Li, C., Wang, X., Wang, C.: Adaptive graph convolutional recurrent network for traffic forecasting. In: NeurIPS, vol. 33, pp. 17804–17815 (2020)
2. Cao, L., Wang, B., Jiang, G., Yu, Y., Dong, J.: Spatiotemporal-aware trend-seasonality decomposition network for traffic flow forecasting. In: AAAI **39**, 11463–11471 (2025)
3. Fu, R., Zhang, Z., Li, L.: Using LSTM and GRU neural network methods for traffic flow prediction. In: YAC, pp. 324–328 (2016)
4. Guo, S., Lin, Y., Feng, N., Song, C., Wan, H.: Attention based spatial-temporal graph convolutional networks for traffic flow forecasting. In: AAAI **33**, 922–929 (2019)
5. Guo, S., Lin, Y., Wan, H., Li, X., Cong, G.: Learning dynamics and heterogeneity of spatial-temporal graph data for traffic forecasting. IEEE Trans. Knowl. Data Eng. **34**(11), 5415–5428 (2021)
6. Hua, W., Dai, Z., Liu, H., Le, Q.V.: Transformer quality in linear time. In: ICML, pp. 9099–9117 (2022)
7. Jiang, J., Han, C., Zhao, W.X., Wang, J.: Pdformer: Propagation delay-aware dynamic long-range transformer for traffic flow prediction. In: AAAI **37**, 4365–4373 (2023)
8. Jiang, W., Luo, J.: Graph neural network for traffic forecasting: a survey. Expert Syst. Appl. **207**, 117921 (2022)
9. Jin, D., Huo, C., Shi, J., He, D., Wei, J., Yu, P.S.: Llgformer: Learnable long-range graph transformer for traffic flow prediction. In: WWW (2025)
10. Li, F., et al.: Dynamic graph convolutional recurrent network for traffic prediction: Benchmark and solution. ACM Trans. Knowl. Discov. Data **17**(1), 1–21 (2023)
11. Li, Y., Yu, R., Shahabi, C., Liu, Y.: Diffusion convolutional recurrent neural network: Data-driven traffic forecasting. In: ICLR (2018)
12. Liu, A., Zhang, Y.: An efficient spatial-temporal transformer with temporal aggregation and spatial memory for traffic forecasting. Expert Syst. Appl. **250**, 123884 (2024)
13. Ma, J., et al.: Less but more: Linear adaptive graph learning empowering spatiotemporal forecasting. In: NeurIPS (2025)
14. Ma, X., Tao, Z., Wang, Y., Yu, H., Wang, Y.: Long short-term memory neural network for traffic speed prediction using remote microwave sensor data. Transport. Res. Part C: Emerg. Technol. **54**, 187–197 (2015)
15. Van der Maaten, L., Hinton, G.: Visualizing data using t-SNE. J. Mach. Learn. Res. **9**(11) (2008)
16. Ruan, W., Dang, X., Zhou, Z., Lyu, S., Liang, Y.: Rast: A retrieval augmented spatio-temporal framework for traffic prediction. In: AAAI (2026)
17. Shao, Z., Zhang, Z., Wang, F., Wei, W., Xu, Y.: Spatial-temporal identity: a simple yet effective baseline for multivariate time series forecasting. In: CIKM, pp. 4454–4458 (2022)
18. Song, C., Lin, Y., Guo, S., Wan, H.: Spatial-temporal synchronous graph convolutional networks: A new framework for spatial-temporal network data forecasting. In: AAAI **34**, 914–921 (2020)
19. Tedjopurnomo, D.A., Bao, Z., Zheng, B., Choudhury, F.M., Qin, A.K.: A survey on modern deep neural network for traffic prediction: Trends, methods and challenges. IEEE Trans. Knowl. Data Eng. **34**(4), 1544–1561 (2020)

20. Wright, L., Demeure, N.: Ranger21: a synergistic deep learning optimizer. arXiv preprint arXiv:2106.13731 (2021)
21. Wu, H., Xu, J., Wang, J., Long, M.: Autoformer: Decomposition transformers with auto-correlation for long-term series forecasting. NeurIPS. pp, 22419–22430 (2021)
22. Wu, M., Lin, Y., Jiang, T., Weng, W.: Mhgnet: Multi-heterogeneous graph neural network for traffic prediction. In: ICASSP (2025)
23. Wu, Z., Pan, S., Long, G., Jiang, J., Chang, X., Zhang, C.: Connecting the dots: Multivariate time series forecasting with graph neural networks. In: KDD (2020)
24. Wu, Z., Pan, S., Long, G., Jiang, J., Zhang, C.: Graph wavenet for deep spatial-temporal graph modeling. In: IJCAI, pp, 1907–1913 (2019)
25. Xiao, Z., Fu, X., Zhang, L., Goh, R.S.M.: Traffic pattern mining and forecasting technologies in maritime traffic service networks: a comprehensive survey. IEEE Trans. Intell. Transp. Syst. **21**(5), 1796–1825 (2019)
26. Xu, J., Zhao, C., Yang, J., Huang, Y., Yang, Y., Por, L.Y.: FDDSGCN: Fractional decoupling dynamic spatiotemporal graph convolutional network for traffic forecasting. In: ICASSP (2025)
27. Yu, B., Yin, H., Zhu, Z.: Spatio-temporal graph convolutional networks: A deep learning framework for traffic forecasting. In: IJCAI (2018)
28. Zheng, C., Fan, X., Wang, C., Qi, J.: GMAN: A graph multi-attention network for traffic prediction. In: AAAI **34**, 1234–1241 (2020)

Rule-Grounded Reasoning for Traffic Video Question Answering with Regulation Knowledge Graphs

Daijie Zhu[1], Yuchen Pan[1], Xin Hu[1(✉)], Long Li[2], Zedong Liu[2], Jie Zhao[1], and Xiangyu Song[1]

[1] School of Data Science and Artificial Intelligence, Chang'an University, Shaanxi 710018, China
{zhudaijie,yuchenpan,huxin711,jiezhao,xiangyu.song}@chd.edu.cn
[2] School of Information Engineer, Chang'an University, Shaanxi 710018, China
llchd248@chd.edu.cn

Abstract. Traffic Video Question Answering (TrafficVideoQA) requires not only visual understanding of traffic scenes but also rule-grounded and causal reasoning based on traffic regulations. Existing methods mainly rely on visual cues or unstructured external knowledge, which makes it difficult to model regulatory constraints explicitly and often introduces irrelevant knowledge during retrieval. To address this issue, we propose CATK-VideoQA, a context-aware knowledge-enhanced framework for TrafficVideoQA. Specifically, we construct a Traffic Regulation Knowledge Graph (TRKG) to represent regulation knowledge as structured triples, and design a Joint Contextual Knowledge Retrieval (JCKR) module to retrieve evidence jointly from question intent and scene context. In this way, the model can obtain regulation knowledge that is both semantically relevant and contextually applicable. Experiments on the SUTD-TrafficQA dataset show that CATK-VideoQA achieves high accuracy and consistently improves performance on complex inference tasks.

Keywords: Knowledge Graph · TrafficVideoQA · Context-Aware Reasoning

1 Introduction

Traffic Video Question Answering (TrafficVideoQA) not only requires understanding the vehicles, road environments, and dynamic interactions in traffic videos, but also needs to perform normative reasoning for tasks such as accident attribution, violation judgment, and prevention analysis. Unlike general VideoQA, these questions often cannot be answered from visual content alone, but require the model to determine the applicability of rules, the legality of behaviors, and the responsibility relations among traffic participants. Therefore, effectively incorporating traffic regulation knowledge into video question answering is essential for improving reasoning performance in TrafficVideoQA.

L. Ding et al. (Eds.): APWeb-WAIM 2026, LNCS 16995, pp. 100–115, 2027.
https://doi.org/10.1007/978-981-92-5699-0_7

Existing methods mainly enhance traffic scene understanding through visual representation learning, multimodal alignment, or spatiotemporal modeling [4,11,12,21,32]. However, when facing questions involving regulation constraints and causal reasoning, they still tend to rely on visual co-occurrence patterns or statistical correlations, without explicit support from traffic rules. Although some studies introduce external knowledge [15,25,27,31], such knowledge is usually represented in unstructured text and is therefore insufficient for modeling the conditional constraints and logical dependencies in traffic regulations. In addition, most existing retrieval methods match knowledge based only on question or video, without jointly constraining relevance by both question intent and video scene facts. This often introduces noisy knowledge that is semantically related but not applicable to the current scenario, which weakens reasoning quality. These limitations can be summarized into two major challenges in TrafficVideoQA, namely the knowledge structure challenge and the knowledge retrieval challenge, as illustrated in Fig. 1

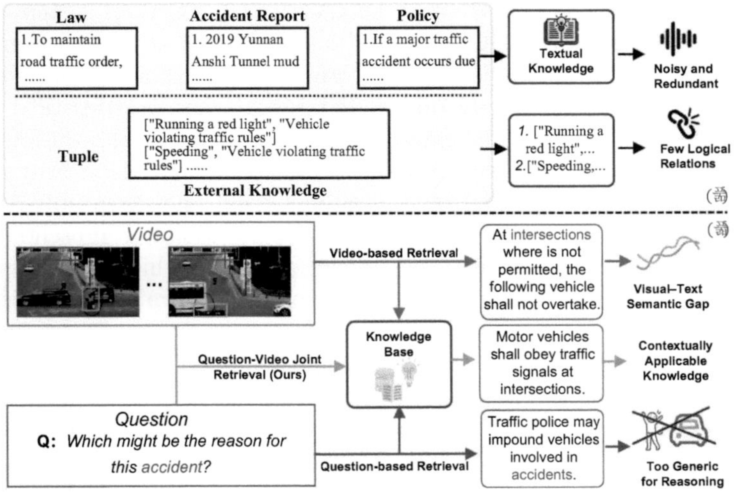

Fig. 1. Two challenges in TrafficVideoQA: (a) weakly structured traffic knowledge with sparse causal relations; (b) existing retrieval mechanisms rely only on textual or video features, making it difficult to obtain accurate knowledge.

To address these issues, we propose CATK-VideoQA, a context-aware knowledge-enhanced reasoning framework for TrafficVideoQA. It constructs a Traffic Regulation Knowledge Graph (TRKG) to represent regulations as structured triples and designs a Joint Contextual Knowledge Retrieval (JCKR) module to retrieve evidence aligned with both question intent and video context. The main contributions are summarized as follows:

- We propose a knowledge-enhanced framework, CATK-VideoQA, which introduces structured knowledge priors to compensate for the lack of domain

knowledge understanding in traditional models and achieve more robust causal reasoning.
- We construct a Traffic Regulation Knowledge Graph (TRKG) and design a Joint Contextual Knowledge Retrieval (JCKR) module, which constrains the retrieval process with question intent and video scene context to avoid noise knowledge unrelated to answering questions.
- Experimental results on the SUTD-TrafficQA dataset validate the effectiveness of the proposed framework, particularly on complex tasks involving normative and causal reasoning. The retrieved triples also provide interpretable knowledge support for answering questions.

2 Related Work

Existing methods mainly improve traffic video understanding through visual representation learning, multimodal alignment, and temporal modeling. Representative methods such as HCRN [18], DualVGR [28], VQAC [17], Tem-Adapter [4], CMCIR [21], and CFMMC-Align [11] have achieved strong performance in object recognition, event understanding, and visual-text alignment. However, these methods still rely largely on explicit visual cues or statistical correlations in videos, and therefore remain limited when answering questions that require background knowledge, implicit relations, and logical constraints. To address this issue, some studies incorporate external knowledge into VideoQA [1,7,9,15,16,20,27]. Nevertheless, such knowledge is usually represented as textual knowledge bases or unstructured rule descriptions, which makes it difficult to explicitly model the conditional dependencies and normative constraints in traffic regulations.

Knowledge graphs are more suitable for representing normative traffic knowledge because they explicitly encode entities, relations, and logical dependencies. Recent advances in large language models have also promoted automatic knowledge graph construction [2,5,13,30], and traffic-related knowledge graphs have been explored in traffic management [10,22,29,33], travel services [6], and traffic event analysis [24]. However, most existing studies focus on graph construction or on general downstream applications, while paying limited attention to knowledge selection for TrafficVideoQA under both question intent and scene facts. To address this limitation, we construct a Traffic Regulation Knowledge Graph and design a retrieval mechanism jointly constrained by question intent and scene caption, providing more accurate rule support for TrafficVideoQA.

3 Traffic Regulation Knowledge Graph

In this section, we introduce the construction of TRKG based on dual-prompt collaboration strategy. The specific process is shown in Fig. 2.

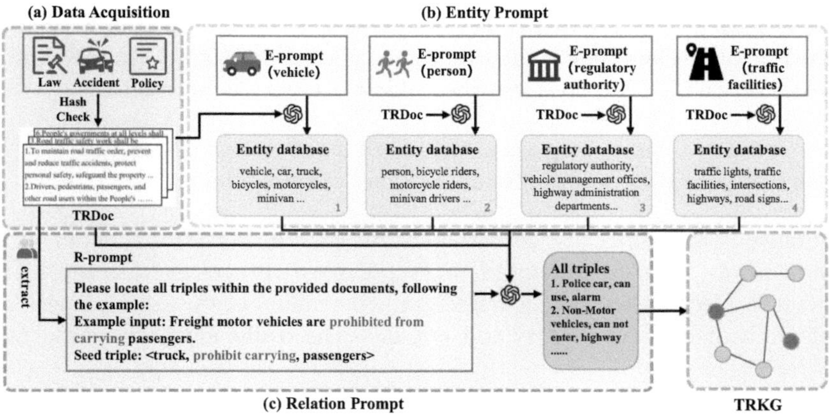

Fig. 2. TRKG construction: (a) cleaning of data; (b) designing Entity Prompt to build the traffic entity database; (c) designing Relation Prompt to obtain triples.

3.1 Data Acquisition and Cleaning

There are significant differences in traffic regulations among countries. This work focus on the Chinese road traffic scenes to carry out video question answering research. Therefore, we build the traffic regulation knowledge graph that adapts to China's traffic rules. First, we collect public traffic regulation documents from the government official website, laws and regulations database, and traffic management departments through the search engine. Subsequently, the documents are cleaned and converted into plain text, and SimHash [23] is employed to remove duplicate entries. Finally, a traffic regulation corpus, denoted as TRDoc $= \{t_1, t_2, ..., t_n\}$, is constructed, where n is the total number of documents.

3.2 Hierarchical Entity Prompt

Traffic entities exhibit significant hierarchical relationships. For instance, the entity *vehicle* can be further subdivided into *car* and *truck*. Traditional methods have difficulty explicitly capturing hierarchical structures among entities. Thus, we design a hierarchical entity prompt (**E-prompts**) strategy for traffic entity extraction as illustrated in Fig. 2(b).

Entity Classification. We categorize traffic entities into two levels: coarse-grained entity and fine-grained entities. For example, the coarse-grained entity *vehicle* is subdivided into the fine-grained entities such as *freight vehicle*, *passenger vehicle* and *specialty vehicle*. We predefine four coarse-grained entities: *person*, *vehicle*, *regulatory authority*, and *traffic facilities*.

Hierarchical Entity Prompt. For each coarse-grained entity, an E-prompt is designed to guide DeepSeek in identifying the corresponding fine-grained entities. For instance, the E-prompt p_v for the *vehicle* category is phrased as:

```
The provided text contains entities related to [vehicle],
such as [car], [truck], etc. Please output these entities.
```

Similarly, E-prompts are constructed for *person*, *regulatory authority*, and *traffic facilities*. These E-prompts $P = \{p_p, p_v, p_r, p_t\}$, together with the TRDoc, are fed into DeepSeek to extract fine-grained traffic entities aligned with each predefined coarse-grained entity and populate the traffic entity database *Dt*.

3.3 Relation Prompt

In traffic scenarios, relationships between entities are often complex and numerous, making it costly to manually define all relationships. Therefore, we design a Relation prompt (**R-prompt**) to guide large language models to automatically identify entity relations and generate structured triples within a constrained entity space, as shown in Fig. 2(c). The specific form of R-prompt is as follows:

```
Please extract all triples within the provided document,
following the example:
Example input: Freight motor vehicles are prohibited from
carrying passengers.
Seed triple output: <truck, prohibit carrying, passengers>
```

Specifically, seed triples are manually extracted from TRDoc and are primarily used to demonstrate to the model how raw regulation texts can be mapped into structured triples. For example, we extract the triple `<truck, prohibit carrying, passengers>` from the original text `Freight motor vehicles are prohibited from carrying passengers`. By including such examples, R-prompt effectively guides the model to recognize complex relations in the traffic scene.

3.4 Triple Extraction

Dual-Prompt Collaborative. We propose a dual-prompt collaborative strategy that simultaneously leverages the E-prompts and R-prompt. Specifically, E-prompts constrain the entity space by identifying and organizing entities into a structured database *Dt*, while the R-prompt operates within this constrained space to generate structured triples. The dual-prompt collaboration strategy fully utilizes the powerful semantic understanding ability of LLMs, significantly improving the efficiency of triplet extraction.

Expert Verification. We invite 10 domain experts with backgrounds in knowledge graphs and traffic laws to independently review the candidate triples. If experts discover errors in certain triples, we trace the errors back to the corresponding extraction module and perform local re-extraction and manual re-validation on the relevant regulation clauses. This process produces a TRKG with over 2,000 entities, 30 relation types, and 700 triples, improving its quality and reliability for retrieval.

4 CATK-VideoQA Methodology

4.1 Overview

The overall CATK-VideoQA architecture is shown in Fig. 3. Given a traffic video sequence V, a natural language question Q, a set of answer candidates A and TRKG $\mathcal{G} = \{(s, r, o)\}$, CATK-VideoQA predicts the answer with the highest matching score, denoted as $\bar{a}$. The task is formally defined as follows:

$$\bar{a} = \underset{a \in A}{\operatorname{argmax}} score_n(a \mid V, Q, \mathcal{G}; \theta). \tag{1}$$

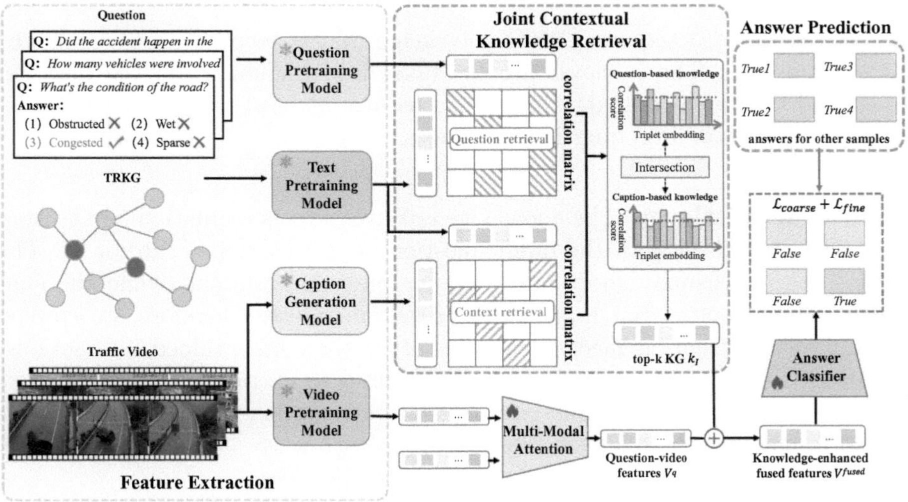

Fig. 3. Overview of the proposed CATK-VideoQA model. The model consists of three modules: feature extraction, JCKR, and answer prediction. Given video and question inputs, JCKR retrieves top-k triples from the TRKG based on both question and caption. The retrieved knowledge is then fused with multimodal features to produce knowledge-enhanced representations for answer prediction.

4.2 Feature Extraction

We employ pretrained visual and textual encoders to obtain the initial multimodal features. For a traffic video V, we uniformly sample 8 frames and use CLIP [26] to extract appearance feature $f_{V^a} = \{f_{V^a_{i,j}} \mid j = 1, \ldots, N_a\} \in R^{B \times N_a \times d_a}$ and motion features $f_{V^m} = \{f_{V^m_{i,j}} \mid j = 1, \ldots, N_m\} \in R^{B \times N_m \times d_m}$, The question feature is denoted as $f_Q = \{Q_{i,j} \mid j = 1, \ldots, N_t\} \in R^{B \times N_t \times d_t}$. The four candidate answer features are represented as $A^c = \{A^{c,n}_{i,j} \mid j = 1, \ldots, N_{ans}\} \in R^{B \times N_{ans} \times d_t}$, $n = 1, 2, 3, 4$, B is the batch size, and $i = 1, \ldots, B$. N_a, N_m, N_t, and N_{ans} denote the token size of the appearance, motion, question, and answer features, while d_a, d_m, and d_t refer to the feature dimension. The knowledge triple feature is denoted as $f_{\mathcal{G}} \in R^{N \times d_t}$, where N is the number of triples.

In addition, to bridge the semantic gap between visual scenes and regulation knowledge, each input video is converted into a textual caption C using a pretrained video captioning model. We sample representative video frames from each video and use LLaVA-1.5 [19] to generate textual scene captions. The generated caption is encoded as the scene-caption feature $f_C \in R^{B \times N_c \times d_t}$, where N_c is caption token size.

4.3 Joint Contextual Knowledge Retrieval

The JCKR aims to acquire TRKG knowledge that is helpful in answering the current question. The retrieval process takes into account both the question intent and the video context, which helps reduce retrieval ambiguity caused by querying solely based on questions or videos.

Knowledge Retriever. The knowledge retriever selects regulation triples from the TRKG based on both the input question Q and the video caption C. The question text is usually short but contains questioning intent, while the caption is rich in content but may contain irrelevant noise. Therefore, we employ the multihead attention mechanism to capture their fine-grained interactions. Specifically, question-to-caption attention is used to extract the scene context that is most relevant to the question intent, while caption-to-question attention is used to enhance the question representation with scene-aware semantic cues. The two interaction results are formulated as:

$$C_\gamma = \mathrm{MHAttn}(W^c_Q f_Q, W^c_K f_C, W^c_V f_C), \tag{2}$$

$$Q_\gamma = \mathrm{MHAttn}(W^q_Q f_C, W^q_K f_Q, W^q_V f_Q). \tag{3}$$

Subsequently, the knowledge triple features are subjected to row-wise normalization to obtain $\tilde{\mathcal{G}}$. We separately compute the cosine similarities between the knowledge features and the question features, as well as the caption features:

$$S_q = Q_\gamma \cdot \tilde{\mathcal{G}}^\top, S_c = C_\gamma \cdot \tilde{\mathcal{G}}^\top. \tag{4}$$

Finally, we retrieve the top-k indices based on the similarity scores S_q and S_c. We empirically set the number of retrieved triples to k=15, as it provides a good balance between retrieval coverage and noise. The choice is based on validation experiments discussed in Sect. 5.4. We take the intersection of the knowledge features selected based on S_q and S_c to obtain the final video-question related knowledge features, denoted as $\mathcal{G}_I$.

If the intersection contains fewer than k triples, we supplement it with the highest-scoring triples from the union of the two retrieval sets to ensure a fixed number of retrieved triples.

Multimodal Integration. To facilitate multimodal feature fusion, the appearance and motion features are first projected into a unified feature space, and the appearance features are average-pooled to match the token length of the motion features. For the retrieved knowledge features $\mathcal{G}_I$, we apply max aggregation along the triple dimension to obtain a global knowledge feature, which highlights the most informative knowledge signals while suppressing noisy evidence. The aggregated knowledge feature is then expanded to align with the dimensionality of the video features, denoted as $\mathcal{G}_{expand}$.

To model the interaction between the question and video, we employ a bidirectional attention mechanism, where the two modalities alternately serve as query and key-value pairs. $\mathbf{V^{qa}}$ and $\mathbf{V^{qm}}$ denote the question-guided appearance and motion features, respectively, and $\mathbf{V^{va}}$ and $\mathbf{V^{vm}}$ denote the appearance-guided and motion-guided question features. $\mathbf{V}^{appearance}$ is obtained by concatenating $\mathbf{V^{qa}}$ and $\mathbf{V^{va}}$, while $\mathbf{V}^{motion}$ is obtained by concatenating $\mathbf{V^{qm}}$ and $\mathbf{V^{vm}}$. The final question-video feature V^q is obtained through weighted fusion:

$$\mathbf{V}^q = \alpha \cdot \mathbf{V}^{appearance} + \beta \cdot \mathbf{V}^{motion}, \tag{5}$$

$\mathcal{G}_{expand}$ is fused with the question-video feature $\mathbf{V}^q$ using an MLP network, to obtain knowledge-enhanced multimodal feature $\mathbf{V}^{fused}$.

$$\mathbf{V}^{fused} = \text{MLP}([\mathbf{V}^q; \mathcal{G}_{expand}]). \tag{6}$$

4.4 Answer Prediction

In the answer prediction phase, we design a multimodal answer classification approach based on feature alignment. Specifically, given the knowledge-enhanced fused feature $\mathbf{V}^{fused}$ and a candidate answer set A^c, we first zero-pad the answer features so that their length N_{ans} is aligned with the video feature length N_m, resulting in a_i.

Subsequently, we calculate the similarity scores of aligned answer features a_i and fused features $\mathbf{V}^{fused}$.

$$score_n = \text{sim}(\mathbf{V}^{fused}, a_i^\top) \in R^B. \tag{7}$$

Finally, the answer $\overline{a}$ corresponding to the highest similarity score is selected as the final prediction.

$$\overline{a} = \arg \max_{n \in \{1,2,3,4\}} score_n. \tag{8}$$

Loss Function. We optimize the model using a hierarchical contrastive learning objective to enhance alignment between knowledge-enhanced representations and candidate answers.

Following [11], we define positive and negative samples. **Positive sample set:** The similarity between the knowledge-enhanced video features V^{fused} and correct answers, including: coarse-grained similarity s^+ and fine-grained similarity s_t^+. **Negative sample set:** Similarity s_j^- between the correct answers of other samples in the same batch and similarity s_m^- between other incorrect options in the same question.

The overall objective consists of a coarse-grained loss and a fine-grained loss:

$$\mathcal{L}_{coarse} = -\frac{1}{B}\sum_{m=1}^{B} \log \frac{\exp(s^+/\tau)}{\exp(s^+/\tau) + \sum_{j \in N_{inter}} \exp\left(s_j^-/\tau\right) + \sum_{m \in N_{intra}} \exp\left(s_m^-/\tau\right)}, \tag{9}$$

$$\mathcal{L}_{fine} = -\frac{1}{B}\frac{1}{N_m + N_t}\sum_{m=1}^{B}\sum_{t=1}^{N_m+N_t} \log \frac{\exp(s_t^+/\tau)}{\exp(s_t^+/\tau) + \sum_{j \in N_{inter}} \exp\left(s_{t,j}^-/\tau\right) + \sum_{m \in N_{intra}} \exp\left(s_{t,m}^-/\tau\right)}, \tag{10}$$

$$\mathcal{L}_{total} = \mathcal{L}_{coarse} + \mathcal{L}_{fine}, \tag{11}$$

where τ is a temperature parameter and N_{inter} represents the correct answers for other samples in the same batch, while N_{intra} denotes the incorrect options for the current question.

The coarse-grained loss $\mathcal{L}_{coarse}$ ensures the overall consistency of the semantic space, while the fine-grained loss $\mathcal{L}_{fine}$ provides detailed support for global representations. By jointly optimizing the global semantic structure and local feature mappings, the knowledge-enhanced features relevant to video question answering can more effectively contribute to answer prediction, thereby improving predictive accuracy.

5 Experiments

5.1 Experiment Setting

We evaluate CATK-VideoQA on SUTD-TrafficQA, which contains 10,080 traffic videos and 62,535 QA pairs split into 56,460 training and 6,075 testing pairs across six reasoning types. We use accuracy as the evaluation metric, defined as the proportion of questions for which the predicted answer matches the ground-truth option. Following CFMMC-Align, we train the model with Adam for 100 epochs, using a learning rate of 2e-4, batch size 64, and a single RTX 3060 GPU.

Table 1. Performance comparison of this model with other baseline methods on the SUTD-TrafficQA dataset. Note that the best-performing method is displayed in bold, while the second-best result is underlined.

Category	methods	Basic	Attribution	Introspection	Counterfactual	Forecasting	Reverse	ALL
		(3595)	(1625)	(148)	(185)	(223)	(299)	(6075)
VideoQA	HCRN [18]	34.2	50.3	33.4	40.7	44.6	50.1	36.3
	VQAC [17]	34.0	49.4	34.4	39.7	38.6	49.7	36.0
	DualVGR [28]	33.9	50.6	33.4	41.4	41.6	50.6	36.1
	ATP [3]	–	–	–	–	–	–	35.6
	CLIP+Unsupervised [26]	25.6	28.8	22.8	30.8	20.1	34.0	26.5
	CLIP+LORA [14]	38.7	38.1	34.5	37.9	38.7	36.7	38.3
	CLIP+Adapter [8]	35.8	32.1	33.1	42.3	32.0	35.4	34.8
TrafficVideoQA	Eclipse [32]	–	–	–	–	–	–	37.1
	TK-QC [27]	–	–	-	–	–	–	49.2
	MDIF [12]	37.1	53.2	39.2	47.6	**50.6**	51.5	38.9
	CMCIR [21]	34.6	43.9	35.8	48.1	39.9	46.5	38.3
	Tem-Adapter [4]	46.0	47.7	34.5	55.0	36.5	44.6	46.0
	Traffic-MLLM [31]	46.5	41.6	19.7	39.2	39.1	43.9	44.1
	CFMMC-Align [11]	46.7	58.3	36.5	56.2	42.6	56.5	50.2
	Ours	**48.5**(+1.8)	**60.5**(+2.2)	**40.6**(+4.1)	**61.1**(+4.9)	47.5	**60.2**(+3.7)	**52.4**(+2.2)

5.2 Comparison with Baseline Methods

As shown in Table 1, the results of the SUTD-TrafficQA dataset highlight the advantages of our proposed model in the TrafficVideoQA task. Compared with general VideoQA methods such as HCRN, VQAC, DualVGR, and CLIP based variants, CATK-VideoQA shows significant advantages in some question categories. This result indicates that baseline methods primarily relying on visual co-occurrence patterns or general multimodal alignment are insufficient for TrafficVideoQA task, as accurate answers often depend on external regulatory knowledge and inference constraints specific to the scene.

Compared with the TrafficVideoQA baselines, especially the latest CFMMC-Align model, our ALL metric performance has improved by 2.2%, and we have significant advantages in inference intensive categories such as Counterfactual, Introspection, and Reverse. This indicates that the proposed method is more suitable for handling complex reasoning in traffic scenarios. The experimental results suggest that integrating domain-specific prior knowledge enhances causal reasoning and interpretability in traffic scenarios. Overall, these findings suggest that combining structured domain knowledge with tailored optimization strategies is an effective approach to advancing TrafficVideoQA research.

5.3 Ablation Study

Tables 2 and 3 report the ablation results of CATK-VideoQA in terms of overall accuracy. As shown in Table 2, using either question-guided retrieval or caption-guided retrieval alone already improves the model, while combining both yields the best overall performance (52.4%). This result indicates that the question offers cues that are more directly related to the reasoning target, whereas the caption supplies scene-specific contextual evidence. Their combination therefore enables more reliable knowledge retrieval for TrafficVideoQA. Table 3 shows that using either coarse- or fine-grained loss alone reduces performance, while their combination achieves the best accuracy of 52.4%. This suggests that the coarse-grained loss promotes global semantic consistency, while the fine-grained loss improves local cross-modal alignment. Their joint optimization thus produces more discriminative multimodal representations for answer prediction.

Table 2. Ablation study on question-based and caption-based knowledge retrieval.

Q-KG	C-KG	$\mathcal{L}_{coarse}$	$\mathcal{L}_{fine}$	ALL
✓		✓	✓	51.5
	✓	✓	✓	50.9
✓	✓	✓	✓	**52.4**

Table 3. Ablation study on coarse-grained and fine-grained contrastive losses.

Q-KG	C-KG	$\mathcal{L}_{coarse}$	$\mathcal{L}_{fine}$	ALL
✓	✓	✓		49.6
✓	✓		✓	48.1
✓	✓	✓	✓	**52.4**

5.4 Sensitivity Analysis

Table 4. Performance comparison across different knowledge configurations on the SUTD-TrafficQA dataset.

Models	ALL(%)
Base	49.5
w/ Textual Knowledge	50.3
w/ TRKG	52.4

Effect of Knowledge Representation. Table 4 evaluates the impact of different knowledge representations on TrafficVideoQA performance. Without external knowledge, the Base model achieves 49.5% accuracy. Replacing it with unstructured textual knowledge brings only a limited gain (50.3%), whereas using the proposed TRKG further improves performance to 52.4%. This demonstrates that structured regulation knowledge provides more effective support for TrafficVideoQA than unstructured text, especially for modeling rule constraints and causal relations.

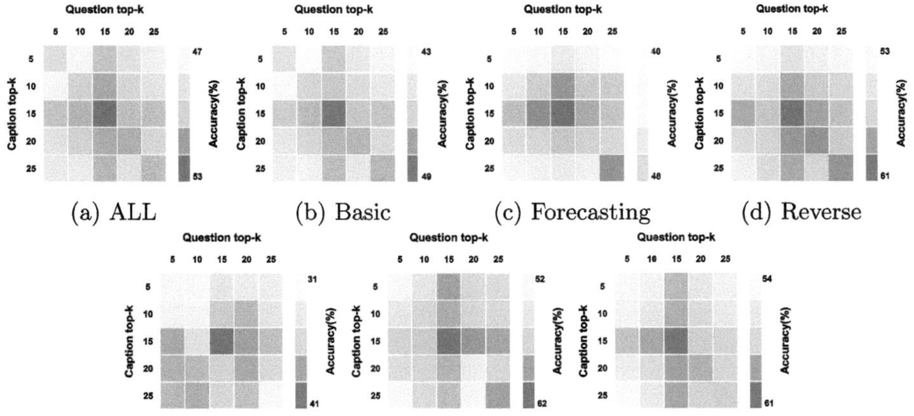

(a) ALL (b) Basic (c) Forecasting (d) Reverse

(e) Introspection (f) Counterfactual (g) Attribution

Fig. 4. Influence of the number of retrieved triples (top-k) on model accuracy.

The Impact of top-k on Knowledge Graph Retrieval. We further analyze the effect of the number of retrieved question- and caption-based triples on model performance. As shown in Fig. 4a, increasing top-k does not consistently improve accuracy: too few triples provide insufficient evidence, while too many introduce noisy knowledge. In addition, better performance is generally obtained when the numbers of question-based and caption-based triples are kept balanced. The best result is achieved when both branches use top-k=15, which provides a good trade-off between knowledge coverage and retrieval noise.

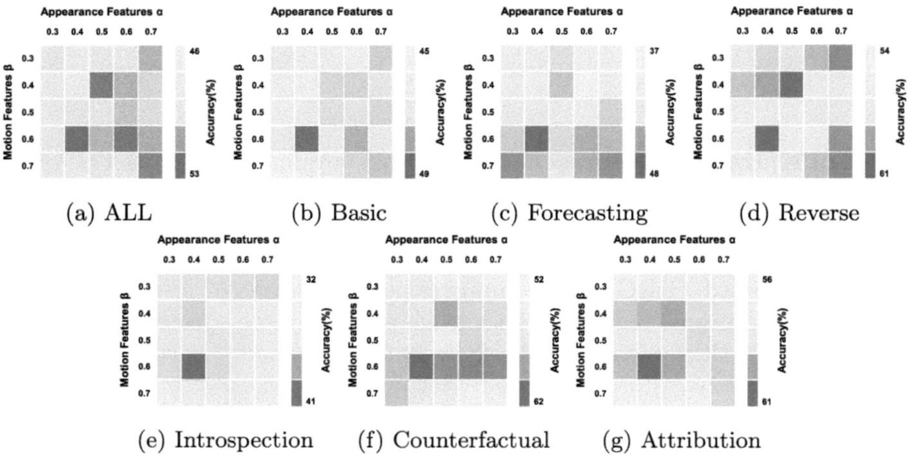

Fig. 5. Effect of fusion ratios between appearance and motion features on accuracy across different reasoning tasks. Darker colors indicate higher accuracy.

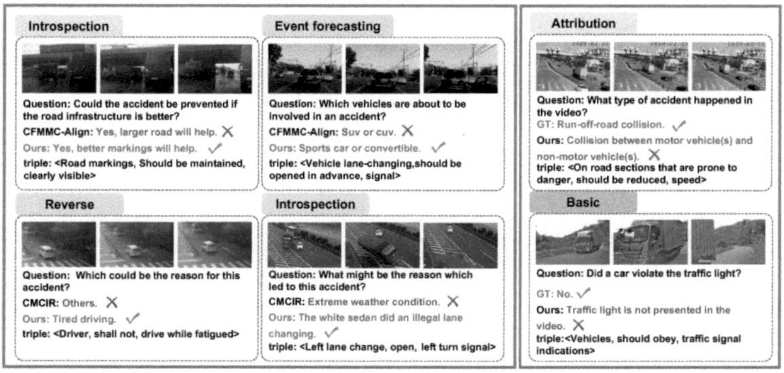

Fig. 6. Visualization of reasoning examples from the SUTD-TrafficQA dataset.

Fusion Parameters for Video Appearance Features and Motion Features. We analyze the impact of fusion ratios between appearance and motion features. As shown in Fig. 5, the best overall performance is achieved at a ratio of 0.4 (appearance) and 0.6 (motion), indicating that motion features play a more important role in TrafficVideoQA. However, the optimal ratio varies across tasks. Basic questions benefit more from higher appearance weights, reflecting their reliance on spatial semantics. In contrast, reasoning-intensive tasks achieve better performance with higher motion weights, highlighting the importance of temporal dynamics and object interactions. Overall, appearance features provide semantic grounding, while motion features contribute more to complex reasoning. Their effective combination is therefore critical for TrafficVideoQA.

Visualization. Figure 6 presents examples from the SUTD-TrafficQA dataset. CATK-VideoQA achieves more accurate results on reasoning-intensive tasks. Although errors may occur in some cases, TRKG still provides useful and interpretable evidence for rule-grounded reasoning beyond visual-only alignment.

6 Conclusion

In this paper, we propose CATK-VideoQA, a context-aware knowledge-enhanced framework for TrafficVideoQA. By integrating TRKG with the JCKR module, the model retrieves regulation knowledge aligned with both question intent and scene context. Experiments on SUTD-TrafficQA show consistent improvements, particularly on complex reasoning tasks, demonstrating the effectiveness of context-aware knowledge retrieval for rule-grounded reasoning. Future work will further exploit graph topology in TRKG and validate CATK-VideoQA on more TrafficVideoQA datasets.

Acknowledgments. This work is supported by "National Key R&D Program of China" (No. 2024YFB4303400), National Natural Science Foundation of China (62407007, 62502051), Fundamental Research Funds for the Central Universities, CHD (300102404105), Shaanxi postdoctoral research project (2025BSHEDZZ022) and Postdoctoral Fellowship Program of CPSF (GZC20251101).

References

1. Agarwal, A., Gawade, S., Azad, A.P., Bhattacharyya, P.: Kitlm: domain-specific knowledge integration into language models for question answering. https://doi.org/10.48550/arXiv.2308.03638. arXiv preprint arXiv:2308.03638 (2023)
2. Bosselut, A., Rashkin, H., Sap, M., Malaviya, C., Celikyilmaz, A., Choi, Y.: Comet: commonsense transformers for automatic knowledge graph construction. https://doi.org/10.18653/v1/p19-1470. arXiv preprint arXiv:1906.05317 (2019)
3. Buch, S., Eyzaguirre, C., Gaidon, A., Wu, J., Fei-Fei, L., Niebles, J.C.: Revisiting the "video" in video-language understanding. In: 2022 IEEE/CVF CVPR, pp. 2907–2917 (2022). https://doi.org/10.1109/CVPR52688.2022.00293

4. Chen, G., et al.: Tem-adapter: adapting image-text pretraining for video question answer. In: Proceedings of the IEEE/CVF International Conference on Computer Vision, pp. 13945–13955 (2023). https://doi.org/10.1109/iccv51070.2023.01282
5. Chen, X., Shrivastava, A., Gupta, A.: Neil: extracting visual knowledge from web data. In: Proceedings of the IEEE International Conference on Computer Vision, pp. 1409–1416 (2013). https://doi.org/10.1109/iccv.2013.178
6. Chi, H., Wang, B., Ge, Q., Huo, G.: Knowledge graph-based enhanced transformer for metro individual travel destination prediction. J. Adv. Transp. **2022**(1), 8030690 (2022). https://doi.org/10.1155/2022/8030690
7. Etzioni, O., Banko, M., Soderland, S., Weld, D.S.: Open information extraction from the web. Commun. ACM **51**(12), 68–74 (2008). https://doi.org/10.1145/1409360.1409378
8. Gao, P., et al.: Clip-adapter: better vision-language models with feature adapters. Int. J. Comput. Vision **132**(2), 581–595 (2024). https://doi.org/10.1007/s11263-023-01891-x
9. Garcia, N., Otani, M., Chu, C., Nakashima, Y.: Knowit vqa: answering knowledge-based questions about videos. In: Proceedings of the AAAI Conference on Artificial Intelligence, vol. 34, pp. 10826–10834 (2020). https://doi.org/10.1609/aaai.v34i07.6713
10. Giannakopoulou, K., Kontogiannis, S., Papastavrou, G., Zaroliagis, C.: A cloud-based time-dependent routing service. In: Sellis, T., Oikonomou, K. (eds.) ALGOCLOUD 2016. LNCS, vol. 10230, pp. 41–64. Springer, Cham (2017). https://doi.org/10.1007/978-3-319-57045-7_4
11. Guo, K., et al.: Cfmmc-align: coarse-fine multi-modal contrastive alignment network for traffic event video question answering. TCSVT **34**(11), 10538–10550 (2024). https://doi.org/10.1109/tcsvt.2024.3409453
12. Guo, W., Zi, L., Cong, X.: Mdif: a multimodal dynamic inference framework for traffic video question answering. Appl. Intell. **55**(16), 1087 (2025)
13. Hao, S., et al.: Bertnet: harvesting knowledge graphs with arbitrary relations from pretrained language models. https://doi.org/10.18653/v1/2023.findings-acl.309. arXiv preprint arXiv:2206.14268 (2022)
14. Hu, E.J., et al.: Lora: low-rank adaptation of large language models. In: ICLR, vol. 1, no. 2, p. 3 (2022). https://doi.org/10.48550/arXiv.2106.09685
15. Jin, W., Zhao, Z., Li, Y., Li, J., Xiao, J., Zhuang, Y.: Video question answering via knowledge-based progressive spatial-temporal attention network. ACM Trans. Multimedia Comput. Commun. Appl. (TOMM) **15**(2s), 1–22 (2019). https://doi.org/10.1145/3321505
16. Jin, Y., Niu, G., Xiao, X., Zhang, J., Peng, X., Yu, J.: Knowledge-constrained answer generation for open-ended video question answering. In: Proceedings of the AAAI Conference on Artificial Intelligence, vol. 37, pp. 8141–8149 (2023). https://doi.org/10.1609/aaai.v37i7.25983
17. Kim, N., Ha, S.J., Kang, J.W.: Video question answering using language-guided deep compressed-domain video feature. In: Proceedings of the IEEE/CVF International Conference on Computer Vision, pp. 1708–1717 (2021). https://doi.org/10.1109/iccv48922.2021.00173
18. Le, T.M., Le, V., Venkatesh, S., Tran, T.: Hierarchical conditional relation networks for video question answering. In: Proceedings of the IEEE/CVF Conference on Computer Vision and Pattern Recognition, pp. 9972–9981 (2020). https://doi.org/10.1109/cvpr42600.2020.00999

19. Liu, H., Li, C., Li, Y., Lee, Y.J.: Improved baselines with visual instruction tuning. In: Proceedings of the IEEE/CVF Conference on Computer Vision and Pattern Recognition, pp. 26296–26306 (2024). https://doi.org/10.1109/cvpr52733.2024.02484
20. Liu, H., Singh, P.: Conceptnet–a practical commonsense reasoning tool-kit. BT Technol. J. **22**(4), 211–226 (2004). https://doi.org/10.1023/b:bttj.0000047600.45421.6d
21. Liu, Y., Li, G., Lin, L.: Cross-modal causal relational reasoning for event-level visual question answering. IEEE Trans. Pattern Anal. Mach. Intell. **45**(10), 11624–11641 (2023). https://doi.org/10.1109/tpami.2023.3284038
22. M. Keller, R.: Building a knowledge graph for the air traffic management community. In: Companion Proceedings of The 2019 World Wide Web Conference, pp. 700–704 (2019). https://doi.org/10.1145/3308560.3317706
23. Manku, G.S., Jain, A., Sarma, A.D.: Detecting near-duplicates for web crawling. In: The Web Conference (2007). https://doi.org/10.1145/1242572.1242592
24. Muppalla, R., Lalithsena, S., Banerjee, T., Sheth, A.: A knowledge graph framework for detecting traffic events using stationary cameras. In: Proceedings of the 2017 ACM on Web Science Conference, pp. 431–436 (2017). https://doi.org/10.1145/3091478.3162384
25. Qasemi, E., Francis, J.M., Oltramari, A.: Traffic-domain video question answering with automatic captioning. https://doi.org/10.48550/arXiv.2307.09636. arXiv preprint arXiv:2307.09636 (2023)
26. Radford, A., et al.: Learning transferable visual models from natural language supervision. In: International Conference on Machine Learning, pp. 8748–8763. PmLR (2021). https://doi.org/10.48550/arXiv.2103.00020
27. Sun, X., Dai, Y., Wang, Y., Ma, W., Lin, X.: Video question answering via traffic knowledge database and question classification. Multimedia Syst. **30**(1), 14 (2024). https://doi.org/10.1007/s00530-023-01240-5
28. Wang, J., Bao, B.K., Xu, C.: Dualvgr: a dual-visual graph reasoning unit for video question answering. IEEE Trans. Multimedia **24**, 3369–3380 (2022). https://doi.org/10.1109/TMM.2021.3097171
29. Wang, X., Wang, J., Han, J.: Knowledge graph construction for railway electrical accident analysis. In: 2019 MLBDBI, pp. 214–219. IEEE (2019). https://doi.org/10.1109/mlbdbi48998.2019.00048
30. West, P., et al.: Symbolic knowledge distillation: from general language models to commonsense models. https://doi.org/10.18653/v1/2022.naacl-main.341. arXiv preprint arXiv:2110.07178 (2021)
31. Xiu, W., Lu, Q., Li, X., Hu, C., Sun, S.: Traffic-mllm: a spatio-temporal mllm with retrieval-augmented generation for causal inference in traffic. https://doi.org/10.48550/arXiv.2509.11165. arXiv preprint arXiv:2509.11165 (2025)
32. Xu, L., Huang, H., Liu, J.: Sutd-trafficqa: a question answering benchmark and an efficient network for video reasoning over traffic events. In: Proceedings of the IEEE/CVF Conference on Computer Vision and Pattern Recognition, pp. 9878–9888 (2021). https://doi.org/10.1109/cvpr46437.2021.00975
33. Zeng, J., Tang, J.: Combining knowledge graph into metro passenger flow prediction: a split-attention relational graph convolutional network. Expert Syst. Appl. **213**, 118790 (2023). https://doi.org/10.1016/j.eswa.2022.118790

Spatio-Temporal Graph Prompt Interaction for Cross-Region Traffic Speed Forecasting

Kun Chen[1], Lei Zhang[1(✉)], Yutong Wu[2], Bailong Liu[1], Fuyang Zhang[3], and Zixin Zhang[4]

[1] School of Computer Science and Technology/School of Artificial Intelligence, China University of Mining and Technology,Xuzhou 221116, Jiangsu, China
{12204209,zhanglei,liubailong}@cumt.edu.cn

[2] School of Electrical Engineering and Computer Science, The University of Queensland, Brisbane, QLD 4072, Australia
wyatttwillage@gmail.com

[3] Beijing University of Posts and Telecommunications, Beijing, China
zhangfuyang@bupt.edu.cn

[4] School of Electrical Engineering, China University of Mining and Technology, Xuzhou 221116, Jiangsu, China
15223524@cumt.edu.cn

Abstract. Accurate cross-region traffic speed forecasting remains challenging because traffic dynamics exhibit non-stationary temporal patterns, heterogeneous road-network topologies, and region-dependent distribution shifts. Existing spatio-temporal prompt learning methods usually rely on unified prompts or static fusion, limiting their ability to encode structured temporal and spatial priors and capture fine-grained spatio-temporal coupling. To address these limitations, we propose Spatio-Temporal Graph Prompt Interaction (STGPI), a prompt-based adaptation framework that constructs graph-structured prompts for traffic speed forecasting. STGPI introduces a Multi-scale Temporal Graph Prompt to capture local, periodic, and trend dependencies, and a Multi-relational Spatial Graph Prompt to encode physical and semantic road-network associations. The two prompts are projected into a shared feature space and integrated through bidirectional cross-attention, enabling temporal evolution patterns and spatial topologies to mutually inform target-domain adaptation. Experiments on METR-LA, PEMS-BAY, and PEMS07(M) demonstrate that STGPI achieves competitive forecasting performance with parameter-efficient cross-region adaptation.

Keywords: traffic speed forecasting · prompt learning · spatio-temporal graph prompt

1 Introduction

Traffic speed forecasting is fundamental to Intelligent Transportation Systems, supporting congestion mitigation, route planning, and traffic management [1].

L. Ding et al. (Eds.): APWeb-WAIM 2026, LNCS 16995, pp. 116–131, 2027.
https://doi.org/10.1007/978-981-92-5699-0_8

Yet urban speed data are highly non-stationary and heterogeneous in both time and space. Temporally, speed dynamics reflect short-term fluctuations, periodicity, and unexpected events; spatially, they propagate through directed road networks and long-range semantic relations. Because these coupled patterns vary across urban environments, models trained in one region often degrade when transferred to another. This makes cross-region adaptation a central challenge for practical traffic forecasting deployment [2].

Early traffic forecasting methods relied on statistical and kernel-based models, including ARIMA and SVR [3,4]. However, their stationarity assumptions and limited nonlinear capacity restrict high-dimensional traffic modeling. Deep spatio-temporal graph neural networks (STGNNs), which integrate graph neural networks with sequence models such as TCNs and Transformers, have become the dominant paradigm [5–7]. Representative models, including DCRNN, STGCN, and MTGNN, capture road-network dependencies and temporal evolution through graph convolution and gating mechanisms [8–10]. Nevertheless, most end-to-end models still assume similar train/test distributions and can overfit source-domain statistics. Full fine-tuning can adapt them to a target region, but it is costly and may cause catastrophic forgetting.

Prompt learning provides a parameter-efficient alternative by adapting frozen pre-trained models with a small set of learnable task- or domain-specific parameters [11]. Recent spatio-temporal prompting methods have shown promise for target-domain adaptation, but two limitations remain. First, temporal and spatial prompts are often constructed as independent vectors or tokens, providing weak structural guidance from graph topology. Second, prompt injection usually relies on static addition or concatenation, with little explicit bidirectional interaction between temporal and spatial prompts. These limitations motivate a structure-aware prompt framework that jointly models target-domain temporal patterns, spatial relations, and their coupling during cross-region adaptation.

Contributions. To address these challenges, we propose Spatio-Temporal Graph Prompt Interaction (STGPI), a cross-region traffic speed forecasting framework that represents target-domain temporal and spatial priors as graph-structured prompts. Unlike prompt methods that mainly optimize unstructured prompt embeddings or use static prompt injection, STGPI separately constructs temporal and spatial prompt graphs and explicitly models their bidirectional interaction.

- We design a structure-aware prompt generation mechanism that separates multi-scale temporal dependencies from multi-relational spatial associations. MTGP captures local, periodic, and trend patterns from target-domain historical observations, while MSGP encodes physical topology and semantic neighborhood relations.
- We develop a prompt alignment and bidirectional interaction module that allows temporal prompts to condition spatial prompt aggregation and spatial prompts to condition temporal pattern selection, thereby modeling fine-grained spatio-temporal coupling during adaptation.

- We conduct cross-region adaptation experiments in which the model is pre-trained on METR-LA and adapted to PEMS-BAY and PEMS07(M). The results show that STGPI achieves competitive forecasting performance with controlled additional trainable parameters.

2 Related Work

Traffic Speed Forecasting. Traffic speed forecasting predicts future traffic states from historical observations. Early statistical and deep sequence models struggle to capture nonlinear spatio-temporal dependencies and the non-Euclidean topology of road networks [3,12,13]. Spatio-temporal graph neural networks (STGNNs) have therefore become a mainstream paradigm for jointly modeling temporal dynamics and irregular spatial structures, as exemplified by STGCN and DCRNN [8,9]. Subsequent studies further introduced adaptive graph learning, such as Graph WaveNet, to alleviate the limitations of incomplete or inaccurate predefined graphs [14]. More recently, Transformer-based models have improved long-range dependency modeling [15], while large-scale pre-training has been explored to enhance generalization across cities [16,17]. Despite these advances, cross-region transfer remains challenging due to heterogeneous road topologies and dynamic distribution shifts, where direct transfer often degrades performance [2]. Although pre-training can improve transferability, adapting to new regions still typically relies on costly full fine-tuning, which increases computational overhead and may impair previously acquired transferable knowledge. Therefore, we focus on practical cross-region adaptation under realistic computational constraints.

Prompt Learning. Prompt learning is a parameter-efficient fine-tuning strategy that adapts frozen pre-trained models by optimizing a small set of learnable continuous embeddings, and has recently been extended to spatio-temporal tasks [11]. Existing studies mainly follow two directions: generative prompting (e.g., GPD [18]) and embedding-based prompt tuning (e.g., PromptST [19], FlashST [20], and UniST [21]). These methods have shown promise for spatio-temporal adaptation and universal urban prediction, but they usually rely on prompt tokens, unified prompt embeddings, or static prompt injection. As a result, they do not explicitly construct separate graph-structured prompts for multi-scale temporal dependencies and multi-relational spatial associations. Edge-prompt methods further demonstrate the value of prompt learning on graph-structured data [22], but they are not designed for cross-region traffic speed forecasting, where target-domain temporal patterns, physical road topology, semantic sensor correlations, and source-to-target adaptation must be modeled jointly. STGPI addresses this gap by constructing temporal and spatial prompt graphs from target-domain training data and aligning them through bidirectional prompt interaction.

3 Definitions

Definition 1 (Road Network Graph) $G = (V, E, A)$ denotes a directed road network, where $V = \{v_1, \ldots, v_N\}$ is the set of traffic sensors, $E \subseteq V \times V$ is the set of directed edges describing traffic connectivity, and $A \in \mathbb{R}^{N \times N}$ is the corresponding adjacency matrix.

Definition 2 (Traffic Speed Sequence) Let $x_{i,t}$ denote the traffic speed observed at sensor i at time t. For the i-th sensor and a historical window of length H, the speed sequence within the interval $[t-H+1, t]$ is defined as $x_{i,t-H+1:t} = [x_{i,t-H+1}, x_{i,t-H+2}, \ldots, x_{i,t}] \in \mathbb{R}^{H \times C}$, where $C = 1$. The historical input sequence for all sensor nodes is defined as:

$$X_{t-H+1:t} = [x_{1,t-H+1:t}; \ldots; x_{N,t-H+1:t}] \in \mathbb{R}^{N \times H \times C} \tag{1}$$

Definition 3 (Traffic Speed Forecasting) Traffic speed forecasting aims to forecast the future speed sequence for H_{out} time steps based on the historical window $X_{t-H+1:t}$. This task utilizes a backbone model $f_\theta(\cdot)$, whose parameters are trainable during pre-training but remain mostly fixed during prompt tuning, to generate the forecast:

$$\widehat{Y} = f_\theta(X_{t-H+1:t}, G), \quad \widehat{Y} \in \mathbb{R}^{N \times H_{\text{out}} \times 1} \tag{2}$$

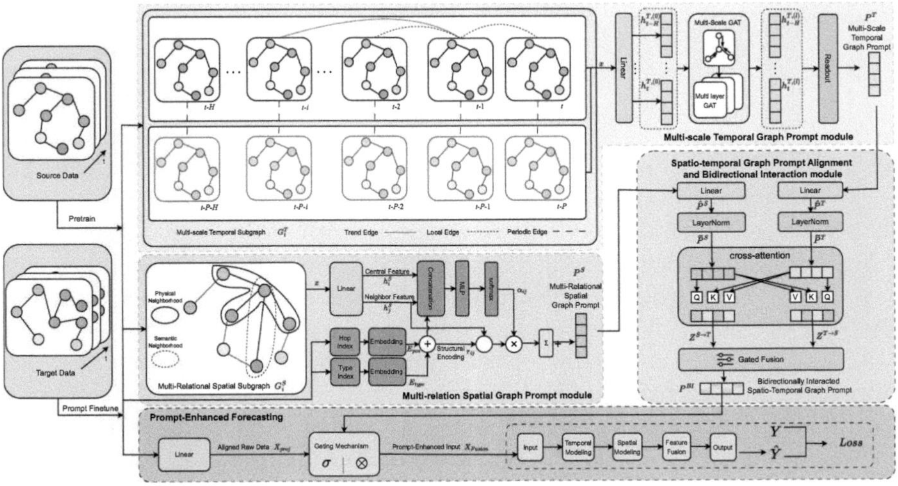

Fig. 1. Overall structure of STGPI method

4 Methodology

4.1 Framework of STGPI

STGPI adopts an established STGNN as the backbone, while updating only a selected subset of backbone components during prompt tuning. As shown in Fig. 1, the framework contains four components: the Multi-scale Temporal Graph Prompt (MTGP) Module, the Multi-relational Spatial Graph Prompt (MSGP) Module, the alignment and bidirectional interaction module, and the forecasting module. MTGP converts the historical window into a temporal graph with local, periodic, and trend edges to produce temporal prompts. MSGP builds local spatial subgraphs from physical topology and semantic similarity, and uses structure-aware attention to produce spatial prompts. The alignment and bidirectional interaction module projects both prompts into a shared space and models their two-way dependency by bidirectional cross-attention. The resulting spatio-temporal prompt is fused with the original input and fed into the backbone for forecasting.

STGPI is designed for cross-region adaptation rather than cold-start or zero-shot deployment. Specifically, target-domain historical observations from the training split are used to pre-construct semantic neighbors and trend edges, after which prompt tuning is performed on the same target-domain training data.

4.2 Multi-scale Temporal Graph Prompt Module

Traffic speed contains short-term, periodic, and long-range dependencies. To encode them explicitly, we build a multi-scale temporal subgraph for time t:

$$G_t^T = (V_t^T, E_t^T) \tag{3}$$

where V_t^T and E_t^T are the temporal node and edge sets. Let $\mathcal{T}$ be the set of global time indices. The node set is $V_t^T = V_{\text{curr}} \cup V_{\text{ctx}}$, where $V_{\text{curr}} = \{\tau \in \mathcal{T} \mid t-H+1 \leq \tau \leq t\}$ denotes the current historical window and $V_{\text{ctx}} = \{\tau - P \mid \tau \in V_{\text{curr}}\}$ denotes the corresponding periodic timestamps, with P the period span.

We define three edge types. For $\tau_a, \tau_b \in V_{\text{curr}}$, a local edge is added if $1 \leq |\tau_a - \tau_b| \leq K_{\text{local}}$. Trend edges are constructed using similarity statistics estimated only from the target-domain training split. Specifically, for non-adjacent nodes in V_{curr}, a trend edge is added when the cosine similarity between their historical traffic-speed profiles exceeds the threshold δ. For each $\tau \in V_{\text{curr}}$, we connect it with its periodic counterpart $\tau - P \in V_{\text{ctx}}$ to model periodic dependence. The resulting trend-edge construction rule is fixed after preprocessing and is applied without accessing validation or test observations.

An L-layer GAT is used to encode G_t^T. The initial feature of node τ for sensor i is

$$h_{i,\tau}^{T,(0)} = \phi(x_{i,\tau}) \tag{4}$$

where $x_{i,\tau}$ is the speed observation and $\phi(\cdot)$ projects the scalar input to a d_T-dimensional space. The layer-wise update is

$$h_{i,\tau}^{T,(l)} = \sigma\left(\sum_{\tau' \in \mathcal{N}^T(\tau)} \alpha_{\tau,\tau'}^{(l)} W_T h_{i,\tau'}^{T,(l-1)}\right) \tag{5}$$

where W_T is the learnable transformation matrix, $\sigma(\cdot)$ is the activation function, $\alpha_{\tau,\tau'}^{(l)}$ is the attention coefficient, and $\mathcal{N}^T(\tau)$ is the neighborhood connected by local, trend, or periodic edges. After L layers, we apply a weighted readout over V_{curr} to obtain the temporal prompt:

$$P_{i,t}^T = \sum_{\tau \in V_{\text{curr}}} \beta_{i,\tau} h_{i,\tau}^{T,(L)} \tag{6}$$

where $\beta_{i,\tau}$ is an adaptive readout weight.

4.3 Multi-relational Spatial Graph Prompt Module

Traffic speed depends on both the physical road topology and semantic correlations among road segments with similar dynamics. To model both, for each center node v_i we construct a multi-relational spatial subgraph

$$G_i^S = (V_i^S, E_i^S) \tag{7}$$

which is fixed once built, while node features vary with time. Its node set is

$$V_i^S = \{v_i\} \cup V_i^{\text{phy}} \cup V_i^{\text{sem}} \tag{8}$$

where V_i^{phy} is obtained by a K_{phy}-hop search on the road graph, i.e., it contains nodes whose shortest-path distance to v_i satisfies $1 \leq d_G(i,j) \leq K_{\text{phy}}$. The semantic neighbor set V_i^{sem} is constructed offline by computing pairwise similarities between sensors' historical speed sequences on the target-domain training split, retaining the top-M most similar nodes for each v_i, and caching the resulting sparse neighbor index.

For each selected neighbor v_j, we add an edge (v_j, v_i) and label it according to whether it is selected from the physical or semantic neighbor set. To distinguish relation types, we encode each pair (v_i, v_j) by

$$r_{ij} = E_{\text{pos}}\left(d_G(i,j)\right) + E_{\text{type}}\left(t(i,j)\right) \tag{9}$$

where $d_G(i,j)$ is the hop distance and $t(i,j)$ is the edge type. The historical sequence of node v_j in $[t-H+1, t]$ is projected as

$$h_{j,t}^S = \psi(x_{j,t-H+1:t}) \tag{10}$$

where $\psi(\cdot)$ maps the sequence to a d_S-dimensional representation.

We then compute structure-aware attention

$$e_{ij} = \text{LeakyReLU}\left(a^{\top}\left[W_S h_{i,t}^S \| W_S h_{j,t}^S \| r_{ij}\right]\right) \tag{11}$$

$$\alpha_{ij} = \frac{\exp(e_{ij})}{\sum_{v_k \in V_i^S} \exp(e_{ik})} \tag{12}$$

where W_S is the feature mapping matrix and a is the attention parameter vector. The aggregated subgraph representation is

$$s_{i,t}^S = \sum_{v_j \in V_i^S} \alpha_{ij}\left(W_S h_{j,t}^S + r_{ij}\right) \tag{13}$$

and the spatial prompt is

$$P_{i,t}^S = W_s s_{i,t}^S \tag{14}$$

where W_s is the output projection matrix.

4.4 Spatio-Temporal Graph Prompt Alignment and Bidirectional Interaction Module

The temporal prompt and spatial prompt emphasize different semantics and may have different feature dimensions and distributions, so direct fusion is sub-optimal. At time t, let $P_t^S \in \mathbb{R}^{N \times d_S}$ and $P_t^T \in \mathbb{R}^{N \times d_T}$ denote the global spatial and temporal prompt matrices over all N sensors. We first project them into a shared d-dimensional space:

$$\hat{P}_t^T = P_t^T W^T + b^T, \hat{P}_t^S = P_t^S W^S + b^S \tag{15}$$

where $W^T \in \mathbb{R}^{d_T \times d}$ and $W^S \in \mathbb{R}^{d_S \times d}$ are learnable projection matrices. We then apply LayerNorm to reduce distribution mismatch:

$$\widetilde{P}_t^T = \text{LayerNorm}(\hat{P}_t^T), \widetilde{P}_t^S = \text{LayerNorm}(\hat{P}_t^S) \tag{16}$$

Next, we model two-way spatio-temporal interaction with bidirectional cross-attention:

$$\text{Attn}(Q, K, V) = \text{softmax}\left(\frac{QK^{\top}}{\sqrt{d}}\right)V, \tag{17}$$

$$Z_t^{T \to S} = \text{Attn}\left(\widetilde{P}_t^S, \widetilde{P}_t^T, \widetilde{P}_t^T\right), \quad Z_t^{S \to T} = \text{Attn}\left(\widetilde{P}_t^T, \widetilde{P}_t^S, \widetilde{P}_t^S\right) \tag{18}$$

Here, $Z_t^{T \to S}$ captures temporal pattern selection conditioned on spatial structure, while $Z_t^{S \to T}$ captures spatial dependence conditioned on temporal evolution.

Because the relative importance of the two directions varies across contexts, we fuse them with an adaptive gate:

$$g^{BI} = \text{sigmoid}\left(\left(Z_t^{T \to S} \| Z_t^{S \to T}\right) W_g + b_g\right) \tag{19}$$

$$P_t^{BI} = g^{BI} \odot Z_t^{T \to S} + (1 - g^{BI}) \odot Z_t^{S \to T} \tag{20}$$

where $W_g \in \mathbb{R}^{2d \times d}$, b_g are learnable parameters, and $P_t^{BI} \in \mathbb{R}^{N \times d}$ is the final spatio-temporal prompt.

4.5 Prompt-Enhanced Forecasting and Prompt Tuning

We use spatio-temporal prediction models as the backbone. Given the historical input $X_{t-H+1:t} \in \mathbb{R}^{N \times H \times C}$, we expand P_t^{BI} along the time dimension to obtain $P_{\text{exp}} \in \mathbb{R}^{N \times H \times d}$, and project $X_{t-H+1:t}$ to the same feature space as $X_{proj} \in \mathbb{R}^{N \times H \times d}$. The prompt-enhanced input is constructed by gated fusion:

$$X_{\text{Fusion}} = (1 - g^F) \odot P_{\text{exp}} + g^F \odot X_{proj} \tag{21}$$

where g^F is generated from the prompt and projected historical features.

The enhanced input is then fed into the backbone for forecasting:

$$\widehat{Y} = f_\theta (X_{\text{Fusion}}, G) \tag{22}$$

where $\widehat{Y} \in \mathbb{R}^{N \times H_{\text{out}} \times 1}$, H_{out} is the forecasting horizon, and G is the road-network graph. During prompt tuning, we freeze a large portion of the backbone parameters and update prompt-related parameters together with selected normalization-related components.

Let N, d, and L denote the number of sensors, prompt hidden dimension, and GAT layers, respectively. Let K_T be the number of edges in each temporal subgraph and $K_S = K_{\text{phy}} + M$ the average number of spatial neighbors. Omitting linear projections, MTGP and MSGP cost $O(NLK_Td)$ and $O(NLK_Sd)$, respectively, while the dense bidirectional prompt interaction costs $O(N^2d)$. Since semantic neighbors and trend edges are precomputed on the target training split and cached, the main extra inference overhead comes from graph-prompt generation and cross-attention, consistent with Table 4.

5 Experiments

5.1 Datasets

We conduct experiments on METR-LA, PEMS-BAY, and PEMS07(M). Table 1 summarizes their key statistics.

Table 1. Dataset description and statistical information

Dataset	Nodes	Edges	Time Steps	Time Interval
METR-LA	207	1515	34,272	5 min
PEMS-BAY	325	2369	52,116	5 min
PEMS07(M)	228	340	12,672	5 min

5.2 Baseline Models

We compare STGPI with representative baselines, including STGCN [9], MTGNN [10], GTS [23], ST-WA [24], STWave [25], FlashST [20], and DTAN [26].

5.3 Experimental Settings

All experiments are conducted on a workstation equipped with an AMD Ryzen 7 9700X CPU and an NVIDIA GeForce RTX 5070Ti GPU. The software environment includes Python 3.10.19, PyTorch 2.9.0, and CUDA 12.8. For STGPI, the prompt hidden dimension is set to 32, the number of GAT layers is set to 4, and the initial learning rate is 0.001. Each dataset is split into training, validation, and test sets with a ratio of 7:1:2. We adopt a cross-region adaptation protocol: the forecasting backbone is first pre-trained on METR-LA as the source domain, and then adapted to each target domain. We use PEMS-BAY and PEMS07(M) as target datasets. For each target dataset, only historical observations from the target training split are used to pre-construct semantic-neighbor indices and trend-edge statistics. The same target training split is then used for prompt tuning, while validation and test samples are reserved for model selection and final evaluation and are never used during offline graph construction. We use the past one hour (12 time steps) to predict traffic speeds in the next one hour. Forecasting performance is evaluated using MAE (Mean Absolute Error), RMSE (Root Mean Square Error), and MAPE (Mean Absolute Percentage Error).

Table 2. Comparison of cross-region adaptation results on PEMS-BAY and PEMS07(M) under the training protocols used by different methods.

Model	PEMS-BAY									PEMS07(M)		
	Horizon 3			Horizon 6			Horizon 12			Average		
	MAE	RMSE	MAPE(%)	MAE	RMSE	MAPE(%)	MAE	RMSE	MAPE(%)	MAE	RMSE	MAPE(%)
STGCN	1.35	2.91	2.88	1.78	4.00	3.79	2.05	4.69	4.92	2.92	5.57	7.37
MTGNN	**1.30**	2.81	2.80	1.65	3.76	3.73	1.93	4.45	**4.44**	2.58	5.16	6.39
GTS	1.33	2.87	2.84	1.66	3.78	3.69	1.97	4.57	4.68	2.60	5.25	6.48
ST-WA	1.35	2.84	2.85	1.67	3.79	3.81	1.98	4.52	4.63	2.64	5.37	6.76
STWave	1.35	2.82	2.77	1.65	3.71	**3.64**	**1.92**	**4.39**	4.51	2.59	5.32	6.42
FlashST	1.36	2.90	2.85	1.69	3.74	3.80	1.97	4.53	4.75	2.61	5.29	6.63
DTAN	1.33	2.84	2.79	1.68	3.82	3.72	1.95	4.50	4.55	2.66	5.46	6.93
STGPI	1.32	**2.78**	**2.75**	**1.64**	**3.70**	3.65	**1.92**	4.42	4.45	**2.51**	**5.12**	**6.26**

5.4 Comparison with Baseline Models

Table 2 reports the cross-region adaptation results on PEMS-BAY and PEMS07(M), where the best and second-best results are highlighted in bold and underlined, respectively. We compare STGPI with prompt-based and full fine-tuning baselines under their corresponding adaptation protocols. STGPI and FlashST adapt the source-pretrained backbone via prompt tuning for 25 epochs, while the other source-pretrained baselines are adapted by full fine-tuning for up to 100 epochs with early stopping. All backbones are pre-trained

Table 3. Comparison of target-only training, source-pretrained full fine-tuning, and source-pretrained STGPI adaptation across different backbone models on PEMS-BAY and PEMS07(M).

Model	PEMS07(M)	PEMS-BAY		
	Average	Horizon 3	Horizon 6	Horizon 12
	MAE/RMSE/MAPE(%)	MAE/RMSE/MAPE(%)	MAE/RMSE/MAPE(%)	MAE/RMSE/MAPE(%)
MTGNN	2.63/5.35/6.52	1.33/2.80/2.81	1.66/3.77/3.79	1.95/4.50/4.62
w/Finetune	2.58(2)/5.16(3)/6.39(8)	**1.30(1)**/2.81(2)/2.80(2)	1.65(1)/3.76(3)/3.73(5)	1.93(2)/4.45(4)/**4.44(3)**
STGPI	**2.51(1)/5.12(2)/6.26(5)**	1.32(2)/**2.78(2)/2.75(3)**	**1.64(2)/3.70(2)/3.65(3)**	**1.92(1)/4.42(3)**/4.45(3)
STGCN	2.97/5.55/7.31	1.39/2.98/2.95	1.85/4.32/4.18	2.08/4.63/4.81
w/Finetune	2.92(5)/5.57(11)/7.37(7)	**1.35(1)/2.91(5)**/2.88(6)	**1.78(4)/4.00(5)**/3.97(8)	2.05(2)/**4.60(4)**/4.92(7)
STGPI	**2.81(3)/5.49(5)/7.18(9)**	1.37(1)/2.94(3)/**2.85(4)**	1.83(3)/4.12(5)/**3.81(4)**	**2.02(4)**/4.69(7)/**4.72(4)**
DTAN	2.70/5.42/6.86	1.35/2.89/2.87	1.68/3.81/3.75	1.98/4.53/4.59
w/Finetune	2.66(3)/5.46(4)/6.98(6)	**1.33(1)/2.84(3)/2.79(3)**	1.68(1)/3.82(2)/**3.72(3)**	1.95(1)/4.50(3)/4.55(2)
STGPI	**2.61(1)/5.35(2)/6.69(5)**	1.35(1)/2.85(2)/2.81(1)	**1.67(1)/3.81(1)**/3.79(2)	**1.95(2)/4.46(3)/4.52(2)**

on METR-LA for 100 epochs, and the learning rate for full fine-tuning is selected from $\{1 \times 10^{-3}, 3 \times 10^{-3}, 5 \times 10^{-4}\}$.

As shown in Table 2, STGPI remains competitive on both target datasets and achieves the best or second-best results on most horizons and metrics. These gains are consistent with its graph-structured prompt design. MTGP captures temporal patterns similar to the current traffic state, MSGP links physically distant but semantically correlated sensors, and the bidirectional interaction module further couples the temporal and spatial prompts.

Table 3 further compares target-only training, source-pretrained full fine-tuning, and source-pretrained STGPI adaptation across MTGNN, STGCN, and DTAN. As shown in Fig. 2, validation performance generally plateaus within about 25 epochs during prompt tuning; therefore, we set the prompt-tuning budget to 25 epochs. The results are reported as mean (std) over three random seeds, where, for example, 5.11(3) denotes 5.11 ± 0.03. *w/Finetune* denotes full fine-tuning of the pre-trained model on the target dataset. STGPI achieves comparable or better mean performance than full fine-tuning on most metrics while updating only prompt modules and selected backbone components. However, it is not uniformly superior in every case. These results indicate that STGPI is better viewed as a competitive and stable adaptation strategy, rather than a universal replacement for full fine-tuning.

5.5 Model Efficiency Analysis

Table 4 compares full fine-tuning and STGPI in target-domain adaptation time, inference time, and trainable parameters. The results show that the efficiency advantage of STGPI mainly lies in target-domain adaptation. Compared with full fine-tuning, STGPI updates only prompt-related parameters and a selected subset of backbone parameters, which reduces adaptation time and trainable parameters, especially for larger backbone models. However, its inference latency is higher than full fine-tuning because graph-prompt generation and bidirectional prompt interaction are still executed during forecasting. This trade-off makes STGPI more suitable for scenarios where adaptation cost, trainable-parameter budget, and rapid deployment to a new region are more important than the lowest possible inference latency. For latency-sensitive large-scale ITS deployment, sparse prompt interaction, cached prompt components, and graph partitioning are promising ways to reduce this overhead.

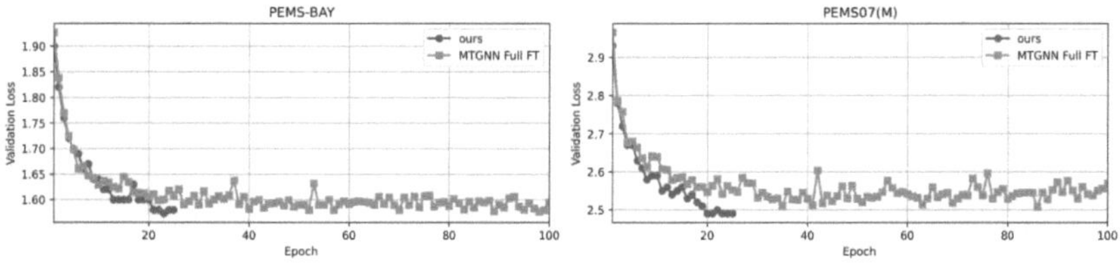

Fig. 2. Convergence curves of STGPI and MTGNN.

Table 4. Efficiency and parameter comparison between full fine-tuning and our method across different backbones.

Backbone	Method	Total Time (s) on PEMS07(M)	Total Time (s) on PEMS-BAY	Inference Time (s) (PEMS07(M)/PEMS-BAY)	Trainable Parameters (PEMS07(M)/PEMS-BAY)	Prompt-only Parameters
MTGNN	Full FT	780	5059	**0.34/2.23**	434,108/573,484	–
	STGPI	**367**	**1750**	1.55/9.62	**380,512/518,640**	41,636
STGCN	Full FT	426	2201	**0.82/4.35**	333,604/395,781	–
	STGPI	**370**	**2037**	1.61/9.47	**129,253/166,501**	41,636
DTAN	Full FT	2689	18529	**1.51/11.05**	454,155/569,682	–
	STGPI	**457**	**2898**	1.98/13.28	**197,610/199,550**	41,636

5.6 Ablation Study

These experiments are designed to validate the contribution of each component in STGPI. We conduct ablations on PEMS07(M). Unlike METR-LA, which contains complete weekly periodicity, PEMS07(M) includes only weekday data and thus exhibits clear temporal pattern discontinuities and distribution shifts. This setting provides a more stringent testbed for assessing the effectiveness of the prompt components in STGPI. We consider three variants: w/o MTGP removes the Multi-scale Temporal Graph Prompt; w/o MSGP removes the Multi-relational Spatial Graph Prompt; w/o Interaction keeps both prompts but simply adds them together.

As reported in Table 5, the full STGPI achieves the best performance. The Multi-scale Temporal Graph Prompt models temporal dependencies as structured prompts on multi-scale temporal subgraphs. It explicitly captures short-term lag effects, periodicity, and trend patterns. After removing it, the model can only rely on the spatial prompt and the backbone itself to compensate temporal dynamics indirectly, which weakens its ability to understand temporal variations in traffic speed. The Multi-relational Spatial Graph Prompt constructs spatial subgraphs with both physical and semantic neighborhoods, and injects priors through structural positional encodings so that the model can distinguish different spatial relations. Removing it leads to a smaller degradation than w/o MTGP, suggesting that our method is more sensitive to temporal modeling in this transfer setting. The w/o Interaction variant uses simple summation for fusion. The performance drop is not necessarily large, because the two prompts still provide structured priors. However, their complementary information is not fully exploited without interaction, which results in a consistent gap to STGPI. Overall, the Multi-scale Temporal Graph Prompt, the Multi-relational Spatial Graph Prompt, and the Spatio-Temporal Graph Prompt Alignment and Bidirectional Interaction Module all play important roles in improving traffic speed forecasting performance.

Table 5. Ablation Results of STGPI on the PEMS07(M) Dataset

	MAE	RMSE	MAPE(%)
w/o MTGP	2.62	5.29	6.52
w/o MSGP	2.58	5.21	6.45
w/o Interaction	2.54	5.15	6.31
STGPI	**2.51**	**5.12**	**6.26**

5.7 Impact of Key Hyperparameters

(1) Prompt hidden dimension d: The prompt hidden dimension determines the information capacity of prompts. It reflects the dimensionality of the semantic space where raw traffic speeds are mapped to encode temporal and spatial priors. As shown in Fig. 3, we evaluate $d \in \{16, 32, 64, 128\}$ and analyze the trends of MAE, MAPE, and RMSE on PEMS07(M) and PEMS-BAY datasets. The results indicate that increasing d generally reduces the forecasting loss, but the improvement is gradual. When $d = 32$, the model achieves the best overall performance, suggesting that this dimension is sufficient to form an effective feature space. As d further increases, performance fluctuates. A large d increases the number of prompt parameters and may introduce redundant noise in cross-domain prompt tuning. Considering both representation capacity and parameter efficiency, we finally set the prompt hidden dimension to 32.

(2) Number of GAT layers: GAT learns attention coefficients to quantify the importance of each edge under the current semantics. As shown in Fig. 4, when the number of layers increases from 2 to 4, MAE, RMSE, and MAPE consistently decrease, indicating that deeper layers help capture temporal dependencies more

effectively. When the number of layers increases to 5, the benefit diminishes, suggesting that overly deep propagation can hurt performance. Therefore, we use a 4-layer GAT in the MTGP.

(3) Numbers of physical and semantic neighbors: The physical neighbor number K_{phy} and the number of semantic neighbors control the spatial receptive field of the prompt module from two complementary perspectives. A too small K_{phy} limits the modeling of local topological dependencies, while a too large K_{phy} may introduce weakly related nodes and dilute useful local interactions. Similarly, too few semantic neighbors are insufficient to capture latent similarity patterns across nodes, whereas too many semantic neighbors tend to introduce noisy semantic relations and reduce the discriminability of the prompt space. Based on the validation results, we set $K_{\text{phy}} = 2$ and the number of semantic neighbors to 5, which achieves a good balance between informative context aggregation and noise control.

(4) Trend-edge threshold δ: The threshold δ controls the sparsity of trend edges in MTGP. A smaller δ introduces more trend edges but may include noisy correlations, whereas a larger δ yields a sparser temporal graph and may miss useful long-range temporal patterns. We select δ according to validation performance on the target-domain validation split and set $\delta = 0.75$ in all experiments. A more systematic sensitivity study of δ will be explored in future work.

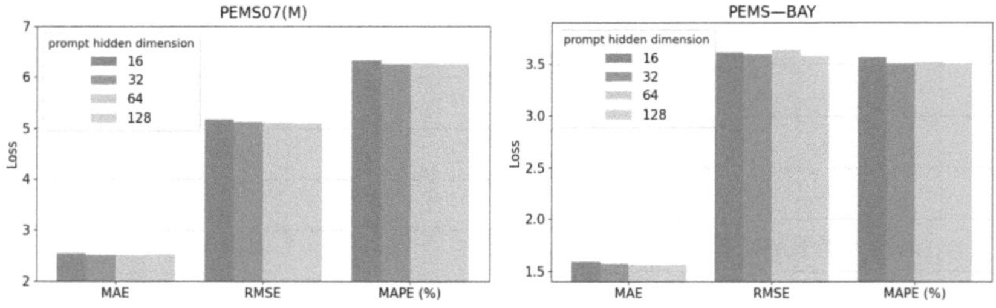

Fig. 3. The impact of prompt hidden dimension size on PEMS-BAY and PEMS07(M) datasets

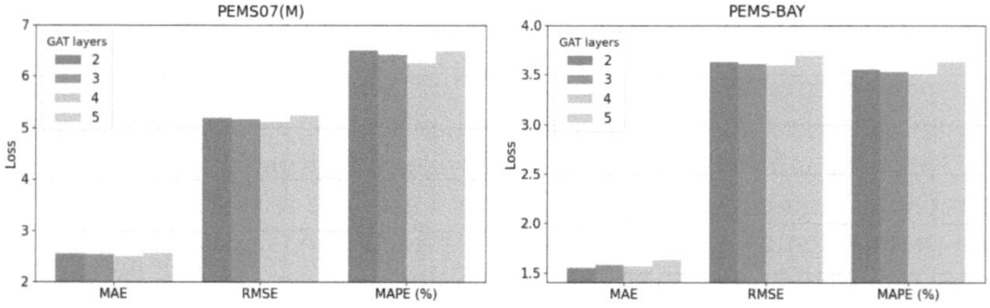

Fig. 4. The impact of GAT layers on PEMS-BAY and PEMS07(M) datasets

6 Conclusion

In this work, we propose a traffic speed forecasting method driven by spatio-temporal graph prompt interaction. STGPI adopts a well-established spatio-temporal graph neural network as backbone, introduces a Multi-scale Temporal Graph Prompt and a Multi-relational Spatial Graph Prompt, and designs a prompt alignment and bidirectional interaction mechanism to adapt to regional traffic patterns with competitive adaptation performance. The method keeps most backbone parameters fixed and tunes prompt-related modules together with a subset of backbone parameters, which enables practical adaptation to the target domain. Experimental results show that STGPI achieves stable and competitive forecasting performance on multiple real-world traffic datasets.

Despite its competitive adaptation performance, STGPI still relies on offline preprocessing to construct trend edges and semantic neighborhoods from target-domain training data. Because these graph structures are fixed after preprocessing, they may not immediately reflect abrupt distribution shifts caused by incidents, temporary traffic controls, or road closures. In addition, our experiments are conducted on standard traffic benchmarks containing hundreds of sensors, while larger ITS networks may require more scalable implementations. Future work will explore lightweight online graph-prompt updating, sparse prompt interaction, and graph partitioning to improve scalability and responsiveness.

References

1. Vlahogianni, E.I., Karlaftis, M.G., Golias, J.C.: Short-term traffic forecasting: where we are and where we're going. Transp. Res. Part C Emerg. Technol. **43**, 3–19 (2014). https://doi.org/10.1016/j.trc.2014.01.005
2. Zhang, Y., Wang, X., Yu, X., Sun, Z., Wang, K., Wang, Y.: Drawing informative gradients from sources: a one-stage transfer learning framework for cross-city spatiotemporal forecasting. In: Proceedings of the AAAI Conference on Artificial Intelligence, vol. 39, pp. 1147–1155 (2025). https://doi.org/10.1609/aaai.v39i1.32102
3. Makridakis, S., Hibon, M.: ARMA models and the box-Jenkins methodology. J. Forecast. **16**(3), 147–163 (1997)
4. Drucker, H., Burges, C.J.C., Kaufman, L., Smola, A.J., Vapnik, V.N.: Support vector regression machines. In: Advances in Neural Information Processing Systems, vol. 9, pp. 155–161 (1996)
5. Zhou, J., et al.: Graph neural networks: a review of methods and applications. AI Open **1**, 57–81 (2020). https://doi.org/10.1016/j.aiopen.2021.01.001
6. Bai, S., Kolter, J.Z., Koltun, V.: An empirical evaluation of generic convolutional and recurrent networks for sequence modeling. arXiv preprint arXiv:1803.01271 (2018). https://doi.org/10.48550/arXiv.1803.01271
7. Vaswani, A., et al.: Attention is all you need. In: Advances in Neural Information Processing Systems, vol. 30, pp. 5998–6008 (2017)
8. Li, Y., Yu, R., Shahabi, C., Liu, Y.: Diffusion convolutional recurrent neural network: data-driven traffic forecasting. In: International Conference on Learning Representations (2018)

9. Yu, B., Yin, H., Zhu, Z.: Spatio-temporal graph convolutional networks: a deep learning framework for traffic forecasting. In: Proceedings of the Twenty-Seventh International Joint Conference on Artificial Intelligence, pp. 3634–3640 (2018). https://doi.org/10.24963/ijcai.2018/505
10. Wu, Z., Pan, S., Long, G., Jiang, J., Chang, X., Zhang, C.: Connecting the dots: multivariate time series forecasting with graph neural networks. In: Proceedings of the 26th ACM SIGKDD International Conference on Knowledge Discovery & Data Mining, pp. 753–763 (2020). https://doi.org/10.1145/3394486.3403118
11. Lester, B., Al-Rfou, R., Constant, N.: The power of scale for parameter-efficient prompt tuning. In: Proceedings of the 2021 Conference on Empirical Methods in Natural Language Processing, pp. 3045–3059 (2021). https://doi.org/10.18653/v1/2021.emnlp-main.243
12. Ma, X., Tao, Z., Wang, Y., Yu, H., Wang, Y.: Long short-term memory neural network for traffic speed prediction using remote microwave sensor data. Transp. Res. Part C Emerg. Technol. **54**, 187–197 (2015). https://doi.org/10.1016/j.trc.2015.03.014
13. Zhang, J., Zheng, Y., Qi, D.: Deep spatio-temporal residual networks for citywide crowd flows prediction. In: Proceedings of the AAAI Conference on Artificial Intelligence, vol. 31, pp. 1655–1661 (2017). https://doi.org/10.1609/aaai.v31i1.10735
14. Wu, Z., Pan, S., Long, G., Jiang, J., Zhang, C.: Graph WaveNet for deep spatial-temporal graph modeling. In: Proceedings of the Twenty-Eighth International Joint Conference on Artificial Intelligence, pp. 1907–1913 (2019). https://doi.org/10.24963/ijcai.2019/264
15. Liu, H., et al.: Spatio-temporal adaptive embedding makes vanilla transformer SOTA for traffic forecasting. In: Proceedings of the 32nd ACM International Conference on Information and Knowledge Management, pp. 4125–4129 (2023). https://doi.org/10.1145/3583780.3615160
16. Li, Z., et al.: UrbanGPT: spatio-temporal large language models. In: Proceedings of the 30th ACM SIGKDD Conference on Knowledge Discovery and Data Mining, pp. 5351–5362 (2024). https://doi.org/10.1145/3637528.3671578
17. Li, Z., Xia, L., Shi, L., Xu, Y., Yin, D., Huang, C.: Open spatio-temporal foundation models for traffic prediction. ACM Trans. Intell. Syst. Technol. 3773912 (2025). https://doi.org/10.1145/3773912
18. Yuan, Y., Shao, C., Ding, J., Jin, D., Li, Y.: Spatio-temporal few-shot learning via diffusive neural network generation. In: International Conference on Learning Representations (2024)
19. Zhang, Z., et al.: PromptST: prompt-enhanced spatio-temporal multi-attribute prediction. In: Proceedings of the 32nd ACM International Conference on Information and Knowledge Management, pp. 3195–3205 (2023). https://doi.org/10.1145/3583780.3615016
20. Li, Z., Xia, L., Xu, Y., Huang, C.: FlashST: a simple and universal prompt-tuning framework for traffic prediction. In: Proceedings of the 41st International Conference on Machine Learning. Proceedings of Machine Learning Research, vol. 235, pp. 28978–28988 (2024)
21. Yuan, Y., Ding, J., Feng, J., Jin, D., Li, Y.: UniST: a prompt-empowered universal model for urban spatio-temporal prediction. In: Proceedings of the 30th ACM SIGKDD Conference on Knowledge Discovery and Data Mining, pp. 4095–4106 (2024). https://doi.org/10.1145/3637528.3671662
22. Fu, X., He, Y., Li, J.: Edge prompt tuning for graph neural networks. In: International Conference on Learning Representations (2025)

23. Shang, C., Chen, J., Bi, J.: Discrete graph structure learning for forecasting multiple time series. In: International Conference on Learning Representations (2021)
24. Cirstea, R.G., Yang, B., Guo, C., Kieu, T., Pan, S.: Towards spatio-temporal aware traffic time series forecasting. In: Proceedings of the IEEE 38th International Conference on Data Engineering, pp. 2900–2913 (2022). https://doi.org/10.1109/ICDE53745.2022.00262
25. Fang, Y., et al.: When spatio-temporal meet wavelets: Disentangled traffic forecasting via efficient spectral graph attention networks. In: Proceedings of the IEEE 39th International Conference on Data Engineering, pp. 517–529 (2023). https://doi.org/10.1109/ICDE55515.2023.00046
26. Cao, C.Y., Bao, Y.X., Hou, Y., Shi, Q.: Traffic speed prediction network based on multi-view spatio-temporal graph convolution network. Comput. Electr. Eng. **127**, 110558 (2025). https://doi.org/10.1016/j.compeleceng.2025.110558

Neural Networks and Learning

Balancing Informativeness and Learnability: Difficulty-Stratified Active CoT Distillation

Liangyu Wei[1], Baohang Zhou[1], Kehui Song[1], Xiaohan Ma[2], Tae-Sun Chung[2], Joon-Young Paik[3], and Rize Jin[1(✉)]

[1] Tiangong University, Tianjin 300387, China
jinrize@tiangong.edu.cn
[2] Ajou University, Suwon 16499, Republic of Korea
[3] Chungnam National University, Daejeon 34134, Republic of Korea

Abstract. Chain-of-Thought (CoT) distillation enables the transfer of complex reasoning prowess from large teacher models to compact students. However, its efficacy is often bottlenecked by inefficient data utilization and a misalignment between rationale complexity and student capacity. To address this, we transition from passive to active learning (AL) and propose Difficulty-Stratified Active Distillation (DSAD), which leverages uncertainty as a proxy for instance difficulty to optimize sample acquisition. Unlike standard AL that often biases training toward extreme outliers, DSAD partitions the unlabeled pool into difficulty-based strata. By performing stratified sampling, DSAD ensures that the student first consolidates foundational reasoning patterns before tackling high-complexity challenges, thereby shielding the model from outlier-induced instability. Extensive experiments on mathematical and commonsense reasoning benchmarks demonstrate that DSAD consistently outperforms both random and AL baselines. Notably, DSAD recovers 90% of full-dataset performance using as little as 30% to 50% of the data, offering a principled pathway for stable and cost-efficient reasoning transfer.

Keywords: Chain-of-Thought Distillation · Active Learning · Difficulty-Stratified Sampling

1 Introduction

Chain-of-Thought (CoT) distillation research has predominantly focused on improving the generalization and reasoning capabilities of small models by transferring structured reasoning traces from large language models, rather than addressing the challenge of learning effectively from limited labeled data. A representative early effort is Distilling Step-by-Step (DSS) [11], which formulates CoT distillation as a multi-task learning problem, training student models to jointly predict task labels and generate intermediate reasoning steps. By explicitly supervising both outcomes and rationales, DSS demonstrates that small

L. Ding et al. (Eds.): APWeb-WAIM 2026, LNCS 16995, pp. 135–149, 2027.
https://doi.org/10.1007/978-981-92-5699-0_9

models can achieve strong reasoning performance with fewer training examples. Nevertheless, DSS assumes access to a fixed set of reasoning annotations and primarily investigates how to better utilize limited data, without considering how such data should be selected or acquired. Subsequent work has further explored alternative formulations of CoT distillation to enhance alignment between reasoning and prediction. For example, mutual information maximization approaches reinterpret CoT distillation [21] from an information-theoretic perspective, aiming to maximize mutual information between rationale generation and final answer prediction. This formulation encourages tighter coupling between reasoning processes and task outcomes, leading to improved distillation effectiveness. However, despite its conceptual novelty, this line of work remains within a passive learning paradigm, relying entirely on pre-collected datasets and offering no mechanism for prioritizing or selecting samples that are most informative for the student model. Other studies focus on structural decomposition of reasoning to improve student model performance. SCoTD [12], for instance, decomposes complex reasoning problems into sequences of simpler subproblems and employs separate models for decomposition and solving. This approach enables small models to benefit from more fine-grained supervision and improves reasoning robustness across tasks. Nevertheless, similar to prior methods, SCoTD operates on static training corpora and does not address how training data should be actively curated or filtered to maximize learning efficiency.

Taken together, existing CoT distillation methods share a common, yet often overlooked, assumption: reasoning annotations are treated as a static and exogenous resource. While these approaches innovate in how reasoning supervision is structured, decomposed, or optimized, they remain confined to a passive learning framework. This paradigm ignores the critical question of how to strategically select or acquire high-value samples. Such a limitation is particularly severe in realistic low-resource settings, where LLM API calls for CoT rationales are costly, and a naive reliance on all available samples often introduces redundant supervision or misaligned complexity, leading to inefficient or unstable learning [14].

In this paper, we take a step toward addressing this gap by introducing Difficulty-Stratified Active Distillation (DSAD), a cost-efficient framework for active Chain-of-Thought distillation. Instead of selecting samples solely based on uncertainty, DSAD explicitly regulates the difficulty distribution of acquired samples by partitioning the unlabeled pool into easy, medium, and hard strata according to uncertainty scores, and performing stratified sampling under a fixed annotation budget. This design mitigates the well-known hard-sample bias of uncertainty-based active learning and promotes more stable reasoning skill acquisition in low-resource regimes. We instantiate DSAD with standard uncertainty criteria, including MNLP, LC, and BALD, and evaluate it under both Standard CoT and Prefix CoT distillation paradigms. Extensive experiments on mathematical, commonsense, and natural language inference benchmarks demonstrate that DSAD consistently improves sample efficiency and learning stability over conventional uncertainty-based baselines, highlighting the importance of explicitly regulating difficulty when actively acquiring CoT supervision. DSAD complements DSS by extending CoT distillation from a passive supervision setting to an active, difficulty-stratified acquisition framework.

2 Related Work

2.1 Chain-Of-Thought Distillation

Chain-of-Thought (CoT) distillation aims to transfer step-by-step reasoning processes from large teacher models to smaller student models, enabling effective multi-step inference while substantially reducing computational cost [9]. Early work on CoT distillation fine-tunes student models using teacher-generated reasoning chains, demonstrating that large language models can serve as effective reasoning teachers [10]. Building upon this paradigm, stepwise and progressive approaches further decompose complex reasoning into simpler intermediate steps, allowing student models to gradually acquire structured reasoning capabilities [6].

Beyond step decomposition, several studies focus on improving the robustness and generalization of distilled reasoning. Explanation-based methods leverage rationales generated by large language models as auxiliary supervision to enhance the reasoning ability of smaller models [13]. Cascaded distillation frameworks further condition answer prediction on decomposed or intermediate reasoning chains, improving reasoning generalizability across tasks [3]. More recently, large-scale systems such as DeepSeek-R1 exploit CoT-distilled data as bootstrapping signals for reinforcement learning, demonstrating the scalability of reasoning supervision in training advanced language models [4].

Despite their effectiveness, existing CoT distillation [5] methods predominantly operate under a passive learning paradigm, assuming access to a fixed and precollected set of reasoning annotations. These approaches lack mechanisms for selectively acquiring informative reasoning chains and therefore do not address the challenge of efficiently obtaining high-value CoT supervision under limited annotation budgets.

2.2 Active Learning

Active learning (AL) aims to reduce annotation cost by iteratively selecting the most informative unlabeled instances for supervision. Classical uncertainty-based strategies, including Maximum Normalized Log-Probability (MNLP), Least Confidence (LC), and Bayesian Active Learning by Disagreement (BALD), remain widely adopted due to their simplicity and effectiveness [19]. Complementary to uncertainty sampling, diversity-driven methods select representative subsets that better cover the input space, such as core-set selection based on geometric coverage [18].

Recent advances revisit active learning in the context of large pretrained language models, extending the traditional selection paradigm toward LLM-based querying, generation, and annotation [22]. These approaches demonstrate that

LLMs can actively participate in both data acquisition and supervision, significantly reducing human annotation costs. In parallel, active learning has also been explored for generative settings by integrating clustering and knowledge distillation, enabling more inclusive and balanced data acquisition under distributional skew [8].

Despite these advances, prior work has primarily focused on improving downstream task performance or data representativeness, without addressing the targeted acquisition of reasoning-chain annotations. Moreover, uncertainty-based AL strategies are known to suffer from hard-example bias in low-resource regimes, where overly difficult samples dominate the query process and impede stable learning [15]. To our knowledge, no existing approach has yet integrated active learning with CoT distillation to enable student models to autonomously identify, balance, and acquire high-value reasoning traces under limited annotation budgets. Our work fills this gap by introducing a difficulty-stratified active CoT distillation framework that explicitly mitigates hard-sample bias while enabling cost-efficient reasoning supervision.

3 Difficulty-Stratified Active Distillation

We introduce the three active learning acquisition strategies used in our CoT distillation framework: MNLP (Maximum Normalized Log-Probability) [17], LC (Least Confidence) [2], and BALD (Bayesian Active Learning by Disagreement) [7], as well as our proposed Difficulty-Stratified Sampling. The whole framework of DSAD is shown in Fig. 1. These acquisition functions are used to identify the most valuable samples from the unlabeled pool that can most effectively enhance the student model's reasoning ability. We denote the full training set as $\mathcal{D} = \{(x_i, y_i, r_i)\}$ where x_i is the input text, y_i is the final answer, r_i is its corresponding chain of thought. Active learning selects 1% of the samples as the initial labeled set $\mathcal{D}_0 \subset \mathcal{D}$ and treats the remaining samples as the unlabeled pool $\mathcal{U} = \mathcal{D} \setminus \mathcal{D}_0$. In our experiments, we mask the labels and rationales in $\mathcal{U}$, and reveal them only when a sample is selected, thereby simulating the

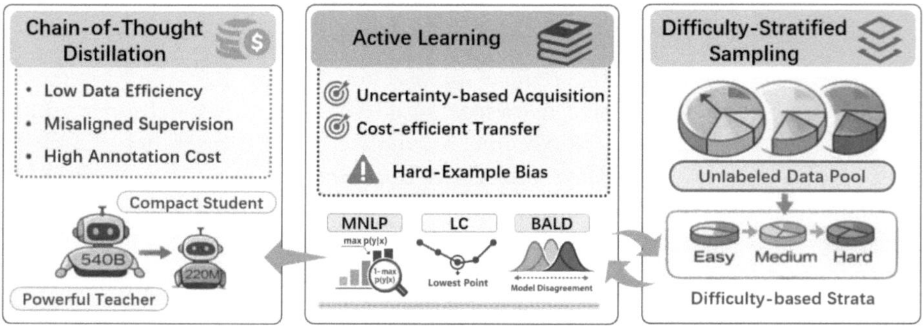

Fig. 1. Overview of Difficulty-Stratified Active Learning for Chain-of-Thought Distillation.

incremental annotation setting in practice [18]. For any input x, we denote the student model's auto-regressive generation probability as:

$$p_\theta(y_t \mid y_{<t}, x) \tag{1}$$

where $y = (y_1, \ldots, y_T)$ is the generated sequence, and T is its length. All acquisition functions defined below are based on these probabilities.

3.1 Maximum Normalized Log-Probability

MNLP quantifies uncertainty by evaluating the student model's average log-likelihood of the generated output sequence. Given an input x, the predicted sequence is:

$$\hat{y} = (\hat{y}_1, \hat{y}_2, \ldots, \hat{y}_T). \tag{2}$$

To prevent longer reasoning chains from being unfairly penalized, MNLP computes a length-normalized negative log-probability:

$$\phi_{\text{MNLP}}(x) = -\frac{1}{T}\sum_{t=1}^{T} \log p_\theta(\hat{y}_t \mid \hat{y}_{<t}, x) \tag{3}$$

where $\log(p_\theta(\hat{y}_t \mid \hat{y}_{<t}, x))$ is the log-probability of generating the t-th token, given the input x and previously generated tokens $\hat{y}_{<t}$. A larger value of ϕ_{MNLP} indicates lower model confidence and thus higher uncertainty. This formulation provides a sequence-level uncertainty measure that aggregates token-wise predictive confidence over the entire generated output. By normalizing the cumulative log-likelihood by the sequence length T, MNLP mitigates the inherent bias toward shorter generations, which would otherwise receive artificially higher likelihood scores.

From active learning perspective, the inputs associated with larger $\phi_{\text{MNLP}}(x)$ correspond to instances for which the student model consistently assigns low conditional probabilities in generated tokens. Such instances indicate regions of the input space where the model's current parameters fail to provide confident explanations, and are therefore more likely to yield informative supervision signals when selected for further distillation or annotation.

3.2 LC-Based Uncertainty Sampling

While MNLP provides a sequence-level confidence estimate by aggregating token log-likelihoods, uncertainty during autoregressive generation may also manifest locally at particular decoding steps. To capture such token-level uncertainty, we adopt the Least Confidence (LC) criterion, which measures how strongly the model prefers its most likely next-token prediction at each generation step. Formally, given the vocabulary $\mathcal{V}$, we compute:

$$\phi_{\text{LC}}(x) = \frac{1}{T}\sum_{t=1}^{T}\left(1 - \max_{v\in\mathcal{V}} p_\theta(v \mid \hat{y}_{<t}, x)\right) \tag{4}$$

where $\max_{v \in \mathcal{V}} p_\theta(v \mid \hat{y}_{<t}, x)$ denotes the maximum predicted probability among all candidate tokens at step t, which can be interpreted as the model's instantaneous confidence under its current conditional context. Consequently, the term $1 - \max_{v \in \mathcal{V}} p_\theta(\cdot)$ quantifies the degree of ambiguity at that step: when the predictive distribution is peaked, the maximum probability is large and the LC contribution is small; when the distribution is flat, the maximum probability decreases and LC increases, indicating greater uncertainty.

A key advantage of LC lies in its ability to directly capture the confidence margin between the most probable token and the remaining vocabulary mass, making it sensitive to step-level uncertainty arising from ambiguous or difficult reasoning transitions. Even when the final generated sequence appears plausible, low-confidence intermediate steps can signal locally unstable decisions that are valuable for further training.

Computationally, LC is efficient to obtain, as it requires only a single decoding pass by extracting the maximum next-token probability at each step, without additional sampling or model evaluations. This property makes LC particularly suitable for large-scale active data selection.

3.3 Bayesian Active Learning by Disagreement

While MNLP and LC estimate predictive uncertainty, BALD measures epistemic uncertainty by computing the mutual information between the output y and model parameters θ. Unlike confidence-based criteria that rely on a single predictive distribution, BALD explicitly captures uncertainty arising from insufficient or ambiguous parameter estimation.

This distinction is particularly important in the context of data-efficient learning, where the student model may encounter regions of the input space that are weakly supported by the current training set. In such cases, epistemic uncertainty provides a principled signal for identifying samples that are most informative for refining the model's internal representations, rather than merely correcting low-confidence predictions. Using Monte Carlo dropout to approximate parameter sampling, BALD is formulated as:

$$\phi_{\text{BALD}}(x) = H(\mathbb{E}_\theta[p_\theta(y \mid x)]) - \mathbb{E}_\theta[H(p_\theta(y \mid x))] \tag{5}$$

where $H(\cdot)$ denotes entropy, $\mathbb{E}_\theta$ is the expectation over stochastic forward passes and $\mathbb{E}_\theta[p_\theta(y \mid x)]$ is the averaged predictive distribution. The first term assesses overall prediction uncertainty after averaging and the second term evaluates the mean uncertainty of individual model samples. A large gap between the two terms indicates strong disagreement among model instances, thus signifying high epistemic uncertainty.

From an information-theoretic perspective, BALD prioritizes samples whose labels are expected to yield the greatest reduction in posterior uncertainty over model parameters. This property makes BALD especially suitable for active distillation, as such samples tend to expose deficiencies in the student model's reasoning capabilities rather than surface-level prediction errors. By focusing on parameter-level disagreement, BALD complements sequence-level and token-level confidence metrics, offering a comprehensive characterization of uncertainty in generative reasoning tasks.

3.4 Difficulty-Stratified Sampling

Pure uncertainty sampling [17] tends to over-select extremely difficult samples, leading to unbalanced learning. Such samples are often associated with ambiguous reasoning paths, noisy annotations, or atypical input patterns, which may destabilize training when selected excessively.

This issue is particularly pronounced in generative reasoning tasks, where high-uncertainty sequences may correspond to long, compositional chains of thought that exceed the current capacity of the student model. Consequently, naively prioritizing only the most uncertain instances can result in inefficient use of annotation or distillation budgets.

To mitigate this bias, we introduce a difficulty-stratified sampling mechanism. Given an uncertainty scorer $\phi(\cdot)$, each unlabeled sample x_i receives a score $s_i = \phi(x_i)$. We then compute the 25th and 75th percentiles of the scores of unlabeled pool $\mathcal{S} = \{s_i | i = 1, 2, \ldots, |\mathcal{U}|\}$:

$$\tau_{\text{low}} = \text{Percentile}(\mathcal{S}, 25), \quad \tau_{\text{high}} = \text{Percentile}(\mathcal{S}, 75). \tag{6}$$

Based on these thresholds, all samples are partitioned into three difficulty strata:

$$\begin{cases} \mathcal{E} = \{i \mid s_i \leq \tau_{\text{low}}\}, \\ \mathcal{M} = \{i \mid \tau_{\text{low}} < s_i \leq \tau_{\text{high}}\}, \\ \mathcal{H} = \{i \mid s_i > \tau_{\text{high}}\}. \end{cases} \tag{7}$$

Eventually, given a sampling budget k, we draw:

$$q_{\mathcal{E}} = \left\lfloor \frac{k}{4} \right\rfloor, \quad q_{\mathcal{M}} = \left\lfloor \frac{k}{2} \right\rfloor, \quad q_{\mathcal{H}} = k - q_{\mathcal{E}} - q_{\mathcal{M}} \tag{8}$$

samples from the easy, medium, and hard strata respectively.

This allocation strategy reflects a deliberate trade-off between exploration and stability. Easy samples reinforce foundational reasoning patterns, medium-difficulty samples support steady skill acquisition, and hard samples challenge the model with informative yet demanding cases. By ensuring balanced exposure across difficulty levels, the proposed scheme prevents overfitting to extreme uncertainty regimes while maintaining sufficient pressure for model improvement.

Importantly, difficulty stratification is agnostic to the specific uncertainty metric employed. As a result, it can be seamlessly combined with MNLP, LC, or BALD, yielding a unified framework that integrates uncertainty estimation with curriculum-aware data selection. This design promotes stable optimization and improved sample efficiency in active Chain-of-Thought distillation.

3.5 Distillation Procedure

We adopt the same rationale-based distillation framework as Distilling Step-by-Step (DSS) to transfer reasoning knowledge from a large teacher model to a smaller student model. Specifically, the teacher is prompted with Chain-of-Thought (CoT) demonstrations to generate both final answers and intermediate rationales, which serve as supervision signals for the student. The student model is trained in a multi-task manner to generate either task labels or rationales conditioned on task-specific prefixes, sharing parameters across both objectives. This joint training encourages the student to acquire intermediate reasoning patterns while maintaining standard task performance.

Importantly, the distillation process itself remains unchanged from DSS. Our contribution lies in the sample selection stage prior to distillation, where difficulty-stratified active sampling is applied to improve the efficiency and stability of DSS-style knowledge transfer under limited annotation budgets.

4 Experiments

4.1 Experimental Setting

Datasets. We evaluate DSAD on three representative benchmarks: e-SNLI [1] for natural language inference, CQA [20] for commonsense reasoning, and SVAMP [16] for arithmetic word problems. These tasks cover a broad spectrum of reasoning complexity. Dataset statistics are summarized in Table 1.

Table 1. Statistics of Datasets

Dataset	Train	Validation	Test
CQA	8,766	975	1,221
SVAMP	720	80	200
e-SNLI	549,367	9,842	9,824

Setup and Baselines. We employ the 540B-parameter PaLM as the teacher LLM and a 220M-parameter T5 as the student. Our framework is built upon the DSS [11] protocol, supporting both Standard CoT (S-CoT) and Prefix CoT (P-CoT) distillation. We compare DSAD against: (1) Random sampling, (2) Vanilla AL (MNLP, LC, BALD), and (3) DSAD-enhanced variants of these strategies.

Implementation Details. Training is conducted on a single NVIDIA RTX 4090 GPU using mixed precision. The training hyperparameters are set as follows: a learning rate of 5×10^{-5}, a batch size of 16, and a task loss weight α= 0.5. Our experiments employ active learning strategies based on three uncertainty measures MNLP, LC, and BALD—combined with difficulty-stratified sampling using a ratio of easy:medium:hard = 1:2:1. Starting from an initial 1% labeled set, the training data is progressively expanded to 5%, 10%, 20%, 30%, 50%, 70%, and 90% of the full dataset. Each configuration is averaged over three random seeds to ensure statistical significance.

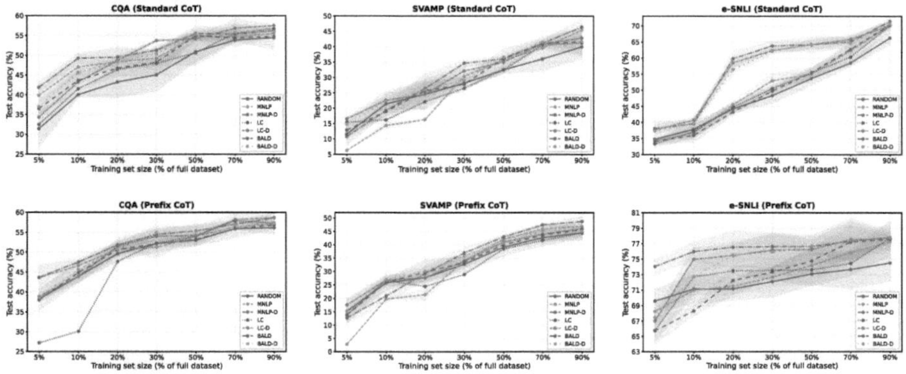

Fig. 2. Learning curves of Standard CoT (S-CoT) and Prefix CoT (P-CoT) distillation on CQA, SVAMP, and e-SNLI using seven data selection strategies as the proportion of labeled training data increases from 5% to 90%, illustrating the impact of uncertainty-based active learning and difficulty-stratified sampling on sample efficiency and performance stability.

4.2 Results

Main Results. We compare seven sampling strategies, including Random, MNLP, LC, BALD, and their difficulty-stratified variants. The main results are reported in Table 2, with overall trends shown in Fig. 2.Without difficulty stratification, conventional uncertainty-based methods do not consistently outperform Random sampling in low-data regimes, and may even underperform in some cases. In contrast, incorporating difficulty-stratified sampling consistently improves performance across all datasets. Among all methods, the MNLP based difficulty-aware strategy (MNLP-D, 1:2:1) achieves the best results in most settings. Notably, using only around 30% of the training data, MNLP-D recovers approximately 90% of the performance obtained with the full dataset, demonstrating its effectiveness in reducing CoT annotation costs.

The Role of Difficulty Distribution. We examine the effect of difficulty allocation policies on difficulty-stratified active distillation by instantiating DSAD with the MNLP-based uncertainty scorer (MNLP-D) and varying the sampling ratios across easy, medium, and hard strata. As shown in Fig. 3, different ratios lead to clear performance differences under limited annotation budgets, indicating that the difficulty distribution of selected samples plays a non-negligible

Table 2. Test accuracy (mean ± standard deviation) of student models distilled under Standard CoT (S-CoT) and Prefix CoT (P-CoT) frameworks on CQA, SVAMP, and e-SNLI, comparing random sampling, uncertainty-based active learning methods (MNLP, LC, BALD), and their difficulty-stratified variants (MNLP-D, LC-D, BALD-D) across 5%, 10%, and 90% labeled data budgets. Boldface indicates the best-performing strategy within each dataset–budget–distillation setting.

Method		CQA			SVAMP			e-SNLI		
		5%	10%	90%	5%	10%	90%	5%	10%	90%
S-CoT	RANDOM	31.42±4.80	43.26±0.60	53.88±3.00	11.58±3.80	21.43±3.04	40.03±3.70	34.76±0.09	37.81±2.34	66.26±2.08
	MNLP	39.87±1.70	47.05±2.33	55.52±0.01	6.32±0.01	14.40±0.92	45.50±0.01	34.30±0.96	36.69±1.65	70.04±0.01
	MNLP-D	**41.88±1.30**	**49.28±1.26**	56.20±0.90	10.79±0.60	19.27±1.90	**46.46±2.84**	**38.08±2.42**	39.56±0.95	**71.49±0.50**
	LC	32.48±0.39	41.52±0.01	56.75±0.01	15.46±0.01	16.20±0.54	41.30±1.90	33.36±1.32	37.12±1.80	70.12±1.26
	LC-D	34.32±0.79	43.26±0.60	**57.55±0.21**	**16.54±0.62**	**22.61±2.80**	42.86±1.53	37.63±1.47	**40.67±0.90**	70.21±1.14
	BALD	36.52±1.39	43.67±2.53	54.58±0.15	12.91±1.49	18.96±1.45	41.64±4.40	34.12±0.85	35.95±2.12	70.35±0.93
	BALD-D	37.01±1.56	45.61±1.37	56.00±1.41	14.83±2.03	22.36±0.98	41.81±4.23	37.34±0.68	39.76±1.18	70.63±1.72
P-CoT	RANDOM	38.27±0.54	43.92±1.39	56.17±1.59	15.25±4.26	25.82±2.40	44.55±2.09	69.60±1.53	71.22±1.86	74.50±2.38
	MNLP	43.57±0.01	46.60±0.01	57.16±0.89	2.82±0.03	19.79±0.01	46.96±0.01	68.25±1.26	70.99±0.64	77.26±1.16
	MNLP-D	**43.68±3.08**	**47.52±0.76**	58.64±1.26	12.76±2.31	20.89±2.41	**48.74±1.82**	**74.04±0.97**	**75.96±1.25**	**77.82±0.55**
	LC	27.21±0.19	30.13±0.01	57.33±1.32	13.91±0.01	26.76±0.01	44.44±2.88	65.78±1.32	72.71±2.36	77.73±2.22
	LC-D	38.87±0.66	43.92±1.39	**58.72±0.76**	**17.58±2.31**	**26.85±2.24**	46.10±2.64	67.03±1.24	74.97±1.52	77.63±1.09
	BALD	38.04±2.55	44.87±2.59	56.83±1.03	13.82±1.92	26.01±1.26	45.69±2.90	65.75±1.76	68.31±0.63	77.79±0.45
	BALD-D	38.55±1.23	45.64±2.11	57.35±0.40	15.33±1.32	27.01±1.39	45.19±0.91	67.47±0.88	72.69±1.30	77.56±1.72

role in CoT distillation. Among all configurations, the 2:1:1 ratio consistently yields higher accuracy and more stable learning curves across datasets, suggesting that moderately emphasizing easier samples supports reliable optimization and gradual reasoning skill acquisition. In contrast, strategies biased toward harder samples or uniform allocation exhibit less stable or inferior performance, motivating explicit difficulty regulation in active CoT distillation.

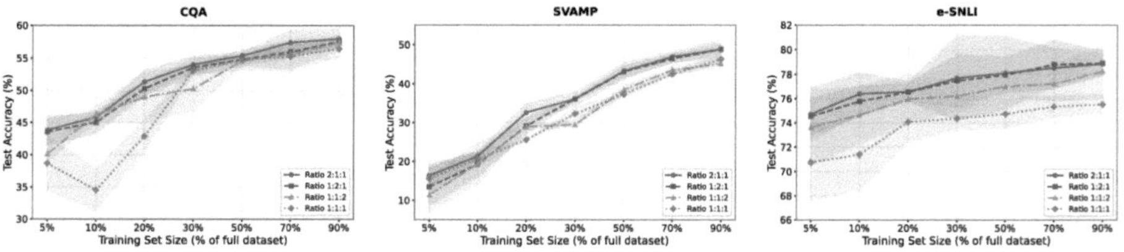

Fig. 3. Effect of different difficulty stratification ratios on S-CoT distillation performance across three datasets, showing how varying the proportions of easy, medium, and hard samples influences learning dynamics under limited annotation budgets.

Impact of Initialization. We further investigate whether student model initialization is necessary for effective difficulty-stratified active CoT distillation. Here, initialization refers to a brief warm-up stage in which the student model is trained on a small labeled seed set (1% of the data) prior to active sample acquisition, rather than to model pretraining. This warm-up allows the student to form an initial task understanding and to produce more calibrated uncertainty estimates during acquisition. To assess its impact, we compare difficulty-stratified active distillation with and without initialization under the P-CoT setting across all datasets (Fig. 4). The results exhibit a dataset-dependent pattern: initialization yields substantial and consistent improvements on e-SNLI, while its effect on CQA and SVAMP is comparatively limited. This suggests that for tasks involving more complex linguistic inference and explanation generation, a brief warm-up phase can enhance uncertainty calibration and guide more effective sample selection.

Importantly, although initialization can be beneficial in certain settings, it is not strictly required for DSAD to function effectively. Even without an explicit warm-up stage, difficulty-stratified active distillation consistently outperforms baseline strategies, demonstrating robustness to different starting conditions and applicability in practical low-resource scenarios.

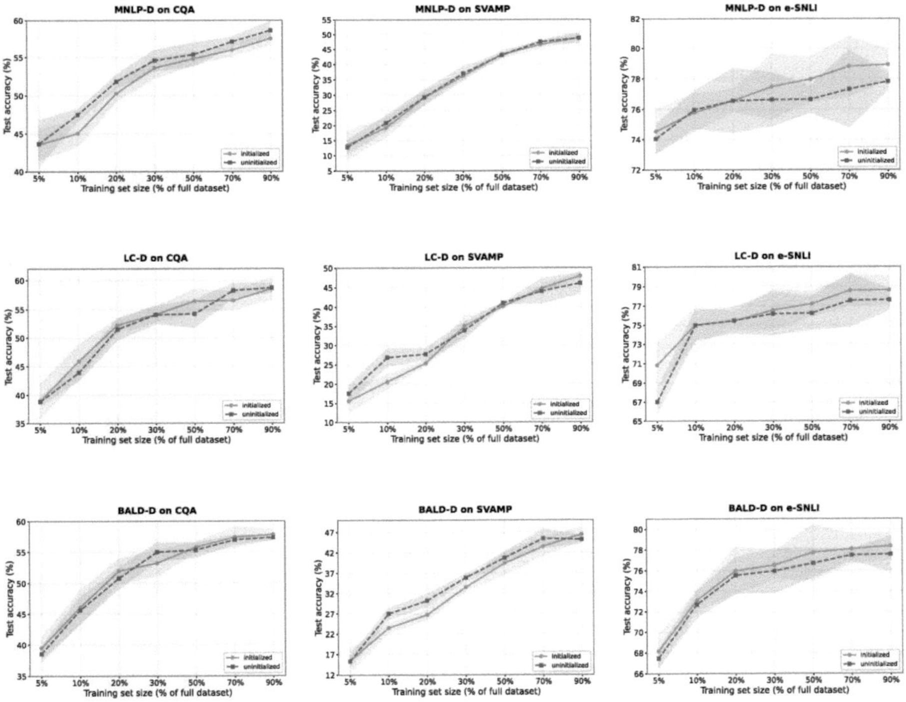

Fig. 4. Impact of student model initialization on MNLP-, LC-, and BALD-based difficulty-stratified active CoT distillation under the P-CoT setting, evaluated across CQA, SVAMP, and e-SNLI.

4.3 Analysis

Why Difficulty Regulation Matters? Empirical results demonstrate that explicit difficulty regulation substantially enhances active CoT distillation under limited annotation budgets. Purely uncertainty-based acquisition often over-selects extremely uncertain samples, which typically involve long or noisy reasoning chains beyond the student model's capacity. Difficulty-stratified sampling mitigates this issue by balancing exposure to easy, medium, and hard instances. This design enables the student to first consolidate core reasoning patterns while remaining exposed to informative challenges, resulting in more stable optimization and improved sample efficiency in low-resource settings.

Interplay Between Uncertainty and Difficulty. Difficulty stratification complements uncertainty-based acquisition by explicitly regulating the difficulty distribution of selected samples, transforming a purely exploratory strategy into a curriculum-aware selection process. This mechanism is agnostic to the specific uncertainty metric, explaining its consistent effectiveness across MNLP-, LC-, and BALD-based strategies. We emphasize that difficulty stratification is not an alternative to uncertainty estimation, but a regulation mechanism that constrains uncertainty-driven acquisition according to the student's learning stage. While uncertainty identifies potentially informative samples, difficulty regulation determines their learnability, enabling a balance between exploration and stability in low-resource settings. By preventing extreme uncertainty from dominating early acquisition, DSAD promotes more reliable optimization and gradual reasoning skill formation.

Table 3. Comparison of different CoT granularity for the same problem generated by different methods.

Dataset	Method	Generated Output
CQA	RANDOM	Standing up requires muscle strength, and muscle fatigue can make it difficult to remain standing, causing someone to sit back down. ✗
CQA	MNLP-D	Standing up too quickly can disrupt balance, making a person feel unsteady and require sitting down again to regain stability. ✓
SVAMP	RANDOM	Since Jack received 6 emails in the morning and 3 in the afternoon, and the total is 10 for the day, all numbers are combined, yielding $6 + 3 + 10 = 19$ as the evening count. ✗
SVAMP	LC-D	The daily total is fixed. After 6 emails in the morning and 3 in the afternoon, the evening count is the remainder. So the number of emails received in the evening is $10 - (6 + 3) = 1$. ✓

Task Dependence and Practical Implications. The impact of student model initialization further reveals the task-dependent nature of active CoT distillation. For linguistically complex tasks such as e-SNLI, a brief warm-up phase improves uncertainty calibration and leads to more effective acquisition, whereas its effect is less pronounced on tasks where the student can rapidly acquire task-specific competence. Together, these findings suggest that effective active CoT distillation requires not only identifying uncertain samples, but also regulating their difficulty distribution in accordance with the student's learning stage, offering a practical guideline for cost-efficient reasoning supervision.

Granularity Case Study. CQA Question: After standing up I had to sit right back down, why would I feel like this? Choices: train, effort, balance, feet, muscles. SVAMP Question: Jack received 3 emails in the afternoon, 6 emails in the morning and some more in the evening. If he received a total of 10 emails in the day. How many emails did Jack receive in the evening? Answer: $10-(6+3) = 1$.

In Table 3, RANDOM sampling tends to induce superficial and error-prone reasoning, whereas difficulty-stratified methods generate structurally correct explanations by better capturing the underlying problem constraints.

5 Conclusion

This paper presents Difficulty-Stratified Active Distillation (DSAD), a framework that optimizes sample acquisition for CoT distillation. While traditional distillation relies on passive data regimes, DSAD reformulates uncertainty as a proxy for instance difficulty, enabling a transition toward a difficulty-aware active learning strategy. We empirically demonstrate that DSAD consistently outperforms competitive baselines across mathematical and commonsense reasoning benchmarks, recovering 90% of teacher performance using only 30%–50% of the training data. Our study reveals that for efficient knowledge transfer, matching data complexity to the student's evolving capacity is more critical than information volume, offering a cost-effective solution for distilling complex reasoning into compact, deployable models.

Acknowledgements. This work was supported by the Tianjin Science and Technology Program funded by Tianjin Municipal Science and Technology Bureau under Grant No. 25ZXSFSN00100.

References

1. Camburu, O.M., Rocktäschel, T., Lukasiewicz, T., Blunsom, P.: e-snli: natural language inference with natural language explanations. In: Proceedings of the 2018 Conference of the North American Chapter of the Association for Computational Linguistics, pp. 953–963 (2018)

2. Culotta, A., McCallum, A.: Reducing labeling effort for structured prediction tasks. In: Proceedings of the Twentieth National Conference on Artificial Intelligence (AAAI-05), vol. 1, pp. 746–751. AAAI Press (2005)
3. Dai, C., Li, K., Zhou, W., Hu, S.: Improve student's reasoning generalizability through cascading decomposed cots distillation (2024). https://arxiv.org/abs/2405.19842
4. DeepSeek-AI, Guo, D., et al.: Deepseek-r1: incentivizing reasoning capability in LLMs via reinforcement learning (2025). https://arxiv.org/abs/2501.12948
5. Do, C.T., Doddipatla, R., Knill, K.: Effectiveness of chain-of-thought in distilling reasoning capability from large language models (2025). https://arxiv.org/abs/2511.05184
6. Fu, Y., Peng, H., Ou, L., Sabharwal, A., Khot, T.: Specializing smaller language models towards multi-step reasoning (2023). https://arxiv.org/abs/2301.12726
7. Gal, Y., Islam, R., Ghahramani, Z.: Deep bayesian active learning with image data (2017). https://arxiv.org/abs/1703.02910
8. Hassan, S., Sicilia, A., Alikhani, M.: An active learning framework for inclusive generation by large language models (2024). https://arxiv.org/abs/2410.13641
9. Hinton, G., Vinyals, O., Dean, J.: Distilling the knowledge in a neural network (2015). https://arxiv.org/abs/1503.02531
10. Ho, N., Schmid, L., Yun, S.Y.: Large language models are reasoning teachers (2023). https://arxiv.org/abs/2212.10071
11. Hsieh, C.Y., et al.: Distilling step-by-step! outperforming larger language models with less training data and smaller model sizes. In: Rogers, A., Boyd-Graber, J., Okazaki, N. (eds.) Findings of the Association for Computational Linguistics: ACL 2023. pp. 8003–8017. Association for Computational Linguistics, Toronto, Canada (2023). https://doi.org/10.18653/v1/2023.findings-acl.507, https://aclanthology.org/2023.findings-acl.507/
12. Li, L.H., Hessel, J., Yu, Y., Ren, X., Chang, K.W., Choi, Y.: Symbolic chain-of-thought distillation: small models can also "think" step-by-step (2024). https://arxiv.org/abs/2306.14050
13. Li, S., et al.: Explanations from large language models make small reasoners better (2022). https://arxiv.org/abs/2210.06726
14. Li, X., et al.: MoDE-CoTD: chain-of-thought distillation for complex reasoning tasks with mixture of decoupled LoRA-experts. In: Calzolari, N., Kan, M.Y., Hoste, V., Lenci, A., Sakti, S., Xue, N. (eds.) Proceedings of the 2024 Joint International Conference on Computational Linguistics, Language Resources and Evaluation (LREC-COLING 2024). pp. 11475–11485. ELRA and ICCL, Torino, Italia (2024). https://aclanthology.org/2024.lrec-main.1003/
15. Lowell, D., Lipton, Z.C., Wallace, B.C.: Practical obstacles to deploying active learning. In: Inui, K., Jiang, J., Ng, V., Wan, X. (eds.) Proceedings of the 2019 Conference on Empirical Methods in Natural Language Processing and the 9th International Joint Conference on Natural Language Processing (EMNLP-IJCNLP), pp. 21–30. Association for Computational Linguistics, Hong Kong, China (2019). https://doi.org/10.18653/v1/D19-1003, https://aclanthology.org/D19-1003/
16. Patel, A., Bhattamishra, S., Goyal, M., Das, R.: Svamp: a structured dataset of arithmetic word problems. In: Findings of the Association for Computational Linguistics: EMNLP 2021, pp. 1537–1545 (2021)

17. Ru, D., et al.: Active sentence learning by adversarial uncertainty sampling in discrete space. In: Cohn, T., He, Y., Liu, Y. (eds.) Findings of the Association for Computational Linguistics: EMNLP 2020, pp. 4908–4917. Association for Computational Linguistics, Online (2020). https://doi.org/10.18653/v1/2020.findings-emnlp.441, https://aclanthology.org/2020.findings-emnlp.441/
18. Sener, O., Savarese, S.: Active learning for convolutional neural networks: a core-set approach (2018). https://arxiv.org/abs/1708.00489
19. Settles, B.: Active learning literature survey. Tech. Rep. TR1648, University of Wisconsin–Madison (2009). http://digital.library.wisc.edu/1793/60660
20. Talmor, A., Herzig, J., Lourie, N., Berant, J.: Commonsenseqa: a question answering challenge targeting commonsense knowledge. In: Proceedings of the 2019 Conference of the North American Chapter of the Association for Computational Linguistics, pp. 4149–4158 (2019)
21. Wang, P., Wang, Z., Li, Z., Gao, Y., Yin, B., Ren, X.: SCOTT: self-consistent chain-of-thought distillation. In: Rogers, A., Boyd-Graber, J., Okazaki, N. (eds.) Proceedings of the 61st Annual Meeting of the Association for Computational Linguistics (Volume 1: Long Papers), pp. 5546–5558. Association for Computational Linguistics, Toronto, Canada (2023). https://doi.org/10.18653/v1/2023.acl-long.304, https://aclanthology.org/2023.acl-long.304/
22. Xia, Y., Mukherjee, S., Xie, Z., Wu, J., Li, X., et al.: From selection to generation: a survey of LLM-based active learning. In: Che, W., Nabende, J., Shutova, E., Pilehvar, M.T. (eds.) Proceedings of the 63rd Annual Meeting of the Association for Computational Linguistics (Volume 1: Long Papers), pp. 14552–14569. Association for Computational Linguistics, Vienna, Austria (2025). https://doi.org/10.18653/v1/2025.acl-long.708, https://aclanthology.org/2025.acl-long.708/

CLEEF: A Contrastive Learning-Based Embedding Enhancement Framework with Triple-Level Adaptive Selection

Jingyu Zhang[1], Liqiang Xie[1], Zhijie Zhu[1], Wenheng Li[1], and Qianzhen Zhang[2(✉)]

[1] School of Computer Science and Technology, Changsha University of Science and Technology, Changsha 410076, China
{zhangzhang,xlq,zhuzhijie920,24208051819}@csust.edu.cn
[2] National Key Laboratory of Information Systems Engineering, National University of Defense Technology, Changsha 410073, China
zhangqianzhen18@nudt.edu.cn

Abstract. In recent years, numerous knowledge graph embedding (KGE) enhancement methods have been proposed to improve link prediction performance. However, their applicability to different triples and training robustness are still limited. Existing KGE enhancement methods still suffer from two key challenges: (1) the same enhancement is applied to all triples, whereas not all triples are suitable for enhanced reasoning; (2) when distinguishing different inference modes, imbalanced positive-negative distributions hinder the effective capture of discriminative differences among samples. To address these issues, we propose CLEEF, a contrastive learningbased framework for KGE enhancement. CLEEF dynamically adapts inference strategies for different triples while remaining robust to severe sample distribution imbalance. ***For first challenge***, CLEEF employs contrastive learning to distinguish the representations of prediction triples under base and enhanced inference modes, and further trains a lightweight binary classifier to dynamically select the more appropriate inference strategy for each triple. ***For second challenge***, we introduce a high-quality negative sample augmentation strategy that improves representation learning under imbalanced sample distributions by incorporating a small number of informative negative samples. Extensive experiments are conducted on three widely used benchmark datasets for knowledge graph completion. The experimental results show that CLEEF improves performance over both the base models and existing enhancement methods across multiple metrics, while remaining compatible with different KGE models and enhancement strategies.

Keywords: Knowledge graph · Contrastive learning · Knowledge graph embedding · Reasoning system

L. Ding et al. (Eds.): APWeb-WAIM 2026, LNCS 16995, pp. 150–166, 2027.
https://doi.org/10.1007/978-981-92-5699-0_10

1 Introduction

Knowledge graph embedding (KGE) models have achieved remarkable success in knowledge graph completion tasks and have been widely applied to various downstream applications, such as recommendation systems [28], question answering [13], and information retrieval [9]. Traditional KGE models, including TransE [2], RotatE [17], and HAKE [30], learn low-dimensional vector representations for entities and relations through designed scoring functions, and assign scores to measure the correctness of triples. Building upon these models, a variety of enhancement frameworks and training strategies have been proposed to further improve the expressive power of KGE models, such as utilizing additional structural or semantic information [6], modifying training objectives [32], or alleviating noise and sparsity issues through more effective sample construction and utilization [18]. These methods typically provide extra learning signals or constraints without altering the underlying scoring functions, thereby enhancing the robustness and generalization ability of the learned embeddings.

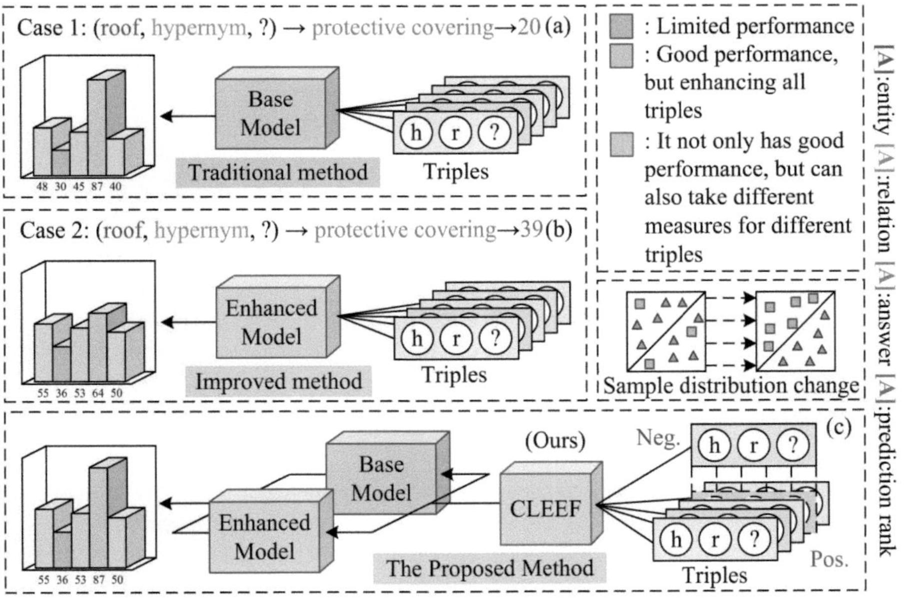

Fig. 1. Mainstream KGE methods and our proposed CLEEF. Combining (a) and (b), it can be seen that the enhancement model applies identical enhancement strategy to all tasks. However, not all tasks are suitable for enhancement. (c) illustrates the solution of our proposed CLEEF to improve KGE enhancement.

However, existing KGE enhancement methods suffer from two major limitations. ***(1) Inflexible Enhancement Strategies.*** Most enhancement approaches apply the same enhancement or regularization strategy to all triples.

In practice, not all triples benefit from enhancement. Some triples are more suitable for the inference patterns of the original base models, and blindly enforcing enhanced reasoning on them may introduce noise or even degrade performance. As illustrated in Figs. 1(a) and 1(b), although using enhanced models generally yields better link prediction results than relying solely on base models, there still exist a small number of prediction triples for which enhanced strategies are not appropriate, leading to inferior performance compared with the base models. ***(2) Insufficient Adaptability for Imbalanced Sample Distributions.*** When distinguishing between two inference modes (i.e., suitable or unsuitable for enhancement), if a mini-batch is dominated by samples from a single class, it will result in extremely insufficiency of positive or negative samples, and contrastive learning struggles to capture fine-grained differences among samples. Consequently, the learned embeddings lack sufficient discriminative power. As illustrated in Figs. 1(a) and 1(b), when treating samples suitable for enhancement as positive and those unsuitable as negative, the number of positive samples exceeds that of negative samples, leading to an imbalanced sample distribution.

To address the aforementioned challenges, we propose CLEEF, a contrastive learningbased embedding enhancement framework with triple-level adaptive selection. ***First, to solve Inflexible Enhancement Strategies***, CLEEF dynamically employs inference strategies for different triples. Specifically, CLEEF uses contrastive learning to distinguish between different prediction tasks and trains a binary classifier to predict whether a triple is more suitable for base or enhanced inference during the prediction phase. ***Second, to tackle Insufficient Adaptability for Imbalanced Sample Distributions***, we introduce a high-quality negative sample augmentation strategy. This strategy improves contrastive learning by adding negative samples. These samples are easy for the base model but challenging for the enhanced model. Thereby, CLEEF effectively handles severe imbalances in positive and negative sample distributions. The main contributions of this work are summarized as follows:

- We propose CLEEF, a general contrastive learningbased framework for KGE enhancement, which achieves dynamic utilization of inference strategies for different triples.
- A frequency matrix is designed to capture entity co-occurrence patterns, complemented by a high-quality negative sample augmentation strategy.
- Extensive experiments are conducted on three public benchmark datasets. Experimental results demonstrate that CLEEF consistently outperforms both the original base models and existing enhancement methods across multiple evaluation metrics, while also exhibiting strong compatibility.

2 Related Work

2.1 Knowledge Graph Embedding

Knowledge graph embedding (KGE) represents entities and relations in low-dimensional spaces for link prediction, and has been extensively studied. Translational models treat relations as transformations in the embedding space.

TransE [2] models relations as vector translations, RotatE [17] extends this idea to complex-space rotations, DualE [3] unifies translation and rotation via dual quaternions, and HAKE [30] models hierarchical relations using polar coordinates. Semantic matching–based models score triples by measuring entity–relation compatibility. DistMult [27] and ComplEx [20] adopt bilinear scoring functions, ConvE [5] introduces convolutional interaction modeling, and PairRE [4] represents relations with paired vectors to improve expressiveness. Graph neural network–based approaches incorporate neighborhood information into entity representations. R-GCN [15] applies relational graph convolutions, CompGCN [21] jointly updates entities and relations through composition, A2N [1] introduces attention mechanisms, and SE-GNN [8] leverages semantic evidence. Transformer-based methods such as SimKGC [24] encode entity and relation descriptions as text using pre-trained language models and apply contrastive learning to improve representation discrimination. Most existing KGE models employ a fixed inference strategy for all triples. CLEEF complements these methods by adaptively utilizing different inference modes at the triple level.

2.2 Enhanced Knowledge Graph Embedding

In recent years, researchers have sought to improve knowledge graph completion performance from the perspective of model enhancement. CAKE [14] enhances negative sampling and multi-view prediction by incorporating a commonsense view. PUDA [19] alleviates false negative and data sparsity issues through positiveunlabeled learning combined with adversarial data augmentation. REP [22] integrates graph structural information into pre-trained embeddings via relation-aware embedding propagation. AnKGE [29] enhances the inductive capability of KGE models through analogical reasoning. KGDM [11] reformulates entity prediction as conditional generation using denoising diffusion probabilistic models to capture multiple relation semantics. Most of these methods adopt static and uniform enhancement strategies, assuming that all triples can benefit equally from enhancement. In contrast, this work further explores enhancement suitability at the triple level and enables dynamic selection of inference strategies.

2.3 Contrastive Learning

Recent studies have adopted contrastive learning as an effective paradigm for representation learning in knowledge graph–related tasks. HyperCL [12] employs multi-view contrastive learning to align entity representations across semantic views, while CENET [26] introduces historical contrastive learning to characterize different reasoning patterns in temporal settings. In addition, contrastive objectives have been used to enrich supervision or improve robustness through entity-level perturbations or ranking-aware signals[23, 31].Along this line, this work also leverages contrastive learning to enhance representation discrimination. Specifically, contrastive objectives are formulated at the triple level to distinguish prediction representations under different inference modes, and are integrated with mechanisms that explicitly account for imbalanced positive and negative samples during optimization.

3 Methods

In this section, we elaborate on the proposed CLEEF framework in detail, which consists of four main components in Fig. 3: **Triplet-level Inference Suitability Modeling** (i.e., data preparation), **Supervised Contrastive Learning**, **Binary Classifier Training** and **Link Prediction**.

3.1 Triplet-Level Inference Suitability Modeling

In our proposed CLEEF framework, both supervised contrastive learning and binary classifier training depend on knowing which inference mode suits each triple. Without this guidance, the model may apply a uniform strategy across all triples. This risks biased predictions on samples that do not benefit from the enhanced inference mode. Thus, constructing the target matrix forms a critical step in our approach. Its primary goal is to assign each triple a label that indicates suitability for the enhanced inference mode. Moreover, we introduce a frequency matrix to capture associations among entities. This offers structural guidance for subsequent optimization of embedding representations.

Consider the knowledge graph $G = (\mathcal{E}, \mathcal{R}, \mathcal{T})$, in which $\mathcal{E}$ denotes the entity set, $\mathcal{R}$ denotes the relation set, and $\mathcal{T}$ is the triple set. For each triple $(h, r, t) \in \mathcal{T}$, we perform either head or tail entity prediction. The inference mode determines whether the enhanced inference mode benefits the triple. Specifically, we compare the ranking produced by the enhanced model $\text{rank}_{\text{enhanced}}(h, r, t)$ against the base model's ranking $\text{rank}_{\text{base}}(h, r, t)$. The triple receives a positive label if the enhanced ranking outperforms the base ranking. Otherwise, it is marked as unsuitable for the enhanced inference mode.

Thus, the target matrix for head entity prediction Y_h is defined as follows:

$$Y_h = \begin{cases} 1, & \text{if } \text{rank}_{\text{enhanced}}(h, r, t) \leq \text{rank}_{\text{base}}(h, r, t) \\ 0, & \text{otherwise} \end{cases}. \tag{1}$$

Similarly, the target matrix for tail entity prediction Y_t is:

$$Y_t = \begin{cases} 1, & \text{if } \text{rank}_{\text{enhanced}}(h, r, t) \leq \text{rank}_{\text{base}}(h, r, t) \\ 0, & \text{otherwise} \end{cases}. \tag{2}$$

We denote the target matrices as Y_h for head entity prediction and Y_t for tail entity prediction. These matrices direct the subsequent training and inference processes within our framework.

Moreover, we construct a frequency matrix to capture entity co-occurrence patterns. In knowledge graphs, entities that frequently appear together typically reveal underlying semantic links. For instance, the repeated co-occurrence of *Beijing* and *China* suggests a capital-country relationship. This co-occurrence information supplies additional semantic signals for embedding learning. It enables the model to better capture relational patterns (Fig. 2).

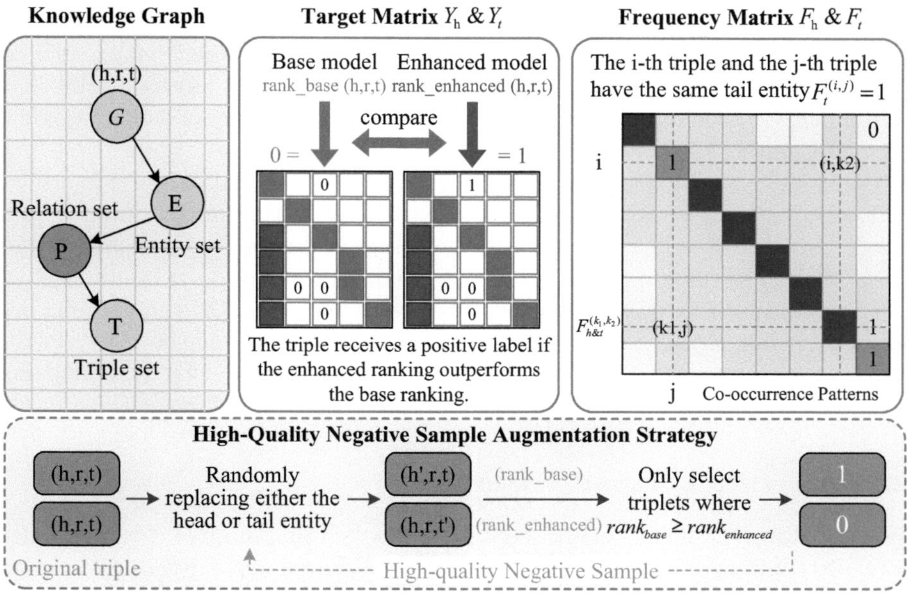

Fig. 2. The CLEEF workflow for constructing the target matrix and frequency matrix.

Accordingly, we construct entity frequency matrices for head and tail entities, denoted as $\mathbf{F}_h \in \mathbb{R}^{|\mathcal{T}| \times |\mathcal{E}|}$ and $\mathbf{F}_t \in \mathbb{R}^{|\mathcal{T}| \times |\mathcal{E}|}$, respectively.

For the head-entity frequency matrix $\mathbf{F}_h$, the element at row i and column j, denoted as $F_h^{(i,j)}$, is defined as follows: if the head entity h_i of a triple shares the same head entity with another triple $(h_k, r_k, t_k) \in \mathcal{T}$, and the tail entity t_k of that triple equals the j-th entity e_j, then $F_h^{(i,j)} = 1$; otherwise, $F_h^{(i,j)} = 0$. Formally, we have:

$$F_h^{(i,j)} = \begin{cases} 1, & \text{if } (h_i = h_k \text{ and } t_k = e_j) \in (h_k, r_k, t_k) \in \mathcal{T} \\ 0, & \text{otherwise} \end{cases}. \tag{3}$$

Similarly, the tail-entity frequency matrix $\mathbf{F}_t$ is constructed based on tail entity co-occurrence. Specifically, there is:

$$F_t^{(i,j)} = \begin{cases} 1, & \text{if } (t_i = t_k \text{ and } h_k = e_j) \in (h_k, r_k, t_k) \in \mathcal{T} \\ 0, & \text{otherwise} \end{cases}. \tag{4}$$

The frequency matrices $\mathbf{F}_h$ and $\mathbf{F}_t$ supply explicit entity association signals to downstream modules. Additionally, they enable the model to capture local structural features of the knowledge graph. Thus, this supports the optimization of embedding representations.

To address the difficulty of contrastive learning in capturing discriminative differences when negative samples are insufficient, we design a high-quality negative sample augmentation strategy based on model performance discrepancies. Specifically, we compare the prediction results of a base model $\mathcal{M}_{\text{base}}$ and an enhanced model $\mathcal{M}_{\text{enhanced}}$ on candidate samples, and select those samples that are difficult for the enhanced model but easy for the base model as high-quality negative samples.

Concretely, for each original triple (h, r, t), we generate candidate samples by randomly replacing either the head or tail entity, resulting in corrupted triples (h', r, t) or (h, r, t'). These candidates are then evaluated by both models to obtain their corresponding ranking scores, denoted as $\text{rank}_{\text{base}}$ and $\text{rank}_{\text{enhanced}}$. A candidate negative sample is considered valid and added to the training set only when $\text{rank}_{\text{enhanced}} > \text{rank}_{\text{base}}$. This strategy ensures that the newly introduced negative samples are sufficiently challenging, thereby effectively encouraging the model to learn more discriminative feature representations.

3.2 Supervised Contrastive Learning

The core objective of the supervised contrastive learning module is to construct more discriminative embedding representations based on existing knowledge graph triples, thereby providing effective support for subsequent precise reasoning. This module is not trained independently; instead, it is guided by the previously constructed target matrix, which specifies triples suitable for enhanced reasoning, enabling contrastive learning to focus on informative samples while avoiding interference from irrelevant or noisy triples.

Specifically, for each triple (h, r, t) in the knowledge graph, the model first constructs a query representation $\mathbf{q}$ that integrates multiple sources of information. Rather than a simple information concatenation, this representation is formed by concatenating the head entity embedding $\mathbf{e}_h$, relation embedding $\mathbf{r}$, and frequency embedding $\mathbf{f}$, as follows:

$$\mathbf{q} = [\mathbf{e}_h; \mathbf{r}; \mathbf{f}]. \tag{5}$$

Among these components, the construction of the frequency embedding $\mathbf{f}$ is particularly critical. It is derived from the frequency matrix $\mathbf{F}$, which captures entity co-occurrence relationships (using either the head-entity frequency matrix $\mathbf{F}_h$ or the tail-entity frequency matrix $\mathbf{F}_t$, depending on the assigned task). Specifically, the frequency matrix is first normalized using a softmax function, followed by a linear transformation with a weight matrix $\mathbf{W}_f$, and finally passed through a tanh activation function:

$$\mathbf{f} = \tanh(\mathbf{W}_f \cdot \text{softmax}(\mathbf{F})) . \tag{6}$$

Given the query representation $\mathbf{q}$, the model further refines the representation space through a contrastive projection layer:

$$\mathbf{z} = \mathbf{W}_c \cdot \mathbf{q}. \tag{7}$$

To learn the principle of pulling together similar samples and pushing apart dissimilar ones, we optimize the model using a supervised contrastive loss $\mathcal{L}_{\text{spc}}$. For each sample i in a mini-batch, its positive sample set is defined as:

$$\mathcal{P}(i) = \{j \in \mathcal{B} : y_i = y_j,\ j \neq i\}. \tag{8}$$

The supervised contrastive loss is formulated as:

$$\mathcal{L}_{\text{spc}} = \frac{1}{N}\sum_{i=1}^{N}\frac{1}{|\mathcal{P}(i)|}\sum_{j\in\mathcal{P}(i)}\left[-\log\frac{\exp(\mathbf{z}_i\cdot\mathbf{z}_j/\tau)}{\sum_{k\neq i}\exp(\mathbf{z}_i\cdot\mathbf{z}_k/\tau)}\right], \tag{9}$$

where N denotes the batch size.

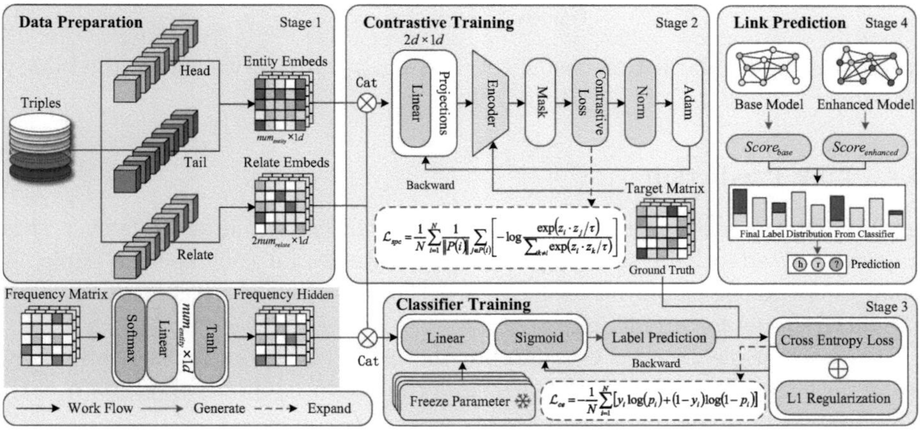

Fig. 3. The overall framework of CLEEF. It consists of four steps from training to prediction: data preparation, contrastive training, classifier training, and link prediction.

3.3 Binary Classifier Training

To enable adaptive inference at the triple level, a binary classifier is designed to determine whether a given triple should adopt the enhanced reasoning mode. Given the query representation $\mathbf{q}$, which is shared with the contrastive learning module, the classifier produces the following probability:

$$p = \sigma\big(\text{Oracle}(\mathbf{q})\big), \tag{10}$$

where Oracle(·) denotes the classifier and $\sigma(\cdot)$ is the sigmoid function. This probability directly guides the selection of the inference mode during training.

To optimize the binary classifier, we use a cross-entropy loss function. Given a set of training samples, the classifier is trained by minimizing the cross-entropy between the predicted probability p and the target label y, where the label is 1 for triples suitable for enhancement and 0 for those that are not:

$$\mathcal{L}_{\text{CE}} = -\frac{1}{N}\sum_{i=1}^{N}\left[y_i \log(p_i) + (1 - y_i)\log(1 - p_i)\right], \tag{11}$$

where N is the batch size, p_i is the predicted probability for the i-th sample, and y_i is the true label.

To prevent overfitting, a regularization term is added to penalize large weights in the binary classifier. The total loss function combines the cross-entropy loss and the regularization term:

$$\mathcal{L}_{\text{reg}} = \lambda \|\mathbf{w}_{\text{oracle}}\|_1, \tag{12}$$

$$\mathcal{L}_{\text{oracle}} = \mathcal{L}_{\text{CE}} + \mathcal{L}_{\text{reg}}, \tag{13}$$

where λ is the regularization coefficient, and $\mathbf{w}_{\text{oracle}}$ are the weights of the binary classifier.

3.4 Link Prediction

In CLEEF, the task of predicting the missing tail entity t in a triple (h, r, t) is improved by adaptively selecting inference strategies for each specific triple. A binary classifier is employed to decide whether to utilize the base model or the enhanced model for prediction.

For each triple (h, r, t), we compute the prediction score for the tail entity using both the base model $f_{\text{base}}(h, r, t)$ and the enhanced model $f_{\text{enhanced}}(h, r, t)$. The final score is computed as follows:

$$score = \alpha \cdot f_{\text{base}}(h, r, t) + (1 - \alpha) \cdot f_{\text{enhanced}}(h, r, t). \tag{14}$$

Here, α represents the weight predicted by the binary classifier, determining the relative contribution of the enhanced model. The final prediction selects the tail entity t' that maximizes the score. This adaptive strategy enables CLEEF to selectively apply enhancements, improving prediction performance while maintaining stability under imbalanced samples.

4 Experiments

In this section, from the systematic evaluation of CLEEF, we mainly answer the following research questions: **RQ1**. Does the CLEEF framework consistently improve link prediction performance across various knowledge graph embedding models? **RQ2**. Can CLEEF be seamlessly integrated with existing enhancement methods, while maintaining their benefits? **RQ3**. Do the key components of CLEEF, including the frequency matrix, enhanced negative sampling, and inference selection module, contribute significantly to its overall effectiveness? **RQ4**. How does CLEEF impact the representation distribution generated by contrastive learning, and in what way do enhanced negative samples affect representation separability?

Table 1. Hyperparameters for our proposed CLEEF model.

Hyperparameters	FB15k-237	WN18RR	NELL-995
Contrastive Learning LR	1e-3	1e-4	1e-3
Contrastive Learning Epochs	30	30	30
Batch Size	1024	1024	1024
Valid Epochs	5	5	5
Binary Classifier LR	1e-3	1e-3	1e-3
Binary Classifier Epochs	20	20	20
Dropout	0.4	0.4	0.4
LeakyReLU	0.2	0.2	0.2
L1 Regularization Parameter	0.01	0.01	0.01
Temperature	0.05	0.05	0.05
Negative Ratio	0.4	0.4	0.4
Weight Decay	1e-5	1e-5	1e-5
Gradient Clipping	1	1	1
Embedding Dimension	512	512	512

Table 2. The statistics of different datasets for ablation study.

Dataset	#Ent	#Rel	#Train	#Valid	#Test
WN18RR	40,943	11	86,835	3,034	3,134
FB15k-237	14,541	237	272,115	17,535	20,466
NELL-995	75,492	200	123,370	15,000	15,838

4.1 Experimental Settings

Implementation Details. All experiments are conducted on a Linux server equipped with an Intel(R) Xeon(R) Gold 6330 CPU, an NVIDIA L20 GPU with 48 GB memory, and 16 GB DDR4 RAM. Hyperparameters are selected via grid search (Table 1).

Dataset Descriptions. All tested methods are evaluated on three benchmarks: FB15k-237, WN18RR, and NELL-995 (Table 2). FB15k-237 and WN18RR focus on dense relations and lexical semantics, while NELL-995 has sparse, noisy relations. These datasets enable a thorough evaluation of model performance across different relational structures.

Evaluation Metrics. In this study, we testify model performance using standard evaluation metrics for the knowledge graph link prediction tasks. The primary metrics include Mean Reciprocal Rank (MRR) and Hits@k, which assess the model's performance in entity prediction from different perspectives.

Table 3. Link prediction results on FB15k-237 and WN18RR. The best results are in bold, and the second-best results are underlined.

Method	FB15k-237				WN18RR			
	MRR	Hit@1	Hit@3	Hit@10	MRR	Hit@1	Hit@3	Hit@10
Conventional KGE								
TransE [2]	0.317	0.223	0.352	0.504	0.224	0.022	0.390	0.520
ANALOGY [10]	0.256	0.165	0.290	0.436	0.405	0.363	0.429	0.474
RotatE [17]	0.336	0.244	0.370	0.524	0.473	0.428	0.491	0.564
HAKE [30]	0.349	0.252	0.385	0.545	0.496	0.452	0.513	0.580
Rot-Pro [16]	0.344	0.246	0.383	0.540	0.457	0.397	0.482	0.577
PairRE [4]	0.348	0.254	0.384	0.539	0.455	0.413	0.469	0.539
DualE [3]	0.365	0.268	0.400	0.559	0.492	0.444	0.513	0.584
UltraE [25]	0.338	0.247	0.363	0.514	0.483	0.425	0.491	0.555
GNN-based KGE								
R-GCN [15]	0.249	0.151	0.264	0.417	-	-	-	-
A2N [1]	0.317	0.232	0.348	0.486	0.450	0.420	0.460	0.510
CompGCN [21]	0.355	0.264	0.390	0.535	0.479	0.443	0.494	0.546
SE-GNN [8]	0.365	0.271	0.399	0.549	0.484	0.446	0.509	0.572
Enhanced KGE								
CAKE [14]	0.321	0.227	0.355	0.515	-	-	-	-
PUDA [19]	0.369	0.268	0.408	0.578	0.481	0.436	0.498	0.582
REP [22]	0.354	0.262	0.388	0.540	0.488	0.439	0.505	0.588
KGPCL [7]	0.357	0.266	0.392	0.541	0.485	0.445	0.498	0.558
AnKGE-HAKE [29]	0.385	0.288	0.428	0.572	0.500	0.454	0.515	0.587
KGDM [11]	**0.520**	**0.423**	**0.566**	**0.708**	**0.516**	<u>0.457</u>	<u>0.519</u>	<u>0.593</u>
CLEEF-AnKGE-HAKE (ours)	<u>0.398</u>	<u>0.302</u>	<u>0.440</u>	<u>0.581</u>	<u>0.513</u>	**0.465**	**0.531**	**0.604**

Table 4. Compatibility evaluation results on FB15k-237 and WN18RR. The better results are in bold.

Method	FB15k-237				WN18RR				NELL-995			
	MRR	Hit@1	Hit@3	Hit@10	MRR	Hit@1	Hit@3	Hit@10	MRR	Hit@1	Hit@3	Hit@10
AnKGE-HAKE	0.385	0.288	0.428	0.572	0.500	0.454	0.515	0.587	-	-	-	-
CLEEF-AnKGE-HAKE	**0.398**	**0.302**	**0.440**	**0.581**	**0.513**	**0.465**	**0.531**	**0.604**	-	-	-	-
CAKE	0.321	0.227	0.355	0.515	-	-	-	-	0.543	0.477	0.583	**0.655**
CLEEF-CAKE	**0.334**	**0.241**	**0.362**	**0.532**	-	-	-	-	**0.547**	**0.482**	**0.586**	0.654

4.2 Main Performance Results (RQ1)

A diverse set of mainstream KGE models are evaluated as baselines, applying the proposed CLEEF framework to each for performance comparisons. Specifically, we first consider traditional KGE models, including TransE, ANALOGY, RotatE, HAKE, Rot-Pro, PairRE, and DualE, which are primarily based on classical mechanisms such as translation, rotation, or bilinear interactions. Additionally, we test graph neural networkbased models (i.e., R-GCN, A2N, CompGCN, and SE-GNN), which excel at capturing higher-order neighborhood information in knowledge graphs. Furthermore, CLEEF is combined with existing enhancement methods, including CAKE, PUDA, REP, AnKGE-HAKE, and KGDM, to evaluate its performance in improved enhancement settings. As shown in Table 3, CLEEF-AnKGE-HAKE achieves the best or second-best results on both FB15k-237 and WN18RR across most metrics. On FB15k-237, it reaches MRR 0.398, Hit@1 0.302, Hit@3 0.440, and Hit@10 0.581, outperforming the original AnKGE-HAKE and all conventional/GNN baselines. Similar improvements appear on WN18RR. These results demonstrate that CLEEF effectively boosts link prediction. We do not compare with transformer-based methods such as SimKGC, as CLEEF is a plug-and-play optimization layer for structural KGE enhancement, while SimKGC targets text-rich scenarios using pre-trained language models.Although KGDM reports higher MRR on FB15k-237, our CLEEF is built on AnKGE-HAKE. Since KGDM has no open-source code, direct integration was impossible. Nevertheless, CLEEF-AnKGE-HAKE still outperforms KGDM on WN18RR. Given CLEEF's strong compatibility (Table 2), we expect further gains if applied to KGDM.

4.3 Compatibility Results (RQ2)

To evaluate the compatibility of the CLEEF framework with existing enhancement methods, we conduct experiments using two representative strategies, AnKGE-HAKE and CAKE, across multiple benchmark datasets. This experimental setup enables a comprehensive assessment of CLEEF's performance under different relational structures and data characteristics. As shown in Table 4, CLEEF consistently enhances performance when applied on top of both enhancement strategies. Specifically, CLEEF-AnKGE-HAKE surpasses the original AnKGE-HAKE on all evaluation metrics for both FB15k-237 and WN18RR.

Similarly, CLEEF-CAKE yields further improvements over CAKE on both FB15k-237 and NELL-995. These experimental results suggest that CLEEF effectively leverages the benefits introduced by different enhancement strategies while adapting to their inference behavior. Overall, the results demonstrate that CLEEF exhibits strong compatibility with a wide range of enhancement methods across diverse datasets. By adaptively selecting suitable inference strategies, CLEEF remains effective even when the base model already incorporates other enhancement techniques, validating its better robustness and plug-and-play nature.

4.4 Ablation Studies (RQ3)

To evaluate the contribution of each component in the CLEEF framework, we conduct ablation studies on the FB15k-237 dataset using CLEEF-AnKGE-HAKE as the base model. Specifically, three variants are assessed by eliminating the frequency matrix (*w/o fre*), negative sample augmentation (*w/o neg*), and the binary classifier (*w/o ora*), and compare the results with the complete model. As shown in Table 5, the complete model outperforms all variants across all metrics, including MRR, Hits@1, Hits@3, and Hits@10. Removing the frequency matrix results in a noticeable performance drop, underscoring its critical role in capturing entity co-occurrence patterns and improving the model's understanding of the graph structure. Similarly, excluding negative sample augmentation also degrades performance, indicating that high-quality negative samples are essential for effective training and accurate representation learning. Among all components, the removal of the binary classifier causes the most significant performance decline. This highlights the importance of the classifier in dynamically determining whether a triple is suitable for enhanced inference, avoiding the drawbacks of applying a uniform enhancement strategy across all triples. Overall, these findings confirm that each component positively contributes to the CLEEF framework, with their combined effects leading to more reliable and robust link prediction performance.

Table 5. Ablation studies of CLEEF on FB15k-237 and WN18RR.

Method	FB15k-237				WN18RR			
	MRR	Hit@1	Hit@3	Hit@10	MRR	Hit@1	Hit@3	Hit@10
CLEEF-AnKGE-HAKE	**0.398**	**0.302**	0.440	0.581	0.513	0.465	**0.531**	**0.604**
CLEEF-AnKGE-HAKE *w/o fre*	0.388	0.290	0.431	0.575	0.501	0.458	0,525	0,591
CLEEF-AnKGE-HAKE *w/o neg*	0.385	0.289	0.429	0.570	0.500	0.455	0.522	0.589
CLEEF-AnKGE-HAKE *w/o ora*	0.376	0.280	0.417	0.560	0.499	0.453	0.515	0.587

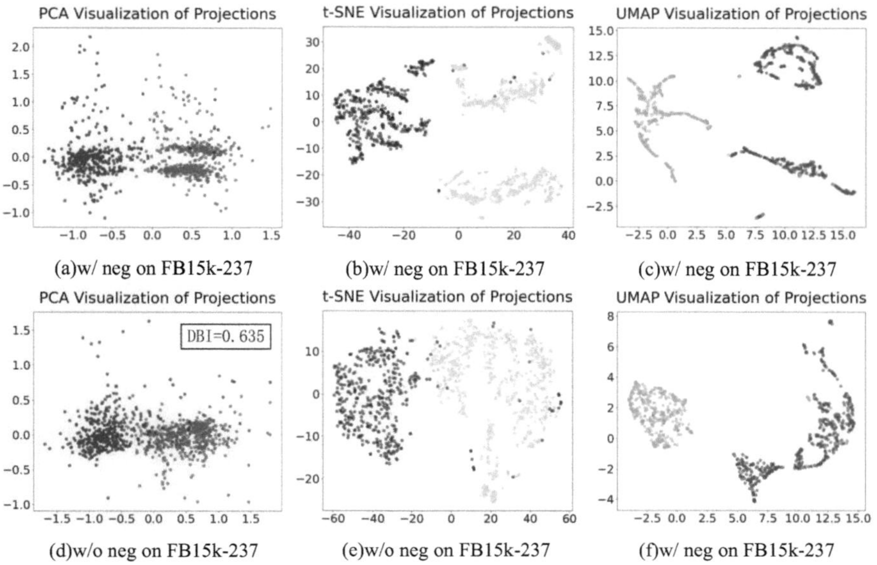

Fig. 4. PCA, t-SNE and UMAP visualizations of triple embeddings on FB15k-237 under different negative sampling settings. Points with the same color indicate triples assigned to the same inference mode.

4.5 Embedding Visualization (RQ4)

To analyze the effect of enhanced negative samples in the CLEEF framework, we visualize triple embeddings on FB15k-237 after contrastive learning using PCA, t-SNE and UMAP. We compare the distributions with and without enhanced negative samples (*w/o neg* and *w/ neg*), where different colors indicate two types of triples. As illustrated in Fig. 4, embeddings learned without enhanced negatives show loose structures and noticeable overlap between two triple types, which hinders their separation and weakens subsequent binary classification. When enhanced negative samples are introduced, the embeddings exhibit clearer inter-class separation. Although one triple type forms multiple sub-clusters, this phenomenon does not conflict with the task objective, which focuses on distinguishing between the two triple types rather than enforcing compact intra-class clustering. DBI scores are collected for both sample settings in the experiments. While the *w/o neg* case yields a lower DBI value, this metric fails to capture the improved discriminability observed in the *w/ neg* setting. The emergence of sub-clusters increases DBI, yet the separation between the two triple types is substantially strengthened, revealing the limitation of DBI in this scenario. Overall, these embedding visualizations indicate that enhanced negative samples reshape the embedding space by improving inter-class separability. Despite the imperfect alignment between clustering metrics and task objectives, the observed distributions provide clear evidence that CLEEF facilitates more stable and reliable adaptive enhancement.

5 Conclusion

This paper introduces CLEEF, a general framework based on contrastive learning for enhancing knowledge graph embeddings. By modeling the outputs of both base and enhanced models as complementary views of the same triple, CLEEF adaptively integrates different inference modes, thus avoiding indiscriminate enhancement. Experimental results on well-known benchmark datasets show that CLEEF can seamlessly integrate with a variety of embedding models and existing enhancement techniques, consistently yielding stable performance improvements. CLEEF provides a simple yet flexible solution for enhancing link prediction, and in future research directions CLEEF can be extended to larger knowledge graphs and other graph-based reasoning tasks.

Acknowledgments.. This work is supported by the National Natural Science Foundation of China (No. 62402064), the Hunan Provincial Key Research and Development Program (Nos. 2024JK2005 and 2026AQ2032), the Natural Science Foundation of Hunan Province, China, (Nos. 2023JJ30054 and 2026JJ81155), the Research Foundation of Education Bureau of Hunan Province, China, (No. 23B0303), the Postgraduate Practice Innovation Project of Changsha University of Science and Technology (No. CLSJCX25070).

References

1. Bansal, T., Juan, D., Ravi, S., McCallum, A.: A2N: attending to neighbors for knowledge graph inference. In: ACL, pp. 4387–4392 (2019)
2. Bordes, A., Usunier, N., García-Durán, A., Weston, J., Yakhnenko, O.: Translating embeddings for modeling multi-relational data. In: NIPS, pp. 2787–2795 (2013)
3. Cao, Z., Xu, Q., Yang, Z., Cao, X., Huang, Q.: Dual quaternion knowledge graph embeddings. In: AAAI, pp. 6894–6902 (2021)
4. Chao, L., He, J., Wang, T., Chu, W.: Pairre: Knowledge graph embeddings via paired relation vectors. In: ACL/IJCNLP, pp. 4360–4369 (2021)
5. Dettmers, T., Minervini, P., Stenetorp, P., Riedel, S.: Convolutional 2D knowledge graph embeddings, pp. 1811–1818 AAAI (2018)
6. Guo, W., Wang, X., Chen, J., Li, Z., Chen, Z.: Ontology-enhanced knowledge graph completion using large language models. In: ISWC, vol. 16140, pp. 61–80 (2025)
7. Li, J., et al.: Knowledge graph pooling and unpooling for concept abstraction. In: COLING, pp. 5364–5374 (Jan 2025)
8. Li, R., et al.: How does knowledge graph embedding extrapolate to unseen data: A semantic evidence view. In: AAAI, pp. 5781–5791 (2022)
9. Li, Z., Ao, Y., He, J.: Sphere: Expressive and interpretable knowledge graph embedding for set retrieval. In: SIGIR, pp. 2629–2634 (2024)
10. Liu, H., Wu, Y., Yang, Y.: Analogical inference for multi-relational embeddings. In: ICML, vol **70**, 2168–2178 (2017)
11. Long, X., Zhuang, L., Li, A., Wei, J., Li, H., Wang, S.: KGDM: A diffusion model to capture multiple relation semantics for knowledge graph embedding. In: AAAI, pp. 8850–8858 (2024)

12. Lu, Y., Yu, W., Jing, X., Yang, D.: Hypercl: A contrastive learning framework for hyper-relational knowledge graph embedding with hierarchical ontology. In: ACL, pp. 2918–2929 (2024)
13. Ma, C., Chen, Y., Wu, T., Khan, A., Wang, H.: Large language models meet knowledge graphs for question answering: Synthesis and opportunities. In: EMNLP, pp, 24578–24597 (2025)
14. Niu, G., Li, B., Zhang, Y., Pu, S.: CAKE: A scalable commonsense-aware framework for multi-view knowledge graph completion. In: ACL, pp. 2867–2877 (May 2022)
15. Schlichtkrull, M.S., Kipf, T.N., Bloem, P., van den Berg, R., Titov, I., Welling, M.: Modeling relational data with graph convolutional networks. In: ESWC, vol. 10843, pp. 593–607 (2018)
16. Song, T., Luo, J., Huang, L.: Rot-pro: Modeling transitivity by projection in knowledge graph embedding. In: NeurIPS, pp. 24695–24706 (2021)
17. Sun, Z., Deng, Z., Nie, J., Tang, J.: Rotate: Knowledge graph embedding by relational rotation in complex space. In: ICLR (2019)
18. Takamoto, M., Oñoro-Rubio, D., Rim, W.B., Maruyama, T., Kotnis, B.: Optimal embedding guided negative sample generation for knowledge graph link prediction. CoRR **abs/2504.03327** (2025)
19. Tang, Z., et al.: Positive-unlabeled learning with adversarial data augmentation for knowledge graph completion. In: IJCAI, pp. 2248–2254 (2022)
20. Trouillon, T., Welbl, J., Riedel, S., Gaussier, É., Bouchard, G.: Complex embeddings for simple link prediction. In: ICML, vol. 48, pp. 2071–2080 (2016)
21. Vashishth, S., Sanyal, S., Nitin, V., Talukdar, P.P.: Composition-based multi-relational graph convolutional networks. In: ICLR (2020)
22. Wang, H., et al.: Simple and effective relation-based embedding propagation for knowledge representation learning. In: IJCAI, pp. 2755–2761 (2022)
23. Wang, J., et al.: Improving the robustness of knowledge-grounded dialogue via contrastive learning. In: AAAI, pp. 19135–19143 (2024)
24. Wang, L., Zhao, W., Wei, Z., Liu, J.: SimKGC: Simple contrastive knowledge graph completion with pre-trained language models. ACL. pp, 4281–4294 (2022)
25. Xiong, B., et al.: Ultrahyperbolic knowledge graph embeddings. In: KDD, pp. 2130–2139 (2022)
26. Xu, Y., Ou, J., Xu, H., Fu, L.: Temporal knowledge graph reasoning with historical contrastive learning. In: AAAI, pp. 4765–4773 (2023)
27. Yang, B., Yih, W., He, X., Gao, J., Deng, L.: Embedding entities and relations for learning and inference in knowledge bases. In: ICLR (2015)
28. Yang, Y., Huang, C., Xia, L., Huang, C.: Knowledge graph self-supervised rationalization for recommendation. In: KDD, pp. 3046–3056 (2023)
29. Yao, Z., Zhang, W., Chen, M., Huang, Y., Yang, Y., Chen, H.: Analogical inference enhanced knowledge graph embedding. In: AAAI, pp. 4801–4808 (2023)
30. Zhang, Z., Cai, J., Zhang, Y., Wang, J.: Learning hierarchy-aware knowledge graph embeddings for link prediction. In: AAAI, pp. 3065–3072 (2020)

31. Zhu, T., Jung, M.C., Clark, J.: Generalized contrastive learning for multi-modal retrieval and ranking. In: WWW pp. 661–670 (2025)
32. Zhu, Y., Zhang, W., Liu, Z., Chen, M., Liang, L., Chen, H.: Croppable knowledge graph embedding. In: ACL, pp. 11818–11835 (2025)

Empower Label Propagation in Heterogeneous Information Networks

Keqi Zhou[1], Zhiqiong Wang[2], Jinyi Chen[1], Xian Zhang[1], and Junchang Xin[1,3(✉)]

[1] School of Computer Science and Engineering, Northeastern University, Shenyang 110819, China
{chenjinyi,zhangxian}@stumail.neu.edu.cn, xinjunchang@mail.neu.edu.cn
[2] College of Medicine and Biological Information Engineering, Northeastern University, Shenyang 110819, China
wangzq@bmie.neu.edu.cn
[3] Key Laboratory of Big Data Management and Analytics (Liaoning Province), Northeastern University, Shenyang, China

Abstract. As a particularly potential method to deal with complex information, the effective and stable label propagation algorithm is expected to handle heterogeneous information networks (HINs), which contain richer structures and more diversified information. Therefore, an empower HIN motif-aware label propagation method is proposed in this paper. Specifically, to improve the effectiveness, motifs are identified to capture higher-order relations among nodes of same type in HINs. And a topology enhancement method for HIN label propagation is studied, which combines motifs with the lower-order relations of HINs to fully utilize the networks' information. Additionally, the randomness of HIN label propagation is reduced by developing a novel label updating rule based on the influence of nodes and a node ranking method to identify the result more effectively and stably. Finally, comparative experiments and case study on multiple real-world HINs demonstrate the superiority and applicability of the proposed method in community detection, similarity search.

Keywords: Label propagation · Heterogeneous information networks · Higher-order · Motif · Stability

1 Introduction

Label propagation [22] is one of the powerful classic methods for vertex label inference in networks (or graphs). This algorithm is implemented through an iterative process of receiving the labels of adjacent vertices, updating its own labels, and feeding back new labels to its neighbors [31]. The label propagation method has become an important foundation for network structure analysis and has demonstrated significant advantages in multiple fields. A large number of studies [7,10,21,24] have been conducted on the label propagation of traditional

L. Ding et al. (Eds.): APWeb-WAIM 2026, LNCS 16995, pp. 167–183, 2027.
https://doi.org/10.1007/978-981-92-5699-0_11

homogeneous graphs, and all these methods are based on the same type of nodes. The label propagation method can effectively explain the composition, function of the network and the behavior of nodes in the network, and is applied in community detection, similarity search, etc.

Heterogeneous information networks (HINs) involve multiple object types and connectivity relationships [25], and can be used to model the relationships between different objects, such as bibliographic and business networks [30]. Figure 1a depicts a HIN of DBLP network, which represents the relationships between entities of different types including authors (i.e., $a_1, \cdots, a_4$), papers (i.e., $p_1, \cdots, p_4$), and conferences (i.e., c_1, c_2). Specifically, if an edge connects an author and a paper, it means the author wrote it. If an edge connects a paper and a conference, it means the paper was presented at the conference. Although the label propagation method has been widely applied in traditional homogeneous networks [11,18], it is not applicable to HINs that contain multiple types of nodes and edges. For example, in the HIN of DBLP network, it is difficult for two authors to be grouped into the same group due to the lack of direct connections. Furthermore, with the scale expansion of HINs, the processing requirements are demanding, and therefore, introducing efficient label propagation methods is critical. Therefore, studying the problem of label propagation over HINs is essential. Study [15] applies label propagation to HINs. Although the method based on label propagation has the characteristics of simplicity and efficiency, the high-order structural features in HINs are often ignored, and the instability problem of label propagation in HINs still needs to be solved urgently.

(a) HIN (b) Two meta-paths

Fig. 1. An example of HIN and its meta-paths

Studies have shown that higher-order connectivity patterns (e.g., motifs) are essential for understanding, controlling, and regulating the basic structural behavior of many complex systems [19,29]. In homogeneous networks, Li et al. proposed a weighted label propagation method by motifs to capture higher-order connectivity patterns [13]. However, motifs of traditional homogeneous graph structures are unsuitable for HINs. Liu et al. attempted to apply label propagation methods to community detection in HINs [15], but the method only focused on the lower-order structure of the networks (the connectivity between the same entity types through a meta-path), the connectivity revealed by the higher-order features is ignored. Defining motifs over HINs is nontrivial, since vertices of the same type (e.g., authors in the DBLP network) may not be connected directly. Spurred by the existing limitations, this paper introduces a topology enhancement method for HIN label propagation combining motif-based higher-order relations with lower-order relations of HINs.

In addition, the instability of label propagation is a major but unsolved issue in HINs [5]. Whether it is a traditional homogeneous network or HIN, the inherent randomness in the label propagation process will significantly affect the stability of the identified community structure. Therefore, under the same conditions, each label propagation may produce different results [1] due to the influence of random node update order and random tie-breaking. Thus, to solve the shortcomings of the label propagation method, Li et al. [10] determined the order of label updates by calculating the information transmission power of nodes. Reference [1] proposed a CSLPR algorithm based on node ranking to improve the certainty and stability of label propagation. Although the existing methods solve the instability problem of label propagation method in the homogeneous graphs, there is still a lack of effective strategies to improve the stability of label propagation in HINs.

Spurred by these concerns, this paper proposes an empower HIN motif-aware label propagation (HINMLP) method to label target type nodes with categories. Firstly, motifs are identified to capture higher-order relations among nodes of same type in HINs. Then, a topology enhancement method for HIN label propagation is studied. This new method explores and fully uses motif-based higher-order network features, effectively fuses lower-order and higher-order structural information to obtain a reweighted network, and performs label propagation on the newly obtained network. In addition to lower-order connectivities, higher-order connectivities can provide more information about the network structure. Then, the label propagation method is further optimized, aiming to solve the main shortcomings regarding the instability of label propagation in HINs. The proposed technique uses network topology to rank the importance of nodes before starting the label propagation. It then begins label propagation to the network's important nodes according to the nodes's ranking importance, improving the stability of the results. In addition, by integrating the degree of closeness between nodes and the influence of nodes into the label update process, the proposed model allows for effective and efficient label propagation. Finally, HINMLP is compared with other methods on the real-world HINs, and the advancement of the proposed method is verified.

The following is a summary of this study's main contributions:

1. Motifs are identified to capture higher-order relations among nodes of same type in HINs. Defining motify over HINs is nontrivial, since vertices of the same type may not be connected directly.
2. A topology enhancement method for HIN label propagation is proposed, which combines motifs with the lower-order relations of HINs. Various relationships among target objects and network topology information of HINs are fully utilized.

3. A novel label propagation strategy is proposed, which takes into account for the first time to reduce randomness of label propagation in HINs. We design a new label updating rule and combine node ranking in the process of propagation. While ensuring efficiency, the stability of label propagation is improved.
4. Comparative experiments and case study on DBLP, Yelp, ACM and DTI real-world HINs demonstrate that the performance of proposed HINMLP is significantly better than that of the other methods.

2 Preliminaries

In this paper, we study in HINs and introduce several concepts as follows.

Definition 1. HIN. An information network $G = \{V, E\}$ is a graph composed of the node (object) set V and edge (relation) set E. The node type mapping function is $\psi : V \rightarrow T$, and the edge type mapping function is $\tau : E \rightarrow R$. Each node $v \in V$ belongs to a specific node type $\psi(v) \in T$, and each edge $e \in E$ belongs to a specific edge type $\tau(e) \in R$. If the information network has a number of node types $|T| > 1$ or a number of edge types $|R| > 1$, then the information network is called a HIN.

Definition 2. HIN schema. Given a HIN $G = \{V, E\}$ with mappings $\psi : V \rightarrow T$ and $\tau : E \rightarrow R$, its schema S is a graph defined over node types T and edge types from R, i.e., $S = \{T, R\}$. The HIN schema shows all the allowable edge types between its node types.

Definition 3. Meta-path [25]**.** The meta-path P is a path $T_1 \xrightarrow{R_1} T_2 \xrightarrow{R_2} T_3 \cdots \xrightarrow{R_l} T_{l+1}$ defined on a HIN schema $S = \{T, R\}$, where l is the length of the meta-path. For example, path $a_1 \rightarrow p_1 \rightarrow c_1 \rightarrow p_2 \rightarrow a_3$ in Fig. 1 is a path instance of meta-path P_2=(APCPA).

In this paper, we aim to study label propagation in HINs, label specific type (called target type) nodes with categories and analyze clusters for vertices of target type. To connect two vertices with the target type, we adopt symmetric meta-paths. The main challenge of this problem lies in the heterogeneity of the network, making it difficult to directly apply the method of homogeneous networks. To maintain the adjacency between nodes of the same type, we define the concept of P-pair and P-Graph as follows.

Definition 4. *P*-pair. In HIN $G = \{V, E\}$, if nodes $u \in V$and $v \in V/u$ can be connected by a meta-path instance of P, then (u, v) is a P-pair or u and v are P-neighbors. Note that all the meta-paths mentioned in this paper are symmetric. For example, nodes a_1 and a_2 in Fig. 1 can be connected via a meta-path instance $a_1 \rightarrow p_1 \rightarrow c_1 \rightarrow p_3 \rightarrow a_2$ of meta-path P_2=(APCPA), and (a_1, a_2) is a P-pair.

Definition 5. *P*-Graph. Given a HIN G and a symmetric meta-path P, the P-graph is a homogeneous graph G_P so that each P-pair of G corresponds to an edge in G_P. Figure 2b illustrates the P_1-Graph of a HIN in Fig. 2a under the P_1=(APA) meta-path in Fig. 1b.

3 Proposed Methods

In this section, motifs are mined to capture higher-order relations among nodes of same type in HINs first. Then, a weighted network is reconstructed containing the higher- and lower-order topology structures to fully utilize HIN information. Second, to reduce the randomness of label propagation in HINs, a new label updating rule and a node ranking method are considered to divide the target node based on the reconstructed network.

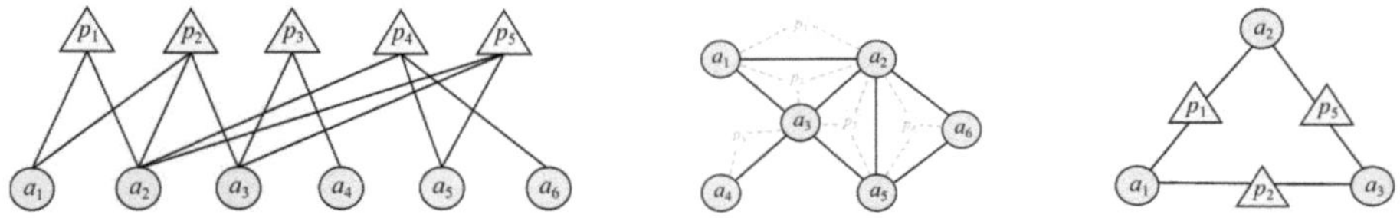

(a) Example of HIN (b) P_1-graph (c) Triangle

Fig. 2. The visualizations of construction process

3.1 Motif-Based Higher-Order Structure Mining in HINs

The similarity matrix is calculated based on the meta-path, and the motif-based hypergraph is constructed using triangle motifs. Then, a new network containing the higher- and lower-order topology structure of HIN is reconstructed by combining the hypergraph and similarity matrix.

The similarity in network construction affects label the target node in the HINs. If there are more instances of meta-path between two target nodes, the two target nodes are always more similar and more likely to be placed in the same cluster. Therefore, this paper measures the similarity of target nodes based on meta-path counting. Precisely, given a meta-path P, to calculate the similarity between target nodes, the counting-based similarity matrix of a meta-path is computed using the commuting matrix [25]. In the DBLP network, as depicted in Fig. 1a, A, P, and C are different node types. Assuming all authors A are regarded as target node types, the meta path is P_2, as illustrated in Fig. 1b. The matrix W_{AP} is a weighted adjacency matrix constructed based on A-type and P-type nodes, and the weighted adjacency matrices W_{PC}, W_{CP}, and W_{PA} are built similarly. Finally, the commuting matrix $W_P = W_{AP}W_{PC}W_{CP}W_{PA}$ based on P_2=(APCPA) is obtained, where $(W_P)_{ij}$ represents the number of meta-path instances connecting any two type A nodes. The commuting matrix reflects the connectivity information of the original lower-order topology in the HINs. By calculating the similarities between the target nodes of type A along meta path P_2, a similarity matrix R_P can be obtained. Similarly, similarity matrices of other meta-paths can be calculated using this method.

Motif plays a crucial role in revealing the networks's structure [19], and therefore, it is necessary and essential to mine higher-order structures based on motifs.

This paper suggests obtaining a triangle extension by replacing the edge with a P-pair in HINs. Precisely, given a meta-path P, if two of the three nodes form a P-pair, then the three nodes form a triangle. For example, in the HIN of Fig. 2a, a_1, a_2, and a_3 regarding P_1=(APA) form a triangle in Fig. 2c because any two are P_1-pair. This indicates that a_1, a_2, and a_3 have a solid social relationship, thus providing more information for label nodes. A triangle consisting of a_1, a_2, and a_3 can be generalized to a triangle motif, which is a higher-order structure composed of multiple nodes. Triangle motifs naturally exist in real-world networks (especially social networks) and have several advantages when establishing the structural characteristics of HIN: (1)Strong local connections can be captured, and the triangle indicates that three nodes are closely connected and stable, suggesting a greater degree of influence and trust. (2)Compared with larger motifs, triangle motifs have higher computational efficiency and require less computing power for analysis. (3)The triangle motif represents the characteristics of HIN at a higher level, reducing the gap between global and local characteristics. The triangle motif is defined as follows.

Definition 6. Triangle motif. Given a HIN and a meta-path P, if any two of the three nodes u, v, and w form a P-pair, then the three nodes (u, v, w) form a triangle motif M.

For nodes of a particular type T_i, a G_P can be obtained under a meta-path P; that is, for each P-pair in the HIN, an edge is added between the two nodes. Thus, the triangles in each G_P correspond to the triangle motifs in the HIN. By introducing the triangle motif adjacency matrix W_M [3] to represent the triangle motif-based hypergraph, which emphasizes the higher-order connectivity between nodes, W_M can be calculated as follows:

$$W_M(i,j) = \sum_{i,j \in V, \psi(i)=\psi(j)=T_i} 1(i,j \ occur \ in \ M) \quad (1)$$

The weight of $W_M(i,j)$ represents the number of instances of the triangle motif M containing both node i and node j $(i \neq j)$, and W_M is a weighted matrix. The greater the edge weights, the closer the connectivity between the nodes. Figure 3 presents the calculation process based on a triangle motif hypergraph. The edge connecting nodes a_2 and a_3, and the edge connecting nodes a_2 and a_5 are contained in two triangle motifs, so their weights in W_M are 2. The edge connecting nodes a_3 and a_4 is not contained in any triangle motif, while the remaining edges are contained in one triangle motif, giving them the weight of 1 in W_M.

A similar matrix R_P containing the original lower-order topology must be embedded to avoid isolated nodes in the higher-order connectivity pattern based on the triangle motif adjacency matrix. So, the new weighted network is redesigned. For each meta-path P, a new weighted network W_P^M is obtained by embedding W_M into R_P. It should be noted that W_P^M fully considers the structural information between nodes, i.e., the higher- and lower-order topology of HIN. The weight of $W_P^M(i,j)$ measures the closeness between nodes i and j.

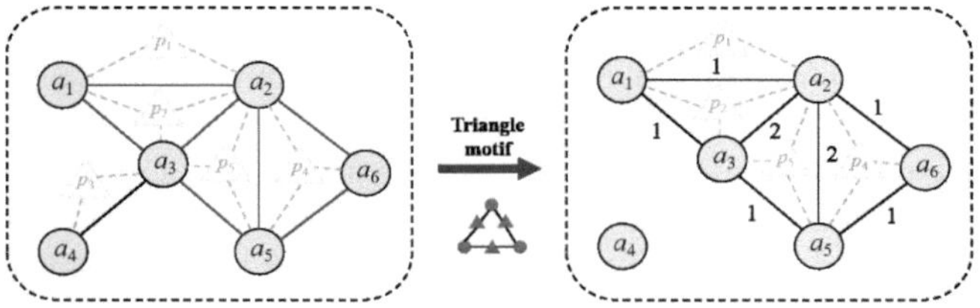

Fig. 3. Construction of the triangle motif-based hypergraph

Given that the greater the weight, the more intimate the two target objects are, the weight of edge should be considered when performing label propagation.

3.2 Empower HIN Label Propagation Strategy

HIN Label propagation is carried out after obtaining the new weighted network W_P^M to label the target nodes. To solve the instability of the label propagation method in HINs, nodes are sorted according to topological features in the pre-processing stage of the proposed method. In study [1], the authors pointed out that communities are formed around important nodes, and low-importance nodes select their suitable communities over time in existing social networks. Therefore, the proposed method updates labels in ascending order of target node importance. Our method employs RDC (Ranking by Degree and being the Core) local sorting to consider the structure features of the new weighted network. Then, according to the order, label propagation starts from low-importance target nodes to high-importance target nodes.

Each target node will receive several labels from its neighbors in the new weighted network W_P^M during label propagation, and deciding which label to use is critical. Current label propagation methods assume that nodes directly accept their neighbors' labels during label propagation. However, influential nodes are more likely to spread to their neighbors and receive relatively weak influence from other nodes [2]. Therefore, the influential nodes are more important, while the weak nodes have no impact. For instance, an internet celebrity has a more substantial effect on the masses, so it is imperative to identify the influence of nodes in the network. The node degree of the reconstructed weighted network is used as the node's influence, reflecting the degree centrality of the lower- and higher-order topologies while having lower computational complexity than other algorithms. Formula (2) calculates the impact degree of node u on v, that is, the acceptance degree of v from u, where $d(u)$ is the degree of u in W_P^M.

$$D_{v \leftarrow u} = \frac{d(u)}{d(u) + d(v)} \tag{2}$$

During the label initialization phase, each node is assigned a unique label, using the number of the graph node as the initial node label. Reference [13] points out that synchronous update strategy is prone to label oscillation, especially in bipartite networks. Therefore, this paper adopts the asynchronous update mode. Specifically, when performing label selection, the connectivity strength between the two target objects and the acceptance degree of the label are considered. This is achieved by assigning vote scores to the neighbors' labels that affect the node's label update. Firstly, the nodes with the same label l in the neighbors of node v are computed as follows:

$$\Gamma(v,l) = \{x | x \in \Gamma(v) \wedge L(x) = l\} \tag{3}$$

where $\Gamma(v)$ is the set of neighbors of node v, and $L(x)$ is the label of node x. Suppose that j neighbors of node v with label l are got and the j neighbors are $n_0, n_1, \cdots, n_{j-1}$. The voting score of label l is:

$$S_l(v) = \sum_{t=0}^{j-1} (W_P^M)_{v,n_t} D_{v \leftarrow n_t} \tag{4}$$

where $(W_P^M)_{v,n_t}$ represents the weight of an edge between nodes v and n_t, which is used to measure the closeness between nodes v and n_t, and $D_{v \leftarrow n_t}$ is the label acceptance degree of node v from the neighbor node n_t. After obtaining all adjacent node labels of the target node and the corresponding voting values of these labels, each target node selects the label with the highest score as the new label. For example, target node's label is updated in the new weighted network in Fig. 4. The orange nodes have label X, the green nodes have label Y. The proposed algorithm selects the label of node a_4 by computing the voting score of the label of connect neighbors to the node a_4, $S_X(a_4) = 3 * 0.43 + 1 * 0.2 = 1.49$, $S_Y(a_4) = 3 * 0.33 + 4 * 0.33 = 2.31$(reserve two decimal fractions). Therefore, node a_4 selects label Y due to higher score than other.

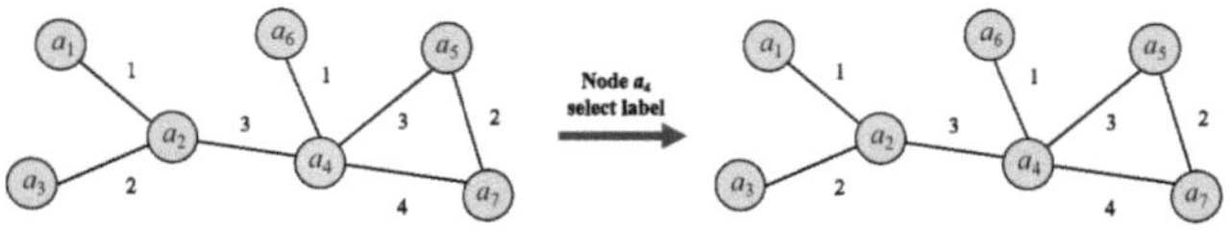

Fig. 4. Calculating the label voting score of node a_4

Algorithm 1 presents the proposed label propagation method in HINs. Each node is assigned an initial label with its number, t is the number of iterations (line 1), and a new weighted graph W_P^M (line 2) for the specified meta-path is obtained using the method mentioned above. The importance of nodes is ranked using RDC, and label propagation starts from the low-importance nodes according to the ranking (line 3). The voting scores of the neighbors' labels that affect the node's label update are calculated according to equations (3) and (4). The most suitable label, which has the maximum voting score, is selected for updating the node label (lines 7-8). When the label of each node in the network no longer changes or the maximum number of iterations T is reached, the label propagation stops. When the label propagation terminates, the labels can detect the cluster structure, and every connected subgraph structure that shares the same label is considered a cluster. In some cases, target nodes in HINs are connected through multiple meta-paths. Thus, to evaluate the various relationships among target nodes, consensus clustering, and aggregation [8] are used to detect groups. The weighted networks of multiple meta-paths are detected respectively, and then the aggregation concept is further introduced to construct the consensus graph based on various groups. Finally, label propagation is rerun on the consensus graph to obtain the final clusters. In summary, the proposed method can obtain more stable and accurate results than the primary label propagation method.

Algorithm 1: HIN Label propagation strategy

Input: HIN $G(V, E)$, target node type T_h, the meta-path P, the maximum number of iterations T

Output: Label assignment vector ξ of target nodes

Initialize the label assignment vector: $\xi^{(t)}(i) = i, \forall i \in \{1, 2, \cdots, n\}$ and set $t = 0$;

Obtain the re-weighted network W_P^M;

vQueue $\leftarrow$ Nodes are sorted according to the ascending order of importance RDC;

while $t < T$ **do**

    $t \leftarrow t + 1$;

    for *node* $i \in$ *vQueue* **do**

        Calculate a value for every obtained label according to equations (3) and (4);

        Choose the most suitable label l as its new label, $\xi^{(t)}(i) \leftarrow l$;

    if $\xi^{(t)}(i) = \xi^{(t-1)}(i), \forall i \in \{1, 2, \cdots, n\}$ **then**

        break;

Obtain label assignment vector $\xi = \xi^{(t)}$;

return Label assignment vector ξ of target nodes ;

Complexity. Let n and m be the number of nodes and edges respectively, k be the average degree of nodes. The time complexity of sorting nodes and calculating influence is $O(kn)$. The time complexity of label propagation is approximately linearly distributed, assuming the number of iterations is T. Thus, the time complexity of the proposed HIN Label propagation method is $O(Tm + kn)$.

4 Experiments

In this section, the HINMLP method is compared with the baseline methods on real-wold datasets to demonstrate the performance of HINMLP method in various evaluation metrics. Furthermore, a case study was conducted to verify the effectiveness of the proposed method.

4.1 Data Description

The proposed method is evaluated on four datasets [9,28] as follows. Their statistics such as the vertex types and edge types are reported in Table 1.

DBLP. The HIN generated based on DBLP includes author name (A), conference name (C), and paper title (P). These objects are regarded as HIN nodes. The authors (target nodes) are labeled with categories considering the meta-paths A-P-A and A-P-C-P-A.

Yelp. This is a business recommendation service company, and a HIN that includes user (U), business (B), and service (S) is generated. These objects are regarded as HIN nodes. The businesses (target nodes) are labeled with categories considering the meta-paths B-U-B and B-S-B.

ACM. The HIN established based on ACM includes three types of nodes: author (A), paper (P), and subject (S). The papers (target nodes) are labeled with categories considering meta-paths P-A-P and P-S-P.

DTI. This drug-target interaction HIN without true category labels was randomly selected from the data of the drug-target sharing platform [26]. The sample dataset mainly contains two types of node drug (D) and target (T). The drugs (target nodes) are labeled with categories considering meta-path D-T-D.

Table 1. Datasets used in our experiments

Dataset	Node type	Edge type	Meta-path
DBLP	Author (A) Paper (P) Conference (C)	Author - Paper Paper - Conference	APA APCPA
Yelp	User (U) Business (B) Service (S)	Business - User Business - Servicer	BUB BSB
ACM	Author (A) Paper (P) Subject (S)	Paper - Author Paper - Subject	PAP PSP
DTI	Drug (D) Target (T)	Drug - Target	DTD

4.2 Baselines and Evaluation Metrics

Four comparison methods have been adopted to evaluate the advancement of the HINMLP method. (1) HINLPClus [15] is the latest label propagation method in HINs. (2) SClump [14] is based on spectral clustering, which maps each target object to a vector and then performs clustering based on these vectors. (3) MWLP [13] is a label propagation method and we adopt the label updating rule of MWLP. (4) Mp2vec++ (shorthands for metapath2vec++) [6] is network embedding methods for HINs that use meta-paths.

The evaluation process adopted is as follows: (1) Three evaluation metrics verify the effectiveness of HINMLP by Purity [23], normalized mutual information (NMI) [16] and adjusted rand index (ARI) [4]. (2) The running time is compared to verify the efficiency. (3) The stability is evaluated using standard deviation. (4) Modularity [20] is used to measure the cluster quality.

4.3 Effectiveness and Efficiency Study

Against Baseline Algorithms. The HINLPClus, SClump, MWLP, Mp2 vec++ and HINMLP methods are run on the DBLP, Yelp and ACM datasets. The corresponding Purity, NMI, and ARI comparison results are presented in Fig. 5a-5c, respectively. In addition, the running time is tested and compared in Fig. 5d, where each final run time presented is the average.

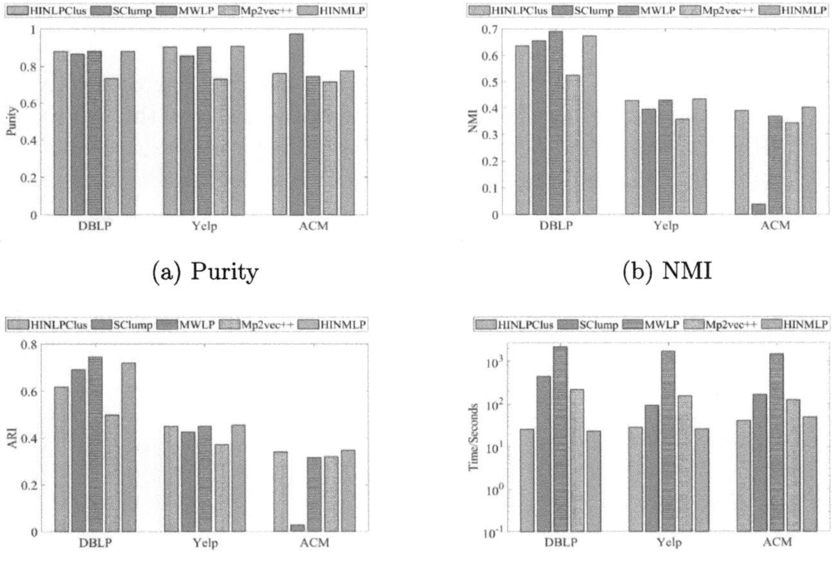

(a) Purity

(b) NMI

(c) ARI

(d) Running time

Fig. 5. Performance comparison of different methods in real-world networks

Figure 5a-5c highlights that the evaluation metrics of the HINMLP method are the best. However, there are special cases that require further explanation. For ACM, although the Purity value of the SClump method is higher than that of other methods, the NMI and ARI values are very low, indicating that the result is not close to the real category. For Yelp, since the number of nodes passed by the target nodes connected through the meta-path is too small, the target nodes may form connected components when they form a new weighted network. Hence, the difference in the experimental results is not apparent. However, the stability of the HINMLP method is better, (see Sect. 4.4). Although the proposed HINMLP method does not provide the best results in all real-world datasets, it achieves the best overall performance.

Figure 5d illustrates the processing time of the above methods, demonstrating that the running time of HINMLP method is the shortest. The running time of HINLPClus is also relatively short because it mainly depends on the convergence rate of the label propagation process, which is very fast. It can be found that although the MWLP method has better performance on DBLP, the running time is too long. This is because MWLP requires a lot of time to calculate the vote score when performing label selection, thus, the running time is higher than that of the other methods. Overall, Purity, NMI, ARI, and running time demonstrate that the HINMLP method can achieve higher precision and efficiency.

Ablation Analysis. In order to further verify the advancement of proposed method, ablation experiments are conducted on DBLP, HINMLP is compared against its variants. Specifically, HINMLP-No does not integrate triangle motif-based higher-order connectivities or include the impact between nodes in the label selection. HINMLP-Mo only considers higher-order connectivities, HINMLP-P only incorporates the impact between nodes into the label selection, and HINMLP considers both. The corresponding results are depicted in Fig. 6. It highlights that although HINMLP-No has a higher Purity than the other methods, the NMI and ARI are lower. Moreover, the result is not close to the real categories. In contrast, all evaluation metrics of HINMLP provide the best overall performance, demonstrating that its improvements combined with higher-order connectivities based on the triangle motif are effective, and it is necessary to incorporate the impact between nodes into the label selection.

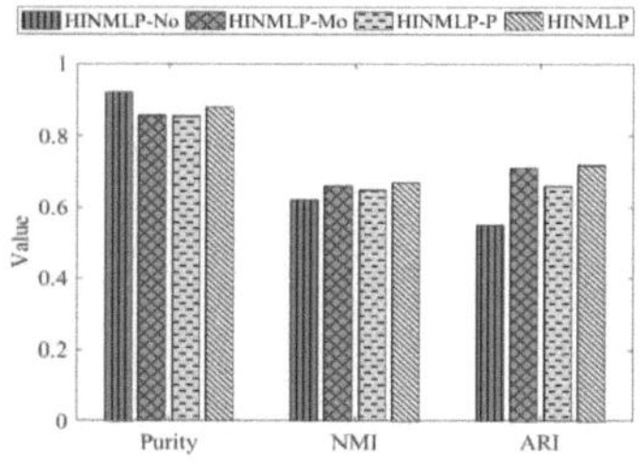

Fig. 6. Comparison variants

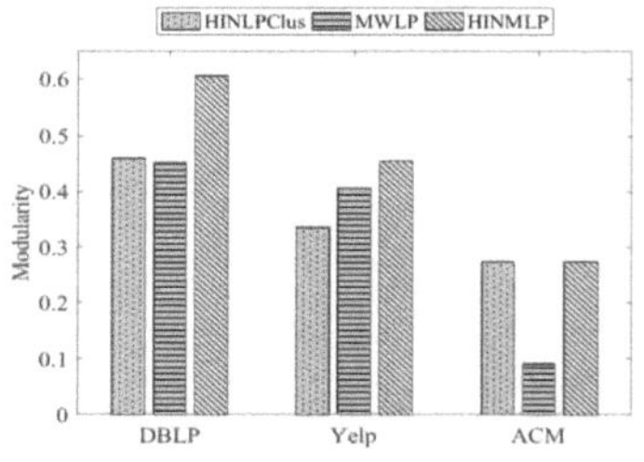

Fig. 7. Modularity comparison

4.4 The Comparison on Stability and Quality

In order to verify that the HINMLP method can reduce the inherent instability of the label propagation method, HINLPClus, MWLP, and HINMLP are adopted and repeated 20 times on the three real datasets. Standard deviation (SD) is used to evaluate stability, with a smaller SD demonstrating better stability. The SD results (the SD values are reserved to four decimal places) for Purity, NMI, and ARI on DBLP, Yelp, and ACM are reported in Table 2, respectively.

Table 2 reveal that the SD value of the HINMLP method is better than other methods based on label propagation, which indicates that HINMLP is the most stable among the competitor methods. This is because HINMLP defines an explicit node update order when node labels are updated, thus improving stability. Moreover, it is found that the neighbor nodes of a node have different impacts on the label update of the node. Therefore, the new voting strategy reduces the probability of the same node's voting score and overcomes the randomness of label propagation. In summary, HINMLP has higher stability.

Modularity measures the quality of community in the networks. Figure 7 presents the modularity values of all competitor methods based on label propagation, revealing that, HINMLP obtains significantly better community quality on real datasets.

Table 2. SD results of different methods in real-world networks

	Purity			NMI			ARI		
Method	DBLP	Yelp	ACM	DBLP	Yelp	ACM	DBLP	Yelp	ACM
HINLPClus	0.0258	0.0000	0.0076	0.0369	0.0002	0.0061	0.0818	0.0002	0.0032
MWLP	0.0000	0.0004	0.0121	0.0002	0.0004	0.0094	0.0001	0.0002	0.0054
HINMLP	0.0000	0.0000	0.0000	0.0000	0.0000	0.0001	0.0000	0.0000	0.0000

4.5 Case Study and Visualization

DTI is a Drug-Target Interaction HIN. We verify the effectiveness of the proposed method in this paper through case studies on the DTI dataset. Three cases were selected from the relevant drugs for research, and the similarities between the query node and other nodes with the same label were determined based on pathsim.

Table 3 lists the three queried drugs and the top five most similar drugs, and the similarity measurement scores among them. Take the query of drug with the number 801 as an example, the first five drug nodes corresponding to 801 in the table all act on the target node with the number 4471 in practical applications. For the top two drug nodes, they still act on the target node with the number 4446 simultaneously. Similar results can also be obtained when querying other drug nodes.

Table 3. Case study of similarity search in DTI Data

	2759		801		832	
Rank	Drug	Score	Drug	Score	Drug	Score
1	907	1.0	2810	1.0	1568	1.0
2	879	1.0	2012	1.0	1570	1.0
3	2360	1.0	2909	0.67	2596	1.0
4	482	0.8	606	0.67	775	1.0
5	2097	0.67	824	0.67	1101	1.0

Figure 8a to 8c respectively show the subgraphs composed of query nodes 2759, 801, and 832, the corresponding drug nodes labeled in the same category by the proposed method in this paper. In the graphs, each edge corresponds to a P-pair, indicating the connection between drug nodes through the meta-path D-T-D, that is, the drug nodes have common interaction target nodes. By observation, it can be seen that the nodes in the figure form tight connections, and have a more stable structure. Meanwhile, Sects. 4.3 and 4.4 prove the superiority of the method proposed in this paper, which can effectively and efficiently detect communities.

Therefore, the result of labeling node categories by the HIN label propagation method proposed in this paper can find drugs with similar effects in practical applications, assist in the query of similar nodes and identify a better and more stable community structure.

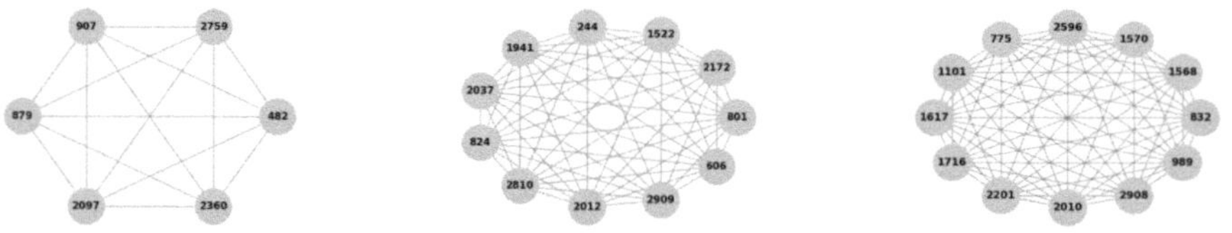

(a) Subgraph of 2759 (b) Subgraph of 801 (c) Subgraph of 832

Fig. 8. The visualizations of network detected by HINMLP

5 Related Work

Motif in Graphs. Initially introduced in [19], motifs represent higher-order relationships in homogeneous graphs. These local connectivity patterns, which occur frequently, are instrumental in generating varied clustering results at a global scale. Research in complex networks extends beyond lower-order to high-order network features, thereby garnering significant attention for motif-based features [27,29]. Li et al. [11] have explored higher-order topologies through extracting network motifs, which facilitates improved cluster in networks. In reference [12], a novel edge enhancement method for motif-aware community detection was introduced, enhancing the performance of state-of-the-art techniques. Madhulika et al. [18] proposed the H-LPMC method, which combines the high-order structure of motif with the initial topology, improving the accuracy of label-based community detection. However, most existing methods concentrate on homogeneous networks with same type vertices, neglecting the heterogeneity in HINs.

Label Propagation. Originally introduced in reference [22], the label propagation method has garnered considerable attention due to its near-linear time complexity. Despite its popularity, label propagation inherently suffers from instability. Recent advancements aim to mitigate the limitation. Specifically, Liu et al. [17] have developed a community detection strategy that integrates the influence of seed nodes with neighborhood similarity to enhance the stability. Study [1] proposed a method based on the node ranking to improve the stability of the label propagation. These improvements have traditionally focused on homogeneous networks. Addressing HINs, Liu et al. [15] have proposed a community detection method utilizing label propagation. Despite these advancements, the instability issue of label propagation in HINs remains unresolved. This paper explores effective strategies to improve the stability of label propagation in HINs.

6 Conclusion

This paper studies an effective, efficient, and stable HINMLP method for HINs. First, motifs are identified to capture higher-order relations among nodes of same type in HINs. Second, a topology enhancement method is proposed by integrating motifs with the original network and considering various relationships between the target objects. This way, the network structure is observed from lower- and higher-order perspectives to enhance topological information usage. Then, to overcome the instability of label propagation methods in HINs, the importance of nodes is sorted, and the connectivity strength and the influence of nodes are integrated into the label updating rule. Finally, the experimental results show that HINMLP is superior to the competitor methods regarding several quality metrics and running time. Meanwhile, HINMLP can effectively reduce instability in the label propagation process.

Acknowledgments. The work is supported by National Natural Science Foundation of China (62432003, 92567205) and the Fundamental Research Funds for the Central Universities (N25BJD013).

Disclosure of Interests. The authors declare that they have no known competing interests that could have appeared to influence the work reported in this paper.

References

1. Aghaalizadeh, S., Afshord, S.T., Bouyer, A., Anari, B.: Improving the stability of label propagation algorithm by propagating from low-significance nodes for community detection in social networks. Computing **104**(1), 21–42 (2022)
2. Aral, S., Walker, D.: Identifying influential and susceptible members of social networks. Science **337**(6092), 337–341 (2012)
3. Bedi, P., Sharma, C.: Community detection in social networks. WIREs Data Mining Knowl. Discov. **6**(3), 115–135 (2016)
4. Benson, A.R., Gleich, D.F., Leskovec, J.: Higher-order organization of complex networks. Science **353**(6295), 163–166 (2016)
5. Berahmand, K., Bouyer, A.: LP-LPA: A link influence-based label propagation algorithm for discovering community structures in networks. Int. J. Mod. Phys. B **32**(06), 1850062 (2018)
6. Dong, Y., Chawla, N.V., Swami, A.: metapath2vec: Scalable representation learning for heterogeneous networks. In: SIGKDD, pp. 135–144. ACM (2017)
7. Ge, Z., Yang, Y., Du, Z.: Integrated self-supervised label propagation for label imbalanced sets. Appl. Intell. **54**(17–18), 8525–8544 (2024)
8. Hmimida, M., Kanawati, R.: Community detection in multiplex networks: a seed-centric approach. Netw. Heterogeneous Media **10**(1), 71–85 (2015)
9. Hu, B., Fang, Y., Shi, C.: Adversarial learning on heterogeneous information networks. In: SIGKDD, pp. 120–129 (2019)
10. Li, C., Chen, H., Li, T., Yang, X.: A stable community detection approach for complex network based on density peak clustering and label propagation. Appl. Intell. **52**(2), 1188–1208 (2022)
11. Li, C., Tang, Y., Tang, Z., Cao, J., Zhang, Y.: Motif-based embedding label propagation algorithm for community detection. Int. J. Intell. Syst. **37**(3), 1880–1902 (2022)
12. Li, P.Z., Huang, L., Wang, C.D., Lai, J.H.: Edmot: An edge enhancement approach for motif-aware community detection. In: SIGKDD, pp. 479–487 (2019)
13. Li, P., Huang, L., Wang, C., Lai, J., Huang, D.: Community detection by motif-aware label propagation. ACM Trans. Knowl. Discov. Data **14**(2), 22:1–22:19 (2020)
14. Li, X., Kao, B., Ren, Z., Yin, D.: Spectral clustering in heterogeneous information networks, pp. 4221–4228. AAAI Press (2019)
15. Liu, D., Li, L.: A label propagation based node clustering algorithm in heterogeneous information networks. IEEE Access **9**, 132631–132640 (2021)
16. Liu, L., Xu, L., Wangy, Z., Chen, E.: Community detection based on structure and content: A content propagation perspective. In: IEEE International Conference on Data Mining, pp. 271–280 (2015)
17. Liu, M., Yang, J., Guo, J., Chen, J.: A label propagation community discovery algorithm combining seed node influence and neighborhood similarity. Knowl. Inf. Syst. **66**(4), 2625–2649 (2024)
18. Madhulika, K., Sabharwal, P., S.: Hybrid label propagation based on motifs and similarity measures for community detection. Knowl. Inf. Syst. **67**(11), 10989–11014 (2025)
19. Milo, R., Shen-Orr, S., Itzkovitz, S., Kashtan, N., Chklovskii, D., Alon, U.: Network motifs: simple building blocks of complex networks. Science **298**(5594), 824–827 (2002)

20. Newman, M.E.J., Girvan, M.: Finding and evaluating community structure in networks. Phys. Rev. E **69**(2 Pt 2), 026113 (2004)
21. Ni, Q., Wang, J., Tang, Z.: Degree and betweenness-based label propagation for community detection. J. Comb. Optim. **49**(2), 21 (2025)
22. Raghavan, U.N., Albert, R., Kumara, S.: Near linear time algorithm to detect community structures in large-scale networks. Phys. Rev. E-Stat., Nonlinear, Soft Matter Phys. **76**(3), 036106 (2007)
23. Sahoo, N., Callan, J., Krishnan, R., Duncan, G., Padman, R.: Incremental hierarchical clustering of text documents. In: Proceedings of the 15th ACM International Conference on Information and Knowledge Management, pp. 357–366 (2006)
24. Sun, L.: Density peaks clustering based on label propagation and k-mutual-nearest neighbors. IEEE Trans. Emerg. Topics Comput. Intell. **9**(2), 1830–1842 (2025)
25. Sun, Y., Han, J., Yan, X., Yu, P.S., Wu, T.: Pathsim: meta path-based top-k similarity search in heterogeneous information networks. Proc. VLDB Endow. **4**(11), 992–1003 (2011)
26. Tang, J., Tanoli, Z.U.R., Ravikumar, B., Alam, Z., Aittokallio, T.: Drug target commons: a community effort to build a consensus knowledge base for drug-target interactions. Cell Chem. Biol. **25**(2), 224-229.e2 (2018)
27. Teng, X., Luo, X., Liu, J.: Transcending modularity: a memetic algorithm combining triangle motif and edge information for community detection. Appl. Soft Comput. **175**, 113082 (2025)
28. Wang, X., et al.: Heterogeneous graph attention network. In: The World Wide Web Conference, pp. 2022–2032 (2019)
29. Yang, S., Xiao, R.: Enhancing the global and local robustness of networks: a network motif-based approach. Commun. Nonlinear Sci. Numer. Simul. **140**, 108439 (2025)
30. Yang, Y., Fang, Y., Lin, X., Zhang, W.: Effective and efficient truss computation over large heterogeneous information networks. In: ICDE, pp. 901–912 (2020)
31. Zhang, W., Shang, R., Jiao, L.: Large-scale community detection based on core node and layer-by-layer label propagation. Inf. Sci. **632**, 1–18 (2023)

FedSketchFair: Efficient and Fair Federated Learning Under Domain Skew via Sketch-Based Aggregation

Yuheng Chen, Meifan Zhang(✉), and Lihua Yin

Cyberspace Institute of Advanced Technology, Guangzhou University, Guangzhou, China
2112433018@e.gzhu.edu.cn, {zhangmf,yinlh}@gzhu.edu.cn

Abstract. Federated learning often encounters domain skew, where clients share a common task but draw data from different distributions. To achieve balanced performance across domains, recent approaches adopt consistency-aware aggregation. This strategy filters conflicting updates based on directional alignment and weights client contributions using geometric distances. However, these geometric evaluations require preserving both gradient directions and magnitudes. Transmitting full-precision models incurs high communication costs. Traditional compression methods such as quantization or sparsification lose magnitudes or disrupt coordinates, which harms the geometric fidelity needed for fairness. To address this limitation, we propose FedSketchFair, which selectively compresses large layers via Count Sketch, a hash-based linear data structure that preserves L_2 norms and inner products in expectation. The fixed-size structure keeps updates from different clients aligned in the compressed space. This allows the server to track directional consistency through gradient signs, estimate distances, and perform aggregation directly without decompression. To reduce the noise introduced by sketching, we keep small layers with fewer parameters uncompressed and apply parameter-level consistency filtering. Experiments on PACS, Office-Caltech, and DomainNet show that FedSketchFair achieves balanced per-domain accuracy and remains competitive with uncompressed baselines under strict communication budgets.

Keywords: Federated learning · Fairness · Gradient compression · Count Sketch · Domain skew

1 Introduction

Federated learning with heterogeneous data often encounters domain skew when clients share a learning task but sample from different underlying distributions. Standard aggregation algorithms can bias the global model toward majority domains, degrading performance on minority ones. We focus on domain fairness, where the goal is to reduce performance imbalance across domains without sacrificing communication efficiency.

L. Ding et al. (Eds.): APWeb-WAIM 2026, LNCS 16995, pp. 184–198, 2027.
https://doi.org/10.1007/978-981-92-5699-0_12

Mitigating domain skew relies on evaluating the geometric relationships between client updates. Specifically, the server must enforce update consistency by filtering conflicting gradient directions to prevent cancellation, and estimate how different the updates are by measuring distances between updates to dynamically balance client influence. While tracking gradient directions requires stable gradient signs, estimating client divergence relies heavily on preserving these geometric metrics, particularly L_2 norms and inner products. For example, FedHeal [6] uses millions of uncompressed parameters to compute exact distances, which supports fairness-aware aggregation but incurs substantial communication (392 MB per round for VGG19 [18]).

To address this communication bottleneck, conventional works apply quantization [1] or sparsification [18]. However, these traditional compression strategies fail to simultaneously satisfy the requirements of consistency-aware aggregation. Aggressive quantization, such as 1-bit signSGD, discards relative magnitudes. This forces a choice between transmitting massive models to compute fairness metrics or applying compression that damages geometric fidelity.

We leverage Count Sketch [4], a fixed-size probabilistic data structure that uses randomized linear projections. Unlike conventional compression, Count Sketch preserves inner products and L_2 norms in expectation, providing a statistical basis for estimating distances. Its linearity and uniform size also keep updates from different clients aligned in the compressed space. This combination enables the server to track sign consistency and estimate distances in the compressed domain, allowing a tunable trade-off between accuracy and communication cost.

We propose **FedSketchFair**, a unified framework that combines sketch-based compression with consistency-aware aggregation to selectively filter conflicting client updates in the compressed domain. To balance efficiency and precision, our framework applies Count Sketch only to large layers. We keep small layers with fewer parameters uncompressed because they are more sensitive to noise, as shown in SK-Gradient [9]. The server then tracks gradient alignment with a new metric called Sign Update Consistency (SUC). We use update signs as a consistency proxy: a unit whose sign agrees with its historical majority direction is treated as more stable, while oscillating directions are filtered. We track SUC at two granularities: cell-level (referring to the individual entries in the sketch table) for sketched large layers, and parameter-level for uncompressed small layers. Distance estimation and masked weighting for large layers also happen in the compressed domain, without reconstructing full-precision updates. This design reduces communication while keeping the information needed for domain fairness.

The contributions of this paper are summarized as follows:

- **A Sketch-Based Framework for Fair FL.** We propose FedSketchFair, a unified framework that enables consistency-aware aggregation under strict communication constraints without reconstructing full-precision gradients.
- **Compressed-Domain Fairness.** We design compressed-domain fairness mechanisms, incorporating cell- and parameter-level SUC, mask-based fil-

tering, and distance-based weighting, that operate without accessing full-precision updates.
- **Evaluation across Heterogeneous Domains.** Experiments on PACS, Office-Caltech, and DomainNet show that FedSketchFair improves worst-domain performance while maintaining overall accuracy under matched communication budgets.

2 Related Work

2.1 Communication-Efficient Federated Learning

Traditional communication-efficient FL methods predominantly rely on quantization (e.g., QSGD [1]) or sparsification (e.g., DGC [18], top-k [26]). While these methods reduce network traffic, they often introduce non-linear distortions that disrupt the geometric relationships (e.g., inner products and relative magnitudes) needed for evaluating domain conflicts. Although techniques like signSGD [2] transmit only signs, they are highly sensitive to domain skew and often fail to preserve fairness. In contrast, Count Sketch [4,7,9] preserves inner products and heavy hitters via linear projections. Building on this property, we selectively sketch large layers and perform masking based on cell- or parameter-level SUC. We then use these compressed-domain signals for momentum-normalized weighting, reducing traffic while retaining essential fairness constraints.

Error-feedback mechanisms can reduce the optimization bias of aggressive compression [12], but they do not directly supply the distance and consistency statistics required by fairness-aware aggregation.

2.2 Fairness in Federated Learning

Recent studies have shown that sketch-based data structures are effective and memory-efficient for measuring data heterogeneity and distribution divergence across clients in one pass [19]. Building upon this insight, we leverage sketches not just for compression, but as a vehicle for consistency-aware aggregation.

Fairness in FL addresses performance gaps caused by domain skew and is framed as performance, individual/group, and collaborative fairness. Tilted and worst-case objectives (q-FFL [17], AFL [22], TERM [14]) reweight losses toward minority domains. Drift and variance control (FedProx [16], SCAFFOLD [11]) stabilizes local updates and improves balance. Robust fair aggregation methods such as FedHeal [6] add consistency or diversity constraints, typically with full-precision communication. Under strong compression, noise and bias alter effective weights and the stability of tilted objectives, complicating fairness. We integrate cell- and parameter-level SUC, mask-based filtering, and momentum-normalized weighting with selective sketching to preserve fairness under tight bandwidth.

2.3 Relation to Personalization and Other Paradigms

Personalization methods such as Ditto [15] improve each client's local model by maintaining client-specific objectives or correction terms. Parameter-efficient FL further reduces communication through trainable adapters such as LoRA [27,30]. These approaches are complementary to FedSketchFair, which keeps a shared global model and focuses on fair aggregation when the server only observes compressed updates.

One-shot FL [8] removes multi-round communication, and recent variants use data-free distillation or generative proxy data to handle heterogeneity [5,10,21, 31,32]. FedSketchFair instead follows iterative FL and reduces per-round traffic while preserving compressed-domain geometric signals for domain fairness.

3 Preliminaries

Federated Learning. Following a typical federated learning setup [11,16,20], we consider M clients (indexed by m). Each client m holds private data $\mathcal{D}_m = \{(x_i, y_i)\}_{i=1}^{N_m}$, where N_m denotes the local data size. The optimization objective is to minimize the global loss:

$$\min_{\mathbf{w}} F(\mathbf{w}) = \sum_{m=1}^{M} p_m f_m(\mathbf{w}), \tag{1}$$

where $f_m(\mathbf{w}) = \frac{1}{N_m} \sum_{i=1}^{N_m} \ell(x_i, y_i; \mathbf{w})$ and p_m is the aggregation weight with $\sum_{m=1}^{M} p_m = 1$.

Domain Skew. In heterogeneous federated learning, domain skew arises when the marginal distribution of labels $P(y)$ is aligned across clients, while the conditional feature distribution given labels varies across domains [13,23,24,33]. Formally,

$$P_m(x \mid y) \neq P_n(x \mid y) \quad \text{while} \quad P_m(y) = P_n(y). \tag{2}$$

Sketch-Based Compression

Count Sketch Construction [4]. For an input vector $\mathbf{g} \in \mathbb{R}^d$, the sketch requires choosing a depth r and a width k (denoted as k_i for layer i). It utilizes r pairwise independent hash functions $h_j : [d] \to [k]$ and sign functions $s_j : [d] \to \{-1, +1\}$ for $j = 1, \ldots, r$ [3]. We initialize a sketch table $C \in \mathbb{R}^{r \times k}$ to zeros. For each coordinate index $u \in [d]$ with value g_u, the table is updated as:

$$C_{j, h_j(u)} \leftarrow C_{j, h_j(u)} + s_j(u)\, g_u, \quad j = 1, \ldots, r. \tag{3}$$

Query estimator (generic): for any sketch table C and index u [4],

$$Q(C, u) = \text{median}_{j \in [r]} \left(s_j(u)\, C_{j, h_j(u)} \right), \quad u \in [d]. \tag{4}$$

The sketch vector is obtained by stacking the rows of the table: $S(\mathbf{g}) := \text{vec}(C) \in \mathbb{R}^{r \times k}$. In expectation [29],

$$\mathbb{E}\left[\langle S(\mathbf{g}_1), S(\mathbf{g}_2) \rangle\right] = \langle \mathbf{g}_1, \mathbf{g}_2 \rangle, \quad \mathbb{E}\left[\|S(\mathbf{g})\|_2^2\right] = \|\mathbf{g}\|_2^2. \tag{5}$$

These properties enable similarity and aggregation on sketches [29]. Linearity [29]:

$$S(a\,\mathbf{x} + b\,\mathbf{y}) = a\,S(\mathbf{x}) + b\,S(\mathbf{y}), \quad a, b \in \mathbb{R}. \tag{6}$$

4 Methodology

We describe FedSketchFair and summarize the key notation in Table 1.

Table 1. Key notations used in this paper.

Notation	Description
W^t, w_m^t	Global / Client model at round t
p_m^t, $q_{m,i}^t$	Client momentum weight / Final aggregation weight
Δw_m^t	Model update of client m
$l_{m,i}$, $c_{m,i}$	Sign consistency tracker / SUC score
τ	SUC filtering threshold
d_m	Client divergence distance
λ	Layer-size classification threshold
β	Momentum update parameter
ρ	Compression ratio
r, k_i	Sketch depth / Sketch width of layer i
S, C	Count Sketch vector / table
mask^t	Binary filtering mask vector

4.1 System Overview

We combine selective compression with consistency-aware aggregation under domain skew and keep consistency and weighting in the compressed domain to reduce communication and aggregation bias. Low-consistency units, specifically sketch cells or raw parameters, are masked by thresholding to reduce conflicting updates and support domain fairness.

As illustrated in Fig. 1, the proposed workflow consists of five sequential steps:

- **Step 1 (Classify).** We classify the model layers into "large" and "small" categories based on a predefined parameter-size threshold λ. Layers exceeding λ are sketched, while smaller ones remain uncompressed.
- **Step 2 (Sketch Construction).** Clients upload fixed-size sketches for large layers, giving a predictable per-round communication budget.
- **Step 3 (Sign Update Consistency).** The server evaluates Sign Update Consistency (SUC) at the cell-level for large sketched layers, and at the parameter-level for small uncompressed layers. Using the statistical stability

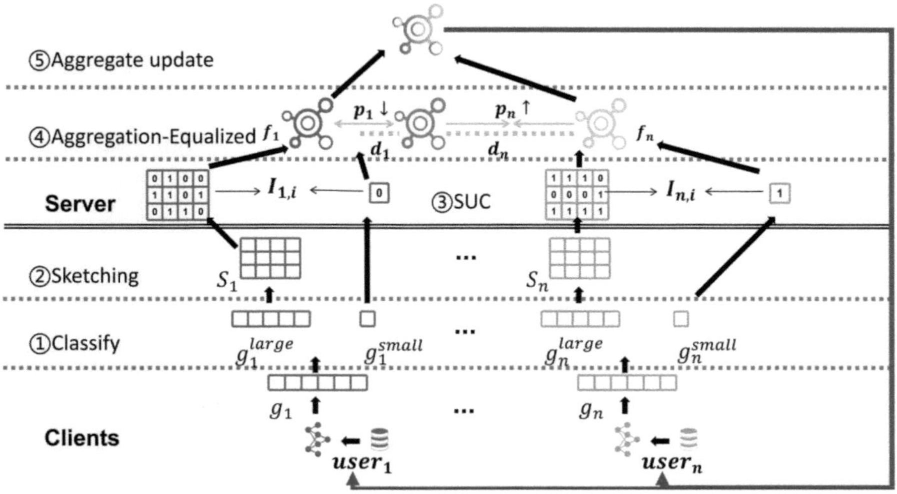

Fig. 1. Architecture of FedSketchFair.

of Count Sketch, directional consistency is estimated directly in the compressed domain without reconstruction. This produces binary filtering masks without requiring decompression.

- **Step 4 (Aggregation Equalization)**. To quantify client divergence and balance domain contributions, the server estimates Euclidean distances between the compressed updates. It then applies momentum (β) to compute the dynamic aggregation weights for each client.
- **Step 5 (Aggregated Update)**. Finally, the server aggregates the masked and weighted updates, broadcasting the resulting global model increment to all clients for local restoration.

4.2 Selective Compression

We adopt a static layer-wise scheme to save communication, keep fairness operations in the compressed domain, and limit approximation error. Define the small/large layer sets as $\mathcal{I}_{\text{small}} = \{i \mid L_i < \lambda\}$ and $\mathcal{I}_{\text{large}} = \{i \mid L_i \geq \lambda\}$. The sketch width is $k_i = \lceil \frac{L_i}{r \cdot \rho} \rceil$, yielding a sketch shape of (r, k_i), where L_i is the number of parameters in layer i. Small layers are sent uncompressed; large layers use Count Sketch with a shared hash/sign table $H = \{(h_j, s_j)\}_{j=1}^{r}$ (depth r) and width k_i, so each large layer has sketch size $\approx L_i/\rho$ under target ratio ρ [3].

Count Sketch cell updates and coordinate queries are given by Eqs. (3) and (4). These properties (Eqs. (6), (5)) enable SUC evaluation, distance estimation, and weighted aggregation on sketches without decompression [29]. The per-round communication budget can be approximated as $\mathcal{B} \approx \sum_{i \in \mathcal{I}_{\text{small}}} L_i + \frac{1}{\rho} \sum_{i \in \mathcal{I}_{\text{large}}} L_i$.

4.3 Sketch Restore

After masked aggregation, the server obtains aggregated sketches S_i^{agg}. Clients restore approximate dense updates with Eq. (4) using the shared hash/sign table H, setting $C := C^{agg}$. The restored update is applied to the model, $W^{t+1} = W^t + \widehat{\Delta w}^t$. By linearity (Eq. (6)), aggregate-then-restore equals restore-then-aggregate in expectation; collision noise is controlled by (r, k_i). Only the final model update uses restoration.

4.4 Consistency and Client Weighting

Evaluating statistics in the sketched domain inherently introduces hash collision noise. However, recent advances in private federated learning suggest that adaptive statistics tracking via linear sketches can control compression error even under high compression rates [28]. Motivated by this evidence, we design an aggregation scheme that separates local consistency selection from global client-level weighting to further stabilize training under heterogeneous domains.

Granular Sign Consistency. To filter unstable directions and retain consistent ones without decompression, we evaluate SUC at two specific granularities corresponding to our selective compression strategy: cell-level for large sketched layers, and parameter-level for small uncompressed layers. We maintain cumulative sign consistency per unit (either a sketch cell or a raw parameter) recursively:

$$l_{m,i}^t \leftarrow \frac{t\, l_{m,i}^{t-1} + I(\Delta w_{m,i}^t \geq 0)}{t+1}, \tag{7}$$

which tracks the empirical frequency of non-negative update directions up to round t, where $I(\cdot)$ denotes the indicator function and the loop starts from $t = 0$. The transmitted update is $\Delta w_{m,i}^t = w_{m,i}^t - W_i^t$ for uncompressed small layers and $\Delta w_{m,i}^t = \mathrm{vec}(C_{m,i}^t)$ for sketched large layers. By sketch linearity, sign consistency is computed on the transmitted updates via $I(\Delta w_{m,i}^t \geq 0)$ without decompression. The SUC score $c_{m,i}^t$ is then defined as $l_{m,i}^t$ if $\Delta w_{m,i}^t \geq 0$, and $1 - l_{m,i}^t$ otherwise. Thus, $c_{m,i}^t$ measures whether the current update agrees with the historical majority direction of the same parameter or sketch cell. Thresholding with $I(c_{m,i}^t \geq \tau)$ filters oscillating directions caused by domain skew and keeps the more consistent trajectories.

Impact of Hash Collisions on Sign Consistency. Neural network updates typically exhibit a heavy-tailed distribution, where a small fraction of coordinates with large magnitudes (known as heavy hitters) dominate the optimization direction [18]. According to the Count Sketch theory [4], the estimation error for a coordinate u can be bounded, with high probability, by the L_2 norm of the tail components: $|\hat{g}_u - g_u| \leq \mathcal{O}(1/\sqrt{k})\|\mathbf{g}_{-v}\|_2$, where k is the sketch width and $\mathbf{g}_{-v}$ is the residual vector after removing the top-v largest elements. Since

SUC relies exclusively on the sign of the updates, a hash collision alters $\text{sign}(g_u)$ only if the accumulated noise exceeds the true magnitude ($|\hat{g}_u - g_u| > |g_u|$). For heavy hitters, their magnitudes are expected to dominate this tail-noise term ($|g_u| \gg \mathcal{O}(1/\sqrt{k})\|\mathbf{g}_{-v}\|_2$), making their signs more stable than near-zero coordinates. Collisions may still flip the signs of tail coordinates; in our method these unstable coordinates are further suppressed by historical SUC thresholding. Thus, the compressed sign signal remains informative in practice, while a full convergence guarantee for non-convex FL under sketch collisions remains future work.

Client-Level Momentum Weighting. To prevent performance collapse on minority domains, we reduce imbalance in client distances to the global model. Using the masked sketch vectors, we estimate this client divergence in the compressed domain as $d_m = \sum_i \|I(c^t_{m,i} \geq \tau) \odot \Delta w^t_{m,i}\|_2^2$. This provides a communication-efficient proxy for exact model-level distance evaluation (similar to full-precision constraints used in [6]), allowing us to update the client aggregation weights via momentum (β):

$$\tilde{p}^t_m = (1-\beta)p^{t-1}_m + \beta \frac{d_m}{\sum_{j=1}^M d_j}, \quad p^t_m = \frac{\tilde{p}^t_m}{\sum_{j=1}^M \tilde{p}^t_j}, \tag{8}$$

Euclidean distance in the compressed domain is statistically unbiased, as it can be expanded into inner products and L_2 norms: $\|\mathbf{x}-\mathbf{y}\|_2^2 = \|\mathbf{x}\|_2^2 + \|\mathbf{y}\|_2^2 - 2\langle \mathbf{x}, \mathbf{y}\rangle$, where each term is preserved in expectation by the sketch properties defined in Eq. (5).

Finally, aggregation applies consistency masking and weights:

$$W^{t+1}_i = W^t_i + \sum_{m=1}^{M} q^t_{m,i} \odot \Delta w^t_{m,i}, \quad q^t_{m,i} = \frac{I(c^t_{m,i} \geq \tau)\, p^t_m}{\sum_{j=1}^M I(c^t_{j,i} \geq \tau)\, p^t_j}. \tag{9}$$

where $\odot$ denotes the Hadamard (element-wise) product. The denominator dynamically excludes clients whose updates are masked out for a specific parameter. This acts as a parameter-level client dropout, ensuring that the masked zero-values do not artificially dilute the magnitudes of valid updates from other domains.

In the rare event where all clients are masked for a specific parameter (making the denominator zero), we default to the previous global state by setting the update for that coordinate to zero.

Algorithm Description. Clients perform local training for K epochs, compute updates, and selectively sketch large layers using Count Sketch [4] at ratio ρ under threshold λ, while keeping small layers uncompressed. The server updates SUC consistency, thresholds with τ to form a mask vector, estimates client distances and momentum update weights p^t with parameter β, derives aggregation weights q^t, aggregates masked sketches, broadcasts the aggregate, and clients restore the global update.

Algorithm 1. FedSketchFair: Selective Compression and Fair Aggregation

Input: $T, K, M, W^0, \rho, \lambda, H, \tau, \beta$, initialize $p_m^{-1} = 1/M$, $l_{m,i}^{-1} = 0$
for $t = 0$ to $T - 1$ **do**
  Client (parallel for $m = 1, \ldots, M$**):**
  $w_m^t \leftarrow W^t$
  LocalUpdate($w_m^t, \mathcal{D}_m$) for K epochs
  $\Delta w_m^t \leftarrow w_m^t - W^t$
  $\mathcal{S}_m \leftarrow$ SelectiveSketch($\Delta w_m^t; \lambda, \rho, H$)
  Server:
  for each client $m \in \{1, \ldots, M\}$ **do**
    $(c_{m,i}^t, l_{m,i}^t) \leftarrow$ SUCUpdate($l_{m,i}^{t-1}, \mathcal{S}_m$)
    mask$_m^t \leftarrow$ Threshold($c_{m,i}^t; \tau$)
    $d_m \leftarrow$ ClientDistance($\mathcal{S}_m$, mask$_m^t$)
  end for
  for each client $m \in \{1, \ldots, M\}$ **do**
    $\tilde{p}_m^t \leftarrow (1 - \beta) p_m^{t-1} + \beta \frac{d_m}{\sum_{j=1}^M d_j}$
  end for
  $p^t \leftarrow$ Normalize($\{\tilde{p}_m^t\}_{m=1}^M$)
  $q^t \leftarrow$ AggregationWeights($\{$mask$_m^t\}, \{p_m^t\}$)
  $\mathcal{S}^{agg} \leftarrow$ MaskedAggregate($\{\mathcal{S}_m\}, q^t$)
  Broadcast($\mathcal{S}^{agg}$)
  Client (parallel for $m = 1, \ldots, M$**):**
  $\widehat{\Delta w}^t \leftarrow$ Restore($\mathcal{S}^{agg}, H$)
  $W^{t+1} \leftarrow W^t + \widehat{\Delta w}^t$
end for

5 Experiments

We evaluate FedSketchFair on diverse multi-domain FL benchmarks to address three key questions: the impact of compression ratios on performance, fairness under high compression, and computation/communication efficiency. We test on PACS, Office-Caltech, and DomainNet, which represent different degrees of domain heterogeneity.

5.1 Experimental Setup

Datasets: We evaluate on PACS [13] (4 domains), Office-Caltech [24] (4 domains), and DomainNet [23] (6 domains). Each client is one domain, inducing domain skew.

Implementation: We use VGG19 [25] trained with SGD and test $\rho \in \{8, 64, 512\}$. Following SK-Gradient [9], we set the layer-size threshold to $\lambda = 2^{15}$ to avoid sketching small layers where collision noise and sketching overhead are less favorable. The sketch depth r controls collision tolerance and is fixed across datasets; the layer width is set as $k_i = \lceil L_i/(r\rho) \rceil$ to meet each target compression ratio. Budgets are matched by adjusting rounds of uncompressed baselines

Table 2. Comparison of VGG19 accuracy (%) on different datasets under matched communication budgets.

ρ	Method	Office-Caltech					PACS					DomainNet						
		A	C	D	W	Avg	P	A	C	S	Avg	C	I	P	Q	R	S	Avg
8	FedAvg	88.52	73.73	83.26	83.79	82.56	37.50	76.37	73.68	66.08	63.40	51.33	14.26	18.40	42.60	36.06	23.80	31.07
	FedProx	87.57	73.26	79.52	85.43	81.09	31.25	58.22	80.70	71.35	60.38	31.86	11.93	22.06	45.30	30.22	31.49	28.81
	FedHeal	78.79	50.85	88.88	90.46	77.09	34.13	62.44	67.83	80.90	61.33	35.11	9.47	10.42	55.40	24.89	26.19	26.91
	SG	85.95	55.29	72.22	79.36	73.66	31.73	77.63	66.66	85.15	65.30	38.58	9.10	13.63	63.00	35.65	35.96	32.65
	DGC	79.69	53.17	72.22	83.33	72.19	33.17	75.10	67.25	80.40	63.98	37.89	10.94	14.63	58.30	36.27	34.40	32.07
	Ours	88.76	65.56	86.11	95.23	**85.90**	50.48	85.23	82.45	83.91	**75.52**	50.86	17.95	23.94	65.80	46.82	40.33	**40.95**
64	FedAvg	54.12	40.35	58.33	58.73	52.88	27.40	38.39	44.44	33.66	35.97	5.79	3.69	4.21	5.40	3.89	2.59	5.16
	FedProx	48.45	35.53	69.44	66.66	55.02	25.48	38.81	40.93	34.92	35.03	6.14	4.79	6.09	10.00	4.61	4.05	5.95
	FedHeal	74.22	34.21	77.77	57.14	60.83	27.40	47.67	48.53	27.63	37.81	4.75	4.42	4.32	15.50	5.02	2.28	6.05
	SG	79.38	61.40	83.33	82.53	76.66	41.82	75.52	63.74	86.68	66.94	43.56	13.16	16.07	63.30	39.54	36.59	35.37
	DGC	83.50	54.82	88.88	74.60	75.45	32.69	75.52	68.42	77.63	63.56	35.92	13.65	14.96	60.40	34.83	38.25	33.00
	Ours	85.56	62.71	88.88	92.06	**82.30**	54.80	88.60	83.62	84.92	**77.99**	52.37	19.18	25.94	67.30	52.15	44.38	**43.55**
512	FedAvg	10.82	11.84	13.88	14.28	12.71	28.36	35.44	30.40	20.85	28.76	2.78	3.19	2.21	2.00	3.17	2.39	2.62
	FedProx	12.88	16.66	13.88	9.52	13.24	21.15	29.95	40.35	36.68	32.03	2.31	2.46	2.66	3.10	2.86	2.07	2.58
	FedHeal	17.52	11.84	13.88	14.28	14.82	20.19	36.28	50.29	27.38	33.53	2.54	3.69	3.10	3.60	3.07	2.18	3.03
	SG	86.08	54.82	72.22	82.53	73.91	32.21	74.26	67.83	83.91	64.55	39.62	11.93	14.41	62.70	37.60	36.90	33.86
	DGC	79.38	64.91	63.88	85.71	73.47	37.50	69.19	58.47	78.89	61.01	35.22	12.54	15.52	62.10	36.37	32.64	32.40
	Ours	87.11	70.61	91.66	99.98	**87.34**	54.80	86.07	87.13	86.93	**78.73**	51.68	16.48	21.72	70.10	46.82	46.98	**42.30**

(FedAvg [20], FedProx [16], FedHeal [6]) to equal the transmitted bytes of compressed methods (DGC [18], SK-Gradient [9], Ours).

5.2 Accuracy Comparison and Analysis Across Datasets

Table 2 shows that FedSketchFair remains accurate under tight communication budgets across all datasets. At the budget corresponding to $\rho = 512$, FedAvg decreases to 12.71% on Office-Caltech and 2.62% on DomainNet, whereas our method maintains 87.34% and 42.30%, respectively. On PACS, FedSketchFair surpasses the best baseline (SK-Gradient) by over 10% at $\rho = 8$ and sustains 78.73% accuracy at $\rho = 512$, outperforming FedAvg by 49.97%.

Fairness Metric Analysis: We assess fairness by worst-domain accuracy and the min-max domain gap. On PACS at $\rho = 512$, FedAvg yields only 20.85% worst-domain accuracy, whereas FedSketchFair raises it to 54.80% and narrows the min-max domain gap (Fig. 2). This indicates that our method avoids sacrificing minority domains for average accuracy.

ResNet-18 Results: To verify full-convergence behavior (Table 3), we evaluate a pre-trained ResNet-18 on PACS. FedSketchFair achieves the highest average accuracy of 94.50%, improves the difficult *Sketch* domain over FedAvg (91.70% vs. 73.36%), and requires only 2.90 MB traffic per round at $\rho = 64$, a 96.6% reduction over dense baselines.

Table 3. Performance and communication overhead on PACS using pre-trained ResNet-18 at full convergence with $\rho = 64$.

Method	Photo	Art	Cartoon	Sketch	Avg (%)	Traffic (MB)
FedAvg	84.61	91.13	99.41	73.36	87.13	85.32
FedProx	86.53	89.02	99.41	81.15	89.03	85.32
FedHeal	91.34	90.71	98.24	88.19	92.12	85.32
SG	92.30	91.56	98.83	88.94	92.91	2.90
DGC	90.86	94.09	98.83	90.20	93.49	4.21
Ours	94.23	93.24	98.83	91.70	**94.50**	**2.90**

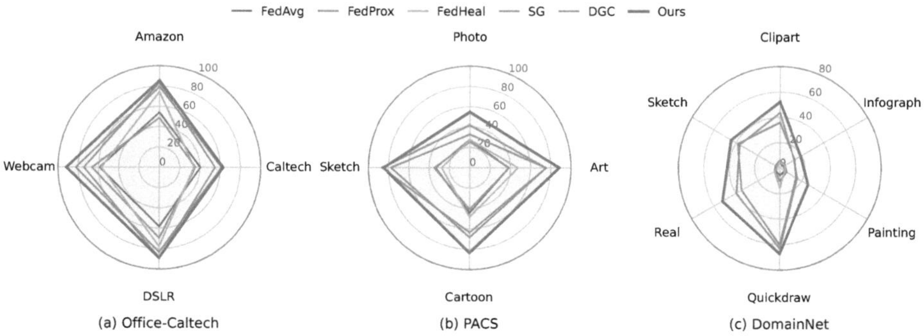

Fig. 2. Per-domain accuracy comparison at $\rho = 64$.

5.3 Communication Cost and Time

We further evaluate communication and computation efficiency in Fig. 3. At $\rho = 512$, uncompressed baselines incur substantial overheads of 532.659 MB/round (FedAvg 0.9676 s; FedProx 1.0265 s; FedHeal 1.0226 s), whereas DGC reduces the traffic to 2.081 MB (0.8215 s). Both SK-Gradient (SG) and our method achieve the lowest traffic of 1.183 MB. Our approach matches SG's communication efficiency, with only a small ∼0.03 s computational overhead from SUC masking and weighting.

5.4 Ablation Study

Table 4 evaluates the individual contributions of SUC and Sketch at a compression ratio of $\rho = 64$. **Component Analysis:**

- **Baseline.** Without enhancements, the system matches FedAvg at $\rho = 64$, yielding 52.88%, 35.97%, and 5.16% on Office-Caltech, PACS, and DomainNet.
- **SUC-only:** Adding the fairness mechanism provides moderate improvements (+7.95% on Office-Caltech, +1.84% on PACS), suggesting that fairness constraints alone are insufficient under severe domain skew.

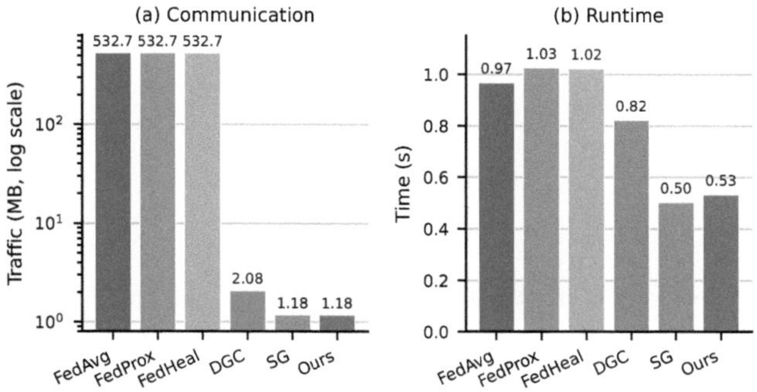

Fig. 3. Per-round communication traffic and runtime at $\rho = 512$.

- **Sketch-only:** Compression alone yields substantial gains (+23.78% on Office-Caltech, +30.21% on DomainNet) by allowing more global updates under the same budget.
- **FedSketchFair (both):** Combining SUC and Sketch yields the best results among the evaluated variants (e.g., 82.30% on Office-Caltech), indicating that the two components are complementary.

Table 4. Ablation study on per-domain accuracy at $\rho = 64$ (%).

SUC	Sketch	Office-Caltech					PACS					DomainNet						
		A	C	D	W	Avg	P	A	C	S	Avg	C	I	P	Q	R	S	Avg
		54.12	40.35	58.33	58.73	52.88	27.40	38.39	44.44	33.66	35.97	5.79	3.69	4.21	5.40	3.89	2.59	5.16
✓		74.22	34.21	77.77	57.14	60.83	27.40	47.67	48.53	27.63	37.81	4.75	4.42	4.32	15.50	5.02	2.28	6.05
	✓	79.38	61.40	83.33	82.53	76.66	41.82	75.52	63.74	86.68	66.94	43.56	13.16	16.07	63.30	39.54	36.59	35.37
✓	✓	**85.56**	**62.71**	**88.88**	**92.06**	**82.30**	**54.80**	**88.60**	**83.62**	**84.92**	**77.99**	**52.37**	**19.18**	**25.94**	**67.30**	**52.15**	**44.38**	**43.55**

5.5 Hyperparameter Analysis

Tables 5 and 6 evaluate the sensitivity to the consistency threshold τ and momentum coefficient β.

Consistency Threshold τ Analysis: The consistency threshold τ controls filtering strength. A small τ retains more updates, while a large τ can discard useful directions under sketch noise. The favorable range is τ = 0.3–0.4, with the best accuracy of 87.02% at $\tau = 0.4$.

Momentum Coefficient β Analysis: The momentum β controls the response speed of client weights. Smaller values smooth the weights, whereas larger values react faster but may amplify transient sketch errors. Table 6 shows the best performance at $\beta = 0.4$ (87.53%).

Table 5. Threshold τ on Office-Caltech ($\rho = 512$)

τ	0.1	0.2	0.3	0.4	0.5
AVG ↑	86.01	84.87	85.99	**87.02**	81.71

Table 6. Momentum β on Office-Caltech ($\rho = 512$)

β	0.2	0.4	0.6	0.8	1.0
AVG ↑	84.79	**87.53**	82.84	85.27	84.84

Parameter Selection Guideline: In practice, we recommend fixing ρ and λ, choosing a small sketch depth r that gives stable median estimates within the bandwidth, and initializing τ in 0.3–0.4 and β around 0.4. The method is not tuning-free: too strict a threshold (e.g., $\tau = 0.5$) or overly reactive momentum can reduce accuracy.

6 Conclusion

FedSketchFair mitigates domain skew via selective compression and compressed-domain consistency-based client weighting, reducing communication while preserving the information needed for filtering and weighting updates. By sketching only large layers, it keeps local compute latency small relative to the bandwidth savings. Across three multi-domain benchmarks, it consistently outperforms baselines under matched communication budgets. Specifically, on Office-Caltech at high compression ($\rho = 512$), FedAvg accuracy decreases to 12.71%, while FedSketchFair maintains 87.34%, balancing minority domains. This behavior stems from SUC masking and momentum weighting, which stabilize aggregation under severe heterogeneity. Future work includes extending this framework to broader federated learning scenarios and studying its integration with formal privacy guarantees, such as differential privacy.

Acknowledgments. This research was funded by Joint Funding Special Project for Guangdong-Hong Kong Science and Technology Innovation 2024A0505040027; NSFC grant 62202113.

Disclosure of Interests. The authors have no competing interests to declare.

References

1. Alistarh, D., Grubic, D., Li, J., Tomioka, R., Vojnovic, M.: QSGD: Communication-efficient SGD via gradient quantization and encoding. In: Advances in Neural Information Processing Systems (NeurIPS), pp. 1709–1720 (2017)
2. Bernstein, J., Wang, Y.X., Azizzadenesheli, K., Anandkumar, A.: signSGD: Compressed optimisation for non-convex problems. In: International Conference on Machine Learning (ICML), pp. 560–569 (2018)
3. Carter, J.L., Wegman, M.N.: Universal classes of hash functions. J. Comput. Syst. Sci. **18**(2), 143–154 (1979)

4. Charikar, M., Chen, K., Farach-Colton, M.: Finding frequent items in data streams. In: International Colloquium on Automata, Languages, and Programming (ICALP), pp. 693–703 (2002)
5. Chen, H., et al.: FedBiP: Heterogeneous one-shot federated learning with personalized latent diffusion models. In: IEEE/CVF Conference on Computer Vision and Pattern Recognition (CVPR), pp. 30440–30450 (2025)
6. Chen, Y., Huang, W., Ye, M.: Fair federated learning under domain skew with local consistency and domain diversity. In: IEEE/CVF Conference on Computer Vision and Pattern Recognition (CVPR), pp. 12077–12086 (2024)
7. Cormode, G., Muthukrishnan, S.: An improved data stream summary: the count-min sketch and its applications. J. Algorithms **55**(1), 58–75 (2005)
8. Guha, N., Talwalkar, A., Smith, V.: One-shot federated learning. arXiv preprint arXiv:1902.11175 (2019)
9. Gui, J., Song, Y., Wang, Z., He, C., Huang, Q.: SK-Gradient: Efficient communication for distributed machine learning with data sketch. In: IEEE 39th International Conference on Data Engineering (ICDE), pp. 2372–2385 (2023)
10. Heinbaugh, C.E., Luz-Ricca, E., Shao, H.: Data-free one-shot federated learning under very high statistical heterogeneity. In: International Conference on Learning Representations (ICLR) (2023)
11. Karimireddy, S.P., Kale, S., Mohri, M., Reddi, S.J., Stich, S.U., Suresh, A.T.: SCAFFOLD: Stochastic controlled averaging for federated learning. In: International Conference on Machine Learning (ICML), pp. 5132–5143 (2020)
12. Karimireddy, S.P., Rebjock, Q., Stich, S., Jaggi, M.: Error feedback fixes signSGD and other gradient compression schemes. In: International Conference on Machine Learning (ICML), pp. 3252–3261 (2019)
13. Li, D., Yang, Y., Song, Y.Z., Hospedales, T.M.: Deeper, broader and artier domain generalization. In: IEEE International Conference on Computer Vision (ICCV), pp. 5542–5550 (2017)
14. Li, T., Beirami, A., Sanjabi, M., Smith, V.: Tilted empirical risk minimization. In: International Conference on Learning Representations (ICLR). (2021)
15. Li, T., Hu, S., Beirami, A., Smith, V.: Ditto: Fair and robust federated learning through personalization. In: International Conference on Machine Learning (ICML), pp. 6357–6368 (2021)
16. Li, T., Sahu, A.K., Zaheer, M., Sanjabi, M., Talwalkar, A., Smith, V.: Federated optimization in heterogeneous networks. In: Proceedings of Machine Learning and Systems (MLSys), pp. 429–450 (2020)
17. Li, T., Sanjabi, M., Beirami, A., Smith, V.: Fair resource allocation in federated learning. In: International Conference on Learning Representations (ICLR) (2020)
18. Lin, Y., Han, S., Mao, H., Wang, Y., Dally, W.J.: Deep gradient compression: Reducing the communication bandwidth for distributed training. In: International Conference on Learning Representations (ICLR), (2018)
19. Liu, Z., Xu, Z., Coleman, B., Shrivastava, A.: One-pass distribution sketch for measuring data heterogeneity in federated learning. In: Advances in Neural Information Processing Systems (NeurIPS) (2023)
20. McMahan, B., Moore, E., Ramage, D., Hampson, S., Agüera y Arcas, B.: Communication-efficient learning of deep networks from decentralized data. In: Artificial Intelligence and Statistics (AISTATS), pp. 1273–1282 (2017)
21. Mendieta, M., Sun, G., Chen, C.: Navigating heterogeneity and privacy in one-shot federated learning with diffusion models. In: IEEE/CVF Winter Conference on Applications of Computer Vision (WACV), pp. 2601–2610 (2025)

22. Mohri, M., Sivek, G., Suresh, A.T.: Agnostic federated learning. In: International Conference on Machine Learning (ICML), pp. 4615–4625 (2019)
23. Peng, X., Bai, Q., Xia, X., Huang, Z., Saenko, K., Wang, B.: Moment matching for multi-source domain adaptation. In: IEEE/CVF International Conference on Computer Vision (ICCV), pp. 1406–1415 (2019)
24. Saenko, K., Kulis, B., Fritz, M., Darrell, T.: Adapting visual category models to new domains. In: European Conference on Computer Vision (ECCV), pp. 213–226. (2010)
25. Simonyan, K., Zisserman, A.: Very deep convolutional networks for large-scale image recognition. In: International Conference on Learning Representations (ICLR) (2015)
26. Stich, S.U., Cordonnier, J.B., Jaggi, M.: Sparsified SGD with memory. In: Advances in Neural Information Processing Systems (NeurIPS), pp. 4452–4463 (2018)
27. Sun, Y., Li, Z., Li, Y., Ding, B.: Improving LoRA in privacy-preserving federated learning. In: International Conference on Learning Representations (ICLR) (2024)
28. Ullah, E., Choquette-Choo, C.A., Kairouz, P., Oh, S.: Private federated learning with autotuned compression. In: International Conference on Machine Learning (ICML), pp. 34668–34708 (2023)
29. Woodruff, D.P.: Sketching as a tool for numerical linear algebra. Found. Trends® Theor. Comput. Sci. **10**(1–2), 1–157 (2014)
30. Yan, Y., Feng, C.M., Zuo, W., Goh, R.S.M., Liu, Y., Zhu, L.: Federated residual low-rank adaptation of large language models. In: International Conference on Learning Representations (ICLR) (2025)
31. Yang, M., Su, S., Li, B., Xue, X.: One-shot heterogeneous federated learning with local model-guided diffusion models. In: International Conference on Machine Learning (ICML), pp. 71157–71176 (2025)
32. Zhang, J., et al.: DENSE: Data-free one-shot federated learning. In: Advances in Neural Information Processing Systems (NeurIPS), vol. 35, pp. 21414–21428 (2022)
33. Zhao, Y., Li, M., Lai, L., Suda, N., Civin, D., Chandra, V.: Federated learning with non-IID data. arXiv preprint arXiv:1806.00582 (2018)

Trajectory Management

Direction-Guided Conditional Denoising for Uncertainty-Aware Pedestrian Trajectory Prediction

Yongfei Ye[1(✉)], Zichen Wang[2], Shilei Kuang[1,2], and Senzhang Wang[2]

[1] China United Network Communications Group Co., Ltd. Jiangxi Branch, Nanchang, China
yongfeiye@chinaunicom.cn, kuangsl@csu.edu.cn
[2] Central South University, Changsha, China
{zcwang0422,szwang}@csu.edu.cn

Abstract. Pedestrian trajectory prediction is critically important in intelligent transportation systems, but remains challenging due to the complexity of interpersonal interactions and the inherent uncertainty of pedestrian behaviors. This paper proposes a Direction-guided Conditional Denoising (DgCD) model for more effective pedestrian trajectory prediction. Specifically, DgCD first constructs a polar coordinate system that is centered on the target pedestrian and divides the surrounding space into directional sectors to better capture the interaction differences. A motion encoding module is then adopted to fuse the historical trajectories with the direction-guided interaction features. To model the uncertainty of pedestrian behaviors, a multimodal framework with latent variable sampling and self-attention is proposed to generate diverse future trajectories. Finally, a conditional denoising module is proposed to refine the predictions in the residual space, which can further improve the prediction accuracy and consistency. Extensive experiment conducted on real dataset show that the proposed DgCD achieves superior performance compared with existing SOTA baselines in the complex multi-pedestrian scenarios.

Keywords: pedestrian trajectory prediction · multimodality · diffusion model · uncertainty modeling

1 Introduction

With the rapid development of urbanization and intelligent transportation systems, technologies such as autonomous driving and intelligent surveillance have become increasingly important. In the complex urban traffic environments, frequent interactions between pedestrians and vehicles require intelligent systems to predict future behaviors for safe and efficient decision-making. Therefore, pedestrian trajectory prediction has received significant research attention recently,

Y. Ye and Z. Wang—These authors contributed equally to this work.

L. Ding et al. (Eds.): APWeb-WAIM 2026, LNCS 16995, pp. 201–215, 2027.
https://doi.org/10.1007/978-981-92-5699-0_13

as it can provide key prior information for many tasks including path planning, collision avoidance, and behavior understanding [5,13].

Pedestrian trajectory prediction aims to infer the future motion from historical trajectories of a target pedestrian and its neighbors. Compared with vehicles, pedestrian motion is more flexible and uncertain, as it is influenced by both individual intentions and social interactions [10,15]. In crowded scenes, pedestrians need to adjust their speed or direction in real time to avoid collisions, while in open spaces, their motion is relatively stable (Fig. 1).

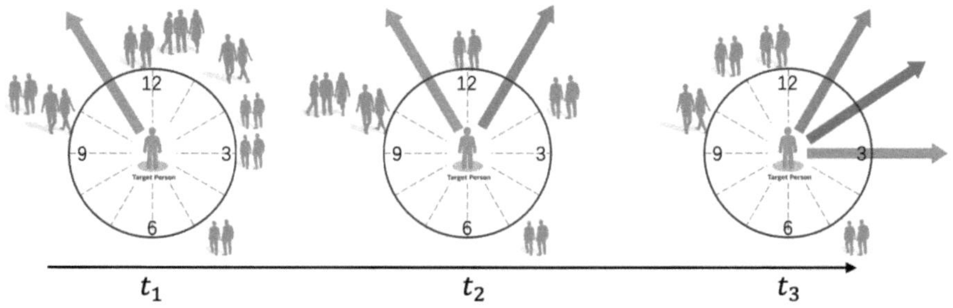

Fig. 1. Illustration of pedestrian interactions at different time steps

In recent years, deep learning-based pedestrian trajectory prediction methods have been extensively studied and achieved significant performance improvement compared with traditional machine learning methods. Early RNN- and LSTM-based approaches [25] can effectively capture the temporal dependencies, but struggle to capture the complex multi-agent interactions. To address this issue, social pooling [1], graph neural networks, and attention mechanisms [23] have been introduced to address this problem. However, these methods still largely rely on global or isotropic aggregation, limiting their ability to model the directional interaction differences. In addition, pedestrian trajectories are highly multi-modal. Therefore, generative models such as VAEs [4], GANs [6], and diffusion models [8] have been widely used to produce diverse future motions recently. Despite these advances, key challenges remain as the interaction effects are direction-dependent and often oversimplified. First, pedestrian behavior usually involves both intention uncertainty and stochastic variation, which are rarely disentangled by existing works. Second, prediction errors tend to accumulate in existing works, which requires further refinement.

To address these issues, this paper proposes a Direction-guided Conditional Denoising (DgCD) model to more effectively predict the pedestrian trajectory with high uncertainty. Specifically, a polar coordinate system is first constructed around the target pedestrian, and his/her surrounding space is divided into directional sectors to explicitly model the interaction differences between the pedestrians. Then, historical motion and direction-guided features are fused into a unified representation. A multi-modal latent variable framework is also introduced to capture the intention uncertainty of the pedestrians. Specifically, it first predicts the intermediate key points, and then interpolates the other points to form a full trajectory. Finally, a conditional denoising module is proposed to refine the predicted trajectories in residual space.

The primary contributions of this paper are summarized as follows.

- A direction-guided interaction modeling method is proposed to explicitly capture the spatial heterogeneity among the neighbor pedestrians.
- A multi-modal trajectory generation framework is proposed to model the diverse future motion patterns of the pedestrians.
- A conditional denoising-based refinement module is proposed to further improve the prediction accuracy and stability by reducing the prediction uncertainty.

2 Related Work

Currently, pedestrian trajectory prediction methods can be briefly categorized into kinematics-based methods, traditional machine learning-based methods, and deep learning-based methods. Next, we will provide a brief review on these methods.

Kinematics-based methods treat pedestrians as independent agents governed by physical laws and predict future trajectories using motion states such as velocity and acceleration. For example, [7] proposed the Social Force Model to describe the interactive forces among pedestrians, while [11] extended it with a long acceleration formulation to avoid collision. A major limitation of this type of method is that they heavily rely on strong physical assumptions, and therefore their performance is usually limited in complex scenarios.

Traditional machine learning-based methods generally leverage the historical trajectories and behavioral intentions for future trajectory prediction. [12] proposed a context-aware dynamic Bayesian network, and [2] used Bayesian inference to model the future motion of the pedestrians. These methods can perform well for short-term prediction (12 s), but their prediction performance may degrade significantly for longer prediction (35 s). With the advances in deep learning technologies, deep learning-based methods have become dominant in pedestrian trajectory prediction due to their strong feature representation learning capabilities. For example, [1] introduced Social Pooling based on LSTM encoding to model interactions, while [18] proposed a spatiotemporal graph convolutional network to capture spatial-temporal dependencies.

Traditional deterministic methods output a single future trajectory, while real-world prediction motion is inherently uncertain. How to effectively model the uncertainty to improve the prediction robustness has attracted rising research attention recently. [20] improved sampling efficiency via knowledge distillation and deterministic sampling. [3] introduced an intent-aware diffusion framework to decouple the intention and the motion uncertainty. [17] proposed a "leapfrog" initialization strategy to directly learn the multi-modal distributions and reduce the denoising steps.

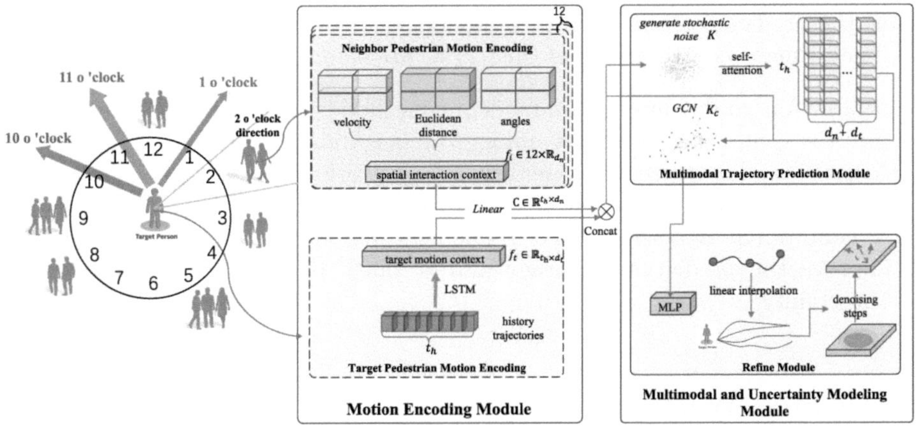

Fig. 2. Framework of the proposed DgCD model.

3 Problem Definition

The pedestrian trajectory prediction task aims to infer the future motion of a target pedestrian (i.e., agent) over a time horizon based on its historical trajectory and the trajectories of his/her surrounding pedestrians (i.e., agents). Formally, for the i-th agent, let $X^i = [p^i_{-t_h+1}, \dots, p^i_0] \in \mathbb{R}^{t_h \times 2}$ denote his/her observed historical trajectory, where $p^i_t \in \mathbb{R}^2$ represents the 2D position (x_t, y_t) at time t. Let $\mathcal{N}$ denote the set of the neighboring agents. Their historical trajectories are represented as $X_{\mathcal{N}} = [X^{N_1}, \dots, X^{N_L}] \in \mathbb{R}^{L \times t_h \times 2}$, where L is the number of neighbors and $X^{N_l} \in \mathbb{R}^{t_h \times 2}$ is the trajectory of the l-th neighbor. Our goal is to predict the future trajectory of the target agent over t_f steps, denoted as $\hat{Y} \in \mathbb{R}^{t_f \times 2}$. Due to the motion uncertainty issue, multiple plausible future trajectories may exist. Therefore, the model needs to output K possible future trajectories $\{\hat{Y}_1, \hat{Y}_2, \dots, \hat{Y}_K\}$, where $\hat{Y}_k \in \mathbb{R}^{t_f \times 2}$.

4 Methodology

Figure 2 illustrates the overall framework of the proposed DgCD, which consists of a motion encoding module and a multi-modal and uncertainty modeling module. Specifically, the motion encoding module includes a target pedestrian motion encoder and a neighboring pedestrian feature encoder. The multi-modal and uncertainty modeling module comprises a multi-modal trajectory prediction module and a refinement module. Next, we will introduce DgCD in detail.

4.1 Motion Encoding Module

The motion encoding module aims to extract high-level representations from the historical trajectories, capturing both the individual motion patterns and their social interactions. It consists of three parts: the target pedestrian motion encoding module, the neighbor pedestrian feature encoding module, and the historical motion context construction.

Target Pedestrian Motion Encoding Module. This module encodes the historical trajectory of the target pedestrian X^i into high-dimensional motion features for interaction modeling and prediction. The trajectory is first embedded into a feature space as follows,

$$f_t = f_{\text{embed}}(X^i), \tag{1}$$

where $f_t \in \mathbb{R}^{t_h \times d_t}$ with t_h as the observation length and d_t as the feature dimension. The embedding function f_{embed} is a two-layer MLP with ReLU and tanh activations.

To enhance feature expressiveness, an outer product is applied at each time step to capture second-order interactions across feature channels, preserving richer structural information than linear mappings. The resulting features are pooled for dimensionality reduction while retaining salient responses, then flattened and linearly projected to obtain the final motion representation. This design captures not only basic motion patterns but also velocity changes, directional variations, and local dynamics, providing a richer context for subsequent interaction modeling and trajectory prediction.

Neighbor Pedestrian Feature Encoding Module. In multi-pedestrian scenarios, the future motion of a target pedestrian is influenced by both its own dynamics and the surrounding neighbors. Hence, modeling the motion states of neighboring pedestrians is essential.

Sector-based spatial partitioning. A polar coordinate system is constructed with the target pedestrian as the origin, and the surrounding space is evenly divided into 12 sectors. The relative position of a neighboring pedestrian j with respect to the target i is represented by the angle $\theta^{(j)} \in [0, 2\pi)$:

$$\theta^{(j)} = \text{atan2}(p_t^j - p_t^i), \tag{2}$$

where p_t^j denotes the position of pedestrian j at time step t.

Intra-sector interaction feature statistics. Multiple neighbors may fall within the same sector, and their collective motion influences the target pedestrian. To capture this effect, statistical features are computed for each sector. Specifically, the average velocity, the average distance to the target pedestrian, and the relative orientation of neighbors are used to characterize the interaction pattern in that direction.

Let the 12 sectors be denoted as $\{s_1, s_2, \ldots, s_{12}\}$, where $|s_i|$ is the number of neighbors in sector s_i, and f^i represents the corresponding sector-level interaction feature. We propose to construct the *speed feature*, the *distance feature*, the *angle feature* as follows.

Speed Feature. Pedestrians often adjust their motion (e.g., slowing down or avoiding) based on the speeds of nearby individuals. Thus, neighbor velocity is informative for trajectory prediction. We compute the average velocity of neighbors within each sector to capture the overall motion tendency as follows,

$$f^i_{\text{vel}} = \frac{1}{|s_i|} \sum_{j \in s_i} \left| p^j_0 - p^j_{-t_h+1} \right| * 2, \tag{3}$$

where p^j_0 and $p^j_{-t_h+1}$ denote the positions of the j-th neighbor at the current time step and the beginning of the observation window, respectively.

Distance Feature. The influence of neighbors depends on their distance to the target pedestrian. Closer individuals generally exert stronger effects. To capture this, we compute the average Euclidean distance within each sector as follows,

$$f^i_{\text{dis}} = \frac{1}{|s_i|} \sum_{j \in s_i} \left| p^i_0 - p^j_0 \right|_2, \tag{4}$$

where p^i_0 denotes the current position of the target pedestrian.

Angle Feature. Discretizing space into sectors may lose fine-grained directional information. To compensate, we compute the average relative angle of neighbors within each sector as follows,

$$f^i_{\text{dir}} = \frac{1}{|s_i|} \sum_{j \in s_i} \theta(j), \tag{5}$$

where $\theta(j)$ is the polar angle of neighbor j relative to the target pedestrian.

By combining the above features, the sector-level representation is defined as follows,

$$f^i = \begin{cases} g_{\text{embed}}(\mathbf{0}), & |s_i| = 0; \\ g_{\text{embed}}\left((f^i_{\text{vel}}, f^i_{\text{dis}}, f^i_{\text{dir}})^\top\right), & \text{otherwise.} \end{cases} \tag{6}$$

where g_{embed} is a two-layer MLP with ReLU and tanh activations, mapping the aggregated features into a high-dimensional space.

Historical Motion Context Construction. As described above, the historical motion feature of the target pedestrian is denoted as $f_t \in \mathbb{R}^{t_h \times d_t}$, and the neighboring interaction features are represented as $f^i \in \mathbb{R}^{d_n}$ for each sector, forming the overall representation $f \in \mathbb{R}^{12 \times d_n}$.

To align the temporal dimension, a linear layer projects f into $f \in \mathbb{R}^{t_h \times d_n}$. The target motion feature f_t and the transformed neighbor feature are then concatenated along the feature dimension to form the historical motion context $c \in \mathbb{R}^{t_h \times (d_t + d_n)}$. This context feature jointly encodes the target's motion and surrounding interactions, providing a more comprehensive representation of the dynamic environment for subsequent trajectory prediction.

4.2 Multi-modal and Uncertainty Modeling Module

In multi-pedestrian scenarios, future trajectories are jointly influenced by historical motion and spatio-temporal interactions with surrounding pedestrians. Therefore, effective spatio-temporal modeling is essential for capturing these dependencies.

However, pedestrian motion is inherently uncertain, as similar historical contexts may result in different behaviors, such as moving straight, detouring, or changing speed. To model this uncertainty, we decompose it into motion uncertainty and intention uncertainty within a multimodal framework.

Motion Uncertainty Modeling. Even with identical historical states input, the future motion of a pedestrian may vary stochastically. To model this, a latent variable is sampled from a standard Gaussian distribution as follows,

$$z \sim \mathcal{N}(0, I), \tag{7}$$

where $z \in \mathbb{R}^{T_{\text{obs}} \times d_z}$. It captures the random variations in the future motion.

A nonlinear mapping $\phi(\cdot)$ then projects z into the same feature space as the context as follows,

$$h_z = \phi(z) \in \mathbb{R}^{T_{\text{obs}} \times d}, \tag{8}$$

Finally, the latent embedding is fused with the historical context to form the input for spatio-temporal modeling as follows,

$$h_{\text{motion}} = [h_z; c] \in \mathbb{R}^{T_{\text{obs}} \times d}. \tag{9}$$

Spatio-Temporal Attention Encoding. To model the temporal dependencies in historical trajectories and spatial interactions among pedestrians, we adopt a Transformer-based self-attention mechanism to encode the fused motion context. Specifically, the fused feature $h_{\text{motion}} \in \mathbb{R}^{t_h \times d}$ is projected into Query, Key, and Value representations: $Q = cW_Q$, $K = cW_K$, and $V = cW_V$, where W_Q, W_K, and W_V are learnable matrices. A multi-head self-attention mechanism is then applied to capture interactions in different feature subspaces as follows,

$$\text{Attention}(Q_i, K_i, V_i) = \text{softmax}\left(\frac{QK^T}{\sqrt{d_k}}\right)V, \tag{10}$$

$$\text{head}_i = \text{Attention}(Q_i, K_i, V_i), \tag{11}$$

The outputs of all heads are concatenated and linearly projected to obtain the final representation as follows,

$$h = \text{Concat}(\text{head}_1, \ldots, \text{head}_h)W_o, \tag{12}$$

where head_i denotes the i-th attention head and W_o is the output projection matrix.

Through multi-head attention, the model jointly captures the temporal dynamics and the spatial interactions, yielding a compact spatio-temporal representation C for subsequent multi-modal trajectory prediction.

Intention Uncertainty Modeling. To model intention uncertainty, we introduce k_m motion-style branches in the decoding stage, where each branch represents a potential motion pattern (e.g., straight, left turn, right turn, acceleration, or deceleration). Given the fused representation h, each branch independently predicts future motion via a dedicated decoder as follows,

$$y_k^{\text{key}} = \text{Decoder}_k(h), \tag{13}$$

where $k = 1, 2, \ldots, K$ and Decoder_k denotes a nonlinear mapping function. All branches share a common backbone for feature extraction while using separate heads for mode-specific outputs, enabling multi-modal trajectory prediction.

Intermediate Goal Point Modeling for Future Trajectories. Instead of directly regressing full future trajectories, we first predict intermediate goal points. Following [16], we assume pedestrians have implicit long-term intentions (e.g., destinations or waypoints), and model future motion as a sequence guided by these goals. This formulation better aligns with historical motion patterns and reduces prediction complexity.

Given a prediction horizon t_f, we estimate n_{key} intermediate goal points. After linear transformation of y_k^{key}, the output is formulated as $Y^{\text{key}} \in \mathbb{R}^{K \times n_{\text{key}} \times D}$, where K is the number of motion modes, n_{key} is the number of intermediate goals, and $D = 2$ denotes 2D coordinates.

Full Trajectory Construction. Since intermediate goal points only cover part of the future time steps, the complete trajectory is reconstructed from them. To maintain temporal consistency, the last observed point p_0 is added as an anchor as follows,

$$\tilde{Y}^{\text{key}} = \{p_0, y_1, \ldots, y_{n_{\text{key}}}\}. \tag{14}$$

This design avoids discontinuities between predicted and observed trajectories. Given the intermediate goals, piecewise linear interpolation is applied. For two adjacent goals y_i and y_{i+1} at time steps t_i and t_{i+1}, the position at time t is

$$p(t) = y_i + \frac{t - t_i}{t_{i+1} - t_i}(y_{i+1} - y_i). \tag{15}$$

By applying interpolation over all segments, the complete trajectory is obtained as $Y^{\text{inter}} \in \mathbb{R}^{K \times T_{\text{pred}} \times D}$.

This interpolation process is deterministic: it does not introduce additional randomness or new motion modes, but only expands the existing intermediate goal-based patterns into full temporal trajectories. Therefore, the number of trajectory modes remains K at this stage.

Conditional Denoising Trajectory Refinement Module. Although intermediate goal prediction and interpolation can produce reasonable trajectories, deviations from ground truth may still exist due to model and data limitations. To address this, we introduce a conditional diffusion model (DDPM) for refinement. Instead of generating trajectories from pure Gaussian noise, the model operates in residual space. Let Y^{inter} and Y^{gt} denote the interpolated and ground-truth trajectories. The residual is defined as

$$R = Y^{\text{gt}} - Y^{\text{inter}}. \tag{16}$$

The diffusion model learns the residual distribution conditioned on the following formula,

$$\text{cond} = [X, X_{\mathcal{N}}, Y^{\text{inter}}], \tag{17}$$

where X is the target pedestrian history and $X_{\mathcal{N}}$ denotes neighboring trajectories.

During training, Gaussian noise is added to the residual as follows,

$$R_t = \sqrt{\bar{\alpha}_t}\, r + \sqrt{1 - \bar{\alpha}_t}\, \epsilon, \tag{18}$$

where $\epsilon \sim \mathcal{N}(0, I)$. The model is trained to predict the noise: $\epsilon_\theta(R_t, t, \text{cond})$ with the following objective,

$$L = \mathbb{E}\left[\|\epsilon - \epsilon_\theta(R_t, t, c)\|^2\right]. \tag{19}$$

During inference, the model starts from Gaussian noise: $R_T \sim \mathcal{N}(0, I)$ and progressively denoises it via

$$R_{t-1} = \frac{1}{\sqrt{\alpha_t}}\left(R_t - \frac{1 - \alpha_t}{\sqrt{1 - \bar{\alpha}_t}}\epsilon_\theta(R_t, t, c)\right) + \sigma_t z, \tag{20}$$

where z is random noise.

Finally, the refined trajectory is obtained as

$$\hat{Y} = Y^{\text{inter}} + \hat{R}. \tag{21}$$

Overall, the framework follows a two-stage process: coarse multi-modal trajectory generation and residual diffusion-based refinement, improving both accuracy and realism while preserving diversity.

5 Experiment

5.1 Dataset

We evaluate the proposed method on the ETH-UCY pedestrian trajectory prediction benchmark, which comprises five real-world scenes (ETH, Hotel, Univ, Zara1, and Zara2) collected in Zurich, Switzerland (ETH) and Zakynthos, Greece (UCY). The benchmark covers diverse environments, including campuses, streets, and crowded pedestrian areas, with trajectories exhibiting various motion patterns such as straight walking, turning, and collision avoidance. All trajectories are represented in a global coordinate system, and evaluation results are reported in meters.

A leave-one-out cross-validation protocol is adopted in evaluation, where the model is trained on four scenes and tested on the remaining one scene. The observation length is set to $t_h = 8$ frames (3.2 s), and the prediction horizon is $t_f = 12$ frames (4.8 s), with a sampling interval of $\Delta t = 0.4$ s.

5.2 Experiment Setup

We implement the proposed DgCD in PyTorch on an NVIDIA GeForce RTX 3090 GPU. Intermediate goal points are set at frames 0, 6, and 11. The maximum number of neighbors is limited to 50, and the surrounding space is divided into 12 polar sectors. The latent noise dimension is set to 16, and the feature dimension is set to 128. The model is trained for 500 epochs using the Adam optimizer with a learning rate of 1×10^{-3}. In the refinement module, the diffusion process runs 50 steps.

Two standard metrics, Average Displacement Error (ADE) and Final Displacement Error (FDE), are used to evaluate performance over a 4.8-second horizon. Their definitions are given as follows,

$$\mathrm{ADE} = \frac{1}{NT_f} \sum_{i=1}^{N} \sum_{t=T+1}^{T_f} \left\| Y_i^t - \hat{Y}_i^t \right\|_2, \tag{22}$$

$$\mathrm{FDE} = \frac{1}{N} \sum_{i=1}^{N} \left\| Y_i^{T+T_f} - \hat{Y}_i^{T+T_f} \right\|_2, \tag{23}$$

where N denotes the total number of test samples, and Y_i^t and $\hat{Y}_i^t$ represent the ground-truth and predicted coordinates of the i-th pedestrian at time step t, respectively.

5.3 Baselines

We compare DgCD with the following baseline models.

- Social-GAN [6]: It generates diverse trajectories via a GAN framework by using MLP pooling for interaction modeling and a discriminator for uncertainty learning.
- Sophie [19]: It extends Social-GAN by incorporating scene context and an attention-based interaction module.
- CGNS [14]: It models trajectory distributions in a conditional latent space and optimizes via variational divergence minimization.
- Social-LSTM [1]: It uses LSTMs for individual motion encoding and pooling for interaction modeling to generate probabilistic trajectories.

- NMMP [9]: It introduces neural message passing to explicitly model agent interactions with separate motion and interaction branches.
- STAR [26]: It combines spatio-temporal Transformers with graph convolution and external memory for stable trajectory prediction.
- SGCN [22]: It builds sparse interaction graphs via self-attention and applies graph convolution for adaptive relation modeling.
- PECNet [16]: It predicts endpoints first, and then generates multi-modal trajectories with a truncation-based diversity strategy.
- Trajectron++ [21]: It ises a graph-based recurrent architecture to model heterogeneous agents and interactions.
- TAGG [24]: It employs directed attention graphs and trajectory heatmaps to enhance interaction modeling and prediction accuracy.

5.4 Performance Comparison Result

Table 1 shows the performance comparison result among the proposed DgCD with various baseline models on the ETH-UCY dataset (ETH, Hotel, Univ, Zara1, Zara2). One can see from the table that DgCD shows consistent performance improvements across all scenes. In terms of ADE and FDE (lower is better), DgCD achieves an average performance of 0.21 and 0.38, respectively, outperforming all the baselines and demonstrating stronger capability in modeling pedestrian interactions and motion uncertainty.

Table 1. Performance comparison on the ETH-UCY dataset in terms of ADE and FDE

Model	ETH	Hotel	Univ	Zara1	Zara2	AVG
Social-GAN	0.81/1.52	0.72/1.61	0.60/1.26	0.34/0.69	0.42/0.84	0.58/1.18
Sophie	0.70/1.43	0.76/1.67	0.54/1.24	0.30/0.63	0.38/0.78	0.54/1.15
CGNS	0.62/1.40	0.70/0.93	0.48/1.22	0.32/0.59	0.35/0.71	0.49/0.97
Social-LSTM	1.09/2.35	0.79/1.76	0.67/1.40	0.47/1.00	0.56/1.17	0.72/1.54
NMMP	0.61/1.08	0.33/0.63	0.52/1.11	0.32/0.66	0.43/0.85	0.41/0.82
STAR	0.36/0.65	0.17/0.36	0.31/0.62	0.29/0.52	0.22/0.46	0.26/0.53
SGCN	0.63/1.03	0.32/0.55	0.37/0.70	0.29/0.53	0.25/0.45	0.37/0.65
PECNet	0.54/0.87	0.18/0.24	0.35/0.60	0.22/0.39	0.17/0.30	0.29/0.48
Trajectron++	0.61/1.02	0.19/0.28	0.30/0.54	0.24/0.42	0.18/0.32	0.30/0.51
TAGG	0.51/0.68	0.25/0.44	0.30/0.50	0.24/0.42	0.16/0.27	0.29/0.46
DgCD	**0.28/0.48**	**0.17/0.33**	**0.28/0.51**	**0.19/0.32**	**0.13/0.23**	**0.21/0.38**

On ETH, DgCD reduces ADE by about 65.4% and 74.3% compared with Social-GAN and Social-LSTM, and outperforms STAR by 22.2%, which shows significantly performacne improvements. On Hotel, DgCD achieves comparable performance to STAR with slightly better FDE, indicating stable behavior in simpler scenarios. On Univ, DgCD reduces ADE by 21.6% over SGCN, showing better adaptability to complex interactions. On Zara1, DgCD outperforms PECNet and Trajectron++ with ADE reductions of 13.6% and 20.8%, respectively. On Zara2, DgCD achieves the best results, reducing ADE and FDE by 18.8% and 14.8% compared to TAGG, rspectviely, demonstrating strong robustness under stochastic motion.

Overall, DgCD consistently outperforms STAR, TAGG, and Trajectron++ across all scenarios, with particularly significant performance gains in complex interactive environments, highlighting its effectiveness in modeling pedestrian interactions and multi-modal motion.

5.5 Ablation Study

To evaluate the contribution of each component in the DgCD model to trajectory prediction performance, we next conduct ablation study by comparing the full version DgCD with its three model variants as follows.

- **Without Partition**: DgCD removes the sector-based partitioning (i.e., the number of sectors is set to 1).
- **Withour Multi-modal**: DgCD removes the multi-modal trajectory prediction module.
- **Without Diff**: DgCD removes the conditional denoising module.

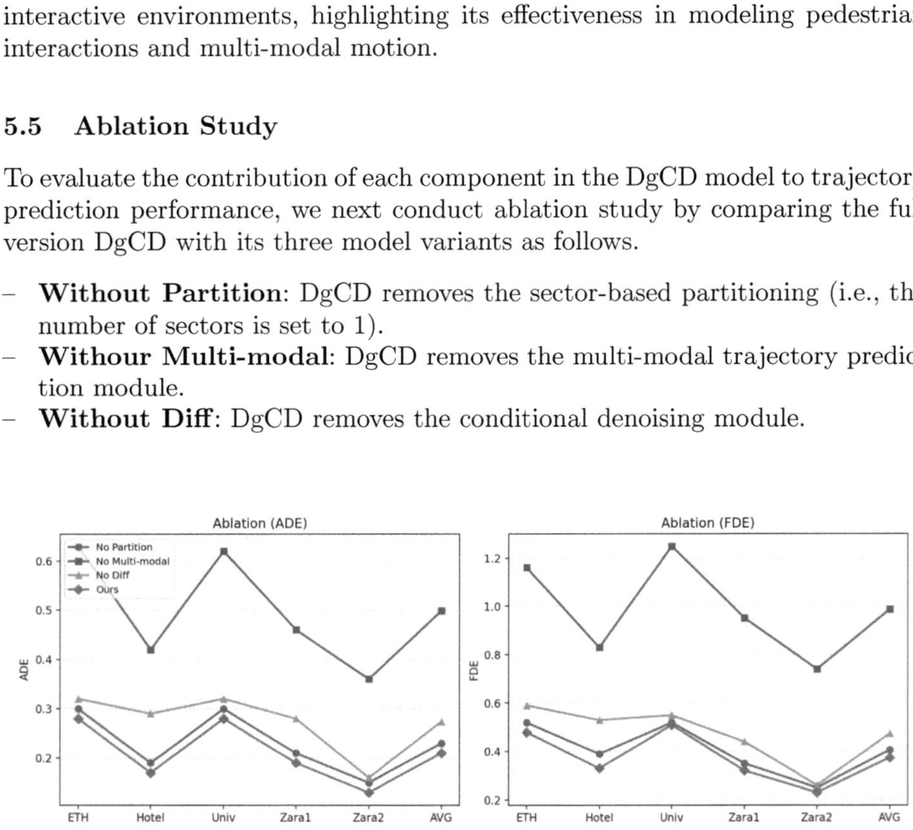

Fig. 3. Ablation study results on five sub-datasets

The results are shown in Fig. 3. Each component contributes to the overall performance. Removing the sector-based partitioning (No Partition) consistently degrades prediction accuracy, demonstrating the effectiveness of direction-guided interaction modeling. The largest performance drop occurs without the multimodal module (No Multi-modal), highlighting the importance of modeling multiple plausible futures and trajectory uncertainty. Removing the conditional denoising module (No Diff) also leads to a noticeable decline, confirming the benefit of residual refinement. Overall, the full model achieves the best performance across all datasets, validating the complementary roles of direction-guided interaction modeling, multimodal prediction, and conditional denoising.

5.6 Case Study

To further show the effectiveness of the DgCD, we further provide a case study in this subsection. Figure 4 shows the prediction results on four representative scenes (ETH, Hotel, Zara1, and Univ). The blue solid line denotes the observed trajectory, the green dashed line is the ground truth, the red dashed line indicates the best prediction, and the light red dashed lines represent other candidate trajectories. One can see that DgCD effectively captures motion trends and interaction effects, producing predictions that closely match the ground truth.

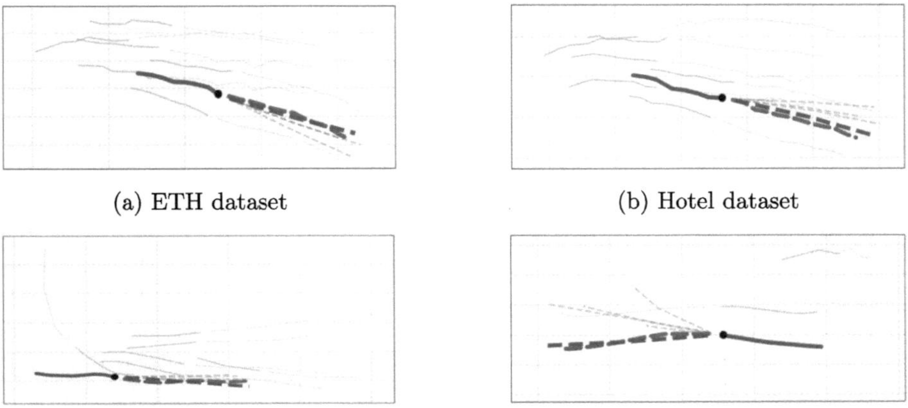

(a) ETH dataset

(b) Hotel dataset

(c) Zara1 dataset

(d) Zara2 dataset

Fig. 4. Visualization results of DgCD on different datasets. The blue solid line denotes the target pedestrian's historical trajectory, the green dashed line the ground-truth future trajectory, and the red dashed line the best predicted trajectory. Red dash-dotted lines represent other predicted trajectories, while gray solid and dashed lines denote the historical and ground-truth future trajectories of neighboring pedestrians, respectively. (Color figure online)

In scenes (a) and (d) with strong interactions, the model accurately captures turning behaviors influenced by nearby pedestrians. In scene (c), where interactions are weak, the prediction nearly overlaps with the ground truth, indicating stable performance. In scene (b), where multiple future paths exist, the best prediction remains accurate while other candidates reflect alternative motion patterns, demonstrating DgCD is able to represent uncertainty.

6 Conclusion

This paper investigates uncertainty-aware pedestrian trajectory prediction and proposes a direction-guided conditional denoising framework (DgCD) to improve accuracy and robustness in complex scenarios. The model encodes the target pedestrian's historical trajectory and constructs a pedestrian-centered polar coordinate system, where neighboring motion features are aggregated within directional sectors to capture direction-aware interactions. These features are fused into a unified motion context. Stochastic latent variables are introduced to model multimodal futures and generate diverse motion patterns. Intermediate trajectory points are predicted and linearly interpolated to form complete trajectories, followed by a conditional denoising module for residual refinement. Experiments on real-world datasets demonstrate that DgCD effectively models trajectory uncertainty and achieves strong performance.

Acknowledgement. This work was supported by the National Natural Science Foundation of China (NSFC) under Grant No. 62572489.

References

1. Alahi, A., Goel, K., Ramanathan, V., Robicquet, A., Fei-Fei, L., Savarese, S.: Social LSTM: Human trajectory prediction in crowded spaces. In: Proceedings of the IEEE Conference On Computer Vision And Pattern Recognition, pp. 961–971 (2016)
2. Best, G., Fitch, R.: Bayesian intention inference for trajectory prediction with an unknown goal destination. In: IEEE/RSJ International Conference on Intelligent Robots and Systems (IROS), pp. 5817–5823. IEEE (2015)
3. Chen, X., Zhang, H., Zhao, F., Hu, Y., Tan, C., Yang, J.: Intention-aware vehicle trajectory prediction based on spatial-temporal dynamic attention network for internet of vehicles. IEEE Trans. Intell. Transp. Syst. **23**(10), 19471–19483 (2022)
4. Cinelli, L.P., Marins, M.A., Da Silva, E.A.B., Netto, S.L.: Variational methods for machine learning with applications to deep networks, vol. 15, Springer (2021)
5. Fu, Z., Jiang, K., Xie, C., Xu, Y., Huang, J., Yang, D.: Summary and reflections on pedestrian trajectory prediction in the field of autonomous driving. IEEE Transactions on Intelligent Vehicles (2024)
6. Gupta, A., Johnson, J., Fei-Fei, L., Savarese, S., Alahi, A.: Social GAN: Socially acceptable trajectories with generative adversarial networks. In: Proceedings of the IEEE Conference on Computer Vision and Pattern Recognition, pp. 2255–2264 (2018)
7. Helbing, D., Molnar, P.: Social force model for pedestrian dynamics. Phys. Rev. E **51**(5), 4282 (1995)
8. Ho, J., Jain, A., Abbeel, P.: Denoising diffusion probabilistic models. Adv. Neural. Inf. Process. Syst. **33**, 6840–6851 (2020)
9. Hu, Y., Chen, S., Zhang, Y., Gu, X.: Collaborative motion prediction via neural motion message passing. In: Proceedings of the IEEE/CVF Conference on Computer Vision and Pattern Recognition, pp. 6319–6328 (2020)

10. Jiang, J., Yan, K., Xia, X., Yang, B.: A survey of deep learning-based pedestrian trajectory prediction: challenges and solutions. Sensors **25**(3), 957 (2025)
11. Karamouzas, I., Heil, P., Van Beek, P., Overmars, M.H.: A predictive collision avoidance model for pedestrian simulation. In: International workshop on motion in games, pp. 41–52. Springer (2009)
12. Kooij, J.F.P., Schneider, N., Flohr, F., Gavrila, D.M.: Context-based pedestrian path prediction. In: European Conference on Computer Vision, pp. 618–633. Springer (2014)
13. Korbmacher, R., Tordeux, A.: Review of pedestrian trajectory prediction methods: Comparing deep learning and knowledge-based approaches. IEEE Trans. Intell. Transp. Syst. **23**(12), 24126–24144 (2022)
14. Li, J., Ma, H., Tomizuka, M.: Conditional generative neural system for probabilistic trajectory prediction. In: IEEE/RSJ International Conference on Intelligent Robots and Systems (IROS), pp. 6150–6156 IEEE (2019)
15. Liu, Y., Ye, Z., Wang, R., Li, B., Sheng, Q.Z., Yao, L.: Uncertainty-aware pedestrian trajectory prediction via distributional diffusion. Knowl.-Based Syst. **296**, 111862 (2024)
16. Mangalam, K., et al.: It is not the journey but the destination: Endpoint conditioned trajectory prediction. In: European Conference on Computer Vision, pp. 759–776. Springer (2020)
17. Mao, W., Xu, C., Zhu, Q., Chen, S., Wang, Y.: Leapfrog diffusion model for stochastic trajectory prediction. In: Proceedings of the IEEE/CVF Conference on Computer Vision and Pattern Recognition, pp. 5517–5526 (2023)
18. Mohamed, A., Qian, K., Elhoseiny, M., Claudel, C.: Social-STGCNN: A social spatio-temporal graph convolutional neural network for human trajectory prediction. In: Proceedings of the IEEE/CVF Conference on Computer Vision and Pattern Recognition, pp. 14424–14432 (2020)
19. Sadeghian, A., Kosaraju, V., Sadeghian, A., Hirose, N., Rezatofighi, H., Savarese, S.: Sophie: An attentive GAN for predicting paths compliant to social and physical constraints. In: Proceedings of the IEEE/CVF Conference on Computer Vision and Pattern Recognition, pp. 1349–1358 (2019)
20. Salimans, T., Ho, J.: Progressive distillation for fast sampling of diffusion models. arXiv preprint arXiv:2202.00512 (2022)
21. Salzmann, T., Ivanovic, B., Chakravarty, P., Pavone, M.: Trajectron++: Dynamically-feasible trajectory forecasting with heterogeneous data. In: European Conference on Computer Vision, pp. 683–700. Springer (2020)
22. Shi, L., et al.: SGCN: Sparse graph convolution network for pedestrian trajectory prediction. In: Proceedings of the IEEE/CVF Conference on Computer Vision and Pattern Recognition, pp. 8994–9003 (2021)
23. Vaswani, A., et al.: Attention is all you need. In: Advances in Neural Information Processing Systems, vol. 30 (2017)
24. Wang, R., Hu, Z., Song, X., Li, W.: Trajectory distribution aware graph convolutional network for trajectory prediction considering spatio-temporal interactions and scene information. IEEE Trans. Knowl. Data Eng. **36**(8), 4304–4316 (2023)
25. Xue, H., Huynh, D.Q., Reynolds, M.: SS-LSTM: A hierarchical LSTM model for pedestrian trajectory prediction. In: IEEE Winter Conference on Applications of Computer Vision (WACV), pp. 1186–1194. IEEE (2018)
26. Yu, C., Ma, X., Ren, J., Zhao, H., Yi, S.: Spatio-temporal graph transformer networks for pedestrian trajectory prediction. In: European Conference on Computer Vision, pp. 507–523. Springer (2020)

EVT^2: Efficient and Verifiable Trajectory Top-k Queries in Hybrid-Storage Blockchains

Yusen Mao[1], Zhongming Yao[2], Junchang Xin[1,3(✉)], Chenchen Yan[1], Yumeng Song[2], Zhongzhong Jiang[1], and Zhiqiong Wang[1]

[1] Northeastern University, Shenyang, China
{maoyusen,yanchenchen}@stumail.neu.edu.cn,
{xinjunchang,zzjiang}@mail.neu.edu.cn, wangzq@bmie.neu.edu.cn
[2] Aalborg University, Aalborg, Denmark
{zyao,yumengs}@cs.aau.dk
[3] Key Laboratory of Big Data Management and Analytics (Liaoning Province), Northeastern University, Shenyang, China

Abstract. With the exponential growth of trajectory data, outsourcing trajectory storage and query processing to third-party service providers has become a common practice. However, this model may introduce data distortion issues, such as incomplete or tampered query results. To address this problem, existing studies typically incorporate blockchain systems for trusted storage and employ Authenticated Data Structures (ADSs) to enable verifiable query processing. Nevertheless, for trajectory Top-k queries, existing ADS-based approaches suffer from low efficiency in verifying result completeness, mainly because they require complex pruning over numerous spatial and temporal attributes. To tackle this challenge, we propose EVT^2, a verifiable trajectory Top-k query framework designed for hybrid-storage blockchain systems. Specifically, we design two spatiotemporally decoupled authenticated data structures: an interval tree–based temporal ADS (ITTA) and a GTree-based spatial ADS (GTSA). These structures effectively reduce the complexity of pruning during verification, thereby improving the efficiency of result completeness verification. Based on these structures, we further develop a verifiable Top-k query mechanism. Experiments on two real-world trajectory datasets demonstrate that EVT^2 achieves orders-of-magnitude improvements in both query performance and verification efficiency compared with state-of-the-art approaches.

Keywords: Trajectory · Verifiable Queries · Top-k Queries · Blockchain

1 Introduction

In recent years, trajectory data has been widely applied in many fields, such as traffic planning [1], logistics dispatch [2], and personalized services [3]. Consequently, efficient management and in-depth analysis of trajectory data have

L. Ding et al. (Eds.): APWeb-WAIM 2026, LNCS 16995, pp. 216–232, 2027.
https://doi.org/10.1007/978-981-92-5699-0_14

become essential requirements in many industrial applications. However, with the continuous growth of trajectory data, storing and querying such large-scale data consumes substantial computing and storage resources. Currently, the mainstream solution is to outsource the storage and query processing of trajectory data to third-party servers [3,4]. Nevertheless, this outsourcing model introduces potential security risks, as third-party servers may return tampered query results [5–8], which undermines the trustworthiness of data services.

To address this issue, blockchain-based hybrid storage systems [5–7,9,10] have been proposed as a new architecture for trusted third-party services. These systems leverage the security, transparency, and immutability of blockchain to provide a verification mechanism for query processing. Specifically, the data owner submits the raw data and the authenticated data structure (ADS) to the service provider while uploading the digest of the ADS to the blockchain. When a query is executed, the server returns the query results along with the corresponding verification objects (VOs). The client then computes a digest based on the returned results and VOs, and compares it with the digest stored on the blockchain to verify whether the results have been tampered with. Owing to the advantages of blockchain-based hybrid storage systems, this approach is naturally suitable for verifiable trajectory Top-k queries processing.

Despite these advances, existing schemes [5–7,10,11] cannot efficiently support trajectory Top-k queries. A trajectory Top-k query is a typical personalized data service that retrieves the top k trajectories that best match given conditions from massive trajectory datasets. Since the query results directly affect the quality of higher-level analysis, decision-making, and scheduling, such queries require strong guarantees on the accuracy and integrity of the returned results. Therefore, how to efficiently and reliably verify the correctness of query results returned by third-party servers remains a critical challenge. To address this pressing problem, we design a novel verifiable framework for trajectory Top-k queries by integrating authenticated data structures and verification mechanisms, enabling efficient, secure and trustworthy query processing. However, this design introduces two key practical challenges.

Challenge I: How to design ADSs for verifiable trajectory Top-k queries? Unlike traditional index structures, ADSs integrate cryptographic hashes into their internal structure to support queries verification. The temporal and spatial attributes of the index for trajectory Top-k queries are mutually constrained, and traditional indexes integrate these two attributes into a unified index structure. A large number of pruning operations are required during Top-k query processing, which can be readily implemented with existing query indexes (e.g., 3DR-tree [30]). However, when cryptographic attributes are embedded to ensure the completeness verification of pruning boundaries, a substantial amount of redundant boundary verification information is generated, which significantly impairs both query efficiency and verification efficiency.

Challenge II: How to support efficient verifiable trajectory Top-k queries based on ADSs? Besides ADSs construction, how to realize efficient query and verification using ADSs remains an urgent problem. Trajectory

Top-k queries involve extensive index pruning: pruned intermediate nodes need completeness verification, while results only exist in leaf nodes, causing redundant hash aggregation and low verification efficiency. Furthermore, using cryptographic hashing to prove all entries after the k-th rank are inferior is inefficient, due to the lack of a unified verification boundary. Finally, limited by the continuous property of hash chains, traditional ADSs cannot generate verifiable objects in parallel for Top-k queries, which becomes a major efficiency bottleneck.

To address these challenges, we introduce a novel framework for **E**fficient and **V**erifiable **T**rajectory **T**op-k queries, called $\texttt{EVT}^2$. To address Challenge I, we design two ADSs based on interval tree (ITTA) and GTree (GTSA), which encrypt and store the temporal and spatial information of trajectory data separately. Since trajectory Top-k queries jointly evaluate spatial and temporal performance, ITTA and GTSA are logically related. To avoid locally optimal but globally inferior results, we use ITTA to filter valid trajectories by temporal information and pre-filter candidates for GTSA, which guarantees that all road nodes in GTSA results meet the temporal requirement. Meanwhile, we delegate spatial completeness verification to the client, which uses a lightweight road network index for neighbor queries and ensures no trajectory is missed.

To address Challenge II, In ITTA, we construct a minimal subtree that covers all traversed index nodes to avoid redundant hash computations. In GTSA, we separate the underlying trajectory datas from the index, so that verification objects can be generated and verified in parallel, which improves query and verification efficiency. Finally, we send the scores of the filtered trajectories to the client, which simplifies the logic of result completeness verification. The main contributions are summarized as follows:

- We present $\texttt{EVT}^2$, a framework for verifiable trajectory Top-k queries over hybrid-storage blockchain, and design ITTA and GTSA. To the best of our knowledge, this work is the first to employ ADSs for supporting verifiable trajectory Top-k queries.
- We design efficient query and verification algorithms based on ITTA and GTSA to significantly enhance the overall efficiency of both query execution and query results verification.
- We conduct extensive experiments against other state-of-the-art indexes, demonstrating $\texttt{EVT}^2$'s high efficiency in query and verification.

Section 2 reviews the related work. Section 3 provides some preliminaries. Section 4 introduces the proposed ADSs and thread model. Section 5 introduces query and verification processing. Section 6 and 7 give security analysis and performance evaluation, respectively. Section 8 presents a conclusion.

2 Related Work

Hybrid-Storage Blockchain System. Hybrid-storage blockchain system has emerged as a mainstream method to slove blockchain storage pressure. The multi-replica storage mechanism of traditional blockchains ensures data reliability [15–17], but redundant storage [18,19] becomes prominent when handling large-scale incremental data like road network trajectories. In recent years, some studies adopt this storage paradigm to address the problem of query verification ensuring query verifiability while alleviating the storage burden of blockchain. Wang et al. [14]. propose the vChain+ reducing single-node storage capacity and enabling verifiable boolean range queries. Futher, Li et al. [5] introduce the MVPTree avoiding result mismatches and omissions during subgraph matching. Li et al. [6] propose the MP-DAG for graph data to efficiently handle keyword queries. Wu et al. [7] propose the PAGB architecture to address the issues of privacy leakage and excessive storage costs in cloud-based graph queries. Zhou et al. [20] introduce the RGB-Trie to verify SPARQL queries on decentralized knowledge graphs. Cui et al. [21] propose a virtual keyword forest to facilitate secure and reliably verifiable query processing in hybrid-storage blockchains. However, existing researches still lack an applicable scheme for secure and verifiable trajectory Top-k queries.

Top- *k* Query. Top-k query is a core method in data management and information retrieval. This query technique filters the k optimal results from large-scale datasets based on rules, and is widely applied to scenarios like e-commerce recommendation and intelligent transportation. Zhong et al. [22] propose GTree accelerating road network neighbor queries by partitioning subgraphs based on edge weights and pre-storing distance matrices. Futher, Chung et al. [23] propose the FANN-PHL algorithm reduces the computational complexity of neighbor queries in road networks. Xu et al. [24] introduce the KNN-index prestores high-frequency query results to optimize index size and query latency. Li et al. [25] propose the TD-H2H adopts a time-attribute-based pruning strategy to enhance the neighbor query efficiency of moving objects in time-dependent road networks. Qi et al. [26] introduce the NNA algorithm retrieving neighbor trajectory points of query points is an order of magnitude faster than traditional methods. However, existing studies only focus on query efficiency and ignore the verification of result . Since trajectory data is mostly stored in third-party databases, trustworthy queries are essential. Moreover, the characteristics of trajectory data bring verification challenges, and existing methods fail to meet requirements.

3 Preliminaries

3.1 Trajectory Top-*k* Queries

Raw trajectories consist of a series of GPS points $p = ((x, y), t)$, where (x, y) denotes longitude and latitude [27,28], and t is the timestamp.

Definition 1. A **road network** is modeled as an undirected weighted graph $G = (V, E, W)$, where V denotes the vertex set of road intersections, E is the edge set and each edge represents a road segment, and W is the weight set representing physical length of road segments.

Figure 1 shows a road network with 15 intersections and 16 segments. For example, vertex v_4 has to incident connecting it to vertices v_3 and v_9.

Definition 2. A **trajectory** $Tr = \langle (v_0, t_0), (v_1, t_1), \ldots, (v_m, t_m) \rangle$ is obtained by map-matching a raw trajectory onto a road network $G = (V, E, W)$, such that $v_k \in V$ and $(v_{k-1}, v_k) \in E$, and $0 \le k \le m$. Specifically, each pair (v_i, t_i) indicates that the moving object is located at vertex $v_i \in V$ at time t_i.

Example 1. In Fig. 1, 12 dashed lines with different colors represent trajectories $\{Tr_1, \ldots, Tr_{12}\}$. Specifically, Tr_3, Tr_5 consist of four vertices.

Top-k queries have been recognized as fundamental operations in database systems [29]. Accordingly, they have analogous applications in trajectory queries, which retrieve the k trajectories that best match the query criteria.

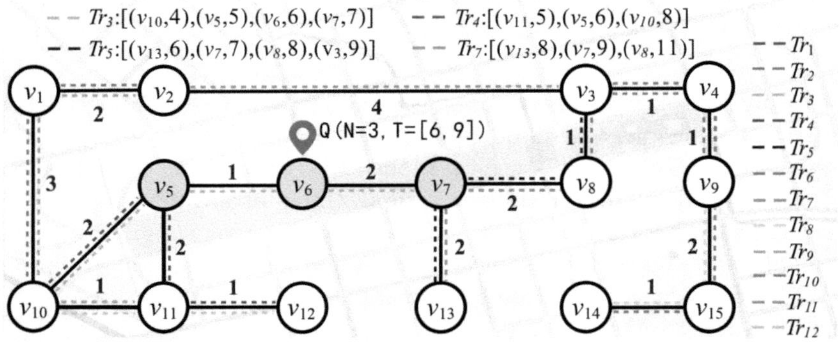

Fig. 1. Example trajectories in a road network.

Definition 3. Given a query anchor point v_q, a spatial neighbor count n, a timestamp t_q, a time interval radius Δt, and a threshold k, a **trajectory Top-*k* query** $q = (v_q, n, t_q, \Delta t, k)$ returns k trajectories sorted by scoring mechanism.

Scoring Mechanism. V_{near} denotes the set of spatial neighbors of the query anchor point, let d_i denote the shortest path distance between vertex v_i and anchor point, and $d_m = \max_{v_i \in V_{\text{near}}} d_i + 1$. The spatial weight of v_i is defined as:

$$w_i = \begin{cases} \frac{d_m - d_i}{\sum_{v_j \in V_{\text{near}}} (d_m - d_j)}, & v_i \in V_{\text{near}} \\ 0, & otherwise \end{cases} \tag{1}$$

where $\sum_{v_i \in V_{\text{near}}} w_i = 1$ and $w_0 > w_1 > \cdots > w_m > 0$, $m = |V_{\text{near}}|$. Building on this, for a trajectory tr passing v_i at timestamp t_p, the spatiotemporal point score is calculated as:

$$S_p(t, v_i) = w_i \cdot \begin{cases} e^{-\alpha(t_p - t_q)^2/(2\Delta t)^2}, & t_p \in [t_q - \Delta t, t_q + \Delta t] \\ 0, & \text{otherwise} \end{cases} \tag{2}$$

where $\alpha > 0$ is a tunable temporal sensitivity parameter (Larger α means stricter time matching). The spatial distance of a trajectory to a point depends on its minimum distance [3] to the point, likewise for spatiotemporal distance, the total comprehensive score of trajectory tr is defined as:

$$S(tr) = \max\{S_p(t, v_i) \mid v_i \in V\} \tag{3}$$

Example 2. Continuing Example 1, consider the Top-2 query $q = (v_6, 3, 7.5, 1.5, 2)$. As shown in Fig. 1, starting from the query point v_6, two neighbors v_5 and v_7 are identified, with trajectories matching the query time, and these three vertices form a small spatial region. The trajectories passing through this region are Tr_3, Tr_4, Tr_5, and Tr_7. By the scoring mechanism the two trajectories are determined to be Tr_3, Tr_5.

3.2 Verifiable Query Methods

Authenticated data structures enable verification of the soundness and completeness of data, in which Merkle trees serves as a classic example.

Definition 4. A **Merkle tree** is a binary tree-based ADS built over dataset $\mathcal{D} = \{d_1, \ldots, d_n\}$ with the following properties: (i) Leaf nodes store $h_i = hash(d_i)$ $(1 \le i \le n)$; (ii) Non-leaf nodes store $h = hash(h_{\text{left}} \mid h_{\text{right}})$, where $h_{\text{left}}, h_{\text{right}}$ are the hash values of the left and right child nodes respectively, and $\mid$ denotes concatenation; (iii) The roothash value uniquely represents characterizes $\mathcal{D}$.

4 System Model and ADSs

4.1 System Model and Threat Model

Hybrid-Storage Blockchain System Model. As shown in Fig. 2, the system involves four types of participants. (i) *Data owners (DO)* generate raw trajectory data, they entrust data to third-party servers. (ii) *Service providers (SP)* store the raw data off-chain and offer query services. (iii) *Clients* initiate queries and receive the query results. (iv) *Blockchain System* maintains an on-chain root digest based on the raw data.

First, the DO constructs ADSs over raw trajectory datas, provides it to the SP, and writes the root digests into the blockchain for query verification. When a client initiates a Top-k query, the SP retrieves results via ITTA and GTSA, and returns them to the client with verification objects I-VO and G-VO. The client reconstructs the root digests from the results and two VOs, compares them to the blockchain-stored digests to check for malicious result tampering, and finally scores the filtered trajectories to select the top k.

4.2 Road Trajectory Temporal ADS

Construction. Traditional road network trajectory indexes integrate spatiotemporal attributes into a single structure. A trajectory traverses multiple road network nodes with corresponding timestamps, and the rapid growth of trajectory data causes index inflation. These redundant timestamps degrade query and verification efficiency, because determining whether a trajectory meets the query time interval requires checking all nodes on the trajectory one by one. To solve this problem, we propose ITTA based on an interval tree, which only stores the start and end times of each trajectory. This scheme reduces storage overhead, improves query and verification efficiency, and avoids embedding temporal attributes into the spatial index.

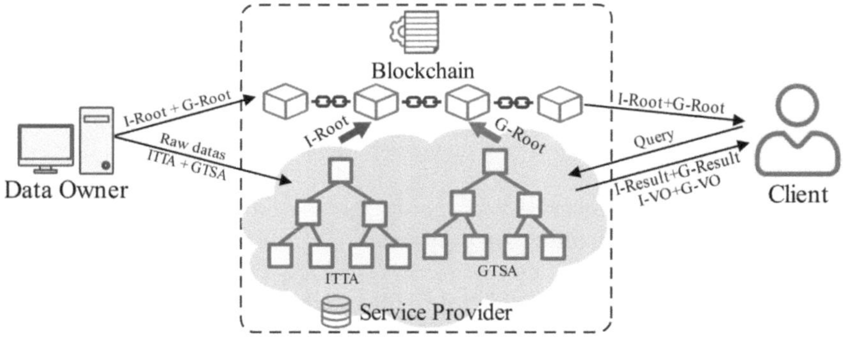

Fig. 2. Authenticated Query Framework in Hybrid-Storage Blockchain.

Definition 5. Given a set of trajectories $S_{Tr} = \{Tr_1, Tr_2, \ldots, Tr_n\}$ where each Tr_i has a sequence of road network nodes and their associated timestamps (v_k, t_k), a **interval tree-based temporal ADS (ITTA)**, Tt is recursively represented as a balanced binary tree:

$$Tt = \begin{cases} (h(Tr_i), [t, t'], h(Ps_i), Ht(Tt)) & \text{if } Tt \text{ is a leaf node} \\ (h(Tr_i), t_{\min}, t_{\max}, h(Ps_i), Ht(Tt), (Tt_l, Tt_r)), & \text{Otherwise} \end{cases}$$

where $h(Tr_i)$ is the hash value of a trajectory Tr_w, which can uniquely identify the trajectory; $t_{\min}$ is the minimum timestamp among all nodes in the tree Tt; $t_{\max}$ is the maximum timestamp among all nodes in the tree Tt; $[t, t']$ is a temporal range, where t is the start time of Tr_i and t' is the end time of Tr_i; $h(Ps_i)$ is the set of road network nodes traversed by the trajectory; Tt_l and Tt_r are the left and right subtrees of Tt, respectively; $Ht(Tt)$ is the hash value of the node:

$$Ht(Tt) = \begin{cases} h(Tr_i) \| [t, t'] \| Ps_i & \text{if } Tt \text{ is a leaf node} \\ h(Tr_i) \| [t, t'] \| t_{\min} \| t_{\max} \| Ps_i \| Ht(Tt_l) \| Ht(Tt_r). & \text{Otherwise} \end{cases}$$

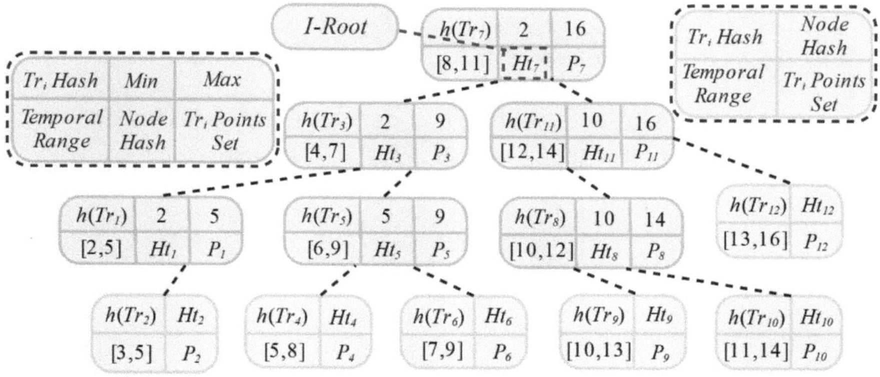

Fig. 3. An example of ITTA.

Update. In ITTA, inserting a new interval transaction involves three core steps. First, insert the interval into the red-black tree-based interval tree, which may maintain balance via left or right rotations and recoloring. Second, update the Max and Min fields of affected nodes upward along the insertion path. Finally, recompute the hash values bottom-up along the path, generate the updated I-Root at the top, and ensure data completeness and soundness.

4.3 Road Trajectory Spatial ADS

Construction. The spatial verifiable index is inspired by GTree, however, as GTree is a nearest neighbor query index built on road network nodes, its query verification lacks clear boundaries, thus making the verification of result completeness relatively complex. To address this issue, we decompose the spatial index into two components, the client-side stored index only contains road network information, while the server-side stored index integrates trajectory data and has complete hash properties. Based on this design, we entrust the task of query completeness verification to the client, and the server is responsible for providing the basis for trajectory soundness verification. For the server-side index, we incorporate the design philosophy of the Merkle Bucket Tree into the construction of its hash properties, and optimize the storage scheme of this index with parallel query and verification capabilities.

Definition 6. Given road network $G = (V, E, W)$ and trajectories $S_{Tr} = \{Tr_1, \ldots, Tr_n\}$, a **GTree-based spatial ADS (GTSA)**, Tg is defined recursively as multiway tree:

$$Tg = \begin{cases} (D_g, B_g, H_g, V_g^l, \{(v, L_{Tr_v}, H_v) \mid v \in V_g^l\}) & \text{if } Tg \text{ is a leaf node} \\ (D_g, B_g, H_g, \{Tg_1, \ldots, Tg_k\}), & \text{Otherwise} \end{cases}$$

where D_g is distance matrix of Tg, store the inter-node distances of boundary nodes; B_g stores boundary road nodes set of Tg; L_{Tr_v} stores trajectories at road node v; V_g^l is road nodes set in leaf Tg; H_v is the hash value of L_{Tr_v}; $\{Tg_1, \ldots, Tg_k\}$ is children of non-leaf Tg; H_g is the hash value of Tg:

$$H_g(Tg) = \begin{cases} h(H_{v_1} \parallel \cdots \parallel H_{v_m}) & \text{if } Tg \text{ is a leaf node} \\ h(H_g(Tg_1) \parallel \cdots \parallel H_g(Tg_k)). & \text{Otherwise} \end{cases}$$

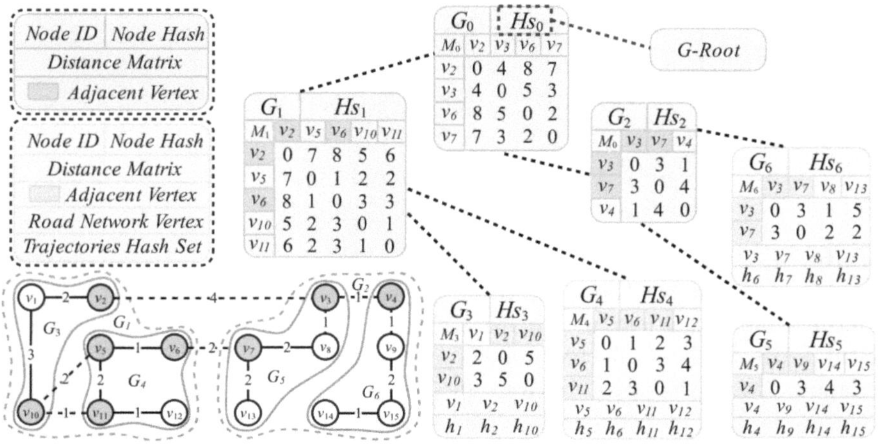

Fig. 4. An example of binary GTSA.

Update. Updating a new trajectory transaction in GTSA involves three main steps. First, insert the trajectory into the corresponding leaf nodes of the spatial index based on the road network nodes it traverses. Second, update the hash attributes of the road network nodes where the trajectory is inserted. Finally, recompute the updated index buckets and perform bottom-up aggregation along the index tree to generate a new G-Root, ensuring the consistency and verifiability of the entire spatial index.

5 Query and Verification

5.1 ITTA and GTSA Query

Temporal Query. Temporal index query logic: Generate a query interval from the specified timestamp, then start root-to-node pre-order traversal. For each node, verify subtree max and min fields to check for overlaps with the query interval. If no overlap, terminate subtree query and return boundary verification info. If overlap exists, check if the node trajectory interval meets the query interval, return trajectory data as results (I-Result) and record traversed vertices when satisfied, else return the interval as verification information (I-VO). Collected nodes act as the candidate set C for spatial index queries.

Example 3. As Fig.3 shows, for query interval $[6, 9]$, pre-order traversal starts at root. The root has temporal range $[2, 16]$ (overlapping query) and trajectory interval $[3, 5]$, so its trajectory info is returned, followed by left and right subtree search. Tr_3 (range $[2, 9]$, overlap exists) with trajectory $[4, 7]$ returns info. Tr_1 (range $[2, 5]$, no overlap) prunes left child and returns boundary value 5. Tr_2, Tr_4, Tr_5 follow Tr_3's logic. Tr_{11} (range $[10, 16]$, no overlap) is pruned safely, returning boundary value 10. Finally, I-VO is a local index tree without pending verification info and $C = \{v_1, v_2, v_3, v_4, v_5, v_7, v_8, v_9, v_{11}, v_{12}, v_{13}, v_{14}\ v_{15}\}$.

Spatial Query. Based on the GTree index, given a road network anchor point and a road network neighbor count n, we select the nearest n road network points from the candidate points filtered by the time index, return their trajectories (G-Result), and take the paths from these road network points to the root node as the verification information (G-VO).

Example 4. As shown in Fig. 4, given the query anchor v_6, a road network neighbor count $n = 3$, and the query candidate set C, the GTree query logic identifies the top n nearest road network points as v_5, v_6, v_7, and returns the trajectory information passing through these three road network points.

Filtering. Result sets R_t and R_s are received from ITTA and GTSA, respectively. However, R_t contains trajectories that fail to satisfy spatial constraints, while R_s includes those violating temporal constraints. To address this, the client computes the intersection of the two sets as $R' = R_t \cap R_s$, thereby ensuring all trajectories in R' meet both spatial and temporal constraints. Subsequently, by the scoring mechanism is employed to select the top k trajectories from R'.

Example 5. Continuing Example 3 and Example 4, $R_t = \{Tr_3, Tr_4, Tr_5, Tr_6, Tr_7\}$ and $R_s = \{Tr_3, Tr_4, Tr_5, Tr_7\}$. $R' = R_t \cap R_s = \{Tr_3, Tr_4, Tr_5, Tr_7\}$. Through the scoring mechanism Tr_3 and Tr_5 are filtered.

5.2 Verification of Query Results

Once the query execution is completed, the system must verify the soundness and completeness of the result before it can be trusted.

The time index verification on the client side consists of three phases: first, inserting the I-Result into the I-VO; second, verifying all inserted timestamps to prevent the I-Result from being tampered with, which would otherwise enable the client to still aggregate a valid root hash while the reconstructed tree is inconsistent with the query path tree; third, aggregating the new root hash of this partial tree in a bottom-up manner and comparing it with the I-Root maintained on the blockchain.

The verification logic of the spatial index first uses the lightweight road network index stored locally on the client to verify the completeness of the nearest road network points retrieved by the server, then embeds G-Result into G-VO to efficiently validate the soundness of trajectory results, because query completeness verification is not required here, distributed verification can be performed directly, and finally the aggregated new digest is compared with the G-Root maintained in the blockchain.

6 Security Analysis

The security of our trajectory Top-k query algorithm is guaranteed by Authenticated Data Structures (ADSs) and blockchain: the off-chain ADS root digest is securely anchored on-chain. Under secure cryptographic primitives, any ADS malicious tampering will be inconsistent with the on-chain digest and detected by clients. Against two typical attacks from the SP, our scheme provides the following security guarantees:

Soundness: If the SP tampers, forges or discards query results from ITTA or GTSA, the immutable sequential correlations among trajectory, road network and temporal information are maintained by hash chains. Due to the bottom-up aggregation mechanism of ADS, any unauthorized modification breaks the hash chain integrity. Thus, the hash recomputed by the client will mismatch the on-chain root digest, enabling immediate detection of such malicious behaviors.

Completeness: If the SP deliberately omits key road network nodes to return incomplete trajectories, the client can verify node integrity using its local lightweight road network index. If the SP forges the I-VO of ITTA for malicious pruning, the client can validate it by checking time interval constraints during hash aggregation. The client performs all aggregation and filtering locally as the service beneficiary. Since it gains no benefit from result forgery, it has no incentive to act maliciously.

Table 1. Trajectory query time (s).

Dataset		Chengdu					Xi'an				
Spa	Tem	1min	10min	30min	1h	2h	1min	10min	30min	1h	2h
5	GKQ	3.930	4.239	2.505	2.985	1.505	1.238	1.220	1.590	1.232	1.238
	EVT^2	**0.485**	**0.493**	**0.456**	**0.438**	**0.383**	**0.121**	**0.120**	**0.159**	**0.211**	**0.294**
10	GKQ	10.36	11.28	6.258	6.349	4.804	2.396	2.324	1.945	1.309	1.311
	EVT^2	**0.566**	**0.568**	**0.561**	**0.577**	**0.529**	**0.158**	**0.181**	**0.213**	**0.237**	**0.294**
15	GKQ	17.71	18.81	10.36	8.536	5.299	3.474	3.395	2.008	1.419	1.449
	EVT^2	**0.702**	**0.776**	**0.702**	**0.683**	**0.612**	**0.174**	**0.168**	**0.217**	**0.275**	**0.336**
20	GKQ	18.13	18.28	16.57	9.816	7.345	3.353	3.435	2.085	1.496	1.488
	EVT^2	**0.827**	**0.898**	**0.955**	**0.781**	**0.688**	**0.222**	**0.214**	**0.251**	**0.212**	**0.366**
30	GKQ	41.59	39.65	23.82	15.49	16.05	4.199	3.979	2.510	1.703	1.846
	EVT^2	**1.287**	**1.154**	**1.266**	**1.095**	**0.902**	**0.261**	**0.257**	**0.268**	**0.315**	**0.382**

7 Experiment

7.1 Experimental Settings

Implementation Details. We implement the service provider and client in python 3.10.11, and implement ADSs in C++14. The provider runs on Intel Core i9, 2.67GHz, 16GB RAM and client on Intel Core i7, 2.60GHz, 16GB RAM. Our blockchain is built on Ethereum, with a 16-node private network deployed on VMware 17.5.2 with Ubuntu 22.04.

Datasets. Two real-world online car-hailing trajectory datasets are used: Chengdu (284,608 trajectories, Oct 1Nov 30, 2018) with a partial road network of 8,882 edges and 5,725 vertices, averaging 773 points per trajectory; and Xi'an (53,739 trajectories, Oct 131, 2018) with a partial road network of 8,651 edges and 3,946 vertices, averaging 1,730 points per trajectory.

Baseline. ***GTree Top-k Query (GKQ)*** embeds temporal and verification attributes into the traditional GTree to support verifiable trajectory Top-k queries.

7.2 Query Performance

We evaluate the trajectory query performance of EVT^2 and baseline on the Chengdu and Xi'an datasets. The road network nearest neighbor query range is set as $n \in \{5, 10, 15, 20, 30\}$. Query anchors are randomly sampled from all region. The temporal radius range is set as $t \in \{1min, 10min, 30min, 1h, 2h\}$.

Table 1 reports the trajectory query time under different spatial thresholds and temporal ranges on both datasets. EVT^2 demonstrates significantly lower query times than GKQ. In the best-case scenario EVT^2 achieves an order-of-magnitude performance improvement. This is because: (i) GKQ stores spatio-temporal attributes and checks each trajectory timestamp against the query interval. In contrast, EVT^2 queries ITTA to filter trajectories meeting temporal constraints. (ii) For Top-k spatial queries, GKQ searches from anchor points and incurs redundant computation in filtering road nodes. However, EVT^2 queries ITTA to filter road nodes containing trajectories that meet time constraints. (iii) GKQ needs to write a large amount of verification information to ensure the optimality of the returned k trajectories.

Figures 5(a) and (b) show the query time composition of EVT^2 on Chengdu and Xi'an datasets with temporal radius 2h and 30min and varying spatial neighbor ranges. Spatial index query time increases with the number of spatial neighbors, as more road nodes need to be queried. Spatial query dominates the total time, since trajectories are stored on all passed road nodes, causing redundant retrieval of duplicates.

Figures 5(c) and (d) show the query time composition of EVT^2 on Chengdu and Xi'an datasets with spatial neighbors 5 and 10 under different temporal radius. As the temporal radius increases, temporal index query time rises because

Table 2. Trajectory verification time (s).

Dataset		Chengdu					Xi'an				
Spa	Tem	1min	10min	30min	1h	2h	1min	10min	30min	1h	2h
5	GKQ	56.11	59.61	32.46	35.62	19.56	16.30	16.57	15.59	15.78	15.92
	EVT^2	**0.602**	**0.624**	**0.561**	**0.545**	**0.500**	**0.107**	**0.101**	**0.123**	**0.177**	**0.221**
10	GKQ	161.6	174.3	87.33	86.29	62.99	39.77	34.37	27.19	16.74	16.72
	EVT^2	**0.704**	**0.755**	**0.695**	**0.747**	**0.754**	**0.144**	**0.152**	**0.173**	**0.186**	**0.229**
15	GKQ	306.8	310.9	141.9	127.8	69.23	60.30	54.85	27.42	18.12	17.80
	EVT^2	**0.878**	**0.933**	**0.955**	**0.817**	**0.764**	**0.167**	**0.185**	**0.202**	**0.241**	**0.250**
20	GKQ	338.5	314.4	255.78	142.6	98.14	58.40	55.61	28.69	19.00	18.69
	EVT^2	**1.035**	**1.139**	**1.327**	**1.277**	**0.843**	**0.222**	**0.215**	**0.217**	**0.263**	**0.274**
30	GKQ	766.5	733.3	425.5	264.2	266.2	65.85	62.04	34.90	22.94	22.76
	EVT^2	**1.660**	**1.612**	**1.826**	**1.300**	**1.165**	**0.275**	**0.271**	**0.273**	**0.313**	**0.349**

more matching trajectories require larger I-VO. Spatial index query time is unstable, since the temporal index changes the road node candidate set and trajectory counts different.

7.3 Verification Performance

We evaluate the trajectory verification performance of EVT^2 and baseline on the Chengdu and Xi'an datasets. The road network nearest neighbor query range is set as $n \in \{5, 10, 15, 20, 30\}$. Query anchors are randomly sampled from all region. The temporal radius range is set as $t \in \{1min, 10min, 30min, 1h, 2h\}$.

Table 2 reports the verification time of trajectory queries under different spatial thresholds and temporal ranges, on both datasets. EVT^2 consistently demonstrates significantly, in most cases achieving two orders of magnitude improvement. This is because: (i) GKQ incurs extra computation for Top-k spatial completeness verification, while EVT^2 offloads this task and trajectory scoring to the lightweight client-side index, reducing redundant verification. (ii) GKQ verifies all timestamps of a trajectory during validation, while EVT^2 quickly validates temporal attributes using the minimal verification subtree of ITTA.

Figures 6(a) and (b) show the verification time composition of EVT^2 on Chengdu and Xi'an datasets with temporal radius 2h and 30min and varying spatial neighbors. Temporal verification time cost is constant due to the fixed I-VO, while spatial verification time increases with more trajectory datas and road nodes need to verify.

Figures 6(c) and (d) show the verification time composition of EVT^2 on Chengdu and Xi'an datasets with spatial neighbors 5 and 10 under different temporal radius. Temporal verification time cost rises with more trajectories and larger T-VOs. Spatial verification time is unstable for the same reason, fluctuating with query results.

Figures 7(a) and (b) show the VO size of EVT^2 and GKQ on Chengdu and Xi'an datasets with varying spatial neighbors. GKQ (purple curve) uses the right axis. EVT^2 reduces VO size by one order of magnitude. On Xi'an dataset, GKQ's VO size stabilizes at 10 neighbors, as all road nodes lie in the same GTree leaf.

Figures 7(c) and (d) shows the VO sizes of EVT^2 and GKQ on Chengdu and Xi'an datasets with varying temporal radius. The VO size of EVT^2 is one order of magnitude smaller than GKQ. The G-VO size is unstable, since different temporal radius retrieve different road nodes with various trajectory counts. GKQ's VO size decreases in both datasets, because a larger temporal radius brings matching nodes closer to anchors and reduces verified filtered node.

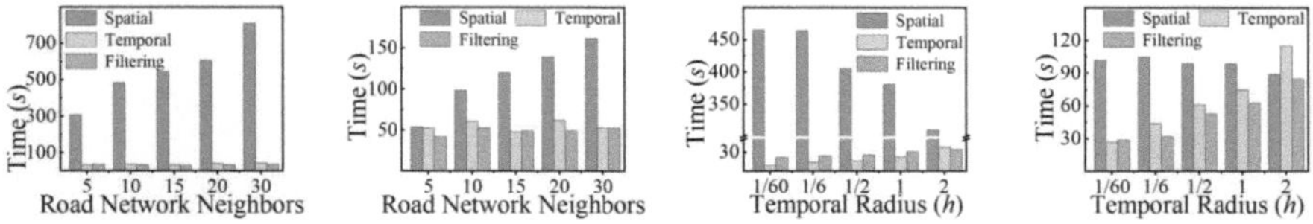

(a) Chengdu-S (b) Xi'an-S (c) Chengdu-T (d) Xi'an-T

Fig. 5. Spatial and temporal impact on query time.

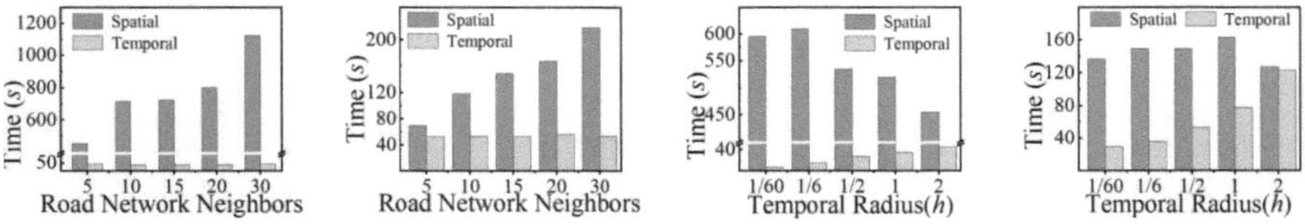

(a) Chengdu-S (b) Xi'an-S (c) Chengdu-T (d) Xi'an-T

Fig. 6. Spatial and temporal impact on verification time.

7.4 ADS Maintenance Cost

We evaluate the maintenance cost of ITTA and GTSA in EVT^2 from four dimensions: construction time, storage cost, update time, and cost on Ethereum.

Figures 8(a) and (b) show the construction time and storage cost of EVT^2 and GKQ, with the Chengdu dataset evaluated on 3, 7, 15, 31, 61 day data and the Xi'an dataset on 3, 7, 15, 21, 31 day data. Bar charts illustrate storage cost and line charts illustrate construction time. We find EVT^2 outperforms GKQ in both metrics, because it adopts a spatio-temporal separated dual-index that effectively reduces redundant trajectory data.

Figures 8(c) and (d) show the ADS update time when inserting 100, 500, 1000, 2000 and 5000 additional trajectories after initial construction. The ADS are initialized with 30-day Chengdu dataset and 15-day Xi'an dataset, respectively. $\texttt{EVT}^2$ outperforms the baseline on both datasets. This is because GKQ stores trajectory temporal sequences in a sequential list with $O(N)$ time complexity. In contrast, our method separates temporal information into ITTA, reducing the complexity to $O(\log N)$ and cutting redundant timestamp storage.

Uploading the two SHA256 root digests of ADS to Ethereum incurs an average end-to-end delay of around 3 s and a gas cost of 35,884. By concatenating them into one SHA256 hash, we maintain the delay at around 3 s while reducing gas consumption to 28,615. These results prove the minimal overhead of $\texttt{EVT}^2$ on Ethereum, owing to two factors: only a small amount of summary data is updated each time, and trajectory updates are submitted in batches, which reduces blockchain interaction frequency.

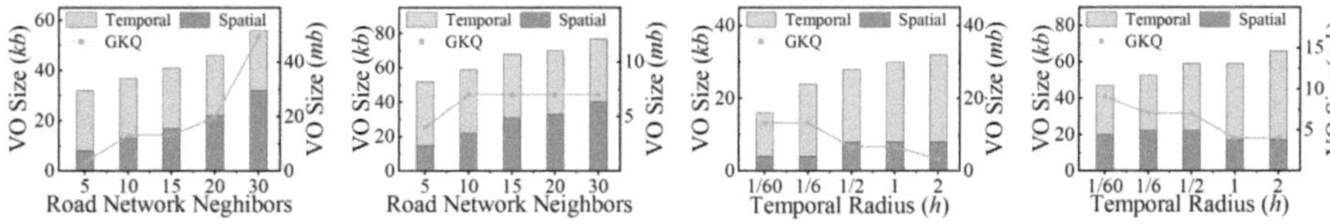

(a) Chengdu-S (b) Xi'an-S (c) Chengdu-T (d) Xi'an-T

Fig. 7. Spatial and temporal impact on VO size.

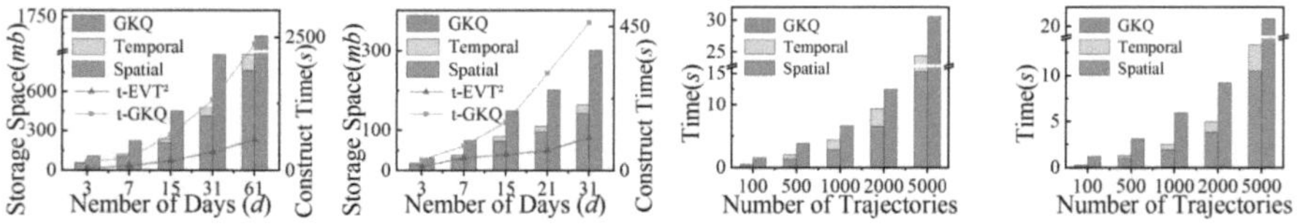

(a) Chengdu Size (b) Xi'an Size (c) Chengdu Time (d) Xi'an Time

Fig. 8. Index size, construction and update time.

8 Conclusion

We propose $\texttt{EVT}^2$, the first framework to support verifiable trajectory Top-k queries in hybrid storage systems. Our design of ITTA and GTSA enables efficient and trustworthy query processing over outsourced trajectory data. Experimental results demonstrate that $\texttt{EVT}^2$ significantly outperforms existing methods, delivering up to an order-of-magnitude gain in query efficiency and two-orders-of magnitude in verification efficiency. For future work, extending the $\texttt{EVT}^2$ framework to support dynamic verifiable trajectory Top-k queries represents a promising research direction.

Acknowledgement. The work is supported by National Natural Science Foundation of China (62432003, 92567205) and the Fundamental Research Funds for the Central Universities (N25BJD013).

References

1. Yuan, J., et al.: T-drive: driving directions based on taxi trajectories. In: Proceedings of the SIGSPATIAL International Conference on Advances in Geographic Information Systems, pp. 99–108 (2010)
2. Kong, F., Li, J., Jiang, B., Wang, H., Song, H.: Trajectory optimization for drone logistics delivery via attention-based pointer network. IEEE Trans. Intell. Transp. Syst. **24**(4), 4519–4531 (2022)
3. Shang, S., Ding, R., Zheng, K., Jensen, C.S., Kalnis, P., Zhou, X.: Personalized trajectory matching in spatial networks. VLDB J. **23**(3), 449–468 (2014)
4. Kong, Q., Zhang, S., Lu, R., Bao, H., Chen, B., Xu, S.: Achieving privacy-preserving trajectory query in geospatial information systems with outsourced cloud. IEEE Trans. Serv. Comput. **17**(4), 1354–1368 (2024)
5. Li, S., Zhang, Z., Xiao, J., Zhang, M., Yuan, Y., Wang, G.: Authenticated Keyword Search on Large-Scale Graphs in Hybrid-Storage Blockchains. In: IEEE International Conference on Data Engineering, pp. 1958–1971 (2024)
6. Li, S., Zhang, Z., Zhang, M., Yuan, Y., Wang, G.: Authenticated subgraph matching in hybrid-storage blockchains. In: IEEE International Conference on Data Engineering, pp. 1986–1998 (2024)
7. Wu, H., Li, Z., Song, R., Xiao, B.: Enabling privacy-preserving and efficient authenticated graph queries on blockchain-assisted clouds. IEEE Trans. Knowl. Data Eng. **35**(9), 9728–9742 (2023)
8. Zhang, C., Xu, C., Wang, H., Xu, J., Choi, B.: Authenticated keyword search in scalable hybrid-storage blockchains. In: IEEE International Conference on Data Engineering, pp. 996–1007 (2021)
9. Yao, Z., et al.: VGQ: enabling Verifiable Graph Queries on Blockchain Systems. In: IEEE International Conference on Data Engineering, pp. 3602–3614 (2025)
10. Zhou, W., Cai, Y., Peng, Y., Wang, S., Ma, K., Li, F.: VeriDB: An SGX-based verifiable database. In: Proceedings of the International Conference on Management of Data, pp. 2182–2194 (2021)
11. Yao, Z., Wang, Z., Wen, L., Hao, K., Xu, J.: Efficient blockchain data trusty provenance based on the W3C PROV model. In: International Conference on Advanced Data Mining and Applications, pp. 61–76 (2023)
12. Wang, S., Bao, Z., Culpepper, J.S., Cong, G.: A survey on trajectory data management, analytics, and learning. ACM Comput. Surv. **54**(2), 1–36 (2021)
13. Xu, C., Zhang, C., Xu, J.: vChain: enabling verifiable boolean range queries over blockchain databases. In: Proceedings of the International Conference on Management of Data, pp. 141–158 (2019)
14. Wang, H., Xu, C., Zhang, C., Xu, J., Peng, Z., Pei, J.: vChain+: optimizing verifiable blockchain boolean range queries. In: IEEE International Conference on Data Engineering, pp. 1927–1940 (2022)
15. Du, Z., Pang, X., Qian, H.: PartitionChain: a scalable and reliable data storage strategy for permissioned blockchain. IEEE Trans. Knowl. Data Eng. **35**(4), 4124–4136 (2021)

16. Yao, Z., Xin, J., Hao, K., Wang, Z., Zhu, W.: Learned-index-based semantic keyword query on blockchain. Mathematics **11**(9), 2055 (2023)
17. Hao, K., Xin, J., Wang, Z., Yao, Z., Wang, G.: Efficient and secure data sharing scheme on interoperable blockchain database. IEEE Trans. Big Data **9**(4), 1171–1185 (2023)
18. Wen, L., Wang, Z., Cui, T., Shi, C., Li, B., Yao, Z.: A Fine-Grained Verification Method for Blockchain Data Based on Merkle Path Sharding. In: International Conference on Advanced Data Mining and Applications, pp. 620–632 (2023)
19. Boughdiri, M., Abdellatif, T., Guegan, C.G.: A systematic literature review on blockchain storage scalability. IEEE Access (2025)
20. Zhou, E., et al.: VeriDKG: a Verifiable SPARQL Query Engine for Decentralized Knowledge Graphs. Proc. VLDB Endowment **17**(4), 912–925 (2023)
21. Cui, N., Wang, D., Li, J., Zhu, H., Yang, X., Xu, J.: Towards dynamic boolean range query over hybrid-storage blockchains: a secure and reliably verifiable framework. In: IEEE International Conference on Data Engineering, pp. 1664–1676 (2025)
22. Zhong, R., Li, G., Tan, K.-L., Zhou, L.: G-tree: an efficient index for KNN search on road networks. In: Proceedings of the ACM International Conference on Information & Knowledge Management, pp. 39–48 (2013)
23. Chung, M., Hyun, S.J., Loh, W.-K.: Efficient exact k-flexible aggregate nearest neighbor search in road networks using the M-tree. arXiv preprint arXiv:2106.05620 (2021)
24. Wang, Y., Yuan, L., Zhang, W., Lin, X., Chen, Z., Liu, Q.: Simpler is more: efficient top-k nearest neighbors search on large road networks. arXiv preprint arXiv:2408.05432 (2024)
25. Li, J., Ni, C., He, D., Li, L., Xia, X., Zhou, X.: Efficient kNN query for moving objects on time-dependent road networks. VLDB J. **32**(3), 575–594 (2023)
26. Qi, S., Sacharidis, D., Bouros, P., Mamoulis, N.: Snapshot and continuous points-based trajectory search. GeoInformatica **21**(4), 669–701 (2017)
27. Lou, Y., Zhang, C., Zheng, Y., Xie, X., Wang, W., Huang, Y.: Map-matching for low-sampling-rate GPS trajectories. In: Proceedings of the 17th ACM SIGSPATIAL International Conference on Advances in Geographic Information Systems, pp. 352–361 (2009)
28. Yu, X., Zhu, S., Ren, Y.: Continuous trajectory similarity search with result diversification. Futur. Gener. Comput. Syst. **143**, 392–400 (2023)
29. Davidson, S., Khanna, S., Milo, T., Roy, S.: Top-k and clustering with noisy comparisons. ACM Trans. Database Syst. **39**(4), 1–39 (2014)
30. Xu, J., Güting, R.H., Gao, Y.: Continuous k nearest neighbor queries over large multi-attribute trajectories: a systematic approach. GeoInformatica **22**(4), 723–766 (2018)

Spatial Relation Modeling for Trajectory-User Linking via Dual-View Graph Learning

Zida Liu[1], Lei Zhang[1(✉)], Yutong Wu[2], Bailong Liu[1], and Yuhan Min[1]

[1] School of Computer Science and Technology / School of Artificial Intelligence, China University of Mining and Technology, Xuzhou 221116, Jiangsu, China
{zhanglei,liubailong}@cumt.edu.cn

[2] School of Electrical Engineering and Computer Science, The University of Queensland, Brisbane 4072, QLD, Australia

Abstract. Trajectory-user linking (TUL) is a task that aims to match anonymous trajectories to their corresponding users, which is essential for understanding complex human mobility patterns. However, existing methods often rely on predefined graph construction rules and static edge weights, making it challenging to capture deep semantic relationships between spatial regions and dynamic interactions between trajectories. To overcome these limitations, we propose a dual-view learning framework for spatial relation modeling in TUL, called DVG-SRM. From the grid-level perspective, we model spatial relationships between regions by considering both physical transition patterns and semantic consistency derived from hierarchical point-of-interest (POI) category representations. From the trajectory-level perspective, we model the interaction relations between trajectories through relation graph construction and refinement, utilizing learnable edge importance estimation and neighborhood-aware denoising. By integrating graph convolution and hierarchical spatio-temporal attention, we learn more discriminative trajectory representations. Experiments on the Foursquare-NYC and Foursquare-TKY datasets demonstrate that the proposed method consistently outperforms strong baseline models.

Keywords: Trajectory-user linking · dual-view learning · spatial relation modeling · graph neural networks · hierarchical POI representation

1 Introduction

The rapid growth of mobile networks has generated vast amounts of trajectory data. Due to privacy concerns, many trajectories are anonymized, complicating trajectory-based analysis. To address this, researchers introduced the trajectory-user linking (TUL) task, aiming to associate anonymous trajectories with their corresponding users [1,2].

L. Ding et al. (Eds.): APWeb-WAIM 2026, LNCS 16995, pp. 233–248, 2027.
https://doi.org/10.1007/978-981-92-5699-0_15

Early TUL methods employed sequence-based architectures, such as RNNs [1], VAEs [2], and attention mechanisms [3]. These methods struggle to capture long-range dependencies and overlook spatial relationships. With the advent of graph neural networks (GNNs), recent approaches like GNNTUL [8], AttnTUL [10], and TULMGAT [11] have shifted towards graph-based modeling. Despite these advances, two challenges remain: (1) most methods rely on physical adjacency or transition statistics, failing to model deep semantic relationships between functionally similar but distant regions; (2) static graph structures and fixed edge weights hinder the differentiation of interaction strengths and the suppression of noisy co-occurrences.

To address these challenges, we introduce *Trajectory-User Linking Based on Dual-View Spatial Relation Modeling* (DVG-SRM). Unlike existing GNN-based methods (e.g., GNNTUL, AttnTUL, TULMGAT) that rely on single-view homogeneous graphs and static weights, DVG-SRM differentiates itself in two aspects. First, our grid-level view incorporates hierarchical POI category representations to discover latent semantic connections, overcoming the limitations of adjacency-based construction. Second, our trajectory-level view dynamically refines interaction edges via learnable importance estimation and neighborhood filtering, effectively suppressing noise. By integrating these dual-view graphs with hierarchical spatio-temporal attention, DVG-SRM learns highly discriminative representations.

The main contributions of this paper are:

- We propose DVG-SRM, the first framework to explicitly model spatial relations for TUL from both grid-level semantic and trajectory-level dynamic interaction perspectives, distinguishing it from single-view GNN methods.
- We design a grid-level strategy using hierarchical POI category representations and semantic-consistency gating to capture deep functional similarities beyond physical adjacency.
- We develop an adaptive trajectory-level strategy that dynamically refines inter-trajectory relations via learnable importance estimation and neighborhood filtering to mitigate data noise.
- Extensive experiments on Foursquare-TKY and NYC datasets demonstrate that DVG-SRM significantly outperforms existing sequence-based and GNN-based baselines.

2 Related Work

The task of trajectory-user linking (TUL) focuses on learning user mobility patterns from check-in data. Early sequential models, such as TULER [1], DeepTUL [3], and MainTUL [4], utilized RNNs and attention mechanisms to process point-of-interest (POI) sequences but struggled with sparse data. To mitigate this, latent representation and generative models like TULVAE [2], AdattTUL [5], and TGAN [6] were proposed. While improving generalization, they largely overlooked spatial topological information.

To address this, graph neural networks (GNNs) have emerged to explicitly model spatial and interaction relations. Approaches like GNNTUL [8], AttnTUL [10], and recent advanced graph models (e.g., S^2TUL [9], TULMGAT [11], HGTUL [12]) significantly enhance spatio-temporal dependency learning. However, despite improved spatial modeling, many current graph-based methods rely on grid-based space partitioning for simplification. This approach fails to effectively incorporate the functional semantics of spatial units, thereby limiting their ability to capture deeper semantic relationships between spatial regions.

3 Preliminaries

Let $\mathcal{U} = \{u_1, u_2, \ldots, u_N\}$ denote the set of users, where u_i represents the i-th user and $|\mathcal{U}|$ denotes the total number of users.

Definition 1 (Trajectory). A trajectory is a sequence of spatio-temporal points $\langle(t_1, \ell_1), (t_2, \ell_2), \ldots, (t_m, \ell_m)\rangle$ generated by user u_i in chronological order during a certain time interval τ, which is denoted by $Tr_{u_i}^{\tau}$.

Definition 2 (POI Category Hierarchy). POI categories are usually organized in a tree-structured hierarchy. Categories lying on the same root-to-leaf path tend to share similar semantic attributes. For example, along the path "Food and Drink → Restaurant → Chinese Restaurant → Noodle Shop", the categories are semantically correlated.

Definition 3 (Hierarchical Enhanced POI Category Representation). Let $\mathcal{C} = \{c_1, c_2, \ldots, c_J\}$ denote the set of POI categories, where c_j represents the j-th POI category and J denotes the total number of POI categories. The hierarchical enhanced POI category representation corresponding to category c_j is denoted by $\mathbf{p}_j$.

Trajectory-User Linking Task. Given a set of anonymous trajectories $\mathcal{T}_r$ generated by users in $\mathcal{U}$ and the corresponding linked trajectories $\mathcal{T}_r^u$, the goal is to learn a mapping function $f : \mathcal{T}_r \rightarrow \mathcal{U}$, which links each anonymous trajectory to its corresponding user.

4 Methodology

This section presents DVG-SRM, which contains five components: grid-level spatial relation modeling, trajectory-level spatial relation modeling, graph convolution, hierarchical spatio-temporal attention, and trajectory-user linking. DVG-SRM models spatial relations from two complementary views, namely the grid-level view and the trajectory-level view. Based on the learned dual-view relations, graph convolution and hierarchical spatio-temporal attention are employed to learn discriminative trajectory representations, which are finally used for trajectory-user linking (Fig. 1).

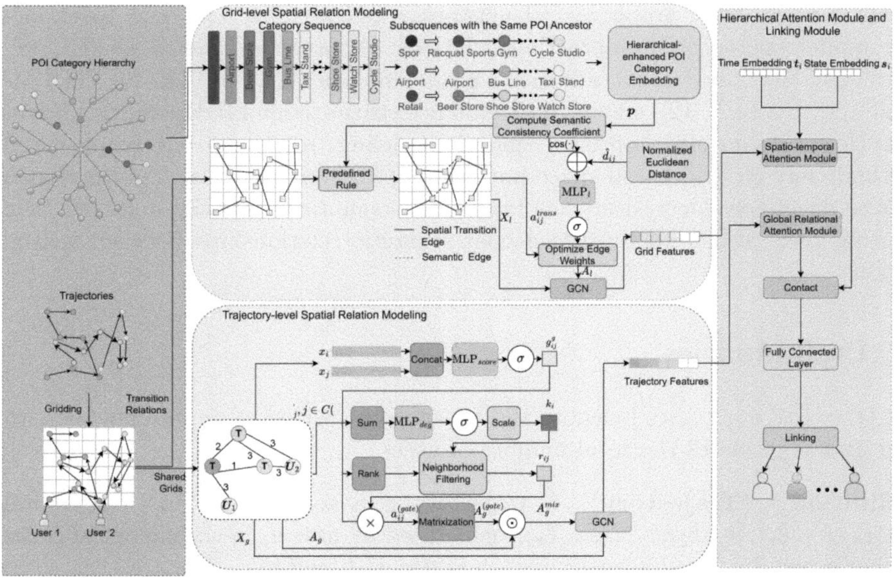

Fig. 1. Overall Structure of DVG-SRM Model

4.1 Grid-Level Spatial Relation Modeling

Hierarchical Enhanced POI Category Embedding. Traditional embedding methods often ignore the hierarchical structure and semantic relations among POI categories. In practice, POI categories are usually organized as a hierarchy, where categories on the same path share similar semantics and leaf-level categories provide finer-grained information.

To model such hierarchical semantics, the original trajectories are first divided into sub-trajectories with the same POI ancestors. Each category c_i is initialized with an embedding $\mathbf{e}_i \in \mathbb{R}^d$. Then, its ancestor category set $A(c_i)$ is constructed, including c_i itself. For each category $c_j \in A(c_i)$, the semantic relevance score between c_i and c_j is computed by

$$s(c_i, c_j) = \mathbf{u}_a^\top \tanh\left(\mathbf{W}_a \begin{bmatrix} \mathbf{e}_i \\ \mathbf{e}_j \end{bmatrix} + \mathbf{b}_a\right), \tag{1}$$

where $\mathbf{W}_a \in \mathbb{R}^{r \times 2d}$ is the weight matrix, and $\mathbf{b}_a \in \mathbb{R}^r$ and $\mathbf{u}_a \in \mathbb{R}^r$ are the bias and weight vectors, respectively.

The attention weight of each ancestor category is then computed as

$$\alpha_{ij} = \frac{\exp(s(c_i, c_j))}{\sum_{c_k \in A(c_i)} \exp(s(c_i, c_k))}. \tag{2}$$

Based on these weights, the hierarchical representation of category c_i is obtained by

$$\mathbf{p}_i = \sum_{c_j \in A(c_i)} w_j \alpha_{ij} \mathbf{e}_j, \tag{3}$$

where $w_j = \exp(-\gamma d_j)$, d_j denotes the hierarchical distance between c_j and c_i, and γ is a learnable scalar.

After obtaining the hierarchical embeddings, a GRU is used to model deep interactions among categories in each sub-sequence. Given a sub-sequence with representation $\mathbf{p} = (\mathbf{p}_1, \mathbf{p}_2, \dots, \mathbf{p}_n)$, the hidden feature vector is computed as

$$\mathbf{h} = \mathrm{GRU}(\mathbf{p}). \tag{4}$$

To further enhance representation learning, masked category prediction (MCP) is adopted as a pretraining task. For each sub-sequence, 15% of categories are randomly selected for masking. Each selected category c_i^m is replaced by the [MASK] token with probability 80%, by a random category token with probability 10%, and remains unchanged with probability 10%. The masked sub-sequence is then fed into stacked Transformer layers, where $\mathbf{h}$ serves as the token embedding and the category index serves as the positional embedding. The prediction for the masked category is computed as

$$\hat{\mathbf{p}}_i = \mathrm{softmax}(\mathbf{W}_{\mathrm{MCP}} \mathbf{o}_i^m + \mathbf{b}_{\mathrm{MCP}}), \tag{5}$$

where $\mathbf{W}_{\mathrm{MCP}} \in \mathbb{R}^{|C| \times d^o}$ and $\mathbf{b}_{\mathrm{MCP}} \in \mathbb{R}^{|C|}$ are the classification parameters, and $\hat{\mathbf{p}}_i$ denotes the predicted category distribution.

The model is trained with cross-entropy loss:

$$\mathcal{L} = \sum_{b=1}^{B} \left(-\frac{1}{|M_s^b|} \sum_{c_i^m \in M_s^b} \sum_{j=1}^{|C|} y_{i,j} \log \hat{p}_{i,j} \right), \tag{6}$$

where $y_{i,j}$ is the one-hot label, $\hat{p}_{i,j}$ is the predicted probability, and M_s denotes the set of masked categories.

Semantic-Guided Construction of the Grid-Level Spatial Graph. To facilitate the construction of the grid-level spatial graph, the geographic space of trajectories is discretized into grids. Specifically, given a grid size s, the whole geographic space is divided into n grids. Accordingly, a grid mapping function $f_g : \ell_i \rightarrow g_i$ is defined, so that each trajectory

$$T_r = \langle (t_1, \ell_1), (t_2, \ell_2), \dots, (t_m, \ell_m) \rangle$$

can be mapped into a grid sequence

$$T_r' = \langle (t_1, g_1), (t_2, g_2), \dots, (t_m, g_m) \rangle.$$

Meanwhile, the hierarchical POI category embedding method is used to obtain the fused representation of each POI category together with its related ancestor information. For each grid, the hierarchical enhanced POI category representation is computed by weighted aggregation based on visit frequency.

To capture the spatial correlations among locations in trajectories, we first construct a graph

$$G_l = (V_l, E_l),$$

where each grid corresponds to a node in G_l, and an edge in E_l indicates the existence of a transition relation between two grids. Furthermore, semantic association edges are introduced to compensate for the missing semantic relations that cannot be captured by physical topology alone. Specifically, if the Geographic distance between two grids is smaller than or equal to a predefined threshold λ_1, and the cosine similarity between their hierarchical enhanced POI representations is larger than or equal to θ, a connection is established even if no physical transition exists between them. The connection rule is defined as

$$e_{ij} = \begin{cases} 1, & \text{if } (lon_i - lon_j)^2 + (lat_i - lat_j)^2 \leq \lambda_1 \text{ and } \cos(\mathbf{p}_i, \mathbf{p}_j) \geq \theta, \\ 0, & \text{otherwise,} \end{cases} \tag{7}$$

where lon and lat denote the longitude and latitude of trajectory points, respectively, and $\mathbf{p}_i$ and $\mathbf{p}_j$ denote the hierarchical enhanced POI embeddings of two different grids.

Semantic-Guided Edge Reweighting. To make the hierarchical enhanced POI category representations not only supplement grid connectivity but also directly affect edge weights, we further design a semantic-guided edge reweighting mechanism. Specifically, for a candidate edge between grid i and grid j, the model first constructs a multi-dimensional edge feature vector, including the semantic-consistency coefficient computed from the hierarchical enhanced POI representations $\mathbf{p}_i$ and $\mathbf{p}_j$, and the normalized Euclidean distance $\hat{d}_{ij}$. Then, to control the influence of semantic information on edge strength, the above features are concatenated and fed into an MLP to generate a gating score $g^l_{ij} \in (0, 1)$:

$$g^l_{ij} = \sigma\Big(\text{MLP}_l\left(\left[\cos(\mathbf{p}_i, \mathbf{p}_j), \hat{d}_{ij}\right]\right)\Big), \tag{8}$$

where $\sigma(\cdot)$ denotes the sigmoid function.

Based on this, the final edge weight is obtained by fusing the physical transition feature with the gated semantic similarity:

$$a^l_{ij} = \log(1 + a^{trans}_{ij}) + g^l_{ij} \cdot \frac{1 + \cos(\mathbf{p}_i, \mathbf{p}_j)}{2}, \tag{9}$$

where a^l_{ij} denotes the edge weight between grid i and grid j, a^{trans}_{ij} denotes the transition count between grid i and grid j, and g^l_{ij} is the gating score used to control the influence strength of the hierarchical enhanced POI category representations on local edge weights.

The adjacency matrix A_l of the grid-level spatial graph G_l is constructed by a^l_{ij}, and the feature matrix X_l is composed of one-hot positional vectors. The hierarchical enhanced POI category representation corresponding to each grid is further concatenated in the graph convolution module as part of the graph input.

4.2 Trajectory-Level Spatial Relation Modeling

Construction of the Trajectory-Level Spatial Graph. The trajectory-level spatial graph is constructed to model the correlations among trajectories as well as the associations between users and trajectories. In the trajectory relation graph

$$G_g = (V_g, E_g),$$

each node in V_g can represent either a trajectory or a user. If two trajectories share at least one grid, an edge is established between them. In addition, an edge is established between each linked trajectory and its corresponding user. The edge weight between two trajectory nodes is defined as the number of shared grids, while the edge weight between a user node and its linked trajectory node is defined as the maximum weight between that trajectory node and other trajectory nodes, so as to strengthen the relation between a user and its trajectory, as follows:

$$a_{ij}^g = |\Omega_i \cap \Omega_j|, \tag{10}$$

where Ω_i denotes the set of grids visited by trajectory i, and a_{ij}^g denotes the number of shared grids between trajectory i and trajectory j.

We use A_g and X_g to define the adjacency matrix and feature matrix of the trajectory relation graph, respectively. Specifically, the visited grids of each node are encoded as a multi-hot vector whose length equals the number of grids, and then projected into a low-dimensional space through a learnable linear layer to obtain X_g.

Edge-Importance Learning and Neighborhood Filtering. To further enhance the expressive capability of trajectory-level spatial relations and suppress noisy interactions, we optimize the constructed trajectory-level spatial graph through edge-importance learning and neighborhood filtering. For each candidate edge (i, j), the edge gating score is defined as

$$s_{ij} = \mathrm{MLP}_{score}([\mathbf{x}_i \,\|\, \mathbf{x}_j]), \tag{11}$$

$$g_{ij}^g = \sigma(s_{ij}), \tag{12}$$

where $\|$ denotes concatenation and $\sigma(\cdot)$ is the Sigmoid function. The resulting gating coefficient g_{ij}^g is used to quantify the relevance strength of an edge to the trajectory-user linking task.

Next, we estimate the number of neighbors connected to each node as

$$k_i = k_{\min} + (k_{\max} - k_{\min}) \cdot \sigma(\mathrm{MLP}_{deg}(h_i)), \tag{13}$$

$$h_i = \sum_{j \in C(i)} a_{ij}^g, \tag{14}$$

where k_i denotes the adaptive neighborhood size of trajectory i, and $k_{\min}$ and $k_{\max}$ denote the lower and upper bounds of the neighborhood size under the condition that the number of neighbors is sufficient. If the number of neighbors of trajectory i is smaller than $k_{\min}$, then k_i is set to the actual number of neighbors. Here, $\sigma(\cdot)$ is the Sigmoid function, and h_i is obtained by summing the edge weights over the candidate edge set $C(i)$ of trajectory i.

Then, the neighboring edges of trajectory i are ranked in descending order according to the gating score g_{ij}^{g} to obtain the rank d_{ij} of neighbor j. We compute the edge gate coefficient r_{ij} as

$$r_{ij} = 1 - \frac{1}{2}\left(1 + \tanh\left(\frac{d_{ij} - k_i}{\lambda_2}\right)\right), \tag{15}$$

where λ_2 is a temperature parameter controlling the smoothness of the transition window. This equation constructs a smooth transition window centered at the adaptive threshold k_i, making the truncation operation differentiable and thus allowing gradients to jointly optimize the scoring network and the neighborhood-threshold prediction network through backpropagation.

Then, the edge gate coefficient r_{ij} is multiplied by the edge gating score g_{ij}^{g} to obtain

$$a_{ij}^{(gate)} = r_{ij} \cdot g_{ij}^{g},$$

which is used to update the adjacency matrix A_g. To preserve the relation strength carried by the shared grids while suppressing noisy edge propagation, the matrix $A_g^{(gate)}$ composed of $a_{ij}^{(gate)}$ is multiplied element-wise with A_g, resulting in the updated adjacency matrix

$$A_g^{(mix)} = A_g^{(gate)} \odot A_g.$$

4.3 Graph Convolution

Graph Convolution on the Grid-Level Spatial Graph. To model spatial adjacency and enhance grid semantics, graph convolution is performed on the grid-level spatial graph with hierarchical enhanced POI category representations as semantic node features:

$$H_l^{(k+1)} = \text{ReLU}\left(\tilde{D}_l^{-\frac{1}{2}} \tilde{A}_l \tilde{D}_l^{-\frac{1}{2}} H_l^{(k)} W_l^{(k)}\right), \tag{16}$$

where $W_l^{(k)}$ is the trainable weight matrix, $\tilde{A}_l = A_l + I$, and $\tilde{D}_{l,ii} = \sum_j \tilde{A}_{l,ij}$. The initial node embedding is

$$H_l^{(0)} = \alpha \cdot X_l \oplus \beta \cdot E_{POI}, \tag{17}$$

where X_l is the feature matrix, E_{POI} is the hierarchical enhanced POI representation, and α, β are trainable scalars.

Graph Convolution on the Trajectory-Level Spatial Graph. To learn discriminative features for trajectory similarity and user–trajectory association, graph convolution is further performed on the trajectory relation graph:

$$H_g^{(k+1)} = \text{ReLU}\left(\tilde{D}_g^{-\frac{1}{2}} \tilde{A}_g \tilde{D}_g^{-\frac{1}{2}} H_g^{(k)} W_g^{(k)}\right), \tag{18}$$

where $\tilde{A}_g = A_g^{(mix)} + I$ and $W_g^{(k)}$ is the trainable weight matrix. The initial embedding is defined as $H_g^{(0)} = X_g$.

4.4 Hierarchical Spatio-Temporal Attention Network

Following AttnTUL [10], we adopt a hierarchical spatio-temporal attention network to model spatial dependency, temporal context, and long-term temporal dependency in trajectories. The module consists of a semantic encoder and a temporal self-attention encoder. The semantic encoder fuses temporal, motion-state, and grid-level embeddings, and then applies positional encoding, multi-head attention, and max-pooling to obtain the local trajectory representation. The temporal self-attention encoder computes inter-trajectory relevance based on trajectory-level relation embeddings, uses Sparsemax [14] to generate sparse attention weights, and performs weighted aggregation to obtain the global trajectory representation.

4.5 Trajectory-User Linking Layer

The goal of the linking layer is to obtain the probability distribution over users. Specifically, the local representation z_i^l and the global representation z_i^g of each trajectory are first concatenated to form a higher-level representation. This higher-level representation is then projected through a fully connected layer into a vector of dimension $|\mathcal{U}|$, as follows:

$$y_i = \left(W_c \begin{bmatrix} z_i^l \\ z_i^g \end{bmatrix} + b_c \right), \tag{19}$$

where $W_c \in \mathbb{R}^{|\mathcal{U}| \times 2d}$ is the trainable weight matrix, $b_c \in \mathbb{R}^{|\mathcal{U}|}$ is the bias vector, and y_i denotes the probability that trajectory T_i belongs to a given user.

To train the model, the cross-entropy loss is adopted and optimized using backpropagation. The loss function is defined as

$$\mathcal{L}(\Theta) = -\frac{1}{\zeta} \sum_{i=1}^{\zeta} \mathbf{c}_i^* \log(\text{softmax}(\mathbf{y}_i)) + \frac{\lambda_{reg}}{2} \|\Theta\|_2^2, \tag{20}$$

where $\mathbf{c}_i^*$ is the true one-hot label vector of trajectory T_i, ζ denotes the number of training trajectories, Θ denotes the set of all trainable parameters, and λ_{reg} is the hyperparameter of L_2 regularization used to alleviate overfitting.

5 Experiments

5.1 Datasets and Evaluation Metrics

We evaluate the proposed method on two real-world check-in datasets collected from Foursquare, namely Foursquare-TKY and Foursquare-NYC. For each user, all check-ins are chronologically concatenated into a long trajectory and then further segmented into multiple sub-trajectories with a fixed interval of 6 h. Table 1 summarizes the statistics of the two datasets, where $|\mathcal{U}|$ denotes the number of users, C denotes the number of check-in records, T denotes the number of trajectories, $POIS$ denotes the number of POIs, and $\bar{len}$ denotes the average trajectory length.

Table 1. Dataset description and statistical information.

Dataset	$\|\mathcal{U}\|$	C	T	POIs	$\bar{len}$
Foursquare-NYC	82	19795	5101	7611	4
Foursquare-TKY	492	103697	26237	19531	4

The TUL task can be regarded as a multi-class classification problem. Following prior work, we adopt ACC@K, Macro-P, Macro-R, and Macro-F1 as the evaluation metrics. Macro-F1 is the harmonic mean of Macro-P and Macro-R over all classes. ACC@K is defined as

$$\text{ACC@K} = \frac{\text{number of trajectories whose true labels appear in the top-K predictions}}{\text{total number of trajectories}}. \tag{21}$$

5.2 Baselines and Experimental Settings

Baselines. We compare DVG-SRM with the following representative baselines.

- **TULER** [1]: TULER has three variants: TULER-G based on GRU, TULER-L based on LSTM, and Bi-TULER based on bidirectional LSTM.
- **TULVAE** [2]: This method addresses the TUL problem in a semi-supervised framework with a variational autoencoder, making use of large-scale unlabeled data to alleviate data sparsity.
- **DeepTUL** [3]: DeepTUL is one of the first methods to exploit multi-periodic mobility patterns for trajectory-user linking.
- **DPLink** [7]: DPLink is an advanced method for linking heterogeneous mobility data and users.
- **GNNTUL** [8]: GNNTUL is one of the earliest TUL models based on graph neural networks.
- **TULMGAT** [11]: TULMGAT improves TUL performance through a multi-scale graph attention network.

Data Preprocessing. To ensure the quality of the datasets and improve the reproducibility of our results, we applied a rigorous data preprocessing pipeline. First, to eliminate ambient noise, we filtered out inactive users with fewer than

10 check-in records and unrepresentative POIs visited fewer than 5 times. Second, all raw check-in records were chronologically sorted for each user. To construct meaningful trajectory segments, we partitioned the continuous check-in streams into sub-trajectories. If the time gap between two consecutive check-ins exceeds 6 h, the sequence is automatically split. Furthermore, excessively short trajectories containing fewer than 3 points were discarded to ensure sufficient sequence context. Finally, for spatial gridding, the geographic bounding box of each dataset was partitioned into equal-sized grids to map raw GPS coordinates to discrete grid indices.

Implementation Details and Hyperparameter Tuning. Trajectories were partitioned into training (60%), validation (20%), and testing (20%). Baselines follow their original settings. For DVG-SRM, we optimized parameters on the validation set to maximize Macro-F1. As detailed in Sect. 5.5, the POI embedding dimension, grid size, and $k_{\max}$ were searched over $\{40, 60, 80, 100, 120\}$, $\{40, 80, 120, 160, 200\}$m, and $\{20, 30, 40, 50, 60\}$, respectively. The optimal grid size and $k_{\max}$ were 40 m and 50 for NYC, and 120 m and 30 for TKY, with an optimal POI dimension around 80. Remaining static settings include: trajectory embedding dimension 128, $\theta = 0.75$, 30-minute window, 2 GCN layers, and 3 self-attention layers (4 heads). Models were optimized via Adam (batch size 16, lr 5×10^{-3}) for up to 80 epochs with early stopping (patience 10) and a fixed random seed for reproducibility.

5.3 Overall Performance

The comparison results between DVG-SRM and the baseline methods are reported in Table 2.

Several observations can be made from Table 2. Early methods such as TULER [1] and TULVAE [2] mainly focus on the spatial embedding of trajectory points, but they ignore spatio-temporal interactions and do not explicitly model users' multi-period mobility patterns, resulting in relatively limited performance. DPLink [7] enhances cross-domain consistency through attention-based fusion of heterogeneous mobility data. DeepTUL [3] improves the modeling of multi-period mobility patterns by introducing attention mechanisms over historical trajectories, and therefore shows better performance than earlier sequence-based models. GNNTUL [8] further improves the performance by extracting high-order spatio-temporal information through graph neural networks. AttnTUL [10] refines this process by integrating hierarchical spatio-temporal attention, which enables more accurate modeling of local and global dependencies. On top of AttnTUL, DVG-SRM further introduces hierarchical enhanced POI category representations and explicitly models semantic associations among neighboring grids, thereby alleviating the information fragmentation caused by spatial discretization and achieving more accurate trajectory-user linking.

Table 2. Comparison of DVG-SRM and baseline methods on Foursquare-NYC and Foursquare-TKY.

Datasets	Methods	ACC@1	ACC@5	Macro-P	Macro-R	Macro-F1
NYC	TULER-L	46.93%	62.32%	48.45%	41.32%	44.59%
	TULER-G	46.74%	62.15%	46.35%	40.21%	43.06%
	Bi-TULER	46.23%	61.61%	47.37%	41.28%	44.13%
	TULVAE	45.19%	60.82%	45.03%	39.12%	41.87%
	DeepTUL	47.72%	63.23%	49.51%	42.84%	45.93%
	DPLink	46.52%	64.32%	46.72%	43.08%	44.82%
	GNNTUL	47.58%	63.85%	46.65%	44.33%	45.46%
	TULMGAT	53.03%	68.50%	52.17%	49.12%	50.59%
	DVG-SRM	**55.94%**	**71.05%**	**57.24%**	**52.34%**	**54.59%**
TKY	TULER-L	43.89%	54.32%	37.29%	31.51%	34.16%
	TULER-G	43.69%	54.14%	35.24%	30.49%	32.68%
	Bi-TULER	43.28%	54.39%	36.12%	31.23%	33.50%
	TULVAE	42.23%	52.87%	34.25%	29.64%	31.78%
	DeepTUL	44.51%	55.12%	37.58%	32.35%	34.77%
	DPLink	43.68%	56.27%	35.44%	32.51%	33.91%
	GNNTUL	44.69%	55.78%	35.62%	33.62%	34.60%
	TULMGAT	49.62%	59.19%	40.27%	37.42%	38.80%
	DVG-SRM	**52.42%**	**61.36%**	**44.54%**	**40.23%**	**42.28%**

5.4 Ablation Study

To verify the effectiveness of different modules in DVG-SRM, we conduct an ablation study on the Foursquare-TKY dataset.The complete model is denoted as DVG-SRM, and its variants are defined as follows.

- **DVG-SRM-L**: removing the gating mechanism in the grid-level spatial graph;
- **DVG-SRM-G**: removing the adaptive edge-learning mechanism in the trajectory-level spatial graph;
- **DVG-SRM-N**: removing both mechanisms;
- **DVG-SRM**: the complete model.

Table 3 reports the performance of DVG-SRM and its variants on Foursquare-TKY. DVG-SRM consistently outperforms all ablated variants, confirming the effectiveness of both mechanisms. Compared with DVG-SRM-L, the complete model better captures latent semantic relations among grids. Compared with DVG-SRM-G, its performance gain indicates that adaptive edge learning effectively strengthens informative trajectory interactions and suppresses noisy relations. Moreover, the inferior performance of DVG-SRM-N further shows that

Table 3. Performance comparison between DVG-SRM and its variants on Foursquare-TKY.

Variant	ACC@1	ACC@5	Macro-P	Macro-R	Macro-F1
DVG-SRM-L	49.51%	60.12%	39.51%	37.21%	38.33%
DVG-SRM-G	49.77%	59.25%	40.36%	38.21%	39.26%
DVG-SRM-N	50.26%	59.49%	41.49%	40.28%	40.88%
DVG-SRM	52.42%	61.36%	44.54%	40.23%	42.28%

the two mechanisms complement each other in improving trajectory-user linking performance.

The complete model consistently outperforms all ablated variants, which confirms the effectiveness of both the adaptive grid-level graph optimization and the adaptive trajectory-level relation learning mechanism.

5.5 Parameter Analysis

Embedding Dimension of Hierarchical Enhanced POI Representations. We first analyze the influence of the embedding dimension of hierarchical enhanced POI category representations. The embedding dimension is selected from $\{40, 60, 80, 100, 120\}$, and the corresponding trends on ACC@1, ACC@5, and Macro-F1 are shown in Fig. 2. The results on both datasets indicate that when the embedding dimension exceeds 80, the model accuracy begins to decrease.

Grid Size. We further analyze the impact of grid size. The grid size is selected from $\{40, 80, 120, 160, 200\}$ meters. As illustrated in Fig. 2, the performance on Foursquare-TKY first increases and then decreases as the grid size grows, whereas on Foursquare-NYC the performance tends to decrease as the grid size increases. Therefore, the grid size is set to 120 meters for Foursquare-TKY and 40 meters for Foursquare-NYC.

Maximum Neighborhood Size in Adaptive Edge Learning. Finally, we investigate the effect of the maximum neighborhood size $k_{\max}$ in the adaptive edge-learning mechanism. The value of $k_{\max}$ is selected from $\{20, 30, 40, 50, 60\}$. As shown in Fig. 2, the best performance on Foursquare-TKY is achieved when $k_{\max} = 30$, while on Foursquare-NYC the best performance is obtained when $k_{\max} = 50$.

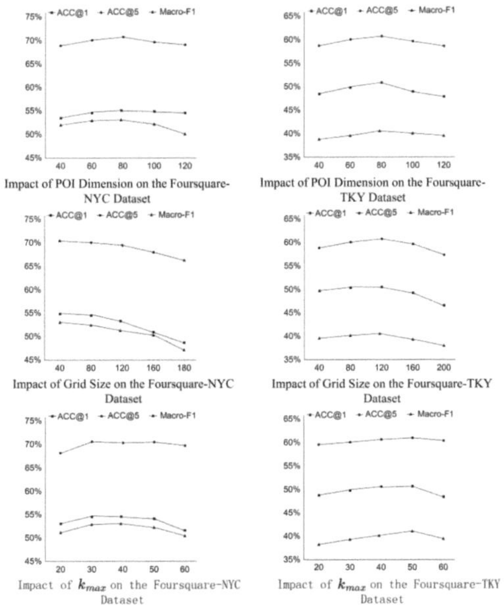

Fig. 2. Impact of Key Parameters

5.6 Scalability and Complexity Analysis

The time complexity of DVG-SRM mainly stems from dual-view graph convolutions, costing $\mathcal{O}(|V_l|d^2+|E_l|d)$ and $\mathcal{O}(|V_g|d^2+|E_g|d)$ respectively, and the hierarchical attention, costing $\mathcal{O}(N \log N \cdot d)$ where N is the sequence length. Crucially, our neighborhood filtering strictly bounds the maximum node degree to $k_{\max}$, ensuring the edge count $|E_g|$ grows linearly rather than quadratically. Regarding memory footprint, we implement sparse matrix representations for A_l and A_g, reducing the space complexity from a prohibitive $\mathcal{O}(|V|^2)$ to $\mathcal{O}(|V|+|E|)$. Together with grid-based spatial partitioning that limits the spatial vocabulary size, these algorithmic optimizations allow DVG-SRM to efficiently scale to massive real-world datasets, such as Foursquare-TKY, without encountering out-of-memory (OOM) errors.

6 Conclusion

This paper addresses the challenges faced by existing trajectory-user linking (TUL) methods, particularly in the area of spatial graph learning. Traditional approaches often rely on predefined graph structures and static edge weights, which limits their ability to capture complex inter-grid relationships and dynamic interactions between trajectories. To overcome these limitations, we propose a novel approach, *Spatial Relation Modeling for Trajectory-User Linking via Dual-View Graph Learning* (DVG-SRM).

DVG-SRM simultaneously models spatial relations from two complementary perspectives: the grid-level and trajectory-level. At the grid level, it integrates regional functional semantics and physical transition patterns to better capture latent associations and refine edge weights. At the trajectory level, DVG-SRM introduces learnable edge-importance estimation and neighborhood filtering to enhance inter-trajectory relations and mitigate noisy connections. Additionally, graph convolution and spatio-temporal attention mechanisms are employed to improve trajectory representation learning, leading to better user linking performance.

Our experiments on two real-world check-in datasets, Foursquare-NYC and Foursquare-TKY, demonstrate that DVG-SRM outperforms several strong baseline methods, highlighting its effectiveness in trajectory-user linking tasks.

References

1. Gao, Q., Zhou, F., Zhang, K., Trajcevski, G., Zhang, F.: Identifying human mobility via trajectory embeddings. In: Proceedings of the 26th International Joint Conference on Artificial Intelligence (IJCAI), pp. 1689–1695 (2017)
2. Zhou, F., Gao, Q., Trajcevski, G., Zhang, K., Zhong, T., Zhang, F.: Trajectory-user linking via variational autoencoder. In: Proceedings of the 27th International Joint Conference on Artificial Intelligence (IJCAI), pp. 3212–3218 (2018)
3. Miao, C., Wang, J., Yu, H., Zhang, W., Qi, Y.: Trajectory-user linking with attentive recurrent network. In: Proceedings of the 19th International Conference on Autonomous Agents and MultiAgent Systems, pp. 878–886 (2020)
4. Chen, W., Li, S., Huang, C., Yu, Y., Jiang, Y., Dong, J.: Mutual distillation learning network for trajectory-user linking. arXiv preprint arXiv:2205.03773 (2022)
5. Gao, Q., Zhang, F., Yao, F., Li, A., Mei, L., Zhou, F.: Adversarial mobility learning for human trajectory classification. IEEE Access **8**, 20563–20576 (2020)
6. Zhou, F., Yin, R., Trajcevski, G., Zhang, K., Wu, J., Khokhar, A.: Improving human mobility identification with trajectory augmentation. GeoInformatica **25**(3), 453–483 (2021)
7. Feng, J., Zhang, M., Wang, H.: DPLink: user identity linkage via deep neural network from heterogeneous mobility data. In: Proceedings of the World Wide Web Conference, pp. 459–469 (2019)
8. Zhou, F., Chen, S., Wu, J.: Trajectory-user linking via graph neural network. In: ICC 2021-IEEE International Conference on Communications, pp. 1–6 (2021)
9. Deng, L., Sun, H., Zhao, Y., Liu, S., Zheng, K.: S2TUL: a semi-supervised framework for trajectory-user linking. In: Proceedings of the Sixteenth ACM International Conference on Web Search and Data Mining, pp. 375–383 (2023)
10. Chen, W., Huang, C., Yu, Y., Jiang, Y., Dong, J.: Trajectory-user linking via hierarchical spatio-temporal attention networks. ACM Trans. Knowl. Discov. Data **18**(4), 1–22 (2024)
11. Li, Y., Sun, T., Shao, Z., Zhen, Y., Xu, Y., Wang, F.: Trajectory-user linking via multi-scale graph attention network. Pattern Recogn. **158**, 110978 (2025)
12. Chang, F., Zhu, X., Hu, Z., Qin, Y.: HGTUL: a hypergraph-based model for trajectory user linking. In: Mei, Y., Qian, C., Bai, Q., Xue, B., Khanna, S. (eds.) Pacific Rim International Conference on Artificial Intelligence. LNCS, vol. 16451, pp. 314–329. Springer, Singapore (2025). https://doi.org/10.1007/978-981-95-7075-1_21

13. Devlin, J., Chang, M.-W., Lee, K., Toutanova, K.: BERT: pre-training of deep bidirectional transformers for language understanding. In: Proceedings of NAACL-HLT, pp. 4171–4186 (2019)
14. Martins, A., Astudillo, R.: From softmax to sparsemax: a sparse model of attention and multi-label classification. In: Proceedings of the 33rd International Conference on Machine Learning, pp. 1614–1623 (2016)
15. Peters, B., Niculae, V., Martins, A.F.T.: Sparse sequence-to-sequence models. arXiv preprint arXiv:1905.05702 (2019)

STMixMamba: A Lightweight Hybrid Model for User Trajectory Forecasting in Location-Based Services

Meishan Chen[1], Wei He[1(✉)], Yonghui Xu[2], Wei Fang[3], and Lizhen Cui[1,2]

[1] School of Software, Shandong University, Jinan, China
202435315@mail.sdu.edu.cn, hewei@sdu.edu.cn
[2] Joint SDU-NTU Centre for Artificial Intelligence Research (C-FAIR), Shandong University and Nanyang Technological University, Jinan, China
{202199000029,clz}@sdu.edu.cn
[3] Shandong Province Key Laboratory of Independent and Reliable Computing Technology and Equipment, Jinan, China
fangwei@chaoyue.com.cn

Abstract. User trajectory forecasting is foundational for location-based services such as point-of-interest recommendation systems and mobile crowdsourcing platforms. These services demand both high accuracy and real-time efficiency in modeling users' movement trajectories, which form complex multivariate spatio-temporal sequences. However, the heterogeneity, nonstationarity, and sparsity of trajectory data make it challenging to simultaneously capture fine-grained and long-term dependencies, as well as cross-variate interactions, within a unified framework that maintains low computational complexity. To address these issues, we propose *STMixMamba*, a lightweight hybrid model that synergistically fuses multi-layer perceptron stacks and bidirectional parameter-enhanced Mamba blocks. This model captures both long- and short-term spatio-temporal dependencies alongside cross-variate interactions, achieving linear complexity—a critical advantage for real-world deployment. Furthermore, *STMixMamba* effectively incorporates contextual semantics and auxiliary information through dynamic spatio-temporal and shared adaptive embeddings. Extensive experiments on real-world datasets demonstrate that *STMixMamba* achieves state-of-the-art performance. Ablation studies further validate its rational design by systematically comparing hybrid architectures integrated via different fusion strategies.

Keywords: User trajectory · Temporal dependencies · Spatio-temporal correlations · MLPs · Mamba blocks

1 Introduction

The popularity of mobile smart devices has driven the rapid development of location-based services (LBS), making user trajectory forecasting a critical task

L. Ding et al. (Eds.): APWeb-WAIM 2026, LNCS 16995, pp. 249–265, 2027.
https://doi.org/10.1007/978-981-92-5699-0_16

in applications such as point-of-interest (POI) recommendation [4] and mobile crowdsourcing (MC) [10]. In POI recommendation, user historical check-ins are used to suggest potentially appealing locations that users may be interested in; in MC platforms, such as ride-hailing and food delivery, predicting the trajectories of service providers and requesters helps improve service matching efficiency. Real-world user trajectories form multivariate long-range spatio-temporal sequences with complex dynamic characteristics, including long- and short-term spatio-temporal dependencies, cross-variate interactions, and rich contextual semantics. Simultaneously capturing these elements is crucial for gaining a comprehensive understanding of the intrinsic dynamic properties of trajectory sequences. However, the heterogeneity, nonstationarity, and sparsity of trajectory data, combined with the need for high accuracy and real-time performance, present significant challenges. These challenges have made user trajectory forecasting in LBS an active research focus.

Given the significance of user trajectory forecasting across diverse domains, this topic has remained a major research focus. Traditional statistical and machine learning models [2,8] primarily capture single-scale temporal patterns, limiting their ability to handle nonlinear spatio-temporal characteristics. Subsequent deep learning approaches, including RNN-based [14], CNN-based [20], and GNN-based models [7], have improved the modeling of short-term spatio-temporal dependencies via neural networks. Transformer-based models [15,18,25], leveraging self-attention mechanisms to capture global dependencies, have since become mainstream. Recently, linear-complexity models have achieved promising performance in spatio-temporal forecasting. In particular, TSMixer [3], which relies on stacked MLPs, has outperformed many Transformers on standard benchmarks, demonstrating the effectiveness of simplified architectures. Meanwhile, Mamba [5] with its content-aware reasoning capability, models long-term dependencies at linear complexity and has emerged as a powerful alternative to Transformers for long-sequence forecasting [17]. However, existing linear-complexity models have limited ability to model bidirectional and long-range dependencies due to unidirectional state propagation, and also show insufficient capacity for spatial and temporal structure modeling.

Despite the preceding efforts and progress, user trajectory forecasting still faces vitally inherent challenges: (1) *How to capture both long- and short-term spatio-temporal dependencies alongside complex cross-variate interactions?* RNN-based, CNN-based, and GNN-based models struggle to capture long-term dependencies due to gradient vanishing, limited receptive fields, and reliance on static graphs [14,16,20]. Transformers lack local inductive bias, limiting accurate modeling of fine-grained dependencies [6]. MLP-based linear models focus on short-term patterns within local windows, overlooking long-term dependencies [17]. Meanwhile, existing Mamba-based models tend to prioritize the modeling of temporal dependencies at the expense of both fine-grained local detail capture and coordinated spatio-temporal feature extraction, resulting in inherently limited spatial adaptability [1,17]. (2) *How to guarantee low complexity while accurately modeling intricate nonlinear multivariate interactions?* Existing mainstream methods struggle to balance the two core requirements of model performance and computational efficiency in multivariate sequence modeling. GNN-based models suffer from severely limited large-scale scalability due to prohibitive computational and memory overhead of iterative neighborhood message passing [16], and Transformer's inherent quadratic computational cost grows quickly with sequence length, limiting their use in long-sequence scenarios. Lightweight linear-complexity models such as stacked MLP architectures and unidirectional state space models like Mamba address computational efficiency issues, yet suffer from new limitations in expressive power and fail to accurately capture fine-grained nonlinear interactions among multivariate variables [1].

To address the above challenges, we propose *STMixMamba*, a unified lightweight hybrid architecture that captures both long- and short-term spatio-temporal dependencies alongside cross-variate interactions with linear complexity. It solves key issues in user trajectory forecasting, including the disconnection between short-term patterns and long-range dependencies, high model complexity, and the decoupling of spatial and temporal features, enabling efficient and accurate prediction. Inspired by TSMixer [3], *STMixMamba* integrates two core complementary modules: MLP-stacked spatio-temporal-feature mixer layers for fine-grained short-term pattern capture, and bidirectional parameter-enhanced Mamba blocks with a dual dynamic-fixed parameter design for global long-range dependency modeling. This hybrid framework breaks the inherent limitations of mainstream paradigms: it compensates for Mamba's insufficient short-term fine-grained modeling, mitigates the weak long-range dependency capture of linear MLP-based models, and avoids the prohibitive quadratic complexity of Transformers. Specifically, our end-to-end pipeline proceeds as follows: First, the RevIN normalization layer eliminates input distribution shift. Then the Tile Map System (TMS) [11] is used for efficient spatial location encoding, paired with dynamic spatio-temporal and shared adaptive embeddings to learn contextual semantic features. Next, the spatio-temporal mixer layer, consisting of time, spatial and feature mixing branches, extracts fine-grained local spatio-temporal patterns and cross-variate information. Following this, the bidirectional parameter-enhanced Mamba blocks model global long-term spatio-temporal dependencies via bidirectional scanning. They use input-dependent dynamic parameters for noise filtering and adaptive information selection, and fixed parameters to learn universal spatio-temporal patterns. Dropout and residual connections are introduced throughout the network to improve training stability and generalization. Finally, the temporal projection layer and inverse RevIN normalization generate the trajectory forecasts. Our contributions are summarized as follows:

- We propose *STMixMamba*, a lightweight linear-complexity hybrid architecture for trajectory forecasting, which fuses MLP stacks and bidirectional parameter-enhanced Mamba blocks to jointly capture long- and short-term spatio-temporal dependencies and cross-variate interactions, breaking the accuracy-efficiency trade-off of existing methods.

- We design a local window-shared lightweight all-MLP mixer layer to constrain parameter growth to linear scale, with a dynamic selection mechanism to reduce redundant computation while capturing fine-grained local patterns.
- We optimize vanilla Mamba with spatio-temporal reversal bidirectional scanning to break its inherent causal constraint, and introduce data-agnostic fixed parameters to capture universal patterns, enabling robust long-range spatio-temporal modeling with mitigated overfitting for trajectory forecasting.
- We conduct extensive experiments on real-world datasets to verify the state-of-the-art performance of *STMixMamba*, with ablation studies confirming the effectiveness of each core component.

The rest of the article is organized as follows. Section 2 gives a brief overview of the work related to user trajectory forecasting models. Section 3 describes the problem definition and introduces our proposed *STMixMamba* in detail. Section 4 presents the experimental results and analysis. Section 5 summarizes this work.

2 Related Work

Recent research has shifted from suboptimal traditional statistical and machine learning models [2,8] to deep learning methods such as RNN-based, CNN-based, and GNN-based models [7,14,20]. Despite progress, these models still face limitations in the complexity and accuracy of long-term spatio-temporal dependency modeling. Transformers [18,24,25] effectively capture long-sequence global dependencies via self-attention mechanism, but the quadratic computational complexity inherent in self-attention severely hinders their practical deployment in real-time or large-scale forecasting scenarios. Furthermore, their lack of inductive bias impairs the capture of fine-grained patterns, while excessive trainable parameters even induce overfitting on datasets with limited available samples [6].

Linear complexity models such as TSMixer [3] outperform Transformers in spatio-temporal forecasting by capturing spatio-temporal dependencies and cross-variate information via all-MLP linear mixer layers [23]. However, MLP's local receptive field limits long-term dependency modeling, and its data-independent parameters lack selectivity, leading to suboptimal performance in spatio-temporal forecasting scenarios with sparsity, heterogeneity, and nonstationarity [1,17]. State Space Models (SSMs) overcome the limitations of Transformers and MLPs, gaining attention for strong long-sequence modeling capability with linear complexity [17]. As a representative SSM, Mamba [5] has been widely applied in natural language processing, computer vision, and multimodality. However, existing Mamba-based models focus on general multivariate time series, failing to balance low complexity and coordinated modeling of spatio-temporal features. Mamba's selective state space smooths out short-term high-frequency fluctuations and overlooks fine-grained details, resulting in limited short-term pattern modeling capability. Nevertheless, Mamba's superior performance in long-sequence dependency modeling motivates us to further explore its potential for user trajectory forecasting with complex spatio-temporal dynamics.

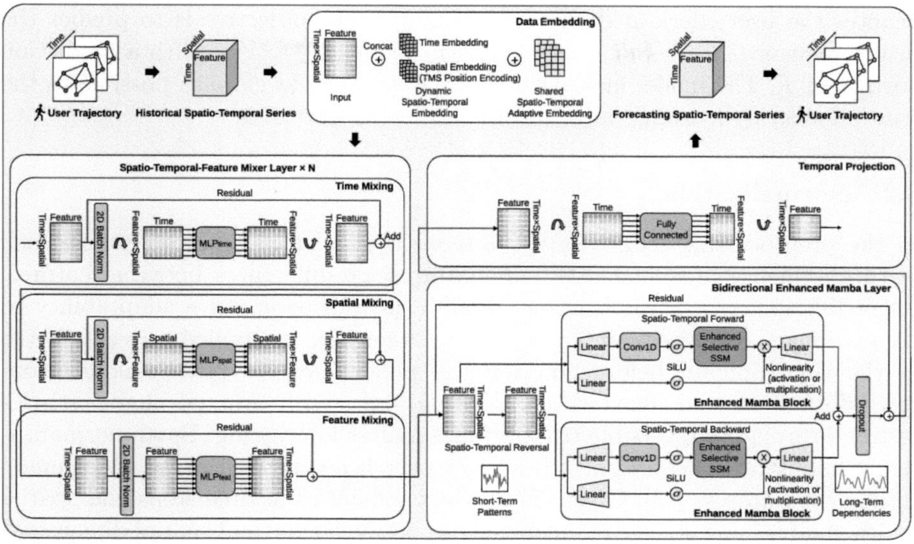

Fig. 1. The overall architecture of STMixMamba. The data embedding encodes contextual semantics and auxiliary information. The MLP-stacked spatio-temporal-feature mixer layer captures fine-grained spatio-temporal patterns and cross-variate interactions. The bidirectional enhanced Mamba layer models long-term spatio-temporal dependencies and global spatial correlations via two parameter-enhanced Mamba blocks in opposite directions. The temporal projection layer generates forecasts via linear transformation.

3 Method

In this section, we first define the user trajectory forecasting problem and then detail STMixMamba, with its overall architecture illustrated in Fig. 1. First, the input data are normalized and pass through data embedding to learn contextual semantics and auxiliary information. Next, the spatio-temporal-feature mixer layer captures fine-grained spatio-temporal correlations and cross-variate interactions. Then, the bidirectional parameter-enhanced Mamba layer further models long-term spatio-temporal dependencies and global spatial correlations. Dropout and residual connections are added to mitigate overfitting and facilitate deep network training. Finally, the temporal projection layer generates the final trajectory forecasts.

3.1 Problem Definition

User trajectory forecasting in LBS aims to accurately predict future visit locations based on user historical check-ins. User check-in trajectories form multivariate long-term spatio-temporal sequences. Given the historical sequence $\boldsymbol{X}_h = \{\boldsymbol{x}_1, \boldsymbol{x}_2, \ldots, \boldsymbol{x}_L\} \in \mathbb{R}^{L \times S \times C_{in}}$, where L is the lookback window length, S is the spatial dimension, C_{in} is the number of feature channels, and $\boldsymbol{x}_t \in \mathbb{R}^{S \times C_{in}}$

denotes the user check-in data at timestamp t, the objective is to predict the future sequence $\boldsymbol{X}_f = \{\boldsymbol{x}_{L+1}, \boldsymbol{x}_{L+2}, \ldots, \boldsymbol{x}_{L+T}\} \in \mathbb{R}^{T \times S \times C_{out}}$ with a prediction horizon of T. The model makes the forecast value $\hat{\boldsymbol{x}}_t$ as close as possible to the true value $\boldsymbol{x}_t$ by learning patterns of historical trajectories.

3.2 Normalization

In the preprocessing stage, we use Z-score normalization to standardize each feature sequence independently, eliminating scale differences between features. Reversible instance normalization (RevIN), proven to improve adaptability to nonstationary sequences and forecast accuracy [9], is applied to each batch in the time domain before entering the mixer layer to remove nonstationary information and alleviate distribution shift, with original characteristics restored through a reversible transformation after forecasting. Batch normalization demonstrates significant advantages over layer normalization on common time series datasets [13]. Given the distinct semantics of time steps and spatial nodes, maintaining structure independence between time and spatial dimensions is crucial to avoid information mixing and loss. In the mixer layer, 2D batch normalization is applied to eliminate scale differences between time steps and features, as well as spatial nodes and features, improving training stability and generalization.

3.3 Data Embedding

We use TMS [11] to encode the spatial locations of user check-in trajectories and flatten geographic coordinates based on the Mercator Projection. The precision of geographic data is determined by the level of detail, where a higher level denotes a more accurate geographic location. We set the spatial detail level to 17 and employ 256×256 pixel tiles to achieve fine-grained spatial grid partitioning. For user check-in trajectories, the latitude and longitude coordinates of check-ins are first mapped to unique quadkeys via TMS, with the quadkey length equal to the detail level. A sliding window of size 4 is then used to convert the quadkeys into n-gram sequences as spatial embeddings. Geographically adjacent locations share longer overlapping quadkey prefixes, which accurately characterize spatial proximity and trajectory position features, enabling the model to effectively capture spatial correlations.

User interests and behavior patterns of trajectories evolve dynamically over time and space, requiring models to capture contextual semantics and auxiliary information for learning spatio-temporal features. We use dynamic spatio-temporal embedding to weight extracted time and spatial characteristics via time intervals, spatial distances, and access frequency, generating a context-aware representation $\boldsymbol{X}_{e_1} \in \mathbb{R}^{L \times S \times d_{e_1}}$ through nonlinear fusion. The dynamic embedding of spatial attributes and temporal dynamics enhance the model's representation capacity and spatio-temporal adaptability, improving forecast accuracy.

The high sparsity of spatio-temporal data may cause overfitting on low-frequency check-ins. To address this issue, we adopt shared spatio-temporal adaptive embedding that provides a learnable global shared embedding matrix $\boldsymbol{X}_{e_2} \in \mathbb{R}^{L \times S \times d_{e_2}}$ as a model parameter, initialized with the Xavier uniform initialization, and generates context-adaptive embeddings for each location via embedding lookup. This embedding utilizes static priors to learn initial spatio-temporal correlations, capturing global location semantics to mitigate data sparsity. Through training optimization, it captures collaborative patterns among nodes to learn dynamic spatio-temporal interactions.

By concatenating dynamic spatio-temporal embedding $\boldsymbol{X}_{e_1}$, shared adaptive embedding $\boldsymbol{X}_{e_2}$, and the original input $\boldsymbol{X} \in \mathbb{R}^{L \times S \times C_{in}}$, we obtain the spatial-temporal representation $\boldsymbol{X}_e \in \mathbb{R}^{L \times S \times V}$ as the input of the mixer layer:

$$\boldsymbol{X}_e = \text{Concat}([\boldsymbol{X} || \boldsymbol{X}_{e_1} || \boldsymbol{X}_{e_2}]) \tag{1}$$

3.4 Spatio-Temporal-Feature Mixer Layer

The all-MLP spatio-temporal-feature mixer layer comprises time mixing, spatial mixing, and feature mixing with MLPs applied alternately along corresponding dimensions. Time mixing uses a single-layer MLP (fully connected layer, activation function, Dropout), sharing time-step-dependent fixed weights across spatial and feature dimensions to learn fine-grained temporal patterns along the time domain. Spatial mixing adopts two-layer MLPs (fully connected layer, activation function, Dropout, another fully connected layer followed by Dropout), sharing weights across time and feature dimensions to model spatial correlations along the spatial domain. Feature mixing follows the same structure as spatial mixing, sharing weights across time and spatial dimensions to capture cross-variate interactions along the feature domain.

Notably, the MLP weights for time, spatial, and feature mixing adopt cross-dimensional parameter sharing, where each matrix is stored as a single copy per mixer layer and globally reused across all elements of the other two dimensions without per-unit duplication. Since each mixing branch's parameter scale depends solely on its corresponding dimension L, S, or V without cross-dimensional weight replication, a single mixer layer yields additive parameter complexity $O(L + S + V)$, fundamentally eliminating the multiplicative parameter explosion $O(LSV)$ inherent in naive non-sharing architectures. This design facilitates cross-dimensional parallel computation, reduces model complexity, and mitigates overfitting, forming the core of the lightweight linear-scaling property. Moreover, it enables sharing and adaptive fusion of learned representations across time, spatial, and feature dimensions. The interleaving structure of three modules extracts single-dimensional information within MLP local windows, capturing fine-grained spatio-temporal patterns and cross-variate interactions with linear complexity, while the decoupled design mitigates noise interference.

Fusing information from the three modules via residual connections yields the output of mixer layer $\boldsymbol{X}_{mix} \in \mathbb{R}^{L \times S \times V}$. The above process is as follows:

$$\begin{aligned}\boldsymbol{X}_{norm1} &= \text{2D-Norm}(\boldsymbol{X}_e),\\ \boldsymbol{X}_t &= \sigma(\boldsymbol{X}_{norm1}^{\mathrm{T}} \boldsymbol{W}_t + \boldsymbol{b}_t),\\ \boldsymbol{X}_{time} &= \boldsymbol{X} + \text{Drop}(\boldsymbol{X}_t^{\mathrm{T}}),\end{aligned} \tag{2}$$

$$\begin{aligned}\boldsymbol{X}_{norm2} &= \text{2D-Norm}(\boldsymbol{X}_{time}),\\ \boldsymbol{X}_{dps1} &= \text{Drop}\big(\sigma(\boldsymbol{X}_{norm2}^{\mathrm{T}} \boldsymbol{W}_{s1} + \boldsymbol{b}_{s1})\big),\\ \boldsymbol{X}_{dps2} &= \text{Drop}\big((\boldsymbol{X}_{dps1} \boldsymbol{W}_{s2} + \boldsymbol{b}_{s2})^{\mathrm{T}}\big),\\ \boldsymbol{X}_{spatial} &= \boldsymbol{X}_{time} + \boldsymbol{X}_{dps2},\end{aligned} \tag{3}$$

$$\begin{aligned}\boldsymbol{X}_{norm3} &= \text{2D-Norm}(\boldsymbol{X}_{spatial}),\\ \boldsymbol{X}_{dpf1} &= \text{Drop}\big(\sigma(\boldsymbol{X}_{norm3} \boldsymbol{W}_{f1} + \boldsymbol{b}_{f1})\big),\\ \boldsymbol{X}_{dpf2} &= \text{Drop}(\boldsymbol{X}_{dpf1} \boldsymbol{W}_{f2} + \boldsymbol{b}_{f2}),\\ \boldsymbol{X}_{mix} &= \boldsymbol{X}_{spatial} + \boldsymbol{X}_{dpf2},\end{aligned} \tag{4}$$

where $\boldsymbol{W}_t \in \mathbb{R}^{L \times L}$, $\boldsymbol{W}_{s1} \in \mathbb{R}^{S \times H_1}$, $\boldsymbol{W}_{s2} \in \mathbb{R}^{H_1 \times S}$, $\boldsymbol{W}_{f1} \in \mathbb{R}^{V \times H_2}$, $\boldsymbol{W}_{f2} \in \mathbb{R}^{H_2 \times V}$, $\boldsymbol{b}_t \in \mathbb{R}^{L}$, $\boldsymbol{b}_{s1} \in \mathbb{R}^{H_1}$, $\boldsymbol{b}_{s2} \in \mathbb{R}^{S}$, $\boldsymbol{b}_{f1} \in \mathbb{R}^{H_2}$, $\boldsymbol{b}_{f2} \in \mathbb{R}^{V}$. H_1 and H_2 denote the hidden sizes of spatial-mixing and feature-mixing MLPs, respectively. Moderately increasing them enhances the model's nonlinear representation capacity to capture more complex correlations. 2D-Norm$(\cdot)$ is 2D batch normalization, $\sigma(\cdot)$ is ReLU activation, and Drop$(\cdot)$ is Dropout. The transpose operation $(\cdot)^{\mathrm{T}}$ yields $\boldsymbol{X}_{norm1}^{\mathrm{T}} \in \mathbb{R}^{V \times S \times L}$ in time mixing and$\boldsymbol{X}_{norm2}^{\mathrm{T}} \in \mathbb{R}^{L \times V \times S}$ in spatial mixing. STMixMamba includes N mixer layers.

3.5 Bidirectional Enhanced Mamba Layer

SSM uses continuous-time differential equations to map the input one-dimensional function or sequence $x(t) \in \mathbb{R}$ to the output $y(t) \in \mathbb{R}$ through a latent state $h(t) \in \mathbb{R}^N$, defined as follows:

$$\begin{aligned}h'(t) &= \boldsymbol{A}h(t) + \boldsymbol{B}x(t),\\ y(t) &= \boldsymbol{C}h(t),\end{aligned} \tag{5}$$

where $\boldsymbol{A} \in \mathbb{R}^{N \times N}$, $\boldsymbol{B} \in \mathbb{R}^{N \times D}$, and $\boldsymbol{C} \in \mathbb{R}^{D \times N}$ are learnable matrices. N and D are the state expansion factor and dimension factor. The continuous parameters $(\varDelta, \boldsymbol{A}, \boldsymbol{B})$ are discretized to $(\overline{\boldsymbol{A}}, \overline{\boldsymbol{B}})$ through zero-order hold and time sampling at intervals of $\varDelta$. The formula of the discrete SSM is as follows:

$$\begin{aligned}h_t &= \overline{\boldsymbol{A}}h_{t-1} + \overline{\boldsymbol{B}}x_t,\\ y_t &= \boldsymbol{C}h_t,\end{aligned} \tag{6}$$

where $\overline{\boldsymbol{A}} = \exp(\varDelta\boldsymbol{A})$ and $\overline{\boldsymbol{B}} = (\varDelta\boldsymbol{A})^{-1}(\exp(\varDelta\boldsymbol{A}) - \boldsymbol{I}) \cdot \varDelta\boldsymbol{B}$, h_t and x_t are the latent state and input vector at time t, respectively. The discrete SSM fuses the properties of RNN and CNN, enabling global convolution for parallel training and linear recurrence for fast sequential inference to achieve linear complexity.

Structured State Space Model (S4), a SSM variant, uses HiPPO to initialize $\overline{\boldsymbol{A}}$ to enhance long-term dependency modeling. Building on S4, Mamba introduces a dynamic selection mechanism that parameterizes $\overline{\boldsymbol{B}}$, $\overline{\boldsymbol{C}}$, and Δ as input-dependent functions of x_t to selectively propagate or forget information, and employs a hardware-aware parallel algorithm for recurrent scanning to capture long-sequence dependencies with linear complexity. The parameterization process is as follows:

$$\begin{aligned} \overline{\boldsymbol{B}} &\rightarrow s_B(x_t) = \text{Linear}_N(x_t), \\ \overline{\boldsymbol{C}} &\rightarrow s_C(x_t) = \text{Linear}_N(x_t), \\ \Delta &\rightarrow s_\Delta(x_t) = \text{softplus}\big(\text{Broadcast}_D(\text{Linear}_1(x_t))\big), \end{aligned} \tag{7}$$

where $\text{Linear}_d(\cdot)$ denotes linear projection to dimension d and the activation function $\text{softplus}(\cdot) = \log(1 + \exp(\cdot))$.

However, fully input-dependent parameters tend to trigger overfitting when modeling high-noise, sparse trajectory data, as such parameters excessively fit idiosyncratic noise of individual check-in samples rather than capturing intrinsic regularities. To address this, we propose a parameter-enhanced Mamba block that incorporates data-independent fixed parameters ($\boldsymbol{B_0}, \boldsymbol{C_0}$) and retains original input-dependent dynamic parameters, forming a dual-parameter collaborative learning mechanism with feature decoupling. Specifically, fixed parameters ($\boldsymbol{B_0}, \boldsymbol{C_0}$) are optimized via global training across entire sequences to learn universal spatio-temporal patterns. In parallel, the dynamic parameters capture specific characteristics of the current check-in and selectively filter information to eliminate redundant noise and invalid sparse signals. This dual dynamic-fixed parameter mechanism explicitly decouples sequence universality and current check-in specificity, enhancing representation capacity and alleviating overfitting. The parameters of the improved Mamba block are as follows:

$$\begin{aligned} \overline{\boldsymbol{B}} &= \text{Linear}_N(x_t) + \boldsymbol{B_0}, \\ \overline{\boldsymbol{C}} &= \text{Linear}_N(x_t) + \boldsymbol{C_0}. \end{aligned} \tag{8}$$

Due to the global planning characteristics and noncausal semantics of user trajectories, Mamba's unidirectional modeling fails to capture global spatial correlations and reverse temporal dependencies where future check-in intentions influence current behavior. To address this, we design a bidirectional enhanced Mamba layer by integrating two improved Mamba blocks. Forward scanning captures sequential temporal dependencies and local spatial correlations, while backward scanning inverts both time and spatial dimensions to capture reverse temporal patterns and nonsequential global spatial correlations. This spatio-temporal joint reversal design maintains Mamba's linear complexity and overcomes unidirectional causal limitations, enhancing global spatio-temporal interaction and long-term dependency modeling capabilities.

In this layer, the output tensor $\boldsymbol{X}_{mix} \in \mathbb{R}^{L \times S \times V}$ of the mixer layer is reshaped into matrix $\boldsymbol{X}_{mix} \in \mathbb{R}^{(L \times S) \times V}$ through matrixization and fed into Mamba blocks, unifying temporal and spatial information into a single dimension to better capture spatio-temporal interactions. The bidirectional parameter-enhanced Mamba blocks model long-term dependencies and global spatial correlations with linear complexity and enable real-time responses to forecasting. The outputs of the Mamba blocks are aggregated, reshaped to the original dimensions to separate temporal and spatial information, and processed via Dropout and a residual connection to generate $\boldsymbol{X}_{mamba} \in \mathbb{R}^{L \times S \times V}$. The above process is as follows:

$$\begin{aligned} \overline{\boldsymbol{X}}_{mix} &= \text{Reshape}(\boldsymbol{X}_{mix}), \\ \boldsymbol{X}_{forward} &= \text{Linear}_V\big(\text{Mamba}\big(\text{Linear}_{d\_model}(\overline{\boldsymbol{X}}_{mix})\big)\big), \\ \overline{\boldsymbol{X}}_{rev} &= \big(\text{Reversal}(\overline{\boldsymbol{X}}_{mix})\big), \\ \boldsymbol{X}_{backward} &= \text{Linear}_V\big(\text{Mamba}\big(\text{Linear}_{d\_model}(\overline{\boldsymbol{X}}_{rev})\big)\big), \\ \overline{\boldsymbol{X}}_{mamba} &= \text{Reshape}\big(\text{Linear}_V(\boldsymbol{X}_{forward} + \boldsymbol{X}_{backward})\big), \\ \boldsymbol{X}_{mamba} &= \boldsymbol{X}_{mix} + \text{Drop}(\overline{\boldsymbol{X}}_{mamba}), \end{aligned} \tag{9}$$

where *d_model* is the model dimension of Mamba block. The input data are linearly transformed from the original feature dimension V to *d_model* before entering the hidden state space and projected back to V after output.

3.6 Temporal Projection

In the temporal projection layer, the output $\boldsymbol{X}_{res} \in \mathbb{R}^{L \times S \times V}$ of the Mamba layer is transposed to $\boldsymbol{X}_{res}^{\mathrm{T}} \in \mathbb{R}^{V \times S \times L}$ to apply the fully connected linear layer along the time domain, learning temporal patterns and mapping the input sequence length L to the target prediction length T. The output is then transposed back to generate the final prediction $\boldsymbol{X}_{pred} \in \mathbb{R}^{T \times S \times V}$. The layer formula is as follows:

$$\boldsymbol{X}_{pred} = \left(\boldsymbol{X}_{res}^{\mathrm{T}} \boldsymbol{W}_p + \boldsymbol{b}_p\right)^{\mathrm{T}}, \tag{10}$$

where $\boldsymbol{W}_p \in \mathbb{R}^{L \times T}$ and $\boldsymbol{b}_p \in \mathbb{R}^{T}$.

4 Experiments

In this section, we conduct comparative experiments on benchmark datasets to evaluate the forecasting performance of our proposed STMixMamba and perform ablation studies to validate its rational design and component contributions.

4.1 Experimental Setting

Datasets. We conduct experiments on real-world public datasets, including user check-in trajectory datasets T-Drive [21,22], NYC [19], and TKY [19], as well as multivariate long-term spatio-temporal series datasets Electricity, Traffic, and ETT (ETTh1, ETTm1). T-Drive contains the trajectories of 10,357 Beijing taxis from February 2 to February 8, 2008, including taxi IDs, timestamps, and latitude-longitude coordinates. NYC and TKY from LBS Foursquare contain 227,428 check-ins in New York and 573,703 check-ins in Tokyo from April 12, 2012 to February 16, 2013, respectively, with attributes covering user IDs, POI

IDs, category IDs, timestamps, geographic coordinates, and semantic information such as venue categories. Following the standard experimental protocol [18], ETT datasets are split into training, validation, and test sets at a 6:2:2 ratio, while all other datasets adopt a 7:1:2 split ratio.

Baselines. Our model is compared with 5 state-of-the-art models, including TSMixer [3], FEDformer [25], Autoformer [18], Informer [24], and TFT [12].

Metrics and Implementation Details. We used MSE and MAE metrics to evaluate the model, with lower values indicating higher prediction accuracy. The experiments were conducted on NVIDIA RTX 3090 (24 GB) GPUs with Ubuntu 20.04. We followed TSMixer's experimental setups [3] with a batch size of 32, a random seed of 0, and the ADAM optimizer, and trained all models for up to 100 epochs with early stopping after 5 epochs without validation improvement. The models proposed in this paper were run according to TSMixer's best hyperparameters, and the four hyperparameters related to Mamba, namely basic model dimension (d_model), state space dimension (d_state), local convolution width (d_conv), and dimension expansion factor (expand), were initialized by preliminary tuning and optimized via grid search based on validation metrics during training. All results were obtained under fixed hyperparameter settings.

4.2 Performance Comparison

Table 1 presents model performance comparisons, with the best results in bold and the second-best underlined. Experimental results demonstrate that our model STMixMamba achieves the best performance, while TSMixer exhibits the second-best results. Specifically, on T-Drive dataset, STMixMamba reduces average MSE from 0.128 (TSMixer) to 0.116 and MAE from 0.263 to 0.247. On NYC dataset, it achieves average reductions of 24.7% in MSE and 18.5% in MAE over the Autoformer baseline. Similar improvements are observed on other datasets, indicating STMixMamba's strong capability in modeling sparse, high-noise long-sequence user trajectory data. To intuitively show STMixMamba's forecasting performance, we visualize the results of STMixMamba and the second-best TSMixer on Electricity and Traffic datasets. We randomly select one variable for each dataset. As shown in Fig. 2, the blue line represents the groundtruth and the orange line represents the forecasts, showing that STMixMamba's predictions are closer to actual values.

Mixer layers leverage MLPs to capture fine-grained spatio-temporal patterns and cross-variate interactions. Parameter-enhanced Mamba blocks utilize input-dependent dynamic parameters to accumulate historical information in latent states and filter noise, modeling long-term dependencies beyond local MLP window limits, while using fixed parameters ($\boldsymbol{B}_0, \boldsymbol{C}_0$) to learn universal sequence characteristics and mitigate overfitting induced by dynamic parameters. The selective state space resets states at abrupt time points to prioritize short-term fluctuation modeling and avoid prediction lag while reducing the sensitivity of

Table 1. Experimental results of STMixMamba and baselines for long-term forecasting in LBS. For spatio-temporal series datasets, we set the lookback length $L = 512$ and forecast length $T \in \{96, 192, 336, 720\}$. For user check-in datasets, $L = 24$ and $T \in \{3, 12, 24\}$.

Models		STMixMamba		TSMixer		FEDformer		Autoformer		Informer		TFT	
Metric		MSE	MAE	MSE	MAE	MSE	MAE	MSE	MAE	MSE	MAE	MSE	MAE
ETTh1	96	**0.362**	**0.395**	0.363	0.396	0.376	0.415	0.435	0.446	0.941	0.769	0.674	0.634
	192	**0.400**	**0.419**	0.402	0.420	0.423	0.446	0.456	0.457	1.007	0.786	0.858	0.704
	336	**0.422**	**0.436**	**0.422**	0.437	0.444	0.462	0.486	0.487	1.038	0.784	0.900	0.731
	720	**0.449**	**0.467**	0.450	0.468	0.469	0.492	0.515	0.517	1.114	0.857	0.745	0.666
	Avg	**0.408**	**0.429**	0.409	0.430	0.428	0.454	0.473	0.477	1.025	0.799	0.794	0.684
ETTm1	96	**0.280**	**0.336**	0.283	0.337	0.326	0.390	0.510	0.492	0.626	0.560	0.752	0.626
	192	**0.323**	**0.362**	0.325	0.363	0.365	0.415	0.514	0.495	0.725	0.619	0.752	0.649
	336	**0.357**	**0.382**	0.359	0.383	0.392	0.425	0.510	0.492	1.005	0.741	0.810	0.674
	720	**0.420**	**0.415**	**0.420**	0.416	0.446	0.458	0.527	0.493	1.133	0.845	0.849	0.695
	Avg	**0.345**	**0.374**	0.347	0.375	0.382	0.422	0.515	0.493	0.872	0.691	0.791	0.661
Electricity	96	**0.129**	**0.227**	0.130	0.228	0.186	0.302	0.196	0.313	0.304	0.393	0.295	0.376
	192	**0.147**	**0.243**	0.148	0.244	0.197	0.311	0.211	0.324	0.327	0.417	0.327	0.397
	336	**0.160**	**0.260**	0.163	0.261	0.213	0.328	0.214	0.327	0.333	0.422	0.298	0.380
	720	**0.190**	0.289	0.191	**0.287**	0.233	0.344	0.236	0.342	0.351	0.427	0.338	0.412
	Avg	**0.157**	**0.254**	0.158	0.255	0.207	0.321	0.214	0.327	0.329	0.415	0.315	0.391
Traffic	96	**0.379**	**0.267**	0.382	0.268	0.576	0.359	0.597	0.371	0.733	0.410	0.678	0.362
	192	**0.400**	**0.277**	0.402	0.278	0.610	0.380	0.607	0.382	0.777	0.435	0.664	0.355
	336	**0.418**	**0.292**	0.419	0.293	0.608	0.375	0.623	0.387	0.776	0.434	0.679	0.354
	720	**0.450**	**0.306**	0.451	**0.306**	0.621	0.375	0.639	0.395	0.827	0.466	0.610	0.326
	Avg	**0.412**	**0.285**	0.414	0.286	0.604	0.372	0.617	0.384	0.778	0.436	0.658	0.349
T-Drive	3	**0.072**	**0.185**	0.079	0.199	0.083	0.204	0.088	0.212	0.085	0.208	0.091	0.219
	12	**0.117**	**0.250**	0.129	0.267	0.135	0.275	0.140	0.284	0.138	0.280	0.145	0.290
	24	**0.158**	**0.306**	0.176	0.324	0.185	0.333	0.193	0.342	0.189	0.338	0.198	0.348
	Avg	**0.116**	**0.247**	0.128	0.263	0.134	0.271	0.140	0.279	0.137	0.275	0.145	0.286
NYC	3	**0.060**	**0.168**	0.066	0.185	0.073	0.194	0.075	0.203	0.076	0.198	0.081	0.211
	12	**0.102**	**0.230**	0.113	0.254	0.128	0.272	0.138	0.288	0.134	0.288	0.146	0.297
	24	**0.168**	**0.302**	0.187	0.337	0.206	0.354	0.222	0.368	0.216	0.363	0.233	0.381
	Avg	**0.110**	**0.233**	0.122	0.258	0.136	0.273	0.146	0.286	0.142	0.283	0.153	0.296
TKY	3	**0.075**	**0.189**	0.088	0.215	0.093	0.222	0.099	0.234	0.095	0.228	0.103	0.242
	12	**0.120**	**0.256**	0.138	0.285	0.149	0.289	0.156	0.302	0.152	0.296	0.162	0.309
	24	**0.163**	**0.310**	0.187	0.342	0.202	0.358	0.215	0.373	0.208	0.365	0.220	0.380
	Avg	**0.119**	**0.252**	0.138	0.281	0.148	0.290	0.157	0.303	0.152	0.296	0.162	0.310

fixed MLP weights in mixer layers, thereby enhancing dynamic adaptability and real-time performance. Bidirectional scanning overcomes causal limitations to capture global spatio-temporal correlations. By fusing spatio-temporal features from mixer layers and Mamba blocks, the residual connection ensures information transmission and mitigates gradient vanishing. Overall, STMixMamba achieves superior or competitive performance across all datasets, confirming that its component synergy and functional complementarity design effectively capture both long- and short-term spatio-temporal features while maintaining linear complexity, thus handling the core challenges of user trajectory forecasting. For real-time LBS scenarios, such as POI recommendation and ride-hailing mobility scheduling, the performance gain achieved without sacrificing inference efficiency carries clear practical significance.

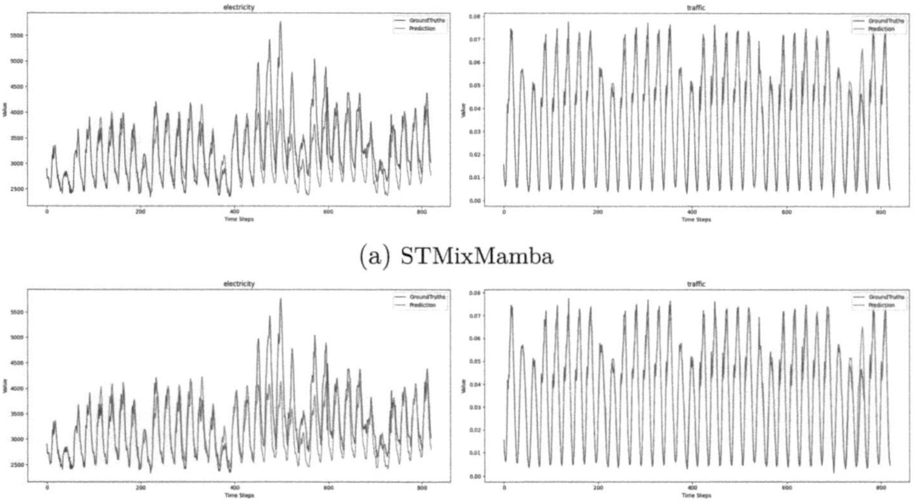

(a) STMixMamba

(b) TSMixer

Fig. 2. Comparison of forecasts between STMixMamba and TSMixer on two datasets when the lookback length is 512 and the forecast length is 720.

4.3 Ablation Study

To validate the effectiveness of STMixMamba components, we conducted ablation experiments on Electricity, T-Drive, NYC and TKY datasets. As shown in Table 2, 'w/o Mamba' denotes the removal of Mamba blocks, 'w/o Parameter' denotes the removal of fixed parameters in enhanced Mamba blocks, 'w/o Residual' denotes the removal of the residual connection, and 'w/o TM', 'w/o SM', and 'w/o FM' denote the removal of the temporal, spatial and feature mixing modules, respectively. Furthermore, we design two variants with different internal fusion methods for the mixer layer MLPs and Mamba blocks and compare their performance. Variant 1 transposes the mixer layer output to swap spatio-temporal and feature dimensions before feeding it into Mamba blocks to evaluate Mamba's long-term spatio-temporal dependency modeling capability.

Variant 2 replaces MLPs in the mixer layer with parameter-enhanced Mamba blocks to investigate whether Mamba can substitute MLPs in capturing fine-grained spatio-temporal dependencies and cross-variate interactions.

The ablation results show that STMixMamba with all components achieves the best performance and significantly outperforms the two variants, demonstrating its rational design and the contribution of each component. As shown in Fig. 3, we visualize partial ablation results on NYC and TKY user trajectory datasets. The transposition of Variant 1 causes Mamba blocks to model along the feature dimension rather than spatio-temporal dimension, validating Mamba's role in capturing long-term spatio-temporal dependencies. The replacement of Variant 2 weakens fine-grained pattern extraction capability due to noise-smoothing tendency of selective state space and introduces parameter redundancy, validating that MLP-stacked mixer layers effectively capture short-term spatio-temporal dependencies and cross-variate interactions.

Table 2. Results of ablation experiments on four datasets.

Models		STMixMamba		w/o Mamba		w/o Parameter		w/o Residual		w/o TM		w/o SM		w/o FM		Variant 1		Variant 2	
Metric		MSE	MAE	MSE	MAE	MSE	MAE	MSE	MAE	MSE	MAE	MSE	MAE	MSE	MAE	MSE	MAE	MSE	MAE
Electricity	96	**0.129**	**0.227**	0.136	0.238	0.130	**0.227**	0.843	0.760	0.132	0.231	**0.129**	**0.227**	0.130	**0.227**	0.130	0.228	0.136	0.232
	192	**0.147**	**0.243**	0.168	0.272	0.148	**0.243**	0.851	0.763	0.149	0.245	**0.147**	**0.243**	0.151	**0.243**	0.148	0.244	0.151	0.244
	336	**0.160**	**0.260**	0.162	0.261	0.161	**0.260**	0.863	0.766	**0.160**	**0.260**	**0.160**	**0.260**	0.167	**0.260**	0.163	0.264	0.167	0.261
	720	**0.190**	**0.289**	0.217	0.318	0.191	**0.289**	0.889	0.775	0.195	0.292	**0.190**	**0.289**	0.206	0.296	0.194	0.292	0.209	0.300
	Avg	**0.157**	**0.254**	0.171	0.272	**0.157**	0.255	0.861	0.766	0.159	0.257	**0.157**	**0.254**	0.164	0.257	0.159	0.257	0.166	0.259
T-Drive	3	**0.072**	**0.185**	1.831	1.002	0.890	0.653	1.128	0.770	49.31	5.260	101.5	7.611	8.270	1.977	2.933	1.183	3.486	1.392
	12	**0.117**	**0.250**	1.964	0.998	0.249	0.368	0.549	0.516	61.48	5.187	75.97	6.170	1.189	0.766	0.615	0.546	0.732	0.649
	24	**0.158**	**0.306**	5.345	1.816	1.521	0.949	0.882	0.678	66.00	5.859	167.0	10.93	6.047	1.711	2.876	1.260	3.408	1.492
	Avg	**0.116**	**0.247**	3.047	1.272	0.887	0.657	0.853	0.655	58.93	5.436	114.8	8.235	5.169	1.485	2.142	0.996	2.542	1.178
NYC	3	**0.060**	**0.168**	2.104	0.982	4.023	1.295	1.706	0.935	31.93	4.291	53.48	5.773	15.68	2.805	7.806	1.767	15.68	2.805
	12	**0.102**	**0.230**	9.724	1.967	9.239	1.861	6.986	1.668	9.112	2.019	12.93	2.344	8.623	1.910	8.796	1.888	8.623	1.910
	24	**0.168**	**0.302**	6.951	1.769	7.104	1.742	1.919	0.939	11.47	2.284	25.74	3.774	14.78	2.807	7.096	1.906	14.78	2.807
	Avg	**0.110**	**0.233**	6.260	1.572	6.789	1.633	3.537	1.180	17.50	2.865	30.71	3.963	13.03	2.507	7.900	1.854	13.03	2.507
TKY	3	**0.075**	**0.189**	4.067	1.336	4.387	1.394	4.343	1.396	5.649	1.689	7.341	1.877	3.003	1.156	7.378	1.850	8.856	2.123
	12	**0.120**	**0.256**	6.165	1.680	5.045	1.531	3.262	1.227	2.924	1.180	3.477	1.275	2.915	1.175	3.865	1.325	4.638	1.589
	24	**0.163**	**0.310**	5.421	1.474	5.087	1.490	4.606	1.480	3.197	1.212	6.573	1.683	4.000	1.362	6.788	1.785	8.146	2.052
	Avg	**0.119**	**0.252**	5.218	1.497	4.840	1.472	4.070	1.368	3.923	1.360	5.797	1.612	3.306	1.231	6.010	1.654	7.213	1.921

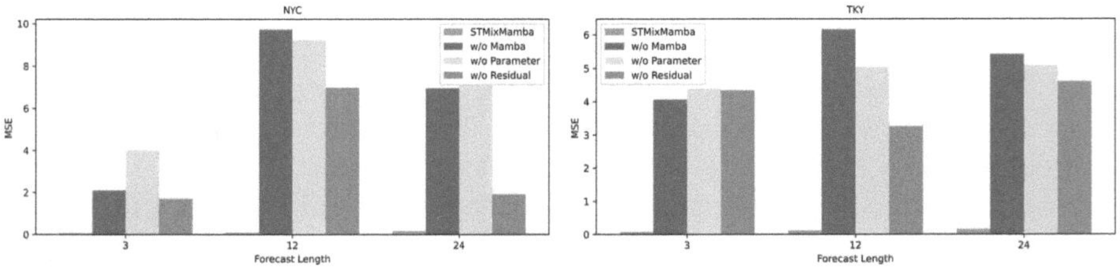

Fig. 3. Performance comparison of module ablation on NYC and TKY datasets.

4.4 Complexity Analysis

STMixMamba achieves linear complexity in both parameter count and inference computation. Its computational cost relies on two core modules: (1) spatio-temporal-feature mixer layers based on stacked MLPs, which attain linear parameter growth via cross-dimension weight sharing and avoid pairwise temporal interaction causing quadratic computation; (2) bidirectional enhanced Mamba layers capturing long-term dependencies via linear selective state space scanning, where bidirectional propagation introduces only constant-factor overhead and maintains linear time complexity with respect to sequence length L. The overall N-layer stacked architecture exhibits a complexity of $O(NLSV)$, scaling linearly with L, in contrast to the quadratic complexity $O(L^2SV)$ of self-attention. This efficient design inherently enables lightweight deployment for real-time LBS.

Under the standard setup on NYC dataset with a prediction horizon $T = 24$, STMixMamba has roughly 230K trainable parameters and 30 ms average per-batch inference latency. It achieves a 2–4$\times$ inference speedup over Transformer-based baselines and introduces only marginal overhead compared with TSMixer, validating its lightweight design for real-time LBS deployment.

5 Conclusion

In this paper, we propose STMixMamba, a lightweight hybrid architecture internally fusing MLP-stacked spatio-temporal-feature mixer layers and bidirectional parameter-enhanced Mamba blocks for user trajectory forecasting in LBS. STMixMamba models both long- and short-term spatio-temporal dependencies and cross-variate interactions through synergistic collaboration among its components, achieving high-precision prediction with linear complexity and addressing the core challenges in trajectory forecasting. Experiments proved that STMixMamba achieved superior performance, and its favorable accuracy-efficiency trade-off provides a lightweight and high-precision solution for real-time deployment in practical location-based services.

Acknowledgments. This work was partially supported by Shandong Provincial Key Research and Development Program under Grant No. 2024CXGC010101 and Shandong Provincial Natural Science Foundation under Grant No. ZR2023LZH008.

References

1. Alkilane, K., He, Y., Lee, D.H.: MixMamba: time series modeling with adaptive expertise. Inf. Fusion **112**, 102589 (2024)
2. Box, G.E., Jenkins, G.M., Reinsel, G.C., Ljung, G.M.: Time series analysis: forecasting and control. John Wiley & Sons (2015)
3. Chen, S.A., Li, C.L., Yoder, N., Arik, S.O., Pfister, T.: TSMixer: an all-MLP architecture for time series forecasting. arXiv preprint arXiv:2303.06053 (2023)

4. Chen, W., et al.: Next-POI recommendation via spatial-temporal knowledge graph contrastive learning and trajectory prompt. IEEE Trans. Knowl. Data Eng. (2025)
5. Gu, A., Dao, T.: Mamba: linear-time sequence modeling with selective state spaces. arXiv preprint arXiv:2312.00752 (2023)
6. Han, S., Xun, Y., Cai, J., Yang, H., Li, Y.: DyGraphformer: transformer combining dynamic spatio-temporal graph network for multivariate time series forecasting. Neural Netw. **181**, 106776 (2025)
7. Hu, J., Zheng, T., Peng, L., Teng, F., Du, S., Li, T.: LightST: a simplifying spatio-temporal graph neural network for traffic flow forecasting. IEEE Trans. Big Data (2025)
8. Jin, X., Zhang, Y., Yao, D.: Simultaneously Prediction of Network Traffic Flow Based on PCA-SVR. In: Liu, D., Fei, S., Hou, Z., Zhang, H., Sun, C. (eds.) ISNN 2007. LNCS, vol. 4492, pp. 1022–1031. Springer, Heidelberg (2007). https://doi.org/10.1007/978-3-540-72393-6_121
9. Kim, T., Kim, J., Tae, Y., Park, C., Choi, J.H., Choo, J.: Reversible instance normalization for accurate time-series forecasting against distribution shift. In: International Conference on Learning Representations (2021)
10. Li, Y., Wang, Y., Wang, P., Wang, W., Tong, X.: A real-time route prediction-based multiobjective task allocation for opportunistic mobile crowdsensing. IEEE Trans. Comput. Soc. Syst. **12**(5), 2549–2561 (2025)
11. Lian, D., Wu, Y., Ge, Y., Xie, X., Chen, E.: Geography-aware sequential location recommendation. In: Proceedings of the 26th ACM SIGKDD International Conference on Knowledge Discovery & Data Mining, pp. 2009–2019 (2020)
12. Lim, B., Arık, S.Ö., Loeff, N., Pfister, T.: Temporal fusion transformers for interpretable multi-horizon time series forecasting. Int. J. Forecast. **37**(4), 1748–1764 (2021)
13. Nie, Y., Nguyen, N.H., Sinthong, P., Kalagnanam, J.: A time series is worth 64 words: long-term forecasting with transformers. arXiv preprint arXiv:2211.14730 (2022)
14. Tang, J., et al.: Deep spatio-temporal dependent convolutional LSTM network for traffic flow prediction. Sci. Rep. **15**(1), 11743 (2025)
15. Vaswani, A., et al.: Attention is all you need. Adv. Neural Inf. Process. Syst. **30** (2017)
16. Wang, X., Liu, L.: STGNet: a spatio-temporal graph neural network for motion prediction in autonomous driving. Neurocomputing, 133063 (2026)
17. Wang, Z., et al.: Is mamba effective for time series forecasting? Neurocomputing **619**, 129178 (2025)
18. Wu, H., Xu, J., Wang, J., Long, M.: Autoformer: decomposition transformers with auto-correlation for long-term series forecasting. Adv. Neural. Inf. Process. Syst. **34**, 22419–22430 (2021)
19. Yang, D., Zhang, D., Zheng, V.W., Yu, Z.: Modeling user activity preference by leveraging user spatial temporal characteristics in LBSNS. IEEE Trans. Syst., Man, Cybern.: Syst. **45**(1), 129–142 (2014)
20. Yang, S., Wu, Q., Li, Z., Wang, K.: PSTCGCN: principal spatio-temporal causal graph convolutional network for traffic flow prediction. Neural Comput. Appl. **37**(20), 14751–14764 (2025)
21. Yuan, J., Zheng, Y., Xie, X., Sun, G.: Driving with knowledge from the physical world. In: Proceedings of the 17th ACM SIGKDD International Conference on Knowledge Discovery and Data Mining, pp. 316–324 (2011)

22. Yuan, J., et al.: T-Drive: driving directions based on taxi trajectories. In: Proceedings of the 18th SIGSPATIAL International Conference on Advances in Geographic Information Systems, pp. 99–108 (2010)
23. Zeng, A., Chen, M., Zhang, L., Xu, Q.: Are transformers effective for time series forecasting? In: Proceedings of the AAAI Conference on Artificial Intelligence, vol. 37, pp. 11121–11128 (2023)
24. Zhou, H., et al.: Informer: beyond efficient transformer for long sequence time-series forecasting. In: Proceedings of the AAAI Conference on Artificial Intelligence, vol. 35, pp. 11106–11115 (2021)
25. Zhou, T., Ma, Z., Wen, Q., Wang, X., Sun, L., Jin, R.: FEDformer: frequency enhanced decomposed transformer for long-term series forecasting. In: International Conference on Machine Learning, pp. 27268–27286. PMLR (2022)

Video and Image Processing

Dense Audio-Visual Event Localization with Bidirectional Temporal Cross-Modal Alignment and Boundary-Aware Cross-Scale Collaboration

Lingling Zi, Xiaoyan Zeng(✉), and Xin Cong

Chongqing Normal University, Chongqing, China
{zll,cx}@cqnu.edu.cn, 2024210516093@stu.cqnu.edu.cn

Abstract. Dense audio-visual event localization aims to localize all events that are simultaneously audible and visible in long untrimmed videos and estimate their precise start and end times. Compared to traditional audio-visual event localization, this task more closely resembles real-world scenarios but faces challenges such as dense event distribution, multi-category overlap, cross-modal temporal misalignment, and significant variations in event durations. Existing methods typically employ synchronous interaction or simple fusion of audio-visual sequences, making it difficult to capture the bidirectional temporal evolution of events and lacking targeted modeling for boundary information transmission across different scales. To address this, we propose a dense audio-visual event localization method based on bidirectional temporal cross-modal alignment and cross-scale boundary collaboration. A bidirectional temporal cross-modal alignment module is designed to establish cross-modal correspondences in both forward history evolution and backward future verification directions. A cross-scale boundary collaboration module is also designed, utilizing cross-scale alignment, left and right translation, and difference modeling to enhance the discriminative representation of event boundaries. Our experimental results on the UnAV-100 dataset demonstrate that the proposed method achieves excellent performance at multiple tIoU thresholds and exhibits particularly strong robustness in high tIoU boundary constraints and complex, dense scenes.

Keywords: Dense audio-visual event localization · Cross-modal alignment · Boundary collaboration

1 Introduction

Audio and vision are two crucial modalities for understanding real-world events. Many events in natural scenes are both visible and audible, such as speech, passing vehicles, and musical performances. Therefore, jointly modeling audio-visual information is important for video event understanding [1–6]. Early audio-visual event localization methods mainly focused on short videos and usually assumed

L. Ding et al. (Eds.): APWeb-WAIM 2026, LNCS 16995, pp. 269–283, 2027.
https://doi.org/10.1007/978-981-92-5699-0_17

that each video contained only one dominant event [1–4,18,20]. However, real-world videos are often long and untrimmed, containing multiple dense or even overlapping events. Dense audio-visual event localization aims to identify all events that are simultaneously visible and audible in such videos and predict their temporal boundaries [7–9].

Despite recent progress, this task still faces several challenges. Dense events often involve complex contextual dependencies, and relying solely on local convolutions or undirected self-attention makes it difficult to simultaneously leverage these two complementary approaches [10–13,15,34]. Second, audio and visual signals are not always strictly synchronized in real videos, and direct fusion at the same temporal position may introduce cross-modal confusion [3,6,9,16,24]. Third, multi-scale features may produce inconsistent boundary responses for the same event, leading to temporal localization shifts [12–14,26,28–30].

To address these issues, we propose BTA-BC based on the DAVEL baseline [7]. The proposed method mainly consists of two modules: a bidirectional temporal cross-modal alignment module and a cross-scale boundary collaboration module. The former models event context from both forward and backward directions and aligns audio-visual features under direction-consistent temporal contexts. The latter performs cross-scale temporal alignment, compensates for boundary offsets using neighboring-scale information, and highlights potential boundary regions through inter-scale differences. Together, these modules improve temporal dependency modeling, alleviate audio-visual misalignment, and enhance boundary localization. Experiments on the UnAV-100 dataset show that BTA-BC achieves superior performance under multiple tIoU thresholds.

The main contributions of this paper are summarized as follows:

- We propose BTA-BC for dense audio-visual event localization, targeting temporal dependencies, cross-modal misalignment, and boundary inconsistency.
- We design a bidirectional temporal cross-modal alignment module to model event context in both forward and backward directions and reduce audio-visual information mismatch.
- We design a cross-scale boundary collaboration module to calibrate event boundaries by cross-scale alignment, local shift compensation, and inter-scale difference modeling.

2 Related Work

Audio-visual event localization focuses on finding events that can be observed in both visual frames and audio signals. Most early studies worked on short videos and treated this problem as event classification at the clip level. Prior methods have improved audio-visual matching by using dual attention, cross-modal relation modeling, positive sample propagation, semantic co-attention, relation modulation, and event-specific preference learning [1–4,16–19]. These methods perform well in short-video settings, but they are usually designed for scenarios where events are sparse and have simple temporal structures. Dense audio-visual event localization is more difficult because the model needs to find all audio-visual events in long untrimmed videos and predict accurate start and end times [7–9]. In this setting, several events may appear close to each other or overlap in time, so the model needs reliable audio-visual matching and accurate temporal boundary prediction.

Cross-modal modeling plays an important role in audio-visual understanding. Many existing methods combine audio and visual features through feature concatenation, gated fusion, or cross-modal attention [17,21,22,24]. Cross-modal attention is widely used because it allows one modality to select useful information from the other modality [3,16,23,24]. However, many existing interaction methods assume that audio and visual signals are aligned at the same temporal position. This assumption is not always true in real videos. For example, a sound may occur before or after the corresponding visual action, and visual cues may become unclear due to occlusion or background interference. As a result, directly matching audio and visual features at the same time step may introduce incorrect information. Our bidirectional temporal cross-modal alignment module addresses this issue by building audio-visual correspondences in both forward and backward temporal contexts, which makes cross-modal interaction more stable for temporally misaligned events.

Multi-scale temporal modeling is also crucial for event localization. Feature pyramids are commonly used for action localization and dense event localization; they can represent events of varying durations. [14,15,25–28,30]. Features at fine temporal scales keep more detailed timing information and are useful for short events and boundary changes. Features at coarse temporal scales cover longer temporal ranges and provide stronger semantic information. Many existing methods combine multi-scale features by upsampling, concatenation, or top-down aggregation [25,36,37]. However, event boundaries from different scales may not be well aligned because downsampling and semantic aggregation can shift boundary responses. If these features are directly fused, the boundary errors may be passed to the final prediction. Our boundary-aware cross-scale collaboration module reduces this problem by using temporal alignment, local shift compensation, and cross-scale difference modeling to refine boundary features and improve localization accuracy.

3 Methodology

3.1 Problem Formulation

Given an untrimmed audio-visual video, we divide it into T consecutive temporal segments. The visual and audio inputs of the t-th segment are denoted as V_t and A_t, respectively, and the whole video is represented as $\{(V_t, A_t)\}_{t=1}^{T}$. The goal of dense audio-visual event localization is to predict all events that occur simultaneously in audio and visual modalities, including their categories and temporal boundaries.

For a given video, the annotation set is defined as $Y = \{y_n = (t_{s,n}, t_{e,n}, c_n)\}_{n=1}^{N}$, where N is the number of events, $t_{s,n}$ and $t_{e,n}$ are the start and end times of the n-th event, and c_n is its category. For each temporal location t, the model predicts the category probability $p(c_t)$ and the distances to the start and end boundaries, denoted as $d_{s,t}$ and $d_{e,t}$. Thus, the prediction is $\hat{y}_t = (d_{s,t}, d_{e,t}, p(c_t))$, and the final category and boundaries are obtained by

$$\hat{c}_t = \arg\max p(c_t), \quad \hat{t}_{s,t} = t - d_{s,t}, \quad \hat{t}_{e,t} = t + d_{e,t}. \tag{1}$$

3.2 Framework Overview

The overall framework of BTA-BC is shown in Fig. 1. It contains four components: unimodal feature embedding, bidirectional temporal cross-modal alignment, boundary-aware cross-scale collaboration, and multi-scale decoding. First, audio and visual features are projected into a unified space and enhanced by unimodal temporal encoders. Then, bidirectional temporal cross-modal alignment models audio-visual interactions in both forward and backward temporal contexts. After that, boundary-aware cross-scale collaboration calibrates boundary representations across different temporal scales. Finally, classification and boundary regression heads predict event categories and category-aware temporal boundaries.

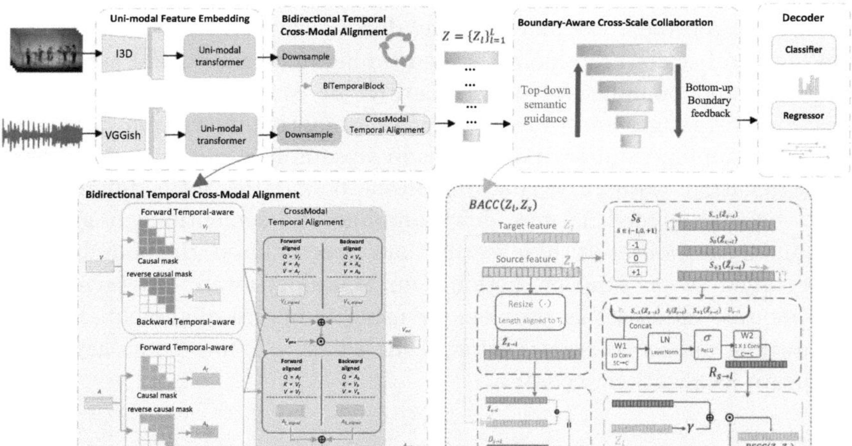

Fig. 1. BTA-BC model architecture.

3.3 Unimodal Feature Embedding

Given $\{(V_t, A_t)\}_{t=1}^{T}$, we extract initial visual and audio features following the baseline method [7]. The visual branch uses a two-stream I3D model to extract RGB and optical flow features [31,33], while the audio branch adopts

VGGish [32]. The extracted features are denoted as $v = \{f_t^v\}_{t=1}^T \in \mathbb{R}^{T \times d_v}$ and $a = \{f_t^a\}_{t=1}^T \in \mathbb{R}^{T \times d_a}$. Since they are extracted by different pre-trained models, we project them into a unified embedding space:

$$F_0^V = \text{Conv}_V(v), \quad F_0^A = \text{Conv}_A(a). \tag{2}$$

where $F_0^V, F_0^A \in \mathbb{R}^{T \times D}$, and D denotes the unified feature dimension. To further capture temporal dependencies within each modality, we employ unimodal temporal encoders:

$$F^V = \text{Trans}_V(F_0^V), \quad F^A = \text{Trans}_A(F_0^A). \tag{3}$$

where Trans_V and Trans_A denote the temporal encoding processes for visual and audio modalities. The obtained F^V and F^A are used as inputs to the following bidirectional temporal cross-modal alignment module.

3.4 Bidirectional Temporal Cross-Modal Alignment Module

Dense audio-visual events usually exhibit temporal continuity, while audio and visual signals are not always strictly synchronized. Therefore, the model needs to capture both past-to-current event evolution and future-to-current event verification, while establishing cross-modal correspondences in temporal contexts [16,24,34].

Given the visual feature F_l^V and audio feature F_l^A at the l-th scale, we construct forward and backward temporal representations. The forward branch uses a causal mask, while the backward branch uses a reverse causal mask:

$$F_l^{m,f} = \text{ForwardAttn}(F_l^m), \quad F_l^{m,b} = \text{BackwardAttn}(F_l^m), \quad m \in \{V, A\}. \tag{4}$$

where m denotes the modality type. $F_l^{V,f}$ and $F_l^{V,b}$ are the forward and backward visual features, while $F_l^{A,f}$ and $F_l^{A,b}$ are the corresponding audio features.

Then, we perform cross-modal alignment under direction-consistent temporal contexts:

$$\begin{aligned}
\bar{F}_l^{V,f} &= \text{Align}(F_l^{V,f}, F_l^{A,f}), \\
\bar{F}_l^{V,b} &= \text{Align}(F_l^{V,b}, F_l^{A,b}), \\
\bar{F}_l^{A,f} &= \text{Align}(F_l^{A,f}, F_l^{V,f}), \\
\bar{F}_l^{A,b} &= \text{Align}(F_l^{A,b}, F_l^{V,b}), \\
\text{Align}(X, R) &= X + \text{MHA}(X, R, R).
\end{aligned} \tag{5}$$

Here, $\text{Align}(X, R)$ aligns feature X to the reference feature R by cross-attention, where X is used as the query and R is used as the key and value. This enables one modality to absorb temporally related and semantically consistent information from the other modality [23,24,35].

After alignment, we introduce a modality gating mechanism [21] to adaptively fuse audio and visual features:

$$\begin{aligned} g_l &= \sigma\left(\text{Conv}\left([F_l^{V,f}; F_l^{V,b}]\right)\right), \\ \hat{F}_l^V &= g_l \odot \left(\bar{F}_l^{V,f} + \bar{F}_l^{V,b}\right), \\ \hat{F}_l^A &= (1 - g_l) \odot \left(\bar{F}_l^{A,f} + \bar{F}_l^{A,b}\right). \end{aligned} \tag{6}$$

where $\sigma(\cdot)$ denotes the Sigmoid function, The gate is generated from bidirectional visual features and is used to adaptively control the contribution of visual and audio information.

To model events with different durations, we apply bidirectional temporal cross-modal alignment at multiple scales:

$$(\hat{F}_{l+1}^V, \hat{F}_{l+1}^A) = \text{BTCA}(\hat{F}_l^V, \hat{F}_l^A), \quad l = 1, 2, \ldots, L-1. \tag{7}$$

where BTCA denotes bidirectional temporal cross-modal alignment. The audio and visual features at each scale are concatenated to form a multi-scale audio-visual feature pyramid:

$$Z_l = \text{Concat}(\hat{F}_l^V, \hat{F}_l^A), \quad Z = \{Z_l\}_{l=1}^L, \quad Z_l \in \mathbb{R}^{B \times C \times T_l}. \tag{8}$$

Here, Z_l denotes the fused feature at the l-th scale. Shallow features capture fine-grained boundaries, while deep features provide long-range semantic context.

3.5 Boundary-Aware Cross-Scale Collaboration

Although multi-scale features provide complementary information, event boundaries may be misaligned across scales due to downsampling and semantic aggregation. To address this issue, we design a Boundary-Aware Cross-Scale Collaboration (BACC) module to enhance boundary representations through temporal alignment, local shifts, and scale-difference modeling.

Given the target-scale feature Z_l and the source-scale feature Z_s, BACC first resamples Z_s to the temporal length of Z_l.

Inspired by the concept of time-shift modeling [38], three non-circular shifted candidates are constructed to compensate for cross-scale boundary offsets. Meanwhile, a difference response is computed to highlight potential boundary regions:

$$\begin{aligned} \bar{Z}_{s\to l} &= \text{Resize}(Z_s, T_l), \quad \bar{Z}_{s\to l} \in \mathbb{R}^{B \times C \times T_l}, \\ \bar{Z}_{s\to l}^{\delta} &= S_\delta(\bar{Z}_{s\to l}), \quad \delta \in \{-1, 0, +1\}, \\ D_{s\to l} &= \left|Z_l - \bar{Z}_{s\to l}\right|. \end{aligned} \tag{9}$$

where Resize$(\cdot)$ denotes temporal resampling, and S_δ denotes non-circular temporal shifting. $D_{s\to l}$ measures the difference between the target and source features at the same temporal position.

The target feature, shifted source features, and difference response are concatenated along the channel dimension:

$$H_{s\to l} = [Z_l, \bar{Z}^{-1}_{s\to l}, \bar{Z}^{0}_{s\to l}, \bar{Z}^{+1}_{s\to l}, D_{s\to l}], \quad H_{s\to l} \in \mathbb{R}^{B\times 5C\times T_l}. \tag{10}$$

Based on $H_{s\to l}$, a lightweight residual calibration network generates a correction term and injects it into the target-scale feature [39]:

$$R_{s\to l} = W_2\big(\phi(\mathrm{LN}(W_1(H_{s\to l})))\big), \quad \mathrm{BACC}(Z_l, Z_s) = (Z_l + \gamma R_{s\to l}) \odot M_l. \tag{11}$$

where W_1 reduces the channel dimension from $5C$ to C, W_2 is a 1×1 convolution, $\phi(\cdot)$ denotes the ReLU activation, γ is a learnable scaling factor, and M_l is the valid temporal mask.

We further adopt a two-stage collaboration strategy. The first stage propagates high-level semantics to shallow features, while the second stage feeds calibrated boundary cues back to deep features:

$$\begin{aligned} \hat{Z}_L &= Z_L, \quad \hat{Z}_l = \mathrm{BACC}(Z_l, \hat{Z}_{l+1}), \quad l = L-1, L-2, \ldots, 1, \\ G_1 &= \hat{Z}_1, \quad G_l = \mathrm{BACC}(\hat{Z}_l, G_{l-1}), \quad l = 2, 3, \ldots, L. \end{aligned} \tag{12}$$

Finally, the model obtains the boundary-calibrated multi-scale feature pyramid $G = \{G_l\}_{l=1}^{L}$, which combines semantic context and fine-grained boundary cues.

3.6 Decoder

For the feature G_l at the l-th scale, the decoder contains a classification head and a boundary regression head. Following the dense prediction paradigm [10, 41], they predict event probabilities and boundary distances at each temporal location:

$$P_l = \mathrm{ClsHead}(G_l), \quad O_l = \mathrm{RegHead}(G_l). \tag{13}$$

Here, P_l is the classification result, and O_l is the category-aware boundary regression result. For temporal position t, the predicted boundary of the k-th category is

$$\hat{b}^k_{l,t} = \left(c_{l,t} - d^{s,k}_{l,t},\ c_{l,t} + d^{e,k}_{l,t}\right), \tag{14}$$

where $c_{l,t}$ is the temporal coordinate, and $d^{s,k}_{l,t}$ and $d^{e,k}_{l,t}$ are the predicted distances to the start and end boundaries. Category-aware regression is adopted to better handle temporally overlapping events.

During training, the model is optimized with a joint classification and boundary regression loss:

$$\mathcal{L} = \alpha \sum_t \mathcal{L}_{cls} + \beta \sum_t I_t \mathcal{L}_{reg}. \tag{15}$$

where $\mathcal{L}_{cls}$ is the Focal Loss [42], $\mathcal{L}_{reg}$ is the generalized IoU loss [43], I_t indicates whether an event exists at the current position, and α and β are balancing coefficients.

During inference, candidate event segments are generated from classification probabilities and regressed boundary distances. Soft-NMS [44] is applied to suppress highly overlapping predictions.

4 Experiments

4.1 Experimental Setups

Dataset. Experiments are conducted on the official UnAV-100 dataset [7], which contains 10,790 untrimmed videos and 100 audio-visual event categories. Each video contains about 2.8 event instances on average, and different events may overlap in time. Following the official split, the training, validation, and test sets are divided with a ratio of 3:1:1.

Evaluation Metric. Following previous works [7–9], we use mean Average Precision (mAP) as the main metric. mAP is reported under temporal IoU thresholds from 0.5 to 0.9 with an interval of 0.1, denoted as $[0.5 : 0.1 : 0.9]$. We also report the average mAP over $[0.1 : 0.1 : 0.9]$, denoted as Avg.

Implementation Details. For fair comparison, we use the same feature extraction settings as the baseline [7]. The visual branch uses RGB and optical flow features extracted by a pre-trained two-stream I3D network [31], while the audio branch uses VGGish features [32]. Both modalities are resampled or padded to the maximum length $T = 224$. The unimodal temporal encoding layer number is set to $L_s = 2$, and the multi-scale temporal modeling layer number is set to $L_c = 6$. The model is trained for 40 epochs with a batch size of 4 using AdamW.

Table 1. Comparison between BTA-BC and Prior methods.

Method	0.5	0.6	0.7	0.8	0.9	Avg.
TadTR [11]	30.4	27.1	23.3	19.4	14.3	29.4
ActionFormer [10]	43.5	39.4	33.4	27.3	17.9	42.2
TriDet [12]	46.2	–	–	–	–	44.4
DAVEL [7]	50.6	45.8	39.8	32.4	21.1	47.8
CCNET [8]	51.9	47.2	41.5	34.1	23.0	49.2
LOCO [9]	52.8	47.6	41.1	33.3	21.9	49.5
BTA-BC	**52.9**	**47.8**	**41.6**	**34.3**	**23.7**	**49.8**

4.2 Comparison to Prior Works

To evaluate the effectiveness of BTA-BC, we compare it with representative temporal action localization and dense audio-visual event localization methods. As shown in Table 1, BTA-BC achieves the best performance under all tIoU thresholds, with an Avg. mAP of 49.8%. Compared with DAVEL [7], BTA-BC improves Avg. mAP by 2%. It also outperforms LOCO [9] by 0.3% in Avg. mAP, with larger gains at high tIoU thresholds. These results indicate that BTA-BC

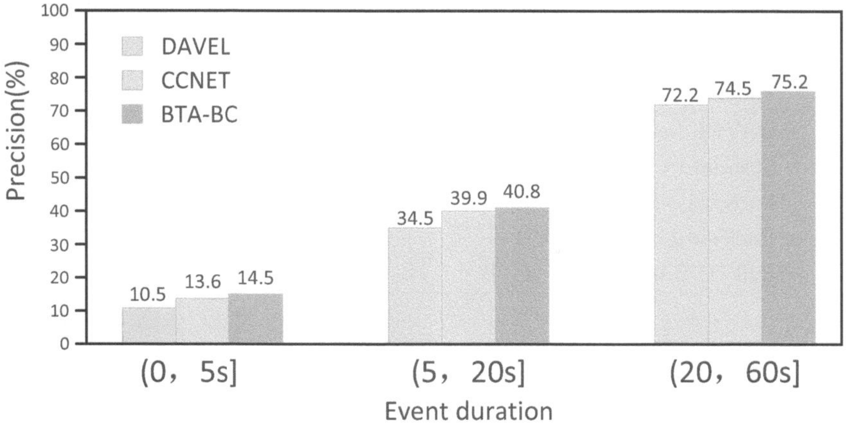

Fig. 2. Localization results for various durations.

improves audio-visual temporal modeling and boundary localization, especially under strict tIoU thresholds.

To evaluate localization under different event durations, we divide the UnAV-100 test events into short $(0s, 5s]$, medium $(5s, 20s]$, and long $(20s, 60s]$ groups. An event is regarded as correctly localized when its category is correct and its tIoU is larger than 0.5. As shown in Fig. 2, BTA-BC achieves the best performance in all duration groups, obtaining 14.5%, 40.8%, and 75.2% on short, medium, and long events, respectively. The gains are more obvious for short and medium events, showing that BTA-BC better captures fine-grained boundaries.

Table 2. Ablation study of the core modules in BTA-BC.

BTCA	BACC	0.5	0.6	0.7	0.8	0.9	Avg.
✓	×	52.4	47.2	40.8	33.4	21.9	49.2
×	✓	51.5	47.4	40.9	33.8	22.8	48.7
✓	✓	**52.9**	**47.8**	**41.6**	**34.3**	**23.7**	**49.8**

4.3 Ablation Studies

To verify the effectiveness of BTCA and BACC, we conduct ablation studies, as shown in Table 2. When only BTCA is used, the model achieves 49.2% Avg. mAP, showing that bidirectional temporal modeling improves audio-visual interaction. When only BACC is used, the model obtains 48.7% Avg. mAP and performs better at tIoU = 0.9, indicating that BACC helps refine event boundaries. With both modules, the full model achieves the best performance, demonstrating their complementarity.

Table 3. Fine-grained ablation study of bidirectional temporal cross-modal alignment. BACC is disabled for all variants.

Variant	Direction	CMA	0.5	0.6	0.7	0.8	0.9	Avg.
DAVEL baseline	none	×	50.6	45.8	39.8	32.4	21.1	47.8
Standard CMA	non-dir	✓	51.4	46.8	40.5	32.8	20.4	48.2
Forward-only BTCA	F	✓	52.1	47.6	41.0	33.1	20.8	48.7
Backward-only BTCA	B	✓	52.2	47.2	40.6	33.5	20.9	48.6
Full BTCA	F+B	✓	52.4	47.2	40.8	33.4	21.9	49.2

Table 3 provides a fine-grained analysis of the temporal direction and cross-modal alignment design in BTCA, where BACC is disabled for all variants to isolate the contribution of BTCA. Compared with the DAVEL baseline, the Standard CMA baseline improves the Avg. mAP from 47.8% to 48.2%, indicating that standard audio-visual cross-modal alignment is beneficial. However, Standard CMA does not explicitly distinguish forward and backward temporal dependencies. By introducing direction-aware temporal modeling, the forward-only and backward-only variants further improve the Avg. mAP to 48.7% and 48.6%, respectively, showing that both historical temporal context and future verification cues are useful for dense audio-visual event localization. Full BTCA achieves the best Avg. mAP of 49.2% and the best performance at the strict tIoU threshold of 0.9, demonstrating that forward and backward temporal contexts are complementary. Compared with Standard CMA, Full BTCA brings a 1.0% Avg. mAP improvement, suggesting that the gain of BTCA comes not merely from cross-modal interaction, but from direction-aware bidirectional temporal cross-modal alignment.

Table 4. Boundary error analysis between predictions and ground truth.

Metric	w/o BACC	w/ BACC	Reduction
Start Error	1.01 s	0.85 s	15.8%
End Error	1.12 s	0.89 s	20.5%
Center Error	0.83 s	0.65 s	21.6%
Duration Error	1.65 s	1.41 s	14.7%

To evaluate the impact of BACC on boundary localization, we conduct a boundary error analysis between matched predictions and ground-truth events. A prediction is matched with a ground truth if they have the same category and their tIoU is larger than 0.5. As shown in Table 4, BACC consistently reduces all boundary errors. These results show that cross-scale boundary collaboration helps the model capture boundary transitions more accurately.

Table 5. Parameter and computational cost analysis of BTA-BC and its variants. FLOPs are measured under the same input setting.

Method	Params (M)	FLOPs (G)	Avg. mAP
DAVEL baseline	139.54	27.0	47.8
+ BTCA	313.2	27.8	49.2
+ BACC	173.1	27.1	48.7
BTA-BC	346.7	27.9	49.8

4.4 Parameter and Computational Cost Analysis

Table 5 reports the parameter size and computational cost of BTA-BC and its variants under the same profiling protocol. Compared with the DAVEL baseline, introducing BTCA improves the Avg. mAP from 47.8% to 49.2%, showing that bidirectional temporal cross-modal alignment is the main contributor to the performance gain. This improvement comes with an increase in parameters, mainly due to the additional forward and backward temporal alignment branches. However, the FLOPs increase moderately from 27.0G to 27.8G, indicating that the extra computation introduced by BTCA is still controlled under the same input setting. When only BACC is used, the model improves the Avg. mAP from 47.8% to 48.7%, while the FLOPs only increase from 27.0G to 27.1G. This suggests that BACC provides an efficient boundary-aware refinement with limited computational overhead. Moreover, combining BTCA and BACC further improves the Avg. mAP to 49.8%, demonstrating that BACC is complementary to BTCA rather than being a redundant component. Overall, BTA-BC achieves the best localization performance with a reasonable accuracy-computation tradeoff, although the bidirectional temporal cross-modal alignment module introduces additional parameters.

4.5 Visualization Results

Figure 3 shows qualitative localization results of BTA-BC. Different colored segments denote different event categories, and the red dashed boxes indicate regions where events are dense or boundaries are ambiguous. Compared with the baseline, BTA-BC produces predictions closer to the ground truth and better separates adjacent events. These results show that BTA-BC can better handle dense events, similar categories, and ambiguous boundaries.

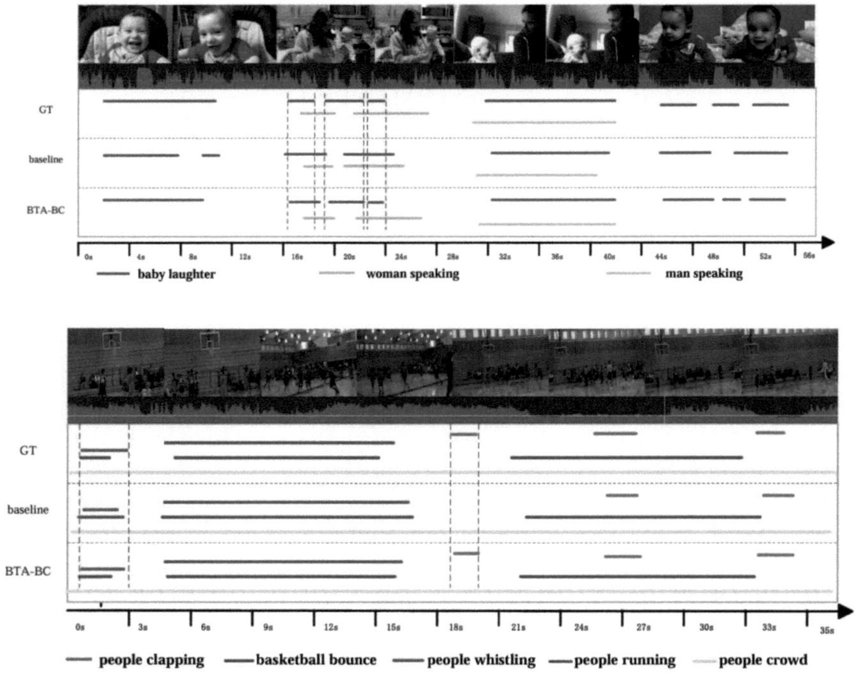

Fig. 3. Qualitative results of BTA-BC in the dense audio-visual event localization task.

5 Conclusion

This paper studies dense audio-visual event localization, which aims to localize all audible and visible events in long untrimmed videos. To address complex temporal dependencies, audio-visual misalignment, and cross-scale boundary inconsistency, we propose BTA-BC with two core modules: bidirectional temporal cross-modal alignment and boundary-aware cross-scale collaboration. The former captures event contexts from both forward and backward directions and aligns audio-visual features under direction-consistent temporal contexts. The latter calibrates event boundaries by using local shifts and cross-scale difference responses, enabling more accurate boundary localization.

Experiments on the UnAV-100 dataset show that BTA-BC outperforms existing methods, especially under strict boundary constraints and for events with different durations. These results demonstrate the effectiveness and robustness of the proposed method.

Acknowledgments. We are deeply grateful to the anonymous reviewers for their insightful comments and valuable suggestions, which have been highly beneficial in improving our manuscript. This work was supported by the Humanities and Social Sciences Program of Chongqing Municipal Education Commission (Grant No. 25SKGH071).

References

1. Tian, Y., Shi, J., Li, B., Duan, Z., Xu, C.: Audio-Visual Event Localization in Unconstrained Videos. In: Ferrari, V., Hebert, M., Sminchisescu, C., Weiss, Y. (eds.) ECCV 2018. LNCS, vol. 11206, pp. 252–268. Springer, Cham (2018). https://doi.org/10.1007/978-3-030-01216-8_16
2. Wu, Y., Zhu, L., Yan, Y.: Dual attention matching for audio-visual event localization. In: Proceedings of the IEEE/CVF International Conference on Computer Vision, pp. 6292–6300 (2019)
3. Xu, H., Zeng, R., Wu, Q.: Cross-modal relation-aware networks for audio-visual event localization. In: Proceedings of the 28th ACM International Conference on Multimedia, pp. 3893–3901 (2020)
4. Zhou, J., Zheng, L., Zhong, Y.: Positive sample propagation along the audio-visual event line. In: Proceedings of the IEEE/CVF Conference on Computer Vision and Pattern Recognition, pp. 8436–8444 (2021)
5. Wu, Y., Yang, Y.: Exploring heterogeneous clues for weakly-supervised audio-visual video parsing. In: Proceedings of the IEEE/CVF Conference on Computer Vision and Pattern Recognition, pp. 1326–1335 (2021)
6. Lamba, J., Akula, J., Dabral, R.: Cross-modal learning for audio-visual video parsing. arXiv preprint arXiv:2104.04598 (2021)
7. Geng, T., Wang, T., Duan, J.: Dense-localizing audio-visual events in untrimmed videos: a large-scale benchmark and baseline. In: Proceedings of the IEEE/CVF Conference on Computer Vision and Pattern Recognition, pp. 22942–22951 (2023)
8. Zhou, Z., Zhou, J., Qian, W., et al.: Dense audio-visual event localization under cross-modal consistency and multi-temporal granularity collaboration. In: Proceedings of the AAAI Conference on Artificial Intelligence, vol. 39, no. 10, pp. 10905–10913 (2025)
9. Xing, L., Qu, H., Yan, R.: Locality-aware cross-modal correspondence learning for dense audio-visual events localization. arXiv preprint arXiv:2409.07967 (2024)
10. Zhang, C.L., Wu, J., Li, Y.: ActionFormer: localizing moments of actions with transformers. In: Avidan, S., Brostow, G., Cissé, M., Farinella, G.M., Hassner, T. (eds.) European Conference on Computer Vision, LNCS, vol. 13664, pp. 492–510. Springer, Cham (2022). https://doi.org/10.1007/978-3-031-19772-7_29
11. Liu, X., Wang, Q., Hu, Y., et al.: End-to-end temporal action detection with transformer. IEEE Trans. Image Process. **31**, 5427–5441 (2022)
12. Shi, D., Zhong, Y., Cao, Q.: TriDet: temporal action detection with relative boundary modeling. In: Proceedings of the IEEE/CVF Conference on Computer Vision and Pattern Recognition, pp. 18857–18866 (2023)
13. Lin, T., Zhao, X., Su, H., Wang, C., Yang, M.: BSN: Boundary Sensitive Network for Temporal Action Proposal Generation. In: Ferrari, V., Hebert, M., Sminchisescu, C., Weiss, Y. (eds.) ECCV 2018. LNCS, vol. 11208, pp. 3–21. Springer, Cham (2018). https://doi.org/10.1007/978-3-030-01225-0_1
14. Lin, T., Liu, X., Li, X.: BMN: boundary-matching network for temporal action proposal generation. In: Proceedings of the IEEE/CVF International Conference on Computer Vision, pp. 3889–3898 (2019)
15. Zhao, C., Thabet, A.K., Ghanem, B.: Video self-stitching graph network for temporal action localization. In: Proceedings of the IEEE/CVF International Conference on Computer Vision, pp. 13658–13667 (2021)
16. Xuan, H., Zhang, Z., Chen, S., et al.: Cross-modal attention network for temporal inconsistent audio-visual event localization. In: Proceedings of the AAAI Conference on Artificial Intelligence, vol. 34, no. 1, pp. 279–286 (2020)

17. Xue, C., Zhong, X., Cai, M., et al.: Audio-visual event localization by learning spatial and semantic co-attention. IEEE Trans. Multimedia **25**, 418–429 (2021)
18. Wang, H., Zha, Z.J., Li, L., et al.: Semantic and relation modulation for audio-visual event localization. IEEE Trans. Pattern Anal. Mach. Intell. **45**(6), 7711–7725 (2022)
19. Ge, S., Jiang, Z., Yin, Y.: Learning event-specific localization preferences for audio-visual event localization. In: Proceedings of the 31st ACM International Conference on Multimedia, pp. 3446–3454 (2023)
20. Mo, S., Tian, Y.: Multi-modal grouping network for weakly-supervised audio-visual video parsing. Adv. Neural. Inf. Process. Syst. **35**, 34722–34733 (2022)
21. Arevalo, J., Solorio, T., Montes-y-Gómez, M., et al.: Gated multimodal units for information fusion. arXiv preprint arXiv:1702.01992 (2017)
22. Perez, E., Strub, F., De Vries, H., et al.: FiLM: visual reasoning with a general conditioning layer. In: Proceedings of the AAAI Conference on Artificial Intelligence, vol. 32, no. 1 (2018)
23. Vaswani, A., Shazeer, N., Parmar, N.: Attention is all you need. Adv. Neural. Inf. Process. Syst. **30** (2017)
24. Tsai, Y.H.H., Bai, S., Liang, P.P.: Multimodal transformer for unaligned multimodal language sequences. In: Proceedings of the 57th Annual Meeting of the Association for Computational Linguistics, pp. 6558–6569 (2019)
25. Lin, T.Y., Dollár, P., Girshick, R.: Feature pyramid networks for object detection. In: Proceedings of the IEEE Conference on Computer Vision and Pattern Recognition, pp. 2117–2125 (2017)
26. Xu, H., Das, A., Saenko, K.: R-C3D: region convolutional 3D network for temporal activity detection. In: Proceedings of the IEEE International Conference on Computer Vision, pp. 5783–5792 (2017)
27. Zhao, Y., Xiong, Y., Wang, L.: Temporal action detection with structured segment networks. In: Proceedings of the IEEE International Conference on Computer Vision, pp. 2914–2923 (2017)
28. Xu, M., Zhao, C., Rojas, D.S.: G-TAD: sub-graph localization for temporal action detection. In: Proceedings of the IEEE/CVF Conference on Computer Vision and Pattern Recognition, pp. 10156–10165 (2020)
29. Lin, C., Xu, C., Luo, D.: Learning salient boundary feature for anchor-free temporal action localization. In: Proceedings of the IEEE/CVF Conference on Computer Vision and Pattern Recognition, pp. 3320–3329 (2021)
30. Gao, Z., Cui, X., Zhuo, T.: Temporal action localization with multi-temporal scales. arXiv preprint arXiv:2208.07493 (2022)
31. Carreira, J., Zisserman, A.: Quo vadis, action recognition? a new model and the kinetics dataset. In: Proceedings of the IEEE Conference on Computer Vision and Pattern Recognition, pp. 6299–6308 (2017)
32. Hershey, S., Chaudhuri, S., Ellis, D.P.W.: CNN architectures for large-scale audio classification. In: IEEE International Conference on Acoustics, Speech and Signal Processing (ICASSP), pp. 131–135. IEEE (2017)
33. Teed, Z., Deng, J.: RAFT: Recurrent All-Pairs Field Transforms for Optical Flow. In: Vedaldi, A., Bischof, H., Brox, T., Frahm, J.-M. (eds.) ECCV 2020. LNCS, vol. 12347, pp. 402–419. Springer, Cham (2020). https://doi.org/10.1007/978-3-030-58536-5_24
34. Zhang, P., Wang, J., Wan, M., et al.: Audio-visual event localization with dual temporal-aware scene understanding and image-text knowledge bridging. Complex Intell. Syst. **11**(1), 15 (2025)

35. Carion, N., Massa, F., Synnaeve, G.: End-to-end object detection with transformers. In: Vedaldi, A., Bischof, H., Brox, T., Frahm, JM. (eds.) European Conference on Computer Vision. LNCS, vol. 12346, pp. 213–229. Springer, Cham (2020). https://doi.org/10.1007/978-3-030-58452-8_13
36. Liu, S., Qi, L., Qin, H., et al.: Path aggregation network for instance segmentation. In: Proceedings of the IEEE Conference on Computer Vision and Pattern Recognition, pp. 8759–8768 (2018)
37. Tan, M., Pang, R., Le, Q.V.: EfficientDet: scalable and efficient object detection. In: Proceedings of the IEEE/CVF Conference on Computer Vision and Pattern Recognition, pp. 10781–10790 (2020)
38. Lin, J., Gan, C., Han, S.: TSM: temporal shift module for efficient video understanding. In: Proceedings of the IEEE/CVF International Conference on Computer Vision, pp. 7083–7093 (2019)
39. He, K., Zhang, X., Ren, S.: Deep residual learning for image recognition. In: Proceedings of the IEEE Conference on Computer Vision and Pattern Recognition, pp. 770–778 (2016)
40. Ba, J.L., Kiros, J.R., Hinton, G.E.: Layer normalization. arXiv preprint arXiv:1607.06450 (2016)
41. Tian, Z., Shen, C., Chen, H.: FCOS: fully convolutional one-stage object detection. In: Proceedings of the IEEE/CVF International Conference on Computer Vision, pp. 9627–9636 (2019)
42. Lin, T.Y., Goyal, P., Girshick, R.: Focal loss for dense object detection. In: Proceedings of the IEEE International Conference on Computer Vision, pp. 2980–2988 (2017)
43. Rezatofighi, H., Tsoi, N., Gwak, J.Y.: Generalized intersection over union: a metric and a loss for bounding box regression. In: Proceedings of the IEEE/CVF Conference on Computer Vision and Pattern Recognition, pp. 658–666 (2019)
44. Bodla, N., Singh, B., Chellappa, R.: Soft-NMS-improving object detection with one line of code. In: Proceedings of the IEEE International Conference on Computer Vision, pp. 5561–5569 (2017)

High-Confidence Cross-Modal Guided Multimodal Manipulated Media Detection and Localization

Kexin Zhang[1,2](✉)

[1] Nanjing University of Science and Technology, Nanjing 210094, China
224127011309@njust.edu.cn
[2] ABC Institute, Rupert-Karls-University Heidelberg, Heidelberg, Germany

Abstract. The task of Detecting and Grounding Multi-Modal Media Manipulation (DGM4) aims to classify manipulation types and localize tampered regions across both images and text through cross-modal interactions. However, existing approaches often neglect the reliability of individual modalities, which can adversely affect the detection and localization performance. To address this limitation, we propose a Cross-Modal Guided Manipulation Detection and Localization (CMGMDL) framework. CMGMDL incorporates two core components: the Guidance Module (GM) and the Filter Refinement Module (FRM), each tailored to the specific requirements of classification and localization tasks. The FRM preserves high-confidence features while filtering and enhancing low-confidence features, thereby constructing a more reliable representation for the classification task. Specifically, the GM leverages predictions from high-confidence regions in the target modality to refine predictions in the source modality, guided by cross-modal feature similarity for the localization task. Experimental results demonstrate that CMGMDL outperforms existing state-of-the-art methods by a substantial margin.

Keywords: Multi-modal manipulated media detection · Cross-modal interaction · Image-text similarity · Guidance Module · Filter Refinement Module

1 Introduction

The rapid advancement of generative artificial intelligence (AIGC) has facilitated the widespread adoption of generative adversarial networks and diffusion models for producing highly realistic synthetic media. This trend has substantially accelerated the spread of misinformation, posing significant cybersecurity threats [5, 9].

To address this issue, considerable efforts have been devoted to media manipulation detection. Early studies primarily focused on single-modality scenarios [20]. In the visual domain, manipulated images can be identified through the analysis of frequency characteristics [3], spatial inconsistencies [6], and pixel-level anomalies [4, 25]. In the textual domain, factors such as writing styles [16],

L. Ding et al. (Eds.): APWeb-WAIM 2026, LNCS 16995, pp. 284–298, 2027.
https://doi.org/10.1007/978-981-92-5699-0_18

readability scores [1], and consistency with world knowledge [21] are considered key indicators for evaluating textual credibility. With the increasing prevalence of multi-modal manipulated media [10,14,23], DGM4 has emerged as a prominent research focus. This task not only facilitates fine-grained classification but also enables the grounding of manipulated regions across both visual and textual modalities [11].

Existing studies on DGM4 aim to categorize manipulation types and localize tampered regions through cross-modal interactions. However, despite notable progress, current methods still face several critical challenges: (1) Neglect of unreliable modality interference. Specifically, current approaches often fail to assess the reliability of visual and textual modalities prior to cross-modal interaction. (2) Lack of task-specific adaptation. Although RamDG [19] enhances modality reliability by integrating the knowledge of celebrity attribute profiles and IDseq [13] reduces the impact of tampered images via a tampering indicator generator, these methods do not fully account for the distinct requirements of classification versus localization tasks.

In response to the aforementioned challenges, we propose a Cross-Modal Guided Manipulation Detection and Localization (CMGMDL) framework, which mitigates the misleading influence of low-confidence modalities during cross-modal interaction while adapting to task-specific requirements. We first estimate confidence scores for each patch and token. In classification tasks, we employ FRM to retain high-confidence features and enhance low-confidence features, thus generating reliable visual and textual features. Based on these features, we perform reliable cross-modal fusion to improve classification performance. For localization tasks, we develop GM to refine visual and textual grounding. The core idea of cross-modality guidance is that if one modality provides reliable and relevant information, predictions in the other modality can be improved by leveraging inter-modal similarity [2]. Although cross-modal confidence guidance and attention gating mechanisms have been widely applied in the fields of computer vision and cross-modal retrieval, few studies have yet applied them to the domain of manipulated media detection to filter out unreliable modality guidance. Specifically, our main contributions are threefold:

(1) Task-oriented cross-modal guidance. We propose the CMGMDL framework to address the misleading influence from unreliable modalities by designing task-specific modality guidance strategies.

(2) GM for localization refinement. GM dynamically refines patch and token predictions using cross-modal similarity and confidence scores, ensuring that guidance originates from reliable signals without discarding potentially useful semantic cues.

(3) Experimental results demonstrate that the proposed method consistently outperforms all the state-of-the-art methods and exhibits strong robustness.

2 Related Works

With the introduction of the DGM4 dataset by HAMMER [17], subsequent studies have gradually shifted toward detecting and grounding multimodal media manipulation [22]. To facilitate fine-grained detection and localization, several studies focus on designing fine-grained alignment objectives. ASAP [24] extends the conventional imagetext contrastive learning framework by incorporating additional contrastive losses between imagecaption pairs and imageexplanatory text pairs. CSCL [11] models both inter-modal and intra-modal consistency. RamDG [19] proposes Celebrity-News Contrastive Learning (CNCL) to align the semantics of authentic celebrity information with corresponding news content. In addition, other studies incorporate auxiliary information to achieve more precise localization of fine-grained tampered regions. UFAFormer [12] enhances the detection of visual forgery artifacts by integrating frequency-domain information. To mitigate interference caused by referencing forged images in token grounding tasks, IDseq [13] fuses predicted bounding boxes of forged faces with textual features and feeds them into a text decoder to localize tampered tokens.

Unlike prior works that either ignore modality reliability [17,19,24] or only prevent interference from tampered images [13], CMGMDL explicitly distinguishes the distinct requirements of classification and localization.

3 Method

3.1 Overview

The architecture of our model is illustrated in Fig. 1. The image and text are processed by an image encoder E_V and a text encoder E_T, respectively. The vision-language contrastive learning loss (L_{vlcl}) facilitates cross-modal alignment. Subsequently, in the High-Confidence Modality Guidance phase, the GM generates refined patch predictions ($\overline{P_{pat}}$) and refined token predictions ($\overline{P_{tok}}$). Finally, the FRM produces enhanced visual features (V_e) and enhanced textual features (T_e) by filtering out unreliable modality features, while the Rectify Module leverages these enhanced features and refined predictions to correct misleading cross-modal information.

3.2 Vision-Language Contrastive Learning

We initially process image I through image encoder E_V, yielding image embeddings v=$\{v^{cls}, v^{pat}\}$. Concurrently, the text T is encoded by the text encoder E_T to extract text embeddings, denoted as t=$\{t^{cls}, t^{tok}\}$. Subsequently, a vision-language contrastive learning loss L_{vlcl} is employed to encourage the embeddings of authentic imagetext pairs to be closer in the shared feature space, while pushing apart those of manipulated or semantically mismatched pairs. L_{vlcl} is formulated as follows:

$$\begin{aligned}
L_{vlcl} &= \frac{1}{2}L_{it} + \frac{1}{2}L_{ti}, \\
L_{it} &= -\frac{1}{b}\log\frac{\exp\left(S\left(I,T^{+}\right)\right)}{\sum_j \exp\left(S\left(I,T^{-}\right)\right)}, \\
L_{ti} &= -\frac{1}{b}\log\frac{\exp\left(S\left(T,I^{+}\right)\right)}{\sum_j \exp\left(S\left(T,I^{-}\right)\right)},
\end{aligned} \tag{1}$$

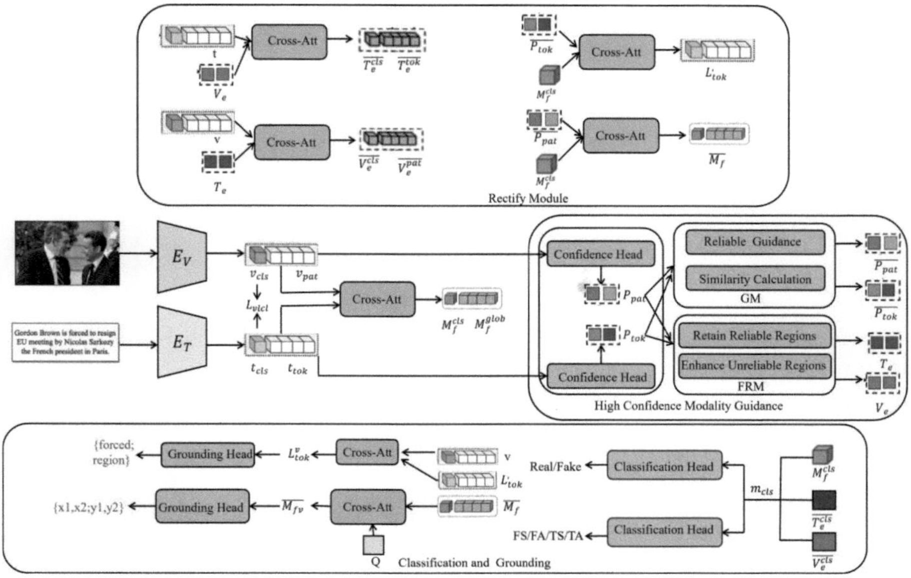

Fig. 1. The overall architecture of CMGMDL. "FS", "FA", "TS", and "TA" denote Face Swap, Face Attribute, Text Swap, and Text Attribute, respectively. "cls" refers to the [CLS] token of the features. The cross-attention mechanism enables cross-modal information interaction and rectification.

where b is the batch size, I represents the set of image tokens, T^+ refers to text tokens from the corresponding unmanipulated pair, T^- comprises all remaining text tokens in the batch. The definitions of T, I^+, I^- are similar.

3.3 Confidence Estimate

We feed image patches and tokens into a classification head that predicts whether each patch or token has been manipulated. The classification head consists of three linear layers, and we derive the confidence score for each patch and token from its output.

Specifically, let $P^i_{pat} \in [0, 1]$ denote the predicted probability that the i-th patch is manipulated, and $P^j_{tok} \in [0, 1]$ denote the corresponding probability for the j-th token. The confidence scores are defined as the complement of these probabilities:

$$\begin{aligned} cof^i_{pat} &= 1 - P^i_{pat}, \\ cof^j_{tok} &= 1 - P^j_{tok}, \end{aligned} \tag{2}$$

This formulation follows the principle that a lower predicted manipulation probability indicates higher reliability. The confidence loss encourages the model to produce reliable probability estimates for each patch and token, formulated as a binary cross-entropy loss:

$$
\begin{aligned}
L_{cof} &= L_{pat} + L_{tok}, \\
L_{pat} &= -\sum_{1}^{N}[y_{pat}^{i} \log{(P_{pat}^{i})} + (1 - y_{pat}^{i}) \log(1 - P_{pat}^{i})], \\
L_{tok} &= -\sum_{1}^{M}[y_{tok}^{j} \log{(P_{tok}^{j})} + (1 - y_{tok}^{j}) \log(1 - P_{tok}^{j})],
\end{aligned} \tag{3}
$$

where y_{pat}^{i} is the ground-truth label indicating whether the i-th patch has been manipulated, and y_{tok}^{j} is the ground-truth label for the j-th token.

3.4 Guidance Module

As illustrated in Fig. 2, GM dynamically refines predictions in the source modality by leveraging the confidence scores of both patches and tokens and the cross-modal similarity matrix between two modalities. For clarity, we illustrate this process using image patch prediction refinement as an example, where the visual modality serves as the source and the textual modality acts as the target.

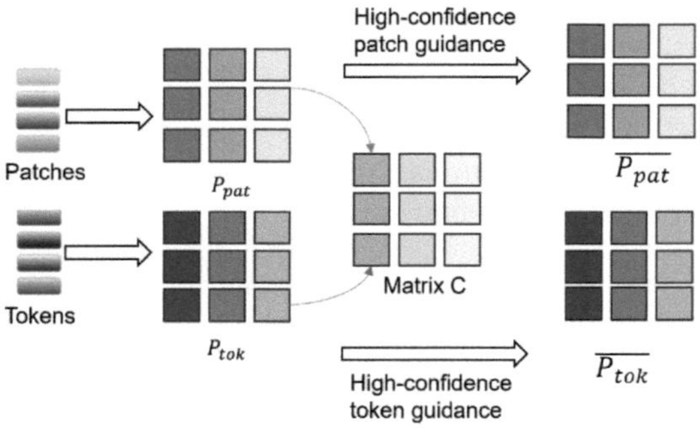

Fig. 2. The process of cross-modal guidance in GM.

Initially, we obtain the cross-modal similarity matrix $C \in \mathbb{R}^{M \times N}$, where each element $c_{mn} \in C$ measures the semantic similarity between the m-th image patch and the n-th textual token. Specifically, the similarity is computed via cosine similarity between normalized embeddings:

$$
\begin{aligned}
\hat{v} &= \frac{v}{\|v\|_2}, \\
\hat{t} &= \frac{t}{\|t\|_2}, \\
C &= \hat{v} \cdot \hat{t}^{\top},
\end{aligned} \tag{4}
$$

where $\hat{v}$ and $\hat{t}$ represent the normalized image feature vector and text feature vector, respectively. $|\cdot|_2$ denotes the L_2 norm computed along the feature dimension for each patch or token independently. With the similarity matrix and token confidence, we apply cross-modal patch prediction guidance based on the principle that each patch prediction is linked to its most similar token, which bridges the two modalities. Furthermore, cross-modal guidance is triggered only when the confidence of the referred token is higher than the confidence threshold and that of the corresponding patch. Finally, we refine the ith patch prediction based on the prediction of the referred jth token and the similarity matrix C. The refined prediction of the ith patch is:

$$\overline{P_{pat}^{i}} = \begin{cases} P_{pat}^{i} * w_{trans} * c_{ij} \ , & cof_{tok}^{j} > cof_{\theta} \text{ and } cof_{tok}^{j} > cof_{pat}^{i} \\ P_{pat}^{i} & , \text{ otherwise} \end{cases} \quad (5)$$

where w_{trans} is the transfer weight, cof_{θ} is the confidence threshold, and c_{ij} is the similarity score between the ith patch and the corresponding jth token. The selection of optimal values for w_{trans} and cof_{θ} will be discussed in the experimental section. The refinement scheme prevents the detrimental influence of low-confidence tokens on patch predictions. Following the same procedure, we obtain the refined prediction for each token, denoted as $\overline{P_{tok}^{j}}$.

3.5 Filter Refinement Module

FRM Architecture. The Filter Refinement Module (FRM) is devised to generate reliable and discriminative features for cross-modal classification tasks. Unlike localization tasks, classification is highly sensitive to noisy features; hence, FRM is explicitly designed to suppress unreliable features while retaining and enhancing informative content.

As illustrated in Fig. 3, given the visual features $v \in \mathbb{R}^{B \times N \times D}$ and the corresponding patch-wise confidence scores $cof_{pat} \in \mathbb{R}^{B \times N}$, we first feed them into a gating network. The gate network consists of two linear layers interleaved with ReLU and Dropout, followed by a Sigmoid activation, producing patch-wise gating weights w_g. This gating mechanism adaptively modulates the contribution of each patch, such that high-confidence features are retained as:

$$V_h = w_g * v \quad (6)$$

To recover potentially informative content from low-confidence regions, we send the original visual features into the enhancement network. The enhancement network, denoted as Enhance($\cdot$), is a two-layer feedforward network with residual LayerNorm and GELU activation. The enhanced low-confidence features are computed as:

$$V_l = (1 - w_g) * \text{Enhance}(v) \quad (7)$$

Finally, the refined representation for downstream classification is obtained by fusing high-confidence and enhanced low-confidence features:

$$V_e = V_h + V_l \quad (8)$$

An analogous procedure is employed to obtain T_e.

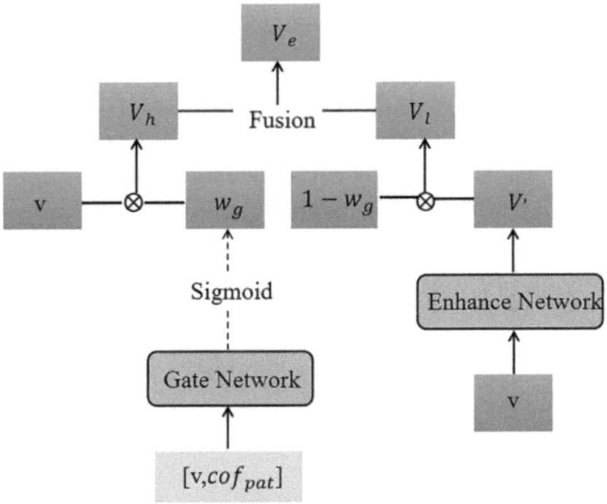

Fig. 3. Schematic illustration of the FRM.

FRM Training Objectives. To supervise FRM, we define a routing loss that aligns the gating behavior with the confidence scores while promoting feature retention and enhancement. The training loss comprises three complementary components:

(1)Consistency Loss. We enforce consistency between the gating weights and the estimated confidence scores:

$$L_c = \|w_g - cof_{pat}\|_F^2 \tag{9}$$

(2)Retention Loss. High-confidence features should be preserved after gating. To align the retained features with confidence scores while ensuring dimensional consistency, we first compute the *per-patch* feature norm. Specifically, we perform normalization on V_h by its channel-wise L_2 norm, calculated along the feature dimensions on a per-patch basis, and then compare the normalized features with the scalar confidence score.

$$L_r = \left\| \frac{V_h}{\|v\|_2 + \epsilon} - cof_{pat} \right\|_F^2 \tag{10}$$

Here, $|.|_2$ denotes the L_2 norm computed along the feature dimension for each patch, and ϵ is a small stabilizer. This ensures numerical stability.

(3) Enhancement Loss. Low-confidence features are expected to receive stronger enhancement. The enhancement loss is defined as:

$$L_e = \left\| \frac{V_l}{\|v\|_2 + \epsilon} - (1 - cof_{pat}) \right\|_F^2 \tag{11}$$

This term encourages the network to inversely modulate features according to confidence scores, effectively decoupling reliable and unreliable feature representations.

The final routing loss for visual modality combines these objectives:

$$L_{irouter} = L_c + L_r + L_e \tag{12}$$

Analogously, we define the routing loss for textual features as $L_{trouter}$, and the overall FRM routing loss is:

$$L_{router} = L_{irouter} + L_{trouter} \tag{13}$$

3.6 Rectify Module

Classification Task. We fuse T_e generated by FRM with the visual features v via a cross-attention mechanism to obtain refined visualtextual representations $\overline{V_e} = \{\overline{V_e^{cls}}, \overline{V_e^{tok}}\}$:

$$\begin{aligned} Attention(Q, K, V) &= Softmax(K^T Q/\sqrt{D})V, \\ \overline{V_e} &= Attention(v, T_e, T_e), \end{aligned} \tag{14}$$

Similarly, the textualvisual representations $\overline{T_e} = \{\overline{T_e^{cls}}, \overline{T_e^{pat}}\}$ are obtained by reversing the roles of the two modalities in the same cross-attention formulation. Enabling cross-modal interaction between FRM-refined features allows the model to suppress misleading information propagation across modalities.

Localization Task. First, **v** and **t** are fed into cross-attention to obtain the text-image correlation $M_f = \{M_f^{cls}, M_f^{glob}\}$. Unlike classification, localization is sensitive to fine-grained details, and even manipulated tokens or patches can provide useful cues. Therefore, instead of discarding unreliable information, the localization task corrects erroneous guidance using refined predictions. For the image modality, M_f^{cls} and $\overline{P_{pat}}$ are fused via cross-attention to produce $\overline{M_f}$, which corrects misleading complementary information in M_f^{cls}:

$$\overline{M_f} = Attention(M_f^{cls}, \overline{P_{pat}}, \overline{P_{pat}}) \tag{15}$$

To preserve local details of the original image, we add a residual connection:

$$M_f = M_f + v \tag{16}$$

Similarly, for the text modality, M_f^{cls} is fused with refined token predictions $\overline{P_{tok}}$ to obtain comprehensive textual tampering clues $L_{tok}^{'}$:

$$L_{tok}^{'} = Attention(M_f^{cls}, \overline{P_{tok}}, \overline{P_{tok}}) \tag{17}$$

3.7 Detection and Localization

Visual Grounding. We then apply cross-attention using $\overline{M_f}$ as the key and value with a learnable query Q [8] to obtain $\overline{M_{fv}}$:

$$\overline{M_{fv}} = Attention(Q, \overline{M_f}, \overline{M_f}) \tag{18}$$

Finally,we feed $\overline{M_{fv}}$ into the grounding head to predict bounding boxes. The training objective combines L_1 loss and IoU loss [15]:

$$L_{bbox} = -||P_{gro} - Sigmoid(y_{box})||_1 + L_{IoU}(P_{gro}, Sigmoid(y_{box})) \tag{19}$$

where P_{gro} is the predicted bounding box and y_{box} is the ground-truth.

Fine-Grained Manipulation Type Detection and Binary Classification. We obtain the classification feature m_{cls} by concatenating $\overline{L_e^{cls}}$,$\overline{V_e^{cls}}$,and M_f^{cls}:

$$m_{cls} = concat(\overline{V_e^{cls}}, \overline{T_e^{cls}}, M_f^{cls}) \tag{20}$$

The fused representation m_{cls} is then fed into a classification head to perform both binary classification and fine-grained manipulation type classification. The overall classification loss is defined using cross-entropy as:

$$\begin{aligned} L_{cls} &= L_{2cls} + L_{mcls}, \\ L_{2cls} &= -y_{2cls} log(P_{2cls}), \\ L_{mcls} &= -\sum_{1}^{4} [y_{mcls}^i log(P_{mcls}^i)] \end{aligned} \tag{21}$$

where y_{2cls} denotes binary classification labels and y_{mcls}^i is the label of the ith fine-grained manipulation type. P_{2cls} represents the prediction results of binary classification model. P_{mcls}^i is the probability of the ith manipulation type.

Manipulated Token Grounding. We apply cross-attention to $L_{tok}^{,}$ using $\mathbf{v}$ as the key and value to extract informative cues:

$$L_{tok}^v = Attention(L_{tok}^{,}, v, v) \tag{22}$$

Since L_{tok}^v contains refined token predictions guided by high-confidence patches, it provides comprehensive textual tampering clues. Finally, L_{tok}^v is fed into a token grounding head to predict manipulation probabilities per token. The loss is binary cross-entropy:

$$L_{tok} = -\sum_{i} (y_{tok}^i log(P_{tok}^i)) \tag{23}$$

where y_{tok}^i is the true label of whether the ith token is manipulated, P_{tok}^i is the prediction result of each token.

Overall Training Loss. The overall training loss of CMGMDL is defined as:

$$L = L_{vlcl} + L_{cof} + L_{cls} + L_{tok} + L_{bbox} + L_{router} \tag{24}$$

CMGMDL is optimized by this loss.

4 Experiments

4.1 Datasets and Metrics

The experiments are conducted on SAMM dataset,which comprises 111K original news, 80K swap-manipulated, and 69K attribute-manipulated cases.Additionally,it contains 260,970 carefully crafted semantic-coordinated samples which is similar to real-world cases and it covers Celeb Attributes Portfolio about visual modality and textual modality information. This dataset has four manipulation types: face swap (FS), face attribute (FA), text swap (TS), and text attribute (TA). We choose RamDG [19] as baseline and we align the textual and visual features with Celeb Attributes Portfolio through contrastive learning.

For binary classification, Accuracy (ACC), Area Under the Receiver Operating Characteristic curve (AUC), and Equal Error Rate (EER) are chosen. We adopt the mean Average Precision (mAP), average per-class F1 (CF1), and average overall F1 (OF1) to evaluate fine-grained classification task. We calculate IoU, IoU50, and IoU75 in the visual grounding task. Token grounding results are evaluated via precision, recall, and F1.

4.2 Implement Details

We set the size of the image to 256×256 and pad the length of the text to 50. ViT-B/16 is employed as an image encoder, and Bert-base is employed as a text encoder. In the cross-modal guidance phase, we will select the optimal transfer weight w_{trans} and confidence threshold cof_θ in the parameter analysis section. For optimization, we use AdamW with a learning rate of 1×10^{-6} and weight decay set to 0.02. The model is trained on four Nvidia A100 GPUs with a batch size of 32 for 50 epochs.

Table 1. Comparison of CMGMDL with state-of-the-art methods on the SAMM. ↑ indicates that higher values are better, while ↓ indicates that lower values are better. We conduct comparisons across four tasks: binary classification(Binary Cls), fine-grained manipulation type classification (Multi-Label), image grounding, and token grounding.

Method	Binary Cls			Multi-Label			Image Grounding			Text Grounding		
	AUC↑	EER↓	ACC↑	mAP↑	CF1↑	OF1↑	IoU_{mean}↑	IoU50↑	IoU75↑	Precision↑	Recall↑	F1↑
VILT [7]	96.10	11.02	88.83	96.03	90.21	89.84	65.38	71.91	54.49	77.42	69.78	73.40
HAMMER [17]	97.85	7.80	92.43	97.98	93.77	93.44	77.68	84.41	78.44	85.94	82.74	84.31
HAMMER++ [18]	97.60	7.99	92.26	97.72	93.70	93.34	77.66	84.12	78.62	85.86	82.89	84.35
VIKI [10]	98.01	7.35	92.65	98.03	94.26	93.39	78.57	84.60	78.18	86.01	80.03	84.41
FKA-Owl [14]	98.09	7.19	92.60	-	-	-	-	-	-	-	-	-
RamDG [19]	98.79	5.42	94.66	98.86	95.52	95.33	80.90	87.56	82.00	86.16	83.54	84.83
CMGMDL	**98.84**	**5.27**	**94.81**	**98.89**	**95.67**	**95.48**	**81.74**	**88.39**	**82.49**	85.97	**84.71**	**85.83**

4.3 Performance Comparison

To evaluate the effectiveness of the proposed CMGMDL framework, we conduct comprehensive comparisons with state-of-the-art methods on the SAMM, as presented in Table 1. The results demonstrate that CMGMDL consistently outperforms existing approaches across most evaluation metrics, achieving superior performance. For instance, CMGMDL surpasses all the existing methods in the classification task, achieving 98.84% AUC, 94.81% ACC, 5.27% EER, and 98.89% mAP. This performance gain can be attributed to the FRM, which effectively filters unreliable modal information. Furthermore, in the visual grounding task, CMGMDL achieves improvements of +0.84%,+0.83%, and +0.49% on IoU, IoU50, and IoU75, compared to the recently proposed RamDG. In text grounding, CMGMDL attains the highest F1 score among all compared methods. These results collectively demonstrate that the GM module significantly enhances grounding performance. Although FKA-Owl leverages rich knowledge for fake news judgment and outperforms HAMMER in binary classification, large vision-language models (LVLMs) lack fine-grained extraction capability.

4.4 Ablation Study

Component Ablation. Table 2 highlights the contributions of individual modules within our framework. We remove GM and FRM, respectively. Specifically, the removal of FRM yields a substantial degradation in classification performance, where ACC decreases by 0.17%. Moreover, removing GM decreases IoU50 by 1.65%. This demonstrates the distinct roles of FRM and GM in improving classification precision and grounding performance, respectively.

Table 2. Ablation of the components in our CMGMDL on SAMM.

Tasks	Binary Cls			Multi-Label			Image Grounding			Text Grounding		
	AUC↑	EER↓	ACC↑	mAP↑	CF1↑	OF1↑	IoUmean↑	IoU50↑	IoU75↑	Precision↑	Recall↑	F1↑
w/o GM	98.80	5.37	94.74	98.88	95.57	95.39	80.31	86.74	81.60	86.36	83.18	84.74
w/o FRM	98.69	5.40	94.64	98.81	94.80	94.81	81.71	88.21	**82.70**	85.26	**84.80**	85.08
CMGMDL	**98.84**	**5.27**	**94.81**	**98.89**	**95.67**	**95.48**	**81.74**	**88.39**	82.49	**85.97**	84.71	**85.83**

Effectiveness of L_c ,L_r and L_e Loss. As shown in Table 3, all components of the FRM training are indispensable. Concretely, L_c enforces consistency between the routing weights and the predicted confidence scores. L_r enhances the model's capacity to preserve informative content derived from high-confidence features. L_e facilitates improved feature separation between reliable and unreliable representations. Through the joint effect of these loss functions, FRM is capable of generating trustworthy features that support effective cross-modal interactions.

Table 3. Discussion of the effectiveness of L_c,L_r, and L_e in FRM training on SAMM.

Tasks	Binary Cls			Multi-Label		
	AUC↑	EER↓	ACC↑	mAP↑	CF1↑	OF1↑
CMGMDL	**98.84**	**5.27**	**94.81**	**98.89**	**95.67**	**95.48**
w/o L_c	98.55	5.72	94.24	98.75	95.09	94.91
w/o L_r	98.69	5.40	94.64	98.81	94.80	94.81
w/o L_e	98.80	5.37	94.74	98.88	95.57	95.39

Parameter Analysis. We analyze the impact of w_{trans} and cof_θ, as shown in Tables 4 and 5. Both parameters achieve optimal performance at 0.8. A low w_{trans} yields insufficient cross-modal guidance, while a high value introduces irrelevant interference. Similarly, an excessively large cof_θ weakens cross-modal mutual verification and error correction, whereas a low threshold introduces substantial noise and misleading guidance.

Table 4. w_{trans} value selection in GM on SAMM.

Tasks	Image Grounding			Text Grounding		
	IoUmean↑	IoU50↑	IoU75↑	Precision↑	Recall↑	F1↑
0.6	80.63	87.00	81.74	**86.60**	82.62	84.56
0.8	**81.74**	**88.39**	**82.49**	85.87	84.71	**85.83**
1	81.04	87.46	82.28	82.01	**84.81**	84.73

Table 5. cof_θ value selection in GM.

Tasks	Image Grounding			Text Grounding		
	IoUmean↑	IoU50↑	IoU75↑	Precision↑	Recall↑	F1↑
0.6	80.93	87.86	81.74	86.20	84.29	85.02
0.8	**81.74**	**88.39**	**82.49**	85.87	84.71	**85.83**
0.9	81.64	88.00	82.04	**86.60**	82.62	84.57

4.5 Visualized Results

The visualized results of the detection and grounding tasks are shown in Fig. 4. We select original samples along with samples where both the image and text are manipulated. In the visual grounding task, green regions indicate the ground-truth manipulated areas, while red regions show the predicted boundaries. In the text grounding task, blue regions indicate the ground-truth positions of manipulated tokens, and red regions show the predicted positions. The visualization results demonstrate that our method can accurately localize manipulated regions, indicating that it is robust to manipulations in the referenced modality.

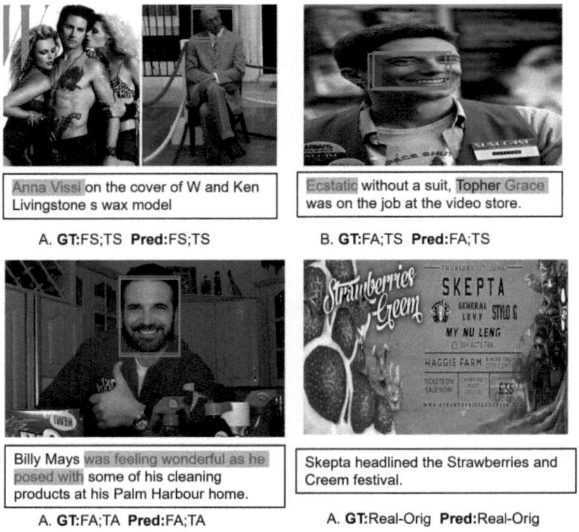

Fig. 4. Visualized results of CMGMDL.GT means the true label, while Pred means the predicted label of the classification task.

5 Conclusion

In this paper, we propose a Cross-Modal Guided Manipulation Detection and Localization (CMGMDL) framework to address modality misguidance in cross-modal interaction and adapt to the requirements of different tasks. Specifically, it consists of GM and FRM. To improve classification performance, FRM employs enhancement and retention to generate reliable cross-modal features. Furthermore, we develop GM to incorporate cross-modal guidance, using modality confidence and cross-modal similarity to refine both visual and textual grounding. The experiments demonstrate the effectiveness of our method, providing valuable insights into multimodal media manipulation detection and localization.

References

1. Aziz, B., Bukhelli, A.: Detecting the manipulation of text structure in text steganography using machine learning. In: Proceedings of the 19th International Conference on Web Information Systems and Technologies, pp. 123–130 (2023)

2. Bin, Y., et al.: Leveraging weak cross-modal guidance for coherence modelling via iterative learning. In: Proceedings of the 32nd ACM International Conference on Multimedia, pp. 4630–4639. ACM (2024)
3. Frank, J., Eisenhofer, T., Schönherr, L., Fischer, A., Kolossa, D., Holz, T.: Leveraging frequency analysis for deep fake image recognition. In: International conference on machine learning, pp. 3247–3258. PMLR (2020)
4. Guillaro, F., Cozzolino, D., Sud, A., Dufour, N., Verdoliva, L.: Trufor: leveraging all-round clues for trustworthy image forgery detection and localization. In: Proceedings of the IEEE/CVF Conference on Computer Vision and Pattern Recognition, pp. 20606–20615 (2023)
5. Jenks, C.J.: Communicating the cultural other: Trust and bias in generative ai and large language models. Applied Linguistics Review **16**(2), 787–795 (2025)
6. Ju, Y., Jia, S., Ke, L., Xue, H., Nagano, K., Lyu, S.: Fusing global and local features for generalized ai-synthesized image detection. In: 2022 IEEE International Conference on Image Processing (ICIP), pp. 3465–3469. IEEE (2022)
7. Kim, W., Son, B., Kim, I.: Vilt: vision-and-language transformer without convolution or region supervision. In: Proceedings of the 38th International Conference on Machine Learning. pp. 5583–5594 (2021)
8. Li, J., Li, D., Savarese, S., Hoi, S.C.H.: Blip-2: bootstrapping language-image pretraining with frozen image encoders and large language models. In: Proceedings of the 40th International Conference on Machine Learning. pp. 19730–19742 (2023)
9. Li, P., Wang, R., Huang, H., He, R., He, Z.: Pluralistic aging diffusion autoencoder. In: Proceedings of the IEEE/CVF International Conference on Computer Vision. pp. 22613–22623 (2023)
10. Li, Q., Gao, M., Zhai, W., Zhang, G., Chen, J., Jeon, G.: Towards multimodal disinformation detection by vision-language knowledge interaction. Information Fusion **102**, 102068 (2024)
11. Li, Y., et al.: Unleashing the potential of consistency learning for detecting and grounding multi-modal media manipulation. In: Proceedings of the IEEE/CVF Conference on Computer Vision and Pattern Recognition. pp. 9242–9252. IEEE (2025)
12. Liu, H., Tan, Z., Chen, Q., Wei, Y., Zhao, Y., Wang, J.: Unified frequency-assisted transformer framework for detecting and grounding multi-modal manipulation. Int. J. Comput. Vision **133**(3), 1392–1409 (2025)
13. Liu, R., Xie, T., Li, J., Yu, L., Xie, H.: Id-seq: decoupled and sequentially detecting and grounding multi-modal media manipulation. In: Proceedings of the 39th AAAI Conference on Artificial Intelligence. pp. 496–504 (2025)
14. Liu, X., et al.: FKA-Owl: advancing multimodal fake news detection through knowledge-augmented LVLMs. In: Proceedings of the 32nd ACM International Conference on Multimedia. pp. 10154–10163. ACM (2024)
15. Rezatofighi, H., Tsoi, N., Gwak, J., Sadeghian, A., Reid, I.D., Savarese, S.: Generalized intersection over union: a metric and a loss for bounding box regression. In: Proceedings of the IEEE/CVF Conference on Computer Vision and Pattern Recognition, pp. 658–666. IEEE (2019)
16. Shah, A., Ranka, P., Dedhia, U., Prasad, S., Muni, S., Bhowmick, K.: Detecting and unmasking ai-generated texts through explainable artificial intelligence using stylistic features. International Journal of Advanced Computer Science & Applications **13**(10), 324–333 (2023)
17. Shao, R., Wu, T., Liu, Z.: Detecting and grounding multi-modal media manipulation. In: Proceedings of the IEEE/CVF Conference on Computer Vision and Pattern Recognition, pp. 6904–6913. IEEE (2023)

18. Shao, R., Wu, T., Wu, J., Nie, L., Liu, Z.: Detecting and grounding multi-modal media manipulation and beyond. IEEE Trans. Pattern Anal. Mach. Intell. **46**(8), 5556–5574 (2024)
19. Shen, J., Wang, Y., Cheng, L., Pu, N., Zhong, Z.: Beyond artificial misalignment: Detecting and grounding semantic-coordinated multimodal manipulations. In: Proceedings of the 33rd ACM International Conference on Multimedia, pp. 11308–11317. ACM (2025)
20. Tan, C., Zhao, Y., Wei, S., Gu, G., Wei, Y.: Learning on gradients: generalized artifacts representation for GAN-generated images detection. In: Proceedings of the IEEE/CVF Conference on Computer Vision and Pattern Recognition. pp. 12105–12114 (2023)
21. Tao, Z., Li, Z., Chen, R., Xi, D., Xu, W.: Unveiling large language models generated texts: A multi-level fine-grained detection framework. Tech. Rep. arXiv arXiv:2410.14231 (2024)
22. Wang, Y., et al.: Detect text forgery with non-forged image features: a framework for detection and grounding of image-text manipulation. In: Proceedings of the 6th Chinese Conference on Pattern Recognition and Computer Vision. vol. 15033, pp. 366–380. Springer, Singapore (2024)
23. Zhang, L.: Detecting multi-modal fake AIGC from the perspective of emotional manipulation purpose. In: 2024 IEEE International Conference on Data Mining Workshops, pp. 33–39. IEEE (2024)
24. Zhang, Z., Wang, Y., Cheng, L., Zhong, Z., Guo, D., Wang, M.: Asap: advancing semantic alignment promotes multi-modal manipulation detecting and grounding. In: Proceedings of the IEEE/CVF Conference on Computer Vision and Pattern Recognition. pp. 4005–4014. IEEE (2025)
25. Zhu, J., et al.: Learning discriminative noise guidance for image forgery detection and localization. In: Proceedings of the AAAI Conference on Artificial Intelligence. vol. 38, pp. 7739–7747 (2024)

LADI: Logic-Aware Dual Injection for Instruction-Guided Image Editing via Structural-Semantic Disentanglement

Wenlei Wang[1], Shuai Xu[1,2(✉)], and Ali Ibrahim Abba[1]

[1] Nanjing University of Aeronautics and Astronautics, Nanjing, China
[2] State Key Laboratory for Novel Software Technology, Nanjing University, Nanjing, China
xushuai7@nuaa.edu.cn

Abstract. Instruction-guided image editing inherently faces a conflict between structural stability and semantic plasticity, often resulting in geometric collapse or attribute bleeding. To address this issue, in this paper, we propose LADI (**L**ogic-**A**ware **D**ual **I**njection), a framework that explicitly disentangles editing into logic-driven planning and dual-stream execution. As a core design, the logic-driven editing planner leverages the Large Multimodal Model (LMM) to bridge the semantic-physical gap, predicting a structural fidelity score to arbitrate geometric rigidity and disentangled semantic tokens for semantic styling. These signals guide a novel dual-stream architecture: the distribution-aware structural injection in the encoder adaptively anchors the geometric skeleton via cross-normalization and spatial gating, while the region-specific parallel semantic injection in the decoder enforces precise attribute binding through masked attention. Extensive experiments on public benchmark datasets demonstrate that LADI achieves the state-of-the-art performance, effectively resolving structural-semantic entanglement.Our source code is available at https://github.com/ei-wang/LADI_edit.

Keywords: Instruction-Guided Image Editing · Disentangled Control · Diffusion Model · Large Multimodal Model

1 Introduction

Instruction-guided image editing has revolutionized content creation, enabling users to manipulate visual content through natural language [5]. Driven by the generation prior from LDM [7], existing studies have made remarkable success on the holistic style transfer and global attribute editing [6]. However, for complex real-world editing demands such as local object replacement or character pose manipulation, existing methods expose a fundamental limitation in the mixture of structural and meaning-making controls. The core challenge is the basic struggle between keeping things in one piece and making sense of things. Most previous works insert editing signal homogeneously into the diffusion backbone

L. Ding et al. (Eds.): APWeb-WAIM 2026, LNCS 16995, pp. 299–313, 2027.
https://doi.org/10.1007/978-981-92-5699-0_19

[19]. Such unified approach processes all instructions homogeneously, failing to distinguish between edits that require strict geometric preservation (e.g., "paint the car red without altering the chassis") and those necessitating structural plasticity (e.g., "turn it into an open-top car", which requires modifying the roof entirely). Consequently, we observe two frequent failure modes: (1) Geometric Rigidity, where strong structural priors suppress necessary shape changes; and (2) Semantic Leakage, where texture modifications inadvertently distort object outlines or bleed into the background. Without an explicit mechanism to arbitrate this trade-off, precise control remains elusive.

We argue that solving this entanglement requires bridging the gap between abstract user intent and concrete generative execution. A robust editing system not only requires an agent to infer how much it needs to be edited, but also an execution that works separately on structure and meaning. To achieve the above objectives, we introduce LADI, a **L**ogic-**A**ware **D**ual **I**njection framework that disentangles structure and semantics through agency. LADI works at two synergistic levels: First, to address reasoning deficiency, we design the Logic-driven Editing Planner (LEP). Unlike standard text encoders that handle all prompts similarly, here we rely on LEP's LMMs reasoning capabilities to serve as an elasticity arbiter [33], which analyzes the instruction to produce a continuous structural fidelity score to decide if there needs to be a tight adherence for substantial structural alteration. Second, to put this plan into practice, we present a Dual-Stream Injection setup to physically separate out control paths from the U-Net. At the encoder side, we inject edges via the distribution-aware structural module, which guides the model to adaptively fix up the shape on demand or play around with restrictions regarding forms while keeping the backbone's pre-trained feature flows untouched. At the decoder side, we operate a region-specific parallel semantic injection. By leveraging the given masks for exact positioning, this module adds in semantic properties such as texture and color only to the designated spot, thus avoiding the typical issues like property loss from the global change.

We believe that by explicitly assigning structural constraints to the encoder and semantic rendering to the decoder, LADI is able to achieve more considerable structural-semantic disentanglement. Our main contributions are as follows:

- In order to resolve the issue of structural stability and semantic plasticity in the instruction-guided image editing task, we propose a novel framework called LADI, which moves beyond superficial text-image alignment to a paradigm of agentic disentanglement, where editing intents are explicitly decoded into quantifiable physical constraints (structural elasticity) and semantic attributes.
- A novel logic-driven editing planner (LEP) is conceived to bridge the semantic-physical gap by translating abstract instructions into quantifiable structural elasticity and disentangled semantic tokens, which further guide the dual-stream injection, where an adaptive structural stream in the encoder is used to regulate geometry, and a masked semantic stream in the decoder is adopted to ensure precise attribute binding.

- Extensive experiments based on two public datasets verify that LADI sets a new state-of-the-art performance against its competitors, particularly in metrics measuring structural consistency (DINO-S) and semantic precision (CLIP-R).

2 Related Work

2.1 Instruction-Guided Image Editing

Instruction-guided image editing aims to manipulate source images based on natural language commands while preserving non-target regions. Early methods, such as Prompt-to-prompt [9] and null-text inversion [8], achieved this by manipulating cross-attention maps during the diffusion process. To enable more intuitive control, InstructPix2Pix (IP2P) [2] introduced a conditional diffusion model fine-tuned on a large-scale dataset of instruction-image triplets, establishing a new paradigm for supervised editing. Subsequent works have focused on expanding the versatility of editing tasks [4,18] or improving data quality [3,10].

In recent times, in the face of intricate or vague directives, MLLMs have been folded within the modification pipeline. Methods like MGIE [5], SmartEdit [12] use LMMs to do instruction reasoning and produce a vivid caption so that it could be used as guidance by diffusion model. But they generally regard the editing procedure as one overall production task and seldom contain specific devices for splitting structure constraints from meaning traits. While DiffEdit [32], which is based on masks and thus only edits local areas while preserving the background, is unable to avoid semantic leakage after its internal shape gets drastically altered. Conflict arises here if such texture alteration distorts an object's geometry unintentionally. In contrast, our proposed LADI framework introduces a Logic-Driven Editing Planner that explicitly arbitrates structural rigidity and semantic elasticity, translating abstract instructions into discrete, disentangled control signals.

2.2 Diffusion Models for Controllable Generation

As highlighted in InstructDiffusion [11], Latent Diffusion Models (LDMs) demonstrate remarkable capabilities in generating photorealistic images by iteratively denoising within a compressed latent space. To extend their applicability, various approaches have been proposed to introduce spatial controllability. ControlNet [13] and T2I-Adapter [14] inject additional structural conditions (e.g., Canny edges, depth maps) into the pre-trained backbone via zero-convolution layers or lightweight adapters, enabling precise spatial alignment [36,37]. More recently, ControlNext [1] simplified this interaction to improve efficiency. Concurrently, tuning-free methods such as MasaCtrl [30] and Plug-and-Play [31] attempt to maintain structural consistency by manipulating mutual self-attention and spatial features.

Despite their success, existing controllable frameworks often apply structural guidance uniformly or rigidly, which may suppress high-level semantic transformations required during editing. In addition, it is also direct injection of an outside feature into the pre-trained features which might shift the distribution of the pretrained feature and then lead to deterioration in generative prior. Addressing these limitations, our method proposes a distribution-aware dual injection strategy. We strategically anchor geometric constraints within the Encoder via a Cross-Normalization mechanism to preserve spatial layout, while creating a parallel stream in the Decoder for semantic rendering. This design, modulated by a predicted elasticity coefficient, ensures that the model can strictly adhere to object boundaries or flexibly adapt geometry based on the editing logic.

3 Methodology

3.1 Problem Formulation

We formulate instruction-guided local editing as a conditional generation task subject to dual constraints. Given a source image $\mathbf{I} \in \mathbb{R}^{H \times W \times 3}$, a natural language instruction T, as well as a binary user mask $\mathbf{M} \in \{0,1\}^{H \times W}$ (which, in practice, can be either user-provided or automatically generated via a standard VLM-guided segmentation strategy), our objective is to synthesize an edited image $\mathbf{I}'$.

This problem is governed by two conflicting objectives: (1) Semantic Alignment: The edited region $\mathbf{M} \odot \mathbf{I}'$ must semantically reflect the instruction T; and (2) Structural Fidelity: The background $(1-\mathbf{M}) \odot \mathbf{I}'$ must strictly preserve the identity of $\mathbf{I}$, while the geometry within $\mathbf{M}$ should possess adaptive elasticity ranging from rigid preservation to plastic deformation based on the logical intent of T. We leverage a pre-trained Latent Diffusion Model (LDM) [17] as the generative backbone, performing the editing in the compressed latent space $\mathbf{z}_0 = \mathcal{E}(\mathbf{I})$.

3.2 Framework of LADI

The overall pipeline of LADI, illustrated in Fig. 1, implements this logic-driven and dual-stream generation process. Building upon the formulation above, we utilize a pre-trained Variational Autoencoder (VAE) [35] to operate on the latent space, performing editing via a diffusion process on the noisy latent $\mathbf{z}_t$. To distinguish control pathways, we denote intermediate feature maps within the U-Net backbone as $\mathbf{h}$ for the Encoder (governing structural layout) and $\mathbf{F}$ for the Decoder (governing semantic rendering).

The execution workflow proceeds sequentially: the Logic-Driven Editing Planner (LEP) first performs intent decoding by analyzing the input tuple $(\mathbf{I}, \mathbf{T}, \mathbf{M})$ alongside historical context to generate a set of disentangled control signals $\mathcal{S} = \{\alpha, \mathbf{T}_{edit}, \mathbf{T}_{loc}, \mathbf{T}_{glo}, \mathbf{T}_{neg}\}$. During the subsequent denoising steps, these signals are physically routed to separate components, where the structural

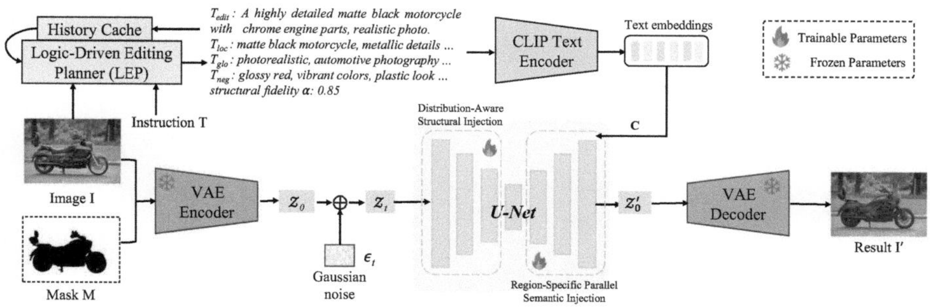

Fig. 1. Overview of the proposed LADI framework. Given a source image and an editing instruction, the Logic-driven Editing Planner (LEP) functions as an elasticity arbitrator, which predicts a structural fidelity score α to regulate geometric rigidity and disentangled semantic tokens. These signals then guide a dual-stream injection process: (1) The Distribution-Aware Structural Injection in the encoder anchors geometric constraints via cross-normalization and spatial gating (modulated by α); (2) The Region-Specific Parallel Semantic Injection in the decoder applies masked attention to strictly bind attributes to the target region.

scalar α and edge features modulate the Encoder features $\mathbf{h}$ to anchor the geometric skeleton, while the semantic tokens are $\mathbf{C}_{sern} = \{\mathbf{C}_{loc}, \mathbf{C}_{glo}\}$ injected into the Decoder features $\mathbf{F}$ via masked attention to render attributes. Finally, the structurally and semantically aligned latent is decoded back to the pixel space to yield the edited result $\mathbf{I}'$.

Logic-Driven Editing Planner (LEP). The Logic-driven Editing Planner (LEP) acts as a state-aware arbitrator, translating abstract intents into precise textual and physical constraints. To ensure consistency across sequential edits, we employ a Reasoning Context Cache $\mathcal{H}_t = \{\mathbf{T}_{edit}^{0:t-1}, \mathbf{E}_{t-1}\}$. Crucially, we store the Structural Edge Map ($\mathbf{E}_{t-1}$) as a geometric anchor to prevent physical drift, and persist the Detailed Editing Instructions ($\mathbf{T}_{edit}$)—rather than ambiguous raw prompts—to retain a high-fidelity semantic memory of the editing trajectory.

Conditioned on this history, the LEP synthesizes a disentangled control set $\mathcal{S}_t = \{\alpha_t, \mathbf{T}_{edit}^t, \mathbf{T}_{loc}^t, \mathbf{T}_{glo}^t, \mathbf{T}_{neg}^t\}$. Beyond predicting the Structural Fidelity Score (α_t) to arbitrate rigidity, the planner rewrites user inputs into a comprehensive Detailed Instruction ($\mathbf{T}_{edit}^t$), generates context-aware Negative Prompts ($\mathbf{T}_{neg}^t$) for classifier-free guidance, and explicitly disentangles descriptions for Local ($\mathbf{T}_{loc}^t$) and Global ($\mathbf{T}_{glo}^t$) attributes. These textual signals are subsequently encoded by the CLIP Text Encoder into embeddings $\{\mathbf{C}_{edit}^t, \mathbf{C}_{loc}^t, \mathbf{C}_{glo}^t, \mathbf{C}_{neg}^t\}$, which are routed to the diffusion backbone to strictly align the structural and semantic generation with the user's evolving intent.

Distribution-Aware Structural Injection. As shown in Fig. 2, to anchor the geometric skeleton, we inject edge-derived features into the U-Net Encoder.

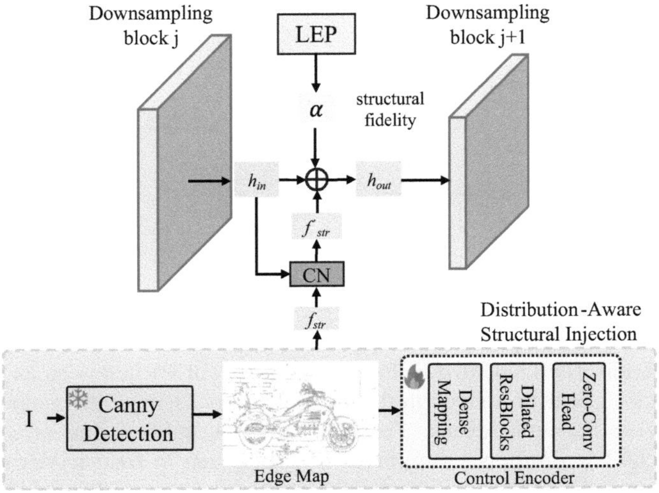

Fig. 2. Illustration of the Distribution-Aware Structural Injection. To robustly anchor geometric constraints, we design a hierarchical Control Encoder comprising an Dense Mapping for feature densification, Dilated ResBlocks for global context aggregation, and a Zero-Conv Head for stable projection. The extracted features $\mathbf{f}_{str}$ are then statistically aligned to the backbone distribution via CN and spatially modulated by the Spatial Gating Map. This mechanism ensures that unmasked regions remain rigidly anchored, while the edit region allows for elastic deformation governed by the planner-predicted fidelity score α.

Since direct injection often disrupts the backbone's pre-trained distribution, we address this via Cross-Normalization (CN) and Adaptive Gating. Let $\mathbf{h}_{in}$ denote the intermediate feature map of a downsampling block, and $\mathbf{f}_{str}$ denote the structural features extracted from the edge map. To statistically align $\mathbf{f}_{str}$ to $\mathbf{h}_{in}$, we first compute the channel-wise statistics. For the k-th channel of any feature map $\mathbf{x}$, the mean μ_k and variance σ_k compute channel-wise mean and standard deviation. [34] Adopting the adaptive instance normalization paradigm, the aligned structural feature $\mathbf{f}'_{str}$ is obtained by:

$$\begin{aligned}\mathbf{f}'_{str} &= \mathrm{CN}(\mathbf{f}_{str} \mid \mathbf{h}_{in}) \\ &= \mu(\mathbf{h}_{in}) + \sigma(\mathbf{h}_{in}) \cdot \frac{\mathbf{f}_{str} - \mu(\mathbf{f}_{str})}{\sqrt{\sigma^2(\mathbf{f}_{str}) + \varepsilon}}\end{aligned}$$

To resolve the stability-plasticity dilemma, the injection is spatially modulated by the predicted fidelity score α. The updated feature is defined as $\mathbf{h}_{out} = \mathbf{h}_{in} + \mathcal{K}(\alpha, M) \odot \hat{\mathbf{f}}_{str}$. Here, $\mathcal{K}(\alpha, \mathbf{M}) = \mathbf{M} \cdot \alpha + (1 - \mathbf{M})$ is the Spatial Gating Map. This formulation ensures that the background (unmasked region) remains rigidly anchored with a gate value of 1.0, while the foreground structural constraints are relaxed or tightened dynamically based on α.

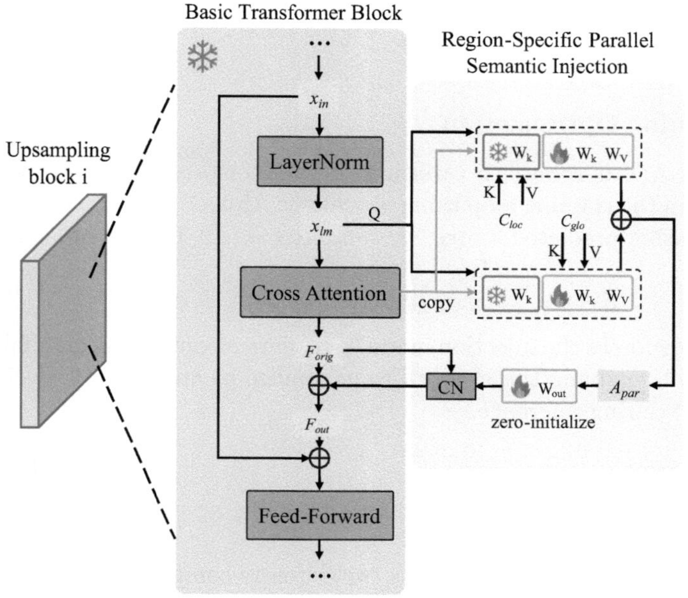

Fig. 3. Illustration of the Region-Specific Parallel Semantic Injection. We introduce a parallel attention branch in the Decoder to inject disentangled semantic tokens. The local stream is strictly constrained by the mask $\mathbf{M}'$ to prevent attribute bleeding. To preserve the generative priors of the pre-trained backbone, the aggregated signal is projected via a Zero-Initialized Layer $\mathbf{W}_{out}$ and rectified by Cross-Normalization before merging, ensuring a seamless and stable integration.

Region-Specific Parallel Semantic Injection. As illustrated in Fig. 3, semantic attributes are rendered in the U-Net Decoder. To prevent attribute bleeding, we introduce a Parallel Semantic Branch with masked attention. Let $\mathbf{x}_{in}$ be the input latent to a Transformer block. We reuse the layer-normalized feature $\mathbf{x}_{lm}$ as the Query ($\mathbf{Q}$) to ensure spatial alignment. The Key ($\mathbf{K}$) and Value ($\mathbf{V}$) matrices are projected from the semantic tokens $\mathbf{C}_{loc}$ and $\mathbf{C}_{glo}$. The parallel attention output is computed as:

$$\begin{aligned}\mathbf{A}_{par} = \mathrm{Attn}(\mathbf{Q}, \mathbf{K}_{loc}, \mathbf{V}_{loc}) \odot \mathbf{M}' \\ +\mathrm{Attn}(\mathbf{Q}, \mathbf{K}_{glo}, \mathbf{V}_{glo}) \ ,\end{aligned} \tag{1}$$

where $\mathbf{M}'$ is the mask resized to the latent resolution.

To merge this signal into the frozen backbone without initial perturbation, we employ a Zero-Convolution Strategy. The aggregated signal is projected by a zero-initialized linear layer $\mathbf{W}_{out}$ and re-aligned via CN using the statistics of the original attention output $\mathbf{F}_{orig}$. The final output is formulated as:

$$\mathbf{F}_{out} = \mathbf{F}_{orig} + \mathrm{CN}\left(\mathbf{W}_{out}(\mathbf{A}_{par}) \mid \mathbf{F}_{orig}\right) \ . \tag{2}$$

Initializing $\mathbf{W}_{out}$ with zeros ensures the model starts training from the robust priors of the base model.

3.3 Training Optimization

To ensure LADI is robust to variations in planner predictions, we decouple the planner from the training loop using Stochastic Alpha Sampling. During training, instead of using predicted scores, we sample $\alpha \sim \mathcal{U}[0,1]$. The objective function is:

$$\mathcal{L} = \mathbb{E}_{\mathbf{z}_0,t,\mathbf{C},\alpha\sim\mathcal{U}[0,1],\epsilon}\left[\|\epsilon - \epsilon_\theta(\mathbf{z}_t,t,\mathbf{C},\alpha,\mathbf{E})\|_2^2\right] . \tag{3}$$

This strategy forces the injection modules to learn a continuous manifold of structural control, enabling the network to generalize to any rigidity level requested by the LEP during inference.

4 Experiments

4.1 Experimental Setup

Datasets. Our evaluation leverages two datasets comprising instruction-image-mask triplets: MagicBrush [3] and UltraEdit [15]. We adhere to the official split for the MagicBrush dataset and adopt an 8:2 training-testing ratio for the UltraEdit dataset [15]. We train our model on the combined training sets of both benchmarks and evaluate performance on their separate test sets. Significantly, this amalgamated corpus encompasses a substantial volume of both single-turn immediate edits and complex multi-turn sequential tasks, providing the necessary breadth to rigorously train our Logic-Driven Planner in long-term context retention and sequential reasoning. Furthermore, the availability of precise ground-truth masks is pivotal, enabling the rigorous training of our Region-Specific Semantic Injection module and allowing us to decouple the model's generative capabilities from potential upstream segmentation errors. To ensure a strictly fair comparison and isolate core editing capabilities from the variance in mask acquisition algorithms, all baseline methods requiring mask inputs in our comparative experiments are provided with the exact same unified ground-truth masks. In practical deployment scenarios, similar to contemporary baselines, our framework effortlessly acquires the binary user mask $\mathbf{M}$ through a standard pipeline combining LLMs with segmentation model.

Evaluation Metrics. We employ a comprehensive metric suite to assess editing quality. Standard metrics include FID for generative fidelity [27], CLIP-Direction (CLIP-D) [22] for global instruction alignment, and LPIPS [28] for background preservation [28]. Crucially, to validate our structural-semantic disentanglement, we utilize two specialized metrics: Region-CLIP (CLIP-R) [23], which measures the similarity between the masked edited region and target text to penalize attribute bleeding; and DINO-Structure Distance (DINO-S) [24–26], which uses DINOv2 features to evaluate geometric integrity, ensuring the model correctly adheres to (or modifies) the structural layout as planned.

Fig. 4. Qualitative comparison across diverse editing scenarios. The editing instructions are written below each row of images. Compared with other methods, our approach (LADI) performs better in accurately locating the edited objects or regions and preserving the detailed information of the input image.

Implementation Details. LADI is implemented using PyTorch with the UltraEdit backbone, integrated with Qwen2.5-VL as the Logic-Driven Editing Planner to generate disentangled control signals. Input images are resized to 512×512 and encoded into latent space via a pre-trained VAE. To preserve the robust generative priors of the diffusion model, we adopt a Parameter-Efficient Fine-Tuning (PEFT) strategy : the U-Net backbone remains frozen, and only the lightweight adapters in the dual-injection streams are optimized using the AdamW optimizer ($lr = 1e-4$) [21]. The model is trained on two NVIDIA RTX 4090 GPUs with a batch size of 8, utilizing Mixed Precision (BF16) and gradient checkpointing to ensure computational efficiency.

4.2 Experimental Results

Qualitative Results. Fig. 4 visually verifies LADI's superiority in arbitrating the stability-plasticity dilemma across diverse editing scenarios. In tasks requiring high semantic plasticity, such as "Turn the car into a wooden sculpture", baselines like IP2P [2] and MGIE [5] suffer from severe attribute bleeding, where the wooden texture inadvertently spills over into the background. LADI, conversely, leverages the Region-Specific Semantic Injection to strictly bind the texture to the car, while the Distribution-Aware Structural Injection (with $\alpha \to 1$) rigidly anchors the wheel geometry, preventing the fine-grained shape distortion observed in FireEdit [16]. Similarly, in tasks demanding high geometric elasticity, such as "Turn a sitting dog into a running wolf", standard methods often struggle to decouple the original pose from the target concept. LADI's Logic-Driven Planner correctly identifies the need for structural relaxation ($\alpha \rightarrow 0$), allowing the Spatial Gating mechanism to release geometric anchors and synthesize a plausible running posture without introducing artifacts or losing identity.

Table 1. Performance of various models (Single-Turn, MagicBrush Dataset)

Model	Category		CLIP-D ↑	CLIP-R ↑	DINO-S ↑	FID ↓	LPIPS ↓
	With Mask Control	With VLM					
IP2P [2]	-	-	0.221	0.819	0.762	20.41	0.182
MagicBrush [3]	-	-	0.226	0.851	0.776	18.04	0.184
UltraEdit [15]	✓	-	0.238	0.853	0.844	13.92	0.216
MGIE [5]	-	✓	0.195	0.776	0.715	15.47	0.254
AnyEdit [4]	✓	✓	0.236	0.862	0.821	13.79	0.167
FireEdit [16]	✓	✓	0.252	0.881	0.858	11.92	0.164
LADI (Ours)	✓	✓	**0.253**	**0.884**	**0.869**	**11.87**	**0.158**

Table 2. Performance of various models (Multi-Turn, UltraEdit Dataset).

Model	Category		CLIP-D ↑	CLIP-R ↑	DINO-S ↑	FID ↓	LPIPS ↓
	With Mask Control	With VLM					
IP2P [2]	-	-	0.185	0.803	0.652	21.16	0.245
MagicBrush [3]	-	-	0.192	0.820	0.678	20.24	0.238
UltraEdit [15]	✓	-	0.170	0.843	0.620	14.95	0.295
MGIE [5]	-	✓	0.215	0.761	0.750	16.66	0.242
AnyEdit [4]	✓	✓	0.220	0.859	0.765	14.89	0.190
FireEdit [16]	✓	✓	0.238	0.874	0.790	12.51	0.180
LADI (Ours)	✓	✓	**0.248**	**0.879**	**0.842**	**12.29**	**0.165**

Quantitative Results. We evaluate our method against current SOTA approaches on the MagicBrush and UltraEdit datasets, and the results are presented in Table 1 and Table 2, where the upward arrows (↑) indicate that the larger the values, the better the performance, and vice versa. In the Single-Turn setting, LADI consistently outperforms competing methods by explicitly avoiding common generative traps. For instance, our superior CLIP-D (0.253) and CLIP-R (0.884) scores confirm that routing semantic tokens via the Region-Specific Semantic Injection strictly confines new attributes to the target zone, stopping the severe attribute bleeding seen in baselines. On the structural front, our Distribution-Aware Structural Injection and Cross-Normalization effectively lock down the geometry, securing the highest DINO-S (0.869) and the lowest LPIPS (0.158). Crucially, because we leveled the playing field by feeding all models the exact same ground-truth masks during evaluation, we can safely rule out mask disparities as the culprit for baseline failures. The structural warping and semantic leakage seen in other methods point directly to fundamental flaws in their unified generative architectures. In contrast, LADI's performance robustly validates the necessity of explicitly disentangling structural anchors from semantic renders.

The performance gap becomes even more pronounced when we shift to Multi-Turn scenarios. Sequential editing notoriously triggers "catastrophic forgetting". As competing models process one edit after another, they progressively erode the original image identity and structural layout—a flaw clearly visible in FireEdit's plummeting DINO-S score of 0.790. LADI, however, maintains an exceptional structural coherence at 0.842. This resilience is entirely driven by our Reasoning Context Cache ($\mathcal{H}_t$). By explicitly storing historical geometric constraints ($\mathbf{E}_{t-1}$) and semantic memory across turns, the Logic-Driven Planner explicitly halts the "identity drift" that typically breaks standard autoregressive editing pipelines.

Beyond automated metrics, human perception remains the ultimate test for image editing. We conduct a comprehensive subjective evaluation involving 50 participants who are asked to blind-rank the multi-turn and single-turn outputs across 60 randomly sampled challenging image-instruction pairs. Reviewers evaluate the results based on two core dimensions: visual plausibility (the naturalness of generated textures without obvious artifacts) and editing accuracy (strict adherence to the prompt while preserving non-target regions). Subjective evaluation further corroborates our quantitative findings, with a 72.15% user preference rate favoring LADI. Human evaluators specifically note that our method preserves critical background structures significantly better than baselines during complex, multi-step tasks.

4.3 Ablation Study

Table 3 breaks down our architecture to prove that every component in the LADI framework carries its own weight. We gradually disable key modules to observe how editing quality degrades, pairing the exact numerical deviations with the geometric shifts visualized in Fig. 5.

We see that replacing LEP with fixed parameters causes a holistic performance drop across the board. As visually captured in Fig. 5, the *w/o* LEP contour uniformly shrinks inwards. Without the dynamic elasticity arbitration provided by the LMMs, the model simply cannot adapt to diverse instruction types, essentially reverting to blind processing. The physical disentanglement streams prove equally critical. When we remove the Distribution-Aware Structural Injection, we observed a precipitous decline in DINO-S, dropping from an optimal 0.865 down to 0.825. This failure is strikingly emphasized by the deep inward collapse on the DINO-S axis. Without explicit edge modulation anchored in the encoder, the diffusion backbone suffers from catastrophic "geometric collapse", losing its ability to preserve fine-grained structures during heavy edits.

Conversely, bypassing the Region-Specific Parallel Semantic Injection severely cripples the model's attribute binding capabilities, dropping the CLIP-R score from 0.882 to 0.846. Figure 5 reflects this as a sharp, targeted contraction on the CLIP-R axis: without masked parallel attention, requested edits bleed wildly into non-target regions. Ultimately, the empirical degradation across all specialized metrics perfectly mirrors the theoretical necessity of our dual-stream, logic-aware design.

Table 3. Ablation Result.

Setting	CLIP-D ↑	CLIP-R ↑	DINO-S ↑	LPIPS ↓
w/o Structural Injection	0.247	0.875	0.825	0.179
w/o Semantic Injection	0.232	0.846	0.861	0.174
w/o LEP	0.241	0.868	0.852	0.166
w/o CN	0.244	0.865	0.855	0.188
Full Model (LADI)	**0.249**	**0.882**	**0.865**	**0.161**

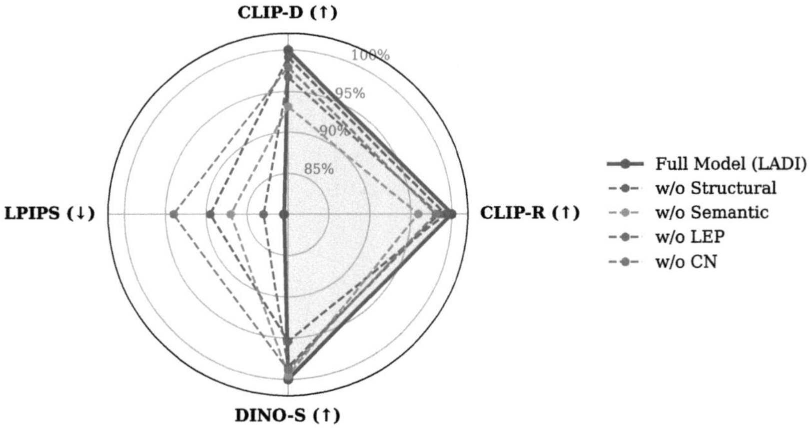

Fig. 5. Radar chart of ablation results. The Full Model (LADI) defines the optimal performance boundary: the outermost perimeter for CLIP-D, CLIP-R, and DINO-S (higher is better), and the innermost anchor for LPIPS (lower is better). Consequently, any inward collapse or outward spike indicates degraded performance.

5 Conclusion

In this paper, we present LADI, a unified framework that effectively resolves the stability-plasticity dilemma in instruction-guided editing. By empowering the generative backbone with a logic-driven editing planner, the editing is executed via a novel dual-stream injection mechanism, which physically isolates geometric anchoring from semantic rendering while maintaining statistical consistency. Extensive evaluations on public benchmark datasets demonstrate that LADI not only establishes a new state-of-the-art in editing fidelity but also exhibits exceptional robustness in sequential and multi-turn scenarios.

Acknowledgements. This work is supported by the Natural Science Foundation of China No. 62302213.

References

1. Peng, B., Wang, J., Zhang, Y., Li, W., Yang, M.-C., Jia, J.: ControlNeXt: powerful and efficient control for image and video generation. arXiv preprint arXiv:2408.06070 (2024)
2. Brooks, T., Holynski, A., Efros, A.A.: InstructPix2Pix: learning to follow image editing instructions. In: IEEE/CVF CVPR, pp. 18392–18402 (2023)
3. Zhang, K., Mo, L., Chen, W., Sun, H., Su, Y.: MagicBrush: A manually annotated dataset for instruction-guided image editing. Adv. Neural. Inf. Process. Syst. **36**, 31428–31449 (2023)
4. Yu, Q., et al.: AnyEdit: mastering unified high-quality image editing for any idea. In: IEEE/CVF CVPR, pp. 26125–26135 (2025)
5. Fu, T.-J., Hu, W., Du, X., Wang, W.Y., Yang, Y., Gan, Z.: Guiding instruction-based image editing via multimodal large language models. In: ICLR (2024)
6. Chen, S.X., Sra, M., Sen, P.: Instruct-CLIP: improving instruction-guided image editing with automated data refinement using contrastive learning. In: IEEE/CVF CVPR, pp. 28513–28522 (2025)
7. Rombach, R., Blattmann, A., Lorenz, D., Esser, P., Ommer, B.: High-resolution image synthesis with latent diffusion models. In: IEEE/CVF CVPR, pp. 10684–10695 (2022)
8. Mokady, R., Hertz, A., Aberman, K., Pritch, Y., Cohen-Or, D.: Null-text inversion for editing real images using guided diffusion models. In: IEEE/CVF CVPR, pp. 6038–6047 (2023)
9. Hertz, A., Mokady, R., Tenenbaum, J., Aberman, K., Pritch, Y., Cohen-Or, D.: Prompt-to-prompt image editing with cross attention control. arXiv preprint arXiv:2208.01626 (2022)
10. Hui, M., et al.: HQ-Edit: a high-quality dataset for instruction-based image editing. In: ICLR (2025)
11. Geng, Z., et al.: InstructDiffusion: a generalist modeling interface for vision tasks. In: IEEE/CVF CVPR, pp. 12709–12720 (2024)
12. Huang, Y., et al.: SmartEdit: exploring complex instruction-based image editing with multimodal large language models. In: IEEE/CVF CVPR, pp. 8362–8371 (2024)
13. Zhang, L., Rao, A., Agrawala, M.: Adding conditional control to text-to-image diffusion models. In: IEEE/CVF ICCV, pp. 3836–3847 (2023)
14. Mou, C., et al.: T2I-Adapter: learning adapters to dig out more controllable ability for text-to-image diffusion models. In: AAAI, vol. **38**, no. 5, pp. 4296–4304 (2024)

15. Zhao, H., et al.: UltraEdit: instruction-based fine-grained image editing at scale. Adv. Neural. Inf. Process. Syst. **37**, 3058–3093 (2024)
16. Zhou, J., et al.: FireEdit: fine-grained instruction-based image editing via region-aware vision language model. In: IEEE/CVF CVPR, pp. 13093–13103 (2025)
17. Ho, J., Jain, A., Abbeel, P.: Denoising diffusion probabilistic models. Adv. Neural. Inf. Process. Syst. **33**, 6840–6851 (2020)
18. Sheynin, S., et al.: EmuEdit: precise image editing via recognition and generation tasks. In: IEEE/CVF CVPR, pp. 8871–8879 (2024)
19. Li, Y., et al.: BrushEdit: all-in-one image inpainting and editing. arXiv preprint arXiv:2412.10316 (2024)
20. Liu, C., Ding, H., Jiang, X.: GRES: generalized referring expression segmentation. In: IEEE/CVF CVPR, pp. 23592–23601 (2023)
21. Runwal, B., Pedapati, T., Chen, P.-Y.: From peft to deft: parameter-efficient fine-tuning for reducing activation density in transformers. In: AAAI, vol. **39**, no. 19, pp. 20218–20227 (2025)
22. Abdal, R., Zhu, P., Femiani, J., Mitra, N., Wonka, P.: CLIP2StyleGAN: unsupervised extraction of stylegan edit directions. In: ACM SIGGRAPH 2022 Conference Proceedings, pp. 1–9 (2022)
23. Radford, A., et al.: Learning transferable visual models from natural language supervision. In: ICML, pp. 8748–8763 (2021)
24. Oquab, M., et al.: DINOv2: learning robust visual features without supervision. arXiv preprint arXiv:2304.07193 (2023)
25. Darcet, T., Oquab, M., Mairal, J., Bojanowski, P.: Vision transformers need registers. arXiv preprint arXiv:2309.16588 (2023)
26. Jose, C., et al.: DINOv2 meets text: a unified framework for image- and pixel-level vision-language alignment. arXiv preprint arXiv:2412.16334 (2024)
27. Heusel, M., Ramsauer, H., Unterthiner, T., Nessler, B., Hochreiter, S.: Gans trained by a two-time-scale update rule converge to a local nash equilibrium. Adv. Neural. Inf. Process. Syst. **30** (2017)
28. Zhang, R., Isola, P., Efros, A.A., Shechtman, E., Wang, O.: The unreasonable effectiveness of deep features as a perceptual metric. In: IEEE/CVF CVPR, pp. 586–595 (2018)
29. Huang, X., et al.: Understanding the planning of LLM agents: a survey. arXiv preprint arXiv:2402.02716 (2024)
30. Cao, M., Wang, X., Qi, Z., Shan, Y., Qie, X., Zheng, Y.: MasaCtrl: tuning-free mutual self-attention control for consistent image synthesis and editing. In: IEEE/CVF ICCV, pp. 22560–22570 (2023)
31. Tumanyan, N., Geyer, M., Bagon, S., Dekel, T.: Plug-and-play diffusion features for text-driven image-to-image translation. In: IEEE/CVF CVPR, pp. 1921–1930 (2023)
32. Couairon, G., Verbeek, J., Schwenk, H., Cord, M.: DiffEdit: diffusion-based semantic image editing with mask guidance. arXiv preprint arXiv:2210.11427 (2022)
33. Liu, H., Li, C., Wu, Q., Lee, Y.J.: Visual instruction tuning. Adv. Neural. Inf. Process. Syst. **36**, 34892–34916 (2023)
34. Huang, X., Belongie, S.: Arbitrary style transfer in real-time with adaptive instance normalization. In: IEEE ICCV, pp. 1501–1510 (2017)
35. Kingma, D.P., Welling, M.: Auto-encoding variational bayes. arXiv preprint arXiv:1312.6114 (2013)

36. Li, Y., et al.: GLIGEN: open-set grounded text-to-image generation. In: IEEE/CVF CVPR, pp. 22511–22521 (2023)
37. Ye, H., Zhang, J., Liu, S., Han, X., Yang, W.: IP-Adapter: text compatible image prompt adapter for text-to-image diffusion models. arXiv preprint arXiv:2308.06721 (2023)

Recognition of Handwritten Python Code in Academic Exam Settings Using a Multi-stage OCR Pipeline

Tuan-Minh Do, Cong-Tam Phan, Hoang-Phuc Mai, Ngoc-Bao-Quang Nguyen, and Cao Vu Bui(✉)

Faculty of Artificial Intelligence, FPT University, Da Nang, Vietnam
vubc@fe.edu.vn

Abstract. Recognizing handwritten source code in academic exam settings is more challenging than ordinary handwritten-text OCR because programming languages require character-level correctness as well as accurate preservation of syntax-critical symbols, punctuation, line order, and indentation. These difficulties are further amplified by diverse handwriting styles, corrections, crossed-out content, and irregular exam-sheet layouts. Therefore, handwritten code recognition should be treated as a structured pipeline problem rather than isolated text transcription.

This paper presents a multi-stage OCR pipeline for syntax-sensitive handwritten Python code recognition. The system integrates YOLO-based line detection, line-status classification, TrOCR-based text recognition, and indentation-aware post-processing for structured code reconstruction. We study auxiliary-data-assisted line detection, line-status classification under imbalanced classes, and several TrOCR adaptation strategies under limited-data conditions. We also compare the adapted recognizer with Azure OCR and Qwen3-VL using a controlled cropped-line evaluation protocol.

Experimental results show that preserving pretrained visual representations while adapting only the autoregressive decoder achieves stronger recognition performance than full-model fine-tuning. In addition, a special-character-weighted loss improves overall recognition robustness while modestly reducing syntax-critical symbol errors. Stage-level and end-to-end evaluations show that the proposed pipeline recovers most valid code lines, while syntax-sensitive recognition errors remain the primary bottleneck among recovered lines.

These findings suggest that handwritten code OCR should be evaluated from a pipeline-level perspective, where detection, filtering, recognition, and structural reconstruction must be analyzed jointly with respect to downstream code usability rather than isolated OCR accuracy alone.

Keywords: Handwritten OCR · Source Code Recognition · Transformer-based OCR · Document Layout Analysis · Python Code Reconstruction

L. Ding et al. (Eds.): APWeb-WAIM 2026, LNCS 16995, pp. 314–328, 2027.
https://doi.org/10.1007/978-981-92-5699-0_20

1 Introduction

Optical character recognition (OCR) for handwritten source code is substantially more challenging than OCR for ordinary handwritten text. In natural language, minor character-level errors may still preserve readability. In contrast, even a single recognition error in source code can break syntax, alter semantics, or render the program invalid. This issue is particularly critical in Python, where indentation, punctuation, operators, and visually similar characters such as `1`, `l`, and `i` directly affect program correctness.

These challenges are amplified in academic exam settings, where students write under time pressure, resulting in diverse handwriting styles, unstable indentation, corrections, crossed-out lines, and ambiguous layouts. Consequently, handwritten code OCR cannot be treated as a simple transcription task. A practical system must identify valid code regions, filter unreliable inputs, preserve structural consistency, and reconstruct usable code.

Recent OCR research has shifted from convolutional recurrent neural networks (CRNNs) to transformer-based models such as TrOCR [16,18]. Although these models achieve strong performance on handwritten-text recognition, they are not specifically designed for syntax-sensitive structured content such as source code, where errors involving brackets, operators, quotation marks, or indentation may invalidate an otherwise readable line.

To address these challenges, we formulate handwritten code OCR as a structured pipeline problem involving line localization, unreliable-line filtering, syntax-sensitive recognition, and indentation-aware reconstruction. We propose a multi-stage OCR pipeline for handwritten Python code in academic exam settings. The pipeline integrates YOLO-based line detection [12,13,19], ResNet18-based line-status classification [7], TrOCR-based text recognition [16], and indentation-aware post-processing for code reconstruction.

We further analyze how errors propagate across the detection, filtering, and recognition stages and influence downstream code reconstruction.

The contributions of this work are summarized as follows:

- We formulate handwritten source-code OCR as a pipeline-level problem involving line localization, unreliable-line filtering, syntax-sensitive recognition, and structural reconstruction.
- We develop a multi-stage OCR pipeline for handwritten Python exam sheets, combining YOLO-based line detection, line-status classification, TrOCR-based recognition, and geometry-based indentation reconstruction.
- We provide stage-level and end-to-end line-level analyses showing how detection, filtering, and recognition errors affect valid-line recovery and transcription quality.
- We investigate TrOCR adaptation under limited handwritten-code data, including adaptation scope, mixed-language training, and a special-character-weighted loss, and compare the adapted recognizer with Azure OCR and Qwen3-VL under a controlled cropped-line evaluation protocol.

2 Related Work

Handwritten text recognition remains challenging because handwriting varies across writers, writing speed, spacing, stroke quality, and scanning conditions. Traditional OCR systems are generally more effective on printed text than on unconstrained handwriting, where character shapes are often ambiguous and segmentation is unreliable. Deep learning approaches, especially CRNN-based recognizers, improve recognition by combining visual feature extraction and sequence modeling [18]. More recent transformer-based models such as TrOCR further improve handwritten-text recognition through large-scale pretraining and attention-based decoding [16].

Handwritten source code recognition introduces additional constraints beyond general handwritten OCR. Source code contains dense punctuation, brackets, operators, and visually similar symbols, while programming languages impose strict syntactic and structural rules. Consequently, even small recognition errors may break syntax or alter program behavior. Earlier work on handwritten Python source code showed that incorporating code-specific grammar and structural constraints improves performance compared with generic handwriting recognition systems [20].

This challenge is particularly evident in educational settings. Islam et al. [11] studied handwritten code recognition for pen-and-paper computer science education using Azure OCR together with indentation recognition and post-OCR correction. Their findings highlight that handwritten code OCR requires both textual and structural correctness, especially for Python, where indentation carries semantic meaning. Complementary to their correction-oriented setting, our work focuses on a full-page OCR pipeline that jointly analyzes line detection, crossed-line filtering, TrOCR adaptation, and end-to-end line recovery.

Recent OCR research also explores pipeline-based systems and general-purpose document understanding models. PreP-OCR integrates document restoration with post-OCR correction to improve recognition on degraded inputs [6]. Commercial OCR systems and VLMs such as Azure OCR, Qwen-VL, and Qwen3-VL demonstrate strong capabilities in OCR and document understanding [1,2,17]. More broadly, document-understanding systems such as Donut [14], Nougat [3], and Pix2Struct [15] combine visual encoding and language modeling for structured document parsing and sequence generation. However, these systems are primarily optimized for printed or semi-structured documents rather than handwritten syntax-sensitive source code with noisy layouts and crossed-out content.

Despite recent progress, most existing approaches focus on isolated text recognition, correction-oriented processing, or general document parsing. In academic exam settings, however, handwritten code OCR must operate as a structured pipeline involving line detection, unreliable-line filtering, syntax-sensitive recognition, and indentation-aware reconstruction. In contrast to prior work, our study evaluates a complete OCR pipeline for handwritten Python exam sheets, integrating line detection, line-status classification, TrOCR adaptation,

OCR/VLM baselines, and indentation-aware reconstruction under a unified pipeline-level evaluation setting.

3 Methodology

3.1 System Overview

The overall pipeline, illustrated in Fig. 1, is designed for handwritten programming-code exam sheets rather than general handwritten notes. Therefore, the system must preserve not only the recognized text content but also the structural properties of source code, such as line order, indentation, and the handling of crossed-out or ambiguous lines.

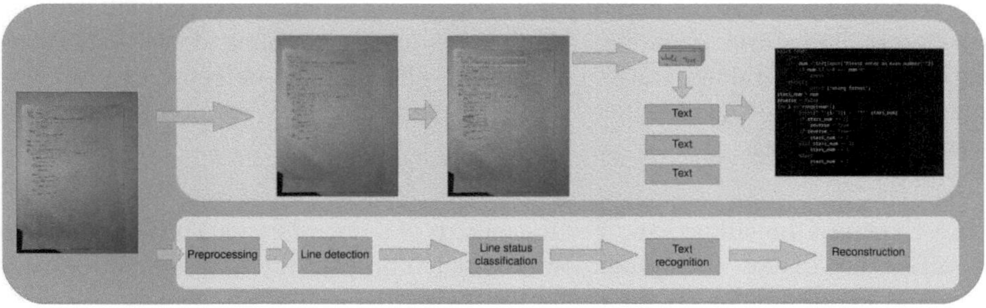

Fig. 1. Overview of the proposed handwritten code OCR pipeline. The system first detects line-level regions from a full-page exam image, filters unreliable lines through line-status classification, performs text recognition using TrOCR, and finally reconstructs structured source code with indentation awareness.

The proposed system consists of four main stages:

1. **Line detection**: locate candidate code-line regions from full-page handwritten exam images.
2. **Line-status classification**: classify each detected line as clean, crossed, or ambiguous.
3. **Text recognition**: recognize the textual content of valid line crops using TrOCR.
4. **Post-processing**: reorder recognized lines and reconstruct indentation-aware source code.

After preprocessing the input page image, the line detection module identifies candidate handwritten code-line regions. Each detected line crop is then passed to the line-status classifier to determine whether it should be used directly, removed, or flagged for review. Crossed-out lines are excluded from recognition, while ambiguous lines can be retained for manual inspection depending on the application setting. Valid line crops are subsequently processed by the TrOCR-based text recognition module. Finally, the recognized line outputs are reordered according to their spatial positions and grouped by indentation level to reconstruct the final source code.

3.2 Models

The proposed pipeline addresses three main learning-based tasks: line detection, line-status classification, and text recognition.

Line Detection. For line detection, we evaluate several YOLO-family detectors, including YOLOv8n, YOLOv10n, and YOLO11n [12,13,19]. These models are selected because line detection in exam sheets requires dense region localization over full-page handwritten inputs. The goal is to identify a detector suitable for dense handwritten line localization in exam-sheet images.

During development, we considered both project-data-only and auxiliary-data-assisted training settings. We also examined one-class and three-class detection formulations, but the final pipeline uses one-class line detection followed by a separate line-status classifier. This choice avoids coupling dense line localization with fine-grained status recognition, allowing the detector to prioritize line recovery while the classifier handles clean/ambiguous/crossed decisions on cropped line images.

Line-Status Classification. For line-status classification, each cropped line is classified into `clean`, `ambiguous`, or `crossed`. This stage removes clearly invalid lines and highlights uncertain inputs for review before OCR.

We compare several convolutional backbones, including ResNet34, ResNet18, MobileNetV3-Small, and DenseNet121 [7,9,10]. The purpose of this comparison is to identify a classifier that is not only accurate but also appropriate for the downstream pipeline. In particular, false positives for the `crossed` class are undesirable because they may remove valid code lines before recognition. The quantitative comparison and final model selection are presented in the experimental section.

Text Recognition. The text recognition stage uses TrOCR, a transformer-based optical character recognition model proposed by Li et al. [16]. TrOCR follows a vision–language encoder–decoder design in which a transformer-based image encoder converts an input text image into visual feature representations, and an autoregressive transformer decoder generates the output character sequence token by token.

A key advantage of TrOCR is that it formulates OCR as a sequence generation problem rather than relying on character-level segmentation. This design allows the model to capture long-range dependencies in text, making it well suited to handwriting recognition, where character shapes may be ambiguous and contextual information is often required for disambiguation.

Because source code contains many symbols, brackets, and punctuation marks, the sequence modeling ability of TrOCR is especially relevant in our setting. Its pretrained encoder–decoder structure also provides a strong foundation for adaptation to handwritten code recognition tasks.

3.3 Post-processing

In this study, the indentation module is used as a lightweight geometry-based reconstruction step rather than a separately optimized learning component. Because Python uses indentation as part of its syntax, line-level OCR outputs must be converted back into structured code. A plain concatenation of recognized lines would not be sufficient. Therefore, we use line geometry to estimate indentation levels. In particular, the left coordinates of detected line boxes are clustered using DBSCAN [5] so that lines with similar horizontal offsets are grouped as belonging to the same indentation level. These clusters are then mapped to indentation depths during code reconstruction.

DBSCAN is suitable for this step because it groups points according to local density and does not require the number of clusters to be specified in advance. This is useful in our setting, where the number of indentation levels can vary across exam pages and noisy detections may appear as outliers. The post-processing stage remains computationally lightweight, yet it is essential for making the OCR output usable as code rather than only as raw text.

3.4 Training Strategy

The learning-based modules are trained using task-specific strategies according to their roles in the pipeline. For line detection, we adopt a progressive two-stage training strategy to balance generalization and domain adaptation. In the first stage, the detector is trained on a mixed dataset combining the auxiliary handwritten-line dataset and the project-specific code-line dataset, allowing the model to learn general line-level cues such as spacing, alignment, stroke continuity, and page layout. In the second stage, the detector is further adapted using only the project-specific dataset to specialize the model toward handwritten exam sheets.

For line-status classification, the classifier is trained independently as a supervised three-class model with the labels `clean`, `ambiguous`, and `crossed`. This stage filters unreliable line crops before text recognition.

For text recognition, we adopt TrOCR-base and compare three adaptation scopes: full fine-tuning, partial encoder–decoder fine-tuning, and decoder-only fine-tuning, where the visual encoder is frozen and only the autoregressive decoder is updated. After selecting the most suitable adaptation scope, we further investigate curriculum-based fine-tuning, augmentation-enhanced fine-tuning, and a special-character-weighted loss. Curriculum learning first uses cleaner samples before training on the full dataset, while augmentation applies moderate image transformations to improve robustness without distorting syntax-critical symbols.

In the special-character-weighted setting, the token-level loss assigns higher penalties to code-specific symbols:

$$\mathcal{L}_{\mathrm{SC}} = -\frac{1}{T}\sum_{t=1}^{T} w(y_t)\log p_t(y_t), \qquad w(y_t) = \begin{cases} \lambda, & \text{if } y_t \in \mathcal{S}, \\ 1, & \text{otherwise.} \end{cases}$$

Here, T is the output sequence length, y_t is the ground-truth token, and $p_t(y_t)$ is its predicted probability. The set $\mathcal{S}$ contains syntax-critical symbols such as brackets, colons, quotation marks, commas, and operators, while λ controls their relative penalty. In our experiments, $\lambda = 3.0$. Special-character errors are computed from insertions, deletions, and substitutions involving symbols in $\mathcal{S}$ after sequence alignment.

4 Experimental Results

4.1 Dataset

We use two datasets in this study. The first is an auxiliary handwritten-line dataset containing approximately 1200 handwritten sheet images [8]. This dataset is used only for detector pretraining. Since the project-specific dataset is relatively small, auxiliary pretraining helps the detector learn general handwritten-line patterns, such as line spacing, stroke continuity, text alignment, and page-level layout, before being adapted to handwritten code exam sheets. Representative samples from this auxiliary dataset are shown in Fig. 2.

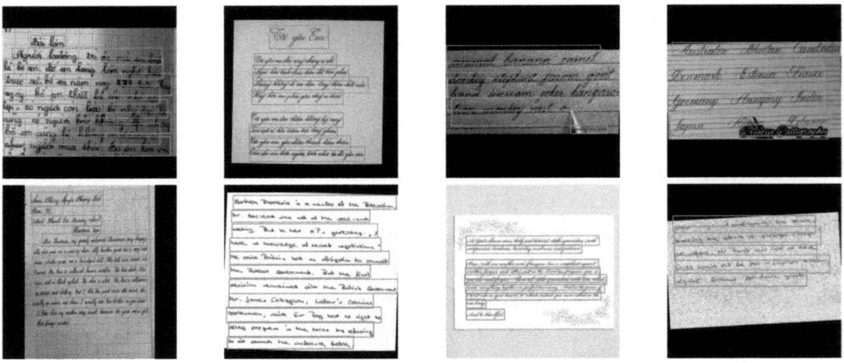

Fig. 2. Representative samples from the auxiliary line-detection dataset used for detector pretraining.

The second dataset is the project-specific handwritten-code dataset, constructed by combining our collected programming exam sheets with samples from a publicly available handwritten code dataset [4]. The resulting dataset contains 143 full-page handwritten code sheets, including 105 Python sheets and 38 C/C++ sheets. Although the main target is Python code recognition, C/C++ sheets are included to increase handwriting and code-symbol diversity, since these languages share many visual patterns such as brackets, operators, punctuation marks, and variable expressions.

After preprocessing and line extraction, the project dataset yields 2225 line-level images annotated into three line-status classes: `clean`, `ambiguous`, and `crossed`. For text recognition, 1896 line-level images are retained after excluding crossed-out lines and samples whose handwriting is too unclear for reliable transcription.

To avoid line-crop leakage, all project-specific data splits are performed at the sheet level rather than the line-crop level. Specifically, the 143 exam sheets are divided into training, validation, and test sets using a 7:1:2 ratio. As a result, all line crops extracted from the same sheet are assigned to the same split. An overview of the project dataset is shown in Fig. 3.

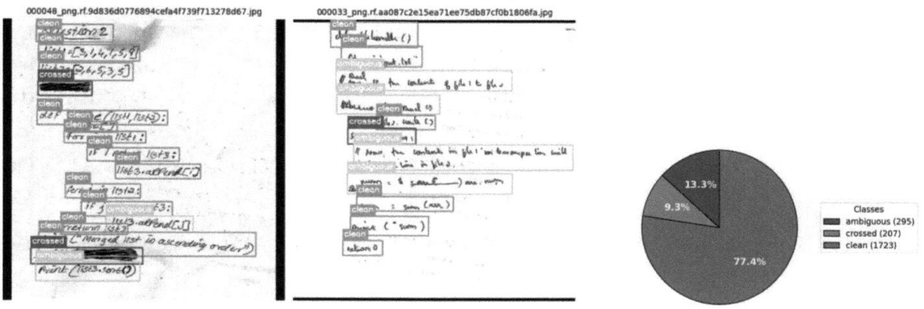

(a) Representative samples. (b) Line-status distribution.

Fig. 3. Overview of the project dataset.

4.2 Evaluation Protocol

To preserve evaluation integrity, all splits are performed at the sheet level so that line crops from the same exam sheet do not appear across training and evaluation partitions.

Stage-level evaluation is conducted using task-specific metrics. Line detection is evaluated using Precision, Recall, mAP@50, and mAP@50–95. Line-status classification is evaluated using Accuracy, Precision, Recall, and F1-score. Text recognition is evaluated using mean line-level character error rate (CER), exact match (EM), and special-character error count where applicable.

In addition to stage-level evaluation, we report end-to-end line-level metrics for the full OCR pipeline. The end-to-end evaluation starts from full-page exam images and uses ground-truth `clean` and `ambiguous` lines as evaluation targets, while crossed-out lines are excluded. Predicted lines classified as `crossed` are also removed before matching. The remaining predicted lines are matched to ground-truth lines using greedy one-to-one IoU-based matching with a threshold of 0.5. Line Recovery Rate measures the proportion of evaluated ground-truth lines that are successfully matched after detection and filtering. E2E Mean CER and E2E EM are computed only over successfully recovered lines. These recognition metrics are therefore conditional on successful line recovery and are intended to measure recognition quality on retained line crops rather than penalize missed detections. Missed valid lines are captured separately by the Line Recovery Rate.

4.3 Line Detection Results

All YOLO variants are trained using the two-stage strategy described in Sect. 3.4. Here, we report the final adapted detectors used in the downstream OCR pipeline, rather than a separate ablation of the auxiliary pretraining stage.

Table 1 compares the YOLO variants on the project-specific code-line evaluation set. YOLO11n achieves the highest recall, mAP@50, and mAP@50–95, indicating the strongest overall detection coverage and localization quality. Compared with YOLOv8n, YOLO11n improves recall from 0.949 to 0.954 and mAP@50–95 from 0.537 to 0.565, while YOLOv8n retains a 0.030 precision advantage. This shows a trade-off between YOLOv8n's more conservative predictions and YOLO11n's stronger line recovery and localization performance.

Table 1. Comparison of final adapted YOLO variants for line detection on the code-line dataset.

Model	Precision	Recall	mAP@50	mAP@50–95
YOLOv8n	**0.947**	0.949	0.963	0.537
YOLOv10n	0.833	0.796	0.878	0.497
YOLO11n	0.917	**0.954**	**0.970**	**0.565**

The advantage of YOLO11n over YOLOv10n is more substantial, with gains of 0.158 in recall, 0.092 in mAP@50, and 0.068 in mAP@50–95. Since missed code lines cannot be recovered by later recognition stages, YOLO11n is selected for the final pipeline to prioritize line recovery and localization quality, despite its lower precision than YOLOv8n.

4.4 Line Classification Results

To provide a detailed evaluation of line-status classification, we compute macro-averaged precision, recall, and F1-score from the test-set confusion matrices. The results are summarized in Table 2.

The corresponding confusion matrices are shown in Fig. 4 to illustrate class-level behavior across the evaluated backbones.

The results reveal a trade-off between overall accuracy and class balance. While ResNet18 achieves the highest test accuracy, ResNet34 obtains the best macro F1-score, indicating more balanced performance across classes. ResNet18 improves accuracy by 0.0312 over ResNet34 and by 0.0044 over DenseNet121, whereas ResNet34 improves macro F1 by 0.0367 over ResNet18.

Class-level behavior shows that the `clean` class is easier to recognize, whereas the `ambiguous` class remains challenging and is often confused with `clean`. This

Table 2. Line-status classification performance computed from the test-set confusion matrices.

Backbone	Accuracy	Precision	Recall	F1
ResNet34	0.8036	0.7201	**0.7322**	**0.7213**
ResNet18	**0.8348**	0.6992	0.6837	0.6846
MobileNetV3-Small	0.8013	**0.7356**	0.6111	0.6435
DenseNet121	0.8304	0.6981	0.6660	0.6732

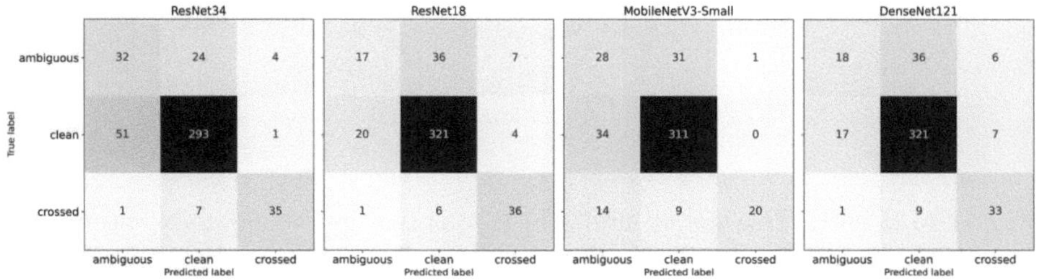

Fig. 4. Confusion matrices of the line-status classification backbones on the test set.

behavior is expected, as the ambiguous class serves primarily as a warning signal for uncertain inputs rather than a strict classification target. In contrast, false positives for the `crossed` class are particularly harmful because they may remove valid code lines before the OCR stage.

Overall, ResNet18 is selected for the final pipeline because it provides the highest overall accuracy with a lightweight architecture and favorable behavior for downstream OCR usage. ResNet34 remains stronger under macro F1-score and may be preferable when class-balanced performance is prioritized.

4.5 Text Recognition Results

Table 3 reports the line-level recognition results.

We first analyze the behavior of TrOCR under different adaptation strategies. Direct use of the pretrained model is insufficient, achieving a CER of 0.9052 and an EM of only 0.0096. This reflects a substantial domain gap between generic OCR pretraining and handwritten code, where punctuation, indentation-related spacing, and visually similar characters are more critical than in ordinary text recognition. Full-model fine-tuning improves EM but increases CER, indicating less stable sequence generation when both the visual encoder and decoder are updated on the limited handwritten-code dataset. In contrast, decoder-only fine-tuning achieves better performance. This suggests that preserving pretrained visual representations while adapting the sequence-generation component is more suitable for this setting.

Among the decoder-based extensions, the special-character-weighted loss achieves the best overall performance, reducing CER to 0.2403 and improv-

Table 3. Line-level recognition performance under TrOCR adaptation strategies and external baselines.

Category	Method	CER	EM	Special-char. Errors
Pretrained baseline	Pretrained TrOCR	0.9052	0.0096	–
Adaptation scope	Full-model fine-tuning	1.1049	0.2347	–
	Partial encoder–decoder fine-tuning	0.3954	0.1672	–
	Decoder-only fine-tuning	0.2737	0.2540	173
Decoder-only extensions	Curriculum-based fine-tuning	0.3006	0.2476	–
	Augmentation-enhanced fine-tuning	0.3061	0.2444	–
	Special-character-weighted loss	**0.2403**	**0.2701**	**169**
Off-the-shelf baseline	Azure OCR [17]	0.4399	0.0514	–
	Qwen3-VL [2]	0.3771	0.1286	–

ing EM to 0.2701. This result supports the motivation that handwritten code recognition should not treat all characters equally. Errors on brackets, colons, quotation marks, and operators can directly affect code correctness, even when the overall character-level error appears moderate. The reduction in special-character error count is modest, from 173 to 169, so the main effect should be interpreted as improved overall line-level recognition robustness rather than a large isolated reduction in symbol errors.

We further compare the proposed recognizer with off-the-shelf systems, including Azure OCR [17] and Qwen3-VL [2]. External OCR/VLM baselines are evaluated at the same line level using the same cropped inputs and normalized ground-truth annotations as the adapted TrOCR models. No task-specific fine-tuning, prompt engineering, or post-processing is applied to Azure OCR or Qwen3-VL; therefore, these systems serve as external reference points rather than directly optimized competitors.

Although Qwen3-VL performs better than Azure OCR, both models remain behind the proposed method on handwritten code. Under this controlled cropped-line setting, the proposed model achieves substantially lower CER and higher EM than Qwen3-VL, suggesting that general OCR/VLM systems may capture parts of the text but still fail to preserve complete code-line correctness.

Overall, the results demonstrate that handwritten code OCR requires not only general text recognition capability but also explicit adaptation to symbol-level and structural constraints.

4.6 Effect of Mixed-Language Code Data

To examine the role of non-Python code sheets, we compare recognition performance under different training-data and checkpoint-selection settings. All results in Table 4 are evaluated on the same held-out test set.

Compared with Python-only training, mixed-language training improves recognition performance on the same held-out test set. When selected using the Python validation subset, the mixed-language model reduces CER from 0.3377

Table 4. Effect of mixed-language training data and checkpoint selection on line-level recognition performance.

Training data	Checkpoint selection	CER	EM	Python CER	Python EM
Python only	Python validation subset	0.3377	0.2251	0.3257	0.2287
Mixed language	Python validation subset	0.2725	0.2669	0.2593	0.2752
Mixed language	Mixed validation set	**0.2403**	**0.2701**	**0.2312**	**0.2829**

to 0.2725 and improves EM from 0.2251 to 0.2669; the Python-specific CER and EM also improve. Selecting the mixed-language model using the full mixed validation set yields the best reported performance. However, this comparison changes both the amount of training data and the validation criterion used for checkpoint selection. Therefore, the results should be interpreted as practical evidence that mixed-language code data is useful in this limited-data setting, rather than as a fully controlled analysis of programming-language effects.

4.7 End-To-End Evaluation

To evaluate the complete OCR pipeline, we perform end-to-end testing on full-page handwritten exam sheets. As described in Sect. 4.2, ground-truth `clean` and `ambiguous` lines are matched to retained predictions after lines classified as `crossed` are removed. Table 5 summarizes the resulting line-level performance.

Table 5. End-to-end line-level performance of the proposed OCR pipeline. Recognition metrics are computed only on successfully recovered lines.

Metric	Value
Line Recovery Rate	0.9051
Mean CER on recovered lines	0.2642
EM on recovered lines	0.3306

The Line Recovery Rate of 0.9051 indicates that most valid code lines are retained after detection and filtering. Among successfully recovered lines, the mean CER is 0.2642 and the EM is 0.3306, showing that exact transcription remains challenging despite relatively strong upstream coverage. The difference between CER and EM reflects the strict character-level correctness required by source code, where a single error in a bracket, colon, operator, or quotation mark may invalidate an otherwise readable line. The higher EM than in the recognition-only evaluation does not indicate an intrinsic improvement in the recognizer, because the end-to-end protocol evaluates a different subset after detection, filtering, and matching exclude some difficult lines.

5 Discussion

The experiments lead to three main observations.

First, recognition remains the primary bottleneck in the proposed pipeline. Although line detection and line-status classification achieve reasonable performance, the usability of reconstructed code is still strongly affected by recognition errors, particularly on punctuation, brackets, operators, quotation marks, and visually similar characters. Common failure cases include missing brackets, incorrect colons, merged symbols, and inconsistent quotation marks under dense or unclear handwriting. The comparison with Azure OCR and Qwen3-VL further suggests that general-purpose OCR and VLM systems are insufficient for syntax-sensitive handwritten code recognition without task-specific adaptation.

Second, adaptation strategy plays an important role in recognition quality. Preserving pretrained visual representations while adapting only the decoder produces more stable behavior than full encoder–decoder fine-tuning, suggesting that excessive visual adaptation may be harmful under limited handwritten-code data. The special-character-weighted loss improves overall recognition robustness by emphasizing syntax-critical symbols, although the isolated reduction in special-character errors remains modest. In addition, the mixed-language analysis indicates that C/C++ sheets provide useful handwriting and symbol-level variation for Python-code recognition, although this result should be interpreted as practical evidence in a limited-data setting rather than a fully controlled language-effect study.

Third, handwritten code OCR should be viewed as a pipeline-level problem rather than an isolated recognition task. Errors are not equally harmful across stages: missed detections remove code lines before recognition, incorrectly classifying valid lines as `crossed` may discard useful content, and small symbol-level errors may still invalidate an entire code line. The end-to-end evaluation supports this observation by showing that the pipeline recovers most valid lines, while exact line-level reconstruction remains challenging. Furthermore, indentation-aware reconstruction is evaluated only qualitatively in this study, indicating the need for more rigorous structural evaluation metrics.

Despite these findings, the study has several limitations. The dataset remains relatively small and may not fully represent handwriting diversity in real exam settings. In addition, although end-to-end line-level metrics are reported, the evaluation does not directly measure syntax validity, code executability, or AST-level correctness. Future work should therefore investigate larger datasets, stronger structural reconstruction methods, and syntax-aware evaluation metrics for handwritten code understanding.

6 Conclusion

This paper presented a multi-stage OCR pipeline for handwritten Python code recognition in academic exam settings. The proposed system combines line detection, line-status classification, transformer-based text recognition, and indentation-aware post-processing for structured code reconstruction.

Experimental results show that text recognition remains the primary bottleneck in the pipeline, with performance strongly affected by adaptation strategy and syntax-sensitive symbol recognition. Decoder-only fine-tuning provides more stable adaptation than full-model fine-tuning, while the proposed special-character-weighted loss improves overall recognition robustness. Comparisons with Azure OCR and Qwen3-VL further highlight the limitations of general-purpose OCR and VLM systems for handwritten code recognition.

End-to-end evaluation shows that the pipeline recovers most valid code lines, although exact reconstruction remains challenging. These findings support a pipeline-level perspective on handwritten code OCR, where detection, filtering, recognition, and reconstruction should be evaluated jointly with respect to downstream code usability.

Future work will focus on improving robustness to difficult handwriting, enhancing structural reconstruction, and developing syntax-aware evaluation metrics for code executability and AST-level correctness.

References

1. Bai, J.: Qwen-VL: a versatile vision-language model for understanding, localization, text reading, and beyond. arXiv preprint arXiv:2308.12966 (2023)
2. Bai, S.: Qwen3-VL technical report. arXiv preprint arXiv:2511.21631 (2025)
3. Blecher, L., Cucurull, G., Scialom, T., Stojnic, R.: Nougat: neural optical understanding for academic documents. In: Proceedings of the Twelfth International Conference on Learning Representations (2024).https://openreview.net/forum?id=fUtxNAKpdV
4. Devika12312: Handwritten code dataset. https://huggingface.co/datasets/devika12312/handwritten_code_dataset (2023). Accessed: 29 Jun 2026
5. Ester, M., Kriegel, H.P., Sander, J., Xu, X.: A density-based algorithm for discovering clusters in large spatial databases with noise. In: Proceedings of the Second International Conference on Knowledge Discovery and Data Mining, pp. 226–231 (1996)
6. Guan, S., et al.: PreP-OCR: a complete pipeline for document image restoration and enhanced OCR accuracy. In: Proceedings of the 63rd Annual Meeting of the Association for Computational Linguistics (Volume 1: Long Papers). pp. 15413–15425. Association for Computational Linguistics, Vienna, Austria (2025). https://doi.org/10.18653/v1/2025.acl-long.749
7. He, K., Zhang, X., Ren, S., Sun, J.: Deep residual learning for image recognition. In: Proceedings of the IEEE Conference on Computer Vision and Pattern Recognition, pp. 770–778 (2016)
8. Hoang: vnh-detection-binh.v1i dataset. https://universe.roboflow.com/hoang-r9hhb/vnh-detection-binh.v1i (2024). Accessed: 29 Jun 2026
9. Howard, A., et al.: Searching for MobileNetV3. In: Proceedings of the IEEE/CVF International Conference on Computer Vision. pp. 1314–1324 (2019)
10. Huang, G., Liu, Z., van der Maaten, L., Weinberger, K.Q.: Densely connected convolutional networks. In: Proceedings of the IEEE Conference on Computer Vision and Pattern Recognition. pp. 4700–4708 (2017)

11. Islam, M.S., Doumbouya, M.K.B., Manning, C.D., Piech, C.: Handwritten code recognition for pen-and-paper CS education. In: Proceedings of the Eleventh ACM Conference on Learning @ Scale. pp. 200–210. L@S '24, Association for Computing Machinery, New York, NY, USA (2024). https://doi.org/10.1145/3657604.3662027
12. Jocher, G., Chaurasia, A., Qiu, J.: Ultralytics yolov8 (2023). https://github.com/ultralytics/ultralytics
13. Jocher, G., Qiu, J.: Ultralytics yolo11 (2024). https://github.com/ultralytics/ultralytics
14. Kim, G., et al.: OCR-free document understanding transformer. In: Computer Vision – ECCV 2022: 17th European Conference, Tel Aviv, Israel, October 23–27, 2022, Proceedings, Part XXVIII. pp. 498–517. Springer (2022). https://doi.org/10.1007/978-3-031-19815-1_29
15. Lee, K., et al.: Pix2Struct: screenshot parsing as pretraining for visual language understanding. In: Proceedings of the 40th International Conference on Machine Learning. Proceedings of Machine Learning Research, vol. 202, pp. 18893–18912. PMLR (2023)
16. Li, M., et al.: TrOCR: transformer-based optical character recognition with pre-trained models. In: Proceedings of the AAAI Conference on Artificial Intelligence. vol. 37, pp. 13094–13102 (2023). https://doi.org/10.1609/aaai.v37i11.26538
17. Microsoft: azure AI document intelligence. https://learn.microsoft.com/en-us/azure/ai-services/document-intelligence/ (2024). Accessed: 29 Jun 2026
18. Shi, B., Bai, X., Yao, C.: An end-to-end trainable neural network for image-based sequence recognition and its application to scene text recognition. IEEE Trans. Pattern Anal. Mach. Intell. **39**(11), 2298–2304 (2017). https://doi.org/10.1109/TPAMI.2016.2646371
19. Wang, A., et al.: YOLOv10: real-time end-to-end object detection. In: Advances in Neural Information Processing Systems. vol. 37, pp. 107984–108011. Curran Associates, Inc. (2024). https://doi.org/10.52202/079017-3429
20. Zhi, Q., Metoyer, R.A.: Recognizing handwritten source code. In: Proceedings of the 43rd Graphics Interface Conference. pp. 163–170. GI '17, Canadian Human-Computer Communications Society, Waterloo, CAN (2017). https://doi.org/10.20380/GI2017.21

Special Track

Adaptive Retrieval Over Dual-Layer Graph Memory for Multi-hop Question Answering

Yaru Zhao, Zhitao Chen, Xueyao Zhang, and Binyang Li(✉)

University of International Relations, Beijing, China
{zhaoyaru,chen,xyzhang,byli}@uir.edu.cn

Abstract. Multi-hop question answering remains challenging for retrieval-augmented generation because success depends not only on retrieving relevant evidence, but also on deciding how retrieval should continue as partial evidence accumulates. Existing graph-based RAG methods provide useful corpus structure, while agentic RAG methods enable iterative retrieval, yet current systems still lack an effective mechanism for transitioning between semantic grounding and relational exploration during inference. We present AgentGraph-RAG, a graph-native agentic RAG framework for multi-hop question answering. AgentGraph-RAG constructs a Dual-Layer Cognitive Graph that unifies chunk-level semantic memory and entity-level relational memory in a single heterogeneous structure. At inference time, an LLM controller operates over a hybrid action space comprising keyword search, semantic search, graph hopping, and full-chunk reading to accumulate evidence under a fixed budget. Experiments on MuSiQue, 2WikiMultiHopQA, and HotpotQA show that AgentGraph-RAG achieves the best results in our controlled comparison set. Relative to the strongest baseline, it improves average LLM Accuracy from 79.9% to 87.2% and average Contain Accuracy from 86.7% to 95.8%. Ablations further show that both memory layers and the graph-hop action are critical, indicating that the gains arise from the interaction between dual-layer graph memory and adaptive retrieval control. Overall, the results support a view of multi-hop RAG as sequential decision making over structured memory rather than retrieval over ranked candidates alone.

Keywords: Retrieval-Augmented Generation · Multi-hop Question Answering · LLM Agents · Graph Retrieval

1 Introduction

Large language models (LLMs) have substantially advanced open-domain question answering, but they still rely on external retrieval when the required knowledge is long-tail, compositional, or absent from parametric memory. Retrieval-augmented generation (RAG) addresses this limitation by grounding generation

Y. Zhao and Z. Chen—These authors contributed equally to this work.

L. Ding et al. (Eds.): APWeb-WAIM 2026, LNCS 16995, pp. 331–342, 2027.
https://doi.org/10.1007/978-981-92-5699-0_21

in retrieved evidence. While retrieving a small set of passages is often sufficient for single-hop questions, multi-hop question answering is more difficult: the model must identify an initial clue, update the retrieval target as new evidence appears, and synthesize an answer across multiple steps.

The challenge is therefore not only what to retrieve, but also how retrieval should continue after partial evidence has been observed. In many existing RAG systems, retrieval is still treated primarily as a ranking problem. In multi-hop QA, however, effective inference requires retrieval control: the model must decide whether to broaden the search semantically, pivot to a newly surfaced entity, inspect a full passage for verification, or stop with an answer. Without such control, the system either over-retrieves or depends heavily on unusually strong first-hop recall.

Prior work addresses parts of this problem, but not the transition structure required for multi-hop retrieval. Graph-based RAG methods enrich the retrieval substrate with graphs, trees, or hierarchies [1–6], improving access to corpus structure but often relying on fixed expansion rules or passive inference-time strategies. Iterative and agentic RAG methods introduce multiple rounds of retrieval and reasoning [7–12], but many still operate over flat memories or fixed workflows. Recent graph-agent systems such as GeAR and DAVIS further suggest that structured retrieval and adaptive control are natural complements [13,14]. What remains under-specified is how to design a memory–action interface that lets the model move effectively between semantic grounding and relational continuation during inference.

We address this gap with AgentGraph-RAG, a graph-native agentic RAG framework for multi-hop question answering. AgentGraph-RAG constructs a Dual-Layer Cognitive Graph that couples chunk-level semantic context with entity-level relational structure in a single heterogeneous memory. It then exposes this memory through a Hybrid Retrieval Action Space comprising keyword search, semantic search, graph hopping, and full-chunk reading. A budgeted ReAct-style controller [15] selects among these actions according to the current evidence state and decides when to stop.

We evaluate AgentGraph-RAG on MuSiQue, 2WikiMultiHopQA, and HotpotQA. Across these benchmarks, AgentGraph-RAG achieves the strongest results in our controlled comparison set. Ablation studies further show that removing either memory layer or disabling the graph-specific traversal action causes substantial degradation, indicating that the gains arise from the interaction between dual-layer graph memory and adaptive retrieval control.

Our contributions are as follows:

- We formulate multi-hop RAG as budgeted evidence accumulation over heterogeneous memory, instantiated with a dual-layer graph that integrates chunk-level semantic evidence and entity-level relational structure.
- We propose a graph-native retrieval interface for LLM agents that unifies keyword search, semantic retrieval, graph traversal, and full-chunk reading within a single action space.

- We demonstrate consistent improvements on three multi-hop QA benchmarks and show through graph and tool ablations that the gains come from the interaction between structured memory and adaptive retrieval control.

2 Related Work

Graph-Structured Retrieval. Graph-structured retrieval augments flat chunk indexing with explicit corpus organization. Prior work has introduced entity-centric summaries, hierarchical abstractions, and graph-based memory to improve retrieval over complex evidence spaces [1–6]. The shared intuition is that richer structure can improve recall and support reasoning over dispersed evidence. Our work is closely related to this line, but differs in emphasis: rather than focusing only on how to build a stronger retrieval substrate, we study how that substrate should be exposed at inference time so that the model can move between semantic lookup and relational continuation during multi-hop retrieval.

Iterative and Agentic RAG. A separate line of work improves RAG through iterative retrieval and reasoning. FLARE triggers retrieval during generation [7]; IRCoT interleaves reasoning and retrieval [8]; Self-RAG and RA-ISF introduce self-reflection and iterative feedback [9,10]; and MCTS-RAG explores tree-search-style inference with retrieval [11]. These methods show that retrieval benefits from adaptive multi-step inference, but many still assume flat memories or fixed interaction patterns with the retriever. In contrast, our focus is on the coupling between iterative control and a graph-native memory interface.

Graph-Agent Hybrids. Recent graph-agent systems further narrow the gap between structured retrieval and adaptive inference [13,14,16]. This line of work is closest to ours, as it treats graph structure not only as an index but also as an interactive reasoning substrate. Our method differs in explicitly factoring retrieval into dual-layer memory and action-based control, and our ablations are designed to test this factorization directly.

3 Method

3.1 Problem Formulation

Let $\mathcal{C} = \{c_1, \ldots, c_N\}$ be a corpus segmented into chunks, and let q be a question whose answer depends on a latent multi-hop evidence chain. Unlike single-shot RAG, the appropriate retrieval granularity is not known in advance: early steps may require semantic recall over chunks, while later steps may require following entity relations or reading full chunks for verification. We model inference as budgeted evidence accumulation. At step t, the system maintains an evidence state

$$S_t = (q, H_t, B_t), \tag{1}$$

where H_t is the current evidence buffer and B_t is the remaining budget. The system selects an action $a_t \in \mathcal{A} \cup \{\textsc{answer}\}$, receives an observation o_t, and updates the evidence buffer as $H_{t+1} = H_t \cup o_t$. Conceptually, the goal is to maximize answer quality while controlling retrieval cost:

$$\tau^* = \arg\max_{\tau} \mathbb{E}\big[R_{\text{ans}}(\tau) - \lambda C(\tau)\big], \tag{2}$$

where $\tau = (a_1, o_1, \ldots, a_T, o_T)$ is a retrieval trajectory, R_{ans} denotes final answer quality, and $C(\tau)$ denotes inference cost. We do not optimize this objective directly; instead, our system approximates it with a budgeted LLM controller operating over an explicit action space.

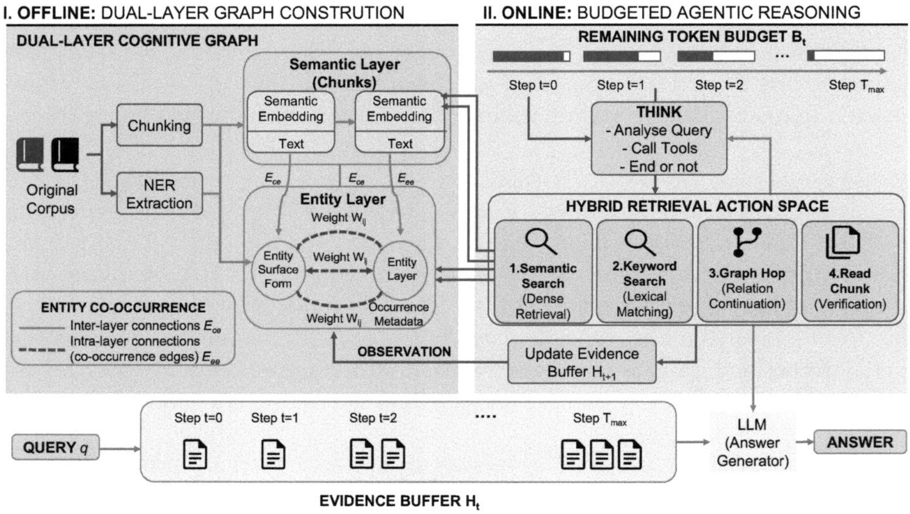

Fig. 1. Overview of AgentGraph-RAG. In the offline stage, the corpus is organized into a dual-layer graph that captures chunk-level semantic memory and entity-level relational memory. In the online stage, the agent iteratively retrieves evidence from this graph before generating the final answer.

3.2 Overview

Figure 1 illustrates the overall pipeline of AgentGraph-RAG. In the offline stage, we build a heterogeneous graph that provides two complementary views of the corpus: chunk nodes preserve semantic context, whereas entity nodes encode relational structure. In the online stage, this graph is exposed to an LLM agent through retrieval tools that share a unified output schema. The agent iteratively selects actions, gathers evidence, and either continues retrieval or returns an answer within a fixed budget. The design follows three principles: separating memory from policy, enabling transitions across retrieval granularities, and reserving expensive full-chunk reading for verification. Under this view, the graph serves not merely as an index, but as a navigable memory over which retrieval actions are executed.

3.3 Dual-Layer Cognitive Graph

We represent memory as a heterogeneous graph

$$G = (V_c \cup V_e, E_{ce} \cup E_{ee}), \tag{3}$$

where V_c is the set of chunk nodes and V_e is the set of entity nodes.

Chunk Layer. Each chunk node $c_i \in V_c$ stores the chunk title, raw text, and a dense embedding for semantic retrieval. This layer provides semantic grounding and supports broad recall when the next hop is not yet tied to a specific entity.

Entity Layer. Each entity node $e_j \in V_e$ stores the entity surface form, type, and occurrence metadata. Entities are extracted with a transformer-based NER model, retaining informative categories such as PERSON, ORG, GPE, LOC, EVENT, WORK_OF_ART, and DATE.

Edges. Containment edges connect chunks and entities:

$$E_{ce} = \{(c_i, e_j) \mid e_j \text{ appears in } c_i\}. \tag{4}$$

Co-occurrence edges connect entity pairs that appear in the same chunk:

$$E_{ee} = \{(e_i, e_j) \mid \exists c_k,\ e_i \in c_k \land e_j \in c_k\}, \tag{5}$$

with weight

$$w_{ij} = \sum_k \mathbf{1}[e_i \in c_k \land e_j \in c_k]. \tag{6}$$

This representation is intentionally lightweight. It avoids dependence on a curated external knowledge graph while preserving explicit transitions between semantic evidence and relational evidence. In practice, chunk nodes often anchor early retrieval, whereas entity nodes become more useful once an intermediate clue has been identified.

3.4 Hybrid Retrieval Action Space

The agent interacts with the graph through four tools that support complementary retrieval behaviors. Specifically, `keyword_search` takes a set of keywords, matches them against entity names, and returns chunks containing the matched entities; it is particularly effective when the question includes explicit lexical anchors such as names, titles, or aliases. In contrast, `semantic_search` takes a free-form query and retrieves the top-k chunks based on cosine similarity over chunk embeddings, making it useful when lexical overlap is limited or when the next clue must be inferred semantically. To support multi-hop exploration over relational structure, `graph_hop` takes an entity name as input and returns neighboring entities ranked by co-occurrence weight, allowing the agent to inspect plausible next-hop candidates without reformulating the entire query. Finally, `read_chunk` takes a chunk identifier and returns the full chunk text. Since search actions usually provide sufficient context for planning, full-chunk reading is primarily used for verification, disambiguation, and final grounding. All tools return outputs in a shared structured format containing retrieved content, provenance, and token usage. The controller selects actions according to the current evidence state,

$$a_t = \arg\max_{a \in \mathcal{A}} P(a \mid q, H_t, G), \tag{7}$$

where the distribution is induced implicitly by the LLM through in-context decision making rather than a separately trained policy.

3.5 Agentic Evidence Accumulation

The controller follows a ReAct-style loop [15], alternating between reasoning over the current evidence state and invoking retrieval tools until the question appears answerable or the budget is exhausted. Rather than adhering to a fixed tool order, it can flexibly adapt its retrieval strategy to the evolving evidence state: for example, it may begin with semantic retrieval, switch to graph traversal after identifying an intermediate entity, and then read a full chunk for verification. This design allows the agent to combine semantic matching, relational exploration, and direct evidence grounding within a unified budgeted inference process.

Algorithm 1: Budgeted Agent Execution

Input : question q, graph memory G, maximum tool-iteration budget $T_{\max}$
Output : final answer

```
/* Initialization                                                    */
Initialize message history with system instructions and q
Initialize evidence buffer H_0 ← ∅
for t ← 1 to T_max do
    if token budget exhausted then
        force answer generation from current evidence
        break
    Query the LLM with the current message history and tool schema
    if no tool call is returned then
        return generated answer
    for each returned tool call do
        Execute the tool on G
        Append the observation to the message history
        Update evidence buffer H_t
return generated answer
```

Conceptually, inference can be viewed as a partially observable budgeted decision process: the agent only has access to the evidence accumulated so far, and each tool call trades additional cost for potentially more informative observations. Although we do not explicitly learn this policy, the formulation clarifies the decision structure that AgentGraph-RAGapproximates at inference time, while the forced-answer fallback ensures bounded tool use and keeps generation aligned with the budgeted setting.

4 Experiments

4.1 Experimental Setup

We evaluate AgentGraph-RAG on three widely used multi-hop QA benchmarks: 2WikiMultiHopQA [17], HotpotQA [18], and MuSiQue [19]. These datasets cover complementary reasoning patterns, ranging from explicit compositional hops to distractor-heavy evidence synthesis. In particular, MuSiQue is useful for stress-testing retrieval control because many of its questions cannot be resolved from a single semantically similar passage. All experiments use the benchmark-associated document collections provided with each dataset, after preprocessing them into chunks, rather than an unrestricted web-scale index. We therefore study adaptive multi-hop retrieval in a controlled benchmark setting and do not claim that these results alone establish superiority under fully open-web retrieval.

We compare AgentGraph-RAG against two groups of baselines. The first group consists of *LLM Only* and *Vanilla RAG*, which measure the performance of standard prompting and single-shot retrieval. The second group includes stronger graph-based methods, namely LightRAG [4], HippoRAG2 [3], and LinearRAG [20]. These baselines represent graph-enhanced retrieval systems that do not employ the same graph-native action interface and adaptive control mechanism as AgentGraph-RAG. We report two evaluation metrics: *LLM Accuracy*, which uses an auxiliary judge model to determine whether a predicted answer is semantically correct, and *Contain Accuracy*, which checks whether the answer contains a normalized supporting fact. We report both because the former emphasizes semantic equivalence, whereas the latter is more sensitive to explicit support.

Unless otherwise stated, all generation-related components, including answer generation and LLM-as-judge evaluation, use `qwen3.5-flash` with temperature 0.0, while dense retrieval uses `qwen3-4B` embeddings. Within the controlled comparison set, we normalize the generation backend, embedding backend, and evaluation pipeline across methods whenever their design permits such standardization. The agent is limited to 15 tool iterations and a total budget of 128,000 tokens. Chunks are constructed with size 500 and overlap 50, and entity extraction is performed with spaCy `en_core_web_trf`. All experiments are run on a single NVIDIA RTX 4090. We also reviewed several recent graph-agent and multi-hop RAG systems from external reports, including GeAR, DAVIS, HiGraAgent, TAG, and RAG-RL [6,12–14,16]. However, because their reported setups are not fully aligned with our judge protocol, metric definitions, retrieval scope, or runtime budget, we do not include them in the main leaderboard. Accordingly, our strongest performance claim is restricted to the controlled comparison set evaluated in this paper.

5 Results and Analysis

5.1 Main Results

Table 1 presents the main results. Within the controlled comparison set, AgentGraph-RAG achieves the best performance on all three datasets under both evaluation metrics. Compared with LinearRAG, the strongest baseline in this setting, AgentGraph-RAG improves average LLM Accuracy from 79.9 to 87.2 and average Contain Accuracy from 86.7 to 95.8.

The improvement is especially pronounced on MuSiQue, where AgentGraph-RAG surpasses LinearRAG by 11.1 points in LLM Accuracy. Since MuSiQue is designed to reduce shortcutting through surface-level similarity, this gain suggests that the advantage of AgentGraph-RAG lies not only in stronger first-hop retrieval, but also in more effective control over subsequent evidence acquisition after an initial clue is identified. More broadly, the comparison highlights the distinct contributions of retrieval, graph structure, and adaptive control. Vanilla RAG improves over the bare LLM, confirming the value of external retrieval, while graph-enhanced baselines further demonstrate the benefit of structured memory for multi-hop reasoning. Building on these gains, AgentGraph-RAG delivers a further substantial improvement, indicating that graph structure alone is insufficient when retrieval remains passive or constrained to a limited interaction pattern.

Table 1. Main results on three multi-hop QA benchmarks. LLM = LLM Accuracy; Cont = Contain Accuracy.

Method	MuSiQue		2Wiki		HotpotQA		Average	
	LLM	Cont	LLM	Cont	LLM	Cont	LLM	Cont
Vanilla Baselines								
LLM Only	55.2	57.9	50.1	55.4	62.8	57.3	56.0	56.9
Vanilla RAG	62.9	69.0	63.8	71.1	75.2	71.9	67.3	70.7
Graph-Enhanced Retrieval								
LightRAG	58.2	63.1	77.4	74.9	71.6	74.6	69.1	70.9
HippoRAG2	65.7	74.2	82.8	**93.5**	88.3	**90.5**	78.9	86.1
LinearRAG	**68.3**	**79.7**	**86.0**	91.2	**85.5**	89.3	**79.9**	**86.7**
Agentic Graph Retrieval								
AgentGraph-RAG	79.4	95.3	89.5	98.8	92.6	93.3	87.2	95.8

5.2 Additional Baselines

To improve literature coverage beyond the controlled comparison set, we also review several additional graph-agent and multi-hop RAG systems from prior reports. Table 2 summarizes the most relevant methods and indicates whether they are directly comparable under our evaluation protocol. These additional baselines broaden literature coverage, but they also highlight an important limitation of cross-paper comparison: recently published systems often differ in datasets, metric definitions, judging pipelines, retrieval scope, or runtime budget. We therefore do not claim an unconditional head-to-head win over every published baseline. Instead, we make two narrower claims. First, AgentGraph-RAG is the strongest method within our controlled comparison set. Second, relative to these additional reported systems, AgentGraph-RAG remains numerically competitive while operating under an explicit budgeted control policy.

Table 2. Additional baselines from prior reports.

Method	Venue	Reported result	Comparable
GeAR [13]	Findings ACL 2025	>10% MuSiQue gain with lower token/iteration cost.	No
DAVIS [14]	Findings EMNLP 2025	Competitive multi-hop QA on HotpotQA and MuSiQue.	No
HiGraAgent [16]	Findings EACL 2026	85.3% average accuracy on HotpotQA, 2Wiki, and MuSiQue.	Partially
TAG [6]	Findings EACL 2026	Strong long-context multi-hop QA with 0.033% extra parameters.	No
RAG-RL [12]	Findings EACL 2026	Improved answer and citation accuracy under distractors.	No
AgentGraph-RAG (Ours)	This paper	87.2 average LLM Accuracy and 95.8 average Contain Accuracy under our protocol.	Yes

5.3 Ablation Studies

We next examine whether the gains of AgentGraph-RAG come from its memory design, its retrieval actions, or the interaction between the two. Table 3 isolates the contribution of the memory design by comparing the full model with two reduced variants: *semantic layer only* and *entity layer only*. Removing either layer leads to a substantial drop in performance, while the full dual-layer graph remains clearly best on both metrics.

Table 3. Ablation of the Dual-Layer Cognitive Graph (average across datasets).

Configuration	Avg. LLM	Avg. Cont
Full dual-layer graph	87.2	95.8
Semantic layer only	81.4	91.3
Entity layer only	78.1	87.8

This pattern is consistent with the intended division of labor between the two memory layers. The chunk layer provides high-recall semantic anchoring, especially in the early stage of reasoning when the agent must identify a plausible evidence chain, whereas the entity layer supports relational continuation once a useful intermediate entity has been surfaced. Removing either layer therefore breaks a key transition in the retrieval process: the agent can either retrieve broadly without a reliable mechanism for continuing the hop, or traverse entity relations without sufficient semantic grounding to start from the right context. Table 4 complements this analysis by ablating the retrieval action space one tool at a time. Among all tools, `graph_hop` is the most critical; removing it reduces average LLM Accuracy from 87.2 to 78.0. This finding suggests that the advantage of AgentGraph-RAG does not come merely from wrapping an agent loop around generic retrieval, but from providing an explicit relational action that allows the agent to continue an evidence chain rather than repeatedly restart retrieval from scratch.

Table 4. Tool-level ablation of the Hybrid Retrieval Action Space (average across datasets).

Configuration	Avg. LLM	Avg. Cont
Full AgentGraph-RAG	**87.2**	**95.8**
Remove `keyword_search`	83.7	92.6
Remove `semantic_search`	82.3	91.3
Remove `graph_hop`	78.0	88.2
Remove `read_chunk`	81.1	90.1

The remaining tools also make distinct contributions. Removing `semantic_search` hurts more than removing `keyword_search`, which is expected when the next clue is semantically related but not lexically explicit. Removing `read_chunk` also causes a large performance drop, indicating that compact search outputs are sufficient for planning but not for robust verification and answer grounding. Overall, the ablation results support the full combination of dual-layer memory and complementary retrieval actions, rather than a single stronger retriever or a single richer memory structure.

5.4 Interaction and Error Analysis

A key question is whether AgentGraph-RAG offers benefits beyond a simple combination of a graph index and a generic ReAct agent. Ablation results show that its performance stems from the interaction between the dual-layer graph memory and the controller. Removing `graph_hop` consistently degrades performance, while replacing the dual-layer memory with single-layer variants also reduces accuracy. These results indicate that neither graph memory nor agentic control alone is sufficient for effective multi-hop retrieval.

Inference operates under fixed iteration and token budgets. Lightweight retrieval actions support planning and exploration, whereas `read_chunk` is mainly used for evidence verification and answer grounding. The forced-answer fallback guarantees termination within the predefined budget. Although graph traversal currently relies on static co-occurrence-based neighbor ranking, the controller dynamically decides when graph exploration is required.

Trajectory analysis reveals three common failure modes: incorrect first-hop entity selection, traversal drift toward irrelevant neighbors, and premature answer generation from insufficient evidence. Future improvements may focus on more reliable entity anchoring, query-aware graph traversal, and stronger evidence verification before answer generation.

6 Discussion and Conclusion

We presented AgentGraph-RAG, a graph-native agentic RAG framework for multi-hop question answering. By coupling a Dual-Layer Cognitive Graph with a Hybrid Retrieval Action Space, AgentGraph-RAG enables an LLM controller to flexibly alternate among semantic grounding, relational exploration, and full-context verification during inference. Experiments on MuSiQue, 2WikiMulti-HopQA, and HotpotQA demonstrate consistent improvements over our controlled comparison set. Ablation studies further show that these gains arise from the interaction between the dual-layer graph memory and the retrieval controller, rather than from graph structure or agentic iteration alone. More broadly, our results suggest that multi-hop retrieval is better viewed as a sequential decision-making process over structured memory rather than simply ranking candidate passages. This perspective highlights the importance of combining a navigable memory representation with adaptive retrieval actions to support effective multi-hop reasoning.

Acknowledgment. This research was supported in part by the Beijing Natural Science Foundation under Grant 4262075, the Funds for Fundamental Research Funds for the Central Universities, University of International Relations under Grant 3262026T87, 3262026T23 and the Open Foundation of State key Laboratory of Networking and Switching Technology (Beijing University of Posts and Telecommunications)(SKLNST-2026-1-05).

References

1. Sarthi, P., Abdullah, S., Tuli, A., et al.: Raptor: recursive abstractive processing for tree-organized retrieval. In: Proceedings of the International Conference on Learning Representations (ICLR) (2024)
2. Edge, D., Trinh, H., Cheng, N.: From local to global: a graph rag approach to query-focused summarization. arXiv preprint arXiv:2404.16130 (2024)
3. Gutiérrez, B.J., Shu, Y., Gu, Y., et al.: HippoRAG: neurobiologically inspired long-term memory for large language models. In: Advances in Neural Information Processing Systems (NeurIPS), vol. 37 (2024)

4. Guo, Z., Xia, L., Yu, Y., et al.: LightRAG: simple and fast retrieval-augmented generation. arXiv preprint arXiv:2410.05779 (2024)
5. Yuntong, H., Lei, Z., Zhang, Z., Pan, B., Ling, C., Zhao, L.: GRAG: graph retrieval-augmented generation. In: Findings of the Association for Computational Linguistics: NAACL 2025, pp. 4145–4157 (2025)
6. Qing, P., Diao, X., Ma, C., Hassanpour, S., Vosoughi, S.: Tailoring memory granularity for multi-hop reasoning over long contexts. In: Findings of the Association for Computational Linguistics: EACL 2026, pp. 3648–3666 (2026)
7. Jiang, Z., et al.: Active retrieval augmented generation. In: Proceedings of the 2023 Conference on Empirical Methods in Natural Language Processing, pp. 7969–7992 (2023)
8. Trivedi, H., Balasubramanian, N., Khot, T., Sabharwal, A.: Interleaving retrieval with chain-of-thought reasoning for knowledge-intensive multi-step questions. In: Proceedings of the 61st Annual Meeting of the Association for Computational Linguistics (Volume 1: Long Papers), pp. 10014–10037 (2023)
9. Asai, A., Zeqiu, W., Wang, Y., Sil, A., Hajishirzi, H.: Self-RAG: learning to retrieve, generate, and critique through self-reflection. In: International Conference on Learning Representations 2024, pp. 9112–9141 (2024)
10. Liu, Y., et al.: RA-ISF: learning to answer and understand from retrieval augmentation via iterative self-feedback. In: Findings of the Association for Computational Linguistics: ACL 2024, pp. 4730–4749 (2024)
11. Hu, Y., Zhao, Y., Zhao, C., Cohan, A.: MCTS-RAG: enhancing retrieval-augmented generation with monte carlo tree search. arXiv preprint arXiv:2503.20757 (2025)
12. Huang, J., et al.: Tackling distractor documents in multi-hop QA with reinforcement and curriculum learning. In: Findings of the Association for Computational Linguistics: EACL 2026, pp. 5548–5561 (2026)
13. Shen, Z., et al.: Gear: graph-enhanced agent for retrieval-augmented generation. In: Findings of the Association for Computational Linguistics: ACL 2025, pp. 12049–12072 (2025)
14. Dinh, M.P., Syed, M., Yankoski, M.G., Ford, T.W.: DAVIS: Planning agent with knowledge graph-powered inner monologue. In: Findings of the Association for Computational Linguistics: EMNLP 2025, pp. 16490–16505 (2025)
15. Yao, S., et al.: React: synergizing reasoning and acting in language models. arXiv preprint arXiv:2210.03629 (2022)
16. Luu, H., Nguyen, L., Pham, T., Pham, H., Quan, T.: HiGraAgent: dual-agent adaptive reasoning over hierarchical knowledge graph for open domain multi-hop question answering. In: Findings of the Association for Computational Linguistics: EACL 2026, pp. 1193–1217 (2026)
17. Ho, X., Nguyen, A.K.D., Sugawara, S., Aizawa, A.: Constructing a multi-hop QA dataset for comprehensive evaluation of reasoning steps. In: Proceedings of the 28th International Conference on Computational Linguistics, pp. 6609–6625 (2020)
18. Yang, Z., et al.: HotpotQA: a dataset for diverse, explainable multi-hop question answering. In: Proceedings of the 2018 Conference on Empirical Methods in Natural Language Processing, pp. 2369–2380 (2018)
19. Trivedi, H., Balasubramanian, N., Khot, T., Sabharwal, A.: Musique: multihop questions via single-hop question composition. Trans. Assoc. Comput. Linguist. **10**, 539–554 (2022)
20. Zhuang, L., et al.: LinearRAG: linear graph retrieval augmented generation on large-scale corpora. arXiv preprint arXiv:2510.10114 (2025)

EviDS-KG: A Conflict-Aware Psychiatric Knowledge Graph Benchmark with Dempster–Shafer Evidence Representation

Kang Yao[1,2], Congcong Tian[3], Quanbo Cheng[1,2], Zhijie Ren[1,2], Weiwei Fu[2(✉)], and Jinjiang Cui[2]

[1] School of Biomedical Engineering (Suzhou), Division of Life Science and Medicine, University of Science and Technology of China, Suzhou, China
{yaokang,renzhijie}@mail.ustc.edu.cn,qbcheng@ustc.edu

[2] Suzhou Institute of Biomedical Engineering and Technology, Chinese Academy of Sciences, Suzhou, China
{fuww,cuijj}@sibet.ac.cn

[3] Faculty of Computing, Harbin Institute of Technology, Harbin, China
24b903119@stu.hit.edu.cn

Abstract. Psychiatric knowledge graphs (KGs) support retrieval, reasoning, and language-model augmentation, but their relations are often conditioned on population, comorbidity, temporality, dosage, outcome definition, and source quality. Binary triples and scalar confidence scores hide whether uncertainty comes from missing evidence, weak applicability, or direct disagreement. We introduce EviDS-KG, a conflict-aware psychiatric KG benchmark whose atomic unit is a qualified evidence bucket with Dempster–Shafer (DS) support, opposition, ignorance, and conflict. The benchmark release contains 1,532 entities, 18 relations, 30,052 reviewed buckets, 32,567 source-linked snippets, 60,104 type-constrained negatives, 2,721 conflict-NLI pairs, and 14,998 Chinese colloquial utterances. It supports link prediction, conflict NLI, edge calibration, and colloquial retrieval. Experiments show that graph-structured and path-oriented link predictors reach MRR 0.704, outperforming classical KGE baselines whose best MRR is 0.149; DS features achieve the strongest conflict-NLI macro-F1 of 0.843 among evaluated baselines; and EviDS-KG+DSIR achieves the best calibration Brier score (0.20879), with a matched-K audit reducing a simple evidence-presence shortcut. Together, the results show strong gains in link prediction, conflict NLI, and calibration, with competitive colloquial retrieval performance.

Keywords: Knowledge graph benchmark · psychiatric NLP · evidence theory

1 Introduction

Knowledge graphs organize biomedical entities and support retrieval, reasoning, and language-model augmentation. Most KG benchmarks treat a triple as

L. Ding et al. (Eds.): APWeb-WAIM 2026, LNCS 16995, pp. 343–354, 2027.
https://doi.org/10.1007/978-981-92-5699-0_22

observed, hidden, or negative. This abstraction is useful for factual relations but brittle for psychiatric knowledge: *treats*, *worsens*, *associated-with*, and *contraindicates* may change with population, phase, comorbidity, dosage, endpoint, temporality, and study design.

Existing biomedical KGs and uncertain KGE methods provide coverage and ranking machinery, but they usually compress evidence into a binary edge or a scalar plausibility score. A single score cannot distinguish unreviewed ignorance, weak applicability, and direct opposition from reliable sources. These states require different actions, making psychiatric KG evaluation a benchmark-design problem as much as a model-design problem.

To address this gap, we propose EviDS-KG. Each qualified edge bucket stores a DS mass vector over the binary frame $\Theta = \{+, -\}$:

$$(m_+, m_-, m_\Theta, K),$$

where m_+ is support, m_- is opposition, m_Θ is unresolved mass, and K is the conflict coefficient accumulated during fusion. The benchmark also exposes belief $\mathrm{Bel} = m_+$, plausibility $\mathrm{Pl} = m_+ + m_\Theta$, and pignistic probability $\mathrm{BetP} = m_+ + 0.5m_\Theta$. The central idea is simple: psychiatric KG evaluation should preserve the evidence state that produces an edge label instead of hiding it inside scalar confidence. Figure 1 illustrates the shift.

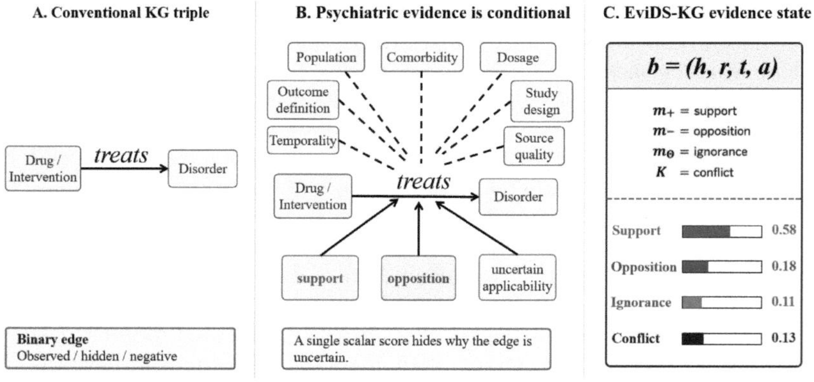

Fig. 1. Psychiatric KG evidence states. A binary KG edge hides whether uncertainty comes from missing evidence, conditional applicability, or direct opposition; EviDS-KG keeps these states explicit.

The paper follows the standard benchmark line: define the evidence unit, construct a controlled benchmark release, and evaluate whether common model families can exploit the preserved evidence state. Our contributions are as follows.

1. We introduce EviDS-KG, a psychiatric KG benchmark with DS-native qualified edge buckets, source-linked evidence, and explicit support, opposition, ignorance, and conflict.

2. We provide a reproducible construction protocol and four tasks: link prediction, conflict NLI, edge-evidence calibration, and colloquial-to-clinical retrieval.
3. We report broad baselines, the DSIR calibrator, and a matched-K audit showing that calibration gains come from reviewed evidence states rather than a trivial evidence-availability cue.

2 Related Work

Biomedical KGs such as UMLS [2], Hetionet [11], PrimeKG [4], and mental-health KGs [22] organize entities and relations at scale. Uncertain and geometric KGE methods, including KG2E [10], UKGE [5], and BoxE [1], model plausibility or uncertainty. Their outputs remain mostly binary, categorical, or scalar. EviDS-KG instead makes polarity, applicability, provenance independence, and conflict coefficients part of the evaluation target.

Dempster–Shafer theory [6,14] and transferable belief models [15] store mass on support, opposition, and the unresolved frame. Truth-discovery methods and knowledge vaults aggregate noisy claims [7,20], and LLMs reduce KG candidate-generation cost [23]. In psychiatry, disagreement is often conditional evidence rather than noise, so EviDS-KG keeps source anchoring, applicability, and conflict as audited fields.

Calibration methods such as temperature scaling, Platt scaling, and isotonic regression [8,12,21] repair scalar probabilities after training. Clinical evidence frameworks [9] motivate our quality, applicability, and inconsistency reporting.

3 Benchmark Design

3.1 Problem Setting

Let $\mathcal{E}$ be psychiatric entities and $\mathcal{R}$ be evidence-sensitive relations. Instead of evaluating only triples (h, r, t), EviDS-KG evaluates qualified buckets

$$b = (h, r, t, \mathbf{a}),$$

where $\mathbf{a}$ records population, condition, temporality, outcome, and source context. Bucket b has reviewed evidence items $\mathcal{S}_b = \{s_1, \ldots, s_n\}$; each item stores a source-linked snippet, polarity in $\{+, -, ?\}$, reliability discount, provenance identifier, and uncertainty reason. Labels are curated release labels, not claims of clinical truth.

The qualifier vector is part of the identifier, not auxiliary metadata. Two buckets with the same (h, r, t) but different population or endpoint qualifiers are evaluated separately, because psychiatric evidence may support one qualified claim and oppose another. This also makes abstention meaningful for under-specified or out-of-scope buckets.

3.2 Evidence Buckets

The bucket design keeps a candidate relation and its applicability conditions together. Evidence items are source-linked snippets or terminology-derived statements, discounted by source design, population match, endpoint clarity, and textual certainty. Figure 2 connects qualifiers, evidence items, provenance de-duplication, and DS fusion.

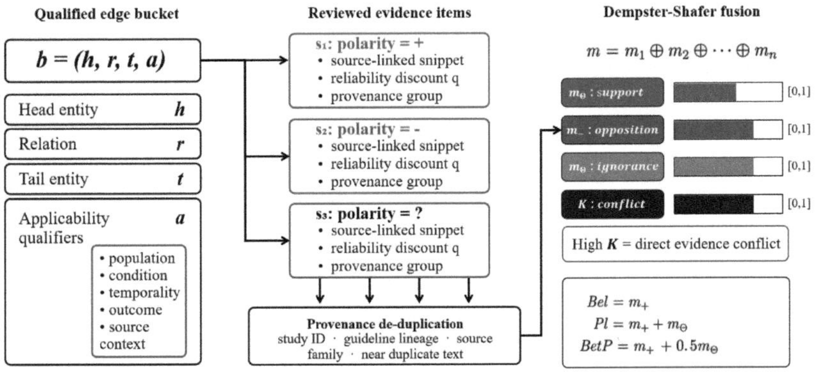

Fig. 2. DS-native evidence bucket. A qualified edge bucket groups reviewed evidence items, de-duplicates provenance, and fuses the resulting masses into support, opposition, ignorance, and conflict.

With reliability q, a positive item assigns q to $\{+\}$ and $1-q$ to Θ; an opposing item does the same for $\{-\}$; unresolved evidence assigns mass to Θ. Provenance groups define the units that enter DS fusion. Dependence is determined by source family, study identifier, guideline lineage, citation ancestry, and documented reuse; near-duplicate text is used only as a cue for checking provenance, not as a stand-alone merge rule.

Polarity and reliability are annotated independently. A reliable source may still contribute mainly to ignorance if its population, dosage, or outcome mismatches the bucket; conversely, a weaker source can contribute directional support with larger residual mass on Θ. This prevents weak applicability from being mistaken for weak truth.

3.3 Dempster Fusion

For two basic probability assignments m_1 and m_2 on $\Theta = \{+, -\}$, Dempster's rule is

$$(m_1 \oplus m_2)(A) = \frac{1}{1-K} \sum_{B \cap C = A} m_1(B) m_2(C), \quad A \neq \emptyset. \tag{1}$$

Here $K = \sum_{B \cap C = \emptyset} m_1(B) m_2(C)$ denotes the conflict coefficient. We retain K as a benchmark field instead of absorbing it into a scalar confidence. High-conflict buckets remain visible to downstream tasks.

3.4 Mass Assignment and Provenance Discounting

Mass assignment is rule-governed and independent of test labels. Source types receive reliability priors, discounted toward m_Θ when population, condition, temporality, or endpoint only partly matches the target bucket. Weak applicability therefore becomes ignorance rather than weak support. Correlated items are merged within provenance groups before fusion, while separately sourced near-duplicates remain distinct groups. Released fields keep item masses, group identifiers, fused state, and discount reasons for inspection or replacement.

3.5 Construction Workflow

Figure 3 summarizes the construction pipeline. Ontology seeds and relation schemas are expanded into candidates; reviewed evidence is source-anchored, grouped by provenance, assigned DS masses, and exported to tasks. Candidate generation is separated from evidence commitment: a bucket enters the reviewed release only after entity normalization, relation checking, source anchoring, polarity review, and provenance grouping. The same bucket identifiers are reused across link prediction, NLI, calibration, and retrieval .

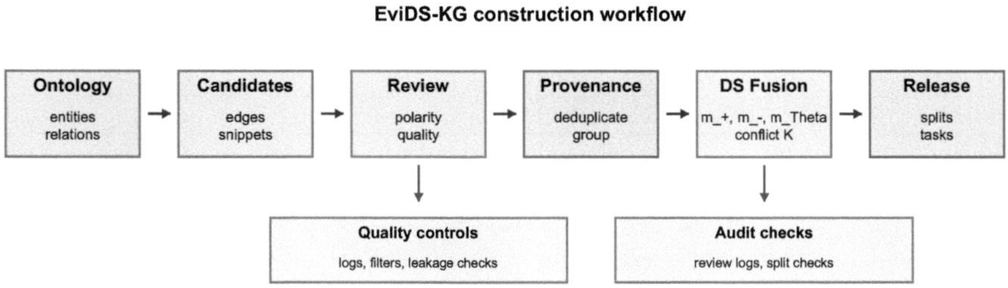

Fig. 3. EviDS-KG construction workflow. The workflow shows where expert review, provenance grouping, DS fusion, split control, and benchmark tasks enter the release pipeline.

3.6 Expert Review and Release Boundary

Reviewers record polarity, applicability, source quality, and uncertainty reasons while blind to model predictions and split membership. Negative triples are type-constrained corruptions screened against known positives, near-duplicate evidence, and expert-plausible alternatives. Adjudication focuses on disagreements that change the DS state, such as polarity conflict, population mismatch, endpoint mismatch, temporality mismatch, and source-quality disagreement.

3.7 Annotation Cost, Scalability, and Reproducibility

Expert review is the main cost. A two-pass workflow checks source fit, entity span, relation type, polarity, and disputed qualifiers; logs store decision reasons such as insufficient evidence, population mismatch, outcome mismatch, and direct opposition. Automated candidate generation, near-duplicate detection, and source grouping provide scale, while polarity, applicability, and reliability remain expert-reviewed.

3.8 Split and Shortcut Controls

The split protocol reduces shortcut learning. Link-prediction splits are relation-stratified and filtered against known reviewed buckets; NLI examples hide label-encoding metadata; near-duplicate templates do not cross partitions; retrieval uses entity-level separation where possible; and calibration negatives are type-compatible and screened against plausible positives. Empty-evidence indicators and conflict-K values are audit variables, not hidden leakage channels (Tables 1, 2, 4 and 5).

Table 1. EviDS-KG benchmark scale and split statistics. Supported and opposing bucket counts partition the reviewed edge buckets; conflict buckets report an orthogonal diagnostic subset where reviewed evidence contains both support and opposition.

Component	Count	Role in the benchmark
Entities	1,532	Disorders, symptoms, drugs, interventions, populations, outcomes
Relations	18	Psychiatric and evidence-sensitive relation types
Evidence snippets	32,567	Source-linked evidence sentences or statements
Supported buckets	27,928	Buckets with net support under reviewed evidence
Opposing buckets	2,124	Reviewed buckets with explicit negative/opposing evidence
Conflict buckets	2,602	Orthogonal diagnostic subset with support–opposition evidence
Type-constrained negatives	60,104	Plausible evaluation corruptions
NLI sentence pairs	2,721	Support / conditional-conflict / opposition diagnostics
Chinese colloquial utterances	14,998	Consultation-to-clinical retrieval queries
Reviewed LP split	21,038 / 4,507 / 4,507	
Negative LP split	42,072 / 9,015 / 9,017	
Average conflict K	0.038	
Average ignorance m_Θ	0.317	

Table 2. Benchmark tasks and the evidence property each task is designed to probe.

Task	Prediction target	Evidence-specific question
Link prediction	Rank missing heads or tails for psychiatric triples	Does the graph require multi-hop reasoning beyond local KGE geometry?
Conflict NLI	Classify evidence-pair relation as support, conditional conflict, or opposition	Do text models recover evidence direction rather than only lexical similarity?
Edge calibration	Estimate reviewed-bucket probability for a candidate edge	Does conflict-stratified calibration change probability estimates relative to scalar post-hoc maps?
Colloquial retrieval	Map Chinese consultation utterances to clinical concepts	Do evidence features help bridge informal user language and curated concepts?

4 Benchmark Tasks

EviDS-KG exposes four tasks over the same evidence release. They share dictionaries, relation schemas, provenance groups, and split identifiers, while testing ranking, evidence direction, calibration, and concept access.

Link prediction. Given a query $(h, r, ?, \mathbf{a})$ or $(?, r, t, \mathbf{a})$, a model ranks type-compatible candidate entities from $\mathcal{E}$. Evaluation uses filtered MR, MRR, and Hits@k after removing other known reviewed edge buckets. DS masses are optional attributes, so the split also supports standard KGE and GNN baselines.

Conflict NLI. Given two source-linked evidence sentences (u, v), the model predicts $y \in \{\text{support}, \text{conditional conflict}, \text{opposition}\}$. Structured metadata that directly encodes the label is hidden. The task is diagnostic: it tests whether models recover evidence direction and conditionality rather than only surface similarity.

Edge-evidence calibration. Given a bucket b, optional DS variables, and a backbone score s_b, the model outputs $\hat{p}_b \in [0, 1]$, a calibrated probability that b belongs to the reviewed evidence release rather than to a type-constrained corruption set. This probability is calibrated to benchmark labels, not to medical ground truth.

Conflict-stratified DSIR. For edge calibration we include DSIR, a validation-fixed DS-aware calibrator. It fits a global isotonic map g and local maps g_j in conflict buckets induced by K; a test example in bucket j uses $\hat{p}_i =$

$(1 - \lambda_j)g_j(x_i) + \lambda_j g(x_i)$ with $\lambda_j = \exp(-n_j/n_0)$. Sparse buckets replace g_j by their empirical prior. All thresholds and shrinkage constants are fixed before test evaluation.

Colloquial-to-clinical retrieval. Given a Chinese colloquial consultation utterance z, the model ranks clinical concepts from the KG dictionary. Relevance labels are curated concept mappings, and multiple concepts may be correct. The task tests whether evidence-aware representations bridge everyday descriptions and curated clinical concepts.

5 Experiments

Following APWeb-WAIM benchmark style, we ask four RQs: **RQ1** whether standard KGE solves link prediction or multi-hop reasoning is needed; **RQ2** whether DS variables improve support/conflict/ opposition recognition; **RQ3** whether conflict-aware evidence improves calibration; and **RQ4** whether the resource supports Chinese colloquial-to-clinical retrieval.

All results use the fixed split files in Sect. 3. Link prediction is filtered against known reviewed buckets, NLI models do not receive label-encoding metadata, and calibration baselines are evaluated against expert-reviewed release labels.

5.1 Evaluation Protocol

The baseline suite covers translational, bilinear, complex-valued, rotational, uncertain, and box-based models [1,3,5,10,16,17,19]. We also include graph/path reasoning methods [13,18,24]. Link prediction uses filtered MR, MRR, Hits@1, and Hits@10; conflict NLI uses macro-F1 and accuracy; calibration uses ECE and Brier score; and retrieval uses NDCG, Hit@k, and MRR. We use paired bootstrap for close comparisons, and $\pm$ denotes repeated-run standard deviation. In the matched-K audit, corruption negatives receive relation-matched pseudo conflict-K values, preventing evidence absence from acting as a negative shortcut (Fig. 4).

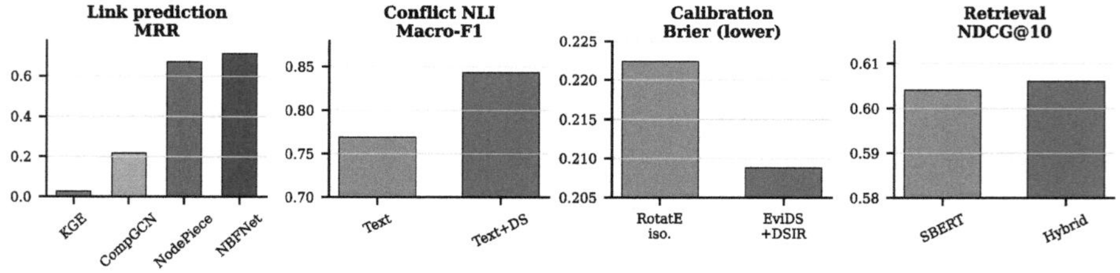

Fig. 4. Compact view of the main experimental signals. The panels summarize the link-prediction, conflict-NLI, calibration, and retrieval trends reported in Tables 3–6.

Table 3. Filtered link-prediction baselines on EviDS-KG. Values are mean±std over three seeds. Graph-structured and path-oriented models outperform classical KGE baselines, indicating that this split stresses relational context beyond local pairwise embedding geometry.

Model	MR↓	MRR↑	H@1↑	H@10↑
TransE	78.4±3.6	0.1042±0.0041	0.0526±0.0027	0.2018±0.0074
DistMult	91.7±4.9	0.0925±0.0038	0.0451±0.0025	0.1846±0.0069
ComplEx	84.3±4.2	0.1127±0.0045	0.0589±0.0030	0.2145±0.0078
RotatE	69.8±3.1	0.1368±0.0052	0.0754±0.0035	0.2517±0.0086
KG2E	80.6±3.8	0.1084±0.0040	0.0558±0.0028	0.2072±0.0071
UKGE	76.9±3.5	0.1186±0.0046	0.0632±0.0031	0.2264±0.0080
BoxE	66.5±2.9	0.1493±0.0055	0.0831±0.0037	0.2678±0.0089
CompGCN	126.4±18.2	0.2317±0.0453	0.2049±0.0478	0.3042±0.0421
NodePiece	34.8±4.5	0.6526±0.0278	0.6314±0.0310	0.7165±0.0246
NBFNet	39.6±7.9	**0.7041±0.0349**	**0.6682±0.0425**	**0.8276±0.0204**

5.2 Link Prediction

Answer to RQ1. Table 3 shows a clear separation. Classical KGE methods now reach up to MRR 0.1493 with BoxE, while CompGCN improves further and NodePiece and NBFNet reach much higher MRRs. NBFNet obtains the best MRR 0.7041 ± 0.0349 and Hits@10 0.8276 ± 0.0204. These results suggest that EviDS-KG is difficult for local pairwise geometry alone and rewards models that exploit richer graph structure or path-oriented relational context.

Table 4. Conflict NLI diagnostic. The majority-class row is deterministic and is reported as a single value; learned models report mean±std. Adding DS features gives the best macro-F1 in this split.

Method	Macro-F1	Accuracy
Majority class	0.267	0.670
TF-IDF + logistic regression	0.766±0.037	0.835±0.009
Char-CNN NLI	0.700±0.031	0.845±0.007
RoBERTa-wwm + MLP	0.769±0.048	0.869±0.006
Focal-RoBERTa	0.753±0.046	0.844±0.015
RoBERTa + DS features	**0.843±0.008**	**0.880±0.009**

Table 5. Chinese colloquial-to-clinical concept retrieval. The hybrid evidence-aware representation leads on NDCG@1, NDCG@10, Hit@1, and MRR, while SBERT gives the highest Hit@10.

Method	NDCG@1	NDCG@10	Hit@1	Hit@10	MRR
BM25 char n-gram	0.222±0.079	0.418±0.056	0.222±0.079	0.671±0.036	0.365±0.061
Char-CNN dense	0.056±0.011	0.296±0.011	0.056±0.011	0.662±0.007	0.212±0.013
SBERT multilingual	0.384±0.043	0.604±0.037	0.384±0.043	**0.880±0.035**	0.529±0.038
RoBERTa-wwm zero-shot	0.185±0.013	0.411±0.027	0.185±0.013	0.727±0.056	0.336±0.015
EviDS-KG hybrid	**0.394±0.029**	**0.606±0.030**	**0.394±0.029**	0.870±0.036	**0.535±0.030**

5.3 Conflict NLI and Retrieval

Answer to RQ2. RoBERTa plus DS features reaches the best macro-F1 0.843 ± 0.008 and accuracy 0.880 ± 0.009. Paired bootstrap confirms the accuracy gain (95% CI [0.002, 0.019], p=0.0136), showing that DS states sharpen evidence-direction recognition.

Answer to RQ4. The hybrid evidence-aware representation is best on NDCG@1, NDCG@10, Hit@1, and MRR, while SBERT remains best on Hit@10. Bootstrap intervals against SBERT cross zero for NDCG@10 and Hit@1, indicating a competitive retrieval signal.

Table 6. Edge-evidence calibration with reliability audit. Values are mean±std over five seeds; ±<1e−4 marks nonzero variation below display precision. The matched-K row assigns corruption negatives relation-matched pseudo K values.

Method	ECE↓	Brier↓
Evidence-type prior	0.48334±<1e−4	0.23417±<1e−4
RotatE + temperature scaling	0.02142±0.00488	0.22296±0.00016
RotatE + isotonic regression	0.00686±0.00217	0.22238±0.00012
RotatE + Platt scaling	0.00237±0.00143	0.22217±<1e−4
Focal calibration	0.02406±0.00448	0.22320±0.00024
EviDS-KG+DSIR (default)	**0.00143±0.00060**	**0.20879±0.00012**
RotatE+DSIR (matched-K audit)	0.00685±0.00188	0.22264±0.00022

5.4 Edge-evidence Calibration

Answer to RQ3. Reviewed buckets carry evidence states and type-constrained corruptions serve as hard non-reviewed candidates. Scalar post-hoc maps on RotatE cluster around Brier 0.222; EviDS-KG+DSIR reaches 0.20879 ± 0.00012, the best score in Table 6. Paired bootstrap against RotatE isotonic regression gives CI $[-0.0143, -0.0129]$ with $p<0.001$. In the matched-K audit, a RotatE+DSIR variant returns Brier 0.22264 ± 0.00022, showing that the gain comes from reviewed evidence states plus conflict-stratified mapping.

5.5 Leakage and Shortcut Controls

Conflict-aware resources are vulnerable to metadata, evidence-presence, source duplication, and easy negatives. EviDS-KG hides label fields, groups evidence by source lineage, and screens corruptions. Models are rewarded for using reviewed evidence states, not for memorizing metadata.

6 Discussion, Limitations, and Ethics

EviDS-KG establishes an evidence protocol for psychiatric KG evaluation. Preserving DS states separates local KGE from multi-hop reasoning, improves NLI evidence-direction labels, and gives the DSIR calibrator the best reliability on reviewed buckets. Each bucket links snippets, provenance groups, qualifiers, and a DS state, so uncertainty becomes an auditable signal rather than a hidden failure mode.

The release boundary is explicit: labels are curated release labels, missing triples may still be true, and negatives are screened evaluation alternatives. The matched-K audit separates genuine evidence-state utility from generic calibration. LLMs are used only for candidate generation, private patient records are excluded, and clinical deployment requires independent validation.

7 Conclusion

We introduced EviDS-KG, a DS-native psychiatric KG benchmark that preserves support, opposition, ignorance, and conflict on qualified edge buckets. The release turns psychiatric evidence into a reproducible evaluation object by tying each label to qualifiers, source-linked snippets, provenance groups, DS masses, and shortcut controls. Across four tasks, explicit evidence states support more auditable psychiatric KG evaluation than scalar triple confidence alone.

The results also show where progress matters: local KGE geometry is not enough, multi-hop paths are valuable, DS features sharpen evidence direction, and DSIR improves reliability when conflict is preserved. EviDS-KG therefore provides a useful testbed for psychiatric KG reasoning, evidence-aware retrieval, and trustworthy clinical NLP.

References

1. Abboud, R., Ceylan, I., Lukasiewicz, T., Salvatori, T.: Boxe: A box embedding model for knowledge base completion. In: NeurIPS (2020)
2. Bodenreider, O.: The Unified Medical Language System (UMLS): integrating biomedical terminology. Nucleic Acids Res. **32**(suppl_1), D267–D270 (2004)
3. Bordes, A., Usunier, N., García-Durán, A., Weston, J., Yakhnenko, O.: Translating embeddings for modeling multi-relational data. In: NeurIPS (2013)
4. Chandak, P., Huang, K., Zitnik, M.: Building a knowledge graph to enable precision medicine. Nat. Sci. Data **10** (2023)
5. Chen, X., Chen, M., Shi, W., Sun, Y., Zaniolo, C.: Embedding uncertain knowledge graphs. In: AAAI (2019)
6. Dempster, A.P.: Upper and lower probabilities induced by a multivalued mapping. Ann. Math. Stat. **38**(2), 325–339 (1967)
7. Dong, X.: Knowledge vault: a web-scale approach to probabilistic knowledge fusion. In: KDD (2014)
8. Guo, C., Pleiss, G., Sun, Y., Weinberger, K.Q.: On calibration of modern neural networks. In: ICML (2017)
9. Guyatt, G.H., et al.: GRADE: an emerging consensus on rating quality of evidence and strength of recommendations. BMJ **336**, 924–926 (2008)
10. He, S., Liu, K., Ji, G., Zhao, J.: Learning to represent knowledge graphs with Gaussian embedding. In: CIKM (2015)
11. Himmelstein, D.S., Lizee, A., Hessler, C., et al.: Systematic integration of biomedical knowledge prioritizes drugs for repurposing. eLife **6** (2017)
12. Platt, J.: Probabilistic outputs for support vector machines and comparisons to regularized likelihood methods. In: Advances in Large Margin Classifiers (1999)
13. Schlichtkrull, M., Kipf, T., Bloem, P., van den Berg, R., Titov, I., Welling, M.: Modeling relational data with graph convolutional networks. In: ESWC (2018)
14. Shafer, G.: A Mathematical Theory of Evidence. Princeton University Press (1976)
15. Smets, P.: The combination of evidence in the transferable belief model. IEEE Trans. Pattern Anal. Mach. Intell. **12**(5), 447–458 (1990)
16. Sun, Z., Deng, Z.H., Nie, J.Y., Tang, J.: Rotate: Knowledge graph embedding by relational rotation in complex space. In: ICLR (2019)
17. Trouillon, T.: Complex embeddings for simple link prediction. In: ICML (2016)
18. Vashishth, S., Sanyal, S., Nitin, V., Talukdar, P.: Composition-based multi-relational graph convolutional networks. In: ICLR (2020)
19. Yang, B., Yih, S.W.T., He, X., Gao, J., Deng, L.: Embedding entities and relations for learning and inference in knowledge bases. In: ICLR (2015)
20. Yin, X., Han, J., Yu, P.S.: Truth discovery with multiple conflicting information providers on the web. IEEE TKDE (2008)
21. Zadrozny, B., Elkan, C.: Obtaining calibrated probability estimates from decision trees and naive Bayesian classifiers. In: ICML (2001)
22. Zhang, Y.: A context-aware knowledge graph for mental disorders with millions of relationships. Nat. Commun. (2023)
23. Zhu, Y.: LLMS as knowledge graph builders: a survey. IEEE TKDE (2024)
24. Zhu, Z., Zhang, Z., Xhonneux, L.P., Tang, J.: Neural bellman-ford networks: a general graph neural network framework for link prediction. In: NeurIPS (2021)

Diagnosing Override Regimes in Multi-hop RAG Choosers: Decision-Relevant AUC and Rescue-Hurt Geometry

Qihui Li[1(✉)], Haodong Lu[1], and Ruixin Kang[2]

[1] Nanyang Technological University, Singapore, Singapore
{E250069,HAODONG003}@e.ntu.edu.sg
[2] Xiamen University Malaysia, Sepang, Malaysia
ait2109086@xmu.edu.my

Abstract. RAG *chooser* architectures routinely report healthy out-of-fold (OOF) discrimination on *is-this-candidate-correct?*, yet exhibit a *chooser-EM plateau*: ranking signal fails to convert into top-1 exact-match (EM) gains over a strong default expert. This is a diagnostic study of why. On a learning-to-defer override pipeline with five feature groups on 2WikiMultihopQA with a Qwen3-8B backbone (n=1000) we introduce a *decision-relevant-AUC* metric and a *rescue-hurt geometry.* We use the pipeline as a diagnostic probe rather than as a proposed new chooser; the three findings below characterise when override-style evaluation is deployable. **(1) Decision-relevant signal collapse**: on rescue-vs-hurt rows decision-AUC is near random (0.575, bootstrap 95% CI $[0.49, 0.66]$, straddling chance) while aggregate OOF AUC is a misleadingly healthy 0.72; the rescue: hurt asymmetry (63:119) imposes a negative structural ceiling, and the headline ΔEM is 0.0 pp ($[+0.0, +0.7]$). **(2) Evidence features are non-contributory**: a drop-one ablation shows only answer/query-shape features carry the OOF signal; dropping NLI, Dempster-Shafer cross-support, support, or witness agreement *raises* AUC. **(3) No headroom under shared context**: two external judges given both cells' top-5 passages (no gold) – DeepSeek-V3 (ΔEM $= -1.4$ pp) and GPT-4o (-0.1 pp, overrides balanced 40:41) – both fail the pre-committed deployment bar, with a k=5 self-consistency arm ruling out a single-shot artefact. A Mistral cross-backbone slice shows the same diagnostic also *identifies* a deployable retrieval-aligned regime (decision-AUC 0.92, +3.0 pp at 13% override). We recommend override-style RAG chooser evaluations report decision-relevant AUC and rescue-vs-hurt geometry alongside standard ranking metrics.

Keywords: multi-hop question answering · retrieval-augmented generation · selective prediction · learning to defer · Dempster-Shafer · evaluation protocol · deployment diagnostics

L. Ding et al. (Eds.): APWeb-WAIM 2026, LNCS 16995, pp. 355–368, 2027.
https://doi.org/10.1007/978-981-92-5699-0_23

1 Introduction

Multi-hop question answering with retrieval-augmented generation (RAG) often produces several plausible candidate answers from distinct pipeline configurations – different retrieval strategies, different aggregation rules, different numbers of hops. A common next step in both research [12,17] and production is to train a *chooser*: a learned controller that looks at side-channel evidence (passage-level NLI, retrieval support, cross-retriever belief, backbone agreement) and selects one candidate per question. The chooser is then evaluated on exact match (EM) against the strongest single-pipeline baseline.

A recurring pattern is that chooser OOF AUC on is-this-candidate-correct? is healthy (≥ 0.7) while the resulting chooser-EM barely exceeds the best-single-cell default, commonly read as a signal that the chooser is *almost* working and needs richer features, a stronger model, or more data.

In this paper we argue that this interpretation is structurally mistaken for the class of override-style RAG choosers we study. We adopt the learning-to-defer framing of Mozannar and Sontag [12]: we fix the strongest single expert as the *default*, we designate one or more weaker experts as *challengers*, and we learn a binary gate that decides, per-question, whether to override the default with the challenger. On 2WikiMultihopQA with a Qwen3-8B backbone and three candidate cells drawn from a controlled retrieval matrix, we run a pre-committed evaluation of this architecture with 19 features spanning five conceptual groups: answer/query shape, retrieval support, NLI-based evidence, Dempster-Shafer cross-support between retrievers [4], and witness-cell agreement. We then audit the result from four angles: all three decision pairs in the 3×2 cell matrix, a drop-one feature-group ablation, a calibration / risk-coverage analysis, and a multi-seed + bootstrap CI pass on the headline number.

Contributions. Our contributions are diagnostic:

1. **Decision-relevant signal collapse.** We identify a sharp divergence between candidate-level OOF AUC (the popular diagnostic, 0.72–0.78 across three pairs) and *decision-relevant AUC* restricted to rescue-vs-hurt rows (0.55–0.66), the only rows that change the EM. On the main pair the rescue pool (63) is smaller than the hurt pool (119), imposing a negative structural ceiling independent of the gate's modelling choices.
2. **Evidence features are non-contributory in the override decision.** A drop-one ablation shows only answer/query shape carries the OOF signal (-17 AUC points when dropped); dropping NLI, support, DS cross-support, or witness-agreement *raises* OOF AUC. The null is tight across five CV seeds and a 1000-sample paired bootstrap (ΔEM 95% CI $[+0.0, +0.7]$ pp), with no risk-coverage operating point – including an in-sample-optimistic oracle – beating the default.
3. **No headroom under shared context.** Two external judges on the same holdout, given both cells' top-5 passages but no gold, both fail to clear the pre-committed deployment bar: DeepSeek-V3 yields ΔEM $= -1.4$ pp (95%

CI $[-3.2, +0.5]$) and GPT-4o yields ΔEM $= -0.1$ pp ($[-1.8, +1.6]$, overrides balanced 40:41); a k=5 self-consistency arm confirms this is not a single-shot artefact. Under this retrieved context even stronger external judges extract no deployable headroom, consistent with the feature-side diagnostics in (1) and (2). A Mistral-7B slice provides the positive counterpart: decision-relevant AUC is high (0.924) and a corridor-constrained threshold yields +3.0 pp at 13% override rate, showing the same diagnostics separate deployable and non-deployable regimes.

The rest of the paper is organised as follows. Section 2 fixes the evaluation protocol, the cell matrix, the override architecture, and the feature schema. Section 3 establishes the OOF-vs-decision-AUC split (contribution 1). Section 4 runs the drop-one feature-group ablation (contribution 2). Section 5 quantifies the tightness of the null using multi-seed, bootstrap, and risk-coverage analyses. Section 6 reports the judge-oracle arm; Sects. 7–8 test regime separation. Section 9 positions the results against the RAG-chooser and selective-prediction literature.

Positioning. Override-style RAG choosers descend from side-channel correctness predictors (Self-RAG [1], CRAG [17]) and from the learning-to-defer line of Madras et al. [11] and Mozannar and Sontag [12]; our analysis tools build on standard calibration [6] and selective-prediction [5] diagnostics. Unlike that work, we ask not whether a chooser ranks candidates well but whether its ranking lies on the *outcome-changing* rows; §9 details the comparison.

2 Setup

2.1 Benchmark and Backbone

All experiments in the main body are on 2WikiMultihopQA [7] dev split, $n = 1000$ held-out questions drawn once and frozen for the entire study. The backbone is Qwen3-8B (`Qwen/Qwen3-8B`), an 8B-scale Qwen instruction-tuned model wired through an IRCoT-style multi-hop loop [14]. Retrieval is BM25 over the 2Wiki corpus with a holdout v3 bucketing to prevent query-passage contamination across splits.

2.2 Candidate Cells

We fix three candidate cells from a retrieval–aggregation matrix, sharing retriever and generator but differing in the fusion rule and the commit-control rule; their per-cell EM on the frozen $n = 1000$ holdout is in Table 1, with G the strongest (the default in our main pair).

The oracle rows give a hard upper bound on any chooser that picks one of C, D, G per question.

Table 1. Per-cell EM and coverage on 2Wiki-Qwen $n = 1000$. Cell G is the default in the main override pair.

Cell	n	Coverage	EM_{all}	$\text{EM}_{\text{covered}}$
C (DS-fusion + conflict-gate)	1000	1.000	0.315	0.315
D (concat-fusion + conflict-gate)	1000	0.998	0.363	0.364
G (concat-fusion + fixed-default control)	1000	0.999	0.371	0.371
Oracle $\{C, D, G\}$	1000	–	0.441	–
Oracle $\{C, G\}$	1000	–	0.434	–

2.3 Override Architecture

Following Mozannar and Sontag [12] we adopt an asymmetric learning-to-defer formulation:

$$\hat{y}(x) = \begin{cases} \text{challenger}(x) & \text{if } s(x) \geq \tau^\star \\ \text{default}(x) & \text{otherwise} \end{cases}, \tag{1}$$

where $s(x) \in [0, 1]$ is a learned override score and $\tau^\star$ a scalar threshold: the default is kept unless $s(x) \geq \tau^\star$. Unlike a symmetric arg max-over-k chooser, this has a designated default and an asymmetric loss surface.

Protocol. We train the gate only on disagreement rows (challenger $\neq$ default after normalisation; ties are trivially label-0). $\tau^\star$ is selected by sweeping all unique *OOF* scores (plus an above-max sentinel) on the full $n = 1000$ hold-out – ties included – so a deployable gate must show its gain on the whole set; we break ties toward the highest τ (fire as rarely as possible). OOF scores drive both AUC and $\tau^\star$; in-fold and full-fit scores never. A configuration "passes" iff (a) $\Delta\text{EM} \geq 1.5\,\text{pp}$, (b) paired McNemar $p < 0.05$, and (c) override rate $\in [5\%, 30\%]$, all locked before any model is fit.

2.4 Features

The gate consumes 19 scalar features in five conceptual groups, audited uniformly in §4; deltas are *challenger – default* where a per-cell quantity exists. The Dempster-Shafer (DS) group is a principled *feature-form* choice, not an end-to-end method claim: per-passage NLI margins induce a basic probability assignment, sources are combined under the Shafer discount and Denoeux's cautious conjunctive rule [4] (idempotent, robust to shared-corpus correlation; definitions [13]), and the fused state is reduced to one scalar margin. Whether a well-formed DS feature yields override deployability is the empirical question answered – negatively here – in §3–§6.

- **Answer/query shape (8):** answer length and is-year; question length, has-year, and four question-type one-hots.

- **Retrieval support/confidence (4):** retrieved count, support fraction, answer logprob, and supporting-passage count.
- **NLI evidence (4):** entailment and contradiction deltas, taking max and mean over passages (DeBERTa-v3 MNLI/FEVER/ANLI; answer vs. each retrieved passage).
- **DS cross-support (2):** cautious-rule cross-support and coverage margins, scoring each cell's answer against the *other* cell's passages – evidence independent of the cell's own retrieval bias.
- **Witness agreement (1):** whether the third cell (D for C-vs-G) agrees with the challenger.

2.5 Model Family

We use a single gradient-boosted tree classifier (LightGBM, 200 estimators, max depth 3, 7 leaves, learning rate 0.05, min child samples 10). These hyperparameters are imported from a prior Phase B chooser ablation with no retuning – deliberately – to keep the present study consistent with already-reported numbers. 5-fold OOF CV with a fixed random seed.

2.6 Seven Diagnostic Passes

Table 2 summarizes the seven passes. P1–P5 interrogate the Qwen3-8B/2Wiki override gate; P6–P7 test transfer across a backbone and a benchmark. Each pass reuses the pre-committed pipeline of §2.3.

Table 2. Seven diagnostic passes and their verdicts.

Pass	Diagnostic	Verdict
P1	OOF vs. decision AUC	**No.** OOF 0.72–0.78; decision 0.55–0.66.
P2	Feature-group ablation	**Only shape helps;** other feature groups do not improve decision signal.
P3+P4	Seed, bootstrap, family, and curve oracle	**Tight null.** ΔEM CI $[+0.0, +0.7]$ pp; LR/LGBM/XGBoost $\leq +0.1$ pp.
P5	External judge headroom	**None.** DeepSeek-V3 -1.4 pp; GPT-4o -0.1 pp.
P6	Cross-backbone check	**Deployable.** Mistral decision-AUC 0.92; +3.0 pp at 13% rate.
P7	Cross-benchmark check	**Rate ceiling.** MAGIC gives +15–17 pp on disagreements but exceeds the rate corridor.

3 P1: OOF AUC vs Decision-relevant AUC

Figure 1 previews the three main findings.

Table 3 reports the three-pair decision matrix. The first observation is that OOF AUC is in the 0.72–0.78 range across all pairs – a number that would be read, in most chooser-ablation tables, as "the model is learning something useful".

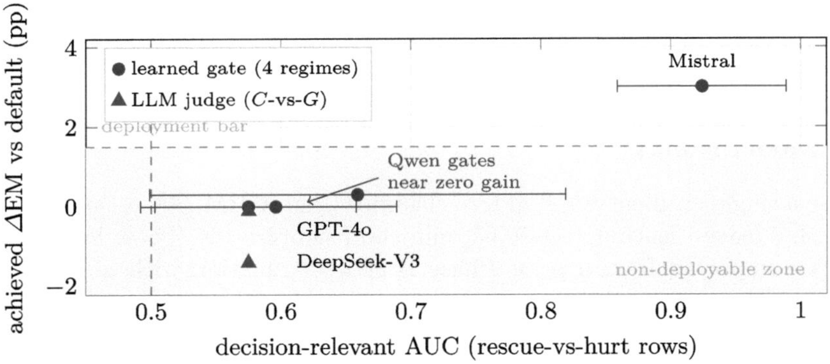

Fig. 1. The diagnostic separates regimes. Decision-relevant AUC versus achieved ΔEM: Qwen gates and LLM judges sit below the deployment bar, while Mistral crosses it. Horizontal bars are bootstrap 95% CIs; dashed lines mark random AUC and the +1.5 pp deployment margin. The C-vs-G oracle ceiling is reported in Table 3; MAGIC is a distinct rate-ceiling regime (§8).

Table 3. Three-pair decision matrix on 2Wiki-Qwen ($n = 1000$). Rescue counts challenger-correct/default-wrong cases; Hurt counts the reverse. OOF AUC uses all non-tie trainable rows, while decision-AUC uses only outcome-changing rows, i.e., Rescue ∪ Hurt (brackets: bootstrap 95% CI, B=2000). Best ΔEM is the pair-specific oracle upper bound obtained by overriding exactly all rescue cases; no learned gate on these features is expected to attain it.

Pair	EM_{chal}	EM_{def}	Rescue	Hurt	OOF AUC	**Dec. AUC**	Best ΔEM	Actual ΔEM	Rate
C-vs-G	0.315	0.371	63	119	0.719	**0.575** [.49,.66]	+6.3	+0.0	0.0%
D-vs-G	0.363	0.371	19	27	0.776	**0.659** [.49,.81]	+1.9	+0.3	2.4%
C-vs-D	0.315	0.363	56	104	0.735	**0.596** [.50,.69]	+5.6	+0.0	0.0%

The decision-relevant AUC tells a different story. Restricted to the rescue ∪ hurt rows – i.e. the only rows whose outcome can be changed by the gate – AUC is in the 0.55–0.66 range. On the main pair the decision-AUC is 0.575 (bootstrap 95% CI $[0.49, 0.66]$, *straddling* the 0.5 random baseline), on a pool of only $63 + 119 = 182$ rows.

Table 4. Drop-one feature-group ablation on C-vs-G ($n = 1000$). Each row zeros all columns in one named group, then reruns OOF evaluation with the same 19-column schema. #live counts columns not zeroed; ΔOOF is the absolute OOF-AUC change from the all-feature baseline.

Dropped group	#live	OOF AUC	ΔOOF	**Dec. AUC**	ΔEM	Verdict
(none)	19	0.719	–	0.575	+0.0	FAIL
answer_shape	10	**0.545**	**−0.174**	**0.495**	+0.0	FAIL
support	14	0.737	+0.018	0.597	+0.1	FAIL
nli	14	0.754	+0.035	0.599	+0.3	FAIL
ds_cross_support	17	0.735	+0.016	0.587	+0.0	FAIL
agreement	17	0.732	+0.013	0.584	+0.0	FAIL

Interpretation. The inflated OOF AUC is dominated by the agreement-tie bulk (both cells right, or both wrong), where ranking is trivial and the decision has no consequence; the rescue-vs-hurt subset – where the gate earns or loses EM – is exactly where discrimination is near random. We therefore recommend chooser papers report decision-relevant AUC alongside OOF AUC: the two diverge by 14–20 AUC points on a pipeline that looks healthy. The pool is also asymmetric – on C-vs-G the rescue:hurt ratio is 63:119, so even an oracle gate recovers only 6.3 pp and any imperfect gate strictly less.

Three-pair replication. Each pair runs the full pre-committed pipeline of §2.3 end-to-end (same features, hyperparameters, 5-fold OOF stacking, $\tau^\star$ selection, and gate criteria), not three AUC re-measurements of one model. Both auxiliary pairs fail – D-vs-G at ΔEM = +0.3 pp, rate 2.4% (below the floor); C-vs-D at 0.0 pp, rate 0.0% – and the OOF/decision gap persists on all three (0.72–0.78 vs 0.57–0.66). The chooser-EM plateau is therefore not an artefact of a particular challenger/default assignment.

4 P2: Drop-One Feature-Group Ablation

Table 4 holds the main pair (C-vs-G) fixed and zeros the columns of one feature group at a time. The aggregate number to read is the decision AUC column.

The ablation has three takeaways. **Only answer_shape carries the OOF signal**: zeroing the eight shape features collapses OOF AUC 0.719→0.545 (random) and decision-AUC 0.575 → 0.495 (below chance). **NLI, support, DS cross-support, and witness agreement do not contribute**: dropping any leaves OOF AUC indistinguishable from baseline, and the OOF deltas are positive (+0.013 to +0.035), meaning the model ranks marginally *better* without them. This is consistent with these evidence signals acting as near-irrelevant features that the tree partially overfits. **No group makes the gate pass**: the best Actual ΔEM is +0.3 pp (drop NLI), still failing the ΔEM and McNemar gates. The claim is narrow – no marginal signal *on the override decision for this pair under the pre-committed gate*; value in candidate ranking or abstention is not contested.

Table 5. Seed variance and paired bootstrap CI on C-vs-G $n = 1000$.

Source	OOF AUC	Dec. AUC	ΔEM (pp)	Override rate	McNemar p
Seed 0	0.719	0.575	+0.0	0.0%	1.00
Seed 1	0.694	0.589	+0.0	0.0%	1.00
Seed 2	0.674	0.551	+0.0	0.0%	1.00
Seed 3	0.736	0.588	+0.0	0.0%	1.00
Seed 4	0.706	0.571	+0.0	0.0%	1.00
Mean ± s.d.	0.706 ± 0.021	0.575 ± 0.014	0.00 ± 0.00	–	–
Bootstrap 1000×, 95% CI on ΔEM:				[+0.00, +0.70] pp	

5 P3 + P4: Structural Ceiling

5.1 Calibration and Curve-oracle

We compute 10-bin ECE (decision-relevant subset and full holdout) and the *curve oracle* – the maximum chooser EM over all unique OOF thresholds, chosen in-sample, a deliberately optimistic upper bound. Two points. **The gate is poorly calibrated**: decision-subset ECE is 0.23–0.33 (full-holdout 0.18–0.27), far worse than a calibrated classifier; post-hoc temperature or isotonic scaling would lower ECE but create no new rescue rows. **No threshold rule saves the main pair**: the curve-oracle EM on C-vs-G equals the default (0.371) even under in-sample optimisation over all ~1000 thresholds (same for C-vs-D); only D-vs-G has a tiny positive region (+0.3 pp) that still fails the gate.

5.2 Multi-seed and Bootstrap

Table 5 reports the five-seed sweep on C-vs-G and a 1000-sample paired bootstrap CI on the seed-0 holdout, re-selecting $\tau^\star$ inside each resample (so the CI reflects variance in both the pick and the per-qid outcomes).

All five seeds give exactly ΔEM = 0.00 pp at zero override; the bootstrap 95% CI upper bound is +0.70 pp, less than half the pre-committed +1.5 pp margin. The null is tight and reproducible.

5.3 Classifier Family Robustness

The main-line gate uses LightGBM; to check the plateau is not a family artefact, Table 6 refits the C-vs-G gate on the identical 19-feature matrix with LightGBM (depth-3, 200 trees), L_2 logistic regression, and XGBoost (depth-3, 200 trees).

Logistic regression is the strongest family by OOF AUC (+4.8 points over LightGBM), yet its ΔEM is +0.1 pp with a single override: the extra ranking signal lands on agreement-tie rows, not on rescue candidates. XGBoost matches LightGBM's verdict exactly. The plateau is a property of the feature matrix and the rescue-hurt geometry, not of the learner.

Table 6. Cross-family override-gate results on C-vs-G $n = 1000$. Same feature matrix, same 5-fold OOF, same $\tau^\star$ selection on the full holdout. All three families fail the pre-committed gate.

Family	OOF AUC	$\tau^\star$	ΔEM (pp)	Rate	Verdict
LightGBM	0.719	1.92 (never)	+0.0	0.0%	FAIL
Logistic L_2	**0.767**	0.895	+0.1	0.1%	FAIL
XGBoost	0.759	1.92 (never)	+0.0	0.0%	FAIL

Table 7. External-judge diagnostic on C-vs-G ($n = 1000$). Each judge sees both cells' top-5 passages and both answers, but no gold answer; decoding is single-shot at T=0. Good/Bad/Neutral counts whether a judge's override helps, hurts, or leaves EM unchanged. Neither judge clears the pre-committed deployment bar.

Quantity	DeepSeek-V3	GPT-4o
Override rate (picks C)	21.3%	24.7%
Tie rate (explicit)	52.2%	55.5%
Malformed rate	0.0%	0.0%
Good / Bad / Neutral overrides	35/49/129	40/41/166
Default-G EM	0.371	0.371
Judge-chooser EM	0.357	0.370
ΔEM vs G (pp)	−1.4	−0.1
Bootstrap 95% CI on ΔEM	$[-3.2, +0.5]$	$[-1.8, +1.6]$
McNemar p vs G	0.156	1.00

6 P5: LLM-Judge Headroom

Passes P1–P4 interrogate the *feature gate*. One question they cannot answer from inside the gate is whether the per-row decision was *recoverable in principle* given the retrieved context: if it was, a sufficiently expressive reasoner should pick the better candidate at a rate yielding ΔEM $\gg 0$ over default-G; if not, the retrieved context itself is the bottleneck, and features derived from the same context are unlikely to close the gap.

Design. On the same $n = 1000$ holdout each question sees the union of C's and G's top-5 retrieved passages (deduped, capped at 8), both committed answers, and nothing else (gold hidden). The judge returns one of {`choose_C`, `choose_G`, `tie`}; ties and malformed responses default to G. We run *two judge families* single-shot at $T = 0$, prompt diff-locked: DeepSeek-V3 and GPT-4o. A judge "recovers headroom" only if it clears the same pre-committed bar as the gate (ΔEM ≥ 1.5 pp, McNemar $p < 0.05$, rate $\in [5\%, 30\%]$).

Outcome. Table 7 reports both judges, and neither clears the bar. DeepSeek-V3 lands at ΔEM $= -1.4$ pp ($p = 0.16$): among its 213 overrides the good/bad ratio is *inverted* (35:49), so it moves on average in the wrong direction. GPT-4o – stronger and from a different family – lands at ΔEM $= -0.1$ pp ($p = 1.0$) with overrides almost exactly balanced (40:41): it gains and loses in equal measure. Both exercise the full three-way space at 0% malformed, so the null is not a refusal artefact.

Table 8. Cross-backbone check on the same 2Wiki slice ($n = 500$, offset 200); both backbones self-extract short answers before scoring. "Uncon." reports the original threshold sweep with no rate cap; "Corr." reports the best threshold inside the pre-committed $[5\%, 30\%]$ rate corridor. Each cell is ΔEM / rate; brackets give bootstrap 95% CIs for decision-AUC.

Backbone	EM_C/EM_G	R/H	OOF	Dec. AUC	Uncon.	Corr.
Qwen3-8B	.398/.414	42/50	.599	**.534** [.41, .65]	+0.6/24.6%	+0.6/24.6%
Mistral-7B-v0.2	.082/.082	24/24	.868	**.924** [.85, .98]	+3.4/40.0%	+3.0/13%

Robustness. Two checks confirm the null is not fragile. (i) *Self-consistency*: a $k = 5$ majority vote (GPT-4o, $T = 0.7$) on a capped $n = 200$ slice reproduces the single-shot ΔEM with the same decisive overrides (16:8) – not a sampling artefact. (ii) *Subset sensitivity*: on that same favourable $n = 200$ slice both judges look positive (GPT-4o +4.0 pp, DeepSeek-V3 +0.5 pp) yet regress to $-0.1/-1.4$ pp at $n = 1000$ – the judge-side analogue of the OOF-vs-decision-AUC gap, where a small, favourably-sampled decision pool inflates apparent headroom that vanishes at scale.

We read this as: under this shared retrieved-context bundle, even stronger external judges – across two families and two sampling regimes – reach no deployable headroom over the default. We do not claim a context-set ceiling in general, only that on this holdout, under this retrieval regime, and for this pair, features based on the same Qwen C-vs-G evidence have no visible headroom to close.

7 Cross-backbone Regime Check

On the same slice ($n = 500$, offset 200) we swap Qwen for Mistral-7B-Instruct-v0.2; both backbones self-extract their verbose commits (T=0) before EM. Table 8 reports both the unconstrained-$\tau^\star$ verdict and the deployment-constrained verdict (best $\tau^\star$ inside the $[5\%, 30\%]$ corridor). Qwen has rescue < hurt (42:50) with decision-AUC straddling random; no corridor-internal point reaches the +1.5 pp margin. Mistral has a balanced pool (24:24) with decision-AUC strictly above random; the best corridor-internal point (at rate 13%) delivers +3.0 pp (16:1, $p \approx 3{\times}10^{-4}$). The unconstrained threshold fires too often, producing the same kind of rate failure later seen on MAGIC. The asymmetry tracks the top-passage entailment–EM correlation (+0.06 Qwen vs +0.29 Mistral): Qwen depends far less on retrieved evidence.

Table 9. MAGIC cross-benchmark: the same pre-committed override gate on both decision pairs. $n = 150$; LightGBM; 5-fold OOF. The McNemar column counts good/bad discordant overrides.

Pair (MAGIC)	OOF AUC	ΔEM (pp)	Rate	Good/Bad	Verdict
B-vs-A	0.714	+15.3	92.0%	25/2	FAIL (rate)
E-vs-D	0.781	+16.7	47.3%	26/1	FAIL (rate)

8 Cross-benchmark: MAGIC Single-Hop-Conflict

To test whether the plateau is a 2Wiki multi-hop artefact, we replicate the pipeline on MAGIC [9], an inter-context conflict benchmark. We use its single-hop conflict split ($n = 150$, two passages per question, retrieval closed), so any lift must adjudicate the two cells' *answers* under identical context. The run keeps the same Qwen3-8B backbone, the same four cells forming pairs B-vs-A and E-vs-D, and the same 19-feature gate and pre-committed corridor. MAGIC therefore fails for a different reason: the overrides improve EM and pass McNemar, but the gate would have to fire outside the allowed rate corridor (Table 9).

The outcome is qualitatively different from 2Wiki but reaches the same verdict. On both pairs the challenger dominates by +15 to +17 EM points, discordant rows favouring override 25:2 and 26:1 (McNemar $p < 10^{-5}$); yet the gate fails the rate ceiling, wanting to fire on 92%/47% of rows. Operationally this mirrors 2Wiki – there ΔEM is flat because rescue rows are scarce; here it is large because rescue rows are the majority – but the same corridor flags both as out-of-spec. The distinction is visible only when rescue-hurt geometry is paired with the operating-rate window; OOF AUC alone cannot discriminate them.

9 Related Work

RAG choosers, deferral, and calibration. RAG side-channel discriminators such as Self-RAG [1], CRAG [17], inter-passage verification [3], and semantic-evidence fact verifiers [8] predict candidate correctness from retrieval and LLM signals, then report both OOF AUC and downstream EM. Decision-relevant AUC asks how much of that ranking signal lies on outcome-changing rows. Our asymmetric gate inherits the learning-to-defer view of Madras et al. [11] and Mozannar and Sontag [12]; related work studies calibrated deferral [16] and multiple-expert deferral [15]. The architectural distinction matters: a symmetric arg max chooser or listwise ranker [2] lacks an explicit rescue-vs-hurt accounting. Our operating-rate and curve-oracle analyses use standard calibration [6] and selective-prediction risk-coverage tools [5].

Evidence and judge diagnostics. Dempster-Shafer belief functions have been used for retriever late-fusion and cautious conflict handling [4]; here DS enters only as a feature-side cross-support margin, so our drop-one null does not address DS as late-fusion or abstention. LLM judges are also widely used to evaluate RAG outputs despite concerns about consistency and bias [10]. We use the judge oracle only as a diagnostic arm (§6): two families (DeepSeek-V3, GPT-4o) at temperature 0, no gold, with a $k=5$ self-consistency check and the full override/tie/malformed distribution reported.

10 Discussion and Conclusion

We studied a 19-feature LightGBM override gate on 2WikiMultihopQA with a Qwen3-8B backbone. Under a pre-committed gate on ΔEM, McNemar p, and override rate, it fails consistently across three decision pairs, five seeds, a paired bootstrap, ablations, and a risk-coverage oracle. The diagnosis is threefold. First, **decision-relevant signal collapse**: OOF AUC (0.72) hides a near-random decision-AUC (0.575, CI $[0.49, 0.66]$), and rescue: hurt asymmetry (63:119) imposes a negative structural ceiling. Second, only answer/query-shape features contribute: the other groups leave $\Delta\text{EM} = 0.0\,\text{pp}$ (CI $[+0.0, +0.7]$). Third, **no headroom under shared context**: two external judges given both cells' top-5 passages, DeepSeek-V3 ($-1.4\,\text{pp}$) and GPT-4o ($-0.1\,\text{pp}$, balanced 40:41), both fail the deployment bar, with a $k=5$ self-consistency arm confirming robustness to sampling.

The +0.15 OOF-vs-decision AUC gap lives on rows whose outcome the gate cannot change. The Qwen plateau, the judge no-headroom (§6), the MAGIC rate-ceiling (§8), and the Mistral retrieval-aligned case (§7) occupy different operating regimes on the same two axes: decision-relevant AUC and override rate. The same diagnostic also *identifies* a deployable Mistral setting (+3.0 pp at 13% rate), suggesting gate utility tracks how much retrieval evidence explains backbone correctness. Conclusions are scoped to override-style gates; a symmetric chooser or listwise ranker [2] could reach higher EM. We offer decision-relevant AUC and rescue-vs-hurt geometry as inexpensive additions to override-style RAG chooser ablation tables.

References

1. Asai, A., Wu, Z., Wang, Y., Sil, A., Hajishirzi, H.: Self-rag: learning to retrieve, generate, and critique through self-reflection. In: ICLR (2024)
2. Burges, C.J.: From RankNet to LambdaRank to LambdaMART: an overview. Microsoft Research, MSR-TR-2010-82 Tech. Rep (2010)
3. Chen, B., Wan, S., Ye, X., Zhao, C.: Inter-passage verification for multi-evidence multi-answer QA. In: Findings of the Association for Computational Linguistics: ACL 2025, pp. 6811–6829. Association for Computational Linguistics, Vienna, Austria (2025)
4. Denoeux, T.: Conjunctive and disjunctive combination of belief functions induced by non distinct bodies of evidence. Artif. Intell. **172**(2–3), 234–264 (2008). https://doi.org/10.1016/j.artint.2007.05.008
5. Geifman, Y., El-Yaniv, R.: Selective classification for deep neural networks. In: NeurIPS (2017)
6. Guo, C., Pleiss, G., Sun, Y., Weinberger, K.Q.: On calibration of modern neural networks. In: ICML (2017)
7. Ho, X., Duong Nguyen, A.K., Sugawara, S., Aizawa, A.: Constructing a multi-hop QA dataset for comprehensive evaluation of reasoning steps. In: COLING (2020)
8. Indrehus, K., Vannebo, C., Pop, R.: SemQA: evaluating evidence with question embeddings and answer entailment for fact verification. In: Proceedings of the Eighth Workshop on Fact Extraction and VERification (FEVER), pp. 184–200. Association for Computational Linguistics, Vienna, Austria (2025)
9. Lee, J., Lee, K., Kim, T.: MAGIC: a multi-hop and graph-based benchmark for inter-context conflicts in retrieval-augmented generation. In: Findings of the Association for Computational Linguistics: EMNLP 2025, pp. 8783–8803. Association for Computational Linguistics, Suzhou, China (2025)
10. Liu, S., et al.: Judge as a judge: improving the evaluation of retrieval-augmented generation through the judge-consistency of large language models. In: Findings of the Association for Computational Linguistics: ACL 2025, pp. 5788–5807. Association for Computational Linguistics, Vienna, Austria (2025)
11. Madras, D., Pitassi, T., Zemel, R.: Predict responsibly: Improving fairness and accuracy by learning to defer. In: NeurIPS (2018). https://openreview.net/forum?id=SJUX_MWCZ
12. Mozannar, H., Sontag, D.: Consistent estimators for learning to defer to an expert. In: Proceedings of the 37th International Conference on Machine Learning (ICML) (2020)
13. Shafer, G.: A Mathematical Theory of Evidence. Princeton University Press (1976)
14. Trivedi, H., Balasubramanian, N., Khot, T., Sabharwal, A.: Interleaving retrieval with chain-of-thought reasoning for knowledge-intensive multi-step questions. In: ACL (2023)
15. Verma, R., Barrejón, D., Nalisnick, E.: Learning to defer to multiple experts: Consistent surrogate losses, confidence calibration, and conformal ensembles. In: Proceedings of the 26th International Conference on Artificial Intelligence and Statistics (AISTATS). PMLR, vol. 206 (2023)

16. Verma, R., Nalisnick, E.: Calibrated learning to defer with one-vs-all classifiers. In: Proceedings of the 39th International Conference on Machine Learning (ICML). PMLR, vol. 162 (2022)
17. Yan, S.Q., Gu, J.C., Zhu, Y., Ling, Z.H.: Corrective retrieval augmented generation. arXiv preprintarXiv:2401.15884 (2024)

Graph Structure Purification: A Two-Stage Defense Against Structural Adversarial Attacks on GNN-Based Network Intrusion Detection Systems

Manh-Huy Dang(✉), Xuan-Trang Phan-Thi, Thanh-Thao Truong, Hung-Chen Truong, and Thanh-Nam Tran

College of Digital Technology and Artificial Intelligence, Nam Can Tho University, 168 Nguyen Van Cu Street, An Binh Ward, Can Tho City, Viet Nam
{dmhuy,ptxtrang,ttthao,thchen,ttnam}@nctu.edu.vn

Abstract. GNN-based network intrusion detection systems (NIDS) are vulnerable to structural adversarial attacks that inject spurious edges to camouflage malicious nodes via message-passing manipulation. Existing purification defenses require $\mathcal{O}\left(N^2\right)$ computation, incompatible with real-time deployment. We propose Graph Structure Purifier (GSP), a two-stage defense combining SimHash-based LSH candidate filtering in $\mathcal{O}(N \cdot b \cdot t)$ with a contrastively trained Metric Scorer for per-edge trust scoring. Evaluated on CIC-IDS2017 (GCN and GAT, five seeds, PGD attack), GSP recovers GCN F1-macro from 4.2% to 34.7% ($\varepsilon = 0.05$) — 8.3× relative increase (+30.5 pp. absolute) — outperforming Jaccard, GNNGuard-S, and RobGCN ($p < 0.05$, Wilcoxon). All configurations exceed 150,000 flows/s with ≤132 ms latency. Ablation confirms LSH as the dominant contributor (7.6× GCN F1 recovery).

Keywords: Graph Neural Networks · Network Intrusion Detection · Adversarial Robustness · Graph Structure Purification · Locality-Sensitive Hashing · Metric Learning · Problem Space Attacks

1 Introduction

Network intrusion detection systems (NIDS) constitute a cornerstone of modern cybersecurity infrastructure, tasked with real-time identification of malicious traffic flows among a high-volume stream of benign communications. Deep learning approaches have progressively displaced hand-crafted signatures, with convolutional and recurrent architectures achieving strong detection rates on benchmark datasets [9, 20]. More recently, Graph Neural Networks (GNNs) have attracted considerable attention for NIDS owing to their ability to explicitly model the relational topology between hosts, ports, and protocol

L. Ding et al. (Eds.): APWeb-WAIM 2026, LNCS 16995, pp. 369–380, 2027.
https://doi.org/10.1007/978-981-92-5699-0_24

interactions [1, 31]. By representing network traffic as a dynamic graph — nodes corresponding to IP addresses and edges to communication flows — GNNs capture higher-order dependencies invisible to per-flow classifiers, yielding improvements across distributed attack patterns such as DDoS, port scanning, and botnet command-and-control [16, 23].

Despite their promise, GNN-based detectors exhibit a fundamental vulnerability: their core message-passing operation $h_v^{(l+1)} = \sigma\left(W^{(l)} \cdot \mathrm{AGG}\left(\left\{h_u^{(l)} : u \in \mathcal{N}(v)\right\}\right)\right)$ processes all neighbors identically. An adversary who can insert a single spurious edge between a malicious node and a benign, high-degree hub forces the GNN to blend the hub's "clean" representation into the attacker's embedding, effectively camouflaging the intrusion in the feature space. This structural adversarial attack is not merely a theoretical threat: packet injection is a trivially achievable operation in contested network segments, and several works have demonstrated that even a small injection budget ($\varepsilon \leq 5\%$ of edges) causes catastrophic F1-macro degradation exceeding 30 percentage points for standard GCN models [28, 34].

A critical distinction exists between Feature Space and Problem Space threat models [11, 22]. Feature Space attacks allow free adjacency manipulation including edge deletion — infeasible without infrastructure-level access. The Problem Space constraint limits adversaries to adding edges, with each injected flow necessarily updating both endpoint feature vectors, preventing attacks that manipulate topology without affecting observable traffic statistics.

Latency bottleneck. Production NIDS at edge routers must sustain 10^5–10^6 [14]. Existing purification methods (Pro-GNN [13], SVD-GCN [8]) require $\mathcal{O}(N^2)$ computation per snapshot — latencies on the order of seconds for $N \approx 20,000$-node graphs, making them impractical for real-time deployment.

Our contributions. This paper addresses both challenges through a principled two-stage defense. Specifically, our contributions are:

1. **Problem Space Attack Formalization.** Threat model with three physical constraints: add-only edge injection, bounded budget $\varepsilon \cdot \mid \mathcal{E} \mid$, and semantic consistency of injected flows.
2. **Graph Structure Purifier (GSP).** Two-stage pipeline: SimHash-based LSH in $\mathcal{O}(N \cdot b \cdot t)$ for candidate pair filtering, followed by a contrastively trained Metric Scorer for per-edge trust scoring and pruning.
3. **Practical Deployment.** Adversarial training occurs offline; online inference uses only the lightweight LSH + Metric filter with Spatial Median Aggregation, keeping latency below 132 ms and throughput above 150,000 flows/s.
4. **Empirical Evaluation.** Evaluated on CIC-IDS2017 (GCN and GAT, five seeds, PGD at $\varepsilon \in \{0.01, 0.05, 0.10, 0.20\}$) with Wilcoxon signed-rank tests; CICIoT2023 validates scalability. GSP outperforms all baselines (No Defense, Jaccard, GNNGuard-S, RobGCN).

Network management applicability. Within the FCAPS model, GSP addresses the Security dimension as a pre-filtering layer upstream of SIEM platforms, deployable at network edge nodes or SDN controllers for real-time structural anomaly triage [14]. Its retrainable, domain-transferable design applies across enterprise, carrier-grade, and IoT managed environments.

2 Related Work

GNN-based NIDS. GNNs have been applied to network intrusion detection through flow-graph representations. Koroniotis et al. [16] demonstrated that structured statistical flow features substantially improve multi-class attack identification in IoT environments. Lo et al. [18] introduced E-GraphSAGE, an inductive GNN-based IDS with strong generalization to unseen attack types; Caville et al. [4] extended this to self-supervised pre-training for zero-day detection. Ring et al. [23] surveyed NIDS datasets, establishing evaluation taxonomies widely adopted in subsequent GNN-NIDS research.

Adversarial attacks on GNNs. Zügner et al. [33] formulated targeted node-level adversarial perturbation as a bilevel optimization; subsequent work generalized this to untargeted attacks [28], RL-based edge perturbation [7], and meta-learning perturbations [34]. Zügner and Günnemann [35] established certifiable robustness bounds; Geisler et al. [10] showed that scale and expressiveness alone cannot compensate for the absence of explicit defense. Following Madry et al. [19], we use PGD as an upper-bound threat model, acknowledging per Biggio and Roli [3] that real attackers rarely have direct gradient access. Sun et al. [25] provides a comprehensive taxonomy of attacks and defenses.

Graph purification and structure defense. Jin et al. [13] proposed Pro-GNN (joint low-rank structure optimization), and Entezari et al. [8] SVD-based cleaning; both require $\mathcal{O}(N^2)$ computation. Zhang and Zitnik [30] proposed GNNGuard (per-layer Pearson edge pruning at $\mathcal{O}(N^2 \cdot F)$); Zhu et al. [32] proposed RobGCN (Gaussian feature reparameterization). Jaccard preprocessing [27] is limited to binarized features, unsuitable for continuous flow statistics. For robust aggregation, the Weiszfeld algorithm [29] provides geometric median computation with provable breakdown-point guarantees; we adopt Spatial Median Aggregation as a second defense layer [17]. LSH [5, 12] enables sub-quadratic candidate selection, applied to scalable graph matching [2] and GCN training [6]; our use for adversarial edge candidate generation is novel, with theoretical analysis in Sect. 4.2.

3 Preliminaries and Problem Formulation

3.1 Graph-Based NIDS

Let $\mathcal{G} = (\mathcal{V}, \mathcal{E}, \boldsymbol{X})$ be a network traffic graph: $\mathcal{V}$ is IP address nodes ($N = |\mathcal{V}|$), $\mathcal{E}$ is communication flow edges, and $\boldsymbol{X} \in \mathbb{R}^{N \times F}$ encodes statistical flow features (byte counts, packet rate, inter-arrival time, entropy, etc.). We construct k-NN graphs ($k = 10$) over $W = 20{,}000$-flow sliding windows ($N \in [15,000, 25,000]$, $\approx 200,000$ edges).

A GNN backbone $f_\theta : \mathcal{G} \rightarrow \{0, \ldots, C-1\}^N$ maps each node to a class label, where C is the number of traffic classes (e.g., $C = 9$ for CIC-IDS2017: eight attack categories plus benign). In the GCN formulation [15], each layer computes:

$$h_v^{(l+1)} = \sigma\left(W^{(l)} \sum_{u \in \mathcal{N}(v) \cup \{v\}} \frac{1}{\sqrt{d_u d_v}} h_u^{(l)}\right)$$

where $d_v = | \mathcal{N}(v) |$ is the node degree. The GAT formulation [26] replaces mean aggregation with learned attention coefficients α_{uv}:

$$h_v^{(l+1)} = \sigma\left(\sum_{u \in \mathcal{N}(v) \cup \{v\}} \alpha_{uv}^{(l)} W^{(l)} h_u^{(l)}\right)$$

Both formulations are vulnerable when the adjacency matrix $\boldsymbol{A}$ is perturbed by adversarial edges.

3.2 Problem Space Threat Model

We adopt a Problem Space threat model [11, 28]: the adversary seeks ΔA maximizing $\mathcal{L}(f_\theta(\mathcal{G} \oplus \Delta \boldsymbol{A}), y)$ subject to add-only injection ($\Delta \boldsymbol{A}_{ij} \geq 0$, C1), bounded budget $\|\Delta \boldsymbol{A}\|_0 \leq \varepsilon \mid \mathcal{E} \mid$ (C2), and semantic consistency (C3): each injected edge updates endpoint features as $\boldsymbol{x}'_u = \boldsymbol{x}_u + \lambda \mid \boldsymbol{x}_u - \boldsymbol{x}_v \mid$, preventing topology manipulation without observable traffic changes. PGD provides an upper-bound implementation (Sect. 5).

4 Proposed Method: Graph Structure Purifier

4.1 Architecture Overview

Figure 1 illustrates the GSP pipeline. During online inference, an incoming graph snapshot $\mathcal{G}_t$ is passed through:

1. **Stage 1 — LSH Filter**: Candidate edge pairs are generated in $\mathcal{O}(N \cdot b \cdot t)$ via SimHash bucketing.
2. **Stage 2 — Metric Scorer**: Per-edge trust weights $w(u, v)$ are computed via a contrastively trained MLP; edges with $w(u, v) < \tau$ are pruned.
3. **GNN Backbone** with Spatial Median Aggregation on the cleaned graph $\hat{\mathcal{G}}_t$.

Offline adversarial training additionally generates PGD attacks under Problem Space constraints to train the Metric Scorer to distinguish adversarial from legitimate edges.

4.2 Stage 1: LSH-Based Candidate Filtering

Motivation. Adversarial edges overwhelmingly connect nodes with dissimilar statistical profiles, creating semantic mismatches detectable by locality-sensitive comparison at $\mathcal{O}(N \cdot b \cdot t)$ cost vs. $\mathcal{O}(N^2)$ for exhaustive evaluation.

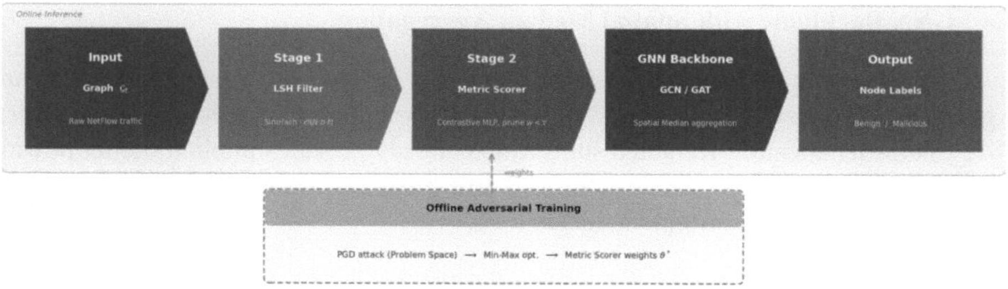

Fig. 1. GSP online inference pipeline. The offline training loop (dashed) uses PGD attacks under Problem Space constraints to train the Metric Scorer

SimHash construction. For each table $k \in \{1, \ldots, t\}$, let $\boldsymbol{r}_{k,1}, \ldots, \boldsymbol{r}_{k,b} \sim \mathcal{N}(0, \boldsymbol{I}_F)$ be b random Gaussian projection vectors drawn independently per table (ensuring inter-table independence required for the collision probability analysis below). The code vector of node v under table k is:

$$\boldsymbol{c}_k(v) = \left[\operatorname{sgn}\left(\boldsymbol{r}_{k,1}^T \boldsymbol{x}_v\right), \ldots, \operatorname{sgn}\left(\boldsymbol{r}_{k,b}^T \boldsymbol{x}_v\right)\right] \in \{-1, +1\}^b$$

Candidate generation and edge mask. For each table k, node pairs (u, v) with $\boldsymbol{c}_k(u) = \boldsymbol{c}_k(v)$ join candidate set $\mathcal{C}_{\text{cand}}$. Existing edges not in $\mathcal{C}_{\text{cand}}$ are immediately removed; those in $\mathcal{C}_{\text{cand}}$ proceed to Stage 2.

4.3 Stage 2: Metric-Based Edge Scoring

Metric Scorer Architecture. Given the candidate pairs from Stage 1, the Metric Scorer g_ψ computes per-edge trust weights. It consists of a three-layer MLP encoder:

$$z_v = \frac{g_\psi(\boldsymbol{x}_v)}{\|g_\psi(\boldsymbol{x}_v)\|_2} \in \mathbb{R}^{d_z}$$

where $d_z = 64$ is the embedding dimension. The Metric Scorer then computes trust weights via an exponential similarity function:

$$w(u, v) = \exp\left(-\frac{\|z_u - z_v\|_2}{\tau}\right) \in (0, 1]$$

where $\tau > 0$ is a temperature hyperparameter controlling the sharpness of the scoring function.

Contrastive Training. The Metric Scorer is trained offline to assign high scores to same-class node pairs and low scores to cross-class pairs, using the contrastive loss:

$$\mathcal{L}_{\text{metric}} = \sum_{(u,v)\in\mathcal{E}_+} \|z_u - z_v\|_2^2 + \sum_{(u,v)\in\mathcal{E}_-} \max\left(0, m - \|z_u - z_v\|_2\right)^2$$

where $\mathcal{E}_+$ and $\mathcal{E}_-$ are same-class and cross-class edge pairs respectively, and $m = 1.0$ is the contrastive margin.

Adaptive Pruning. Edges with $w(u, v) < \tau_{\text{prune}}$ (default $\tau_{\text{prune}} = 0.5$) are removed; the threshold can be tuned to trade off false-drop rate against adversarial edge retention.

4.4 GNN Backbone with Spatial Median Aggregation

Even after purification, some adversarial edges may survive. We apply Spatial Median Aggregation (Weiszfeld algorithm [29]) to the GCN backbone as a second defense layer; GAT retains its attention-weighted sum, which already provides implicit outlier down-weighting. The geometric median achieves a 40% breakdown point for $k = 10$ neighbors [29], versus zero for the arithmetic mean.

4.5 Offline Adversarial Training

The Min-Max objective is optimized by alternating PGD attack steps (gradient ascent on $\mathcal{L}$ under constraints C1–C3, with feature updates $\widetilde{\boldsymbol{X}} \leftarrow \boldsymbol{X} + \lambda \cdot \mid \boldsymbol{X}[\text{src}] - \boldsymbol{X}[\text{dst}] \mid$ for injected edges) and defense steps (minimizing $\mathcal{L}(f_\theta(\pi_\phi(\mathcal{G} \oplus \Delta \boldsymbol{A}^*)), y)$), jointly training the purifier to remove adversarial edges while preserving clean-graph accuracy.

5 Experimental Evaluation

5.1 Datasets and Experimental Setup

Datasets. We use two publicly available network traffic benchmarks:

- **CIC-IDS2017** [24]: Five-day PCAP capture, 78 flow features, 9 classes (8 attacks + benign). Severe class imbalance (benign >80%) depresses F1-macro; used for all evaluation phases.
- **CICIoT2023** [21]: Large-scale IoT benchmark, 33 attack types across 7 categories, 46 features; 9-class balanced subset. Used for clean-traffic baseline and latency benchmarking.

Graph Construction. k-NN graphs (k = 10), cosine similarity, W = 20,000-flow windows; $N \in [15,000, 25,000]$ nodes.

Backbones. GCN (2 layers, 64-dim, dropout 0.3) and GAT (2 layers, 4 heads, 64-dim, dropout 0.3). Training. Up to 60 epochs, early stopping (patience 10), Adam (lr 10^{-3}, wd 5×10^{-4}), five seeds (42, 123, 456, 789, 2024). GSP hyperparameters. LSH: $b = 8$, $t = 10$; Metric Scorer: 3-layer MLP (64–64-64), $\tau = 1.0$, $m = 1.0$, 15 epochs, $\tau_{\text{prune}} = 0.5$; Spatial Median: $T = 5$ Weiszfeld iterations. Attack. PGD (10 steps, step 0.01, $\lambda = 0.1$), $\varepsilon \in \{0.01, 0.05, 0.10, 0.20\}$. Defenses. No Defense; Jaccard [27]; GNNGuard-S [30]; RobGCN [32]; GSP (ours). Metrics. F1-macro (primary), F1-weighted, Accuracy, AUC-ROC.

5.2 Baseline Clean-Traffic Performance

Table 1 reports performance on clean (unattacked) graphs. GCN achieves $\text{F1}_M = 35.1 \pm 0.5\%$ on CIC-IDS2017 and $49.4 \pm 2.2\%$ on CICIoT2023; GAT achieves $35.8 \pm 1.7\%$ and $47.4 \pm 0.3\%$ respectively.

Table 1. Baseline clean-traffic performance (mean ± std., five seeds)

Dataset	Backbone	$F1_M$ (%)	$F1_W$ (%)	Acc (%)	AUC
CIC-IDS2017	GCN	35.1 ± 0.5	84.6 ± 0.7	78.7 ± 0.9	98.9 ± 0.4
CIC-IDS2017	GAT	35.8 ± 1.7	82.6 ± 1.9	76.1 ± 2.6	98.4 ± 0.4
CICIoT2023	GCN	49.4 ± 2.2	78.7 ± 2.7	79.7 ± 2.1	99.0 ± 0.1
CICIoT2023	GAT	47.4 ± 0.3	76.0 ± 0.2	78.1 ± 0.1	98.9 ± 0.0

The $F1_M$/$F1_W$ gap reflects severe class imbalance (benign >80%; Infiltration <0.1%); near-perfect AUC (98.4–99.0%) confirms discriminative capability. F1-macro is the primary metric for its sensitivity to rare attack class degradation; note that a model assigning all nodes to benign achieves F1-macro ≈ 11%, so values of 35–49% represent genuine multi-class capability.

5.3 Attack Vulnerability Analysis

Table 2 quantifies F1-macro degradation under PGD attack at four budgets. We report the mean F1-drop ($\Delta F1_M = F1_M^{clean} - F1_M^{attack}$) across five seeds.

Table 2. F1-macro drop (%) under PGD structural attack on CIC-IDS2017. Higher values indicate greater attack success (mean ± std., five seeds)

Backbone	$\varepsilon = 0.01$	$\varepsilon = 0.05$	$\varepsilon = 0.10$	$\varepsilon = 0.20$
GCN	11.8 ± 2.8	30.9 ± 1.0	31.1 ± 1.0	31.6 ± 1.0
GAT	0.1 ± 1.7	1.9 ± 1.7	32.2 ± 1.1	32.1 ± 1.5

Key observations: GCN drops 11.8% at $\varepsilon = 0.01$, saturating at 30.9% ($\varepsilon = 0.05$), confirming mean aggregation is disrupted by modest budgets. GAT resists at $\varepsilon \leq 0.05$ (0.1–1.9%) but collapses at $\varepsilon = 0.10$ (32.2%), motivating GSP as a universal defense for both architectures.

5.4 Defense Effectiveness

Table 3 compares the F1-macro of the defended model under PGD attack at the representative budget $\varepsilon = 0.05$, evaluated against four baselines: No Defense, Jaccard, GNNGuard-S, and RobGCN. Significance marker ($*p < 0.05$) denotes one-sided Wilcoxon signed-rank tests with H1: GSP > baseline.

Clean-graph F1 is 35.1 ± 0.5% (GCN) and 35.8 ± 1.7% (GAT) for all preprocessing defenses and No Defense; GSP preserves clean-graph performance within ±0.5 pp.

Table 3. Defense F1-macro (%) under PGD ($\varepsilon = 0.05$) on CIC-IDS2017 (mean std., five seeds). *$p < 0.05$ vs. GSP (one-sided Wilcoxon signed-rank test)

Backbone	No defense	Jaccard	GNNGuard-S	RobGCN	GSP (ours)
GCN	4.2 ± 1.1	4.2 ± 1.1	20.7 ± 2.0	16.2 ± 2.3	**34.7 ± 0.9**
GAT	33.9 ± 1.9	33.9 ± 1.9	34.5 ± 1.8	16.0 ± 2.9	**35.7 ± 1.8**

Key Findings:

1. **GSP provides dramatic GCN recovery**: F1 rises from 4.2% to 34.7% — **8.3x relative increase (+30.5 pp)**, near-complete recovery to clean-graph baseline (35.1%). Jaccard provides **zero benefit** ($p < 0.05$): injected edges exhibit semantic inconsistency detectable only by the learned metric.
2. **GSP improves GAT** (33.9% → 35.7%, $p < 0.05$) by removing residual edges that attention fails to down-weight; at $\varepsilon \geq 0.10$ (Table 2), GSP is equally critical for GAT.
3. **GNNGuard-S achieves intermediate recovery** (20.7%, $p < 0.05$); **RobGCN performs poorly** (16.2%/16.0%, $p < 0.05$) — Gaussian feature reparameterization targets feature perturbations, not structural edge injections.
4. **GSP preserves clean-graph performance** within ±0.5 pp., confirming negligible false-drop of legitimate edges.

5.5 Latency and Throughput Analysis

Table 4 reports inference latency and throughput of GCN and GAT with and without GSP on both datasets.

Table 4. Inference latency and throughput (mean ± std. across five graph windows, three timing repeats per window; throughput reported as mean)

Dataset	Backbone	Mode	Throughput (flows/s)	Latency (ms)
CIC-IDS2017	GCN	Without GSP	609,182	32.9 ± 12.2
CIC-IDS2017	GCN	With GSP	359,336	55.8 ± 25.4
CIC-IDS2017	GAT	Without GSP	257,837	77.8 ± 23.2
CIC-IDS2017	GAT	With GSP	175,808	114.1 ± 48.8
CICIoT2023	GCN	Without GSP	686,758	29.5 ± 5.4
CICIoT2023	GCN	With GSP	288,691	70.3 ± 45.1
CICIoT2023	GAT	Without GSP	274,974	73.8 ± 16.6
CICIoT2023	GAT	With GSP	153,754	132.0 ± 81.0

Analysis: GSP adds 22.9–58.2 ms overhead; all configurations exceed 150,000 flows/s [14]. GCN + GSP provides the optimal robustness-latency trade-off: 34.7% F1 at 55.8 ms and 359 K flows/s, versus GAT+GSP's 114.1 ms for 1 pp. additional gain.

5.6 Ablation Study

Table 5 compares four GSP component configurations on CIC-IDS2017:

- **None**: No defense (raw GNN under PGD attack)
- **LSH Only**: Stage 1 candidate filtering with direct edge removal for non-candidate pairs (no metric scoring)
- **Metric Only**: Stage 2 metric scoring applied to all edges (no LSH pre-filtering)
- **GSP Full**: Both stages combined

Table 5. Ablation study — F1-macro (%) under PGD ($\varepsilon = 0.05$), CIC-IDS2017, mean ± std. over five seeds

Backbone	None	LSH only	Metric only	GSP full
GCN	4.2 ± 1.0	31.9 ± 1.1	21.1 ± 3.9	**33.2 ± 1.0**
GAT	33.9 ± 1.7	35.1 ± 1.7	34.1 ± 1.5	**35.2 ± 1.6**

Note: GSP Full (33.2 ± 1.0%) differs from Table 3 (34.7 ± 0.9%) due to between-run variance from independent ablation retraining, not a method difference.

Findings:

1. **LSH is the dominant contributor for GCN**: restoring F1 from 4.2% to 31.9% (**7.6×, +27.7 pp**), confirming adversarial edges predominantly connect dissimilar nodes.
2. **Metric Only is incomplete (21.1%)**: without LSH pre-filtering, borderline legitimate edges receive low trust scores, increasing false-positive pruning.
3. **GSP Full (33.2%) improves LSH Only (31.9%)** by refining boundary-case edges; **GAT shows small differences across conditions** (33.9–35.2%), reflecting inherent attention robustness at $\varepsilon = 0.05$.

6 Limitations and Future Work

Adversarial evaluation is limited to CIC-IDS2017; extension to CICIoT2023 under full Problem Space simulation remains future work. Pro-GNN [13] and SVD-GCN [8] are excluded due to $\mathcal{O}(N^2)$ cost; GNNGuard-S and RobGCN are statistically outperformed ($p \leq 0.05$), with GNNGuard-S providing intermediate GCN recovery (20.7%). Extension to GraphSAGE/GIN backbones and incremental streaming LSH variants are natural future directions.

7 Conclusion

We presented the Graph Structure Purifier (GSP), a two-stage defense framework for GNN-based network intrusion detection systems against structural adversarial attacks in the Problem Space. By combining $\mathcal{O}(N \cdot b \cdot t)$ LSH-based candidate filtering with learned contrastive edge scoring, GSP achieves near-complete structural purification at throughputs exceeding 150,000 flows/s and latencies below 132 ms. Evaluation on CIC-IDS2017 with GCN and GAT backbones across five random seeds demonstrates that GSP recovers GCN F1-macro from 4.2% to 34.7% under PGD attack ($\varepsilon = 0.05$) — an 8.3× relative increase (+30.5 pp. absolute) — while statistically outperforming all compared baselines (Jaccard, GNNGuard-S, RobGCN) via Wilcoxon signed-rank tests. The ablation study confirms that the LSH stage is the primary contributor (7.6× GCN F1 recovery), with the Metric stage providing incremental refinement, validating the two-stage design. GSP demonstrates a competitive, practical defense framework for adversarially robust, latency-aware GNN-based NIDS deployments at network edge infrastructure, with full attack-and-defense evaluation on CIC-IDS2017 and scalability benchmarking on CICIoT2023.

References

1. Bacciu, D., Errica, F., Micheli, A., Podda, M.: A gentle introduction to deep learning for graphs. Neural Netw. **129**, 203–221 (2020)
2. Bai, Y., Ding, H., Bian, S., Chen, T., Sun, Y., Wang, W.: SimGNN: a neural network approach to fast graph similarity computation. In: ACM International Conference on Web Search and Data Mining (WSDM), pp. 384–392 (2019)
3. Biggio, B., Roli, F.: Wild patterns: ten years after the rise of adversarial machine learning. Pattern Recogn. **84**, 317–331 (2018)
4. Caville, E., Lo, W.W., Layeghy, S., Portmann, M.: Anomal-E: a self-supervised network intrusion detection system based on graph neural networks. Knowl.-Based Syst. **258**, 110030 (2022)
5. Charikar, M.: Similarity estimation techniques from rounding algorithms. In: ACM Symposium on Theory of Computing (STOC) (2002)
6. Chen, J., Ma, T., Xiao, C.: FastGCN: fast learning with graph convolutional networks via importance sampling. In: International Conference on Learning Representations (ICLR) (2018)
7. Dai, H. et al.: Adversarial attack on graph structured data. In: International Conference on Machine Learning (ICML), Proceedings of Machine Learning Research (PMLR), vol. 80, pp. 1115–1124 (2018)
8. Entezari, N., Al-Sayouri, S.A., Darvishzadeh, A., Nikolakopoulos, A.N.: All you need is low (rank): defending against adversarial attacks on graphs. In: ACM Web Search and Data Mining (WSDM) (2020)
9. Ferrag, M.A., Maglaras, L., Moschoyiannis, S., Janicke, H.: Deep learning for cyber security intrusion detection: approaches, datasets, and comparative study. J. Inf. Secur. Appl. **50**, 102419 (2020)
10. Geisler, S., Schmidt, T., Şirin, H., Zügner, D., Bojchevski, A., Günnemann, S.: Robustness of graph neural networks at scale. Adv. Neural Inf. Process. Syst. (NeurIPS). **34** (2021)
11. Grosse, K., Papernot, N., Manoharan, P., Backes, M., McDaniel, P.: Adversarial examples for malware detection. In: European Symposium on Research in Computer Security (ESORICS), vol. 10493, pp. 62–79. Springer LNCS (2017)
12. Indyk, P., Motwani, R.: Approximate nearest neighbors: towards removing the curse of dimensionality. In: ACM Symposium on Theory of Computing (STOC) (1998)
13. Jin, W., Ma, Y., Liu, X., Tang, X., Wang, S., Tang, J.: Graph structure learning for robust graph neural networks. In: ACM SIGKDD Conference on Knowledge Discovery and Data Mining (KDD) (2020)

14. Khraisat, A., Gondal, I., Vamplew, P., Kamruzzaman, J.: Survey of intrusion detection systems: techniques, datasets and challenges. Cybersecurity. **2**(1), 20 (2019)
15. Kipf, T.N., Welling, M.: Semi-supervised classification with graph convolutional networks. In: International Conference on Learning Representations (ICLR) (2017)
16. Koroniotis, N., Moustafa, N., Sitnikova, E.: A new network forensic framework based on deep learning for Internet of Things networks: a particle deep framework. Future Gen. Comput. Syst. (Elsevier). **110**, 91–106 (2020)
17. Li, B., Jha, S., Xin, T., Yao, H.: Reliable representations make a stronger defender: unsupervised structure refinement for robust GNN. In: ACM SIGKDD Conference on Knowledge Discovery and Data Mining (KDD) (2022)
18. Lo, W.W., Layeghy, S., Sarhan, M., Gallagher, M., Portmann, M.: E-GraphSAGE: a graph neural network based intrusion detection system for IoT. In: 2022 IEEE/IFIP Network Operations and Management Symposium (NOMS), pp. 1–9 (2022)
19. Madry, A., Makelov, A., Schmidt, L., Tsipras, D., Vladu, A.: Towards deep learning models resistant to adversarial attacks. In: International Conference on Learning Representations (ICLR) (2018)
20. Mirsky, Y., Doitshman, T., Elovici, Y., Shabtai, A.: Kitsune: an ensemble of autoencoders for online network intrusion detection. In: Network and Distributed System Security Symposium (NDSS) (2018)
21. Neto, E.C.P., Dadkhah, S., Ferreira, R., Zohourian, A., Lu, R., Ghorbani, A.A.: CICIoT2023: a real-time dataset and benchmark for large-scale attacks in IoT environments. Sensors. **23**(13), 5941 (2023)
22. Pitropakis, N., Panaousis, E., Giannetsos, T., Anastasiadis, E., Loukas, G.: A taxonomy and survey of attacks against machine learning. Comput. Sci. Rev. (Elsevier). **34**, 100199 (2019)
23. Ring, M., Wunderlich, S., Scheuring, D., Landes, D., Hotho, A.: A survey of network-based intrusion detection data sets. Comput. Secur. **86**, 147–166 (2019)
24. Sharafaldin, I., Lashkari, A.H., Ghorbani, A.A.: Toward generating a new intrusion detection dataset and intrusion traffic characterization. In: International Conference on Information Systems Security and Privacy (ICISSP) (2018)
25. Sun, L. et al.: Adversarial attack and defense on graph data: a survey. IEEE Trans. Knowl. Data Eng. **35**(8), 7693–7711 (2022)
26. Veličković, P., Cucurull, G., Casanova, A., Romero, A., Lio, P., Bengio, Y.: Graph attention networks. In: International Conference on Learning Representations (ICLR) (2018)
27. Wu, H., Wang, C., Tyshetskiy, Y., Docherty, A., Lu, K., Zhu, L.: Adversarial examples for graph data: deep insights into attack and defense. In: International Joint Conference on Artificial Intelligence (IJCAI) (2019)
28. Xu, K. et al.: Topology attack and defense for graph neural networks: an optimization perspective. In: International Joint Conference on Artificial Intelligence (IJCAI), pp. 3961–3967 (2019)
29. Yin, D., Chen, Y., Kannan, R., Bartlett, P.: Byzantine-robust distributed learning: towards optimal statistical rates. In: International Conference on Machine Learning (ICML), Proceedings of Machine Learning Research (PMLR), vol. 80, pp. 5650–5659 (2018)
30. Zhang, X., Zitnik, M.: GNNGuard: defending graph neural networks against adversarial attacks. Adv. Neural Inf. Process. Syst. (NeurIPS). **33**, 9263–9275 (2020)
31. Zhou, J. et al.: Graph neural networks: a review of methods and applications. AI Open. **1**, 57–81 (2020)
32. Zhu, D., Zhang, Z., Cui, P., Zhu, W.: Robust graph convolutional networks against adversarial attacks. In: ACM SIGKDD Conference on Knowledge Discovery and Data Mining (KDD), pp. 1399–1407 (2019)

33. Zügner, D., Akbarnejad, A., Günnemann, S.: Adversarial attacks on neural networks for graph data. In: ACM SIGKDD Conference on Knowledge Discovery and Data Mining (KDD) (2018)
34. Zügner, D., Günnemann, S.: Adversarial attacks on graph neural networks via meta learning. In: International Conference on Learning Representations (ICLR) (2019)
35. Zügner, D., Günnemann, S.: Certifiable robustness and robust training for graph convolutional networks. In: ACM SIGKDD Conference on Knowledge Discovery and Data Mining (KDD), pp. 1658–1668 (2019)

VeilSearch: Split-Vector Local Differential Privacy for Encrypted Cross-Modal Retrieval

Yingying Qi, Jiabei Wang(✉), Xugong Qin, and Yongbin Zhou(✉)

School of Cyber Science and Engineering, Nanjing University of Science and Technology, Nanjing, China
{qiyingying,wangjiabei,qinxugong,zhouyongbin}@njust.edu.cn

Abstract. Cross-modal retrieval enables expressive search across heterogeneous modalities and is increasingly deployed in untrusted cloud environments. While encrypted-domain retrieval protects sensitive data (e.g., data containing faces and contextual descriptions), structural leakage (e.g., access, search, and rank patterns) remains a critical privacy risk. Existing local differential privacy approaches, such as *LDPfeat*, partially mitigate such leakage but introduce two challenges: feature expansion and high-dimensional semantic distortion. We present *VeilSearch*, a semantic-preserving encrypted retrieval framework for bidirectional image-text search. Its core component, the Split-Vector Generalized Randomized Response (SV-GRR) mechanism, maps high-dimensional embeddings into multiple sub-codebook spaces. This design enlarges the perturbation candidate space while reducing semantic distortion and maintaining 1:1 storage efficiency. Extensive experiments on COCO and Flickr30k show that *VeilSearch* achieves competitive retrieval performance with low overhead, demonstrating a favorable practical privacy-utility trade-off.

Keywords: Cross-modal Retrieval · Local Differential Privacy · Encrypted Retrieval · Pattern Leakage Protection

1 Introduction

Cross-modal retrieval (CMR) enables semantic search across heterogeneous data such as images and text, serving as a core component of modern multimedia systems. Applications including image-text search, multimodal recommendation and visual understanding rely on shared embedding spaces to align visual and textual features. As CMR systems are widely deployed on clouds, sensitive multimodal data with faces and personal preferences is routinely outsourced for storage and computation. Protecting sensitive multi-modal information during outsourced retrieval has become increasingly important.

Encryption effectively protects the raw content of multimedia data in outsourced storage and retrieval. However, as extensively studied in searchable

L. Ding et al. (Eds.): APWeb-WAIM 2026, LNCS 16995, pp. 381–394, 2027.
https://doi.org/10.1007/978-981-92-5699-0_25

encryption (SE) literature [5,12,13], even encrypted systems inevitably leak certain observable interaction patterns during the retrieval process, including access and search patterns. Similar to single-modal text retrieval in SE, cross-modal retrieval in the encrypted domain introduces additional leakages, particularly rank order and fine-grained similarity scores. As demonstrated by the Coordinate Alignment (CA) attack in Sect. 4.1, a semi-honest server can exploit these leakages to infer sensitive user attributes (Table 4). This vulnerability highlights the urgent need for effective pattern protection mechanisms.

Existing defenses for hiding pattern leakage provide limited practical solutions in this setting. Strong cryptographic techniques [7,8,16] offer theoretical security guarantees. However, their substantial computational and communication overhead render them impractical for large-scale, high-dimensional cross-modal retrieval. To overcome these limitations, we propose a hybrid paradigm that integrates cryptographic protection with feature-level perturbation based on local differential privacy (LDP) [3,6]. In this design, the client perturbs extracted embeddings via LDP-based feature perturbation, providing a tunable trade-off between privacy and retrieval recall. Then, the client uses a similarity-preserving encryption scheme to ensure the raw content. The server subsequently performs secure top-k similarity search directly over the encrypted, obfuscated embeddings. A straightforward implementation of LDP-based feature perturbation, such as *LDPfeat* [19], however, faces two practical bottlenecks in high-dimensional cross-modal retrieval.

(1) *Subset-Based Feature Expansion*: *LDPfeat* generates m perturbed outputs for each input feature (based on w-Subset [19] mechanism), resulting in an m-fold increase in storage and communication cost. This subset-based output mechanism increases storage and communication overhead, limiting scalability in large-scale cross-modal databases.

(2) *High-Dimensional Semantic Distortion*: *LDPfeat* builds a fixed-size sampling space $\mathcal{K}$ through global clustering [10] from large-scale public datasets and performs sampling directly in the original high-dimensional feature space. This approach balance preservation probability and semantic coverage. As defined by $p = me^{\varepsilon}/(me^{\varepsilon} + |\mathcal{K}| - m)$, the probability p of retaining the original value drops sharply as $|\mathcal{K}|$ expands to cover high-dimensional features. Conversely, a restricted $|\mathcal{K}|$ fails to provide sufficient semantic granularity, leading to excessive distances between perturbed outputs and true features. Thus, retrieval effectiveness degrades due to insufficient retention probability or semantic distortion.

To address these challenges, we propose *VeilSearch*, a novel privacy-preserving and semantic-aware framework for bidirectional cross-modal retrieval under our hybrid paradigm. It introduces a divide-and-conquer mapping, the split-vector Generalized Randomized Response (SV-GRR) design, achieving zero-expansion storage. By integrating EASPE [14,20], our framework facilitates secure inner-product computation directly on ciphertext, preventing the server from directly observing semantic relationships.

Contributions. The main contributions are summarized as follows:

- *Systematic leakage analysis*: We investigate pattern leakage in encrypted cross-modal retrieval and analyze how access and rank information can be

Table 1. Summary of Notations.

Notation	Description	Notation	Description
$\mathcal{K}$	The sample space of *LDPfeat*.	v_i	A sub-vector of a doc-feature.
$\mathcal{F}_{DB}$	The document feature database.	v_i'	The obfuscated output of a sub-vector.
$\mathcal{F}_Q$	The Query feature database.	K_{search}	The encryption key for features(EASPE).
f_d	The document feature.	$K_{content}$	The encryption key for doc-content.
f_d'	The obfuscated full feature.	$DocEDB$	The encrypted document database.
f_q	The query feature.	$\widehat{f_d}$	The encrypted doc-feature.
M	The number of divided fragments.	$\widehat{f_q}$	The encrypted query feature.
CB_i	The codebook of the i-th sub-vector.		

exploited to infer semantic relationships between queries and documents. We further demonstrate the vulnerability through a Coordinate Alignment attacks under a semi-honest server setting.

- *VeilSearch framework*: We present semantic-preserving encrypted retrieval framework, *VeilSearch*, that integrates LDP-based feature perturbation with ciphertext-domain similarity computation. It factorizes perturbation into local subspaces, yielding a combinatorially enlarged candidate space under constant feature dimensionality. It mitigates pattern leakage in cross-modal encrypted retrieval.
- *Comprehensive evaluation*: We conduct extensive experiments on COCO and Flickr30k datasets in both text-to-image (T2I) and image-to-text (I2T) settings. *VeilSearch* achieves retrieval utility and privacy protection higher than existing LDP-based baselines while maintaining practical efficiency.

2 Preliminary

We build *VeilSearch* upon the foundations of LDP [3,6], Contrastive Language-Image Pretraining (CLIP) [9,18,21], and Enhanced Asymmetric Scalar Product Preserving Encryption (EASPE) [14,20]. Notation is summarized in Table 1.

Local Differential Privacy. LDP allows users to sanitize their data locally before sending it to the server, so the server does not need to be trusted.

Definition 1 (Local Differential Privacy). *A randomized mechanism $\mathcal{M}$ satisfies ε-LDP where $\varepsilon \geq 0$, if and only if for any inputs x_1 and x_2,*

$$\forall y \in Range(\mathcal{M}) : \frac{\Pr[\mathcal{M}(x_1) = y]}{\Pr[\mathcal{M}(x_2) = y]} \leq e^{\varepsilon}, \tag{1}$$

where $Range(\mathcal{M})$ denotes the set of all possible outputs. Conversely, a larger ε loosens the constraint and reduces privacy protection.

Cross-Modal Feature Extraction. CLIP serves as the backbone for cross-modal retrieval. It has two encoders: a query encoder $f_q \leftarrow$

Clip.QueEncode($query$) and a document encoder $f_d \leftarrow$ Clip.DocEncode (doc). After normalization, both representations $\bar{f}_d$ and $\bar{f}_q$ are projected into a shared hypersphere. Its symmetry natively supports bidirectional retrieval tasks, enabling both text-to-image and image-to-text retrieval with the same underlying metric. The semantic similarity is computed as the dot product $S = \bar{f}_d^\top \bar{f}_q$.

Enhanced Asymmetric Scalar Product-Preserving Encryption (EASPE). EASPE [14,20] performs ciphertext-domain inner-product computation. Let $\Omega = (\mathsf{KGen}, \mathsf{FeatEnc}, \mathsf{QueryEnc}, \mathsf{SimComp})$ be a EASPE scheme, where $\mathsf{KGen}(\lambda)$ generates secret key K, $\mathsf{FeatEnc}(K, \bar{f}_d) \rightarrow \hat{f}_d$ encrypts doc-features, $\mathsf{QueryEnc}(K, \bar{f}_q) \rightarrow \hat{f}_q$ encrypts queries, and the inner-product computed in ciphertext by $\mathsf{SimComp}(\hat{f}_d, \hat{f}_q) = \bar{f}_d^\top \cdot \bar{f}_q$ is exactly the same as that in plaintext.

3 System Overview

3.1 System Model

Our system model involves three entities: **(i) Data Owner (DO):** extracts doc-features, obfuscates each feature with LDP, encrypts the obfuscated data, and outsources them to the server. **(ii) Data User (DU):** uploads a trapdoor to search for matched documents from the server. **(iii) Server:** stores encrypted sensitive data, executing secure retrieval to return the top-k results to the DU.

3.2 Threat Model

Consistent with previous work [11,15], we adopt the semi-honest adversary model, where the adversary follows the protocol but attempts to infer underlying sensitive information. Pattern information leakage specifically addresses both access pattern (Def. 2) and rank pattern (Def. 3). The adversary can leverage pattern leakage to reconstruct queries and documents using auxiliary knowledge.

Definition 2 (Access Pattern Leakage). *The access pattern leakage of top-k encrypted retrieval scheme is defined as* $\mathcal{L}_{access}(q) = \{\, i \mid x_i \in \mathrm{TopK}(q, \mathcal{F}_{DB})\,\}$. *That is, the server learns the exact set of identifiers corresponding to the returned top-k results. For any two queries,* $q_a = q_b \Rightarrow \mathcal{L}_{access}(q_a) = \mathcal{L}_{access}(q_b)$.

Definition 3 (Rank Pattern Leakage). *The rank pattern leakage of a top-k encrypted retrieval scheme is defined as* $\mathcal{L}_{rank}(q) = \{(i_j, s_j)\}_{j=1}^{k}$, *where* $i_1 \succ i_2 \succ \cdots \succ i_k$ *denotes the ranked order of the top-k results, and s_j is the similarity score between query q and document. This leak reveals both the rank order and concrete similarity scores of the returned documents with respect to the query.*

3.3 Definition of *VeilSearch*

We present *VeilSearch*, enabling pattern-protected cross-modal encrypted search.

Definition 4 (*VeilSearch*). *A retrieval scheme Σ over encrypted cross-modal data consists of the following three polynomial-time algorithms/protocols.*

- *KeyGen*(λ): *A probabilistic algorithm that takes a security parameter* λ *and outputs two secret key sets* K_Σ.
- *OFeatEnc*($K_\Sigma, \varepsilon, \mathcal{F}_{DB}, \{CB_i\}_{i=1}^{M}, DocDB$): *An algorithm executed by the client that takes as input the secret key* K_Σ, *the privacy budget* ε, *and the sample sets* $\{CB_i\}_{i=1}^{M}$ *and doc-feature dataset* $\mathcal{F}_{DB}$ *to obtain encrypted and obfuscated data* $\widehat{\mathcal{F}}_{DB}$ *and* $DocEDB$.
- *OSearch*($K_\Sigma, f_q; \widehat{\mathcal{F}}_{DB}, DocEDB, k$): *A client-server protocol, where the client takes as input the secret key set* K_Σ, *a query feature* f_q *to generate trapdoors* $\widehat{f}_q$, *while the server takes as input* $\widehat{\mathcal{F}}_{DB}$ *and* $DocEDB$. *At the end of the protocol, the server outputs the matching results* C_{topk}.

Security Goals. (i) Data & Query Confidentiality: The server learns nothing about plaintext content or queries beyond the defined leakage, remaining computationally indistinguishable under $IND-CPA$; (ii)Pattern Privacy: *VeilSearch* mitigates access and rank pattern leakage, ensuring the server cannot recover or exploit the original semantic relationships stored in the ciphertext.

4 Our Construction

4.1 Motivation: Coordinate Alignment Attack

Although encryption can protect the raw content of multimedia data, the server can observe the score matrix $S \in \mathbb{R}^{m \times n}$, where each entry represents the similarity score between a query and a document. To recover the underlying semantic mappings, we identify a powerful inference attack called Coordinate Alignment attack. Assuming the adversary obtains a small fraction of Top-k plaintext $(\mathbf{k}_i, \mathbf{x}_d)$ pairs as background knowledge, the attack exploits both raw similarity scores and ranking order information Top-k $\left\{(id_j, score_j)\right\}_{j=1}^{k}$. The score leakage is caused by encryption algorithm EAPSE.

Phase 1: Keyword-to-Row Alignment. For each row in S, a combined signature is constructed by fusing raw similarity scores and order. The correlation between the combined signatures of kw_i and row r in S is calculated as $\mathrm{corr}(\mathbf{k}_i, \mathbf{s}_r) = \alpha \cdot \rho_{order} + (1-\alpha) \cdot \rho_{score}$, where the mapping from BK to S is determined by $\phi(i) = \arg\max_r \mathrm{corr}(\mathbf{k}_i, \mathbf{s}_r)$. The resulting aligned rows form the set of Seed Rows $\mathcal{R}_{seed}$.

Phase 2: Document-to-Column Recovery. Using $\mathcal{R}_{seed}$ as a shared coordinate system, known documents are projected as sparse vectors on the plaintext side, where values exist only if d appears in the Top-k for kw, otherwise marked as NaN. The document-to-column mappings are recovered through localized correlation alignment. The correlation between the observed dimensions $\mathbf{x}_d|_{\mathrm{obs}}$ (without NaN values) in D_{known} and c in S is calculated as $\psi(d) = \arg\max_c \mathrm{corr}(\mathbf{x}_d|_{\mathrm{obs}}, \mathbf{y}_c|_{\mathrm{obs}})$.

Such leakage is particularly detrimental in cross-modal retrieval, as it allows a semi-honest server to infer sensitive user attributes and visual semantics from

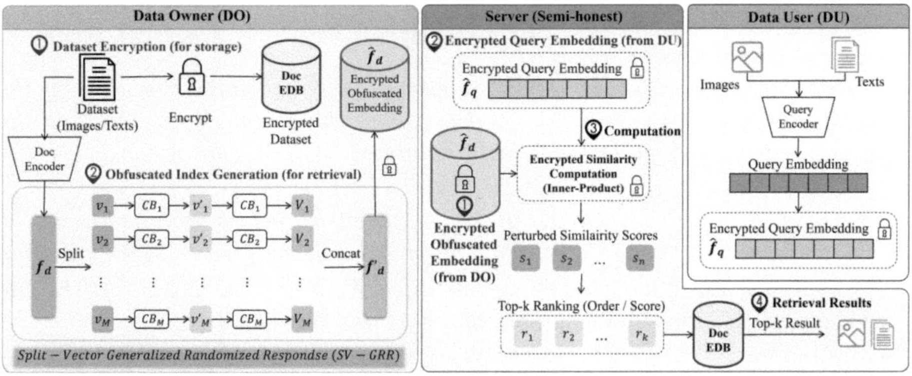

Fig. 1. Overview of the *VeilSearch*.

seemingly innocuous retrieval behaviors (Table 4). To address this critical vulnerability, we propose *VeilSearch*, a novel privacy-preserving framework for bidirectional cross-modal retrieval under our hybrid paradigm. It effectively mitigates both access and rank patterns while maintaining high retrieval utility. To address feature expansion and semantic distortion, *VeilSearch* combine deterministic nearest-anchor mapping with independent GRR on sub-vectors (SV-GRR) , achieving zero-expansion storage while constructing a combinatorially expanded candidate perturbation space. Encryption algorithm EASPE [14,20] facilitates secure inner-product computation directly on ciphertext, shielding underlying semantics from honest-but-curious servers. Systematic privacy analysis confirms that *VeilSearch* maintains a stable privacy bound with retrieval utility.

4.2 *VeilSearch* Scheme

Phase I: System Initialization The DO executes the KeyGen algorithm to output a key set $K_{\Sigma} = (K_{\text{search}}, K_{\text{content}})$. We employ K_{search} for EASPE-based feature encryption, enabling secure inner-product similarity computation over ciphertext. Raw contents are protected via symmetric encryption with K_{content}. Before retrieval, these keys are securely distributed to authorized users.

Phase II: Secure Index Generation To mitigate the feature expansion, the high-dimensional semantic distortion, and maintain retrieval utility, DO transforms raw features f_d into privacy-preserving structures via the SV-GRR mechanism shown in Fig. 1 (left). DO executes the OFeatEnc algorithm to obfuscate the candidate database.

Sub-vector Partitioning and Mapping. To prevent excessive noise injection in the high-dimensional feature space (e.g., 1024-d), we employ a divide-and-conquer strategy (lines 2-6), partitioning f_d into M disjoint sub-vectors v_i. Each v_i is mapped to its nearest anchor v_i' in a pre-trained sub-codebook CB_i. This discretization creates robust semantic anchors and confines the feature space.

Algorithm 1 $\mathsf{OFeatEnc}(K_\Sigma, \varepsilon, \mathcal{F}_{DB}, \{CB_i\}_{i=1}^{M}, DocDB)$

1: Initialize encrypted secure index $\widehat{\mathcal{F}}_{DB} \leftarrow \emptyset$
2: **for all** $f_d \in \mathcal{F}_{DB}$ **do**
3:     $(v_1, v_2, \ldots, v_M) \leftarrow \mathsf{Split}(f_d, M)$ ▷ Sub-vector Partitioning
4:     Initialize an empty array $V \leftarrow [\,]$
5:     **for** $i = 1$ **to** M **do**
6:         $v_i' \leftarrow \mathsf{Nearest}(v_i, CB_i),\ v_i' \in CB_i$ ▷ Deterministic Mapping
7:         Compute $p \leftarrow \dfrac{e^{\varepsilon_i}}{e^{\varepsilon_i} + |CB_i| - 1}$
8:         Draw $b \sim Bernoulli(p)$ ▷ GRR Replacement
9:         $V_i \leftarrow v_i'$, if $b = 1$
10:         $V_i \leftarrow Sample(CB_i \setminus \{v_i'\}, 1)$, otherwise
11:     **end for**
12:     $\widetilde{f}_d \leftarrow \mathsf{Concat}(V_i)$ ▷ Combinatorial Expansion, $|\widetilde{f}_d| = |f_d|$
13:     $\bar{f}_d \leftarrow \mathsf{Normalize}(\widetilde{f}_d)$, replace f_d by $\bar{f}_d$
14:     $\widehat{f}_d \leftarrow \mathsf{EASPE.FeatEnc}(\bar{f}_d, K_{search})$, append $\widehat{f}_d$ into $\widehat{\mathcal{F}}_{DB}$
15: **end for**
16: $\mathsf{DocEDB} \leftarrow \{c \mid c \leftarrow \mathsf{SymEnc}(doc, K_{content}),\ doc \in DocDB\}$
17: Upload $(\widehat{\mathcal{F}}_{DB}, DocEDB)$ to server

Localized Perturbation via GRR. Each v_i' is independently perturbed using the GRR mechanism over CB_i (lines 7-10). By adhering to the privacy budget ε, the mechanism probabilistically retains or flips the centroid. This ensures ε-LDP while restricting semantic distortion to the local sub-codebook CB_i, reducing the risk of excessive semantic distortion observed in global-domain perturbation.

Reconstruction and Normalization. All the perturbed sub-vectors are concatenated and re-normalized. While local codebooks remain small $|CB_i|$, the global vector resides in a theoretically combinatorial space of $|CB_i|^M$, enabling fine-grained semantic representation. Normalization further projects the features onto the unit hypersphere to preserve cosine similarity validity.

Encryption and Upload. Finally, the DO encrypts these features using EASPE. $\mathsf{FeatEnc}(\cdot,\cdot)$ and the raw content via $\mathsf{SymEnc}(\cdot,\cdot)$ (Lines 14-17). Although some combinatorial candidates may not correspond to realistic semantic embeddings, the factorized perturbation still increases perturbation diversity in practice. The feature perturbation process is performed once during index generation and is independent of the database size.

Phase III: Retrieval Protocol. The retrieval phase, denoted as $\mathsf{OSearch}$, enables secure cross-modal matching through an interaction between the DU and the Server (see Fig. 1 (right)). No perturbation processing is required on the side of the DU. This protocol ensures that similarity computation remains confined to the ciphertext domain, shielding both query intent and document content from the server.

$C \rightarrow S$: The client invokes $\mathsf{EASPE.QueEnc}(\cdot,\cdot)$ to generate a search trapdoor $\widehat{f_q}$. This trapdoor facilitates inner-product evaluation against the encrypted index while concealing the original query semantics from the server.

$S \rightarrow C$: Upon receiving $\widehat{f_q}$, the server performs $\mathsf{EASPE.SimComp}(\cdot,\cdot)$ across the obfuscated index $\widehat{\mathcal{F}}_{DB}$. Because the index is perturbed, the server observes similarity scores computed over perturbed embeddings. Finally, the server locates the top-k encrypted documents C_{topk} from $DocEDB$ and returns them to the DU for local decryption.

5 Security Analysis

We provide a security analysis of *VeilSearch* in terms of data and query confidentiality, as well as pattern protection. LDP remains robust under the post-processing property, while EASPE ensures content confidentiality independently.
Data & Query Confidentiality. The data privacy of *VeilSearch* is grounded in the semantic confidentiality of the underlying encryption primitives (Them. 1).

Theorem 1. *The VeilSearch scheme achieves IND-CPA security.*
Proof. The data privacy of VeilSearch is directly reducible to the security of its core primitives. Raw contents are protected via symmetric encryption (e.g., AES) under $K_{content}$*, while features are encrypted using* EASPE *under* K_{search}*. In* EASPE*, internal randomization ensures that ciphertexts are computationally indistinguishable, which is proved in [4, 20]. Consequently, an adversary* $\mathcal{A}$ *without the secret keys can achieve only a negligible advantage in the IND-CPA game:* $Adv_{VeilSearch,\mathcal{A}}^{IND-CPA}(1^\lambda) \leq negl(\lambda)$.

Privacy Analysis of Pattern Protection. *VeilSearch* achieves pattern protection by injecting calibrated noise via LDP.

Theorem 2. *The SV-GRR mechanism satisfies* $\sum \varepsilon_i$*-LDP.*
Proof. Let v *be a sub-vector and* $v' \in CB$ *be its nearest anchor. The mechanism follows the pipeline* $v \xrightarrow{det.} v' \xrightarrow{GRR} V$*. Since the initial mapping is deterministic* $\Pr[V|v] = \Pr[V|v']$*. For any* v_1, v_2 *with anchors* v'_1, v'_2*, the GRR guarantees:*

$$\frac{\Pr[V|v_1]}{\Pr[V|v_2]} = \frac{\Pr[V|v'_1]}{\Pr[V|v'_2]} \leq \frac{e^{\varepsilon_i}/(e^{\varepsilon_i} + |CB| - 1)}{1/(e^{\varepsilon_i} + |CB| - 1)} = e^{\varepsilon_i} \tag{2}$$

By the sequential composition property, the overall privacy budget equals the sum of the sub-vector budgets. Thus, the SV-GRR mechanism satisfies $\sum \varepsilon_i$*-LDP.* □

The original features determine the true similarity matrix and the resulting access and rank patterns. After SV-GRR perturbation, retrieval is performed over a perturbed similarity structure, introducing controlled uncertainty into observable ranking behaviors. While ε-LDP does not formally guarantee retrieval-pattern privacy, it empirically reduces the correlation between observed retrieval patterns and the original semantic structure.

6 Experimental Evaluation

We evaluate *VeilSearch* in terms of efficiency, retrieval effectiveness, and privacy-utility trade-off. Retrieval effectiveness is measured by Recall@k(R@k) under varying ε. We measure retrieval effectiveness using Recall@K at a specific budget that achieves a favorable privacy-utility trade-off. We further assess privacy leakage via CA attack using access, search, and rank pattern leakage, reporting adversarial success rates. All components are implemented in Python and executed on a machine equipped with a 12th Gen Intel® Core^{TM} i7-12700 CPU @ 2.1 GHz and 16 GB RAM. Experiments are conducted on COCO [1] and Flickr30k [2].

Table 2. Phase-wise Execution Time on COCO T2I (ms).

Method	KeyGen	OFeatEnc	OSearch	
			$C \to S$	$S \to C$
LDPfeat	25.70	18350.64	1.34	2821.20
VeilSearch	23.19	6244.09	1.28	903.28

Table 3. Running Time of Two Key Phases on COCO T2I (s).

Phase	Method	m=1	m=2	m=3	m=4	m=5
OFeatEnc	*LDPfeat*	6.24	12.36	18.24	24.94	31.94
	VeilSearch	constant at 6.24				
OSearch($S \to C$)	*LDPfeat*	1.00	1.86	2.82	3.67	4.78
	VeilSearch	constant at 0.90				

6.1 Efficiency Analysis

We first report the execution time of the three-phase, including key generation (KeyGen), feature perturbation and encryption (OFeatEnc), and the search interaction OSearch (both $C \to S$ and $S \to C$). The running time on COCO (5k images/25k texts) and Flickr30k (1k images/5k texts) is under a fixed output subset size $m = 3$ (Table 2). The sample spaces of *LDPfeat* and *VeilSearch* are constructed once offline from the COCO train dataset (118k images) and reused in subsequent experiments. Furthermore, we measure the running time of two dominant phases (Table 3), namely OFeatEnc and OSearch ($S \to C$). The baseline *LDPfeat* scales linearly with output size m, while *VeilSearch* remains constant.

Table 4. Recovery Performance on Flickr30k w/o *VeilSearch* against CA Attack. Results are evaluated under 5%, 10%, and 20% background knowledge. We set $\alpha = 0.7$ to prioritize order over scores, while $\alpha = 0$ serves as the score-only base.

DatasetKnowledge		No. of Recovered Keywords (Correct) (Accuracy Rate of Recovered Keywords) (Correct Keyword Recovery Rate)		No. of Recovered Documents (Correct) (Accuracy Rate of Recovered Documents) (Correct Document Recovery Rate)	
No. of query	No. of doc	Non-private (α=0)	***VeilSearch*** (α=0.7)	Non-private (α=0)	***VeilSearch*** (α=0.7)
250(5%)	776	250(250) (100%) (100%)	241(**10**) 96.40% 4.15%	171(171) 22.04% 100%	139(**0**) 17.91% 0%
500(10%)	912	500 (500) (100%) (100%)	458 (**22**) (91.60%) (4.80%)	397 (397) (43.45%) (100%)	292 (**2**) (32.02%) (0.68%)
1000(20%)	979	1000 (1000) (100%) (100%)	880 (**56**) (88.00%) (3.18%)	722 (722) (73.75%) (100%)	445 (**12**) (45.45%) (2.70%)

Table 5. Recall@K of Obfuscated Methods on COCO and Flickr30k (%).

		COCO (ε=9)						Flickr30k (ε=7)					
		Text-to-Image			Image-to-Text			Text-to-Image			Image-to-Text		
Model	Method	R@1	R@5	R@10	R@1	R@5	R@10	R@1	R@5	R@10	R@1	R@5	R@10
	Non-private	28.28	52.94	64.11	48.08	74.02	74.02	57.34	83.24	90.00	78.60	94.90	94.90
	LDPfeat	6.84	21.60	31.83	12.44	36.32	36.32	8.36	20.58	26.10	15.50	41.70	41.70
RN50	***VeilSearch***	**22.97**	**46.44**	**57.88**	**36.06**	**62.22**	**62.22**	**39.76**	**68.64**	**79.06**	**58.20**	**85.00**	**85.00**
	Non-private	30.37	54.77	66.10	49.98	75.00	75.00	58.72	83.52	90.02	78.60	94.90	94.90
	LDPfeat	7.25	22.76	33.06	13.76	38.36	38.36	10.04	23.10	28.90	14.00	39.80	39.80
ViT-B/32	***VeilSearch***	**26.55**	**50.84**	**62.46**	**32.24**	**58.40**	**58.40**	**33.40**	**62.02**	**73.38**	**50.60**	**78.60**	**78.60**
	Non-private	32.71	57.76	68.23	51.78	76.72	76.72	62.16	85.72	91.90	82.20	96.60	96.60
	LDPfeat	7.50	23.77	33.65	14.74	39.64	39.64	10.42	23.58	29.16	15.90	41.60	41.60
ViT-B/16	***VeilSearch***	**29.20**	**53.43**	**64.26**	**33.84**	**60.76**	**60.76**	**37.98**	**64.90**	**75.84**	**50.60**	**82.70**	**82.70**

6.2 Attack Analysis

The attack jointly exploits access pattern and rank pattern (both score and order). We assume the adversary obtains 5%20% plaintext $(query, docs)$ pairs as background knowledge, which is realistic in semi-honest cloud scenarios where the server may access public or leaked auxiliary data. It achieves near-perfect recovery in the Non-private, while *VeilSearch* substantially degrades attack effectiveness across all scenarios (Table 4).

6.3 Comparative Retrieval Validity

In this section, we evaluate *VeilSearch* against three baselines: (1) Non-private, a non-private CLIP retrieval model (utility upper bound); (2) *LDPfeat* [17], a representative feature-level LDP mechanism; and (3) a recent CMR-SSE scheme [11], which follows the SSE paradigm and performs exact matching, lacking retrieval flexibility. Table 5 reports the R@k under fixed budgets on COCO and Flickr30k.

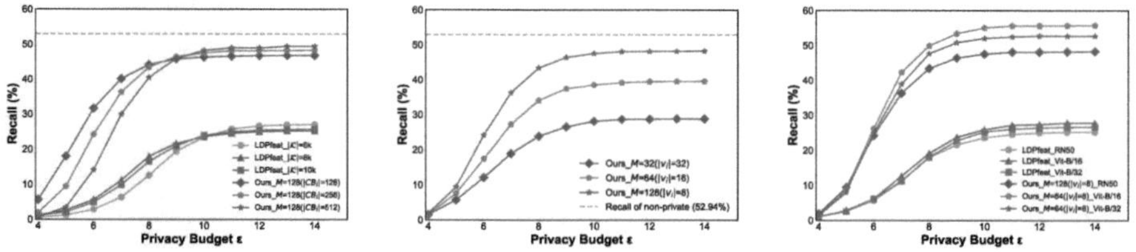

(a) COCO-T2I: Diff-size of sample spaces(RN50). (b) COCO-T2I: Diff-num of vector segment(RN50). (c) COCO-T2I: Different backbone architectures.

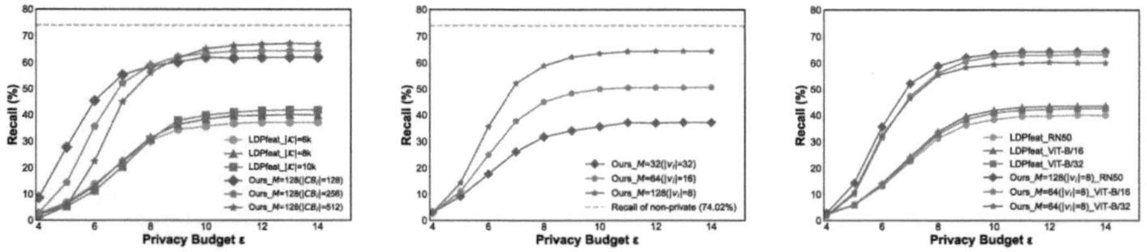

(d) COCO-I2T: Diff-size of sample spaces(RN50). (e) COCO-I2T: Diff-num of vector segment(RN50). (f) COCO-I2T: Different backbone architectures.

Fig. 2. Retrieval performance on COCO (R@5). We evaluate retrieval utility by contrasting *VeilSearch*'s sampling space ($|CB_i|^M$) against *LDPfeat*'s global space ($|\mathcal{K}|$), while analyzing the impact of partition quantity (M) and backbones. Warm and cool tones represent *VeilSearch* and *LDPfeat* baseline, respectively.

Comparison with *LDPfeat*. *VeilSearch* consistently achieves higher retrieval utility under localized perturbation. Specifically, on Flickr30k ($\varepsilon = 7$) with RN50 for T2I, *VeilSearch* (39.76%) represents a nearly 4.8× improvement over *LDPfeat* (8.36%) on R@1. Table 5 demonstrates that *VeilSearch* empirically alleviates the semantic distortion commonly observed under global-domain perturbation.
Approaching Non-private Utility. *VeilSearch* sustains strong semantic consistency, with negligible performance degradation relative to the non-private baseline, and achieves better utility after privacy-preserving perturbation.

6.4 Parameter Sensitivity

Influence of Sampling Space Size. We split the feature into M sub-vectors and build sub-codebooks CB_i via Spherical K-Means [10]. The sampling space

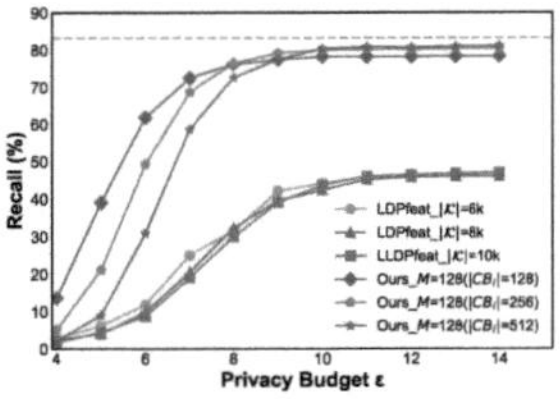

(a) Flickr-T2I: Diff-size of sample spaces(RN50).

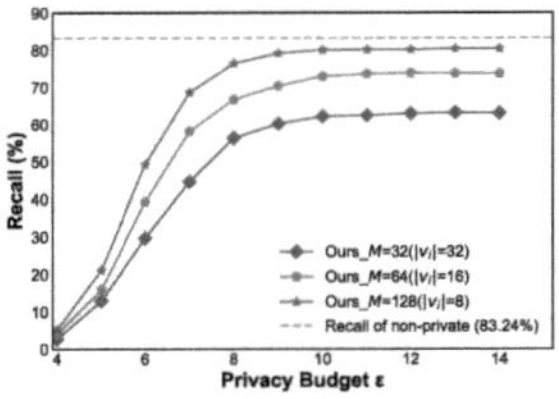

(b) Flickr-T2I: Diff-num of vector segment(RN50).

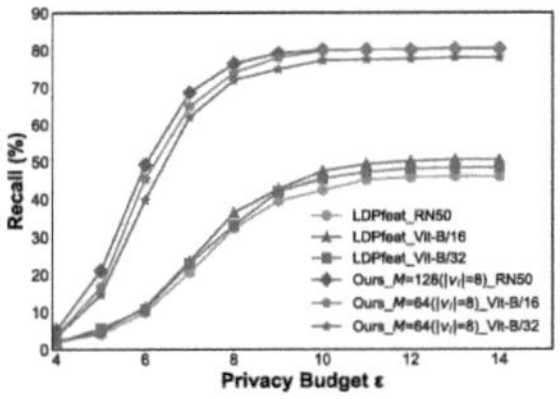

(c) Flickr-T2I: Different backbone architectures.

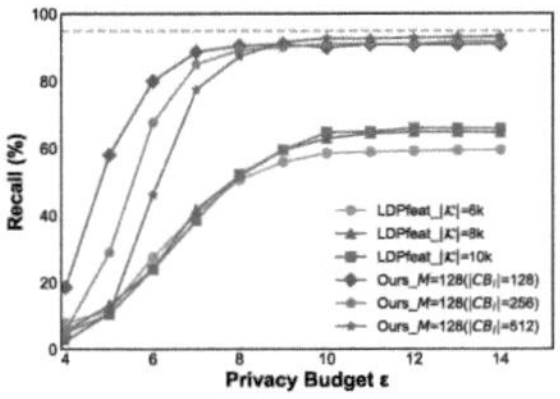

(d) Flickr-I2T: Diff-size of sample spaces(RN50).

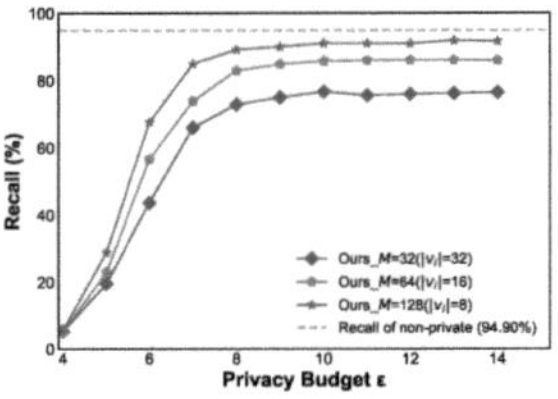

(e) Flickr-I2T: Diff-num of vector segment(RN50).

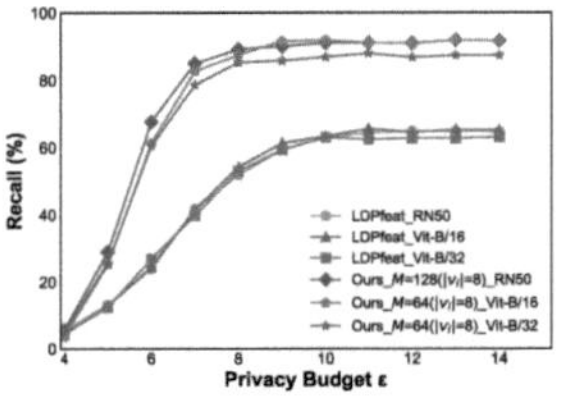

(f) Flickr-I2T: Different backbone architectures.

Fig. 3. Retrieval performance on Flickr30k (R@5). The experimental settings and color schemes are the same as in Fig. 2.

of *Veilsearch* expands exponentially to $|CB_i|^M$. As Fig. 2(a,d) and Fig. 3(a,d), *VeilSearch*($|CB_i|$ = 128/256/512) consistently outperforms *LDPfeat* ($|\mathcal{K}|$ = 6k/8k/10k) across all budget. Results show that our SV-GRR effectively mitigates semantic distortion, ensuring robust and substantial gains.

Influence of Vector Splitting. We investigate the effect of the number of partitions M on RN50 ($|f_d|$=1024 and M=32/64/128). As Fig. 2(b,e) and Fig. 3(b,e), retrieval recall improves monotonically as M increases. A larger M requires extra sub-codebooks, yet the overhead remains linear in the one-time offline clustering.

Robustness to Different backbones. We verify the scalability of *VeilSearch* across diverse backbones, including CNN-based (RN50) and Transformer-based (ViT-B/32, ViT-B/16) models. Compared to *LDPfeat* ($|\mathcal{K}| = 8k$), *VeilSearch* ($|CB_i| = 256$, $|v_i| = 8$) consistently achieves superior R@5 performance, as shown in Fig. 2(c,f) and Fig. 3(c,f). Recall that ε typically is confined within $[0.01, 10]$ for practical usage [17]. Experiments demonstrate that a larger ε quickly reduces the strength of privacy protection. Thus, we adopt $\varepsilon = 9$ for COCO and $\varepsilon = 7$ for Flickr30k, ensuring an optimal trade-off across all tested architectures.

Qualitative comparisons. Figure 4 presents a representative of T2I to illustrate pattern protection. Compared with the CLIP-Native baseline, *VeilSearch* perturbs the access and rank pattern. *VeilSearch* reduces the adversary's ability to infer query semantics from observed rank and access patterns (Table 4).

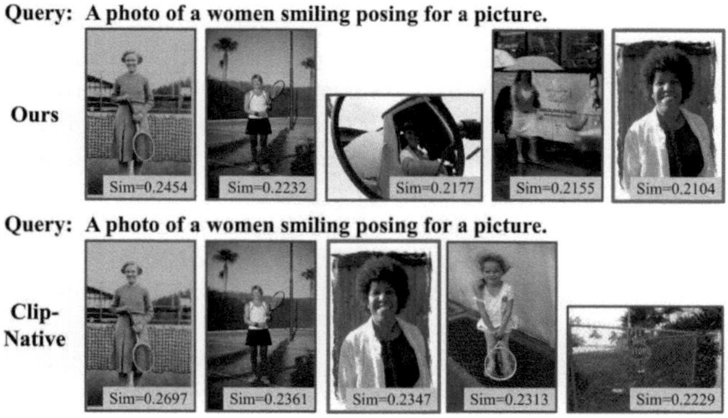

Fig. 4. Qualitative comparison with CLIP-Native. The green frame is the ground-truth image. *VeilSearch* (Color figure online) effectively perturbs both access pattern (false positive/negative) and rank pattern (order/scores) compared to CLIP-Native.

7 Conclusion

Cloud-based cross-modal retrieval suffers from access and rank leakage, while direct high-dimensional LDP perturbation causes semantic distortion and retrieval degradation. *VeilSearch* introduces a novel perturbation framework via SV-GRR, leveraging combinatorial factorization of perturbation spaces while maintaining 1:1 storage and communication efficiency, achieving a favorable privacy-utility balance. Future work will investigate incremental codebook updates and adaptive privacy budgeting for lower privacy costs and better scalability.

Acknowledgments. This work was supported by the Yunnan Provincial Major Science and Technology Special Plan Projects (202502AD080008), National Natural Science Foundation of China (No.62302226, No.62302224, No.62502207) and Yunnan Provincial New R&D Institution Cultivation Project (202404BQ040148).

Disclosure of Interests. The authors have no competing interests to declare that are relevant to the content of this article.

References

1. Coco. https://cocodataset.org/
2. Flickr. https://github.com/BryanPlummer/flickr30k_entities
3. Agarwal, S., Kamath, G., Majid, M., Mouzakis, A., Silver, R., Ullman, J.R.: Private mean estimation with person-level differential privacy. In: SODA, pp. 1–62 (2025)
4. Bernard, O., Joye, M., Smart, N.P., Walter, M.: Drifting towards better error probabilities in fully homomorphic encryption schemes. In: EUROCRYPT, pp. 181–211 (2025)
5. Cash, D., Grubbs, P., Perry, J., Ristenpart, T.: Leakage-abuse attacks against searchable encryption. In: CCS, pp. 668–679 (2015)

6. Fang, H., Chen, L., Liu, S.: Further study on frequency estimation under local differential privacy. In: USENIX Security, pp. 2771–2787 (2025)
7. Garimella, G., Goff, B., Miao, P.: Computation efficient structure-aware psi from incremental function secret sharing. In: CRYPTO, pp. 309–345 (2024)
8. Goldreich, O., Ostrovsky, R.: Software protection and simulation on oblivious rams. J. ACM (JACM) **43**(3), 431–473 (1996)
9. Guo, H., et al.: Towards natural language-based document image retrieval: New dataset and benchmark. In: CVPR, pp. 29722–29732 (2025)
10. Hornik, K., Feinerer, I., Kober, M., Buchta, C.: Spherical k-means clustering. J. Stat. Softw. **50**, 1–22 (2012)
11. Huang, W., Wang, X., Zhu, D., Ma, X., Ma, J.: When multimedia meets security: privacy-preserving cross-modal retrieval for large-scale data. IEEE Trans. Inf. Forensics Secur. **21**, 319–332 (2025)
12. Islam, M.S., Kuzu, M., Kantarcioglu, M.: Access pattern disclosure on searchable encryption: ramification, attack and mitigation. In: NDSS, pp. 1–15 (2012)
13. Langhout, T.J., Chen, H., Liang, K.: File-injection attacks on searchable encryption, based on binomial structures. In: ESORICS, pp. 424–443 (2024)
14. Lin, W., Wang, K., Zhang, Z., Chen, H.: Revisiting security risks of asymmetric scalar product preserving encryption and its variants. In: ICDCS, pp. 1–10 (2017)
15. Ma, C., Jia, C., Du, R., Ha, G., Li, M.: Privacy-preserving searchable encryption based on anonymization and differential privacy. In: ICWS, pp. 371–382 (2024)
16. Martins, P., Sousa, L., Mariano, A.: A survey on fully homomorphic encryption: an engineering perspective. CSUR **50**(6), 1–33 (2017)
17. Pittaluga, F., Zhuang, B.: LDP-feat: image features with local differential privacy. In: ICCV, pp. 17580–17590 (2023)
18. Qin, X., et al.: Clip is almost all you need: Towards parameter-efficient scene text retrieval without OCR. In: CVPR, pp. 24873–24883 (2025)
19. Wang, T., Zhang, X., Feng, J., Yang, X.: A comprehensive survey on local differential privacy toward data statistics and analysis. Sensors **20**(24), 7030 (2020)
20. Yang, Y., Miao, Y., Choo, K.K.R., Deng, R.H.: Lightweight privacy-preserving spatial keyword query over encrypted cloud data. In: ICDCS, pp. 392–402 (2022)
21. Zeng, G., et al.: Focus, distinguish, and prompt: unleashing clip for efficient and flexible scene text retrieval. In: ACM MM, pp. 2525–2534 (2024)

Special Track

CorrTie: Correction-Aware Tie-Breaking for Active Learning with Vision-Language Models

Duc Tai Phan, Tri Nguyen Thai, Khoa Minh Nguyen, Nhut Minh Nguyen, and Duc Ngoc Minh Dang(✉)

AiTA Lab, Faculty of Information Technology, FPT University, Ho Chi Minh City, Vietnam
{ducptse194683,tritnse194607,khoanmse184909,nhutnmse184534}@fpt.edu.vn, ducdnm2@fe.edu.vn

Abstract. Vision-language models (VLMs) provide strong transferable representations for visual recognition, but adapting them to downstream image classification tasks remains challenging when labeled data are scarce. Active learning (AL) reduces annotation cost by selecting informative unlabeled samples for oracle labeling; however, most AL strategies use oracle feedback only to expand the labeled training set. The correction event between a model prediction and the oracle label is usually not reused to guide future acquisition. To address this limitation, we propose Correction-aware Tie-breaking (CorrTie), a lightweight post-acquisition reranker for AL with VLMs. CorrTie keeps the base AL strategy unchanged and uses past oracle corrections to estimate class-wise correction risk. This risk is then used to rerank near-tie candidates while preserving the original acquisition ranking as the primary signal. Experiments with CoOp prompt learning on four image classification benchmarks and five base AL strategies show that CorrTie improves the average accuracy by +7.14, +3.74, and +0.66 percentage points at the 1%, 2%, and 5% annotation budgets, respectively. These results indicate that oracle corrections can serve not only as supervision for prompt learning, but also as useful feedback for future active sample acquisition.

Keywords: Vision-language models · Active learning · Prompt learning · Image classification · Reranking

1 Introduction

Vision-language models (VLMs) have recently become a powerful paradigm for visual recognition by aligning visual and textual representations in a shared embedding space. A representative example is Contrastive Language-Image Pre-training (CLIP) [12], which enables zero-shot recognition by comparing image features with textual class descriptions. Despite their strong transferability, adapting VLMs to domain-specific or fine-grained image classification tasks

L. Ding et al. (Eds.): APWeb-WAIM 2026, LNCS 16995, pp. 397–407, 2027.
https://doi.org/10.1007/978-981-92-5699-0_26

remains challenging when labeled data are scarce, since high-quality annotations are often expensive and time-consuming to obtain.

Prompt learning provides an efficient adaptation strategy by optimizing a small set of learnable prompt parameters while keeping most of the pre-trained VLM fixed. Methods such as Context Optimization (CoOp) [17], Visual Prompt Tuning (VPT) [6], Multi-modal Prompt Learning (MaPLe) [7], and Adaptive Prompt Tuning (APT) [3] have shown the effectiveness of this paradigm. However, prompt learning still depends heavily on the quality of labeled samples, making sample selection important when annotation budgets are limited.

Active learning (AL) addresses this issue by selecting a small subset of unlabeled samples for oracle annotation. Existing AL strategies estimate the usefulness of samples from different perspectives. Uncertainty-based methods prioritize low-confidence samples [9,16], diversity-based methods aim to cover the feature space [14], and hybrid methods combine informativeness and representativeness [1,10,11]. For example, Batch AL by Diverse Gradient Embeddings (BADGE) [1] selects diverse and uncertain samples in gradient space, Graph Convolutional Network-based AL (GCNAL) [4] exploits sample relationships, and Calibrated Entropy-weighted Clustering (CEC) improves AL for VLMs through calibrated uncertainty and clustering [13]. Despite their differences, these methods mainly rely on the current model state to rank unlabeled samples.

However, AL naturally produces another signal that is often underutilized. Before annotation, the current VLM assigns each selected sample a predicted class; after annotation, the oracle provides the true label. The mismatch between these two labels forms a correction event, indicating where the current prompt learner is unreliable. If samples predicted as a particular class are frequently corrected by the oracle, future samples predicted as that class may deserve higher acquisition priority. Existing AL strategies typically use oracle labels only to update the labeled set, whereas this correction signal is not explicitly reused in future selection.

To address this limitation, we propose Correction-aware Tie-breaking (CorrTie), a lightweight plug-in reranker for AL with VLMs. CorrTie keeps the base AL strategy unchanged and adds a correction-aware reranking step after candidate acquisition. Specifically, a base strategy first produces a candidate ranking from the unlabeled pool, and CorrTie estimates class-wise correction risk from previous prediction-label mismatches to reorder candidates that are close in the original ranking. In this way, CorrTie preserves the base acquisition preference while using oracle correction history to resolve near-ties.

The key design of CorrTie is conservative reranking. Rather than replacing the base strategy's acquisition score, CorrTie applies correction risk only within near-tie groups, preventing the correction signal from dominating the acquisition process. CorrTie also introduces no additional learnable acquisition model; it only maintains a lightweight memory of previously selected samples, their predicted classes, oracle labels, and correction indicators. This makes CorrTie simple to implement as a post-acquisition module for annotation-efficient VLM adaptation.

The main contributions of this work are summarized as follows:

- We propose CorrTie, a plug-in correction-aware tie-breaking reranker for AL with VLMs.
- We introduce a lightweight oracle correction memory that estimates class-wise correction risk from previous prediction-label mismatches.
- We design a conservative reranking mechanism that uses correction risk to reorder only near-tie candidates, thereby preserving the original acquisition behavior while incorporating past oracle feedback.
- We evaluate CorrTie across four image classification benchmarks, five AL strategies, and three annotation budgets. Experimental results show average improvements of +7.14, +3.74, and +0.66 percentage points (pp) at the 1%, 2%, and 5% budgets, respectively.

The remainder of this paper is organized as follows. Section 2 reviews related work on VLMs, prompt learning, and AL. Section 3 presents the proposed CorrTie method. Section 4 describes the experimental settings. Section 5 reports and discusses the experimental results. Finally, Sect. 6 concludes the paper and outlines future directions.

2 Related Work

2.1 Vision-Language Models and Prompt Learning

VLMs have become a strong foundation for visual recognition by aligning images and natural language in a shared embedding space. CLIP is a representative VLM that learns transferable visual representations from large-scale image-text supervision and enables zero-shot recognition through textual class descriptions [12]. Despite this strong generalization ability, adapting VLMs to downstream tasks remains challenging when labeled data are limited, especially for domain-specific or fine-grained image classification.

Prompt learning has been widely used as an efficient adaptation strategy for VLMs. CoOp replaces hand-crafted prompts with learnable context vectors while keeping the pre-trained backbone fixed [17]. VPT adapts the visual encoder using learnable prompt tokens [6], while MaPLe jointly learns prompts for both vision and language branches [7]. APT further uses visual guidance to adapt textual prompts for fine-grained few-shot learning [3]. Although these methods reduce the cost of full fine-tuning, their performance still depends on the quality of the labeled samples, making active sample selection important when annotation budgets are limited.

2.2 Active Learning for Image Classification

AL aims to improve model performance while reducing annotation cost by selecting informative unlabeled samples for oracle labeling. Existing AL strategies are commonly based on uncertainty, diversity, or both. Entropy-based selection prioritizes samples with uncertain predictions [16], while Core-set selection focuses on covering the feature space by minimizing the distance between unlabeled samples and the labeled set [14]. Hybrid methods such as BADGE combine uncertainty and diversity in gradient space [1]. GCNAL further exploits sample relationships through graph-based modeling [4].

Recent studies have extended AL to VLM-based recognition. CEC addresses the miscalibration issue of VLM predictions by combining calibrated uncertainty, neighborhood information, and clustering-based selection [13]. These methods mainly design acquisition scores or selection rules based on the current model state. However, after oracle annotation, the mismatch between the model prediction and the true label also reveals a correction signal. CorrTie differs from standard acquisition strategies by using this past correction information as a post-acquisition reranking signal, while keeping the original candidate ranking as the primary selection signal.

3 Methodology

Figure 1 illustrates the proposed CorrTie framework. CorrTie is designed as a post-acquisition reranking module for AL with VLMs. Instead of replacing the base AL strategy, CorrTie receives a candidate ranking from the base strategy, estimates correction risk from previous oracle feedback, and uses this signal to rerank near-tie candidates before annotation. The selected samples are then annotated by the oracle and used to update both the labeled set and the correction memory.

3.1 Problem Setup

We consider pool-based AL for C-class image classification. At round t, let $\mathcal{D}_L^{(t)}$ and $\mathcal{D}_U^{(t)}$ denote the labeled set and unlabeled pool, respectively. Given a query budget K, the goal is to select K samples from $\mathcal{D}_U^{(t)}$ for oracle annotation. The annotated samples are then added to $\mathcal{D}_L^{(t)}$ and removed from $\mathcal{D}_U^{(t)}$.

As shown in the first stage of Fig. 1, CorrTie starts from a candidate ranking produced by a base AL strategy $\mathcal{A}$. For each candidate image x, CorrTie also uses the class predicted by the current prompt learner before annotation, denoted by $\hat{c}^{(t)}(x)$. The candidate ranking is defined as:

$$\mathcal{R}^{(t)} = \mathcal{A}\left(\mathcal{D}_U^{(t)}, \mathcal{D}_L^{(t)}\right) = (x_1, x_2, \ldots, x_M), \tag{1}$$

where $M \geq K$ is the number of candidates considered before final query selection. Earlier candidates in $\mathcal{R}^{(t)}$ have higher acquisition priority. CorrTie refines this ranking and selects the first K samples from the reranked list.

3.2 Correction Memory and Risk Estimation

In standard AL, oracle labels are usually used only to expand the labeled set for subsequent training. CorrTie additionally uses prediction-label mismatches

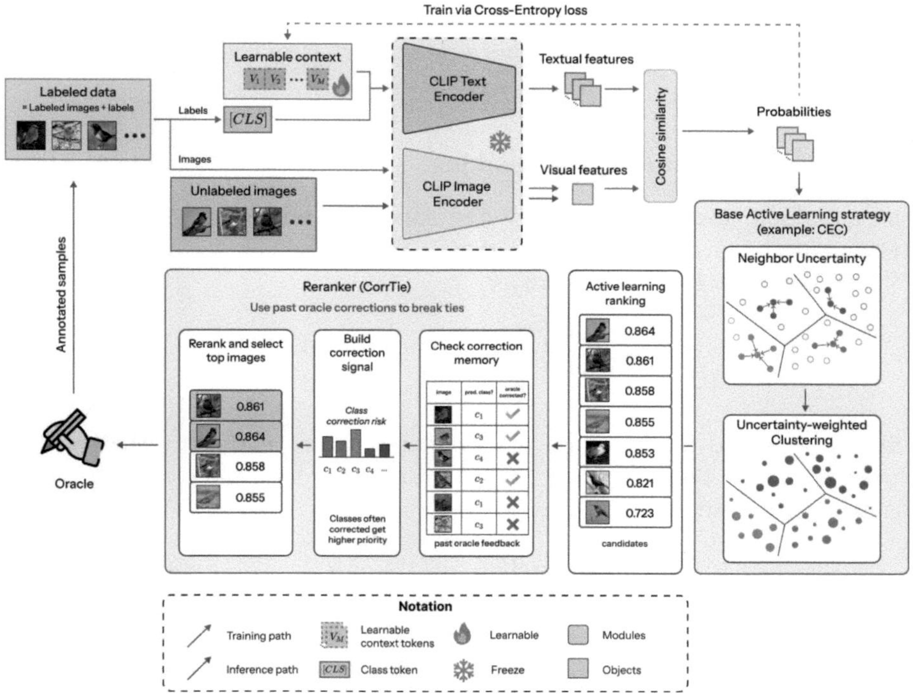

Fig. 1. Overview of the CorrTie framework. A base AL strategy first produces a candidate ranking from the unlabeled pool. CorrTie then uses correction memory from previous oracle feedback to estimate class-wise correction risk and rerank near-tie candidates before oracle annotation and prompt learning.

as correction signals. This feedback path corresponds to the correction memory component in Fig. 1. For a selected sample x_i with oracle label y_i, the correction indicator is defined as:

$$e_i = \mathbf{1}\left(\hat{c}^{(t)}(x_i) \neq y_i\right), \tag{2}$$

where $e_i = 1$ indicates that the model prediction is corrected by the oracle, and $e_i = 0$ indicates that the prediction matches the oracle label. CorrTie maintains a lightweight correction memory that stores, for each previously queried sample, its predicted pseudo-class $\hat{c}_i$ and correction indicator e_i:

$$\mathcal{M}^{(t)} = \{(\hat{c}_i, e_i)\}. \tag{3}$$

This memory is updated after each oracle annotation step, so the correction signal used at round t comes only from previous labeled feedback.

For each predicted class c, CorrTie computes the class-wise correction risk as:

$$R_c^{(t)} = \frac{\sum_{(\hat{c}_i, e_i) \in \mathcal{M}^{(t)}} \mathbf{1}(\hat{c}_i = c)\, e_i}{\sum_{(\hat{c}_i, e_i) \in \mathcal{M}^{(t)}} \mathbf{1}(\hat{c}_i = c) + \epsilon}, \tag{4}$$

where $\epsilon = 10^{-8}$ is used for numerical stability. A higher $R_c^{(t)}$ indicates that samples previously predicted as class c were more frequently corrected by the oracle.

3.3 Correction-Aware Tie-Breaking

The reranking stage in Fig. 1 keeps the candidate ranking from the base AL strategy as the primary acquisition signal. For a candidate x_j at position j in $\mathcal{R}^{(t)}$, we define its base-rank score as:

$$B(x_j) = \begin{cases} 1, & M = 1, \\ 1 - \frac{j-1}{M-1}, & M > 1. \end{cases} \tag{5}$$

This score assigns larger values to candidates ranked earlier by the base AL strategy. CorrTie then combines the base-rank score with the correction risk of the candidate's predicted class:

$$F^{(t)}(x_j) = \alpha B(x_j) + (1 - \alpha) R^{(t)}_{\hat{c}^{(t)}(x_j)}, \tag{6}$$

where $\alpha \in [0, 1]$ controls the balance between the base ranking and the correction history. A larger α keeps CorrTie closer to the base AL strategy, while a smaller α gives more influence to previous oracle corrections.

To avoid over-modifying the base acquisition behavior, CorrTie uses $F^{(t)}(x_j)$ only to reorder candidates within near-tie groups, as illustrated by the tie-breaking step in Fig. 1. Two adjacent candidates are assigned to the same near-tie group when:

$$|B(x_j) - B(x_{j+1})| < \delta. \tag{7}$$

Within each near-tie group, candidates are sorted in descending order of $F^{(t)}(x_j)$. The groups are then concatenated in their original order, and the first K candidates are selected for oracle annotation. Algorithm 1 summarizes the overall query procedure shown in Fig. 1.

4 Experimental Settings

We evaluate CorrTie on four image classification benchmarks: Describable Textures Dataset (DTD) [5], Caltech101 [2], Fine-Grained Visual Classification of Aircraft (FGVC-Aircraft) [8], and University of Central Florida 101 (UCF101) [15]. These datasets cover texture recognition, generic object classification, fine-grained aircraft classification, and action recognition. Images are preprocessed using the default CLIP transformation. We use CLIP ViT-B/16 [12] as the frozen VLM backbone and CoOp [17] as the prompt learner. During acquisition, the current prompt learner is used to produce predictions for unlabeled candidates. After oracle annotation, the selected samples are added to the labeled set, and the prompt learner is optimized on the updated labeled set.

Algorithm 1. CorrTie query strategy.

Require: $\mathcal{D}_L^{(0)}$, $\mathcal{D}_U^{(0)}$, rounds T, query budget K, candidate count $M \geq K$, base AL strategy $\mathcal{A}$, hyperparameters α, δ, ϵ
Ensure: Updated prompt learner and correction memory $\mathcal{M}$
Initialize $\mathcal{M}^{(0)} \leftarrow \emptyset$
for $t = 0$ **to** $T - 1$ **do**
  Obtain candidate ranking $\mathcal{R}^{(t)} = (x_1, \ldots, x_M)$ using $\mathcal{A}$ as in Eq. (1)
  Predict $\hat{c}^{(t)}(x_j)$ for each $x_j \in \mathcal{R}^{(t)}$
  Compute class-wise correction risks $R_c^{(t)}$ using Eq. (4)
  Compute $B(x_j)$ and $F^{(t)}(x_j)$ using Eqs. (5)–(6)
  Form near-tie groups using Eq. (7)
  Sort each group by descending $F^{(t)}(x_j)$
  Concatenate groups and select the first K candidates
  Query oracle labels and update $\mathcal{D}_L^{(t+1)}$, $\mathcal{D}_U^{(t+1)}$
  Update $\mathcal{M}^{(t+1)}$ using Eq. (2)
  Optimize the prompt learner on $\mathcal{D}_L^{(t+1)}$
end for

We apply CorrTie to five base AL strategies: Random, Entropy [16], BADGE [1], GCNAL [4], and CEC [13]. For each base strategy, CorrTie receives the candidate ranking produced by that strategy and reranks near-tie candidates using correction risk. The annotation budget ratio is set to $b(\%) \in \{1, 2, 5\}$ of the training pool, and each budget is converted into a fixed query size K. CorrTie uses $\alpha = 0.5$, $\delta = 0.05$, and $\epsilon = 10^{-8}$ in all experiments. Each experiment is repeated over three random seeds, 1, 10, and 100, and results are reported as mean top-1 accuracy with standard deviation. For each base AL strategy, we report the accuracy after applying CorrTie, with the signed change in accuracy relative to the original base strategy shown in parentheses. The Average row reports the mean across the four datasets for each base AL strategy. When discussing the overall gain at each budget, we further average the signed changes across the five base strategies. The implementation is available at https://github.com/TaiDuc1001/CorrTie.

5 Experimental Results

5.1 Quantitative Results

Table 1 shows the main results of CorrTie with CoOp prompt learning. Each entry shows the top-1 accuracy after applying CorrTie to a base AL strategy, while the value in parentheses denotes the signed accuracy change relative to the original base strategy. Therefore, a positive value indicates that CorrTie improves the corresponding base strategy, whereas a negative value indicates that the reranking step reduces performance in that setting.

The averaged results show that CorrTie is most beneficial under low annotation budgets. At the 1% budget, CorrTie improves the average accuracy of all five base strategies, with signed changes of +7.10, +9.17, +7.97, +6.97, and

Table 1. Results for CoOp prompt learning with signed change annotations. Classification accuracy is reported after applying CorrTie, and the value in parentheses denotes the signed accuracy change in percentage points (pp) relative to the original base strategy. Columns indicate the base AL strategy to which CorrTie is applied. **Bold** indicates the largest signed change, and underlining indicates the second-largest signed change among active selection methods. Zero-shot results are reported as references and are excluded from the ranking.

Dataset	$b(\%)$	Random	Entropy [16]	BADGE [1]	GCNAL [4]	CEC [13]	Zero-shot
DTD	1	45.98% (+7.58 pp)	**46.57% (+11.37 pp)**	45.98% (+5.78 pp)	45.98% (+7.18 pp)	48.23% (+0.33 pp)	44.30%
	2	48.80% (+4.60 pp)	**48.03% (+7.13 pp)**	49.72% (+2.82 pp)	49.65% (+4.85 pp)	50.00% (-2.80 pp)	
	5	53.25% (-0.85 pp)	**50.96% (+1.66 pp)**	54.79% (-1.41 pp)	53.47% (-1.53 pp)	55.02% (-3.18 pp)	
Caltech101	1	88.26% (+0.06 pp)	**91.27% (+5.17 pp)**	88.26% (+0.06 pp)	88.26% (-0.14 pp)	90.78% (+2.08 pp)	91.30%
	2	90.30% (+1.90 pp)	**91.84% (+2.54 pp)**	91.09% (+1.29 pp)	90.09% (+0.29 pp)	91.13% (+2.13 pp)	
	5	92.80% (+1.70 pp)	**92.31% (+2.91 pp)**	93.71% (+1.51 pp)	93.12% (+0.72 pp)	93.84% (+1.04 pp)	
FGVC-Aircraft	1	24.57% (+6.17 pp)	23.51% (+3.81 pp)	**24.57% (+6.77 pp)**	24.57% (+6.17 pp)	24.23% (+3.93 pp)	24.90%
	2	25.43% (+4.23 pp)	23.91% (+1.91 pp)	**25.09% (+4.39 pp)**	25.32% (+4.12 pp)	25.95% (+3.65 pp)	
	5	**28.14% (+2.14 pp)**	25.56% (+0.86 pp)	27.44% (+1.74 pp)	27.01% (+0.71 pp)	28.74% (+1.64 pp)	
UCF101	1	69.97% (+14.57 pp)	69.42% (+16.32 pp)	**69.97% (+19.27 pp)**	69.97% (+14.67 pp)	69.16% (+11.56 pp)	64.30%
	2	70.90% (+4.30 pp)	69.34% (+7.24 pp)	**72.15% (+8.45 pp)**	70.67% (+6.77 pp)	71.97% (+4.97 pp)	
	5	74.98% (+1.18 pp)	72.94% (+0.14 pp)	**76.60% (+1.30 pp)**	74.13% (+1.03 pp)	76.18% (-0.02 pp)	
Average	1	57.20% (+7.10 pp)	**57.69% (+9.17 pp)**	57.20% (+7.97 pp)	57.20% (+6.97 pp)	58.10% (+4.48 pp)	56.20%
	2	58.86% (+3.76 pp)	**58.28% (+4.71 pp)**	59.51% (+4.24 pp)	58.93% (+4.01 pp)	59.76% (+1.99 pp)	
	5	62.29% (+1.04 pp)	**60.44% (+1.39 pp)**	63.14% (+0.79 pp)	61.93% (+0.23 pp)	63.45% (-0.13 pp)	

+4.48 pp for Random, Entropy, BADGE, GCNAL, and CEC, respectively. Averaging these changes across the five strategies gives an overall gain of +7.14 pp. This is the greatest improvement among the three budgets, suggesting that correction-aware reranking is most useful when the labeled set is still small, and the current prompt learner makes more correctable prediction errors.

At the 2% budget, CorrTie still improves all five base strategies in the average row, but the overall gain decreases to +3.74 pp. The largest average signed change is obtained with Entropy (+4.71 pp), followed by BADGE (+4.24 pp) and GCNAL (+4.01 pp). At the 5% budget, the overall signed change further decreases to +0.66 pp. In this setting, CorrTie still improves Random, Entropy, BADGE, and GCNAL on average, but slightly reduces the average result of CEC by -0.13 pp. These results indicate that CorrTie does not uniformly improve across all high-budget settings; rather, its benefit diminishes as the labeled set grows and the base acquisition ranking becomes more reliable.

It is also important to distinguish the highest accuracy after CorrTie from the largest signed change. For example, in the average row, CEC-based ranking gives the highest accuracy after CorrTie at the 1%, 2%, and 5% budgets, reaching 58.10%, 59.76%, and 63.45%, respectively. However, the largest signed changes are obtained by Entropy at all three budgets. This means that CorrTie can provide the largest relative correction to weaker or more unstable acquisition rankings, while strategies with stronger original rankings may still achieve higher final accuracy but smaller gains.

At the dataset level, CorrTie provides especially large gains on UCF101 and FGVC-Aircraft. On UCF101 at the 1% budget, the signed changes reach +19.27 pp for BADGE, +16.32 pp for Entropy, and +14.67 pp for GCNAL. On

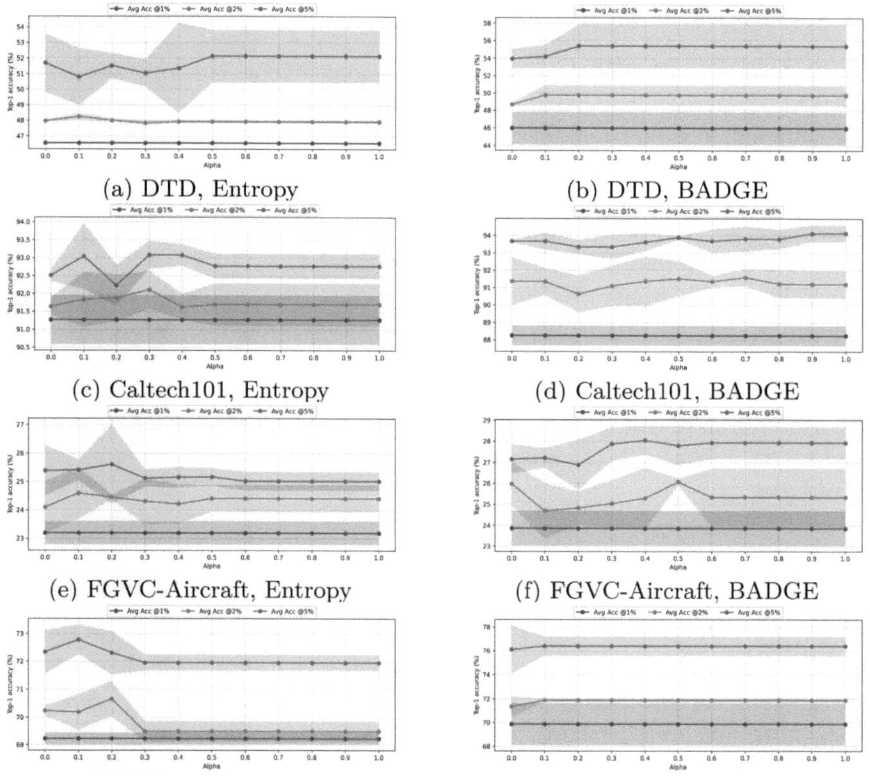

(a) DTD, Entropy (b) DTD, BADGE

(c) Caltech101, Entropy (d) Caltech101, BADGE

(e) FGVC-Aircraft, Entropy (f) FGVC-Aircraft, BADGE

(g) UCF101, Entropy (h) UCF101, BADGE

Fig. 2. Sensitivity analysis of the CorrTie trade-off coefficient α. Top-1 accuracy is reported at annotation budgets of 1%, 2%, and 5% across four datasets and two base AL strategies.

FGVC-Aircraft, all five base strategies obtain positive signed changes across all three budgets. This suggests that correction memory is useful in settings where the prompt learner repeatedly confuses visually similar classes or action categories. In contrast, DTD shows a more mixed pattern. CorrTie improves all five base strategies at the 1% budget and most strategies at the 2% budget, but at the 5% budget, it decreases the performance of Random, BADGE, GCNAL, and CEC. This may indicate that class-wise correction risk is less reliable for texture recognition, where correction patterns may not align as clearly with semantic class-level errors.

Overall, the quantitative results support the use of oracle correction feedback as an additional acquisition signal, especially in early AL rounds. However, the results also show that CorrTie should be interpreted as a conservative reranking module rather than a universally beneficial replacement for base acquisition strategies. Its effect depends on the annotation budget, dataset characteristics, and the quality of the original candidate ranking.

5.2 Sensitivity Analysis

Figure 2 shows the effect of the trade-off coefficient α using Entropy and BADGE as base AL strategies. The parameter α balances the base-rank score and correction risk: smaller values emphasize correction history, while larger values keep CorrTie closer to the original candidate ranking. The 1% curves are nearly flat in most settings, since the correction memory is still limited in the earliest AL stage. At the 2% and 5% budgets, the effect of α becomes more visible, but the best value varies across datasets and base strategies.

Overall, the sensitivity analysis does not indicate a single universally optimal α. Some settings benefit from stronger correction influence, while others are more stable when the base ranking remains dominant. Values around $\alpha = 0.4$–0.5 provide a reasonable balance across the tested settings, preserving the base acquisition ranking while still allowing correction risk to affect near-tie decisions. Therefore, we use $\alpha = 0.5$ as a fixed default rather than tuning it separately for each dataset.

6 Conclusion

In this paper, we propose CorrTie, a lightweight correction-aware tie-breaking reranker for AL with VLMs. Instead of replacing the base acquisition strategy or introducing an additional acquisition model, CorrTie operates after candidate ranking and uses past oracle corrections to refine near-tie decisions. The proposed method maintains a correction memory from previous prediction-label mismatches, estimates class-wise correction risk, and combines this signal with the original base ranking through a conservative reranking rule. Experiments with CoOp prompt learning show that CorrTie improves averaged performance under limited annotation budgets, particularly in early AL rounds where correction feedback provides useful information about the current model's failure patterns. The results also indicate that the benefit of CorrTie depends on the reliability of correction memory, dataset characteristics, and the quality of the original candidate ranking, leaving room for future work on more fine-grained correction modeling, adaptive trade-off selection, and broader evaluation across prompt learners, VLM backbones, and AL settings.

References

1. Ash, J.T., Zhang, C., Krishnamurthy, A., Langford, J., Agarwal, A.: Deep batch active learning by diverse, uncertain gradient lower bounds. In: International Conference on Learning Representations (2020)
2. Bansal, M., Kumar, M., Sachdeva, M., Mittal, A.: Transfer learning for image classification using vgg19: caltech-101 image data set. J. Ambient. Intell. Humaniz. Comput. **14**(4), 3609–3620 (2023)

3. Brouwer, E., van Woerden, J., Burghouts, G., Valdenegro-Toro, M., Zullich, M.: Adaptive prompt tuning: vision guided prompt tuning with cross-attention for fine-grained few-shot learning. In: Proceedings of the 20th International Joint Conference on Computer Vision, Imaging and Computer Graphics Theory and Applications, pp. 114–125. SCITEPRESS - Science and Technology Publications (2025)
4. Caramalau, R., Bhattarai, B., Kim, T.K.: Sequential graph convolutional network for active learning. In: 2021 IEEE/CVF Conference on Computer Vision and Pattern Recognition (CVPR), pp. 9578–9587 (2021)
5. Cimpoi, M., Maji, S., Kokkinos, I., Mohamed, S., Vedaldi, A.: Describing textures in the wild. In: 2014 IEEE Conference on Computer Vision and Pattern Recognition, pp. 3606–3613 (2014)
6. Jia, M., et al.: Visual prompt tuning. In: Computer Vision - ECCV 2022: 17th European Conference. Tel Aviv, Israel, Proceedings, Part XXXIII, pp. 709–727. Springer-Verlag, Berlin, Heidelberg (2022)
7. Khattak, M.U., Rasheed, H., Maaz, M., Khan, S., Khan, F.S.: Maple: multi-modal prompt learning. In: 2023 IEEE/CVF Conference on Computer Vision and Pattern Recognition (CVPR), pp. 19113–19122 (2023)
8. Maji, S., Kannala, J., Rahtu, E., Blaschko, M., Vedaldi, A.: Fine-grained visual classification of aircraft. Tech. rep., arXiv (2013)
9. Phan, D.T., Nguyen, N.M., Dang, D.N.M.: DAAL: dual ambiguity in active learning for object detection with yoloe. In: Proceedings of the 17th International Conference on Management of Digital Ecosystem (MEDES 2025). ACM, Ho Chi Minh City, Vietnam (2025)
10. Phan, D.T., Nguyen, N.M., Nguyen, K.P., Pham, T., Dang, D.N.M.: ALMUS: enhancing active learning for object detection with metric-based uncertainty sampling. In: 2025 25th Asia-Pacific Network Operations and Management Symposium (APNOMS), pp. 1–6 (2025)
11. Phan, D.T., et al.: From object difficulty to image scoring: a strategy for active learning in object detection. Knowl. Based Syst. **342**, 115946 (2026)
12. Radford, A., et al.: Learning transferable visual models from natural language supervision. In: Meila, M., Zhang, T. (eds.) Proceedings of the 38th International Conference on Machine Learning. Proceedings of Machine Learning Research, vol. 139, pp. 8748–8763. PMLR (18–24 Jul 2021)
13. Safaei, B., Patel, V.M.: Active learning for vision-language models. In: 2025 IEEE/CVF Winter Conference on Applications of Computer Vision (WACV), pp. 4902–4912 (2025)
14. Sener, O., Savarese, S.: Active learning for convolutional neural networks: a core-set approach. In: International Conference on Learning Representations (2018)
15. Soomro, K., Zamir, A.R., Shah, M.: UCF101: a dataset of 101 human actions classes from videos in the wild. CoRR abs/1212.0402 (2012)
16. Wang, D., Shang, Y.: A new active labeling method for deep learning. In: 2014 International Joint Conference on Neural Networks (IJCNN), pp. 112–119 (2014)
17. Zhou, K., Yang, J., Loy, C.C., Liu, Z.: Learning to prompt for vision-language models. Int. J. Comput. Vis. **130**(9), 2337–2348 (2022)

DACMRec: A Dual-Level Augmented Contrastive Meta-Learning Model for Next POI Recommendation

RuYue Wang[1], Wei He[1,2](✉), and Zhen Feng[3](✉)

[1] School of Software, Shandong University, 1500 Shunhua Road, Jinan 250101, Shandong, China

[2] Joint SDU-NTU Centre for Artificial Intelligence Research (C-FAIR), Jinan 250101, Shandong, China

hewei@sdu.edu.cn

[3] Jinan Inspur Data Technology Co., Ltd., Jinan, China

fengzh@inspur.com

Abstract. Next POI recommendation, a popular application paradigm for personalized location-based services, has emerged as a prominent research focus in service computing. However, data sparsity and few-shot problems severely hinder models from capturing complex spatiotemporal dependencies and dynamic user preferences, especially for cold-start users with limited check-in records. Although recent studies have attempted to mitigate these challenges via contrastive learning or meta-learning, two critical limitations remain unaddressed. First, mainstream contrastive learning-based methods predominantly rely on single-view data augmentation, which inevitably distorts intrinsic spatiotemporal semantics and fails to model high-order interaction topology. Second, existing meta-learning paradigms for few-shot recommendation are decoupled from robust spatiotemporal representation learning, lacking deep synergy between contrastive pre-training and meta-optimization. To bridge these gaps, we propose *DACMRec*, a novel Dual-level Augmented Contrastive Meta-Learning model for next POI recommendation. Specifically, we design a dual-level augmentation strategy that preserves spatiotemporal semantic integrity while modeling high-order interaction topology, enabling the learning of generalizable user mobility representations. We further construct a deeply coupled contrastive meta-learning framework to synergize robust representation learning and fast meta-adaptation. Extensive experiments on real-world check-in datasets demonstrate that *DACMRec* outperforms state-of-the-art methods across various sparsity levels and in few-shot scenarios.

Keywords: Next POI recommendation · Contrastive learning · Meta learning · Spatio-temporal context · Graph neural network

L. Ding et al. (Eds.): APWeb-WAIM 2026, LNCS 16995, pp. 408–424, 2027.
https://doi.org/10.1007/978-981-92-5699-0_27

1 Introduction

Next Point-of-Interest (POI) recommendation is a fundamental task in Location-based services (LBS). However, its performance is often bottlenecked by extreme data sparsity in user-POI interactions, which is driven by the long-tail distribution of real-world human mobility (e.g., up to 99.35% sparsity in the NYC dataset). This severe sparsity makes it difficult for existing models to capture complex spatiotemporal dependencies and personalized preferences, especially for users with limited check-in records.

To address this, various approaches have been explored. Graph neural networks (e.g., EEDN [18], HCCF [1]) rely on neighborhood aggregation but struggle with multi-hop propagation in highly sparse matrices. Attention mechanisms (e.g., STAN [14], DRAN [19]) excel at sequential modeling but often fail to mine deep global spatial associations. While contrastive learning (e.g., CL4SRec [22], SGL [21]) has recently been introduced to extract self-supervised signals, mainstream single-level augmentations tend to distort intrinsic spatiotemporal semantics and destroy essential high-order topological structures.

Beyond overall sparsity, the few-shot cold-start problem for new and long-tail users remains a critical challenge. Most models suffer severe performance drops when interaction records are extremely scarce. Although meta-learning has been applied to enhance few-shot generalization, existing methods generally lack a deep synergy between meta-optimization and robust spatiotemporal representation learning. This decoupling restricts their ability to construct relevant meta-tasks and adapt quickly in dynamic LBS scenarios.

To bridge these gaps, we propose *DACMRec*, a Dual-level Augmented Contrastive Meta-Learning model. Our framework first utilizes a dual-level self-supervised contrastive mechanism to extract structural and semantic invariance from user trajectories, alleviating representation degradation under extreme sparsity and capturing generalizable mobility priors. Concurrently, we integrate a contrastive prior-guided meta-learning strategy to enable fast personalized adaptation for few-shot cold-start users. By tightly coupling robust representation learning with meta-optimization, DACMRec better captures both stable preferences and dynamic mobility patterns under highly sparse settings. The main contributions of this paper are summarized as follows:

- We propose a structure-feature dual-level augmented contrastive learning mechanism, which constructs complementary topological and semantic views via SVD-based graph reconstruction and controllable feature noise injection, effectively alleviating representation degradation under extreme data sparsity.
- We design a FOMAML-based few-shot cold-start adaptation strategy deeply integrated with the contrastive module, which embeds contrastive-learned mobility priors into model initialization to enable fast personalized adaptation with extremely limited interaction data.
- Extensive experiments conducted on multiple real-world datasets have validated the effectiveness of our method. The results demonstrate that its performance consistently ranks among the best in the industry and confirm the contributions of both data augmentation and meta-learning strategies.

2 Related Work

2.1 Contrastive Learning

Contrastive learning has been widely explored to tackle data sparsity in recommendation systems by constructing positive and negative pairs. Recent studies have applied it to collaborative filtering [27,30] and sequential recommendation [11,29]. Typically, these methods rely on structure-level augmentations, such as node and edge dropout in SGL [21] and KGCL [23], or feature-level noise injection as seen in SimGCL [25]. However, in sparse user-POI interaction graphs, random dropout operations often destroy essential topological structures, which might worsen the cold-start issue rather than solve it.

2.2 Meta Learning

To handle the cold-start and few-shot problems, meta-learning has been introduced to recommendation models to enable fast adaptation. Early works like MeLU [6] applied MAML [4] to multi-layer perceptrons, while MAMO [2] and TaNP [8] incorporated memory modules and neural processes, respectively. More recent methods have shifted to graph-based structures, such as MetaHIN [12], PAM [15], and adaptive subgraph models [7], to capture richer semantic priors. Despite these advances, applying standard meta-learning on large-scale spatiotemporal graphs requires computing second-order Hessian matrices. This usually leads to GPU memory overflow and limits the scalability of the models in real-world LBS applications.

2.3 Next POI Recommendation

Deep learning methods for next POI recommendation mostly model sequential check-ins via RNNs or attention networks, including ST-RNN [9], STGN [26], and STAN [14]. To capture high-order user-POI relations, GNNs like NGCF [17] and LightGCN [5] are widely adopted. Building on this, recent models try to incorporate adaptive spatial signals [16,20,28] or use prompt-guided spatiotemporal encoding [10,13]. Compared with the above studies, we propose to perturb both the graph structure and node features instead of relying on a single view. By combining this dual-level strategy with meta-learning, our method aims to maintain representation robustness even when check-in records are extremely scarce.

3 Preliminaries

To clearly illustrate the proposed model framework, we first formally define the key concepts and mathematical notations used throughout this paper. The primary notations are summarized in Table 1.

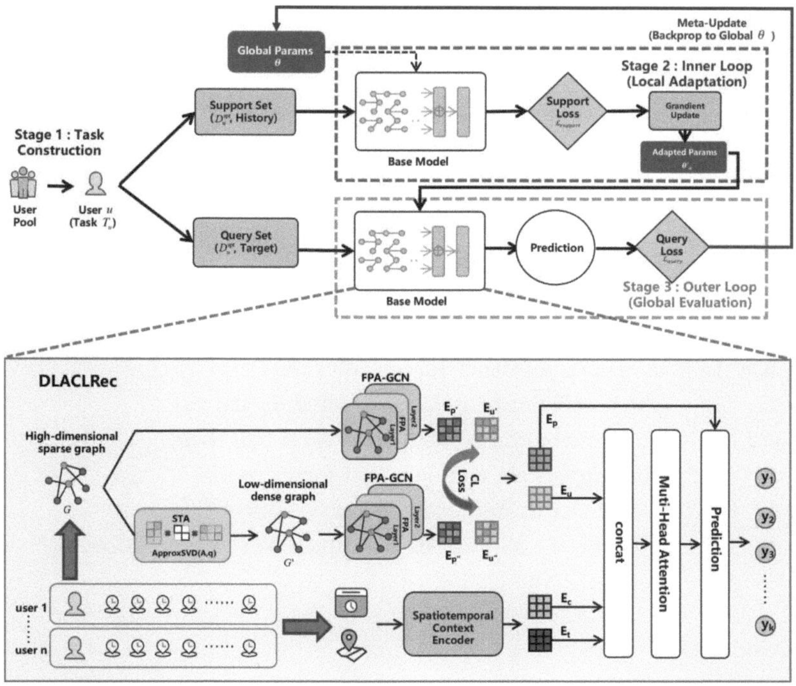

Fig. 1. The overall framework of the proposed DACMRec. The architecture integrates a base learner (DLACLRec) into a meta-learning optimization framework. DLACLRec extracts robust user-POI representations via dual-level (structural and feature) augmented contrastive learning, and models dynamic behaviors using spatio-temporal context and sequence prediction. Furthermore, the FOMAML-based meta-learning framework formulates recommendations as independent meta-tasks, enabling rapid personalized adaptation for few-shot cold-start users.

3.1 User Check-in Sequence

For each user $u \in \mathcal{U}$, their historical check-in records are arranged in chronological order to form the user's check-in sequence S_u, which is defined as:

$$S_u = \{r_{u,1}, r_{u,2}, \dots, r_{u,n}\} \tag{1}$$

where n is the length of the sequence. Each check-in record $r_{u,i}$ can be represented as a tuple:

$$r_{u,i} = (u, p_i, t_i, c_i) \tag{2}$$

This indicates that user u visited POI $p_i \in \mathcal{P}$ at timestamp $t_i \in \mathcal{T}$, and the geographical coordinate of this POI is $c_i = (lat_i, lon_i)$ representing latitude and longitude.

Table 1. Summary of Key Notations

Notation	Definition
$\mathcal{U}, \mathcal{P}$	Set of users and set of Point-of-Interests (POIs)
$\mathcal{T}, \mathcal{C}$	Set of timestamps and geographical coordinates
r	A single check-in record
S_u	The check-in sequence of user u
$\mathcal{G}$	The global user-POI interaction graph
$\tilde{\mathcal{G}}$	The low-dimensional graph after STA
$\mathbf{A}$	Original adjacency matrix of $\mathcal{G}$
$\tilde{\mathbf{A}}_{SVD}$	Low-rank adjacency matrix after STA
$\mathcal{T}_u$	The specific meta-task constructed for user u
$p(\mathcal{T})$	The distribution of meta-tasks across all users
$\mathcal{D}_u^{spt}, \mathcal{D}_u^{qry}$	The support set and query set for meta-task $\mathcal{T}_u$
θ	Global shared initialization parameters of the model
θ'_u	User-specific parameters fine-tuned on the support set $\mathcal{D}_u^{spt}$

3.2 User-POI Interaction Graph

Based on the global interaction matrix, we construct a bipartite user-POI interaction graph $\mathcal{G}$:

$$\mathcal{G} = (\mathcal{V}, \mathcal{E}) \tag{3}$$

where the node set $\mathcal{V} = \mathcal{U} \cup \mathcal{P}$ contains all user nodes and POI nodes. The edge set $\mathcal{E}$ represents the interaction relationships between users and POIs. Specifically, if user u has visited POI p, an edge $e_{u,p} \in \mathcal{E}$ is established between them; otherwise, no edge exists.

4 Model

This chapter introduces the proposed dual-level augmented contrastive meta-learning model for next POI recommendation, as illustrated in Fig. 1. The model consists of a base learner (DLACLRec) and a meta-learning optimization framework. DLACLRec integrates three core modules: dual-level data augmentation, spatio-temporal embedding, and check-in sequence prediction. Specifically, the augmentation module applies structural and feature-level perturbations to extract robust user-POI representations under limited interaction data. The embedding module utilizes a geocoder to encode geographical and temporal contexts, which the sequence module then fuses to better capture dynamic user behavioral patterns. Furthermore, the meta-learning framework formulates the recommendation process as independent meta-tasks. By employing a First-Order Approximate Meta-Learning mechanism for global optimization and local fine-tuning, it facilitates rapid personalized adaptation with sparse historical records, thereby mitigating the cold-start challenge for long-tail and new users.

4.1 Spatiotemporal Context Encoding

To accurately capture the physical spatial dependencies and temporal dynamics of user movements, we encode multi-source contexts into dense representations. Instead of merely using discrete POI IDs, which lack spatial awareness, we incorporate geographical and temporal embeddings.

For spatial encoding, we map each POI's coordinates to a Quadkey in a hierarchical tile system. Hard grid division often introduces a boundary effect, causing spatially adjacent POIs to be assigned completely different higher-level Quadkeys. To mitigate this issue, we extract the Quadkeys of both the POI's center grid and its 8 neighboring grids. These 9 Quadkeys are serialized using an N-gram algorithm and fed into a Stacked Self-Attention Network. An average pooling operation is then applied to aggregate the neighborhood context, yielding a robust and spatially continuous geographical embedding $e_{p,c}$.

For temporal encoding, the continuous timestamp is mapped to discrete slots (e.g., hours of the day and days of the week) to obtain a temporal embedding $e_{p,t}$. Finally, for the i-th check-in step, the comprehensive representation x_i is formed by fusing the user's long-term preference embedding e_u, the spatial embedding, and the temporal embedding:

$$x_i = e_u + e_{p,c} + e_{p,t} \tag{4}$$

This fused representation explicitly encodes spatial continuity and temporal periodicity, providing a comprehensive context for subsequent sequence modeling without requiring massive parameter overhead.

4.2 Dual-Level Augmented Contrastive Learning

In highly sparse LBS scenarios, extreme data sparsity severely limits the model's ability to capture accurate collaborative signals. Existing graph-based recommendation methods often rely on single-level data augmentation (e.g., random node or edge dropping) to construct contrastive views. However, in POI recommendation, such random perturbations tend to destroy essential spatiotemporal semantics and crucial high-order topological structures, leading to unstable representation learning. To address the extreme sparsity while preserving semantic integrity, we propose a dual-level augmented contrastive learning module that constructs complementary views from both structural and feature perspectives.

Structure-Level SVD Augmentation (STA) To extract global spatial correlations and filter out localized sparsity-induced noise without disrupting the primary topology, we perform Singular Value Decomposition (SVD) on the original user-POI adjacency matrix $\mathbf{A}$. By retaining the highest singular values q, we construct an approximated low-rank graph $\tilde{\mathbf{A}}_{SVD}$:

$$\mathbf{A} = U\Sigma V^T, \quad \tilde{\mathbf{A}}_{SVD} = U_q \Sigma_q V_q^T \tag{5}$$

where Σ_q is a diagonal matrix containing the top-q largest singular values, and U_q and V_q contain the corresponding singular vectors. This truncated matrix $\tilde{\mathbf{A}}_{SVD}$ serves as the structure-augmented view, ensuring that the dominant global collaborative signals are preserved while random interaction noise is smoothed out.

Feature-Level Perturbation Augmentation (FPA) To further enhance the model's robustness against feature noise, we inject random controlled noise directly into the embedding space. For a node representation e in the feature space, the augmented view e' is generated by introducing Gaussian noise:

$$e' = e + \epsilon, \quad \epsilon \sim \mathcal{N}(0, \sigma^2 I) \tag{6}$$

where ϵ is drawn from a Gaussian distribution with a zero mean and variance σ^2, and I is the identity matrix. This continuous perturbation maintains semantic consistency while increasing the diversity of local feature spaces, preventing the model from overfitting to specific sparse interaction patterns. By feeding the original graph and the augmented views into the LightGCN encoder, we obtain multi-view representations. Ultimately, we apply the InfoNCE loss to maximize the mutual information between the same node across different views, significantly alleviating the representation degradation caused by extreme data sparsity.

Contrastive Loss We employ a contrastive learning objective to distinguish the representations of the same node under different views from those of other nodes. By aligning the embeddings of the same node in the original graph $\mathcal{G}$ and the augmented graph $\mathcal{G}'$, the model establishes consistency constraints across views.

For any user node u, its representations e_u and e'_u from $\mathcal{G}$ and $\mathcal{G}'$ form a positive pair, while the representations of other users form negative pairs. The user-side contrastive loss is defined using the InfoNCE formulation:

$$\mathcal{L}_{CL}^{(u)} = \sum_{u \in \mathcal{U}} -\log \frac{\exp(s(e_u, e'_u)/\tau)}{\sum_{v \in \mathcal{U}} \exp(s(e_u, e'_v)/\tau)} \tag{7}$$

where $s(\cdot, \cdot)$ denotes the cosine similarity function, and τ is the temperature parameter. Similarly, the POI-side contrastive loss is defined as:

$$\mathcal{L}_{CL}^{(p)} = \sum_{p \in \mathcal{P}} -\log \frac{\exp(s(e_p, e'_p)/\tau)}{\sum_{g \in \mathcal{P}} \exp(s(e_p, e'_g)/\tau)} \tag{8}$$

The final comprehensive contrastive loss is the average of the user and POI contrastive losses:

$$\mathcal{L}_{CL} = \frac{1}{2}\left(\mathcal{L}_{CL}^{(u)} + \mathcal{L}_{CL}^{(p)}\right) \tag{9}$$

4.3 Sequence Prediction and Recommendation

Building upon the spatiotemporal context, we employ a Multi-Head Self-Attention (MHSA) mechanism to capture dynamic user preferences and complex sequential dependencies without relying on rigid Markov assumptions. For the sequence representations X, the h-th attention head is computed as:

$$head_h = \text{Attention}(XW_Q^{(h)}, XW_K^{(h)}, XW_V^{(h)}) \tag{10}$$

where W_Q, W_K, and W_V are learnable projection matrices. By concatenating the outputs of all heads, the model adaptively weighs the relevance of historical check-ins to the current prediction.

To optimize the personalized ranking of POIs, we utilize the Bayesian Personalized Ranking (BPR) loss, which maximizes the margin between the observed POI i and an unobserved negative POI j. We unify the BPR loss with the contrastive loss $\mathcal{L}_{CL}$ derived from our dual-level augmentation module to form the comprehensive task loss $\mathcal{L}_{task}$:

$$\mathcal{L}_{task} = \sum_{(u,i,j)\in\mathcal{O}} -\ln\sigma(\hat{y}_{u,i} - \hat{y}_{u,j}) + \lambda\mathcal{L}_{CL} + \lambda_{reg}\|\Theta\|^2 \tag{11}$$

where $\mathcal{O}$ denotes the training triplets, $\sigma(\cdot)$ is the sigmoid function, λ balances the contrastive signal, and λ_{reg} is the L_2 regularization weight for all trainable parameters Θ.

4.4 FOMAML-Based Meta-Optimization

While the dual-level contrastive learning mitigates overall data sparsity, long-tail users with extremely limited interactions still suffer from the cold-start problem under conventional global optimization paradigms. To endow the model with rapid personalized adaptation capabilities, we embed the aforementioned recommendation framework into a First-Order Model-Agnostic Meta-Learning architecture.

We formulate the recommendation process for each user u as an independent meta-task $\mathcal{T}_u$. For each task, the check-in sequence is chronologically partitioned into a support set $\mathcal{D}_u^{spt}$ for task-specific adaptation and a query set $\mathcal{D}_u^{qry}$ for global generalization evaluation.

Inner Loop (Fast Adaptation): During the inner loop, the model initializes with the globally shared parameters θ. It evaluates the task loss $\mathcal{L}_{task}^{\mathcal{D}_u^{spt}}$ on the support set. Specifically, this support loss integrates the BPR loss evaluated on the implicit feedback of the support set, the contrastive loss $\mathcal{L}_{CL}$ (calculated via Eq. 9) for maintaining graph structural consistency, and the L_2 regularization term, formulated as:

$$\mathcal{L}_{task}^{\mathcal{D}_u^{spt}} = \mathcal{L}_{BPR}(\mathcal{D}_u^{spt}) + \lambda\mathcal{L}_{CL} + \lambda_{reg}\|\Theta\|^2 \tag{12}$$

Then, the model performs a lightweight gradient descent step using this comprehensive loss to obtain the user-specific parameters θ'_u:

$$\theta'_u = \theta - \alpha \nabla_\theta \mathcal{L}_{task}^{\mathcal{D}_u^{spt}}(\theta) \tag{13}$$

where α is the inner learning rate. This step allows the model to swiftly capture local individualized preferences with minimal interaction records.

Outer Loop (Global Meta-Update): Standard MAML involves computing second-order Hessian matrices during the outer loop, which causes severe memory overflow and computational bottlenecks when applied to deep spatiotemporal graphs. To overcome this, we employ FOMAML, which approximates the meta-gradient by dropping the computationally expensive second-order derivative term. The global parameters θ are updated by evaluating the task loss on the query set using the adapted parameters θ'_u:

$$\theta \leftarrow \theta - \beta \left(\sum_{\mathcal{T}_u \sim p(\mathcal{T})} \nabla_{\theta'_u} \mathcal{L}_{task}^{\mathcal{D}_u^{qry}}(\theta'_u) + \lambda \nabla_\theta \mathcal{L}_{CL}(\theta) \right) \tag{14}$$

where β is the meta learning rate, and $p(\mathcal{T})$ is the task distribution. By alternating between local adaptation and global meta-updates, the framework learns a highly sensitive initialization parameter space, enabling precise POI sequence recommendations for cold-start users.

Table 2. Statistics of the Evaluation Datasets

Dataset	Users	POIs	Check-ins	Sparsity
Gowalla	3930	8745	590,850	99.49%
Brightkite	4218	9042	1,048,575	99.88%
TKY	2293	7870	447,076	99.33%
NYC	1083	5130	147,729	99.35%

5 Experiments

In this section, we conduct extensive experiments on four real-world datasets to evaluate the effectiveness of the proposed DACMRec framework. We aim to answer how our model performs against state-of-the-art baselines and how each proposed component contributes to its superiority in extreme sparsity and few-shot scenarios.

5.1 Experimental Settings

Datasets. We evaluate our model on four widely used LBS datasets: Gowalla, Brightkite, TKY, and NYC. These datasets exhibit extreme interaction sparsity, as shown in Table 2. To ensure data quality, we filter out users and POIs with fewer than 10 interactions. For the meta-learning setup, we chronically sort each user's trajectory, using the most recent check-ins as the test set and splitting the remaining historical records into support and query sets for task formulation.
Evaluation Metrics. We adopt two standard evaluation metrics: Recall@K and NDCG@K (with K set to 10 and 20) to evaluate the coverage and ranking quality of the recommendation lists, respectively.
Baselines. To thoroughly evaluate DACMRec, we compare it with six state-of-the-art baselines across four categories: (1) **General Graph Recommendation:** LightGCN [5], which extracts representations via lightweight graph convolution without non-linearities. (2) **Contrastive Learning:** SimGCL [25], which alleviates sparsity by introducing uniform noise into the embedding space. (3) **Sequential Recommendation:** SHAN [24] and FEARec [3], which capture dynamic user intents via hierarchical attention and frequency-domain autocorrelation, respectively. (4) **Meta-Learning Frameworks:** MAML [4] and MeLU [6], which focus on fast personalization in cold-start scenarios via bi-level gradient updates and MLP-based meta-optimization.

5.2 Performance

The overall performance comparison is presented in Table 3. DACMRec consistently outperforms all baselines across all four datasets. Notably, compared to the strongest baseline, FEARec, our framework achieves significant improvements, with a maximum boost of 8.70% in NDCG@10 on the Brightkite dataset.

This performance leap is primarily attributed to DACMRec successfully breaking the limitations of single-paradigm architectures. While pure graph models like LightGCN lack few-shot adaptive fine-tuning capabilities, and traditional meta-learning methods like MeLU lose high-order spatial topological information by relying on MLPs, our framework deeply integrates global graph structure awareness with local personalization. Furthermore, compared to sequence models (SHAN, FEARec) that struggle when explicit historical interactions are scarce, our dual-level contrastive augmentation robustly mines underlying self-supervised signals.

5.3 Ablation Study

To verify the contributions of key components, we compare DACMRec with four degraded variants: 1) **w/o meta**: removes the meta-learning optimization; 2) **w/o cl**: removes the entire contrastive learning framework; 3) **w/o svd**: removes the structure-level augmentation; 4) **w/o noise**: removes the feature-level perturbation. The results are summarized in Table 4 and visualized in Fig. 2.

Table 3. Performance Comparison with Baselines on Four Datasets

Dataset	Metric	LightGCN	SimGCL	SHAN	MAML	MeLU	FEARec	DACMRec	Improv.
Gowalla	Recall@10	0.0815	0.0882	0.0834	0.0792	0.0915	0.1002	**0.1052**	+4.99%
	NDCG@10	0.0412	0.0453	0.0426	0.0385	0.0482	0.0541	**0.0583**	+7.76%
	Recall@20	0.1064	0.1145	0.1082	0.1023	0.1186	0.1265	**0.1315**	+3.95%
	NDCG@20	0.0487	0.0531	0.0498	0.0452	0.0561	0.0618	**0.0652**	+5.50%
Brightkite	Recall@10	0.0863	0.0915	0.0881	0.0824	0.0963	0.1042	**0.1103**	+5.85%
	NDCG@10	0.0441	0.0476	0.0452	0.0411	0.0508	0.0563	**0.0612**	+8.70%
	Recall@20	0.1125	0.1198	0.1142	0.1065	0.1245	0.1311	**0.1364**	+4.04%
	NDCG@20	0.0523	0.0564	0.0531	0.0488	0.0594	0.0642	**0.0691**	+7.63%
TKY	Recall@10	0.0905	0.0954	0.0912	0.0865	0.0995	0.1082	**0.1124**	+3.88%
	NDCG@10	0.0482	0.0515	0.0493	0.0454	0.0543	0.0618	**0.0650**	+5.17%
	Recall@20	0.1184	0.1256	0.1205	0.1142	0.1302	0.1351	**0.1385**	+2.51%
	NDCG@20	0.0565	0.0602	0.0574	0.0532	0.0631	0.0684	**0.0713**	+4.23%
NYC	Recall@10	0.0762	0.0814	0.0785	0.0741	0.0862	0.0945	**0.0985**	+4.23%
	NDCG@10	0.0384	0.0416	0.0392	0.0365	0.0445	0.0502	**0.0541**	+7.76%
	Recall@20	0.0995	0.1068	0.1021	0.0963	0.1124	0.1196	**0.1245**	+4.09%
	NDCG@20	0.0452	0.0488	0.0461	0.0423	0.0521	0.0575	**0.0615**	+6.95%

Table 4. Ablation Study on Four Datasets

Dataset	Metric	w/o meta	w/o cl	w/o svd	w/o noise	DACMRec
Gowalla	Recall@10	0.1030	0.0945	0.1005	0.0945	**0.1052**
	NDCG@10	0.0565	0.0488	0.0542	0.0518	**0.0583**
	Recall@20	0.1285	0.1168	0.1252	0.1215	**0.1315**
	NDCG@20	0.0632	0.0542	0.0608	0.0575	**0.0652**
Brightkite	Recall@10	0.1075	0.0965	0.1042	0.1008	**0.1103**
	NDCG@10	0.0584	0.0502	0.0558	0.0531	**0.0612**
	Recall@20	0.1332	0.1205	0.1298	0.1256	**0.1364**
	NDCG@20	0.0665	0.0572	0.0638	0.0605	**0.0691**
TKY	Recall@10	0.1124	0.0995	0.1095	0.1052	**0.1124**
	NDCG@10	0.0650	0.0572	0.0632	0.0605	**0.0650**
	Recall@20	0.1359	0.1232	0.1334	0.1285	**0.1385**
	NDCG@20	0.0708	0.0632	0.0692	0.0665	**0.0713**
NYC	Recall@10	0.0666	0.0782	0.0924	0.0865	**0.0985**
	NDCG@10	0.0410	0.0452	0.0512	0.0485	**0.0541**
	Recall@20	0.0804	0.1025	0.1185	0.1112	**0.1245**
	NDCG@20	0.0444	0.0498	0.0582	0.0545	**0.0615**

As shown, removing the meta-learning module (**w/o meta**) causes a severe performance drop on the extremely sparse NYC dataset, with Recall@10 falling from 0.0985 to 0.0666. This indicates that in cold-start scenarios, relying solely on contrastive learning is insufficient; meta-learning is essential to capture personalized features via adaptive fine-tuning.

Conversely, on the TKY dataset, removing meta-learning has a more marginal impact, whereas removing the contrastive framework (**w/o cl**) drops Recall@10 to 0.0995. The more severe performance collapse on NYC compared to TKY—despite their similar overall sparsity levels (99.35% vs. 99.33%)—is likely due to NYC's extremely small user base (only 1,083 users), which creates a more extreme cold-start condition. This suggests that when the user base and collaborative edges are slightly more abundant (as in TKY), the graph's collaborative signals are inherently more robust. In such cases, the generalization and anti-noise capabilities provided by contrastive learning become the decisive factors for optimal performance.

5.4 Further Analysis

Impact of Data Sparsity. To test robustness, we reduced the check-in data for each user to 80%, 60%, and 40%. Sequence models (such as SHAN) exhibited a sharp decline in performance when data retention dropped to 40%, revealing their extreme reliance on rich historical interaction data. In contrast, DACMRec

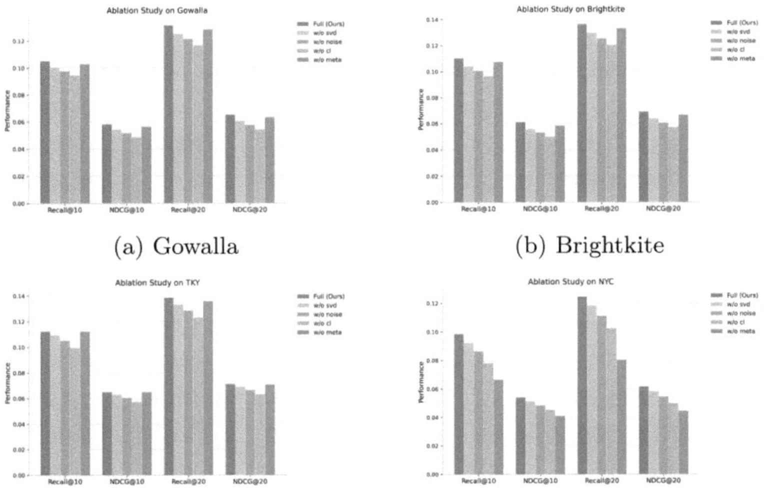

(a) Gowalla (b) Brightkite

(c) TKY (d) NYC

Fig. 2. Ablation study on four datasets.

maintained the smoothest decay curve. This robustness stems from the self-supervised signals provided by dual-level augmented contrastive learning, which enables the model to continuously extract topological information even when a large number of explicit edges are removed. Figure 3 illustrates the impact of data sparsity, demonstrating the model's robustness under extreme conditions.

To investigate the specific impact of multi-head attention mechanisms on feature capture capabilities in sequence modeling, this paper conducted hyper-parameter sensitivity experiments on the dataset for attention head counts Head Value = 1, 2, 4, 8, 16. Figure 4 illustrates the performance trends of the model across various evaluation metrics. As shown in the figure, when the number of heads is small, the model's ability to capture the representational space of users' multi-level travel intentions is limited, resulting in low recommendation accuracy. As the number of heads increases, the model begins to simultaneously capture spatiotemporal dependencies across different subspaces, with performance peaking at Head=8. However, when the number of heads was further increased to 16, all performance metrics showed a certain degree of decline. This is primarily because, in highly sparse cold-start recommendation scenarios, blindly expanding the number of attention heads introduces an excessive number of learnable parameters, causing the model to rapidly overfit on the limited dataset.

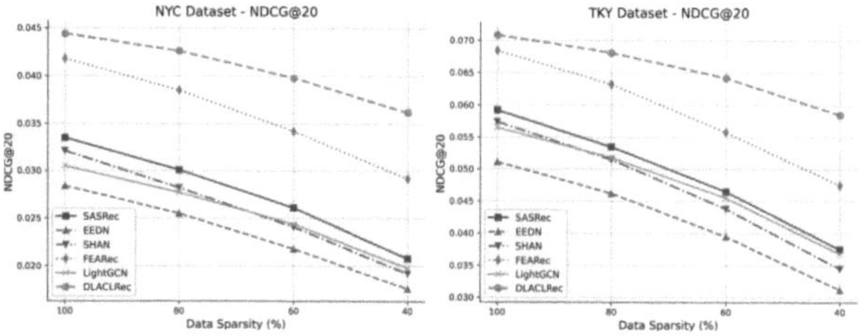

Fig. 3. Impact of data sparsity.

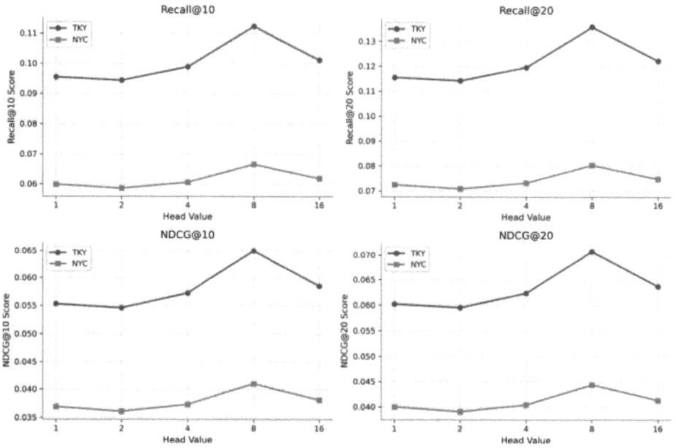

Fig. 4. Impact of multi-head attention heads.

6 Conclusion

In this paper, we propose DACMRec, a next-POI recommendation model integrating dual-level augmented contrastive learning and meta-learning, aimed at tackling the pervasive challenges of extreme data sparsity and cold-start in Location-Based Services.By introducing a dual-level augmented contrastive learning module, which applies SVD truncation at the structural level and injects noise at the feature level, the model effectively extracts robust and valuable collaborative signals while preserving critical spatiotemporal semantics.

Furthermore, we formulate the recommendation process as independent meta-tasks, optimized via a FOMAML mechanism. This endows the model with rapid adaptation capabilities, enabling it to deliver precise personalized recommendations for long-tail users relying on only minimal interaction data. Extensive experiments on four real-world datasets demonstrate that DACMRec consistently outperforms state-of-the-art baseline methods.

For future work, we plan to extend the proposed framework in two promising directions. First, we will incorporate multi-modal LBS data (e.g., textual reviews and social networks) and explore the integration of Large Language Models to further enrich the semantic representations of POIs. Second, we noted the emergence of excellent concurrent works in 2025. We plan to conduct deep comparative studies and integrations between DACMRec and these latest state-of-the-art architectures.

Disclosure of Interests. The authors have no competing interests to declare that are relevant to the content of this article.

Acknowledgment. This work was partially supported by Shandong Provincial Natural Science Foundation under Grant No. ZR2023LZH008 and Shandong Provincial Key Research and Development Program under Grant No. 2024CXGC010101.

References

1. Chen, M., Huang, C., Xia, L., Wei, W., Xu, Y., Luo, R.: Heterogeneous graph contrastive learning for recommendation. In: Proceedings of the Sixteenth ACM International Conference on Web Search and Data Mining, pp. 544–552 (2023)
2. Dong, M., Yuan, F., Yao, L., Xu, X., Zhu, L.: Mamo: memory-augmented meta-optimization for cold-start recommendation. In: Proceedings of the 26th ACM SIGKDD International Conference on Knowledge Discovery & Data Mining, pp. 688–697 (2020)
3. Du, X., et al.: Frequency enhanced hybrid attention network for sequential recommendation. In: Proceedings of the 46th International ACM SIGIR Conference on Research and Development in Information Retrieval, pp. 78–88 (2023)
4. Finn, C., Abbeel, P., Levine, S.: Model-agnostic meta-learning for fast adaptation of deep networks. In: International Conference on Machine Learning, pp. 1126–1135. PMLR (2017)
5. He, X., Deng, K., Wang, X., Li, Y., Zhang, Y., Wang, M.: LightGCN: simplifying and powering graph convolution network for recommendation. In: Proceedings of the 43rd International ACM SIGIR Conference on Research and Development in Information Retrieval, pp. 639–648 (2020)
6. Lee, H., Im, J., Jang, S., Cho, H., Chung, S.: Melu: meta-learned user preference estimator for cold-start recommendation. In: Proceedings of the 25th ACM SIGKDD International Conference on Knowledge Discovery & Data Mining, pp. 1073–1082 (2019)
7. Lei, S., et al.: Feature-structure adaptive completion graph neural network for cold-start recommendation. In: Proceedings of the AAAI Conference on Artificial Intelligence, vol. 39, pp. 12022–12030 (2025)
8. Lin, X., Wu, J., Zhou, C., Pan, S., Cao, Y., Wang, B.: Task-adaptive neural process for user cold-start recommendation. In: Proceedings of the Web Conference 2021, pp. 1306–1316 (2021)
9. Liu, Q., Wu, S., Wang, L., Tan, T.: Predicting the next location: a recurrent model with spatial and temporal contexts. In: Proceedings of the AAAI Conference on Artificial Intelligence, vol. 30, (2016)
10. Liu, S., at al.: STGIN: spatial-temporal graph interaction network for large-scale POI recommendation. In: Proceedings of the 32nd ACM International Conference on Information and Knowledge Management, pp. 4120–4124 (2023)
11. Liu, Z., Chen, Y., Li, J., Yu, P.S., McAuley, J., Xiong, C.: Contrastive self-supervised sequential recommendation with robust augmentation. arXiv preprint arXiv:2108.06479 (2021)

12. Lu, Y., Fang, Y., Shi, C.: Meta-learning on heterogeneous information networks for cold-start recommendation. In: Proceedings of the 26th ACM SIGKDD International Conference on Knowledge Discovery & Data Mining, pp. 1563–1573 (2020)
13. Luo, Y., Duan, H., Liu, Y., Chung, F.L.: Timestamps as prompts for geography-aware location recommendation. In: Proceedings of the 32nd ACM International Conference on Information and Knowledge Management, pp. 1697–1706 (2023)
14. Luo, Y., Liu, Q., Liu, Z.: STAN: spatio-temporal attention network for next location recommendation. In: Proceedings of the web conference 2021, pp. 2177–2185 (2021)
15. Luo, Y., et al.: Online item cold-start recommendation with popularity-aware meta-learning. In: Proceedings of the 31st ACM SIGKDD Conference on Knowledge Discovery and Data Mining, pp. 927–937 (2025)
16. Rao, X., et al.: Next point-of-interest recommendation with adaptive graph contrastive learning. IEEE Trans. Knowl. Data Eng., (2024)
17. Wang, X., He, X., Wang, M., Feng, F., Chua, T.S.: Neural graph collaborative filtering. In: Proceedings of the 42nd international ACM SIGIR Conference on Research and Development in Information Retrieval, pp. 165–174 (2019)
18. Wang, X., Fukumoto, F., Cui, J., Suzuki, Y., Li, J., Yu, D.: Eedn: Enhanced encoder-decoder network with local and global context learning for poi recommendation. In: Proceedings of the 46th International ACM SIGIR Conference on Research and Development in Information Retrieval, pp. 383–392 (2023)
19. Wang, Z., Zhu, Y., Liu, H., Wang, C.: Learning graph-based disentangled representations for next poi recommendation. In: Proceedings of the 45th International ACM SIGIR Conference on Research and Development in Information Retrieval, pp. 1154–1163 (2022)
20. Wang, Z., Zhu, Y., Wang, C., Ma, W., Li, B., Yu, J.: Adaptive graph representation learning for next poi recommendation. In: Proceedings of the 46th International ACM SIGIR Conference on Research and Development in Information Retrieval, pp. 393–402 (2023)
21. Wu, J., et al.: Self-supervised graph learning for recommendation. In: Proceedings of the 44th International ACM SIGIR Conference on Research and Development in Information Retrieval, pp. 726–735 (2021)
22. Xie, X., et al.: Contrastive learning for sequential recommendation. In: 2022 IEEE 38th International Conference on Data Engineering (ICDE), pp. 1259–1273. IEEE (2022)
23. Yang, Y., Huang, C., Xia, L., Li, C.: Knowledge graph contrastive learning for recommendation. In: Proceedings of the 45th International ACM SIGIR Conference on Research and Development in Information Retrieval, pp. 1434–1443 (2022)
24. Ying, H., et al.: Sequential recommender system based on hierarchical attention network. In: IJCAI International Joint Conference on Artificial Intelligence (2018)
25. Yu, J., Yin, H., Xia, X., Chen, T., Cui, L., Nguyen, Q.V.H.: Are graph augmentations necessary? simple graph contrastive learning for recommendation. In: Proceedings of the 45th International ACM SIGIR Conference on Research and Development in Information Retrieval, pp. 1294–1303 (2022)
26. Zhao, P., et al.: Where to go next: a spatio-temporal gated network for next poi recommendation. IEEE Trans. Knowl. Data Eng. **34**(5), 2512–2524 (2020)
27. Zhou, C., Ma, J., Zhang, J., Zhou, J., Yang, H.: Contrastive learning for debiased candidate generation in large-scale recommender systems. In: Proceedings of the 27th ACM SIGKDD Conference on Knowledge Discovery & Data Mining, pp. 3985–3995 (2021)

28. Zhou, H., Xu, J., Zhu, Q., Liu, C.: Disentangled graph debiasing for next poi recommendation. In: Proceedings of the 48th International ACM SIGIR Conference on Research and Development in Information Retrieval, pp. 1779–1788 (2025)
29. Zhou, K., et al.: S3-rec: self-supervised learning for sequential recommendation with mutual information maximization. In: Proceedings of the 29th ACM International Conference on Information & Knowledge Management, pp. 1893–1902 (2020)
30. Zhou, X., Sun, A., Liu, Y., Zhang, J., Miao, C.: SelfCF: a simple framework for self-supervised collaborative filtering. ACM Transactions on Recommender Systems **1**(2), 1–25 (2023)

Hierarchical Prototype Reasoning Network for Few-Shot and Zero-Shot Learning

Tu Nguyen Anh[1(✉)], Nhan Huu Tran[2], and Vinh Dinh Nguyen[2]

[1] FPT School of Business and Technology, FPT University, Can Tho City, Vietnam
tu26ms43072@fsb.edu.vn

[2] Faculty of Information Technology, FPT University, Can Tho City, Vietnam
NhanTHCE181655@fpt.edu.vn, vinhnd29@fe.edu.vn

Abstract. We propose the **Hierarchical Prototype Reasoning Network (HPRN)**, a lightweight unified framework for few-shot and zero-shot learning. HPRN decomposes visual representations into coarse and fine subspaces for hierarchical prototype matching, refined iteratively by a GRU module with entropy-driven early stopping. A learnable scalar balances prototype and reasoning outputs; CLIP text embeddings are projected into the same space for seamless zero-shot inference. HPRN achieves **74.17%** on CIFAR-FS and **69.07%** on mini-ImageNet (5-way 1-shot, DenseNet-121, 7.93M parameters), and **90.55% F1** on Aero-Eyes, with zero-shot accuracy within 1.12% of the few-shot baseline. Monitorable activation patterns localize 79.7% of misclassifications for failure diagnosis.

Keywords: Few-shot learning · Zero-shot learning · Prototype networks · Hierarchical feature learning · Aerial object detection

1 Introduction

Few-shot learning enables recognition of novel categories from only a handful of labeled examples, where annotation is costly or infeasible. Despite impressive progress on standard benchmarks [1,2,6], current approaches still face three major limitations that hinder real-world adoption.

First, limited decision transparency: Most methods rely on opaque embeddings [2,3], hindering feature attribution and uncertainty quantification.

Second, monolithic representations: Existing techniques typically collapse multi-scale visual information into a single-level embedding [1,3], discarding the natural hierarchical structure of objects by merging global shape and local texture into a single signal, reducing discriminative power. Even strong baselines such as [4,5] operate within this single-level paradigm.

Third, fragmented handling of few-shot and zero-shot regimes: Few-shot and zero-shot learning are often treated as separate problems [13,14], preventing natural integration of visual examples with semantic knowledge from

L. Ding et al. (Eds.): APWeb-WAIM 2026, LNCS 16995, pp. 425–439, 2027.
https://doi.org/10.1007/978-981-92-5699-0_28

language models. A truly unified framework should handle both regimes without requiring architectural changes.

We introduce **HPRN** (Hierarchical Prototype Reasoning Network), a lightweight **unified framework** that handles both few-shot and zero-shot inference within a single architecture without any structural modification. HPRN is based on the mutual reinforcement between hierarchical prototype spaces and iterative GRU refinement: decomposing features into coarse and fine subspaces sharpens the context signal guiding GRU refinement, while entropy-driven early stopping adapts computation to query difficulty. This integration enables three capabilities simultaneously: (1) hierarchical feature decomposition into coarse and fine subspaces for multi-scale prototype matching; (2) a GRU-based reasoning module [21] with entropy-driven early stopping that refines ambiguous predictions; and (3) learnable text-to-visual alignment that projects CLIP [13] embeddings directly into the same prototype space, enabling a seamless transition from zero-shot to few-shot inference.

HPRN exposes prototype distances and binarized activation patterns ($|\rho| \leq 0.158$) for failure diagnosis, localizing prototype–reasoning conflicts responsible for 79.7

2 Related Work

Few-shot learning aims to classify novel categories from limited labeled examples. HPRN targets three underexplored aspects: enhanced decision inspection, hierarchical multi-scale representations, and unified few-shot and zero-shot inference.

2.1 Metric-Based Few-Shot Methods

Prototypical Networks [1], Matching Networks [2], and Relation Networks [3] established the episodic learning paradigm, with recent CNN-based methods (FEAT [7], COSOC [9]) reaching 62–69% on mini-ImageNet. HPRN advances this line by decomposing prototypes into hierarchical coarse/fine subspaces, yielding +3.47% over distance-only baselines.

2.2 Meta-Learning Approaches

MAML [6] and MetaOptNet [10] optimize for fast task adaptation, while transformer-based FewTURE [11] reaches 72.40% using 29M parameters and large-scale self-supervised pre-training. HPRN achieves 69.1% on mini-ImageNet with only 7.93M parameters and standard ImageNet pre-training, making it suitable for settings where computational resources and pre-training data are constrained.

2.3 Zero-Shot Learning and Vision-Language Models

CLIP [13] and prompt-tuning methods (CoOp [14], CLIP-Adapter [23]) achieve strong zero-shot accuracy but are not designed to seamlessly incorporate visual support examples. HPRN bridges this gap by projecting CLIP text embeddings into the hierarchical prototype space, achieving 71.28% zero-shot accuracy on CIFAR-FS, only 1.12% below the few-shot baseline within the same unified architecture.

2.4 Interpretability and Inspection Methods

Concept Bottleneck Models [15] require manual concept definitions; neural-symbolic approaches rely on structured scene representations unavailable in standard benchmarks. HPRN learns intermediate representations end-to-end without requiring manual annotations.

3 Methodology

3.1 Problem Formulation

For N-way K-shot learning, each episode $\mathcal{E} = (\mathcal{S}, \mathcal{Q})$ consists of a support set $\mathcal{S} = \{(\boldsymbol{x}_i^s, y_i^s)\}_{i=1}^{N\times K}$ and a query set $\mathcal{Q} = \{(\boldsymbol{x}_j^q, y_j^q)\}_{j=1}^{M}$, where $M = 15$ and $\boldsymbol{x}_i^s \in \mathbb{R}^{3\times 32\times 32}$ for CIFAR-FS. The episodic loss follows [1,2]:

$$\mathcal{L} = \frac{1}{M}\sum_{j=1}^{M} \mathcal{L}_{\text{CE}}(f_\theta(\boldsymbol{x}_j^q, \mathcal{S}), y_j^q) + \lambda_{\text{reg}}\mathcal{L}_{\text{reg}} \tag{1}$$

3.2 Architecture Overview

Figure 1 illustrates HPRN's pipeline. Backbone features are projected into coarse/fine subspaces; prototypes are matched via Euclidean distance; a GRU module refines predictions with entropy-driven early stopping; learnable $\gamma \approx 0.79$ fuses both signals. For zero-shot inference, CLIP text embeddings replace visual prototypes via a learned MLP projection.

3.3 Hierarchical Feature Extraction

The backbone is pre-trained on ImageNet [18] and fine-tuned during meta-training at a lower learning rate. We evaluate both ResNet18 [16] and DenseNet-121 [17] as backbone choices. Two parallel projection layers map the backbone feature $\boldsymbol{f}$ into hierarchical representations:

$$\boldsymbol{F}_c = \text{LayerNorm}(\text{ReLU}(W_c\boldsymbol{f} + \boldsymbol{b}_c)) \in \mathbb{R}^{128}, \quad \boldsymbol{F}_f = \text{LayerNorm}(\text{ReLU}(W_f\boldsymbol{f} + \boldsymbol{b}_f)) \in \mathbb{R}^{128} \tag{2}$$

Both are L2-normalized: $\boldsymbol{F} \leftarrow \boldsymbol{F}/(\|\boldsymbol{F}\|_2 + 10^{-8})$.

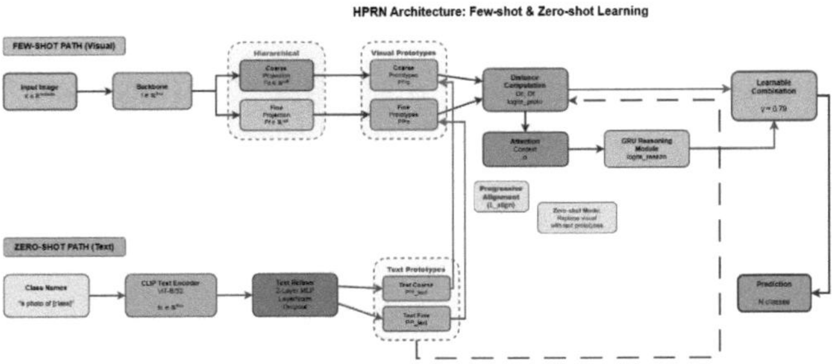

Fig. 1. Overview of HPRN. Backbone features are split into coarse and fine 128-d subspaces for hierarchical prototype matching. A GRUCell (64-d input, 256-d hidden state) refines predictions with entropy driven early stopping and fuses them with prototype logits via learnable $\gamma \approx 0.79$. CLIP text embeddings enable zero-shot inference through the same prototype space.

3.4 Prototype Computation and Distance Matching

Class prototypes are computed by mean-pooling support features, then L2-normalized:

$$\boldsymbol{P}_c^{(1)} = \frac{1}{K} \sum_{i:y_i^s=c} \boldsymbol{F}_{c,i}^s, \quad \boldsymbol{P}_c^{(2)} = \frac{1}{K} \sum_{i:y_i^s=c} \boldsymbol{F}_{f,i}^s, \quad \boldsymbol{P}_c^{(\cdot)} \leftarrow \boldsymbol{P}_c^{(\cdot)} / \|\boldsymbol{P}_c^{(\cdot)}\|_2 \tag{3}$$

Coarse and fine Euclidean distance matrices $D_c^{(1)}, D_f^{(2)} \in \mathbb{R}^{n_q \times N}$ are combined via a learnable mixing weight $\lambda_{\text{mix}} \in [0, 1]$, initialized at 0.5 and converging to 0.558 after training:

$$D = \lambda_{\text{mix}} \cdot D_c^{(1)} + (1 - \lambda_{\text{mix}}) \cdot D_f^{(2)}, \qquad \text{logits}_{\text{proto}} = -D/\tau \tag{4}$$

where $\tau = 0.0907$.

3.5 Attention-Weighted Context Construction

We compute separate soft attention distributions over all N prototypes:

$$w_{\text{coarse}} = \text{softmax}(-D_c^{(1)}/\tau), \quad w_{\text{fine}} = \text{softmax}(-D_f^{(2)}/\tau) \tag{5}$$

Fused via λ_{mix}:

$$w^{(\text{fused})} = \lambda_{\text{mix}} \cdot w_{\text{coarse}} + (1 - \lambda_{\text{mix}}) \cdot w_{\text{fine}} \in \mathbb{R}^{n_q \times N} \tag{6}$$

The context vector is:

$$\boldsymbol{\alpha} = w^{(\text{fused})} [\boldsymbol{P}_c^{(1)}; \boldsymbol{P}_c^{(2)}]_{c=1}^N \in \mathbb{R}^{n_q \times d_\alpha} \tag{7}$$

where $d_\alpha = d_c + d_f = 256$ and $[\cdot;\cdot]$ denotes concatenation.

3.6 Adaptive Iterative Refinement Module

A two-layer MLP extracts a compact rule vector from the context vector $\boldsymbol{\alpha} \in \mathbb{R}^{n_q \times 256}$:

$$\boldsymbol{z} = \text{Dropout}_{p=0.1}\left(\text{ReLU}(\text{LayerNorm}(W_1\boldsymbol{\alpha} + \boldsymbol{b}_1))\right) \tag{8}$$

$$\boldsymbol{R} = W_2\boldsymbol{z} + \boldsymbol{b}_2 \in \mathbb{R}^{n_q \times 64} \tag{9}$$

where the rule extraction MLP has architecture 256 → 64 → 64. A binarized representation is derived exclusively for post-hoc monitoring (Sect. 5.8); it is not used in the forward pass:

$$\boldsymbol{R}_{\text{bin}} = \mathbf{1}[\sigma(\boldsymbol{R}) > 0.5] \tag{10}$$

The GRUCell receives the continuous rule vector $\boldsymbol{R} \in \mathbb{R}^{n_q \times 64}$ as input at each step, with hidden state dimension 256 initialized from the context vector: $\boldsymbol{h}_0 = \boldsymbol{\alpha} \in \mathbb{R}^{n_q \times 256}$. The hidden state is updated for $i \in \{1, \ldots, k_{\max}\}$ steps:

$$\boldsymbol{h}_i = \text{GRUCell}(\boldsymbol{R},\ \boldsymbol{h}_{i-1}) \tag{11}$$

Intermediate logits are computed via $\text{logits}_i = \text{MLP}_{\text{pred}}(\boldsymbol{h}_i)$, where the predictor MLP has architecture 256 → 128 → N.

Entropy-driven early stopping quantifies average prediction uncertainty at step i:

$$\mathcal{U}_i = -\frac{1}{n_q}\sum_{j=1}^{n_q}\sum_{c=1}^{N} p_{i,j,c}\log(p_{i,j,c} + 10^{-8}) \tag{12}$$

where $p_{i,j,c} = \text{softmax}(\text{logits}_{i,j})_c$. Reasoning terminates if $\mathcal{U}_i < \delta = 0.5$ or i reaches $k_{\max} = 4$; $\delta \in [0.4, 0.6]$ yields <0.3% accuracy variation on held-out episodes.

After reasoning completes, all hidden states $\boldsymbol{H} = [\boldsymbol{h}_0, \ldots, \boldsymbol{h}_T]$ are aggregated via learned attention weights $\boldsymbol{a} = \text{softmax}(\text{MLP}_{\text{attn}}([\boldsymbol{H};\ \tilde{\boldsymbol{R}}]))$, where $\tilde{\boldsymbol{R}}$ denotes $\boldsymbol{R}$ broadcast across time steps:

$$\boldsymbol{y} = \sum_{t=0}^{T} \boldsymbol{a}_t\boldsymbol{h}_t, \qquad \text{logits}_{\text{reason}} = \text{MLP}_{\text{pred}}(\boldsymbol{y}) \tag{13}$$

3.7 Learnable Prototype-Reasoning Combination

A learnable scalar θ, initialized at 0.5, controls fusion via $\gamma = \sigma(\theta)$:

$$\text{logits}_{\text{final}} = \gamma \cdot \text{logits}_{\text{proto}} + (1 - \gamma) \cdot \text{logits}_{\text{reason}} \tag{14}$$

After training, $\gamma \approx 0.79$, confirming prototype matching as the primary signal (79%) with GRU refinement handling ambiguous cases (21%).

3.8 Design Rationale

Euclidean distance is faster than Earth Mover's Distance [8] and scale-invariant after L2 normalization. GRU supports adaptive stopping with half the parameters of a Transformer. Projection dimension $d_c = d_f = 128$ balances expressiveness and efficiency: 64-d degrades accuracy by 1.9% while 256-d adds 80% parameters for only 0.3% gain.

3.9 Regularization Strategies

To encourage diverse prototype representations, we introduce two auxiliary losses. The diversity loss penalizes cosine similarity between class prototypes:

$$\mathcal{L}_{\text{div}} = \frac{1}{N(N-1)} \sum_{i \neq j} |\text{cos\_sim}(\boldsymbol{P}_i, \boldsymbol{P}_j)|, \quad \lambda_{\text{div}} = 0.1 \tag{15}$$

The orthogonality loss enforces near-orthonormal prototypes:

$$\mathcal{L}_{\text{ortho}} = \|\boldsymbol{P}^\top \boldsymbol{P} - I_N\|_F^2, \quad \lambda_{\text{ortho}} = 0.05 \tag{16}$$

Both losses operate on L2-normalized prototypes to prevent trivial collapse.

3.10 Zero-Shot Learning via Text Alignment

For zero-shot inference, CLIP ViT-B/32 encodes class descriptions (e.g., "a photo of [class_name]"):

$$\boldsymbol{t}_c = \text{CLIP}_{\text{text}}(\text{description}) \in \mathbb{R}^{512} \tag{17}$$

A two-layer MLP (LayerNorm–ReLU–Dropout$_{0.1}$) projects $\boldsymbol{t}_c$ into the prototype space:

$$\boldsymbol{P}_{\text{text},c} = W_2(\text{Dropout}(\text{LayerNorm}(\text{ReLU}(W_1 \boldsymbol{t}_c)))) \in \mathbb{R}^{d_c + d_f} \tag{18}$$

where $W_1 \in \mathbb{R}^{512 \times 512}$, $W_2 \in \mathbb{R}^{256 \times 512}$. The output is split into $\boldsymbol{P}^{(1)}_{\text{text},c}$ (first 128-d) and $\boldsymbol{P}^{(2)}_{\text{text},c}$ (last 128-d), then L2-normalized.

Visual and text prototypes are aligned during training via a progressive loss:

$$\mathcal{L}_{\text{align}} = \frac{1}{N} \sum_{c=1}^{N} \|[\boldsymbol{P}_c^{(1)}; \boldsymbol{P}_c^{(2)}] - \boldsymbol{P}_{\text{text},c}\|_2^2 \tag{19}$$

Importantly, $\mathcal{L}_{\text{align}}$ is computed exclusively over training-split classes; CLIP text embeddings for test classes are never exposed to visual prototype supervision during training, ensuring no test-class leakage in the zero-shot evaluation. $\lambda_{\text{align}}(e)$ increases linearly from 0.5 to 3.0 over training epochs. Total loss:

$$\mathcal{L}_{\text{total}} = \mathcal{L}_{\text{CE}} + \lambda_{\text{div}} \mathcal{L}_{\text{div}} + \lambda_{\text{ortho}} \mathcal{L}_{\text{ortho}} + \lambda_{\text{align}}(e) \mathcal{L}_{\text{align}} \tag{20}$$

Table 1. Optimal Hyperparameters from Bayesian Search

Parameter	Range	CIFAR-FS	mini-ImageNet
d_c, d_f	{64, 128}	128	128
τ	[0.08, 0.25]	0.0907	0.0907
λ_{mix}	[0.3, 0.7]	0.558	0.558
k_{max}	{3, 4, 5}	4	4
LR (main)	[3e-4, 3e-3]	8.65e-4	8.65e-4
λ_{ortho}	[0.01, 0.05]	0.05	0.0394
λ_{align}	[0.5, 3.0]	1.5	0.5

50 trials, Ax Platform, expected improvement acquisition, seed 42.

4 Experimental Setup

4.1 Datasets and Tasks

We evaluate HPRN on CIFAR-FS [19], mini-ImageNet [20], and Aero-Eyes [12]. CIFAR-FS and mini-ImageNet follow the standard 64/16/20 train/val/test split and are evaluated under the 5-way 1-shot setting with 15 queries per episode. Aero-Eyes formulates aerial object tracking as a 2-way target versus background classification task under severe class imbalance and challenging variations in altitude, illumination, and occlusion. Each episode uses six support images comprising three target views and three background frames.

4.2 Training Configuration

CIFAR-FS and mini-ImageNet. Adam [22] with OneCycleLR ($\eta_{\text{main}} = 8.65 \times 10^{-4}$), gradient clipping 1.0; 10 epochs (CIFAR-FS), 5 epochs (mini-ImageNet). Standard augmentation: flips, crops, jitter; ImageNet normalization.

Aero-Eyes. Adam [22] with CosineAnnealingLR ($T_{\max} = 15$, $\eta_{\min} = 10^{-5}$), $\eta_{\text{main}} = 10^{-3}$, $\eta_{\text{backbone}} = 10^{-4}$, gradient clipping 1.0, 15 epochs, 150 episodes per epoch. Strong augmentation covers rotation $\pm 180°$, scale 0.7–1.3×, perspective $\pm 15\%$, flips, and color jitter to handle aerial viewpoint variation.

4.3 Hyperparameter Search Strategy

Bayesian optimization (Ax Platform, 50 trials) identifies robust architectural parameters that transfer across datasets; only regularization weights require minor tuning (Table 1).

4.4 Statistical Validation and Implementation

All results are reported over 600 test episodes (9,000 total predictions) with 95% confidence intervals and Welch's t-test significance at $p < 0.05$, using random seed 42. Experiments run in PyTorch 2.0.1 on an NVIDIA RTX 3050 with 4GB VRAM. Training CIFAR-FS takes approximately 45 minutes over 10 epochs, with 26ms per episode at inference. Aero-Eyes training runs for 3.5 h over 15 epochs, with per-video inference taking around 38 s.

Table 2. CIFAR-FS 5-Way 1-Shot Results

Method	Backbone	Params	Acc (%)
Matching Network	Conv-4	0.11M	35.74 ± 0.79
Relation Network	Conv-4	0.23M	35.02 ± 1.26
Prototypical Net	Conv-4	0.11M	57.64 ± 0.07
Baseline++	ResNet-18	11.18M	55.28 ± 0.83
Simple CNAPS	ResNet-18	11.44M	57.64 ± 0.06
HPRN (ResNet-18)	ResNet-18	**12.03M**	**72.40 ± 0.91**
HPRN (DenseNet-121)	DenseNet-121	**7.93M**	**74.17 ± 0.82**

Table 3. mini-ImageNet 5-Way 1-Shot Comparison

Method	Backbone	Pretrain	Params	Acc (%)
Classical Methods:				
Matching Network	Conv-4	None	0.11M	43.56 ± 0.84
MAML	Conv-4	None	0.11M	48.70 ± 1.84
Prototypical Net	Conv-4	None	0.11M	49.42 ± 0.78
Relation Network	Conv-4	None	0.23M	50.44 ± 0.82
Baseline++	ResNet-18	ImgNet	11.2M	51.87 ± 0.77
Advanced CNN Methods (ImageNet pretrain):				
MetaOptNet	ResNet-12	ImgNet	12.4M	62.64 ± 0.61
SimpleShot	ResNet-18	ImgNet	11.2M	62.85 ± 0.20
FEAT	ResNet-12	ImgNet	12.4M	62.96 ± 0.19
DeepEMD	ResNet-12	ImgNet	12.5M	65.91 ± 0.82
FRN	ResNet-12	ImgNet	12.5M	66.45 ± 0.19
COSOC	ResNet-12	ImgNet	12.5M	69.28 ± 0.49
Vision Transformers (Large-scale self-supervised pretrain):				
EASY	ViT-Small	DINO	22.1M	74.33 ± 0.38
FewTURE	Swin-Tiny	MIM	29.0M	72.40 ± 0.78
HPRN (ResNet-18)	ResNet-18	ImgNet	12.03M	67.39 ± 0.45
HPRN (DenseNet-121)	DenseNet-121	ImgNet	**7.93M**	**69.07 ± 0.52**

ImgNet: ImageNet-1K supervised; DINO: self-supervised ViT; MIM: masked image modelling

5 Results and Analysis

5.1 Few-Shot Learning Performance

Table 2 reports CIFAR-FS 5-way 1-shot results. HPRN with ResNet18 achieves 72.40%, surpassing Prototypical Networks [1] by 14.76%; DenseNet-121 further improves to 74.17% (CV=1.11%). Table 3 shows that on mini-ImageNet, HPRN-DenseNet achieves 69.07%, closely matching COSOC at 69.28% while using 37% fewer parameters. ViT-based methods reach 72.40–74.33% but rely on 22.1–29.0M parameters and large-scale self-supervised pre-training, placing them in a different resource regime.

5.2 Zero-Shot Learning Capability

Replacing visual support prototypes with CLIP-derived text embeddings [13] yields 71.28% zero-shot accuracy on CIFAR-FS, only 1.12% below the few-shot result of 72.40%, demonstrating that the hierarchical prototype space successfully bridges the visual–semantic gap.

5.3 Cross-Dataset Generalization

Using shared architectural parameters ($d_c = d_f = 128$, $\tau = 0.0907$, $\lambda_{\text{mix}} = 0.558$, $k_{\text{max}} = 4$) without any dataset-specific tuning, HPRN achieves 72.18% on CIFAR-FS and 65.47% on mini-ImageNet, 0.22% below the CIFAR-FS optimum and 3.60% below the mini-ImageNet optimum, suggesting that architectural parameters transfer well across datasets while regularization weights benefit from per-dataset tuning.

5.4 Aero-Eyes Aerial Tracking Challenge

HPRN is applied in a 2-way binary classification setting. The support set for each video consists of six images: three target references and three background frames sampled from the beginning, middle, and end of the sequence. The core architecture remains unchanged, while five adaptations during inference address the aerial video domain, with hierarchical prototype matching serving as the primary discriminative mechanism. Specifically, temporal smoothing reduces frame noise but cannot recover from incorrect prototype decisions, adaptive thresholding adjusts decision boundaries from HPRN outputs, and curriculum learning stabilizes training without modifying inference. The discriminative gain therefore stems from hierarchical prototype matching, which produces embeddings robust to viewpoint and scale variations before subsequent processing.

Multi-Scale Inference and Augmentation. Predictions are ensembled over three resolutions (224, 320, 448 px) with weights $\boldsymbol{w} = [1.0, 1.2, 1.5]/3.7$. Training augmentation (rotation $\pm 180°$, scale 0.7–1.3×, perspective $\pm 15\%$, flips, color jitter) provides viewpoint robustness.

Temporal Smoothing. A 7-frame median filter (window size selected by grid search over $\{3, 5, 7\}$ on the training split):

$$p_{\text{smooth}}(t) = \text{median}_{i \in [t-3,\, t+3]}\, p_{\text{ensemble}}(i) \tag{21}$$

Adaptive Thresholding. Let p_{90} denote the 90th percentile of p_{smooth} for a given video. The scaling factor α is:

$$\alpha = \begin{cases} 0.7 & \text{if } p_{90} < 0.4 \\ 1.0 & \text{if } 0.4 \leq p_{90} \leq 0.8 \\ 1.2 & \text{if } p_{90} > 0.8 \end{cases} \tag{22}$$

and $t_{\text{video}} = t_{\text{base}} \times \alpha$ with $t_{\text{base}} = 0.5$.

Curriculum Learning. Videos ranked by difficulty $d_v = 1 - r_{\text{pos}}$; training set expands over 15 epochs:

$$\mathcal{V}_{\text{train}}(e) = \begin{cases} 50\% \text{ easiest} & \text{if } e \leq 4 \\ 75\% \text{ easiest} & \text{if } 5 \leq e \leq 9 \\ \text{all videos} & \text{if } e \geq 10 \end{cases} \tag{23}$$

Table 4 shows HPRN achieves 95.62% accuracy and 90.55% F1 over 80,729 frames, outperforming the ResNet18 baseline by +10.55% accuracy and +18.45% F1. The high precision (97.86%) reflects conservative prototype-distance predictions that suppress false alarms under severe class imbalance. Table 5 reports per-video results; Fig. 2 illustrates correct classifications under viewpoint and lighting variation.

Table 4. Aero-Eyes Challenge Results (14 videos, 80,729 frames)

Method	**Acc**	**Prec**	**Rec**	**F1**
ResNet18 Baseline	85.07%	67.43%	77.46%	72.10%
HPRN (Ours)	**95.62%**	**97.86%**	**84.25%**	**90.55%**
Improvement	**+10.55%**	**+30.43%**	**+6.79%**	**+18.45%**

Table 5. Per-Video Performance on Aero-Eyes

Video ID	Frames	Acc (%)	Prec (%)	F1 (%)
Lifering_0	4,697	99.7	99.8	99.5
WaterBottle_0	4,998	99.5	98.7	98.8
Backpack_0	10,466	98.1	99.2	96.7
MobilePhone_0	6,410	94.1	98.8	75.7
WaterBottle_1	6,774	85.2	99.7	80.9
Jacket_0	5,085	82.1	100.0	35.9
(8 remaining)	*42,299*	*F1: 86.7–97.7%*		
Overall	**80,729**	**95.62**	**97.86**	**90.55**

Jacket_0: extreme camouflage, 100% precision but 78% of targets missed.

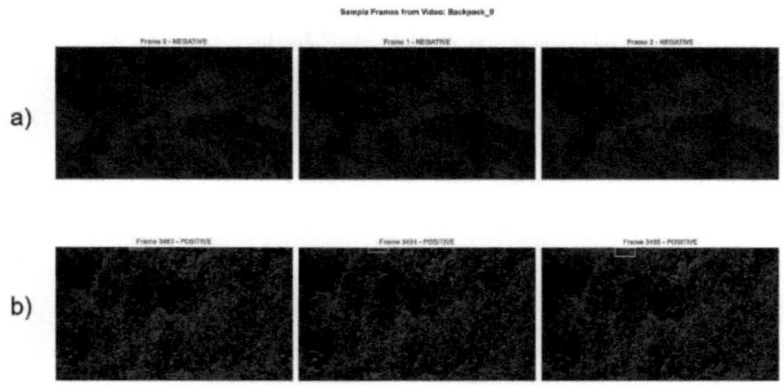

Fig. 2. Aero-Eyes Backpack_0 (F1: 96.7%). **(a)** Correct negative classification. **(b)** Correct positive classification under viewpoint/scale/lighting variation. Multi-scale ensemble (224 × 320 × 448) + 7-frame median filtering.

5.5 Ablation Studies

Table 6 quantifies each component's contribution. The reasoning module contributes the largest gain (+3.47%); removing hierarchical decomposition costs 2.63%; the diversity loss accounts for 1.76%; and fixing $\gamma = 0.5$ costs 1.39%. Early stopping has negligible impact (−0.13%), confirming that most queries converge well before $k_{\max}$.

5.6 Backbone Comparison

Among five backbones evaluated on CIFAR-FS 5-way 1-shot, DenseNet-121 achieves the best accuracy–efficiency trade-off at 74.17% ± 0.82% with 7.93M parameters (CV = 1.11%), significantly outperforming ResNet-18 at 72.40% ($p = 0.0127$, Welch's t-test). MobileNetV2 offers the smallest footprint (3.27M parameters) at 73.04%, while ResNet-50 and EfficientNet-B0 provide no meaningful accuracy gain over DenseNet-121 despite higher parameter counts.

Table 6. Component Ablation on CIFAR-FS

Component	Removed	Accuracy
Full HPRN	—	72.40%
– Hierarchical decomp.	Single 256-d	69.77% (−2.63%)
– Diversity loss	No Div	70.64% (−1.76%)
– Reasoning module	$\gamma = 1$	68.93% (−3.47%)
– Early stopping	Always $k = 4$	72.27% (−0.13%)
– Learnable γ	Fixed $\gamma = 0.5$	71.01% (−1.39%)

$\gamma = 1$: prototype only; $\gamma = 0$: reasoning only.

5.7 Computational Efficiency

Table 7 reports the trainable parameter breakdown. The core few-shot pipeline requires 585K trainable parameters with DenseNet-121 (excluding the text refiner, 395K, active only during zero-shot alignment; 980K total trainable), with inference at 26ms per episode on an RTX 3050 with 4GB VRAM.

Table 7. Trainable Parameter Breakdown (DenseNet-121 backbone)

Component	Params	%
Projection layers (1024 → 128 coarse + fine, with LayerNorm)	262,912	26.8%
GRUCell (input: 64-d $\boldsymbol{R}$; hidden: 256-d)	247,296	25.2%
Text refiner (512 → 512 → 256, zero-shot alignment only)	395,008	40.3%
Predictor MLP (256 → 128 → N)	33,541	3.4%
Rule extraction MLP (256 → 64 → 64)	20,736	2.1%
Attention MLP (320 → 64 → 1)	20,609	2.1%
Learnable scalar γ	1	<0.1%
Total trainable (DenseNet-121)	**980,103**	100%
DenseNet-121 features (frozen)	6,953,856	—
Total model (DenseNet-121)	**7,933,959**	—

ResNet18 variant: projection 131,840; total trainable 849,031; total model 12,026,569.

5.8 Inspection Capability and Failure Analysis

Among 64 activation dimensions, 57.8% activate frequently with weak prediction correlation (max $|\rho| = 0.158$), confirming enhanced inspection without overclaiming formal interpretability. Early stopping yields 35% computational savings; 79.7% of misclassifications stem from prototype–reasoning disagreement where the fixed γ prevents correction of confident but incorrect prototype decisions, as illustrated in Fig. 3.

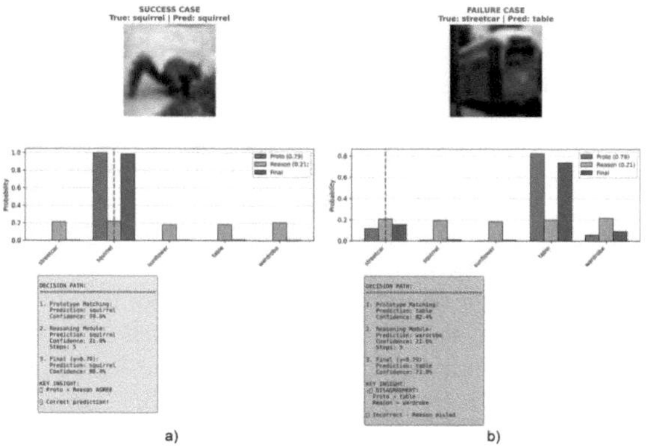

Fig. 3. Decision path comparison. **(a) Success:** squirrel classified correctly (proto 99.6%, final 98.4%). **(b) Failure:** streetcar misclassified as "table" (proto 82.4%) despite reasoning predicting "wardrobe"; fixed $\gamma = 0.79$ locks in the wrong prototype prediction.

6 Conclusion

HPRN unifies few-shot and zero-shot learning via hierarchical prototype matching and GRU iterative refinement. With 7.93M parameters, it achieves 74.17% on CIFAR-FS, 69.07% on mini-ImageNet, 90.55% F1 on Aero-Eyes, and zero-shot accuracy within 1.12% of the few-shot baseline, with monitorable activation patterns supporting auditable inference.

References

1. Snell, J., Swersky, K., Zemel, R.: Prototypical networks for few-shot learning. Adv. Neural Inf. Process. Syst., vol. 30, pp. 4077–4087. Curran Associates (2017). https://doi.org/10.48550/arXiv.1703.05175
2. Vinyals, O., Blundell, C., Lillicrap, T., Kavukcuoglu, K., Wierstra, D.: Matching networks for one shot learning. Adv. Neural Inf. Process. Syst., vol. 29, pp. 3630–3638. Curran Associates (2016). https://doi.org/10.48550/arXiv.1606.04080
3. Sung, F., Yang, Y., Zhang, L., Xiang, T., Torr, P.H.S., Hospedales, T.M.: Learning to compare: relation network for few-shot learning. In: Proceedings of the IEEE/CVF Conference on Computer Vision and Pattern Recognition (CVPR), pp. 1199–1208. IEEE (2018). https://doi.org/10.48550/arXiv.1711.06025
4. Chen, W.Y., Liu, Y.C., Kira, Z., Wang, Y.C.F., Huang, J.B.: A closer look at few-shot classification. In: International Conference on Learning Representations (ICLR) (2019). https://doi.org/10.48550/arXiv.1904.04232
5. Wang, Y., Chao, W.L., Weinberger, K.Q., van der Maaten, L.: SimpleShot: revisiting nearest-neighbor classification for few-shot learning. arXiv preprint arXiv:1911.04623 (2019). https://doi.org/10.48550/arXiv.1911.04623
6. Finn, C., Abbeel, P., Levine, S.: Model-agnostic meta-learning for fast adaptation of deep networks. In: Proceedings of the 34th International Conference on Machine Learning (ICML), vol. 70, pp. 1126–1135. PMLR (2017). https://doi.org/10.48550/arXiv.1703.03400

7. Ye, H.J., Hu, H., Zhan, D.C., Sha, F.: Few-shot learning via embedding adaptation with set-to-set functions. In: Proceedings of the IEEE/CVF Conference on Computer Vision and Pattern Recognition (CVPR), pp. 8805–8814. IEEE (2020). https://doi.org/10.1109/CVPR42600.2020.00883
8. Zhang, C., Cai, Y., Lin, G., Shen, C.: DeepEMD: few-shot image classification with differentiable earth mover's distance and structured classifiers. In: Proceedings of the IEEE/CVF Conference on Computer Vision and Pattern Recognition (CVPR), pp. 12200–12210. IEEE (2020). https://doi.org/10.1109/CVPR42600.2020.01222
9. Luo, X., et al.: Rectifying the shortcut learning of background for few-shot learning. Adv. Neural Inf. Process. Syst., vol. 34, pp. 13073–13085. Curran Associates (2021)
10. Lee, K., Maji, S., Ravichandran, A., Soatto, S.: Meta-learning with differentiable convex optimization. In: Proceedings of the IEEE/CVF Conference on Computer Vision and Pattern Recognition (CVPR), pp. 10649–10657. IEEE (2019). https://doi.org/10.1109/CVPR.2019.01091
11. Hiller, M., Ma, R., Harandi, M., Drummond, T.: Rethinking generalization in few-shot classification. Adv. Neural Inf. Process. Syst., vol. 35, pp. 3582–3595. Curran Associates (2022). https://doi.org/10.52202/068431-0259
12. Zalo AI Challenge Team: Aero-Eyes: finding and Rescuing with AI-Powered Drones. Zalo AI Challenge Benchmark (2025)
13. Radford, A., et al.: Learning transferable visual models from natural language supervision. In: Proceedings of the 38th International Conference on Machine Learning (ICML), vol. 139, pp. 8748–8763. PMLR (2021). https://doi.org/10.48550/arXiv.2103.00020
14. Zhou, K., Yang, J., Loy, C.C., Liu, Z.: Learning to prompt for vision-language models. Int. J. Comput. Vision **130**, 2337–2348 (2022). https://doi.org/10.1007/s11263-022-01653-1
15. Koh, P.W., et al.: Concept bottleneck models. In: Proceedings of the 37th International Conference on Machine Learning (ICML), vol. 119, pp. 5338–5348. PMLR (2020). https://doi.org/10.48550/arXiv.2007.04612
16. He, K., Zhang, X., Ren, S., Sun, J.: Deep residual learning for image recognition. In: Proceedings of the IEEE/CVF Conference on Computer Vision and Pattern Recognition (CVPR), pp. 770–778. IEEE (2016). https://doi.org/10.1109/CVPR.2016.90
17. Huang, G., Liu, Z., Pleiss, G., van der Maaten, L., Weinberger, K.Q.: Convolutional networks with dense connectivity. IEEE Trans. Pattern Anal. Mach. Intell. **44**(12), 8704–8716 (2022). https://doi.org/10.1109/TPAMI.2019.2918284
18. Deng, J., Dong, W., Socher, R., Li, L.J., Li, K., Fei-Fei, L.: ImageNet: a large-scale hierarchical image database. In: Proceedings of the IEEE/CVF Conference on Computer Vision and Pattern Recognition (CVPR), pp. 248–255. IEEE (2009). https://doi.org/10.1109/CVPR.2009.5206848
19. Krizhevsky, A.: Learning multiple layers of features from tiny images, University of Toronto (2009). Technical Report
20. Ravi, S., Larochelle, H.: Optimization as a model for few-shot learning. In: International Conference on Learning Representations (ICLR) (2017)
21. Cho, K., et al.: Learning phrase representations using RNN encoder-decoder for statistical machine translation. In: Proceedings of the 2014 Conference on Empirical Methods in Natural Language Processing (EMNLP), pp. 1724–1734. ACL (2014). https://doi.org/10.3115/v1/D14-1179

22. Kingma, D.P., Ba, J.: Adam: a method for stochastic optimization. In: International Conference on Learning Representations (ICLR) (2015). https://doi.org/10.48550/arXiv.1412.6980
23. Gao, P., et al.: CLIP-Adapter: Better vision-language models with feature adapters. arXiv preprint arXiv:2110.04544 (2021). https://doi.org/10.48550/arXiv.2110.04544

Impact of DICOM Preprocessing Strategies on Chest X-Ray Abnormality Detection

Thi-Bich-Tra Le, Ngoc-Duy Le, Tuan-Minh Do, Trung-Nguyen Hoang, Ly-Minh-Hoang Tran, and Thi-Thu-Hong Phan(✉)

AIT Laboratory, Faculty of Artificial Intelligence, FPT University Da Nang, Da Nang 550000, Vietnam
{tralthb,hongptt11}@fe.edu.vn

Abstract. Chest X-ray abnormality detection is an important task in computer-aided diagnosis. Although modern object detectors have been widely applied to this problem, DICOM preprocessing is often treated as a fixed technical conversion step, while its role as an experimental factor has received limited attention. Different preprocessing strategies may alter image contrast and lesion visibility, potentially affecting detection performance. This paper presents a controlled comparison of DICOM preprocessing strategies for chest X-ray abnormality detection on the VinDr-CXR dataset. We evaluate Raw min-max normalization, VOI LUT processing, Percentile Clipping, CLAHE, Histogram Equalization, and Adaptive Percentile normalization across three detector families: YOLOv8, Faster R-CNN, and RT-DETR. We further investigate three-channel combined preprocessing representations constructed from the best-performing individual methods to examine whether complementary intensity views improve detection performance. Detection performance varies substantially across preprocessing strategies, with mAP@0.5 ranging from 19.22% to 35.58% depending on detector architecture and preprocessing choice. Moderate signal-preserving methods generally provide more stable performance, whereas aggressive enhancement may amplify irrelevant structures and reduce localization accuracy. These findings suggest that DICOM preprocessing should be treated as a model-dependent design choice rather than a fixed technical conversion step in medical object detection pipelines.

Keywords: Chest X-ray · DICOM preprocessing · Object detection · YOLOv8 · Faster R-CNN · RT-DETR

1 Introduction

Chest X-ray (CXR) imaging is widely used for screening and diagnosing thoracic abnormalities due to its accessibility and efficiency. Recent advances in deep learning have enabled various object detection architectures, including

L. Ding et al. (Eds.): APWeb-WAIM 2026, LNCS 16995, pp. 440–455, 2027.
https://doi.org/10.1007/978-981-92-5699-0_29

YOLO [11], Faster R-CNN [14], and DETR-based models [3,22], to achieve strong performance in automatic abnormality localization for CXR images.

However, unlike natural images, CXR images are typically stored in DICOM format with high-bit-depth intensity values, while most deep learning frameworks operate on standard 8-bit images. Therefore, DICOM preprocessing is required before training, where different preprocessing strategies may substantially alter image contrast, intensity distribution, and structural visibility. Methods such as Histogram Equalization and CLAHE [23] may improve local lesion visibility but can also amplify noise and irrelevant anatomical structures, potentially affecting localization performance and false-positive behavior.

Although many studies focus on detector architectures and training strategies, preprocessing is often treated as a fixed technical step rather than an important experimental factor. In addition, prior studies mainly evaluate preprocessing methods independently, while the effect of combining multiple preprocessing operations for chest X-ray object detection remains underexplored.

The objective of this study is to provide a controlled evaluation of the impact of DICOM preprocessing strategies on chest X-ray abnormality detection using YOLOv8, Faster R-CNN, and RT-DETR on the VinDr-CXR dataset, and to investigate whether combining complementary preprocessing methods improves detection performance. The main contributions of this study are summarized as follows:

- We systematically compare multiple DICOM preprocessing methods for chest X-ray abnormality detection.
- We investigate both single and three-channel combined preprocessing strategies to assess the benefit of complementary intensity views.
- We evaluate these preprocessing strategies across YOLOv8, Faster R-CNN, and RT-DETR under consistent experimental settings.
- We demonstrate that the effectiveness of DICOM preprocessing depends on the detector architecture.

The remainder of this paper is organized as follows. Section 2 reviews related work. Section 3 presents the methodology. Section 4 reports the experimental results. Section 5 discusses the findings, and Sect. 6 concludes the paper.

2 Related Work

Deep learning-based object detection has been widely applied in chest X-ray (CXR) analysis for localizing thoracic abnormalities. Recent studies have explored various one-stage, two-stage, and transformer-based detection frameworks to improve abnormality localization under challenges such as low contrast, anatomical overlap, and small lesion size [1,2].

Among one-stage detectors, YOLO-based architectures are widely adopted due to their efficiency and real-time inference capability. Specialized variants such as YOLO-CXR [9] and NSEC-YOLO [21] have been proposed to improve small lesion localization in chest X-ray images through enhanced feature extraction and noise suppression mechanisms. Other one-stage detectors [6,7,12,17,18] further improve dense object detection through focal optimization, anchor-free prediction but have not been applied widely to the CXR field.

Two-stage detectors such as Faster R-CNN [14], Mask R-CNN [10], and R-FCN [4] utilize region proposal-based detection pipelines for object localization in computer vision tasks.

More recently, transformer-based detectors have attracted increasing attention for their ability to model global contextual relationships. DETR [3] introduced an end-to-end Transformer-based object detection framework that eliminates handcrafted anchor design and non-maximum suppression. Subsequent variants such as DINO [20] and RT-DETR [22] further improved optimization stability, convergence speed, and real-time inference performance for modern object detection tasks.

Chest X-ray images are typically stored in DICOM format, requiring preprocessing before being used in deep learning pipelines. Preprocessing methods such as histogram equalization (HE) [8] and CLAHE [23] are commonly applied to enhance image contrast and improve lesion visibility. Recent studies have shown that preprocessing can significantly influence model performance and generalization in chest X-ray analysis. Dapamede et al. [5] demonstrated that VOI LUT transformation improves robustness and generalizability. Similarly, Singthongchai and Wangkhamhan [15] showed that adaptive normalization and histogram standardization can improve training stability and cross-dataset performance. These findings suggest that contrast enhancement and intensity normalization strongly affect feature visibility and representation learning in deep learning models. However, most existing studies mainly evaluate preprocessing methods independently and focus on classification tasks, while the effect of combining multiple preprocessing operations on modern object detection models for chest X-ray abnormality localization remains underexplored.

3 Methodology

Figure 1 illustrates the overall experimental workflow of this study.

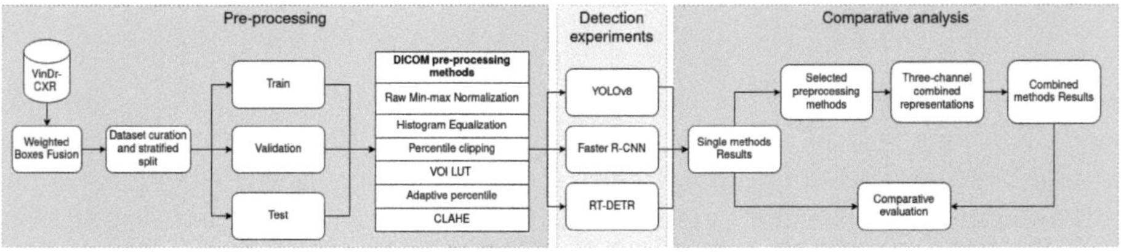

Fig. 1. Overview of the experimental pipeline for evaluating single and combined DICOM preprocessing strategies across different object detection architectures.

The pipeline consists of three main stages: preprocessing, detection experiments, and comparative analysis. In the preprocessing stage, the VinDr-CXR annotations are first curated, and Weighted Boxes Fusion is applied to merge highly overlapping training boxes before constructing the stratified train, validation, and test splits. Multiple DICOM preprocessing strategies are then applied to generate different intensity representations of the same chest X-ray images.

In the detection stage, each preprocessing variant is evaluated independently using three representative detector architectures: YOLOv8, Faster R-CNN, and RT-DETR. The training and evaluation settings are kept consistent within each detector family so that the observed performance differences mainly reflect the effect of DICOM preprocessing. In the comparative analysis stage, the single-preprocessing results are first analyzed to identify strong and stable methods. These selected methods are then used to construct three-channel combined representations, which are further evaluated and compared with the single-method results using standard object detection metrics.

3.1 DICOM Preprocessing Methods

We compare several representative DICOM preprocessing methods, including Normalization, VOI LUT Processing, Percentile Clipping, CLAHE, Histogram

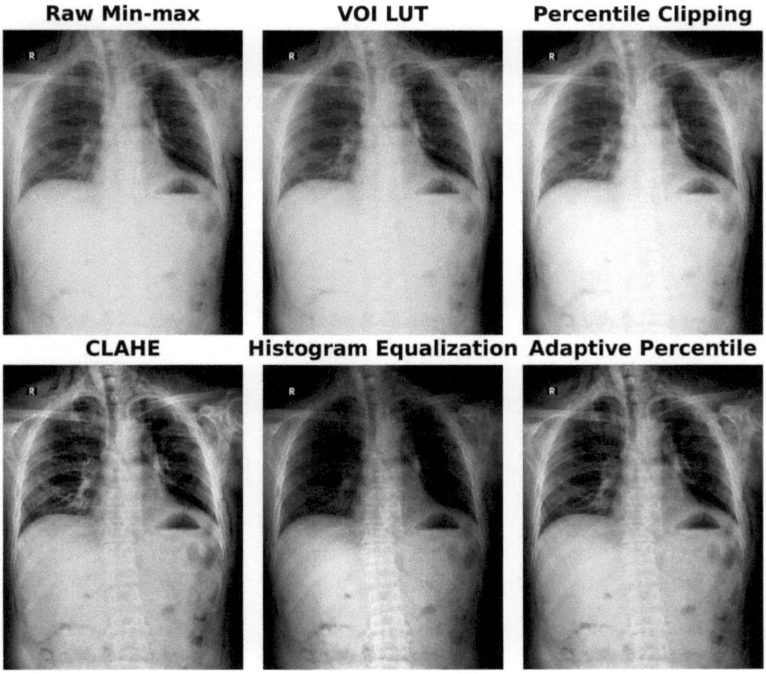

Fig. 2. Visual comparison of DICOM preprocessing methods.

Equalization, and Adaptive Percentile normalization. Figure 2 illustrates the visual appearance of these individual preprocessing outputs.

Based on the initial experimental results, the four best-performing and most stable methods were selected for combination-based experiments. Instead of applying these methods sequentially, we construct three-channel combined representations, where each channel corresponds to the output of a different preprocessing method. This design allows the detector to receive complementary intensity representations of the same DICOM image.

3.1.1 Raw Min-Max Normalization

In this method, the raw DICOM pixel array is directly normalized into an 8-bit grayscale image using image-wise min-max normalization:

$$I_{\text{norm}} = \frac{I - I_{\text{min}}}{I_{\text{max}} - I_{\text{min}}} \times 255 \tag{1}$$

This approach does not use additional DICOM metadata or radiology-specific intensity transformation, making it a simple baseline preprocessing strategy.

3.1.2 VOI LUT Processing

VOI LUT (Value of Interest Look-Up Table) processing applies radiology-oriented intensity transformation using viewing parameters stored in the DICOM metadata before image normalization. This step aims to emphasize clinically relevant intensity regions and improve visual contrast for chest abnormalities.

After VOI LUT transformation, the image is normalized into an 8-bit grayscale range using min-max normalization.

Compared with direct raw normalization, this approach attempts to preserve clinically meaningful contrast more effectively.

3.1.3 Percentile Clipping

Percentile-based clipping is applied to reduce the influence of extreme intensity outliers. Let p_l and p_h denote the lower (0.5th percentile) and upper (99.5th percentile) thresholds, respectively. The clipped image I_c is computed as

$$I_c(x) = \min(\max(I(x), p_l), p_h) \tag{2}$$

The clipped image is then normalized into the range $[0, 255]$ using Eq. (1).

Percentile clipping is robust to extreme intensity values caused by noise or acquisition artifacts, producing more stable intensity distributions across images.

3.1.4 Adaptive Percentile Normalization

Percentile clipping normalization Eq. (2) was first applied to suppress extreme intensity outliers where the 0.5th and 99.5th percentiles were used as clipping thresholds.

The clipped image was then normalized using adaptive statistical normalization:

$$I_{norm}(x, y) = \frac{I_c(x, y) - \mu_{orig}}{\sigma_{orig}} \cdot \sigma_{target} + \mu_{target} \quad (3)$$

where μ_{orig} and σ_{orig} denote the mean and standard deviation of the clipped image. This approach aims to reduce intensity variations across images while producing more consistent intensity distributions.

3.1.5 Contrast Limited Adaptive Histogram Equalization (CLAHE)

Each chest X-ray image was first windowed and normalized into an 8-bit grayscale image. For images with MONOCHROME1 photometric interpretation, intensity inversion was applied to ensure consistent brightness representation.

The windowing operation was defined as

$$I_{windowed} = \text{clip}(I, c - \tfrac{w}{2}, c + \tfrac{w}{2}) \quad (4)$$

where c and w denote the window center and window width, respectively.

The normalized image was computed as

$$I_{norm} = \frac{I_{windowed} - (c - \frac{w}{2})}{w} \times 255 \quad (5)$$

To enhance local contrast, Contrast Limited Adaptive Histogram Equalization (CLAHE) was applied with a clip limit of 2.0 and a tile grid size of 8×8. This step aims to improve the visibility of subtle pathological regions while reducing excessive noise amplification.

Finally, the processed image was converted into a three-channel representation and resized to 512×512 pixels for model training.

3.1.6 Histogram Equalization

For comparison, a global contrast enhancement approach based on Histogram Equalization (HE) was also applied. Each DICOM image was first normalized into an 8-bit grayscale image using min-max normalization Eq. (1)

Global histogram equalization was then performed as

$$I_{he} = \text{HE}(I_{norm}) \quad (6)$$

Unlike CLAHE, which enhances contrast locally, histogram equalization applies a global intensity transformation that may improve overall contrast but can also amplify noise in homogeneous regions.

Finally, the processed image was converted into a three-channel representation and resized to 512×512 pixels for model training.

3.2 Detection Models

To examine whether the impact of preprocessing remains consistent across different detector architectures, we consider three representative object detection models, including a one-stage detector, a two-stage detector, and a transformer-based detector.

3.2.1 YOLOv8

is a representative one-stage object detector developed by Ultralytics [11]. It directly predicts bounding boxes and class probabilities in a single forward pass, without a separate region proposal stage. With its anchor-free design and decoupled detection head, YOLOv8 provides an efficient balance between detection accuracy and inference speed, making it suitable for real-time and medical image detection tasks.

3.2.2 Faster R-CNN

is a representative two-stage object detector that first generates candidate object regions using a Region Proposal Network (RPN) and then performs object classification and bounding box refinement [14]. Its two-stage design provides accurate localization, making it well suited for medical image analysis tasks such as lesion detection in chest X-ray images.

3.2.3 RT-DETR

is a real-time transformer-based object detection framework [22] built upon the DETR paradigm [3]. RT-DETR performs end-to-end object detection through direct bounding box prediction using bipartite matching. By leveraging multi-scale self-attention mechanisms, the architecture effectively captures global contextual information, which is particularly beneficial for medical image analysis involving complex thoracic abnormalities.

4 Experimental Results

4.1 Dataset

We evaluate the three detectors using the VinDr-CXR dataset [13], which contains 18,000 CXR images in DICOM format. Figure 3 illustrates representative

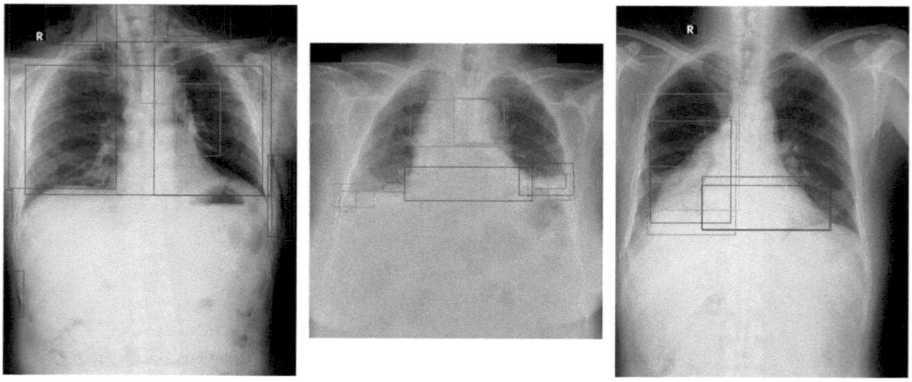

Fig. 3. Representative DICOM chest X-ray images with bounding-box annotations from the VinDr-CXR dataset.

Table 1. Class-wise annotation distribution of the curated VinDr-CXR dataset.

Class	Annotations	Class	Annotations
Pleural thickening	4348	Pleural effusion	1914
Pulmonary fibrosis	3731	Interstitial Lung Disease	1060
Aortic enlargement	3655	Infiltration	1039
Other lesion	2817	Calcification	986
Cardiomegaly	2730	Consolidation	561
Nodule/Mass	2177	Atelectasis	328
Lung Opacity	2127	Pneumothorax	156

DICOM CXR images with corresponding bounding-box annotations from the dataset.

Following the abnormality grouping and normal-case balancing strategies motivated by Zhang et al. [21], we focus on 14 thoracic abnormality categories and group the 8 less frequent findings into a single "Other lesion" class. To reduce the dominance of normal cases, we retained all images containing at least one targeted abnormality and randomly selected 1,000 "No finding" images. This curation process yielded a final dataset of 6,471 images. Instead of using the original official VinDr-CXR split, we constructed a custom stratified 70/10/20 split on the curated dataset to ensure consistent evaluation across preprocessing methods. Stratification was performed based on image-level abnormality labels to preserve class distribution across splits. The resulting split contains 4,529 training images, 647 validation images, and 1,295 independent test images.

The class-wise annotation distribution of the curated dataset is reported in Table 1.

Because the original VinDr-CXR training annotations include bounding boxes provided independently by multiple radiologists, highly overlapping boxes of the same class may represent repeated annotations of the same lesion. Following recent CXR lesion detection studies that use box-fusion strategies for annotation or localization refinement [9,19], we applied Weighted Boxes Fusion (WBF) [16] to aggregate highly overlapping training boxes of the same class. Boxes were merged when their IoU exceeded 0.5, while spatially separated boxes were kept as distinct lesions.

This step was applied only to the training annotations of the original dataset to reduce duplicate supervision signals. Therefore, WBF is used as a heuristic annotation aggregation strategy for training rather than as a modification of the validation or test ground truth.

4.2 Training Configuration

For fair comparison, all preprocessing methods are evaluated under the same training protocol for each detector. The same dataset split (70/10/20), input resolution, training epochs, optimizer settings, and evaluation protocol are used across all experiments. Only the DICOM preprocessing strategy is changed.

All experiments were conducted on an NVIDIA RTX A6000 GPU using the VinDr-CXR dataset with an input resolution of 512×512. Each model was trained for 50 epochs under the same experimental setting to ensure consistency across preprocessing methods.

For the one-stage detector, we employed the YOLOv8n architecture implemented using the Ultralytics framework and initialized with pretrained weights. The two-stage detector was Faster R-CNN with a pretrained ResNet-50-FPN backbone, whereas the transformer-based detector was RT-DETR-L initialized with pretrained weights.

For all detectors, the AdamW optimizer is used with an initial learning rate of 1×10^{-4} and a batch size of 8. During training, the same data augmentation pipeline is applied across all experiments, consisting of random horizontal flipping, shift-scale-rotate transformation, brightness and contrast adjustment, and blur augmentation. The checkpoint achieving the highest validation mAP@0.5 was selected for final evaluation on the independent test set.

4.3 Evaluation Metrics

We evaluate detection performance using precision, recall, and mean Average Precision (mAP). Precision measures the proportion of predicted bounding boxes that are correct, while recall measures the proportion of ground-truth objects that are successfully detected. The main metric is mAP@0.5, where a predicted bounding box is considered correct if its Intersection over Union (IoU) with the ground-truth box is at least 0.5. We also report mAP@0.5:0.95 to evaluate localization quality under stricter IoU thresholds.

4.4 Effect of Single Preprocessing on Detection Models

Table 2 summarizes the effect of single DICOM preprocessing methods on YOLOv8, Faster R-CNN, and RT-DETR.

Across all detectors, preprocessing has a clear but architecture-dependent impact on detection performance. RT-DETR achieves the best overall performance under most preprocessing settings, especially with Raw min-max normalization, which obtains the highest mAP@0.5 (34.81%) and mAP@0.5:0.95 (17.31%). YOLOv8 remains competitive across several preprocessing methods, while Faster R-CNN shows lower mAP values but relatively stable recall.

Among single preprocessing methods, Percentile clipping provides the best mAP@0.5 for YOLOv8 (31.21%) and Faster R-CNN (21.68%), suggesting that suppressing extreme intensity values can improve localization for detectors that rely strongly on local features or region proposal quality. VOI LUT achieves the highest recall for both YOLOv8 (36.14%) and Faster R-CNN (26.27%), indicating that DICOM-aware intensity transformation may help recover more abnormal regions.

Table 2. Effect of DICOM preprocessing on different detectors (%).

Detector	Preprocessing Method	Precision	Recall	mAP@0.5	mAP@0.5:0.95
YOLOv8	Raw min-max	36.63	34.89	30.96	**15.66**
	VOI LUT	36.93	**36.14**	30.68	15.46
	Percentile clipping	**39.30**	34.75	**31.21**	15.56
	CLAHE	35.66	34.17	29.80	14.87
	Histogram Equalization	36.02	34.05	30.28	15.07
	Adaptive percentile	27.96	23.69	19.76	8.18
Faster R-CNN	Raw min-max	25.41	25.41	19.22	8.19
	VOI LUT	25.41	**26.27**	20.72	8.76
	Percentile clipping	**26.91**	25.52	**21.68**	**9.33**
	CLAHE	26.31	25.21	20.60	8.92
	Histogram Equalization	25.71	25.54	20.79	9.11
	Adaptive percentile	23.81	23.69	20.79	8.18
RT-DETR	Raw min-max	**44.26**	**39.24**	**34.81**	**17.31**
	VOI LUT	43.66	38.87	34.09	17.07
	Percentile clipping	43.61	38.56	33.88	16.90
	CLAHE	43.03	37.56	33.85	16.65
	Histogram Equalization	41.28	38.48	31.75	15.88
	Adaptive percentile	30.16	26.30	20.51	8.36

In contrast, RT-DETR performs best with Raw min-max normalization. This suggests that transformer-based detection may benefit from preserving the original global intensity structure, since attention-based feature aggregation can be affected by strong local enhancement or distribution shifts.

CLAHE and Histogram Equalization provide mixed results. Although these methods enhance visual contrast, they do not consistently improve detection performance and may amplify ribs, vessels, or background structures, leading to localization ambiguity. Adaptive percentile normalization causes a clear performance drop for YOLOv8 and RT-DETR, suggesting that overly aggressive normalization may disrupt stable intensity relationships in chest X-ray images.

Overall, the results indicate that effective DICOM preprocessing should balance lesion visibility and anatomical consistency. Moderate, signal-preserving methods such as Percentile clipping, VOI LUT, and Raw min-max normalization are generally more reliable than aggressive contrast enhancement or adaptive normalization.

4.5 Effect of Combined Preprocessing on Detection Models

Following the single-preprocessing experiments, we selected four representative methods– normalization, VOI LUT, Percentile Clipping, and CLAHE–because

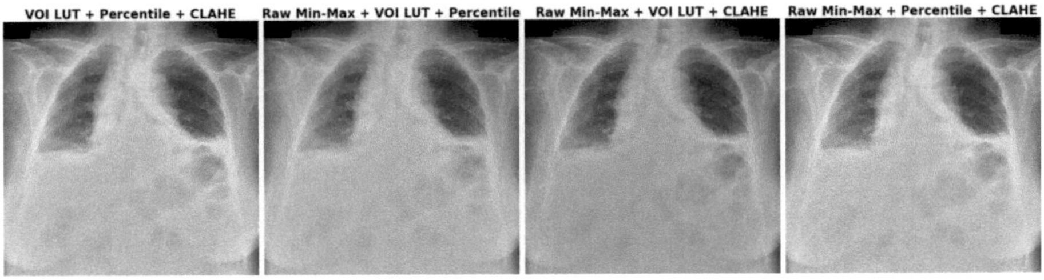

Fig. 4. Visual examples of three-channel combined preprocessing representations. Each color channel corresponds to the output of a different DICOM preprocessing method applied to the same image.

Table 3. Effect of combining multiple DICOM preprocessing methods on different detectors (%).

Detector	Preprocessing Combination	Precision	Recall	mAP@0.5	mAP@0.5:0.95
YOLOv8	Raw min-max + VOI LUT + Percentile	36.73	35.38	30.77	15.22
	Raw min-max + VOI LUT + CLAHE	36.87	34.53	30.43	15.12
	Raw min-max + Percentile + CLAHE	**37.22**	**36.06**	**31.25**	**15.53**
	VOI LUT + Percentile + CLAHE	36.54	35.22	30.33	15.04
Faster R-CNN	Raw min-max + VOI LUT + Percentile	25.66	27.27	27.87	12.20
	Raw min-max + VOI LUT + CLAHE	28.46	28.46	28.02	11.90
	Raw min-max + Percentile + CLAHE	**27.68**	**27.67**	**29.15**	**12.43**
	VOI LUT + Percentile + CLAHE	24.43	26.19	26.27	11.59
RT-DETR	Raw min-max + VOI LUT + Percentile	**44.46**	38.83	**35.58**	**18.11**
	Raw min-max + VOI LUT + CLAHE	41.23	37.61	33.89	16.72
	Raw min-max + Percentile + CLAHE	38.80	34.76	31.02	15.21
	VOI LUT + Percentile + CLAHE	41.19	**38.95**	33.91	16.88

they showed relatively stable performance across the three detector architectures and achieved competitive mAP@0.5 results, as reported in Table 2. Specifically, these methods consistently showed competitive and relatively stable detection performance across the evaluated detectors.

These methods were combined by constructing three-channel image representations, where each channel corresponds to the output of a different preprocessing method, as illustrated in Fig. 4. This design enables the model to access multiple complementary intensity transformations of the same DICOM image, instead of relying on a single preprocessing pipeline. We focus on combinations of three out of the four selected methods to maintain a standard three-channel input format, allowing straightforward integration into existing detection frameworks without modifying the input structure, while avoiding the additional complexity and potential redundancy that may arise from increasing the input dimensionality beyond three channels.

The results show that the effectiveness of combined preprocessing varies substantially across models and does not consistently outperform the best individual methods. Table 3 summarizes the performance of the combined three-channel preprocessing representations across the three detectors.

For YOLOv8, the three-channel combined representations show negligible improvement over the best individual preprocessing methods. The best combination, Raw min-max + Percentile + CLAHE, achieves 31.25% mAP@0.5 and 36.06% recall, which are almost identical to the best single-method results obtained with Percentile clipping (31.21% mAP@0.5) and VOI LUT (36.14% recall). Thus, these results do not provide strong evidence that complementary multi-channel preprocessing substantially improves YOLOv8 performance under the current experimental setting.

In contrast, Faster R-CNN benefits more clearly from the combined representations. The best configuration, Raw min-max + Percentile + CLAHE, improves mAP@0.5 from 21.68% with the best single method to 29.15%, while also increasing recall to 27.67%. This indicates that complementary intensity views may improve proposal generation by making abnormal regions more distinguishable from surrounding anatomical structures.

For RT-DETR, the benefit of combined preprocessing depends on whether the representation preserves global intensity consistency. The Raw min-max + VOI LUT + Percentile combination achieves the best mAP@0.5 of 35.58%, improving over the best single method, Raw min-max normalization, which obtains 34.81%. However, combinations involving CLAHE generally produce lower mAP@0.5, suggesting that strong local contrast enhancement may introduce distracting texture patterns and reduce localization accuracy.

The results indicate that the effect of preprocessing is strongly architecture-dependent. Percentile clipping is the most effective single method for YOLOv8 and Faster R-CNN, while Raw min-max normalization performs best for RT-DETR. For combined three-channel representations, Faster R-CNN shows the largest improvement, YOLOv8 shows only marginal gains, and RT-DETR benefits mainly from signal-preserving combinations. These findings suggest that DICOM preprocessing should be selected according to detector architecture rather than treated as a fixed conversion step.

4.6 Qualitative Results

Figure 5 presents a visual comparison of detection outputs obtained using different preprocessing pipelines against the ground-truth annotations. The qualitative results provide visual evidence consistent with the quantitative findings, showing that preprocessing can change lesion visibility and detection behavior.

When applying only Raw min-max normalization, the image appears relatively low in contrast, and some anatomical boundaries are less clearly separated. As observed in Fig. 5, the detector identifies Cardiomegaly but does not clearly detect the annotated Aortic enlargement in this example. The prediction also includes a Lung Opacity region near the right lower lung area, suggesting that low-contrast representations may make it more difficult to distinguish subtle abnormalities from surrounding anatomical structures.

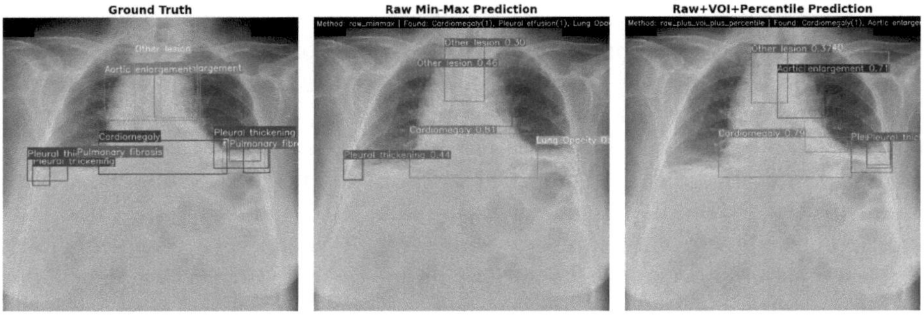

Fig. 5. Qualitative comparison of detection results. The combined Raw min-max + VOI LUT + Percentile representation produces a detection more consistent with the annotated Aortic enlargement than standalone Raw min-max normalization. This example is for qualitative illustration only.

In contrast, the combined representation based on Raw min-max, VOI LUT, and Percentile clipping appears to improve the visibility of mediastinal contours and upper thoracic structures. This representation enables the detector to identify Aortic enlargement in this example and produces outputs that are more consistent with several annotated regions. These observations are consistent with the quantitative trend in Table 3, suggesting that a three-channel representation combining global intensity preservation, DICOM-aware windowing, and outlier suppression may provide a more suitable input representation for complex lesion detection.

This example illustrates the trade-off between preserving the original radiographic appearance and enhancing lesion-relevant contrast. Effective preprocessing should improve clinically relevant visibility without introducing distracting anatomical noise or artificial artifacts.

5 Discussion

The experimental results show that DICOM preprocessing noticeably affects CXR abnormality detection, and its impact varies across detector architectures.

Among single preprocessing methods, Percentile Clipping achieves the best mAP@0.5 for YOLOv8 and Faster R-CNN, reaching 31.21% and 21.68%, respectively. VOI LUT obtains the highest recall for these two detectors, suggesting that DICOM-aware intensity transformation may improve lesion sensitivity. For RT-DETR, Raw min-max normalization performs best among single methods, achieving 34.81% mAP@0.5 and 17.31% mAP@0.5:0.95. This suggests that transformer-based detectors may benefit more from preserving the original global intensity structure than from strong contrast enhancement.

CLAHE and Histogram Equalization show inconsistent effects, possibly because contrast enhancement can amplify ribs, vessels, and background noise. Adaptive Percentile performs the weakest for YOLOv8 and RT-DETR, indicating that aggressive normalization may distort useful radiographic information.

For combined preprocessing, the effect is also architecture-dependent. YOLOv8 shows only a marginal gain, increasing from 31.21% to 31.25% mAP@0.5, while Faster R-CNN improves more clearly from 21.68% to 29.15%. RT-DETR achieves the best overall result with Raw min-max + VOI LUT + Percentile, reaching 35.58% mAP@0.5 and 18.11% mAP@0.5:0.95.

Overall, no single preprocessing method is universally optimal. Percentile Clipping and Raw min-max normalization are reliable single-method choices under the evaluated setting, while combined preprocessing appears more beneficial for Faster R-CNN and RT-DETR than for YOLOv8.

This study has several limitations. First, the experiments were conducted on a curated subset of VinDr-CXR using a custom stratified split, so the results should be interpreted as controlled within-study comparisons rather than direct state-of-the-art comparisons. Second, each configuration was evaluated using a fixed split and a single training run; repeated runs with multiple random seeds are needed to assess statistical robustness. Third, although Weighted Boxes Fusion was used following previous CXR lesion detection studies to reduce highly overlapping training annotations, this study did not include an ablation analysis comparing training with and without annotation fusion. Finally, this study focuses on a single dataset. Future work will evaluate the proposed preprocessing strategies on additional public chest X-ray datasets collected from different institutions to further assess their robustness and cross-dataset generalization.

6 Conclusion

This paper presented a controlled comparison of DICOM preprocessing strategies for chest X-ray abnormality detection on the VinDr-CXR dataset using YOLOv8, Faster R-CNN, and RT-DETR. The results show that preprocessing significantly affects detection performance, with the most effective strategy depending on the detector architecture. Percentile Clipping performs best for YOLOv8 and Faster R-CNN, while Raw min-max normalization is the strongest single method for RT-DETR. Combined preprocessing provides limited benefit for YOLOv8 but improves performance for Faster R-CNN and achieves the best overall RT-DETR result with the Raw min-max + VOI LUT + Percentile combination. These findings highlight that DICOM preprocessing should be treated as an important design choice in medical object detection rather than a fixed technical conversion step. Future work will focus on cross-dataset validation and adaptive preprocessing strategies for different abnormality types.

References

1. Ait Nasser, A., Akhloufi, M.A.: A review of recent advances in deep learning models for chest disease detection using radiography. Diagnostics **13**(1), 159 (2023). https://doi.org/10.3390/diagnostics13010159
2. Çallı, E., Sogancioglu, E., van Ginneken, B., van Leeuwen, K.G., Murphy, K.: Deep learning for chest x-ray analysis: a survey. Med. Image Anal. **72**, 102125 (2021). https://doi.org/10.1016/j.media.2021.102125

3. Carion, N., Massa, F., Synnaeve, G., Usunier, N., Kirillov, A., Zagoruyko, S.: End-to-end object detection with transformers. In: Vedaldi, A., Bischof, H., Brox, T., Frahm, J.-M. (eds.) ECCV 2020, Part I. LNCS, vol. 12346, pp. 213–229. Springer, Cham (2020). https://doi.org/10.1007/978-3-030-58452-8_13
4. Dai, J., Li, Y., He, K., Sun, J.: R-FCN: object detection via region-based fully convolutional networks. Adv. Neural Inf. Process. Syst. **29**, 379–387 (2016). https://proceedings.neurips.cc/paper/2016/hash/577ef1154f3240ad5b9b413aa7346a1e-Abstract.html
5. Dapamede, T., Li, F., Khosravi, B., Purkayastha, S., Trivedi, H., Gichoya, J.: DICOM LUT is a key step in medical image preprocessing towards AI generalizability. J. Imaging Inform. Med. **38**(5), 3040–3048 (2025). https://doi.org/10.1007/s10278-025-01418-5
6. Duan, K., Bai, S., Xie, L., Qi, H., Huang, Q., Tian, Q.: Centernet: keypoint triplets for object detection. In: 2019 IEEE/CVF International Conference on Computer Vision (ICCV), pp. 6568–6577 (2019). https://doi.org/10.1109/ICCV.2019.00667
7. Ge, Z., Liu, S., Wang, F., Li, Z., Sun, J.: YOLOX: exceeding YOLO series in 2021. CoRR abs/2107.08430 (2021). https://arxiv.org/abs/2107.08430
8. Gonzalez, R.C., Woods, R.E.: Digital Image Processing, 3rd edn. Pearson Prentice Hall, Upper Saddle River, NJ (2008)
9. Hao, S., Li, X., Peng, W., Fan, Z., Ji, Z., Ganchev, I.: YOLO-CXR: a novel detection network for locating multiple small lesions in chest x-ray images. IEEE Access **12**, 156003–156019 (2024). https://doi.org/10.1109/ACCESS.2024.3482102
10. He, K., Gkioxari, G., Dollár, P., Girshick, R.: Mask R-CNN. In: Proceedings of the IEEE International Conference on Computer Vision (ICCV), pp. 2961–2969 (2017). https://doi.org/10.1109/ICCV.2017.322
11. Jocher, G., Chaurasia, A., Qiu, J.: Ultralytics YOLOv8 (2023). https://github.com/ultralytics/ultralytics
12. Lin, T.Y., Goyal, P., Girshick, R., He, K., Dollár, P.: Focal loss for dense object detection. In: 2017 IEEE International Conference on Computer Vision (ICCV), pp. 2999–3007 (2017). https://doi.org/10.1109/ICCV.2017.324
13. Nguyen, H.Q., Lam, K., Le, L.T., et al.: VINDR-CXR: an open dataset of chest x-rays with radiologist's annotations. Sci. Data **9**(1), 429 (2022). https://doi.org/10.1038/s41597-022-01498-w
14. Ren, S., He, K., Girshick, R., Sun, J.: Faster R-CNN: towards real-time object detection with region proposal networks. IEEE Trans. Pattern Anal. Mach. Intell. **39**(6), 1137–1149 (2017). https://doi.org/10.1109/TPAMI.2016.2577031
15. Singthongchai, J., Wangkhamhan, T.: Adaptive normalization enhances the generalization of deep learning model in chest x-ray classification. J. Imaging **12**(1) (2026). https://doi.org/10.3390/jimaging12010014
16. Solovyev, R., Wang, W., Gabruseva, T.: Weighted boxes fusion: ensembling boxes from different object detection models. Image Vis. Comput. **107**, 104117 (2021). https://doi.org/10.1016/j.imavis.2021.104117
17. Tan, M., Pang, R., Le, Q.V.: Efficientdet: scalable and efficient object detection. In: 2020 IEEE/CVF Conference on Computer Vision and Pattern Recognition (CVPR), pp. 10778–10787 (2020). https://doi.org/10.1109/CVPR42600.2020.01079
18. Tian, Z., Shen, C., Chen, H., He, T.: FCOS: fully convolutional one-stage object detection. In: Proceedings of the IEEE/CVF International Conference on Computer Vision (ICCV), pp. 9626–9635 (2019). https://doi.org/10.1109/ICCV.2019.00972

19. Yao, J., Guo, Z., Zhang, X., Yan, N., Wang, Q., Yu, W.: Cross-domain lung opacity detection via adversarial learning and box fusion. Sci. Rep. **14**, 31353 (2024). https://doi.org/10.1038/s41598-024-82719-7
20. Zhang, H., et al.: DINO: DETR with improved denoising anchor boxes for end-to-end object detection. In: The Eleventh International Conference on Learning Representations (2023). https://openreview.net/forum?id=3mRwyG5one
21. Zhang, X., Liu, L., Yang, X., Liu, L., Peng, W.: NSEC-YOLO: real-time lesion detection on chest x-ray with adaptive noise suppression and global perception aggregation. J. Radiat. Res. Appl. Sci. (2025). https://doi.org/10.1016/j.jrras.2024.101281
22. Zhao, Y., et al.: DETRs beat YOLOs on real-time object detection. In: 2024 IEEE/CVF Conference on Computer Vision and Pattern Recognition (CVPR), pp. 16965–16974 (2024). https://doi.org/10.1109/CVPR52733.2024.01605
23. Zuiderveld, K.: Contrast Limited Adaptive Histogram Equalization, pp. 474–485. Academic Press Professional, Inc., USA (1994)

Persistence-Aware Reward Design for Closed-Loop Reinforcement Learning-Based Network Intrusion Defense

Yen Vy Trinh Nguyen, Le Binh Ho, Tuan Anh Pham, Hoang Tri Nguyen, and Hoang Dinh Mai(✉)

FPT University, Ho Chi Minh City, Vietnam
{vytnyse183776,binhhlse183564,anhptse183403,trinhse183413}@fpt.edu.vn, dinhmh@fe.edu.vn

Abstract. Reward function design is a critical but underspecified problem in reinforcement learning-based network intrusion defense. Existing approaches either derive rewards from ground-truth labels, making them structurally equivalent to supervised losses, or rely on sparse compromise penalties that provide insufficient gradient during the prolonged reconnaissance and exploitation phases preceding an attack's detection. We propose a Persistence-Aware Reward (PAR) architecture that decomposes the reward signal into four interpretable components: a detection bonus whose severity ordering is inspired by NIST SP 800-61r2 incident handling priorities, an action-cost ladder encoding the principle of least privilege, a service-damage penalty derived from operational feedback rather than inference-time labels, and five session-aware shaping terms that couple reward to per-IP temporal context. The shaping terms govern a Redirect-to-Block escalation trajectory driven by evidence accumulated across a 15-step observation window, penalising both premature blocking and oscillatory de-escalation. Under rigorous online validation in a parameterised synthetic IP-traffic simulator, the full PAR configuration achieves 95.34% attack mitigation alongside a low benign intervention rate of 0.175%. Transferred without retraining to a closed-loop Mininet/Containernet testbed where non-Allow actions are enforced as real iptables rules, the policy consistently maintains its structured escalation behavior across varying environment configurations. These results show that dense, session-aware reward design enables graduated multi-step defense strategies that binary or sparse reward designs do not naturally express.

Keywords: Reinforcement Learning · Reward Shaping · Network Intrusion Defense · Proximal Policy Optimization · Closed-Loop Security

L. Ding et al. (Eds.): APWeb-WAIM 2026, LNCS 16995, pp. 456–467, 2027.
https://doi.org/10.1007/978-981-92-5699-0_30

1 Introduction

Modern cyber attacks are increasingly adaptive, multi-stage, and automated, outpacing static signature-based intrusion detection systems [6]. Deep reinforcement learning (DRL) offers a principled alternative: rather than matching traffic against fixed rules, an RL agent learns a defense policy through interaction with an environment, receiving a reward signal that encodes both threat response quality and operational response cost [9].

The effectiveness of DRL-based intrusion defense depends critically on the reward function. Poorly specified rewards produce policies that maximise proxy metrics, such as raw detection accuracy, while failing to encode operationally important properties such as graduated response, false-positive control, and long-horizon persistence [1]. Reward design for cyber defense is harder than for many classical RL benchmarks: the environment is partially observable, attack sessions span many timesteps, ground-truth labels are unavailable during deployment, and over-response against benign users must be balanced against under-response against persistent attackers.

Existing RL-IDS rewards mostly follow either label-derived objectives or sparse compromise penalties, which can collapse the policy into a supervised-like classifier or provide too little gradient for long-horizon response. This paper addresses this gap with a dense, session-aware reward architecture.

The main contributions of this paper are summarized as follows:

1. We introduce a reward-source taxonomy for RL-IDS: label-derived, structure-derived, and effect-derived rewards.
2. We propose PAR, a dense reward composed of an effect-derived base component and five session-aware shaping terms conditioned on per-IP temporal context.
3. We validate PAR through algorithm benchmarking, reward ablation, policy-behaviour analysis, and public-dataset transfer evaluation, while clarifying the simulator-to-deployment setting.

2 Related Work

Potential-based shaping is a classical RL result: Ng et al. [5] show that shaping of the form $F(s, a, s') = \gamma\Phi(s') - \Phi(s)$ preserves the set of optimal policies under standard assumptions, whereas arbitrary shaping terms can change the induced policy ranking. In cyber-defense RL, sparse mission-success rewards [3] and label-derived objectives [4,7] remain common, but they provide limited gradient for long-horizon response and often reduce training to a supervised-like objective. PAR differs by directly encoding operational knowledge into an interpretable, effect-derived reward with session-aware terms. Table 1 positions PAR relative to these paradigms.

Table 1. Reward paradigm taxonomy for RL-IDS and cyber-defense RL.

Paradigm	Source	Dense?	Session-aware?
Label-derived	label	Yes	No
Structure-derived	data	Yes	No
Dynamic threat score	rule	Yes	No
Sparse compromise penalty	system	No	No
PAR	**effect**	**Yes**	**Yes**

3 Problem Formulation

We model network defense as a partially observable Markov decision process $\langle S, A, P, R, \gamma, \Omega, O\rangle$, where the agent observes $o_t \in \Omega$ instead of the true state $s_t \in S$.

State and Observation Spaces. The environment state encodes the full traffic and session context for each active IP, including packet statistics, payload features, accumulated evidence, and enforcement state. At each 1-second timestep, the agent receives a 34-dimensional observation vector:

$$o_t = [f_t \parallel \tau_t \parallel e_{t-1}] \in [0,1]^{34}, \tag{1}$$

where $f_t \in [0,1]^{20}$ contains network-traffic features summarising the current state, $\tau_t \in [0,1]^{10}$ encodes per-IP temporal state, and $e_{t-1} \in [0,1]^4$ is a delayed effect vector:

$$e_{t-1} = [\rho_{\text{web}}, \rho_{\text{honeypot}}, \rho_{\text{presence}}, d_{\text{service}}]. \tag{2}$$

Here, ρ_{web} is the web-hit ratio, ρ_{honeypot} is the honeypot-hit ratio, ρ_{presence} indicates whether the source remains active, and d_{service} is the simulator's composite service-damage score derived from the delayed effect collector.

Action Space. The agent selects one of four discrete actions: Allow, RateLimit, Redirect, and Block. RateLimit applies token-bucket limiting, Redirect sends traffic to a honeypot for Layer 7 evidence collection, and Block installs a DROP rule. During training and simulator evaluation, action effects are computed analytically by the simulator. During Mininet/Containernet deployment validation, non-Allow actions are translated into real `iptables` rules inside the router namespace.

Discount Factor. We use $\gamma = 0.995$ to reflect long-horizon attack sessions spanning 15–20 observation windows. This contrasts with static dataset RL formulations that set $\gamma \approx 0$ because consecutive samples have little sequential structure [4].

4 Persistence-Aware Reward

4.1 Design Goals

PAR targets four operational requirements: detection quality, mitigation effect, persistence cost, and operational safety. The reward must reinforce correct threat response, reflect observed consequences of actions, penalise sustained under-response, and avoid over-response against benign traffic.

4.2 Reward Equation

The total reward is

$$r_t = \underbrace{B_{\text{action}} - C_{\text{action}} - 0.12 d_{\text{service}}}_{r_{\text{base}}} \\ + \underbrace{r_{\text{osc}} + r_{\text{stab}} + r_{\text{ramp}} + r_{\text{persist}} + r_{\text{premature}}}_{r_{\text{shape}}}, \quad (3)$$

clipped to $[-1, 1]$ before the PPO update. The base component captures instantaneous utility, while the shaping component encodes session continuity.

4.3 Component Interpretation

Detection Bonus. B_{action} maps traffic type and action pairs to scalar rewards. Its severity ordering is inspired by NIST SP 800-61r2 incident handling priorities [2], while the scalar magnitudes are empirically calibrated for the training environment. Table 2 gives the values used in the simulator training experiments.

Table 2. Detection bonus B_{action} used to construct the training reward. Traffic type is a simulator-side reward label, not an input exposed to the deployed policy.

Traffic type	Action	B_{action}
DDoS/Port Scan	Block	+0.30
DDoS/Port Scan	Allow	−0.50
Brute Force/SQLi/XSS	Redirect	+0.35
Brute Force/SQLi/XSS	Allow	−0.40
Benign	Block	−0.60

Training/Inference Clarification. B_{action} is a handcrafted reward lookup table used only during training to construct the reward signal. In this paper, the *traffic type* in Table 2 refers to a simulator-side label that is available to the reward constructor while building the training objective; it is not an observation feature that the deployed policy receives at inference time. At deployment, the frozen policy does not access traffic-type labels or reward components; it selects actions solely from the observation vector o_t, temporal state τ_t, and delayed effect vector e_{t-1}. Thus, the label-free claim applies to policy inference, not to the supervised construction of the training reward inside the simulator. In other words, the reward constructor may use traffic-type information during training, but the learned policy itself is evaluated from observation and effect signals only.

Action-Cost Ladder. $C_{\text{action}} \in \{0.00, 0.01, 0.04, 0.15\}$ for Allow, RateLimit, Redirect, and Block, respectively, matching the simulator implementation. This ladder encodes least privilege: stronger interventions must be justified by stronger evidence.

Service-Damage Penalty. In the simulator, d_{service} is the delayed effect score, computed from attack confidence, web exposure, presence, and honeypot redirection. Concretely, the implementation uses a clipped composite of attack confidence, web-hit ratio, presence ratio, and honeypot-hit ratio, which we denote here as a simulated service-damage score:

$$d_{\text{service}} = \text{clip}\Big(0.7\,\text{attack\_conf}\,\text{web\_hit\_ratio} + 0.3\,\text{attack\_conf}\,\text{presence\_ratio}\,(1 - \text{honeypot\_hit\_ratio}),\ 0,\ 1\Big). \tag{4}$$

The coefficient 0.12 in Eq. 3 was chosen to keep a roughly 3:1 ratio between the maximum detection bonus and maximum damage penalty, preventing damage avoidance from dominating threat response.

Session-Aware Shaping Terms. r_{osc} penalises oscillatory de-escalation while damage remains elevated. r_{stab} rewards holding a contextually correct action. r_{ramp} creates a progressive gradient toward Block near the end of the 15-step escalation window. r_{persist} rewards sustained Block once the block-ready flag is latched and attacker presence remains active. $r_{\text{premature}}$ penalises Block before sufficient evidence accumulates.

PAR is an engineering-driven reward specification rather than a potential-based shaping function. Because r_{persist} and r_{ramp} depend on history-dependent variables such as window length and block-ready state, we do not claim policy invariance under arbitrary transition dynamics. Instead, PAR encodes the desired Observe → Redirect → Block protocol as soft constraints.

5 Experimental Setup

5.1 Environment

We consider two experimental settings. First, a training and evaluation simulator implements the online PPO training loop and produces the numerical results reported in Sects. 6.1–6.3. Each episode contains 16 synthetic IP endpoints: 4 benign, 2 noisy-normal, and 10 attack endpoints spanning SYN Flood, Port Scan, Brute Force, SQLi, and XSS. The simulator uses round-robin scheduling with a session block size of zero, a missing-data probability of 0.01, a drift magnitude of 0.12, and an episode length of 320 steps. Effect feedback is generated by the simulator's analytic effect function rather than by a live HTTP/Nginx deployment collector.

Second, a Mininet/Containernet deployment testbed is used to validate the frozen trained policy under closed-loop execution, rather than for online PPO training. In this setting, non-Allow actions are enforced as real `iptables` rules inside the router namespace via container execution tools.

The evaluation protocol uses PPO with four vectorized environments, five training seeds, and the optimal reward checkpoint selected for evaluation. To ensure strict reproducibility, the associated replication artifacts–including the automated ablation training pipelines, data aggregation scripts, and a public evidence manifest recording seeds, evaluation episodes, and metric definitions–will be made available upon publication. Domain randomization is applied to reduce overfitting to nominal attack parameters.

5.2 RL Algorithm and Hyperparameters

We train PPO [8] with four parallel environments, a rollout length of 2048, a batch size of 128, and a linear learning-rate schedule from 3×10^{-4} to 6×10^{-5} over 500,000 timesteps. The policy and value networks use architectures $\pi : [256, 128]$ and $V : [256, 256, 128]$, respectively. The entropy coefficient is set to 0.05 and the clipping parameter to 0.15. Algorithm benchmarking is conducted over five training seeds with 30 evaluation episodes per seed.

5.3 Reward Baselines

We evaluate four reward configurations under PPO:

- **R1 Binary:** a label-derived $+1/-1$ reward that matches the per-step optimal action.
- **R2 Base only:** $r_t = r_{\text{base}}$, without session-aware shaping.
- **R3 No persistence/ramp:** the full PAR reward without r_{persist} and r_{ramp}.
- **R4 Full PAR:** the complete reward defined in Eq. 3.

6 Results

6.1 Algorithm Benchmark

Table 3 reports PPO, DQN, and A2C under full PAR. Fig. 1 illustrates the temporal distribution of these actions across attack session phases.

PPO achieves a mitigation-to-benign-harm ratio of 544.8, which is 7.6× higher than DQN and 126.42× higher than A2C. DQN attains slightly higher raw mitigation but intervenes more often on benign traffic, yielding a lower mitigation-to-harm tradeoff. A2C achieves competitive mitigation but incurs substantially higher benign harm, consistent with its short rollout buffer being insufficient to cover the suppress-and-return cycle following a Block action.

Table 3. Algorithm benchmark under full PAR. Values are means over 5 seeds and 30 evaluation episodes.

Algo	Mean reward	Attack mitig. (%)	Exact (%)	Dmg AUC	Benign interv. (%)
PPO	58.80	95.34	90.81	0.0644	0.175
DQN	60.71	99.54	92.26	0.0583	1.39
A2C	24.46	95.97	85.59	0.0764	22.27

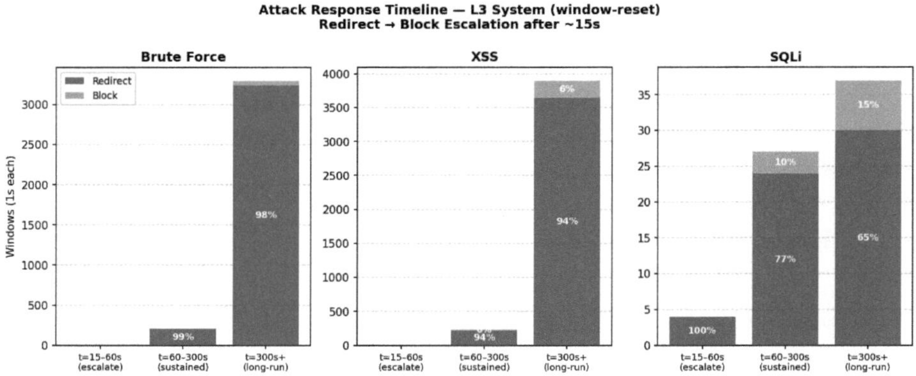

Fig. 1. Attack response timeline under PAR on CIC-IDS2018 Friday multi-attack data.

6.2 Reward Ablation

Table 4 reports the R1–R4 ablation study under PPO to evaluate the independent contribution of each reward component. The empirical results demonstrate that incorporating session-aware shaping fundamentally alters the benign-intervention tradeoff, and the resulting escalation dynamics are evaluated using per-session denominators to accurately capture long-horizon threat trajectories.

Table 4. Reward ablation under PPO. Mitigation and benign intervention are per labelled window; escalation and premature block are per L7 IP session in the traceable rerun pipeline.

Config	Attack mitig. (%)	Benign interv. (%)	Escalation (%)	Prem. block (%)
R1 Binary	99.97	0.04	0.00	0.00
R2 Base only	99.51	0.04	0.00	0.00
R3 No persistence/ramp	99.56	0.03	0.08	0.00
R4 Full PAR	95.34	0.18	89.33	10.67

Three key findings follow. First, effect-derived base rewards improve benign safety over binary label-derived rewards. Second, adding session-aware shaping is essential to establish the intended escalation pathway. Third, the persistence and ramp terms remain the primary drivers of the Redirect → Block pathway, as the full PAR variant shows substantially higher escalation than the simpler variants under strict evaluation constraints.

6.3 Policy Behaviour

The learned policy produces differentiated escalation rates across attacks (Table 5), indicating an implicit decision structure rather than a uniform always-Block response.

Table 5. Escalation rates under full PAR.

Attack	Escalation	Interpretation
SQLi	79%	21% neutralised by honeypot
XSS	99%	Classified critically severe
Brute Force	82%	Some truncated by rate limit
Overall	85%	Mean over L7 attacks
Premature	15%	Block before full evidence

6.4 Out-of-Distribution Validation

The trained policy was evaluated without retraining on CIC-IDS2017 and CSE-CIC-IDS2018 to assess zero-shot transfer under distribution shift. Because these are static datasets, they do not validate the full closed-loop reward mechanism: agent actions do not causally alter future traffic or service-damage feedback. On CIC-IDS2017, the policy achieves 100.0% mitigation with zero false positives for SYN Flood traffic across n = 1,169 windows. The cross-dataset accuracy comparison is shown in Fig. 2, and the CSE-CIC-IDS2018 Friday Multi-Attack results are summarized in Table 6.

Figure 3 compares the prediction accuracy of the three processing layers. L1 represents the raw PPO policy, L2 incorporates AI-Agent validation, and L3 applies the Window-Reset mechanism. Brute Force and XSS maintain near-perfect accuracy throughout the pipeline. SQLi reaches only 71.6% because highly obfuscated payloads are attenuated by CRS-942 before entering the RL decision process. Therefore, the reduced SQLi accuracy reflects a limitation of the dataset and preprocessing pipeline rather than of the proposed PAR reward architecture.

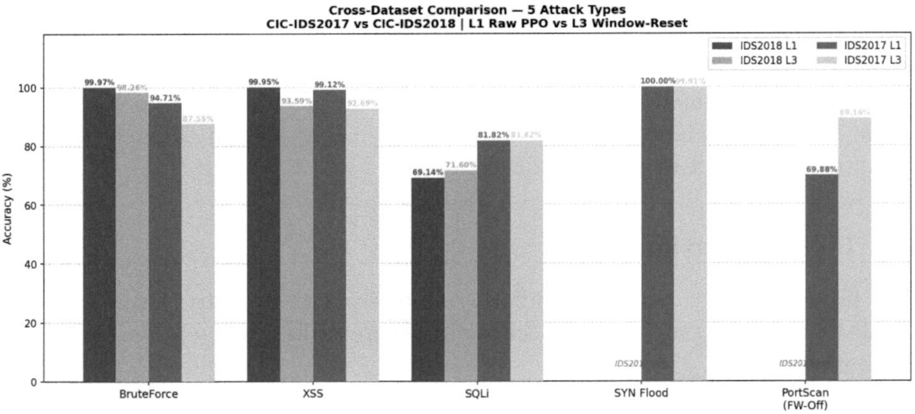

Fig. 2. Cross-dataset accuracy comparison for five attack types. IDS2018 values are shown for Brute Force, XSS, and SQLi.

Table 6. OOD results on CSE-CIC-IDS2018 Friday Multi-Attack.

Class	n	Accuracy	Mitigation
Benign	1,702	98.0%	–
Brute Force	3,510	100.0%	100.0%
XSS	4,136	100.0%	100.0%
SQLi	81	71.6%	71.6%
Total	9,429	99.4%	–

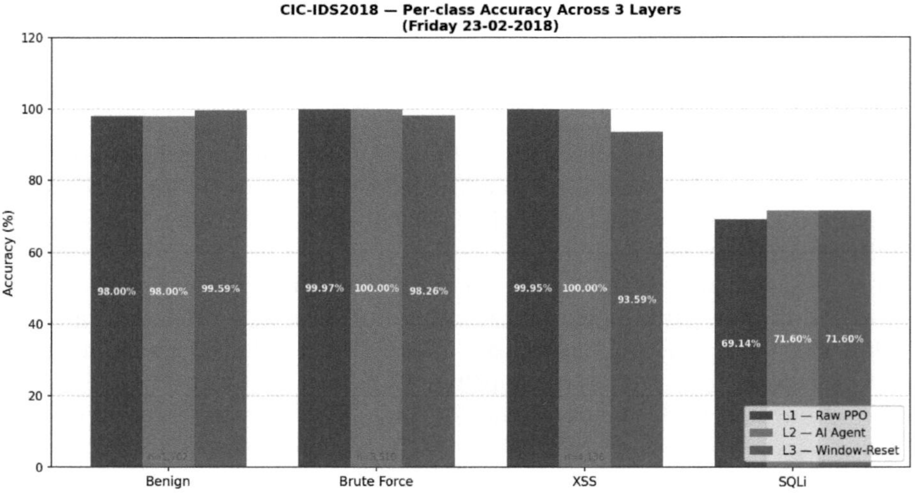

Fig. 3. Per-class accuracy across three processing layers on CSE-CIC-IDS2018 Friday.

7 Discussion

7.1 Reward Design as the Primary Policy Driver

The ablation results confirm that reward design, not algorithm choice alone, determines whether an RL-IDS agent learns a graduated defense strategy. While absolute empirical metrics are sensitive to validation environments and specific pipeline configurations, the core architectural importance of session-aware shaping for structured escalation behavior remains clear and robust. This strongly supports the view that the underlying reward taxonomy serves as the primary driver of operational policy behavior.

7.2 Effect-Derived vs. Label-Derived Reward

R2 replaces label-derived feedback with an effect-derived service signal and improves benign safety relative to R1. This supports the paper's main distinction: deployment-aligned rewards should be grounded in effects of actions rather than static labels. However, during training the detection bonus still uses traffic-type information to construct reward, so the implementation is best described as hybrid label-informed training reward with label-free inference. At deployment, the learned policy uses only observations and does not access traffic labels.

7.3 Limitations and Future Work

Four limitations bound the current evaluation. First, the R1–R4 reward ablation is conducted under PPO only. Although PPO, DQN, and A2C are benchmarked under full PAR, extending the full ablation to DQN and A2C is necessary to determine whether shaping benefits are algorithm-agnostic; the present paper therefore does not claim algorithm-agnosticity. Second, the current empirical evidence is derived from five training seeds and 30 evaluation episodes per seed. While this provides a consistent baseline to track policy behaviors, scaling the experiment to a larger seed volume is necessary to compute tight 95% confidence intervals and establish strong statistical robustness; a broader parametric study will report seed-level and episode-level confidence intervals for mitigation, benign intervention, and escalation metrics. Third, the reward coefficients are hand-tuned for the current traffic mix. To transition this framework toward operational environments, a critical next step involves conducting a systematic sensitivity analysis over key reward weights and thresholds (such as the persistence bonus, premature-block penalty, damage coefficient, action-cost ladder, and escalation-window length) to confirm policy stability under plausible threat perturbations. Fourth, PAR is not potential-based and does not guarantee policy invariance under arbitrary transition dynamics.

Beyond these primary limitations, several additional future directions are important for deployment and evaluation. The current evaluation does not yet characterise benign workload diversity or host-level entropy, which are necessary to understand whether learned policies generalise beyond the current traffic mix.

Additional SQL injection (SQLi) experiments would also increase sample size and stress-test the reward design under a broader application-layer adversary. Rollout horizon and session length should be treated as deployment requirements: short replay or buffer horizons can disproportionately harm A2C by degrading advantage estimates across longer session trajectories.

Finally, the current setup does not address SQLi obfuscation or the operational limitations of CRS-942 in this environment. Future work should investigate obfuscation-resistant detection strategies and quantify the gaps that appear when application-layer patterns are altered, especially for a CRS signature-based layer that may have brittle coverage against crafted payloads.

7.4 Relation to Companion System Work

This paper focuses specifically on reward design and reward ablation. Companion system work from the same project line focuses on deployment pipeline, feature extraction, and enforcement architecture. The independent contribution here is the reward-source taxonomy and the empirical isolation of PAR components.

8 Conclusion

We presented PAR, a persistence-aware reward architecture for RL-based network intrusion defense. PAR combines an effect-derived base reward with five session-aware shaping terms that encode a graduated Observe → Redirect → Block protocol. A PPO policy trained online in a parameterised simulator achieves high mitigation with low benign intervention and transfers without retraining to a Mininet/Containernet deployment testbed. In the updated evaluation, the full PAR variant achieves 95.34% attack mitigation with 0.175% benign intervention, and omitting persistence/ramp shaping materially alters escalation behavior. These results validate dense, session-aware reward design as a dependable and practical mechanism for learning multi-step, production-aligned defense policies in autonomous network infrastructure.

Declarations

Data Availability. CIC-IDS2017 and CSE-CIC-IDS2018 are publicly available from the Canadian Institute for Cybersecurity. Simulation code, trained model weights, and evaluation scripts will be released upon publication.

Competing Interests. The authors declare no competing interests.

References

1. Bates, A., Haack, J., Sherburne, M.: Reward shaping for happier autonomous cyber security agents. In: AAAI Workshop on Artificial Intelligence for Cyber Security (2023)

2. Cichonski, P., Millar, T., Grance, T., Scarfone, K.: Computer security incident handling guide. Technical report, Special Publication 800-61 Revision 2, National Institute of Standards and Technology (2012). https://doi.org/10.6028/NIST.SP.800-61r2
3. Hammar, K., Stadler, R.: Learning security strategies through game play and optimal stopping. IEEE Trans. Netw. Serv. Manag. **21**(2), 1750–1768 (2024). https://doi.org/10.1109/TNSM.2023.3324525
4. Lopez-Martin, M., Carro, B., Sanchez-Esguevillas, A.: Application of deep reinforcement learning to intrusion detection. Expert Syst. Appl. **141**, 112963 (2020). https://doi.org/10.1016/j.eswa.2019.112963
5. Ng, A.Y., Harada, D., Russell, S.: Policy invariance under reward transformations: theory and application to reward shaping. In: Proceedings of the 16th International Conference on Machine Learning (ICML), pp. 278–287 (1999)
6. Nguyen, T.T., Reddi, V.J.: Deep reinforcement learning for cyber security: a survey. IEEE Trans. Neural Netw. Learn. Syst. **34**(8), 3779–3795 (2023). https://doi.org/10.1109/TNNLS.2021.3121870
7. Otoum, S., Kantarci, B., Mouftah, H.T.: Adaptively supervised and intrusion-aware data aggregation for wireless sensor clusters in critical infrastructures. IEEE Trans. Industr. Inf. **20**(1), 130–139 (2024). https://doi.org/10.1109/TII.2023.3267648
8. Schulman, J., Wolski, F., Dhariwal, P., Radford, A., Klimov, O.: Proximal policy optimization algorithms. arXiv preprint arXiv:1707.06347 (2017), https://arxiv.org/abs/1707.06347
9. Sewak, M., Sahay, S.K., Rathore, H.: Deep reinforcement learning in the advanced cybersecurity threat detection and protection. Inf. Syst. Front. **25**(2), 589–611 (2023). https://doi.org/10.1007/s10796-022-10267-2

Special Track

A Multi-LLM Collaborative Framework for Chemical Warehouse Safety Assessment with Knowledge Distillation

Li Xu(✉)

Shanghai Key Laboratory of Trustworthy Computing, East China Normal University, Shanghai 200062, China
71275902017@stu.ecnu.edu.cn

Abstract. Ensuring safe co-storage of hazardous chemicals in warehouses is a critical yet largely manual task, hampered by non-standardized product names and incomplete safety data. We present an end-to-end AI-assisted system that addresses this challenge through four core components: (1) a multi-LLM cross-validation framework that standardizes chemical names and resolves inter-model conflicts without manual ground truth; (2) a PubChem-based enrichment pipeline that augments resolved entities with structured hazard attributes; (3) a rule-based safety evaluation engine that assesses pairwise chemical compatibility across warehouse locations; and (4) a knowledge distillation pipeline that transfers cloud-LLM extraction capability to a local model for offline SDS processing. Applied to real-world inventory data from a chemical logistics company—751 products and 383 warehouse locations—our system achieves 52.6% CAS coverage with a 93.1% conflict arbitration success rate; relative to a Qwen-only baseline, cross-validation corrects hallucinated identifiers a single model cannot self-detect, reducing strictly incompatible co-storage locations by 60%. The distilled local model further reaches 57.98% field extraction accuracy on held-out SDS documents, outperforming zero-shot inference by 7.2 pp in scalar accuracy (21.2 pp in set F1) while enabling fully offline deployment.

Keywords: Chemical safety · Warehouse management systems · Large language models · Information integration · Knowledge distillation · Hazard assessment

1 Introduction

Warehouse Management Systems (WMS) are central to chemical logistics, yet most deployments lack the ability to enforce chemical co-storage regulations automatically [13]. Regulatory standards such as GB 15603 [9] and GHS [11] define hazard categories and segregation rules that require knowing the precise chemical identity of every stored product. In practice, however, inventory data is highly heterogeneous: product names combine trade names, abbreviated

L. Ding et al. (Eds.): APWeb-WAIM 2026, LNCS 16995, pp. 471–483, 2027.
https://doi.org/10.1007/978-981-92-5699-0_31

formulas, and transliterations, making reliable linkage to standardised chemical databases—and thus to safety classifications—both difficult and error-prone.

The information management challenge is threefold. First, no single structured database provides full coverage of industrial trade products [6]. Second, AI-based extraction from product names produces hallucinated identifiers that cannot be detected without cross-referencing. Third, Safety Data Sheet (SDS) documents—the authoritative source of chemical hazard data—are scattered across heterogeneous formats and remain largely disconnected from WMS records, creating a persistent information silo.

While individual components such as chemical NER, database validation and rule-based compatibility checking are well studied, we are not aware of a deployed system that combines them into an annotation-free, end-to-end pipeline for ambiguous Chinese industrial inventories; our contribution is therefore primarily one of system integration, with the multi-LLM cross-validation design tailored to hallucination suppression in a safety-critical setting as the main methodological novelty. In this paper, we present such a system that addresses all three challenges, and make the following contributions:

- We design a **multi-LLM cross-validation pipeline** that integrates outputs from two large language models to resolve naming ambiguities, achieving 52.6% CAS coverage and a 93.1% conflict arbitration success rate without manual annotation (Sect. 4).
- We develop a **five-tier conflict arbitration mechanism** that verifies extracted identifiers against authoritative sources (PubChem, CAS Common Chemistry [1]), correcting 88.9% of AI-hallucinated CAS numbers (Sect. 4.3).
- We build an **automated safety assessment engine** that evaluates pairwise chemical compatibility using a layered rule set derived from GB 15603 and NFPA 491M, flagging 9 of 383 warehouse locations as requiring immediate remediation (Sect. 5).
- We close the SDS information silo via **knowledge distillation**: a local 7B model fine-tuned on cloud-LLM extractions achieves 57.98% field accuracy and enables fully offline SDS processing, outperforming zero-shot inference by 7.2 pp in scalar accuracy and 21.2 pp in set F1 (Sect. 6).

2 Related Work

2.1 Warehouse Management and Chemical Safety Information Systems

Warehouse Management Systems (WMS) coordinate inventory tracking, location management, and logistics operations [13]. For chemical warehouses, safety enforcement requires linking inventory records to hazard classifications defined by GHS [11] and national standards such as GB 15603 [9], yet most commercial WMS platforms treat chemical identifiers as free-text strings without automated validation or compatibility checking. Prior hazard-information work builds structured databases [6] and incompatibility rule sets but assumes chemical identities are already known and standardised; we instead address the upstream data quality problem—resolving ambiguous product names to canonical identifiers—as a prerequisite for safety enforcement.

2.2 Chemical Named Entity Recognition

Chemical named entity recognition (NER) is a prerequisite for automated chemical information processing. Early systems relied on dictionary lookup and hand-crafted rules; transformer-based models have since substantially improved recall on non-standard and abbreviated chemical names. Isazawa and Cole [4] proposed a unified BERT-based model achieving F_1 of 89.7 on the CHEMDNER benchmark and 88.0 on the Matscholar corpus within the ChemDataExtractor framework. Curated corpora such as BC5CDR [7] have further driven domain-specific NER research. However, these supervised approaches require annotated training data and struggle with trade names and abbreviated product identifiers prevalent in industrial inventories, motivating our annotation-free, LLM-based approach.

2.3 LLM-Based Information Extraction

Large language models (LLMs) have emerged as powerful zero-shot tools for information extraction, offering strong generalization across domains without task-specific training data [14], and schema-constrained prompting (e.g. JSON output) further improves extraction quality on domain-specific documents [12]. Our work extends this paradigm by querying two LLMs in parallel and using inter-model agreement to validate extractions without human-labelled ground truth.

2.4 Safety Data Sheet Processing

Prior work on SDS processing has combined rule-based extraction with machine learning classifiers [10]. Khan et al. [5] developed a multi-step ML system achieving precision of 0.96–0.99 on five administrative SDS fields (product name, manufacturer, revision date, etc.) across 150,000 annotated documents. However, these approaches target fixed-format metadata fields, whereas extracting *semantic safety attributes* (GHS hazard class, flash point, incompatible substances) from unstructured SDS text remains underexplored, particularly for Chinese industrial documents— the gap our distillation pipeline addresses.

2.5 Knowledge Distillation for NLP

Parameter-efficient fine-tuning methods such as LoRA [3] enable cost-effective adaptation of large language models to narrow domains with limited labelled data. Knowledge distillation [2] complements this by transferring teacher-LLM capabilities into compact student models. We combine both to adapt a 7B-parameter model for offline SDS attribute extraction, using cloud-LLM outputs as supervision.

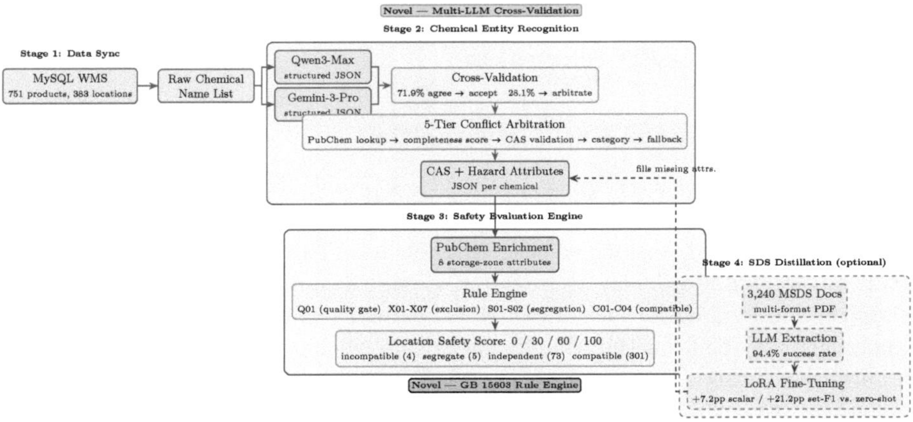

Fig. 1. End-to-end pipeline for chemical warehouse safety assessment. Highlighted panels mark the components emphasized in this work.

3 System Overview

Figure 1 shows the four-stage pipeline of our system. Stage 1 synchronizes warehouse inventory data from a remote MySQL database, producing a list of raw product names. Stage 2 queries two LLMs in parallel to standardize each name to its canonical CAS number and enriches the resolved entities with structured hazard attributes via PubChem. Stage 3 applies a layered rule engine to evaluate pairwise chemical compatibility across all co-located products. The optional Stage 4 supplements Stage 2 coverage by extracting safety attributes directly from supplier SDS documents and distilling this capability into a local model for offline use.

Data Architecture. The system is built on a three-layer data store. The *operational layer* is a MySQL database maintained by the company's existing WMS, holding product records (goods_id, name, quantity, location) that are synchronised into a local SQLite instance at Stage 1. The *knowledge layer* aggregates resolved chemical entities, PubChem attributes (molecular formula, flash point, GHS hazard tags), and SDS-derived safety fields into a unified schema that serves the rule engine. The *document layer* comprises the 3,240 historical SDS files that feed the distillation pipeline, each layer being updated independently.

Dataset. Experiments use real data from a chemical logistics company: 751 distinct products across 383 warehouse locations and 3,240 historical SDS documents (MSDS format, the legacy Chinese industrial standard equivalent to SDS under GHS). Product names are highly non-standardized, mixing Chinese trade names, abbreviated formulas, and transliterations.

4 Chemical Entity Recognition and Attribute Enrichment

4.1 Multi-LLM Standardization

Given a raw product name, we query Qwen3-Max (`qwen3-max-2025-09-23`) and Gemini-3-Pro (`gemini-3-pro-high`) in parallel using a unified prompt that requests the canonical chemical name, CAS Registry Number, physical state, GHS hazard tags, and flash point. We refer to these as "Qwen" and "Gemini" throughout. Both are accessed via their respective cloud APIs with default decoding settings (`max_tokens` = 2000).[1] Both models are instructed to return only valid JSON with no additional commentary; a condensed schema is shown below:

```
Given the chemical product name "{name}", return a JSON object:
{
  "canonical_name": "<IUPAC or common name>",
  "cas_number":     "<CAS Registry Number or null>",
  "physical_state": "<solid|liquid|gas|unknown>",
  "flash_point_c":  <number or null>,
  "ghs_hazard_tags": ["<GHS class>", ...],
  "incompatible_with": ["<substance>", ...]
}
```

4.2 Cross-Validation and Conflict Detection

Let r_Q and r_G denote the responses from Qwen and Gemini. The primary consistency signal is *CAS agreement*, $\text{Agree}(r_Q, r_G) = \mathbb{1}[\text{CAS}(r_Q) = \text{CAS}(r_G)]$; when it holds, the result is accepted directly. Among the 256 products for which both models returned a CAS number, 71.9% (184) showed complete agreement and were accepted directly; the remaining 28.1% (72) exhibited conflicting CAS numbers and were forwarded to the five-tier arbitration stage.

4.3 Five-Tier Conflict Arbitration

For conflicting responses, we apply a five-tier decision procedure:

1. **PubChem CID Lookup**: query both candidate CAS numbers in PubChem; accept the one that resolves to a valid compound.
2. **Information Completeness Score**: score each candidate across 10 safety-relevant fields $f_1, \ldots, f_{10}$ (GHS classification, flash point, hazard tags, etc.):

$$S(r) = \sum_{i=1}^{10} \mathbb{1}\left[f_i(r) \neq \emptyset\right] \quad (1)$$

   Select the response with the higher score $S(r)$.

[1] Model roles differ by stage: the cloud models Qwen3-Max and Gemini-3-Pro (joined by Claude for the SDS teacher panel of Sect. 6) handle standardization and proxy-label extraction, while the local Qwen2.5-7B-Instruct student and Qwen3.5-4B zero-shot baseline (offline via Ollama) are deliberately small for on-premise SDS processing.

3. **CAS Common Chemistry Validation**: verify each candidate against the CAS Common Chemistry API to flag AI-hallucinated entries not present in the official registry.
4. **Category Consistency**: use GHS hazard tag agreement as a tiebreaker when CAS numbers differ.
5. **Conservative Fallback**: if all tiers fail, mark the entity as unresolved and assign it to independent storage.

Among the 72 conflicting pairs, 93.1% (67 of 72) were resolved by Tier 1–4; the remaining 5 cases had both candidate CAS numbers absent from PubChem and were left unresolved. We define this 93.1% *arbitration success rate* as the fraction of conflicts for which the procedure yielded a single accepted CAS number validated against PubChem/CAS Common Chemistry—i.e. *conflict resolution against authoritative registries*, not verified correctness against an expert-annotated ground truth, which is unavailable for this inventory (cf. the manual-audit limitation in Sect. 6). Separately, CAS Common Chemistry validation across all candidate CAS numbers identified 27 hallucinated entries (format-valid CAS numbers that do not exist in the official registry); 24 of the 27 (88.9%) were corrected by the complementary model's output, and the remaining 3 were left unresolved.

Precision–Recall Complementarity. A key empirical finding is that Qwen and Gemini exhibit complementary precision–recall trade-offs. Gemini achieves higher recall (51.4% CAS coverage vs. 35.3% for Qwen), while Qwen achieves higher precision (mean PubChem quality score 7.92 vs. 7.74 for Gemini on a 10-point scale), reflecting a conservative "return only when confident" behaviour. Consequently, Qwen contributes 9 unique identifications that Gemini misses, raising the joint coverage from 51.4% to 52.6% (Fig. 2). We stress that the principal value of the multi-LLM design is not this marginal +1.2 pp coverage gain but cross-validation itself: it exposes the 27 hallucinated CAS numbers that a single model cannot self-detect and, via arbitration, prevents them from propagating into the false safety alerts quantified in Sect. 5 (Qwen-only: 10 incompatible locations vs. 4 for the joint system).

5 Safety Evaluation Engine

5.1 Chemical Feature Engineering

Each resolved chemical entity is enriched with PubChem attributes [6] and assigned to one of eight storage zones (e.g., *flammable*, *corrosive*, *water-reactive*) based on its hazard tags and flash point.

5.2 Pairwise Compatibility Assessment

The rule engine evaluates each pair (a, b) of chemicals sharing a warehouse location through four decision phases:

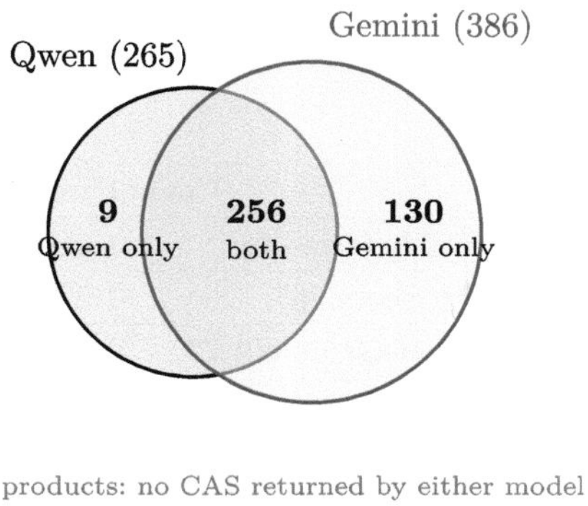

Fig. 2. Product-level CAS coverage overlap. Of the 256 products with a CAS from both models, 184 (71.9%) agreed and 72 entered arbitration; the joint system covers 9+256+130 = 395 products (52.6%).

1. **Data Quality Gate (Q01)**: pairs where either entity has a goods-level completeness score < 0.3 (a pre-computed $[0, 1]$ field coverage ratio, distinct from the CAS-candidate score $S(r)$ in Eq. 1) are classified as *independent* (insufficient data to judge).
2. **Exclusion Rules (X01–X07)**: seven hard constraints derived from GB 15603 and NFPA 491M [8], covering oxidizer/reducer, water-reactive/liquid, and unstable compound interactions.
3. **Segregation Rules (S01–S02)**: two zone-conflict rules requiring physical separation. S01 fires when both chemicals belong to different non-general hazard zones; S02 fires when one chemical belongs to a high-risk zone (*flammable_high* or *reactive*) and the other is in general storage.
4. **Compatibility Rules (C01–C04)**: conditions under which co-storage is explicitly permitted.

The four-verdict output (*incompatible / segregate / independent / compatible*) maps to an ordinal location-level safety score (0, 30, 60, 100); a location takes the minimum (worst) score over its pairs.

5.3 Results

Of the 383 warehouse locations, 99 held two or more distinct products and therefore required pairwise evaluation, yielding 308 chemical pairs in total. Table 1 summarizes the location-level results.

Nine locations (2.3%) require immediate attention. Table 2 shows the triggering frequency of each rule category across the 308 evaluated chemical pairs. Rule X04 (water-reactive substances co-stored with liquids) accounts for 43 of the 70 flagged pairs (61.4%), the dominant hazard here (e.g. Location C3-3-1, where aluminium trichloride and phosphorus pentoxide sit alongside liquid acids).

Violation Analysis. Of the 9 locations requiring attention, 4 are strictly incompatible (safety score 0) and 5 require physical segregation (score 30). All 4 incompatible cases involve water-reactive curing agents (isocyanate-based or silicone

Table 1. Safety evaluation results across 383 warehouse locations. *284 single-product locations are included in the Compatible count (no co-storage risk by definition; no pairwise evaluation required).

Verdict	Count	Percentage
Incompatible (score 0)	4	1.0%
Segregate (score 30)	5	1.3%
Independent (score 60)	73	19.1%
Compatible (score 100)	301*	78.6%

Table 2. Rule trigger counts across 308 evaluated chemical pairs. Q01 and the default fallback together account for 211 *independent* verdicts (68.5%).

Rule	Description	Pairs	Verdict
X04	Water-reactive substance co-stored with liquid	43	Incompatible
S01	Two chemicals from different non-general hazard zones	24	Segregate
S02	High-risk zone (*flammable_high/reactive*) co-located with general storage	3	Segregate
C01–C04	Explicitly permitted co-storage conditions	27	Compatible
Q01/fallback	Insufficient attribute data for judgement	211	Independent

crosslinker compounds) stored alongside liquid solvents or acidic compounds—a violation of Rule X04. The 5 segregation cases involve chemicals from different hazard zones, most commonly flammable liquids co-located with toxic compounds. These violations are operationally actionable: the rule engine outputs per-location relocation recommendations, specifying which product should be moved and to which compatible storage zone.

Unresolved-Risk Exposure. The *independent* verdict denotes *unknown*, not *safe*: it is issued when at least one chemical lacks sufficient attributes (Q01/fallback) to apply any exclusion rule. This affects 211 of 308 evaluated pairs (68.5%) and 73 of 383 locations (19.1%), driven by the 47.4% of products without a PubChem-resolved CAS number. Because an unresolved pair could in principle hide an incompatibility, the 9 flagged locations are a *lower bound* on true risk. As a conservative upper bound, treating every independent location as potentially unsafe raises the at-risk count from 9 (2.3%) to 82 (21.4%) of locations. The true value lies between these bounds and cannot be tightened without more attribute coverage—which is precisely the data gap that the on-demand SDS extraction of Sect. 6 is designed to close, rather than a limitation of the rule logic itself.

Ablation: Impact of Data Quality. Table 3 compares three input configurations. Replacing cross-validated data with Qwen-only input raises the strictly incompatible location count from 4 to 10 (+150%), demonstrating that hallucinated CAS numbers propagate directly into false safety alerts. Gemini-only input produces the same 4 incompatible locations as the joint system, yet flags 7 segregation-required locations (vs. 5 for joint), suggesting arbitration also reduces false segregation alerts even when CAS coverage is similar.

Table 3. Ablation: single-model vs. cross-validated pipeline. "Incompatible Locs." counts locations with safety score 0 (strictly incompatible pairs); the joint system additionally flags 5 segregation-required locations (score 30), totalling 9 locations requiring immediate attention.

Configuration	CAS Coverage	Incompatible Locs.	Arbitration Acc.
Qwen only	35.3%	10	—
Gemini only	51.4%	**4**	—
Joint (ours)	**52.6%**	**4**	**93.1%**

6 SDS-Based Knowledge Distillation

6.1 Motivation

A key limitation of Stage 2 is its high *independent* verdict rate (68.5%), arising from insufficient PubChem coverage for 47.4% of products. We address this by extracting safety attributes directly from supplier SDS documents—an alternative path that does not rely on CAS-to-PubChem resolution.

6.2 LLM Extraction Pipeline (Phase 1)

We parse the 3,240 SDS documents using `pdfplumber`; 704 files were unreadable (scanned images or corrupted PDFs) and excluded, leaving 2,536 machine-readable documents. We locate the six key GHS sections (§1, §2, §7, §9, §10, §14) via keyword matching and query three cloud LLMs (Qwen, Gemini, and Claude) in parallel to extract structured `SdsExtractedRecord` JSON; the response with the highest field completeness score (Eq. 1) is retained as the proxy label. Of the 2,536 machine-readable documents, 2,393 (94.4%) yielded valid extractions.

Ablation (Matching Experiment). Linking extracted records to warehouse products via CAS and fuzzy name matching achieved only 27.0% coverage (203/751), leaving the 68.5% *independent* rate unchanged from the Stage 2 baseline. This reflects a structural disconnect between the historical SDS library and current inventory—stale documents for out-of-stock products, missing filings for newly introduced ones, and unreliable name matching between purchase orders and SDS headers. Moreover, of the 203 matched products only 21 (2.8% of inventory) yielded net new attributes, the rest already being complete from Stage 2—insufficient to move the *independent* rate. This motivates on-demand extraction at registration time, which avoids all three issues and removes the dependency on a pre-matched SDS library.

6.3 Knowledge Distillation to Local Model (Phase 2)

We construct a distillation dataset of 1,633 (input, output) pairs—SDS section text paired with the corresponding cloud-LLM extractions—and fine-tune `Qwen2.5-7B-Instruct` using LoRA [3] (rank 16, $\alpha = 32$, 3 epochs).

Table 4. Model comparison on the 163-sample held-out set. Parse failure = fraction of outputs not valid JSON (failed outputs are assigned all-null values and excluded from accuracy; Pre-LoRA accuracy is thus over only 7.4% of samples, shown only to confirm fine-tuning is a prerequisite for structured output). Scalar Acc. and Set F1 are simple averages over the 11 scalar and 2 set fields.

Model	Parse Failure	Scalar Acc.	Set F1
Pre-LoRA base (Qwen2.5-7B)	92.6%	1.46%	0.80%
Zero-shot (Qwen3.5-4B)	**1.2%**	50.79%	28.69%
Distilled/LoRA (ours)	12.3%	**57.98%**	**49.88%**

Table 5. Per-field extraction accuracy: distilled model vs. zero-shot baseline, both evaluated on the same 163-sample held-out set. GT = non-null ground-truth count. Averages are simple (unweighted) means over all 11 scalar/2 set fields.

Field	Type	GT	Distilled	Zero-shot
CAS number	Scalar	78	53.8%	64.1%
Danger level	Scalar	163	57.7%	14.1%
Signal word	Scalar	122	63.1%	18.9%
Physical state	Scalar	132	75.8%	11.4%†
Flash point	Scalar	46	45.7%	58.7%
Boiling point	Scalar	41	48.8%	65.9%
Ventilation req.	Scalar	142	78.9%	85.2%
Keep sealed	Scalar	127	72.4%	87.4%
UN number	Scalar	130	48.5%	55.4%
Packing group	Scalar	99	42.4%	45.5%
Transport class	Scalar	130	50.8%	52.3%
GHS pictograms	Set F1	163	48.0%	0.4%†
Incompatible mat.	Set F1	146	51.8%	57.0%
Avg. scalar			**57.98%**	50.79%
Avg. set F1			**49.88%**	28.69%

6.4 Evaluation

Table 4 summarizes format compliance and accuracy across the three configurations, all on the same 163-sample held-out set (exact match vs. cloud-LLM proxy labels). The pre-LoRA base model (Qwen2.5-7B without fine-tuning) failed to produce valid JSON in 92.6% of cases, confirming that format compliance is itself a learned behaviour. The distilled model's 12.3% parse failure rate—higher than the zero-shot model's 1.2%—reflects a known LoRA trade-off: fine-tuning on structured output templates reduces output diversity but can introduce formatting regressions on edge-case SDS layouts not covered by the training distribution. Table 5 gives the per-field breakdown.

† The zero-shot model often returns these fields in Chinese while labels use English, causing near-total exact-match failure on GHS pictograms (0.4%) and partial failure on physical state (11.4%) despite semantic correctness. This highlights a **format consistency** advantage of fine-tuning: LoRA aligns output style

with the label distribution (+7.2 pp scalar, +21.2 pp set F1 over zero-shot), and the distilled model runs fully offline at 4.3 s per document.

Per-field Analysis. The distilled model performs strongest on fields with structured, low-entropy values: physical state (75.8%), ventilation requirement (78.9%), and keep-sealed flag (72.4%). These are binary or categorical fields where fine-tuning on domain-specific labels is most effective. Performance is weaker on fields requiring numeric parsing or cross-document reasoning (Table 5): flash point suffers from inconsistent unit representation, and UN number involves long lookup tables the 7B model has not fully memorised. On these numeric and lookup fields the zero-shot model is in fact more accurate, likely because they rely on chemical domain knowledge better retained in the larger pre-training mixture than enforced by fine-tuning on proxy labels. This suggests a practical deployment strategy with an explicit safety guardrail: use the distilled model for categorical and flag fields where format consistency is paramount, but route the numeric and lookup fields on which it trails zero-shot—notably flash point, boiling point, UN number, CAS number and incompatible materials—to a cloud-API or human-review fallback rather than trusting the local output, so that the 12.3% parse failures and numeric errors never silently enter a safety verdict.

Limitations. Evaluation accuracy is measured against cloud-LLM extractions used as proxy labels rather than human-annotated ground truth, introducing a potential circularity: the student model is rewarded for reproducing teacher outputs, including any systematic errors the teacher makes. To partially validate proxy label quality, we manually annotated 30 held-out SDS samples; signal word labels achieved 87.5% agreement with human annotation, supporting the reliability of the danger-level field used in safety rule evaluation. Human-annotated benchmarks covering all fields remain important future work.

7 Conclusion

We presented an end-to-end system for AI-assisted chemical warehouse safety assessment that integrates annotation-free multi-LLM cross-validation (93.1% arbitration success), PubChem-based hazard enrichment, a GB 15603/NFPA 491M rule engine with quantified safety scores, and SDS knowledge distillation into a local 7B model (57.98% field accuracy, +7.2 pp over zero-shot) for offline use.

Limitations and Future Work. The 68.5% *independent* verdict rate reflects incomplete chemical attribute coverage rather than algorithmic limitations, and—as quantified in Sect. 5—leaves a residual risk exposure of up to 82 locations (21.4%) that our 9 active alerts do not bound from above; closing this gap is a safety priority, not merely future work. The primary remedy is to deploy the distilled local model for *on-demand* SDS extraction—triggered when a new product is first registered rather than applied in batch—to progressively raise attribute coverage without requiring a pre-existing, matched SDS library. The LLM panel can also be extended to additional frontier models for broader cross-validation coverage. Planned evaluation extensions include comparison against non-LLM baselines (PubChem synonym search, fuzzy CAS matching, dictionary normalization) and a larger expert-annotated audit stratified over high-risk chemicals and unresolved products.

A Complete Rule Engine Specification

Table 6 specifies every rule of the safety engine (Sect. 5), evaluated in strict priority order (gate → exclusion → segregation → compatibility → default); the first matching rule fixes the verdict and exclusion rules are symmetric in (a, b). Tag abbreviations: *ox* = oxidizer, *fl* = flammable, *red* = reducing agent, *ac* = corrosive acid, *ba* = corrosive base, *wr* = water-reactive, *ru* = reactive/unstable; *fp* = flash point (°C), *cs* = completeness score $[0, 1]$, *dl* = danger level. The *Principle* column names each rule's hazard-class principle; the rule set as a whole derives from GB 15603 [9] and NFPA 491M [8], which give segregation and reaction principles rather than pairwise tag predicates, so we map no individual rule to a specific clause. Storage zones (S01–S02) follow the highest-priority match-

Table 6. Full rule specification (Conf. = H/M/L rule confidence; verdict scores: incompatible 0, segregate 30, independent 60, compatible 100). Tag abbreviations are defined in the text above.

ID	Trigger condition (attributes & thresholds)	Verdict/Conf.	Principle
Phase 0—Data quality gate			
Q01	either side $cs < 0.3$	independent/L	—
Q02	either side tags= {none} yet $dl > 0$	independent/L	—
Phase 1—Exclusion (red-line, symmetric)			
X01	$ox \wedge fl$	incompatible/H	oxidizer–fuel
X02	$ox \wedge red$	incompatible/H	oxidizer–reducer
X03	$ac \wedge ba$	incompatible/H	acid–base
X04	$wr \wedge$ state=liquid	incompatible/M	water-reactive release
X05	$ru \wedge ox$	incompatible/H	unstable–oxidizer
X06	$ru \wedge ac$	incompatible/M	acid-catalysed decomp.
X07	$fl \wedge fl \wedge$ both $fp < 23$	incompatible/M	flammable load
Phase 2—Segregation (zone conflict)			
S01	zones differ, neither *general*	segregate/M	zone conflict
S02	one *general*, other *flammable_high*/*reactive*	segregate/M	zone conflict
Phase 3—Compatibility (all four required)			
C01	both $dl = 0$	compatible/L	conservative
C02	both tags $\in \{\{\text{none}\}, \emptyset\}$		
C03	both zone = *general*		
C04	both $cs \geq 0.5$		
Phase 4—Default: no rule fires → independent/M (score 60)			

ing class: *reactive* > *flammable_high* (*fp* < 23 °C) > *flammable* > *oxidizer* > *corrosive* > *water_reactive* > *toxic* ($dl \geq 2$) > *general.*

References

1. CAS: CAS Common Chemistry: an open community resource for basic chemical information. J. Chem. Inf. Model. (2021). https://commonchemistry.cas.org
2. Hsieh, C.Y., et al.: Distilling step-by-step! Outperforming larger language models with less training data and smaller model sizes. In: Findings of the Association for Computational Linguistics: ACL 2023, pp. 8003–8017 (2023). https://aclanthology.org/2023.findings-acl.507
3. Hu, E.J., et al.: LoRA: low-rank adaptation of large language models. In: Proceedings of the International Conference on Learning Representations (ICLR) (2022). https://arxiv.org/abs/2106.09685
4. Isazawa, T., Cole, J.M.: Single model for organic and inorganic chemical named entity recognition in ChemDataExtractor. J. Chem. Inf. Model. **62**(5), 1207–1213 (2022). https://doi.org/10.1021/acs.jcim.1c01199
5. Khan, M., Penfield, J., Suman, A., Crowell, S.: A machine learning driven automated system to extract multiple information fields from safety data sheet documents. Heliyon **11**, e42215 (2025). https://doi.org/10.1016/j.heliyon.2025.e42215
6. Kim, S., Chen, J., Cheng, T., Gindulyte, A., He, J., He, S., Li, Q., Shoemaker, B.A., Thiessen, P.A., Yu, B., et al.: PubChem 2023 update. Nucleic Acids Res. **51**(D1), D1373–D1380 (2023). https://doi.org/10.1093/nar/gkac956
7. Li, J., et al.: Biocreative V CDR task corpus: a resource for chemical disease relation extraction. Database **2016** (2016). https://doi.org/10.1093/database/baw068
8. Association, N.F.P.: NFPA 491M: Manual of hazardous chemical reactions. Technical report, National Fire Protection Association, Quincy, MA (1991)
9. National Standardization Administration of China: GB 15603–2022: General requirements for safe storage of hazardous chemicals. Technical report, National Standardization Administration of China (2022)
10. Suman, A., Khan, M., Talreja, V., et al.: A machine learning driven automated system for safety data sheet indexing. Sci. Rep. **14**, 4415 (2024). https://doi.org/10.1038/s41598-024-55231-1
11. United Nations: Globally harmonized system of classification and labelling of chemicals (GHS), 9th revised edition. Technical report, United Nations (2021). https://unece.org/transport/dangerous-goods/ghs-rev9-2021
12. Wang, X., et al.: InstructUIE: multi-task instruction tuning for unified information extraction. arXiv preprint arXiv:2304.08085 (2023)
13. Zhang, Z., Yuan, S., Yu, M., Mannan, M.S., Wang, Q.: A hazard index for chemical logistic warehouses with modified flammability rating by machine learning methods. ACS Chem. Health Saf. **27**(3), 190–197 (2020). https://doi.org/10.1021/acs.chas.9b00026
14. Zhou, W., Zhang, S., Gu, Y., Chen, M., Poon, H.: UniversalNER: targeted distillation from large language models for open named entity recognition. In: Proceedings of the International Conference on Learning Representations (ICLR) (2024). https://arxiv.org/abs/2308.03279

A Weakly Supervised Approach to Student–Major Fit Prediction Using Latent Behavioral Factors

Tuan Phong Tran(✉), Van Vu Nguyen, Quang Ha Nguyen, and Thuy Hang Nguyen

FPT University, Hanoi, Viet Nam
{phongtt35,nguyenvv4,hanq11,hangnt169}@fpt.edu.vn

Abstract. The selection of an appropriate academic major remains a critical challenge in higher education, particularly in early-stage decision-making where explicit ground truth for student–major fit is unavailable. Existing approaches primarily rely on academic performance or psychometric assessments, which often fail to capture behavioral patterns associated with long-term success. This paper proposes a data-driven framework for predicting student–major fit by integrating latent behavioral representation with weakly supervised label construction. Behavioral survey responses are transformed into low-dimensional latent factors using Exploratory Factor Analysis (EFA), capturing persistence and cognitive processing traits. A composite proxy label is constructed by combining normalized academic performance, self-assessed skill, and perceived fit, with redundancy mitigated through residualization and variance-based weighting. Experiments on a dataset of undergraduate students using Logistic Regression, Random Forest, Support Vector Machine, and XGBoost show that behavioral features consistently outperform traditional background features, achieving an F1-score of up to 0.61. Although statistical significance is not observed, large effect sizes indicate strong practical relevance. These findings highlight the importance of behavioral factors in modeling student–major alignment and demonstrate the potential of data-centric approaches for scalable, web-based educational analytics under weak supervision.

Keywords: Educational Data Mining · Learning Analytics · Weakly Supervised Learning · Behavioral Modeling · Data-Centric AI · Feature Representation · Student Modeling · E-learning Analytics

1 Introduction and Related Work

Selecting an appropriate academic major is a critical decision in higher education, particularly for first-year students who often have limited domain knowledge and self-awareness. Poor alignment between students and their chosen majors has been associated with lower academic performance, reduced engagement, and higher dropout risk [1, 4]. Consequently, predicting student–major fit has become an important topic in educational data mining and learning analytics.

L. Ding et al. (Eds.): APWeb-WAIM 2026, LNCS 16995, pp. 484–494, 2027.
https://doi.org/10.1007/978-981-92-5699-0_32

Existing student modeling approaches mainly rely on academic records or psychometric assessments. Grade prediction methods typically exploit historical academic performance [8], while psychological assessments focus on interests and personality traits. Although informative, these approaches often overlook behavioral patterns that reflect how students learn and interact with educational tasks over time.

Recent studies have demonstrated that behavioral features, including persistence, engagement, and learning strategies, are strong predictors of academic outcomes and frequently outperform traditional demographic and academic background variables [2, 5, 6, 13, 14]. These findings have motivated the adoption of behavioral analytics in learning analytics systems and early-warning applications [7, 15]. However, relatively little research has explicitly addressed student–major fit prediction, and existing studies generally employ predefined feature representations that may not capture latent behavioral characteristics [9].

Another challenge is the lack of explicit ground truth for student–major fit. Unlike academic performance, student–major alignment cannot be directly observed and must instead be inferred from multiple indirect indicators. This naturally leads to a weakly supervised learning setting, where proxy labels are constructed from noisy signals. Recent work highlights the importance of principled label construction in improving model reliability [16, 17]. Meanwhile, composite indicator methods and regression-based residualization provide statistically grounded techniques for integrating multiple correlated indicators while reducing redundancy [10–12].

To improve feature representation, dimensionality reduction techniques such as Exploratory Factor Analysis (EFA) have been widely adopted to uncover latent behavioral constructs from survey data [18]. Such latent representations have also been shown to improve the predictive performance and interpretability of educational machine learning models [14, 19].

Motivated by these challenges, this paper proposes a data-driven framework for student–major fit prediction by integrating latent behavioral representation with weakly supervised label construction. Behavioral survey responses are transformed into latent factors using EFA, while a composite proxy label is generated by combining academic performance, self-assessed skill, and perceived fit through residualization and variance-based weighting. We evaluate the proposed framework using Logistic Regression, Random Forest, Support Vector Machine, and XGBoost. Experimental results show that latent behavioral features consistently outperform traditional background features, highlighting their practical value for student–major fit prediction under weak supervision.

The main contributions of this work are threefold: (1) a weakly supervised framework for student–major fit prediction without explicit ground-truth labels; (2) an interpretable latent behavioral representation based on EFA; and (3) empirical evidence demonstrating the superior predictive value of behavioral characteristics over conventional background features.

2 Methodology

This study proposes a data-centric pipeline for student–major fit prediction consisting of four stages: (1) data preprocessing, (2) latent behavioral feature extraction, (3) weakly supervised label construction, and (4) predictive modeling (Fig. 1). The framework emphasizes feature representation and label quality rather than model complexity.

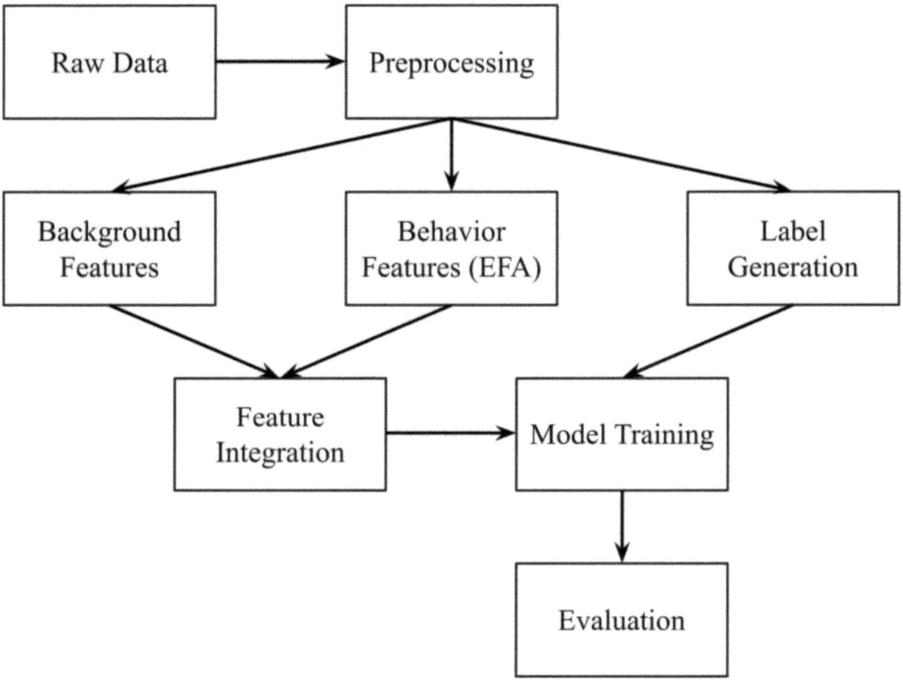

Fig. 1. Overall pipeline of the proposed approach for student-major fit prediction

2.1 Data Collection and Preprocessing

The dataset was collected from 213 undergraduate students through a structured survey, including three types of information: (i) academic background, (ii) behavioral responses, and (iii) current academic status. Background features (6–8 variables) capture prior exposure to STEM-related subjects, programming experience, and project involvement. Behavioral responses consist of 14 Likert-scale items designed to reflect persistence, engagement, and cognitive processing strategies (Table 1).

Incomplete responses were removed, numerical variables were normalized to the range [0,1] using min–max scaling, and categorical variables were one-hot encoded to ensure consistency across heterogeneous feature types.

Table 1. Summary of dataset and feature groups

Category	Features	Description
Background	6–8	STEM, alignment, experience
Behavioral	14 → 2	Likert → EFA factors
Label	3	GPA, Skill, Fit
Samples	213	Students

2.2 Latent Behavioral Feature Extraction

Exploratory Factor Analysis (EFA) was applied to derive latent behavioral representations from the survey responses. Data suitability was confirmed by a Kaiser–Meyer–Olkin (KMO) value of 0.881 and a significant Bartlett's test of sphericity ($p < 0.001$). Based on the Kaiser criterion and scree plot analysis (Fig. 2), two latent factors were retained.

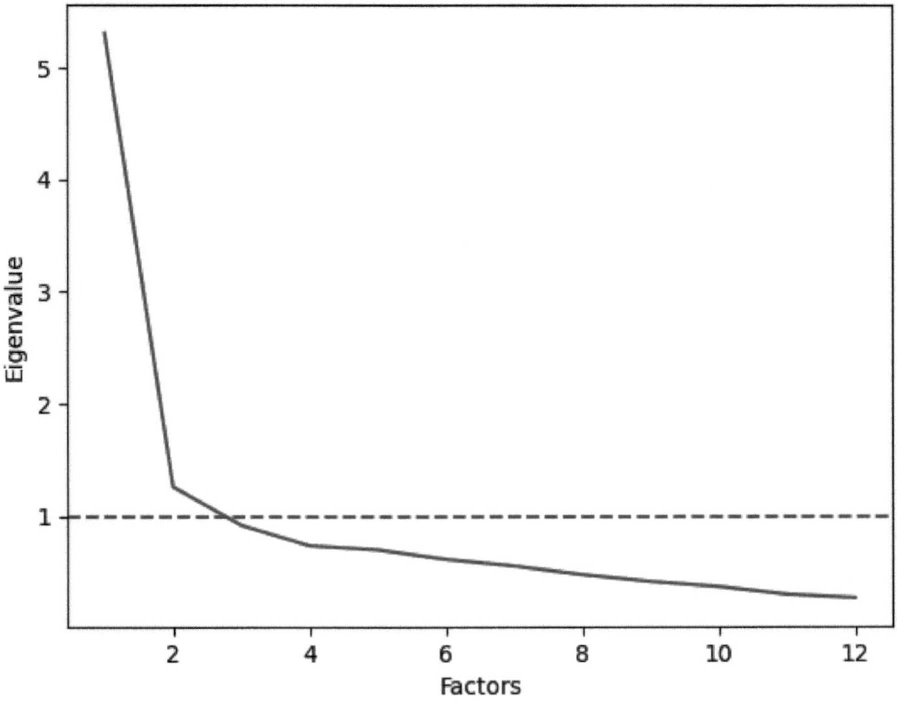

Fig. 2. Scree plot for factor selection

Promax rotation was employed to allow correlated behavioral constructs. Items with factor loadings below 0.5 were excluded, resulting in two interpretable dimensions:

(1) persistence-driven engagement and analytical depth, and (2) structured cognitive processing (Table 2).

Table 2. Rotated factor loadings (Promax) for behavioral items

Behavioral item	Factor 1	Factor 2
Spend hours solving a problem	0.92	
Persist until finding a solution	0.74	
Optimize systems for better performance	0.68	
Think in terms of cause–effect ("if…then…")	0.58	
Curious about how systems work internally		0.72
Understand errors rather than fix quickly		0.53
Think in step-by-step procedures		0.79
Build systems piece by piece		0.78

Cronbach's alpha values of 0.781 and 0.775 indicate acceptable internal consistency. The resulting factor scores were used as behavioral features in the predictive models.

2.3 Weakly Supervised Label Construction

Since explicit ground-truth labels for student–major fit is unavailable, a composite proxy label was constructed from three complementary indicators: GPA, self-assessed skill, and perceived major fit.

After min–max normalization, Pearson correlation analysis revealed a strong correlation between skill and perceived fit ($r = 0.7686$). To eliminate redundant information, perceived fit was residualized with respect to skill using Ordinary Least Squares (OLS):

$$\text{fit}_{res} = \text{Fit} - (\alpha + \beta \cdot \text{Skill})$$

A composite FitScore is then defined as a weighted sum of the normalized components:

$$\text{FitScore} = \mathrm{w}_1 \cdot \text{GPA} + \mathrm{w}_2 \cdot \text{Skill} + \mathrm{w}_3 \cdot \text{fit}_{\text{res}}$$

Weights (w_i) were determined proportionally to feature variance to reflect relative information contributions and to avoid heuristic selection:

$$\mathrm{w}_\mathrm{i} = \frac{\text{Var}(\mathrm{x}_\mathrm{i})}{\text{Var}(\text{GPA}) + \text{Var}(\text{Skill}) + \text{Var}(\text{fit}_{\text{res}})}$$

Finally, the continuous FitScore was converted into a binary label using the 60th percentile threshold:

$$Label = \begin{cases} 1, \textit{if } FitScore > \tau \\ 0, \textit{otherwise} \end{cases} \quad where\ \tau = P_{60}(FitScore)$$

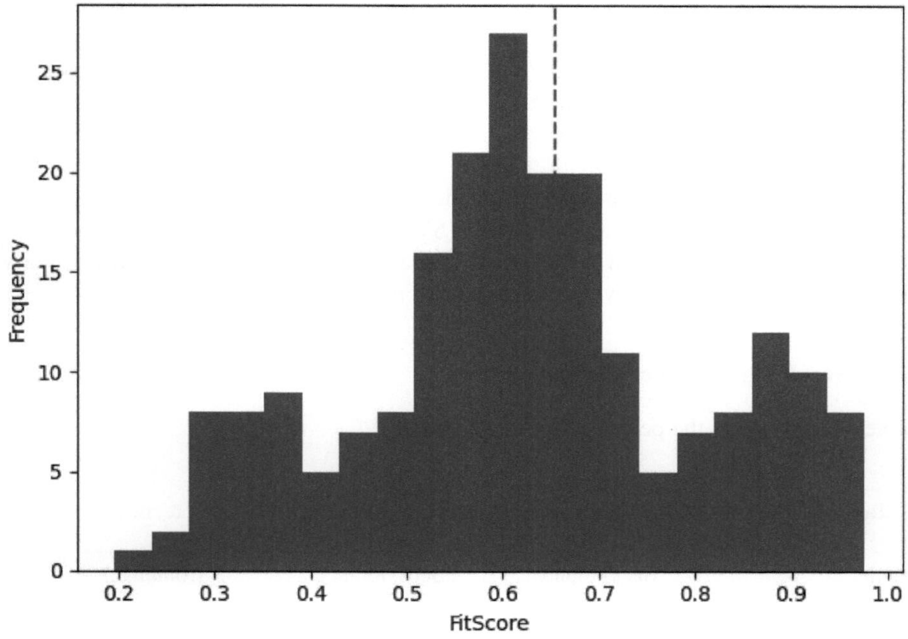

Fig. 3. Distribution of FitScore and threshold selection

The distribution of the FitScore and the selected threshold are illustrated in Fig. 3. Sensitivity analysis showed consistent behavior across alternative percentile thresholds, while the P60 threshold provided a balanced emphasis on high-fit instances.

2.4 Predictive Modeling

Four machine learning models were evaluated: Logistic Regression, Random Forest, Support Vector Machine (RBF kernel), and XGBoost. Rather than optimizing individual models, these algorithms were used to compare the predictive value of three feature sets: background features, latent behavioral factors, and their combination.

Performance was evaluated using stratified 5-fold cross-validation. The primary evaluation metric was the F1-score, complemented by accuracy, precision, and recall. To ensure reproducibility, all experiments were conducted with a fixed random seed. Statistical significance was assessed using paired t-tests, while effect sizes were reported to evaluate the practical relevance of observed differences.

3 Experiments

This section evaluates the effectiveness of the proposed data-centric framework, with a focus on assessing the contribution of different feature groups and the robustness of the learned representations across multiple models.

3.1 Experimental Setup

Experiments were conducted on the dataset of 213 undergraduate students using the feature representations and proxy labels described in Sect. 2. Three feature configurations were evaluated: (i) background features, (ii) latent behavioral features extracted by EFA, and (iii) their combination.

Four classifiers were considered: Logistic Regression (LR), Random Forest (RF), Support Vector Machine with an RBF kernel (SVM), and XGBoost (XGB). Performance was evaluated using stratified 5-fold cross-validation with the F1-score as the primary metric. Fixed random seeds were used to ensure reproducibility.

3.2 Overall Performance Comparison

Table 3 summarizes the performance of all models.

Table 3. Performance comparison across models and feature sets (F1-score, mean ± std)

Model	Background	Behavioral (EFA)	Combined
Logistic regression	0.400 ± 0.106	0.569 ± 0.118	0.611 ± 0.134
Random forest	0.420 ± 0.130	0.559 ± 0.093	0.535 ± 0.097
SVM (RBF)	0.412 ± 0.115	0.573 ± 0.102	0.584 ± 0.110
XGBoost	0.431 ± 0.121	0.598 ± 0.089	0.590 ± 0.095
Majority baseline	0.000 ± 0.000	–	–

Across all models, latent behavioral features consistently outperform background features. For example, Logistic Regression improves from 0.400 to 0.569, while XGBoost increases from 0.431 to 0.598. Adding background features yields mixed results: Logistic Regression benefits from the combined representation, whereas Random Forest and XGBoost show no consistent improvement, suggesting that background variables may introduce redundant information.

3.3 Statistical Analysis

Statistical comparisons were performed using paired t-tests on the cross-validation results (Table 4). For Random Forest, behavioral features outperform background features with a large effect size (Cohen's d = 1.18), although statistical significance is not reached ($p = 0.077$), likely due to the limited sample size. In contrast, the combined feature set does not significantly improve over behavioral features alone ($p = 0.069$, Cohen's d = −0.21), indicating that adding background variables provides only marginal benefit.

Although moderate variation is observed across cross-validation folds, the ranking of feature configurations remains consistent across models, indicating that the learned behavioral representations are robust.

Table 4. Statistical comparison between feature configurations

Comparison	t-value	p-value	Cohen's d
Behavior vs. Background	2.36	0.077	1.18
Combined vs. Behavior	−1.82	0.69	−0.21

3.4 Feature Importance Analysis

Feature importance analysis using Random Forest further confirms the dominance of behavioral information. The two latent behavioral factors contribute most to model predictions, whereas background variables exhibit comparatively low importance (Fig. 4).

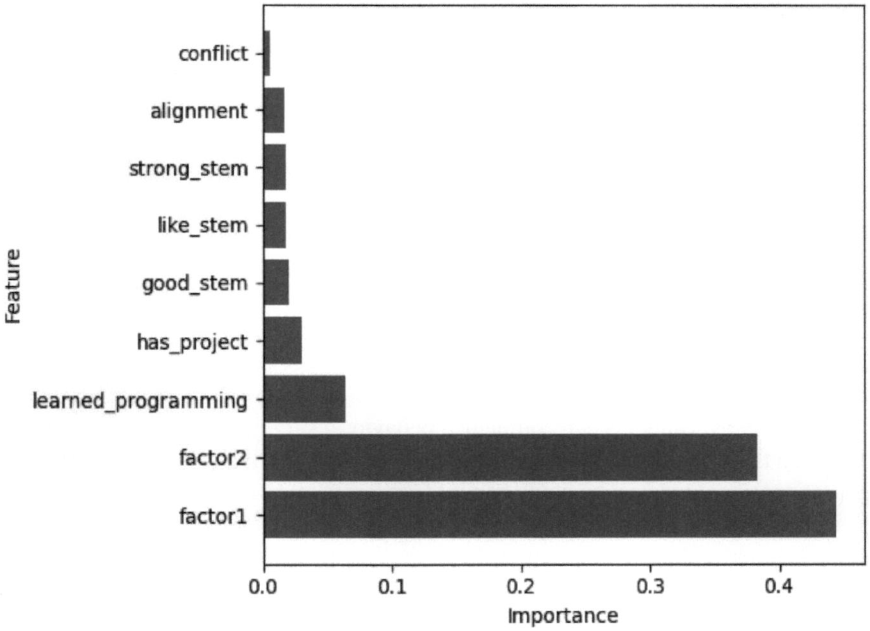

Fig. 4. Feature importance from Random Forest model

This observation aligns with the hypothesis that student–major fit is more strongly associated with how students engage with learning tasks rather than their prior academic exposure.

4 Discussion and Limitations

4.1 Discussion

The experimental results consistently show that latent behavioral factors provide stronger predictive signals for student–major fit than traditional academic background features. Across all evaluated models, behavioral representations derived from Exploratory Factor Analysis achieved better performance, suggesting that students' learning behaviors capture information beyond prior academic achievement. The results also indicate that combining behavioral and background features does not consistently improve prediction, implying that effective feature representation is more important than simply increasing the number of input variables.

These findings support a data-centric perspective, where improvements in feature representation and label quality can substantially enhance predictive performance without relying on increasingly complex learning algorithms. The extracted latent behavioral factors provide interpretable representations of persistence and cognitive processing, while the proposed weakly supervised framework enables statistically grounded learning despite the absence of explicit ground-truth labels.

An important methodological contribution of this study is the formulation of student–major fit as a weakly supervised learning problem. Because true student–major alignment cannot be directly observed, a composite proxy label was constructed by integrating academic performance, self-assessed skill, and perceived fit using residualization and variance-based weighting. Although this strategy inevitably introduces label noise and should be regarded as an approximation rather than a definitive measure of student–major fit, it provides a practical and scalable solution for learning from real-world educational data where ground-truth labels are unavailable.

From an application perspective, the proposed framework can be integrated into web-based educational platforms as a decision-support tool for major recommendation and academic advising. Students can complete a behavioral survey and receive personalized feedback on their compatibility with a chosen major, while advisors may use prediction results to identify students who could benefit from early intervention. At the institutional level, aggregated predictions can support curriculum evaluation, monitor student–major alignment across cohorts, and contribute to improving student retention and learning outcomes.

4.2 Limitations

This study has several limitations. First, the dataset is relatively small ($N = 213$), which may limit statistical power and the generalizability of the findings despite the use of cross-validation and effect size analysis. Second, the behavioral variables are derived from self-reported surveys and may not fully reflect actual learning behaviors. Incorporating interaction logs from learning management systems or other digital learning traces could improve behavioral measurement.

Finally, student–major fit is modeled using a composite proxy label because explicit ground-truth labels are unavailable. Although residualization and variance-based weighting help reduce redundancy among the component variables, the resulting labels remain approximations of an inherently latent construct. Consequently, the reported performance should be interpreted within the context of weakly supervised learning and further validated using longitudinal or independently annotated datasets.

5 Conclusion and Future Work

This study proposed a weakly supervised framework for predicting student–major fit by combining latent behavioral representations with composite proxy label construction. Experimental results show that behavioral factors consistently outperform traditional academic background features, highlighting the importance of data-centric feature representation and label design for educational prediction under limited supervision.

Future work will focus on validating the framework using larger, multi-institution, and longitudinal datasets to improve its generalizability and to assess the long-term validity of the proposed proxy labels. In addition, richer behavioral representations derived from learning management system interaction logs, digital learning traces, and advanced representation learning techniques, including deep learning and large language models, will be investigated to further enhance prediction performance and personalized academic support.

References

1. Saa, A.A.: Educational data mining and students' performance prediction. Data Sci. J. (2023)
2. Waheed, H., et al.: Predicting academic performance using deep learning. Comput. Educ. **161**, 104–124 (2020)
3. Al-Shehri, M.A., et al. Machine learning in higher education: a systematic review. Educ. Sci. (2025)
4. Romero, C., Ventura, S.: Educational data mining: a review. IEEE Trans. Syst. Man Cybern. **40**(6), 601–618 (2010)
5. Hussain, A., et al.: Student engagement predictions in online learning environments. PLoS One. (2023)
6. Liu, Y., et al.: Combining Behavioral and Academic Data for Student Modeling. Springer (2024)
7. Xu, J., Recker, K. Early Warning Systems for Identifying at-Risk Students. (2022)
8. Elbadrawy, A., Karypis, G.: Domain-Aware Grade Prediction and Top-N Course Recommendation. RecSys (2016)
9. Doe, J., et al.: Predicting student major using machine learning. arXiv. (2018)
10. Nardo, M., et al.: Handbook on Constructing Composite Indicators. OECD (2008)
11. Hyndman, R.J., Fan, Y.: Sample quantiles in statistical packages. Am. Stat. (1996)
12. Seber, G.A.F., Lee, A.J.: Linear Regression Analysis. Wiley (2003)
13. Chen, X., Zou, D., Xie, H.: Behavioral analytics in educational data mining: a review of recent advances. IEEE Access. (2023)
14. Li, Y., Chen, L., Wang, M.: Modeling student learning behaviors for performance prediction in online education. Comput. Educ.: Artif. Intell. (2024)
15. Baker, R.S., Inventado, P.S.: Educational data mining and learning analytics: applications to early warning systems. J. Learn. Anal. (2023)
16. Zhou, Z.-H.: A brief introduction to weakly supervised learning. Natl. Sci. Rev. (2018)
17. Zhang, C., et al.: Data-centric AI: perspectives and challenges. ACM Comput. Surv. (2024)

18. Kline, P.: Exploratory and Confirmatory Factor Analysis in Behavioral Research. Routledge (updated edition)
19. Nguyen, T., et al.: Interpretable machine learning for student modeling using latent behavioral features. Expert Syst. Appl. (2025)

Assessing Uncertainty in Stock Returns: A Gaussian Mixture Distribution-Based Method

Yanlong Wang[1,2], Jian Xu[1], Hongkang Zhang[1], Shao-Lun Huang[1], Danny Dongning Sun[2(✉)], and Xiao-Ping Zhang[1]

[1] Tsinghua Shenzhen International Graduate School, Tsinghua University, Beijing, China
xpzhang@ieee.org
[2] Pengcheng Laboratory, Shenzhen, China
sundn@pcl.ac.cn

Abstract. Modeling the uncertainty of stock returns is fundamental to risk management and decision making in financial markets, yet remains challenging due to the latent, time-varying, and heterogeneous nature of return distributions across thousands of assets. Traditional GARCH-family models rely on restrictive parametric assumptions and struggle to capture nonlinear information effects and cross-asset heterogeneity, while existing deep learning approaches typically produce point forecasts and do not directly characterize predictive uncertainty. To address these limitations, we propose a deep mixture density framework that models next-day return distributions as a Gaussian mixture, jointly capturing short-term fluctuations and non-traditional features such as skewness and heavy tails. The framework integrates a Transformer-based encoder for time-series forecasting over technical indicators with a learnable stock-code embedding branch, and fuses both representations to output mixture weights, means, and variances under a maximum-likelihood objective. In addition, the learned embeddings enable a complementary analysis of uncertainty similarity across assets through low-dimensional visualization, providing an interpretable view of stocks sharing similar risk profiles. We conduct extensive experiments on 3,226 stocks from the Chinese A-share main board over five years, comparing against a broad set of GARCH-family baselines. Results show that the proposed method delivers more accurate distributional and volatility forecasts, with particularly pronounced gains during high-volatility regimes, and remains stable across repeated training runs. By unifying distributional forecasting, cross-sectional representation learning, and uncertainty-oriented interpretability, our framework offers a practical tool for volatility modeling, portfolio risk assessment, and data-driven decision support in financial applications.

Keywords: Stock return uncertainty · Gaussian mixture distribution · Mixture density network · Volatility forecasting · Deep learning · Chinese A-shares

L. Ding et al. (Eds.): APWeb-WAIM 2026, LNCS 16995, pp. 495–507, 2027.
https://doi.org/10.1007/978-981-92-5699-0_33

1 Introduction

Accurate forecasting of stock returns and their uncertainty is central to financial risk management and investment decisions. Because return prediction is inherently uncertain, modeling the conditional return distribution is often more informative than a point forecast, but this distribution is latent, time-varying, and shaped by nonlinear information effects, which makes it hard to recover and relate to information-flow dynamics. As a result, many traditional approaches rely on single parametric forms such as normal or t-distributions and summarize risk through scalar indicators.

Volatility is a key proxy for uncertainty in financial markets [21]. The mixture distribution hypothesis links volatility to cumulative information flow [7], and related studies further emphasize delayed price adjustment under liquidity constraints and sequential information arrival [8]. Prior work also connects return dynamics to information uncertainty [14]. GARCH-type models remain the standard tool for volatility forecasting and capture clustering effects well (e.g., [22]), but their assumptions can limit performance under strong nonlinearity, multivariate dependence, and cross-asset heterogeneity [10].

Machine learning can learn nonlinear structures that are difficult to capture with classical linear models [13]. Many studies report gains in return prediction across multiple asset classes (e.g., [24]). Deep learning methods, including Transformer variants, are particularly effective for complex sequential data [17].

The uncertainty literature uses multiple proxies, including variance risk premium [3], forecast disagreement [2], and volatility-of-volatility [4]. More generally, uncertainty quantification aims to characterize predictive distributions conditioned on available information [1].

In this work, we use deep learning to predict the dynamic distribution of asset returns and to explore the nonlinear relationship between information flow and price volatility. Specifically, we model the return distribution as a Gaussian mixture and predict its parameters via the output layer of a deep network. Unlike single parametric forms such as Gaussian or t-distributions, which often fail to capture the return distribution in a given period [15], a Gaussian mixture can represent a much wider range of shapes. This mixture-distribution methodology has proven useful for asset pricing [20] and can be optimized via maximum likelihood estimation [16], but computational constraints and the optimization challenges of mixture models have limited its use in this domain.

Our proposed model is designed to handle time-series data while distinguishing between individual stock identities. It processes indicator data with a Transformer with modules tailored for sequential information [23], and separately encodes stock identifiers into a vector space via a code embedding network. A fusion network then combines both outputs to predict the parameters of a Gaussian mixture distribution, yielding the predicted return distribution; we refer to this model as MDNe and present its full structure in Fig. 2. A version without the code embedding component, denoted MDN, serves as a control. To assess what MDNe learns about return uncertainty, we further map the code-embedding outputs to two dimensions via t-SNE [18] and visualize the resulting clustering of uncertainty features across stocks.

Our empirical analysis uses all Chinese A-share main-board stocks from 2018 to 2022. The dataset includes daily prices, volume, 10 information-flow indicators (Table 1), and realized range volatility from 5-minute intraday data. We evaluate forecasting quality with MSE, QLIKE, and CRPS [12] against GARCH-family baselines.

- **Distributional deep framework.** We build a Transformer-based model with stock-code embeddings and a fusion network that outputs a Gaussian mixture distribution, explicitly modeling the dynamic evolution of return distributions under nonlinear market structure.
- **Embedding-based uncertainty analysis.** We learn stock representations with code embeddings and use t-SNE to visualize uncertainty similarity, providing an interpretable view of shared risk patterns across assets.
- **Risk modeling and empirical validation.** We assess uncertainty step by step over time and show, through comparisons with GARCH-family models, that the proposed method improves volatility-forecasting accuracy in practice.

2 Dataset and Method

2.1 Data Source

We collected data for all A-share main board listed companies in China from January 2018 to December 2022. The dataset was divided as follows: data samples from 2018 to 2020 were used as the training set to optimize the model parameters, while data samples from 2021 to 2022 served as the test set to verify the out-of-sample performance of the trained model. Additionally, for the deep learning model, we selected six-month data samples from the second half of 2020 as the validation set to adjust hyperparameters and prevent overfitting. Since the GARCH model and its variants have fewer hyperparameters, no separate validation set was used for them.

To meet the requirements of GARCH models, which need sufficient sample points for each stock, we excluded stocks listed or delisted in the past two years, resulting in a final dataset of 3226 stock samples. For the deep learning model, we constructed 10 distinct technical indicators based on daily trading volume and price data from these stocks. The detailed formulas for these indicators can be found in Table 1, which capture information from both volume and price data across time and cross-sectional dimensions.

In addition, we used intraday data with a 5-min frequency to compute the realized range volatility (RRV) as described in Eq. (1).

$$\mathrm{RRV}_t = \frac{1}{4\log(2)} \sum_{i=1}^{n} (\log(\mathrm{H}_{i,t}) - \log(\mathrm{L}_{i,t}))^2, \tag{1}$$

Table 1. Summary of indicators.

Indicator	Formula	Description
RANK60	Rank(close, 60)	Percentile of current close in past 60-day close prices.
BETA5	Slope(close, 5)/close	Rate of close-price change over past 5 days, normalized by latest close.
BETA20	Slope(close, 20)/close	Rate of close-price change over past 20 days, normalized by latest close.
CNTD60	UP60 − DOWN60	Difference between the percentages of up and down days over past 60 days.
MIN5	Min(low, 5)/close	Minimum low over past 5 days, normalized by latest close.
MIN10	Min(low, 10)/close	Minimum low over past 10 days, normalized by latest close.
KLEN	(high-low)/open	Intraday price range normalized by opening price.
STD5	Std(close, 5)/close	5-day close-price standard deviation, normalized by latest close.
VMA5	Mean(volume, 5)/volume	5-day average volume, normalized by latest volume.
VSTD10	Std(volume, 10)/volume	10-day volume standard deviation, normalized by latest volume.

where $\mathrm{H}_{i,t}$ and $\mathrm{L}_{i,t}$ respectively present the highest and lowest prices observed in interval $i = 1, ..., n$ on day t. The RRV serves as a reliable proxy for the actual volatility, which actually cannot be directly measured. Specifically, the RRV represents the cumulative volatility derived from the amplitude within each time interval throughout the day. Previous research by [6] demonstrates the proximity of the RRV to actual volatility, affirming its validity as a substitute.

2.2 Gaussian Mixture Distribution

It is well known that individual stock return distributions in general deviate from normal or t-distributions, exhibiting more complex patterns such as bimodality or skewness. The Gaussian mixture distribution is a powerful statistical tool that accurately captures and represents the shape of data distributions by combining multiple Gaussian distributions, making it well-suited for characterizing complex distributions of financial asset returns. Its effectiveness is supported by [11], who concluded that the mixture distribution can effectively approximate various types of return distributions. In this paper, we adopt the Gaussian mixture distribution as the model for the stock returns.

The variable $x_t \in \mathbb{R}$ represents the space of return values at time step t. The basic mathematical form of a Gaussian mixture distribution $\mathrm{Q}_t(x_t)$, which models the distribution of returns, is a weighted sum of multiple Gaussian distributions as expressed on Eq. (2). Each Gaussian distribution is defined by its mean $\mu_{i,t}$, standard deviation $\sigma_{i,t}$, and is weighted by $w_{i,t}$ to form $\mathrm{Q}_t(x_t)$. These weights sum to 1, ensuring that the entire mixture distribution is a valid representation of the probability distribution. Specifically, the mixture distribution takes the form:

$$\mathrm{Q}_t(x_t) = \sum_{i=1}^{n} w_{i,t} \cdot \mathcal{N}(\mu_{i,t}, \sigma_{i,t}), \qquad \sum_{i=1}^{n} w_{i,t} = 1. \tag{2}$$

where $t = 1, 2, 3, \ldots, m$ represents the time steps, $Q_t(x_t)$ represents the distribution of returns at time t, x_t represents the return value, $w_{i,t}$ represents the weight of the i-th Gaussian component, $\mu_{i,t}$ represents the mean of the i-th Gaussian component, and $\sigma_{i,t}$ represents the standard deviation of the i-th Gaussian component. The parameter n represents the number of Gaussian components.

Consider a mixture of five one-dimensional Gaussian distributions as an example. In Fig. 1, the dotted lines in different colors represent the individual Gaussian distributions, while the solid line shows the probability density function of the Gaussian mixture distribution formed by these components. It is evident that the weighted sum of these components, with specific weights, results in a uniquely defined Gaussian mixture distribution. By varying the weights, the mixture distribution can exhibit a range of non-traditional distribution patterns.

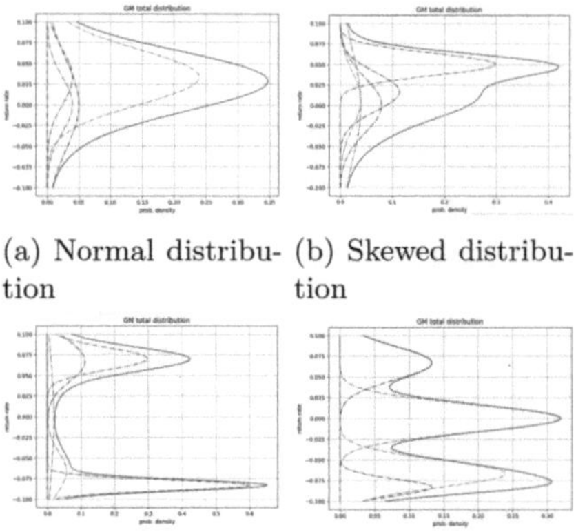

(a) Normal distribution (b) Skewed distribution (c) Bimodal distribution (d) Multimodal distribution

Fig. 1. Examples of return densities generated by a five-component Gaussian mixture: (a) near-normal, (b) skewed, (c) bimodal, and (d) multimodal.

The variance of the Gaussian mixture distribution σ_t^2 serves as a key measure of the distribution's volatility, calculated based on the variance and mean of each component's Gaussian distribution. This can be computed using Eq. (3):

$$\sigma_t^2 = \sum_{i=1}^{n} w_{i,t} \cdot (\mu_{i,t}^2 + \sigma_{i,t}^2) - \left(\sum_{i=1}^{n} w_{i,t} \cdot \mu_{i,t} \right)^2 .. \quad (3)$$

The variance expression follows from the mixture mean and second moment:

$$\mu_t = \int_{-\infty}^{\infty} x f_t(x)\, dx = \sum_{i=1}^{n} w_{i,t} \int_{-\infty}^{\infty} x f_{i,t}(x)\, dx = \sum_{i=1}^{n} w_{i,t} \mu_{i,t}. \quad (4)$$

$$\mathrm{E}[X^2] = \int_{-\infty}^{\infty} x^2 f_t(x)\, dx = \sum_{i=1}^{n} w_{i,t} \int_{-\infty}^{\infty} x^2 f_{i,t}(x)\, dx = \sum_{i=1}^{n} w_{i,t}(\mu_{i,t}^2 + \sigma_{i,t}^2). \quad (5)$$

By the law of total variance:

$$\sigma_t^2 = \mathrm{E}[X^2] - \mu_t^2 = \sum_{i=1}^{n} w_{i,t} \cdot (\mu_{i,t}^2 + \sigma_{i,t}^2) - \left(\sum_{i=1}^{n} w_{i,t} \cdot \mu_{i,t} \right)^2 . \quad (6)$$

2.3 Model Architecture

We use a mixture density network to predict the conditional distribution of next-day returns rather than only a point estimate. The architecture combines a Transformer-based encoder for time-series indicators, instantiated as Crossformer [23], with a stock-code embedding branch, then fuses both representations to output Gaussian mixture parameters.

Crossformer is chosen as a representative Transformer variant for time-series modeling because it captures both temporal and cross-dimensional dependencies effectively. This setup allows the model to represent nonlinear return dynamics while keeping uncertainty estimation explicit in the output layer.

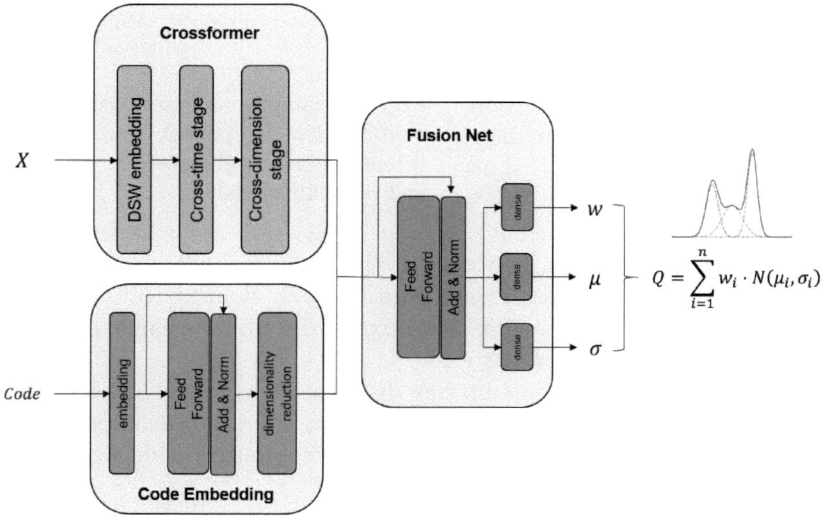

Fig. 2. Network structure of MDNe. The indicator branch (Crossformer) and code-embedding branch are fused to output Gaussian mixture parameters w, μ, and σ.

Following the mixture density network framework of [5], we integrate Crossformer and code embeddings for conditional return-distribution forecasting. As shown in Fig. 2, the Crossformer branch takes ten technical indicators $X \in \mathbb{R}^{C \times T}$, where C is the number of indicators and T is the historical window length.

In parallel, each stock code is mapped to an integer index and then to a dense embedding vector through a learnable embedding layer. This branch captures stock-specific characteristics that are difficult to infer from time-series indicators alone.

The two branch outputs are fused and passed to the prediction head, which outputs mixture weights, means, and standard deviations. Model parameters are estimated by maximum likelihood, equivalently by minimizing negative log-likelihood:

$$\min_{\theta} \mathcal{L} = \min_{\theta} - \sum_{k=1}^{m} \log \left(Q(y|x_k; \theta) \right) \tag{7}$$

subject to

$$w_i(x;\theta) \geq 0, \quad \sigma_i(x;\theta) > 0, \quad \sum_{i=1}^{n} w_i(x;\theta) = 1, \tag{8}$$

where

$$Q(y|x;\theta) = \sum_{i=1}^{n} w_i(x;\theta) \mathcal{N}(y|\mu_i(x;\theta), \sigma_i(x;\theta)), \tag{9}$$

$$\mathcal{N}(y|\mu_i, \sigma_i) = \frac{1}{\sqrt{2\pi\sigma_i^2}} \exp\left(-\frac{(y-\mu_i)^2}{2\sigma_i^2} \right). \tag{10}$$

In (7), m is the number of training samples, x denotes model inputs, and θ denotes trainable parameters. The output vectors (w, μ, σ) define the Gaussian mixture distribution of returns; their length is determined by the number of mixture components n. In the experiments, we set $n = 9$.

2.4 Code Embedding and T-SNE Visualization

Because the model is trained on thousands of stocks, we include stock-code embeddings to represent persistent cross-sectional characteristics. As illustrated in Fig. 3, each stock code is tokenized, mapped to a learnable dense vector, and trained jointly with the forecasting objective.

To interpret the learned representation, we project embeddings into two dimensions via t-SNE [18] and color each point by risk-related attributes. Embedding spaces are known to encode meaningful similarity structures [19], and here stocks with similar uncertainty-related attributes tend to cluster together, providing a complementary interpretation of the model outputs.

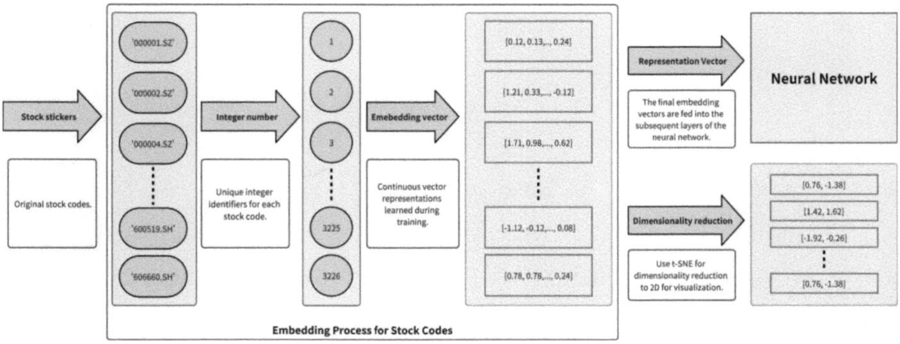

Fig. 3. Stock code embedding workflow: stock identifiers are tokenized, mapped to dense vectors, and then used by downstream prediction or visualization modules.

3 Empirical Results

3.1 Evaluation Setup

We evaluate the proposed MDNe (MDN with code embeddings) against a control MDN without embeddings to isolate the embedding contribution.

We compare both deep models with GARCH, GJR-GARCH, APARCH, and TARCH, all set to univariate form with $p = q = 1$ and zero-mean returns; this focuses the comparison on volatility modeling rather than mean dynamics or model-order complexity, without biasing MSE/QLIKE computation.

Evaluation uses MSE, QLIKE, and CRPS. MSE/QLIKE measure deviations between predicted volatility and RRV, while CRPS measures consistency between predicted return distributions and realized returns.

The sample contains price and volume data for 3,226 A-share main-board stocks listed in China before 2020, split into 2018–2020 for training (with the second half of 2020 held out for validation and hyperparameter tuning) and 2021–2022 for out-of-sample testing. MDN/MDNe are trained as one pooled network over all stocks to capture cross-stock patterns, whereas GARCH-family models are fitted separately per stock; both are updated annually under an expanding-window setup (e.g., 2022 forecasts use 2018–2021 as training data) to keep the test window strictly out-of-sample. Volatility forecast curves for representative stocks are shown in Fig. 4.

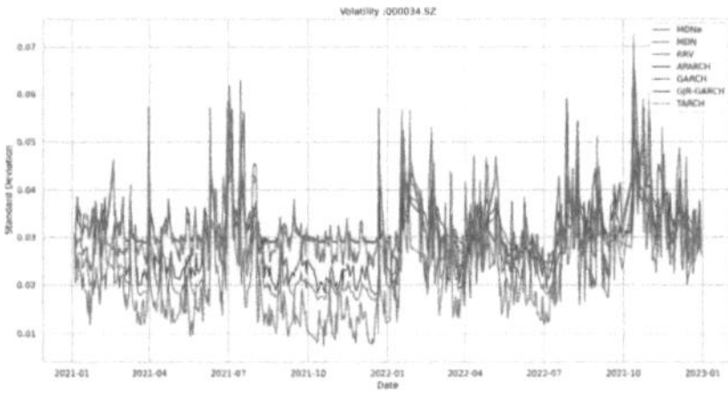

(a) stock code:000034.SZ

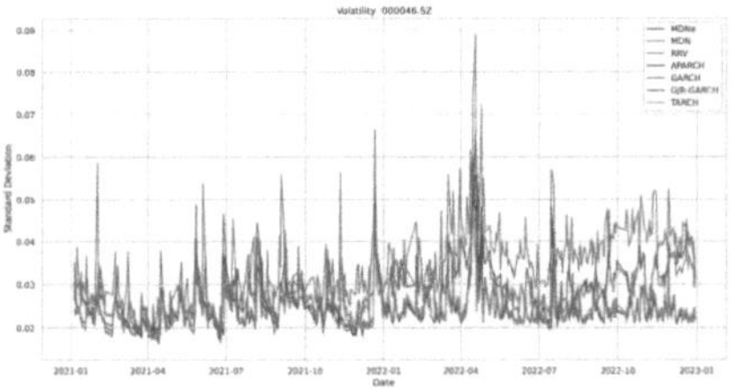

(b) stock code:000046.SZ

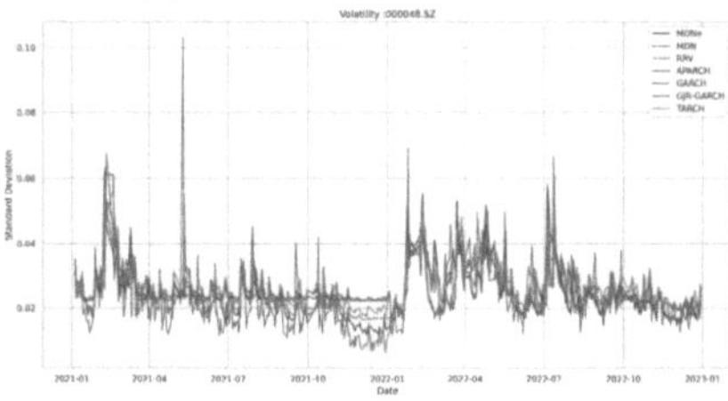

(c) stock code:000048.SZ

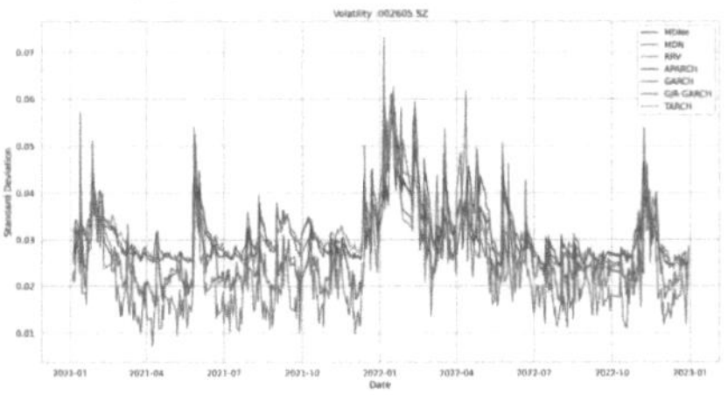

(d) stock code:002605.SZ

Fig. 4. Volatility forecasts for four sample stocks. MDN/MDNe track the RRV proxy more closely than GARCH-family baselines, especially during short-term fluctuations.

As shown in Fig. 4, MDN and MDNe produce trajectories closer to RRV than GARCH-family models for most short-term movements. We next verify this pattern over all stocks with quantitative metrics.

3.2 Evaluation Results

The overall results in Table 2 show that MDNe achieves the lowest average loss on all three metrics (CRPS, MSE, and QLIKE).

Table 2. Evaluation of out-of-sample volatility forecasts.

Forecasting horizon	MDNe	MDN	GARCH	GJR-GARCH	APARCH	TARCH
Total stock average:						
CRPS (%)	**1.4683**	1.4701	1.4856	1.4862	1.4881	1.4865
MSE	**0.7233**	0.7526	0.8942	0.8539	1.1537	0.8896
QLIKE	**1.8501**	1.8553	1.8657	1.8661	1.8664	1.8650
10% quantile:						
CRPS (%)	1.0358	**1.0335**	1.0502	1.0518	1.0522	1.0518
MSE	0.3542	0.3825	0.3597	0.3789	**0.3528**	0.3607
QLIKE	**1.5976**	1.6072	1.6070	1.6089	1.6054	1.6064
20% quantile:						
CRPS (%)	1.1786	**1.1733**	1.2002	1.1999	1.1988	1.1989
MSE	**0.4425**	0.4515	0.4710	0.4848	0.4675	0.4668
QLIKE	**1.7039**	1.7077	1.7111	1.7119	1.7111	1.7117
50% quantile:						
CRPS (%)	1.4675	**1.4659**	1.4819	1.4824	1.4835	1.4831
MSE	0.6512	**0.6474**	0.7559	0.7620	0.7568	0.7292
QLIKE	1.8685	**1.8683**	1.8803	1.8802	1.8791	1.8789
80% quantile:						
CRPS (%)	**1.7652**	1.7722	1.7878	1.7855	1.7877	1.7858
MSE	**0.9645**	0.9703	1.1662	1.1856	1.1744	1.1396
QLIKE	2.0329	**2.0325**	2.0384	2.0396	2.0403	2.0383
90% quantile:						
CRPS (%)	**1.9406**	1.9489	1.9556	1.9563	1.9565	1.9566
MSE	**1.1790**	1.2288	1.4662	1.4816	1.4860	1.4589
QLIKE	2.1154	**2.1125**	2.1256	2.1263	2.1295	2.1257

Notes. Bold values indicate the best (lowest-loss) model in each row.

At low-volatility quantiles, MDN can occasionally match or slightly outperform MDNe. As volatility increases, MDN/MDNe tend to achieve lower losses than GARCH-family models, and MDNe attains the best CRPS and MSE in most quantiles. Overall, the results are consistent with stronger performance of distributional deep models under high-uncertainty regimes.

To further assess whether these loss differences are systematic, we report Diebold-Mariano (DM) test statistics [9] for MSE and QLIKE losses. For each stock-day in the test window we compute a per-observation loss differential between the two compared models, pool the differentials across stocks and days, and apply the standard DM statistic with a heteroskedasticity- and autocorrelation-consistent (HAC) long-run variance estimator to account for residual serial correlation. Positive statistics indicate that the column model has lower loss than the row model; the reported p-values are uncorrected pairwise tests, and the consistent direction observed across all baselines indicates that the conclusions are not driven by a single comparison.

Table 3. Diebold-Mariano test results.

Forecasting horizon	MDNe	MDN	GARCH	GJR-GARCH	APARCH
MSE Loss					
MDN	12.44**				
GARCH	84.29**	72.8**			
GJR-GARCH	87.84**	75.62**	22.82**		
APARCH	21.83**	21.16**	15.50**	14.78**	
TARCH	42.02**	38.65**	12.62**	9.04**	−14.41**
QLIKE Loss					
MDN	42.23**				
GARCH	134.88**	109.19**			
GJR-GARCH	138.59**	113.08**	20.69**		
APARCH	129.76**	107.43**	17.26**	6.17**	
TARCH	120.80**	96.08**	−17.38**	−32.82**	−28.99**

Notes. Positive values indicate better performance of the column model.
** indicates $p < 0.01$.

As reported in Table 3, findings are broadly consistent across MSE and QLIKE: most pairwise comparisons favor MDNe, and many of these differences are significant at the 1% level.

3.3 Similarity of Return Uncertainty

To provide an interpretable view of learned stock representations, we project code embeddings to two dimensions using t-SNE and color points by risk-related attributes. This visualization highlights cross-asset similarity patterns in uncertainty space.

For visualization, each attribute is converted to a relative ranking $c_i = r_i/S$, where c_i is the color value for stock i, r_i is its rank on the selected attribute, and S is the number of stocks.

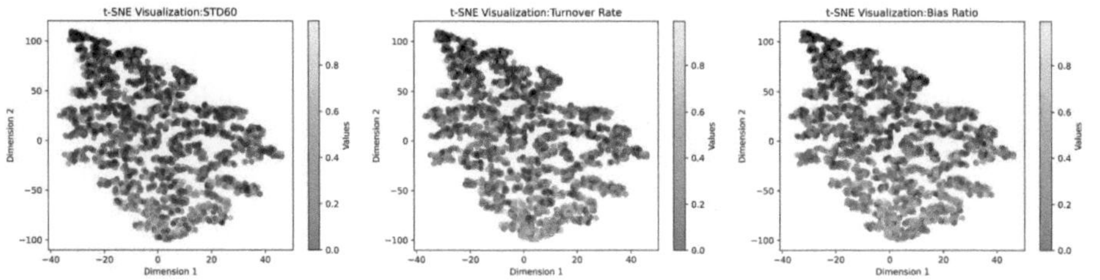

(a) STD60. (b) Turnover rate. (c) Bias ratio.

Fig. 5. t-SNE map of learned stock embeddings colored by STD60, turnover rate, and bias ratio. Nearby points typically share similar risk attributes.

Since t-SNE is designed to preserve local neighborhoods [18], the smooth color gradients in Fig. 5, rather than a random color pattern, indicate that stocks close in the learned embedding space tend to share similar values on each risk attribute. We therefore treat this view as an interpretability-oriented analysis that complements the quantitative CRPS/MSE/QLIKE results.

3.4 Robustness Analysis

We evaluate robustness by training MDN and MDNe for 30 independent runs and comparing CRPS distributions. We focus on deep models because stochastic optimization and initialization can affect performance. As shown in Fig. 6, MDNe is both more accurate (lower median CRPS) and more stable (narrower spread), indicating stronger robustness than MDN.

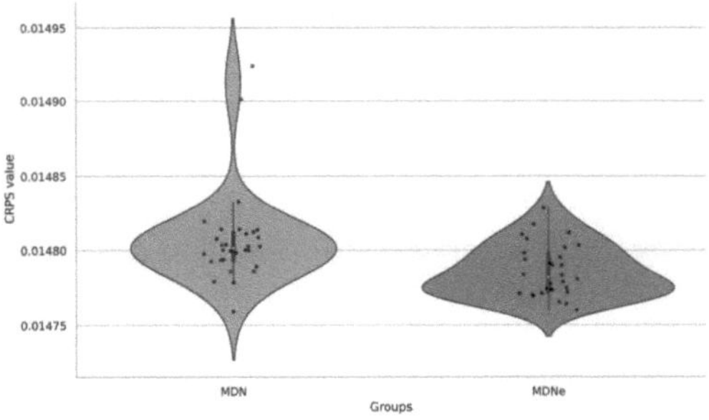

Fig. 6. CRPS distributions over 30 runs. MDNe has a lower median and a tighter spread than MDN.

4 Conclusion

This study models stock return uncertainty with a Gaussian-mixture deep framework and evaluates both volatility accuracy and distributional calibration. On Chinese A-share data, the proposed method outperforms GARCH-family baselines across key metrics, with stronger gains in high-volatility regimes. The embedding-based t-SNE analysis further provides an interpretable view of uncertainty similarity across assets. Overall, integrating deep learning with distributional modeling improves practical uncertainty quantification for financial risk management.

Acknowledgements. This work was supported in part by the Shenzhen Ubiquitous Data Enabling Key Lab under Grant ZDSYS20220527171406015, and in part by the Tsinghua Shenzhen International Graduate School-Shenzhen Pengrui Endowed Professorship Scheme of Shenzhen Pengrui Foundation.

References

1. Abdar, M., et al.: A review of uncertainty quantification in deep learning: techniques, applications and challenges. Inf. Fusion **76**, 243–297 (2021)
2. Anderson, E.W., Ghysels, E., Juergens, J.L.: The impact of risk and uncertainty on expected returns. J. Financ. Econ. **94**(2), 233–263 (2009)
3. Bali, T.G., Zhou, H.: Risk, uncertainty, and expected returns. J. Financ. Quant. Anal. **51**(3), 707–735 (2016)
4. Baltussen, G., Van Bekkum, S., Van Der Grient, B.: Unknown unknowns: uncertainty about risk and stock returns. J. Financ. Quant. Anal. **53**(4), 1615–1651 (2018)
5. Bishop, C.: Mixture Density Networks. Workingpaper, Aston University (1994)
6. Christensen, K., Podolskij, M.: Realized range-based estimation of integrated variance. J. Econometrics **141**(2), 323–349 (2007)
7. Clark, P.K.: A subordinated stochastic process model with finite variance for speculative prices. Econometrica **41**(1), 135–155 (1973)
8. Darolles, S., Le Fol, G., Mero, G.: Mixture of distribution hypothesis: analyzing daily liquidity frictions and information flows. J. Econometrics **201**(2), 367–383 (2017). Dec
9. Diebold, F.X., Mariano, R.S.: Comparing predictive accuracy. J. Bus. Econ. Stat. **13**(3), 253–263 (1995)
10. Engle, R.: Dynamic conditional correlation: a simple class of multivariate generalized autoregressive conditional heteroskedasticity models. J. Bus. Econ. Stat. **20**(3), 339–350 (2002)
11. Giacomini, R., Gottschling, A., Haefke, C., White, H.: Mixtures of t-distributions for finance and forecasting. J. Econometrics **144**(1), 175–192 (2008). May
12. Gneiting, T., Raftery, A.E.: Strictly proper scoring rules, prediction, and estimation. J. Am. Stat. Assoc. **102**(477), 359–378 (2007)
13. Gu, S., Kelly, B., Xiu, D.: Empirical asset pricing via machine learning. Rev. Financ. Stud. **33**(5), 2223–2273 (2020)
14. Han, B., Hong, D., Warachka, M.: Forecast accuracy uncertainty and momentum. Manage. Sci. **55**(6), 1035–1046 (2009)
15. Han, C.: Bimodal characteristic returns and predictability enhancement via machine learning. Manage. Sci. **68**(10), 7701–7741 (2022)
16. Jagabathula, S., Subramanian, L., Venkataraman, A.: A conditional gradient approach for nonparametric estimation of mixing distributions. Manage. Sci. **66**(8), 3635–3656 (2020)
17. Leippold, M., Wang, Q., Zhou, W.: Machine learning in the Chinese stock market. J. Financ. Econ. **145**(2, Part A), 64–82 (2022)
18. Maaten, L.v.d., Hinton, G.: Visualizing data using t-SNE. J. Mach. Learn. Res. **9**(86), 2579–2605 (2008)
19. Mikolov, T., Chen, K., Corrado, G.S., Dean, J.: Efficient estimation of word representations in vector space (2013)

20. Rachev, S., SenGupta, A.: Laplace-weibull mixtures for modeling price changes. Manage. Sci. **39**(8), 1029–1038 (1993)
21. Ross, S.A.: Information and volatility: the no-arbitrage martingale approach to timing and resolution irrelevancy. J. Financ. **44**(1), 1–17 (1989)
22. Zakoian, J.M.: Threshold heteroskedastic models. J. Econ. Dyn. Control **18**(5), 931–955 (1994)
23. Zhang, Y., Yan, J.: Crossformer: transformer utilizing cross-dimension dependency for multivariate time series forecasting. In: International Conference on Learning Representations (2023)
24. Zhou, Y., Fan, J., Xue, L.: How much can machines learn finance from Chinese text data? Manag. Sci. (2024)

Diagnosing Domain Shift in Wav2Vec2-Based Cross-Corpus Speech Emotion Recognition

Hoang-Anh-Hong Trinh and Tran-Ngoc-Tran Le(✉)

FPT University, Greenwich Vietnam, Ho Chi Minh campus, Hanoi, Vietnam
hongthagcs230008@fpt.edu.vn, tranltn2@fe.edu.vn

Abstract. Cross-corpus speech emotion recognition (SER) remains a persistent challenge due to distributional mismatch across datasets in terms of speakers, recording conditions, and expression styles. We present a rigorous diagnostic benchmark for cross-corpus SER, providing the community with a reproducible evaluation framework and systematic evidence of the factors driving domain shift in self-supervised speech encoders. Concretely, we construct a unified four-corpus benchmark from RAVDESS, TESS, SAVEE, and CREMA-D (13,174 utterances) with a fully documented preprocessing and augmentation pipeline, and conduct a comprehensive comparison of spectrogram-based CNN baselines, hybrid CNN–RNN and CNN–LSTM models, and fine-tuned Wav2Vec2 under in-domain, leave-one-dataset-out (LODO), and 2v2 cross-corpus evaluation protocols. While Wav2Vec2 achieves strong in-domain accuracy (0.96 on 3-way sentiment, 0.76 on 8-way emotion), cross-corpus accuracy degrades to 0.38–0.43 in LODO and collapses toward random guessing in several 2v2 configurations, even with aggressive class balancing and data augmentation. Parameter-efficient fine-tuning improves computational efficiency but does not fundamentally address this bottleneck. These results provide strong evidence that domain shift, rather than model capacity or class imbalance, is the primary obstacle to robust cross-corpus SER and that our benchmark establishes a reproducible foundation for developing the next generation of domain-invariant and adaptation-aware architectures.

Keywords: Speech emotion recognition · Cross-corpus generalization · Domain shift · Wav2Vec2 · Diagnostic benchmark

1 Introduction

Speech emotion recognition (SER) is a key component in affect-aware technologies such as conversational agents, telehealth platforms, call center analytics, and social robots. Unlike sentiment analysis, which relies primarily on lexical content, SER focuses on acoustic cues including prosody, spectral shape, and voice quality that reflect underlying affective states. A large body of work has

L. Ding et al. (Eds.): APWeb-WAIM 2026, LNCS 16995, pp. 508–519, 2027.
https://doi.org/10.1007/978-981-92-5699-0_34

reported high recognition accuracy on individual benchmark corpora, yet most evaluations assume that training and test data share the same recording conditions and speaker characteristics, an assumption that rarely holds in realistic deployment scenarios.

Traditional SER systems typically adopt a pipeline of preprocessing, handcrafted acoustic feature extraction, and classical classification. Studies combining prosodic and spectral descriptors such as MFCC, LPC, energy, zero crossing rate, and pitch with models like SVM, kNN, random forest, Gaussian Naive Bayes, or multilayer perceptrons have achieved impressive in-domain performance, often exceeding ninety-five percent accuracy on controlled datasets [2,5,7,8]. However, these approaches struggle to generalise across speakers, languages, and corpora, since manually engineered features tend to capture dataset specific artefacts rather than domain-invariant emotional patterns.

Deep learning has advanced SER by learning representations directly from time frequency inputs. Convolutional models operating on Mel or log Mel spectrograms, sometimes followed by recurrent layers such as LSTM or GRU, consistently outperform traditional pipelines on single corpora [1,3,11,12]. On this combined dataset, sentiment-level CNN RNN and CNN LSTM architectures achieved test accuracies of approximately eighty-three percent and eighty-one percent, with strong area under the curve scores, demonstrating that deep models can learn robust features when training and test distributions are aligned.

More recently, self-supervised transformer models such as Wav2Vec2 have been adapted to SER by fine-tuning pre-trained encoders on labelled emotion data [4]. These models learn contextualised representations directly from raw waveforms and frequently surpass CNN and LSTM baselines on in-domain benchmarks. Parameter-efficient fine-tuning strategies, including partial layer updating and mixed precision training, have been proposed to reduce computational cost while preserving accuracy [9]. Despite these advances, empirical studies consistently show that SER models, including transformer-based ones, degrade markedly when evaluated in cross corpus settings where training and test corpora differ in accent, demographics, recording environment, and emotional acting style [6,10]. Existing work on cross corpus SER has focused mainly on handcrafted or spectrogram features with adversarial or transfer learning methods, and there is limited evidence on how Wav2Vec2-based SER behaves under systematic cross-domain stress tests.

This paper presents a diagnostic study of domain shift in Wav2Vec2-based cross corpus SER. Building on a unified four-corpus benchmark that merges RAVDESS, TESS, SAVEE, and CREMA D, we design a standardised preprocessing and augmentation pipeline and compare spectrogram-based CNN baselines, hybrid CNN RNN and CNN LSTM sentiment models, and Wav2Vec2-based emotion and sentiment classifiers. We then evaluate the strongest models under leave-one-dataset-out (LODO) and two-versus-two (2v2) training and testing protocols in order to quantify how performance degrades when the target corpus is unseen during training. Rather than proposing a new adaptation algorithm, our goal is to clarify where current methods fail and to identify the factors that must be addressed by future domain-invariant and adaptation-aware architectures.

Our contributions are threefold:

- We construct a unified four-corpus SER benchmark by merging RAVDESS, TESS, SAVEE, and CREMA-D into a 13,174-utterance dataset with a fully documented preprocessing and augmentation pipeline and a reproducible evaluation protocol that includes in-domain, leave-one-dataset-out (LODO), and two-versus-two (2v2) regimes.
- We perform a comprehensive comparison of spectrogram-based CNN baselines, hybrid CNN–RNN and CNN–LSTM sentiment models, and Wav2Vec2-based emotion and sentiment classifiers on the unified corpus, quantifying in-domain performance across feature types and architectures and confirming that Wav2Vec2 offers strong in-domain accuracy [1,3,4,12].
- We conduct detailed cross-corpus evaluations of Wav2Vec2-based SER under LODO and 2v2 protocols, showing that accuracy typically falls to the range 0.38–0.46 in LODO experiments and can approach random guessing in some 2v2 configurations even with class balancing and data augmentation, which indicates that domain shift, rather than model capacity or class imbalance, is the primary bottleneck for real-world deployment [6,10]. We analyse these results in terms of corpus differences and fine-tuning strategies, thereby outlining concrete requirements for future domain-invariant and adaptation-aware SER models.

2 Related Work

2.1 Traditional and Deep Learning Approaches to SER

Early SER systems combined hand-crafted acoustic descriptors, including MFCC, pitch, energy, and zero-crossing rate, with classical classifiers such as SVM, MLP, and random forest, achieving strong in-domain performance but limited cross-corpus generalisation due to their reliance on dataset-specific feature artefacts [2,7]. Deep learning substantially advanced the field by enabling end-to-end learning from time–frequency representations: CNN models operating on log-Mel spectrograms learn local spectral patterns, while hybrid CNN–RNN and CNN–LSTM architectures additionally capture longer-range temporal dynamics, consistently outperforming traditional pipelines on single-corpus benchmarks [1,3]. Further improvements have been demonstrated through architectures combining dilated convolutions, residual connections, and attention mechanisms, as well as spatial pyramid pooling, confirming that richer representational capacity benefits in-domain SER when sufficient labelled data are available [11,12]. Nevertheless, both traditional and spectrogram-based deep models remain sensitive to distributional shift across corpora, since their learned representations tend to encode dataset-specific acoustic characteristics rather than domain-invariant emotional structure.

2.2 Self-supervised and Transformer-Based SER

Recent advances in self-supervised learning have led to transformer-based speech encoders such as Wav2Vec2, which learn contextualised representations directly from raw waveforms. These models are pre-trained on large quantities of unlabelled audio using contrastive or masked prediction objectives, and can then be fine-tuned on downstream tasks with relatively modest labelled datasets [4]. In the context of SER, fine-tuning Wav2Vec2 has been shown to outperform many conventional CNN and LSTM baselines on corpora such as RAVDESS, EMO-DB, and IEMOCAP, achieving substantial gains in accuracy and robustness on in-domain evaluations [4].

However, full fine-tuning of all transformer layers is computationally expensive and may cause the model to specialise too strongly to corpus-specific characteristics. Recent work therefore explores parameter-efficient fine-tuning strategies tailored to SER, including freezing most of the encoder and updating only the upper layers, employing low-rank adaptation, and using mixed-precision training to reduce memory consumption and training time [9]. Empirical results indicate that partial fine-tuning of higher transformer blocks can retain most of the performance of full fine-tuning while significantly improving efficiency, making transformer-based SER more accessible for real-world deployment [9]. Nevertheless, existing evaluations remain largely limited to single-corpus or randomly shuffled splits, leaving open questions about how these models behave under strong cross-corpus domain shift.

2.3 Cross-Corpus SER and Domain Adaptation

Cross-corpus SER aims to train models on one or more source datasets and generalise to target datasets with different speakers, recording conditions, and annotation protocols, a setting that more closely reflects dataset-level variability. Latif et al. showed that naively trained deep models suffer significant degradation when tested on unseen corpora, and proposed progressively discriminative transfer networks such as ADDi and sADDi, which use adversarial discriminators to encourage domain-invariant emotional representations without requiring labelled target data [10]. Gideon et al. introduced ADDoG and MADDoG, which iteratively align feature distributions across corpora via adversarial learning in a "meet-in-the-middle" representation space, yielding improved cross-dataset robustness in noisy and in-the-wild conditions [6]. These works highlight that distribution mismatch, rather than model capacity, is the dominant challenge in cross-corpus SER and that explicit domain adaptation is often necessary to bridge the gap.

Despite this progress, most cross-corpus studies have focused on handcrafted features or spectrogram-based deep models, and there is relatively little evidence on how self-supervised transformer encoders behave under comparable evaluation protocols. Moreover, prior work often reports results on limited combinations of datasets or under less stringent splitting strategies, making it difficult to disentangle the effects of class imbalance, augmentation, and architectural choices from intrinsic domain shift. Our study complements this literature by focusing specifically on Wav2Vec2-based SER in a multi-corpus setting, quantifying cross-corpus degradation under leave-one-dataset-out and two-versus-two protocols and diagnosing the extent to which domain shift remains the primary bottleneck even when using powerful pre-trained encoders.

3 Datasets and Preprocessing

We construct a unified English SER corpus by merging four widely used acted emotion datasets: RAVDESS, TESS, SAVEE, and CREMA-D. The combined corpus contains 13,174 utterances after cleaning and preprocessing, covering a diverse range of speakers, recording conditions, and elicited emotions. Table 1 summarises the key characteristics of each corpus.

Table 1. Overview of the four emotional speech corpora used in this study

Dataset	Speakers	Emotions	Utterances	Notes
RAVDESS	24	7	2,452	North American English, studio recorded
TESS	2	7	2,800	Female speakers, Canadian English
SAVEE	4	7	480	Male British English
CREMA-D	91	6	7,442	Diverse accents, crowd-sourced
Combined	–	8	13,174	Unified corpus after cleaning

All audio is subjected to a standardised preprocessing pipeline implemented in Python using Librosa and related libraries. First, every recording is resampled to 22,050 Hz to enforce a consistent temporal resolution while preserving the frequency range relevant for speech and affective cues. Coarse silence trimming with a 30 dB threshold below the peak amplitude removes leading and trailing silence, which reduces irrelevant segments and computational cost. To suppress background noise, Wiener filtering is applied as an adaptive denoising method that attenuates steady-state noise while preserving prosodic and spectral patterns essential for emotion recognition. A finer trimming stage with a 25 dB threshold eliminates residual low-energy artefacts and refines speech boundaries. Finally, peak amplitude normalisation scales each waveform to the range $[-1, 1]$, preventing the models from exploiting loudness differences between speakers or datasets instead of emotion-related structure.

The preprocessing pipeline operates over a speaker-wise directory structure to maintain dataset integrity and to support speaker-independent splits. According to the implementation logs, all 13,174 recordings were processed successfully, with an average reduction in signal duration of approximately 18 percent due to silence removal and an estimated improvement in signal-to-noise ratio of about 3–5 dB. These operations yield a uniform, noise-reduced corpus that is suitable for both spectrogram-based and waveform-based modelling.

To improve generalisation and mitigate class imbalance, stochastic audio augmentation is applied on-the-fly during training but never on validation or test data, in order to avoid information leakage. For waveform-based models, the transformations include additive white Gaussian noise with signal-to-noise ratios between 10 and 20 dB, pitch shifting by up to two semitones, and time stretching with factors between 0.9 and 1.1. For spectrogram-based models, SpecAugment-style frequency and time masking is employed on log-Mel spectrograms, which introduces local occlusions in the time–frequency plane while preserving global structure. After preprocessing, the unified corpus is partitioned into disjoint training, validation, and test splits using speaker-independent criteria, forming a consistent basis for all subsequent experiments on CNN, hybrid, and Wav2Vec2-based SER models.

4 Models and Training Protocol

4.1 Spectrogram-Based CNN Baselines

Following prior work systematically comparing waveform, MFCC, and log-Mel inputs for CNN classifiers [1,3], we adopt log-Mel spectrograms as the primary representation, as they consistently yield the highest accuracy among CNN input variants while preserving both spectral shape and temporal evolution in a format well suited to convolutional models. The baseline CNN consists of three convolutional blocks, each followed by max-pooling, batch normalisation, and non-linear activation, culminating in a global average pooling layer and a fully connected softmax classifier. To better exploit temporal structure, a sliding-window variant segments spectrograms into overlapping 128×128 patches with 10% overlap, with clip-level predictions obtained by probability averaging over windows. This model achieves approximately 59% accuracy on eight-way emotion classification, with strong performance on neutral and surprise but frequent confusion among happy, sad, and fearful, reflecting overlapping acoustic patterns in these categories (Fig. 1).

4.2 Sentiment-Level CNN–RNN, CNN–LSTM, and CNN–ResNet

To reduce label noise and evaluate performance on coarser affective dimensions, we group the eight emotion labels into three sentiment classes: Positive (happy, surprised), Moderate (neutral, calm), and Negative (sad, angry, fearful, disgust).[1] On this sentiment-aggregated corpus, we train three hybrid architectures: CNN–RNN, CNN–LSTM, and CNN–ResNet—all operating on log-Mel spectrogram inputs with a shared convolutional front-end. The CNN–RNN model applies a time-distributed CNN followed by a bidirectional GRU; CNN–LSTM

[1] The assignment of *surprised* to the Positive class follows its acoustic profile in acted corpora, where high arousal and rising prosodic contours make it perceptually similar to happy; surprise is acknowledged to be ambiguously valenced in psychological literature [13].

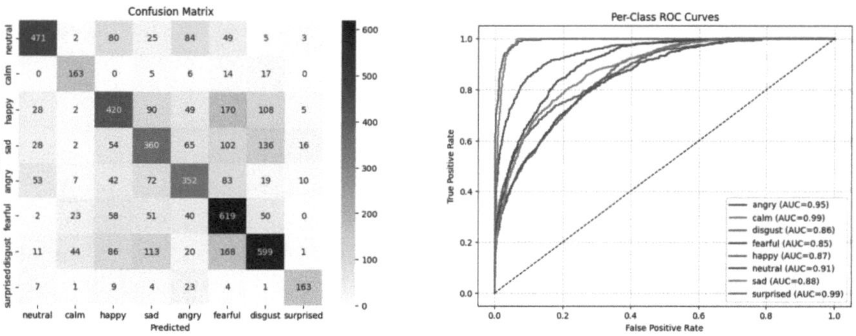

Fig. 1. Sliding-window spectrogram CNN: row-normalized confusion matrix (left) and per-class ROC curves (right).

replaces GRU with bidirectional LSTM for stronger long-range modelling at higher computational cost; CNN–ResNet employs a residual CNN backbone on colour-mapped spectrograms for higher representational capacity. Table 2 summarises results on the sentiment-aggregated corpus.

Table 2. Sentiment-level performance of hybrid CNN architectures.

Model	Accuracy	Macro–F1	Macro–Precision	AUC (avg.)	Notes
CNN–RNN	0.83	0.83	0.83	>0.90	Best overall trade-off
CNN–LSTM	0.81	0.81	0.81	>0.90	Higher training cost
CNN–ResNet	0.76	0.7612	0.7627	>0.8	Overfitting risk

CNN–RNN achieves the best accuracy–complexity trade-off with balanced precision and recall across all three sentiment classes; CNN–ResNet underperforms slightly but may benefit from additional training data or stronger regularisation.

4.3 Wav2Vec2 Fine-Tuned Models

For transformer-based baselines, we fine-tune a Wav2Vec2-base encoder with a task-specific classification head for both eight-way emotion recognition and three-class sentiment classification on the unified corpus [4]. The encoder consists of a convolutional feature extractor followed by a stack of transformer blocks that produce contextualised frame-level representations. A global pooling layer aggregates frame embeddings into a fixed-size utterance representation, which feeds a fully connected layer with softmax output.

All audio is resampled to 16 kHz and normalised before being passed to the Wav2Vec2 feature extractor. We initialise from a publicly available Base checkpoint and fine-tune using the Adam optimiser with a learning rate of 3 ×

10^{-5}, batch size of 32, and up to 50 epochs, employing early stopping based on validation loss [4]. Mixed-precision (FP16) training is used to reduce memory consumption and accelerate optimisation. For the main experiments, we adopt full fine-tuning where all transformer layers are updated, and we additionally explore parameter-efficient variants that freeze lower layers and update only the upper blocks and classification head, in line with recent work on efficient SER fine-tuning [9].

The eight-way emotion model is trained on the unified, speaker-independent split and evaluated using accuracy, macro-averaged F1-score, and per-class precision and recall. The sentiment model uses the same encoder but a three-class output layer and is trained on the sentiment-grouped labels. In-domain results confirm that Wav2Vec2-based models outperform spectrogram CNN baselines on both emotion and sentiment tasks, providing a strong foundation for the subsequent cross-corpus evaluations reported in Sect. 5 (Table 3).

Table 3. In-domain performance of Wav2Vec2-based SER on the unified corpus.

Task	Accuracy	Notes
8-way emotion	0.76	Strong performance on calm and angry; happy and surprise remain challenging.
3-way sentiment	0.96	High precision and recall across all sentiment classes.

Parameter-efficient fine-tuning variants that freeze lower Wav2Vec2 layers and update only the upper blocks and classification head exhibit in-domain accuracy within a few percentage points of full fine-tuning, while substantially reducing training time and memory consumption. However, as discussed in Sect. 5, these strategies have only marginal impact on cross-corpus robustness, indicating that computational efficiency can be improved without fundamentally altering the sensitivity of the model to domain shift.

5 Cross-Corpus Evaluation

We evaluate cross-corpus robustness of the Wav2Vec2-based SER models using two complementary protocols: leave-one-dataset-out (LODO) and two-versus-two (2v2) training and testing. Both settings are designed to simulate realistic deployment scenarios in which the target corpus differs systematically from the training data, a regime known to expose severe domain shift in prior SER work [6,10].

5.1 Leave-One-Dataset-Out (LODO) Evaluation

In the LODO protocol, the model is trained on three of the four datasets and evaluated on the remaining unseen dataset. This process is repeated four times so that each corpus serves once as the held-out target. The same Wav2Vec2-based architecture and training configuration used for in-domain experiments are retained, including class balancing through augmentation on the training partitions. Table 4 summarises the results in terms of accuracy, macro-averaged precision, recall, and F1-score for each target dataset.

Table 4. LODO evaluation of Wav2Vec2-based SER with class balancing and augmentation.

Test dataset	Accuracy	Precision	Recall	F1
RAVDESS	0.43	0.38	0.43	0.36
TESS	0.40	0.66	0.40	0.37
SAVEE	0.38	0.53	0.38	0.34
CREMA-D	0.36	0.53	0.36	0.40

Despite the strong in-domain performance of Wav2Vec2-based models, LODO accuracy collapses to approximately 0.36–0.43 across target corpora, with F1-scores in the mid-0.30 s. This represents a substantial degradation compared with single-corpus or pooled evaluations and confirms that class balancing and augmentation alone do not resolve cross-corpus mismatch. The relatively higher precision on TESS and CREMA-D suggests that some emotion categories remain separable in the target distributions, but the low recall indicates that many target instances fall outside the learned decision regions. These findings are consistent with earlier reports that deep models trained on one corpus or a pool of corpora often fail to generalise to unseen datasets without explicit domain adaptation [6, 10].

5.2 Two-Versus-Two (2v2) Evaluation

To further probe distribution shift, we adopt a 2v2 protocol in which two datasets are used for training and the remaining two are reserved for testing. This setting is more challenging than LODO because both the language and recording conditions of the test corpora may differ substantially from the training pair. We explore all ordered combinations of two training and two test datasets and report accuracy, macro precision, and macro F1-score in Table 5.

The 2v2 results expose an even more severe form of domain shift than LODO. Some train/test pairs, such as CREMA-D + SAVEE training with RAVDESS + TESS testing or CREMA-D + RAVDESS training with SAVEE + TESS testing, retain moderate accuracy around 0.36–0.38 and F1-scores above 0.30, suggesting that these corpus pairs share partially compatible acoustic and expressive characteristics. In contrast, other configurations collapse to near-random performance: training on CREMA-D + TESS and testing on RAVDESS + SAVEE yields an accuracy of 0.122, and training on RAVDESS + SAVEE and testing on CREMA-D + TESS yields an accuracy of 0.039 with F1 close to zero.

Table 5. 2v2 cross-corpus evaluation for Wav2Vec2-based SER.

Train datasets	Test datasets	Accuracy	Precision	F1
CREMA+D + SAVEE	RAVDESS + TESS	0.383	0.391	0.311
CREMA+D + TESS	RAVDESS + SAVEE	0.122	0.026	0.042
SAVEE + TESS	CREMA+D + RAVDESS	0.305	0.351	0.268
CREMA+D + RAVDESS	SAVEE + TESS	0.365	0.563	0.366
RAVDESS + SAVEE	CREMA+D + TESS	0.039	0.002	0.003
RAVDESS + TESS	CREMA+D + SAVEE	0.194	0.470	0.215

This extreme variability indicates that cross-corpus generalisation strongly depends on the specific combination of training and test datasets. Pairs that mix corpora with similar recording setups or acting styles, such as CREMA-D with RAVDESS, tend to transfer better, whereas combinations that span large differences in accent, demographic profiles, or microphone characteristics exhibit almost no transfer at all. The asymmetry between certain train–test pairs further suggests that the direction of transfer matters: learning from more diverse or noisy corpora does not automatically guarantee robustness when transferring to more controlled datasets, and vice versa. Overall, the 2v2 evaluation underscores that even powerful self-supervised encoders remain highly sensitive to domain shift in SER and that explicit mechanisms for domain-invariant representation learning or adaptation are required to achieve reliable cross-corpus performance [6,10].

6 Discussion

The empirical results highlight that domain shift is the dominant failure mode for Wav2Vec2-based SER in cross-corpus settings. Although the model attains strong in-domain accuracy on the unified corpus, LODO and 2v2 evaluations reveal that performance degrades sharply when the target dataset is unseen during training, with accuracy approaching random guessing in several 2v2 configurations despite extensive class balancing and augmentation. This pattern indicates that the learned representations remain strongly tied to corpus-specific characteristics rather than capturing domain-invariant emotional structure, consistent with prior observations on cross-corpus SER [6,10].

Several factors contribute to this shift. At the corpus level, accent and pronunciation differences (North American English in RAVDESS and TESS, British English in SAVEE, and diverse accents in CREMA-D), divergent speaker demographics (four male speakers in SAVEE versus ninety-one diverse actors in CREMA-D), and heterogeneous recording conditions (studio versus crowd-sourced environments) collectively distort the marginal distribution of acoustic features and make it difficult for the model to disentangle speaker identity from emotion. At the modelling level, full fine-tuning of all Wav2Vec2 layers amplifies corpus specialisation: while it maximises in-domain performance, it causes the model to overfit the joint distribution of speakers, recording conditions, and acting styles present in the training data. Parameter-efficient strategies that freeze lower layers partially mitigate this effect but do not eliminate cross-corpus degradation [6,10].

Adversarial and discrepancy-based methods such as ADDi, sADDi, ADDoG, and MADDoG directly address distribution mismatch by encouraging domain-invariant feature alignment [6,10], and our results suggest that similar mechanisms are necessary when fine-tuning self-supervised speech encoders for SER if cross-corpus robustness is a priority. To contextualise the observed degradation, Table 6 compares our baselines against published adversarial UDA results; direct comparison is approximate due to differences in dataset splits, label sets, and evaluation metrics.

Table 6. Contextual comparison with published cross-corpus SER methods. † Results from original papers; UAR = unweighted average recall, approximately equivalent to accuracy on balanced test sets.

Method	Type	Corpus setting	Metric†
ADDoG [6]†	Adversarial domain gen.	IEMOCAP→MSP-Improv (3-cl.)	UAR: 0.444–0.474
MADDoG [6]†	Multi-corpus adversarial	IEMOCAP + MSP + PRI-ORI	UAR: 0.462–0.481
ADDi/sADDi [10]†	Adversarial dual discrim.	IEMOCAP/MSP/EmoDB	UAR: 0.48–0.56
Wav2Vec2 ours (LODO)	No adaptation	4-corpus, 8-class	Acc: 0.36–0.43
Wav2Vec2 ours (2v2)	No adaptation	4-corpus, 8-class	Acc: 0.039–0.383

The gap between our non-adaptive baseline (LODO 0.36–0.43 on 8-class) and adversarial UDA methods (UAR 0.44–0.56 on 3–4 class tasks) suggests that explicit domain-invariant mechanisms could recover 8–15 percentage points of the observed degradation, reinforcing that adaptation-aware fine-tuning of self-supervised encoders is a well-motivated direction for future work.

7 Conclusion

This paper presented a diagnostic study of domain shift in Wav2Vec2-based cross-corpus SER using a unified four-corpus benchmark (RAVDESS, TESS, SAVEE, and CREMA-D). Fine-tuned Wav2Vec2 achieves strong in-domain accuracy (0.96 on 3-way sentiment, 0.76 on 8-way emotion) but degrades sharply under LODO (0.36–0.43) and collapses toward random guessing in several 2v2 configurations, providing clear evidence that domain shift, not model capacity or class imbalance, is the primary bottleneck for cross-corpus deployment. Parameter-efficient fine-tuning improves computational efficiency but does not fundamentally address this bottleneck. These findings motivate future work on integrating adversarial or discrepancy-based domain adaptation objectives directly into the fine-tuning of self-supervised encoders, exploring domain-conditioned architectures such as multi-task learning or mixture-of-experts, and combining uncertainty estimation with domain-aware training to enable reliable out-of-distribution detection in heterogeneous deployment scenarios.

References

1. Ahmed, M.: An ensemble deep learning framework for speech emotion recognition. IEEE Access (2021)
2. Aouani, H.: Speech emotion recognition using handcrafted acoustic features and classical classifiers. J. Intell. Syst. (2020)
3. Barhoumi, W., BenAyed, Y.: Deep architectures for speech emotion recognition: a comparative study. Expert Syst. Appl. (2024)
4. Chen, L.W., Rudnicky, A.: Exploring wav2vec 2.0 fine tuning for improved speech emotion recognition. In: ICASSP 2023-2023 IEEE International Conference on Acoustics, Speech and Signal Processing (ICASSP), pp. 1–5. IEEE (2023)
5. Chowdhury, N.: Hybrid 1D-CNN and CNN-BiLSTM for speech emotion recognition. In: Proceedings of the IEEE Conference on Acoustics, Speech, and Signal Processing (2025)
6. Gideon, J.: Learning emotional representations from speech with ADDoG and MADDoG. In: Proceedings of the Interspeech (2019)
7. Hema, R.: Comparing traditional and CNN-based speech emotion recognition. Int. J. Comput. Appl. (2023)
8. Kaloub, A., Elgabar, M.: Multi-feature extraction for Arabic speech emotion recognition. Int. J. Speech Technol. (2025)
9. Lashkarashvili, N., Wu, W., Sun, G., Woodland, P.C.: Parameter efficient fine-tuning for speech emotion recognition and domain adaptation. In: ICASSP 2024-2024 IEEE International Conference on Acoustics, Speech and Signal Processing (ICASSP), pp. 10986–10990. IEEE (2024)
10. Latif, S.: Progressively discriminative transfer network for cross-corpus speech emotion recognition. IEEE Trans. Affect. Comput. (2022)
11. Madarina, N.: Spectrogram-based speech emotion recognition with CNN and spatial pyramid pooling. Neural Comput. Appl. (2023)
12. Meng, D.: Speech emotion recognition using 3D log-mel spectrograms and dilated CNN-BiLSTM. Knowl. Based Syst. (2019)
13. Plutchik, R.: A general psychoevolutionary theory of emotion. In: Theories of Emotion, pp. 3–33. Elsevier (1980)

REM-CaR: Retrieval-Augmented Generation Enhanced Medical Case-Based Reasoner

Zhiliang Li[1,2], Beihong Jin[1,2](✉), Yuhui Chen[3,4], Tao Gong[3,4], and Yu Fu[5]

[1] Institute of Software, Chinese Academy of Sciences, Beijing, China
Beihong@iscas.ac.cn
[2] University of Chinese Academy of Sciences, Beijing, China
[3] Department of Neurology, Beijing Hospital, Beijing, China
[4] National Center of Gerontology, Institute of Geriatric Medicine, Chinese Academy of Medical Sciences, Beijing, China
[5] Department of Neurology, Peking University Third Hospital, Beijing, China

Abstract. Currently, large language models (LLMs) have exhibited impressive generalizability but remain incompetent for high-stakes medical applications due to domain-specific hallucinations. To mitigate hallucinations and enhance medical reasoning, current approaches widely adopt either chain-of-thought or retrieval-augmented generation on LLMs. However, they are often insufficient in terms of reasoning capability. Furthermore, existing approaches largely overlook case-based reasoning, thereby ignoring empirical patient histories that are fundamental to real-world clinical decision-making. In this paper, we propose REM-CaR (Retrieval-augmented generation-Enhanced Medical Case-based Reasoner), a novel framework that fundamentally restructures the LLM reasoning process by dynamically synergizing knowledge retrieval with case-based guidance. REM-CaR designs an uncertainty-aware dynamic retrieval mechanism that monitors the evolving inference state of the backbone LLM, fetching explicit medical facts purely on demand to minimize noise. Meanwhile, it integrates implicit clinical experience from similar historical cases to provide critical reasoning anchors. Extensive experimental results demonstrate the superiority of our proposed framework. Notably, REM-CaR reduces prediction errors by up to 43.31% on the specialized stroke prognosis task and improves accuracy by up to 18.38% on the medication recommendation task for multi-specialty diseases, establishing a reliable paradigm for LLM-driven clinical applications.

Keywords: Large Language Models · Case-Based Reasoning · Retrieval-Augmented Generation · Chain-of-Thought

1 Introduction

In recent years, large language models (LLMs) have achieved strong performance in language understanding and generation in general domains [1]. Driven by

L. Ding et al. (Eds.): APWeb-WAIM 2026, LNCS 16995, pp. 520–533, 2027.
https://doi.org/10.1007/978-981-92-5699-0_35

advances in model scaling and instruction tuning [3], these models have demonstrated enhanced capabilities beyond text generation, including improved performance on tasks requiring multi-step reasoning [11]. Their capability to capture broad linguistic patterns enables them to perform well across a wide range of open-ended tasks, particularly in zero-shot settings where task variability is high.

However, when applied to high-stakes, knowledge-intensive domains such as clinical medicine, LLMs suffer from hallucinations, generating factually inconsistent or unsupported content [24]. Existing approaches mainly address this issue through either chain-of-thought (CoT), which decomposes complex problems into step-by-step reasoning [20], or retrieval-augmented generation (RAG), which grounds model outputs with external factual knowledge [19].

Despite their individual merits, how to seamlessly integrate reasoning with RAG remains an open and critical challenge. Relying solely on CoT reasoning within the model in knowledge-intensive domains might amplify hallucinations, as the verbose intermediate reasoning leads to long contexts in which model performance typically degrades [15]. Conversely, conventional RAG approaches typically operate in a "retrieve-then-generate" manner [12]. Prepending massive amounts of retrieved documents before generation often introduces noise, distracting the LLM and disrupting its logical reasoning trajectory. Therefore, it is essential to develop a mechanism that tightly integrates the on-demand retrieval of external knowledge with the state deduction of internal reasoning.

Meanwhile, combining LLMs with case-based reasoning (CBR) has emerged as an attractive paradigm [22], particularly in medical scenarios. Clinical decision-making is a complex process that integrates established medical guidelines with practical experience [14]. To tailor abstract medical knowledge to individual patients, physicians often complement objective facts by consulting historical patient cases with similar symptoms, functional statuses, and disease progressions. Unlike RAG, which provides explicit, macro-level medical facts, CBR offers implicit, micro-level clinical experience. Therefore, integrating CBR into the LLM reasoning process can provide contextual relevance for diagnostic and prognostic predictions, offering a novel way to enhance reasoning capabilities and prediction reliability.

Motivated by the potential benefits of unifying these paradigms, we propose REM-CaR (Retrieval-augmented generation-Enhanced Medical Case-based Reasoner), a novel framework that fundamentally restructures the reasoning process by combining dynamic knowledge retrieval with case-based guidance. The main contributions of this work are threefold:

- We propose REM-CaR, a medical reasoning framework that fuses canonical medical facts with empirical patient cases to mirror the decision process of human physicians.
- We design an uncertainty-aware dynamic retrieval mechanism. By monitoring the internal reasoning state, REM-CaR fetches critical information on demand, effectively minimizing the noise interference and context fragmentation that are inherent in static retrieval approaches.

- We conduct extensive experiments on both knowledge-intensive and reasoning-intensive medical tasks, demonstrating that REM-CaR consistently outperforms other baselines and generalizes effectively across diverse clinical scenarios.

2 Related Work

When LLMs are applied to the medical field, they face heightened requirements for up-to-date knowledge and reliable reasoning. To address knowledge limitations, RAG integrates external authoritative sources to complement parametric memory [6]. For example, MedRAG [25] proposes a unified RAG framework that integrates diverse authoritative medical corpora to significantly enhance the factual accuracy of LLMs in complex clinical question answering. i-MedRAG [26] enhances medical knowledge retrieval by decomposing complex medical questions into multiple sub-queries, enabling more comprehensive exploration of relevant evidence. MedGraphRAG [23] structures medical knowledge into hierarchical graphs with top-down precise retrieval and bottom-up response refinement, thereby enabling evidence-grounded medical generation.

Orthogonal to retrieval-based approaches, CoT prompting improves complex decision-making by eliciting explicit reasoning processes [18,20]. For instance, CoMT [9] emulates human diagnostic reasoning by decomposing procedures, improving the accuracy of medical report generation while mitigating hallucinations. What is more, a recent approach introduces an interactive self-reflection framework that integrates knowledge acquisition and answer generation to alleviate hallucinations in medical generative QA systems [8].

While RAG provides explicit macro-level facts and CoT structures the deductive process, clinical decision-making fundamentally relies on experiential knowledge. CBR offers a natural paradigm to ground LLM reasoning in human-aligned clinical practice by recalling similar past experiences. Recently, the synergy of CBR and LLMs has attracted substantial attention [5]. Implementing the CBR cycle with LLMs has been shown to significantly reduce hallucinations compared to standard prompting [21]. In the medical field, hybrid CBR-LLM approaches, such as the explainable hip fracture classification system [16], demonstrate the considerable practical value of using historical patient cases as reasoning anchors.

Compared to existing approaches, which typically treat reasoning and retrieval as independent steps, our work explores a more integrated approach. We propose a framework that dynamically combines case-based retrieval and external knowledge acquisition with the step-by-step reasoning process of the LLM, aiming to provide on-demand context for complex clinical decision-making and reduce potential hallucinations.

3 Method

We first formalize the task of this paper. Given a case repository $\mathcal{P}$ and a knowledge base $\mathcal{K}$, our goal is to design a reasoning workflow that enables an LLM to leverage both sources to generate an answer y for a patient query q, formed by concatenating the patient's medical record and question. Here, $\mathcal{P} = \{p_1, p_2, \ldots, p_N\}$ denotes a repository of N historical patient records, while $\mathcal{K}$ contains standardized medical knowledge, such as clinical guidelines and disease mechanisms.

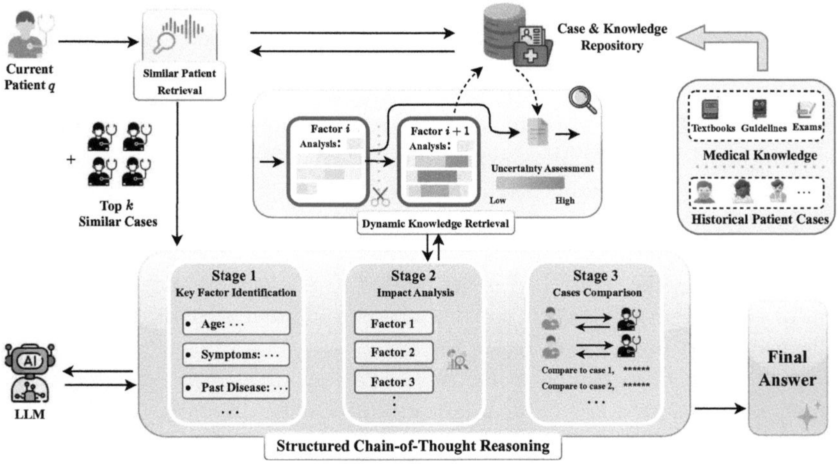

Fig. 1. Overall Framework

The proposed framework is illustrated in Fig. 1, and consists of three key components:

1. **Similar Patient Retrieval**: Clinically similar historical cases are retrieved from the case repository based on the patient's medical record.
2. **Structured Chain-of-Thought Reasoning**: Step-wise medical reasoning is conducted through a structured reasoning template that organizes key stages such as information extraction, causal analysis, and case comparison.
3. **Dynamic Knowledge Retrieval**: External medical knowledge is dynamically retrieved during reasoning according to the uncertainty of the designated output generated by the LLM to supplement missing information.

3.1 Similar Patient Retrieval

We construct a case vector database $D_{\mathcal{P}}$ by combining global patient semantics with key medical entities to improve case retrieval.

For each patient record p_i, we obtain a global embedding $e^{(i)}_{patient}$ and entity embeddings $\{e^{(i,1)}_{entity}, \cdots, e^{(i,n)}_{entity}\}$, where medical entities are extracted using named entity recognition. The final patient representation is computed as $h(p_i) = \frac{1}{2}\left(e^{(i)}_{patient} + \frac{1}{n}\sum_{j=1}^{n} e^{(i,j)}_{entity}\right)$, and the resulting embedding is stored in $D_{\mathcal{P}}$.

During inference, the medical record p_t of the target patient is encoded using the same procedure, and the top-k most similar cases are retrieved from $D_{\mathcal{P}}$ using cosine similarity, thus forming $\mathbf{p} = \arg\text{top-k}_{h(p_i)\in D_{\mathcal{P}}} \cos(h(p_t), h(p_i))$.

3.2 Structured Chain-of-Thought Reasoning

We design a structured reasoning workflow that guides the LLM through clinically inspired step-by-step reasoning to construct a causally grounded CoT from patient data. The reasoning process consists of three sequential stages:

- **Key Factor Identification**: The LLM is prompted to extract key clinical factors (e.g., demographics, symptoms, and medical history) strictly from the patient record without introducing additional assumptions. These factors provide the basis for subsequent reasoning while reducing interference from irrelevant information.
- **Impact Analysis**: The LLM is demanded to analyze the potential contribution of each identified factor to the patient's clinical outcome through medically grounded factor-level reasoning.
- **Similar Case Comparison**: Retrieved patient cases are compared with the target patient across key clinical factors to identify clinically relevant similarities and differences, providing additional evidence for diagnosis or prognosis.

Finally, the above analyses are fed into the LLM to generate the answer y, which is typically a diagnostic or prognostic prediction.

3.3 Uncertainty-Aware Dynamic Knowledge Retrieval

The **Impact Analysis** stage relies on external medical knowledge to infer relationships between clinical factors and outcomes. We therefore devise an uncertainty-aware dynamic retrieval mechanism that monitors factor-level uncertainty during reasoning.

Factor-Level Perplexity Monitoring. To enable fine-grained monitoring during reasoning, we design a factor-level perplexity-based detection strategy.

Let the batch sent to the LLM be $\mathcal{Q} = \{q_1, q_2, \cdots, q_B\}$. During generation, reasoning is produced incrementally through chunked streaming generation with chunk length l. The chunk generated at the j-th step for query q_i is denoted as $\mathbf{c}_{i,j} = \{c_{i,j}^{(1)}, c_{i,j}^{(2)}, \cdots, c_{i,j}^{(l)}\}$, where $c_{i,j}^{(r)}$ $(r \in [1, l])$ denotes a generated token. The chunk $\mathbf{c}_{i,j}$ controls generation granularity but does not necessarily align with structured reasoning units.

Under the structured prompting constraints, the reasoning associated with each factor is delimited by the tags < FACTOR > and < /FACTOR >. For the m-th factor of query q_i, the complete reasoning unit is defined as $F_{i,j,m} = \text{Fetch}\left(\cup_j \mathbf{c}_{i,j}, m\right)$, where Fetch() extracts from tokens the m-th factor whose start and end positions are determined by the locations of the m-th tags < FACTOR > and < /FACTOR > (see Fig. 2).

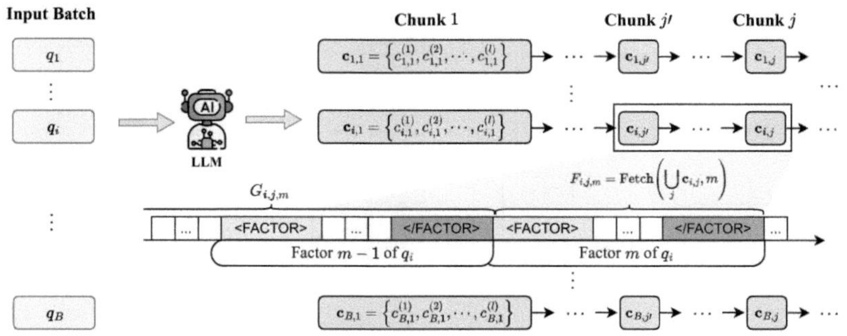

Fig. 2. Relationship Between Generation Chunks and Factor-Level Reasoning Units

Given q_i, let $G_{i,j,m}$ denote the generated tokens preceding $F_{i,j,m}$. For each reasoning unit $F_{i,j,m}$, token-level log probabilities are accumulated during generation:

$$\ell_{i,j,m}^{(t)} = \log p\left(LLM(q_i \oplus G_{i,j,m} \oplus x^{(<t)}) = x^{(t)}\right) \tag{1}$$

where $x^{(t)}$ is the t-th token in $F_{i,j,m}$.

The average perplexity of $F_{i,j,m}$ is computed as:

$$\text{PPL}(F_{i,j,m}) = \exp\left(-\frac{1}{|F_{i,j,m}|}\sum_{t=1}^{|F_{i,j,m}|} \ell_{i,j,m}^{(t)}\right) \tag{2}$$

Based on this measurement, a factor-level uncertainty indicator is defined as:

$$I_{\text{uncertain}}(F_{i,j,m}) = \begin{cases} 1, & \text{if PPL}(F_{i,j,m}) > \tau \\ 0, & \text{otherwise.} \end{cases} \tag{3}$$

Here τ denotes a predefined perplexity threshold. Dynamic knowledge retrieval is triggered only when a factor-level reasoning unit is identified as uncertain and the query still has remaining retrieval budget.

Knowledge Retrieval Triggered by High Perplexity. At the end of each generation step j, factor-level reasoning units with high perplexity are selected for knowledge retrieval. Given the reasoning unit $F_{i,j,m}$ and the generation context $G_{i,j,m}$, an LLM generates a retrieval query using the query generation prompt $\mathcal{G}_{query}$. All queries $\{\text{Query}_{i,j,m}\}$ generated at the same step are aggregated and executed in parallel.

The dynamic knowledge retrieval component returns raw knowledge $K_{i,j,m}$, and $K_{i,j,m}$ is further compressed to $\hat{K}_{i,j,m}$ by an LLM using the knowledge compression prompt $\mathcal{G}_{compress}$. The compressed knowledge is wrapped with the special `<KNOWLEDGE>` tags and injected into the generation context: $G_{i,j,m} \leftarrow G_{i,j,m} \oplus$ (`<KNOWLEDGE>`$\hat{K}_{i,j,m}$`</KNOWLEDGE>`). After injection, generation resumes with the augmented context (Fig. 3).

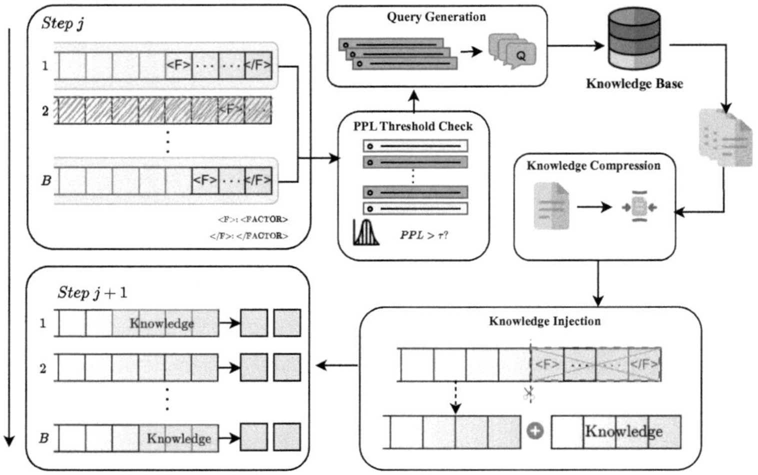

Fig. 3. Dynamic Knowledge Injection Pipeline

4 Experimental Evaluation

4.1 Experimental Setup

First of all, we equip REM-CaR with Qwen2.5-7B-Instruct [27] as the backbone LLM and BGE-M3 [2] as the text embedder. Next, we construct external knowledge base using the following knowledge sources:

- **Clinical Guidelines**: Clinical guidelines provide evidence-based standards for diagnosis and treatment. Using GraphRAG [4], we structure these documents into a medical knowledge graph covering diseases, symptoms, examinations, and treatments.
- **Textbooks**: Textbooks are segmented into semantically coherent units, from which DeepSeek [13] extracts core medical concepts, standardizes them into structured entries, and stores the entries in ChromaDB for efficient retrieval.
- **Medical Exam Questions**: QA datasets (e.g., MedQA [10]) are converted into declarative knowledge statements using DeepSeek, embedded with BGE-M3, and stored in ChromaDB, reducing structural bias and facilitating integration with other sources.

We evaluate REM-CaR on two medical tasks that target clinical specialist reasoning and clinical generalist reasoning, respectively. Specifically, we employ the following two data sets:

- **Stroke Dataset**: The self-built dataset consists of 836 electronic health records, each of which includes activities of daily living (ADL) scores at admission, chief complaints, and relevant examination results. Among them, 501 records are used to construct the case repository, while the remainder are used for predicting stroke patients' ADL scores at discharge based on admission data. The collection of data in the self-built stroke dataset has been approved by the institutional review board (IRB) of the hospital.

- **DialMed Dataset** [7]: The dataset contains multi-turn doctor-patient dialogs, covering a total of 16 common diseases and 70 corresponding medications. We use 9,605 dialogs to construct the case repository, and 1,199 dialogs as the test set to recommend medications to patients.

For the above medical tasks, we adopt grid search to select the optimal hyperparameter values in REM-CaR. Ultimately, the chunk length l is set to 100, the retrieved number of similar cases k is set to 3, and the perplexity threshold τ is set to the 98th percentile for ADL prediction and the 99th percentile for medication recommendation, corresponding to the top 2% and 1% most uncertain samples, respectively.

Table 1. Main Results

Method	Stroke		DialMed
	MAE(↓)	MSE(↓)	Accuracy(↑)
Direct Generation	15.70(↓42.48%)	380.86	0.6263(↑18.38%)
Retrieval-Based Generation	15.93(↓43.31%)	365.47	0.6422(↑15.45%)
CoT-Enhanced Generation	<u>12.93</u>(↓30.16%)	<u>283.23</u>	<u>0.6564</u>(↑12.95%)
REM-CaR	**9.03**	**194.68**	**0.7414**

Gray numbers indicate the relative improvement of REM-CaR over each baseline.

4.2 Performance Comparison

To evaluate the effectiveness of the proposed framework in medical reasoning tasks, we compare it against the following baselines:

- **Direct Generation**: The backbone LLM generates answers based solely on the original input, without leveraging external knowledge or structured reasoning.
- **Retrieval-Based Generation**: The backbone LLM generates answers using inputs augmented with externally retrieved medical knowledge. For the stroke dataset, we adopt a query decomposition strategy following i-MedRAG, where the clinical context is converted into sub-questions for retrieval.
- **Chain-of-Thought (CoT)-Enhanced Generation**: The backbone LLM performs explicit multi-step reasoning before generating the final answer, following the same reasoning chain design as our framework.

The main results are shown in Table 1. Compared to the direct generation method, the retrieval-based generation method improves accuracy on the knowledge-intensive medication recommendation task by 2.54%, and degrades performance on the reasoning-oriented ADL prediction task (results in a 1.46%

higher MAE). The degradation may be due to the fact that the stroke dataset involves relatively long clinical contexts, where adding retrieved knowledge further increases input length and may dilute the model's attention to patient-specific signals. The CoT-enhanced method yields stable improvements across both scenarios, increasing the accuracy of the medication recommendation task by 4.81% and reducing ADL prediction error by 17.64%, compared to the direct generation method. Our proposed framework achieves an 18.38% accuracy boost for the medication recommendation task over the direct generation method, and a 43.31% error reduction for the ADL prediction task over the retrieval-based generation method. These results collectively demonstrate that our framework, which seamlessly integrates structured CoT with external knowledge retrieval and similar-case referencing, can resolve complex medical scenarios.

4.3 Ablation Study

To evaluate the effectiveness of individual components within our proposed framework, we conduct a comprehensive ablation study by systematically removing specific components. Notably, removing the CoT component inherently disables the dynamic knowledge retrieval component, as it relies on the CoT process. Furthermore, an additional variant (i.e., variant IV) utilizing a static retrieval strategy is introduced to evaluate the uncertainty-based dynamic knowledge retrieval.

Table 2. Results of Ablation Study

Method	Components			Stroke		DialMed
	Cases[1]	CoT[2]	Knowledge[3]	MAE(↓)	MSE(↓)	Accuracy(↑)
REM-CaR	✓	✓	$\mathcal{D}$	**9.03**	**194.68**	**0.7414**
Variant I	✓	✓	×	9.56(↓5.54%)	<u>215.99</u>	<u>0.7173</u>(↑3.36%)
Variant II	✓	×	×	11.45(↓21.14%)	249.37	0.7039(↑5.33%)
Variant III	×	✓	$\mathcal{D}$	12.63(↓28.50%)	260.26	0.7080(↑4.72%)
Variant IV	✓	✓	$\mathcal{S}$	<u>9.36</u>(↓3.53%)	217.46	0.7039(↑5.33%)

[1] Cases: Similar Patient Retrieval; [2] CoT: Structured Chain-of-Thought Reasoning;
[3] Knowledge: Knowledge Retrieval; * $\mathcal{D}$: Dynamic; $\mathcal{S}$: Static.
Gray numbers indicate the relative improvement of REM-CaR over each baseline.

The evaluation results are shown in Table 2. By comparing our REM-CaR with its ablated variants (including variants I, II, and III), we can quantify the contribution of each component, and find that the similar patient retrieval component and the structured CoT reasoning component exert comparable effects on performance.

Moreover, comparing the performance of variant I with that of variant II, we find a disparity in the effectiveness of the reasoning mechanism across the two tasks. Specifically, the medication recommendation task is not significantly affected by the presence or absence of the reasoning mechanism, whereas adding the reasoning mechanism significantly improves performance on the ADL prediction task. To analyze the underlying causes, we visualize the patient embeddings using UMAP [17] ($n_{neighbors} = 20$, $min_{dist} = 0.1$), where the points denoting patient embeddings are colored by discharge ADL scores for the ADL prediction task and by integer-encoded disease types for the medication recommendation task. As shown in Fig. 4, samples from the DialMed dataset form distinct categorical clusters with clear boundaries, whereas those from the stroke dataset exhibit a dispersed, heterogeneous space. From Fig. 4, we infer that in the medication recommendation task, once similar cases are retrieved, they are directly served as decision cues due to the high consistency of clinical features among these cases; simple inference mechanisms are of limited use. In contrast, in the ADL prediction task, the retrieved cases yield only fragmented references. Therefore, explicit reasoning is essential to capture complex differences across various factors, which helps to achieve accurate predictions. The results above indicate that the effectiveness of explicit reasoning mechanisms is influenced by the quality of similar cases. When similar cases are not sufficiently similar, CoT plays a more significant role. In other words, the similar patient retrieval component and the structured CoT reasoning component are complementary in terms of clinical decision-making.

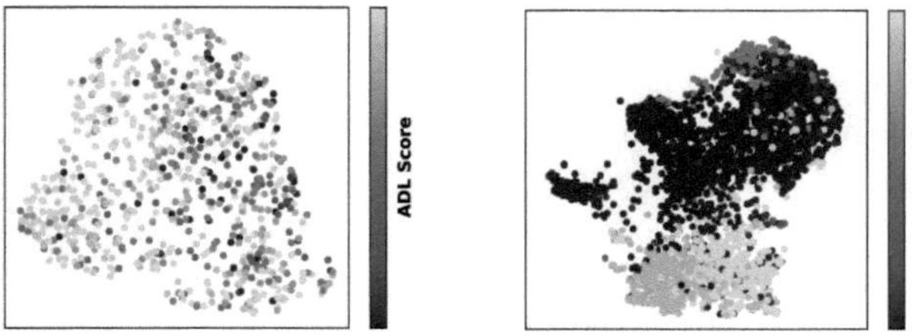

(a) Stroke Dataset (b) DialMed Dataset

Fig. 4. Visualization of Patient Embeddings

Furthermore, from the 1st, 2nd and 5th lines in Table 2, we find that our complete framework outperforms variants I and IV, showing that dynamic retrieval consistently yields superior performance over non-retrieval and static retrieval.

To elucidate the performance gap among non-retrieval, static retrieval, and dynamic retrieval, we conduct a sample-level analysis on two test sets.

For the medication recommendation task on the DialMed test set, we conduct pairwise comparisons between variant I and variant IV, as well as between variant IV and REM-CaR. Compared to variant I, variant IV corrects 103 previously incorrect predictions but simultaneously disrupts 119 correct ones. Interestingly, the effect of static retrieval is inconsistent across settings. While it improves performance on the stroke test set, it degrades performance on the DialMed test set. This suggests that static retrieval introduces high variability rather than consistent gains. Its effectiveness is highly sensitive to the input context, particularly when the input becomes long due to the combination of CoT and similar cases. In such cases, additional retrieved knowledge may dilute salient signals or introduce misaligned information, leading to unpredictable performance changes. In contrast, dynamic retrieval mitigates this issue by selectively incorporating external knowledge, resulting in more stable and consistent improvements.

For the ADL prediction task on the stroke test set, we employ DeepSeek as an LLM judge to evaluate the medical reasoning trajectories generated by both strategies. Specifically, we randomly order the outputs of REM-CaR and variant IV to eliminate positional bias. Dynamic retrieval achieves a 70.4% win rate over static retrieval, demonstrating its superior coherence, robust causal reasoning, and stricter adherence to clinical standards.

4.4 Case Study

We select two examples from the DialMed test set to demonstrate the advantage of our framework in detail.

This first example, shown on the left of Fig. 5, demonstrates that baseline methods, including direct generation, retrieval-based generation, and CoT-enhanced generation, fail to predict the ground-truth medication (Erythromycin) for a patient with chronic rhinitis and mucosal erosion. Although the CoT-enhanced baseline correctly reasons that treatments should promote nasal mucosal repair and avoid severe side effects, its final recommendation exhibits a faithfulness hallucination, where the generated answer does not remain consistent with its own reasoning process. Instead of following the derived rationale, it recommends generic treatments such as Budesonide, a corticosteroid that may worsen nasal dryness and bleeding in patients with mucosal erosion. This failure likely stems from insufficient coverage of such fine-grained clinical patterns in both the LLM's parametric knowledge and general-purpose knowledge bases. Moreover, the retrieval-based method recommends the anti-allergy medication Ebastine despite the absence of evidence for allergic rhinitis. In contrast, our CBR-based framework retrieves clinically similar historical cases and transfers their treatment rationale to the target patient, enabling the correct identification of the nuanced medication. This case highlights the effectiveness of CBR in compensating for knowledge gaps.

Another example is shown on the right of Fig. 5. For a patient with "yellow phlegm" (purulent sputum), variant II struggles with the noise of multiple cases retrieved, resulting in an incorrect composite prescription. In contrast, REM-CaR first retrieves explicit medical knowledge (<KNOWLEDGE>) that indicates that appropriate antibiotics should be selected for such symptoms. This retrieved knowledge acts as a strong logical constraint during the subsequent analysis. Guided by this medical principle, the backbone LLM aligns the target patient with the most consistent historical case (i.e., Case 1) based on closely matching symptoms like a high fever and a sore throat, and accurately transfers its antibiotic treatment logic. Consequently, REM-CaR predicts the exact ground-truth medication (Levofloxacin), demonstrating that REM-CaR

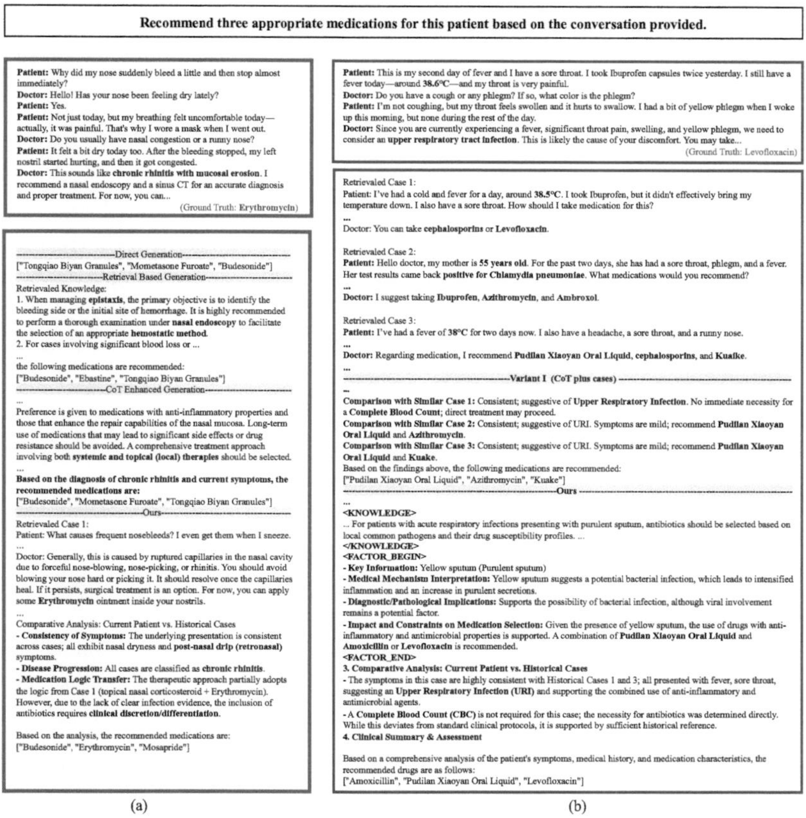

Fig. 5. Examples from DialMed Test Set

can leverage retrieved knowledge to identify the optimal reference among multiple historical cases.

5 Conclusion

To address the unreliable reasoning of LLMs in medical scenarios, we propose REM-CaR, a framework that seamlessly integrates structured chain-of-thought reasoning, case comparison, and uncertainty-driven dynamic retrieval. REM-CaR is capable of providing supplementary knowledge for knowledge-intensive tasks (e.g., medication recommendation) and performing multi-step causal inference for reasoning-intensive tasks (e.g., stroke prognostic prediction). Experimental results show that REM-CaR outperforms conventional baselines relying solely on either retrieval-only or reasoning-only mechanisms. Most importantly, our work highlights the significance of dynamically coupling knowledge acquisition with the reasoning process to support clinical decision-making.

Acknowledgements. This work is supported by the National Natural Science Foundation of China (No. 62172394, No. 62072450) and the Basic Research Program of ISCAS (No. ISCAS-JCMS-202305).

References

1. Achiam, J., et al.: GPT-4 technical report. arXiv preprint arXiv:2303.08774 (2024)
2. Chen, J., Xiao, S., Zhang, P., Luo, K., Lian, D., Liu, Z.: M3-embedding: multi-linguality, multi-functionality, multi-granularity text embeddings through self-knowledge distillation. In: Findings of the Association for Computational Linguistics: ACL 2024, pp. 2318–2335 (2024)
3. Chung, H.W., et al.: Scaling instruction-finetuned language models. J. Mach. Learn. Res. **25**(70), 1–53 (2024)
4. Edge, D., et al.: From local to global: a graph RAG approach to query-focused summarization. arXiv preprint arXiv:2404.16130 (2024)
5. Floyd, M.W., Leake, D., Ménager, D.H., Watson, I., Wilkerson, K.: Levels of AI memory - and case-based ways for LLMs to ascend them. In: CEUR Workshop Proceedings, vol. 3993, pp. 2–14 (2025)
6. Gao, Y., et al.: Retrieval-augmented generation for large language models: a survey. arXiv preprint arXiv:2312.10997 **2**(1), 32 (2023)
7. He, Z., et al.: DialMed: a dataset for dialogue-based medication recommendation. In: Proceedings of the 29th International Conference on Computational Linguistics, pp. 721–733 (2022)
8. Ji, Z., Yu, T., Xu, Y., Lee, N., Ishii, E., Fung, P.: Towards mitigating LLM hallucination via self reflection. In: Findings of the Association for Computational Linguistics: EMNLP 2023, pp. 1827–1843 (2023)
9. Jiang, Y., et al.: CoMT: chain-of-medical-thought reduces hallucination in medical report generation. In: ICASSP 2025-2025 IEEE International Conference on Acoustics, Speech and Signal Processing (ICASSP), pp. 1–5. IEEE (2025)
10. Jin, D., Pan, E., Oufattole, N., Weng, W.H., Fang, H., Szolovits, P.: What disease does this patient have? A large-scale open domain question answering dataset from medical exams. Appl. Sci. **11**(14), 6421 (2021)
11. Kojima, T., Gu, S.S., Reid, M., Matsuo, Y., Iwasawa, Y.: Large language models are zero-shot reasoners. In: Advances in Neural Information Processing Systems, vol. 35, pp. 22199–22213 (2022)
12. Lewis, P., et al.: Retrieval-augmented generation for knowledge-intensive NLP tasks. In: Advances in Neural Information Processing Systems, vol. 33, pp. 9459–9474 (2020)
13. Liu, A., et al.: DeepSeek-V3. 2: pushing the frontier of open large language models. arXiv preprint arXiv:2512.02556 (2025)
14. Liu, G., Zhang, Y., Liu, X., Yao, Q.: Case-based reasoning enhances the predictive power of LLMs in drug-drug interaction. arXiv preprint arXiv:2505.23034 (2025)
15. Liu, N.F., et al.: Lost in the middle: how language models use long contexts. Trans. Assoc. Comput. Linguist. **12**, 157–173 (2024)
16. Queipo-de Llano, E., Ciurcau, M., Paz-Olalla, A., Díaz-Agudo, B., Recio-García, J.A.: Explainable classification system for hip fractures: a hybrid CBR+LLM surrogate approach. In: CEUR Workshop Proceedings, vol. 3708, pp. 65–80 (2024)
17. McInnes, L., Healy, J., Saul, N., Grossberger, L.: UMAP: uniform manifold approximation and projection. J. Open Source Softw. **3**(29), 861 (2018)

18. Muennighoff, N., et al.: s1: simple test-time scaling. In: Proceedings of the 2025 Conference on Empirical Methods in Natural Language Processing, pp. 20286–20332 (2025)
19. Neha, F., Bhati, D., Shukla, D.K.: Retrieval-augmented generation (RAG) in healthcare: A. Comprehensive review. AI **6**(9), 226 (2025)
20. Wei, J., et al.: Chain-of-thought prompting elicits reasoning in large language models. In: Advances in Neural Information Processing Systems, vol. 35, pp. 24824–24837 (2022)
21. Wilkerson, K., Leake, D.: On implementing case-based reasoning with large language models. In: Recio-Garcia, J.A., Orozco-del-Castillo, M.G., Bridge, D. (eds.) International Conference on Case-Based Reasoning, pp. 404–417. Springer, Cham (2024). https://doi.org/10.1007/978-3-031-63646-2_26
22. Wiratunga, N., et al.: CBR-RAG: case-based reasoning for retrieval augmented generation in LLMs for legal question answering. In: Recio-Garcia, J.A., Orozco-del-Castillo, M.G., Bridge, D. (eds.) International Conference on Case-Based Reasoning, pp. 445–460. Springer, Cham (2024). https://doi.org/10.1007/978-3-031-63646-2_29
23. Wu, J., et al.: Medical graph RAG: evidence-based medical large language model via graph retrieval-augmented generation. In: Proceedings of the 63rd Annual Meeting of the Association for Computational Linguistics (Volume 1: Long Papers), pp. 28443–28467 (2025)
24. Xia, Z., Xu, J., Zhang, Y., Liu, H.: A survey of uncertainty estimation methods on large language models. In: Findings of the Association for Computational Linguistics: ACL 2025, pp. 21381–21396 (2025)
25. Xiong, G., Jin, Q., Lu, Z., Zhang, A.: Benchmarking retrieval-augmented generation for medicine. In: Findings of the Association for Computational Linguistics: ACL 2024, pp. 6233–6251 (2024)
26. Xiong, G., Jin, Q., Wang, X., Zhang, M.: Improving retrieval-augmented generation in medicine with iterative follow-up questions. In: Biocomputing 2025: Proceedings of the Pacific Symposium, pp. 199–214. World Scientific (2024)
27. Yang, A., et al.: Qwen2. 5 technical report. arXiv e-prints pp. arXiv–2412 (2024)

Special Track

FLESC: Flexible Stripeless Erasure Coding Scheme for In-Memory Storage Systems

Xiao Li[1(✉)], Guiwen Luo[1], Yaqiang Zhang[1], Yaqian Zhao[1], and Jing Wang[2]

[1] IEIT SYSTEMS Co., Ltd., Jinan 250101, China
{lixiao09,luoguiwen,zhangyaqiang,zhaoyaqian}@ieisystem.com
[2] East China Normal University, Shanghai 200062, China
wangjing@cs.ecnu.edu.cn

Abstract. Erasure coding schemes play a critical role in fault-tolerant distributed storage. Traditional stripe-based schemes face limitations in low-latency in-memory storage; the recently proposed stripeless scheme Nos imposes constraints on cluster sizes. This paper introduces FLExible Stripeless erasure Coding (FLESC) scheme, which generalizes Symmetric Balanced Incomplete Block Design (SBIBD) and introduces a virtual node layer, decoupling coding parameters from physical topology, enabling deployment on arbitrary cluster sizes and tolerating node failures. Experiments show FLESC achieves competitive read/write performance, maintains low latency, and supports previously infeasible configurations.

Keywords: Erasure coding · In-memory storage · Stripeless design · Fault tolerance

1 Introduction

Erasure coding provides fault tolerance and durability in distributed storage [16,19]. Historically, storage systems were optimized for databases on hard disk drives (HDDs) and solid-state drives (SSDs). However, the growth of interactive e-commerce and social media has elevated latency-sensitive small objects to first-class revenue generators. This shift has driven the rise of in-memory storage systems, which eliminate disk I/O bottlenecks by keeping data in dynamic random-access memory (DRAM). Because DRAM is volatile and large-scale clusters suffer frequent failures, erasure coding is a fundamental requirement.

Erasure coding schemes are commonly implemented via two *stripe* modes. *Intra-object striping* divides a single object into fragments distributed across nodes; *inter-object striping* groups multiple objects into one stripe.

Nos [8] pioneered an inter-object data placement scheme that bypasses stripe modes, eliminating data splitting and placement overheads. Nos at its core utilizes Symmetric Balanced Incomplete Block Design (SBIBD) as a primary-to-backup affinity matrix, tolerating up to $p < k$ node failures in a cluster of

L. Ding et al. (Eds.): APWeb-WAIM 2026, LNCS 16995, pp. 537–550, 2027.
https://doi.org/10.1007/978-981-92-5699-0_36

$v = k^2 - k + 1$ nodes, where k denotes the number of objects encoded into each parity. Since v is rigidly determined by k, Nos is far less flexible than conventional schemes like the Reed-Solomon (RS) codes.

This paper proposes FLESC (/flesk/), a flexible erasure coding scheme, to address Nos' flexibility issue. Our contributions are summarized as follows:

(i) We generalize Nos by proving fault tolerance of SBIBD matrices with arbitrary λ, enabling the FLESC subsystem with flexible parameter selection.
(ii) We propose the FLESC full system that accommodates arbitrary cluster sizes through a virtual node layer, decoupling coding parameters from physical cluster size.
(iii) We introduce a virtual node migration mechanism that handles changes to physical nodes without requiring global data movement.

2 Background and Related Work

Erasure Coding Schemes. A systematic erasure coding scheme is characterized by two parameters (k, p): objects are partitioned into k data fragments and then p parity fragments are added, tolerating up to p failures. The collection of these $(k + p)$ fragments forms a *stripe*. To ensure fault tolerance, fragments within the same stripe must reside on different nodes.

Stripe Modes. Based on object size and application scenarios, data objects are either divided into smaller fragments, or grouped into larger fragments before encoding.

Intra-object striping partitions a single object into multiple data and parity fragments distributed across nodes. Its drawback is that reading or writing requires contacting multiple nodes, increasing I/O fanout and network strain.

Inter-object striping groups multiple objects into a single stripe without splitting individual objects. It offers lower I/O fanout when an entire object resides on one node, but recovery may require accessing data from multiple objects. Object-to-stripe mapping can be *static* (e.g., via hashing, simple but may cause load imbalance) or *dynamic* (via a metadata server, more adaptive but introduces a bottleneck).

For in-memory storage with lightweight, low-latency data, both stripe modes introduce overheads, motivating stripeless approaches.

SBIBD. An SBIBD is a binary $v \times v$ matrix $A = (A_{ij})_{v \times v}$ characterized by three parameters (v, k, λ) such that [1,8,11]: (i) Every row and every column of A contains exactly k ones (and $v - k$ zeros); (ii) Any two distinct rows share exactly λ columns with entry one; (iii) The three parameters in SBIBD are mutually constrained by

$$v = \frac{k(k-1)}{\lambda} + 1. \tag{1}$$

The identity (1) follows from double-counting row/column pairs of ones. A necessary condition for the existence of an SBIBD is given by the Bruck-Ryser-Chowla theorem [1,3]. Constructive techniques are discussed in [4,11,18]. By reordering the rows, all diagonal entries of the SBIBD can be made zero. As an example, an (11, 6, 3)-SBIBD is presented in Fig. 1.

	c_0	c_1	c_2	c_3	c_4	c_5	c_6	c_7	c_8	c_9	c_{10}
r_0	0	0	1	1	1	1	0	1	1	0	0
r_1	0	0	1	0	0	1	1	1	0	1	1
r_2	1	1	0	0	1	1	1	1	0	0	0
r_3	1	1	1	0	0	1	0	0	1	1	0
r_4	1	1	1	1	0	0	0	1	0	0	1
r_5	0	1	0	1	0	0	1	1	1	1	0
r_6	1	0	0	0	1	0	0	1	1	1	1
r_7	1	0	0	1	0	1	1	0	1	0	1
r_8	0	1	0	1	1	1	0	0	0	1	1
r_9	0	1	1	0	1	0	1	0	1	0	1
r_{10}	1	0	1	1	1	0	1	0	0	1	0

Fig. 1. An (11, 6, 3)-SBIBD.

Related Work *Erasure coding schemes for in-memory storage.* XOR-based codes and Reed-Solomon codes [14] are the most widely deployed families. A line of work has investigated applying erasure coding schemes to in-memory key-value storage systems. Cocytus [2], EC-Cache [13], MemEC [21], BCStore [10] are the representatives. Some systems target at remote memory, for instances, Hydra [9], Carbink [22], Nos [8]. These systems are either stripe-based, which can introduce placement and management overheads, or face limitations in flexibility when adapting to varying cluster sizes and object distributions.

Systems that Mix Replication and Erasure Coding. Large-scale systems often use a phased approach where data is initially stored with replication, and later encoded using erasure coding in the background. The representative implementations include f4 from Facebook [12], HDFS [17], HACFS [20] and RCStor [15]. These systems utilize the performance of replication for hot data, and the space efficiency of erasure coding for warm or cold data.

3 Motivation

This paper is motivated by the flexibility limitations of Nos, a stripeless erasure coding scheme for in-memory storage. Nos allows nodes to independently replicate data and locally XOR k replicas in the background to generate parities, eliminating the rigid "striping" required by classical codes.

Nos interprets a $(v, k, 1)$-SBIBD as a primary-to-backup affinity matrix, and $A_{ij} = 1$ implies objects with a primary copy on node i are replicated to backup node j. This establishes a replication pattern across a cluster of $v = k^2 - k + 1$

nodes, ensuring any two primary nodes share at most one backup node. Nos can tolerate $p < k$ simultaneous node failures. A "write" operation requires only $p+2$ parallel replications—including the original object on its primary node—followed by local XOR operations, so the encoding overhead is marginal.

Nevertheless, these benefits come with intrinsic limitations such as: (i) *Infeasibility for large k.* Nos requires $v \approx k^2$ nodes. If $k \geq 100$, this implies tens of thousands of nodes; (ii) *Strict restriction on cluster size.* Cluster size v must be k^2-k+1; (iii) *Fixed number of cluster nodes.* Nos adopts a static data-placement policy, the cluster cannot adjust its size in response to workload changes.

These limitations stem from $(v, k, 1)$-SBIBD constraints. Nos maps v one-to-one to physical servers, imposing mathematical constraints directly on hardware topology. Two complementary directions can be explored to address the limitations: (i) Relaxing the requirement on the dimension parameter v by allowing $\lambda > 1$. (ii) Introducing virtual nodes to decouple mathematical parameters from physical hardware.

SBIBD with Relaxed Parameters. Nos enforces that no two primary nodes share more than one common backup nodes. Therefore, Nos adopts SBIBDs with $\lambda = 1$. We argue that $\lambda = 1$ is overly stringent. Recovery only needs the weaker guarantee that after p failures, at least one surviving node can disambiguate the lost objects. Allowing $\lambda > 1$ preserves this property while unlocking a wider family of (v, k, λ)-SBIBDs, where v grows as $O(k^2/\lambda)$ instead of $k^2 - k + 1$, scaling to "wide-stripe" scenarios with moderate k.

Virtual Nodes. Nos directly uses the SBIBD matrix as its primary-to-backup affinity matrix, imposing a constraint on the number of physical nodes. Instead, FLESC employs virtual consistent hashing—an extension of classical consistent hashing—to split each physical node into evenly distributed "virtual nodes". By introducing a virtual node layer, the constraints on the physical cluster size can be eliminated. This approach also supports on-demand addition or removal of physical nodes without global data migration.

By combining these two ideas, we propose FLESC. The detailed coding scheme is presented in the following section.

4 FLESC Coding Scheme

FLESC is a flexible stripeless coding scheme for any physical cluster with $n \geq v$ nodes. It is parameterized by (n, v, k, p, λ) and tolerates p node failures under

$$n \geq v = \frac{k(k-1)}{\lambda} + 1, \text{ and } k \geq \lambda(p-1) + 2. \tag{2}$$

The scheme consists of a subsystem over v virtual nodes and a full system that extends this design to the actual n physical nodes.

4.1 Subsystem

A subsystem has v virtual nodes (indexed from 0 to $v - 1$), which are logical entities for analysis, not physical machines. The primary-backup affinity matrix is a (v, k, λ)-SBIBD matrix A (rows/columns indexed from 0). For any node j, *replication source set* $S_j = \{i \mid A_{ij} = 1\}$ (primary nodes replicating to j); for any node i, *replication target set* $T_i = \{j \mid A_{ij} = 1\}$ (nodes storing replicas of objects whose primary is on i). Both sets have size k.

The FLESC subsystem is parameterized by (v, k, p, λ), with the constraint

$$k \geq \lambda(p - 1) + 2. \tag{3}$$

Here (v, k, λ) are parameters of the underlying SBIBD satisfying (1), and p denotes the maximum number of node failures the subsystem can tolerate. Figure 2 shows the two-step encoding scheme for the subsystem:

(i) *Replication placement.* Each object is initially stored on its primary node. Every primary node has k replication target nodes. For each object, randomly select $q = \lambda(p - 1) + 2$ nodes from these k target nodes and send its replicas to them. Since the diagonal entries of the underlying SBIBD are 0, a primary node never replicates an object to itself.

(ii) *Parity computation.* Each node, while serving as a primary node for some objects, also acts as a backup node by receiving replicas from its replication source set. It buffers incoming replicas until it has received at least one replica from each of its k replication source nodes. It then XORs these k independent replicas into a single parity and discards the original replicas.

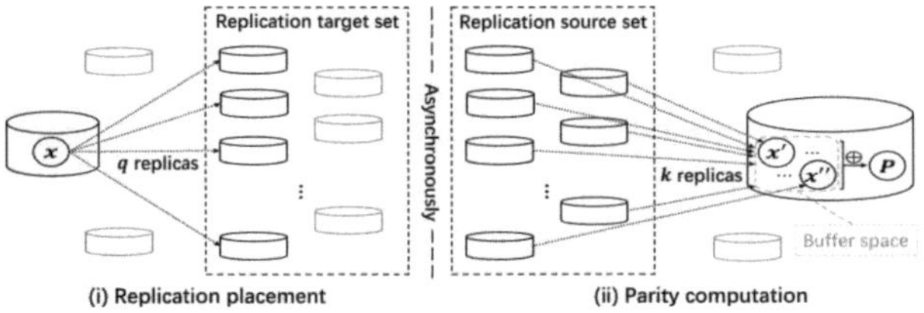

Fig. 2. Two steps of the FLESC subsystem.

The workflow is identical to Nos except for the number of replicas per object. In fact, when $\lambda = 1$, $q = p + 1$, FLESC subsystem reduces to Nos.

When some nodes fail, the objects whose primary copies reside on these nodes become inaccessible and need to be restored from surviving backup nodes. The fault-tolerant guarantee of the FLESC subsystem is formalized as follows.

Proposition 1. *Suppose data objects are stored on FLESC subsystem with parameters (v, k, p, λ) satisfying (1)(3). When at most p nodes fail, all objects on these failed nodes can be successfully recovered.*

Proof. Without loss of generality, assume that p nodes fail, including node 0. We prove that any object x primarily stored on node 0 can be recovered.

A parity P of object x is the XORed result of x and other $k-1$ objects, $P = x \oplus x_1 \oplus \cdots \oplus x_{k-1}$. If P and all objects except x are alive, then x can be recovered as $x = P \oplus x_1 \oplus \cdots \oplus x_{k-1}$. In this case, we say x is *directly recoverable*.

For the subsequent argument, we introduce two notions:

(i) A parity P is said to *encode* an object x, if x is one of the k objects that are XORed to compute P.
(ii) A node j is *associated* with node i, if node j belongs to the replication target set of node i. This is equivalent to $A_{ij} = 1$.

We proceed by deriving a contradiction. Suppose x cannot be recovered. In particular, it cannot be recovered directly. Then every parity that encodes x must either (i) be lost, or (ii) encode at least one other lost object. Moreover, each living parity that encodes x must encode at least one additional lost object y that, in turn, cannot be recovered directly. Clearly, such y belongs to some failed node $i \neq 0$.

Let $\mathcal{P}$ be the set of all parities that encode x, then $|\mathcal{P}| = q$ and all these parities reside on different nodes. Suppose f of these parities are lost, and the remaining $q-f$ of them are alive, where $0 \leq f \leq q-1$. Let $\mathcal{F}$ be the set of f failed nodes that store the f lost parities, $|\mathcal{F}| = f$. Each of the remaining $q-f$ alive parities encodes at least one failed object not located on node 0.

Pick one such failed object y for each alive parity and let $\mathcal{Y}$ denote the set of these picked failed objects, then $|\mathcal{Y}| = q - f$.

Consider all ordered pairs (y, P) with $y \in \mathcal{Y}$ and P a parity that encodes y. There are $(q-f)q$ such pairs in total. For a specific pair (y, P), let i be the primary node of y, which has failed, and let j be the node that stores the corresponding P. By the property of SBIBDs, for any failed node $i \neq 0$, set $\mathcal{Y}$ has at most λ objects on node i. This is because each object y and x share one parity, while node i and node 0 have at most λ common replication target nodes. We will use this result in the following proof.

To prevent direct recovery of any $y \in \mathcal{Y}$, every pair (y, P) must fall into one of the following cases:

(i) **Parity P is on failed node 0.** Each $y \in \mathcal{Y}$ can contribute one such pair, so at most $q-f$ pairs arise here.
(ii) **Parity P is on some node j that is associated with at least two failed nodes (one is node i).** For a specific y on failed node i and any other failed node $\ell \neq i$, there are at most λ parities that encode both y and some object on node ℓ. With $p-1$ choices for ℓ, each y has at most $\lambda(p-1)$ parities that encode both object y on node i and an object on node ℓ. Summing over all $y \in \mathcal{Y}$ gives an upper bound of $\lambda(p-1)(q-f)$ pairs.
(iii) **Parity P is on a failed node $j \neq 0$ that is associated with exactly one failed node (namely node i).** All nodes in $\mathcal{F}$ are associated with node 0, so $j \notin \mathcal{F}$. There are $p-f-1$ possible nodes j left. Each such j is associated with only one failed node i, and node i contains at most λ objects

y in $\mathcal{Y}$. Moreover, each object y has exactly one parity on node j. Hence each fixed j contributes at most λ pairs, for a total of at most $\lambda(p-f-1)$ pairs.

These three cases cover all pairs that prevent direct recovery of y (possibly with overlap). The total number of such pairs is at most $(q-f)+\lambda(p-1)(q-f)+\lambda(p-f-1)$. Subtracting this from the total number of pairs, we have

$$\begin{aligned} &q(q-f)-[(q-f)+\lambda(p-1)(q-f)+\lambda(p-f-1)] \\ =&[q-\lambda(p-1)-1](q-f)-\lambda(p-f-1). \end{aligned} \tag{4}$$

If $q \leq \lambda(p-1)+1$, the result in (4) is non-positive. If $q=\lambda(p-1)+2$, the result in (4) simplifies to $(\lambda-1)f+2>0$.

Hence, when the number of replicas is set to the minimum permissible value $q=\lambda(p-1)+2$, at least one pair (y, P) survives, and does not fall into any of the obstructive categories. Consequently, parity P is on a live node that is associated with exactly one failed node (the node storing y), so y can be recovered directly.

Based on the above discussion, at least one alive parity P that encodes x has the property that every other object contributing to P can be directly recovered. Consequently, x itself can also be reconstructed. □

4.2 Full System

Based on the FLESC subsystem over v virtual nodes, we can realize the FLESC full system with parameters (n, v, k, p, λ) for any cluster of n physical nodes given $n \geq v$, while tolerating p simultaneous failures.

Virtual Node Layer. Label physical nodes $0, \ldots, n-1$. Each node i hosts v virtual nodes $(i, 0), \ldots, (i, v-1)$, giving nv virtual nodes in total, each hosted on one physical node for its I/O, backups, and parity.

Partition the nv virtual nodes into n subsystems of v nodes, using FLESC. For tolerance, one subsystem's v nodes must be on v distinct physical nodes; a membership table enforces this by listing (i, j) per subsystem with no duplicate i. Migration must not co-locate two nodes of the same subsystem.

Initial partition: (i, j) maps to subsystem $m=\lfloor(jn+i)/v\rfloor$, distributing across $0, \ldots, n-1$ (others possible; Fig. 3 shows $(n, v, k, p, \lambda)=(4,3,2,1,1)$).

If at most p physical nodes fail, each subsystem has at most p failed virtual nodes; thus each subsystem and the whole cluster restores all lost objects.

Addition of Physical Nodes. The FLESC full system supports flexible addition and removal of physical nodes while retaining the ability to tolerate any p simultaneous physical node failures.

When a new physical node is added, some virtual nodes can be migrated from the original physical nodes to the newly added one, and only the objects, replicas and parities on these virtual nodes are supposed to be migrated accordingly.

Suppose the newly added physical node is labeled as node i. The workflow of virtual nodes migration is as follows:

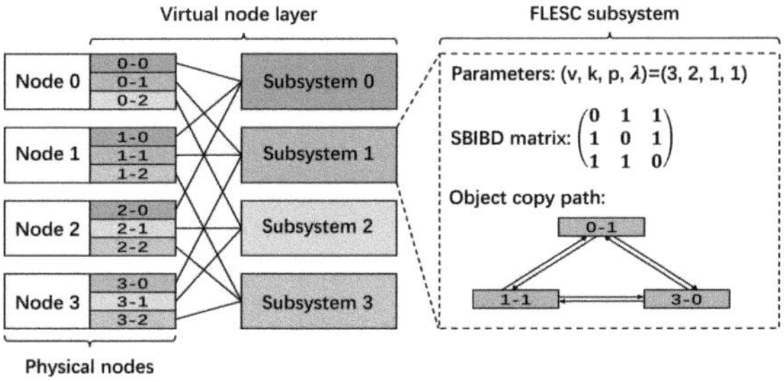

Fig. 3. Virtual node layer: mapping physical nodes to FLESC subsystems. Example: $(n, v, k, p, \lambda) = (4, 3, 2, 1, 1)$.

(i) Pick a physical node i_0 that currently hosts v_0 virtual nodes $(i_0, 0)$, $(i_0, 1)$, $\cdots$, $(i_0, v_0 - 1)$. Suppose there are currently v virtual nodes on physical node i. Check that the virtual node $(i_0, v_0 - 1)$ does not belong to the same subsystem as any virtual node residing on node i. If the check passes, move virtual node $(i_0, v_0 - 1)$ to physical node i and label it (i, v), and update the membership table of the subsystem to which this virtual node belongs. If the check fails, stop migrating from physical node i.

(ii) For the remaining physical nodes that require data migration, perform the previous procedure sequentially.

Removal of Physical Nodes. Conversely, a physical node can be removed as long as the remaining number of nodes is no less than the number of virtual nodes per subsystem. All virtual nodes on the departing node are relocated to suitable surviving nodes. Data on unaffected virtual nodes remains intact.

Let the departing node be physical node i, currently hosting v virtual nodes $(i, 0), (i, 1), \cdots, (i, v - 1)$. For each virtual node (i, j) in ascending order:

(i) scan the remaining physical nodes. For each candidate physical node i_0 that currently hosts v_0 virtual nodes, check whether any of those v_0 nodes belongs to the same subsystem as virtual node (i, j). The first physical node i_0 for which the check is negative (i.e., no subsystem conflict) receives the virtual node, and relabel it as (i_0, v_0). Meanwhile, update the membership table of the subsystem to which this virtual node belongs.

(ii) Proceed to the next virtual node of the departing host and repeat the previous procedure.

Figure 4 illustrates the process of migration after adding a physical node, and Fig. 5 illustrates the process of migration after removing a physical node.

4.3 Discussion

FLESC eliminates the limitations of Nos outlined in Sect. 3. The advantage of FLESC is its ability to deploy stripeless erasure coding schemes on clusters of

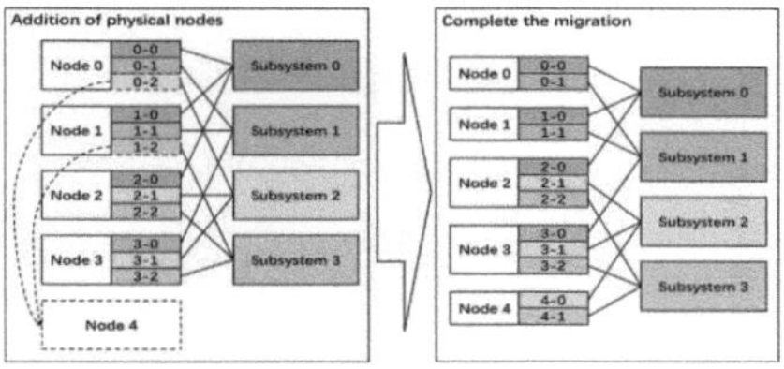

Fig. 4. Add one physical node to the 4 physical nodes cluster and complete the migration.

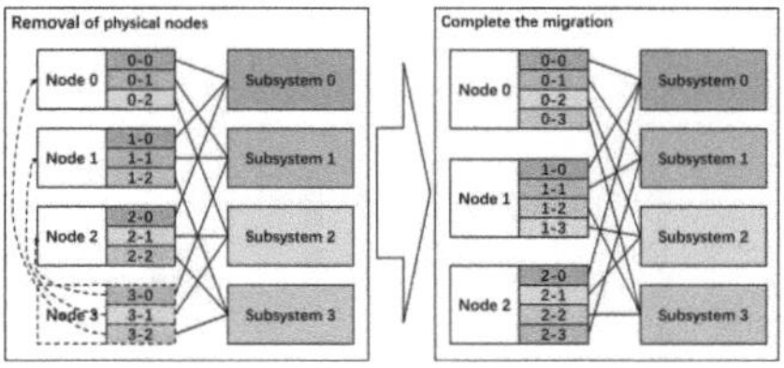

Fig. 5. Remove one physical node from the 4 physical nodes cluster and complete the migration.

any size and to accommodate arbitrary stripe widths. Moreover, FLESC can achieve the addition or removal of physical nodes under the static data placement policy by modifying the mapping between the virtual node layer and the physical cluster. The benefits come with trade-offs. FLESC's shortcoming is the additional bandwidth cost. Throughput decreases significantly when $\lambda > 1$.

5 Evaluation

We modified the `Nostor` code [7] and conducted experiments to test the read/write performance, the applicable scope and the fault recovery characteristics of FLESC.

5.1 Experiment Environment

We evaluate FLESC on CloudLab [6]. The test environment is based on several c6525-25g server nodes. The specific configuration is as follows,

- **CPU**: 1×16-core AMD 7302P, running at 3.0 GHz,
- **RAM**: 128GB (8×16 GB 3200 MT/s),
- **NIC**: Mellanox ConnectX-5 Ex 25Gb,
- **OS**: Ubuntu 24.04.2 LTS, kernel version 6.8.

Baseline. We also tested the following systems for comparison:

- `Nostor`: The implementation of Nos [8]. It uses XOR operation to generate parities.
- `Cocytus`: A representative stripe-based inter-object erasure-coded in-memory object storage system [2]. It uses RS code to generate parities.
- `Repl`: Create $p + 1$ replicas of an object to achieve fault tolerance.

Evaluations use two configurations $(n, k, p) = (7, 3, 1)$ and $(13, 4, 2)$, with n physical nodes. FLESC is tested with various λ (per-experiment). Its SBIBD dimension $v = k(k-1)/\lambda + 1$. When $v = n$, we assign v virtual nodes per physical node and apply FLESC full system to compare with `Nostor`, which uses (k, p) and $v = n$. `Cocytus` uses (k, p) for RS coding; `Repl` uses only p.

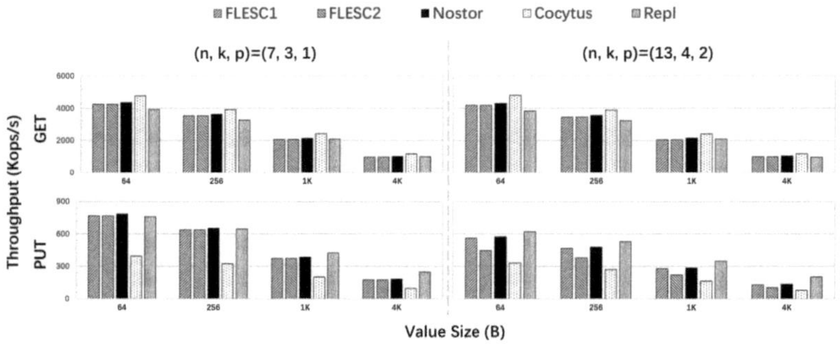

Fig. 6. Performance of 100%-GET and 100%-PUT microbenchmarks.

5.2 Benchmarks

We evaluate FLESC with the following benchmarks:

- 100%-GET and 100%-PUT microbenchmarks with fixed value sizes;
- YCSB [5] A, B and D (C is equivalent to 100%-GET).

Figure 6 shows the throughput of systems under 100%-GET & 100%-PUT workloads and both parameter configurations, where FLESC1 corresponds to $\lambda = 1$ and FLESC2 corresponds to $\lambda = 2$.

For GET operations, the measured read bandwidth of all systems is fairly close. FLESC performs two hash-table lookups per read while the other three systems perform only one. Under the two configurations, the read throughput of FLESC is about 83.6% of that of the best system, and is about 95.8% of `Nostor`.

For PUT, `Repl` has highest throughput (simple replication). `Nostor` and FLESC1 follow; their throughput drops with value size: at 64B they achieve 92.4% and 90.2% of Repl's rate, at 4KB fall to 66.8% and 63.9%; the small gap is due to FLESC1's extra virtual-physical lookup. Under (7,3,1), FLESC2 matches Nostor (both send $q = 2$ replicas). Under (13,4,2), FLESC2's throughput is only 76.4%–81% of Nostor's, because $q = \lambda(p-1) + 2 = 4$ vs. $p + 1 = 3$, increasing write traffic. `Cocytus` has poorest write performance (38.7%–53.5% of Repl), likely due to synchronous updates of data and parity.

Figure 7 shows latency-thpt curves with $(n, k, p) = (13, 4, 2)$ and 64B values. For GET, `Nostor`'s curve also represents `Cocytus` and `Repl`, while FLESC1's curve represents FLESC2 as well. All systems deliver highly similar performance. For PUT, FLESC1, `Nostor` and `Repl` have the lowest latencies. FLESC2 has similar latencies under normal situations, but it reaches the throughput limit more quickly because it has more replicas. `Cocytus` has much higher latencies and lower throughputs due to its high I/O fanout.

`Nostor` has shown that the parameter k has little influence on the performance of stripeless erasure coding schemes, because primary-backup replications and parity updates are performed asynchronously [8].

We study λ's effect on FLESC write performance. Figure 8 shows 100%-PUT throughput for $(n, k) = (31, 6)$ with varied p, λ. Two trends: (1) for fixed

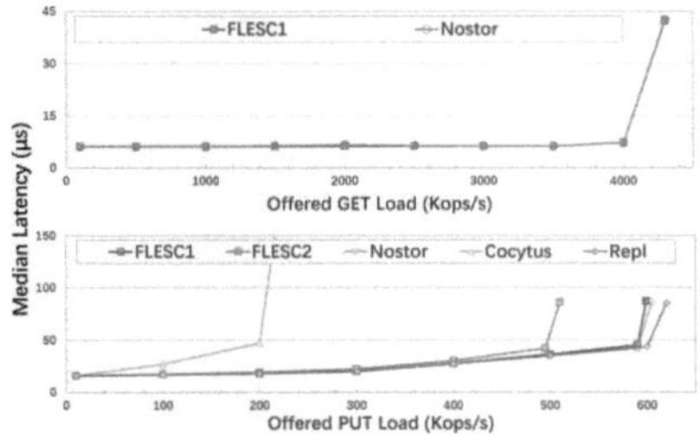

Fig. 7. Latency-throughput curves under GET and PUT microbenchmarks.

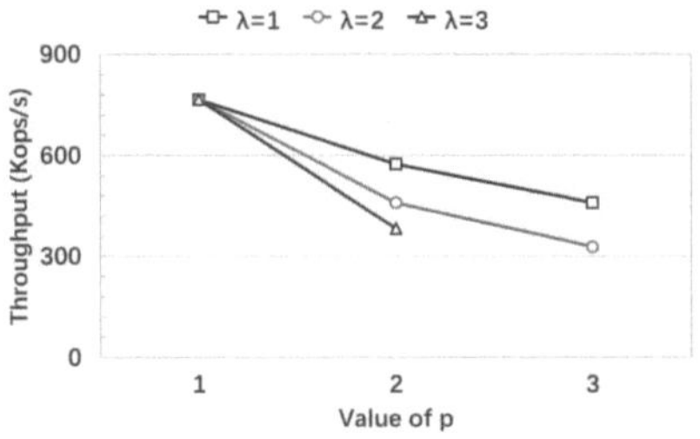

Fig. 8. Performance with different (p, λ) configurations.

λ, throughput drops as p increases, with diminishing marginal loss, since $q = \lambda(p-1)+2$ grows linearly with p; (2) larger λ accelerates the drop.

- For $\lambda = 1$, raising p from 1 to 2 and 2 to 3 reduces the throughput by 24.3% and 20.6%, respectively.
- For $\lambda = 2$, the corresponding drops are 41.2% and 28.8%.
- For $\lambda = 3$, the first drop already reaches roughly 50% (the case $(\lambda, p) = (3, 3)$ yields $q = 8 > k = 6$ and is therefore invalid for FLESC).

Figure 9 shows the performance of YCSB workloads. For YCSB-A, B, D, the throughput of FLESC1 is 95.7% to 98.8% of that of `Nostor`.

These experiments show that FLESC delivers similar throughput and latency to `Nostor`. Next we illustrate that FLESC demonstrates greater flexibility.

5.3 Cluster Size Compatibility

We conduct this experiment to validate that FLESC can be deployed on clusters with arbitrary numbers of physical nodes—the very motivation behind FLESC.

Figure 10 shows, for 64B values and fixed $p = 2$, how read/write throughput varies with the number of physical nodes. The experiment employed the same subsystem parameters $(v, k, p, \lambda) = (7, 3, 2, 1)$. The virtual-to-physical mapping is adjusted for different number of physical nodes.

`Nostor` is run with $(k, p) = (3, 2)$ when $n = 7$ and $(4, 2)$ when $n = 13$. It cannot be instantiated for $n = 9$ or 11 because no SBIBD exists for those settings. `Cocytus` uses ReedSolomon coding with $(k, p) = (3, 2)$ throughout.

For $7 \leq n \leq 13$, FLESC read bandwidth is $\sim$ 97% of `Nostor`'s, 87.3%–92.8% of `Cocytus`'s, and 1.08×–1.17× `Repl`'s. Write throughput is 96%–101% of `Nostor`'s, 1.89×–2.06× `Cocytus`'s, and essentially equal to `Repl`'s. Crucially, FLESC supports previously impossible $n = 9, 11$, extending `Nostor`'s scheme to any cluster size.

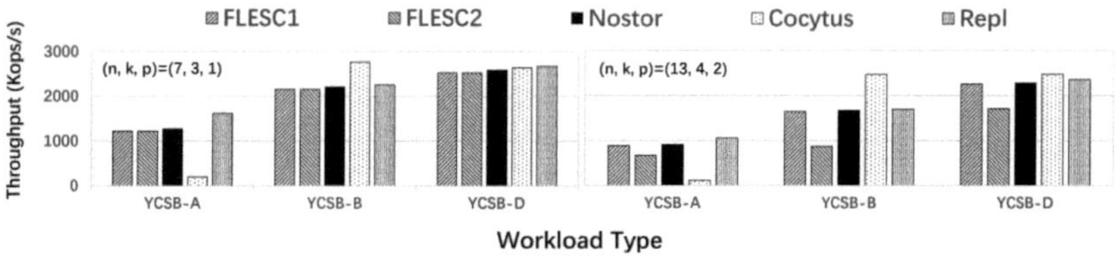

Fig. 9. Performance of YCSB workloads.

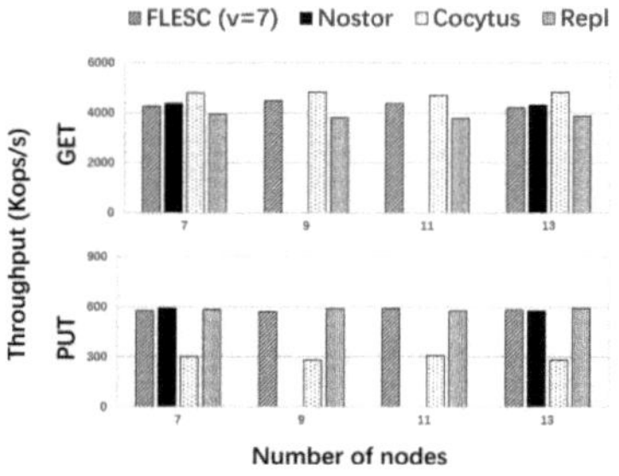

Fig. 10. Performance with different numbers n of physical nodes.

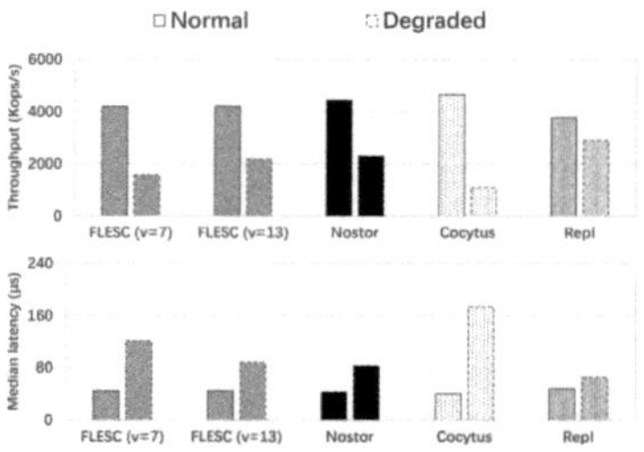

Fig. 11. Recovery performance with $(n, k, p) = (13, 4, 2)$.

5.4 Recovery Performance

We fail and reboot two servers at 64B to measure degraded read bandwidth and latency. Figure 11 compares the impaired cluster with the failure-free baseline. `Nostor`, `Cocytus` and `Repl` use $(n, k, p) = (13, 4, 2)$; FLESC is evaluated with $(n, v, k, p, \lambda) = (13, 7, 3, 2, 1)$ and $(13, 13, 4, 2, 1)$.

`Repl` suffers the smallest impact from the failure (-23.3% bandwidth,$+36.3\%$ latency), since it merely fetches an intact replication without any decoding. `Cocytus` shows the worst performance(-76.5% bandwidth, $+332.9\%$ latency) due to the expensive matrix-multiplication recovery algorithm.

FLESC and `Nostor` fall between `Repl` and `Cocytus`. FLESC with $v = 13$ (-48.3% bw, $+97.2\%$ lat) matches `Nostor` (-48.2% bw, $+94.6\%$ lat), but $v = 7$ suffers more (-62.6% bw, $+170.5\%$ lat), likely due to more parities inserted into the hash table ($(q/k)\times$ objects). For $\lambda = 1$, $(v, k) = (7, 3)$ degrades more than $(13, 4)$. Thus, FLESC should set v as close to n as possible to maximize k and reduce degraded-read impact.

6 Conclusion

This paper presents FLESC, a flexible stripeless erasure coding scheme for in-memory storage that scales to any cluster size. It uses SBIBD to select replication targets and builds a fault-tolerant subsystem. It further incorporates the virtual node layer to build the full system supporting arbitrary cluster size and dynamic node changes, maximizing resource utilization while ensuring tolerance.

Experiments show FLESC's competitive throughput, low latency, and seamless adaptability.

Acknowledgements. This work was supported by Key R&D Program of Shandong Province, China (No. 2024CXPT066).

Disclosure of Interests. The authors have no competing interests to declare that are relevant to the content of this article.

References

1. Bruck, R.H., Ryser, H.J.: The nonexistence of certain finite projective planes. Can. J. Math. **1**(1), 88–93 (1949)
2. Chen, H., et al.: Efficient and available in-memory KV-store with hybrid erasure coding and replication. ACM Trans. Storage (TOS) **13**(3), 1–30 (2017)
3. Chowla, S., Ryser, H.J.: Combinatorial problems. Can. J. Math. **2**, 93–99 (1950)
4. Colbourn, C.J.: CRC Handbook of Combinatorial Designs. CRC Press (2010)
5. Cooper, B.: Yahoo! cloud serving benchmark (YCSB). https://github.com/brianfrankcooper/YCSB
6. Duplyakin, D., et al.: The design and operation of CloudLab. In: 2019 USENIX Annual Technical Conference (USENIX ATC 19), pp. 1–14 (2019)
7. Gao, J.: Nos: Source code repository (2025). https://github.com/IcicleF/Nos. Accessed 16 Dec 2025
8. Gao, J., Shu, J., Yan, B., Zhang, Y., Huang, K.: Stripeless data placement for erasure-coded in-memory storage. In: 19th USENIX Symposium on Operating Systems Design and Implementation (OSDI 25), pp. 821–838 (2025)
9. Lee, Y., Al Maruf, H., Chowdhury, M., Cidon, A., Shin, K.G.: Hydra: resilient and highly available remote memory. In: 20th USENIX Conference on File and Storage Technologies (FAST 22), pp. 181–198 (2022)
10. Li, S., Zhang, Q., Yang, Z., Dai, Y.: BCStore: bandwidth-efficient in-memory KV-store with batch coding. In: Proceedings of IEEE MSST (2017)
11. Lindner, C.C., Rodger, C.A.: Design Theory. Chapman and Hall CRC (2017)
12. Muralidhar, S., et al.: f4: Facebook's warm BLOB storage system. In: 11th USENIX Symposium on Operating Systems Design and Implementation (OSDI 14), pp. 383–398 (2014)
13. Rashmi, K., Chowdhury, M., Kosaian, J., Stoica, I., Ramchandran, K.: EC-Cache: load-balanced, low-latency cluster caching with online erasure coding. In: 12th USENIX Symposium on Operating Systems Design and Implementation (OSDI 16), pp. 401–417 (2016)
14. Reed, I.S., Solomon, G.: Polynomial codes over certain finite fields. J. Soc. Ind. Appl. Math. **8**(2), 300–304 (1960)
15. Shan, Y., Chen, K., Gong, T., Zhou, L., Zhou, T., Wu, Y.: Geometric partitioning: explore the boundary of optimal erasure code repair. In: Proceedings of the ACM SIGOPS 28th Symposium on Operating Systems Principles, pp. 457–471 (2021)
16. Shen, Z., et al.: A survey of the past, present, and future of erasure coding for storage systems. ACM Trans. Storage **21**(1), 1–39 (2025)
17. Shvachko, K., Kuang, H., Radia, S., Chansler, R.: The hadoop distributed file system. In: 2010 IEEE 26th Symposium on Mass Storage Systems and Technologies (MSST), pp. 1–10. IEEE (2010)

18. Stinson, D.R.: Combinatorial designs: constructions and analysis. ACM SIGACT News **39**(4), 17–21 (2008)
19. Weatherspoon, H., Kubiatowicz, J.D.: Erasure coding vs. replication: a quantitative comparison. In: International Workshop on Peer-to-Peer Systems, pp. 328–337. Springer, Berlin, Heidelberg (2002). https://doi.org/10.1007/3-540-45748-8_31
20. Xia, M., Saxena, M., Blaum, M., Pease, D.A.: A tale of two erasure codes in HDFS. In: 13th USENIX Conference on File and Storage Technologies (FAST 15), pp. 213–226 (2015)
21. Yiu, M.M., Chan, H.H., Lee, P.P.: Erasure coding for small objects in in-memory KV storage. In: Proceedings of the 10th ACM International Systems and Storage Conference, pp. 1–12 (2017)
22. Zhou, Y., et al.: Carbink: fault-tolerant far memory. In: 16th USENIX Symposium on Operating Systems Design and Implementation (OSDI 22), pp. 55–71 (2022)

MADRQ: A Multi-agent Demonstration-Guided Framework for Multi-dimensional Range Query Optimization

Yabin Liu and Chaokun Wang(✉)

School of Software, Tsinghua University, Beijing 100084, China
liu-yb23@mails.tsinghua.edu.cn, chaokun@tsinghua.edu.cn

Abstract. Multi-dimensional range queries retrieve tuples that satisfy multiple range predicates over different attributes and commonly arise in analytical workloads with correlated predicates and complex joins. Such query patterns are motivated by applications including spatial search, e-commerce filtering, financial analytics, and IoT data exploration. Optimizing them remains challenging because correlated predicates and large join spaces weaken cardinality estimation and restrict plan exploration. Although learned optimizers improve individual components, they often rely on costly training and still search only a narrow candidate space. To address these issues, this paper proposes MADRQ, a multi-agent demonstration-guided optimization framework for multi-dimensional range queries. MADRQ starts from the database default plan, retrieves a demonstration, generates constrained local modifications in a hint-based intermediate representation, and ranks legal candidates through white-box legality filtering and LLM evaluation. Experiments on representative relational benchmarks show that MADRQ delivers consistent execution-time improvements over optimizer-centric baselines. Ablation studies further confirm the contribution of demonstration retrieval, database statistics, legality filtering, and LLM-based evaluation.

Keywords: Multi-dimensional range queries · Large language model · Query optimization · Multi-agent systems

1 Introduction

Multi-dimensional range queries are an important query pattern in database systems and data-intensive applications. They retrieve tuples that satisfy multiple range predicates over different attributes, often under strong correlations, skewed distributions, and evolving workloads. These query patterns are motivated by scenarios such as scientific data exploration and also arise in applications including geographic search, e-commerce filtering, and IoT analytics. In such settings,

L. Ding et al. (Eds.): APWeb-WAIM 2026, LNCS 16995, pp. 551–565, 2027.
https://doi.org/10.1007/978-981-92-5699-0_37

the performance depends not only on index support, but also on whether the query optimizer can choose effective access paths, join orders, and physical operators.

Optimizing these queries is challenging primarily due to two reasons. First, there is no single linear order that preserves interactions across dimensions, so classical one-dimensional structures such as B^+-trees cannot fully capture multi-attribute predicate patterns, especially when queries involve complex joins and aggregations. Furthermore, query optimizers often naively assume attribute independence; when attributes are actually strongly correlated, cardinality estimation errors compound rapidly up the query plan tree and mislead optimization decisions [9,11,12]. Second, real workloads are dynamic. Continuous data updates and distribution shifts quickly render pre-computed database statistics and cost models obsolete. As a result, the optimizer must jointly reason about predicate selectivity, access-path selection, join order, and intermediate-result size.

Traditional optimizers rely on dynamic programming and cost-based search to enumerate candidate plans [1,21]. Although this paradigm remains highly influential, its effectiveness is bounded by the quality of statistics and the ability to explore a rapidly growing plan space [17]. Learned approaches improve subtasks such as cardinality estimation and join ordering, but many of these methods require expensive offline training, frequent retraining, or specialized architectures that are difficult to integrate into a general-purpose optimizer. Large language models (LLMs) provide a new alternative because they can compare structurally different plans with strong contextual reasoning [23,25]. However, direct end-to-end plan generation with LLMs remains risky because unrestricted outputs may be semantically inconsistent, physically invalid, or difficult to map into executable database plans.

Driven by these observations, we propose a non-intrusive design paradigm: rather than replacing the native optimizer, we augment it with a controllable framework that leverages historical optimization knowledge, broadens the candidate exploration space, and strictly enforces database legality constraints. This rationale inspires our integration of demonstration-guided reasoning with a multi-agent architecture. Specifically, historical demonstrations provide valuable optimization priors for similar queries, while specialized agents decouple the complex optimization workflow into distinct stages of retrieval, exploration, and evaluation.

To this end, we propose MADRQ, a multi-agent demonstration-guided optimization framework for multi-dimensional range queries. MADRQ starts from the database default plan, retrieves a relevant demonstration, generates constrained local modifications in a hint-based intermediate representation, and ranks only legal candidates through a legality-aware evaluation pipeline. In this way, it combines the reasoning flexibility of LLMs with the strict execution semantics required by database engines.

In summary, this paper makes the following contributions.

1. We propose MADRQ, a practical and controllable multi-agent optimization framework that combines LLM reasoning with explicit database constraints through three coordinated stages: demonstration retrieval, plan exploration, and plan evaluation.
2. We design a contrastive query-plan retrieval mechanism and a hint-based intermediate representation that support demonstration-guided optimization through constrained local modifications.
3. We design a legality-aware evaluation pipeline that pairs rule-based verification with LLM-based candidate comparison, reducing the risk of adopting non-executable or invalid plans.
4. We conduct experiments on representative relational benchmarks to show consistent improvements of MADRQ over optimizer-centric baselines, and to validate the effectiveness of its core components.

2 Background and Related Work

This section reviews related work on multi-dimensional range-query optimization and identifies the limitations of existing methods.

2.1 Traditional Query Optimization Methods

Traditional optimization methods for multi-dimensional range queries focus on two core areas: index structure design and query plan generation.

Index Design. Early approaches relied on composite B^+-trees, ordering attributes by selectivity to maximize prefix-based pruning [21]. While this principle remains the default in mainstream databases, composite indexes have limitations in supporting non-prefix range queries. To address this limitation, multi-dimensional indexes such as R-trees [7] and GiST [8] were developed to support arbitrary attribute combinations and mixed-type queries. However, they suffer from high maintenance overhead, often taking 2–3 times longer to update than B^+-tree under intensive write workloads. For dynamic workloads, later studies explored adaptive indexing [22], which dynamically adjusts index priorities based on historical query frequencies. However, these methods rely heavily on extensive query logs and adapt poorly to cold starts or sudden workload shifts.

Query Plan Generation. Plan generation involves cooperative optimization of conditional filter ordering and index selection to balance plan optimality and generation efficiency. Traditional approaches utilize heuristics, dynamic programming, or evolutionary algorithms to prune the search space. For instance, greedy strategies [6] order predicates by estimated intermediate result sizes to prevent data explosion. However, such heuristics are highly sensitive to cardinality estimation and skewed data distributions can cause severe estimation errors, leading to suboptimal execution orders. Alternatively, genetic algorithms [2] can approximate optimal plans within polynomial time, but they remain strictly bounded by the accuracy of the cost models.

In summary, traditional optimization methods have two common limitations. First, they rely heavily on static statistical information, such as cardinality and histograms. Under dynamic data distributions or complex range predicates, outdated statistics frequently lead to index misselection and suboptimal plans. Second, they lack the ability to reuse historical query experience, requiring the recalculation of index priorities or plan generation for each multi-field query, resulting in wasted computation, especially under high-frequency workloads with many repetitive queries.

2.2 Learned Query Optimization Methods

Recent research has introduced Machine Learning and Deep Learning to reduce the dependence on static statistics and manually designed heuristics. These efforts primarily span three dimensions: cost prediction and index selection, multi-dimensional learned indexes, and end-to-end plan generation.

Cost Prediction and Index Selection. Machine Learning models are employed to capture non-linear correlations between attributes that traditional cost models often miss. For cost prediction, Krishnan et al. [10] use online algorithms on historical execution data to predict future query costs; however, this approach struggles to generalize to unseen attribute combinations. For index selection, Lulf et al. [15] employ Random Forests to determine whether to use composite or single-column indexes. Yet, this method only makes binary usage decisions and ignores the crucial step of optimizing attribute ordering within the index. Chen et al. [3] further model associations among attributes, indexes, and data with Graph Convolutional Networks (GCNs), generating representations that guide index usage.

Multi-dimensional Learned Indexes. Because traditional indexes are typically workload-agnostic, they often bottleneck on skewed data. To address this problem, Flood [19] co-optimizes the index structure and data layout for specific workloads, significantly improving the read performance. However, Flood struggles with highly skewed queries or strongly correlated dimensions. Tsunami [5] mitigates this problem by introducing a lightweight Grid Tree that partitions space into non-overlapping regions to capture dimension correlations, thereby reducing both query latency and index size. For spatial data, LISA [13] maps multi-dimensional keys to one-dimensional features using specialized mapping functions and local models, offering a novel approach to spatial range queries.

End-to-End Plan Generation. Deep learning methods attempt to directly generate execution plans through end-to-end modeling. RTOS [26] formulates query optimization as a reinforcement learning problem, using a Tree-LSTM to encode query conditions and iteratively merge sub-plans into a complete join tree. To address information loss in long-sequence condition encoding, TESSM [4] uses selective state space models (Tree-Mamba) for join order selection, though its high computational overhead limits practical deployment.

While ML and DL techniques successfully reduce reliance on static statistics and improve execution efficiency, they suffer from two major drawbacks. First, they incur high training and maintenance costs, as learned indexes and deep networks require massive amounts of training data and frequent retraining to adapt to data drift. Second, their generalization capabilities are inherently limited, often leading to severe performance degradation when encountering novel or shifting workloads.

2.3 LLM-Based Query Optimization Methods

Recent breakthroughs in Large Language Models (LLMs) offer a new paradigm for optimizing multi-dimensional range queries. By leveraging their advanced semantic understanding and logical reasoning capabilities, LLMs can help reason about complex predicate correlations and plan alternatives. Current research in this area primarily focuses on two directions: prompt engineering and end-to-end plan generation.

Prompt Engineering. Effective prompts help adapt general-purpose LLMs to query optimization. Pourreza et al. [20] integrate explicit schema information and range-condition rules into prompts, providing the structural context needed to identify constraint boundaries. To impart optimization knowledge without retraining, Nan et al. [18] employ few-shot prompting techniques. By embedding high-quality examples into the context window, they enable LLMs to learn useful optimization patterns through analogy and in-context learning. Because LLMs are also prone to generating invalid or suboptimal structures, Liu et al. [14] propose a negative-example-guided approach. This method uses contrastive signals to suppress hallucinations and help the model avoid erroneous patterns such as severe index misselection.

End-to-End Plan Generation. End-to-end plan generation approaches formulate query optimization directly as a sequence generation task, translating raw SQL inputs into complete physical execution plans. Tan et al. [23] introduce LLM-QO, utilizing supervised instruction tuning to train LLMs to explicitly mimic the step-by-step reasoning logic of traditional database optimizers. However, this framework incurs substantial computational overhead during the fine-tuning phase and requires vast amounts of domain-specific training pairs. To balance generation efficiency with plan accuracy, Yao et al. [25] propose LLMOpt, which adopts a two-stage generate-and-filter framework. In this design, the LLM first generates a diverse set of candidate query plans, which are subsequently evaluated and pruned by a dedicated filtering module to ensure basic structural validity before execution.

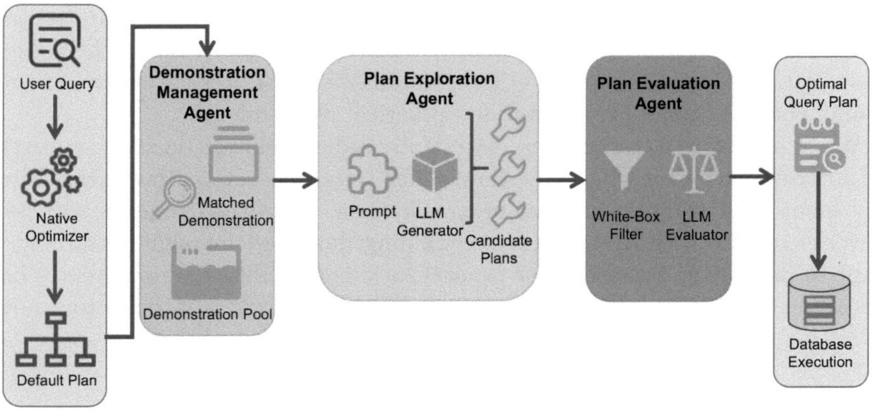

Fig. 1. Overall workflow of MADRQ.

While LLM-based approaches provide significant advantages, such as reducing reliance on static database statistics and reducing training data requirements through few-shot learning, they still face critical deployment challenges. The high inference and API costs of LLMs make them economically impractical for large-scale, highly concurrent query workloads. Furthermore, these models currently lack deep physical integration with the underlying database engines. Consequently, the execution plans generated by LLMs that appear theoretically optimal may lack execution semantics, causing them to be rejected or encounter severe bottlenecks in actual database systems. Motivated by these limitations, our goal is not to replace the optimizer with an unrestricted generator, but to build a constrained and practically deployable optimization loop around the native database engine.

3 Design of MADRQ

3.1 Overview

We present MADRQ, a multi-agent demonstration-guided optimization framework for multi-dimensional range queries. The design goal of MADRQ is to combine the reasoning flexibility of LLMs with the control requirements of a database optimizer. To achieve this goal, MADRQ decomposes optimization into three coordinated stages: demonstration retrieval, candidate-plan exploration, and candidate-plan evaluation. Given an input query Q, the database first produces a default physical plan, which is then converted into a structured hint sequence compatible with `pg_hint_plan`. The demonstration management agent retrieves one relevant historical demonstration, the plan exploration agent proposes constrained local modifications around the default plan, and the plan evaluation agent filters and ranks candidate plans before execution. Figure 1 shows the overall workflow.

The decomposition is motivated by three considerations. First, unconstrained end-to-end plan generation with an LLM is difficult to control in a large physical plan space. Second, explicit stage boundaries make the optimization pipeline easier to interpret, debug, and replace modularly. Third, the decomposition allows optimization-relevant database knowledge to be injected where it is most useful: demonstrations guide exploration, action constraints preserve executability, and white-box checks remove invalid outputs. In this sense, MADRQ follows the broader idea of role specialization in LLM agents [24], but grounds each role in database semantics. The multi-agent decomposition is therefore functionally motivated rather than cosmetic: it lets retrieval, constrained generation, and legality-aware comparison use different inputs, constraints, and verification mechanisms within one optimization loop. Rather than synthesizing a full plan from scratch, MADRQ starts from the native optimizer output and explores better alternatives incrementally. Compared with a single-agent formulation that directly emits a full plan, this design is easier to constrain, debug, and align with database execution semantics.

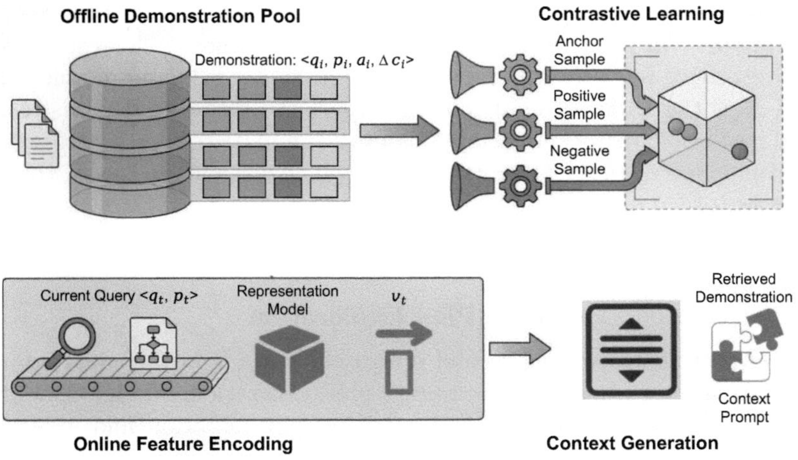

Fig. 2. Construction and retrieval pipeline of the demonstration management agent.

3.2 Demonstration-Guided Retrieval

Demonstration Pool. The first design challenge is how to provide optimization priors that are relevant to the current query-plan state. General-purpose LLMs are strong at reasoning, but they do not natively encode the fine-grained experience needed for physical query optimization. MADRQ addresses this issue with a demonstration management agent that maintains a structured demonstration pool, in which each demonstration is represented as

$$D_i = \langle q_i, p_i, a_i, \Delta c_i \rangle, \tag{1}$$

where q_i is a historical SQL query, p_i is its initial plan, a_i is an effective plan-modification action, and Δc_i measures the relative latency reduction achieved by that modification.

Contrastive Learning. To retrieve a demonstration that is useful for the current query-plan pair $\langle q_t, p_t \rangle$, we encode the query and its default plan jointly. The encoder is trained with contrastive learning so that query-plan pairs benefiting from similar optimization strategies are embedded close to each other in the representation space. For each anchor pair $\langle q, p \rangle$, we form a positive sample $\langle q^+, p^+ \rangle$ from a historical demonstration that leads to the strongest improvement, and a negative sample $\langle q^-, p^- \rangle$ from a demonstration associated with degraded performance. The encoder is trained by minimizing the following loss:

$$\mathcal{L} = -\log \frac{\exp(\mathrm{sim}(v_t, v_{pos})/\tau)}{\sum_{j=1}^{N} \left(\exp(\mathrm{sim}(v_t, v_{pos_j})/\tau) + \exp(\mathrm{sim}(v_t, v_{neg_j})/\tau)\right)}, \quad (2)$$

where v_t denotes the representation of the current query-plan pair, v_{pos} denotes the representation of its positive sample, v_{pos_j} and v_{neg_j} denote the representations of the j-th positive and negative samples in the batch, respectively, τ is the contrastive temperature hyperparameter, $\mathrm{sim}(\cdot,\cdot)$ denotes cosine similarity, and N is the batch size. At inference time, the retrieved demonstration is inserted into the exploration prompt. Figure 2 summarizes the construction and retrieval pipeline of the demonstration management agent. In effect, this stage converts historical optimization experience into query-specific guidance for the next stage.

3.3 Constrained Candidate Plan Exploration

Plan Representation. The second design challenge is how to support useful LLM exploration without unconstrained plan generation. MADRQ addresses this challenge with a hint-based intermediate representation and a restricted action space. We serialize the default plan into a hint sequence that exposes only the physical decisions most relevant to optimization: scan type, join operator, and global join order. For example, single-table access paths are represented by hints such as `SeqScan(A)` or `IndexScan(A)`; local join operators are represented by hints such as `HashJoin(A B)` or `NestLoop(A B)`; the global join order is represented by a `Leading` hint such as `Leading(((A B) C))`. The representation provides a common interface across LLM prompting, action application, and database execution.

Constrained Action Space. Rather than asking the LLM to produce a complete physical plan, we define a discrete action space $\mathcal{A}$ with three action types:

1. **Order swap** `Swap`(R_i, R_j) changes the relative positions of two relations, R_i and R_j, in the `Leading` structure.

2. **Scan override** `Override_Scan`(R_i, m_s) replaces the access path of relation R_i with a target scan method m_s, for example, changing a sequential scan to an index scan.
3. **Join override** `Override_Join`(R_i, R_j, m_j) replaces the physical join operator used for joining relations R_i and R_j with a target join method m_j, for example, changing a nested loop join to a hash join.

The LLM is only allowed to emit actions from this predefined set. As a result, candidate plans remain local modifications of a valid seed plan, which makes them easier to verify and compare.

Prompt Construction. The plan exploration prompt is built from four high-level ingredients: (1) a task instruction that asks the model to reduce plan cost through valid local modifications, (2) a retrieved demonstration from the demonstration management agent, (3) the current query-plan pair together with selected database statistics, and (4) a strict output format that requires structured actions rather than free-form text. In the deployed system, these ingredients are organized into a unified prompt template with six explicit blocks: a task-description block, an action-space block, a hard-constraints block, a demonstration block, a current-query-plan-context block, and an output-instruction block. The hard-constraints block explicitly forbids non-existent relations, illegal join pairs, unavailable indexes, and semantically inconsistent rewrites, while the output-instruction block requires the model to produce a small number of independently executable action sets. The plan exploration agent applies the generated actions to the default hint sequence to construct a set of candidate plans. As a result, this stage expands the candidate space around the native optimizer output without losing structural control.

3.4 Plan Evaluation

The final design challenge is how to compare candidate plans without accepting invalid or semantically inconsistent outputs. MADRQ addresses this issue with a plan evaluation agent and a legality-aware evaluation pipeline that combines white-box filtering with LLM-based selection.

White-Box Legality Filtering. Each candidate plan is checked against three classes of constraints:

1. **Metadata constraints**: all referenced tables, columns, indexes, and join keys must exist and be available.
2. **Generation constraints**: every candidate must be derived from valid actions in $\mathcal{A}$ and may only modify operators or relations present in the current plan.
3. **Structural constraints**: the `Leading` structure must match the set of base tables in the query without duplication, omission, or obvious join inconsistencies.

Candidates that fail any check are pruned immediately.

Candidate Selection. After filtering, up to M legal candidates are retained. The plan evaluation agent then forms a unified evaluation set by combining these candidates with the database default plan. The evaluation prompt includes the original SQL query, core database statistics, and the hint sequences of all legal plans. The LLM compares access paths, join order, and physical operators across all candidates and selects the best legal candidate for execution. In this way, the final stage preserves the comparative strength of LLM reasoning while ensuring that only executable plans reach the database.

4 Evaluation

4.1 Experimental Setup

MADRQ is implemented in Python on top of PostgreSQL. We use a PostgreSQL hinting extension to expose and enforce hint-based plan modifications. The experiments are conducted on Ubuntu 16.04.7 LTS with an Intel Xeon E5-2630 CPU and 315 GB memory, using Python 3.10.

In the experiments reported here, the generic LLM component of MADRQ is instantiated with GPT-4o through the OpenAI API. We keep the LLM backend fixed across all experiments and use stage-specific prompt templates: the exploration stage uses the six-block prompt described in Sect. 3, while the evaluation stage compares the default plan with up to M legal candidates in a shared prompt. The exploration stage generates $R = 8$ candidate action sets for each query, after which legality filtering retains at most $M = 4$ candidates for final comparison. GPT-4o decoding uses temperature = 1.0 and top-p = 1.0, corresponding to the default OpenAI API settings.

We evaluate on two widely used benchmarks. JOB contains 33 complex join queries over IMDB data and is particularly sensitive to join ordering and access-path decisions. TPC-H contains 22 decision-support query templates and represents a more regular analytical workload. We use JOB and TPC-H as controlled relational benchmarks that stress join ordering and access-path selection under complex predicate interactions. These benchmarks do not fully cover specialized workloads such as spatial queries or streaming IoT applications, but they still reflect the core optimization challenges targeted by MADRQ. We compare MADRQ with the PostgreSQL native optimizer and Bao [16]. We choose Bao as the main learned baseline because, like MADRQ, it augments rather than replaces the native PostgreSQL optimizer, making the comparison structurally aligned. We also conduct ablations by removing demonstration retrieval (w/o Demo), database statistics (w/o Stat), and the LLM-based evaluation stage (w/o Eval-LLM). In addition, we analyze the effect of the white-box legality module by removing validity filtering (w/o Validity) and measuring the proportion of hallucinated candidate plans. Unless otherwise stated, the number of generated action groups is set to $R = 8$ and the maximum number of retained legal candidates is set to $M = 4$.

Table 1. Overall execution-time comparison (seconds)

Dataset	Method	Mean	Median	75th	95th
JOB	PostgreSQL	14.81	3.88	8.27	58.03
	Bao	12.24	**3.06**	6.68	48.27
	MADRQ	**11.08**	3.11	**6.52**	**42.33**
TPC-H	PostgreSQL	7.18	0.74	1.58	86.44
	Bao	6.96	0.74	1.55	84.02
	MADRQ	**6.59**	**0.72**	**1.49**	**79.84**

4.2 Overall Results

Table 1 reports execution-time statistics. MADRQ improves over both PostgreSQL and Bao on the reported aggregate metrics for the two benchmarks. On JOB, mean latency drops from 14.81 s to 11.08 s, a relative reduction of 25.2%. On TPC-H, the gain is smaller but remains consistent on the reported aggregates, with mean latency decreasing from 7.18 s to 6.59 s. The larger gain on JOB is expected because JOB contains harder multi-join queries with a larger search space. In this setting, demonstration-guided exploration and unified candidate evaluation are more likely to find better alternatives than the native optimizer alone.

Bao already improves over PostgreSQL, indicating that learning-based candidate selection is useful even when the underlying optimizer is kept intact. However, Bao remains limited by the quality and diversity of its candidate plan space. A plausible explanation for the additional gain of MADRQ is that it explicitly expands the candidate set with demonstration-guided local modifications and compares all legal alternatives, including the default plan, in a shared evaluation context. Figure 3 shows the same overall pattern in normalized form, with MADRQ outperforming the baselines more clearly on JOB than on TPC-H.

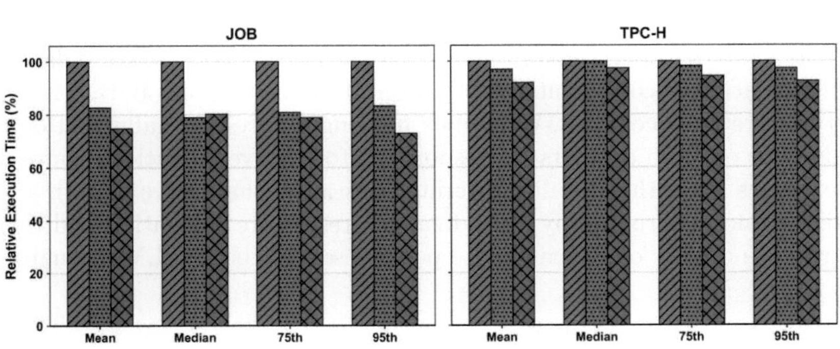

Fig. 3. Normalized performance relative to PostgreSQL.

4.3 Impact of Major Components

Table 2 shows that removing any major component of MADRQ degrades the performance. The largest drop comes from removing demonstration retrieval, which raises mean execution time to 12.73 s on JOB and 7.05 s on TPC-H. This result indicates that the demonstration is important for steering the LLM toward transferable and workload-aware modifications. Removing database statistics also hurts the performance because the model loses signals about selectivity and cost-sensitive operator choices. Replacing the LLM-based final ranking with the native cost model causes a smaller but still consistent degradation, suggesting that candidate generation contributes most of the gain, while the evaluator adds complementary benefits. Taken together, these experimental results suggest that the benefit of MADRQ comes from the staged combination of retrieval, constrained exploration, and legality-aware evaluation rather than from any single component in isolation.

Table 2. Ablation results (mean execution time in seconds)

Method	JOB	TPC-H
w/o Demo	12.73	7.05
w/o Stat	12.41	6.92
w/o Eval-LLM	<u>11.96</u>	<u>6.79</u>
MADRQ	**11.08**	**6.59**

4.4 Effect of Legality Filtering

Beyond end-to-end performance, we examine whether white-box legality filtering improves the candidate quality. To this end, we construct a variant without legality filtering (w/o Validity) and measure hallucinated candidates caused by metadata errors, illegal join pairs, or inconsistent `Leading` structures. We report the hallucination ratio before filtering, the residual ratio after filtering, and the corresponding relative reduction.

Table 3 shows that a substantial fraction of LLM-generated candidates violate hard database constraints before filtering, especially on JOB, where join structures are more complex. White-box filtering reduces the hallucination ratio to below 3% on both datasets, corresponding to relative reductions above 91%. These results show that legality filtering does more than serve as a final safeguard: it removes structurally invalid candidates before evaluation and thereby improves the quality of the candidate pool presented to the LLM evaluator.

4.5 End-to-End Overhead

A practical concern for LLM-assisted optimization is whether the execution-time savings can offset additional planning overhead. Table 4 separates planning

Table 3. Effect of legality filtering on hallucinated candidate plans

Dataset	Before filtering	After filtering	Reduction
JOB	29.7%	2.1%	92.9%
TPC-H	21.4%	1.8%	91.6%

time from execution time. MADRQ has the highest planning overhead because it includes demonstration retrieval, action generation, legality checking, and unified plan comparison. Even so, it achieves the best reported end-to-end runtime on both benchmarks, although the margin on TPC-H is small. The effect is clearest on JOB, where savings from better execution plans compensate for the additional planning cost.

Table 4. End-to-end runtime analysis (seconds)

Dataset	Method	Planning	Execution	End-to-End
JOB	PostgreSQL	0.05	14.81	14.86
	Bao	0.28	12.24	12.52
	MADRQ	0.76	11.08	**11.84**
TPC-H	PostgreSQL	0.03	7.18	7.21
	Bao	0.17	6.96	7.13
	MADRQ	0.51	6.59	**7.10**

Taken together, these results suggest that MADRQ is best viewed as a framework for expensive analytical queries, including complex multi-dimensional range queries, where the extra planning time can be offset by substantial execution-time savings. For extremely short point queries, the benefit is expected to be smaller.

5 Conclusion

This paper presented MADRQ, a controllable multi-agent framework for improving optimizer-generated plans for analytical queries with multiple predicates and complex joins. By separating demonstration retrieval, constrained plan exploration, and legality-aware plan evaluation, MADRQ combines LLM reasoning with explicit database constraints in a controllable optimization loop. The experiments on two representative relational benchmarks demonstrate consistent improvements over PostgreSQL and Bao, while ablation studies confirm the contribution of each major component. Taken together, these results suggest that multi-agent orchestration is a practical direction for bringing LLM reasoning into query optimization without sacrificing executability. Future work will extend MADRQ to more complex query types and explore more adaptive multi-agent coordination strategies.

Acknowledgments. This work is supported in part by the National Natural Science Foundation of China (No. 62372264 and No. 92467203) and Sina Weibo Corp. Chaokun Wang is the corresponding author.

References

1. Astrahan, M.M., et al.: System R: relational approach to database management. ACM Trans. Database Syst. **1**(2), 97–137 (1976)
2. Bennett, K.P., Ferris, M.C., Ioannidis, Y.E.: A Genetic Algorithm for Database Query Optimization. University of Wisconsin-Madison Department of Computer Sciences, Tech. rep. (1991)
3. Chen, J., et al.: Efficient join order selection learning with graph-based representation. In: Proceedings of the 28th ACM SIGKDD Conference on Knowledge Discovery and Data Mining, pp. 97–107 (2022)
4. Chu, Y., Liu, Y., Zhang, Y., Hou, X., Yu, L., Peng, Z.: TESSM: tree-based selective state space models for efficient join order selection learning. In: Proceedings of the 33rd ACM International Conference on Information and Knowledge Management, pp. 374–383 (2024)
5. Ding, J., Nathan, V., Alizadeh, M., Kraska, T.: Tsunami: a learned multidimensional index for correlated data and skewed workloads. Proc. VLDB Endowment **14**(2), 74–86 (2020)
6. Fegaras, L., Maier, D.: Optimizing object queries using an effective calculus. ACM Trans. Database Syst. **25**(4), 457–516 (2000)
7. Guttman, A.: R-Trees: a dynamic index structure for spatial searching. In: Proceedings of the 1984 ACM SIGMOD International Conference on Management of Data, pp. 47–57 (1984)
8. Hellerstein, J.M., Naughton, J.F., Pfeffer, A.: Generalized search trees for database systems. In: Proceedings of the 21st International Conference on Very Large Data Bases, pp. 562–573. Morgan Kaufmann (1995)
9. Kipf, A., Kipf, T., Radke, B., Leis, V., Boncz, P.A., Kemper, A.: Learned cardinalities: estimating correlated joins with deep learning. In: Conference on Innovative Data Systems Research (2019)
10. Krishnan, P.: Online Prediction Algorithms for Databases and Operating Systems. Brown University (1995)
11. Krishnan, S., Yang, Z., Goldberg, K., Hellerstein, J., Stoica, I.: Learning to optimize join queries with deep reinforcement learning. arXiv preprint arXiv:1808.03196 (2018)
12. Leis, V., Gubichev, A., Mirchev, A., Boncz, P., Kemper, A., Neumann, T.: How good are query optimizers, really? Proc. VLDB Endowment **9**(3), 204–215 (2015)
13. Li, P., Lu, H., Zheng, Q., Yang, L., Pan, G.: LISA: a learned index structure for spatial data. In: Proceedings of the 2020 ACM SIGMOD International Conference on Management of Data, pp. 2119–2133 (2020)
14. Liu, J., Mozafari, B.: GenRewrite: query rewriting via large language models. arXiv preprint arXiv:2403.09060 (2024)

15. Lülf, C., Martins, D.M.L., Salles, M.A.V., Zhou, Y., Gieseke, F.: Fast search-by-classification for large-scale databases using index-aware decision trees and random forests. Proc. VLDB Endowment **16**(11), 2845–2857 (2023)
16. Marcus, R., Negi, P., Mao, H., Tatbul, N., Alizadeh, M., Kraska, T.: Bao: making learned query optimization practical. In: Proceedings of the 2021 International Conference on Management of Data, pp. 1275–1288 (2021)
17. Marcus, R., Negi, P., Mao, H., Zhang, C., Alizadeh, M., Kraska, T., Papaemmanouil, O., Tatbul, N.: Neo: a learned query optimizer. Proc. VLDB Endowment **12**(11), 1705–1718 (2019)
18. Nan, L., et al.: Enhancing text-to-SQL capabilities of large language models: a study on prompt design strategies. In: Findings of the Association for Computational Linguistics: EMNLP 2023, pp. 14935–14956 (2023)
19. Nathan, V., Ding, J., Alizadeh, M., Kraska, T.: Learning multi-dimensional indexes. In: Proceedings of the 2020 ACM SIGMOD International Conference on Management of Data, pp. 985–1000 (2020)
20. Pourreza, M., Rafiei, D.: DIN-SQL: decomposed in-context learning of text-to-SQL with self-correction. In: Advances in Neural Information Processing Systems, vol. 36, pp. 34123–34139. Curran Associates, Inc (2023)
21. Selinger, P.G., Astrahan, M.M., Chamberlin, D.D., Lorie, R.A., Price, T.G.: Access path selection in a relational database management system. In: Proceedings of the 1979 ACM SIGMOD International Conference on Management of Data, pp. 23–34 (1979)
22. Sun, J., Li, G.: An end-to-end learning-based cost estimator. Proc. VLDB Endowment **13**(3), 307–319 (2019)
23. Tan, J., et al.: Can large language models be query optimizer for relational databases? Proc. ACM Manage. Data **3**(6), 1–28 (2025)
24. Xi, Z., et al.: The rise and potential of large language model based agents: a survey. Sci. China Inf. Sci. **68**(2), 121101 (2025)
25. Yao, Z., Li, H., Zhang, J., Li, C., Chen, H.: A query optimization method utilizing large language models. arXiv preprint arXiv:2503.06902 (2025)
26. Yu, X., Li, G., Chai, C., Tang, N.: Reinforcement learning with tree-LSTM for join order selection. In: 2020 IEEE 36th International Conference on Data Engineering, pp. 1297–1308. IEEE (2020)

Panel-Aware Best-of-K Selection for Mental-Health Support Dialogue

Kang Yao[1,2], Quanbo Cheng[1,2], Zhijie Ren[1], Weiwei Fu[2(✉)], and Jinjiang Cui[2]

[1] School of Biomedical Engineering (Suzhou), Division of Life Science and Medicine, University of Science and Technology of China, Suzhou, China
{yaokang,renzhijie}@mail.ustc.edu.cn, qbcheng@ustc.edu

[2] Suzhou Institute of Biomedical Engineering and Technology, Chinese Academy of Sciences, Suzhou, Jiangsu, China
{fuww,cuijj}@sibet.ac.cn

Abstract. Best-of-K selection improves dialogue generation by choosing a final response from multiple candidates. In mental-health support dialogue, however, a pooled verifier can discard useful expert-specific preferences before selection. We propose **PanelCover-BoK**, a panel-aware coverage selection framework for Mandarin support dialogue. The method estimates role-level utilities, projects them through dialogue-state features, and selects a K-response set with a robust coverage objective that balances average panel utility and the least-covered expert role. On an 800-dialogue expert-evaluation set, PanelCover-BoK is the best-performing evaluated system among reproduced planners, retrieval baselines, prompt-only LLM systems, and direct LLM responses. Blind expert preference evaluation shows that PanelCover-BoK wins 57.1%–63.6% of non-tied pairwise comparisons and maintains tie-aware win rates above 0.545. Mechanism analysis, held-out expert scoring, and backbone transfer are consistent with the interpretation that the gains are attributable to preserving expert-specific alternatives before final selection.

Keywords: Mental-health dialogue · Best-of-K selection · Panel-aware optimization · Expert preference modeling

1 Introduction

Best-of-K generation has become a practical way to improve dialogue systems. A generator produces several candidate responses, and a verifier chooses the candidate with the highest estimated quality. In mental-health support dialogue, this verifier also determines which professional priorities guide the response seen by the user.

Support quality is inherently multi-perspective. A safety-oriented reviewer may prefer caution in ambiguous risk contexts; a client-experience reviewer may

K. Yao and Q. Cheng—These authors contributed equally to this work.

L. Ding et al. (Eds.): APWeb-WAIM 2026, LNCS 16995, pp. 566–576, 2027.
https://doi.org/10.1007/978-981-92-5699-0_38

favor validation and continuity; a CBT-oriented support reviewer may prefer concrete next steps. These differences reflect distinct professional priorities rather than arbitrary label noise, so a useful selector should exploit expert agreement while preserving role-specific signal.

Most Best-of-K systems collapse this signal too early. A pooled Bradley–Terry (BT) verifier averages expert judgments into a single scalar utility and then selects the response that is best for the average. This is simple and often effective, but it can prefer a compromise response while discarding a candidate set that contains strong options for different expert roles. The key issue is the order of operations: *pool before selecting* is not equivalent to *select per expert before averaging*. The latter naturally induces a coverage objective over a candidate set.

We treat this as a selection problem. Given a dialogue context and a fixed strategy-conditioned candidate bank, the goal is to choose a small candidate set that covers expert-specific preferences and then materialize one response from that set. We formalize panel-aware coverage, derive a coverage-dividend measure that quantifies what pooled selection loses, and optimize the induced objective with exact enumeration in the current seven-strategy action space.

We instantiate the framework with **PanelCover-BoK**, which combines a shared strategy-conditioned response bank, multi-dimensional expert utility models, robust coverage optimization, and a panel-state final selector. In planner-style comparisons, the candidate generator is held fixed, isolating the selection rule.

Our contributions are as follows:

1. We formalize panel-aware Best-of-K selection as a coverage optimization problem and identify when pooled and panel-aware selection can disagree.

2. We propose PanelCover-BoK, an exact-enumeration panel coverage algorithm with state-conditioned utility projection and risk-aware feasibility constraints.

3. We establish the best performance among the evaluated baselines under a blind 800-dialogue expert protocol, comparing against reproduced planners, retrieval systems, prompt-only LLM variants, and direct LLM responses.

4. We provide evidence from mechanism analysis, ablation, held-out expert scoring, and backbone transfer, supporting the interpretation that the improvement is driven by coverage selection.

2 Related Work

Emotional-Support and Mental-Health Dialogue. Emotional-support and mental-health support dialogue research has introduced datasets and models for empathy, supportive conversations, and strategy-aware support [8,16]. Later work studies mixed strategies, lookahead planning, state transition, knowledge grounding, LLM preference bias, and LLM-oriented evaluation [2,4,5,18,22,23]. Our work focuses on the selection layer that decides which candidate response should be surfaced when several expert perspectives are relevant.

Best-of-K Selection and Learned Verifiers. Best-of-K selection and learned verifiers are widely used in instruction following, preference optimization, and reasoning evaluation [7,12]. LLM judges and preference models are sensitive to prompt design and benchmark construction [6,9]; we study a complementary source of sensitivity: how the verifier represents multiple expert views before response selection.

Disagreement-Aware and Perspectivist NLP. Perspectivist NLP argues that annotator disagreement can encode meaningful variation rather than mere noise [3,19]. Multi-annotator preference modeling, including BT-style ranking models [1], provides tools for preserving such variation. We extend this idea from label aggregation to Best-of-K dialogue selection, where the timing of aggregation changes which response is selected.

Safety-Sensitive Dialogue Evaluation. Safety-sensitive dialogue evaluation considers risk detection, crisis-oriented support cues, privacy, and appropriate boundaries [17,20]. We handle safety as both an evaluation dimension and a feasibility constraint, without treating the system output as diagnosis or clinical intervention.

3 Panel-Aware Coverage Selection

3.1 Task Formulation

Let x denote a dialogue context and let $\mathcal{A}$ be a finite set of strategy labels:

$$\mathcal{A} = \{\text{QUESTION}, \text{REFLECTION}, \text{EMPATHY}, \text{REFRAME}, \\ \text{SUMMARIZATION}, \text{ACTION\_SUGGESTION}, \text{SAFETY\_REFERRAL}\}.$$

A SAFETY_REFERRAL label denotes a risk-aware supportive response pattern, such as encouraging help-seeking or appropriate resources; it is not a diagnosis, crisis-service decision, or clinical intervention. A shared generator maps each context–strategy pair (x, a) to a cached response $r(x, a)$. A planner selects a strategy subset $S \subseteq \mathcal{A}$ with $|S| \leq K$, inducing the response set

$$R_S(x) = \{r(x, a) : a \in S\}. \tag{1}$$

The selection problem is to choose S so that the induced candidate set covers the preferences of a panel of expert roles, while still allowing a single final response to be materialized.

3.2 Pooled Selection Vs. Panel Coverage

Let E be the set of expert roles and let $u_e(x, a) \in [0, 1]$ be the probability-normalized utility that expert e assigns to response $r(x, a)$. A pooled verifier averages expert utilities and then chooses the best response:

$$P(S \mid x) = \max_{a \in S} \frac{1}{|E|} \sum_{e \in E} u_e(x, a). \tag{2}$$

Panel-aware coverage reverses this order by first taking each expert's best response from the set and then averaging:

$$F(S \mid x) = \frac{1}{|E|} \sum_{e \in E} \max_{a \in S} u_e(x, a). \tag{3}$$

The pooled objective rewards a single response that is good for the average expert. The panel objective rewards a set that contains strong responses for different expert roles.

Coverage Property. For fixed utilities, $F(S \mid x)$ is a monotone submodular set function. Adding a candidate cannot decrease any expert's maximum utility, and the marginal gain for expert e, $\max(0, u_e(x,a) - \max_{b \in S} u_e(x,b))$, decreases as S grows. Averaging over experts preserves submodularity, connecting panel-aware selection to classical coverage optimization [11]. Larger action spaces could use greedy approximations; our seven-strategy setting permits exact enumeration.

The difference between the two objectives is the coverage dividend:

$$C(S \mid x) = F(S \mid x) - P(S \mid x) \geq 0. \tag{4}$$

It is zero when expert views select the same response or when $|S| = 1$, and it increases when different experts prefer different candidates. For two systems S and T, pooled and panel-aware selection disagree when

$$\big[P(S \mid x) - P(T \mid x)\big] \cdot \big[F(S \mid x) - F(T \mid x)\big] < 0. \tag{5}$$

Equivalently, a system with lower pooled utility can win under panel coverage if

$$C(S \mid x) - C(T \mid x) > P(T \mid x) - P(S \mid x). \tag{6}$$

This condition gives a concrete criterion for when a pooled verifier changes the ordering of Best-of-K systems.

3.3 Multi-Dimensional Expert Utility

Expert utilities are estimated from blind pairwise judgments. The selector uses the core dimension set

$$\mathcal{D} = \{\textit{overall, helpfulness, empathy, specificity,} \\ \textit{actionability, appropriateness, safety}\}.$$

For each expert role e and dimension $d \in \mathcal{D}$, we fit a regularized BT model that assigns a score $\ell_{e,d}(x, a)$ to response $r(x, a)$. Since raw logits from different expert–dimension models need not share an absolute scale, we aggregate only BT-induced pairwise probabilities within the same dialogue context:

$$\begin{aligned} p_{e,d}(a \succ b \mid x) &= \sigma\big(\ell_{e,d}(x,a) - \ell_{e,d}(x,b)\big), \\ u_{e,d}(x,a) &= \frac{1}{|\mathcal{A}| - 1} \sum_{\substack{b \in \mathcal{A} \\ b \neq a}} p_{e,d}(a \succ b \mid x). \end{aligned} \tag{7}$$

This gives each response an expected within-cache win probability against the remaining strategy-conditioned candidates on dimension d, without directly averaging raw BT logits across experts or dimensions.

The final expert utility is a state-conditioned projection over dimensions:

$$u_e(x, a) = \sum_{d \in \mathcal{D}} w_d(s(x)) u_{e,d}(x, a), \quad \sum_{d \in \mathcal{D}} w_d(s(x)) = 1. \tag{8}$$

The state vector $s(x)$ represents distress, risk, readiness, alliance, and clarity. Fixed, pre-test state lifts increase safety under risk, empathy under distress, specificity under low clarity, actionability under readiness, and appropriateness under low alliance. The resulting weights are normalized before Eq. 8 is applied.

3.4 Optimization Objective

The plain panel objective in Eq. 3 can still over-serve the majority of the panel. We therefore use a robust coverage objective:

$$J(S \mid x) = (1 - \alpha) \frac{1}{|E|} \sum_{e \in E} \max_{a \in S} u_e(x, a) + \alpha \min_{e \in E} \max_{a \in S} u_e(x, a). \tag{9}$$

The first term maximizes mean panel coverage; the second protects the least-covered expert role. We fix $\alpha = 0.15$. Because the action space is small, exact enumeration gives the optimum of Eq. 9 within the feasible family.

4 PanelCover-BoK

4.1 Overall Workflow

Figure 1 illustrates the workflow. Given a dialogue context, the system estimates dialogue state and risk cues, creates a strategy-conditioned candidate bank, filters infeasible sets with a safety gate, scores candidates with per-role BT utilities and state-conditioned weights, enumerates feasible K-sets, and chooses one response using a panel-state selector.

4.2 Candidate Bank and Feasibility Constraints

All planner-style systems use the same strategy-conditioned candidate bank, so differences come from selecting the K-set rather than writing new responses. The feasibility family $\mathcal{F}(x)$ is context-dependent: severe risk requires the risk-aware SAFETY_REFERRAL support pattern; high distress or low alliance requires support-oriented strategies such as EMPATHY or REFLECTION; low clarity favors information-gathering or SUMMARIZATION.

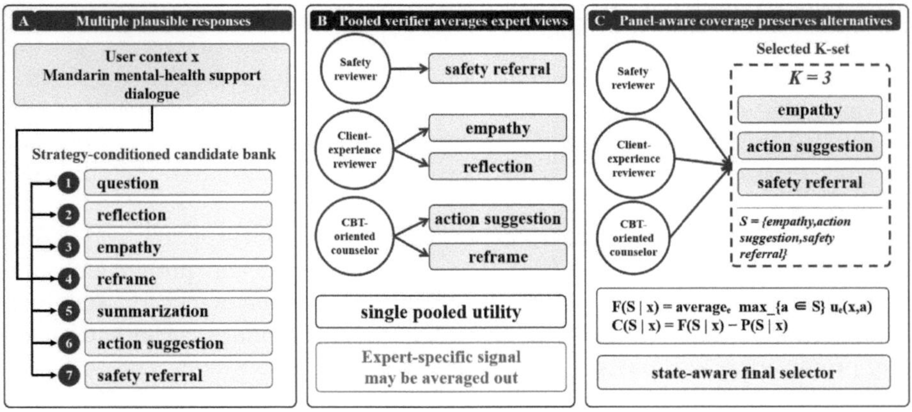

Fig. 1. Overview of PanelCover-BoK. Multiple strategy-conditioned responses are first constructed for the same dialogue context. A pooled verifier can average away expert-specific signals, whereas panel-aware coverage preserves a compact K-set that contains useful alternatives for different expert roles before the state-aware final selector materializes one response.

4.3 Robust Coverage Optimization

For every feasible set $S \in \mathcal{F}(x)$ with $|S| = K$, PanelCover-BoK computes the robust coverage score in Eq. 9. Because $|\mathcal{A}| = 7$ and $K = 3$, the unconstrained search contains only $\binom{7}{3} = 35$ sets. We therefore use exact enumeration:

$$S^*(x) = \underset{S \in \mathcal{F}(x), |S| = K}{\operatorname{argmax}} J(S \mid x). \tag{10}$$

After candidate utilities are computed, the per-context inference cost is $O(|\mathcal{F}(x)|\,|E|K)$, negligible for the seven-strategy setting.

4.4 Panel-State Final Selector

The system outputs one response with a panel-state final selector:

$$a^*(x) = \underset{a \in S^*(x)}{\operatorname{argmax}} \frac{1}{|E|} \sum_{e \in E} u_e(x, a), \quad V_{\text{state}}(x) = r(x, a^*(x)). \tag{11}$$

Thus coverage is optimized before the final state-conditioned role utilities are aggregated.

5 Experiments

We evaluate whether PanelCover-BoK improves blind expert preference, whether panel-aware coverage explains the gain, whether the effect transfers across backbones and held-out roles, and which components matter.

5.1 Data and Baselines

The corpus contains 385,143 training chats, 8,931 development chats, and 8,973 test chats built from Mandarin mental-health support-dialogue resources, including PsyDial, SMILE-style data, CPsyCoun, and KokoroChat-style supportive-dialogue resources [13–15,21]. Expert evaluation uses a separate 800-dialogue held-out set.

Baselines include reproduced planners MISC [18], MultiESC [2], and TransESC [23]; retrieval baselines KEMI [4] and BM25-RAG; and prompt-only references including Qwen-max, Qwen3, Llama3.1-8B, Gemma3-12B, and Self-Refine [10]. Planner-style systems share the same candidate cache and safety gate; prompt-only systems are open-generation references.

5.2 Expert Evaluation Protocol

We use a blind panel with five expert roles. Here, an expert role denotes one role-specific evaluator used for both role-level utility modeling and response-level preference assessment. Each comparison presents anonymized A/B responses in random order; system identity and automatic scores are hidden. The 800-dialogue evaluation set yields 4,000 raw overall-dimension judgments per baseline comparison, corresponding to five role-specific judgments per dialogue. W/L/T counts are reported at this raw judgment level. Conditional win rate removes ties; tie-aware win rate counts ties as 0.5 wins. All reported win rates are rounded to three decimal places.

5.3 Implementation and Statistical Testing

Unless otherwise specified, PanelCover-BoK uses $K = 3$ and $\alpha = 0.15$. Expert utility models are fitted per role and dimension from blind pairwise judgments. The text-input BT extender reconstructs in-panel BT logits with Pearson correlations of 0.789–0.839 across role–dimension models. A 3,847-verdict audit shows that per-expert BT improves log-loss and Kendall τ over pooled BT (0.5175 vs. 0.5234; 0.5789 vs. 0.5673), and panel-state accuracy improves on the highest-disagreement stratum (0.7281 vs. 0.6996, $n = 456$).

For response-level expert evaluation, OR values come from a mixed-effects logistic model on non-tie judgments with dialogue and expert random intercepts. Mechanism analyses use BT-projected set-level scores under matched candidate caches, with context-level bootstrap intervals and sign-flip tests over per-context differences.

5.4 RQ1: Main Expert Preference Results

Figure 2A and Table 1 answer RQ1 under the same blind expert-preference protocol. PanelCover-BoK is preferred over every evaluated baseline: conditional WR ranges from 0.571 to 0.636, tie-aware WR remains above 0.545, and mixed-effects ORs are above one (1.33–1.75). These results make PanelCover-BoK the best-performing system in the evaluated protocol, including against strong direct decoders and Self-Refine.

Dimension-level summaries place the largest gains on helpfulness, specificity, appropriateness, and actionability, while measured empathy, validation, over-advice avoidance, and safety preference are not reduced under the shared safety gate.

Table 1. Blind expert preference results on the 800-dialogue evaluation set. W/L/T counts are raw overall-dimension judgments for PanelCover-BoK against each baseline; each comparison contains five role-specific judgments per dialogue. Conditional WR excludes ties; tie-aware WR counts ties as 0.5 wins. Rates are rounded to three decimal places.

Baseline	W/L/T	Cond. WR	Tie-aware WR	OR
MISC	1,801/1,055/1,144	0.631	0.593	1.70
MultiESC	1,739/1,049/1,212	0.624	0.586	1.66
TransESC	1,745/1,087/1,168	0.616	0.582	1.60
KEMI	1,635/1,081/1,284	0.602	0.569	1.51
BM25-RAG	1,690/1,078/1,232	0.611	0.577	1.57
Qwen-max Direct	1,537/1,095/1,368	0.584	0.555	1.40
Qwen3-14B Direct	1,614/1,094/1,292	0.596	0.565	1.47
Qwen3-8B Direct	1,727/1,069/1,204	0.618	0.582	1.61
Llama3.1-8B Direct	1,821/1,043/1,136	0.636	0.597	1.75
Gemma3-12B Direct	1,771/1,053/1,176	0.627	0.590	1.68
Self-Refine	1,459/1,097/1,444	0.571	0.545	1.33

5.5 RQ2: Pooled vs Panel-Aware Mechanism Analysis

As shown in Fig. 2B, pooled BT-projected selected-response scoring places PanelCover-BoK near parity with representative baselines (0.498–0.507), while panel-aware response scoring yields higher values (0.541–0.562), a coverage gain of +0.043 to +0.056. Direct K-set scoring gives panel-aware WR from 0.527 to 0.549. These results instantiate Eqs. 4–6: the gain comes from preserving candidates that serve different expert roles before the final response is chosen.

5.6 RQ3: Robustness and Transfer

Strict leave-one-expert-out scoring refits the verifier without the held-out role and evaluates under that role's utility; the ranges remain positive for all representative baselines (0.525–0.554). External-role stress tests show the same pattern, especially when the target role emphasizes dimensions represented in the learned panel utility.

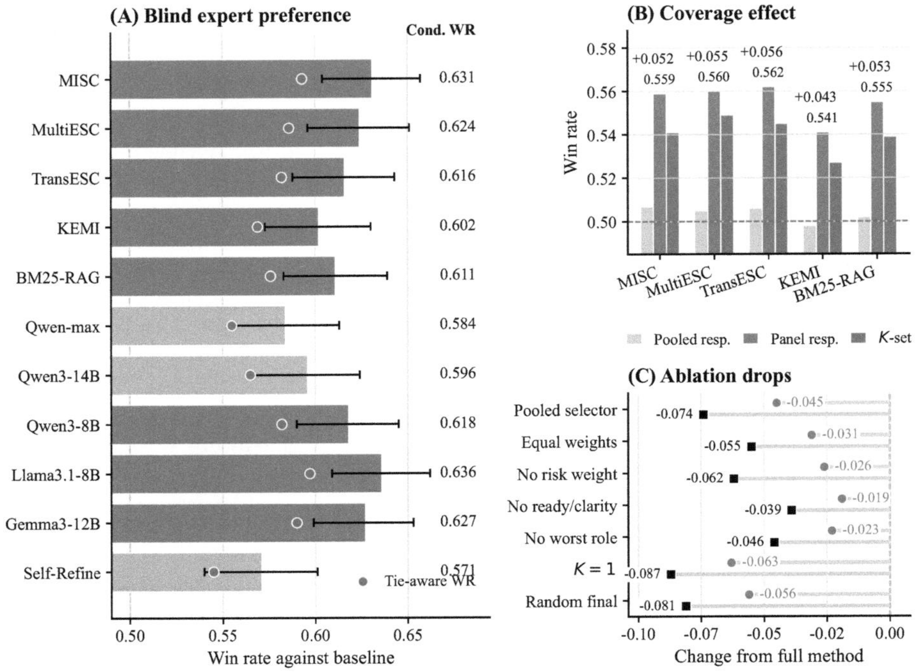

Fig. 2. Experimental evidence for PanelCover-BoK. Panel A reports the same blind expert-preference protocol as Table 1; bars are conditional win rates, orange points are tie-aware win rates, and intervals denote 95% confidence intervals. Panel B compares pooled selected-response scoring, panel-aware selected-response scoring, and direct K-set scoring under matched candidate caches; annotations show the empirical coverage gain from panel-aware response scoring. Panel C shows drops from the full method under component ablations; teal markers are human conditional WR drops and navy markers are high-risk WR drops.

Across five LLM backbones, PanelCover-BoK improves average projected utility by +0.039 over direct decoding and by +0.024 over pooled Best-of-K (Table 2), supporting its role as a transferable selector.

5.7 RQ4: Ablation and Safety Analysis

Figure 2C shows that replacing the panel-state selector with a pooled selector reduces Panel WR by 0.027 and human conditional WR by 0.045. The clearest degradation occurs when the candidate set is collapsed to $K = 1$ or the final selector is randomized, indicating that the main gain comes from preserving and selecting among expert-specific alternatives. A budget sweep gives the same interpretation: average WR rises from 0.516 at $K = 1$ to 0.558 at $K = 3$, then saturates at 0.559 for $K \in \{4, 5\}$.

Table 2. Backbone transfer under matched prompts, candidate budget, and safety gate. Higher projected utility is better.

Backbone	Direct	Pooled Best-of-K	PanelCover-BoK	ΔDirect	ΔPooled
Qwen-max	0.561	0.575	**0.596**	+0.035	+0.021
Qwen3-14B	0.552	0.566	**0.589**	+0.037	+0.023
Qwen3-8B	0.536	0.551	**0.576**	+0.040	+0.025
Llama3.1-8B	0.519	0.532	**0.559**	+0.040	+0.027
Gemma3-12B	0.527	0.543	**0.568**	+0.041	+0.025
Average	0.539	0.553	**0.578**	+0.039	+0.024

6 Discussion and Conclusion

The main algorithmic point is that response selection can benefit from optimizing a candidate set, not only a single-response score. A pooled verifier asks which response is best for an averaged expert. PanelCover-BoK instead keeps a compact set that covers several expert priorities before choosing the final response.

We presented PanelCover-BoK, a panel-aware coverage selection framework for Best-of-K mental-health support dialogue. Experiments on Mandarin support dialogue establish the best performance among the evaluated systems, with gains over reproduced planners, retrieval systems, prompt-only LLM variants, and direct LLM responses. Mechanism analysis, ablation, and transfer results support the interpretation that preserving expert-specific alternatives before final selection improves the response surfaced to the user.

References

1. Bradley, R.A., Terry, M.E.: Rank analysis of incomplete block designs: I. the method of paired comparisons. Biometrika **39**(3/4), 324–345 (1952)
2. Cheng, Y., Liu, W., Li, W.: Improving multi-turn emotional support dialogue generation with lookahead strategy planning. In: Proceedings of EMNLP, pp. 3014–3026 (2022)
3. Davani, A.M., Díaz, M., Prabhakaran, V.: Dealing with disagreements: looking beyond the majority vote in subjective annotations. Transactions of the Association for Computational Linguistics **10**, 92–110 (2022)
4. Deng, Y., Zhang, W., Yuan, Y., Lam, W.: Knowledge-enhanced mixed-initiative dialogue system for emotional support conversations. In: Proceedings of ACL, pp. 4079–4095 (2023)
5. Kang, D., Kim, S., Kwon, T.: Can large language models be good emotional supporter? mitigating preference bias on emotional support conversation. In: Proceedings of ACL, pp. 15232–15261 (2024)
6. Kim, S., Suk, J., Longpre, S.: Prometheus 2: an open source language model specialized in evaluating other language models. In: Proceedings of EMNLP (2024)
7. Lightman, H., Kosaraju, V., Burda, Y.: Let's verify step by step. In: The Twelfth International Conference on Learning Representations (2024)

8. Liu, S., Zheng, C., Demasi, O.: Towards emotional support dialog systems. In: Proceedings of ACL-IJCNLP, pp. 3469–3483 (2021)
9. Liu, Y., Iter, D., Xu, Y.: G-Eval: NLG evaluation using GPT-4 with better human alignment. In: Proceedings of EMNLP, pp. 2511–2522 (2023)
10. Madaan, A., Tandon, N., Gupta, P.: Self-refine: iterative refinement with self-feedback. In: Advances in Neural Information Processing Systems (2023)
11. Nemhauser, G.L., Wolsey, L.A., Fisher, M.L.: An analysis of approximations for maximizing submodular set functions–I. Math. Program. **14**(1), 265–294 (1978)
12. Ouyang, L., Wu, J., Jiang, X.: Training language models to follow instructions with human feedback. In: Advances in Neural Information Processing Systems, vol. 35 (2022)
13. Qi, Z., Kaneko, T., Takamizo, K.: KokoroChat: a japanese psychological counseling dialogue dataset collected via role-playing by trained counselors. In: Proceedings of ACL, pp. 12424–12443 (2025)
14. Qiu, H., He, H., Zhang, S.: SMILE: single-turn to multi-turn inclusive language expansion via ChatGPT for mental health support. In: Findings of EMNLP, pp. 615–636 (2024)
15. Qiu, H., Lan, Z.: PsyDial: a large-scale long-term conversational dataset for mental health support. In: Proceedings of ACL, pp. 21624–21655 (2025)
16. Rashkin, H., Smith, E.M., Li, M., Boureau, Y.L.: Towards empathetic open-domain conversation models: a new benchmark and dataset. In: Proceedings of ACL, pp. 5370–5381 (2019)
17. Sun, H., Zhang, Z., Deng, J.: Safety assessment of Chinese large language models. arXiv preprint arXiv:2304.10436 (2023)
18. Tu, Q., Li, Y., Cui, J.: MISC: a mixed strategy-aware model integrating COMET for emotional support conversation. In: Proceedings of ACL, pp. 308–319 (2022)
19. Uma, A., et al.: Learning from disagreement: a survey. Journal of Artificial Intelligence Research **72**, 1385–1470 (2021)
20. Xie, T., Qi, X., Zeng, Y.: SORRY-bench: systematically evaluating large language model safety refusal behaviors. arXiv preprint arXiv:2406.14598 (2024)
21. Zhang, C., Li, R., Tan, M.: CPsyCoun: a report-based multi-turn dialogue reconstruction and evaluation framework for chinese psychological counseling. In: Findings of ACL, pp. 13947–13966 (2024)
22. Zhao, H., Li, L., Chen, S.: ESC-eval: evaluating emotion support conversations in large language models. In: Proceedings of EMNLP, pp. 15785–15810 (2024)
23. Zhao, W., Zhao, Y., Wang, S., Qin, B.: TransESC: smoothing emotional support conversation via turn-level state transition. In: Findings of ACL. pp. 6725–6739 (2023)

PBSM: A Prediction-Based Switch Migration Framework for Controller Utilization Reduction in Distributed SDN

Firas Zobary(✉)

Wuhan University of Technology, Wuhan, Hubei, China
firas_zobary@hotmail.com

Abstract. Dynamic switch migration is a key mechanism for sustaining controller performance in distributed Software-Defined Networks (SDN), yet existing reactive and predictive schemes share three fundamental limitations: they assume Poisson traffic that ignores real-world burstiness, they predict aggregate controller load while treating the controller as an opaque resource, and they trigger migrations using static thresholds that lag rapid load growth. We present PBSM, a Prediction-Based Switch Migration framework that couples a burst-aware utilization model with architecture-aware prediction and stability-controlled migration. First, we develop an M/G/1 utilization model with Markov-Modulated Poisson Process (MMPP) arrivals and decompose controller overhead into five architecture-specific control-message components (α, β, σ, δ, φ) for Distributed Local-View (D-LV), Distributed Global-View (D-GV), and Hierarchical control planes. Second, an LSTM prediction engine forecasts these five overhead components — not aggregate load — so that the predicted utilization is grounded in the same theoretical model that governs the controller. Third, a migration controller combines a slope-aware dynamic threshold with an oscillation-frequency constraint, and we prove that the maximum controller utilization is non-increasing under the resulting policy. Experiments on the LambdaNet topology with five OpenDaylight controllers show that PBSM triggers migration 5–10 s earlier than state-of-the-art baselines (TDQN, APOP, PBCLR, OQLBA, GLBMF), reduces average controller utilization from 80% to ~70%, achieves MAPE of 0.64–0.95% (versus 2.93–6.02% for ARIMA/SVR), and lowers migration instability by 76.2% relative to ordered selection, at a CPU overhead of only 2.5%.

Keywords: SDN · Load Balancing · Switch Migration

1 Introduction

Centralized SDN controllers face severe scalability pressure as traffic volume and burstiness grow. Distributing the control plane over multiple controllers alleviates the single-point bottleneck, but it creates a new question: when and how should switches be reassigned between controllers so that no controller is overloaded while system stability is preserved? Static switch-to-controller mappings cannot adapt to traffic dynamics and lead to severe load imbalance, whereas naive dynamic mappings introduce oscillations that destabilize the control plane [1, 2].

L. Ding et al. (Eds.): APWeb-WAIM 2026, LNCS 16995, pp. 577–591, 2027.
https://doi.org/10.1007/978-981-92-5699-0_39

Most existing controller utilization studies suffer from three coupled weaknesses. (i) They model arrivals as Poisson with a constant rate, although empirical SDN traffic is bursty, self-similar, and long-range dependent due to IoT microbursts, periodic streaming and topology-synchronization events [3]. (ii) They predict aggregate controller load using a generic time-series model, treating the controller as an opaque resource — so the predictor and the system model are decoupled. (iii) They trigger migrations using a fixed utilization threshold, which detects overload too late under steep load growth and produces back-and-forth oscillations under volatile load.

The central observation of this paper is that these three weaknesses must be fixed jointly. A burst-aware traffic model identifies what the controller really processes; an architecture-aware prediction of those components delivers theoretically grounded forecasts; and a stability-controlled migration policy converts forecasts into actions without harming long-term equilibrium. We develop this integrated view in a framework called PBSM (Prediction-Based Switch Migration). The main contributions are as follows:

1. Burst-aware utilization model. We build an M/G/1 queueing model with Markov–Modulated Poisson Processes (MMPP) arrivals and derive a closed-form decomposition of controller overhead into five architecture-specific control-message components for D-LV, D-GV, and Hierarchical control planes. A burst factor derived from extreme-value statistics rescales the utilization to capture worst-case spikes.
2. Architecture-aware LSTM forecasting. A multi-output LSTM forecasts the five overhead components rather than aggregate load. The predicted utilization is reconstructed by passing the forecast through the same architecture-specific overhead function used in the utilization model, ensuring model–prediction coupling.
3. Slope-aware migration with stability guarantee. A dynamic threshold lowers the migration boundary in proportion to the predicted utilization slope. An oscillation-frequency metric prevents repeated reassignments. We prove that the resulting policy is non-increasing in maximum controller utilization and converges in finite time.

We emphasize that PBSM's novelty lies not in any single component — burst-aware queueing models, LSTM traffic prediction, and dynamic-threshold migration each have precedents in isolation — but in the coupling between them. The ablation confirms this coupling is load-bearing: replacing the five-component forecast with an aggregate-load forecast (same LSTM, same threshold logic) degrades average utilization, and the gain comes from *what* is predicted, not merely that something is predicted.

2 Related Works

The scalability of the Software Defined Networking (SDN) control plane has attracted significant research attention, particularly in relation to controller utilization reduction and dynamic load balancing. Early studies focused on modeling controller utilization and defining scalability metrics for distributed SDN architectures. For example, Karakus et al. [4] introduced one of the earliest scalability metrics for SDN control planes. However, their model assumed static controller processing times even as the network size and traffic intensity increased. Although distributed control plane architectures with multiple controllers can improve scalability and reduce controller utilization [5], most existing deployments rely on static switch–controller mappings that are unable to adapt efficiently to dynamic traffic variations. Consequently, researchers began exploring dynamic switch–controller reassignment mechanisms to improve load balancing during peak traffic conditions [5].

A large body of work uses reactive migration, triggering reassignment only after utilization exceeds a threshold [6–9]. Zhou et al. [10] study resulting load oscillations without a predictive fix; Mayilsamy et al. [11] select controllers below a static threshold, assuming stable traffic; Mokhtar et al. [12] rank controllers by load level. All share the same limitation: decisions follow overload rather than anticipating it, and none adapts thresholds to temporal fluctuations. To reduce migration overhead, other work uses heuristic or optimization-based strategies: Sridevi et al. [13] apply Artificial Bee Colony optimization to select migration targets; Lai et al. [14] propose a best-fit strategy minimizing migration cost; Cello et al. [15] cluster switches by communication pattern, at the cost of higher overhead when whole clusters move. These methods improve efficiency under specific conditions but lack predictive capability under bursty traffic. Prediction-based approaches enable proactive management. Zafar et al. [16] use NLMS prediction for SD-IoT traffic; Zhou et al. [17] propose intelligent switch-to-controller selection without formal utilization modeling; Ul Huque et al. [18] predict flow counts to size the controller pool. Statistical forecasters — ARIMA [19] and Taylor-series expansion [20] — struggle with the nonlinear, long-range-dependent traffic typical of SDN; Xiao et al. [21] combine deep prediction with migration but without queueing-theoretic modeling; Sikder et al. [22] propose a relaxed migration framework to reduce overhead. None couples the predictor to an architecture-specific overhead model — the gap PBSM addresses.

Despite the considerable progress achieved in prediction–based controller load management, several limitations remain unresolved. Most existing approaches rely on simplified queueing models such as M/M/1, which do not accurately represent the non–exponential service times and bursty traffic characteristics commonly observed in practical SDN environments. Furthermore, current studies generally address prediction, migration, utilization modeling, and oscillation control independently rather than integrating them into a unified framework. Therefore, there remains a need for a comprehensive approach that combines accurate controller utilization modeling, prediction–driven switch migration, adaptive threshold mechanisms, and oscillation mitigation to improve the scalability and stability of distributed SDN control planes.

3 Problem Formulation

Let $C = \{c_1, c_2, \ldots, c_n\}$ denote the set of controllers and $S = \{s_1, s_2, \ldots, s_m\}$ the set of switches. A binary variable $x_{ij} \in \{0, 1\}$ encodes the assignment, with $x_{ij} = 1$ if the ith switch is controlled by the jth controller. Each controller has processing capacity μ_j (operations per second) and overhead O_j that depends on the architecture-specific control messages it processes. Controller utilization is:

$$U_j = \frac{O_j}{\mu_j} \tag{1}$$

Optimization Objective. Maintain controller utilization within a safe operating region under dynamic and bursty traffic:

$$\max_{c_j \in C} U_j(t) < T_U, \forall t \tag{2}$$

subject to:

1. Single assignment constraint. Each switch is assigned to exactly one controller:

$$\sum_j x_{ij} = 1, \forall s_i \in S \tag{3}$$

2. Capacity constraint. Controller utilization remains below a threshold:

$$U_j(t) < T_U, \forall c_j \in C \tag{4}$$

3. Migration stability constraint. Switches must not be repeatedly reassigned between the same pair of controllers.
4. Post–migration feasibility. The target controller's utilization after accepting the migrated switch must remain below a safe operating threshold.

Under MMPP-driven burstiness, U_j can rise from a moderate value to saturation within a few sampling intervals. A reactive trigger detects overload after it occurs, so the controller spends the detection-to-migration gap inside the nonlinear region. PBSM instead forecasts the utilization trajectory $U(t + W)$ over a horizon W and triggers migration before constraint (2) is violated.

4 Burst–Aware Utilization Model

4.1 MMPP Arrival and Service Time

This paper adopts the MMPP to model flow arrivals. MMPP consists of a continuous-time Markov chain with Q hidden states, state-specific Poisson arrival rates λ_q, and a transition rate matrix $\boldsymbol{R} = [r_{ij}]$ that governs the switching behavior between states. This matrix governs the temporal dynamics between traffic regimes. MMPP enables: Representation of burst magnitudes via variation in λ_q, modeling of burst durations via state sojourn times, and Preservation of first-order statistics through the average arrival rate:

$$\lambda_{avg} = \sum_{q=1}^{Q} \pi_q \lambda_q \tag{5}$$

where π_q is the stationary probability of being in state q.

For service times (controller processing delays), we generalize the traditional M/M/1 assumption by adopting an MMPP/G/1 queueing framework, in which the arrivals (MMPP) are bursty and non-Poisson traffic. Most of previous studies have primarily modeled controller performance based on throughput and RT using simplified M/M/1 queueing models. However, these models fail to capture the bursty and temporally correlated nature of SDN traffic, which is crucial in large-scale or multi-tenant networks. In contrast, our model leverages the MMPP/G/1 queueing framework, enabling us to better represent the controller's behavior under real-world traffic scenarios.

4.2 Architecture-Specific Overhead Decomposition

OpenFlow uses three message families: Controller-to-Switch, Asynchronous, and Symmetric. We isolate the components that drive controller load and write:

$$O = f(\alpha, \beta, \sigma, \delta, \varphi) \tag{6}$$

where α counts Controller-to-Switch messages (mainly Flow-Mod); β counts Asynchronous messages (mainly Packet-In); σ counts synchronization messages caused by a switch's global flows; δ counts inter-controller synchronization messages for global flows passing through the domain; and φ counts global flows originating in other domains and traversing the local domain. The composition of these terms differs across architecture.

Distributed Local View (D-LV).

Each controller manages only its domain and has no global state. For global flow the controller must consult neighbors, adding extra load. Let γ_n^l be the number of nth domain switches involved in a flow path, $N_{l,n}$ the number of neighbors, h the hosts per switch, and λ_{ij} the host-pair flow rate. The overhead in the nth domain becomes:

$$O = \sum_{k_{start}^n}^{k_{end}^n} (\alpha_k + \beta_k + \sigma_k) + \delta_n^l + \varphi_n^l \times \gamma_n^l \tag{7}$$

with k_{start}^n and k_{end}^n are the range of switch IDs in each domain (n), and $\alpha_k = 3 + \theta_k = 3 + \left(\rho_{l,k} + \rho_{g,k}\right) \times \gamma_n^l$ counts Flow-Mod messages, $\beta_k = \rho_{l,k} + \rho_{g,k}$ counts Packet-In messages, and $\sigma_k = \rho_{g,k} \times N_{l,n}$ counts neighbor-synchronization messages. The constants 3 cover features_request, feature_reply, and set_configuration exchanged at channel setup.

Distributed Global View (D-GV).

All controllers maintain a consistent global view, so per-flow synchronization vanishes ($\sigma_k = 0$). However, periodic background synchronization δ_n^g is needed to preserve consistency and scales quadratically with the number of controllers due to all-to-all coordination. The overhead is:

$$O = \sum_{k_{start}^n}^{k_{end}^n} (\alpha_k + \beta_k) + \delta_n^g + \varphi_n^g \times \gamma_n^g \tag{8}$$

with α_k and β_k as in D-LV but γ_n^g replacing γ_n^l. D-GV pays a quadratic synchronization cost in exchange for optimal routing, whereas D-LV pays an $O(d)$ neighbor-consultation cost but achieves near-linear scaling—formalizing the PACELC consistency-throughput compromise [23] inside the controller-utilization model.

Hierarchical (D-H). Leaf controllers manage local domains, and a root controller mediates global flows. For each global flow the leaf controller exchanges two messages with the root, so $\delta_n^H = 2 \times \varphi_n^H$ and:

$$O = \sum_{k_{start}^n}^{k_{end}^n} (\alpha_k + \beta_k + \sigma_k) + \varphi_n^H \times \left(2 + \gamma_n^H\right) \tag{9}$$

The five-component decomposition (Eqs. 1–9) is the substrate that the prediction engine forecasts. This is the key structural difference from prior predictive migration: PBSM forecasts what the architecture says the controller actually processes, not a generic aggregate.

5 The PBSM Framework

PBSM is a closed-loop pipeline of four modules: a Traffic Monitoring module that samples the five overhead components α, β, σ, δ, φ from each controller; a Utilization Prediction Engine that forecasts those components and reconstructs $U(t + W)$ via (Eqs. 9–11); a Migration Decision module that selects when to migrate (Algorithm 1) and which switch goes where (Algorithm 2); and a Migration Execution module that performs the OpenFlow-level handover. The first three modules are described below; execution follows standard OpenFlow role-change procedures and is omitted for space.

5.1 Multi-output LSTM Prediction Engine

LSTM is selected over ARIMA/SVR because SDN traffic exhibits nonlinear patterns and long-range dependencies that linear and kernel-stationary models cannot capture. The gating mechanism (input, forget, output) preserves long-range information while reacting to bursts. For each controller c_j we feed a historical window H of the five components and predict the next W steps:

$$\begin{bmatrix} \hat{\alpha}_{t+1} & \hat{\beta}_{t+1} & \hat{\sigma}_{t+1} & \hat{\delta}_{t+1} & \hat{\varphi}_{t+1} \\ \hat{\alpha}_{t+2} & \hat{\beta}_{t+2} & \hat{\sigma}_{t+2} & \hat{\delta}_{t+2} & \hat{\varphi}_{t+2} \\ \vdots & \vdots & \vdots & \vdots & \vdots \\ \hat{\alpha}_{t+W} & \hat{\beta}_{t+W} & \hat{\sigma}_{t+W} & \hat{\delta}_{t+W} & \hat{\varphi}_{t+W} \end{bmatrix} = LSTM \begin{bmatrix} \alpha_{t-H} & \beta_{t-H} & \sigma_{t-H} & \delta_{t-H} & \varphi_{t-H} \\ \alpha_{t-H+1} & \beta_{t-H+1} & \sigma_{t-H+1} & \delta_{t-H+1} & \varphi_{t-H+1} \\ \vdots & \vdots & \vdots & \vdots & \vdots \\ \alpha_t & \beta_t & \sigma_t & \delta_t & \varphi_t \end{bmatrix} \tag{10}$$

Predicted utilization is reconstructed using the architecture-specific function from Eqs. 7–9:

$$\hat{U}_{t+W} = \frac{\hat{O}_{t+W}}{\mu} = \frac{f\left(\hat{\alpha}_{t+W}, \hat{\beta}_{t+W}, \hat{\sigma}_{t+W}, \hat{\delta}_{t+W}, \hat{\varphi}_{t+W}\right)}{\mu} \tag{11}$$

where $\hat{O}_{t+W}$ is the predicted overhead at time $t+W$. Reusing the same f as the analytical model is what makes the prediction architecture-aware: a D-LV controller is forecast through the D-LV overhead function and a D-GV controller through its own, so the predictor never confuses synchronization-dominated load with flow-setup load.

5.2 Slope-Aware Threshold and Oscillation Control

A static threshold T_U is adequate under quasi-stationary traffic but delays migration under steep growth. Let:

$$S(t) = \frac{1}{W-1}\sum_{i=1}^{W-1}\left(\hat{U}_{t+i+1} - \hat{U}_{t+i}\right) \tag{12}$$

be the average short-term slope of the predicted utilization. We replace the static boundary with:

$$T_U^{dyn}(t) = T_U - kS(t) \tag{13}$$

where $k > 0$ is a sensitivity coefficient. Under rapid growth (large $S(t)$) the threshold drops and migration is triggered earlier; under stable load $S(t) \approx 0$ the threshold converges back to T_U. The overload condition is $\hat{U}_{t+W} > T_U^{dyn}(t)$.

To prevent reverse migrations, we track an oscillation frequency for switch s between controllers c_i and c_j:

$$O_t^{ij}(s) = \frac{(t-1)\,O_t^{ij}(s) + x_t^{ij}(s)}{t}, t \geq 1 \tag{14}$$

where $x_t^{ij}(s) = 1$ if s oscillated between c_i and c_j at iteration t. A switch is eligible for reassignment only if $O_t^{ij}(s) \leq \zeta$. The range of threshold ζ is [0,1]. We also track the Migration Instability Rate (MIR). This rate measures the frequency at which the switches, after being reassigned to a new controller, return to their previous controller in the next epoch. The high value of this metric indicates instability in the switch assignment process, leading to unnecessary migrations and increased control plane overhead.

$$MIR = \sum_{S_i}\sum_{C_j}\frac{\neg\left(x_{ij}(t) - x_{ij}(t-1)\right)}{|\,S_i\,|} \tag{15}$$

5.3 Algorithms

Algorithm 1 forecasts the first-time step at which controller c_j is predicted to violate $T_U^{dyn}(t)$. Algorithm 2 then solves the joint "which switch/where to migrate" problem with admission control and oscillation filtering. Together they answer the three migration questions — when, which, where — using the same five-component representation.

Algorithm 1**:** Overutilized Controller Prediction

Inputs: $c_j \in C_A$: Controllers set, W: prediction window, T_U: The controller static utilization threshold, μ_{c_j}: Controller processing capacity, Historical overhead components: [α, β, σ, δ, φ] for time steps $[t - H, \ldots, t]$

Outputs: $W_{OH}^{c_j}$: The predicted step in which the controller c_j will be overutilized

Initialize:

$W_{OH}^{c_j} = -1$

$\left[\hat{\alpha}, \hat{\beta}, \hat{\sigma}, \hat{\delta}, \hat{\varphi}\right]_{t+1 \to t+W} \leftarrow$ *trained_model.predict* $([\alpha, \beta, \sigma, \delta, \varphi]_{t - H, \ldots, t})$

for $w = 1$ *to* W **do**

  $\hat{O}_{t+w} \leftarrow f\left(\hat{\alpha}_{t+w}, \hat{\beta}_{t+w}, \hat{\sigma}_{t+w}, \hat{\delta}_{t+w}, \hat{\varphi}_{t+w}\right)$ // Use Eq. 9, 10, 11

  $\hat{U}_{t+w} \leftarrow \hat{O}_{t+w}/\mu_{c_j}$

end for

if $W > 1$ **then**

  $S(t) = \frac{1}{W-1}\sum_{i=1}^{W-1}\left(\hat{U}_{t+i+1} - \hat{U}_{t+i}\right)$ **else** $S(t) = 0$

end if

$T_U^{dyn}(t) = T_U - kS(t)$

for $w = 1$ *to* W **do**

if $\hat{U}_{t+w} > T_U^{dyn}$ **then** $W_{OH}^{c_j} \leftarrow w$; **break**

end for

return $W_{OH}^{c_j}$

Algorithm 2: Switch Migration

(*continued*)

(*continued*)

Inputs: $c_j \in C$: Controllers set, s_i: Set of switches, μ_j: The processing capacity of jth controller
Outputs: *Migration _ plane*
1: **Initialize:** $Migration\_list = \emptyset$
2: **for** each controller $c_j \in C$ **do**
3: $W_{OH}^{C_j} = utilization\_prediction(c_j, W, T_U)$
4: **if** $\left(W_{OH}^{C_j} \neq -1\right)$ **then**
5: $signal = 0$
6: **for** each switch $s_i \in S_{c_j}$ **do**
7: **if** $\left(\hat{U}_{t+W_{OH}}^{j} - \Delta\hat{U}_{t+W_{OH}}^{i} \leq T_U^{dyn} \&\& signal = 0\right)$ **then**
8: add s_i to $Migration\_list$
9: $signal = 1$
10: **end if**
11: **end for**
12: **if** $(signal == 0)$ **then** Switch with the smallest load will be added to
13: $Migration\_list$
14: **end if**
15: **end if**
16: **end for**
17: **While** $Migration\_list \neq \emptyset$ **do**
18: $s_{victim} \longleftarrow$ Select the switch s_i with the smallest W_{OH}
19: $c_{target} \longleftarrow$ Select the controller with lowest load
20: Update $O_t^{j,target}(s_{victim})$ //Eq. 16
21: **if** $O_t^{j,target}(s_{victim}) > \zeta$ **then** select another s_{victim}; continue
22: **for** $c_j \in C$ **do**
23: **if** $\left(\hat{U}_t^{target} + \Delta\hat{U}_t^{victim} < T_U^{dyn}\right)$ **then**
24: Add the connection $(s_{victim} \rightarrow c_{target})$ to $Migration\_plane$
25: Remove s_{victim} from $Migration\_list$
26: **else** select another target controller
27: **end if**
28: **end for**
29: **end while**
30: **return** $Migration\_plane$

6 Stability, Termination and Complexity

Theorem 1 (Non-increasing Maximum Utilization). *Under Algorithm 2, the maximum controller utilization* $U_{max} = max_j U_j$ *is non-increasing across migration iterations, provided the admission-control constraint in line 23 is satisfied.*

Proof (Sketch). Removing this switch reduces the source controller's overhead by ΔO_{victim}, so $U'_{source} = \frac{O_{source} - \Delta O_{victim}}{\mu} < U_{source}$. Admission control ensures $\hat{U}_t^{target} + \Delta \hat{U}_t^{victim} < T_U^{dyn} \leq T_U < 1$. Since only overloaded controllers are sources, $\hat{U}_t^{target} < T_U < U_{source}$, hence $\max\left(\hat{U}_t^{source}, \hat{U}_t^{target}\right) \leq U_{source} = U_{max}$. The oscillation constraint $O_t^{j,target}(s_{victim}) > \zeta$ blocks the reverse migration, preserving the improvement.

Remark. Switch-to-controller assignment is NP-hard in general, so Theorem 1 establishes a monotone descent rather than a global optimum: the policy converges to a local optimum where no single-switch migration further reduces U_{max} without violating stability.

Theorem 2 (Finite Termination). *Algorithm 2 terminates in at most $O(|C|\cdot|S|)$ migrations.*

Proof (Sketch). Each migration strictly reduces the overhead of some source controller while keeping all utilizations bounded by admission control. Since the set of controllers–switch pairs is finite and utilization is bounded in [0, 1], the descent must halt; it halts when either no controller is predicted to exceed T_U^{dyn} within W or no feasible migration exists.

Complexity. Algorithm 1 has time complexity $O(C \bullet W + C \bullet H \bullet D)$ with $D = 5$ components. The pre-trained LSTM has $O(1)$ inference per controller; with fixed W, H, D the complexity is linear in $|C|$. Algorithm 2 is $O(C \bullet S)$ in the worst case. For $C \leq 100$, $W = 10$, $H = 50$, $D = 5$ we observe ~25 k operations per cycle, negligible on modern hardware.

7 Experimental Evaluation

7.1 Setup

We implement PBSM in Python 3.12 on Ubuntu 20.04 (Intel i5-12500H, 16 GB RAM, $P = 2^{30}$ ops/s) and use Mininet with five OpenDaylight controllers over the LambdaNet backbone topology (41 switches, 200 hosts $\approx$ 5 hosts/switch), consistent with [24]. The per-host-pair flow rate is $\lambda_{ij} = 0.1$ req/s. We treat the controller as bottlenecked at $U = 0.8$, in line with standard queueing practice. Each scenario is run 10 times with seed 42; we report mean $\pm$ 95% CI and report paired t-tests with $p < 0.005$.

We compare PBSM against five recent algorithms: TDQN [25], OQLBA [26], APOP [20], PBCLR [16] and GLBMF [27]. For prediction we compare LSTM with ARIMA and SVR. For switch selection we compare against ordered (smallest-load first) and random strategies. LSTM hyperparameters were obtained by grid search on a validation split: learning rate 0.001 (Adam), 5 hidden layers with 2 cells each, 100 epochs, horizon $W = 10$. The dynamic-threshold coefficient $k = 2$ and oscillation threshold $\zeta = 0.6$ were tuned empirically and analyzed in Sect. 7.5. The data was split into training (first 70%), validation (next 15%) and testing (final 15%). All MAPE values are computed on the test partition.

7.2 Effect on Controller Utilization

OpenFlow requests are generated by IPerf and captured with Wireshark to compute utilization via Eqs. 8–11. Under D-GV, c_1, c_2 reach the 80% bottleneck at $t \approx 120$ s; under D-LV they reach it at $t \approx 160$ s because each controller manages a smaller portion of the network and incurs less synchronization. After PBSM activates, the overloaded controllers shed switches before crossing the bottleneck, and the average utilization of previously overloaded controllers drops from 80% to ~70% in both architectures — a 12.5% reduction (Fig. 1).

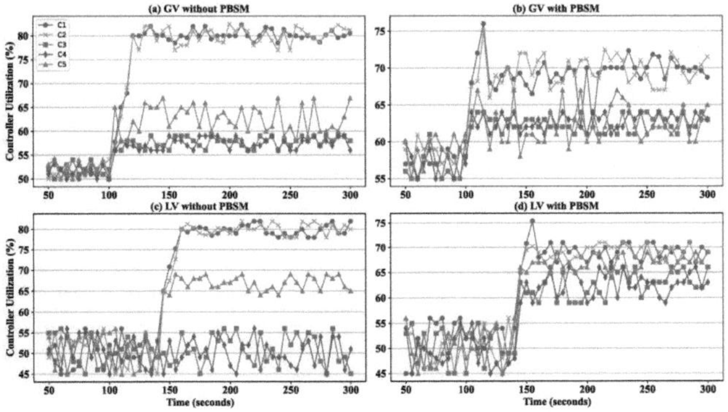

Fig. 1. Different Architectures with and without PBSM

7.3 Migration Trigger Time and Response Time

Figure 2 shows controller utilization around the migration trigger. PBSM triggers at $t=$ 135 s, 5 s earlier than the other predictive baselines (TDQN, APOP, PBCLR at $t=$ 140 s) and 10 s earlier than the reactive baselines (GLBMF, OQLBA at $t=$ 145 s). The early trigger is the combined effect of LSTM forecasting and the slope-aware threshold: when the predicted slope is steep, T_U^{dyn} drops proportionally and migration starts before the controller enters the nonlinear region.

In response-time terms (Fig. 3), PBSM and PBCLR are clustered at the bottom; PBCLR is occasionally lower because it migrates pre-emptively without stability filtering, while PBSM trades a small amount of short-term RT for robustness under bursty traffic. TDQN follows closely but its RL decision step introduces variability. OQLBA and APOP are slightly higher because of the cost of their per-event or profit-evaluation computations. GLBMF reacts last and pays the highest RT during surges (Table 1).

7.4 Prediction Accuracy and Overheads

We evaluate prediction accuracy with MAPE over sampling intervals from 10 to 60 s (Table 2). LSTM outperforms ARIMA and SVR, achieving MAPE between 0.64%

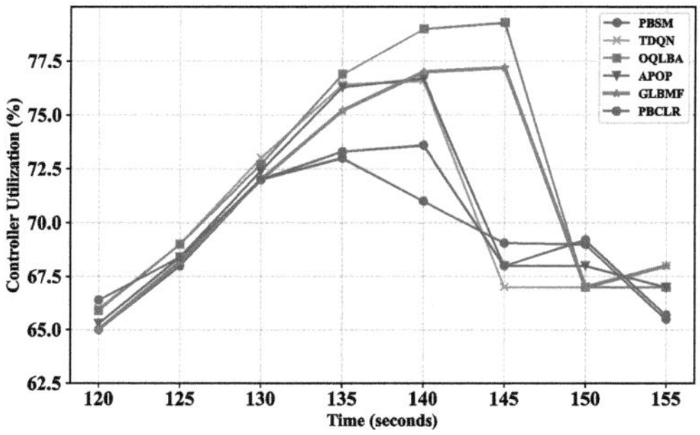

Fig. 2. Comparison of switch migration trigger time

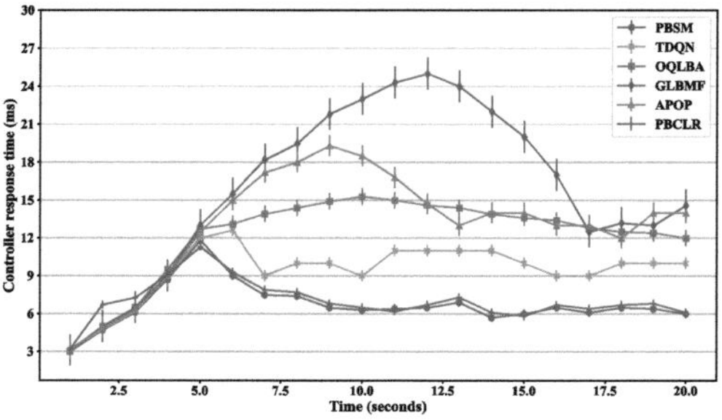

Fig. 3. Average controllers RT during switch migration

Table 1. MAPE values for LSTM, ARIMA and SVR

Sample time	LSTM	ARIMA	SVR
10 s	**0.73**	5.66	3.19
20 s	**0.64**	5.43	2.93
30 s	**0.95**	6.02	3.48
40 s	**0.81**	5.82	3.32
50 s	**0.92**	5.86	3.39
60 s	**0.8**	5.76	3.28

and 0.95% versus 2.93–6.02% for the baselines. ARIMA is the weakest because non-stationary differencing erases trend information; SVR is more flexible but cannot exploit long-range temporal dependencies the way the LSTM gating mechanism does.

Communication and Computational Overhead. Activating PBSM increases total control messages from 12540 to 13130 in D-GV (+4.7%) and 9875 to 10260 in D-LV (+3.9%); bandwidth grows +4.5% (D-GV) and + 3.3% (D-LV), partly offset by fewer Packet-In bursts toward overloaded controllers. CPU utilization grows from 7.3% to

9.8% and memory from 82 MB to 105 MB (+28%), both within standard operating envelopes for SDN controllers.

7.5 Migration Stability and Sensitivity

Compared with the ordered and random switch-selection strategies, PBSM reduces MIR by 76.2% (vs. ordered: 8.4 → 2) and 33.3% (vs. random: 3 → 2), and reduces oscillation count by ~90.2% relative to ordered. Ordered selection picks the smallest-load switch every iteration and shifts it back and forth; random distributes migrations uniformly but cannot exploit traffic structure; PBSM filters by both oscillation history and predicted impact.

Table 2. Sensitivity to dynamic-threshold coefficient k and oscillation threshold ζ

k	Trigger(s)	Util (%)	#Mig	ζ	Util (%)	#Mig	MIR
0.5	140	73	26	0.2	71.8	21	1
1	137	70.8	30	0.4	69.9	27	1.5
2	135	68.5	32	0.6	68.5	32	2
3	132	67.4	41	0.8	67.6	44	3.5
5	130	65.4	55	1.0	66.9	59	5

In terms of thresholds sensitivity, as shown in Table 2, a small k keeps the dynamic threshold close to TU and forfeits early triggering; a large k pulls migrations too early and inflates their number. $k = 2$ balances trigger time and migration count. Similarly, very small ζ blocks necessary reassignments (under-migration) while $\zeta \geq 1$ disables oscillation control and amplifies MIR; $\zeta = 0.6$ is the sweet spot.

7.6 Ablation Study

Table 3 isolates the contribution of each PBSM component. Removing the dynamic threshold pushes the trigger 5 s later and raises utilization from 68.5% to 72.0%, confirming the slope-aware term as the source of early triggering. Disabling oscillation control (MIR) keeps the trigger but nearly doubles migrations (60 vs. 32) and triples MIR (5 vs. 2). Replacing the architecture-specific overhead prediction with aggregate-load prediction degrades utilization to 75.5%, showing that the model–prediction coupling — forecasting the five overhead components rather than the aggregate — is what makes the migration decisions accurate, not merely the LSTM by itself.

Table 3. Ablation Study Results

Method	Trigger time (s)	Avg Util. (%)	#Migrations	MIR (count)
Full PBSM	135	68.5	32	2
w/o Dynamic threshold	140	72	28	2
w/o MIR	135	69	60	5
Aggregated load	137	75.5	35	2

8 Conclusion

We presented PBSM, a prediction-based switch-migration framework whose three components — MMPP/G/1 utilization modeling, architecture-aware overhead forecasting by a multi-output LSTM, and slope-aware stability-controlled migration — are designed to reinforce each other rather than operate in isolation. Forecasting the five architecture-specific overhead components instead of a generic aggregate load couples the predictor to the system model; the slope-aware dynamic threshold converts steep growth into earlier triggers; and the oscillation-frequency constraint, together with admission control, yields a provable non-increasing trajectory of the maximum controller utilization. Experiments on LambdaNet with OpenDaylight show consistent improvements over five recent baselines in trigger time, response time, prediction accuracy and migration stability, at a CPU overhead of 2.5%. Future work will study elastic horizon W, federated training across multi-domain deployments, and joint optimization with northbound application QoS.

References

1. Hu, F., Hao, Q., Bao, K.: A survey on software-defined network and openflow: from concept to implementation. IEEE Commun. Surv. Tutor. **16**(4), 2181–2206 (2014)
2. Kreutz, D., Ramos, F.M.V., Verissimo, P.E., Rothenberg, C.E., Azodolmolky, S., Uhlig, S.: Software-defined networking: a comprehensive survey. Proc. IEEE. **103**(1), 14–76 (2014)
3. Aliyu, A.L., Diockou, J.: An analytical queuing model based on SDN for IoT traffic in 5G. In: International Conference on Advanced Information Networking and Applications, pp. 435–445. Springer (2023)
4. Karakus, M., Durresi, A.: A scalability metric for control planes in software defined networks (sdns). In: 2016 IEEE 30th International Conference on Advanced Information Networking and Applications (AINA), pp. 282–289. IEEE (2016)
5. Naji, H.R., Riyahi, H.: A survey of load balancing approaches based on switch migration in software-defined networks. IET Networks. **14**(1), e70015 (2025)
6. Hamdan, M., et al.: A comprehensive survey of load balancing techniques in software-defined network. J. Netw. Comput. Appl. **174**, 102856 (2021)
7. Neghabi, A.A., Navimipour, N.J., Hosseinzadeh, M., Rezaee, A.: Load balancing mechanisms in the software defined networks: a systematic and comprehensive review of the literature. IEEE Access. **6**, 14159–14178 (2018)

8. Zafar, S., Lv, Z., Zaydi, N.H., Ibrar, M., Hu, X.: DSMLB: dynamic switch-migration based load balancing for software-defined IoT network. Comput. Netw. **214**, 109145 (2022)
9. Belgaum, M.R., Musa, S., Alam, M.M., Su'ud, M.M.: A systematic review of load balancing techniques in software-defined networking. IEEE Access. **8**, 98612–98636 (2020)
10. Zhou, Y., Wang, Y., Yu, J., Ba, J., Zhang, S.: Load balancing for multiple controllers in SDN based on switches group. In: 2017 19th Asia-Pacific Network Operations and Management Symposium (APNOMS), pp. 227–230. IEEE (2017)
11. Mayilsamy, J., Rangasamy, D.P.: Load balancing in software-defined networks using spider monkey optimization algorithm for the internet of things. Wirel. Pers. Commun. **116**(1), 23–43 (2021)
12. Mokhtar, H., Di, X., Zhou, Y., Hassan, A., Ma, Z., Musa, S.: Multiple-level threshold load balancing in distributed SDN controllers. Comput. Netw. **198**, 108369 (2021)
13. Sridevi, K., Saifulla, M.A.: LBABC: distributed controller load balancing using artificial bee colony optimization in an SDN. Peer Peer Netw. Appl. **16**(2), 947–957 (2023)
14. Lai, W.-K., Wang, Y.-C., Chen, Y.-C., Tsai, Z.-T.: TSSM: time-sharing switch migration to balance loads of distributed SDN controllers. IEEE Trans. Netw. Serv. Manag. **19**(2), 1585–1597 (2022)
15. Cello, M., Xu, Y., Walid, A., Wilfong, G., Chao, H.J., Marchese, M.: BalCon: a distributed elastic SDN control via efficient switch migration. In: 2017 IEEE International Conference on Cloud Engineering (IC2E), pp. 40–50. IEEE (2017)
16. Zafar, S., Zafar, B., Hu, X., Zaydi, N.H., Ibrar, M., Erbad, A.: PBCLR: prediction-based control-plane load reduction in a software-defined IoT network. Internet of Things (Netherlands). **24**, 100934 (2023). https://doi.org/10.1016/j.iot.2023.100934
17. Zhou, Y., Ren, B., Xie, J., Luo, L., Guo, D., Zhou, X.: Enable the proactively load-balanced control plane for SDN via intelligent switch-to-controller selection strategy. Comput. Netw. **233**, 109867 (2023)
18. ul Huque, M.T.I., Si, W., Jourjon, G., Gramoli, V.: Large-scale dynamic controller placement. IEEE Trans. Netw. Serv. Manag. **14**(1), 63–76 (2017)
19. Filali, A., Cherkaoui, S., Kobbane, A.: Prediction-based switch migration scheduling for SDN load balancing. In: ICC 2019–2019 IEEE International Conference on Communications (ICC), pp. 1–6. IEEE (2019)
20. Zhong, H., Fan, J., Cui, J., Xu, Y., Liu, L.: Assessing profit of prediction for SDN controllers load balancing. Comput. Netw. **191**, 107991 (2021)
21. Xiao, J., Pan, X., Liu, J., Wang, J., Zhang, P., Abualigah, L.: Load balancing strategy for SDN multi-controller clusters based on load prediction. J. Supercomput. **80**(4), 5136–5162 (2024)
22. Sikder, R., Hossain, M.S., Alenazi, M.J.F., Atiquzzaman, M.: A relaxed and faster switch migration framework to balance the load of distributed control plane in software defined networks. Clust. Comput. **27**(7), 8995–9012 (2024)
23. Khoshaba, O., Grechaninov, V., Molodetska, T., Lopushanskyi, A., Zavertailo, K.: Study of the workspace model in distributed structures using CAP. In: Mathematical Modeling and Simulation of Systems: Selected Papers of 17th International Conference, MODS, November 14–16, 2022, Chernihiv, Ukraine, p. 229. Springer Nature (2023)
24. Internet Topology Zoo [Online]. http://www.topology-zoo.org/dataset.html. Accessed 10 Jan 2026
25. Sharma, A., Balasubramanian, V., Kamruzzaman, J.: A temporal deep Q learning for optimal load balancing in software-defined networks. Sensors. **24**(4), 1216 (2024)
26. Kumari, A., Roy, A., Sairam, A.S.: Optimizing SDN controller load balancing using online reinforcement learning. IEEE Access. **12**, 131591–131604 (2024)
27. Prajapati, U., Chatterjee, B.C., Banerjee, A.: GLBMF: greedy-based load balancing in SDN by reducing switch migrations and prioritizing mice flow traffic. Wirel. Pers. Commun. (2024). https://doi.org/10.1007/s11277-024-10989-5

Structured Similar-Column Retrieval for Long-Tail Column Type Annotation

Changlong Wang, Huimei Tian(✉), Zhixiong Yin, Wenhao Zhao, and Pengjuan Lu

Northwest Normal University, Lanzhou, China
wchlong@nwnu.edu.cn, 2578083579@qq.com

Abstract. Column Type Annotation (CTA) aims to predict semantic types for columns in tables and is a key task in table understanding. Existing approaches usually perform well on high-frequency labels, but they still suffer from class imbalance and data sparsity on long-tail labels. To address this problem, this paper proposes SSCR (Structured Similar-Column Retrieval), a structured similar-column retrieval approach for long-tail CTA. By combining table-level graph modeling with structured similar-column retrieval, SSCR provides richer contextual information for long-tail label prediction. Based on this, two retrieval-enhanced strategies are designed: one is a frequency-aware fusion strategy for long-tail enhancement, and the other is a probabilistic gated selection strategy for overall improvement. Experimental results show that the probabilistic gated selection strategy maintains overall robustness, while the long-tail-oriented fusion strategy achieves improvement on long-tail-related metrics, with Long-tail Acc reaching 0.6489.

Keywords: Table understanding · Column type annotation · Long-tail labels · Table-level graph modeling · Structured similar-column retrieval

1 Introduction

Tabular data widely exists in open data platforms, enterprise databases, and web knowledge resources, and its automated semantic understanding is an important foundation for intelligent table analysis [7]. Column Type Annotation (CTA) aims to assign semantic type labels to target columns in tables and is a key task in table understanding, knowledge integration, and downstream analytics [1]. Recent advances based on pre-trained language models, table-level context modeling, and graph neural networks have substantially improved overall CTA performance. However, these improvements are mainly concentrated on high-frequency labels, while the recognition of low-frequency and long-tail labels remains unstable in real-world scenarios.

The root cause is that label frequencies in practical CTA datasets usually follow long-tail distributions. In widely used datasets such as Turl [3] and

L. Ding et al. (Eds.): APWeb-WAIM 2026, LNCS 16995, pp. 592–604, 2027.
https://doi.org/10.1007/978-981-92-5699-0_40

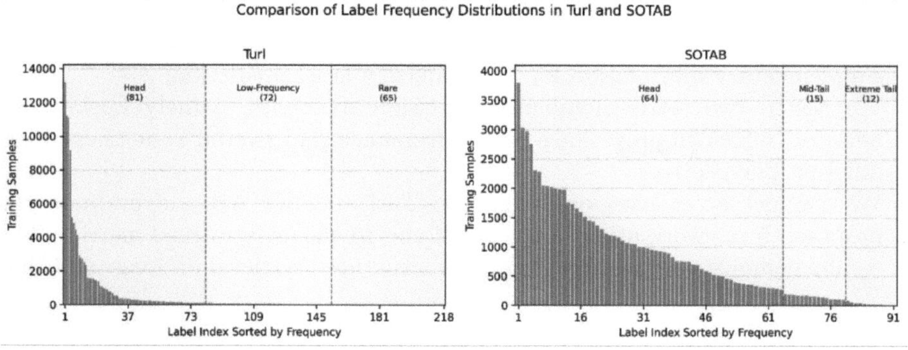

Fig. 1. Label frequency distributions and long-tail partitions on Turl and SOTAB.

SOTAB [8], a small number of head labels contain abundant training samples, whereas many tail labels have only limited observations, as illustrated in Fig. 1. Watchog [10] further points out that such distributions introduce severe class imbalance and data sparsity, which significantly affect tail-label prediction performance. Nevertheless, most existing studies focus on general column annotation or overall performance optimization and do not explicitly treat long-tail CTA as a problem requiring dedicated modeling and evaluation.

Long-tail CTA remains challenging because low-frequency labels usually have limited samples, unstable value patterns, and higher noise levels. Relying solely on local textual features within a target column makes it difficult to learn robust decision boundaries [13]. Although table-level modeling can exploit contextual information from neighboring columns, such information is often insufficient for accurately recognizing rare semantic types. Meanwhile, training corpora contain numerous semantically similar columns that naturally provide prototype-like evidence for low-frequency labels. This observation motivates the use of structured similar-column retrieval as an auxiliary source of information for long-tail prediction.

Based on this observation, we propose SSCR (Structured Similar-Column Retrieval) for long-tail CTA. SSCR combines table-level graph modeling with structured similar-column retrieval from the training corpus, where retrieved prototypes are selected according to semantic similarity, column-value patterns, and table context. Unlike general retrieval methods that introduce external textual knowledge, SSCR focuses on retrieving structurally similar columns that are closer to the target column in semantic role and contextual usage. To effectively utilize the retrieved information, we further design two retrieval-enhanced decision mechanisms: Fusion, a rule-based strategy for long-tail improvement, and Selector, a probabilistic gated strategy for robust overall performance.

The main contributions of this paper are summarized as follows:

- We propose SSCR, a retrieval-enhanced framework that introduces structured similar-column retrieval into table-level graph modeling and provides supplementary information for low-frequency label prediction.
- We design two retrieval-enhanced decision strategies, namely Fusion and Selector, which improve long-tail performance and overall robustness from different perspectives.
- We conduct extensive experiments on Turl and SOTAB and evaluate the proposed framework using both overall and frequency-stratified metrics. The results demonstrate the effectiveness of structured retrieval for long-tail CTA.

2 Related Work

2.1 Column Type Annotation and Table-Level Context Modeling

Semantic type annotation, especially column type annotation, aims to predict semantic labels for columns in relational tables, and is a core preprocessing task in data discovery, data integration, and table understanding. Early representative approaches such as Sherlock [5] formulate CTA as a column-level supervised classification problem and construct neural models based on hand-crafted statistical and semantic features. Later, Sato [14] introduces intra-table context and improves prediction performance by modeling semantic dependencies among columns in the same table.

With the development of pre-trained language models, Turl [3] introduces the pre-training and fine-tuning paradigm into relational table understanding and proposes a structure-aware Transformer encoder. Doduo [11] further feeds the whole table into a unified pre-trained model and jointly handles column type prediction and column relation prediction. In addition to intra-table context, researchers have also begun to explore inter-table information. Reca [12] finds related tables and introduces their columns as inter-table context into target column prediction. GAIT [4] models a table as a graph and explicitly encodes column dependencies through graph neural networks, providing a unified modeling path for intra-table and inter-table information.

The table-level graph modeling component in this paper follows the design idea of GAIT. This paper focuses on long-tail scenarios and further introduces structured similar-column retrieval as supplementary information for low-frequency labels.

2.2 Long-Tail Learning and Class-Imbalanced Learning

Long-tail learning is an important problem in general classification tasks. Focal Loss [9] reduces the influence of easily classified samples and encourages the model to focus on hard examples. Class-Balanced Loss [2] redefines class weights according to the effective number of samples. Decoupling representation learning and classifier learning further demonstrates that stage-wise training is particularly important for tail-class recognition [6].

In the CTA domain, Watchog [10] explicitly points out the class imbalance problem caused by long-tail label distributions and improves tail-class performance through contrastive learning and semi-supervised techniques. However, Watchog primarily relies on contrastive learning to acquire representations from large-scale unlabeled corpora and is particularly suitable for extremely low-resource scenarios. In contrast, this work assumes the availability of a certain amount of labeled data and focuses on enhancing an existing table-level graph model through SSCR. Therefore, the two approaches are complementary in terms of their technical routes.

3 Problem Definition

3.1 Task Definition

Let an input table be denoted as $T = \{c_1, c_2, \ldots, c_n\}$, where c_i denotes the i-th target column and n is the number of target columns in the current table. Each column consists of a column header and several cell values. Given a predefined semantic label set $\mathcal{L} = \{\ell_1, \ell_2, \ldots, \ell_L\}$, the goal of CTA is to predict a semantic type $y_i \in \mathcal{L}$ for each target column.

Let $f(\ell)$ be the frequency of label ℓ in the training set. Labels are divided into high-frequency and low-frequency groups based on $f(\ell)$. Frequency analysis is necessary because overall metrics are often dominated by head labels, while low-frequency labels exhibit substantial internal diversity. Therefore, frequency-stratified evaluation is required.

3.2 Table-Level Long-Tail CTA Setting

Table-level modeling means that when predicting the semantic type of a target column, the model also uses contextual information from other columns in the same table. The prediction remains column-level, but the input includes topic clues, semantic dependencies, and structural constraints from co-occurring columns.

This setting is adopted for two reasons: (1) a column's semantics are often constrained by other columns, e.g., a "name" column can be disambiguated by adjacent "author" or "price" columns; (2) for low-frequency labels, the target column alone is sparse and ambiguous, while intra-table context provides additional semantic support.

4 Method

4.1 Overall Framework

This paper proposes a SSCR framework for long-tail column type annotation.The overall process of SSCR consists of four stages, as illustrated in Fig. 2.

Given an input table T, SSCR uses three types of information for each target column: the content information of the target column itself, the intra-table contextual information provided by other target columns in the same table, and the structured similar-column information retrieved from the training corpus.

Based on these information, SSCR further designs two decision mechanisms to control when and how retrieval information is incorporated into the final prediction. First, the target column is serialized and encoded to obtain an initial

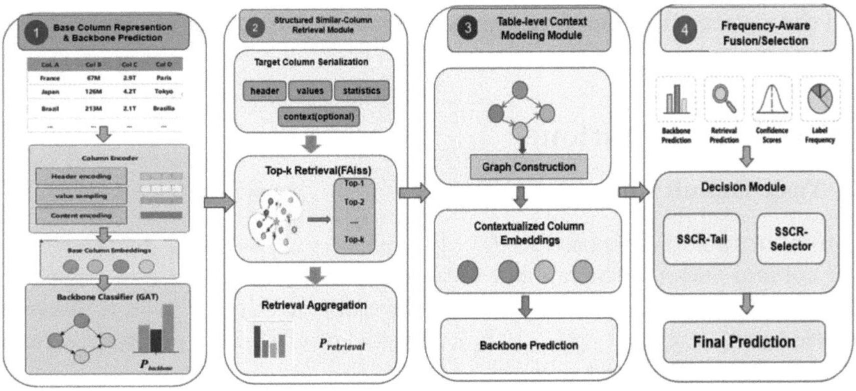

Fig. 2. Overall framework of SSCR.

column-level representation and an initial classification score vector. Second, a column prototype corpus is constructed from the training corpus, and the top-K similar column prototypes are retrieved for each target column. Third, target columns in the same table are modeled as a graph to capture inter-column dependencies. Finally, a frequency-aware fusion module and a probabilistic gated selector generate the final prediction according to the confidence of the core model, the retrieval branch, and label frequency information.

Algorithm 1 summarizes the main procedure of SSCR. Line 1 constructs the column prototype corpus from the training data. Lines 2–6 serialize each target column, perform structured similar-column retrieval, and aggregate retrieved labels to obtain the retrieval prediction. Lines 7–8 construct the table-level graph and generate the core model prediction using the graph backbone. Lines 9–13 apply either Fusion or Selector to determine the final prediction for each target column. Finally, Line 14 returns the predicted semantic types.

Algorithm 1: Summarizes the main procedure of SSCR.

Input: An input table $T = \{c_1, c_2, \ldots, c_n\}$; training corpus $\mathcal{D}_{train}$
Output: Final predictions $\{\hat{y}_i\}_{i=1}^{n}$
Build the column prototype corpus $\mathcal{P}$ from $\mathcal{D}_{train}$;
foreach *target column* $c_i \in T$ **do**
  Serialize the target column and obtain initial scores s_i^0;
  Construct retrieval query q_i and retrieve top-K similar prototypes R_i^K;
  Aggregate retrieved labels to obtain retrieval scores s_i^r;
  Obtain retrieval prediction $\hat{y}_i^{(r)}$ and confidence r_i;
Construct a table-level graph using target columns and initial scores s_i^0;
Apply graph backbone $\mathcal{G}$ to obtain core predictions $\hat{y}_i^{(g)}$, confidence g_i, and margin m_i;
foreach *target column* $c_i \in T$ **do**
  if *Fusion is used* **then**
    Apply the fusion rule to generate final prediction $\hat{y}_i$;
  else
    Compute selector probability and choose between retrieval and core predictions;
return $\{\hat{y}_i\}_{i=1}^{n}$;

4.2 Basic Target-Column Representation and Initial Classification Score Vector

This section constructs the basic semantic representation of the target column and obtains the initial classification score vector through a basic classifier.

Basic Target-Column Representation. Let the i-th target column be denoted as c_i, its column header as h_i, and its cell value sequence as $V_i = \{v_{i1}, v_{i2}, \ldots, v_{im}\}$, where m is the number of retained cell values. Since table columns need to be processed by language models as text sequences, a serialization function is used to concatenate the column header and cell values into textual input: $x_i = \text{Serialize}(h_i, V_i) = [h_i, v_{i1}, v_{i2}, \ldots, v_{im}]$.

Here, Serialize$(\cdot)$ denotes the operation of converting the column header and cell values into a textual representation. This serialization-then-encoding formulation is consistent with the basic idea of table serialization in Doduo: since pre-trained language models take token sequences as input, columns or tables must first be converted into sequential inputs.

Basic Encoder and Initial Prediction Score Vector. For the target column c_i, the serialized text x_i is encoded by the target-column text encoder $E(\cdot)$ to obtain a basic semantic representation $z_i = E(x_i)$. Then, a basic column classifier produces the initial prediction logits over the label space as $s_i^0 = W_0 z_i + b_0$, where W_0 and b_0 denote the weight matrix and bias vector of the basic classifier, respectively. The resulting s_i^0 is used as the initial classification score vector.

4.3 Retrieval Module

Prototype Corpus Construction. To obtain more contextual information about the target column and improve annotation performance, this paper constructs a column prototype corpus $\mathcal{P}$ from table columns in the training corpus. For each labeled column c_j, we extract its column header h_j, cell value set V_j, the header set of the same table H_j, contextual headers C_j excluding itself, and its label y_j. These elements are serialized into a structured column prototype text:$r_j = \text{Serialize}_r(h_j, V_j, H_j, C_j)$.

Different from simply concatenating pure column values, this representation retains three types of structured information: column headers, contextual headers, and column values. Therefore, it is referred to as structured similar-column information.

Each prototype in the corpus is represented as $p_j = (r_j, y_j, f(y_j))$, where $f(y_j)$ denotes the frequency of label y_j in the training set. To reduce the influence of redundant prototypes from high-frequency labels, the prototype corpus is deduplicated to retain a semantically diverse prototype set.

Query and Retrieval. For the column c_i to be predicted, a query text is constructed using the same structured serialization format as the prototypes, i.e., $q_i = \text{Serialize}_q(h_i, V_i, H_i, C_i)$. To map queries and prototypes into the same vector space, a pre-trained sentence embedding model from Sentence-Transformers is used. Let $F(\cdot)$ denote the sentence encoder; then the query vector and prototype vector are given by $e_i^q = F(q_i)$ and $e_j^p = F(r_j)$, respectively.

Nearest-neighbor retrieval is then performed on the vector index to obtain the top-K most similar prototypes:$R_i^K = \text{TopK}(\text{sim}(e_i^q, e_j^p))$,

where $\text{sim}(\cdot)$ denotes the vector similarity function. Each retrieved prototype is associated with its label, frequency, and similarity score. The top-K label information is then aggregated to obtain the retrieval-only prediction.

Let the j-th retrieved prototype have label y_j, similarity score sim_{ij}, and rank position rank_{ij}. The retrieval branch aggregates the information score for each label ℓ as:

$$s_{i,\ell}^r = \sum_{j \in R_i^K,\, y_j = \ell} \text{sim}_{ij} \cdot w_{\text{rank}}(j) \cdot w_{\text{freq}}(\ell), \tag{1}$$

where $w_{\text{rank}}(j)$ is the rank-based weight, $w_{\text{freq}}(\ell)$ is the frequency-based penalty term, and $s_{i,\ell}^r$ is the aggregated score assigned by the retrieval branch to label ℓ. This design suppresses the dominance of high-frequency labels in retrieval results and makes the retrieval branch more oriented toward long-tail prediction.

4.4 Table-Level Context Modeling

Graph Construction. To utilize semantic dependencies among multiple columns in the same table, this paper adopts table-level graph modeling. For a table T, target columns are treated as graph nodes, and a graph $G = (\mathcal{V}, \mathcal{E})$ is constructed, where each node $u_i \in \mathcal{V}$ corresponds to a target column c_i. The initial feature of node u_i is set as $h_i^0 = s_i^0$. For any two target columns c_i and c_j in the same table, if $i \neq j$, an edge $(u_i, u_j) \in \mathcal{E}$ is built. This nearly complete graph represents potential topic consistency, semantic co-occurrence, and structural complementarity among columns in the same table.

Graph Propagation. Let h_i^l denote the representation of node u_i after the l-th graph propagation layer. The node representation is updated as: $h_i^{l+1} = \Phi^l\left(h_i^l, \{h_j^l : u_j \in \mathcal{N}(u_i)\}\right)$, where $\mathcal{N}(u_i)$ denotes the neighbor set of node u_i, and $\Phi^l(\cdot)$ denotes the graph propagation operator of the l-th layer.

After L propagation layers, the core model branch score is obtained through the output layer as $s_i^g = W_g h_i^L + b_g$, where W_g and b_g denote the weight matrix and bias vector of the output layer, respectively.

Training Objective. Let the ground-truth label be y_i. The core model adopts the standard cross-entropy loss:

$$\mathcal{L}_g = -\sum_{i=1}^{N} \log \frac{\exp(s_{i,y_i}^g)}{\sum_{\ell \in \mathcal{L}} \exp(s_{i,\ell}^g)}, \tag{2}$$

where N is the number of target columns in the current batch, $s_{i,\ell}^g$ denotes the score output by the core model for label ℓ on the i-th target column, and s_{i,y_i}^g denotes the prediction score corresponding to the ground-truth label y_i.

4.5 Frequency-Aware Fusion and Probabilistic Gated Selector

Although the retrieval branch is more friendly to long-tail labels, its overall performance is usually lower than that of the core model. Therefore, this paper does not directly replace the core model with retrieval, but designs two frequency-aware decision modules.

Frequency-Aware Fusion. This strategy uses the core model prediction by default. Only when the core model is not sufficiently confident about the current sample and the retrieval branch provides strong information for a tail label, the retrieval branch is allowed to override the core model result. Let g_i denote the top-1 confidence of the core model branch, m_i denote the score margin between the top two candidate labels of the core model branch, r_i denote the top-1 confidence of the retrieval branch, and $\hat{y}_i^{(g)}$ and $\hat{y}_i^{(r)}$ denote the predicted labels given by the core model branch and the retrieval branch for the i-th target column, respectively. Let $\mathcal{L}_{\text{tail}}$ denote the set of tail labels. Given thresholds τ_s, τ_m, and τ_r, the final prediction is defined as:

$$\hat{y}_i = \begin{cases} \hat{y}_i^{(r)}, & g_i < \tau_s,\ m_i < \tau_m,\ r_i \geq \tau_r,\ \hat{y}_i^{(r)} \in \mathcal{L}_{\text{tail}}, \\ \hat{y}_i^{(g)}, & \text{otherwise}. \end{cases} \tag{3}$$

Here, τ_s, τ_m, and τ_r are the core model confidence threshold, the score margin threshold, and the retrieval branch confidence threshold, respectively.

Probabilistic Gated Selector. The second strategy is a probabilistic gated selector. Unlike frequency-aware Fusion, which directly uses manually set thresholds, this strategy trains a lightweight binary selector to learn whether the backbone branch or the retrieval branch should be trusted more for a given sample.

The input feature vector of the selector is defined as:

$$\mathbf{x}_i^{\text{sel}} = \phi\left(g_i, m_i, r_i, \mathbf{1}[\hat{y}_i^{(g)} = \hat{y}_i^{(r)}], f(\hat{y}_i^{(g)}), f(\hat{y}_i^{(r)})\right), \tag{4}$$

where $\phi(\cdot)$ denotes feature concatenation. Here, $\mathbf{1}[\hat{y}_i^{(g)} = \hat{y}_i^{(r)}]$ is an indicator function, which equals 1 when the two branches make the same prediction and 0 otherwise. $f(\hat{y}_i^{(g)})$ and $f(\hat{y}_i^{(r)})$ denote the training-set frequencies of the labels predicted by the two branches, respectively.

Let the selector output the probability of choosing the retrieval branch as $q_i = P(\text{use retrieval} \mid \mathbf{x}_i^{\text{sel}})$. To avoid excessive coverage of high-frequency labels and maintain stable overall performance, this paper adopts a probabilistic gating strategy. Let τ_q denote the selector threshold, and require that the retrieval-predicted label is not a head label. The final prediction is defined as:

$$\hat{y}_i = \begin{cases} \hat{y}_i^{(r)}, & q_i \geq \tau_q \text{ and } \hat{y}_i^{(r)} \notin \mathcal{L}_{\text{head}}, \\ \hat{y}_i^{(g)}, & \text{otherwise}. \end{cases} \tag{5}$$

Compared with frequency-aware fusion, the selector no longer relies only on a small number of fixed thresholds, but learns from the validation set which branch combination is more reliable. At the same time, through the probabilistic gate of "high threshold + non-head label", it avoids large-scale coverage of core model predictions by retrieval information.

5 Experimental Setup

5.1 Datasets

This paper evaluates the proposed method on two public CTA datasets, Turl [3] and SOTAB [8]. Table 1 summarizes their basic statistics. Turl exhibits a pronounced long-tail label distribution, making it well suited for the problem setting of this paper, whereas SOTAB has a relatively weaker long-tail distribution and is used to evaluate the robustness of the proposed method under different label distributions.

This paper constructs frequency-aware multi-column table-level experimental data to ensure that table-level context is available and that the graph modeling scale remains controllable. For the experimental datasets, this paper conducts frequency analysis based on training label frequencies: labels with $f(\ell) \geq 200$ are regarded as head labels, labels with $100 \leq f(\ell) < 200$ are regarded as low-frequency labels, and labels with $f(\ell) < 100$ are regarded as rare labels.

In the experiments, labels with $f(\ell) < 200$ are regarded as long-tail labels, and labels with $f(\ell) < 100$ are regarded as extreme-tail labels.

Table 1. Basic statistics of the Turl and SOTAB datasets

Dataset	Metric	Training	Validation	Testing
Turl	Tables	32,000	4,000	4,000
	Target Columns	110,220	13,717	13,774
	Avg. Target Columns per Table	3.44	3.43	3.44
SOTAB	Tables	17,167	2,290	1,906
	Target Columns	75,540	10,136	7,747
	Avg. Target Columns per Table	4.40	4.43	4.07

5.2 Baselines

The compared methods include three groups:

1. Table-level graph backbone baselines: GAT, GCN, and GGNN. These three methods are all derived from [4].
2. Retrieval method comparison: the two retrieval methods proposed in this paper, Retrieval-overall and Retrieval-tail, are compared.
3. Variants of the proposed method: Fusion for long-tail improvement and Selector for robust overall improvement.

Among them, the table-level graph backbones are used to compare different table-level context modeling methods. The retrieval baselines are used to analyze the effect of structured similar-column retrieval itself. The proposed method variants are used to evaluate the influence of different decision mechanisms on long-tail gains and overall performance.

6 Results and Analysis

6.1 Overall Results

We evaluate all methods on Turl and SOTAB. Table 2 and Table 3 report overall and frequency-stratified metrics. Key observations are as follows.

On Turl, which has a strong long-tail distribution, GAT shows the most stable performance on long-tail buckets. Retrieval-tail achieves notable gains on long-tail metrics, but its overall performance remains lower than the core model, indicating that retrieval is best used as an auxiliary branch. Fusion further improves long-tail performance, while Selector obtains moderate gains with better overall robustness.

On SOTAB, which has a weaker long-tail distribution, the core model alone is already strong, so retrieval brings marginal improvements. Retrieval-tail still helps on extreme-tail labels, but its overall performance lags behind the graph backbone. Fusion and Selector yield only slight gains, confirming that the effectiveness of retrieval enhancement depends on both the dataset's long-tail degree and the core model's strength.

Table 2. Main experimental results on Turl. Ret-tail denotes Retrieval-tail

Metric	GAT	GCN	GGNN	Ret-tail	Fusion	Selector
Micro-F1	0.8127	0.8088	0.8084	0.7143	0.8129	**0.8130**
Macro-F1	0.5910	0.5763	0.5619	0.5329	**0.6069**	0.5913
Weighted-F1	0.8015	0.7982	0.8008	0.7230	**0.8027**	0.8020
Long-tail Acc	0.6318	0.6147	0.5987	**0.6713**	0.6489	0.6361
Extreme-tail Acc	0.6097	0.5875	0.5654	**0.6600**	0.6358	0.6177
Long-tail Macro-F1	0.4398	0.4227	0.4024	**0.4873**	0.4682	0.4433
Extreme-tail Macro-F1	0.3999	0.3822	0.3626	**0.4569**	0.4324	0.4040
Head Acc	**0.8260**	0.8230	0.8238	0.7175	0.8249	**0.8260**

Table 3. Main experimental results on SOTAB.

Metric	GAT	GCN	GGNN	Ret-tail	Fusion	Selector
Micro-F1	0.8970	0.8891	**0.9006**	0.7217	0.8970	0.8970
Macro-F1	0.8543	**0.8604**	0.8401	0.6898	0.8509	0.8516
Weighted-F1	0.8961	0.8891	**0.8988**	0.7161	0.8962	0.8962
Long-tail Acc	0.8371	0.8247	0.8165	0.7814	**0.8392**	**0.8392**
Extreme-tail Acc	**0.8750**	0.8214	0.7143	**0.8750**	**0.8750**	**0.8750**
Long-tail Macro-F1	0.4485	0.4427	0.3605	0.3333	**0.4491**	**0.4491**
Extreme-tail Macro-F1	**0.5137**	0.5040	0.2511	0.4815	**0.5137**	**0.5137**
Head Acc	0.9010	0.8934	**0.9062**	0.7177	0.9009	0.9009

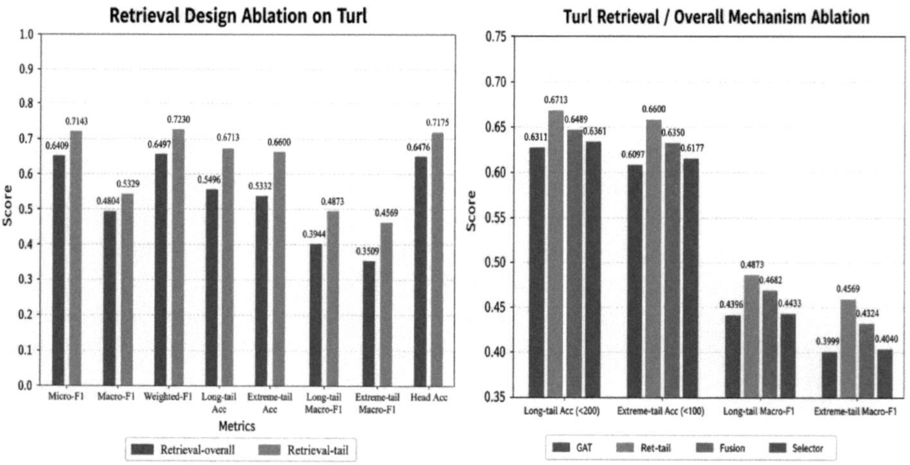

(a) (b)

Fig. 3. Ablation comparison.

6.2 Ablation Study

Since GAT significantly outperforms GCN and GGNN in long-tail scenarios, we use GAT as the core backbone in all ablations. Figure 3 summarizes the results.

Retrieval design, as shown in Fig. 3(a), shows that Retrieval-tail outperforms Retrieval-overall on all long-tail metrics, e.g., Long-tail Acc +0.12 and Extreme-tail Acc +0.13, showing that frequency-based penalty effectively suppresses head-label dominance.

Comparison of enhancement mechanisms, as shown in Fig. 3(b), shows that Ret-tail improves over GAT on four long-tail metrics: Long-tail Acc 0.6318 → 0.6713, Extreme-tail Acc 0.6097 → 0.6600, Long-tail Macro-F1 0.4398 → 0.4873, and Extreme-tail Macro-F1 0.3999 → 0.4569. Fusion is slightly below Ret-tail, indicating that simply fusing retrieval information may introduce noise. Selector performs only slightly above GAT, suggesting that an overly conservative selection mechanism filters out valuable retrieval information for tail classes.

6.3 Efficiency Analysis

SSCR employs a FAISS-based prototype index containing 8,163 structured column prototypes. The retrieval embedding dimension is 384 and the retrieval size is fixed to K=5. Since retrieval is performed over a compact prototype repository, the additional inference overhead is limited and remains practical for medium-scale CTA datasets.

7 Conclusion

This paper investigates long-tail Column Type Annotation (CTA), a practical yet underexplored challenge in table understanding. We propose SSCR, a retrieval-enhanced framework integrating table-level graph modeling, Structured Similar-Column Retrieval, and frequency-aware decision strategies. Experiments on Turl and SOTAB demonstrate that structured retrieval improves long-tail prediction while maintaining competitive overall performance. The results further show that its effectiveness depends on dataset-specific label distributions.

Future work will investigate more effective frequency-aware learning strategies, larger prototype repositories, advanced retrieval mechanisms, broader comparisons with representative CTA systems, and deeper analyses of retrieval efficiency, scalability, and statistical robustness.

Acknowledgment. This work was supported by the National Natural Science Foundation of China under Grant Nos. 62362060 and 72364033.

References

1. Cremaschi, M., Spahiu, B., Palmonari, M.: Survey on semantic interpretation of tabular data: Challenges and directions. arXiv preprint arXiv:2411.11891 (2024)
2. Cui, Y., Jia, M., Lin, T.Y., Song, Y., Belongie, S.: Class-balanced loss based on effective number of samples. In: Proceedings of the IEEE/CVF Conference on Computer Vision and Pattern Recognition, pp. 9268–9277 (2019)
3. Deng, X., Sun, H., Lees, A., Wu, Y., Yu, C.: TURL: Table understanding through representation learning. In: Proceedings of the ACM SIGMOD Record **51**, 33–40 (2022)
4. Hoseinzade, E., Wang, K.: Graph neural network approach to semantic type detection in tables. In: Proceedings of the Pacific-Asia Conference on Knowledge Discovery and Data Mining, pp. 121–133. Springer, Cham (2024). https://doi.org/10.1007/978-981-97-2266-2_10
5. Hulsebos, M., et al.: Sherlock: a deep learning approach to semantic data type detection. In: Proceedings of the 25th ACM SIGKDD International Conference on Knowledge Discovery and Data Mining. pp. 1500–1508 (2019)
6. Kang, B., et al.: Decoupling representation and classifier for long-tailed recognition. arXiv preprint arXiv:1910.09217 (2019)
7. Kayali, M., Lykov, A., Fountalis, I.: Chorus: foundation models for unified data discovery and exploration. arXiv preprint arXiv:2306.09610 (2023)
8. Korini, K., Peeters, R., Bizer, C.: SOTAB: the WDC schema.org table annotation benchmark. In: Proceedings of the CEUR Workshop Proceedings, vol. **3320**, pp. 14–19 (2022)
9. Lin, T.Y., Goyal, P., Girshick, R., He, K., Dollár, P.: Focal loss for dense object detection. In: Proceedings of the IEEE International Conference on Computer Vision, pp. 2980–2988 (2017)
10. Miao, Z., Wang, J.: Watchog: a light-weight contrastive learning based framework for column annotation. In: Proceedings of the ACM on Management of Data **1**, 1–24 (2023)
11. Suhara, Y., et al.: Annotating columns with pre-trained language models. In: Proceedings of the 2022 International Conference on Management of Data. pp. 1493–1503 (2022)
12. Sun, Y., Xin, H., Chen, L.: RECA: related tables enhanced column semantic type annotation framework. In: Proceedings of the VLDB Endowment, vol. 16, pp. 1319–1331 (2023)
13. Wang, X., et al.: Decisive vector guided column annotation. the Pattern Recognition **158**, 110958 (2025)
14. Zhang, D., Suhara, Y., Li, J., Hulsebos, M., Demiralp, Ç., Tan, W.C.: SATO: contextual semantic type detection in tables. arXiv preprint arXiv:1911.06311 (2019)

Special and Industrial Tracks

A LLM-Powered Multi-agent System for Cross-View Integration in Digital Government Systems

Chang Xie[1], Haoyi Shang[3], Canqiang Li[2](✉), and Keman Huang[1](✉)

[1] Renmin University of China, Beijing, China
{xiechang,keman}@ruc.edu.cn
[2] Department of Automation, Tsinghua University, Beijing, China
cq-li18@mails.tsinghua.edu.cn
[3] Nanjing University, Nanjing, China
231250110@smail.nju.edu.cn

Abstract. Improving digital government performance requires the coherent integration of performance (indicator), business, and data views, yet supporting materials are typically expressed in unstructured, inconsistent natural language, making manual consolidation inefficient and unsustainable. To address this cross-view integration challenge, we propose an LLM-powered multi-agent system that automatically (i) extracts performance indicators, business processes, and data associated with business activities (ii) establishes mappings across them, and (iii) generates optimization recommendations to refine both views and mappings. A case study on a smart court project demonstrates the system's effectiveness in producing accurate, explainable, and actionable cross-view integration.

Keywords: LLM-powered multi-agent systems · digital government · performance indicators · business process extraction · cross-view integration · smart court

1 Introduction

Digital government has become a critical pillar of modern governance [1–3], with its value reaffirmed during the COVID-19 pandemic. However, as a complex system engineering task requiring cross-departmental, multi-actor, and long-term coordination, its implementation often suffers from insufficient information sharing, weak resource integration, and limited reuse, causing outcomes to fall short of design expectations [3].

While frameworks such as the Federal Enterprise Architecture (FEA) [2] provide guidance, they lack effective dynamic cross-view integration. Performance, business, and data views remain fragmented, with supporting information scattered across heterogeneous unstructured documents [6]–performance cannot reflect real operations, business cannot map to data, and data cannot support evaluation. Existing approaches are largely ex-post, labor-intensive, and subjective [5].

L. Ding et al. (Eds.): APWeb-WAIM 2026, LNCS 16995, pp. 607–616, 2027.
https://doi.org/10.1007/978-981-92-5699-0_41

This paper proposes an LLM-powered multi-agent approach [9,10] that dynamically integrates the three views(performance, business and data views) via three subsystems: (i) extraction (performance indicators and business/data information), (ii) mapping (linking the views, notably performance-process), and (iii) optimization (recommending improvements to strengthen integration).

2 Related Work

Digital government is widely recognized as a highly complex governance model shaped by multi-level coordination, institutional constraints, technological heterogeneity, and diverse service scenarios, yet still faces major challenges including limited governance capacity, persistent data-sharing and collaboration barriers, fragmented infrastructure, weak lifecycle management, shallow integration of frontier technologies, and underdeveloped performance evaluation systems [15].

While LLMs and multi-agent technologies offer strong language understanding and knowledge extraction capabilities [16], their real-world deployment remains constrained: reliance on static corpora causes outdated information and weak domain alignment, dependence on high-quality data and compute inflates costs, and risks such as hallucinations, vulnerabilities, privacy leakage, and bias amplification persist [18,19], leaving them short of the stability, trustworthiness, and controllability required in complex real-world scenarios [17].

3 A Multi-agent System for Cross-View Integration

To integrate the **performance view** (performance indicators), **business view** (business processes), and **data view** (related data resources across different organizational views), we propose an LLM-powered multi-agent system that automatically analyzes unstructured digital-government documents (Fig. 1). The workflow has three stages:

1. **View Extraction:** a *performance agent* structures indicators into a hierarchy, while a *business and data agent* jointly models process flows (business view) and the data resources associated with each activity (data view).
2. **Cross-View Mapping:** a *mapping agent* establishes explicit links from each indicator to its supporting business activities and data elements.
3. **Solution Optimization:** an *optimization agent* recommends improvements across the three views and their mappings based on the integrated analysis.

This pipeline transforms fragmented text into a structured, cross-view integrated model, enabling a holistic and verifiable understanding of digital government systems.

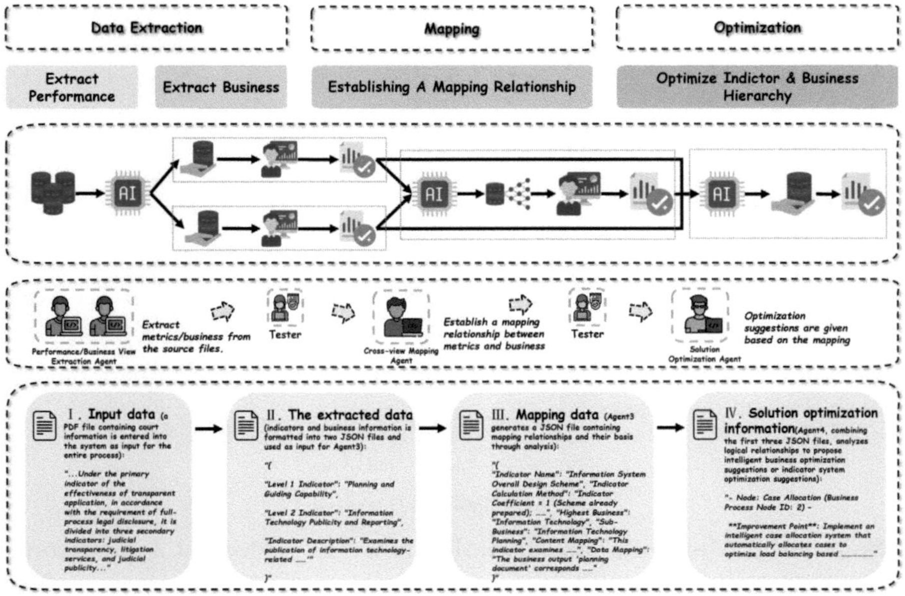

Fig. 1. Architecture of the LLM-powered multi-agent system for cross-view integration in digital government.

3.1 Formal System Definition

We formalize our LLM-powered Multi-Agent Based System as a tuple $S = \langle A, \mathcal{D}, \mathcal{T} \rangle$, where:

- $A = \{a_{\text{ind}}, a_{\text{biz}}, a_{\text{map}}, a_{\text{opt}}\}$ is the set of agents, representing Performance Extraction, Business &Data Extraction, Mapping, and Optimization agents.
- $\mathcal{D} = \{T_{\text{doc}}, D_{\text{ind}}, G_{\text{biz}}, D_{\text{data}}, D_{\text{map}}, S_{\text{opt}}\}$ is the set of core data structures that model the system's information flow: from the initial unstructured documents (T_{doc}) to structured representations of the performance view (a hierarchy of indicators, D_{ind}), the business view (a directed graph of business activities and process sequences, G_{biz}), and the data view (data resources attached to each business activity, D_{data}), the cross-view mappings that connect them (D_{map}), and the final optimization solutions (S_{opt}).
- $\mathcal{T} = \{\tau_{\text{ind}}, \tau_{\text{biz}}, \tau_{\text{map}}, \tau_{\text{opt}}\}$ is the set of task functions corresponding to each agent in A.

Agent and Task Formalization. Each agent $a_i \in A$ is defined as a structure $a_i = \langle M, P_i, \tau_i \rangle$, where M is the core Large Language Model (LLM), P_i is a dedicated prompt module that specifies the agent's role and output format, and $\tau_i \in \mathcal{T}$ is its task function.

The task functions define the core transformations performed by each agent:

$$\tau_{\text{ind}} : T_{\text{doc}} \rightarrow D_{\text{ind}} \tag{1}$$

$$\tau_{\text{biz}} : T_{\text{doc}} \rightarrow (G_{\text{biz}}, D_{\text{data}}) \tag{2}$$

$$\tau_{\text{map}} : (D_{\text{ind}}, G_{\text{biz}}, D_{\text{data}}) \rightarrow D_{\text{map}} \tag{3}$$

$$\tau_{\text{opt}} : (D_{\text{ind}}, G_{\text{biz}}, D_{\text{data}}, D_{\text{map}}) \rightarrow S_{\text{opt}} \tag{4}$$

System Execution Workflow. The system's overall function, F_{sys}, processes an input document T_{doc} to generate a complete, structured analysis. The workflow is executed as follows:

1. **Parallel Extraction:** The system concurrently extracts the performance, business, and data views:

$$D_{\text{ind}} = \tau_{\text{ind}}(T_{\text{doc}}) \tag{5}$$

$$(G_{\text{biz}}, D_{\text{data}}) = \tau_{\text{biz}}(T_{\text{doc}}) \tag{6}$$

2. **Sequential Mapping and Optimization:** The subsequent agents process the outputs in sequence:

$$D_{\text{map}} = \tau_{\text{map}}(D_{\text{ind}}, G_{\text{biz}}, D_{\text{data}}) \tag{7}$$

$$S_{\text{opt}} = \tau_{\text{opt}}(D_{\text{ind}}, G_{\text{biz}}, D_{\text{data}}, D_{\text{map}}) \tag{8}$$

3.2 Agent Implementation Details

Performance View Extraction Agent (a_{ind}). This agent extracts evaluation indicators from design and implementation documents in two stages. **(i) Data Extraction.** PDF files are parsed into plain text via `pypdf`, then a task-specific prompt drives an LLM (Deepseek in this study, with reasoning and structured-output capabilities) to output indicators and their attributes as a Markdown table. **(ii) View Construction.** The Markdown table is converted into a JSON file that preserves the "Level-1 → Level-2 → Level-3" hierarchy and written back to the global state, serving as the deliverable to the mapping agent.

Business & Data View Extraction Agent (a_{biz}). This agent parses unstructured text via Chain-of-Thought (CoT) prompting [11], decomposing the task into three steps. **(i) Business Connection Identification.** Using previously extracted business nodes as context, the agent reanalyzes the text to identify process sequences (from → to). **(ii) Data Dependency Analysis.** The agent further extracts data resources associated with each activity, yielding a process-centered data view that aligns business operations with their underlying data assets. **(iii) View Construction.** The node and relation data are merged into a machine-readable directed graph (JSON), forming the structured business & data view.

Cross-View Mapping Agent (a_{map}). Taking the three JSON views as input, this agent links performance indicators to business activities and data elements via a three-channel strategy: **(i) Performance–Business** matches indicators to business activities by content similarity; **(ii) Performance–Data** leverages the data resources attached to each activity to identify indicator-relevant data elements; **(iii) Structural Enhancement** exploits the process topology and indicator hierarchy as structural cues to refine mappings. To ensure transparency, the agent is prompted to output a justification for each mapping, yielding results that are both accurate and explainable.

Solution Optimization Agent (a_{opt}). Given the three views and their mappings, this agent follows Chain-of-Thought reasoning to refine the system in five steps: **(i)** propose new third-level indicators from the existing structure; **(ii)** add corresponding business activities or links; **(iii)** reconstruct mappings over the expanded views; **(iv)** self-inspect to fix contradictions and coverage gaps; **(v)** export structured tables and JSON. This stage-based design yields verifiable recommendations and supports per-step expert validation, strengthening the alignment of system design with governance objectives.

4 Experimental Results

To verify the effectiveness of our approach, we use a real-world smart court construction project as a case and report the performance of each agent. Ground-truth annotations (covering evaluation tasks) were independently performed by two graduate students with experience in digital government research. Disagreements were resolved through discussion until consensus was reached.

4.1 Application Scenario: Smart Court Project

We use the **Smart Court**, a national judicial modernization initiative, as our case. It features a complex business ecosystem and a hierarchical performance framework spanning areas such as judicial transparency and intelligent service integration, yet its performance, business, and data views are scattered across separate design specifications—an ideal testbed for our framework, applied as follows:

1. **Corpus Ingestion:** The system parses the project document corpus to establish a foundational knowledge base.
2. **Performance View Extraction:** The *performance view extraction agent* formalizes a structured, hierarchical system of performance indicators.
3. **Business & Data Extraction:** Concurrently, the *business & data extraction agent* models workflow topologies and associated data resources.
4. **Cross-View Mapping:** The *mapping modeling agent* employs semantic matching to establish evidentiary links between indicators and business nodes.
5. **Solution Optimization:** The *solution optimization agent* identifies systemic misalignments, generating targeted recommendations for business process and indicator refinement.

4.2 Performance View Extraction Agent

Extraction Example. The agent parses the source PDF via `pypdf` and outputs each indicator as a structured JSON record (name, level, description, calculation method). It additionally infers a "Data Parameter" attribute from the calculation method—e.g., from "Coefficient = 1/0.5/0 (compiled / being compiled / not started)", it derives the parameter "Scheme compilation status" with its three states, exposing the measurable variable behind the indicator and supporting downstream cross-view alignment.

Evaluation Results. We adopt the following metrics to evaluate extraction effectiveness:

- **Precision:** The proportion of extracted fields that are correct.
- **Recall:** The proportion of all ground-truth fields that are successfully captured.
- **F1 Score:** The weighted harmonic mean of precision and recall, comprehensively reflecting overall performance.

$$F1 = 2 \times \frac{\text{Precision} \times \text{Recall}}{\text{Precision} + \text{Recall}} \tag{9}$$

Table 1. Indicator extraction agent evaluation results.

Attribute Type	Precision	Recall	F1 Score
Level 1 Indicator	0.971	1.000	0.985
Level 2 Indicator	1.000	1.000	1.000
Level 3 Indicator	0.971	0.985	0.978

As shown in Table 1, the evaluation results demonstrate that the indicator extraction agent achieves consistently high performance across all hierarchical indicator levels. Specifically, the agent reaches perfect precision and recall (1.000) for extracting Level 2 Indicators. For Level 1 and Level 3 Indicators, all metrics remain exceptionally high, with F1 scores of 0.985 and 0.978, respectively. These results confirm the robustness and reliability of the extraction approach for identifying the core indicator hierarchy.

4.3 Business/Data View Extraction Agent

Business/Data View Example. This agent extracts business activities, associated data, and process relations. For instance, the agent identifies *Case Filing Registration* as a node under the *Adjudication / Case Filing* domain, with inputs "Complaint, Evidentiary Materials, Litigant Information" and outputs "Notice of Case Acceptance, Case Number, Court Summons"; the node connects to the downstream *Case Allocation* node via a sequential flow, with the generated case number serving as the data dependency.

Evaluation Results. To comprehensively evaluate the agent's effectiveness, we assessed the extraction performance for both business/data node attributes and the relations (edges) between them, using Precision, Recall, and F1 Score as core metrics.

The results presented in Table 2 demonstrate the agent's high performance across all extraction tasks. For node attribute extraction, the agent achieved near-perfect precision for business categories and strong performance in identifying associated data elements. Furthermore, it effectively identified both sequential process flows and underlying data dependencies, which is critical for understanding the complete business logic.

Table 2. Business node and relation extraction agent evaluation results.

Extraction Type	Precision	Recall	F1 Score
Node Attributes			
Highest Business	1.000	0.952	0.975
Subdivided Business	1.000	0.947	0.972
Data Element (In/Out)	0.965	0.941	0.953
Relation Types			
Process Sequence	0.973	0.945	0.959
Data Dependency	0.958	0.920	0.939

Overall, the high F1 scores across both node and relation extraction tasks confirm that this agent provides stable and accurate foundational data for subsequent cross-view mapping and process optimization.

4.4 Cross-View Mapping Agent

The following shows a representative automatic mapping result between an indicator and a business activity.

Automated Mapping Result

Indicator Name: Overall Information System Design Plan
Calculation Method: Coefficient: 1 (plan completed); 0.5 (plan in progress); 0 (not started)
Business Classification:

- Highest Business: Informatization
- Subdivision Business: Informatization Planning

Content Mapping: The indicator examines the development of informatization planning. The business description states "establish informatization construction plans", with both involving informatization strategic planning content. Direct correlation.

Data Mapping: Business output "planning documents" corresponds to indicator parameter "plan completion status", with direct data matching.

Accuracy Evaluation. To evaluate the mapping accuracy of the mapping agent, for each pair $(i, b) \in I \times B$ between performance indicators and business activities, binary labels are assigned by both manual annotation and the agent output separately, indicating whether a mapping exists (1: mapping exists; 0: no mapping). We then apply Cohen's kappa coefficient [4] to measure the inter-rater agreement between them.

The κ_{original} value of 0.83940 falls within the $[0.81, 1.00]$ interval, demonstrating that the initial mapping results are almost completely consistent with the manual annotations, confirming the strong performance of the mapping agent.

Building upon this, we further optimized mapping generation by establishing indicator tree relationships and extracting impact relationships between business processes, yielding $\kappa_{\text{optimized}} = 0.86737$. The κ value increased by 0.02797 (approximately 0.03), confirming that this structural enrichment successfully enhances cross-view mapping effectiveness.

4.5 Solution Optimization Agent

Optimization Suggestion Example. The solution optimization agent integrates the three preceding outputs—**performance, business/data, and cross-view mapping**—to generate targeted optimization recommendations.

Solution Optimization Example

New Indicator – *AI-Assisted Trial Decision Support Degree*: examines AI application in trial decisions (case analysis, risk prediction, judgment recommendation); measures the scope and effectiveness of intelligent trial support across all court levels.

New Business – *Intelligent Litigation Guidance Service*: AI-powered guidance covering document templates, case recommendations, result prediction, and mediation suggestions, enabling automation and standardization of the litigation guidance workflow.

New Mapping – *AI-Assisted Trial Decision Support Degree* $\rightarrow$ *Judgment Document Production.* **Content:** AI-assisted decision-making aligns with judgment document generation. **Data:** business inputs "deliberation opinions" and "legal provisions" produce "judgment documents", corresponding to the indicator parameter "number of AI-assisted decisions".

Coverage Evaluation. Some indicators (e.g., "judicial credibility", "social conflict resolution capability") are inherently macro-level and represent aggregated outcomes of multiple processes, making one-to-one mapping infeasible. We thus define four coverage metrics:

$$\mathrm{IC} = \frac{N_{\text{mapped}}}{N_{\text{total}}}, \quad \mathrm{ISC} = \frac{N_{\text{perfect}}}{N_{\text{total}}}, \tag{10}$$

$$\mathrm{BC} = \frac{N_{\text{covered}}}{N_{\text{process}}}, \quad \mathrm{HBC} = \frac{N_{\text{highest\_covered}}}{N_{\text{highest}}} \tag{11}$$

where IC (Indicator Coverage) and ISC (Strong Coverage) measure indicator-to-process mapping (Strong requires direct traceability to an operable activity, single-business dominance and direct performance reflection); BC(Business Coverage) and HBC measure(Highest Business Coverage) whether core / top-level business processes correspond to indicators.

Results. All 68 indicators are mapped (IC = 100%), with ISC = 81%; the 13 weakly mapped ones are macro-level or administrative (e.g., infrastructure). BC reaches 41% (40/98), constrained by fine-grained processes and many-to-one mappings, while HBC reaches 77% (16/21); unmapped top-level categories (e.g., Judicial Research, Supervision) are qualitative or supportive functions resistant to quantification. After incorporating newly proposed indicators and businesses, IC remains 100%, ISC rises to 81.4%, and BC improves to 42.6%, with new links such as "intelligent litigation guidance service", "case filing risk early warning", and "big data trial situation analysis" enhancing overall mapping completeness.

5 Conclusion

This study presents an LLM-powered multi-agent system that automates the extraction, mapping, and optimization of performance, business, and data views for digital government, enabling cross-view integration. The architecture comprises four agents: an *indicator agent* extracts key elements from professional documents; a *business agent* uses chain-of-thought reasoning to transform unstructured text into process-oriented graphs; a *mapping agent* aligns indicators with business steps via semantic and field matching to produce interpretable associations; and an *optimization agent* recommends improvements from both perspectives. Experiments on the smart court case confirm that the system effectively extracts the three views, establishes meaningful cross-view mappings, and generates reasonable optimization directions.

Future work will further validate the proposed framework on more diverse digital government scenarios, investigate its scalability for larger enterprise repositories, compare it with additional baseline methods, and enhance dynamic updating of data and knowledge graphs, multi-agent collaboration, and more structured and interpretable explanations.

Acknowledgements. This work was supported by the National Natural Science Foundation of China under Grant Nos. 62441230 and 62172425, the Scientific Research Innovation Capability Support Project for Young Faculty under Grant No. SRICSPYF-ZY2025001, and the Fundamental Research Funds for the Central Universities and the Research Funds of Renmin University of China under Grant Nos. 22XNKJ04.

References

1. Haug, N., Dan, S., Mergel, I.: Digitally-induced change in the public sector: a systematic review and research agenda. Public Manag. Rev. **26**(7), 1963–1987 (2024)
2. Gong, Y., Yang, J., Shi, X.: Towards a comprehensive understanding of digital transformation in government: analysis of flexibility and enterprise architecture. Gov. Inf. Q. **37**(3), 101487 (2020)
3. Janowski, T.: Digital government evolution: from transformation to contextualization. Gov. Inf. Q. **32**(3), 221–236 (2015)
4. Cohen, J.: A coefficient of agreement for nominal scales. Educ. Psychol. Measur. **20**(1), 37–46 (1960)
5. Milićević, A., Vučković, T., Krstić, D., Ivić, A.: Information systems integration in e-government: a bibliometric analysis approach. In: 2023 22nd International Symposium INFOTEH-JAHORINA (INFOTEH), pp. 1–5. IEEE (2023)
6. Nahri, I., Pinquié, R., Véron, P., Bus, N., Thorel, M.: Extracting structured requirements from unstructured building technical specifications for building information modeling. arXiv preprint arXiv:2508.13833 (2025)
7. Ku, C.H., Iriberri, A., Leroy, G.: Natural language processing and e-government: crime information extraction from heterogeneous data sources. In: Proceedings of the 2008 International Conference on Digital Government Research, pp. 162–170 (2008)
8. Hariguna, T., Ruangkanjanases, A.: Adaptive decision-support system model for automated analysis and classification of crime reports for e-government. J. Appl. Data Sci. **4**(3), 303–316 (2023)
9. Pan, S., Luo, L., Wang, Y., Chen, C., Wang, J., Wu, X.: Unifying large language models and knowledge graphs: a roadmap. IEEE Trans. Knowl. Data Eng. **36**(7), 3580–3599 (2024)
10. Xu, D., et al.: Large language models for generative information extraction: a survey. Front. Comp. Sci. **18**(6), 186357 (2024)
11. Wei, J., et al.: Chain-of-thought prompting elicits reasoning in large language models. In: Advance Neural Information Processing System, vol. 35, pp. 24824–24837 (2022)
12. Landis, J.R., Koch, G.G.: The measurement of observer agreement for categorical data. Biometrics, pp. 159–174 (1977)
13. Gil-García, J.R., Pardo, T.A.: E-government success factors: mapping practical tools to theoretical foundations. Gov. Inf. Q. **22**(2), 187–216 (2005)
14. Bannister, F.: The curse of the benchmark: an assessment of the validity and value of e-government comparisons. Int. Rev. Adm. Sci. **73**(2), 171–188 (2007)
15. Mergel, I., Edelmann, N., Haug, N.: Defining digital transformation: results from expert interviews. Gov. Inf. Q. **36**(4), 101385 (2019)
16. Bommasani, R.: On the opportunities and risks of foundation models. arXiv preprint arXiv:2108.07258 (2021)
17. Chang, Y., et al.: A survey on evaluation of large language models. ACM Trans. Intell. Syst. Technol. **15**(3), 1–45 (2024)
18. Ji, Z., et al.: Survey of hallucination in natural language generation. ACM Comput. Surv. **55**(12), 1–38 (2023)
19. Weidinger, L., et al.: Ethical and social risks of harm from language models. arXiv preprint arXiv:2112.04359 (2021)

A Blockchain-Based Framework for Fine-Grained Fair Data Trading with Verifiable Policy Compliance

Hai Liang[1], Peng Chen[1], Changsong Yang[1,2], Yujue Wang[3(✉)], Yong Ding[1,2], and Qianhong Wu[4]

[1] Guangxi Key Laboratory of Cryptography and Information Security, Guilin University of Electronic Technology, Guilin, China

[2] Lion Rock Labs of Cyberspace Security, Institute of Cyberspace Technology, HKCT Institute of Higher Education, Hong Kong, China

[3] Hangzhou Innovation Institute of Beihang University, Hangzhou, China
wyujue@buaa.edu.cn

[4] School of Cyber Science and Technology, Beihang University, Beijing, China

Abstract. Fine-grained and fair data trading is essential for maximizing data utility, yet its deployment is often constrained by trust deficits and privacy vulnerabilities. Existing schemes struggle to balance transactional fairness with efficiency, frequently defaulting to fully trusted intermediaries. To address these limitations, we propose *FGFDT*, a blockchain-based fair data trading scheme enabled by proxy re-encryption. Specifically, *FGFDT* integrates an optimized *Groth* signature with attribute-based credentials, enabling buyers to specify demand policies and sellers to selectively provide ciphertexts while proving compliance with these policies. Furthermore, we design a proxy re-encryption mechanism for secure, privacy-preserving ciphertext transformation, coupled with a dynamic sequence-based Merkle hash tree (*SMHT*) to support data integrity verification. Theoretical analysis shows that the proposed *FGFDT* scheme is superior to existing related solutions in terms of computational and storage overhead.

Keywords: Fine-grained data trading · fair data trading · blockchain · proxy re-encryption

1 Introduction

In the data-driven digital economy, fine-grained data trading can precisely unlock data utility and protect privacy [21]. However, achieving fair data trading has long been hindered by the mutual distrust between buyers and sellers [18]. Traditional centralized trading platforms [4,23], while attempting to break the trust impasse, inevitably introduce risks such as single points of failure and illegal data resale. To circumvent the shortcomings of centralization, blockchain offers an innovative trading approach [1,10]. In blockchain-based data trading, the buyer

L. Ding et al. (Eds.): APWeb-WAIM 2026, LNCS 16995, pp. 617–630, 2027.
https://doi.org/10.1007/978-981-92-5699-0_42

securely holds funds in a smart contract (*SC*) [8]. The seller stores encrypted, compliant data off-chain, such as the InterPlanetary File System or a cloud server (*CS*) [13], and submits proof of data availability. After verification, the seller submits the correct decryption key to *SC* to automatically trigger fund settlement. This decentralized mechanism effectively resolves the mutual trust dilemma and fundamentally guarantees absolute fairness in trading.

Current data trading schemes struggle to simultaneously guarantee data availability defined as the verification of data existence and integrity without plaintext exposure, data retrievability which ensures that authorized buyers can securely access and decrypt the content and privacy protection. Although existing research has attempted to address these issues, significant shortcomings remain. In terms of availability verification, schemes combining encryption, ZKPs, and public predicate functions, such as hash functions, are often unsuitable for personalized records lacking publicly verifiable predicate functions [11]. Regarding retrievability, blockchain-based re-encryption technology typically relies on an intermediary, which converts ciphertext encrypted by one user's public key into a format decryptable by another user's private key. Crucially, this conversion is performed without the intermediary ever decrypting the original ciphertext [12,15,19,22]. However, this third-party dependency lacks strict oversight of data access, storage and processing [3,7]. Furthermore, even the most advanced blockchain-based fair data trading schemes cannot address privacy risks arising from collusion among dishonest entities, such as data and identity privacy leaks, signature forgery [14,20] and other issues.

1.1 Our Contributions

To address the challenges of data availability, data retrievability and privacy protection, this paper proposes *FGFDT*, a blockchain-based fair and fine-grained data trading scheme. *FGFDT* supports buyers in specifying data needs through demand policies and achieves secure, fair trading with automatic fund transfers via *SC*. To support data availability verification, we constructed an *SMHT* that, unlike traditional Merkle trees relying on static indexes, supports efficient dynamic updates and lightweight proof generation by introducing a dynamic node indexing mechanism. This enables verifiers to confirm data availability without revealing plaintext. Furthermore, we design a proxy re-encryption mechanism to support authorized data retrievability. Security analysis shows that *FGFDT* safeguards data privacy in the process of data trading, while providing identity privacy protection for both parties involved in the process of data trading. Theoretical analysis demonstrate the computation and storage overheads of FGFDT and indicates that they remain comparable to those of existing schemes while supporting signed demand-policy verification and fine-grained data trading.

1.2 Related Works

To ensure the verification of data availability, Zhao et al. [24] combined machine learning with fair data trading, verified data validity through distance metric learning, and used dual authentication signatures to prevent key abuse. However, this solution relies on centralized data preprocessing and is not compatible with the decentralized nature of blockchain. Galteland and Wu [5] designed a blockchain privacy-preserving fair trading protocol, using smart contracts to achieve atomic fund transfers and encrypted commitments to verify the legitimacy of data keys. Nevertheless, the seller must disclose the complete data hash, and fine-grained attribute-level data desensitization is not achieved. Liu et al. [13] proposed a blockchain cloud transparent data marketing solution, which manages anonymous credentials and data availability verification through alliance chains to support fair trading in a decentralized environment. However, it relies on a trusted committee for data verification, which introduces centralization risks.

Regarding the privacy protection of user identity and data, Jung et al. [9] introduced the AccountTrade system, which uses a specialized indexing mechanism to detect malicious buyers and hold them accountable in trading. However, this design does not support selective disclosure or privacy protection of data attributes. Xue et al. [20] combined attribute-based anonymous credentials with a dynamic sequence-based Merkle hash tree, enabling sellers to disclose only buyer-required attributes while hiding hospital identities and users' sensitive information through zero-knowledge proofs. Long et al. [14] presented the BFFDT scheme, which combines pairing-based proxy re-encryption with a dynamic sequence Merkle hash tree to support cross-public-key conversion of encrypted symmetric keys and third-party-assisted fair verification. Although these studies consider data availability verification, privacy protection, and fairness, they still provide limited trust building between trading parties or rely on trusted third parties. Inspired by [14,20], our $FGFDT$ scheme aims to establish a fine-grained, fair, reliable, and secure data trading solution without trusted third-party support.

2 System Model and Requirements

2.1 System Model

Our $FGFDT$ system is composed of five types of entities: the Key Generation Center (KGC), data seller, data buyer, cloud server (CS), and smart contract (SC).

- KGC: KGC is trusted to execute system initialization and key generation correctly.
- Data Seller: A data seller is an individual who owns the data records and wishes to profit from them.

- Data Buyer: A data buyer is responsible for collecting data, such as from government agencies and commercial companies. It only pays for the data records that meet its requirements.
- *CS*: A third-party server with powerful storage capacity. It is primarily responsible for performing ciphertext conversion in proxy re-encryption and storing the signatures submitted by the data buyer, as well as the ciphertext and related verification information submitted by the data seller.
- *SC*: A blockchain-deployed, self-executing code that runs after specific conditions are verified. When these conditions are met, *SC* can automatically transfer funds, ensuring the atomicity of the trading.

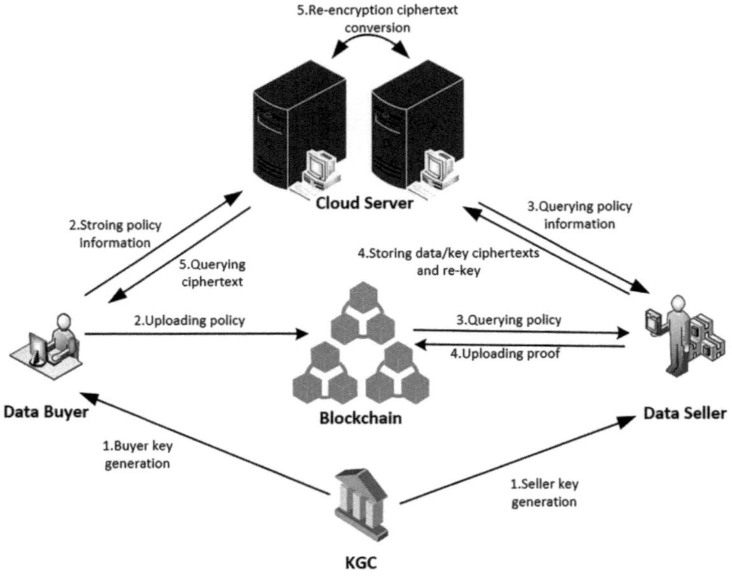

Fig. 1. System model.

As shown in Fig. 1, the data buyer deploys *SC* and defines data policy requirements, such as specific metrics and indicators. Subsequently, the demand policy is recorded in the *SC*, and the corresponding reward is deposited into it. Upon receiving the policy requirements, the data seller first encrypts the data that conforms to the policy using a symmetric key. Then, based on this symmetric key, the seller encrypts the key and generates a one-time re-encryption key, and uploads them along with the data ciphertext and re-encrypted ciphertext to *CS*, while relevant proof is uploaded to *SC*. Upon receiving this information, *CS* securely uses the re-encryption key to transform the symmetric key ciphertext into ciphertext encrypted using the buyer's public key. After obtaining and verifying the relevant proof from *SC*, the buyer retrieves the ciphertext and corresponding data record from *CS*. Subsequently, the buyer uses its private key to recover the symmetric key and further decrypts to obtain the target data. Finally, the buyer submits a confirmation message to *SC*. Once the confirmation is successfully verified, *SC* releases the corresponding data reward to the data seller.

2.2 System Requirements

In *FGFDT* system, *SC* strictly executes its preset logic. A malicious data buyer, after obtaining the required data, may refuse to pay the corresponding reward and try to find out the data seller's real identity.

(1) Data Privacy Protection: During data trading, the seller only discloses the data required by the data buyer, and the usability of the data is verified through data-assisted authentication information. The buyer cannot obtain other undiscovered sensitive information from data records. Furthermore, buyers cannot deduce the seller's private key from the re-encrypted ciphertext.
(2) Identity Privacy Protection: In the process of data trading, other entities should be precluded from deducing the real identities of buyers and sellers via the public key. Moreover, the unlinkability of different trading from the same buyer and seller should be guaranteed to effectively preserve identity privacy. Furthermore, *SC* should not leak the identity privacy of either the data buyer or seller.
(3) Unforgeability: During the process of data trading, the trading policy signature generated by data buyer should be unforgeable, preventing malicious tampering of trading policy.
(4) Trading Fairness: The data seller receives the reward, while the data buyer receives the required data, and this process cannot be interrupted or rolled back.
(5) Fine-grained trading: *FGFDT* should support fine-grained data trading, allowing the seller to provide only specific data that conforms to the trading policy defined by the buyer, without affecting the overall data availability verification.

3 FGFDT Construction

In the *FGFDT* system, the data seller, the data buyer, *CS* and *SC* cooperate to complete the fair data trading. The data buyer creates and deploys *SC*, specifies a demand policy and deposits the corresponding reward into *SC*. Simultaneously, *SC* records the current block timestamp T_{curr} and sets the trading deadline $T_{\text{exp}} = T_{\text{curr}} + \Delta T$, where ΔT is the agreed confirmation window. The seller who possesses data meeting the requirements transacts with the buyer. The *FGFDT* system consists of seven algorithms.

Setup: *KGC* takes the security parameter k as input and defines n as the maximum number of attributes in the data records. It initiates by selecting group G_1, G_2 and G_T with prime order p, a bilinear mapping $e: G_1 \times G_2 \rightarrow G_T$, and generators $g, y \in G_1$ and $\hat{g}, \hat{y} \in G_2$, and six secure cryptographic hash functions, including $H_1 : \{0,1\}^* \rightarrow \mathbb{Z}_p^*$, $H_2 : \{0,1\}^* \rightarrow G_2$, $H_3 : G_2 \rightarrow \mathbb{Z}_p^*$, $H_4 : \{0,1\}^* \rightarrow G_1$, and $H_5 : G_1 \rightarrow \mathbb{Z}_p^*$. Subsequently, KGC randomly selects $x \in \mathbb{Z}_p^*$ and computes the system public key $P_{\text{pub}} = \hat{g}^x$. A secure symmetric encryption algorithm $S = \{Enc, Dec\}$ is selected. Following this, the output public parameters are $par = \{e, G_1, G_2, G_T, p, g, \hat{g}, y, \hat{y}, H_1, H_2, H_3, H_4, H_5, P_{\text{pub}}, S\}$.

SKeyG: The data seller first sends its identity ID_u to KGC. Next, the KGC computes the data seller's partial private key $psk_u = H_4(ID_u)^x$ and returns it. Then, the data seller checks whether

$$e(psk_u, \hat{g}) \stackrel{?}{=} e(H_4(ID_u), P_{\text{pub}}). \tag{1}$$

If so, the seller randomly selects an element $y_u \in \mathbb{Z}_p^*$, computes

$$usk = psk_u \cdot H_4(ID_u)^{y_u}, \tag{2}$$

$$upk = g^{H_5(usk)}, \tag{3}$$

and securely stores the private key usk and publishes the public key upk.

BKeyG: The data buyer first sends its identity ID_b to KGC. Next, the KGC computes the data buyer's partial private key $psk_b = H_4(ID_b)^x$ and returns it. Then, the buyer checks whether

$$e(psk_b, \hat{g}) \stackrel{?}{=} e(H_4(ID_b), P_{\text{pub}}). \tag{4}$$

If so, the data buyer randomly selects an element $y_b \in \mathbb{Z}_p^*$, computes

$$bsk = psk_b \cdot H_4(ID_b)^{y_b}, \tag{5}$$

$$bpk = g^{H_5(bsk)}. \tag{6}$$

and securely stores the private key bsk and publishes the public key bpk.

PolDef: Assume the number of attributes in the data records is l and define the attribute values for each attribute $\{Attr_i\}_{i\in[1,l]}$ as $\{D_i\}_{i\in[1,l]}$.

1. The data buyer defines I as the attributes to be disclosed and $J \subseteq I$ as the attributes whose values must be disclosed before payment. Let JV denote the values corresponding to the attributes in J. For instance, if the buyer collects data related to diabetes and needs to include attributes such as disease, age, diastolic pressure, serum insulin, it would specify $I = \{\text{disease, age, diastolic pressure, serum insulin}\}$, $J = \{\text{disease}\}$, $JV = \{\text{flu}\}$. Assuming the attributes in set I are $\{attr_i\}_{i\in[1,n]}$, and the attributes and attribute values in sets J and JV are $\{attr_j\}_{j\in[1,m]}$ and $\{jv_j\}_{j\in[1,m]}$, respectively, the data buyer knows the data seller possesses the required data by disclosing the attributes in I and the attribute values JV of the attributes in J. Then, it randomly selects $r_1 \in \mathbb{Z}_p^*$, randomizes the public key $bpk' = bpk^{r_1}$, and computes the hash values and signatures for sets I, J and JV as follows:

$$h_I = H_2(attr_1 \| attr_2 \| \cdots \| attr_n), \tag{7}$$
$$h_{JJV} = H_2\big((attr_1 \| jv_1) \| (attr_2 \| jv_2), \| \cdots \| (attr_m \| jv_m)\big) \tag{8}$$
$$R = g^{r_1}, \tag{9}$$
$$\hat{S}_1 = \left(\hat{y} \cdot \hat{g}^{H_5(bsk)}\right)^{\frac{r_1}{r_1 + H_3(h_I)}}, \tag{10}$$
$$\hat{T}_1 = \left(\hat{y}^{H_5(bsk)} \cdot h_I\right)^{\frac{r_1}{r_1 + H_3(h_I)}}, \tag{11}$$
$$\hat{S}_2 = \left(\hat{y} \cdot \hat{g}^{H_5(bsk)}\right)^{\frac{r_1}{r_1 + H_3(h_{JJV})}}, \tag{12}$$
$$\hat{T}_2 = \left(\hat{y}^{H_5(bsk)} \cdot h_{JJV}\right)^{\frac{r_1}{r_1 + H_3(h_{JJV})}}. \tag{13}$$

The buyer obtains the hashes h_I, h_{JJV} and signatures $\{\sigma_I\} = \{R, \hat{S}_1, \hat{T}_1\}$, $\{\sigma_{JJV}\} = \{R, \hat{S}_2, \hat{T}_2\}$.

2. To reduce on-chain storage, the buyer stores $\{h_I, h_{JJV}, \sigma_I, \sigma_{JJV}\}$ in *CS* and obtains the corresponding storage address $addr_1$. It defines the trading policy as $pol = (I, J, JV)$, submits $(addr_1, pol)$ to *SC*, and deposits the corresponding reward into *SC*.

PolVer: In this algorithm, the data seller verifies the authenticity and integrity of *pol* as follows:

$$e\left(R \cdot g^{H_3(h_I)}, \hat{S}_1\right) \stackrel{?}{=} e(g, \hat{y}) \cdot e(bpk', \hat{g}), \tag{14}$$
$$e\left(R \cdot g^{H_3(h_I)}, \hat{T}_1\right) \stackrel{?}{=} e(bpk', \hat{y}) \cdot e(g, h_I), \tag{15}$$
$$e\left(R \cdot g^{H_3(h_{JJV})}, \hat{S}_2\right) \stackrel{?}{=} e(g, \hat{y}) \cdot e(bpk', \hat{g}), \tag{16}$$
$$e\left(R \cdot g^{H_3(h_{JJV})}, \hat{T}_2\right) \stackrel{?}{=} e(bpk', \hat{y}) \cdot e(g, h_{JJV}). \tag{17}$$

If the above equations hold, the policy *pol* is valid and the *PolVer* algorithm outputs 1, otherwise, outputs 0.

Present: In this algorithm, the data seller selects the data records that satisfy the defined policy. Define Π as the index set of attributes in I, and Ω as the index set of attributes in J.

(1) The seller first generates a unique trading identifier $txID$ and computes the hash value $h_{ID} = H_1(txID)$.
(2) It chooses a random number $r_2 \in \mathbb{Z}_p^*$ to randomize the public key, yielding $upk' = upk^{\frac{1}{r_2}}$.
(3) Then, a one-time symmetric key $k \in G_T$ is randomly selected and used to encrypt the data records, producing the ciphertexts $\{CD_i =$

$S.Enc(k, D_i)\}_{i \in \Pi}$. The key k itself is encrypted via upk to generate the ciphertext $CK = \{CK_1, CK_2\}$, where $CK_1 = \hat{g}^{h_{ID} \cdot r_2}$, $CK_2 = k' \cdot e(upk, CK_1)$ and $k' = (k \| H_5(k))$.

(4) Following this, it constructs two SMHTs over $\{CD_i\}_{i \in \Pi}$ and $\{D_i\}_{i \in \Omega}$, obtaining roots h_R and $h_{\hat{R}}$. In SMHT, each node is represented by a tuple consisting of its layer, sequence number, and hash. For an internal node, the hash value is computed from the concatenation of its child-node hashes. Appending a leaf updates only the hashes on its path to the root. To support integrity verification in partial data trading, SMHT further uses Auxiliary Authentication Information (AAI). The AAI contains the sibling hashes required to recompute the root hash from the retrieved partial data. Therefore, the buyer can combine the received data blocks with their corresponding AAI to reconstruct the root hash and verify data integrity. This tuple-based dynamic structure supports scalable append and extraction operations in continuous data trading scenarios.

(5) Subsequently, it generates corresponding auxiliary information sets AAI_Π and AAI_Ω for $\{CD_i\}_{i \in \Pi}$ and $\{D_i\}_{i \in \Omega}$, respectively. This enables the buyer to reconstruct the root hashes h_R and h'_R for integrity verification.

(6) Afterwards, it generates a one-time re-encryption key $rk = e(bpk, \hat{g}^{H_5(usk) \cdot h_{ID}})$ and a zero-knowledge proof π_{ID}, where rk is sent to CS and π_{ID} proves that the trading identifier $txID$ is valid.

(7) After that, CS uses the re-encryption key rk to convert the original ciphertext of the symmetric key k into $CK' = \{CK'_1, CK'_2\}$, where $CK'_1 = CK_1$ and $CK'_2 = CK_2 \cdot rk$.

(8) And then, the seller stores $\{CD_i, (i, Attr_i)\}_{i \in \Pi}, AAI_\Pi, AAI_\Omega, h_R, h'_R, CK', \{D_i\}_{i \in \Omega}, upk'\}$ in the CS and obtains the storage address $addr_2$.

(9) Finally, the seller submits the defined credential $pt = \{addr_2, h_{ID}, \pi_{ID}\}$ to the SC.

PreVer: In this algorithm, the data buyer verifies whether the data obtained meets the policy.

(1) Upon retrieving the credential pt from SC, the data buyer first validates π_{ID} to ensure both the validity and integrity of $txID$. It subsequently decrypts CK' using bsk to get

$$k' = \frac{CK'_2}{e(upk', CK'_1)^{H_5(bsk)+1}}. \tag{18}$$

(2) The buyer then downloads $\{CD_i\}_{i \in \Pi}$ and CK' from the CS via $addr_2$. After verifying that the sequence of CD_i is consistent with the sequence of $Attr_i$ in data records, it reconstructs the $SMHT$ using CD_i and AAI_Π to compute the root node $\widetilde{h}_R$. If $h_R = \widetilde{h}_R$, the data location is confirmed.

(3) Then, it uses k to decrypt $\{CD_i\}_{i\in\Pi}$ to get $\{D_i = S.Dec(k, CD_i)\}_{i\in\Pi}$. Based on $\{D_i\}_{i\in\Omega}$ and AAI_Ω, it reconstructs the *SMHT* to compute the root node hash value $\widetilde{h'_R}$ and verifies data integrity by checking if $h'_R \stackrel{?}{=} \widetilde{h'_R}$.

(4) Upon successful verification, the buyer sends a confirmation message to *SC*, which transfers the reward to the seller and the *PreVer* algorithm outputs 1, otherwise, outputs 0. If no confirmation is received by T_{exp}, *SC* will automatically and forcibly transfer the reward to the seller.

4 Analysis

4.1 Security Analysis

The security analysis of the proposed *FGFDT* scheme relies on the following difficult problem assumption.

Discrete Logarithm (DL) Assumption: Let G be a cyclic group of prime order p, and g be a generator of group G. For an element $y = g^x$ in G, computing $x \in \mathbb{Z}_p$ is difficult.

Theorem 1. *The FGFDT scheme can provide data privacy protection, that is, no adversary can obtain sensitive information in the data records.*

Proof. In the *FGFDT* scheme, a proxy re-encryption mechanism is used to securely convert the symmetric key ciphertext encrypted with the seller's public key into the ciphertext encrypted with the buyer's public key. This approach is an improvement on the scheme proposed by Long et al. [14]. The re-encrypted ciphertext CK' is generated from the original ciphertext CK and the re-encryption key $rk = e(bpk, \hat{g}^{H_5(usk)\cdot h_{ID}})$, where $h_{ID} = H_1(txID)$ is a unique trading identifier hash. When decrypting CK', the buyer uses its private key bsk to compute the key $k = \frac{CK'_2}{e(upk', CK'_1)^{H_5(bsk)+1}}$. Furthermore, the mathematical construction of rk inherits the unidirectionality of the underlying proxy re-encryption scheme [2,16]. Even if the buyer uses its private key bsk to extract the seller's encapsulated parameters $e(g, \hat{g})^{H_5(usk)}$, extracting the original long-term private key usk remains computationally infeasible due to the *DL* assumption. This ensures that the buyer cannot recover the seller's long-term private key based on the transformation parameters exchanged during the trading. Therefore, our *FGFDT* scheme also provides data privacy protection under the *DL* assumption.

Theorem 2. *The FGFDT scheme provides identity privacy protection, meaning that other entities cannot infer the identity of the data buyer and seller from their respective public key. Tradings from the same data buyer and seller cannot be linked. Also, SC does not reveal the identities of the data seller and buyer.*

Proof. In the *FGFDT* scheme, the data buyer and seller blind their public keys by choosing random numbers r_1 and r_2, respectively, resulting in $bpk' = bpk^{r_1}$ and $upk' = upk^{1/r_2}$. Due to the *DL* assumption, no adversary can deduce the original identity of the data buyer and seller from bpk' and upk'. Moreover, each trading independently and randomly selects a symmetric key k and generates a corresponding one-time re-encryption key $rk = e\left(bpk, \hat{g}^{H_5(usk)\cdot h_{ID}}\right)$. Since $h_{ID} = H_1(txID)$ is derived from the unique trading identifier $txID$, the re-encryption keys rk from different trading phases are different. This also prevents an adversary from linking trading to the same data seller. According to Theorem 1, the adversary cannot derive the seller's private key usk. Consequently, the trading of the same data buyer and seller cannot be linked. At the same time, the trading policy signature, and the zero-knowledge proof are all generated or verified off-chain. Only the storage addresses, trading policy *pol*, and credential *pt* are uploaded to SC, without disclosing the identity privacy of the data seller and buyer. Therefore, our $FGFDT$ scheme provides identity privacy protection.

Theorem 3. *The FGFDT scheme can provide unforgeability of the data buyer's trading policy signatures.*

Proof. In the $FGFDT$ scheme, the data buyer's signatures σ_I and σ_{JJV} on the trading policy *pol* are unforgeable under the DL assumption. The signature scheme is improved based on the scheme proposed by Groth [6]. Based on [6, Theorem 2], the scheme by Groth [6] provides unforgeability under the DL assumption. Therefore, our $FGFDT$ scheme can provide unforgeability under the DL assumption, guaranteeing that the trading policy generated by the data buyer cannot be maliciously tampered with.

Theorem 4. *The FGFDT scheme can guarantee fair trading, meaning the data seller obtains the reward when the data buyer obtains the required data, and this process cannot be interrupted or revoked.*

Proof. In the $FGFDT$ scheme, the process of the data trading is similar to the trading process in the scheme proposed by Xue et al. [20]. The data buyer deposits funds into SC for custody, and defines the attribute policy of the required data. Simultaneously, SC sets a timestamp to define the validity period of the data trading, preventing malicious buyers from refusing to send confirmation messages after receiving valid data. After proving possession of the data buyer's desired data, the data seller encrypts the attribute values $\{D_i\}$ to produce the attribute value ciphertexts $\{CD_i\}$, and generates the root nodes h_R and h'_R to ensure data integrity. Finally, a symmetric key k is encrypted using a re-encryption mechanism. After verifying the legitimacy of the re-encryption key rk and the integrity of the data, the data buyer uploads the confirmation message to the SC. Upon receiving a valid confirmation, SC releases the reward to the seller. If no confirmation is received by T_{exp}, SC executes the predefined timeout rule. According to Theorem 1 in [20], the scheme proposed by Xue et al. [20] guarantees fair trading. Therefore, our $FGFDT$ scheme also guarantees fair trading.

Theorem 5. *The FGFDT scheme can support fine-grained data trading.*

Proof. In the *FGFDT* scheme, the data seller achieves fine-grained data trading through *SMHT*. Specifically, the data seller first uses the encrypted attribute value ciphertexts $\{CD_i\}$ as leaf nodes to construct an *SMHT* to obtain the root node hash value h_R. Similarly, a root hash h'_R is obtained based on the attribute values $\{D_i\}$. The data buyer then uses AAI_Π and AAI_Ω to recompute $\widetilde{h}_R$ and $\widetilde{h}'_R$ and verify the integrity of the data records. If the adversary tampers with the data blocks or forges AAI_Π and AAI_Ω, it would lead to incorrect $\widetilde{h}_R$ and $\widetilde{h}'_R$ verification would fail. Therefore, *FGFDT* supports fine-grained data trading.

4.2 Theoretical Analysis

This section compares the computational and storage overheads of all entities. To simplify the analysis process, the costs of scalar multiplication and pairing operations are denoted as T_E and T_P, respectively. Let L_p, L_{G1}, L_{G2}, L_G, L_{T1} and L_{T2} respectively represent the sizes of the elements in $\mathbb{Z}_p^*$, G_1, G_2, the G and G_T elements in the scheme by Long et al. [14], and the G_T elements in *FGFDT* scheme. We adopt the ZKP construction described in [13]. Note that, the computational costs of symmetric encryption and decryption algorithms and hash functions are ignored. Let n be the number of attributes in the data records, where each attribute corresponds to an attribute value, and η represents the number of DPs the data buyer can accept in [20]. The size of the original data and its ciphertext are represented by n_d and n_c respectively.

Table 1. Computation costs in the trading phase

Scheme	KGC	Data buyer	Data seller	SC	CS
Xue et al. [20]	\	$(5\eta + 10)T_E$	$(n + 21)T_E + 18T_P$	$8T_E$	\
Long et al. [14]	\	$2T_E + 7T_P$	$8T_E + T_P$	$2T_E$	\
FGFDT	$4T_P$	$15T_E + 10T_P$	$8T_E + 16T_P$	\	\

Regarding computational overhead during trading, the data buyer and seller interact with *KGC* to generate their key pairs. Each user performs $T_E + 2T_P$, while *KGC* performs $4T_P$ for both users. The buyer incurs $10T_E$ to define and sign the trading policy and $4T_E + 8T_P$ during final verification, resulting in $15T_E + 10T_P$. The seller incurs $7T_E + 14T_P$ for policy verification and re-encryption-key generation, resulting in $8T_E + 16T_P$. Table 1 gives a comparison of the computational costs of the *FGFDT* scheme and the ones by Xue et al. [20] and Long et al. [14] in this phase. As can be seen from Table 1, the off-chain computational cost of *FGFDT* is slightly higher than the schemes by Xue et al. [20] and Long et al. [14]. This is because in our scheme, the seller must authenticate the policy defined by the buyer. However, the schemes of Xue et al. [20] and Long et al. [14] do not take this into account.

Regarding storage overhead during trading, *KGC* stores public parameters that include 2 elements from G_1 and G_2 respectively and system public-private key pair, with a storage cost of $2L_{G1}+3L_{G2}+L_p$. Then the buyer incurs a storage cost of $n_d + 2L_{G1}$ for stores its public-private key pair and the traded data. CS stores the ciphertexts, two authentication paths, two SMHT roots, CK', and the policy-related hashes and signatures, for a total of $n_c + 3L_{G_1} + 4L_{G_2} + L_{T_2} + (2\log_2 n + 4)L_p$.

Table 2. Storage overheads in the trading phase

Scheme	KGC	Data seller	Data buyer	CS	SC
Xue et al. [20]	\	\	$n_d + 3L_{G1} + L_p$	$nL_{G1} + (\eta + 2)L_{G2}$	$11L_{G1} + 2L_{G2} + 6L_p + \|I\| + \|J\| + \|JV\|$
Long et al. [14]	\	\	$n_d + 7L_G + L_{T1} + L_p$	$n_c + (n+1)L_G + L_{T1}$	$(n+7)L_G + 7L_p + \|I\|$
FGFDT	$2L_{G1} + 3L_{G2} + L_p$	\	$n_d + 2L_{G1}$	$n_c + 3L_{G1} + 4L_{G2} + L_{T2} + (2\log_2 n + 4)L_p$	$6L_p + \|I\| + \|J\| + \|JV\|$

SC stores $addr_1$, $addr_2$, h_{ID}, π_{ID}, the policy sets, and the confirmation state, requiring $6L_p+|I|+|J|+|JV|$. As can be seen from Table 2, the storage overhead for both the data buyer and *SC* in this phase is significantly lower than that of Xue et al. [20]. Since the scheme by Long et al. [14] does not protect the trading policy, there is a security issue of potential tampering. In our *FGFDT* scheme, the data buyer signs the trading policy to prevent tampering, so the storage overhead of the *CS* is slightly higher than that of Long et al. [14].

5 Conclusion

This paper presented *FGFDT*, which supports proxy re-encryption-based ciphertext transformation and ensured fine-grained data authenticity by constructing *SMHT* and using improved *Groth* signature. The theoretical analysis verified that *FGFDT* outperformed existing solutions in terms of overhead efficiency while guaranteeing trading fairness, data and identity privacy. Future work will explore blockchain-based fair computation trading schemes and robust on-chain dispute arbitration mechanisms, enabling buyers to obtain reliable and accurate computation results without direct access to the original data, even under highly contested dispute scenarios.

Acknowledgements. This work was supported in part by the National Natural Science Foundation of China under Grants 62572038 and 62562021, the Beijing-Tianjin-Hebei Natural Science Foundation Cooperation Project under Grant 25JJJJC0033, the Guangxi Natural Science Foundation under Grant 2025GXNSFAA069678, the Key Research and Development Program of Guangxi under Grant AB25069266, the Lion Rock Labs of Cyberspace Security under Grant LRL24-1-C003, and the Innovation Project of Guangxi Graduate Education under Grant YCSW2026731.

References

1. Barbhaya, U.R., Vishwakarma, L., Das, D.: ETradeChain: blockchain-based energy trading in local energy market (LEM) using modified double auction protocol. IEEE Trans. Green Commun. Network. **8**(1), 559–571 (2024). https://doi.org/10.1109/TGCN.2023.3307360
2. Blaze, M., Bleumer, G., Strauss, M.: Divertible protocols and atomic proxy cryptography. In: Nyberg, K. (ed.) EUROCRYPT 1998. LNCS, vol. 1403, pp. 127–144. Springer, Heidelberg (1998). https://doi.org/10.1007/BFb0054122
3. Cui, J., Zhang, X., Zhong, H., Zhang, J., Liu, L.: Extensible conditional privacy protection authentication scheme for secure vehicular networks in a multi-cloud environment. IEEE Trans. Inf. Forensics Secur. **15**, 1654–1667 (2020). https://doi.org/10.1109/TIFS.2019.2946933
4. Dixit, A., Singh, A., Rahulamathavan, Y., Rajarajan, M.: FAST DATA: a fair, secure, and trusted decentralized IIoT data marketplace enabled by blockchain. IEEE Internet Things J. **10**(4), 2934–2944 (2023). https://doi.org/10.1109/JIOT.2021.3120640
5. Galteland, Y.J., Wu, S.: Blockchain-based privacy-preserving fair data trading protocol. Cryptology ePrint Archive, Paper 2021/1321 (2021). https://eprint.iacr.org/2021/1321
6. Groth, J.: Efficient fully structure-preserving signatures for large messages. In: Iwata, T., Cheon, J.H. (eds.) ASIACRYPT 2015. LNCS, vol. 9452, pp. 239–259. Springer, Heidelberg (2015). https://doi.org/10.1007/978-3-662-48797-6_11
7. Guo, H., Zhang, Z., Xu, J., An, N., Lan, X.: Accountable proxy re-encryption for secure data sharing. IEEE Trans. Dependable Secure Comput. **18**(1), 145–159 (2021). https://doi.org/10.1109/TDSC.2018.2877601
8. He, D., Ding, K., Chan, S., Guizani, M.: Unknown threats detection methods of smart contracts. IEEE Internet Things J. **11**(3), 4430–4441 (2024). https://doi.org/10.1109/JIOT.2023.3299492
9. Jung, T., et al.: AccountTrade: accountability against dishonest big data buyers and sellers. IEEE Trans. Inf. Forensics Secur. **14**(1), 223–234 (2019). https://doi.org/10.1109/TIFS.2018.2848657
10. Li, S., et al.: BlockExplorer: exploring blockchain big data via parallel processing. IEEE Trans. Comput. **72**(8), 2377–2389 (2023). https://doi.org/10.1109/TC.2023.3248280
11. Li, Y., et al.: ZKCPlus: optimized fair-exchange protocol supporting practical and flexible data exchange. In: Proceedings of the 2021 ACM SIGSAC Conference on Computer and Communications Security, pp. 3002–3021. Association for Computing Machinery, New York, NY, USA (2021). https://doi.org/10.1145/3460120.3484558
12. Lin, Z., Zhou, J., Cao, Z., Dong, X., Choo, K.K.R.: Generalized autonomous path proxy re-encryption scheme to support branch functionality. IEEE Trans. Inf. Forensics Secur. **18**, 5387–5400 (2023). https://doi.org/10.1109/TIFS.2023.3306942
13. Liu, D., Huang, C., Ni, J., Lin, X., Shen, X.S.: Blockchain-cloud transparent data marketing: Consortium management and fairness. IEEE Trans. Comput. **71**(12), 3322–3335 (2022). https://doi.org/10.1109/TC.2022.3150724
14. Long, Y., Peng, C., Chen, Y., Tan, W., Sun, J.: BFFDT: blockchain-based fair and fine-grained data trading using proxy re-encryption and verifiable commitment. IEEE Internet Things J. **11**(23), 38508–38520 (2024). https://doi.org/10.1109/JIOT.2024.3449412

15. Luo, F., Wang, H., Susilo, W., Yan, X., Zheng, X.: Public trace-and-revoke proxy re-encryption for secure data sharing in clouds. IEEE Trans. Inf. Forensics Secur. **19**, 2919–2934 (2024). https://doi.org/10.1109/TIFS.2024.3357240
16. Miao, P., Patranabis, S., Watson, G.: Unidirectional updatable encryption and proxy re-encryption from DDH. In: Boldyreva, A., Kolesnikov, V. (eds.) Public-Key Cryptography — PKC 2023. LNCS, vol. 13940, pp. 368–398. Springer Nature, Switzerland, Cham (2023). https://doi.org/10.1007/978-3-031-31371-4_13
17. Pereira, G.C.C.F., et al.: A family of implementation-friendly BN elliptic curves. J. Syst. Softw. **84**(8), 1319–1326 (2011). https://doi.org/10.1016/j.jss.2011.03.083
18. Song, R., Xiao, B., Song, Y., Guo, S., Yang, Y.: A survey of blockchain-based schemes for data sharing and exchange. IEEE Trans. Big Data **9**(6), 1477–1495 (2023). https://doi.org/10.1109/TBDATA.2023.3293279
19. Wang, F., Cui, J., Zhang, Q., He, D., Gu, C., Zhong, H.: Lightweight and secure data sharing based on proxy re-encryption for blockchain-enabled industrial internet of things. IEEE Internet Things J. **11**(8), 14115–14126 (2024). https://doi.org/10.1109/JIOT.2023.3340567
20. Xue, L., Ni, J., Liu, D., Lin, X., Shen, X.: Blockchain-based fair and fine-grained data trading with privacy preservation. IEEE Trans. Comput. **72**(9), 2440–2453 (2023). https://doi.org/10.1109/TC.2023.3251846
21. Zabelin, D., Yuyama, T., Nakanishi, T.: The world is drowning in data. Why don't we trade it like on a stock exchange? World Econ. Forum (2022). https://www.weforum.org/stories/2022/01/data-trading-stock-exchange/. Accessed 2 July 2026
22. Zhang, J., Su, S., Zhong, H., Cui, J., He, D.: Identity-based broadcast proxy re-encryption for flexible data sharing in VANETs. IEEE Trans. Inf. Forensics Secur. **18**, 4830–4842 (2023). https://doi.org/10.1109/TIFS.2023.3299466
23. Zhang, X., et al.: A data trading scheme with efficient data usage control for industrial IoT. IEEE Trans. Industr. Inf. **18**(7), 4456–4465 (2022). https://doi.org/10.1109/TII.2021.3123312
24. Zhao, Y., Yu, Y., Li, Y., Han, G., Du, X.: Machine learning based privacy-preserving fair data trading in big data market. Inf. Sci. **478**, 449–460 (2019). https://doi.org/10.1016/j.ins.2018.11.028

SADA: Balancing Attack Strength and Visual Fidelity in Unrestricted Adversarial Attacks

Hui Li[1], Yanrong Lu[1(✉)], Wencheng Yang[2], Ji Zhang[2], Taotao Cai[2], and Kaize Shi[2]

[1] College of Safety Science and Engineering, Civil Aviation University of China, Tianjin, China
yr_lu@cauc.edu.cn

[2] School of Science, Engineering and Digital Technologies, University of Southern Queensland, Toowoomba, QLD, Australia

Abstract. Traditional L_p attacks introduce detectable high-frequency noise, while recent diffusion-based unrestricted attacks improve naturalness but struggle to balance attack strength and fidelity, causing semantic drift or background artifacts. We propose Semantically Aware Diffusion Attack (SADA), a framework that generates transferable adversarial examples with semantic consistency and realism. SADA integrates three key strategies: fusing U-Net attention with SAM masks to decouple foreground from background; applying background-aware optimization with adaptive loss and gradient rectification to confine perturbations to semantic regions; and using U-Net gradient alignment to project semantic gradients onto the classifier's discriminative direction for better generalization. Experiments show SADA reduces accuracy from 90.93% to 45.88%–61.42% with high fidelity (FID 60.12–61.1), and resists DiffPure with only 4.4% accuracy recovery, bypassing state-of-the-art defenses. The on-manifold examples expose classifier vulnerabilities and misaligned decision boundaries, promising improved robustness.

Keywords: Adversarial Attack · Diffusion Models · Semantic Consistency · Transferability · Model Robustness · On-manifold

1 Introduction

Early L_p-norm adversarial attacks [10,25] generate unnatural high-frequency noise, leading to poor transferability, weak robustness against defenses, and low visual realism. Recent unrestricted attacks [3,21] instead leverage generative priors for natural perturbations, and diffusion models [13] in particular enable semantic manipulation in latent space [5]. However, these methods face a critical trade-off: stronger attacks tend to drift off the data manifold, while strictly preserving fidelity yields perturbations too weak to cross decision boundaries—a failure to balance "walking on the manifold" with "crossing the boundary" [35].

L. Ding et al. (Eds.): APWeb-WAIM 2026, LNCS 16995, pp. 631–642, 2027.
https://doi.org/10.1007/978-981-92-5699-0_43

This matters because on-manifold examples are stealthier and more resilient to purification defenses (e.g., DiffPure [29]): they exploit non-robust features yet remain statistically natural [15], whereas norm-constrained attacks are easily removed by manifold-projection defenses [26,33].

Confining attacks to semantic regions via a single mask is insufficient: soft attention masks leak background noise, while hard segmentation masks impose rigid boundaries and uniform weighting. This calls for an approach that keeps adversarial samples on (or extremely close to) the data manifold, treating visual quality and semantic consistency as hard prerequisites. To this end, we propose the Semantically Aware Diffusion Attack (SADA), which constrains the perturbation search space to the data manifold and exploits diffusion priors to generate stealthy, high-quality adversarial examples with strong transferability and resistance to purification.

Our contributions are threefold: (1) a dual-stream guidance strategy that reduces semantic drift and weakens manifold-projection defenses; (2) a background aware adversarial optimization strategy that enables precise, fidelity-preserving attacks on semantic regions; (3) a U-Net gradient alignment mechanism that improves black-box success rates without sacrificing image quality.

2 Related Work

2.1 Norm-Bounded Attacks

Norm-bounded attacks optimize perturbations under L_p constraints and underpin adversarial research for their simplicity and white-box efficacy [4,10,19,30,36,46]. To improve black-box transferability, later work integrated priors such as momentum [8], translation invariance [9], and frequency-domain optimization [24]. Nevertheless, the L_p constraint remains fundamentally limiting: the resulting perturbations are often perceptible and lie in low-probability, off-manifold regions, making them easily neutralized by purification-based defenses—motivating a shift from pixel-level noise to on-manifold synthesis.

2.2 Unrestricted Adversarial Attacks

Unrestricted attacks bypass pixel-level noise via semantic transformations of shape, texture, and color [1,2,31,40]; perceptual color-space methods (e.g., PerC-AL [45], NCF [43]) improve naturalness but, relying on rigid distribution modeling, sacrifice transferability. Diffusion models have since redefined the field with strong latent-space priors, yet existing frameworks face a persistent trilemma: ACA [6] lacks structural constraints and drifts semantically, Diff-PGD [42] introduces granular artifacts, and DiffAttack [5] blurs boundaries due to low-resolution guidance. Balancing semantic consistency with attack transferability thus remains open, requiring a framework that keeps samples on the data manifold while ensuring black-box efficacy.

2.3 Data Manifold and Adversarial Defense

The Data Manifold Hypothesis interprets traditional norm-bounded attacks as off-manifold high-frequency noise [35], which allows purification defenses like DiffPure [29] and DensePure [39] to neutralize them via manifold projection. Conversely, on-manifold adversarial examples—characterized by natural statistics and low FID scores [12]-exploit non-robust yet predictive features [15], creating an intractable "blind spot" for current defenses. Since these samples strictly adhere to the manifold's statistical laws, purification mechanisms fail to distinguish them from clean data, preserving their aggressive semantic features.

3 Preliminaries and Problem Definition

3.1 Latent Diffusion Models

The SADA is built on latent diffusion models (LDM) [32], which map the image space $\mathcal{X}$ to a low-dimensional latent space $\mathcal{Z}$ using Variational Autoencoder (VAE). An encoder E maps an input image $x \in \mathbb{R}^{H\times W\times 3}$ to a latent variable $z_0 = E(x)$. The forward diffusion progressively adds noise z_0 to yield z_t, while the reverse process restores z_0 via a denoising U-Net $\epsilon_\theta(z_t, t, C)$ conditioned on C (e.g., a text prompt).

3.2 Image Latent Mapping

We map a real image x into the latent space via deterministic DDIM inversion [34], where the mapping $z_0 \rightarrow z_T$ is:

$$z_{t+1} = \sqrt{\frac{\alpha_{t+1}}{\alpha_t}} z_t + \sqrt{\alpha_{t+1}} \left(\sqrt{\frac{1}{\alpha_{t+1}} - 1} - \sqrt{\frac{1}{\alpha_t} - 1} \right) \cdot \epsilon_\theta(z_t, t, C), \tag{1}$$

with α_t a noise schedule. For text-image alignment, Classifier-Free Guidance (CFG) [14] extrapolates from the unconditional toward the conditional estimate:

$$\tilde{\epsilon}_\theta(z_t, t, C, \varnothing) = \epsilon_\theta(z_t, t, \varnothing) + w\big(\epsilon_\theta(z_t, t, C) - \epsilon_\theta(z_t, t, \varnothing)\big), \tag{2}$$

where $\varnothing$ is the null-text embedding and w the guidance scale. As an extrapolation coefficient, w is not restricted to $[0, 1]$: $w > 1$ (default 7.5) strengthens prompt adherence but, if too large, over-amplifies the conditional direction and corrupts the latent statistics that faithful inversion relies on [27]. We therefore fix $w = 1$ during inversion and apply Null-Text Optimization: we compute a pivot trajectory $\{z_0^*, \ldots, z_T^*\}$ at $w = 1$, then optimize the per-timestep null embedding $\varnothing_t$ to minimize

$$\min_{\varnothing_t} \|z_{t-1}^* - z_{t-1}(z_t, t, C, \varnothing_t)\|_2^2. \tag{3}$$

This yields a latent that is faithful yet editable, serving as the initialization for adversarial perturbation.

3.3 Attack Objective

Given a classifier $f(\cdot)$ and an original image x with ground-truth label y, our goal is to find an adversarial example x_{adv} such that $f(x_{adv}) \neq y$ while preserving perceptual fidelity to x. Unlike pixel-level attacks, SADA searches in latent space: it finds an optimal adversarial latent z_{adv} and decodes it as $x_{adv} = D(z_{adv})$.

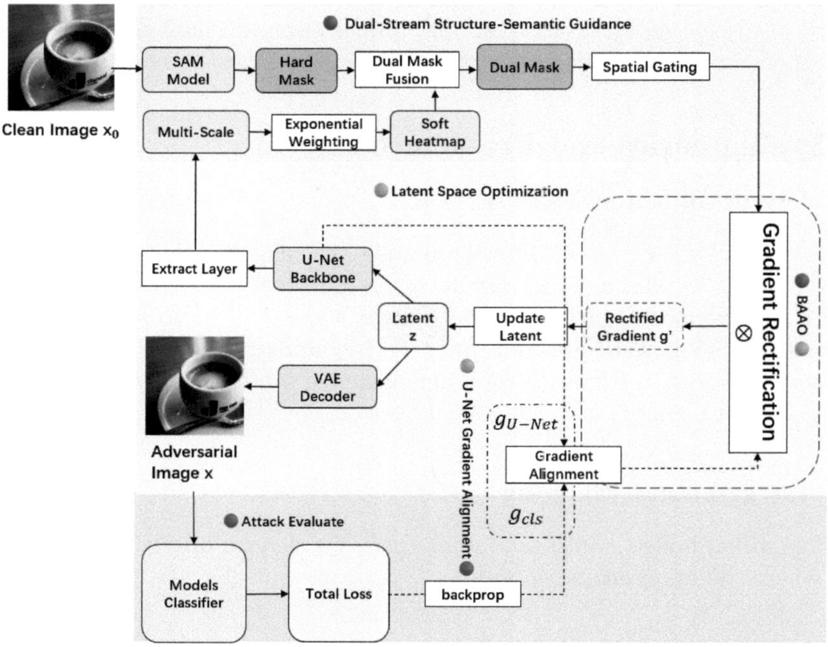

Fig. 1. The SADA pipeline: Dual-Stream Guidance (yellow) for localization, Latent Space Optimization (green; Gradient Alignment and BAAO) for updates, and Attack Evaluation (red) for feedback, iteratively transforming a clean image x_0 into an adversarial image x. (Color figure online)

4 Methodology

4.1 Architecture of the SADA Framework

As shown in Fig. 1, SADA comprises three core modules: Dual-Stream Structure-Semantic Guidance, U-Net Gradient Alignment, and Background-Aware Adversarial Optimization (BAAO). Starting from DDIM inversion of x_0 into latent noise z_t, the dual-stream module localizes the target, U-Net Gradient Alignment calibrates a transferable latent trajectory, and BAAO attacks foregrounds while preserving backgrounds—evaluated on black-box models in a closed feedback loop.

4.2 Dual-Stream Structure-Semantic Guidance

The dual-stream structure-semantic guidance mechanism captures both high-level semantics and low-level boundaries. It comprises a Semantic Stream and Dual-Stream Fusion.

Multi-Scale Attention Fusion (MSAF). At denoising timestep t, we extract attention maps $\{\mathcal{A}_l\}_{l=1}^{L}$ from all U-Net cross-attention layers. Since deeper features are more critical for object localization [11,37], we aggregate them via exponential weighting.

$$\mathcal{M}_{\text{attn}} = \sum_{l=1}^{L} w_l \cdot \text{Blur}(\mathcal{A}_l), \quad \text{where } w_l = \frac{e^{\gamma \cdot l}}{\sum_{k=1}^{L} e^{\gamma \cdot k}} \tag{4}$$

Here, γ controls the contribution of different layers: higher γ emphasizes deeper semantic features. A Gaussian blur $\text{Blur}(\cdot)$ smooths single-layer attention maps to remove noise, yielding a semantically precise heatmap.

Dual-Stream Fusion: Structure Stream and Dual Fusion. We introduce the binary mask $\mathcal{M}_{\text{sam}}$ SAM [17] (1 for foreground, 0 for background) as a structural supplement. The final guidance mask $\mathcal{M}_{\text{guide}}$ is obtained via soft-weighted fusion, combining the semantic heatmap with structural boundaries.

$$\mathcal{M}_{\text{guide}} = \eta \cdot \mathcal{M}_{\text{sam}} + (1 - \eta) \cdot \mathcal{M}_{\text{attn}} \tag{5}$$

$\mathcal{M}_{\text{guide}}$ defines the semantic attack region and is used for loss weighting and gradient control.

4.3 U-Net Gradient Alignment Mechanism

To improve black-box transferability, we extract intermediate features $f_{\text{U-Net}}$ from the U-Net for current latent z_t and compute its semantic gradient $\nabla_z \mathcal{L}_{\text{U-Net}}$. This gradient is projected onto the classifier gradient $\nabla_z \mathcal{L}_{\text{cls}}$ [6]:

$$g_{\text{align}} = \frac{\langle \nabla_z \mathcal{L}_{\text{U-Net}}, \nabla_z \mathcal{L}_{\text{cls}} \rangle}{\|\nabla_z \mathcal{L}_{\text{cls}}\|^2 + \epsilon} \cdot \nabla_z \mathcal{L}_{\text{cls}} \tag{6}$$

The total update gradient combines both:

$$g_{\text{total}} = \nabla_z \mathcal{L}_{\text{cls}} + \lambda_{\text{align}} \cdot g_{\text{align}} \tag{7}$$

This injects U-Net's generalized features into perturbations, enhancing attack transferability.

4.4 Background-Aware Adversarial Optimization (BAAO)

The BAAO strategy consists of a background-sensitive hybrid loss and explicit gradient rectification. The full pipeline is summarized in Algorithm 1.

Background-Sensitive Hybrid Loss. Using guidance mask $\mathcal{M}_{\text{guide}}$, the total loss comprises: adversarial classification Loss maximizes standard cross-entropy; a weighted sum of losses from multiple models [23].

Background-weighted Consistency Loss- decouples pixel and perceptual (LPIPS [44]) losses into foreground and background:

$$\mathcal{L}_{\text{consist}} = \underbrace{\|(x_{\text{adv}} - x) \odot \mathcal{M}_{\text{guide}}\|}_{\text{Foreground}} + \lambda_{\text{bg}} \cdot \underbrace{\|(x_{\text{adv}} - x) \odot (1 - \mathcal{M}_{\text{guide}})\|}_{\text{Background}} \tag{8}$$

with $\lambda_{\text{bg}} > 1$. This concentrates perturbations in semantic cores while suppressing background changes. TV loss is added as a regularization term.

Gradient Rectification Mechanism. We construct a scaling map $S = (1 - \mathcal{M}_{\text{guide}}) \cdot \eta_d + \mathcal{M}_{\text{guide}} \cdot \gamma_a$, where $\eta_d \in [0, 1)$ dampens background updates and $\gamma_a > 1$ amplifies foreground attacks. Gaussian blur smooths S to $\tilde{S}$, and the final latent update gradient is $\hat{g} = g \odot \tilde{S}$. This decouples strong foreground from weak background perturbations, balancing attack potency and stealthiness.

Algorithm 1. Semantically-Aware Diffusion Attack (SADA)

Require: Clean image x, target model f, diffusion model ϵ_θ, prompt P, steps K, step size α

Ensure: Adversarial example x_{adv}

$C \leftarrow \text{TextEncoder}(P)$; $M_{sam} \leftarrow \text{SAM}(x)$
$z \leftarrow \text{DDIM\_Inversion}(x, \epsilon_\theta, C)$
for $k = 0$ to $K - 1$ **do**
  $F_{mid}, A_{maps} \leftarrow \text{U-Net}(z, t_k, C)$
  $M_{guide} \leftarrow \text{Fuse}(M_{sam}, \text{MSAF}(A_{maps}))$ // dual-stream guidance
  $g_{cls} \leftarrow \nabla_z \mathcal{L}_{CE}(f(\text{Decode}(z)), y)$
  $g_{align} \leftarrow \text{Project}(\nabla_z \mathcal{L}_{MSE}(F_{mid}, F_{orig}),\ g_{cls})$ // gradient alignment
  $g_{total} \leftarrow \text{Rectify}(g_{cls} + \lambda_{align}\, g_{align},\ M_{guide})$ // BAAO
  $z \leftarrow z - \alpha \cdot \text{Sign}(g_{total})$
end for
return $x_{adv} \leftarrow \text{Decode}(z)$

---

5 Experiments

The experimental validation comprises four parts: (1) comparing the SADA with mainstream attacks on transferability and stealthiness; (2) evaluating robustness against defenses, especially purification-based methods; (3) assessing image naturalness; (4) ablation study.

Experimental Setup Datasets. 1,000 images from ImageNet validation set [7], following ACA [6], NCF [43], PerC-AL [45], and DiffAttack [5]. This balanced sampling covers ImageNet-1K's label space, ensuring diversity and statistical significance while remaining computationally feasible.

Evaluation Metrics. Top-1 accuracy (attack success) and the Frechet Inception Distance (FID) [12] (visual quality).

Implementation Details. NVIDIA 4090, PyTorch, Stable Diffusion v1.4, DDIM scheduler with $T = 50$.

Attack Evaluation. Compared methods: MI-FGSM [8], TI-FGSM [9], S^2I-FGSM [24], PerC-AL [45], NCF [43], ACA [6], DiffAttack [5] and Diff-PGD [42]. Parameters follow default settings. Metric: model accuracy (ACC, %).

Hyperparameters. Image mapping iterations $N_i = 10$; attack iterations $N_a = 10$ step size $\eta = 0.04$; perturbation budget $k = 0.1$; momentum $\mu = 1.0$; SD v1.4. Prompts generated by LLaVA-NeXT [22]; SAM masks (fallback UPerNet).

5.1 Attacks on Normally Trained Models

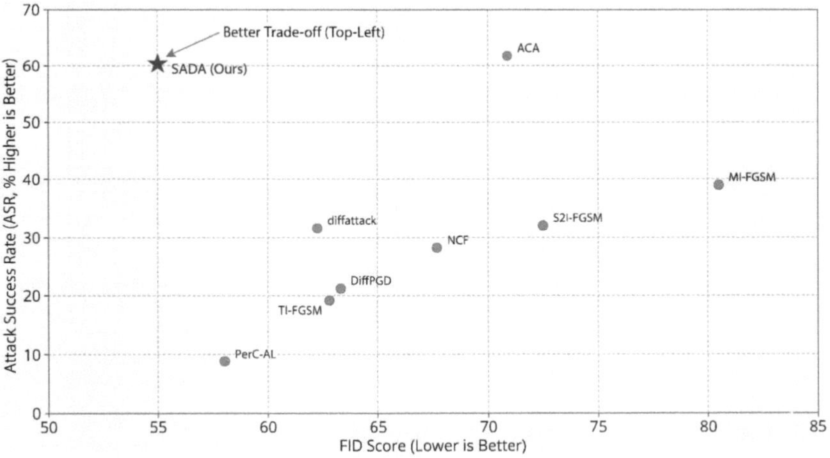

Fig. 2. Pareto-frontier of ASR vs. FID for Inception-v3 based adversarial attacks

Transferability and visual quality (FID) are reported in Table 1. We evaluate the SADA against pixel-based attacks (MI-FGSM [8], TI-FGSM [9], S^2I-FGSM [24]), unrestricted adversarial attacks (PerC-AL [45], NCF [43], ACA [6]), and diffusion-based (DiffAttack [5], Diff-PGD [42]) attacks, using their official optimal settings. Surrogate models: ResNet-50, VGG-19, MobileNet-v2, Inception-v3, ConvNeXt, Swin-B.

Analysis of the Attack-Fidelity Trade-off. Figure 2 shows the Pareto frontier with Inception-v3 as the white-box surrogate. SADA occupies the optimal top-left region, balancing attack success and fidelity: ACA reaches slightly higher ASR but at far worse FID (>70), while PerC-AL attains low FID (~58) yet barely reduces target accuracy. Under matched fidelity, SADA outperforms ACA, DiffAttack, and others, delivering competitive black-box transferability at FID as low as 61.1.

Table 1. Comparison of Different Models Under Various Attacks

Surrogate Model	Attack \ Model	Res-50	VGG-19	Mob-v2	Inc-v3	ConvNeXt	CN-V2-B	Mob-V4	Eff-V2	ViT-B	Swin-B	DeiT-B	DeiT-S	Swin-V2	DeiT-3	MaxViT	Mix-B	Mix-L	AVG	FID
		CNNs								Transformers						MLPs				
-	**Clean**	92.7	88.7	86.9	80.5	97.0	96.1	94.6	85.4	93.7	95.9	94.5	94.0	95.6	95.8	95.5	82.4	76.5	90.9	57.8
Res-50	MI-FGSM	0	19.9	20.2	28.9	57.8	59.5	21.5	31.5	67.3	67	72.4	67	69	74	55	52.2	45.4	50.54	81.2
	TI-FGSM	0	42.4	37.1	46	83.6	85.5	38.5	49	81.6	83.7	84.5	79	85	86	70	66	61.7	67.48	66
	S^2I-FGSM	0	9.2	6.6	18.6	44.1	46	7.5	21	63.9	52	65.9	59	54	67.5	48	45.6	44.3	40.83	79.8
	PerC-AL	92.8	88.8	86.9	80.9	97	96.5	94.7	83.9	94.4	96.1	95.1	94.1	96	96.5	95.7	83.4	77.9	91.12	**57.9**
	NCF	10.1	27.4	28	50.9	75.4	82.8	65.1	66.9	62.3	72.8	70.8	62.6	78.7	82	85	53.1	45.7	63.09	72.4
	ACA	7.2	26.8	25.3	25	40.9	43	36.6	29.6	38.9	40.6	39.7	36.8	42.2	41.9	42.4	26.3	25.5	**35.09**	70.1
	DiffAttack	3.4	23.7	21.7	26.4	39.9	48.3	34.5	36.8	47.4	41.4	46.6	42.5	46.7	53.5	46.1	43.2	45.1	40.24	64.2
	Diff-PGD	2.3	18	18.9	39.2	45.9	59.3	36.9	50.3	69.6	55.4	68.6	66.1	58.9	70.6	56.8	53.5	50.2	51.14	68.1
	SADA(ours)	12.7	45	46.9	41.9	54.3	63.9	58.1	48.8	49.6	54.2	56	53.3	60.5	61.7	62.8	45.9	43.5	52.90	60.12
VGG-19	MI-FGSM	22.7	0	15.4	33.5	53.2	55	16.5	36	73.2	63.3	74.7	68	65	76	51	54.3	48.6	50.40	82.4
	TI-FGSM	44.5	0	32.8	47.4	77.8	79.5	34	49.5	81.4	79.3	83.6	79	81	85	67	64.9	60.3	65.44	66.6
	S^2I-FGSM	17.9	0	11.3	31.8	49.5	51	12	34	74.1	57.9	76	68	59.5	77.5	48	52.6	50.8	48.24	82.9
	PerC-AL	92	84.8	86.7	80.5	97.1	96.5	94.3	84	94.4	95.8	95	93.9	95.6	96.7	95.9	83	77.6	91.19	**57.8**
	NCF	35.2	7.2	29	50.3	79.5	84.8	69.7	67.6	67.2	76.8	76.2	67.7	81.1	83.7	84.7	55.1	48.3	66.06	71.4
	ACA	33.7	5.3	28.9	29.8	46.9	48.7	40.5	30.7	41.8	43.6	42.4	41.4	46.1	46.7	45.1	28.3	28.1	**38.92**	70.4
	DiffAttack	19.1	5.9	18.2	29.1	42.5	48.2	35.2	36.5	51.3	41.7	50	43.3	46.7	54.7	43.1	40.2	39.9	39.98	64
	Diff-PGD	31.5	3.6	26.3	43.9	59	66.8	50.9	58.3	76.8	62.4	77.1	72.5	65.3	78.9	64.3	59.3	55.7	59.31	65
	SADA(ours)	56.4	10.3	49.3	46.8	63	68.2	64.2	52.4	54.9	59.6	59.8	59.8	63.4	65.2	65.7	49.9	45.1	57.73	60.7
Mob-v2	MI-FGSM	26.4	18.7	0	31	62	64	54.2	33	69.5	65.2	71.6	63	67	73	43	46.9	44.4	52.06	76.4
	TI-FGSM	47.2	37.9	0	45.2	83	85	47.6	47.5	79.9	80.9	81.8	76	82	83.5	60	61.7	58.3	66.09	65.6
	S^2I-FGSM	21	13.4	0	27.2	64.3	66	57.9	29.5	74.1	62.6	75.2	68	64	76.5	50	51.4	48.3	53.09	79.4
	PerC-AL	92.1	88.5	86.7	80.7	96.9	96.3	94.8	83.7	94.4	96.1	95.1	93.8	95.4	96.7	96	83.2	78	91.36	**57.8**
	NCF	34.2	27.6	7.5	49.5	77	84.8	68.2	66.4	65.8	74.7	74.6	66.8	79.6	82.2	84.7	53.1	48.1	64.83	71.3
	ACA	33.2	28.9	12.2	30.1	46.2	50.6	40.2	33.5	42	44.5	43.2	40.8	45.2	47.9	46	30.7	26.6	**39.35**	69.9
	DiffAttack	24.7	23.6	1.5	31.5	48.2	55.6	34.3	38.8	49.6	45.3	51.3	45.8	50.6	56.7	47.5	38.8	39.5	42.61	64.3
	Diff-PGD	35.3	10.5	34.9	49.5	46.6	67.6	49.3	60.7	70.5	60.2	76.1	71.9	64.2	75.8	64.8	66.3	59.4	58.04	63.1
	SADA(ours)	60.2	54	10.9	48.2	66.9	73.2	66.1	53.8	58.8	63.4	64.9	62	68.7	69.1	69.4	53.4	50.6	61.42	60.42
Inc-v3	MI-FGSM	42.8	36.6	34.4	0	79.8	81.5	35.5	37	75.3	79.4	78.6	73	81	80	58	56.5	48.9	61.14	80.5
	TI-FGSM	76	70.1	66.7	0.1	93.8	95	67.5	69	88.7	91.2	89.7	88	92	90.5	75	73.8	66.8	80.86	62.8
	S^2I-FGSM	52.3	47.8	43.3	0	86.3	88	44	46.5	80.8	84.1	83.8	78	85	84.5	65	63.5	57.3	68.14	72.5
	PerC-AL	91.3	87.4	85.4	77.1	96.3	95.8	93.5	83.3	94.4	95.8	94.6	93.5	95.3	96	95.2	82.7	77.2	91.11	**58.02**
	NCF	52	42.2	43.9	15.2	86.1	89.6	77	71.2	73.7	82.3	81.2	74.9	86.4	87.8	88.7	60.3	53.9	71.95	67.7
	ACA	32.6	31.7	32.9	12.8	41.8	45.7	39.2	34.6	39	40.1	40.7	38.3	42.9	43.5	43.9	33.5	32.1	**38.28**	70.9
	DiffAttack	60.1	58.3	56.1	13.9	78.6	76.1	67.2	56.6	75.1	75.1	76.1	72.7	75	79.4	77.4	59.5	55.1	68.65	62.24
	Diff-PGD	68.4	62.2	63.5	10.5	89.4	89.2	77.5	69.4	86.9	85.9	86.6	85	86.5	89.5	86.7	71.3	63.8	78.86	63.3
	SADA(ours)	56.1	53.1	51.2	38.2	58.3	64.6	58.7	47	52	54.4	58.9	55	60.3	62.1	63.1	47	44	55.36	61.1
ConvNeXt	MI-FGSM	34.5	22.4	26.5	41.9	0	54	27	43.5	63.4	18	56.5	56	19	58	38	41.4	40.2	40.02	84.5
	TI-FGSM	50.7	37.3	41.1	51.8	0	67.1	42	53	70.9	38.8	68.6	69	40	70	48	52.3	47.2	52.99	73.5
	S^2I-FGSM	13.6	9.6	11.9	20.2	0	64.4	12.5	21	35.4	44.2	31	31	55	32	24	23.2	25.6	28.41	99.4
	PerC-AL	91.6	87.8	86.9	80.6	96.7	96.5	94.1	83.7	94.4	96.2	95	94.2	95.6	96.4	95.9	83.1	78.1	90.63	**57.7**
	NCF	44.2	39.7	39.8	54	40.6	76.4	64	62.1	59.7	62.2	64.5	57.8	69.1	76.2	77.2	52.1	47.5	59.16	67.8
	ACA	26.8	26.9	25.3	24.9	14.4	34.8	30.2	26	32.5	27.5	29.4	29.3	29.4	31.9	31.1	22.3	21	28.08	72.4
	DiffAttack	20.8	24.6	24.8	26.8	2.8	17.4	20.8	24	26.3	13	21.2	25.4	18	23.6	16.7	22.2	25.7	**21.96**	74.4
	Diff-PGD	45.3	39.2	44.8	49.9	12.1	44.3	45.6	54.2	60.3	37.6	54.8	56	33	59.3	46.1	46.3	42.9	47.48	63.9
	SADA(ours)	50.9	50.5	46.3	44.8	18.8	55.6	52.3	44.6	40.5	39.4	47.8	45.9	51.2	52.7	52.5	43.5	40.1	47.41	60.7
Swin-B	MI-FGSM	55.7	42.3	42.7	55.2	42.5	70.6	0.9	65	64.2	64	73.5	66	49	52.4	47.9	40.1	40.6	51.94	72.8
	TI-FGSM	71.9	61.7	56.9	60.2	66	76.3	1.9	72.5	72.2	72	73.7	73	58	61.2	56.9	29.6	29	60.13	65.9
	S^2I-FGSM	47.4	37.8	35.4	45.3	26.8	48.5	1	47	46.2	45	53.1	48	38	39.3	39	47.5	43.7	40.27	68.2
	PerC-AL	91	86.4	84.2	77.7	96.1	95.8	93.3	81.9	93.5	92.7	94	93.7	94.3	96.2	94.3	79.4	74.1	84.45	**58.3**
	NCF	49.8	44	44.2	58.7	68.1	79.2	67.7	64.7	62.4	36.3	64.6	61.2	65	76.9	77.3	52.9	48.9	56.58	66.5
	ACA	29.5	29	27.7	27.1	31.4	36.6	33	28.4	33.7	14.3	31.6	31.7	30.3	35	33.5	23.7	22.4	**27.72**	71.5
	DiffAttack	42.7	44.4	41.9	43.7	34.1	39.8	43.1	41.9	39.2	11.2	34.1	37.5	28	40.4	32.6	37.3	37.1	34.30	66.7
	Diff-PGD	59.8	53.9	53.5	57.2	54.6	62.8	63.3	63.2	66.9	26.8	60	62.6	28.9	67	56.7	54.6	52.4	51.78	62.2
	SADA(ours)	54.3	54.5	50.3	46.8	49.2	59.9	56.7	48	42	17.2	48.4	48.2	54.1	58.1	57.2	45.8	43.2	45.88	60.3

5.2 Attacks on Adversarial Defense Methods

Following Yuan et al. [43] and Long et al. [24], we evaluate robustness against input preprocessing [16,18,20,28,41], adversarially trained models [18,38], and DiffPure [29], using Inc-v3 as the surrogate. The target is Inc-v3 itself for NRP and DiffPure, and follows the official papers otherwise. Results are in Table 2. Table 2 reports black-box transferability against defense methods. The SADA consistently reduces defense model accuracy more than NCF, DiffAttack, and Diff-PGD. Average accuracy across defenses drops to 50.2% (vs. DiffAttack 55.2%, NCF 55.8%, Diff-PGD 59.1%). Against purification-based defenses (DiffPure, NRP), the SADA achieves the best attack, yielding only by 4.4 and 0.4%-point accuracy recovery, respectively—outperforming ACA (6.8% and 0.7%). This shows the SADA effectively bypasses gradient masking and purification.

5.3 Visualization

Qualitative Comparison. Figure 3 compares sample quality. Gradient-based methods (MI-FGSM, TI-FGSM, S^2I-FGSM) introduce obvious high-frequency

Table 2. Robustness on defense approaches. Top-1 accuracy (%) reported.

	HGD	R&P	NIP-r3	RS	Adv-Inc-v3	Inc-v3ens3	Inc-v3ens4	IncRes-v2ens	AVG	Inc-v3normal	NRP	DiffPure
MI-FGSM	77.9	76.8	65.2	62.7	51.1	49.8	53.7	70.5	63.5	0	+5.9	+38.4
TI-FGSM	84.7	86.1	87.0	69.4	66.1	62.4	64.5	76.8	74.6	0.1	+25.8	+55.5
S^2I-FGSM	72.5	76.5	73.3	65.0	51.8	47.0	52.2	67.7	63.3	0	+3.2	+47.0
PerC-AL	95.6	94.4	96.7	74.2	80.8	76.7	75.4	88.6	85.3	7.7	+56.8	+55.9
NCF	71.1	66.4	74.6	**29.0**	48.8	47.2	49.0	60.5	55.8	17.4	+11.0	+14.8
ACA	**47.8**	**46.4**	**46.1**	<u>36.6</u>	**38.1**	**40.2**	**37.8**	**42.1**	**41.9**	12.8	<u>+0.7</u>	<u>+6.8</u>
DiffAttack	62	65.5	70	52.8	<u>46</u>	<u>43.8</u>	43.1	58.3	55.2	13.9	+2.3	+15.9
Diff-PGD	54.7	<u>52.3</u>	<u>47.5</u>	51.1	69.1	61.2	62.5	74.6	59.1	10.5	+39.1	+35.4
SADA(ours)	<u>51.9</u>	53.4	55.1	54.3	46.8	43.9	<u>42.7</u>	<u>53.5</u>	<u>50.2</u>	38.2	**+0.4**	**+4.4**

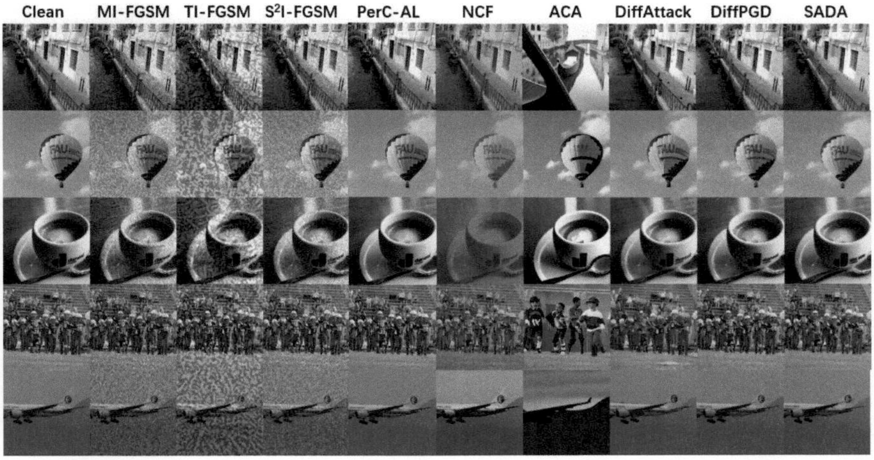

Fig. 3. Visual comparisons among different attacks

noise; PerC-AL improves imperceptibility but sacrifices transferability; NCF produces unnatural color distortion. Among diffusion-based attacks, Diff-PGD suffers from grainy noise, ACA causes semantic shift and over-generation due to weak structural constraints, and DiffAttack produces blurry artifacts from low-resolution soft masks with imprecise object boundaries. In contrast, SADA uses dual-stream guidance with SAM masks to impose precise boundaries and adaptively reconstructs high-frequency details rather than adding noise, thus achieving a better balance of visual imperceptibility and semantic consistency.

5.4 Ablation Study

We evaluate the U-Net gradient alignment mechanism (Figs. 4a, 4b). The U-Net module synergistically improves transferability across architectures: e.g., it lowers Inc-v3 source model accuracy by 5.8% without harming visual quality. FID scores shift closer to the clean baseline (57.8), especially for VGG-19 and Res-50. Thus, U-Net expands the Pareto frontier, enabling more aggressive yet less perceptible examples.

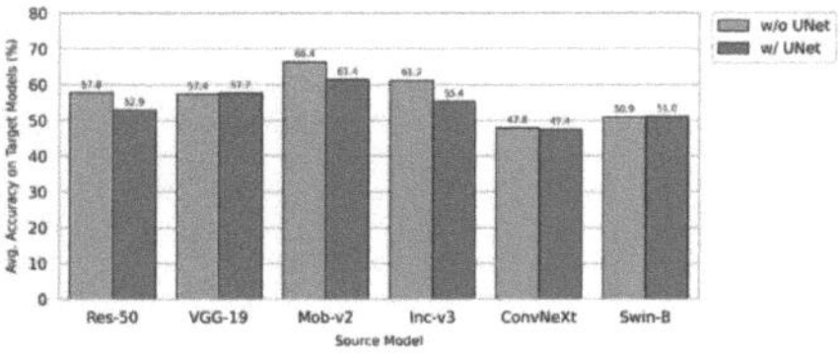

(a) Effectiveness of U-Net module

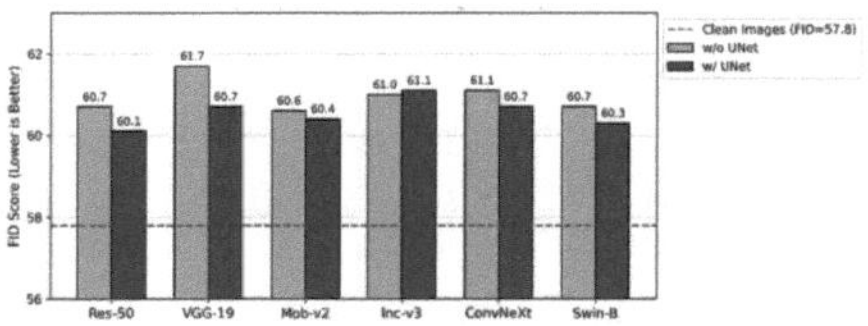

(b) Impact of U-Net on image quality (FID)

Fig. 4. Ablation study of the U-Net gradient alignment module.

6 Conclusion

The SADA advances unrestricted adversarial attacks by resolving the trade-off between imperceptibility and transferability via three core strategies. By constraining perturbations to the natural data manifold, we show that multi-modal models remain vulnerable even within semantically plausible regions. Future work will extend SADA to video attacks, evaluate against certified defenses, and explore its interaction with adversarial training to improve model robustness.

Acknowledgment. We would like to thank all the editors and anonymous reviewers for their helpful advice. This paper is supported by the National Key Research and Development Program of China (2023YFB4302901), National Natural Science Foundation of China (No. 61802276), Tianjin Natural Science Foundation Project (24JCZDJC01000), and the Fundamental Research Funds for the Central Universities of China (No. 3122025091).

References

1. Alaifari, R., Alberti, G.S., Gauksson, T.: ADef: an iterative algorithm to construct adversarial deformations (2018). arXiv preprint arXiv:1804.07729
2. Bhattad, A., Chong, M.J., Liang, K., Li, B., Forsyth, D.A.: Unrestricted adversarial examples via semantic manipulation (2019). arXiv preprint arXiv:1904.06347
3. Brown, T.B., Carlini, N., Zhang, C., Olsson, C., Christiano, P., Goodfellow, I.: Unrestricted adversarial examples (2018). arXiv preprint arXiv:1809.08352
4. Carlini, N., Wagner, D.: Towards evaluating the robustness of neural networks. In: 2017 IEEE Symposium on Security and Privacy (SP), pp. 39–57. IEEE (2017)
5. Chen, J., Chen, H., Chen, K., Zhang, Y., Zou, Z., Shi, Z.: Diffusion models for imperceptible and transferable adversarial attack. PAMI (2024)
6. Chen, Z., Li, B., Wu, S., Jiang, K., Ding, S., Zhang, W.: Content-based unrestricted adversarial attack (2023). arXiv preprint arXiv:2305.10665
7. Deng, J., Dong, W., Socher, R., Li, L.J., Li, K., Li, F.F.: ImageNet: a large-scale hierarchical image database. In: 2009 IEEE Conference on Computer Vision and Pattern Recognition, pp. 248–255. IEEE (2009)

8. Dong, Y., et al.: Boosting adversarial attacks with momentum. In: Proceedings of the IEEE Conference on Computer Vision and Pattern Recognition, pp. 9185–9193 (2018)
9. Dong, Y., Pang, T., Su, H., Zhu, J.: Evading defenses to transferable adversarial examples by translation-invariant attacks. In: Proceedings of the IEEE/CVF Conference on Computer Vision and Pattern Recognition, pp. 4312–4321 (2019)
10. Goodfellow, I.J., Shlens, J., Szegedy, C.: Explaining and harnessing adversarial examples. In: ICLR (2015)
11. Hertz, A., Mokady, R., Tenenbaum, J., Aberman, K., Pritch, Y., Cohen-Or, D.: Prompt-to-prompt image editing with cross-attention control. In: CVPR (2023)
12. Heusel, M., Ramsauer, H., Unterthiner, T., Nessler, B., Hochreiter, S.: GANs trained by a two time-scale update rule converge to a local Nash equilibrium. In: NeurIPS, vol. 30, pp. 6626–6637 (2017)
13. Ho, J., Jain, A., Abbeel, P.: Denoising diffusion probabilistic models. In: Advances in Neural Information Processing Systems, vol. 33, pp. 6840–6851 (2020)
14. Ho, J., Salimans, T.: Classifier-free diffusion guidance. In: NeurIPS 2021 Workshop on Deep Generative Models and Downstream Applications (2021)
15. Ilyas, A., Santurkar, S., Tsipras, D., Engstrom, L., Tran, B., Madry, A.: Adversarial examples are not bugs, they are features (2019)
16. Jia, X., Wei, X., Cao, X., Foroosh, H.: ComDefend: an efficient image compression model to defend adversarial examples. In: Proceedings of the IEEE/CVF Conference on Computer Vision and Pattern Recognition, pp. 6084–6092 (2019)
17. Kirillov, A., et al.: Segment anything. In: ICCV, pp. 4015–4026 (2023)
18. Kurakin, A., et al.: Adversarial attacks and defences competition (2018)
19. Li, X.C., Zhang, X.Y., Yin, F., Liu, C.L.: Decision-based adversarial attack with frequency mixup. IEEE Trans. Inf. Forensics Secur. **17**, 1038–1052 (2022)
20. Liao, F., Liang, M., Dong, Y., Pang, T., Hu, X., Zhu, J.: Defense against adversarial attacks using high-level representation guided denoiser. In: Proceedings of the IEEE/CVF Conference on Computer Vision and Pattern Recognition (CVPR), pp. 1778–1787 (2018)
21. Liu, F., Zhang, C., Zhang, H.: Towards transferable unrestricted adversarial examples with minimum changes. In: 2023 IEEE Conference on Secure and Trustworthy Machine Learning (SaTML), pp. 327–338. IEEE (2023)
22. Liu, H., et al.: LlaVA-NeXT: improved reasoning, OCR, and world knowledge, January 2024. https://llava-vl.github.io/blog/2024-01-30-llava-next/
23. Liu, Y., Chen, X., Liu, C., Song, D.: Delving into transferable adversarial examples and black-box attacks. arXiv preprint arXiv:1611.02770 (2016)
24. Long, Y., et al.: Frequency domain model augmentation for adversarial attack. In: ECCV, pp. 549–566 (2022)
25. Madry, A., Makelov, A., Schmidt, L., Tsipras, D., Vladu, A.: Towards deep learning models resistant to adversarial attacks. In: ICLR (2018)
26. Meng, D., Chen, H.: MagNet: a two-pronged defense against adversarial examples. In: CCS (2017)
27. Mokady, R., Hertz, A., Aberman, K., Pritch, Y., Cohen-Or, D.: Null-text inversion for editing real images using guided diffusion models. In: CVPR, pp. 6038–6047 (2023)
28. Naseer, M., Khan, S., Hayat, M., Khan, F.S., Porikli, F.: A self-supervised approach for adversarial robustness. In: Proceedings of the IEEE/CVF Conference on Computer Vision and Pattern Recognition (CVPR), pp. 262–271 (2020)
29. Nie, W., Guo, B., Huang, Y., Xiao, C., Vahdat, A., Anandkumar, A.: Diffusion models for adversarial purification. In: ICML (2022)

30. Qian, Y., et al.: Enhancing transferability of adversarial examples through mixed-frequency inputs. IEEE Trans. Inf. Forensics Secur. **19**, 7633–7645 (2024)
31. Qiu, H., Xiao, C., Yang, L., Yan, X., Lee, H., Li, B.: SemanticAdv: generating adversarial examples via attribute-conditioned image editing. In: European Conference on Computer Vision, pp. 19–37. Springer (2020)
32. Rombach, R., Blattmann, A., Lorenz, D., Esser, P., Ommer, B.: High-resolution image synthesis with latent diffusion models. In: CVPR, pp. 10684–10695 (2022)
33. Samangouei, P., Kabkab, M., Chellappa, R.: Defense-GAN: protecting classifiers against adversarial attacks using generative models. In: ICLR (2018)
34. Song, J., Meng, C., Ermon, S.: Denoising diffusion implicit models. In: ICLR (2021)
35. Stutz, D., Hein, M., Schiele, B.: Disentangling adversarial robustness and generalization. In: CVPR (2019)
36. Szegedy, C., et al.: Intriguing properties of neural networks (2013). arXiv preprint arXiv:1312.6199
37. Tang, R., et al.: What the DAAM: interpreting stable diffusion using cross attention. In: Proceedings of the 61st Annual Meeting of the Association for Computational Linguistics (Volume 1: Long Papers), pp. 5644–5659 (2023)
38. Tramèr, F., Kurakin, A., Papernot, N., Goodfellow, I., Boneh, D., McDaniel, P.: Ensemble adversarial training: attacks and defenses. In: International Conference on Learning Representations (ICLR) (2018)
39. Xiao, C., Deng, R., Li, B., Yu, F., Liu, M., Song, D.: DensePure: understanding diffusion models towards adversarial robustness. In: International Conference on Learning Representations (ICLR) (2023)
40. Xiao, C., Zhu, J.Y., Li, B., He, W., Liu, M., Song, D.: Spatially transformed adversarial examples. arXiv preprint arXiv:1801.02612 (2018)
41. Xie, C., Wang, J., Zhang, Z., Zhou, Y., Xie, L., Yuille, A.: Mitigating adversarial effects through randomization. In: International Conference on Learning Representations (ICLR) (2018)
42. Xue, H., Araujo, A., Hu, B., Chen, Y.: Diffusion-based adversarial sample generation for improved stealthiness and controllability. In: Advances in Neural Information Processing Systems, vol. 36, pp. 2894–2921 (2023)
43. Yuan, S., Zhang, Q., Gao, L., Cheng, Y., Song, J.: Natural color fool: towards boosting black-box unrestricted attacks. In: Advances in Neural Information Processing Systems, vol. 35, pp. 7546–7560 (2022)
44. Zhang, R., Isola, P., Efros, A.A., Shechtman, E., Wang, O.: The unreasonable effectiveness of deep features as a perceptual metric. In: CVPR, pp. 586–595 (2018)
45. Zhao, Z., Liu, Z., Larson, M.: Towards large yet imperceptible adversarial image perturbations with perceptual color distance. In: CVPR (2020)
46. Zhao, Z., et al.: SAGE: steering the adversarial generation of examples with accelerations. IEEE Trans. Inf. Forensics Secur. **18**, 789–803 (2023)

Sensitive Data Protection for Text-to-SQL Tasks in Large Language Models

Weiwei Yang[1], Junrui Lu[1], Rize Jin[1(✉)], and Joon-Young Paik[2]

[1] Tiangong University, Tianjin 300387, P. R. China
{2431111340,jinrize}@tiangong.edu.cn
[2] Chungnam National University, Daejeon, Republic of Korea
lucadi@cnu.ac.kr

Abstract. Large language models (LLMs) dominate Text-to-SQL tasks thanks to strong language comprehension. Yet domain adaptation demands knowledge distillation and supervised fine-tuning, which usually rely on real business queries full of sensitive information. Direct training on such data brings severe privacy leakage risks. We design a privacy-preserving framework combining data desensitization and knowledge distillation, working in two stages. First, a desensitization pipeline builds rule sets from security standards, uses an LLM to detect sensitive content, and runs context-aware desensitization that retains business logic while wiping private details. Second, a teacher model generates SQL from desensitized text to build high-quality training samples, which fine-tunes a lightweight student model to inherit domain skills without privacy hazards. Experiments show that our pipeline achieves 92.5% sensitive data processing accuracy and cuts costs by 83% over baselines; the student model reaches 91.5% Text-to-SQL accuracy.

Keywords: Text-to-SQL · Large Language Model · Supervised Fine-Tuning · Knowledge Distillation · Data De-identification

1 Introduction

Text-to-SQL links natural language and databases for data analysis and retrieval. Recent large language model (LLM) advances deliver strong general-domain Text-to-SQL performance, as LLMs reliably produce valid SQL for standard schemas thanks to robust language understanding and generation [1–3]. Nevertheless, these models exhibit clear limitations when handling domain-specific database grammars. They frequently produce SQL with syntax errors and logical inconsistencies, which undermines practical application value. Specifically, industrial databases adopt proprietary syntax and custom functions that LLMs fail to comply with, resulting in sharp drops in query accuracy [4,5].

Supervised fine-tuning aligns LLMs with domain database syntax and logic for better SQL generation [6,7]. Yet it raises privacy risks: fine-tuning relies on real business queries holding sensitive corporate and user data, and raw training may leak private information against security rules [8,9]. In response, we

L. Ding et al. (Eds.): APWeb-WAIM 2026, LNCS 16995, pp. 643–654, 2027.
https://doi.org/10.1007/978-981-92-5699-0_44

propose a privacy-preserving fine-tuning framework combining data desensitization and knowledge distillation. We design a dedicated desensitization pipeline to precisely detect and anonymize private data without erasing valuable domain features. Specifically, The DeepSeek-R1 teacher model generates standard SQL from sanitized natural language inputs to build a privacy-safe training corpus, on which the lightweight Qwen2.5-7B student model is fine-tuned to learn domain expertise without touching original sensitive records.

2 Related Work

2.1 Privacy Challenges in Domain-Specific Text-to-SQL

Domain-specific Text-to-SQL fine-tuning faces severe privacy risks, with few targeted systematic privacy solutions in existing research [10,11]. Fine-tuning datasets hold two categories of sensitive data. First, content privacy covers personal IDs, financial and medical records in text queries, violating GDPR [12] and HIPAA [13]. Second, structural privacy includes confidential table names, column schemas and relational constraints that expose core enterprise data architecture [6,7].

Conventional coarse filtering cannot separate private content from reusable domain knowledge, leaving models prone to sensitive data memorization and leakage, which blocks cross-institutional model sharing. No unified end-to-end framework covers desensitization, knowledge decoupling, model tuning and privacy validation. This gap fails to balance privacy, model performance and regulatory compliance [10,11]. The issue worsens for niche databases: labeled samples only reach tens of thousands, standard privacy tools like differential privacy degrade model effectiveness, yet authentic data patterns are essential to learn proprietary SQL syntax.

2.2 Limitations of Traditional Data Desensitization

Traditional data desensitization suffers from two core limitations: it fails to retain original data structural patterns and destroys semantic integrity after modification, which drastically reduces deep learning models' learning efficiency on sanitized datasets. Most existing privacy protection strategies only adopt isolated, simple technical fixes [14], leading to inherent systemic defects. Simple approaches like character masking or direct placeholder replacement break SQL syntactic coherence, weakening the model's generalization ability on training samples. Privacy-sensitive model training demands desensitization methods to strike a balanced tradeoff among structural consistency, semantic fidelity, and downstream task performance. Nevertheless, conventional desensitization lacks the capability to grasp contextual and logical correlations hidden in data, so it cannot produce high-quality training corpora compatible with advanced LLMs.

3 Methodology

Figure 1 depicts the proposed privacy-preserving data desensitization framework. Its components are elaborated one by one in the following subsections.

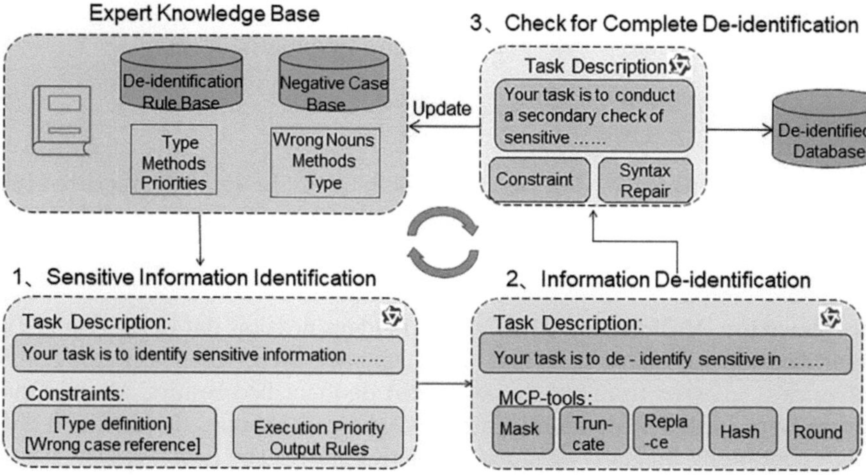

Fig. 1. The proposed privacy-preserving data desensitization framework.

3.1 Database Construction

De-identification Rule Base. As the core guiding document for the entire desensitization process, the content of the desensitization rule base can be formally expressed as: each rule R_i is a triple $R_i = (S_i, M_i, P_i)$, where:

S_i represents the sensitive type. By clearly defining the category to which the information belongs (e.g., $S_i \in \{\text{personal privacy}, \text{trade secrets}, \text{financial data}\}$), it provides a formal basis for the accurate identification of sensitive information.

M_i denotes the desensitization method, covering various operation operators such as $M_i \in \{\text{replacement}, \text{masking}, \text{generalization}, \text{deletion}\}$.

P_i is the priority field. Through preset numerical priorities (e.g., $P_i \in [1, 5]$, where a larger value indicates higher priority), a conflict resolution mechanism $\text{Resolve}(R_a, R_b) = \max(P_a, P_b)$ is constructed to ensure the orderliness of desensitization operations in complex scenarios.

Negative Case Base. If the large model produces flawed de-identification outputs—such as misidentified sensitive data or excessive masking during de-identification audits—we log four core pieces of information: original text (T), input prompt (P), model output (O), and error category (E). These elements form a quadruple tuple to formalize each problematic case, defined as:

$$S = \{T, P, O, E\} \tag{1}$$

Negative cases are converted into targeted training samples to conduct directional fine-tuning, strengthening the model's robustness against boundary and error-prone scenarios. Meanwhile, case analysis insights enable reverse optimization of the de-identification rule base, supplementing differentiated processing rules for special business contexts. This builds a closed-loop improvement pipeline spanning "problem collection (C) → analysis and attribution (A) → model optimization (M) → rule iteration (R)", formulated as:

$$Closed - Loop = C \rightarrow A \rightarrow M \rightarrow R \rightarrow C \quad (2)$$

De-identified Database. The de-identified data will be securely imported into the de-identification database according to predefined data models and storage structures.

Rule Iteration Validation Link. The de-identification database D and the de-identification rule base R form a data feedback loop, where the applicability of rules is inferred from the actual stored de-identified results. Model Optimization Data Link The de-identification database D supplies de-identified data samples containing business scenario characteristics to the negative case base c and the model optimization module M, assisting algorithms in identifying de-identification needs in complex scenarios, i.e.:

$$D = (C + M) \text{ (Data Samples + De-Identified Results)} \quad (3)$$

The above bidirectional interaction mechanism can be abstracted into a unified closed-loop model:

$$D \leftrightarrow (R \oplus C \oplus M) \quad (4)$$

where, $\leftrightarrow$ denotes bidirectional data flow, and $\oplus$ represents the collaborative optimization relationship among the rule base, case base, and model, jointly driving the dynamic evolution of the de-identification system.

3.2 Sensitive Component Identification

In the sensitive information recognition phase, we construct a three-dimensional data-driven prompt input system that integrates the original text, de-identification rule base, and negative case base. This system can be formally represented as:

$$Prompt = f(T, R, C) \quad (5)$$

where T represents the original text (the carrier of information to be processed), R represents the de-identification rule base (a structured set of standards), and C represents the negative case base (a collection of historical error patterns). These three elements are deeply integrated through the function f to form a dual-driven mechanism:

$$f(T, R, C) = RuleMatching(T, R) + ErrorExperience(T, C) \quad (6)$$

where RuleMatching$(T, R) = \sum_{i=1}^{n} \omega_i$ Match (T, r_i) (r_i is the i-th de-identification rule, and ω_i is the rule weight maintained by the rule base); ErrorExperience$(T, C) = \sum_{j=1}^{m} \alpha_j$ Avoid (T, C_i) C_i is the j-th negative case pattern, and α_j is the error pattern weight dynamically adjusted based on case frequency).

To ensure the standardization and consistency of large model processing, we introduce a priority function P and a format constraint function F:

$$NormalizedProcessing = F(P(f(T, R, C))) \tag{7}$$

where P defines the priority strategy for rule conflicts (e.g., $P(r_i) > P(r_j)$ indicates that rule i takes precedence over rule j). F constrains the output format (e.g., F (Output) = Sensitivity Type, Location, Processing Method).

Finally, the normalized prompt is input into the large model M to perform the sensitive information recognition task:

$$RecognitionResult = M(F(P(f(T, R, C)))) \tag{8}$$

This mechanism significantly enhances the model's ability to handle complex scenarios through three-dimensional data fusion and a dual-driven architecture, as shown in Table 1.

Table 1. Privacy-compliant data-driven dual-engine sensitive info ID system.

Task Overview
Your task is to accurately identify and label sensitive information in text according to the following rules. Strictly adhere to the sensitive type definitions, labeling formats, and precautions to avoid omissions, misjudgments, or over-labeling. The labeling must balance the rigor of rule matching with the flexibility of language comprehension
Sensitive Type Definitions [*de-identification database*]
Error Case References [*negative case base*]
Priority Rules: 1. **Longest Match Priority**, 2. **Ambiguity Resolution Rule**
Output Format
- Directly label the original text using the format [**Sensitive Type: Sensitive Content**], preserving the original text format and punctuation
- If no sensitive information is found in the text, return the standard format: **No sensitive content detected**
Verification Mechanism
After labeling, perform further checks against the following steps:
1. **Integrity Check**: Traverse all sensitive types in the [*de-identification database*] to ensure no omissions
2. **Compliance Check**: Verify that all labels conform to the format requirements (e.g., [Type: Content])
3. **Consistency Check**: Compare with similar cases in the [*negative case base*] to avoid repeating similar errors

3.3 Information Desensitization

After extracting and recognizing sensitive information from annotated texts, the LLM proceeds to the critical desensitization execution stage. Real-world production data covers diverse types, each requiring tailored desensitization strategies to avoid destroying inherent data business structures. To enable precise sensitive data processing, our method adopts a hybrid solution combining rules and LLM functional tools, with detailed tool implementations presented in Table 2.

Table 2. Data desensitization tool functions Set.

functions	description	example	param
rounding_off	Rounding of numerical or date data	13:25:15 → 13:00:00; 78.6 → 78	name: in_text, type: string, num. or date
masked	Masking parts of data, such as phone numbers and ID card numbers	152****1234	name: in_text, type: string, ID string
quantization	Adjusting the degree of data distortion through quantization intervals	27 → 30	name: in_text, type: float, num.
truncation	Truncating the tail of the data	010-88886666 → 010	name: in_text, type: float
hash	Mapping the input to a string of fixed length	8 → a17d281c4a	name: in_text, type: string
rerank	Reordering the values of a certain column in the database	22,31,27 → 31,27,22	name: in_list, type: list
encryption	The plaintext and ciphertext formats remain unchanged	15266661234 → 15173459527	name: in_str, type: string

The LLM invokes predefined rules from the rule base and dynamically adjusts processing logic via natural language processing. During computation, semantic parsing analyzes grammatical links between sensitive terms and their context to guarantee intact text syntax after desensitization, before matching suitable desensitization functions. The system then feeds function outputs into multi-turn dialogue prompts (Table 3) to guide the LLM in substituting sensitive content with sanitized equivalents. By tightly integrating rule engines, contextual reasoning and functional tools, the full workflow delivers efficient sensitive data masking while fully preserving original text semantics. The sanitized outputs thus strike a balanced tradeoff between regulatory compliance and textual readability.

Table 3. Privacy-Compliant Data-Driven Dual-Engine Sensitive Info ID System.

First-Round Prompt
Please provide the translation in the following JSON format:
"will call function list": ["function name": "xxx", "function in params": ["param1", "param2"], "reason about call function": "xx", "source text fragment": "" ,]
Text to be desensitized: ..... Analyze the input to determine the desensitization functions required.
Second-Round Prompt
desensitization functions selected in the previous step: Function execution results are as follows: Local execution results of the
"source text fragment": " ", "will call function list": ["function name":"xxx", "function in params": ["param1", "param2"], "reason about call function": "xx", "function run result": " " ,]
The above is the local execution result of the relevant desensitization functions. Please modify the original input according to the transformation results of the desensitization functions, strictly follow the desensitization requirements, output the desensitized text, and output it in JSON format:
"desensitized uttext" : "xxxx"

3.4 Desensitization Result Inspection and Evaluation

Once text de-identification finishes, the method launches automated validation powered by tailored prompt engineering and multi-dimensional verification modules (Table 4). Prompts integrate explicit inspection benchmarks and standardized error reporting guidelines: they list quantitative evaluation metrics including syntax validity and sensitive data masking accuracy, alongside uniform output templates for pinpointing exact error locations. In the validation stage, the LLM first parses sanitized text syntax to check for incomplete sentence structures and illogical modifiers, while a tense consistency algorithm detects cross-sentence logical flaws. The model then re-runs the de-identification rule base for a secondary sweep, verifying full compliance of sensitive data handling, and measures semantic similarity to detect any loss of core meaning caused by masking. Passing samples are archived into the knowledge base. Non-compliant outputs trigger automatic error logging, which stores raw text, full prompt sequences, and categorized error records in the negative case library alongside rule refinement recommendations. This closed feedback loop boosts single-pass de-identification accuracy and fuels iterative rule base updates, establishing a full iterative pipeline: identification → desensitization → inspection → optimization.

Table 4. Privacy-Compliant Data-Driven Dual-Engine Sensitive Info ID System.

Task Overview
The following de-identified text requires secondary inspection to ensure compliance with the de-identification ruleset requirements and semantic integrity. The inspection process must follow priority rules and meticulously record all compliance issues and optimization suggestions
1. Sensitive Information Processing Compliance Check (Priority: High): Verify whether all sensitive types are processed in accordance with the [De-Identification Ruleset v2.3.0]. Focus on investigating easily overlooked de-identification scenarios such as information nested in parentheses or mixed multilingual content
2. Grammar and Semantic Integrity Check (Priority: Medium): Analyze sentence structures to verify the completeness of subject-verb-object structures and the clarity of anaphoric references. Repair context logic breaks caused by de-identification, and check whether numerical generalization preserves critical information such as units and magnitude
3. Format Consistency and Special Scenario Check (Priority: Low): Ensure that the annotation format uniformly uses [Sensitive Type: De-Identified Content]
Qualified results must clearly state: "The de-identification results have passed secondary inspection and comply with the [De-Identification Ruleset v2.3.0] requirements."
Unqualified results must detail the problem location, type, specifics, and rule conflict situations

3.5 Knowledge Distillation

Knowledge distillation constitutes the core stage of model capability transfer, which efficiently transfers SQL generation expertise and optimizes model performance via two core procedures. The first module generates paired training data. It feeds sanitized real-business query texts into the teacher model DeepSeek-R1 to distill its powerful SQL generation knowledge. The workflow proceeds as follows: user queries first undergo thorough desensitization to guarantee privacy protection while retaining intact business semantics for teacher model input.

Leveraging deep semantic comprehension and standardized SQL syntax generation, DeepSeek-R1 outputs precise matching SQL statements, thereby constructing high-quality [query, SQL] paired samples.

The second step is the supervised fine-tuning (SFT) process [15], where the [query, SQL] data pairs generated in the first step serve as training corpus for the "student model" to be optimized. To validate the effectiveness of this approach, we integrated privacy-protected data aligned with real-world business scenarios and used it to train lightweight models. This paper selects Qwen2-7B as the baseline model M for experiments. The training dataset generated via knowledge distillation is denoted as $T = \{q_i, s_i, D_i\}$, where q_1 represents a natural language question, D denotes the corresponding database schema, and s_1 is the target SQL statement for the query and database. The objective of supervised fine-tuning is to minimize the following empirical loss, where L is a loss function quantifying the discrepancy between generated and ground-truth SQL statements, and M^* represents the optimized lightweight model. The formal expression is as follows:

$$\min \sum_{i=1}^{|T|} L\left(M^*\left(\sigma\left(q_i, D_i\right)\right), s_i\right) \tag{9}$$

Table 5. Prompts used.

Task Overview
Your task is to accurately identify and label sensitive information in the text according to the following rules. You must strictly follow the definitions of sensitive types, labeling formats, and precautions to avoid omissions, misjudgments, or over-labeling. The labeling process should balance the strictness of rule matching with the flexibility of language understanding
Sensitive Type Definitions: Refer to the latest version of the [Desensitization Database]
Error Case References: Refer to the typical error types in the [Negative Case Library]
Priority Rules: Longest Match First: When a text segment matches multiple sensitive type definitions, prioritize labeling the longest continuous string
Ambiguity Resolution: When the type cannot be clearly determined, label in the following order of priority: Name > ID Number > Mobile Number > Bank Card Number > Email
Output Format: Output the text after desensitization processing
Verification Mechanism: After labeling, perform a secondary check according to the following steps
Completeness Check: Review all sensitive types in the [Desensitization Database] to ensure no omissions
Compliance Check: Verify that all labels meet the format requirements (e.g., [Type: Content])
Consistency Check: Compare with similar cases in the [Negative Case Library] to avoid repeating the same type of errors
The original content is as follows: ....
Please perform the desensitization operation and provide the desensitized text

4 Experiment

4.1 Test Set Sampling

Following the pipeline in Sect. 3, we distilled 12.3K Text-to-SQL data pairs. Subsequent syntactic validation via an SQL parsing engine confirmed that 11.59K

Table 6. Model comparison of de-identification accuracy and per-sample token cost.

Model	Acc	Cost
deepseek-R1+base_prompt	78.7%	0.0884
deepseek-V3+base_prompt	74.3%	0.068
qwen2.5-32B+base_prompt	65.2%	0.056
qwen2.5-7B+base_prompt	56.4%	0.055
qwen2.5-7B + pipeline (Ours)	92.5%	0.015

pairs were syntactically valid. Among these qualified samples, 10K were allocated for training and 1.59K for evaluation. To further strengthen model robustness, we adopted prompt augmentation by randomly applying diverse system prompts during training. All dataset conversations were converted to the ShareGPT training format, ultimately yielding an expanded corpus of 50K training samples and 8K test samples.

4.2 Settings

We then conducted supervised fine-tuning of Qwen2.5-7B [16] on a single A100 GPU with the prepared training corpus. We fixed the unified dataset sequence length to 8192 to accommodate long input texts, and set the global batch size to 128. The Adam optimizer was adopted, with an initial learning rate of 2e-4 and a minimum learning rate of 1e-5. We applied QLoRA fine-tuning [17], which cuts the number of tunable parameters to boost training efficiency and hardware utilization. All training ran under BF16 precision; this format reduces computation and memory costs while preserving stable numerical accuracy. To validate our de-identification pipeline's performance, we set up comparative experiments. Several mainstream LLMs with basic prompts processed raw data as control groups, with metrics including de-identification accuracy and inference cost recorded in Table 5. Our experimental group leveraged Qwen2.5-7B as the core model powering the full proposed pipeline.

4.3 Main Results

De-identification pipeline results reveal that DeepSeek-R1 [18] achieves the highest accuracy under standalone de-identification prompts yet incurs the highest inference cost. Our proposed pipeline raises de-identification accuracy by 17.5% and cuts the average per-sample token cost by 83% relative to DeepSeek-R1, with even more pronounced performance gains against vanilla Qwen2.5-7B, as detailed in Table 6. All inference cost calculations adopt Alibaba Cloud's official token pricing standards listed in Table 7.

To analyze how each pipeline stage affects overall de-identification efficiency, we carried out ablation studies by removing individual modules: specifically Stage 1 (sensitive term recognition) and Stage 3 (de-identification validation),

Table 7. Alibaba cloud token pricing standard for LLM inference.

Model	Input Token Cost	Output Token Cost
deepseek-R1	0.004/K	0.016/K
deepseek-V3	0.002/K	0.008/K
qwen2.5-32B	0.004/K	0.012/K
qwen2.5-7B	0.005/K	0.001/K

Table 8. Ablation study of pipeline modules on de-identification performance.

Method	Accuracy	Token-Cost
all pipeline	92.5%	0.015
w/o stage1	78.3%	0.012
w/o stage3B	83.7%	0.011

Table 9. Performance comparison of existing models and Qwen2.5-7B trained on desensitized domain data.

Model	deepseek-R1	qwen-2.5 32B	qwen-2.5 7B	qwen-2.5 7B SFT
Accuracy	94.5%	87.6%	65.9%	91.5%

with results summarized in Table 8. The ablation outcomes confirm that Stage 2's pre-localization of sensitive terms is indispensable to reliable de-identification performance.

Finally, we fine-tuned Qwen2.5-7B using the sanitized dataset, with Text-to-SQL performance outcomes listed in Table 9. Experimental results demonstrate that the model trained on desensitized data gains markedly stronger domain-specific SQL generation capacity. This finding validates that our sanitized corpus faithfully retains authentic domain business patterns while eliminating privacy risks, making the entire framework suitable for real industrial deployment.

5 Conclusion

This paper presents an end-to-end privacy-preserving framework with hierarchical desensitization and knowledge distillation to address the privacy-performance-cost trade-off in industrial Text-to-SQL fine-tuning. Evaluations on real enterprise data show that our method improves de-identification accuracy by 17.5% and reduces per-sample token overhead by 83% compared with DeepSeek-R1. Ablation results verify that staged sensitive localization and multi-dimensional inspection effectively preserve authentic domain semantics while eliminating privacy risks. Fine-tuned via QLoRA on Qwen2.5-7B, our lightweight model yields competitive domain SQL generation performance and stable generalization without exposing raw sensitive data. This work fills the research gap in balanced privacy protection and cost efficiency, offering a practical and scalable solution for real-world Text-to-SQL deployment.

Acknowledgment. This work was supported by the Tianjin Science and Technology Program funded by Tianjin Municipal Science and Technology Bureau under Grant No. 25ZXSFSN00100.

References

1. Qin, B., et al.: A survey on text-to-SQL parsing: concepts, methods, and future directions. arXiv preprint arXiv:2208.13629 (2022)
2. Shi, L., Tang, Z., Zhang, N., Zhang, X., Yang, Z.: A survey on employing large language models for text-to-SQL tasks. arXiv preprint arXiv:2407.15186 (2024)
3. Xie, Y., et al.: Decomposition for enhancing attention: improving LLM-based text-to-SQL through workflow paradigm. arXiv preprint arXiv:2402.10671 (2024)
4. Sui, G., et al.: Reboost large language model-based text-to-SQL, text-to-Python, and text-to-function–with real applications in traffic domain. arXiv preprint arXiv:2310.18752 (2023)
5. Peng, X., Zhang, Y., Yang, J., Stevenson, M.: On the security vulnerabilities of text-to-SQL models. arXiv preprint arXiv:2211.15363 (2022)
6. Gou, J., Yu, B., Maybank, S.J., Tao, D.: Knowledge distillation: a survey. Int. J. Comput. Vision **129**(6), 1789–1819 (2021)
7. Cho, J.H., Hariharan, B.: On the efficacy of knowledge distillation. In: Proceedings of the IEEE/CVF International Conference on Computer Vision, pp. 4794–4802 (2019)
8. Fu, W., Wang, H., Gao, C., Liu, G., Li, Y., Jiang, T.: Practical membership inference attacks against fine-tuned large language models via self-prompt calibration. arXiv preprint arXiv:2311.06062 (2023)
9. Gupta, R., Tanwar, S., Al-Turjman, F., Italiya, P., Nauman, A., Kim, S.W.: Smart contract privacy protection using ai in cyber-physical systems: tools, techniques and challenges. IEEE Access **8**, 24746–24772 (2020)
10. Yang, Y., Huang, X., Sang, J.: Exploring the privacy protection capabilities of Chinese large language models. IEEE MultiMedia (2025)
11. Staab, R., Vero, M., Balunovićé, M., Vechev, M.: Beyond memorization: violating privacy via inference with large language models. arXiv preprint arXiv:2310.07298 (2023)
12. Voigt, P., Von dem Bussche, A.: The EU General Data Protection Regulation (GDPR). A Practical Guide, 1st ed., vol. 10, no. 3152676, pp. 10–5555. Springer International Publishing, Cham (2017)
13. Gostin, L.O., Levit, L.A., Nass, S.J.: Beyond the HIPAA Privacy Rule: Enhancing Privacy, Improving Health Through Research (2009)
14. Brown, H., Lee, K., Mireshghallah, F. Shokri, R., Tramèr, F.: What does it mean for a language model to preserve privacy? In: Proceedings of the 2022 ACM Conference on Fairness, Accountability, and Transparency, pp. 2280–2292 (2022)
15. Ouyang, L., et al.: Training language models to follow instructions with human feedback. In: Advances in Neural Information Processing Systems, vol. 35, pp. 27730–27744 (2022)
16. Yang, A., et al.: Qwen2.5 technical report. arXiv preprint arXiv:2412.15115 (2024)

17. Dettmers, T., Pagnoni, A., Holtzman, A., Zettlemoyer, L.: QLoRA: efficient fine-tuning of quantized LLMs. In: Advances in Neural Information Processing Systems, vol. 36, pp. 10088–10115 (2023)
18. Guo, D., et al.: DeepSeek-R1: incentivizing reasoning capability in LLMs via reinforcement learning. arXiv preprint arXiv:2501.12948 (2025)

The First 3D Integrated Web-Based Seft-Visualization Blockchain Structure

Anh-Khoa Ngo-Ho, Hoang-Du Thach, and Anh-Khoi Ngo-Ho(✉)

Faculty of Information Technology, Nam Can Tho University, 168 Nguyen Van Cu Street, An Binh Ward, Can Tho City, Vietnam
{nhakhoa,nhakhoi}@nctu.edu.vn, du220839@stu-dent.nctu.edu.vn

Abstract. The integration of 3D digital assets into the blockchain ecosystem has traditionally been limited to simple storage and metadata association, often referred to as Level 1 and Level 2 implementation. However, the critical challenge of direct, real-time visualization, defined here as Level 3, remains largely unaddressed due to the lack of native rendering support in decentralized environments. This paper proposes a novel, integrated system for the secure visualization of encrypted 3D models triggered by blockchain-based ownership verification. By synthesizing Ethereum-based smart contracts, AES-256-GCM authenticated encryption via the Web Crypto API, and WebGL-based rendering through the model-viewer framework, we establish a secure "Decryption-to-Display" mechanism. Our approach ensures that high-fidelity 3D data is decrypted only within the client's volatile memory using a dynamic Blob URL, effectively bypassing the need for insecure local storage or external software. Experimental results confirm that the proposed system achieves sub-3-s load times and maintains a consistent 60 FPS rendering performance on desktop environments. This research provides a practical framework for on-chain 3D visualization, providing a robust blueprint for secure and intuitive interaction with digital twins and metaverse assets.

Keywords: Blockchain · 3D Visualization · NFT · AES-256-GCM · WebGL · Smart Contracts · IPFS · Decentralized Ownership · Real-time Rendering · Digital Twins

1 Introduction

The rapid evolution of blockchain technology has fundamentally redefined digital ownership, transitioning from simple transactional ledgers to complex, decentralized ecosystems supporting diverse asset classes. Within this digital transformation, 3D digital assets represent a frontier of immense potential, encompassing critical applications ranging from architectural Computer-Aided Design (CAD) models and complex scientific visualizations to high fidelity components within the burgeoning metaverse. While the integration of Non-Fungible Tokens (NFTs) has provided a robust framework for establishing provenance, immutability, and scarcity, the current technological landscape remains disproportionately optimized for 2D media. Existing NFT standards and web-based blockchain interfaces offer native, seamless support for common image formats

L. Ding et al. (Eds.): APWeb-WAIM 2026, LNCS 16995, pp. 655–664, 2027.
https://doi.org/10.1007/978-981-92-5699-0_45

such as WebP, JPEG, and PNG, allowing for immediate visualization and interaction upon ownership verification. However, a significant systemic gap exists regarding the lifecycle of 3D assets. These high-quality 3D assets serve as the foundational input for our proposed web-based blockchain visualization structure. Currently, even when a 3D asset is stored and encrypted on-chain, no standardized interface exists to visualize it immediately after ownership verification, leaving the potential of high dimensional assets largely unrealized.

To understand the necessity of this research, the challenges of 3D integration can be categorized into three distinct evolutionary levels, and the relations between these levels form the core motivation of our work:

- Level 1 (Decentralized Storage): The industry has successfully addressed the storage of 3D models on-chain or through decentralized protocols like the InterPlanetary File System (IPFS). By minting NFTs with associated metadata, developers can link a token to a 3D asset; however, this level lacks the security necessary for exclusive content.
- Level 2 (Encryption and Access Control): This level involves the encryption of files. While owner-based encryption and smart contract verification exist, they typically follow classical cryptographic patterns that secure the data at rest but fail to bridge the gap to a seamless end-user experience.
- Level 3 (Real-time Secure Visualization): This unresolved level, and the primary focus of this study, is the mechanism for direct, real-time 3D visualization directly within the blockchain ecosystem without compromising the security guarantees established in Level 2.

The technical difficulty of Level 3 arises from the lack of native blockchain support for 3D rendering. Unlike 2D assets, which browsers can interpret natively, 3D models require high-performance rendering engines and specific GPU-accelerated environments. Users are frequently subjected to fragmented experiences, forced to leave their secure wallet environments, download large encrypted blobs, and utilize external third-party software to interact with their holdings. This process introduces severe security risks during the file-handling stage and significantly degrades the utility and liquidity of 3D NFTs.

This research addresses these deficiencies by proposing an end-to-end integrated system for the direct visualization of encrypted 3D models triggered by blockchain-based ownership verification. The core innovation lies not in a single new algorithm, but in the novel architectural synthesis of blockchain-based access control, client-side cryptography, and modern web rendering technologies into a cohesive "Decryption-to-Display" workflow. By integrating AES-256-GCM authenticated encryption via the Web Crypto API with WebGL-based rendering through the model-viewer framework, we demonstrate that 3D assets can achieve feature parity with 2D NFTs in terms of accessibility and verification flow. This production-ready solution ensures that 3D assets can be verified, decrypted in-memory, and displayed safely. Consequently, this work establishes a new standard for on-chain 3D visualization systems, enabling creators to guarantee exclusive access to high value 3D content while providing collectors with cryptographically verified ownership experiences that match the intuitiveness of traditional 2D media.

By bridging this gap, our study offers a technical blueprint for future Metaverse and Web 3.0 infrastructures where high-dimensional assets are the primary mode of interaction.

2 Related Work

The conceptual origin of modern blockchain technology is fundamentally rooted in cryptographically secure time-stamping (Haber and Stornetta, 1991), which evolved into decentralized ledgers (Nakamoto, 2008) and complex state machines capable of executing autonomous logic via smart contracts (Wood, 2014). Building upon these foundations, Non-Fungible Tokens (NFTs) have emerged as a protocol for representing unique digital ownership (Chohan, 2021), governed by established standards like EIP-721 (Entriken et al., 2018) and EIP-1155 (Radomski et al., 2018). While these tokens offer vast opportunities across various fields (Zheng et al., 2022), they also introduce critical security vulnerabilities requiring robust evaluation frameworks (Wang et al., 2021; Das et al., 2021). To handle the substantial storage requirements of high-fidelity digital assets, decentralized file systems such as IPFS are frequently employed to provide content-addressed data persistence (Benet, 2014; Nadini et al., 2021).

Recent advancements in artificial intelligence have significantly optimized 3D space reconstruction. Techniques integrating AI-driven neural rendering with geometric methods, as well as 3D Gaussian splatting, now allow for the rapid and high-fidelity generation of 3D models directly from standard RGB videos (Ngo et al., 2025; Ngo-Ho et al., 2026). In the specialized domain of 3D visualization, efficient management of models within a web environment necessitates sophisticated geometric modeling (Botsch et al., 2010), spatial indexing (Meagher, 1982; Guttman, 1984), and multiresolution rendering systems (Rusinkiewicz and Levoy, 2000). The convergence of blockchain architectures and 3D rendering is prominently observed in the development of the Metaverse and digital twins (Gadekallu et al., 2022; Suhail et al., 2022). Extensive surveys highlight the imperative for robust security frameworks in these environments (Wang et al., 2022) amidst persistent systemic challenges regarding scalability (Zheng et al., 2018). Specific applications of this convergence include secure data sharing for 3D printing (Baza et al., 2020), protecting author royalties through digital model watermarking (Nizamuddin et al., 2019), and smart contracts for additive manufacturing (Steger et al., 2018).

Despite the extensive body of work surrounding 3D data storage and Metaverse frameworks, there remains a notable absence of a practical, high-performance solution for the direct, real-time visualization of encrypted 3D models within a web-based blockchain interface. Current methodologies focus heavily on Level 1 storage or Level 2 access control encryption, but they fail to address the critical "Level 3" problem: providing a seamless system from ownership verification to instant rendering. This research significantly differentiates itself by proposing an integrated architecture that utilizes client-side decryption and WebGL-based rendering. Unlike existing frameworks that require external software, this approach enables users to interact with secure 3D assets directly within their decentralized wallet environment.

3 Proposed System Architecture

The core principle of the proposed system architecture is rooted in the orchestration of a "Zero-Knowledge Visualization" system, designed to ensure that raw 3D data is never exposed in its unencrypted state outside the volatile memory of the client's browser. To achieve this, the architecture is structurally divided into verification, cryptographic processing, and in-memory rendering workflows.

Unlike traditional NFT platforms that rely on public decentralized gateways for direct rendering, which often exposes assets to unauthorized scraping, our methodology introduces an intermediate cryptographic verification layer integrated directly into the rendering lifecycle. The fundamental logic is governed by an ownership-driven decryption trigger, where the system treats the user's wallet address as a dynamic cryptographic component to validate access rights before any data is processed.

The operational workflow, as illustrated in Fig. 1, is designed as a four-stage system that transitions the asset from a blockchain state to the WebGL rendering buffer. Initially, the system performs a handshake verification where the frontend interface queries the NFT3D smart contract to confirm if the connected wallet address satisfies the condition:

$$balanceOf\ (TokenID) > 0$$

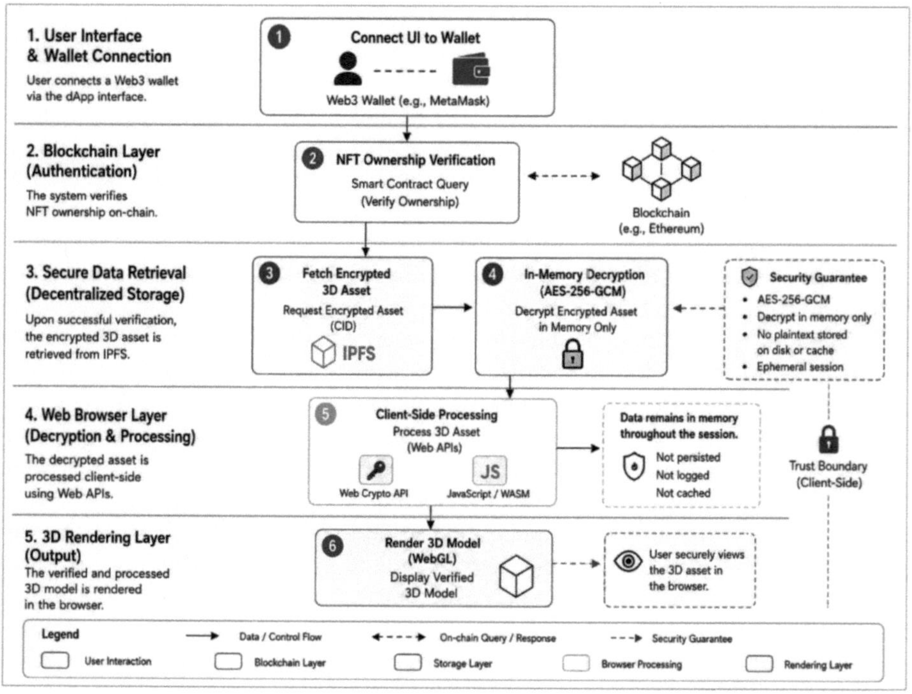

Fig. 1. The proposed integrated system for direct 3D visualization via blockchain ownership verification

To ensure high-fidelity security and performance, we implement a dual-layer cryptographic approach using the Blake2b algorithm for data integrity and AES-256-GCM for authenticated encryption. For any 3D model M represented as a sequence of bytes B, we first compute a unique identifier:

$$H(M) = Blake2b(B, digest_{size} = 32)$$

This offers superior performance on 64-bit platforms and serves as an immutable reference pointer within the Ethereum smart contract. During the encryption phase, the system utilizes AES in Galois/Counter Mode (GCM) to provide both confidentiality and authenticity. Let P be the plaintext 3D file and K be a randomly generated 256-bit symmetric key; the encryption function produces a ciphertext C and an authentication tag T through the relation:

$$(\mathrm{C}, \mathrm{T}) = \mathrm{AES} - \mathrm{GCM}_{\mathrm{K}}(\mathrm{IV}, \mathrm{P}, \mathrm{AAD})$$

where IV is a 96-bit Initialization Vector and AAD represents the TokenID. The inclusion of T is critical, as it ensures that any unauthorized modification to the encrypted model during its transit via IPFS will be detected immediately during the decryption phase, thereby preventing man-in-the-middle attacks on the 3D geometry.

3.1 In-Memory Decryption and Rendering Workflow

Upon successful verification, the encrypted blob C is retrieved from IPFS using the Content Identifier (CID) stored in the contract metadata, while the wrapped encryption key $K_{Wrapped}$ is simultaneously fetched. This wrapped key is a version of the symmetric key K that has been encrypted using a key derived from the owner's address.

The client-side cryptographic processing uses the Web Crypto API, where the user provides a signature to derive the local decryption key, unwrapping $K_{Wrapped}$ to yield K. The final stage is the dynamic injection of the decrypted plaintext P into the browser's memory. By converting the resulting binary data into a Blob URL, the system bypasses the need for local storage and feeds the data directly into the src attribute of a < model-viewer> component. This component leverages WebGL and the device's GPU to execute real-time rendering of the 3D model

This integrated logic ensures that the visualization of 3D assets on the blockchain achieves the same level of accessibility and security as traditional 2D NFTs, formally described in Algorithm 1.

Algorithm 1: Secure Decryption-to-Display System for 3D Assets

1. $owner \leftarrow NFT3D.\ ownerOf(T_{id})$
2. ***if*** $owner \neq U_{addr}$ **then**
3. ***return*** *Exception("Access Denied")*
4. ***end if***
5. $\nabla On - chain\ metadata\ retrieval$
6. $(CID, K_{wrapped}, IV, Tag) \leftarrow Storage3D.\ getMetadata(T_{id})$

$\nabla Off - chain\ encrypted\ data fetching$
$C \leftarrow IPFS.fetch(CID)$
$\nabla Client - side\ key\ derivation\ and\ unwrapping$
$K_{local} \leftarrow DeriveKey(Sig)$
$K \leftarrow UnwrapKey(K_{wrapped}, K_{local})$
$\nabla Authenticated\ Decryption\ (AES - 256 - GCM)$
$P \leftarrow Decrypt_{AES - GCM}(K, C, IV, Tag)$
$\nabla Integrity\ validation$
if $P = \emptyset$ ***then***
  return *Exception ("Data Integrity Violation")*
end if
$\nabla Zero - exposure\ rendering\ preparation$
$U_{blob} \leftarrow CreateVolatileURL(P)$
$WebGL.\ Load((U_{blob})$
return *Success*

4 Implementation Analysis and Discussion

To demonstrate the effectiveness of the proposed method and address the limitations of existing frameworks highlighted in current literature, we conducted comprehensive empirical evaluations. This section details the prototype implementation and evaluates the system across two primary dimensions: smart contract operational costs and in-memory rendering performance.

The backend infrastructure is built upon the Ethereum Sepolia testnet, utilizing Solidity version 0.8.28 to take advantage of enhanced security features and gas-efficient operations. The custom smart contracts were developed to manage ownership verification and store the unique hashes alongside their IPFS Content Identifiers (CIDs), ensuring a strict 1:1 mapping between the on-chain token and the off-chain encrypted file. The experimental frontend utilized a React-based architecture integrated with the Ethers.js library for blockchain state interaction and the Web Crypto API for native cryptographic operations. The implementation of the <model-viewer> component was specifically tuned for WebGL performance, utilizing a custom loading system that intercepts the decrypted binary stream and converts it into a temporary Blob URL, inherently preventing the browser from caching the plaintext data to the local disk.

To assess the economic feasibility of deploying the proposed architecture on an Ethereum-compatible network, we measured the gas consumption for all core smart contract operations during a complete asset lifecycle.

As detailed in Table 1, the total gas required for a complete lifecycle, from initial upload to secondary market transfer, is approximately 805,690 gas. While the prototype estimated cost (~$80.56 on Layer-1 Ethereum) represents a tangible deployment expense, these operations are highly optimized. By separating the heavy 3D data storage (IPFS) from the on-chain metadata pointers, the smart contract footprint is minimized.

Beyond cost efficiency, the system's ability to deliver a seamless user experience was validated through rigorous performance benchmarking. To quantify the real advantage of

Table 1. Estimated Gas Consumption and Transaction Costs for Core Smart Contract Operations

Operation	Gas used (estimated)	ETH equivalent	USD estimated cost*
uploadFile()	182,450	0.00729	$18.23
mintNFT()	245,890	0.00984	$24.60
setPrice()	78,230	0.00313	$7.82
buyNFT()	156,780	0.00627	$15.68
transferFile()	142,340	0.00569	$14.23
Total lifecycle	**805,690**	**0.03222**	**$80.56**

>Note: USD costs are prototype estimates based on a baseline exchange rate of approximately 1 ETH ≈ $2,500 during the testing phase. Actual costs may fluctuate based on network congestion and market volatility.

our "Decryption-to-Display" pipeline against existing paradigms (such as forcing users to download encrypted blobs and use external local software), we evaluated the system using a high-fidelity 50 MB 3D model.

Table 2. System Performance and In-Memory Rendering Metrics (Evaluated on a 50 MB 3D Model)

Metric category	Specific parameter	Evaluated result
Data processing	IPFS upload latency	45–120 s
	IPFS retrieval latency	200–800 ms
	AES-256-GCM encryption	12–25 s
	Client-side decryption	<150 ms
	IPFS cache hit rate	~85%
Rendering (desktop)	First paint time	450 ms
	Total load time	2.9 s
	Rendering frame rate	60 FPS (Stable)
	GPU utilization	35% – 45%

The results in Table 2 confirm that the proposed system successfully bridges the gap between decentralized security and seamless usability. Crucially, the Client-Side Decryption latency is strictly bounded under 150 ms via the Web Crypto API. Compared to traditional baseline approaches (where manual downloading and local decryption often take upwards of 15–30 s), our in-memory pipeline achieves a Total Load Time of just 2.9 s. Furthermore, the rendering engine is highly stable, maintaining a consistent 60 FPS while keeping GPU utilization at a manageable 35%–45%, ensuring that end-users do not experience hardware throttling during visualization.

While the proposed algorithm excels in securing intellectual property and providing a seamless viewing experience, the empirical data highlights inherent limitations that warrant discussion. First, as observed in Table 2, the IPFS Upload Latency (45–120 s) and AES-256-GCM Encryption (12–25 s) times represent a noticeable bottleneck during the initial asset creation phase for creators. Second, based on the cost analysis (Table 1), deploying this system directly on Ethereum Layer-1 incurs significant gas fees (~$80.56 per lifecycle), which could limit mass adoption for lower-value assets. Finally, the system relies entirely on a signature-derived "Wrapped Key"; thus, loss of private key access results in permanent irrecoverability of the 3D visual content.

Future research directions should address these constraints by deploying the smart contracts on Layer-2 (L2) rollups or Layer-3 (L3) application-specific chains to drastically reduce gas costs. Additionally, implementing progressive decryption protocols, where a low-resolution base mesh is decrypted first, followed by background streaming of high-resolution textures, could further mask network retrieval latencies for multi-gigabyte metaverse assets.

5 Conclusion

This research has successfully addressed the critical "Level 3" challenge in the blockchain ecosystem by establishing a novel, integrated system for the direct visualization of encrypted 3D models. Throughout the study, we have demonstrated that the primary barrier to 3D asset adoption was not merely a matter of decentralized storage or basic encryption, but rather the absence of a seamless mechanism to bridge ownership verification with real-time rendering. By synthesizing Ethereum-based smart contracts, AES-256-GCM authenticated encryption, and WebGL-based visualization frameworks, we have provided a technical solution that allows high-fidelity 3D assets to achieve feature parity with traditional 2D NFTs. The proposed architecture ensures that 3D models remain cryptographically secure within decentralized storage while being instantly accessible for interaction within a user's secure wallet environment. Our experimental results confirm that this approach maintains high-performance standards, with sub-3-s load times and consistent 60 FPS rendering on modern web interfaces, effectively proving that security does not need to be sacrificed for user experience.

Looking forward, several promising research directions emerge from this foundation. First, the integration of quantum-resistant cryptographic algorithms, such as CRYSTALS-Kyber, could further future-proof the "Wrapped Key" mechanism against emerging computational threats. Second, the exploration of Layer-3 rollups and specialized Data Availability (DA) layers could reduce gas costs and further minimize the latency of fetching large-scale 3D geometry from decentralized networks. Additionally, the implementation of progressive decryption protocols would allow for the streaming of massive, multi-gigabyte 3D environments, enabling a more immersive and scalable Metaverse. Ultimately, this work contributes to the broader vision of Web 3.0 by transforming the blockchain from a static ledger of ownership into a dynamic, secure, and highly visual medium for digital interaction. The transition from "Level 1" storage to "Level 3" instant visualization marks a significant milestone in the evolution of digital twins and high-dimensional assets, laying the groundwork for a future where the virtual and decentralized worlds are indistinguishable in their intuitiveness and security.

References

Baza, M., et al.: Blockchain-based secure and privacy-preserving data sharing for 3D printing. IEEE Access. **8**, 110833–110848 (2020). https://doi.org/10.1109/ACCESS.2020.3013233

Benet, J.: IPFS - content addressed, versioned, P2P file system. arXiv. (2014) https://arxiv.org/abs/1407.3561

Botsch, M., Kobbelt, L., Pauly, M., Alliez, P., Lévy, B.: Polygon Mesh Processing. CRC Press (2010). https://doi.org/10.1201/b10688

Chohan, U. W. (2021). Non-fungible tokens: blockchains, scarcity, and value. SSRN Electron. J. https://ssrn.com/abstract=3822743

Das, D., Bose, P., Ruaro, N., Kruegel, C., Vigna, G.: Understanding security issues in the NFT ecosystem. arXiv. (2021) https://arxiv.org/abs/2111.08893

Entriken, W., Shirley, D., Evans, J., Sachs, R.: EIP-721: Non-Fungible Token Standard. Ethereum Improvement Proposal No. 721 (2018) https://eips.ethereum.org/EIPS/eip-721

Gadekallu, T.R., et al.: Blockchain for the metaverse: a review. arXiv. (2022) https://arxiv.org/abs/2203.09738

Guttman, A.: R-trees: a dynamic index structure for spatial searching. In: Proceedings of the 1984 ACM SIGMOD International Conference on Management of Data, pp. 47–57. ACM (1984). https://doi.org/10.1145/602259.602266

Haber, S., Stornetta, W.S.: How to time-stamp a digital document. J. Cryptol. **3**(2), 99–111 (1991). https://doi.org/10.1007/BF00196791

Meagher, D.: Geometric modeling using octree encoding. Comput. Graphics Image Process. **19**(2), 129–147 (1982). https://doi.org/10.1016/0146-664X(82)90104-6

Nadini, M., et al.: Mapping the NFT revolution: market trends, trade networks, and visual features. Sci. Rep. **11**(1), 10900 (2021). https://doi.org/10.1038/s41598-021-00053-8

Nakamoto, S. (2008). Bitcoin: A Peer-to-Peer Electronic Cash System, Bitcoin. https://bitcoin.org/bitcoin.pdf

Ngo-Ho, A.K., Ngo-Ho, A.K., Nguyen, T.L.: Automatic 3D space reconstruction system from video using 3D Gaussian splatting. In: Communications in Computer and Information Science, vol. 2713. Springer, Singapore (2026). https://doi.org/10.1007/978-981-95-3355-8_25

Ngo, H.-A.-K., Nguyen, V.-L., Huynh, K.-T., Ngo, H.-A.-K.: Advancing 3D reconstruction: integrating AI-driven neural rendering with geometric techniques for high-fidelity model generation from RGB video. In: Proceedings of the 15th International Conference on Computational Science and Network Intelligence (CSoNet 2025) (2025)

Nizamuddin, N., et al.: Blockchain-based framework for protecting author royalty of 3D-printable digital models. Arabian J. Sci. Eng. **44**, 3849–3866 (2019). https://doi.org/10.1007/s13369-018-03706-0

Radomski, W., Cooke, A., Castonguay, P., Therien, J., Binet, E., Sandford, R.: EIP-1155: Multi Token Standard. Ethereum Improvement Proposal No. 1155 (2018) https://eips.ethereum.org/EIPS/eip-1155

Rusinkiewicz, S., Levoy, M.: QSplat: a multiresolution point rendering system for large meshes. In: Proceedings of the 27th Annual Conference on Computer Graphics and Interactive Techniques (SIGGRAPH), pp. 343–352. ACM (2000). https://doi.org/10.1145/344779.344940

Steger, J., et al.: Secure additive manufacturing with smart contracts. Comput. Ind. **97**, 93–104 (2018). https://doi.org/10.1016/j.compind.2018.02.001

Suhail, S., et al.: Blockchain-based digital twins: research trends, issues, and future challenges. ACM Comput. Surv. **54**(11s), 1–34 (2022). https://doi.org/10.1145/3453165

Wang, Q., Li, R., Wang, Q., Chen, S.: Non-fungible token (NFT): overview, evaluation, opportunities and challenges. arXiv. (2021) https://arxiv.org/abs/2105.07447

Wang, Y., et al.: A survey on metaverse: fundamentals, security, and privacy. IEEE Commun. Surv. Tutorials. **25**(1), 319–352 (2022). https://doi.org/10.1109/COMST.2022.3202047

Wood, G. (2014). Ethereum: A Secure Decentralised Generalised Transaction Ledger. Ethereum Project Yellow Paper. https://ethereum.github.io/yellowpaper/paper.pdf

Zheng, Z., et al.: Blockchain challenges and opportunities: a survey. Int. J. Web Grid Serv. **14**(4), 352–375 (2018). https://doi.org/10.1504/IJWGS.2018.095647

Zheng, Z., Li, S., Chen, J.: A survey: implementations of non-fungible token system in different fields. arXiv. (2022) https://arxiv.org/abs/2209.15288

Demo Track

THESIS-CHECKER: An LLM-Based Configurable Service for Thesis Compliance Review

Ruixiao Huang[1,2], Ruize Gao[1,2], Weilong Ding[1,2(✉)], Zihang Yin[1,2], and Zhuofeng Zhao[1,2]

[1] Beijing Key Laboratory of Key Technologies for AI+ Domain Applications, North China University of Technology, Beijing 100144, China
{dingweilong,2023312120127}@ncut.edu.cn

[2] School of AI & CS, North China University of Technology, Beijing 100144, China

Abstract. Automated thesis compliance checking faces two major challenges: cross-institutional adaptability and reliable long-document analysis. We propose THESIS-CHECKER, a configurable automated review Web service. It adopts a configurable rule-routing mechanism that enables efficient adaptation to different institutional requirements through reusable templates and rule sets. We further design a two-stage multi-model orchestration mechanism: high-concurrency preliminary screening of lightweight tasks, followed by in-depth precision reasoning for complex logic, reducing response latency while improving analysis efficiency. To address LLM inference instability, we introduce stream-based heartbeat monitoring and token-length constraints to resolve interruptions and redundancy. Prototype evaluation demonstrates the practical effectiveness of the proposed service, efficiently completing the review process and providing an extensible framework for standardized thesis management. A demo video of THESIS-CHECKER is available at https://youtu.be/nLh4C0x5rSo.

Keywords: Large Language Models · Thesis Review · Configurable Services · Model Orchestration · Thesis Revision Assistance

1 Introduction

The review of degree theses is an essential part of ensuring the quality of higher education, which primarily relies on manual, page-by-page comparison. In practice, automated thesis compliance review faces three major challenges. (1) High cross-institutional adaptation costs. Existing tools often hard-code rules into software, making it difficult to flexibly adapt to varying detailed requirements when standards change. (2) Stability and efficiency in processing long documents are hard to balance. Traditional rules cannot identify deep logical errors, while directly using a single large language model (LLM) to process long texts leads to high latency and unstable outputs. (3) Existing review tools lack a closed-loop workflow from problem location to precise revision, further hindering the practical application for both students and administrators.

Ruixiao Huang and Ruize Gao contributed equally to this work.

L. Ding et al. (Eds.): APWeb-WAIM 2026, LNCS 16995, pp. 667–670, 2027.
https://doi.org/10.1007/978-981-92-5699-0_46

Recent advances in LLMs have shown promising capabilities in writing assistance and automated assessment [1]. Based on these advances, we develop THESIS-CHECKER, a configurable compliance review service for university theses. Our contributions are as follows.

THESIS-CHECKER is a configurable LLM-based thesis review service dedicated to degree thesis compliance review, and demonstrates practical feasibility in real-world campus scenarios.

- We propose a hybrid review mechanism based on dynamic configuration and task routing. It achieves low-cost cross-institutional adaptation by dispatching review tasks to either local deterministic algorithms or downstream LLMs [2].
- We design a two-stage model orchestration pattern with robustness optimization. Combining high-concurrency preliminary screening with in-depth precision reasoning, it introduces stream-based heartbeat monitoring and token-length constraints to ensure stable long-document processing.
- We validate the practical value of the service in real-world scenarios. THESIS-CHECKER covers the entire review workflow, improving review efficiency by providing in-line annotations and structured quality summaries.

2 Service Overview and Key Modules

THESIS-CHECKER adopts a decoupled modular architecture supported by a Global Configuration Engine, which dynamically injects cross-institutional review templates into the pipeline without modifying the underlying code. As illustrated in Fig. 1, the standardized review process comprises three main phases, including Input and Document Process, Analysis driven by a Rule-Based Deterministic Process, and Dual-File Output. Through this configuration-driven workflow, the service aggregates detection results into dual-format reports, achieving a complete closed loop from specification self-checking to revision assistance.

2.1 Foundation Analysis and Rule Verification Module

In the Input and Document Process stage, a FIFO queue sequences multi-user requests. The service then combines image and table analysis and regular expression-based pattern matching to accurately isolate core content blocks, effectively filtering out background noise. For rule verification, the module employs a task routing architecture based on dynamic rule pool assembly. Secretaries can con-figure templates via a backend portal based on two key dimensions, namely Position Verification, such as cover and abstract, and Category Verification, such as format and content. Consequently, formatting rules are directly scheduled to local deterministic algorithms for precise interception, while complex semantic tasks are extracted as context slices and forwarded to the downstream LLM orchestration module. Finally, the service synchronously outputs results into a Summary Report Dashboard for overall assessment and an Annotated Document View for quick tracing.

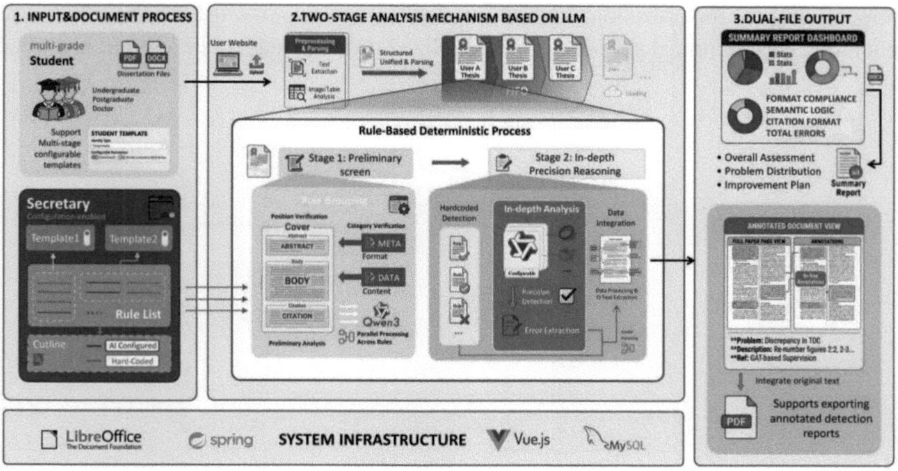

Fig. 1. Overall architecture of THESIS-CHECKER

2.2 Two-Stage Multi-model Orchestration Module

This module resolves engineering pain points of LLMs in processing long documents via a task-driven decoupled architecture. The first stage performs high-concurrency preliminary screening. The server divides the thesis into fine-grained segments and schedules models in parallel to rapidly identify potential non-compliance areas and output issue locations. The second stage conducts in-depth precision reasoning. This stage bifurcates into two parallel execution tracks, including Hardcoded Detection for processing local deterministic format-ting rules and configurable In-depth Analysis for handling complex semantics. Finally, a Data Integration module merges the results from both parallel tracks with the original text via O-Text Extraction to generate precise and context-aware modification suggestions. To address LLM logical hallucinations and inference interruptions [3], we introduce a robustness optimization strategy. In-stead of traditional fixed timeouts, a stream-based heartbeat monitoring mechanism tracks character output in real-time; if generation stagnates, it quickly triggers a parallel retry. Additionally, a token-length-based filtering strategy is applied to the first stage: outputs exceeding preset thresholds trigger an automatic circuit breaker to restart the session, effectively blocking erroneous information spread and ensuring data quality for detailed analysis.

3 Evaluation

To evaluate practical performance, we tested a 31,000-word master's thesis containing 40 figures and 38 references. THESIS-CHECKER completed the comprehensive multi-model analysis within 120 s, significantly outperforming manual checks that typically require tens of minutes. The service accurately identified 40 formatting errors and 23 deep semantic issues, effectively covering common pre-submission deduction items. By compensating for the precision shortcomings of manual reviews, the service offers efficient and stable technical support for standardized thesis management, as demonstrated in Fig. 2.

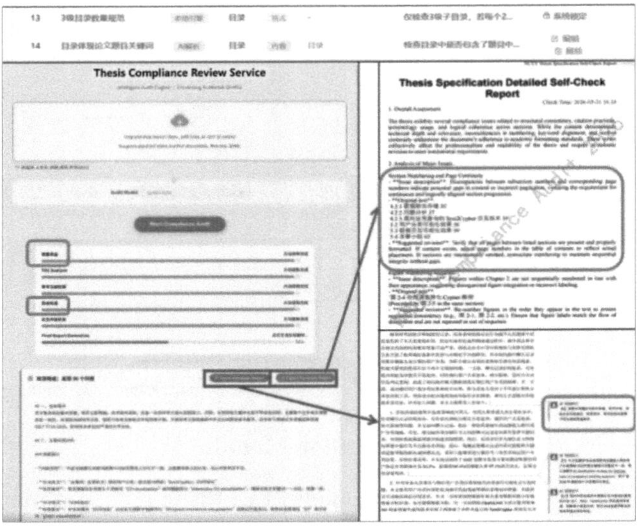

Fig. 2. Demonstration of the review workflow

4 Conclusion

We propose THESIS-CHECKER, an automated degree thesis pre-review service integrating a dynamic configuration engine, rule-based routing, and a robust two-stage LLM orchestration mechanism to efficiently verify formatting and semantic issues. Evaluation on a 31,000-word thesis confirms its efficiency. Future work will focus on expanding multi-institutional templates and optimizing model scheduling strategies.

Acknowledgments. This work was supported by Beijing Key Lab of AI+ Domain Applications (No. 110051360026XN086-12) and National Undergraduate Training Program for Innovation (No. 10805136026XN073-293).

References

1. Xiao, C., Ma, W., Xu, S.X., Zhang, K., Wang, Y., Fu, Q.: From automation to augmentation: large language models elevating essay scoring landscape. arXiv. (2024). https://doi.org/10.48550/arXiv.2401.06431
2. He, H., Ding, W., Zhang, H., Zhao, Z.: A LLMs-based procuratorial service for detecting drug trafficking on digital forensics data. In: 22nd International Conference on Service-Oriented Computing (ICSOC 2024), pp. 254–258 (2024)
3. Yang, Y., Ding, W., Gu, Y., Zhang, H., Wei, W., Gao, H.: Beyond data heterogeneity: a multivariate time series forecasting for energy systems through enhanced Channel fusion in frequency domain. Inf. Fusion. **127**, 103870 (2026)

DySRec: Dynamic Context-Aware Psychometric Scale Recommendation via Multi-Agent Collaboration

Yanzeng Li[1], Xiaoning Cao[1], Jialun Zhong[2], Jianpeng Hu[2], Jiangshan Tan[3,7], Ningning Liu[4], Feng Xiang[5], and Shasha Han[6,7](✉)

[1] Institute of Artificial Intelligence and Future Networks, Beijing Normal University, Zhuhai, China
liyanzeng@bnu.edu.cn
[2] Wangxuan Institute of Computer Technology, Peking University, Beijing, China
[3] Fuwai Hospital, Chinese Academy of Medical Sciences, Beijing, China
[4] Peking University Sixth Hospital, Peking University Institute of Mental Health, Beijing, China
[5] Beijing Malt Butler Technology Co., Ltd, Beijing, China
[6] School of Population Medicine and Public Health, Chinese Academy of Medical Sciences, Beijing, China
hanshasha@pumc.edu.cn
[7] Peking Union Medical College, Beijing, China

Abstract. Selecting psychometric scales requires integrating patient information, behaviors, and dynamic context. Existing systems use static pipelines or predict symptoms from isolated inputs, limiting dynamic assessment and transparent decision-making. We propose DySRec, a multi-agent conversational system for dynamic scale recommendation. DySRec engages users in multi-turn dialogue, models scale selection as a sequential decision process, and coordinates specialized agents for context maintenance, scale recommendation, risk monitoring, and decision logging. It captures semantic, behavioral, and historical signals to dynamically update user representations and compute scale-context compatibility. A closed-loop refinement mechanism guides conversation to elicit missing attributes. We present the prototype design, and the system has been verified in a real-world deployment.

Keywords: Psychometric Scale Recommendation · Multi-Agent System

1 Introduction

Psychometric assessment is central to psychological diagnosis, screening, and intervention planning [12,14]. Standardized scales measure latent constructs such as depression and anxiety, supporting evidence-based decisions [8,13]. However,

Y. Li and X. Cao contributed equally.

L. Ding et al. (Eds.): APWeb-WAIM 2026, LNCS 16995, pp. 671–675, 2027.
https://doi.org/10.1007/978-981-92-5699-0_47

selecting appropriate scales and adapting assessment over time remains challenging: clinicians must continuously integrate utterances, behavioral signals, prior results, and context to update their understanding and determine next steps [3,11]. Most existing automated systems treat psychometric evaluation as static inference, following predefined pipelines or predicting symptom severity from isolated inputs [1,5]. These approaches assume a fixed assessment policy and ignore the dynamic evolution of user states or shifting objectives [10]. Recent LLM-based methods extract nuanced psychological signals from text [6,9], but focus on state estimation rather than adaptive policy planning. Moreover, real clinical practice involves targeted follow-up questions to clarify ambiguous or missing information before administering instruments [2,7], which is a feedback mechanism absent from current systems.

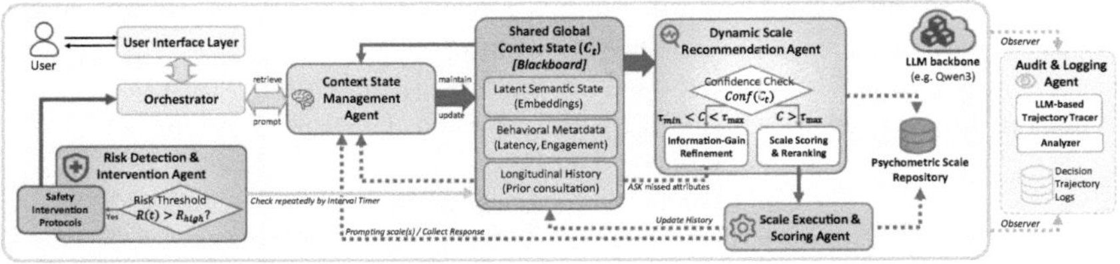

Fig. 1. DySRec architecture. Different arrows represent different data flows; an Orchestrator organizes the workflow and serves as gateway to the user interface; inter-agent communication uses JSON with predefined schema.

We propose DySRec, a *dy*namic, psychometric *s*cale *rec*ommendation framework grounded in multi-agent collaboration. DySRec formulates assessment as sequential decision-making, where specialized agents maintain a shared context state, recommend scales, monitor risk, and log decisions. This decomposition enables explicit modeling of competing objectives, including informativeness, user burden, and safety, while a closed-loop refinement mechanism actively elicits missing attributes to reduce recommendation uncertainty.

2 Methodology and System Architecture

DySRec models psychometric assessment as a sequential decision process $\mathcal{M} = \langle \mathcal{C}, \mathcal{A}, \mathcal{R}, \mathcal{T} \rangle$, where $\mathcal{C}$ is the evolving context state, $\mathcal{A}$ is the scale action space, $\mathcal{R}$ is the risk-aware policy, and $\mathcal{T}$ is the state transition function Fig. 1.

Dynamic Context State. A global context state $C_t = \Phi(u_t, C_{t-1}) \in \mathbb{R}^d$ serves as shared memory, updated by each user utterance u_t. It concatenates LLM-derived semantic embeddings (emotional valence, symptom mentions), behavioral metadata (latency, engagement), and longitudinal history (prior scores, diagnostic trajectories).

Information-Gain Driven Refinement. Before recommendation, the *Recommendation Agent* evaluates state completeness via confidence $Conf(C_t) = 1 - |\{i \in \mathcal{K}_{req} : i \notin C_t\}|/|\mathcal{K}_{req}|$. If $\tau_{min} < Conf(C_t) < \tau_{max}$, a *Refinement Loop* selects the attribute $a^* = \arg\max_a[H(C_t) - \mathbb{E}[H(C_t|a)]]$ maximizing expected information gain, enabling active uncertainty reduction.

Adaptive Scale Scoring and Selection. When $Conf(C_t) > \tau_{max}$, scales are scored as $S_{cand}(s) = \mathbf{w}^\top[A(s), Pr(s)]^\top$, where $A(s)$ is cosine similarity between C_t and the scale's characteristic vector, and $Pr(s)$ favors shorter or complementary instruments. The LLM then re-ranks and filters candidates to yield S_{final}.

Risk-Aware Coordination. A *Risk Agent* computes $R(t) = \sigma(\alpha E_t + \beta K_t + \gamma L_t + \delta S_t) \in [0, 1]$, where E, K, L, S capture emotional volatility, high-risk keywords, linguistic anomalies, and historical severity. If $R(t) > R_{high}$, a hard override triggers immediate clinical intervention.

Multi-Agent Architecture. DySRec adopts Blackboard-style communication [4] where agents read/write a shared versioned context C. Five agents collaborate: **Context State Management** (maintains C, processes refinement), **Dynamic Scale Recommendation** (multi-step selection or missing-attribute feedback), **Risk Detection & Intervention** (estimates risk, can override, halt, and trigger emergency), **Scale Execution & Scoring** (presents scales, auto-scores via JSON schemas, feeds back to C), and **Audit & Logging** (records decisions, risk evaluations, interventions for transparency).

Implementation. We use Qwen3 [15] as the backbone LLM with $\tau_{\min} = 0.2$, $\tau_{\max} = 0.8$, $R_{\text{high}} = 0.85$ (pilot-calibrated with domain experts). DySRec is deployed in "Black Hole Roast", a mobile mental health app serving 5,000+ users with adaptive recommendation across 53 scales Fig. 2.

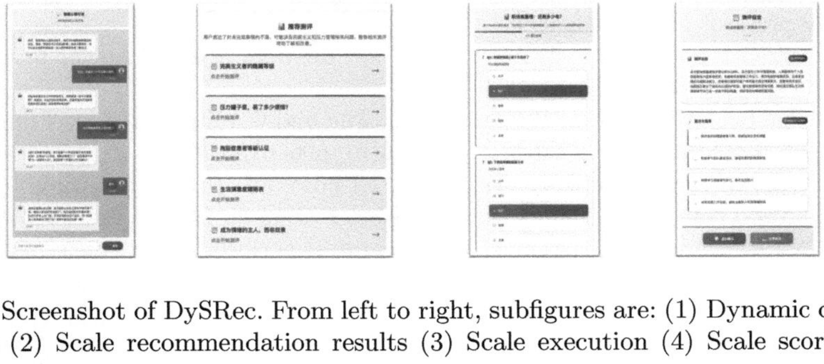

Fig. 2. Screenshot of DySRec. From left to right, subfigures are: (1) Dynamic dialogue process (2) Scale recommendation results (3) Scale execution (4) Scale scoring and interpretation.

3 Conclusion

We introduced DySRec[1], a dynamic context-aware psychometric scale recommendation framework grounded in multi-agent collaboration. By modeling assessment as a sequential decision process, DySRec moves beyond static symptom prediction toward adaptive policy-level reasoning. The system integrates incremental context modeling, adaptive scale scoring, closed-loop information refinement, and safety-driven risk control within an auditable architecture. As a deployed system, DySRec demonstrates how structured agent decomposition and LLM-based semantic modeling can jointly support interactive, transparent, and safety-conscious psychometric workflows.

Acknowledgments. This work was supported by National Natural Science Foundation of China (No. 82304269), the Chinese Academy of Medical Sciences Innovation Fund for Medical Sciences (No. 2023-I2M-3-008) and the Key Research and Development Program of Jiangxi Province (No. 20244AFI92004).

References

1. Calvo, R.A., Milne, D.N., Hussain, M.S., Christensen, H.: Natural language processing in mental health applications using non-clinical texts. Nat. Lang. Eng. **23**(5), 649–685 (2017)
2. DeJonckheere, M., Vaughn, L.M.: Semistructured interviewing in primary care research: a balance of relationship and rigour. Family medicine and community health **7**(2), e000057 (2019)
3. Groth-Marnat, G.: Handbook of psychological assessment. John Wiley & Sons (2009)
4. Han, B., Zhang, S.: Exploring advanced LLM multi-agent systems based on blackboard architecture. arXiv preprint arXiv:2507.01701 (2025)
5. Hilty, D.M., Cheng, Y., Luxton, D.D.: Artificial intelligence and predictive modeling in mental health. In: Digital Mental Health: The Future is Now, pp. 323–350. Springer, Cham (2025). https://doi.org/10.1007/978-3-031-59936-1_13
6. Hua, Y., et al.: Large language models in mental health care: a scoping review. arXiv preprint arXiv:2401.02984 (2024)
7. Kramer, G.P., Bernstein, D.A., Phares, V.: Introduction to clinical psychology, Cambridge University Press (2019)
8. Kroenke, K., Spitzer, R.L., Williams, J.B.: The phq-9: validity of a brief depression severity measure. J. Gen. Intern. Med. **16**(9), 606–613 (2001)
9. Li, S., et al.: A community-codesigned LLM-powered chatbot for primary care: a randomized controlled trial. Nature Health pp. 1–13 (2026)
10. Liu, X., et al.: A comparison of deep learning performance against health-care professionals in detecting diseases from medical imaging: a systematic review and meta-analysis. The lancet digital health **1**(6), e271–e297 (2019)
11. Meyer, G., et al.: Psychological testing and psychological assessment: A review of evidence and issues. Am. Psychol. **56**(2), 128 (2001)

[1] Demo Video: https://vimeo.com/1165370352.

12. Myers, K., Winters, N.C.: Ten-year review of rating scales. i: overview of scale functioning, psychometric properties, and selection. Journal of the American Academy of Child & Adolescent Psychiatry **41**(2), 114–122 (2002)
13. Spitzer, R.L., Kroenke, K., Williams, J.B., Löwe, B.: A brief measure for assessing generalized anxiety disorder: the gad-7. Arch. Intern. Med. **166**(10), 1092–1097 (2006)
14. WHO: ICD-11: international classification of diseases (2022). 11th revision
15. Yang, A., et al.: Qwen3 technical report. arXiv preprint arXiv:2505.09388 (2025)

TraceTG: A Traceable Testing Platform for Developing a Temporal Graph Database Management System

Jinghe Song(✉) and Jiacheng Chen

School of Computer Science and Engineering, Beihang University, XueYuan Road #37, Beijing, China 100191
{songjh,cjcstu}@buaa.edu.cn

Abstract. The development of a database management system requires repeated performance tests across system versions to verify its design and address issues. However, this testing procedure becomes costly and error-prone in the context of temporal graph databases, where workloads, database snapshots, and logs are too large to be managed manually by developers, making issue tracing expensive. Existing benchmark-style evaluations and database-specific testing tools lack support for tracing and reusing such testing artifacts across development iterations in the temporal graph database context. We develop TraceTG, a traceable testing platform for developing temporal graph database management systems. TraceTG organizes each test as a traceable experiment unit and supports database reuse, workload execution, result collection, and historical inspection. The demonstration shows how developers create experiment units, monitor execution pipelines, reuse historical configurations, replay previous testing units, and compare results across database versions.

Keywords: temporal graph database · database development · database testing · performance regression

1 Introduction

Temporal graphs are graph data whose vertices, edges, and attributes evolve over time [1]. The management of such data is crucial for analyzing the dynamics of real-world systems represented by temporal graphs, and many temporal graph data management systems have been developed [2]. During the development of a temporal graph database management system, each new database version must be repeatedly tested on representative datasets and workloads to validate its performance. This process is costly and error-prone: temporal graph datasets are usually large and require a long time to import, update workloads may affect later baselines, and results are hard to reproduce when versions, snapshots, environments, workloads, and logs are recorded separately and managed manually.

L. Ding et al. (Eds.): APWeb-WAIM 2026, LNCS 16995, pp. 676–680, 2027.
https://doi.org/10.1007/978-981-92-5699-0_48

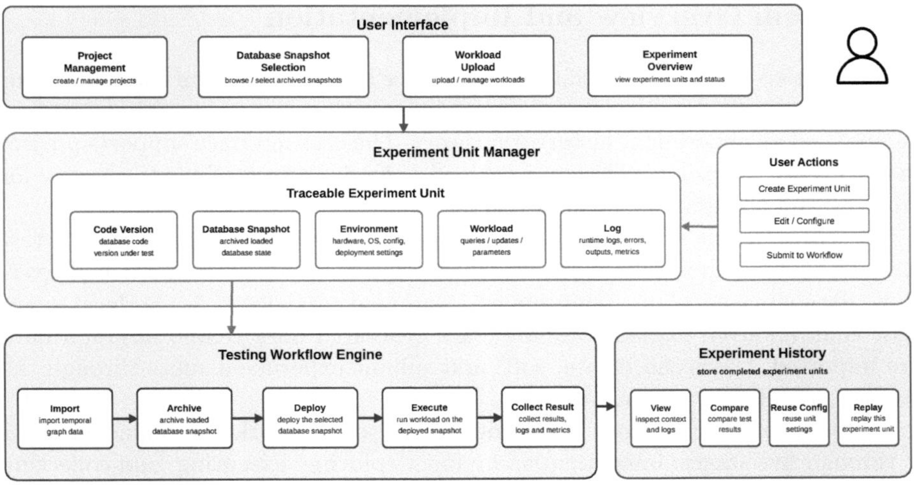

Fig. 1. System architecture of TraceTG.

Existing work mainly supports two kinds of testing practices. The first is performance-oriented evaluation. Temporal graph systems are commonly evaluated by running selected temporal operations, such as snapshot queries, temporal traversal, ingestion, and graph analytics, on synthetic, real, or benchmark-derived datasets and workloads [3–5]. Such evaluations are important for reporting the capability of a temporal graph system, but their results usually lack traceable development contexts, such as the database code version, loaded graph state, environment, workload, and logs. This limits their ability to support iterative temporal graph database development.

The second is database-oriented regression and replay testing. Mature database systems provide regression tests, test frameworks, upgrade validation, and replay-based tools for repeated validation during system development. These tools are effective within their own ecosystems, but they are not directly reusable in our setting. For example, PostgreSQL [6] and MySQL [7] testing frameworks are open-source but tightly integrated with their own source trees, test languages, expected outputs, and server assumptions. Oracle replay-based testing [8] is also tied to the Oracle ecosystem. Therefore, these solutions cannot directly provide a portable testing layer for temporal graph database development.

To address this gap, we develop TraceTG, a traceable testing platform for large-scale temporal graph database development. TraceTG focuses on three objectives: **(1) traceable experiment management**, which binds the code version, database snapshot, environment, workload, and logs into one unit; **(2) snapshot reuse and state management**, which reuses archived loaded database states and restores stable baselines for later tests; and **(3) historical comparison**, which stores completed units and supports result comparison, configuration reuse, and replay.

2 System Overview and Implementation

Figure 1 shows the system architecture of TraceTG. The platform consists of four functional parts: a user interface, an experiment unit manager, a testing workflow engine, and an experiment history repository. The user interface supports project management, snapshot selection, workload upload, and experiment overview for creating and configuring testing tasks.

The experiment unit manager is the core component. It organizes each test as a traceable experiment unit, which binds five types of context: code version, database snapshot, environment, workload, and logs. A database snapshot is an archived loaded database state generated after temporal graph data are imported. Users can create, edit, and submit experiment units through the actions provided by the manager.

After an experiment unit is submitted, the testing workflow engine executes it through five stages: importing, archiving, deploying, executing, and collecting results. The workflow imports temporal graph data, archives the loaded database state as a database snapshot, deploys the selected snapshot, executes the workload, and collects results, logs, and metrics. The completed unit is then stored in the experiment history repository. Developers can inspect previous units, compare test results, reuse historical configurations to define new units, or replay a selected unit for repeated validation.

3 Key Technologies

Traceable Experiment Unit. TraceTG organizes each test as a traceable experiment unit:

$$U = \langle V_s, V_d, E, W, L \rangle,$$

where V_s, V_d, E, W, and L denote the source-code version, database snapshot, execution environment, workload, and logs, respectively. This unit records the testing context required for later inspection, replay, and comparison.

Snapshot Reuse. Temporal graph datasets are often expensive to import repeatedly. TraceTG archives the loaded database state as a reusable snapshot and restores it before later workload execution. For update workloads that modify the database state, TraceTG restores the original snapshot before each run, so comparable tests start from the same baseline. In our measurement on a 106 GB synthetic dataset, a full import into PETGraphDB [1] takes 35,895 s while deploying the archived snapshot takes only 215 s. This yields a 167× speedup per iteration.

Versioned Historical Comparison. TraceTG stores completed experiment units in the history repository and compares them across database versions. For comparable units with the same snapshot and workload, TraceTG compares execution status, running time, outputs, and logs. Developers can use these differences to inspect performance changes and locate possible regressions.

4 Demonstrations

We demonstrate TraceTG in a temporal graph database development scenario. The demonstration shows how developers inspect testing states, monitor execution pipelines, and trace historical results across database versions.

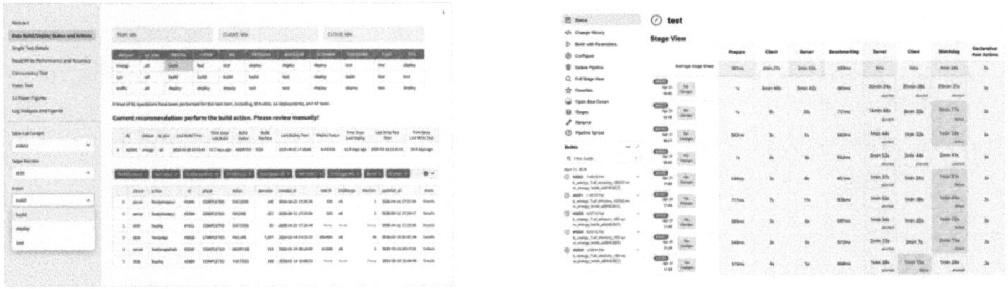

(a) Testing state analysis.

(b) Task execution pipeline.

Fig. 2. GUI of TraceTG.

Testing State Analysis. As shown in Fig. 2(a), the front-end interface summarizes build, deployment, and testing states for different databases and datasets. It also uses historical records to recommend the next action, such as building a version, deploying it, or running a workload.

Automated Pipeline Execution. After the user confirms an action, TraceTG submits the task to the back-end pipeline. Figure 2(b) shows a testing job divided into preparation, client configuration, server deployment, benchmarking, watchdog monitoring, and post-processing actions. The interface reports the duration and status of each stage, helping developers locate failed or aborted steps.

Historical Inspection. All executed tasks are stored as historical records. Developers can inspect previous jobs, compare their status and duration, and open detailed logs when failures occur. The demonstration illustrates how TraceTG can reduce repeated data preparation, preserve experimental context, and support comparison across database versions.

References

1. Song, J., Zuo, Z., Lin, X., Wang, Y., Ma, S.: PETGraphDB: a property evolution temporal graph data management system. arXiv preprint arXiv:2512.05417 (2025)
2. Han, W., et al.: Chronos: a graph engine for temporal graph analysis. In: EuroSys 2014, pp. 1:1–1:14. ACM (2014)

3. Rost, C., et al.: Distributed temporal graph analytics with GRADOOP. VLDB J. **31**, 375–401 (2022)
4. Hou, J., et al.: AeonG: an efficient built-in temporal support in graph databases. Proc. VLDB Endow. **17**(6), 1515–1527 (2024)
5. Püroja, D., Waudby, J., Boncz, P., Szárnyas, G.: The LDBC Social Network Benchmark Interactive workload v2: a transactional graph query benchmark with deep delete operations. Proc. VLDB Endow. **16**(12), 3637–3640 (2023)
6. PostgreSQL Global Development Group: PostgreSQL documentation: regression tests. https://www.postgresql.org/docs/current/regress.html
7. Oracle: MySQL test framework components. https://dev.mysql.com/doc/dev/mysql-server/latest/PAGE_MYSQLTEST_FRAMEWORK_COMPONENTS.html
8. Oracle: Oracle Real Application Testing user's guide. https://docs.oracle.com/en/database/oracle/oracle-database/19/ratug/

iCoLoc: An Interactive System for Spatial Co-location Pattern Mining via LLM-Guided Intent and Contrastive Preference Learning

Xijia Ye, Xinran Xu, Jing Huang, Qi Han, and Xuguang Bao(✉)

Department of Intelligent Science and Technology, Guilin University of Electronic Technology, Guilin, China
baoxuguang@guet.edu.cn

Abstract. Traditional interactive spatial co-location pattern mining (SCPM) systems require users to possess domain expertise and manually select relevant patterns at the initial stage. Moreover, they rely on fixed parameter settings, often generating numerous irrelevant patterns, and cannot adapt to dynamically changing user requirements. This demonstration presents iCoLoc, an end-to-end workbench for non-expert analysts whose core mechanism is contrastive preference learning with re-ranking-without-re-mining. On a Beijing POI benchmark (4,592 instances, 16 categories), users issue natural-language queries; a local LLM cold-start a user vector from fuzzy intent, a PI-based miner generates candidates once, and binary feedback iteratively refines the user representation to re-rank the top-20 results without regenerating the candidate set. In a 10-round simulated interaction study, we compare three ranking variants on the same data and mining settings; the contrastive configuration reaches 0.98 ranking accuracy after feedback accumulates compared with 0.80 (baseline) and 0.86 (feature-weighted) at the final round. This demo shows how non-experts can mine spatial patterns via natural language, without domain expertise.

Keywords: SCPM · spatial data mining · LLMs · contrastive preference learning · intent understanding

1 Introduction

Traditional SCPM [1] focuses on mining frequently co-occurring spatial features (e.g., nearby POIs) but ignores user behavior and preferences. Subsequent studies incorporate high-utility mining [2], graph-based modeling [3], interactive systems [4], and preference-aware filtering [5] to involve users. However, they still rely on fixed parameters and domain expertise, adapt poorly to evolving preferences, and rarely link fuzzy intent or binary feedback to ranking in one session—limiting use by non-expert analysts (e.g., retail screening, urban POI review). To address these gaps, this demonstration presents iCoLoc, whose central mechanism is contrastive preference learning with re-ranking-without-re-mining: a local LLM cold-starts a user vector from fuzzy intent; a PI-based miner generates candidates once; binary feedback then iteratively refines the

L. Ding et al. (Eds.): APWeb-WAIM 2026, LNCS 16995, pp. 681–684, 2027.
https://doi.org/10.1007/978-981-92-5699-0_49

user vector to re-rank the top-20 results without regenerating the candidate set. Rather than returning a static set of patterns, iCoLoc iteratively engages with the user, employing contrastive learning to capture implicit, evolving preferences and LLMs to handle cold-start semantic parsing and initialize the user vector. The demo targets non-experts who explore patterns via language and feedback, without hand-tuning mining parameters.

2 System Overview

iCoLoc is an interactive SCPM system that supports fuzzy natural-language queries as well as human-in-the-loop refinement. The overall system workflow is illustrated in Fig. 1. At runtime, the system loads the POI dataset and model configurations, and then processes user requests through an intent-driven pipeline: (i) LLMs interpret natural language to extract user preferences, which are then used to initialize potentially interesting patterns and a corresponding user vector, (ii) Using a Join-Base algorithm, frequent candidate itemsets are derived, sorted by cosine similarity to the user vector, and the top-20 patterns are offered for user selection, (iii) Users select patterns as either interesting or uninteresting, and the system uses the selected patterns to train a contrastive learning model, thereby refining the user vector to better align with the user's preferences.

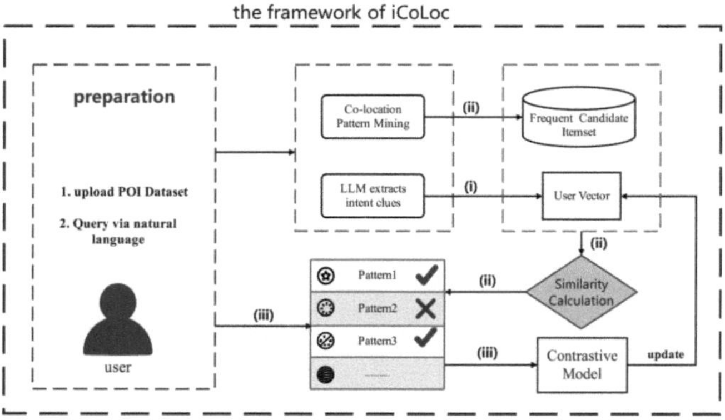

Fig. 1. Architecture of the iCoLoc system

3 Demonstration

The demonstration uses a Beijing POI dataset derived from open geographic features and converted to a uniform JSON schema: 4,592 instances and 16 categories (e.g., Restaurant, Cafe, Supermarket, Cinema, Hospital), each record containing id, type, and planar coordinates (x, y) in a local projected space. The same schema is used for the preloaded demo and for user uploads via the Web UI. For more demonstrations, please refer to https://youtu.be/19WxxZbObKc.

3.1 Analysis of iCoLoc System

Figure 2a shows the complete query process from fuzzy query to result generation. Figure 2b visualizes dataset spatial distribution to reveal geographic data layout and feature spatial correlations. Figure 2c illustrates the parameter input and dataset import interface. Here, users upload JSON files of spatial datasets, which are spatial data files containing feature instances and their corresponding coordinates. Figure 2d presents the manual training module, which displays both training history and configuration parameters. Users can adjust training strategies to obtain ideal training outcomes.

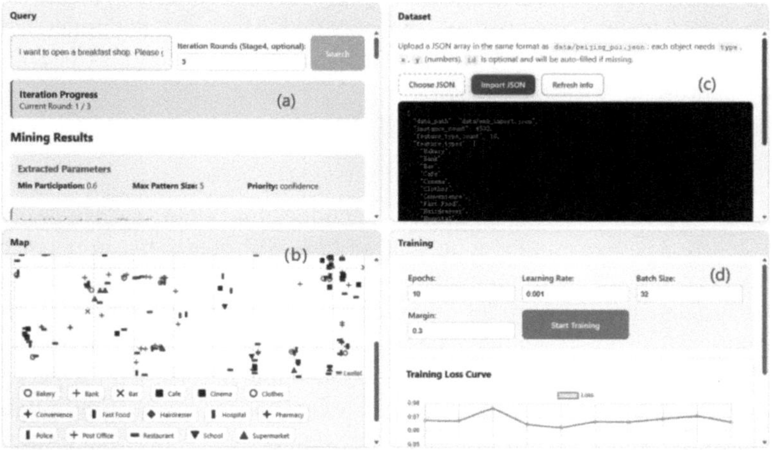

Fig. 2. iCoLoc system overview

3.2 Experimental Evaluation

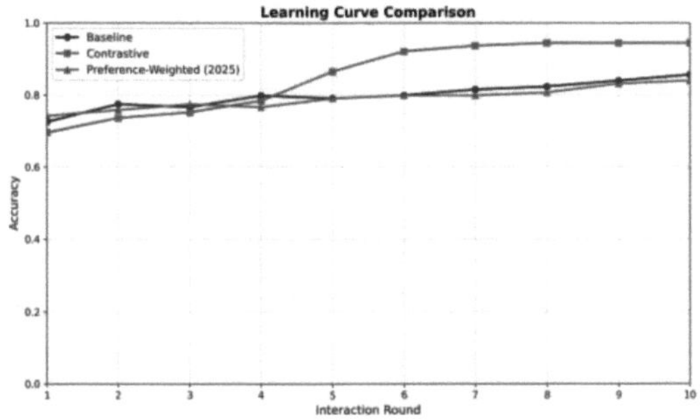

Fig. 3. Efficiency evaluation result

We evaluated iCoLoc against conventional methods in terms of accuracy, comparing it with a baseline approach (iCoLoc without contrastive learning part) and the personalized region-of-interest recommendation method proposed in 2025 [6]. Evaluation uses a synthetic user who prefers patterns containing Restaurant, where the ground truth labels a pattern as relevant if and only if it includes a liked POI type and excludes all disliked types. After a single PI mining pass (participation index 0.6, maximum pattern size 5), one fixed query drives 10 feedback rounds, with five patterns labeled per round. Each round updates the ranker, and accuracy is computed as the fraction of all mined patterns correctly classified at a decision threshold of 0.7. As shown in the 10-round interaction curves in Fig. 3, the contrastive approach exhibits clear "feedback-driven iterative improvement": its metrics start low but, as contrastive learning time accumulates, the model progressively learns more stable user preference boundaries, leading to rapid accuracy gains in later rounds. In contrast, the baseline lacks a learnable projection layer. The preference-weighted method enhances ranking via explicit preference rules, yet its ability to model complex semantic preferences remains inferior to the contrastive preference approach.

4 Conclusion

In this work, we present iCoLoc, an interactive co-location mining system designed for spatial co-location pattern mining. It integrates LLMs with contrastive preference learning to effectively capture user preferences and identify relevant spatial patterns. Unlike traditional systems that require prior user profiles or structured queries, iCoLoc allows non-expert users to express their intent through fuzzy natural-language inputs. Users can also provide simple like/dislike feedback. The system initializes user preference vectors via LLM-based intent parsing and iteratively refines them through contrastive learning, continuously improving the quality of subsequent pattern ranking. Experimental results demonstrate that this human-in-the-loop design achieves superior performance in preference-aware pattern filtering, validating its practical utility in real-world spatial data mining tasks.

Acknowledgments. This work was supported by grants (No.62566016) from the National Natural Science Foundation of China, grants (No. 2025GXNSFAA069551) from the Guangxi Natural Science.

References

1. Zala, A., Patel, J., Patel, D.: A survey on spatial co-location pattern mining. Int. J. Comput. Appl. **96**(19), 1–7 (2014)
2. Wang, J., Liu, Y., Zhang, X.: Mining high-access spatial co-location patterns from location-based service data. Knowl.-Based Syst. **263**, 110331 (2023)
3. Wang, L., Yang, P., Zhou, L.: Graph-based spatial co-location pattern mining with neighborhood modeling. Inf. Sci. **666**, 120407 (2024)
4. Bao, X., Gu, T., Chang, L.: Knowledge-based interactive postmining of user preferred co-location patterns using ontologies. IEEE Trans. Cybern. **52**(9), 9467–9480 (2021)
5. Wang, L., Fang, Y., Zhou, L.: Preference-aware spatial co-location pattern mining: a framework and applications. Expert Syst. Appl. **198**, 116821 (2022)
6. Tang, Q., Xu, S., Wang, Y., Liu, S., Wang, Z., Hua, H.: Personalized region of interest recommendation through adaptive fusion of multi-dimensional user preferences. J. Big Data. **12**, 224 (2025)

PCTR-Miner: A Tourism Route Recommendation System Based on Circular Co-location Pattern Mining

Qi Han, Yao Qin, and Xuguang Bao(✉)

Guilin University of Electronic Technology, Guilin 541004, China
baoxuguang@guet.edu.cn

Abstract. With the rapid growth of online tourism information, tourism route recommendation has become an important technique for transforming scattered attraction data into actionable travel plans and reducing tourists' decision-making burden. Many existing methods generate routes based on sequential models, focusing mainly on route popularity and the visiting order of POIs, while ignoring return trip requirements. In real tourism scenarios, tourists often start from and return to a fixed location, such as a hotel or scenic area entrance. Linear routes may therefore lead to repeated paths or additional detours, reducing the practicality and efficiency of route planning. To address this problem, we present PCTR-Miner, a Personalized Circular Tourism Route Miner system. The system combines non-redundant circular co-location pattern mining with an interactive personalization mechanism to generate circular routes that better meet user needs, thereby improving the feasibility of travel route planning and user satisfaction.

Keywords: Tourism Route Recommendation · Circular Co-location Pattern · Personalized Itinerary Recommendation

1 Introduction

Tourism route planning helps transform fragmented tourism information into practical travel decisions, especially for tourists unfamiliar with a destination. Existing travel route recommendation methods mainly extract linear points of interest (POI) tour sequences from travel data to meet user preferences. For example, Tsai et al. [1] generated personalized visiting sequences using an LSTM-based model, while Bin et al. [2] proposed a personalized route recommendation method using heterogeneous data and sequential pattern mining. However, in actual travel scenarios, tourists need to return to a fixed starting area, such as a hotel, scenic-area entrance, parking lot, or visitor center. Since these methods do not account for return costs, the recommended routes may end far from the starting area, leading to additional travel costs, repeated paths, and inefficient itineraries.

As a branch of spatial data mining, spatial co-location pattern mining aims to reveal frequent and meaningful associations among spatial features, while the circular co-location pattern [3] further describes ordered circular associations based on trajectory

L. Ding et al. (Eds.): APWeb-WAIM 2026, LNCS 16995, pp. 685–689, 2027.
https://doi.org/10.1007/978-981-92-5699-0_50

data. Its circular structure naturally matches circular tourism routes. Therefore, we adopt the graph-based algorithm (GBA) [3] and combine it with non-redundant pattern mining [4] to mine non-redundant circular co-location patterns, thereby overcoming the limitations of linear route models and laying the foundation for personalized circular route recommendations.

On this basis, we propose PCTR-Miner, a personalized circular tourism route recommendation system that mines non-redundant circular patterns and integrates interactive personalization to generate user-oriented recommendations. Unlike traditional methods that produce linear POI sequences, PCTR-Miner recommends circular routes that support multi-attraction visits and natural return to the starting area, thereby reducing return costs, repeated paths, and manual route adjustments.

2 System Overview

The system framework of PCTR-Miner is shown in Fig. 1. It is implemented as a web-based interactive platform that allows users to upload data, configure personalized requirements, execute the recommendation process, and view results. The Web Interaction Layer handles information exchange between the frontend and backend. The backend consists of three layers: the Data Processing Layer, the Circular Pattern Mining Layer, and the Personalized Recommendation Layer, which sequentially perform data preprocessing, circular pattern mining, and personalized route recommendation.

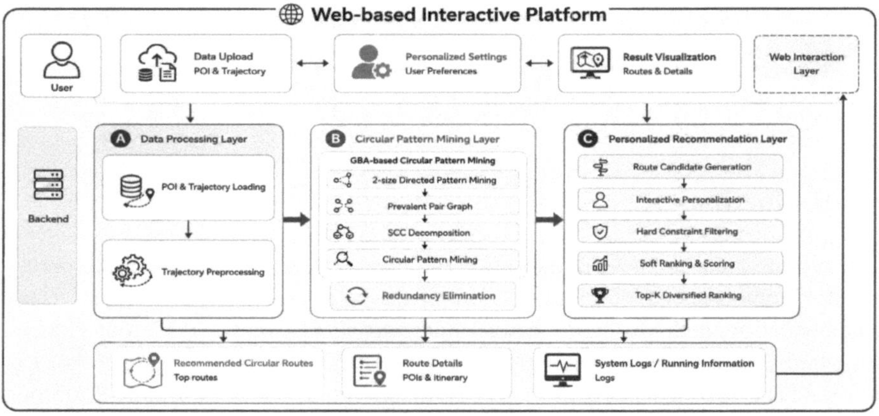

Fig. 1. The framework of PCTR-Miner

The Data Processing Layer is responsible for loading and preprocessing POI data and tourist visit data. It transforms raw visiting records into tourist trajectory data, which are then passed to the mining layer for circular pattern discovery.

The Circular Pattern Mining Layer adopts GBA [3] to mine circular co-location patterns. It first extracts prevalent 2-size directed linear patterns from trajectory sequences and uses them as edges to construct a directed graph. For a 2-size pattern $\langle f_i, f_j \rangle$, its support ratio is defined as:

$$Support\_ratio(\langle f_i, f_j \rangle) = \min\left(\frac{|\ Inst(\langle f_i, f_j \rangle, f_i)\ |}{|\ Inst(f_i)\ |}, \frac{|\ Inst(\langle f_i, f_j \rangle, f_j)\ |}{|\ Inst(f_j)\ |} \right) \tag{1}$$

Then, Tarjan's algorithm [3] is used to identify strongly connected components in the graph, within which candidate cycles are efficiently searched. For a candidate circular pattern $c = \langle f_1, f_2, \ldots, f_k, f_1 \rangle$, its support ratio is calculated as:

$$Support\_ratio(c) = \min_{f_i \in c} \frac{|\ Inst(c, f_i)\ |}{|\ Inst(f_i)\ |} \tag{2}$$

Here, $Inst(f_i)$ denotes all instances of feature f_i, while $Inst(\cdot, f_i)$ denotes the instances of f_i participating in the corresponding linear or circular pattern. After prevalence filtering, we obtain prevalent circular co-location patterns. A redundancy elimination step [4] finally removes circular patterns fully contained in larger ones, resulting in non-redundant circular patterns for route generation

The Personalized Recommendation Layer converts circular patterns into candidate routes and recommends Top-K routes through interactive personalization. Users can configure conditions such as preferred categories, season, starting point, must-visit POIs, and time budget as hard constraints or soft preferences. Hard constraints remove routes that fail to satisfy mandatory requirements, while soft preferences are weighted according to user-defined priorities for scoring and ranking. This design avoids the fixed hard constraints and weight settings used in previous systems, thereby improving the match with user needs.

3 Demonstration Scenarios and Efficiency Evaluation

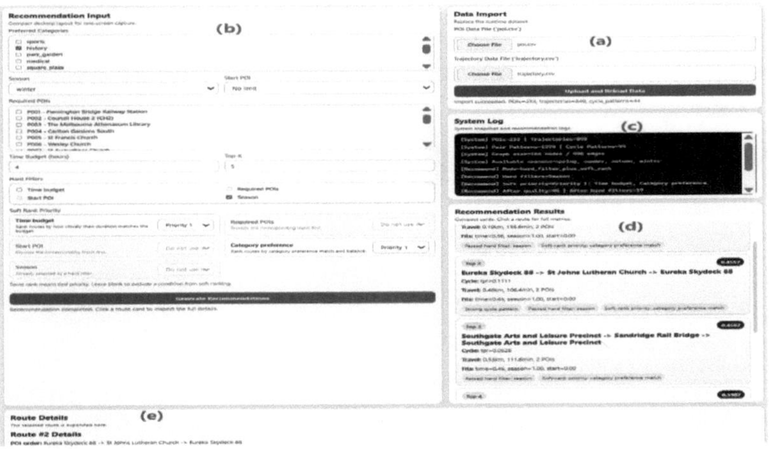

Fig. 2. The demonstration of PCTR-Miner

PCTR-Miner has a user-friendly interface and supports straightforward user interactions. In this demonstration, we use visitor data from Melbourne [5] to demonstrate the functionality and efficiency of PCTR-Miner. The system's source code[1] and video demonstration[2] can be accessed through the links provided.

Demonstration. Figure 2 shows the web interface of PCTR-Miner. Users import data through the data import module in Fig. 2a. Then, in Fig. 2b, they configure personalized conditions and Top-K values, designate selected conditions as hard constraints and the rest as soft constraints, and determine the scoring weights of the soft constraints through ranking. Figure 2c records system logs such as data statistics and runtime status. The ranked circular routes are displayed in Fig. 2d, including scores and matching information, while Fig. 2e presents the detailed POI visiting order for the selected routes.

Efficiency Assessment. PCTR-Miner is compared with PV-PrefixSpan [2] under the same personalized conditions and different support ratio thresholds. In the following formulas, TypeMatch and SeasonMatch are calculated as the proportion of POIs satisfying the personalized requirements in a route to the total POIs of that route. Since both methods are based on co-location pattern mining, support_ratio reflects the popularity of the corresponding route in historical tourist trajectories. As shown in Fig. 3, PCTR-Miner achieves a more stable average match degree for Top-3 routes and generates circular routes for practical travel planning.

$$MatchDegree = \frac{TypeMatch + SeasonMatch + TimeFit + Support\_ratio}{4} \tag{3}$$

$$TimeFit = \max\left(0, 1 - \frac{|\,duration - Tbudget\,|}{Tbudget}\right) \tag{4}$$

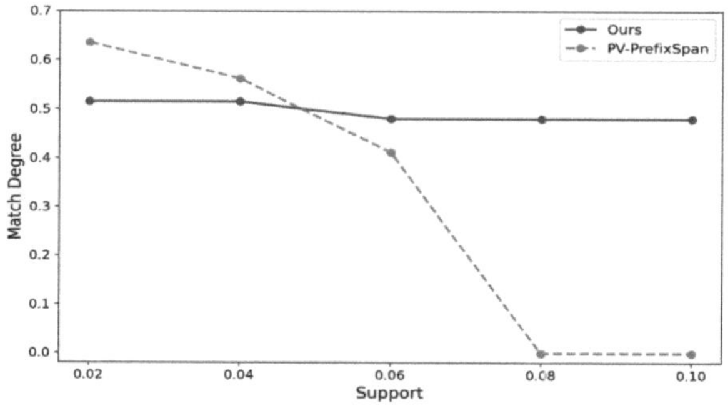

Fig. 3. Average match degree under different support ratio thresholds.

[1] https://github.com/hanqi4831-png/tourism_route_demo
[2] https://youtu.be/tXVzX5iVixY

4 Conclusion

This demonstration presents a circular route recommendation system called PCTR-Miner. This system generates circular routes that meet user needs, addressing the problems of high return costs and insufficient support for circular routes in linear recommendation schemes. PCTR-Miner provides practical route planning support for scenarios requiring a natural return to the starting point, such as urban tourism, scenic spots, and theme parks.

Acknowledgements. This work was supported by grants (No.62566016) from the National Natural Science Foundation of China, grants (No.2025GXNSFAA069551) from the Guangxi Natural Science.

References

1. Tsai, C.Y., Chen, Y.J., Peña, A.S., et al.: A visiting sequence recommendation framework: enhanced by dynamic landmark and stay time. Expert Syst. Appl. **230**, 120662 (2023)
2. Bin, C., Gu, T., Sun, Y., Chang, L.: A personalized POI route recommendation system based on heterogeneous tourism data and sequential pattern mining. Multimed. Tools Appl. **78**, 35135–35156 (2019)
3. Geng, Z., Bao, X.: Spatial circular co-location pattern mining algorithms based on trajectory data. J. Guilin Univ. Electron. Technol. (2025)
4. Bao, X., Lu, J., Gu, T., Chang, L., Xu, Z., Wang, L.: Mining non-redundant co-location patterns. IEEE Trans. Neural Networks Learn. Syst. **33**(11), 6613–6626 (2022)
5. Wang, X., Leckie, C., Chan, J., et al.: Improving personalized trip recommendation by avoiding crowds. In: Proceedings of the 25th ACM International Conference on Information and Knowledge Management, pp. 25–34. ACM, New York (2016)

GCSS-Miner: A Graph-Based Co-location Siting System for EV Charging Piles

Jing Huang, Mingsai Ban, and Xuguang Bao(✉)

Guilin University of Electronic Technology, Guilin 541004, China
baoxuguang@guet.edu.cn

Abstract. Efficient deployment of charging infrastructure is essential for improving charging accessibility and supporting sustainable urban transportation. Traditional electric vehicle (EV) charging pile siting methods mainly rely on density, coverage, and isolated spatial features while overlooking spatial associations among urban Points of Interest (POIs). Such spatial relationships can better capture interaction effects among urban facilities that jointly shape charging demand, and neglecting them may lead to inaccurate identification of high-demand areas. To address this issue, this paper proposes GCSS-Miner, a Graph-based Co-location Siting System for EV charging piles. The system integrates Delaunay triangulation and the Neo4j graph database to mine spatial co-location patterns that describe spatial associations among urban facilities for identifying potential charging demand areas. Experiments on a real-world dataset demonstrate that GCSS-Miner achieves high efficiency and effectiveness, providing effective decision support for EV charging infrastructure deployment and urban planning.

Keywords: EV charging piles · spatial co-location patterns · graph-structure analysis · Delaunay triangulation

1 Introduction

With the rapid growth of new energy vehicles, fairness and efficiency of charging infrastructure deployment have become core concerns [1]. The layout of charging facilities directly affects EV adoption and sustainable urban development. Charging demand is jointly influenced by interactions among residential, commercial, transportation, and other urban facilities rather than isolated factors. Therefore, uncovering spatial relationships among urban facilities is essential for identifying high-demand charging areas. Existing siting methods mainly include GIS-based spatial analysis and machine learning-based demand forecasting. Mhana and Awad [2] combined the analytical hierarchy process (AHP) with GIS for multi-factor site evaluation, while Tan et al. [3] used machine learning with spatial indicators for layout assessment. However, most studies treat urban elements independently and ignore spatial dependencies and co-location patterns among POIs, limiting their ability to capture multi-facility interactions. Previous studies have shown that graph-based spatial analysis effectively captures spatial dependencies overlooked by traditional models [4]. To better support EV charging site selection, this paper

L. Ding et al. (Eds.): APWeb-WAIM 2026, LNCS 16995, pp. 690–694, 2027.
https://doi.org/10.1007/978-981-92-5699-0_51

proposes GCSS-Miner, a graph-based spatial co-location siting system. Unlike standard Delaunay triangulation, which ignores charging-demand heterogeneity, an adaptive edge threshold is introduced:

$$AT_{V_i} = \text{mean}(E_g) + \rho \cdot \frac{\text{STD}_{V_i}}{\text{STD}_g} \cdot \left[\text{mean}(E_{V_i}) - \text{mean}(E_g)\right], \quad \rho = \frac{N_{\text{charging}}}{N_{\text{total}}} \tag{1}$$

where ρ denotes the proportion of charging facilities within the local region; $N_{charging}$ and N_{total} represent the numbers of charging facilities and total POIs, respectively. $\text{mean}(E_{V_i})$ and STD_{V_i} are the mean and standard deviation of local triangle edges around vertex V_i; $\text{mean}(E_g)$ and STD_g are the global mean and standard deviation of all edges in the Delaunay mesh; larger local-global deviation together with the scaling factor ρ in facility-sparse regions raises AT_{V_i} to reserve more long-distance spatial adjacency edges and retain latent demand signals. This mechanism preserves more spatial connections in sparsely served areas and helps to identify potential demand clusters. GCSS-Miner further employs Neo4j for co-location mining to capture spatial interactions and improve siting accuracy.

2 System Overview

The GCSS-Miner architecture is shown in Fig. 1. It follows a three-stage workflow: data loading and processing, spatial analysis and co-location mining for candidate area identification, and result visualization for decision support.

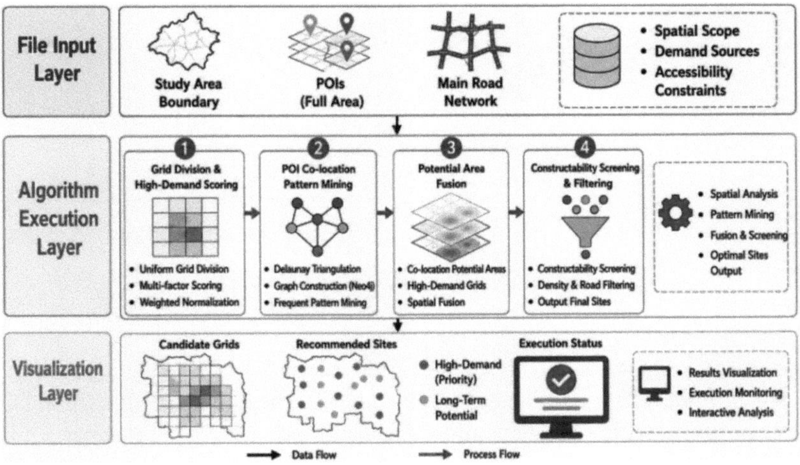

Fig. 1. Framework of GCSS-Miner

File Input Layer. This layer loads the study area boundary, POIs, and main road data to define the spatial scope, demand sources, and accessibility constraints.

Algorithm Execution Layer. It executes four core tasks: first, dividing the study area into uniform grids following the method in Ref. [4] and scoring high-demand grids via weighted normalization; second, mining POI co-location patterns around existing charging piles using Delaunay triangulation and Neo4j [5]; third, fusing co-location-derived potential areas with scored high-demand grids; finally, screening grids for constructability following the multi-criteria evaluation framework of Ref. [2] and filtering by charging pile density and road conditions to output final sites.

Visualization Layer. This layer displays candidate grids and final recommended sites on a map, along with the system execution status.

3 Demonstration Scenario and Efficiency Evaluation

GCSS-Miner provides a user-friendly interface with concise interaction procedures. In this paper, a real-world dataset from Xindu District, Chengdu, is used to demonstrate the system capabilities and efficiency. The source code[1] and video demonstration[2] of this system are accessible via the provided links.

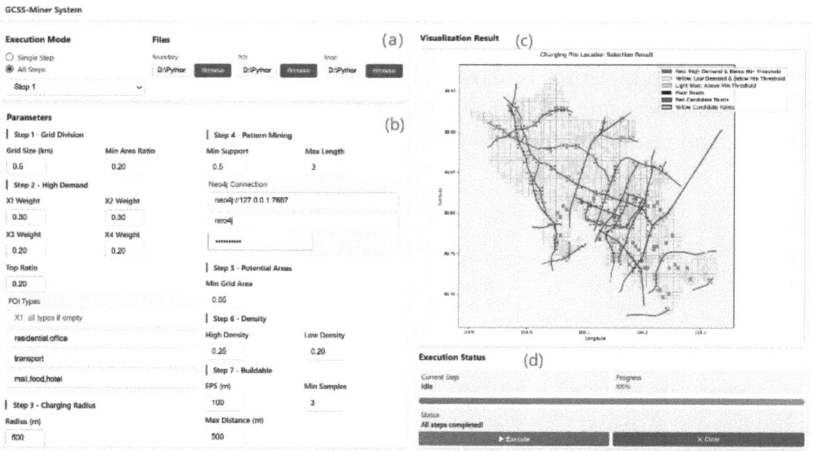

Fig. 2. Demonstration of GCSS-Miner

Demonstration. Figure 2 illustrates the interface and functional demonstration of GCSS-Miner. Figure 2a shows the data upload panel, where datasets for Xindu District, Chengdu are imported for demonstration. Figure 2b presents the parameter configuration panel for setting relevant analysis parameters. Figure 2c visualizes the final siting results, including spatial grids, main roads, and candidate charging pile sites. Red points denote high-demand candidate sites for priority construction, while yellow points represent sites with long-term development potential. Figure 2d displays the operation control and status panel, indicating successful execution without errors.

[1] https://github.com/jinghuang0728/GCSS-Miner.git
[2] https://youtu.be/poi5WCQxSS0.

To evaluate GCSS-Miner's siting performance, we compared it with Decision Tree-based Location Optimization for Charging Facilities (DT-LOCF) [3] under the same grid settings, identical POI dataset and different candidate grid sizes. We adopt the F1 score as the unified evaluation metric, whose simplified calculation formula is defined as:

$$F1 = \frac{2TP}{2TP + FP + FN} \tag{2}$$

where *TP* stands for grids with real charging stations predicted as high-demand zones, *FP* for grids falsely marked high-demand with no piles, and *FN* for grids with stations missed by the model. As Fig. 3 illustrates, both methods' $F1$ scores rise then flatten. Insufficient candidate grids fail to fully cover potential high-demand zones and distort demand characterization; redundant grids introduce noise from low-demand zones. From 200 to 450 candidate grids, GCSS-Miner surpasses the baseline, with the largest advantage at 350 grids. This proves spatial co-location features capture latent demand and deliver stable multi-scale performance. GCSS-Miner boosts EV charging siting precision and robustness to guide urban charging infrastructure planning.

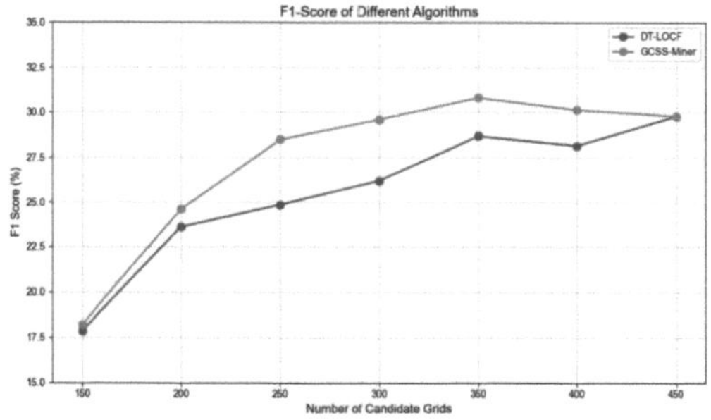

Fig. 3. Efficiency comparison with related literature

4 Conclusion

To address the limitation that existing EV charging pile siting methods ignore spatial interactions among urban facilities, this paper introduces graph-based spatial co-location mining into charging infrastructure planning and presents GCSS-Miner. By combining spatial adjacency construction with graph pattern mining, GCSS-Miner captures facility interactions, improves siting rationality, promotes balanced allocation of charging resources, and thus provides better support for urban infrastructure planning.

Acknowledgments. This work was supported by the National Natural Science Foundation of China (Grant No.62566016) and the Guangxi Natural Science Foundation (Grant No.2025GXNSFAA069551).

References

1. Li, S.: Transportation justice for sustainable cities: an equity review of EV charging infrastructure in China. Sustainable Cities Soc.: Adv. **1**(1), 100010 (2025)
2. Mhana, K.H., Awad, H.A.: An ideal location selection of electric vehicle charging stations: employment of integrated analytical hierarchy process with geographical information system. Sustain. Cities Soc. **107**, 105456 (2024)
3. Tan, J., Ge, X., Qian, J.: Optimization of spatial layout of electric vehicle charging facilities in Kunming based on machine learning. J. Hubei Univ. (Nat. Sci. Ed.). **47**(4), 17–26 (2025)
4. Xie, X., Mao, W., Yang, Z., et al.: A hybrid spatial learning method integrating graph neural networks and explainable AI to understand urban vitality. Sustain. Cities Soc. **134**, 106920 (2025)
5. Wang, J., Ai, T., Wu, W., Xu, H., Li, G.: Graph structure-based spatial co-location pattern mining. Acta Geodaetica et Cartographica Sinica. **53**(4), 724–735 (2024)

SKTQ: A Privacy-Preserving Continuous Spatial Keyword Top-k Query System in Cloud-Fog Environments

Xueling Hu, Yiping Teng(✉), Bingfeng Yu, and Gang Wang

School of Computer Science, Shenyang Aerospace University, Shenyang, China
{huxueling,yubingfeng}@stu.sau.edu.cn, {typ,gangwang}@sau.edu.cn

Abstract. Continuous spatial keyword top-k queries require timely result updates as users move, but outsourcing them to semi-trusted cloud-fog platforms may expose locations, keywords, trajectories, and spatio-textual objects. This paper presents SKTQ, a privacy-preserving continuous query system that integrates encrypted data upload, KASTree-based secure indexing, cloud-fog collaborative processing, safe-zone maintenance, and interactive visualization. SKTQ reuses top-k results inside the safe zone and recomputes them only when necessary. Demonstration on real datasets validates its practical workflow.

Keywords: Spatial Keyword Continuous Query · Privacy Protection · Cloud-Fog Collaborative Architecture

1 Introduction

Continuous spatial keyword top-k queries are important for mobile recommendation and urban navigation because results must be updated as users move. Prior work improves spatial-textual retrieval efficiency [1], maintains continuous query results over dynamic objects [2], and uses fog-assisted privacy-preserving processing, such as PSKF [3] and PRSQ-F [4].Recent studies also explore privacy-preserving spatial range query processing in fog-based IoT environments [5] and weighted spatial keyword queries over encrypted cloud data [6]. However, existing studies mainly focus on individual algorithms or protocols, and still lack an integrated demonstration system that combines secure indexing, encrypted pruning and scoring, safe-zone-based continuous maintenance, and interactive visualization over encrypted spatial-textual data.

We design and implement SKTQ[1,2], an end-to-end privacy-preserving continuous spatial keyword top-k query system in cloud-fog environments. SKTQ integrates a KASTree-based secure hybrid index, cloud-fog collaborative query processing, safe-zone monitoring, and a frontend-backend framework for encrypted

[1] https://github.com/hx0-123/Search.
[2] https://github.com/hx0-123/Search/releases/tag/demo-v1.0.

L. Ding et al. (Eds.): APWeb-WAIM 2026, LNCS 16995, pp. 695–699, 2027.
https://doi.org/10.1007/978-981-92-5699-0_52

data management and query visualization. Demonstrations on real datasets show that SKTQ supports practical continuous top-k query services while protecting locations, keywords, trajectories, and outsourced objects.

2 System Architecture

SKTQ adopts a cloud-fog collaborative architecture for privacy-preserving continuous spatial keyword top-k query processing, as shown in Fig. 1. The data owner encrypts spatial-textual objects and builds secure indexes before outsourcing; the query user submits encrypted continuous queries; the cloud performs secure index search, pruning, safe-zone monitoring, and result aggregation; and fog nodes compute protected spatial-textual scores.

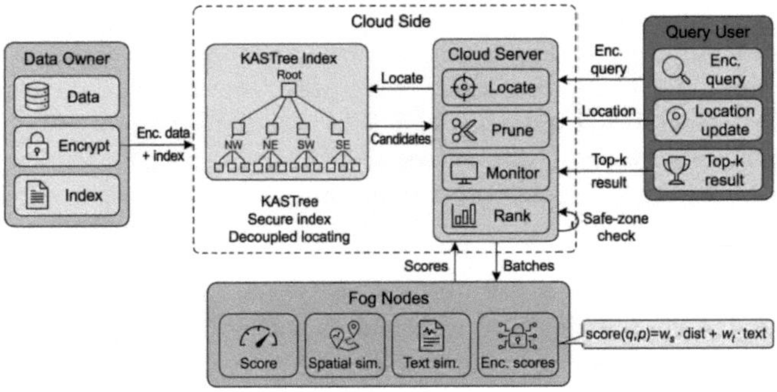

Fig. 1. System Architecture

Under our threat model, we assume trusted data owners and users, honest-but-curious non-colluding cloud and fog nodes [3], and authenticated channels, where the cloud observes encrypted queries, index metadata, candidate region IDs, and ranking results, fog nodes receive encrypted candidates or IDs and scoring values, neither party learns plaintext locations, keywords, trajectories, or scores, and full access-pattern hiding is beyond this prototype.

Data Outsourcing and Secure Index Construction. Each spatial-textual object is represented as$p = \langle p.loc, p.doc \rangle$, where $p.loc$ and $p.doc$ denote its location and keyword set. Before outsourcing, the data owner encrypts sensitive attributes using the Paillier cryptosystem and organizes the encrypted data with KASTree, as shown in Fig. 2. KASTree consists of two coordinated structures: KTree and AssetTree. KTree is a secure storage index that recursively partitions the spatial domain until the number of objects in each leaf node is below a preset threshold. Its leaf nodes store encrypted object identifiers, encrypted locations, encrypted keyword vectors, and encrypted metadata used for pruning. AssetTree is a secure query index with the same partition granularity as KTree, but it does not store plaintext spatial boundaries. Instead, it stores encrypted interval labels

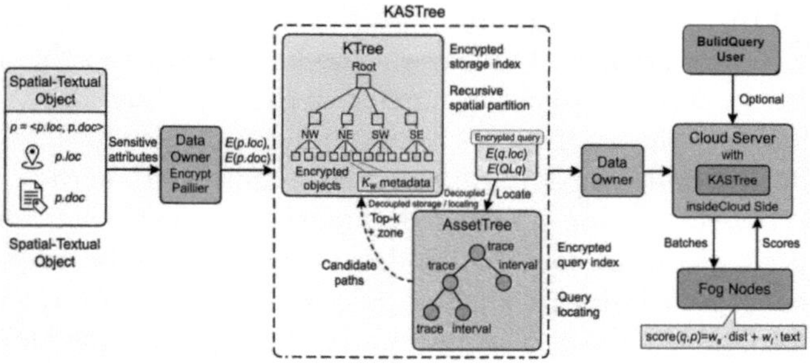

Fig. 2. KASTree

and encrypted traversal traces. During query processing, an encrypted query location or query range is first mapped on AssetTree to obtain an encrypted trace, and the trace is then used to access the candidate leaf nodes in KTree. This design decouples query locating from encrypted data storage, reducing the risk of directly linking query positions with the physical data distribution.

Cloud-Fog Collaborative Query Processing. A query is denoted as $q = \langle q.loc, q.doc, k\rangle$. Given an encrypted query, the cloud uses AssetTree to locate candidate regions, retrieves encrypted candidates from KTree, and prunes irrelevant objects over encrypted metadata. Let p denote a candidate object. The remaining candidates are sent to fog nodes for protected spatial-textual scoring.

For spatial relevance, fog nodes compute the encrypted squared Euclidean distance over $E_{pk}(q.loc)$ and $E_{pk}(p.loc)$, and normalize it as the encrypted spatial similarity $E_{pk}(dist(q,p))$. For textual relevance, let $\mathcal{W} = \{kw_1, \ldots, kw_m\}$ be the global keyword dictionary. The keyword sets $q.doc$ and $p.doc$ are encoded as encrypted binary vectors $E_{pk}(\mathbf{b}_q)$ and $E_{pk}(\mathbf{b}_p)$, where $b_{q,j} = 1$ iff $kw_j \in q.doc$ and $b_{p,j} = 1$ iff $kw_j \in p.doc$. The encrypted keyword intersection and union sizes are computed as

$$E_{pk}(I) = \sum_{j=1}^{m} SM(E_{pk}(b_{q,j}), E_{pk}(b_{p,j})),$$

$$E_{pk}(U) = \sum_{j=1}^{m} \left(E_{pk}(b_{q,j}) + E_{pk}(b_{p,j}) - SM(E_{pk}(b_{q,j}), E_{pk}(b_{p,j}))\right).$$

The encrypted textual similarity is obtained by

$$E_{pk}(text(q,p)) = SDC(E_{pk}(I), E_{pk}(U)).$$

The encrypted overall score is

$$E_{pk}(score(q,p)) = w_s E_{pk}(dist(q,p)) + w_t E_{pk}(text(q,p)),$$

where $w_s + w_t = 1$. Fog nodes return only encrypted scores, and the cloud maintains the Top-k list using SLESS, SMAX, and SEQ [7]. Thus, neither party learns plaintext distances, keyword matches, or relevance scores.

Continuous Query Maintenance. SKTQ maintains a safe zone for each moving query to avoid repeated full secure top-k queries. After the initial query, the safe radius is derived from the current k-th score boundary, the spatial-textual weights, and the maximum textual similarity. Therefore, while the user remains inside the zone, objects outside the maintained candidate boundary cannot exceed the current top-k threshold, and the previous result remains valid. If the encrypted distance from the updated location to the safe-zone center exceeds the encrypted radius, the cloud triggers a new secure query, refreshes candidates, recomputes scores via fog nodes, and updates the result and safe zone.

3 Demonstration

The demonstration presents the SKTQ workflow in a cloud-fog environment through two roles: the data owner, who uploads and encrypts spatial-textual data and constructs secure indexes, and the query user, who submits encrypted map-based queries and receives continuously updated top-k results while moving.

Figure 3 shows the data owner workflow. The data owner uploads a spatial-textual dataset, previews parsed records, and performs local privacy processing, including Paillier-based encryption and secure index construction, before outsourcing encrypted data and indexes to the cloud-fog platform. The interface reports encryption progress, index-building status, and cloud-fog node monitoring information, including node availability, task load, and recent query execution.

(a) Key Generation (b) Data Import (c) Secure Deployment

Fig. 3. Demonstration of Data Upload, Encryption and Storage

Figure 4 shows the mobile user workflow. The user first obtains the public key from the data owner to encrypt query locations and keywords. After loading the key, the user submits encrypted spatial keyword queries by selecting a map location and specifying keywords, query radius, and spatial-textual preference weight. SKTQ returns top-k results as ranked items and map markers, together with distance scores, textual scores, overall scores, user trajectory, and the current safe zone. Results are reused inside the safe zone and refreshed when the user moves outside it.

(a) Key Request (b) Encrypted Query (c) Continuous Update

Fig. 4. Demonstration of Secure Query Authorization, Execution, and Update

4 Conclusion

This paper presented SKTQ, a privacy-preserving continuous spatial keyword top-k query system in cloud-fog environments. SKTQ integrates encrypted data upload, KASTree-based secure indexing, cloud-fog collaborative query processing, safe-zone monitoring, and interactive visualization. The demonstration shows the complete workflow from secure deployment to encrypted query execution and continuous result update, while the repository provides verification materials on real datasets like POI and SINA, with documented workflow records.

Acknowledgement. The work was partially supported by the Shenyang Aerospace University Innovation and Entrepreneurship Plan (D202511202313310178),the Natural ScienceFoundation of Liaoning Province (2025-MS-126), the Youngand Middle-aged Science and Technology Innovation TalentSupport Plan of Shenyang (RC230832).Yiping Teng is the corresponding author.

References

1. Wu, D., et al.: Density-based top-k spatial textual clusters retrieval. IEEE Trans. Knowl. Data Eng. **34**(11), 5263–5277 (2022)
2. Dong, Y., et al.: Continuous top-k spatial-keyword search on dynamic objects. VLDB J. **30**(2), 141–161 (2021)
3. Li, X., et al.: Privacy-preserving top-k spatial keyword queries in fog-based cloud computing. IEEE Trans. Serv. Comput. **16**(1), 504–514 (2023)
4. Tong, Q., Miao, Y., Li, H., Liu, X., Deng, R.H.: Privacy-preserving ranked spatial keyword query in mobile cloud-assisted fog computing. IEEE Trans. Mob. Comput. **22**(6), 3604–3618 (2023)
5. Mahdikhani, H., Lu, R., Shao, J., Ghorbani, A.: Using reduced paths to achieve efficient privacy-preserving range query in fog-based IoT. IEEE Internet Things J. **8**(6), 4762–4774 (2021)
6. Sun, L., Lu, R., Zheng, Y., Shao, J.: Efficient and privacy-preserving weighted nearby-fit spatial keyword query in cloud. IEEE Internet Things J. **12**(12), 20498–20511 (2025)
7. Zhang, S., Ray, S., Lu, R., Zheng, Y., Guan, Y., Shao, J.: Achieving efficient and privacy-preserving dynamic skyline query in online medical diagnosis. IEEE Internet Things J. **9**(12), 9973–9986 (2022)

MMIL-CAD: A Multimodal MIL Visual Analytics System for Clinician-Assisted IBD Diagnosis

Tianya Zhu, Haiwei Pan(✉), Kejia Zhang, Chunling Chen, Yajie Liu, and Xinyu Liu

Harbin Engineering University, Nantong Street 145, Harbin, China
{zhuty,panhaiwei}@hrbeu.edu.cn

Abstract. Web-based medical information systems are increasingly used to support intelligent diagnosis, multimodal data management, and interactive clinical workflows. However, existing computer-assisted diagnostic systems for inflammatory bowel disease (IBD) mainly focus on either single-modal or image-level analysis, and provide limited support for patient-level multimodal data management, prediction review and clinician feedback. To address these limitations, this paper presents MMIL-CAD, a web-based multimodal multi-instance learning (MIL) visual analytics system for clinician-assisted IBD diagnosis. This system integrates endoscopic and intestinal ultrasound (IUS) images of the same patient, and combines MIL with web-based visual analytics. MMIL-CAD supports patient-level prediction, multimodal image review, low-confidence prediction alerts, and clinician feedback within a unified visual analytics workflow. The system enables clinicians to examine multimodal data distributions, review prediction results, and identify low-confidence samples for more efficient patient-level diagnosis, while corrected labels can be further reused for iterative model optimization. Experimental results on real-world IBD datasets demonstrate that MMIL-CAD effectively supports patient-level multimodal analysis and interactive clinical review for clinician-assisted diagnosis.

Keywords: Visual Analytics · Human-Computer Interaction · Inflammatory Bowel Disease · Multi-Instance Learning · Patient-Level Prediction

1 Introduction

Web-based medical information systems are increasingly important for multimodal data management and intelligent clinical workflows. Inflammatory bowel disease (IBD), including Crohn's disease (CD) and ulcerative colitis (UC), typically requires multimodal assessment using both endoscopy and intestinal ultrasound (IUS) [1]. Endoscopy reveals mucosal lesions, while IUS provides complementary information on bowel wall thickness and transmural inflammation. However, both modalities are affected by observer variability, leading to inconsistent disease activity evaluation [2]. In clinical practice, patient examinations often contain varying numbers of multimodal images. Therefore, effective patient-level IBD diagnosis requires integrating data across modalities rather than relying on isolated image-level or single-modal analysis.

L. Ding et al. (Eds.): APWeb-WAIM 2026, LNCS 16995, pp. 700–703, 2027.
https://doi.org/10.1007/978-981-92-5699-0_53

Although computer-assisted diagnostic methods have shown promising performance in recent years, most existing approaches remain image-level [3], and lack effective support for multimodal patient-level review, low-confidence prediction inspection, and annotation refinement. In addition, many systems provide limited visual evidence, clinician interaction, and collaborative clinical review, reducing their interpretability and practicality in real clinical workflows [4].

To address these limitations, this paper presents MMIL-CAD, a multimodal visual analytics system for clinician-assisted IBD diagnosis. The system integrates endoscopic and IUS images of the same patient and combines multimodal multi-instance learning (MIL) [3] with web-based visual analytics. MMIL-CAD supports patient-level prediction, prediction review, multimodal image browsing, and manual label correction within a unified clinical workflow, enabling clinician feedback and iterative dataset refinement. The experimental dataset contains 253 IBD patients, a total of 8253 endoscopic images and 1928 IUS images, along with ultrasound metadata. The system achieved 90.6% overall accuracy in patient-level multi-class classification, with a 0.9038 weighted average F1 score. The main contributions are summarized as follows:

- We present MMIL-CAD, a web-based multimodal visual analytics system that integrates multimodal data management, patient-level prediction, and clinical review into a unified workflow for clinician-assisted IBD diagnosis.
- The system supports patient-level prediction by separately encoding endoscopic and IUS images, aggregating modality-specific image features through MIL pooling, and fusing pooled visual features with structured metadata for classification.
- The system provides interactive interfaces for multimodal image review, low-confidence case inspection, and manual label correction, enabling clinician feedback and iterative dataset refinement.

2 System Architecture

As shown in Fig. 1, MMIL-CAD supports a clinical workflow consisting of multimodal data input, patient-level prediction, interactive review, and clinician feedback. Solid arrows indicate the model prediction workflow, while dashed arrows indicate clinician feedback for iterative refinement.

Endoscopic images, IUS images, and metadata are uploaded via the web interface. The preprocessing module performs data cleaning, normalization, augmentation, and metadata encoding. The backend MIL model performs feature extraction, patient-level aggregation, and multimodal fusion for classification. Prediction results, confidence scores, and images are then presented through the clinical interface for review.

Clinicians can inspect multimodal images, review low-confidence predictions, and manually correct prediction. Corrected annotations and review records are stored in the backend database for subsequent dataset management and iterative model optimization.

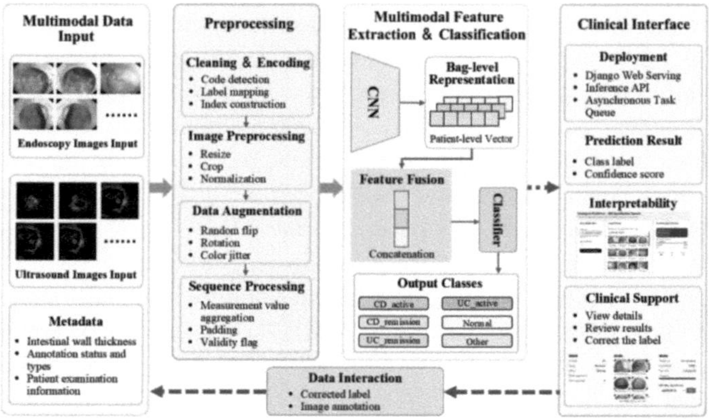

Fig. 1. MMIL-CAD System Architecture

3 Multimodal MIL Model

MMIL-CAD adopts a multimodal MIL framework for IBD classification. The model uses a dual-branch ResNet-18 pre-trained on ImageNet. Each branch encodes one modality into 512-dimensional features and projects them to 256 dimensions. Since each patient contains varying numbers of images, modality-specific features are aggregated through average MIL pooling to obtain fixed-length patient-level representations. The ultrasound metadata, which contains 31 features including bowel wall thickness statistics and annotation quality indicators, is encoded through a separate multilayer perceptron. The pooled visual features and metadata features are concatenated into a unified patient representation for classification. To address class imbalance, the training process incorporates focal loss, weighted sampling, and data augmentation.

4 Demonstration Scenario

The MMIL-CAD system provides a web-based visual analytics platform for clinician-assisted IBD diagnosis. The demonstration scenario follows a clinical workflow including data upload, patient-level prediction, and clinician review. This section introduces four interfaces for patient-level analysis and clinical review.

Homepage Overview. As shown in Fig. 2a, the homepage presents dataset statistics, disease distributions, image distributions, and recent prediction records, helping clinicians quickly identify uncertain cases requiring further inspection.

Patient-Level Prediction. The prediction interface illustrated in Fig. 2b enables clinicians to upload or select patient data for analysis. It presents prediction categories, confidence scores, and multimodal images, enabling interactive multimodal review and patient-level analysis. Low-confidence predictions below a threshold of 0.7 are automatically flagged for clinician review.

Prediction Review and Correction. The recent patients interface shown in Fig. 2c supports prediction inspection and manual label correction, and the corrected labels are saved for iterative optimization of the dataset and improvement of the model.

Model Analysis. Figure 2d provides visual summaries of model performance, including confusion matrices and evaluation metrics, helping clinicians analyze prediction behavior and classification performance.

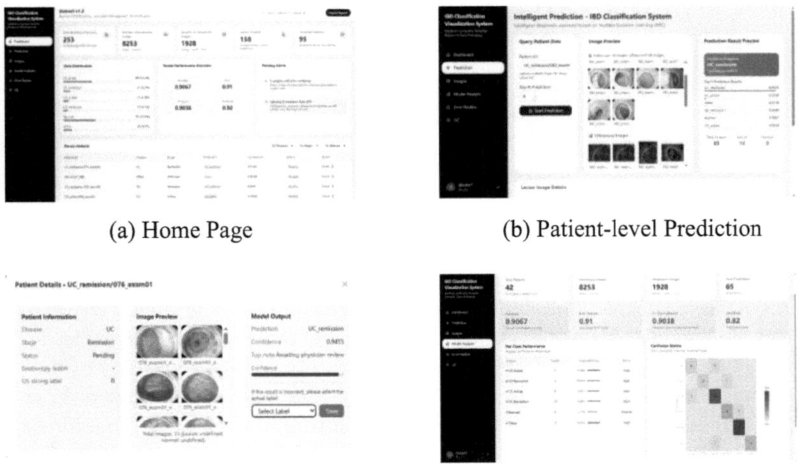

(a) Home Page

(b) Patient-level Prediction

(c) Label Correction

(d) Model Analysis

Fig. 2. MMIL-CAD System Demonstration

5 Conclusion

This paper presents MMIL-CAD, a web-based multimodal visual analytics system for clinician-assisted IBD diagnosis. The system integrates multimodal MIL prediction and clinician feedback into a unified workflow. MMIL-CAD supports patient-level analysis through multimodal image review and prediction review. Future work will focus on collecting larger clinical datasets, improving multimodal MIL strategies, and extending interactive analysis functions for more comprehensive clinical review.

Acknowledgments. This work was supported in part by the National Natural Science Foundation of China under Grant 62072135.

References

1. Iacucci, M., Santacroce, G., Zammarchi, I., et al.: Artificial intelligence and endo-histo-omics: new dimensions of precision endoscopy and histology in inflammatory bowel disease. Lancet Gastroenterol. Hepatol. **9**(8), 758–772 (2024)
2. Hashash, J.G., Ng, F.Y.C., Farraye, F.A., et al.: Inter- and intraobserver variability on endoscopic scoring systems in Crohn's disease and ulcerative colitis: a systematic review and meta-analysis. Inflamm. Bowel Dis. **30**(12), 2217–2226 (2024)
3. Campanella, G., Hanna, M.G., Geneslaw, L., et al.: Clinical-grade computational pathology using weakly supervised deep learning on whole slide images. Nat. Med. **25**(8), 1301–1309 (2019)
4. Topol, E.J.: High-performance medicine: the convergence of human and artificial intelligence. Nat. Med. **25**(1), 44–56 (2019)

IFQAIR-LLM: Intelligent Financial Question Answering Integrated with Intention Recognition Based on Large Language Model

Fangshu Chen, Junjun Sun, Junqi Pan, and Jiahui Wang(✉)

Shanghai Polytechnic University, Shanghai, China
{fschen,jjsun,wangjh}@sspu.edu.cn

Abstract. Large language models have experienced significant growth, but Knowledge Base Question-Answering in finance remains underdeveloped. These systems struggle to accurately identify specific professional question intentions and effectively aggregate information from multiple knowledge points, resulting in suboptimal responses. To address this challenge, we developed the **IFQAIR-LLM: I**ntelligent **F**inancial **Q**uestion-**A**nswering integrated with **I**ntention **R**ecognition based on **L**arge **L**ang-uage **M**odels, which includes intent processing, information retrieval, and interactive learning modules. The intent module enriches the data to extract key information using keywords. A multiroute retrieval method based on an improved knowledge base enables robust semantic recognition. Interactive learning dynamically refines the results, improving the effectiveness of the system. The system can handle complex queries and allows local deployment for data security. Extensive experiments on real financial datasets confirm its effectiveness, with an average prediction accuracy of 91% .

Keywords: KBQA · LLM · Semantic Recognition · Fine Tuning

1 Introduction

With the growing demand for effective access to information resources, Domain Specific Knowledge Base Question Answering (DSKBQA) in finance is becoming popular due to its user-friendliness [1]. However, traditional QA systems that rely on keyword matching cannot provide accurate and in-depth answers in business scenarios supported by knowledge bases [2].

To address this issue, we present an LLM-employing system with three modules [3]. The intent processing module captures user input, enriches its semantics, clarifies user intents, refines queries, standardizes patterns, and matches requirements. There is an information retrieval module considering domain characteristics, using a tuned model and multi-route retrieval for better search and answer

L. Ding et al. (Eds.): APWeb-WAIM 2026, LNCS 16995, pp. 704–708, 2027.
https://doi.org/10.1007/978-981-92-5699-0_54

ranking. The interactive learning module checks the quality of the answer and self-optimizes via feedback to enhance the prompts and embedding models.

In summary, the contributions of this paper can be summarized as follows:

1. We developed the IFQAIR-LLM system integrating intent processing, information retrieval, and interactive learning modules to accommodate vertical domain characteristics.

2. We combined traditional NLP techniques with LLM models to enhance answer precision.

3. To tackle the challenge of intricate user intent recognition in QA systems, we have specifically devised an intent processing module.

2 System Architecture

Figure 1 depicts the overall architecture of IFQAIR-LLM. It comprises three modules: I) intent processing module, II) information retrieval module, and III) interactive learning module.

Intent Processing Module. This module is designed for the financial domain, where questions exhibit professional terms and homogeneous information. **CoT**(Chain-of-Thought) prompts facilitate the interaction between the LLM and users to enhance questions. The users provide specific data, summarize multi-turn information, and integrate contexts to form a clear-intentioned question q'. After the rectification of the intent, q' is transformed into q^*. In parallel, documents are converted into a representation D and their segments are processed accordingly. We adopt Yi-34B-Chat [4] to generate questions Q' after intent processing. We simplify the Information Extraction task, concentrating on NPs(Noun Phrase) and predicates. Split the input, create a stack,

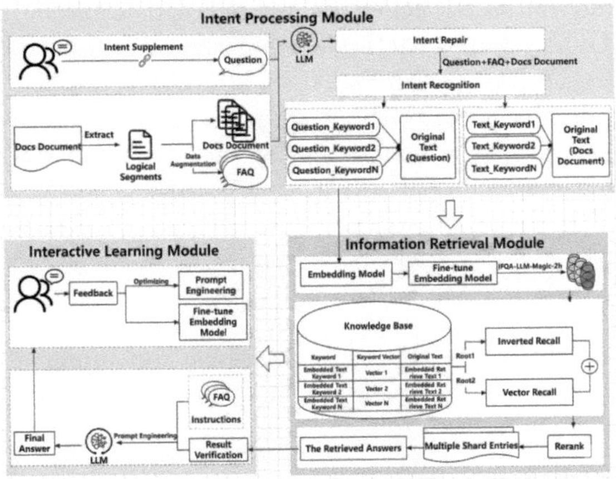

Fig. 1. IFQAIR-LLM System.

perform operations to build a tree with NPs, and extract the NP list NP and the keyword list K.

Information Retrieval Module. This module improves retrieval accuracy by widening the similarity margin between correct and incorrect answers to determine an optimal separation threshold, filtering out low-similarity candidates. We use the bge-large-zh-v1.5 model, fine-tuned with ranked list loss [5], as our embedding model (IFQAIR-LLM-Magic-Zh). Training pairs (X, y) are optimized to learn an embedding function f that increases similarity for positive pairs. After anchor-based sampling and hard negative mining, weighted loss functions are jointly optimized. During retrieval, keywords K are encoded into vectors V, and retrieved information I provides context for LLM inference. To reduce search cost, we align document keywords D with refined query keywords q^*. A hybrid retrieval strategy combines vector-based and BM25 recall, with results merged and re-ranked using Reciprocal Rank Fusion (RRF).

Interactive Learning Module. This module is employed for the enterprise knowledge base. The CO-STAR principle was utilized to design prompts. In experiments, LLM answers were generated with matched text and standard answers. A user feedback mechanism (with scores ranging from 0 to 4) was established for retrieval results. Scores less than 4 were recorded for prompt adjustment, and scores less than 3 were marked as incorrect for embedding model tuning.

For intent processing, Yi-34B-Chat was configured with temperature=0.7, top-p=0.95, and repetition_penalty=1.2. For retrieval, BM25 used $b = 0.75$ and $\gamma = 1.2$, and the embedding model was fine-tuned with ranked list loss. Evaluation was performed on four datasets: Doc (133,239 texts, 3.6GB), FQA1 (11,199 QA pairs, 1.45GB), FQA2 (8,192 pairs, 1GB), and FQA3 (2,589 pairs, 500MB).

As shown in Table 1, our IFQA-LLM consistently outperforms all baseline methods across all datasets, achieving an average accuracy of 0.91. Among the baselines, KGQArr-based methods yield the lowest performance (average accuracy 0.670.69), DEKCOR achieves 0.83, and DBGPT+Yi-34B-Chat reaches 0.90. The results demonstrate that our proposed intent processing, multi-route retrieval, and interactive learning modules effectively enhance the system's capability in complex cross-document financial QA tasks.

3 System Demonstration

In this section, we introduce the core functions and application cases of our system.

As shown in Fig. 2, IFQAIR-LLM platform features a comprehensive dual-interface design comprising an interactive 'QA Chat' and an analytical 'Graphic Evaluation' dashboard. In the 'QA Chat' view, the interface is organized with a left-hand sidebar for managing chat history. The central interaction area uniquely features a detailed 'Intent Analysis' panel, which visualizes the complete preprocessing pipeline. This panel displays the 'Extract Result' and 'Repair Result' JSON data to clarify how entities are identified and abbreviations are resolved (e.g., mapping 'PE' to 'Price-to-Earnings Ratio') to form the 'Repaired Question'. Distinctively, the right side of this panel presents a 'Constituent Syntax Tree', offering a hierarchical visualization of the sentence structure alongside extracted keywords and the final model response. Complementing this, the 'Graphic Evaluation' view provides a visual analysis of system metrics. The left configuration panel enables users to customize experimental settings, including 'Target Dataset', 'Intent Model', and 'Recognition Method'.The main dashboard renders distinct analytical charts based on the customized settings.

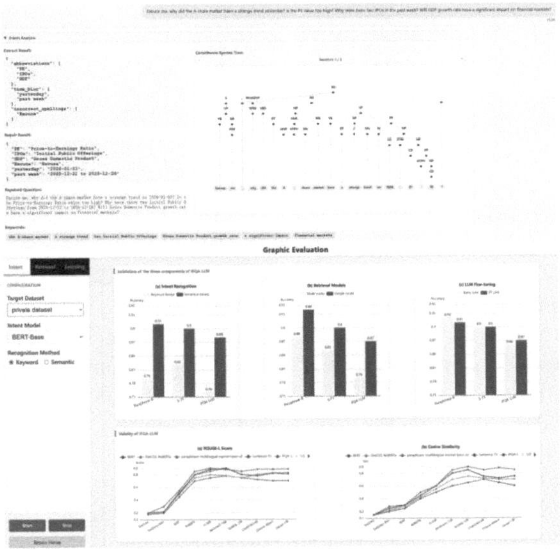

Fig. 2. Web Interfaces of IFQAIR-LLM

Table 1. Performance on different datasets

Methods	Doc accuracy	FQA1	FQA2	FQA3	Avg.
KGQArr+Bert(MLM)	0.77	0.68	0.67	0.65	0.69
KGQArr+RoBerta(MLM)	0.77	0.68	0.67	0.66	0.67
KGQArr+XLnet(PeLM)	0.76	0.66	0.65	0.59	0.67
DEKCOR	0.81	0.85	0.82	0.82	0.83
DBGPT(v0.5.0, Yi-34B-Chat)	**0.92**	0.90	0.89	0.90	0.90
DBGPT(v0.5.0, Tongyi-Finance-14B-Chat)	0.89	0.88	0.89	0.88	0.89
DBGPT(v0.5.0, XuanYuan-13B-Chat)	0.87	0.88	0.86	0.86	0.87
IFQA-LLM (Ours)	0.91	**0.92**	**0.91**	**0.90**	**0.91**

Acknowledgements. The work was supported by National Natural Science Foundation of China (Grant No. 62002216), the Shanghai Sailing Program (Grant No. 20YF1414400), and the Natural Science Foundation of Shanghai (Grant No. 25ZR1402173).

References

1. Zhou, C., Li, Q., Li, C., et al.: A comprehensive survey on pretrained foundation models: a history from BERT to ChatGPT. Int. J. Mach. Learn. Cybern. **15**(3), 1001–1065 (2024). https://doi.org/10.1007/s13042-023-02058-9
2. Zhu, F., Lei, W., Wang, C.: Retrieving and reading: a comprehensive survey on open-domain question answering. arXiv:2101.00774 (2021)
3. Chen, F., Huang, Y., Wang, J., et al.: IFQA-LLM: intelligent intention-driven financial question-answering with large language models. J. Supercomput. **81**(2), 1245–1270 (2025). https://doi.org/10.1007/s11227-024-06672-8
4. Young, A., Chen, B., Li, C.: Yi: Open foundation models by AI (2024). arXiv:2403.04652
5. Wang, X., Hua, Y., Kodirov, E.: Ranked list loss for deep metric learning. In: Proceedings of the IEEE/CVF Conference on Computer Vision and Pattern Recognition (CVPR), pp. 5207–5216. IEEE, New York (2019). https://doi.org/10.1109/CVPR.2019.00535

Author Index

A
Abba, Ali Ibrahim 299
Anh, Tu Nguyen 425

B
Ban, Mingsai 690
Bao, Xuguang 681, 685, 690

C
Cai, Taotao 631
Cao, Xiaoning 671
Chen, Chunling 700
Chen, Fangshu 704
Chen, Jiacheng 676
Chen, Jinyi 167
Chen, Kun 116
Chen, Meishan 249
Chen, Peng 617
Chen, Yuheng 184
Chen, Yuhui 520
Chen, Zhitao 331
Cheng, Quanbo 343, 566
Chung, Tae-Sun 135
Cong, Xin 269
Cui, Jinjiang 343, 566
Cui, Lizhen 249
Cui, Zhihong 83

D
Dang, Duc Ngoc Minh 397
Dang, Manh-Huy 369
Deng, Ling 67
Ding, Weilong 667
Ding, Yong 617
Do, Tuan-Minh 314, 440
Du, Kai 33
Du, Liang 67

F
Fang, Wei 249
Feng, Zhen 408
Fu, Weiwei 343, 566
Fu, Yu 520

G
Gao, Ruize 667
Gong, Tao 520

H
Han, Qi 681, 685
Han, Shasha 671
He, Wei 249, 408
Ho, Le Binh 456
Hoang, Trung-Nguyen 440
Hu, Jianpeng 671
Hu, Xin 100
Hu, Xueling 695
Huang, Jing 681, 690
Huang, Keman 607
Huang, Ruixiao 667
Huang, Shao-Lun 495

J
Jiang, Bo 50
Jiang, Zhongzhong 216
Jin, Beihong 520
Jin, Rize 135, 643

K
Kang, Ruixin 355
Kuang, Shilei 201

L. Ding et al. (Eds.): APWeb-WAIM 2026, LNCS 16995, pp. 709–711, 2027.
https://doi.org/10.1007/978-981-92-5699-0

L
Le, Ngoc-Duy 440
Le, Thi-Bich-Tra 440
Le, Tran-Ngoc-Tran 3, 508
Lei, Kai 18
Leng, Fangling 83
Li, Binyang 331
Li, Canqiang 607
Li, Hui 33, 631
Li, Long 100
Li, Qihui 355
Li, Wenheng 150
Li, Xiao 537
Li, Yanzeng 671
Li, Zhiliang 520
Liang, Hai 617
Liu, Bailong 116, 233
Liu, Baoxu 50
Liu, Hengyu 83
Liu, Ningning 671
Liu, Tanren 18
Liu, Xinyu 700
Liu, Yabin 551
Liu, Yajie 700
Liu, Zedong 100
Liu, Zida 233
Lu, Haodong 355
Lu, Junrui 643
Lu, Pengjuan 592
Lu, Yanrong 631
Luo, Guiwen 537
Luo, Qiong 67

M
Ma, Xiaohan 135
Mai, Hoang Dinh 456
Mai, Hoang-Phuc 314
Mao, Yusen 216
Min, Yuhan 233

N
Ngo-Ho, Anh-Khoa 655
Ngo-Ho, Anh-Khoi 655
Nguyen, Hoang Tri 456
Nguyen, Khoa Minh 397
Nguyen, Ngoc-Bao-Quang 314
Nguyen, Ngoc-Phuong-Linh 3
Nguyen, Nhut Minh 397
Nguyen, Vinh Dinh 425
Nguyen, Van Vu 484
Nguyen, Quang Ha 484
Nguyen, Thuy Hang 484
Nguyen, Yen Vy Trinh 456
Niu, Shanhe 50

P
Paik, Joon-Young 135, 643
Pan, Haiwei 700
Pan, Junqi 704
Pan, Yuchen 100
Pham, Tuan Anh 456
Phan, Cong-Tam 314
Phan, Duc Tai 397
Phan, Thi-Thu-Hong 440
Phan-Thi, Xuan-Trang 369

Q
Qi, Yingying 381
Qin, Xugong 381
Qin, Yao 685
Qiu, Siya 67

R
Ren, Zhijie 343, 566

S
Shang, Haoyi 607
Shao, Mingxing 83
Shi, Kaize 631
Song, Jinghe 676
Song, Kehui 135
Song, Xiangyu 100
Song, Yumeng 216
Sun, Danny Dongning 495
Sun, Junjun 704

T
Tan, Jiangshan 671
Tang, Jing 67
Teng, Yiping 695
Thach, Hoang-Du 655
Thai, Tri Nguyen 397
Tian, Congcong 343
Tian, Huimei 592
Tran, Ly-Minh-Hoang 440
Tran, Nhan Huu 425
Tran, Thanh-Nam 369
Tran, Tuan Phong 484

Trinh, Hoang-Anh-Hong 508
Truong, Hung-Chen 369
Truong, Thanh-Thao 369

V
Vu Bui, Cao 314

W
Wang, Changlong 592
Wang, Chaokun 551
Wang, Gang 695
Wang, Jiabei 381
Wang, Jiahui 704
Wang, Jing 537
Wang, Jingjing 18
Wang, Ruiqi 50
Wang, RuYue 408
Wang, Senzhang 201
Wang, Wenlei 299
Wang, Yanlong 495
Wang, Yuhao 33
Wang, Yujue 617
Wang, Yunxiang 50
Wang, Zhiqiong 167, 216
Wang, Zichen 201
Wei, Liangyu 135
Wu, Qianhong 617
Wu, Yutong 116, 233

X
Xia, Linhan 18
Xiang, Feng 671
Xie, Chang 607
Xie, Liqiang 150
Xin, Junchang 167, 216
Xu, Jian 495
Xu, Li 471
Xu, Qiankang 18
Xu, Shuai 299
Xu, Xinran 681
Xu, Yangnan 83
Xu, Yonghui 249

Y
Yan, Chenchen 216
Yan, Ziwei 18
Yang, Boya 50
Yang, Changsong 617
Yang, Mingzhan 18
Yang, Weiwei 643
Yang, Wencheng 631
Yao, Kang 343, 566
Yao, Zhongming 216
Ye, Xijia 681
Ye, Yongfei 201
Yin, Lihua 184
Yin, Zhixiong 592
Yin, Zihang 667
Yu, Bingfeng 695
Yu, Chengbo 33
Yu, Ge 83
Yu, Minghe 83

Z
Zeng, Chuxuan 67
Zeng, Xiaoyan 269
Zhang, Fuyang 116
Zhang, Hongkang 495
Zhang, Ji 631
Zhang, Jingyu 150
Zhang, Kejia 700
Zhang, Kexin 284
Zhang, Lei 116, 233
Zhang, Meifan 184
Zhang, Qianzhen 150
Zhang, Tiancheng 83
Zhang, Xian 167
Zhang, Xiao-Ping 495
Zhang, Xueyao 331
Zhang, Yaqiang 537
Zhang, Zixin 116
Zhao, Jie 100
Zhao, Wenhao 592
Zhao, Yaqian 537
Zhao, Yaru 331
Zhao, Zhuofeng 667
Zhong, Jialun 671
Zhou, Baohang 135
Zhou, Keqi 167
Zhou, Yongbin 381
Zhu, Daijie 100
Zhu, Tianya 700
Zhu, Zhijie 150
Zi, Lingling 269
Zobary, Firas 577
Zou, Xiangdong 33

MIX
Papier aus verantwortungsvollen Quellen
Paper from responsible sources
FSC® C105338

If you have any concerns about our products,
you can contact us on
ProductSafety@springernature.com

In case Publisher is established outside the EU,
the EU authorized representative is:
Springer Nature Customer Service Center GmbH
Europaplatz 3, 69115 Heidelberg, Germany

Printed by Libri Plureos GmbH
in Hamburg, Germany